TEXAS ESTATE PLANNING STATUTES

WITH COMMENTARY

2015-2017 EDITION

≈

Gerry W. Beyer

Governor Preston E. Smith Regents Professor of Law
Texas Tech University School of Law

authorHOUSE®

AuthorHouse™
1663 Liberty Drive
Bloomington, IN 47403
www.authorhouse.com
Phone: 1 (800) 839-8640

Published by AuthorHouse   08/12/2015

ISBN: 978-1-5049-2927-1 (sc)
ISBN: 978-1-5049-2926-4 (e)

Print information available on the last page.

Any people depicted in stock imagery provided by Thinkstock are models, and such images are being used for illustrative purposes only. Certain stock imagery © Thinkstock.

This book is printed on acid-free paper.

PREFACE

Texas Estate Planning Statutes with Commentary (2015-2017 Edition) is a compilation of Texas statutes which are significant to courses related to estate planning such as Wills & Estates, Trusts, Estate Planning, Estate Administration, Elder Law, and Guardianship. I have included commentary entitled *Statutes in Context* to many sections. These annotations provide background information, explanations, and citations to key cases which should assist you in identifying the significance of the statutes and how they operate.

Most changes made by the 2015 Texas Legislature are shown in red-lined format to make the changes easy for the reader to locate.

Despite my best efforts and those of the publisher, errors may have crept into the text or the *Statutes in Context*. In addition, new cases and legislation make important changes to the law. You may access a list of updates to this work at http://www.ProfessorBeyer.com.

I invite you to assist me in making the next edition of this book even more useful. Please let me know if you detect any problems with this book or have suggestions for future editions. I am especially interested in recommendations regarding other statutes which should be included and areas in which additional commentary would be helpful. You may contact me via e-mail at gwb@ProfessorBeyer.com.

I would like to express my appreciation for the outstanding and invaluable assistance of Ms. Michele Thaetig, Senior Business Assistant, Texas Tech University School of Law in the preparation of this book.

Good luck in your course and in your legal career.

GERRY W. BEYER
August 2015

Summary of Contents

CONTENTS

CONTENTS

CONTENTS

CONTENTS

Chapter 1159. Renting Estate Property **458**

Chapter 1203. Resignation, Removal, or Death of Guardian; Appointment of Successor 484

CONTENTS

CONTENTS

CONTENTS

CONTENTS

SUMMARY OF CHANGES MADE BY
2015 LEGISLATURE

This article reviews the highlights of the legislation enacted by the 2015 Texas Legislature relating to the Texas law of intestacy, wills, estate administration, trusts, and other estate planning matters. The reader is warned that not all recent legislation is presented and not all aspects of each cited statute are analyzed. You must read and study the full text of the legislation before relying on it or using it as authority.

I. INTERFACE BETWEEN PROBATE CODE AND ESTATES CODE

The 2015 Legislature made it clear that the Estates Code is to be treated as an amendment, albeit a huge one, to the Probate Code. Accordingly, if a will refers to "the Probate Code as amended," that reference is deemed to be to the Estates Code. Acts 2015, 84th Leg., ch. 173, § 1, eff. Sept. 1, 2015 (amending Estates Code § 21.002(b)).

II. INTESTATE SUCCESSION

A. Posthumous Heirs

Posthumous heirs must now be in gestation at the time of the intestate's death to obtain inheritance rights. This amendment precludes the use of the decedent's sperm, eggs, or embryos to produce heirs who are born years or decades after the intestate's death. In addition there are no longer different rules for lineal and collateral posthumous heirs. Acts 2015, 84th Leg., ch. 995, § 8, eff. Sept. 1, 2015 (amending Estates Code § 201.056).

B. Determination of Heirship

1. Contents of Application

The contents of the application to declare heirship was changed in several respects including:

- The time of death no longer need be provided; the date of the intestate's death is sufficient.

- Instead of providing the residences of the intestate's heirs, the application must now state the physical addresses of the heirs where service can be had.

- The application must indicate whether each heir is an adult or a minor.

Acts 2015, 84th Leg., ch. 995, § 9, eff. Sept. 1, 2015 (amending Estates Code § 202.005).

2. Service of Citation

Service of citation is not needed on a party who entered an appearance or who has waived citation. Acts 2015, 84th Leg., ch. 995, § 10, eff. Sept. 1, 2015 (amending Estates Code § 202.055) and Acts 2015, 84th Leg., ch. 995, § 11, eff. Sept. 1, 2015 (amending Estates Code § 202.056).

III. WILLS

A. Savings Statute

Texas now has a savings statute which provides that a will is valid in Texas, even if it does not meet the Texas requirements, if it meets the requirements of the jurisdiction where (1) the will was executed, (2) the decedent was domiciled, or (3) the decedent had a place of residence. Acts 2015, 84th Leg., ch. 995, § 13, eff. Sept. 1, 2015 (adding Estates Code § 251.053).

B. One-Step Self-Proving Affidavit

The sequencing of events for the proper use of a self-proving affidavit which is included in the will itself was revised to eliminate the extremely awkward procedure which was previously required. Acts 2015, 84th Leg., ch. 995, § 14, eff. Sept. 1, 2015 (amending Estates Code § 251.1045).

C. Limitation on Court's Authority to Restrict Wills

A court may no longer prohibit a person from revoking an existing will or codicil. Previously, the court was restricted only from preventing a person from executing a new will or codicil. Acts 2015, 84th Leg., ch. 995, §§ 15 & 16, eff. Sept. 1, 2015 (amending Estates Code § 253.001).

D. Forfeiture Clauses

A new subsection provides that forfeiture clauses are unenforceable if there is an existing law which provides that these clauses may not be construed to prevent a beneficiary from enforcing fiduciary duties or seeking a judicial construction of the will. Acts 2015, 84th Leg., ch. 995, § 17, eff. Sept. 1, 2015 (adding Estates Code § 254.005(b)).

E. Divorce and Pour Over Trusts

The provisions of an irrevocable pour over trust in favor of an ex-spouse or a relative of an ex-spouse who is not also a relative of the testator will now be ineffective unless a court order or contract provides otherwise. Instead, the trust will be read as if that person disclaimed his or her interest or, in the case of fiduciary appointments, died before the divorce. Acts 2015, 84th Leg., ch. 378, § 1, eff. Sept. 1, 2015 (amending Estates Code § 123.001).

F. Exoneration

When the Probate Code was recodified, the date on or after which the testator had to execute a will for the no-exoneration presumption to apply was inadvertently dropped. This date, September 1, 2005, was restored. Acts 2015, 84th Leg., ch. 995, § 18, eff. Sept. 1, 2015 (adding Estates Code § 255.304).

G. Class Gifts

Unless the testator's will provides otherwise, a person must be born or in gestation at the time of the testator's death to qualify as a member of a class for purposes of a class gift. Acts 2015, 84th Leg., ch. 995, § 19, eff. Sept. 1, 2015 (adding Estates Code § 255.401). This section, designed to preclude the use of the decedent's sperm, eggs, or embryos to produce class members who are born years or decades after the testator's death, may have an inadvertent impact because the section does not distinguish between immediate gifts (e.g., "to my grandchildren") and postponed gifts (e.g., "to my child for life, and then to my grandchildren"). In the latter case, it is likely the testator intended grandchildren born after the testator's death to be included in the class.

H. Judicial Modification and Reformation

In a major change in Texas law, courts have now been given the authority to modify and reform a will even if the will is unambiguous effectively overruling the Supreme Court of Texas case of *San Antonio Area Foundation v. Lang*, 35 S.W.3d 636 (Tex. 2000), which held that "extrinsic evidence is not admissible to construe an unambiguous will provision." *Id.* at 637. Acts 2015, 84th Leg., ch. 995, § 19, eff. Sept. 1, 2015 (adding Estates Code §§ 255.451-.455).

Below are the key features of how a court may exercise this new power:

- Only a personal representative may petition for modification or reformation; disgruntled beneficiaries and wishful beneficiaries lack standing.

- The court has broad authority to order the personal representative to perform acts which the testator prohibited and to prevent the personal representative from acting as the testator specified.

- The court must have a "good" reason for ordering the modification or reformation such as to make estate administration more efficient, carry out the settlor's tax objectives, assist a beneficiary in qualifying for government benefits, or to correct a scrivener's error but only if there is clear and convincing evidence of the testator's intent.

- The court must modify or reform the will to conform to the "probable" intent of the testator.

- The personal representative has no duty to seek a reformation or modification and is not required to tell the beneficiaries that the personal representative has the ability to seek reformation or modification.

- The personal representative has no liability for failing to seek reformation or modification.

Although these provisions have the laudable goal of carrying out the testator's intent, they have the possibility of preventing a testator from achieving certainty when drafting a will. For example, the testator could write, "I leave $10,000 to X," and later have the court decide that the testator actually meant to leave X $100,000 or that the funds were intended for Y.

IV. ESTATE ADMINISTRATION

A. Application to Probate a Will

1. Eligible Applicants

An independent administrator designated by all of the distributees of the decedent now has standing to file an application to probate the decedent's will and for the appointment of a personal representative. Acts 2015, 84th Leg., ch. 995, § 21, eff. Sept. 1, 2015 (amending Estates Code § 256.051(a)) and Acts 2015, 84th Leg., ch. 995, § 28, eff. Sept. 1, 2015 (amending Estates Code § 301.051).

2. Contents of Application

a. Generally

The applicant no longer needs to state the time of the testator's death; stating the date of death is sufficient. Acts 2015, 84th Leg., ch. 995, § 22, eff. Sept. 1, 2015 (amending Estates Code § 256.052(a)(3)).

b. Lost Will

The applicant no longer needs to state the age and marital status of each of the beneficiaries and heirs when attempting to probate a lost will. Instead, the applicant must now state whether the person is an adult or a minor. Acts 2015, 84th Leg., ch. 995, § 23, eff. Sept. 1, 2015 (amending Estates Code § 256.054(3)) and Acts 2015, 84th Leg., ch. 995, § 26, eff. Sept. 1, 2015 (amending Estates Code § 257.053(3)).

c. Muniment of Title

The applicant no longer needs to state the time of the testator's death; stating the date of death is sufficient. However, the applicant must now provide the physical address where service can be had on the executor named in the will. Acts 2015, 84th Leg., ch. 995, § 25, eff. Sept. 1, 2015 (amending Estates Code § 257.051(a)).

B. Timing for Issuance of Letters

An application for letters may now be filed even after four years from the decedent's death has elapsed if necessary to "prevent real property in a decedent's estate from becoming a danger to the health, safety, or welfare of the general public" provided the applicant is a home-rule municipality that is a creditor of the estate. Acts 2015, 84th Leg., ch. 576, § 1, eff. Sept. 1, 2015 (amending Estates Code § 301.002(b)).

C. Foreign Wills

1. Proof

The method of proving a foreign will and the effectiveness of a self-proving affidavit were clarified to make the probate process easier and more efficient. Acts 2015, 84th Leg., ch. 995, § 24, eff. Sept. 1, 2015 (amending Estates Code § 256.152(b) & (c)).

2. Time of Probate

It is now clear that a foreign will that has already been probated in another state or country may be admitted to probate in Texas even if the application is more than four years after the testator's death. Acts 2015, 84th Leg., ch. 995, § 46, eff. Sept. 1, 2015 (amending Estates Code § 501.001).

D. Application for Letters of Administration

The applicant no longer needs to state the time of the intestate's death; stating the date of death is sufficient. The applicant no longer needs to state the age and marital status of each of the heirs. Instead, the applicant must now state whether each heir is an adult or a minor. Acts 2015, 84th Leg., ch. 995, § 29, eff. Sept. 1, 2015 (amending Estates Code § 301.052(3) & (6)).

E. Notice to Beneficiaries

The affidavit or certificate of the personal representative confirming notice to the beneficiaries no longer needs to contain the addresses of the beneficiaries. Acts 2015, 84th Leg., ch. 995, § 31, eff. Sept. 1, 2015 (amending Estates Code § 308.004(a)).

F. Affidavit in Lieu of Inventory

A personal representative who elects to use the affidavit in lieu of inventory procedure does not need to provide the inventory to beneficiaries who are entitled to $2,000 or less, have already received the property to which they are entitled, or have executed a written waiver. Acts 2015, 84th Leg., ch. 995, § 33, eff. Sept. 1, 2015 (adding Estates Code § 309.056(b-1)).

G. Exempt Property

1. Personal Property Amounts

The amounts of personal property which are exempt from creditors were increased. For a single adult, the amount was raised from $30,000 to $50,000 and for a family, from $60,000 to $100,000. Acts 2015, 84th Leg., ch. 793, § 1, eff. Sept. 1, 2015 (amending Property Code § 42.001(a)).

2. Title if Estate Insolvent

If any exempt property remains in an insolvent estate that was not set aside for the surviving spouse and children, it is now clear that the balance of this exempt property passes in the same manner as other estate property. Acts 2015, 84th Leg., ch. 995, § 38, eff. Sept. 1, 2015 (amending Estates Code § 353.153).

H. Independent Administration

It is now clear that the beneficiaries or heirs may agree to independent administration in separate documents; they do not need to sign the same application. Acts 2015, 84th Leg., ch. 995, § 40, eff. Sept. 1, 2015 (amending Estates Code § 401.002) & Acts 2015, 84th Leg., ch. 995, § 41, eff. Sept. 1, 2015 (amending Estates Code § 401.003(a)).

I. Creditors

1. Duty of Creditor to Possess or Sell

If a creditor in a dependent administration elects or defaults to preferred debt and lien status, and decides to take possession or sell the collateral prior to the maturity of the debt, the creditor must do so within a reasonable time. If the creditor does not, the court may order the property sold free of the debt and the proceeds used to pay the debt. This will assist the estate in obtaining any surplus value the collateral may have over the debt owed. Acts 2015, 84th Leg., ch. 995, § 39, eff. Sept. 1, 2015 (adding Estates Code § 355.1551).

2. Child Support Acceleration

When computing the amount of accelerated child support for which a deceased parent is responsible, the present value of dental health insurance premiums must now be included as well as health insurance premiums. Acts 2015, 84th Leg., ch. 1150, § 9, eff. Sept. 1, 2015 (amending Family Code 154.015(c)(2)).

J. Small Estate Affidavit

The listing of estate assets in a small estate affidavit must now indicate which assets the applicant claims are exempt. Acts 2015, 84th Leg., ch. 1106, § 1, eff. Sept. 1, 2015 (adding § 205.002(b)).

K. Estates of Attorneys

The Legislature added new provisions to address what happens to trust and escrow accounts when a lawyer dies. Acts 2015, 84th Leg., ch. 995, § 45, eff. Sept. 1, 2015 (adding Estates Code Chapter 456). The personal representative now has the authority to enter into a written contract with a Texas lawyer who may then be a signer on the account, determine the proper recipients of the funds in the account, distribute the funds to the proper recipients, and then close the account. If the personal representative is a Texas attorney, the person may takes these steps him- or herself. The financial institution has a duty to comply with the attorney's instructions and is not liable for the actions of the attorney.

V. TRUSTS

A. Trust Protectors

1. Private Trusts

Section 114.0031 was added to provide more detailed coverage of trust protectors in the private trust context. Acts 2015, 84th Leg., ch. 1108, § 2, eff. June 19, 2015 (adding Property Code § 114.0031).

Here are the key features of this new provision:

- The settlor may grant the protector any powers and authority which the settlor desires including, but not limited to, the power to remove and appoint trustees and advisors, the power to modify or amend the trust for tax purposes or to facilitate efficient trust administration, and the power to modify, expand, or restrict the terms of a power of appointment the settlor granted to a beneficiary.

- By default, the trust protector is a fiduciary. However, the settlor may provide that a protector acts in a nonfiduciary capacity.

- The trustee is liable for following the directions of a trust protector only if the trustee's conduct constitutes willful misconduct.

- If the settlor requires the trustee to obtain the consent of a trust protector before acting, the trustee is not liable for any act taken or not taken as a result of the protector's failure to provide the required consent after being requested to do so unless the trustee's actions constitute willful misconduct or gross negligence.

- Unless the settlor provided otherwise, the trustee has no duty to monitor the protector's conduct, to provide advice to or consult with the protector, or tell the beneficiaries that that the trustee would have acted differently from how the protector directed.

- The trustee's actions in carrying out the protector's directions are deemed to be merely administrative actions and are not considered to be the trustee monitoring or participating in actions within the scope of the protector's authority unless there is clear and convincing evidence to the contrary.

2. Charitable Trusts

Section 114.003 which previously covered protectors for all types of trusts is now applicable only to charitable trusts imposing more restrictive rules than the new § 114.0031 provides for private trusts. Acts 2015, 84th Leg., ch. 1108, § 1, eff. June 19, 2015 (amending Property Code § 114.003).

B. Perpetual Care Cemetery Trusts

A perpetual care cemetery trust may now be modified or terminated using the court's deviation powers under Property Code § 112.054. In addition to the grounds in this section, the court may modify the trust "if the income from the fund is inadequate to maintain, repair, and care for the perpetual care cemetery and another source for providing additional contributions to the fund is unavailable." The Banking Commissioner of Texas must consent to any changes before the court may order them. Acts 2015, 84th Leg., ch. 19, §3 , eff. May 15, 2015 (adding Health & Safety Code § 712.0255).

VI. OTHER ESTATE PLANNING MATTERS

A. Transfer on Death Deeds

The 2015 Legislature enacted a Texasized version of the Uniform Real Property Transfer on Death Act joining over a dozen other states that have already done so. Acts 2015, 84th Leg., ch. 841, § 1, eff. Sept. 1, 2015 (adding Estates Code Chapter 114). This Act permits a property owner to designated the new owner of real property upon his or her death in a deed which is property recorded during the owner's lifetime. Below are some of the key features of this Act:

- The property owner must have contractual capacity (not merely testamentary capacity) to execute a TOD deed.

- An agent under a power of attorney may not execute a TOD deed on behalf of the property owner.

- The beneficiary does not need to know about the TOD deed and does not need to have supplied any consideration. However, the beneficiary may disclaim the property following the normal disclaimer procedures.

- The named beneficiary has no legal or equitable interest in the property until the beneficiary survives the property owner by 120 hours.

- The property owner may revoke the TOD deed at any time and does need a reason for so doing.

- The property owner may not make the TOD deed irrevocable.

- The property owner's will cannot revoke or supersede a TOD deed.

- If the property owner names his or her spouse as the beneficiary and then a court issues a final judgment of divorce, the TOD deed is revoked as long as notice of the judgment is recorded before the property owner's death.

- The TOD deed has no legal effect during the property owner's lifetime. For example, the property owner may transfer the property to someone other than the beneficiary even if the transferee has actual knowledge of the TOD deed as long as the transferee records his or her deed before the property owner dies.

- When the property owner dies, creditors with interests in the property are generally treated like other estate creditors.

- When the property owner dies, the property transferred by a TOD deed is subject, as a last resort, to the claims against the estate including allowances in lieu of exempt property and the family allowance.

- The Act provides optional forms a property owner may use to create and revoke TOD deeds.

B. Disclaimers

The Texasized version of the Uniform Disclaimer of Property Interests Act replaces the disclaimer provisions in both the Estates Code and the Trust Code. Acts 2015, 84th Leg., ch. 562, eff. Sept. 1, 2015 (adding Property Code Title 13). Below are some of the significant changes:

- The nine-month deadline to make a disclaimer was removed. There is no longer a time-based deadline for Texas disclaimers although the nine-month rule still applies under Federal law to disclaimers that are made for tax purposes.

- The mechanics of making a disclaimer were simplified. For example, a heir or beneficiary disclaiming an interest no longer needs to file the disclaimer with the court; merely delivering it to the personal representative is normally sufficient.

- Separate provisions govern the disclaimer of different types of property and ownership methods.

- Disclaimers by fiduciaries are expressly covered with rules for different types of fiduciaries clarifying many areas where uncertainty existed under prior law.

For a comprehensive discussion of the Uniform Act, see Glenn M. Karisch, Thomas M. Featherston, Jr., & Julia E. Jonas, *Disclaimers Under the New Texas Uniform Disclaimer of Property Interests Act*, available at http://texasprobate.com/index/2015/6/9/the-new-texas-uniform-disclaimer-of-property-interests-act.html.

C. Multiple Party Accounts

1. Disclosures

The disclosure requirements with which a financial institution must comply were tightened. A financial institution would be wise to use the suggested form and have the customer initial to the right (not to the left, below, or above) of each paragraph to avoid the necessity of complying with additional requirements. Acts 2015, 84th Leg., ch. 85, § 1, eff. Sept. 1, 2015 (amending Estates Code § 113.053). A new section provides similar rules for credit unions which are more like those that previously existed for other financial institutions. Acts 2015, 84th Leg., ch. 85, § 2, eff. Sept. 1, 2015 (adding Estates Code § 113.0531).

2. P.O.D. Accounts

A guardian of the estate or an agent of an original payee may open a P.O.D. account for the ward or principal. Acts 2015, 84th Leg., ch. 378, § 2, eff. Sept. 1, 2015 (adding Estates Code § 113.152(c)).

3. Trust Accounts

The provisions governing trust accounts were clarified to remove previous doubts as to the ability to name an express written trust as the beneficiary of a trust account. Acts 2015, 84th Leg., ch. 255, § 1, eff. May 29, 2015 (amending Estates Code § 113.001).

4. Effect of Divorce

Under most circumstances, provisions of a multiple-party account in favor of an ex-spouse or a relative of the ex-spouse who is not a relative of the decedent will not be effective to transfer the funds to the ex-spouse or ex-spouse's relative. Acts 2015, 84th Leg., ch. 995, § 5, eff. Sept. 1, 2015 (adding Estates Code § 123.151).

5. Access When Depositor Died Intestate

If an intestate dies owning a bank account that has funds which do not pass to another person under the terms of the account, an interested person may apply to the court for an order requiring the financial institution to reveal the balance in the account if 90 days have passed since the intestate died, no letters have been issued, and no petition for the appointment of a personal representative is pending. Acts 2015, 84th Leg., ch. 217, § 1, eff. Sept. 1, 2015 (adding Estates Code Chapter 153). This new procedure will help heirs determine the appropriate administration method for the decedent's estate.

D. Transfers to Minors

The amount that may be transferred to a custodian for the benefit of a minor under certain circumstances has been increased to account for inflation from $10,000 to $25,000. Acts 2015, 84th Leg., ch. 622, eff. Sept. 1, 2015 (amending Property Code § 141.007(c) & 141.008(c)).

E. Misapplication by Fiduciary

The values of property which a fiduciary must have misapplied to be guilty of various offenses were increased to adjust for inflation. For example, the fiduciary now must misapply more than $300,000 to be guilty of a first degree felony rather than $200,000. Acts 2015, 84th Leg., ch. 1251, § 21, eff. Sept. 1, 2015 (amending Penal Code § 32.45(c)).

F. Durable Power of Attorney

If a durable power of attorney is used in a real property transaction that needs to be recorded, the power of attorney must be filed not later than the 30th day after the real property instrument is filed. Acts 2015, 84th Leg., ch. 808, § 1, eff. Sept. 1, 2015 (amending Estates Code § 751.151).

The amendment does not provide the consequences of a late filing. For example, is the underlying real property transaction void or voidable?

G. Directive to Physicians

Minor changes were made to the form for the Texas directive to physicians (living will). Acts 2015, 84th Leg., ch. 435, § 4, eff. Sept. 1, 2015 (amending Health & Safety Code § 166.033).

H. Body Disposition

1. Persons With Authority to Control Disposition

The decedent's personal representative has been added to the list of individuals who have the authority to control the disposition of remains if the decedent did not leave written instructions or name an agent. The priority of the personal representative is after the decedent's adult siblings and before more distant relatives. Acts 2015, 84th Leg., ch. 1103, § 1, eff. Sept. 1, 2015 (amending Health & Safety Code § 711.002(a)). Liability for the costs rests solely on the decedent's estate and not the personal representative individually. Acts 2015, 84th Leg., ch. 1103, § 1, eff. Sept. 1, 2015 (adding Health & Safety Code § 711.002(a-3)).

2. Effect of Divorce

If the decedent divorces an agent after signing the document, the ex-spouse may not make disposition arrangements unless the instrument expressly states that the ex-spouse is to serve regardless of the divorce. Acts 2015, 84th Leg., ch. 1103, § 1, eff. Sept. 1, 2015 (amending Health & Safety Code § 711.002(c)).

3. Clarification of When Agent Signs

Previously, there was some confusion whether the agent must sign the document at the time of execution or only after the decedent dies. The statute now provides that the agent does not need to sign until the agent acts pursuant to the appointment. Acts 2015, 84th Leg., ch. 1103, § 1, eff. Sept. 1, 2015 (amending Health & Safety Code § 711.002(c)).

4. Non-Compliance Damages

If the provider of prepaid funeral contract or other contract providing for funeral arrangements fails to comply with the contract, the provider "is liable for the additional expenses incurred in the disposition of the decedent's remains as a result of the breach of contract." Acts 2015, 84th Leg., ch. 1103, § 1, eff. Sept. 1, 2015 (amending Health & Safety Code § 711.002(g)).

5. Form

The form, which is now optional rather than mandatory, has been changed in several ways including:

- The form is now called "Appointment for Disposition of Remains."

- The spaces for the agent's acceptance of the appointment were moved from the body of the form to the end of the form.

- An explanation that the appointment of a spouse is revoked upon divorce unless the instrument provides otherwise is now included in the form.

Acts 2015, 84th Leg., ch. 1103, § 1, eff. Sept. 1, 2015 (amending Health & Safety Code § 711.002(b)).

I. Self-Help Forms

The Legislature charged the Supreme Court of Texas with the task of promulgating a wide range of self-help forms in English and Spanish, along with plain language instructions, for wills for six common scenarios (e.g., single with no children and married with an adult child), an application for probating a will as a muniment of title, and a small estate affidavit. Each form must state that it is not a substitute for attorney advice. The clerks of the probate courts will have the duty to tell the general public about the forms and the court must accept these forms unless they are completed so poorly that it causes a substantial defect that cannot be fixed. Note that the Spanish versions are for convenience only and cannot be submitted to the probate court. Acts 2015, 84th Leg., ch. 602, § 1, eff. Sept. 1, 2015 (adding Government Code § 22.020).

Additional Source: For an excellent and comprehensive review of the new legislation, I recommend that you consult William D. Pargaman & Craig Hopper, *2015 Texas Estate and Trust Legislative Update* available at http://www.snpalaw.com/resources.

CONVERSION CHART
PROBATE CODE TO ESTATES CODE

Probate Code	Estates Code
2(a) (part)	21.006
2(c)	21.004
3 (part)	22.001
3(a)	22.002
3(b)	22.004
3(c)	22.005
3(d)	22.006
3(e)	22.007
3(f)	22.019
3(g)	22.007
3(h)	22.008
3(i)	22.009
3(j)	22.010
3(k)	22.011
3(l)	22.012
3(m)	22.013
3(o)	22.015
3(p)	22.016
3(q)	22.017
3(r)	22.018
3(s)	22.020, 22.021
3(t)	22.022
3(u)	22.023 repealed
3(v)	22.024
3(w)	22.025
3(x)	22.027
3(z)	22.028
3(aa)	22.031
3(bb)	22.029, 31.001
3(dd)	22.030
3(ee)	22.032
3(ff)	22.034
3(ii)	22.007
3(jj)	22.026
3(kk)	22.003

Probate Code	Estates Code
3(ll)	22.014
3(mm)	22.033
4A	32.001
4B	31.002
4C	32.002
4D	32.003
4E	32.004
4F	32.005
4G	32.006
4H	32.007
5B	34.001
5C	34.002
6	33.001
6A	33.002
6B	33.003
6C	33.004
6D	33.005
8(a)	33.051, 33.052, 33.055
8(b)	33.053, 33.101
8(c)(1)	33.101, 33.102
8(c)(2)	33.103
8(d)	33.104
8(e)	33.054
8A(a)	33.101, 33.102
8A(b)	33.103
8B	33.104
9	54.002
10	55.001
10A(a)	55.051, 55.052
10A(b)	55.053
10B	55.101, 55.102
10C	54.001
11	52.051
11A	53.053
11B	53.054

Probate Code	Estates Code
12(a)	53.051
12(b)	53.052
12(c)	53.052
13	52.001
13(e)	52.051
14	52.002
15	52.052
16	52.003
17	52.004
17A	52.053
18	54.052
19	53.101
20	53.102
21	55.002
22	51.203, 54.051
23	53.105 repealed
24	53.001
25	53.106
26	55.151, 55.152
27	55.201, 55.202, 55.203
28	351.053
29	351.002
31	55.251, 55.252
32	351.001
33(a)	51.001
33(b)	51.001
33(c)	51.002, 51.003
33(d)	51.151
33(e)	51.056
33(f)(1)	51.101, 51.051
33(f)(2)	51.053
33(f)(3)	51.054
33(g)	51.104
33(h)	51.102
33(i)	51.103
33(j)	51.202
34	51.055
34A	53.104
35	51.201

Probate Code	Estates Code
36(a)	351.352, 351.353, 351.354
36(b)	351.355
36B	151.001
36C	151.002
36D	151.003
36E	151.004
36F	151.005
37	101.001, 101.003, 101.051
37A(a)	122.002
37A(b)	122.003
37A(c)	122.101
37A(d)	122.102
37A(e)	122.001
37A(f)	122.103
37A(g)	122.051
37A(h)	122.052-112.055
37A(i)	122.056
37A(j)	122.005
37A(k)	122.004
37A(l)	122.151, 112.152
37A(m)	122.153
37A(n)	122.104
37A(o)	122.105, 122.106
37A(p)	122.057
37B(a)	122.201
37B(b)	122.202, 122.203
37B(c)	122.204
37B(d)	122.205
37B(e)	122.206
37C(a)	255.101
37C(b)	255.102
38(a)	201.001
38(b)	201.002
39	201.102, 201.103
40	201.054
41(a)	201.056
41(b)	201.057
41(c)	201.060

Probate Code	Estates Code
41(d)	201.058, 201.059, 201.061
41(e)	201.062
41(f)	201.062
42(a)	201.051
42(b)(1)	201.052
42(b)(2)	201.053
42(c)	102.001, 353.001
42(d)	201.055
43	201.101
44(a)	201.151
44(b)	201.151
44(c)	201.152
45	201.003
46(a)	101.002, 111.001
46(b)	111.002
47(a)	121.051-121.053
47(b)	121.151
47(c)	121.101, 121.102
47(d)	121.152
47(e)	121.153
47(f)	121.001
47A(a)	123.101
47A(b)	123.102
47A(c)	123.102
47A(d)	123.103
47A(e)	123.103
47A(f)	123.104
48(a)	202.001, 202.002, 202.003 repealed
48(b)	202.006
48(c)	202.003 repealed
49(a)	202.004, 202.005
49(b)	202.007, 202.008
50(a)	202.051, 202.054
50(b)	202.052
50(c)	202.053
50(d)	202.055
50(e)	202.056
51	202.101-202.103

Probate Code	Estates Code
52	203.001
52A	203.002
53(a)	202.151
53(b)	202.009
53(c)	202.009
53A(a)	204.051
53A(b)	204.052
53A(c)	204.053
53A(d)	204.053
53A(e)	204.054
53A(f)	204.055
53A(g)	204.056
53B(a)	204.101
53B(b)	204.102
53B(c)	204.103
53C(a)	204.151
53C(b)	204.152
53C(c)	204.152
53C(d)	204.153
53D	204.201
53E	204.001
54	202.201
55(a)	202.202, 202.203
55(b)	202.204
55(c)	202.205
56	202.206
57	251.001
58(a)	251.002
58(b)	251.002
58(c)	255.002, 255.003
58(d)	255.001
58a	254.001
58b	254.003
58c	255.351
59(a)	251.051, 251.052, 251.102, 251.103, 251.104
59(a-1)	251.1045
59(b)	251.101, 251.104, 251.105

Probate Code	Estates Code
59(c)	251.102, 251.106
59A	254.004
60	251.052, 251.107
61	254.002
62	254.002
63	253.002
64	254.005
67(a)	255.052
67(a)(1)	255.053
67(a)(2)	255.054
67(b)	255.055
67(c)	255.051
67(d)	255.052
67(e)	255.056
68(a)	255.153, 255.154
68(b)	255.152
68(c)	255.152
68(d)	255.152
68(e)	255.151
69(a)	123.001
69(b)	123.001
69(c)	123.002
69A	253.001
70	255.201 repealed
70A(a)	255.252
70A(b)	255.253
70A(c)	255.251
71(a)	252.001, 252.003
71(b)	252.002
71(c)	252.004
71(d)	252.051, 252.052
71(e)	252.101-252.105
71(f)	252.151, 252.152
71(g)	252.153
71A(a)	255.301
71A(b)	255.302
71A(c)	255.303
72(a)	256.002, 301.001, 454.001, 454.002, 454.004, 454.051,

Probate Code	Estates Code
	454.052
72(b)	454.003
73	256.003
74	301.002
75	252.201-252.204
76	256.051, 301.051
77	304.001
78	304.003
79	304.002
80(a)	301.201
80(b)	303.201, 301.202
80(c)	301.203
81(a)	256.052, 256.053
81(b)	256.054
82	301.052
83(a)	256.101
83(b)	256.102
83(c)	256.103
84(a)	256.152
84(b)	256.153
84(c)	256.154
84(d)	256.155
85	256.156
87	256.157
88(a)	256.151, 301.151
88(b)	256.152
88(c)	301.152
88(d)	301.153
88(e)	301.154
89	256.201
89A(a)	257.051, 257.052
89A(b)	257.053
89B	257.054
89C(a)	257.001
89C(b)	257.101
89C(c)	257.102
89C(d)	257.103
90	256.202
91	256.203

Probate Code	Estates Code
92	362.002
93	256.204
94	256.001
95(a)	501.001
95(b)	501.002, 501.003
95(c)	501.003, 503.002, 505.052
95(d)	504.003, 501.004, 501.005
95(e)	501.007
95(f)	501.008
96	503.001, 503.003
97	503.001
98	503.051
99	503.052
100(a)	504.001
100(b)	504.002, 504.004
100(c)	504.003
101	504.051, 504.052
102	504.053
103	502.001
104	502.002
105	501.006
105A(a)	505.001, 505.003
105A(b)	505.004, 505.005
105A(c)	505.002
105A(d)	505.002
105A(e)	505.006
106	505.051
107	505.052
107A(a)	505.101
107A(b)	505.101
107A(c)	505.102
107A(d)	505.103
108	152.001, 152.004
109	152.001
110	152.001
111(a)	152.002
111(b)	152.003
112	152.002

Probate Code	Estates Code
113(a)	152.051
113(b)	152.052
113(c)	152.054
113(d)	152.055
114(a)	152.053
114(b)	152.055
115(a)	152.101
115(b)	152.101
115(c)	152.102
115(d)	152.102
128(a)	258.001, 303.001
128(b)	258.002
128(c)	258.003, 303.002
128A(a)	308.001
128A(a-1)	308.0015
128A(b)	308.002
128A(c)	308.002
128A(d)	308.002
128A(e)	308.003
128A(f)	308.002
128A(g)	308.004
128A(h)	308.004
128B(a)	258.051
128B(b)	258.051
128B(c)	258.051
128B(d)	258.052
128B(e)	258.053
129A	258.101, 303.003
131A(a)	452.001, 452.003
131A(b)	452.002
131A(c)	452.003
131A(d)	452.004
131A(e)	452.005
131A(f)	452.006
131A(g)	452.006
131A(h)	452.006
131A(i)	452.007
131A(j)	452.008
132(a)	452.051

Probate Code	Estates Code
132(b)	452.052
133	452.101, 452.102
134	452.151
135	452.152
137(a)	205.001-205.004
137(b)	205.008
137(c)	205.006
137(d)	205.005
138	205.007
139	451.001
140	451.002
141	451.003
142	451.004
143	354.001
145(a)	none
145(b)	401.001
145(c)	401.002
145(d)	401.002
145(e)	401.003
145(f)	401.004
145(g)	401.003
145(h)	402.001
145(i)	401.004
145(j)	401.004
145(k)	401.004
145(l)	401.004
145(m)	401.004
145(n)	401.004
145(o)	401.001
145(p)	401.005
145(q)	351.351, 401.007
145(r)	401.008
145A	401.006
145B	402.002
145C(a)	402.051
145C(b)	402.052
145C(c)	402.053
145C(d)	402.054
146(a)(1)	403.051

Probate Code	Estates Code
146(a)(2)	403.051
146(a)(3)	403.051
146(a)(4)	403.001
146(a-1)	403.051
146(b)	403.052
146(b-1)	403.053
146(b-2)	403.054
146(b-3)	403.055
146(b-4)	403.056
146(b-5)	403.056
146(b-6)	403.057
146(b-7)	403.058
146(c)	403.0585
147	403.059
148	403.060
149	404.002
149A	404.001
149B	405.001
149C	404.0035, 404.0036, 404.0037
149D	405.003
149E	405.003
149F	405.003
149G	405.011
150	405.008
151(a)	405.004
151(a-1)	405.005
151(b)	405.006
151(c)	405.007
151(d)	405.007
151(e)	405.002
152	405.009
153	405.010
154	404.004
154A	404.005
154A(i)	351.351
155	101.052, 453.001, 453.002
156	101.052, 453.006
160(a)	453.003

Probate Code	Estates Code
160(b)	453.003, 453.004
160(c)	453.003, 453.004
168	453.006-453.008
176	453.005
177	453.009
178(a)	306.001
178(b)	306.002
178(c)	306.001
179	301.101
180	301.153
181	306.003
182	306.004
183	306.005
186	306.007
187	306.006
188	307.001
189	305.002
190(a)	305.051
190(b)	305.052
190(c)	305.053
190(d)	305.054, 305.055
192	305.003, 305.054
194	303.101, 305.106
194(1)	305.151
194(2)	305.151
194(3)	305.152
194(5)	305.154
194(6)	305.155
194(7)	305.156
194(8)(a)	305.157
194(8)(b)	305.156
194(8)(c)	305.156
194(8)(d)	305.156
194(8)(e)	305.158
194(9)	305.159
194(10)	305.201
194(11)	305.202
194(12)	305.201, 305.207
194(13)	305.153

Probate Code	Estates Code
194(14)	305.160
195	305.101
196	305.108
197	305.107, 305.109
198	305.103
199	305.104
200	305.105
201(a)	305.203
201(b)	305.204
201(c)	305.205
202	305.204
203	305.251
204	305.251
205	305.252
206(a)	305.252
206(b)	305.253
207	305.254
208	305.255
209	305.257
210	305.256
211	305.206
212	305.206
213	305.110
214	305.102
215	305.102
216	305.102
217	305.102
218	305.111
220(a)	361.102
220(b)	361.103
220(c)	361.104
220(d)	361.105
220(e)	361.106
220(f)	361.101
220(g)	361.151
221(a)	361.001
221(b)	361.002
221(c)	361.003
221(d)	361.004

Probate Code	Estates Code	Probate Code	Estates Code
221(e)	361.005	242	352.051
221(f)	361.005	243	352.052
221A	56.001	244	352.053
221B	56.002	245	351.003
222(a)(1)	361.051	248	309.001
222(a)(2)	361.054	249	309.003
222(b)	361.052	250	309.051. 309.056
222(c)	361.053	251	309.052
222A	361.054	252	309.053
223	361.152	253	309.002
224	361.153	255	309.054
225	361.153	256	309.101
226	361.154	257	309.102
227	361.155	258	309.103
230	351.101	259	309.104
232	351.102	260	309.055
233(a)	351.151	261	309.151
233(b)	351.152	262	354.051
233(c)	351.152	263	354.052
233(d)	351.152	264	354.053
233(e)	351.153	265	354.054
233A	351.054	266	354.055
234(a)	351.051	267	354.056
234(b)	351.052	268	354.057
235	351.103	269	354.058
238(a)	351.201	270	102.004
238(b)	351.202	271	353.051
238(c)	351.203	272	353.052
238(d)	351.203	273	353.053
238(e)	351.203	274	353.055, 353.056
238(f)	351.202	275	353.054
238(g)	351.204	277	353.151
238(h)	351.205	278	353.152
238(i)	351.205	279	353.153
238A	351.104	280	353.154
239	351.301-351.303	281	353.155
240	307.002	282	102.002
241(a)	352.002-352.004	283	102.003
241(b)	352.001	284	102.005

Probate Code	Estates Code
285	102.006
286	353.101
287	353.102
288	353.101
289	353.103
290	353.104
291	353.105
292	353.106, 353.107
293	353.107
294(a)	308.051
294(b)	308.052
294(c)	308.051
294(d)	308.054
295	308.053
296	308.055
297	308.056
298(a)	355.001, 355.060
298(b)	355.061
299	355.008
301	355.004, 355.059
302	355.007
303	355.006, 355.062
304	355.005
306(a)	355.151
306(b)	355.152
306(c)	355.153
306(c-1)	355.153
306(d)	355.154
306(e)	355.155
306(f)	355.156
306(g)	355.157
306(h)	355.158
306(i)	355.158, 355.159
306(j)	355.158
306(k)	355.160
307	355.003
308	355.002
309	355.051
310	355.052

Probate Code	Estates Code
311	355.053
312(a)	355.054
312(b)	355.055
312(c)	355.056
312(d)	355.057
312(e)	355.058
313	355.064, 355.066
314	355.065
315	355.111
316	355.202
317	355.201
318	355.063
319	355.101
320(a)	355.103
320(b)	355.104
320(c)	355.105
320(d)	355.106
320A	355.110
321	355.108
322	355.102
322A(a)	124.001
322A(b)	124.005
322A(c)	124.006
322A(d)	124.006
322A(e)	124.006
322A()	124.006
322A(g)	124.007
322A(h)	124.008
322A(i)	124.009
322A(k)	124.010
322A(l)	124.003
322A(m)	124.010
322A(n)	124.014
322A(o)	124.015
322A(p)	124.004
322A(q)	124.011
322A(r)	124.012
322A(s)	124.001
322A(t)	124.013

Probate Code	Estates Code	Probate Code	Estates Code
322A(u)	124.015	352(a)	356.651
322A(v)	124.016	352(b)	356.652
322A(w)	124.017	352(c)	356.653
322A(x)	124.002	352(d)	356.654
322A(y)	124.018	352(e)	356.655
322B	355.109	353	356.551
323	355.112	354	356.553-356.555
324	355.203	355	356.552, 356.556
326	355.107	356	356.557
328	355.113	357	356.558
329(a)	351.251	358	356.559
329(b)	351.252	359	357.001
329(c)	351.252, 351.253	360	357.001
331	356.001	361	357.002
332	356.002	362	357.005
333	356.051	363	357.003
334	356.101, 356.102	364	357.004
335	356.151-356.155	365	357.051
336	356.103	366	357.052
337	356.104	367(a)	358.001
338	356.201-356.203	367(b)	358.051
339	356.105	367(c)	358.051-358.060
340	356.257	368(a)	358.101
341	356.251	368(b)	358.102
342	356.252	369(a)	358.151
344	356.253	369(b)	358.151-358.155
345	356.254	370	358.201
345A	356.255	371	358.251-358.254
346	356.256	373(a)	360.001
347	356.601, 356.602	373(b)	360.001
348(a)	356.301, 356.302	373(c)	360.002
348(b)	356.351-356.353	374	360.051
349(a)	356.401	375	360.052
349(b)	356.402	377	360.101
349(c)	356.403	378	360.102
349(d)	356.404	378A(a)	124.052
349(e)	356.405	378A(b)	124.051
350	356.451	378B(a)	310.003
351	356.501, 356.502	378B(b)	310.004

Probate Code	Estates Code	Probate Code	Estates Code
378B(c)	310.004	408(d)	362.013
378B(d)	310.004	409	362.009
378B(g)	310.005	410	362.010
378B(h)	310.001, 310.006	412	362.008
378B(i)	310.002	414	362.052
379	360.251	427	551.001-551.004
380(a)	360.151	428	551.005
380(b)	360.152	429	551.101
380(c)	360.153	430	551.006
380(d)	360.154	431	551.102
380(e)	360.155	432	551.103
380(f)	360.156	433(a)	551.051, 551.052
380(g)	360.157	433(b)	551.052, 551.055
381(a)	360.201	433(c)	551.052, 551.053
381(b)	360.202	433(d)	551.054
381(c)	360.202	436(1)	113.001
381(d)	360.203	436(2)	113.001
382	360.252	436(3)	113.001
384	360.301	436(4)	113.004
385	360.253	436(5)	113.004
386	360.254	436(6)	113.003
387	360.103	436(7)	113.002
398A	351.105	436(8)	113.001
399(a)	359.001	436(9)	113.001
399(b)	359.002	436(10)	113.004
399(c)	359.003, 359.004	436(11)	113.001
399(d)	359.005	436(12)	113.001
400	359.101	436(13)	113.001
401	359.051-359.054	436(14)	113.004
402	359.006	436(15)	113.001
403	359.102	437	113.101
404	362.001	438(a)	113.102
405	362.003, 362.004	438(b)	113.103
405A	362.007	438(c)	113.104
406	362.051	438A(a)	113.004
407	362.005	438A(b)	113.105
408(a)	362.006	438A(c)	113.105
408(b)	362.011	438A(d)	113.154
408(c)	362.012	438A(e)	113.105

Probate Code	Estates Code	Probate Code	Estates Code
438A(f)	113.206, 113.208	460(d)	112.205
438A(g)	113.208	460(e)	112.207
438B	113.106, 113.1541	460(f)	112.201, 112.202
439(a)	113.151	460(g)	112.208
439(b)	113.152	461	112.251-112.253
439(c)	113.153	462	112.002
439(d)	113.155	471	123.051
439A(a)	113.051	472(a)	123.052
439A(b)	113.052	472(b)	123.053
439A(c)	113.053	473(a)	123.054
439A(d)	113.053	473(b)	123.055
440	113.156, 113.157	481	751.001
441	113.158	482	751.002
442	113.251-113.252	483	751.004
443	113.201	484	751.051
444	113.003, 113.005, 113.202	485	751.052
		485A	751.053
445	113.203, 113.207	486	751.054
446	113.204	487	751.055-751.056
447	113.205	487A	751.057
448	113.209	488	751.058
449	113.210	489	751.151
450(a)	111.051, 111.052	489B(a)	751.101
450(b)	111.053	489B(b)	751.102
450(c)	111.051	489B(c)	751.103
451	112.051	489B(d)	751.104
452	112.052	489B(e)	751.104
453	112.151	489B(f)	751.103
454	112.152	489B(g)	751.105
455	112.054	489B(h)	751.106
456(a)	112.035, 112.101	489B(i)	751.005
456(b)	112.102	489B(j)	751.006
456(c)	112.103	490(a)	752.001-752.003, 752.051
456(d)	112.101		
457	112.104	490(b)	752.004
458	112.053, 112.105	491	752.101
459	112.106	492	752.102
460(a)	112.203	493	752.103
460(b)	112.204	494	752.104
460(c)	112.206	495	752.105

Probate Code	Estates Code
496	752.106
497	752.107
498	752.108
499	752.109
500	752.110
501	752.111
502	752.112
503	752.113
504	752.114
505	752.115
506	751.003
601	1002.001
601(1)	1002.002
601(2)	1002.003
601(3)	1002.004
601(4)	1002.005
601(5)	1002.006
601(6)	1002.007
601(7)	1002.009
601(8)	1002.008
601(9)	1002.010
601(10)	1002.011
601(11)	1002.012
601(12)	1002.013
601(12-a)	1002.014
601(13)	1002.016
601(14)	1002.017
601(15)	1002.018
601(16)	1002.019
601(18)	1002.020
601(19)	1002.021
601(20)	1002.022
601(21)	1002.023
601(22)	1002.024
601(23)	1002.028
601(24)	1002.025
601(25)	1002.015
601(27)	1002.026
601(28)	1002.027

Probate Code	Estates Code
601(29)	1002.008
601(30)	1002.029
601(31)	1002.030
602	1001.001,1101.105
603(a)	1001.002
603(b)	1001.003
604	1022.002
605	1022.001
606 repealed	none
606A	1021.001
607 repealed	none
607A	1022.002
607B	1022.003
607C	1022.004
607D	1022.005
607E	1022.006
608	1022.007
609	1022.008
610	1023.001
611	1023.002
612	1023.003
613	1023.004
614	1023.005
615	1023.006
616	1023.007
617	1023.008
618	1023.009
619	1023.010
621	1052.051
622(a)	1053.051
622(b)	1053.052
622(c)	1053.052
623(a)	1052.001
623(b)	1052.051
624	1052.002
625	1052.052
626	1052.003
627	1052.004
627A	1052.053

Probate Code	Estates Code	Probate Code	Estates Code
628	1055.102	646(b)	1054.201
629	1053.101	646(c)	1054.203
630	1053.102	646(d)	1054.005
632(a)	1051.001	646(e)	1054.002
632(b)	1051.001	647	1054.004
632(c)	1051.002, 1051.003	647A(a)	1054.201
632(d)	1051.201	647A(b)	1054.201
632(e)	1051.056	647A(c)	1054.202
632(f)(1)	1051.051	647A(d)	1054.203
632(f)(2)	1051.053	647A(e)	1054.202
632(f)(3)	1051.054	648(a)	1054.102, 1054.105
632(f)(4)	1051.052	648(b)	1054.103
632(g)	1051.154	648(c)	1054.104
632(h)	1051.152	648(d)	1054.104
632(i)	1051.153	648(e)	1054.105
632(j)	1051.252	648(f)	1054.101
633(a)	1051.101	648A(a)	1054.151
633(b)	1051.102	648A(b)	1054.152
633(c)	1051.103	648A(c)	1054.153
633(d)	1051.104	648A(d)	1054.154
633(d)	1051.104	649	1051.253, 1055.101
633(e)	1051.105	650	1053.103
633(f)	1051.104, 1051.106	651	1053.001
633(g)	1051.101	652	1055.053
634	1051.055	653	1056.001
635	1051.251	654	1056.051, 1056.052
636	1151.301	655	1152.001
641	1055.002	656	1152.002
642	1055.001	657	1056.101, 1056.102
643	1055.052	659(a)	1106.001
644	1055.051	659(b)	1106.002
645(a)	1054.051	659(c)	1106.003
645(b)	1054.055	659(d)	1106.003
645(c)	1054.054	660	1106.005
645(d)	1054.055	661	1106.004
645(e)	1054.052	662	1151.002
645(f)	1054.053	663	1106.006
645A	1054.056	665(a)	1155.002
646(a)	1054.001, 1054.003	665(a-1)	1155.004

Probate Code	Estates Code	Probate Code	Estates Code
665(b)	1155.003	676(e)	1104.053
665(c)	1155.006, 1155.007	676(f)	1104.053
665(d)	1155.006, 1155.007	676(g)	1202.002
665 (d-1)	1155.007	677(a)	1104.101, 1104.102
665(g)	1155.002	677(b)	1104.103
665(e)	1155.008	677(c)	1104.103
665(f)	1155.005	677(d)	1104.103
665(h)	1155.001	677(e)	1202.002
665A	1155.051 [repealed]	677A(a)	1104.152
665B	1155.054	677A(b)	1104.152
665C(a)	1155.053	677A(c)	1104.152
665C(b)	1155.053	677A(d)	1104.156
665C(c)	1155.053	677A(e)	1104.160
665C(d)	1155.102	677A(f)	1104.159
665D	1155.052	677A(g)	1104.153
666	1155.101	677A(h)	1104.151
667	1155.103	677A(i)	1104.154
668	1155.152	677A(j)	1104.154
669	1155.151	677B(a)	1104.157
670(a)	1155.201	677B(c)	1104.155
670(b)	1155.202	677B(d)	1104.158
670(c)	1155.202	677B(e)	1104.157
671(a)	1201.001	677B(f)	1104.157
671(b)	1201.002	678	1104.353
671(c)	1201.002	679(a)	1104.202
671(d)	1201.002, 1201.003	679(b)	1104.202
671(e)	1201.004	679(c)	1104.203
672(a)	1201.052	679A(d)	1104.209
672(b)	1201.053	679(e)	1104.207
672(c)	1201.053	679(f)	1104.202, 1104.212
672(d)	1201.054	679(g)	1104.210
672(e)	1201.051	679(h)	1104.211
673	1164.001	679(i)	1104.204
674	1164.002	679(j)	1104.201
675	1151.001	679(k)	1104.205
676(a)	1104.054	679(l)	1104.205
676(b)	1104.051	679A(a)	1104.201
676(c)	1104.052	679A(b)	1104.208
676(d)	1104.053	679A(c)	1104.206

Probate Code	Estates Code	Probate Code	Estates Code
679A(e)	1104.208	694B	1202.052
679A(f)	1104.208	694C(a)	1202.101
680	1104.054	694C(b)	1202.101
681	1104.351-357	694C(c)	1202.102
682	1101.001	694D	1202.151
682A(a)	1103.001, 1103.003	694E	1202.153
682A(a-1)	1103.002	694F	1202.152
682A(a-2)	1103.002	694G	1202.155
682A(b)	1103.004	694H	1202.156
683(a)	1102.001, 1102.004	694I	1202.157
683(b)	1102.002	694J	1202.154
683(c)	1102.005	694K	1202.103
683A	1102.003	694L	1202.102
684(a)	1101.101	695(a)	1203.102
684(b)	1101.101	695A(a)	1203.151
684(c)	1101.101, 1101.102	695A(a-1)	1203.151
684(d)	1101.154	695A(b)	1203.152
684(e)	1101.106	695A(c)	1203.153
685(a)	1101.051	696	1104.301
685(b)	1101.052	696A	1104.251
685(c)	1101.051	696B	1104.253
686	1101.053	697(a)	1104.302, 1104.303
687(a)	1101.103	697(b)	1104.303
687(b)	1101.103	697(c)	1104.304
687(c)	1101.104	697(d)	1104.305
689	1104.002	697(e)	1104.306
690	1104.001	697A(a)	1104.257
692	1101.155	697A(b)	1104.258
693(a)	1101.151	697B(a)	1104.251
693(b)	1101.152	697B(b)	1104.255
693(c)	1101.153	697B(c)	1104.256
693(d)	1101.153	697B(d)	1104.254
693(e)	1101.153	697B(e)	1104.252
694	1202.001	698(a)	1104.402
694A(a)	1202.051	698(a-1)	1104.406
694A(b)	1202.054	698(a-2)	1104.406
694A(c)	1202.054	698(a-3)	1104.406
694A(d)	1202.053	698(a-4)	1104.407
694A(e)	1202.055	698(a-5)	1104.403

Probate Code	Estates Code	Probate Code	Estates Code
698(a-6)	1104.404	709(b)	1105.202
698(b-1)	1104.408	709(c)	1105.203
698(c-1)	1104.410	710	1105.202
698(b)	1104.405	711	1105.251
698(c)	1104.409	712	1105.251
698(d)	1104.411	713	1105.252
698(e)	1104.402	714(a)	1105.252
698(f)	1104.412	714(b)	1105.253
699	1105.002	715	1105.254
700	1105.051	716	1105.255
701	1105.003, 1105.052	717	1105.257
702	1105.101	718	1105.256
702A	1105.102	719	1105.204
703(a)	1105.003, 1105.151	720	1105.204
703(b)	1105.152	721	1105.111
703(c)	1105.153	722	1105.103
703(d)	1105.154	723	1105.103
703(e)	1105.155	724	1105.103
703(f)	1105.156	725	1105.103
703(g)	1105.157	726	1105.112
703(h)	1105.157	727	1154.001
703(i)	1105.157	728	1154.003
703(j)	1105.157	729	1154.051
703(k)	1105.157	730	1154.052
703(l)	1105.158	731	1154.053
703(m)	1105.159	732	1154.002
703(n)	1105.160	733	1154.054
703(o)	1105.161	734	1154.101
703(p)	1105.160, 1105.162	735	1154.102
703(q)	1105.154	736	1154.103
703(r)	1105.163	737	1154.104
703(s)	1105.152	738	1154.055
704	1105.109	739	1154.151
705	1105.108, 1105.110	741(a)	1163.001
706	1105.104	741(b)	1163.002
707	1105.105	741(c)	1163.003, 1163.004
708	1105.106	741(d)	1163.004
708A	1105.107	741(e)	1163.005
709(a)	1105.201	741(f)	1163.005

Probate Code	Estates Code	Probate Code	Estates Code
741(g)	1163.006	759(e)	1203.106
742(a)	1163.051	759(f)	1203.101
742(b)	1163.051	759(g)	1203.201
742(c)	1163.051	759(h)	1203.107
742(d)	1163.051	760(a)	1203.001
742(e)	1163.051	760(b)	1203.002, 1203.102
742(f)	1163.052-1163.054	760(c)	1203.004
743(a)	1163.101	760(d)	1203.005
743(b)	1163.101	760(e)	1203.006
743(c)	1163.103	760(f)	1203.006
743(d)	1163.104	760(g)	1203.003
743(e)	1163.104	760A	1057.001
743(f)	1163.104	760B	1057.002
743(g)	1163.101, 1163.102	761(a)	1203.051
743(h)	1163.102	761(b)	1203.056
743(i)	1163.102	761(c)	1203.052
743(j)	1163.105	761(c-1)	1203.052
744	1163.151	761(d)	1203.053
745	1204.001	761(e)	1203.057
746	1204.051	761(f)	1203.054, 1203.102
747	1204.108	761(g)	1203.055
748	1204.052	762	1203.056
749	1204.101, 1204.102	763	1203.202
750	1204.201	764	1203.202
751	1204.105	765	1203.203
752(a)	1204.106	767	1151.051
752(b)	1204.109	768	1151.101, 1151.151
752(c)	1204.151	769	1151.004
752(d)	1204.152	770(a)	1151.052
753	1204.107	770(b)	1151.053
754	1204.053	770(c)	1151.053
755	1204.002	770(d)	1151.053
756	1204.103	770A	1151.054
757	1204.104	771	1151.152
758	1204.202	776(a-2)	1156.003
759(a)	1203.102	776(a-3)	1156.003
759(b)	1203.103	772	1151.105
759(c)	1203.104	773	1151.104
759(d)	1203.105	774(a)	1151.102

Probate Code	Estates Code	Probate Code	Estates Code
774(b)	1151.103	794	1157.003
775	1151.153	795	1157.002
776(a)	1156.001	796	1157.051
776(a-1)	1156.001	797	1157.052
776(a-2)	1156.002	798	1157.053
776(b)	1156.004	799(a)	1157.054
776A	1156.052	799(b)	1157.055
777	1156.051	799(c)	1157.056
778	1151.003	799(d)	1157.057
779	1151.155	799(e)	1157.058
780	1151.154	800	1157.063, 1157.065
781(a)	1151.201	801	1157.064
781(a-1)	1151.201	802	1157.107
781(a-2)	1151.201	803	1157.201
781(b)	1151.202	804	1157.101
781(c)	1151.202, 1151.203	805(a)	1157.103
782(a)	1151.251	805(b)	1157.103
782(b)	1151.252	805(c)	1157.105
783(a)	1153.001	806	1157.106
783(b)	1153.002	807	1157.202
783(c)	1153.001	808	1157.104
784(a)	1153.003	809	1157.108
784(b)	1153.003	811	1158.001
784(c)	1153.003	812	1158.051
784(d)	1153.003	813	1158.101, 1158.102
784(e)	1153.004	814(a)	1158.151
785	1153.005	814(b)	1158.151, 1158.152
786(a)	1157.001, 1157.060	814(c)	1158.153-1158.155
786(b)	1157.061	815	1158.103
787	1157.008	816	1158.104
788	1157.004, 1157.059	817	1158.201-1158.203
789	1157.007	818	1158.105
790	1157.006, 1157.062	819	1158.257
791	1157.005	820	1158.251
792	1157.102	821	1158.252
793(a)	1157.151	823	1158.253
793(b)	1157.151	824	1158.254
793(c)	1157.152	824A	1158.255
793(d)	1157.153	825	1158.256

Probate Code	Estates Code	Probate Code	Estates Code
826	1158.601, 1158.602	848(a)	1160.101
827(a)	1158.301, 1158.302	848(b)	1160.102
827(b)	1158.351-1158.353	849(a)	1160.151
828(a)	1158.401	849(b)	1160.151
828(b)	1158.402	849(c)	1160.152
828(c)	1158.403	849(d)	1160.153
828(d)	1158.404	849(e)	1160.154
828(e)	1158.405	849(f)	1160.155
829	1158.451	850	1160.201
830	1158.501, 1158.502	851	1160.251-1160.254
831(a)	1158.651	853(a)	1158.701
831(b)	1158.652	853(b)	1158.702,
831(c)	1158.653	853(c)	1158.703
831(d)	1158.654	853(d)	1158.704
832	1158.551	853(e)	1158.705
833	1158.552-1158.556	853(f)	1158.706
835	1158.557	854(a)	1161.001
836	1158.558	854(b)	1161.007
837	1158.559	854(c)	1161.007
839	1159.001	855(a)	1161.002
840	1159.001	855(a-1)	1161.002
841	1159.002	855(b)	1161.003
842	1159.005	855(c)	1161.004
843	1159.003	855(d)	1161.004
844	1159.004	855(e)	1161.004
845	1159.051	855(f)	1161.004
846	1159.052	855(g)	1161.005
847(a)	1160.001	855A	1161.006
847(b)	1160.051	855B(a)	1161.051
847(c)	1160.051	855B(a-1)	1161.051
847(d)	1160.052	855B(b)	1161.052
847(e)	1160.053	855B(c)	1161.053
847(f)	1160.054	855B(d)	1161.054
847(g)	1160.055	855B(e)	1161.052
847(h)	1160.056	857(a)	1161.101
847(i)	1160.056	857(b)	1161.102
847(j)	1160.057, 1160.058	857(c)	1161.104
847(k)	1160.059	857(d)	1161.103
847(m)	1160.060	857(e)	1161.103

Probate Code	Estates Code
857(f)	1161.106
857(g)	1161.103
857(h)	1161.105
857(i)	1161.104
857(j)	1161.106
858(a)	1161.202, 1161.203
858(b)	1161.202
858(c)	1161.205
858(d)	1161.203
858(e)	1161.203
858(f)	1161.203
858(g)	1161.204
860(a)	1161.151
860(b)	1161.152
860(c)	1161.153
860(d)	1161.151
861	1161.203
862	1161.204
865(a)	1162.001
865(b)	1162.002
865(c)	1162.008
865(d)	1162.002
865(f)	1162.004
865A(a)	1162.005
865A(b)	1162.005
865A(c)	1162.006
865A(d)	1162.006, 1162.007
865A(e)	1162.007
865A(f)	1162.008
865A(g)	1162.007
866(a)	1162.051
866(b)	1162.052
866(c)	1162.053
867(a)	1301.057
867(a-1)	1301.051
867(b)	1301.053
867(b-1)	1301.054
867(b-2)	1301.052
867(b-3)	1301.054

Probate Code	Estates Code
867(b-4)	1301.055
867(c)	1301.057
867(d)	1301.057
867(e)	1301.057
867(f)	1301.053, 1301.054, 1301.056
867A	1301.052
868(a)	1301.058, 1301.101
868(b)	1301.102
868(c)	1301.103
868(d)	1301.101
868(e)	1301.102
868(f)	1301.153
868A	1301.152
868B	1301.058
868C	1301.202
869	1301.201
869A	1301.155
869B	1301.002
869C	1301.151
870	1301.203
870A	1301.1535
871	1301.154
872	1301.156
873	1301.204
874	1251.002
875(a)	1251.001
875(b)	1251.001
875(c)	1251.003
875(d)	1251.004
875(e)	1251.005
875(f)(1)	1251.006, 1251.008
875(f)(2)	1251.006
875(f)(3)	1251.006
875(f)(4)	1251.006
875(f)(5)	1251.007
875(f)(6)	1251.009
875(g)	1251.010, 1251.012
875(h)	1251.151
875(i)	1251.013

Probate Code	Estates Code
875(j)	1251.011
875(k)	1251.051
875(l)	1251.052
876	1251.101
877	1251.102
878	1251.152
879	1251.152, 1251.153
881(a)	1252.051
881(b)	1252.051
881(c)	1252.052
881(d)	1252.053
881(e)	1252.054
881A	1252.055
882	1252.001-1252.003
883(a)	1353.002, 1353.003
883(b)	1353.002, 1353.003
883(c)	1353.004
883(d)	1353.005
883(e)	1353.001
883(f)	1353.001
883(g)	1353.004, 1353.005
883(h)	1353.006
883A	1353.103
883B(a)	1353.051
883B(b)	1353.052
883B(c)	1353.051
883B(d)	1353.052
883B(e)	1353.052
883C(a)	1353.101, 1353.102
883C(b)	1353.102
883C(c)	1353.102
883D	1353.151
884	1353.054
884A	1353.053
885(a)	1354.001-1354.003
885(b)	1354.004
885(c)	1354.005
885(d)	1354.006
885(e)	1354.007

Probate Code	Estates Code
885(f)	1354.008
885(g)	1354.009
887(a)	1355.001, 1355.051
887(b)	1355.052
887(c)	1355.102, 1355.103
887(d)	1355.104
887(e)	1355.002
887(f)	1355.105
887(g)	1355.151-1355.154
889(a)	1351.001, 1351.006
889(b)	1351.002
889(c)	1351.003
889(d)	1351.003
889(e)	1351.004
889(f)	1351.005
889A(a)	1352.001
889A(b)	1352.051, 1352.052, 1352.056
889A(c)	1352.053
889A(d)	1352.054
889A(e)	1352.055
889A(f)	1352.054
889A(g)	1352.057, 1352.058
889A(h)	1352.055
889A(i)	1352.055
889A(j)	1352.052
889A(k)	1352.059
890(a)	1351.051
890(b)	1351.052, 1351.053, 1351.057
890(c)	1351.053
890(d)	1351.054
890(e)	1351.054
890(f)	1351.055
890(g)	1351.056
890A(a)	1352.001
890A(b)	1352.101
890A(c)	1352.101, 1352.102, 1352.106
890A(d)	1352.103

Probate Code	Estates Code
890A(e)	1352.104
890A(f)	1352.105
890A(g)	1352.104
890A(h)	1352.104
890A(i)	1352.107
890A(j)	1352.105
890A(k)	1352.108
891(a)	1253.001
891(b)	1253.002
891(c)	1253.003
891(d)	1253.003
892(a)	1253.051
892(b)	1253.052
892(c)	1253.055
892(d)	1253.053
892(e)	1253.053
892(f)	1253.053
892(g)	1253.053
892(h)	1253.056
893	1253.054 repealed
894(a)	1253.101
894(b)	1253.102
894(c)	1253.103
894(d)	1253.102
895(a)	1253.151
895(b)	1253.152
901	1356.001
902	1356.002
903(a)	1356.051, 1356.052
903(b)	1356.051
903(c)	1356.051
903(d)	1356.055
903(e)	1356.053
904(a)	1356.001
904(b)	1356.054
905	1356.056
910	1302.001
911	1302.002
912	1302.003

Probate Code	Estates Code
913	1302.004
914	1302.005
915	1302.007
916	1302.006

CONVERSION CHART
ESTATES CODE TO PROBATE CODE

Estates Code	Probate Code
21.001	new
21.002	new
21.003	new
21.004	2(c)
21.005	new
21.006	2(a)
22.001	3
22.002	3(a)
22.003	3(kk)
22.004	3(b)
22.005	3(c)
22.006	3(d)
22.007	3(e), (g), (ii)
22.008	3(h)
22.009	3(i)
22.010	3(j)
22.011	3(k)
22.012	3(l)
22.013	3(m)
22.014	3(ll)
22.015	3(o)
22.016	3(p)
22.017	3(q)
22.018	3(r)
22.019	3(f)
22.020	3(s)
22.021	3(s)
22.022	3(t)
22.023 repealed	3(u)
22.024	3(v)
22.025	3(w)
22.026	3(jj)
22.027	3(x)
22.028	3(z)
22.029	3(bb)

Estates Code	Probate Code
22.030	3(dd)
22.031	3(aa)
22.032	3(ee)
22.033	3(mm)
22.034	3(ff)
31.001	3(bb)
31.002	4B
32.001	4A
32.002	4C
32.003	4D
32.004	4E
32.005	4F
32.006	4G
32.007	4H
33.001	6
33.002	6A
33.003	6B
33.004	6C
33.005	6D
33.051	8(a)
33.052	8(a)
33.053	8(b)
33.054	8(e)
33.055	8(a)
33.101	8(c)(1), 8A(a)
33.102	8(c)(1), 8A(a)
33.103	8(c)(2), 8A(b)
33.104	8(d), 8B
34.001	5B
34.002	5C
51.001	33(a), (b)
51.002	33(c)
51.003	33(c)
51.051	33(f)(1)

Estates Code	Probate Code
51.052	33(f)(4)
51.053	33(f)(2)
51.054	33(f)(3)
51.055	34
51.056	33(e)
51.101	33(f)(1)
51.102	33(h)
51.103	33(i)
51.104	33(g)
51.151	33(d)
51.201	35
51.202	33(j)
51.203	22
52.001	13
52.002	14
52.003	16
52.004	17
52.051	11, 13(e)
52.052	15
52.053	17A
53.001	24
53.051	12(a)
53.052	12(b), (c)
53.053	11A
53.054	11B
53.101	19
53.102	20
53.103	23
53.104	34A
53.105 repealed	23
53.106	25
53.107	new
54.001	10C
54.002	9
54.051	22
54.052	18
55.001	10
55.002	21
55.051	10A(a)

Estates Code	Probate Code
55.052	10A(a)
55.053	10A(b)
55.101	10B
55.102	10B
55.151	26
55.152	26
55.201	27
55.202	27
55.203	27
55.251	31
55.252	31
56.001	221A
56.002	221B
101.001	37
101.002	46(a)
101.003	37
101.051	37
101.052	155, 156
102.001	42(c)
102.002	282
102.003	283
102.004	270
102.005	284
102.006	285
111.001	46(a)
111.002	46(b)
111.051	450(a), (c)
111.052	450(a)
111.053	450(b)
111.054	new
112.001	new
112.002	462
112.051	451
112.052	452
112.053	456(a), 458
112.054	455
112.101	456(a), (d)
112.102	456(b)
112.103	456(c)

Estates Code	Probate Code	Estates Code	Probate Code
112.104	457	113.157	440
112.105	458	113.158	441
112.106	459	113.201	443
112.151	453	113.202	444
112.152	454	113.203	445
112.201	460(f)	113.204	446
112.202	460(f)	113.205	447
112.203	460(a)	113.206	438A(f)
112.204	460(b)	113.207	445
112.205	460(d)	113.208	438A(f), (g)
112.206	460(c)	113.209	448
112.207	460(e)	113.210	449
112.208	460(g)	113.251	442
112.251	461	113.252	442
112.252	461	113.253	442
112.253	461	114.001	new
113.001	436(1), (2), (3), (8), (9), (11), (12), (13), (15)	114.002	new
113.002	436(7)	114.003	new
113.003	436(6), 444	114.004	new
113.004	436(4), (5), (10), (14), 438A(a)	114.005	new
		114.006	new
113.005	444	114.051	new
113.051	439A(a)	114.052	new
113.052	439A(b)	114.053	new
113.053	439A(c), (d)	114.054	new
113.0531	new	114.055	new
113.101	437	114.056	new
113.102	438(a)	114.057	new
113.103	438(b)	114.101	new
113.104	438(c)	114.102	new
113.105	438A(b), (c), (e)	114.103	new
113.106	438B	114.104	new
113.151	439(a)	114.105	new
113.152	439(b)	114.106	new
113.153	439(c)	114.151	new
113.154	438A(d)	114.152	new
113.1541	438B(c)	121.001	47(f)
113.155	439(d)	121.051	47(a)
113.156	440	121.052	47(a)

Estates Code	Probate Code
121.053	47(a)
121.101	47(c)
121.102	47(c)
121.151	47(b)
121.152	47(d)
121.153	47(e)
122.001	37A(e)
122.002	37A(a)
122.003 repealed	37A(b)
122.004 repealed	37A(k)
122.005 repealed	37A(j)
122.051 repealed	37A(g)
122.052 repealed	37A(h)
122.053 repealed	37A(h)
122.054 repealed	37A(h)
122.055 repealed	37A(h)
122.056 repealed	37A(i)
122.057 repealed	37A(p)
122.101 repealed	37A(c)
122.102 repealed	37A(d)
122.103 repealed	37A(f)
122.104 repealed	37A(n)
122.105 repealed	37A(o)
122.106 repealed	37A(o)
122.107 repealed	new
122.151 repealed	37A(l)
122.152 repealed	37A(l)
122.153 repealed	37A(m)
122.201	37B(a)
122.202	37B(b)
122.203 repealed	37B(b)
122.204	37B(c)
122.205	37B(d)
122.206	37B(e)
123.001	69(a), (b)
123.002	69(c)
123.051	471
123.052	472(a)
123.053	472(b)

Estates Code	Probate Code
123.054	473(a)
123.055	473(b)
123.101	47A(a)
123.102	47A(b), (c)
123.103	47A(d), (e)
123.104	47A(f)
123.151	new
124.001	322A(a), (s)
124.002	322A(x)
124.003	322A(l)
124.004	322A(p)
124.005	322A(b)
124.006	322A(c), (d), (e), (f)
124.007	322A(g)
124.008	322A(h)
124.009	322A(i)
124.010	322A(k), (m)
124.011	322A(q)
124.012	322A(r)
124.013	322A(t)
124.014	322A(n)
124.015	322A(o), (u)
124.016	322A(v)
124.017	322A(w)
124.018	322A(y)
124.051	378A(b)
124.052	378A(a)
151.001	36B
151.002	36C
151.003	36D
151.004	36E
151.005	36F
152.001	108, 109, 110
152.002	111(a), 112
152.003	111(b)
152.004	108
152.051	113(a)
152.052	113(b)
152.053	114(a)

Estates Code	Probate Code	Estates Code	Probate Code
152.054	113(c)	202.053	50(c)
152.055	113(d), 114(b)	202.054	50(a)
152.101	115(a), (b)	202.055	50(d)
152.102	115(c), (d)	202.056	50(e)
153.001	new	202.057	new
153.002	new	202.101	51
153.003	new	202.102	51
201.001	38(a)	202.103	51
201.002	38(b)	202.151	53(a)
201.003	45	202.201	54
201.051	42(a)	202.202	55(a)
201.052	42(b)(1)	202.203	55(a)
201.053	42(b)(2)	202.204	55(b)
201.054	40	202.205	55(c)
201.055	42(d)	202.206	56
201.056	41(a)	203.001	52
201.057	41(b)	203.002	52A
201.058	41(d)	204.001	53E
201.059	41(d)	204.051	53A(a)
201.060	41(c)	204.052	53A(b)
201.061	41(d)	204.053	53A(c), (d)
201.062	41(e), (f)	204.054	53A(e)
201.101	43	204.055	53A(f)
201.102	39	204.056	53A(g)
201.103	39	204.101	53B(a)
201.151	44(a), (b)	204.102	53B(b)
201.152	44(c)	204.103	53B(c)
202.001	48(a)	204.151	53C(a)
202.002	48(a)	204.152	53C(b), (c)
202.003 repealed	48(a), (c)	204.153	53C(d)
202.0025	new	204.201	53D
202.004	49(a)	205.001	137(a)
202.005	49(a)	205.002	137(a)
202.006	48(b)	205.003	137(a)
202.007	49(b)	205.004	137(a)
202.008	49(b)	205.005	137(d)
202.009	53(b), (c)	205.006	137(c)
202.051	50(a)	205.007	138
202.052	50(b)	205.008	137(b)

Estates Code	Probate Code
205.009	new
251.001	57
251.002	58(a), (b)
251.051	59(a)
251.052	59(a), 60
251.053	new
251.101	59(b)
251.102	59(a), (c)
251.103	59(a)
251.104	59(a), (b)
251.1045	59(a-1)
251.105	59(b)
251.106	59(c)
251.107	60
252.001	71(a)
252.002	71(b)
252.003	71(a)
252.004	71(c)
252.051	71(d)
252.052	71(d)
252.101	71(e)
252.102	71(e)
252.103	71(e)
252.104	71(e)
252.105	71(e)
252.151	71(f)
252.152	71(f)
252.153	71(g)
252.201	75
252.202	75
252.203	75
252.204	75
253.001	69A
253.002	63
254.001	58a
254.002	61, 62
254.003	58(b)
254.004	59A
254.005	64

Estates Code	Probate Code
255.001	58(d)
255.002	58(c)
255.003	58(c)
255.051	67(c)
255.052	67(a), (d)
255.053	67(a)(1)
255.054	67(a)(2)
255.055	67(b)
255.056	67(e)
255.101	37C(a)
255.102	37C(b)
255.151	68(e)
255.152	68(b), (c), (d)
255.153	68(a)
255.154	68(a)
255.201 repealed	70
255.251	70A(c)
255.252	70A(a)
255.253	70A(b)
255.301	71A(a)
255.302	71A(b)
255.303	71A(c)
255.304	new
255.351	58c
254.401	new
255.451	new
255.452	new
255.453	new
255.454	new
255.455	new
256.001	94
256.002	72(a)
256.003	73
256.051	76
256.052	81(a)
256.053	81(a)
256.054	81(b)
256.101	83(a)
256.102	83(b)

Estates Code	Probate Code	Estates Code	Probate Code
256.103	83(c)	301.203	80(c)
256.151	88(a)	303.001	128(a)
256.152	84(a), 88(b)	303.002	128(c)
256.153	84(b)	303.003	129A
256.154	84(c)	304.001	77
256.155	84(d)	304.002	79
256.156	85	304.003	78
256.157	87	305.001	new
256.201	89	305.002	189
256.202	90	305.003	192
256.203	91	305.004	new
256.204	93	305.051	190(a)
257.001	89C(a)	305.052	190(b)
257.051	89A(a)	305.053	190(c)
257.052	89A(a)	305.054	190(d), 192
257.053	89A(b)	305.055	190(d)
257.054	89B	305.101	194, 195
257.101	89C(b)	305.102	214, 215, 216, 217
257.102	89C(c)	305.103	198
257.103	89C(d)	305.104	199
258.001	128(a)	305.105	200
258.002	128(b)	305.106	194
258.003	128(c)	305.107	197
258.051	128B(a), (b), (c)	305.108	196
258.052	128B(d)	305.109	197
258.053	128B(e)	305.110	213
258.101	129A	305.111	218
301.001	72(a)	305.151	194(1), (2)
301.002	74	305.152	194(3)
301.051	76	305.153	194(4), (13)
301.052	82	305.154	194(5)
301.101	179	305.155	194(6)
301.151	88(a)	305.156	194(7), (8(b), (c), (d))
301.152	88(c)	305.157	194(8(a))
301.153	88(d), 180	305.158	194(8(e))
301.154	88(e)	305.159	194(9)
301.155	new	305.160	194(14)
301.201	80(a), (b)	305.201	194(10), (12)
301.202	80(b)	305.202	194(11)

Estates Code	Probate Code
305.203	201(a)
305.204	201(b), 202
305.205	201(c)
305.206	211, 212
305.207	194(12)
305.251	203, 204
305.252	205, 206(a)
305.253	206(b)
305.254	207
305.255	208
305.256	210
305.257	209
306.001	178(a), (c)
306.002	178(b)
306.003	181
306.004	182
306.005	183
306.006	187
306.007	186
307.001	188
307.002	240
308.001	128A(a)
308.0015	128A(a-1)
308.002	128A(b), (c), (d), (f)
308.003	128A(e)
308.004	128A(g), (h)
308.051	294(a), (c)
308.052	294(b)
308.053	295
308.054	294(d)
308.055	296
308.056	297
309.001	248
309.002	253
309.003	249
309.051	250
309.052	251
309.053	252
309.054	255

Estates Code	Probate Code
309.055	260
309.056	250(c), (d), (e)
309.057	new
309.101	256
309.102	257
309.103	258
309.104	259
309.151	261
310.001	378B(h)
310.002	378B(i)
310.003	378B(a)
310.004	378B(b), (c), (d)
310.005	378B(g)
310.006	378B(h)
351.001	32
351.002	29
351.003	245
351.051	234(a)
351.052	234(b)
351.053	28
351.054	233A
351.101	230
351.102	232
351.103	235
351.104	238A
351.105	398A
351.151	233(a)
351.152	233(b), (c), (d)
351.153	233(e)
351.201	238(a)
351.202	238(b), (f)
351.203	238(c), (d), (e)
351.204	238(g)
351.205	238(h), (i)
351.251	329(a)
351.252	329(b), (c)
351.253	329(c)
351.301	239
351.302	239

Estates Code	Probate Code
351.303	239
351.351	145(q), 154A(i)
351.352	36(a)
351.353	36(a)
351.354	36(a)
351.355	36(b)
352.001	241(b)
352.002	241(a)
352.003	241(a)
352.004	241(a)
352.051	242
352.052	243
352.053	244
353.001	42(c)
353.051	271
353.052	272
353.053	273
353.054	275
353.055	274
353.056	274
353.101	286, 288
353.102	287
353.103	289
353.104	290
353.105	291
353.106	292
353.107	292, 293
353.151	277
353.152	278
353.153	279
353.154	280
353.155	281
354.001	143
354.051	262
354.052	263
354.053	264
354.054	265
354.055	266
354.056	267

Estates Code	Probate Code
354.057	268
354.058	269
355.001	298(a)
355.002	308
355.003	307
355.004	301
355.005	304
355.006	303
355.007	302
355.008	299
355.051	309
355.052	310
355.053	311
355.054	312(a)
355.055	312(b)
355.056	312(c)
355.057	312(d)
355.058	312(e)
355.059	301
355.060	298(a)
355.061	298(b)
355.062	303
355.063	318
355.064	313
355.065	314
355.066	313
355.101	319
355.102	322
355.103	320(a)
355.104	320(b)
355.105	320(c)
355.106	320(d)
355.107	326
355.108	321
355.109	322B
355.110	320A
355.111	315
355.112	323
355.113	328

Estates Code	Probate Code
355.151	306(a)
355.152	306(b)
355.153	306(c), (c-1)
355.154	306(d)
355.155	306(e)
355.1551	new
355.156	306(f)
355.157	306(g)
355.158	306(h), (i)(1), (j)
355.159	306(i)(2)
355.160	306(k)
355.201	317
355.202	316
355.203	324
356.001	331
356.002	332
356.051	333
356.101	334
356.102	334
356.103	336
356.104	337
356.105	339
356.151	335
356.152	335
356.153	335
356.154	335
356.155	335
356.201	338
356.202	338
356.203	338
356.251	341
356.252	342
356.253	344
356.254	345
356.255	345A
356.256	346
356.257	340
356.301	348(a)
356.302	348(a)

Estates Code	Probate Code
356.351	348(b)
356.352	348(b)
356.353	348(b)
356.401	349(a)
356.402	349(b)
356.403	349(c)
356.404	349(d)
356.405	349(e)
356.451	350
356.501	351
356.502	351
356.551	353
356.552	355
356.553	354
356.554	354
356.555	354
356.556	355
356.557	356
356.558	357
356.559	358
356.601	347
356.602	347
356.651	352(a)
356.652	352(b)
356.653	352(c)
356.654	352(d)
356.655	352(e)
357.001	359, 360
357.002	361
357.003	363
357.004	364
357.005	362
357.051	365
357.052	366
358.001	367(a); new
358.051	367(b), (c)
358.052	367(c)
358.053	367(c)
358.054	367(c)

Estates Code	Probate Code	Estates Code	Probate Code
358.055	367(c)	360.153	380(c)
358.056	367(c)	360.154	380(d)
358.057	367(c)	360.155	380(e)
358.058	367(c)	360.156	380(f)
358.059	367(c)	360.157	380(g)
358.060	367(c)	360.201	381(a)
358.101	368(a)	360.202	381(b), (c)
358.102	368(b)	360.203	381(d)
358.151	369(a), (b)	360.251	379
358.152	369(b)	360.252	382
358.153	369(b)	360.253	385
358.154	369(b)	360.254	386
358.155	369(b)	360.301	384
358.201	370	361.001	221(a)
358.251	371	361.002	221(b)
358.252	371	361.003	221(c)
358.253	371	361.004	221(d)
358.254	371	361.005	221(e), (f)
359.001	399(a)	361.051	222(a)(1)
359.002	399(b)	361.052	222(b)
359.003	399(c)	361.053	222(c)
359.004	399(c)	361.054	222(a)(2), 222A
359.005	399(d)	361.101	220(f)
359.006	402	361.102	220(a)
359.051	401(a), (b), (c), (d)	361.103	220(b)
359.052	401(e)	361.104	220(c)
359.053	401(e)	361.105	220(d)
359.054	401(e)	361.106	220(e)
359.101	400	361.151	220(g)
359.102	403	361.152	223
360.001	373(a), (b)	361.153	224, 225
360.002	373(c)	361.154	226
360.051	374	361.155	227
360.052	375	362.001	404
360.101	377	362.002	92
360.102	378	362.003	405
360.103	387	362.004	405
360.151	380(a)	362.005	407
360.152	380(b)	362.006	408(a)

Estates Code	Probate Code
362.007	405A
362.008	412
362.009	409
362.010	410
362.011	408(b)
362.012	408(c)
362.013	408(d)
362.051	406
362.052	414
401.001	145(b), (o)
401.002	145(c), (d)
401.003	145(e), (g)
401.004	145(f), (i), (j), (k), (l), (m), (n)
401.005	145(p)
401.006	145A
401.007	145(q)
401.008	145(r)
402.001	145(h)
402.002	145B
402.051	145C(a)
402.052	145C(b)
402.053	145C(c)
402.054	145C(d)
403.001	146(a)(4)
403.051	146(a)(1)-(3), (a-1)
403.052	146(b)
403.053	146(b-1)
403.054	146(b-2)
403.055	146(b-3)
403.056	146(b-4), (b-5)
403.057	146(b-6)
403.058	146(b-7)
403.0585	146(c)
403.059	147
403.060	148
404.001	149A
404.002	149
404.003	new
404.0035	149C

Estates Code	Probate Code
404.0036	149C
404.0037	149C
404.004	154
404.005	154A
405.001	149B
405.002	151(e)
405.003	149D, 149E, 149F
405.004	151(a)
405.005	151(a-1)
405.006	151(b)
405.007	151(c), (d)
405.008	150
405.009	152
405.010	153
405.011	149G
405.012	new
451.001	139
451.002	140
451.003	141
451.004	142
452.001	131A(a)
452.002	131A(b)
452.003	131A(a), (c)
452.004	131A(d)
452.005	131A(e)
452.006	131A(f), (g), (h)
452.007	131A(i)
452.008	131A(j)
452.051	132(a)
452.052	132(b)
452.101	133
452.102	133
452.151	134
452.152	135
453.001	155
453.002	155
453.003	160(a), (c)
453.004	160(b), (c)
453.005	176

Estates Code	Probate Code	Estates Code	Probate Code
453.006	156, 168	503.003	96
453.007	168	503.051	98
453.008	168	503.052	99
453.009	177	504.001	100(a)
454.001	72(a)	504.002	100(b)
454.002	72(a)	504.003	95(d)(2), 100(c)
454.003	72(b)	504.004	100(b)
454.004	72(a)	504.051	101
454.051	72(a)	504.052	101
454.052	72(a)	504.053	102
455.001	new	505.001	105A(a)
455.002	new	505.002	105A(c), (d)
455.003	new	505.003	105A(a)
455.004	new	505.004	105A(b)
455.005	new	505.005	105A(b)
455.006	new	505.006	105A(e)
455.007	new	505.051	106
455.008	new	505.052	95(c), 107
455.009	new	505.101	107A(a), (b)
455.010	new	505.102	107A(c)
455.011	new	505.103	107A(d)
455.012	new	551.001	427
456.001	new	551.002	427
456.002	new	551.003	427
456.003	new	551.004	427
456.004	new	551.005	428
456.005	new	551.006	430
501.001	95(a)	551.051	433(a)
501.002	95(b)(1), (2), (c)	551.052	433(a), (b), (c)
501.003	95(b)(1), (2)	551.053	433(c)
501.004	95(d)(1), (2)	551.054	433(d)
501.005	95(d)(1), (2)	551.055	433(b)
501.006	105	551.101	429
501.007	95(e)	551.102	431
501.008	95(f)	551.103	432
502.001	103	751.001	481
502.002	104	751.002	482
503.001	96, 97	751.003	506
503.002	95(c)	751.004	483

Estates Code	Probate Code	Estates Code	Probate Code
751.005	489B(i)	1001.003	603(b)
751.006	489B(j)	1002.001	601
751.051	484	1002.0015	new
751.052	485	1002.002	601(1)
751.053	485A	1002.003	601(2)
751.054	486	1002.004	601(3)
751.055	487(a), (b), (c), (d)	1002.005	601(4)
751.056	487(e)	1002.006	601(5)
751.057	487A	1002.007	601(6)
751.058	488	1002.008	601(8), (29)
751.101	489B(a)	1002.009	601(7)
751.102	489B(b)	1002.010	601(9)
751.103	489B(c), (f)	1002.011	601(10)
751.104	489B(d), (e)	1002.012	601(11)
751.105	489B(g)	1002.013	601(12)
751.106	489B(h)	1002.014	601(12-a)
751.151	489	1002.015	601(25)
752.001	490(a)	1002.016	601(13)
752.002	490(a)	1002.017	601(14)
752.003	490(a)	1002.018	601(15)
752.004	490(b)	1002.019	601(16)
752.051	490(a)	1002.020	601(18)
752.101	491	1002.021	601(19)
752.102	492	1002.022	601(20)
752.103	493	1002.023	601(21)
752.104	494	1002.024	601(22)
752.105	495	1002.025	601(24)
752.106	496	1002.026	601(27)
752.107	497	1002.027	601(28)
752.108	498	1002.028	601(23)
752.109	499	1002.029	601(30)
752.110	500	1002.030	601(31)
752.111	501	1002.031	new
752.112	502	1021.001	606A
752.113	503	1022.001	605
752.114	504	1022.002	605, 607A
752.115	505	1022.003	607B
1001.001	602	1022.004	607C
1001.002	603(a)	1022.005	607D

Estates Code	Probate Code	Estates Code	Probate Code
1022.006	607E	1052.004	627
1022.007	608	1052.051	621, 623(b)
1022.008	609	1052.052	625
1023.001	610	1052.053	627A
1023.002	611	1053.001	651
1023.003	612	1053.051	622(a)
1023.004	613	1053.052	622(b), (c)
1023.005	614	1053.101	629
1023.006	615	1053.102	630
1023.007	616	1053.103	650
1023.008	617	1053.104	new
1023.009	618	1053.105	new
1023.010	619	1054.001	646(a)
1051.001	632(a), (b)	1054.002	646(e)
1051.002	632(c)	1054.003	646(a)
1051.003	632(c)	1054.004	647
1051.051	632(f)(1)	1054.005	646(d)
1051.052	632(f)(4)	1054.006	new
1051.053	632(f)(2)	1054.007	new
1051.054	632(f)(3)	1054.051	645(a)
1051.055	634	1054.052	645(e)
1051.056	632(e)	1054.053	645(f)
1051.101	633(a), (g)	1054.054	645(c)
1051.102	633(b)	1054.055	645(b), (d)
1051.103	633(c)	1054.056	645A
1051.104	633(d), (d-1), (f)	1054.101	648(f)
1051.105	633(e)	1054.102	648(a)
1051.106	633(f)	1054.103	648(b)
1051.151	632(f)(1)	1054.104	648(c), (d)
1051.152	632(h)	1054.105	648(a), (e)
1051.153	632(i)	1054.151	648A(a)
1051.154	632(g)	1054.152	648A(b)
1051.201	632(d)	1054.153	648A(c)
1051.251	635	1054.154	648A(d)
1051.252	632(j)	1054.155	new
1051.253	649	1054.201	646(b), 647A(a), (b)
1052.001	623(a)	1054.202	647A(c), (e)
1052.002	624	1054.203	646(c), 647A(d)
1052.003	626	1055.001	642

Estates Code	Probate Code	Estates Code	Probate Code
1055.002	641	1103.002	682A(a-1), (a-2)
1055.003	new	1103.003	682A(a)
1055.051	644	1103.004	682A(b)
1055.052	643	1104.001	690
1055.053	652	1104.002	689
1055.101	649	1104.051	676(b)
1055.102	628	1104.052	676(c)
1055.151	new	1104.053	676(d), (e), (f)
1056.001	653	1104.054	676(a), 680
1056.051	654	1104.101	677(a)
1056.052	654	1104.102	677(a)
1056.101	657	1104.103	677(b), (c), (d)
1056.102	657	1104.151	677A(h), 677B(a)
1057.001	760A	1104.152	677A(a), (b), (c)
1057.002	760B	1104.153	677A(g)
1101.001	682	1104.154	677A(i), (j)
1101.002	new	1104.155	677B(c)
1101.051	685(a), (c)	1104.156	677A(d)
1101.052	685(b)	1104.157	677B(b), (e), (f)
1101.053	686	1104.158	677B(d)
1101.101	684(a), (b), (c)	1104.159	677A(f)
1101.102	684(c)	1104.160	677A(e)
1101.103	687(a), (b)	1104.201	679(j), 679A(a)
1101.104	687(c)	1104.202	679(a), (b), (f)
1101.105	602	1104.203	679(a), (c), (d)
1101.106	684(e)	1104.204	679(i)
1101.151	693(a)	1104.205	679(k), (l)
1101.152	693(b)	1104.206	679A(c)
1101.153	693(c), (d), (e)	1104.207	679(e)
1101.154	684(d)	1104.208	679A(b), (e), (f)
1101.155	692	1104.209	679A(d)
1101.156	new	1104.210	679(g)
1102.001	683(a)	1104.211	679(h)
1102.002	683(b)	1104.212	679(f)
1102.003	683A	1104.251	696A, 697B(a)
1102.004	683(a)	1104.252	697B(e)
1102.005	683(c)	1104.253	696B
1102.006	new	1104.254	697B(d)
1103.001	682A(a)	1104.255	697B(b)

Estates Code	Probate Code	Estates Code	Probate Code
1104.256	697B(c)	1105.106	708
1104.257	697A(a)	1105.107	708A
1104.258	697A(b)	1105.108	705
1104.301	696	1105.109	704
1104.302	697(a)	1105.110	705
1104.303	697(a), (b)	1105.111	721
1104.304	697(c)	1105.112	726
1104.305	697(d)	1105.151	703(a)
1104.306	697(e)	1105.152	703(b), (s)
1104.351	681	1105.153	703(c)
1104.352	681	1105.154	703(d), (q)
1104.353	678, 681	1105.155	703(e)
1104.354	681	1105.156	703(f)
1104.355	681	1105.157	703(g), (h), (i), (j), (k)
1104.356	681	1105.158	703(l)
1104.357	681	1105.159	703(m)
1104.358	new	1105.160	703(n), (p)
1104.401	new	1105.161	703(o)
1104.402	698(a), (e)	1105.162	703(p)
1104.403	698(a-5)	1105.163	703(r)
1104.404	698(a-6)	1105.201	709(a)
1104.405	698(b)	1105.202	709(b), 710
1104.406	698(a-1), (a-2), (a-3)	1105.203	709(c)
1104.407	698(a-4)	1105.204	719, 720
1104.408	698(b-1)	1105.251	711, 712
1104.409	698(c)	1105.252	713, 714(a)
1104.410	698(c-1)	1105.253	714(b)
1104.411	698(d)	1105.254	715
1104.412	698(f)	1105.255	716
1105.001	new	1105.256	718
1105.002	699	1105.257	717
1105.003	701, 703(a)	1106.001	659(a)
1105.051	700	1106.002	659(b)
1105.052	701	1106.003	659(c), (d)
1105.101	702	1106.004	661
1105.102	702A	1106.005	660
1105.103	722, 723, 724, 725	1106.006	663
1105.104	706	1151.001	675
1105.105	707	1151.002	662

Estates Code	Probate Code	Estates Code	Probate Code
1151.003	778	1154.055	738
1151.004	769	1154.101	734
1151.051	767	1154.102	735
1151.052	770(a)	1154.103	736
1151.053	770(b), (c), (d)	1154.104	737
1151.054	770A	1154.151	739
1151.055	new	1155.001	665(h)
1151.056	new	1155.002	665(a), (g)
1151.101	768	1155.003	665(b)
1151.102	774(a)	1155.004	665(a-1)
1151.103	774(b)	1155.005	665(f)
1151.104	773	1155.006	665(c), (d)
1151.105	772	1155.007	665(d), (d-1)
1151.151	768	1155.008	665(e)
1151.152	771	1155.051 [repealed]	665A
1151.153	775	1155.052	665D
1151.154	780	1155.053	665(C)(a), (b), (c)
1151.155	779	1155.054	665A; 665B
1151.201	781(a), (a-1), (a-2)	1155.101	666
1151.202	781(b), (c)	1155.102	665C(d)
1151.203	781(c)	1155.103	667
1151.251	782(a)	1155.151	669
1151.252	782(b)	1155.152	668
1151.301	636	1155.201	670(a)
1151.351	new	1155.202	670(b), (c)
1152.001	655	1156.001	776(a), (a-1)
1152.002	656	1156.002	776(a-2)
1153.001	783(a), (c)	1156.003	776(a-2), (a-3)
1153.002	783(b)	1156.004	776(b)
1153.003	784(a), (b), (c), (d)	1156.051	777
1153.004	784(e)	1156.052	776A
1153.005	785	1157.001	786(a)
1154.001	727	1157.002	795
1154.002	732	1157.003	794
1154.003	728	1157.004	788
1154.051	729	1157.005	791
1154.052	730	1157.006	790
1154.053	731	1157.007	789
1154.054	733	1157.008	787

Estates Code	Probate Code		Estates Code	Probate Code
1157.051	796		1158.155	814(c)
1157.052	797		1158.201	817
1157.053	798		1158.202	817
1157.054	799(a)		1158.203	817
1157.055	799(b)		1158.251	820
1157.056	799(c)		1158.252	821
1157.057	799(d)		1158.253	823
1157.058	799(e)		1158.254	824
1157.059	788		1158.255	824A
1157.060	786(a)		1158.256	825
1157.061	786(b)		1158.257	819
1157.062	790		1158.301	827(a)
1157.063	800		1158.302	827(a)
1157.064	801		1158.351	827(b)
1157.065	800		1158.352	827(b)
1157.101	804		1158.353	827(b)
1157.102	792		1158.401	828(a)
1157.103	805(a), (b)		1158.402	828(b)
1157.104	808		1158.403	828(c)
1157.105	805(c)		1158.404	828(d)
1157.106	806		1158.405	828(e)
1157.107	802		1158.451	829
1157.108	809		1158.501	830
1157.151	793(a), (b)		1158.502	830
1157.152	793(c)		1158.551	832
1157.153	793(d)		1158.552	834
1157.201	803		1158.553	833
1157.202	807		1158.554	833
1158.001	811		1158.555	833
1158.051	812		1158.556	834
1158.101	813		1158.557	835
1158.102	813		1158.558	836
1158.103	815		1158.559	837
1158.104	816		1158.601	826
1158.105	818		1158.602	826
1158.151	814(a), (b)		1158.651	831(a)
1158.152	814(b)		1158.652	831(b)
1158.153	814(c)		1158.653	831(c)
1158.154	814(c)		1158.654	831(d)

Estates Code	Probate Code	Estates Code	Probate Code
1158.701	853(a)	1161.004	855(c), (d), (e), (f)
1158.702	853(b)	1161.005	855(g)
1158.703	853(c)	1161.006	855A
1158.704	853(d)	1161.007	854(b), (c)
1158.705	853(e)	1161.008	863
1158.706	853(f)	1161.051	855B(a), (a-1)
1159.001	839, 840	1161.052	855B(b), (e)
1159.002	841	1161.053	855B(c)
1159.003	843	1161.054	855B(d)
1159.004	844	1161.101	857(a)
1159.005	842	1161.102	857(b)
1159.051	845	1161.103	857(d), (e), (g)
1159.052	846	1161.104	857(c), (i)
1160.001	847(a); new	1161.105	857(h)
1160.051	847(b), (c)	1161.106	857(f), (j)
1160.052	847(d)	1161.151	860(a), (d)
1160.053	847(e)	1161.152	860(b)
1160.054	847(f)	1161.153	860(c)
1160.055	847(g)	1161.201	858(h)
1160.056	847(h), (i)	1161.202	858(a), (b)
1160.057	847(j)	1161.203	858(a), (d), (e), (f), 861
1160.058	847(j)	1161.204	858(g), 862
1160.059	847(k)	1161.205	858(c)
1160.060	847(m)	1162.001	865(a)
1160.101	848(a)	1162.002	865(b), (d)
1160.102	848(b)	1162.003	865(e)
1160.151	849(a), (b)	1162.004	865(f)
1160.152	849(c)	1162.005	865A(a), (b)
1160.153	849(d)	1162.006	865A(c), (d)
1160.154	849(e)	1162.007	865A(d), (e), (g)
1160.155	849(f)	1162.008	865(c), 865A(f)
1160.201	850	1162.051	866(a)
1160.251	851	1162.052	866(b)
1160.252	851	1162.053	866(c)
1160.253	851	1163.001	741(a)
1160.254	851	1163.002	741(b)
1161.001	854(a)	1163.003	741(c)
1161.002	855(a), (a-1)	1163.004	741(c), (d)
1161.003	855(b)	1163.005	741(e), (f)

Estates Code	Probate Code	Estates Code	Probate Code
1163.006	741(g)	1202.201	new
1163.051	742(a), (b), (cd), (d), (e)	1203.001	760(a)
1163.052	742(f)	1203.002	760(b)
1163.053	742(f)	1203.003	760(g)
1163.054	742(f)	1203.004	760(c)
1163.101	743(a), (b), (g)	1203.005	760(d)
1163.1011	new	1203.006	760(e), (f)
1163.102	743(g), (h), (i)	1203.051	761(a)
1163.103	743(c)	1203.052	761(c), (c-1)
1163.104	743(d), (e), (f)	1203.053	761(d)
1163.105	743(j)	1203.0531	new
1163.151	744	1203.054	761(f)
1164.001	673	1203.055	761(g)
1164.002	674	1203.056	761(b), 762
1201.001	671(a)	1203.057	761(e)
1201.002	671(b), (c), (d)	1203.101	759(f)
1201.003	671(d)	1203.102	695(a), 759(a), 760(b), 761(f)
1201.004	671(e)	1203.103	759(b)
1201.051	672(e)	1203.104	759(c)
1201.052	672(a)	1203.105	759(d)
1201.053	672(b), (c)	1203.106	759(e)
1201.054	672(d)	1203.107	759(h)
1202.001	694	1203.108	695(c), (d), (e)
1202.002	676(g), 677(e)	1203.151	695A(a), (a-1)
1202.051	694A(a)	1203.152	695A(b)
1202.052	694B	1203.153	695A(c)
1202.053	694A(d)	1203.201	759(g)
1202.054	694A(b), (c)	1203.202	695(b), 763, 764
1202.055	694A(e)	1203.203	765
1202.101	694C(a), (b)	1204.001	745
1202.102	694C(c), 694L	1204.002	755
1202.103	694K	1204.051	746
1202.151	694D	1204.052	748
1202.152	694F	1204.053	754
1202.153	694E	1204.101	749
1202.154	694J	1204.102	749
1202.155	694G	1204.103	756
1202.156	694H	1204.104	757
1202.157	694I	1204.105	751

Estates Code	Probate Code		Estates Code	Probate Code
1204.106	752(a)		1253.051	892(a)
1204.107	753		1253.052	892(b)
1204.108	747		1253.053	892(d), (e), (f), (g)
1204.109	752(b)		1253.054 repealed	893
1204.151	752(c)		1253.055	892(c)
1204.152	752(d)		1253.056	892(h)
1204.201	750		1253.101	894(a)
1204.202	758		1253.102	894(b), (d)
1251.001	875(a), (b)		1253.103	894(c)
1251.002	874		1253.151	895(a)
1251.003	875(c)		1253.152	895(b)
1251.004	875(d)		1301.001	new
1251.005	875(e)		1301.002	869B
1251.006	875(f)(1), (2), (3), (4)		1301.051	867(a-1)
1251.007	875(f)(5)		1301.052	867(b-2), 867A
1251.008	875(f)(1)		1301.053	867(b), (f)
1251.009	875(f)(6)		1301.054	867(b-1), (b-3), (f)
1251.010	875(g)		1301.055	867 (b-4)
1251.011	875(j)		1301.056	867(f)
1251.012	875(g)		1301.057	867(a), (b-5), (c), (d), (e)
1251.013	875(i)		1301.058	868(a), 868B
1251.051	875(k)		1301.101	868(a), (d)
1251.052	875(l)		1301.102	868(b), (e)
1251.101	876		1301.103	868(c)
1251.102	877		1301.151	869C
1251.151	875(h)		1301.152	868A
1251.152	878, 879		1301.153	868(f)
1251.153	879		1301.1535	870A
1252.001	882		1301.154	871
1252.002	882		1301.155	869A
1252.003	882		1301.156	872
1252.051	881(a), (b)		1301.201	869
1252.052	881(c)		1301.202	868C
1252.053	881(d)		1301.203	870
1252.054	881(e)		1301.204	873
1252.055	881A		1302.001	910
1253.001	891(a)		1302.002	911
1253.002	891(b)		1302.003	912
1253.003	891(c), (d)		1302.004	913

Estates Code	Probate Code	Estates Code	Probate Code
1302.005	914	1353.006	883(h)
1302.006	916	1353.051	883B(a), (c)
1302.007	915	1353.052	883B(b), (d), (e)
1351.001	889(a)	1353.053	884A
1351.002	889(b)	1353.054	884
1351.003	889(c), (d)	1353.101	883C(a)
1351.004	889(e)	1353.102	883C(a), (b), (c)
1351.005	889(f)	1353.103	883A
1351.006	889(a)	1353.151	883D
1351.051	890(a)	1354.001	885(a)
1351.052	890(b)	1354.002	885(a)
1351.053	890(b), (c); new	1354.003	885(a)
1351.054	890(d), (e)	1354.004	885(b)
1351.055	890(f)	1354.005	885(c)
1351.056	890(g)	1354.006	885(d)
1351.057	890(b)	1354.007	885(e)
1352.001	889A(a), 890A(a)	1354.008	885(f)
1352.051	889A(b)	1354.009	885(g)
1352.052	889A(b), (j)	1355.001	887(a)
1352.053	889A(c)	1355.002	887(e)
1352.054	889A(d), (f)	1355.051	887(a)
1352.055	889A(e), (h), (i)	1355.052	887(b)
1352.056	889A(b)	1355.101	new
1352.057	889A(g)	1355.102	887(c)
1352.058	889A(g)	1355.103	887(c)
1352.059	889A(k)	1355.104	887(d)
1352.101	890A(b), (c)	1355.105	887(f)
1352.102	890A(c)	1355.151	887(g)
1352.103	890A(d)	1355.152	887(g)
1352.104	890A(e), (g), (h)	1355.153	887(g)
1352.105	890A(f), (j)	1355.154	887(g)
1352.106	890A(c)	1356.001	901, 904(a)
1352.107	890A(i)	1356.002	902
1352.108	890A(k)	1356.051	903(a), (b), (c)
1353.001	883(e), (f)	1356.052	903(a)
1353.002	883(a), (b)	1356.053	903(e)
1353.003	883(a), (b)	1356.054	904(b)
1353.004	883(c), (g)	1356.055	903(d)
1353.005	883(d), (g)	1356.056	905

Estates Code	Probate Code
1357.001	new
1357.002	new
1357.003	new
1357.051	new
1357.052	new
1357.053	new
1357.054	new
1357.055	new
1357.056	new
1357.101	new
1357.102	new

I.
BUSINESS AND COMMERCE CODE

Title 1.   Uniform Commercial Code

Chapter 8.   Investment Securities

Subchapter D.   Registration

Statutes in Context
§ 8.402

This section is the source of the erroneous belief that letters testamentary and letters of administration are "good" for only 60 days.

---

§ 8.402.   Assurance that Indorsement or Instruction is Effective

(a) An issuer may require the following assurance that each necessary indorsement or each instruction is genuine and authorized:

(1) in all cases, a guaranty of the signature of the person making an indorsement or originating an instruction, including, in the case of an instruction, reasonable assurance of identity;

(2) if the indorsement is made or the instruction is originated by an agent, appropriate assurance of actual authority to sign;

(3) if the indorsement is made or the instruction is originated by a fiduciary pursuant to Section 8.107(a)(4) or (5), appropriate evidence of appointment or incumbency;

(4) if there is more than one fiduciary, reasonable assurance that all who are required to sign have done so; and

(5) if the indorsement is made or the instruction is originated by a person not covered by another provision of this subsection, assurance appropriate to the case corresponding as nearly as may be to the provisions of this subsection.

(b) An issuer may elect to require reasonable assurance beyond that specified in this section.

(c) In this section:

(1) "Appropriate evidence of appointment or incumbency" means:

(A) in the case of a fiduciary appointed or qualified by a court, a certificate issued by or under the direction or supervision of the court or an officer thereof and dated within 60 days before the date of presentation for transfer; or

(B) in any other case, a copy of a document showing the appointment or a certificate issued by or on behalf of a person reasonably believed by an issuer to be responsible or, in the absence of that document or certificate, other evidence the issuer reasonably considers appropriate.

(2) "Guaranty of the signature" means a guaranty signed by or on behalf of a person reasonably believed by the issuer to be responsible. An issuer may adopt standards with respect to responsibility if they are not manifestly unreasonable.

Amended by Acts 1995, 74th Leg., ch. 962, § 1, eff. Sept. 1, 1995.

Title 3.   Insolvency, Fraudulent Transfers, and Fraud

Chapter 24.   Uniform Fraudulent Transfer Act

Statutes in Context
Chapter 24

A creditor may set aside a transfer if that transfer meets the requirements set forth in the Texas version of the Uniform Fraudulent Transfer Act. This Act frequently comes into play when a donor makes an outright gift or creates a trust which would otherwise restrict the ability of an existing or future creditor to get paid from the transferred property. Note that a disclaimer under Probate Code § 37A or Property Code § 112.010 will not be considered as fraudulent even if the disclaiming beneficiary's intent is to keep the property away from the beneficiary's creditors (definition of "transfer" in § 24.002(12)).

---

§ 24.001.   Short Title

This chapter may be cited as the Uniform Fraudulent Transfer Act.

Amended by Acts 1987, 70th Leg., ch. 1004, § 1, eff. Sept. 1, 1987.

§ 24.002.   Definitions

In this chapter:

(1) "Affiliate" means:

(A) a person who directly or indirectly owns, controls, or holds with power to vote, 20 percent or more of the outstanding voting securities of the debtor, other than a person who holds the securities:

(i) as a fiduciary or agent without sole discretionary power to vote the securities;

or

(ii) solely to secure a debt, if the person has not exercised the power to vote;

(B) a corporation 20 percent or more of whose outstanding voting securities are directly or indirectly owned, controlled, or held with power to vote, by the debtor or a person who directly or indirectly owns, controls, or holds, with power to vote, 20 percent or more of the outstanding voting securities of the debtor, other than a person who holds the securities:

(i) as a fiduciary or agent without sole power to vote the securities; or

(ii) solely to secure a debt, if the person has not in fact exercised the power to vote;

(C) a person whose business is operated by the debtor under a lease or other agreement, or a person substantially all of whose assets are controlled by the debtor; or

(D) a person who operates the debtor's business under a lease or other agreement or controls substantially all of the debtor's assets.

(2) "Asset" means property of a debtor, but the term does not include:

(A) property to the extent it is encumbered by a valid lien;

(B) property to the extent it is generally exempt under nonbankruptcy law; or

(C) an interest in property held in tenancy by the entireties to the extent it is not subject to process by a creditor holding a claim against only one tenant, under the law of another jurisdiction.

(3) "Claim" means a right to payment or property, whether or not the right is reduced to judgment, liquidated, unliquidated, fixed, contingent, matured, unmatured, disputed, undisputed, legal, equitable, secured, or unsecured.

(4) "Creditor" means a person, including a spouse, minor, person entitled to receive court or administratively ordered child support for the benefit of a child, or ward, who has a claim.

(5) "Debt" means a liability on a claim.

(6) "Debtor" means a person who is liable on a claim.

(7) "Insider" includes:

(A) if the debtor is an individual:

(i) a relative of the debtor or of a general partner of the debtor;

(ii) a partnership in which the debtor is a general partner;

(iii) a general partner in a partnership described in Subparagraph (ii) of this paragraph; or

(iv) a corporation of which the debtor is a director, officer, or person in control;

(B) if the debtor is a corporation:

(i) a director of the debtor;

(ii) an officer of the debtor;

(iii) a person in control of the debtor;

(iv) a partnership in which the debtor is a general partner;

(v) a general partner in a partnership described in Subparagraph (iv) of this paragraph; or

(vi) a relative of a general partner, director, officer, or person in control of the debtor;

(C) if the debtor is a partnership:

(i) a general partner in the debtor;

(ii) a relative of a general partner in, a general partner of, or a person in control of the debtor;

(iii) another partnership in which the debtor is a general partner;

(iv) a general partner in a partnership described in Subparagraph (iii) of this paragraph; or

(v) a person in control of the debtor;

(D) an affiliate, or an insider of an affiliate as if the affiliate were the debtor; and

(E) a managing agent of the debtor.

(8) "Lien" means a charge against or an interest in property to secure payment of a debt or performance of an obligation, and includes a security interest created by agreement, a judicial lien obtained by legal or equitable process or proceedings, a common-law lien, or a statutory lien.

(9) "Person" means an individual, partnership, corporation, association, organization, government or governmental subdivision or agency, business trust, estate, trust, or any other legal or commercial entity.

(10) "Property" means anything that may be the subject of ownership.

(11) "Relative" means an individual related by consanguinity within the third degree as determined by the common law, a spouse, or an individual related to a spouse within the third degree as so determined, and includes an individual in an adoptive relationship within the third degree.

(12) "Transfer" means every mode, direct or indirect, absolute o means every mode, direct or indirect, absolute or conditional, voluntary or involuntary, of disposing of or parting with an asset or an interest in an asset, and includes payment of money, release, lease, and creation of a lien or other encumbrance. The term does not include a transfer under a disclaimer filed under Chapter 240, [Section 37A, Texas Probate Code, or Section 112.010,] Property Code.

(13) "Valid lien" means a lien that is effective against the holder of a judicial lien subsequently obtained by legal or equitable process or proceedings.

Amended by Acts 1987, 70th Leg., ch. 1004, § 1, eff. Sept. 1, 1987. Amended by Acts 1993, 73rd Leg., ch. 846, § 2, eff. Sept. 1, 1993; Acts 1997, 75th Leg., ch. 911, § 95, eff. Sept. 1, 1997, Acts 2015, 84th Leg., ch.

562, § 1, eff. Sept. 1, 2015.

§ 24.003. Insolvency

(a) A debtor is insolvent if the sum of the debtor's debts is greater than all of the debtor's assets at a fair valuation.

(b) A debtor who is generally not paying the debtor's debts as they become due is presumed to be insolvent.

~~(c) A partnership is insolvent under Subsection (a) of this section if the sum of the partnership's debts is greater than the aggregate, at a fair valuation, of all of the partnership's assets and the sum of the excess of the value of each general partner's nonpartnership assets over the partner's nonpartnership debts.~~

(d) Assets under this section do not include property that has been transferred, concealed, or removed with intent to hinder, delay, or defraud creditors or that has been transferred in a manner making the transfer voidable under this chapter.

(e) Debts under this section do not include an obligation to the extent it is secured by a valid lien on property of the debtor not included as an asset.

Amended by Acts 1987, 70ᵗʰ Leg., ch. 1004, § 1, eff. Sept. 1, 1987. Amended by Acts 1993, 73ʳᵈ Leg., ch. 570, § 8, eff. Sept. 1, 1993. Subsection (c) repealed by Acts 2013, 83rd Leg., ch. 9, §11, eff. Sept. 1, 2013.

§ 24.004. Value

(a) Value is given for a transfer or an obligation if, in exchange for the transfer or obligation, property is transferred or an antecedent debt is secured or satisfied, but value does not include an unperformed promise made otherwise than in the ordinary course of the promisor's business to furnish support to the debtor or another person.

(b) For the purposes of Sections 24.005 (a)(2) and 24.006 of this code, a person gives a reasonably equivalent value if the person acquires an interest of the debtor in an asset pursuant to a regularly conducted, noncollusive foreclosure sale or execution of a power of sale for the acquisition or disposition of the interest of the debtor upon default under a mortgage, deed of trust, or security agreement.

(c) A transfer is made for present value if the exchange between the debtor and the transferee is intended by them to be contemporaneous and is in fact substantially contemporaneous.

(d) "Reasonably equivalent value" includes without limitation, a transfer or obligation that is within the range of values for which the transferor would have sold the assets in an arm's length transaction.

Amended by Acts 1987, 70ᵗʰ Leg., ch. 1004, § 1, eff. Sept. 1, 1987. Amended by Acts 1993, 73ʳᵈ Leg., ch. 570, § 9, eff. Sept. 1, 1993.

§ 24.005. Transfers Fraudulent as to Present and Future Creditors

(a) A transfer made or obligation incurred by a debtor is fraudulent as to a creditor, whether the creditor's claim arose before or within a reasonable time after the transfer was made or the obligation was incurred, if the debtor made the transfer or incurred the obligation:

(1) with actual intent to hinder, delay, or defraud any creditor of the debtor; or

(2) without receiving a reasonably equivalent value in exchange for the transfer or obligation, and the debtor:

(A) was engaged or was about to engage in a business or a transaction for which the remaining assets of the debtor were unreasonably small in relation to the business or transaction; or

(B) intended to incur, or believed or reasonably should have believed that the debtor would incur, debts beyond the debtor's ability to pay as they became due.

(b) In determining actual intent under Subsection (a)(1) of this section, consideration may be given, among other factors, to whether:

(1) the transfer or obligation was to an insider;

(2) the debtor retained possession or control of the property transferred after the transfer;

(3) the transfer or obligation was concealed;

(4) before the transfer was made or obligation was incurred, the debtor had been sued or threatened with suit;

(5) the transfer was of substantially all the debtor's assets;

(6) the debtor absconded;

(7) the debtor removed or concealed assets;

(8) the value of the consideration received by the debtor was reasonably equivalent to the value of the asset transferred or the amount of the obligation incurred;

(9) the debtor was insolvent or became insolvent shortly after the transfer was made or the obligation was incurred;

(10) the transfer occurred shortly before or shortly after a substantial debt was incurred; and

(11) the debtor transferred the essential assets of the business to a lienor who transferred the assets to an insider of the debtor.

Amended by Acts 1987, 70ᵗʰ Leg., ch. 1004, § 1, eff. Sept. 1, 1987. Amended by Acts 1993, 73ʳᵈ Leg., ch. 570, § 10, eff. Sept. 1, 1993.

§ 24.006. Transfers Fraudulent as to Present Creditors

(a) A transfer made or obligation incurred by a debtor is fraudulent as to a creditor whose claim arose before the transfer was made or the obligation was incurred if the debtor made the transfer or incurred the obligation without receiving a reasonably equivalent value in exchange for the transfer or obligation and the debtor was insolvent at that time or the debtor became insolvent as a result of the transfer or obligation.

(b) A transfer made by a debtor is fraudulent as to a creditor whose claim arose before the transfer was made if the transfer was made to an insider for an antecedent debt, the debtor was insolvent at that time, and the insider had reasonable cause to believe that the debtor was insolvent.

Amended by Acts 1987, 70th Leg., ch. 1004, § 1, eff. Sept. 1, 1987.

§ 24.007. When Transfer is Made or Obligation is Incurred

For the purposes of this chapter:

(1) a transfer is made:

(A) with respect to an asset that is real property other than a fixture, but including the interest of a seller or purchaser under a contract for the sale of the asset, when the transfer is so far perfected that a good faith purchaser of the asset from the debtor against whom applicable law permits the transfer to be perfected cannot acquire an interest in the asset that is superior to the interest of the transferee; and

(B) with respect to an asset that is not real property or that is a fixture, when the transfer is so far perfected that a creditor on a simple contract cannot acquire a judicial lien otherwise than under this chapter that is superior to the interest of the transferee;

(2) if applicable law permits the transfer to be perfected as provided in Subdivision (1) of this section and the transfer is not so perfected before the commencement of an action for relief under this chapter, the transfer is deemed made immediately before the commencement of the action;

(3) if applicable law does not permit the transfer to be perfected as provided in Subdivision (1) of this section, the transfer is made when it becomes effective between the debtor and the transferee;

(4) a transfer is not made until the debtor has acquired rights in the asset transferred; and

(5) an obligation is incurred:

(A) if oral, when it becomes effective between the parties; or

(B) if evidenced by a writing, when the writing executed by the obligor is delivered to or for the benefit of the obligee.

Amended by Acts 1987, 70th Leg., ch. 1004, § 1, eff. Sept. 1, 1987.

§ 24.008. Remedies of Creditors

(a) In an action for relief against a transfer or obligation under this chapter, a creditor, subject to the limitations in Section 24.009 of this code, may obtain:

(1) avoidance of the transfer or obligation to the extent necessary to satisfy the creditor's claim;

(2) an attachment or other provisional remedy against the asset transferred or other property of the transferee in accordance with the applicable Texas Rules of Civil Procedure and the Civil Practice and Remedies Code relating to ancillary proceedings; or

(3) subject to applicable principles of equity and in accordance with applicable rules of civil procedure:

(A) an injunction against further disposition by the debtor or a transferee, or both, of the asset transferred or of other property;

(B) appointment of a receiver to take charge of the asset transferred or of other property of the transferee; or

(C) any other relief the circumstances may require.

(b) If a creditor has obtained a judgment on a claim against the debtor, the creditor, if the court so orders, may levy execution on the asset transferred or its proceeds.

Amended by Acts 1987, 70th Leg., ch. 1004, § 1, eff. Sept. 1, 1987.

§ 24.009. Defenses, Liability, and Protection of Transferee

(a) A transfer or obligation is not voidable under Section 24.005 (a)(1) of this code against a person who took in good faith and for a reasonably equivalent value or against any subsequent transferee or obligee.

(b) Except as otherwise provided in this section, to the extent a transfer is voidable in an action by a creditor under Section 24.008 (a)(1) of this code, the creditor may recover judgment for the value of the asset transferred, as adjusted under Subsection (c) of this section, or the amount necessary to satisfy the creditor's claim, whichever is less. The judgment may be entered against:

(1) the first transferee of the asset or the person for whose benefit the transfer was made; or

(2) any subsequent transferee other than a good faith transferee who took for value or from any subsequent transferee.

(c)(1) Except as provided by Subdivision (2) of this subsection, if the judgment under Subsection (b) of this section is based upon the value of the asset transferred, the judgment must be for an amount equal to the value of the asset at the time of the transfer, subject to adjustment as the equities may require.

(2) The value of the asset transferred is not to be adjusted to include the value of improvements made by a good faith transferee, including:

(A) physical additions or changes to the asset transferred;

(B) repairs to the asset;

(C) payment of any tax on the asset;

(D) payment of any debt secured by a lien on the asset that is superior or equal to the rights of a voiding creditor under this chapter; and

(E) preservation of the asset.

(d)(1) Notwithstanding voidability of a transfer or an obligation under this chapter, a good faith transferee or obligee is entitled, at the transferee's or obligee's election, to the extent of the value given the debtor for the transfer or obligation, to:

(A) a lien, prior to the rights of a voiding creditor under this chapter, or a right to retain any interest in the asset transferred;

(B) enforcement of any obligation incurred; or

(C) a reduction in the amount of the liability on the judgment.

(2) Notwithstanding voidability of a transfer under this chapter, to the extent of the value of any improvements made by a good faith transferee, the good faith transferee is entitled to a lien on the asset transferred prior to the rights of a voiding creditor under this chapter

(e) A transfer is not voidable under Section 24.005(a)(2) or Section 24.006 of this code if the transfer results from:

(1) termination of a lease upon default by the debtor when the termination is pursuant to the lease and applicable law; or

(2) enforcement of a security interest in compliance with Chapter 9 of this code.[1]

(f) A transfer is not voidable under Section 24.006 (b) of this code:

(1) to the extent the insider gave new value to or for the benefit of the debtor after the transfer was made unless the new value was secured by a valid lien;

(2) if made in the ordinary course of business or financial affairs of the debtor and the insider; or

(3) if made pursuant to a good-faith effort to rehabilitate the debtor and the transfer secured present value given for that purpose as well as an antecedent debt of the debtor.

Amended by Acts 1987, 70th Leg., ch. 1004, § 1, eff. Sept. 1, 1987. Amended by Acts 1993, 73rd Leg., ch. 570, § 11, eff. Sept. 1, 1993.

§ 24.010. Extinguishment of Cause of Action

(a) Except as provided by Subsection (b) of this section, a cause of action with respect to a fraudulent transfer or obligation under this chapter is extinguished unless action is brought:

(1) under Section 24.005 (a)(1) of this code, within four years after the transfer was made or the obligation was incurred or, if later, within one year after the transfer or obligation was or could reasonably have been discovered by the claimant;

(2) under Section 24.005 (a)(2) or 24.006 (a) of this code, within four years after the transfer was made or the obligation was incurred; or

(3) under Section 24.006 (b) of this code, within one year after the transfer was made.

(b) A cause of action on behalf of a spouse, minor, or ward with respect to a fraudulent transfer or obligation under this chapter is extinguished unless the action is brought:

(1) under Section 24.005 (a) or 24.006 (a) of this code, within two years after the cause of action accrues, or if later, within one year after the transfer or obligation was or could reasonably have been discovered by the claimant; or

(2) under Section 24.006 (b) of this code within one year after the date the transfer was made.

(c) If a creditor entitled to bring an action under this chapter is under a legal disability when a time period prescribed by this section starts, the time of the disability is not included in the period. A disability that arises after the period starts does not suspend the running of the period. A creditor may not tack one legal disability to another to extend the period. For the purposes of this subsection, a creditor is under a legal disability if the creditor is:

(1) younger than 18 years of age, regardless of whether the person is married; or

(2) of unsound mind.

Amended by Acts 1987, 70th Leg., ch. 1004, § 1, eff. Sept. 1, 1987. Amended by Acts 1993, 73rd Leg., ch. 570, § 12, eff. Sept. 1, 1993.

§ 24.011. Supplementary Provisions

Unless displaced by the provisions of this chapter, the principles of law and equity, including the law merchant and the law relating to principal and agent, estoppel, laches, fraud, misrepresentation, duress, coercion, mistake, insolvency, or other validating or invalidating cause, supplement its provisions.

Amended by Acts 1987, 70th Leg., ch. 1004, § 1, eff. Sept. 1, 1987.

§ 24.012. Uniformity of Application and Construction

This chapter shall be applied and construed to effectuate its general purpose to make uniform the law with respect to the subject of this chapter among states enacting it.

Amended by Acts 1987, 70th Leg., ch. 1004, § 1, eff. Sept. 1, 1987.

§ 24.013. Costs

In any proceeding under this chapter, the court may award costs and reasonable attorney's fees as are equitable and just.

Added by Acts 2003, 78th Leg., ch. 420, § 1, eff. Sept. 1, 2003.

---

[1] Bus. & C. § 9.101 et seq.

II.

BUSINESS ORGANIZATIONS CODE

Title 1. General Provisions

Chapter 2. Purposes and Power of Domestic Entity

Subchapter A. Purposes of Domestic Entity

Statutes in Context
§ 2.106

This provision provides authority for a nonprofit corporation to serve as a trustee. The section does not apply to a nonprofit corporation serving in other fiduciary roles such as the executor of a will.

---

§ 2.106. Power of Nonprofit Corporation to Serve as Trustee.

(a) A nonprofit corporation that is described by Section 501(c)(3) or 170(c), Internal Revenue Code, or a corresponding provision of a subsequent federal tax law, or a nonprofit corporation listed by the Internal Revenue Service in the Cumulative List of Organizations Described in Section 170(c) of the Internal Revenue Code of 1986, I.R.S. Publication 78, or any successor I.R.S. publication, may serve as the trustee of a trust:

(1) of which the nonprofit corporation is a beneficiary; or

(2) benefiting another organization described by one of those sections of the Internal Revenue Code, or a corresponding provision of a subsequent federal tax law, or listed by the Internal Revenue Service in the Cumulative List of Organizations Described in Section 170(c) of the Internal Revenue Code of 1986, I.R.S. Publication 78, or any successor I.R.S. publication.

(b) Any corporation (or person or entity assisting such corporation) described in this section shall have immunity from suit (including both a defense to liability and the right not to bear the cost, burden, and risk of discovery and trial) as to any claim alleging that the corporation's role as trustee of a trust described in this section constitutes engaging in the trust business in a manner requiring a state charter as defined in Section 181.002(a)(9), Finance Code. An interlocutory appeal may be taken if a court denies or otherwise fails to grant a motion for summary judgment that is based on an assertion of the immunity provided in this subsection.

Acts 2003, 78th Leg., ch. 182, § 1, eff. Jan. 1, 2006.

III.
CIVIL PRACTICE AND REMEDIES CODE

Title 2. Trial, Judgment, and Appeal

Subtitle B. Trial Matters

Chapter 15. Venue

Subchapter A. Definitions; General Rules

Statutes in Context
§ 15.007

The venue provisions of the Probate Code trump many of the normal venue provisions contained in the Civil Practice and Remedies Code.

---

§ 15.007. Conflict with Certain Provisions

Notwithstanding Sections 15.004, 15.005, and 15.031, to the extent that venue under this chapter for a suit by or against an executor, administrator, or guardian as such, for personal injury, death, or property damage conflicts with venue provisions under the Estates [Texas Probate] Code, this chapter controls.

Acts 1995, 74th Leg., ch. 138, § 1, eff. Aug. 28, 1995. Acts 2015, 84th Leg., ch. 1236, § 20.001, eff. Sept. 1, 2015.

Subchapter B. Mandatory Venue

Statutes in Context
§ 15.011 & § 15.031

Civil Practice and Remedies Code §§ 15.011 and 15.031 contain venue provisions that may impact the proper location in which to bring a suit involving estates and trusts.

---

§ 15.011. Land

Actions for recovery of real property or an estate or interest in real property, for partition of real property, to remove encumbrances from the title to real property, for recovery of damages to real property, or to quiet title to real property shall be brought in the county in which all or a part of the property is located.

Acts 1985, 69th Leg., ch. 959, § 1, eff. Sept. 1, 1985. Amended by Acts 1995, 74th Leg., ch. 138, § 2, eff. Aug. 28, 1995.

Subchapter C. Permissive Venue

§ 15.031. Executor; Administrator; Guardian

If the suit is against an executor, administrator, or guardian, as such, to establish a money demand against the estate which he represents, the suit may be brought in the county in which the estate is administered, or if the suit is against an executor, administrator, or guardian growing out of a negligent act or omission of the person whose estate the executor, administrator, or guardian represents, the suit may be brought in the county in which the negligent act or omission of the person whose estate the executor, administrator, or guardian represents occurred.

Acts 1985, 69th Leg., ch. 959, § 1, eff. Sept. 1, 1985.

Chapter 16. Limitations

Subchapter A. Limitations of Personal Actions

Statutes in Context
Chapter 16

The comprehensive provisions of Chapter 16 provide statutes of limitations for a variety of causes of action. Section 16.062 is of particular importance because it extends the running of a limitations period for 12 months after the decedent's death, unless a personal representative is appointed sooner in which case the limitations period resumes running at the time the personal representative qualifies. See Probate Code § 146(b-6).

---

§ 16.001. Effect of Disability

(a) For the purposes of this subchapter, a person is under a legal disability if the person is:

(1) younger than 18 years of age, regardless of whether the person is married; or

(2) of unsound mind.

(b) If a person entitled to bring a personal action is under a legal disability when the cause of action ion accrues, the time of the disability is not included in a limitations period.

(c) A person may not tack one legal disability to another to extend a limitations period.

(d) A disability that arises after a limitations period starts does not suspend the running of the period.

Acts 1985, 69th Leg., ch. 959, § 1, eff. Sept. 1, 1985. Amended by Acts 1987, 70th Leg., ch. 1049, § 56, eff. Sept. 1, 1987.

§ 16.002. One-Year Limitations Period

(a) A person must bring suit for malicious prosecution, libel, slander, or breach of promise of marriage not later than one year after the day the cause of action accrues.

(b) A person must bring suit to set aside a sale of property seized under Subchapter E, Chapter 33, Tax Code,[1] not later than one year after the date the property is sold.

Acts 1985, 69th Leg., ch. 959, § 1, eff. Sept. 1, 1985. Amended by Acts 1995, 74th Leg., ch. 1017, § 3, eff. Aug. 28, 1995.

§ 16.003. Two-Year Limitations Period

(a) Except as provided by Sections 16.010, 16.0031, and 16.0045, a person must bring suit for trespass for injury to the estate or to the property of another, conversion of personal property, taking or detaining the personal property of another, personal injury, forcible entry and detainer, and forcible detainer not later than two years after the day the cause of action accrues.

(b) A person must bring suit not later than two years after the day the cause of action accrues in an action for injury resulting in death. The cause of action accrues on the death of the injured person.

Acts 1985, 69th Leg., ch. 959, § 1, eff. Sept. 1, 1985. Amended by Acts 1995, 74th Leg., ch. 739, § 2, eff. June 15, 1995; Acts 1997, 75th Leg., ch. 26, § 2, eff. May 1, 1997. Subsec. (a) amended by Acts 2005, 79th Leg., ch. 97, § 3, eff. Sept. 1, 2005.

§ 16.004. Four-Year Limitations Period

(a) A person must bring suit on the following actions not later than four years after the day the cause of action accrues:

(1) specific performance of a contract for the conveyance of real property;

(2) penalty or damages on the penal clause of a bond to convey real property;

(3) debt;

(4) fraud; or

(5) breach of fiduciary duty.

(b) A person must bring suit on the bond of an executor, administrator, or guardian not later than four years after the day of the death, resignation, removal, or discharge of the executor, administrator, or guardian.

(c) A person must bring suit against his partner for a settlement of partnership accounts, and must bring an action on an open or stated account, or on a mutual and current account concerning the trade of merchandise between merchants or their agents or factors, not later than four years after the day that the cause of action

accrues. For purposes of this subsection, the cause of action accrues on the day that the dealings in which the parties were interested together cease.

Acts 1985, 69th Leg., ch. 959, § 1, eff. Sept. 1, 1985. Amended by Acts 1999, 76th Leg., ch. 950, § 1, eff. Aug. 30, 1999.

§ 16.0045. [Five-Year] Limitations Period For Claims Arising From Certain Offenses

(a) A person must bring suit for personal injury not later than 15 [five] years after the day the cause of action accrues if the injury arises as a result of conduct that violates:

(1) Section 22.011(a)(2) [22.011], Penal Code (sexual assault of a child);

(2) Section 22.021(a)(1)(B) [22.021], Penal Code (aggravated sexual assault of a child);

(3) Section 21.02, Penal Code (continuous sexual abuse of young child or children);

(4) Section 20A.02(a)(7)(A), (B), (C), (D), or (H) or Section 20A.02(a)(8), Penal Code, involving an activity described by Section 20A.02(a)(7)(A), (B), (C), (D), or (H) or sexual conduct with a child trafficked in the manner described by Section 20A.02(a)(7) [20A.02], Penal Code (certain sexual trafficking of a child [persons]); [or]

(5) Section 43.05(a)(2) [43.05], Penal Code (compelling prostitution by a child); or

(6) Section 21.11, Penal Code (indecency with a child).

(b) A person must bring suit for personal injury not later than five years after the day the cause of action accrues if the injury arises as a result of conduct that violates:

(1) Section 22.011(a)(1), Penal Code (sexual assault);

(2) Section 22.021(a)(1)(A), Penal Code (aggravated sexual assault);

(3) Section 20A.02, Penal Code (trafficking of persons), other than conduct described by Subsection (a)(4); or

(4) Section 43.05(a)(1), Penal Code (compelling prostitution).

(c) In an action for injury resulting in death arising as a result of conduct described by Subsection (a) or (b), the cause of action accrues on the death of the injured person.

(d) A [(c) The] limitations period under this section is tolled for a suit on the filing of a petition by any person in an appropriate court alleging that the identity of the defendant in the suit is unknown and designating the unknown defendant as "John or Jane Doe." The person filing the petition shall proceed with due diligence to discover the identity of the defendant and amend the petition by substituting the real name of the defendant for "John or Jane Doe" not later than the 30th day after the date that the defendant is identified to the plaintiff. The limitations period begins running again on the date that the petition is amended.

---

[1] Tax Code § 33.91 et seq.

Added by Acts 1995, 74ᵗʰ Leg., ch. 739, § 1, eff. June 15, 1995. Amended by Acts 2011, 82ⁿᵈ Leg., ch. 1, § 3.01, eff. Sept. 1, 2011, Acts 2015, 84ᵗʰ Leg., ch. 918, § 1, eff. Sept. 1, 2015.

§ 16.005. Action for Closing Street or Road

(a) A person must bring suit for any relief from the following acts not later than two years after the day the cause of action accrues:

(1) the passage by a governing body of an incorporated city or town of an ordinance closing and abandoning, or attempting to close and abandon, all or any part of a public street or alley in the city or town, other than a state highway; or

(2) the adoption by a commissioners court of an order closing and abandoning, or attempting to close and abandon, all or any part of a public road or thoroughfare in the county, other than a state highway.

(b) The cause of action accrues when the order or ordinance is passed or adopted.

(c) If suit is not brought within the period provided by this section, the person in possession of the real property receives complete title to the property by limitations and the right of the city or county to revoke or rescind the order or ordinance is barred.

Acts 1985, 69ᵗʰ Leg., ch. 959, § 1, eff. Sept. 1, 1985.

§ 16.006. Carriers of Property

(a) A carrier of property for compensation or hire must bring suit for the recovery of charges not later than three years after the day on which the cause of action accrues.

(b) Except as provided by Subsections (c) and (d), a person must bring suit for overcharges against a carrier of property for compensation or hire not later than three years after the cause of action accrues.

(c) If the person has presented a written claim for the overcharges within the three-year period, the limitations period is extended for six months from the date written notice is given by the carrier to the claimant of disallowance of the claim in whole or in part, as specified in the carrier's notice.

(d) If on or before the expiration of the three-year period, the carrier brings an action under Subsection (a) to recover charges relating to the service or, without beginning an action, collects charges relating to that service, the limitations period is extended for 90 days from the day on which the action is begun or the charges are collected.

(e) A cause of action regarding a shipment of property accrues on the delivery or tender of the property by the carrier.

(f) In this section, "overcharge" means a charge for transportation services in excess of the lawfully applicable amount.

Acts 1985, 69ᵗʰ Leg., ch. 959, § 1, eff. Sept. 1, 1985.

§ 16.007. Return of Execution

A person must bring suit against a sheriff or other officer or the surety of the sheriff or officer for failure to return an execution issued in the person's favor, not later than five years after the date on which the execution was returnable.

Acts 1985, 69ᵗʰ Leg., ch. 959, § 1, eff. Sept. 1, 1985.

§ 16.008. Architects, Engineers, Interior Designers, and Landscape Architects Furnishing Design, Planning, or Inspection of Construction of Improvements

(a) A person must bring suit for damages for a claim listed in Subsection (b) against a registered or licensed architect, engineer, interior designer, or landscape architect in this state, who designs, plans, or inspects the construction of an improvement to real property or equipment attached to real property, not later than 10 years after the substantial completion of the improvement or the beginning of operation of the equipment in an action arising out of a defective or unsafe condition of the real property, the improvement, or the equipment.

(b) This section applies to suit for:

(1) injury, damage, or loss to real or personal property;

(2) personal injury;

(3) wrongful death;

(4) contribution; or

(5) indemnity.

(c) If the claimant presents a written claim for damages, contribution, or indemnity to the architect, engineer, interior designer, or landscape architect within the 10-year limitations period, the period is extended for two years from the day the claim is presented.

Acts 1985, 69ᵗʰ Leg., ch. 959, § 1, eff. Sept. 1, 1985. Amended by Acts 1997, 75ᵗʰ Leg., ch. 860, § 1, eff. Sept. 1, 1997.

§ 16.009. Persons Furnishing Construction or Repair of Improvements

(a) A claimant must bring suit for damages for a claim listed in Subsection (b) against a person who constructs or repairs an improvement to real property not later than 10 years after the substantial completion of the improvement in an action arising out of a defective or unsafe condition of the real property or a deficiency in the construction or repair of the improvement.

(b) This section applies to suit for:

(1) injury, damage, or loss to real or personal property;

(2) personal injury;

(3) wrongful death;

(4) contribution; or

(5) indemnity.

(c) If the claimant presents a written claim for damages, contribution, or indemnity to the person performing or furnishing the construction or repair work during the 10-year limitations period, the period is extended for two years from the date the claim is presented.

(d) If the damage, injury, or death occurs during the 10th year of the limitations period, the claimant may bring suit not later than two years after the day the cause of action accrues.

(e) This section does not bar an action:

(1) on a written warranty, guaranty, or other contract that expressly provides for a longer effective period;

(2) against a person in actual possession or control of the real property at the time that the damage, injury, or death occurs; or

(3) based on wilful misconduct or fraudulent concealment in connection with the performance of the construction or repair.

(f) This section does not extend or affect a period prescribed for bringing an action under any other law of this state.

Acts 1985, 69th Leg., ch. 959, § 1, eff. Sept. 1, 1985.

§ 16.010. Misappropriation of Trade Secrets

(a) A person must bring suit for misappropriation of trade secrets not later than three years after the misappropriation is discovered or by the exercise of reasonable diligence should have been discovered.

(b) A misappropriation of trade secrets that continues over time is a single cause of action and the limitations period described by Subsection (a) begins running without regard to whether the misappropriation is a single or continuing act.

Added by Acts 1997, 75th Leg., ch. 26, § 1, eff. May 1, 1997.

§ 16.011. Surveyors

(a) A person must bring suit for damages arising from an injury or loss caused by an error in a survey conducted by a registered public surveyor or a licensed state land surveyor:

(1) not later than 10 years after the date the survey is completed if the survey is completed on or after September 1, 1989; or

(2) not later than September 1, 1991, or 10 years after the date the survey was completed, whichever is later, if the survey was completed before September 1, 1989.

(b) If the claimant presents a written claim for damages to the surveyor during the 10-year limitations period, the period is extended for two years from the date the claim is presented.

(c) This section is a statute of repose and is independent of any other limitations period.

Added by Acts 1989, 71st Leg., ch. 1233, § 1, eff. Sept. 1, 1989. Amended by Acts 2001, 77th Leg., ch. 1173, § 1, eff. Sept. 1, 2001.

§ 16.012. Products Liability: Manufacturing Equipment

(a) In this section:

(1) "Claimant," "seller," and "manufacturer" have the meanings assigned by Section 82.001.

(2) "Products liability action" means any action against a manufacturer or seller for recovery of damages or other relief for harm allegedly caused by a defective product, whether the action is based in strict tort liability, strict products liability, negligence, misrepresentation, breach of express or implied warranty, or any other theory or combination of theories, and whether the relief sought is recovery of damages or any other legal or equitable relief, including a suit for:

(A) injury or damage to or loss of real or personal property;

(B) personal injury;

(C) wrongful death;

(D) economic loss; or

(E) declaratory, injunctive, or other equitable relief.

(b) Except as provided by Subsections (c), (d), and (d-1), a claimant must commence a products liability action against a manufacturer or seller of a product before the end of 15 years after the date of the sale of the product by the defendant.

(c) If a manufacturer or seller expressly warrants in writing that the product has a useful safe life of longer than 15 years, a claimant must commence a products liability action against that manufacturer or seller of the product before the end of the number of years warranted after the date of the sale of the product by that seller.

(d) This section does not apply to a products liability action seeking damages for personal injury or wrongful death in which the claimant alleges:

(1) the claimant was exposed to the product that is the subject of the action before the end of 15 years after the date the product was first sold;

(2) the claimant's exposure to the product caused the claimant's disease that is the basis of the action; and

(3) the symptoms of the claimant's disease did not, before the end of 15 years after the date of the first sale of the product by the defendant, manifest themselves to a degree and for a duration that would put a reasonable person on notice that the person suffered some injury.

(d-1) This section does not reduce a limitations period for a cause of action described by Subsection (d) that accrues before the end of the limitations period under this section.

(e) This section does not extend the limitations period within which a products liability action involving the product may be commenced under any other law.

(f) This section applies only to the sale and not to the lease of a product.

(g) This section does not apply to any claim to which the General Aviation Revitalization Act of 1994

(Pub. L. No. 103-298, 108 Stat. 1552 (1994), reprinted in note, 49 U.S.C. Section 40101) or its exceptions are applicable.

Added by Acts 1993, 73ʳᵈ Leg., ch. 5, § 2 eff. Sept. 1, 1993. Amended by Acts 2003, 78ᵗʰ Leg., ch. 204, § 5.01, eff. Sept. 1, 2003.

Subchapter B. Limitations of Real Property Actions

§ 16.021. Definitions

In this subchapter:

(1) "Adverse possession" means an actual and visible appropriation of real property, commenced and continued under a claim of right that is inconsistent with and is hostile to the claim of another person.

(2) "Color of title" means a consecutive chain of transfers to the person in possession that:

(A) is not regular because of a muniment that is not properly recorded or is only in writing or because of a similar defect that does not want of intrinsic fairness or honesty; or

(B) is based on a certificate of headright, land warrant, or land scrip.

(3) "Peaceable possession" means possession of real property that is continuous and is not interrupted by an adverse suit to recover the property.

(4) "Title" means a regular chain of transfers of real property from or under the sovereignty of the soil.

Acts 1985, 69ᵗʰ Leg., ch. 959, § 1. eff. Sept. 1, 1985.

§ 16.022. Effect of Disability

(a) For the purposes of this subchapter, a person is under a legal disability if the person is:

(1) younger than 18 years of age, regardless of whether the person is married;

(2) of unsound mind; or

(3) serving in the United States Armed Forces during time of war.

(b) If a person entitled to sue for the recovery of real property or entitled to make a defense based on the title to real property is under a legal disability at the time title to the property vests or adverse possession commences, the time of the disability is not included in a limitations period.

(c) Except as provided by Sections 16.027 and 16.028, after the termination of the legal disability, a person has the same time to present a claim that is allowed to others under this chapter.

Amended by Acts 1987, 70ᵗʰ Leg., ch. 1049, § 57, eff. Sept. 1, 1987.

§ 16.023. Tacking of Successive Interests

To satisfy a limitations period, peaceable and adverse possession does not need to continue in the same person, but there must be privity of estate between each holder and his successor.

Acts 1985, 69ᵗʰ Leg., ch. 959, § 1, eff. Sept. 1, 1985.

§ 16.024. Adverse Possession: Three-Year Limitations Period

A person must bring suit to recover real property held by another in peaceable and adverse possession under title or color of title not later than three years after the day the cause of action accrues.

Acts 1985, 69ᵗʰ Leg., ch. 959, § 1, eff. Sept. 1, 1985.

§ 16.025. Adverse Possession: Five-Year Limitations Period

(a) A person must bring suit not later than five years after the day the cause of action accrues to recover real property held in peaceable and adverse possession by another who:

(1) cultivates, uses, or enjoys the property;

(2) pays applicable taxes on the property; and

(3) claims the property under a duly registered deed.

(b) This section does not apply to a claim based on a forged deed or a deed executed under a forged power of attorney.

Acts 1985, 69ᵗʰ Leg., ch. 959, § 1, eff. Sept. 1, 1985.

§ 16.026. Adverse Possession: 10-Year Limitations Period

(a) A person must bring suit not later than 10 years after the day the cause of action accrues to recover real property held in peaceable and adverse possession by another who cultivates, uses, or enjoys the property.

(b) Without a title instrument, peaceable and adverse possession is limited in this section to 160 acres, including improvements, unless the number of acres actually enclosed exceeds 160. If the number of enclosed acres exceeds 160 acres, peaceable and adverse possession extends to the real property actually enclosed.

(c) Peaceable possession of real property held under a duly registered deed or other memorandum of title that fixes the boundaries of the possessor's claim extends to the boundaries specified in the instrument.

Acts 1985, 69ᵗʰ Leg., ch. 959, § 1, eff. Sept. 1, 1985. Amended by Acts 1989, 71ˢᵗ Leg., ch. 764, § 1, eff. Sept. 1, 1989.

§ 16.027. Adverse Possession: 25-Year Limitations Period Notwithstanding Disability

A person, regardless of whether the person is or has been under a legal disability, must bring suit not later than 25 years after the day the cause of action accrues to recover real property held in peaceable and adverse possession by another who cultivates, uses, or enjoys the property.

Acts 1985, 69ᵗʰ Leg., ch. 959, § 1, eff. Sept. 1, 1985.

§ 16.028. Adverse Possession With Recorded Instrument: 25-Year Limitations Period

(a) A person, regardless of whether the person is or has been under a legal disability, may not maintain an action for the recovery of real property held for 25 years before the commencement of the action in peaceable and adverse possession by another who holds the property in good faith and under a deed or other instrument purporting to convey the property that is recorded in the deed records of the county where any part of the real property is located.

(b) Adverse possession of any part of the real property held under a recorded deed or other recorded instrument that purports to convey the property extends to and includes all of the property described in the instrument, even though the instrument is void on its face or in fact.

(c) A person who holds real property and claims title under this section has a good and marketable title to the property regardless of a disability arising at any time in the adverse claimant or a person claiming under the adverse claimant.

Acts 1985, 69th Leg., ch. 959, § 1, eff. Sept. 1, 1985.

§ 16.029. Evidence of Title to Land by Limitations

(a) In a suit involving title to real property that is not claimed by this state, it is prima facie evidence that the title to the property has passed from the person holding apparent record title to an opposing party if it is shown that:

(1) for one or more years during the 25 years preceding the filing of the suit the person holding apparent record title to the property did not exercise dominion over or pay taxes on the property; and

(2) during that period the opposing parties and those whose estate they own have openly exercised dominion over and have asserted a claim to the land and have paid taxes on it annually before becoming delinquent for as long as 25 years.

(b) This section does not affect a statute of limitations, a right to prove title by circumstantial evidence under the case law of this state, or a suit between a trustee and a beneficiary of the trust.

Acts 1985, 69th Leg., ch. 959, § 1, eff. Sept. 1, 1985.

§ 16.030. Title Through Adverse Possession

(a) If an action for the recovery of real property is barred under this chapter, the person who holds the property in peaceable and adverse possession has full title, precluding all claims.

(b) A person may not acquire through adverse possession any right or title to real property dedicated to public use.

Acts 1985, 69th Leg., ch. 959, § 1, eff. Sept. 1, 1985.

§ 16.031. Enclosed Land

(a) A tract of land that is owned by one person and that is entirely surrounded by land owned, claimed, or fenced by another is not considered enclosed by a fence that encloses any part of the surrounding land.

(b) Possession of the interior tract by the owner or claimant of the surrounding land is not peaceable and adverse possession as described by Section 16.026 unless:

(1) the interior tract is separated from the surrounding land by a fence; or

(2) at least one-tenth of the interior tract is cultivated and used for agricultural purposes or is used for manufacturing purposes.

Acts 1985, 69th Leg., ch. 959, § 1, eff. Sept. 1, 1985.

§ 16.032. Adjacent Land

Possession of land that belongs to another by a person owning or claiming 5,000 or more fenced acres that adjoin the land is not peaceable and adverse as described by Section 16.026 unless:

(1) the land is separated from the adjacent enclosed tract by a substantial fence;

(2) at least one-tenth of the land is cultivated and used for agricultural purposes or used for manufacturing purposes; or

(3) there is actual possession of the land.

Acts 1985, 69th Leg., ch. 959, § 1, eff. Sept. 1, 1985.

§ 16.033. Technical Defects in Instrument

(a) A person with a right of action for the recovery of real property or an interest in real property conveyed by an instrument with one of the following defects must bring suit not later than two years after the day the instrument was filed for record with the county clerk of the county where the real property is located:

(1) lack of the signature of a proper corporate officer, partner, or company officer, manager, or member;

(2) lack of a corporate seal;

(3) failure of the record to show the corporate seal used;

(4) failure of the record to show authority of the board of directors or stockholders of a corporation, partners of a partnership, or officers, managers, or members of a company;

(5) execution and delivery of the instrument by a corporation, partnership, or other company that had been dissolved, whose charter had expired, or whose franchise had been canceled, withdrawn, or forfeited;

(6) acknowledgment of the instrument in an individual, rather than a representative or official, capacity;

(7) execution of the instrument by a trustee without record of the authority of the trustee or proof of the facts recited in the instrument;

(8) failure of the record or instrument to show an acknowledgment or jurat that complies with applicable law; or

(9) wording of the stated consideration that may or might create an implied lien in favor of the grantor.

(b) This section does not apply to a forged instrument.

(c) For the purposes of this section, an instrument affecting real property containing a ministerial defect, omission, or informality in the certificate of acknowledgment that has been filed for record for longer than two years in the office of the county recorder of the county in which the property is located is considered to have been lawfully recorded and to be notice of the existence of the instrument on and after the date the instrument is filed.

Acts 1985, 69th Leg., ch. 959, § 1, eff. Sept. 1, 1985. Amended by Acts 1993, 73rd Leg., ch. 291, § 1, eff. Sept. 1, 1993. Subsec. (a) amended by and subsec. (c) added by Acts 2007, 80th Leg., ch. 819, § 1, eff. June 15, 2007.

§ 16.034. Attorney's Fees

(a) In a suit for the possession of real property between a person claiming under record title to the property and one claiming by adverse possession, if the prevailing party recovers possession of the property from a person unlawfully in actual possession, the court:

(1) shall award costs and reasonable attorney's fees to the prevailing party if the court finds that the person unlawfully in actual possession made a claim of adverse possession that was groundless and made in bad faith; and

(2) may award costs and reasonable attorney's fees to the prevailing party in the absence of a finding described by Subdivision (1).

(b) To recover attorney's fees, the person seeking possession must give the person unlawfully in possession a written demand for that person to vacate the premises. The demand must be given by registered or certified mail at least 10 days before filing the claim for recovery of possession.

(c) The demand must state that if the person unlawfully in possession does not vacate the premises within 10 days and a claim is filed by the person seeking possession, the court may enter a judgment against the person unlawfully in possession for costs and attorney's fees in an amount determined by the court to be reasonable.

Acts 1985, 69th Leg., ch. 959, § 1, eff. Sept. 1, 1985. Subsec. (a) amended by Acts 2009, 81st Leg., ch. 901, § 1, eff. Sept. 1, 2009.

§ 16.035. Lien on Real Property

(a) A person must bring suit for the recovery of real property under a real property lien or the foreclosure of a real property lien not later than four years after the day the cause of action accrues.

(b) A sale of real property under a power of sale in a mortgage or deed of trust that creates a real property lien must be made not later than four years after the day the cause of action accrues.

(c) The running of the statute of limitations is not suspended against a bona fide purchaser for value, a lienholder, or a lessee who has no notice or knowledge of the suspension of the limitations period and who acquires an interest in the property when a cause of action on an outstanding real property lien has accrued for more than four years, except as provided by:

(1) Section 16.062, providing for suspension in the event of death; or

(2) Section 16.036, providing for recorded extensions of real property liens.

(d) On the expiration of the four-year limitations period, the real property lien and a power of sale to enforce the real property lien become void.

(e) If a series of notes or obligations or a note or obligation payable in installments is secured by a real property lien, the four-year limitations period does not begin to run until the maturity date of the last note, obligation, or installment.

(f) The limitations period under this section is not affected by Section 3.118, Business & Commerce Code.

(g) In this section, "real property lien" means:

(1) a superior title retained by a vendor in a deed of conveyance or a purchase money note; or

(2) a vendor's lien, a mortgage, a deed of trust, a voluntary mechanic's lien, or a voluntary materialman's lien on real estate, securing a note or other written obligation.

Acts 1985, 69th Leg., ch. 959, § 1, eff. Sept. 1, 1985. Amended by Acts 1997, 75th Leg., ch. 219, § 1, eff. May 23, 1997.

§ 16.036. Extension of Real Property Lien

(a) The party or parties primarily liable for a debt or obligation secured by a real property lien, as that term is defined in Section 16.035, may suspend the running of the four-year limitations period for real property liens through a written extension agreement as provided by this section.

(b) The limitations period is suspended and the lien remains in effect for four years after the extended maturity date of the debt or obligation if the extension agreement is:

(1) signed and acknowledged as provided by law for a deed conveying real property; and

(2) filed for record in the county clerk's office of the county where the real property is located.

(c) The parties may continue to extend the lien by entering, acknowledging, and recording additional extension agreements.

(d) The maturity date stated in the original instrument or in the date of the recorded renewal and extension is conclusive evidence of the maturity date of the debt or obligation.

(e) The limitations period under this section is not affected by Section 3.118, Business & Commerce Code.

Acts 1985, 69th Leg., ch. 959, § 1, eff. Sept. 1, 1985.

Amended by Acts 1997, 75th Leg., ch. 219, § 2, eff. May 23, 1997.

§ 16.037. Effect of Extension of Real Property Lien on Third Parties

An extension agreement is void as to a bona fide purchaser for value, a lienholder, or a lessee who deals with real property affected by a real property lien without actual notice of the agreement and before the agreement is acknowledged, filed, and recorded.

Acts 1985, 69th Leg., ch. 959, § 1, eff. Sept. 1, 1985. Amended by Acts 1997, 75th Leg., ch. 219, § 3, eff. May 23, 1997.

§ 16.038. Rescission or Waiver of Accelerated Maturity Date

(a) If the maturity date of a series of notes or obligations or a note or obligation payable in installments is accelerated, and the accelerated maturity date is rescinded or waived in accordance with this section before the limitations period expires, the acceleration is deemed rescinded and waived and the note, obligation, or series of notes or obligations shall be governed by Section 16.035 as if no acceleration had occurred.

(b) Rescission or waiver of acceleration is effective if made by a written notice of a rescission or waiver served as provided in Subsection (c) by the lienholder, the servicer of the debt, or an attorney representing the lienholder on each debtor who, according to the records of the lienholder or the servicer of the debt, is obligated to pay the debt.

(c) Service of a notice under Subsection (b) must be by first class or certified mail and is complete when the notice is deposited in the United States mail, postage prepaid and addressed to the debtor at the debtor's last known address. The affidavit of a person knowledgeable of the facts to the effect that service was completed is prima facie evidence of service.

(d) A notice served under this section does not affect a lienholder's right to accelerate the maturity date of the debt in the future nor does it waive past defaults.

(e) This section does not create an exclusive method for waiver and rescission of acceleration or affect the accrual of a cause of action and the running of the related limitations period under Section 16.035(e) on any subsequent maturity date, accelerated or otherwise, of the note or obligation or series of notes or obligations.

Added by Acts 2015, 84th Leg., ch. 759, § 1, eff. July 17, 2015.

Subchapter C. Residual Limitations Period

§ 16.051. Residual Limitations Period

Every action for which there is no express limitations period, except an action for the recovery of real property, must be brought not later than four years after the day the cause of action accrues.

Acts 1985, 69th Leg., ch. 959, § 1, eff. Sept. 1, 1985.

Subchapter D. Miscellaneous Provisions

§ 16.061. Rights Not Barred

(a) A right of action of this state or a political subdivision of the state, including a county, an incorporated city or town, a navigation district, a municipal utility district, a port authority, an entity acting under Chapter 54, Transportation Code, a school district, or an entity created under Section 52, Article III, or Section 59, Article XVI, Texas Constitution, is not barred by any of the following sections: 16.001-16.004, 16.006, 16.007, 16.021-16.028, 16.030-16.032, 16.035-16.037, 16.051, 16.062, 16.063, 16.065-16.067, 16.070, 16.071, 31.006, or 71.021.

(b) In this section:

(1) "Navigation district" means a navigation district organized under Section 52, Article III, or Section 59, Article XVI, Texas Constitution.

(2) "Port authority" has the meaning assigned by Section 60.402, Water Code.

(3) "Municipal utility district" means a municipal utility district created under Section 52, Article III, or Section 59, Article XVI, Texas Constitution.

Acts 1985, 69th Leg., ch. 959, § 1, eff. Sept. 1, 1985. Amended by Acts 1989, 71st Leg., ch. 2, § 4.02, eff. Aug. 28, 1989; Acts 1993, 73rd Leg., ch. 782, § 1, eff. Aug. 30, 1993; Amended by Acts 1997, 75th Leg., ch. 1070, § 47, eff. Sept. 1, 1997; Amended by Acts 2001, 77th Leg., ch. 1420, § 8.204, eff. Sept. 1, 2001.

§ 16.062. Effect of Death

(a) The death of a person against whom or in whose favor there may be a cause of action suspends the running of an applicable statute of limitations for 12 months after the death.

(b) If an executor or administrator of a decedent's estate qualifies before the expiration of the period provided by this section, the statute of limitations begins to run at the time of the qualification.

Acts 1985, 69th Leg., ch. 959, § 1, eff. Sept. 1, 1985.

§ 16.063. Temporary Absence from State

The absence from this state of a person against whom a cause of action may be maintained suspends the running of the applicable statute of limitations for the period of the person's absence.

Acts 1985, 69th Leg., ch. 959, § 1, eff. Sept. 1, 1985.

§ 16.064. Effect of Lack of Jurisdiction

(a) The period between the date of filing an action in a trial court and the date of a second filing of the same action in a different court suspends the running of the applicable statute of limitations for the period if:

(1) because of lack of jurisdiction in the trial court where the action was first filed, the action is dismissed or the judgment is set aside or annulled in a direct proceeding; and

(2) not later than the 60th day after the date the dismissal or other disposition becomes final, the action is commenced in a court of proper jurisdiction.

(b) This section does not apply if the adverse party has shown in abatement that the first filing was made with intentional disregard of proper jurisdiction.

Acts 1985, 69th Leg., ch. 959, § 1, eff. Sept. 1, 1985.

§ 16.065. Acknowledgment of Claim

An acknowledgment of the justness of a claim that appears to be barred by limitations is not admissible in evidence to defeat the law of limitations if made after the time that the claim is due unless the acknowledgment is in writing and is signed by the party to be charged.

Acts 1985, 69th Leg., ch. 959, § 1, eff. Sept. 1, 1985.

§ 16.066. Action on Foreign Judgment

(a) An action on a foreign judgment is barred in this state if the action is barred under the laws of the jurisdiction where rendered.

(b) An action against a person who has resided in this state for 10 years prior to the action may not be brought on a foreign judgment rendered more than 10 years before the commencement of the action in this state.

(c) In this section "foreign judgment" means a judgment or decree rendered in another state or a foreign country.

Acts 1985, 69th Leg., ch. 959, § 1, eff. Sept. 1, 1985.

§ 16.067. Claim Incurred Prior to Arrival in this State

(a) A person may not bring an action to recover a claim against a person who has moved to this state if the claim is barred by the law of limitations of the state or country from which the person came.

(b) A person may not bring an action to recover money from a person who has moved to this state and who was released from its payment by the bankruptcy or insolvency laws of the state or country from which the person came.

(c) A demand that is against a person who has moved to this state and was incurred prior to his arrival in this state is not barred by the law of limitations until the person has lived in this state for 12 months. This subsection does not affect the application of Subsections (a) and (b).

Acts 1985, 69th Leg., ch. 959, § 1, eff. Sept. 1, 1985.

§ 16.068. Amended and Supplemental Pleadings

If a filed pleading relates to a cause of action, cross action, counterclaim, or defense that is not subject to a plea of limitation when the pleading is filed, a subsequent amendment or supplement to the pleading that changes the facts or grounds of liability or defense is not subject to a plea of limitation unless the amendment or supplement is wholly based on a new, distinct, or different transaction or occurrence.

Acts 1985, 69th Leg., ch. 959, § 1, eff. Sept. 1, 1985.

§ 16.069. Counterclaim or Cross Claim

(a) If a counterclaim or cross claim arises out of the same transaction or occurrence that is the basis of an action, a party to the action may file the counterclaim or cross claim even though as a separate action it would be barred by limitation on the date the party's answer is required.

(b) The counterclaim or cross claim must be filed not later than the 30th day after the date on which the party's answer is required.

Acts 1985, 69th Leg., ch. 959, § 1, eff. Sept. 1, 1985.

§ 16.070. Contractual Limitations Period

(a) Except as provided by Subsection (b), a person may not enter a stipulation, contract, or agreement that purports to limit the time in which to bring suit on the stipulation, contract, or agreement to a period shorter than two years. A stipulation, contract, or agreement that establishes a limitations period that is shorter than two years is void in this state.

(b) This section does not apply to a stipulation, contract, or agreement relating to the sale or purchase of a business entity if a party to the stipulation, contract, or agreement pays or receives or is obligated to pay or entitled to receive consideration under the stipulation, contract, or agreement having an aggregate value of not less than $500,000.

Acts 1985, 69th Leg., ch. 959, § 1, eff. Sept. 1, 1985. Amended by Acts 1991, 72nd Leg., ch. 840, § 2, eff. Aug. 26, 1991.

§ 16.071. Notice Requirements

(a) A contract stipulation that requires a claimant to give notice of a claim for damages as a condition precedent to the right to sue on the contract is not valid unless the stipulation is reasonable. A stipulation that requires notification within less than 90 days is void.

(b) If notice is required, the claimant may notify any convenient agent of the company that requires the notice.

(c) A contract stipulation between the operator of a railroad, street railway, or interurban railroad and an employee or servant of the operator is void if it requires as a condition precedent to liability:

(1) the employee or servant to notify the system of a claim for damages for personal injury caused by negligence; or

(2) the spouse, parent, or child of a deceased employee or servant to notify the system of a claim of death caused by negligence.

(d) This section applies to a contract between a federal prime contractor and a subcontractor, except that the notice period stipulated in the subcontract may be for a period not less than the period stipulated in the prime contract, minus seven days.

(e) In a suit covered by this section or Section 16.070, it is presumed that any required notice has been given unless lack of notice is specifically pleaded under oath.

(f) This section does not apply to a contract relating to the sale or purchase of a business entity if a party to the contract pays or receives or is obligated to pay or receive consideration under the contract having an aggregate value of not less than $500,000.

Acts 1985, 69th Leg., ch. 959, § 1, eff. Sept. 1, 1985. Amended by Acts 1991, 72nd Leg., ch. 840, § 3, eff. Aug. 26, 1991.

§ 16.072. Saturday, Sunday, or Holiday

If the last day of a limitations period under any statute of limitations falls on a Saturday, Sunday, or holiday, the period for filing suit is extended to include the next day that the county offices are open for business.

Acts 1985, 69th Leg., ch. 959, § 1, eff. Sept. 1, 1985.

Subtitle C. Judgments

Chapter 37. Declaratory Judgments

Statutes in Context
§§ 37.001–37.011

Civil Practice and Remedies Code §§ 37.001–37.011 is the Texas version of the Uniform Declaratory Judgments Act. Of particular importance to trusts and estates is § 37.005 which gives the court broad authority to resolve any question which arises in the administration of a trust or estate, including the power to construe wills.

§ 37.001. Definition

In this chapter, "person" means an individual, partnership, joint-stock company, unincorporated association or society, or municipal or other corporation of any character.

Acts 1985, 69th Leg., ch. 959, § 1, eff. Sept. 1, 1985.

§ 37.002. Short Title, Construction, Interpretation

(a) This chapter may be cited as the Uniform Declaratory Judgments Act.

(b) This chapter is remedial; its purpose is to settle and to afford relief from uncertainty and insecurity with respect to rights, status, and other legal relations; and it is to be liberally construed and administered.

(c) This chapter shall be so interpreted and construed as to effectuate its general purpose to make uniform the law of those states that enact it and to harmonize, as far as possible, with federal laws and regulations on the subject of declaratory judgments and decrees.

Acts 1985, 69th Leg., ch. 959, § 1, eff. Sept. 1, 1985.

§ 37.003. Power of Courts to Render Judgment; Form and Effect

(a) A court of record within its jurisdiction has power to declare rights, status, and other legal relations whether or not further relief is or could be claimed. An action or proceeding is not open to objection on the ground that a declaratory judgment or decree is prayed for.

(b) The declaration may be either affirmative or negative in form and effect, and the declaration has the force and effect of a final judgment or decree.

(c) The enumerations in Sections 37.004 and 37.005 do not limit or restrict the exercise of the general powers conferred in this section in any proceeding in which declaratory relief is sought and a judgment or decree will terminate the controversy or remove an uncertainty.

Acts 1985, 69th Leg., ch. 959, § 1, eff. Sept. 1, 1985.

§ 37.004. Subject Matter of Relief

(a) A person interested under a deed, will, written contract, or other writings constituting a contract or whose rights, status, or other legal relations are affected by a statute, municipal ordinance, contract, or franchise may have determined any question of construction or validity arising under the instrument, statute, ordinance, contract, or franchise and obtain a declaration of rights, status, or other legal relations thereunder.

(b) A contract may be construed either before or after there has been a breach.

(c) Notwithstanding Section 22.001, Property Code, a person described by Subsection (a) may obtain a determination under this chapter when the sole issue concerning title to real property is the determination of the proper boundary line between adjoining properties.

Acts 1985, 69th Leg., ch. 959, § 1, eff. Sept. 1, 1985. Subsec. (c) added by Acts 2007, 80th Leg., ch. 305, § 1, eff. June 15, 2007.

§ 37.005. Declarations Relating to Trust or Estate

A person interested as or through an executor or administrator, including an independent executor or administrator, a trustee, guardian, other fiduciary, creditor, devisee, legatee, heir, next of kin, or cestui que trust in the administration of a trust or of the estate of a decedent, an infant, mentally incapacitated person, or insolvent may have a declaration of rights or legal relations in respect to the trust or estate:

(1) to ascertain any class of creditors, devisees, legatees, heirs, next of kin, or others;

(2) to direct the executors, administrators, or trustees to do or abstain from doing any particular act in their fiduciary capacity;

(3) to determine any question arising in the administration of the trust or estate, including

questions of construction of wills and other writings; or

(4) to determine rights or legal relations of an independent executor or independent administrator regarding fiduciary fees and the settling of accounts.

Acts 1985, 69th Leg., ch. 959, § 1, eff. Sept. 1, 1985. Amended by Acts 1987, 70th Leg., ch. 167, § 3.08(a), eff. Sept. 1, 1987. Amended by Acts 1999, 76th Leg., ch. 855, § 10, eff. Sept. 1, 1999.

§ 37.0055. Declarations Relating to Liability for Sales and Use Taxes of Another State

(a) In this section, "state" includes any political subdivision of that state.

(b) A district court has original jurisdiction of a proceeding seeking a declaratory judgment that involves:

(1) a party seeking declaratory relief that is a business that is:

(A) organized under the laws of this state or is otherwise owned by a resident of this state; or

(B) a retailer registered with the comptroller under Section 151.106, Tax Code; and

(2) a responding party that:

(A) is an official of another state; and

(B) asserts a claim that the party seeking declaratory relief is required to collect sales or use taxes for that state based on conduct of the business that occurs in whole or in part within this state.

(c) A business described by Subsection (b)(1) is entitled to declaratory relief on the issue of whether the requirement of another state that the business collect and remit sales or use taxes to that state constitutes an undue burden on interstate commerce under Section 8, Article I, United States Constitution.

(d) In determining whether to grant declaratory relief to a business under this section, a court shall consider:

(1) the factual circumstances of the business's operations that give rise to the demand by the other state; and

(2) the decisions of other courts interpreting Section 8, Article I, United States Constitution.

Added by Acts 2007, 80th Leg., ch. 699, § 1, eff. Sept. 1, 2007.

§ 37.006. Parties

(a) When declaratory relief is sought, all persons who have or claim any interest that would be affected by the declaration must be made parties. A declaration does not prejudice the rights of a person not a party to the proceeding.

(b) In any proceeding that involves the validity of a municipal ordinance or franchise, the municipality must be made a party and is entitled to be heard, and if the statute, ordinance, or franchise is alleged to be unconstitutional, the attorney general of the state must also be served with a copy of the proceeding and is entitled to be heard.

Acts 1985, 69th Leg., ch. 959, § 1, eff. Sept. 1, 1985.

§ 37.007. Jury Trial

If a proceeding under this chapter involves the determination of an issue of fact, the issue may be tried and determined in the same manner as issues of fact are tried and determined in other civil actions in the court in which the proceeding is pending.

Acts 1985, 69th Leg., ch. 959, § 1, eff. Sept. 1, 1985.

§ 37.008. Court Refusal to Render

The court may refuse to render or enter a declaratory judgment or decree if the judgment or decree would not terminate the uncertainty or controversy giving rise to the proceeding.

Acts 1985, 69th Leg., ch. 959, § 1, eff. Sept. 1, 1985.

§ 37.009. Costs

In any proceeding under this chapter, the court may award costs and reasonable and necessary attorney's fees as are equitable and just.

Acts 1985, 69th Leg., ch. 959, § 1, eff. Sept. 1, 1985.

§ 37.010. Review

All orders, judgments, and decrees under this chapter may be reviewed as other orders, judgments, and decrees.

Acts 1985, 69th Leg., ch. 959, § 1, eff. Sept. 1, 1985.

§ 37.011. Supplemental Relief

Further relief based on a declaratory judgment or decree may be granted whenever necessary or proper. The application must be by petition to a court having jurisdiction to grant the relief. If the application is deemed sufficient, the court shall, on reasonable notice, require any adverse party whose rights have been adjudicated by the declaratory judgment or decree to show cause why further relief should not be granted forthwith.

Acts 1985, 69th Leg., ch. 959, § 1, eff. Sept. 1, 1985.

Title 4. Liability in Tort

Chapter 71. Wrongful Death; Survival; Injuries Occurring Out of State

Statutes in Context
§§ 71.001–71.052

Civil Practice and Remedies Code §§ 71.001–71.052 deal with survival and wrongful death actions. The distinction between these two actions is important. A survival action is normally brought by the personal representative of the decedent for damages to which the decedent would have been entitled if the decedent had not died. The decedent may or may not have already filed suit for these damages prior to death. Any recovery is distributed as part of the decedent's estate. On the other hand, a wrongful death action is usually brought by the person(s) specified in § 71.004 (surviving spouse, children, or parents) and any recovery belongs to that person regardless of how the decedent's property would pass under intestacy or by will.

Subchapter A. Wrongful Death

§ 71.001. Definitions

In this subchapter:

(1) "Corporation" means a municipal, private, public, or quasi-public corporation other than a county or a common or independent school district.

(2) "Person" means an individual, association of individuals, joint-stock company, or corporation or a trustee or receiver of an individual, association of individuals, joint-stock company, or corporation.

(3) "Death" includes, for an individual who is an unborn child, the failure to be born alive.

(4) "Individual" includes an unborn child at every stage of gestation from fertilization until birth.

Acts 1985, 69th Leg., ch. 959, § 1, eff. Sept. 1, 1985. Amended by Acts 2003, 78th Leg., ch. 822, § 1.01, eff. Sept. 1, 2003.

§ 71.002. Cause of Action

(a) An action for actual damages arising from an injury that causes an individual's death may be brought if liability exists under this section.

(b) A person is liable for damages arising from an injury that causes an individual's death if the injury was caused by the person's or his agent's or servant's wrongful act, neglect, carelessness, unskillfulness, or default.

(c) A person is liable for damages arising from an injury that causes an individual's death if:

(1) the person is a proprietor, owner, charterer, or hirer of an industrial or public utility plant or of a railroad, street railway, steamboat, stagecoach, or other vehicle for the transportation of goods or passengers; and

(2) the injury was caused by the person's or his agent's or servant's wrongful act, neglect, carelessness, unskillfulness, or default.

(d) A person is liable for damages arising from an injury that causes an individual's death if:

(1) the person is a receiver, trustee, or other person in charge of or in control of a railroad, street railway, steamboat, stagecoach, or other vehicle for the transportation of goods or passengers, of an industrial or public utility plant, or of other machinery; and

(2) the injury was caused by:

(A) the person's wrongful act, neglect, carelessness, unskillfulness, or default;

(B) the person's servant's or agent's wrongful act, neglect, carelessness, unfitness, unskillfulness, or default; or

(C) a bad or unsafe condition of the railroad, street railway, or other machinery under the person's control or operation.

(e) A person is liable for damages arising from an injury that causes an individual's death if:

(1) the person is a receiver, trustee, or other person in charge of or in control of a railroad, street railway, steamboat, stagecoach, or other vehicle for the transportation of goods or passengers, of an industrial or public utility plant, or of other machinery; and

(2) the action could have been brought against the owner of the railroad, street railway, or other machinery if he had been acting as operator.

Acts 1985, 69th Leg., ch. 959, § 1, eff. Sept. 1, 1985.

§ 71.003. Application; Certain Conduct Excepted

(a) This subchapter applies only if the individual injured would have been entitled to bring an action for the injury if the individual had lived or had been born alive.

(b) This subchapter applies whether the injury occurs inside or outside this state.

(c) This subchapter does not apply to a claim for the death of an individual who is an unborn child that is brought against:

(1) the mother of the unborn child;

(2) a physician or other licensed health care provider, if the death is the intended result of a lawful medical procedure performed by the physician or health care provider with the requisite consent;

(3) a person who dispenses or administers a drug in accordance with law, if the death is the result of the dispensation or administration of the drug; or

(4) a physician or other health care provider licensed in this state, if the death directly or indirectly is caused by, associated with, arises out of, or relates to a lawful medical or health care practice or procedure of the physician or the health care provider.

Acts 1985, 69th Leg., ch. 959, § 1, eff. Sept. 1, 1985. Amended by Acts 2003, 78th Leg., ch. 822, § 1.02, eff. Sept. 1, 2003.

§ 71.004. Benefiting From and Bringing Action

(a) An action to recover damages as provided by this subchapter is for the exclusive benefit of the surviving spouse, children, and parents of the deceased.

(b) The surviving spouse, children, and parents of the deceased may bring the action or one or more of those individuals may bring the action for the benefit of all.

(c) If none of the individuals entitled to bring an action have begun the action within three calendar months after the death of the injured individual, his executor or administrator shall bring and prosecute the action unless requested not to by all those individuals.

Acts 1985, 69th Leg., ch. 959, § 1. eff. Sept. 1, 1985.

§ 71.005. Evidence Relating to Marital Status

In an action under this subchapter, evidence of the actual ceremonial remarriage of the surviving spouse is admissible, if it is true, but the defense is prohibited from directly or indirectly mentioning or alluding to a common-law marriage, an extramarital relationship, or the marital prospects of the surviving spouse.

Acts 1985, 69th Leg., ch. 959, § 1. eff. Sept. 1, 1985.

§ 71.0055. Evidence of Pregnancy

In an action under this subchapter for the death of an individual who is an unborn child, the plaintiff shall provide medical or other evidence that the mother of the individual was pregnant at the time of the individual's death.

Added by Acts 2003, 78th Leg., ch. 822, § 1.03, eff. Sept. 1, 2003.

§ 71.006. Effect of Felonious Act

An action under this subchapter is not precluded because the death is caused by a felonious act or because there may be a criminal proceeding in relation to the felony.

Acts 1985, 69th Leg., ch. 959, § 1. eff. Sept. 1, 1985.

§ 71.007. Ineffective Agreement

An agreement between the owner of a railroad, street railway, steamboat, stagecoach, or other vehicle for the transportation of goods or passengers, of an industrial or public utility plant, or of other machinery and an individual, corporation, trustee, receiver, lessee, joint-stock association, or other entity in control of or operating the vehicle, plant, or other machinery does not release the owner or the entity controlling or operating the vehicle, plant, or other machinery from liability provided by this subchapter.

Acts 1985, 69th Leg., ch. 959, § 1. eff. Sept. 1, 1985.

§ 71.008. Death of Defendant

(a) If a defendant dies while an action under this subchapter is pending or if the individual against whom the action may have been instituted dies before the action is begun, the executor or administrator of the estate may be made a defendant, and the action may be prosecuted as though the defendant or individual were alive.

(b) A judgment in favor of the plaintiff shall be paid in due course of administration.

Acts 1985, 69th Leg., ch. 959, § 1. eff. Sept. 1, 1985.

§ 71.009. Exemplary Damages

When the death is caused by the wilful act or omission or gross negligence of the defendant, exemplary as well as actual damages may be recovered.

Acts 1985, 69th Leg., ch. 959, § 1, eff. Sept. 1, 1985.

§ 71.010. Award and Apportionment of Damages

(a) The jury may award damages in an amount proportionate to the injury resulting from the death.

(b) The damages awarded shall be divided, in shares as found by the jury in its verdict, among the individuals who are entitled to recover and who are alive at that time.

Acts 1985, 69th Leg., ch. 959, § 1, eff. Sept. 1, 1985.

§ 71.011. Damages Not Subject to Debts

Damages recovered in an action under this subchapter are not subject to the debts of the deceased.

Acts 1985, 69th Leg., ch. 959, § 1, eff. Sept. 1, 1985.

§ 71.012. Qualification of Foreign Personal Representative

If the executor or administrator of the estate of a nonresident individual is the plaintiff in an action under this subchapter, the foreign personal representative of the estate who has complied with the requirements of Section 95, Texas Probate Code, for the probate of a foreign will is not required to apply for ancillary letters testamentary under Section 105, Texas Probate Code, to bring and prosecute the action.

Added by Acts 1999, 76th Leg., ch. 382, § 1, eff. May 29, 1999.

Subchapter B. Survival

§ 71.021. Survival of Cause of Action

(a) A cause of action for personal injury to the health, reputation, or person of an injured person does not abate because of the death of the injured person or because of the death of a person liable for the injury.

(b) A personal injury action survives to and in favor of the heirs, legal representatives, and estate of the injured person. The action survives against the liable person and the person's legal representatives.

(c) The suit may be instituted and prosecuted as if the liable person were alive.

Acts 1985, 69th Leg., ch. 959, § 1, eff. Sept. 1, 1985.

§ 71.022. Qualification of Foreign Personal Representative

If the executor or administrator of the estate of a nonresident individual is the plaintiff in an action under this subchapter, the foreign personal representative of the estate who has complied with the requirements of Section 95, Texas Probate Code, for the probate of a foreign will is not required to apply for ancillary letters testamentary under Section 105, Texas Probate Code, to bring and prosecute the action.

Added by Acts 1999, 76ᵗʰ Leg., ch. 382, § 2, eff. May 29, 1999.

Subchapter C. Death or Injury Caused by Act or Omission Out of State

§ 71.031. Act or Omission Out of State

(a) An action for damages for the death or personal injury of a citizen of this state, of the United States, or of a foreign country may be enforced in the courts of this state, although the wrongful act, neglect, or default causing the death or injury takes place in a foreign state or country, if:

(1) a law of the foreign state or country or of this state gives a right to maintain an action for damages for the death or injury;

(2) the action is begun in this state within the time provided by the laws of this state for beginning the action;

(3) for a resident of a foreign state or country, the action is begun in this state within the time provided by the laws of the foreign state or country in which the wrongful act, neglect, or default took place; and

(4) in the case of a citizen of a foreign country, the country has equal treaty rights with the United States on behalf of its citizens.

(b) Except as provided by Subsection (a), all matters pertaining to procedure in the prosecution or maintenance of the action in the courts of this state are governed by the law of this state.

(c) The court shall apply the rules of substantive law that are appropriate under the facts of the case.

Acts 1985, 69ᵗʰ Leg., ch. 959, § 1, eff. Sept. 1, 1985. Amended by Acts 1997, 75ᵗʰ Leg., ch. 424, § 3, eff. May 29, 1997.

Chapter 84. Charitable Immunity and Liability

Statutes in Context
§§ 84.001–84.008

A charitable trust originally could not be liable for tort damages because of the doctrine of charitable immunity. In *Howle v. Camp Amon Carter*, 470 S.W.2d 629 (Tex. 1971), the Texas Supreme Court abolished charitable immunity for torts occurring after March 9, 1966. The Charitable Immunity and Liability Act of 1987, contained in Civil Practice and Remedies Code §§ 84.001–84.008, reinstates, in specified circumstances, charitable immunity for volunteers and limits the liability of employees of charities. Note that liability is restricted only for acts of ordinary negligence.

§ 84.001. Name of Act

This Act may be cited as the Charitable Immunity and Liability Act of 1987.

Added by Acts 1987, 70ᵗʰ Leg., ch. 370, § 1, eff. Sept. 1, 1987.

§ 84.002. Findings and Purposes

The Legislature of the State of Texas finds that:

(1) robust, active, bona fide, and well-supported charitable organizations are needed within Texas to perform essential and needed services;

(2) the willingness of volunteers to offer their services to these organizations is deterred by the perception of personal liability arising out of the services rendered to these organizations;

(3) because of these concerns over personal liability, volunteers are withdrawing from services in all capacities;

(4) these same organizations have a further problem in obtaining and affording liability insurance for the organization and its employees and volunteers;

(5) these problems combine to diminish the services being provided to Texas and local communities because of higher costs and fewer programs;

(6) the citizens of this state have an overriding interest in the continued and increased delivery of these services that must be balanced with other policy considerations; and

(7) because of the above conditions and policy considerations, it is the purpose of this Act to reduce the liability exposure and insurance costs of these organizations and their employees and volunteers in order to encourage volunteer services and maximize the resources devoted to delivering these services.

Added by Acts 1987, 70ᵗʰ Leg., ch. 370, § 1, eff. Sept. 1, 1987.

§ 84.003. Definitions

In this chapter:

(1) "Charitable organization" means:

(A) any organization exempt from federal income tax under Section 501(A) of the Internal Revenue Code of 1986[1] by being listed as an exempt organization in Section 501(c)(3) or 501(c)(4) of the code,[2] if it is a corporation, foundation, community chest, church, or fund organized and operated exclusively for charitable, religious, prevention of cruelty to children or animals, youth sports and youth recreational, neighborhood crime prevention or patrol, fire protection or prevention, emergency medical or hazardous material response services, or educational purposes, including

---

[1] 26 U.S.C. § 501(a).
[2] 26 U.S.C. § 501(c)(3), 501(c)(4).

private primary or secondary schools, if accredited by a member association of the Texas Private School Accreditation Commission but excluding fraternities, sororities, and secret societies, or is organized and operated exclusively for the promotion of social welfare by being primarily engaged in promoting the common good and general welfare of the people in a community;

(B) any bona fide charitable, religious, prevention of cruelty to children or animals, youth sports and youth recreational, neighborhood crime prevention or patrol, or educational organization, excluding fraternities, sororities, and secret societies, or other organization organized and operated exclusively for the promotion of social welfare by being primarily engaged in promoting the common good and general welfare of the people in a community, and that:

(i) is organized and operated exclusively for one or more of the above purposes;

(ii) does not engage in activities which in themselves are not in furtherance of the purpose or purposes;

(iii) does not directly or indirectly participate or intervene in any political campaign on behalf of or in opposition to any candidate for public office;

(iv) dedicates its assets to achieving the stated purpose or purposes of the organization;

(v) does not allow any part of its net assets on dissolution of the organization to inure to the benefit of any group, shareholder, or individual; and

(vi) normally receives more than one-third of its support in any year from private or public gifts, grants, contributions, or membership fees;

(C) a homeowners association as defined by Section 528(c) of the Internal Revenue Code of 1986[1] or which is exempt from federal income tax under Section 501(A) of the Internal Revenue Code of 1986 by being listed as an exempt organization in Section 501(c)(4) of the code;

(D) a volunteer center, as that term is defined by Section 411.126, Government Code; or

(E) a local chamber of commerce that:

(i) is exempt from federal income tax under Section 501(a) of the Internal Revenue Code of 1986 by being listed as an exempt organization in Section 501(c)(6) of the code;

(ii) does not directly or indirectly participate or intervene in any political campaign on behalf of or in opposition to any candidate for public office; and

(iii) does not directly or indirectly contribute to a political action committee that makes expenditures to any candidates for public office.

(F) any organization exempt from federal income tax under Section 501(a) of the Internal Revenue Code of 1986 by being listed as an exempt organization in Section 501(c)(3) or 501(c)(5) of the code, if it is an organization or corporation organized and operated exclusively for wildfire mitigation, range management, or prescribed burning purposes.

(2) "Volunteer" means a person rendering services for or on behalf of a charitable organization who does not receive compensation in excess of reimbursement for expenses incurred. The term includes a person serving as a director, officer, trustee, or direct service volunteer, including a volunteer health care provider.

(3) "Employee" means any person, including an officer or director, who is in the paid service of a charitable organization, but does not include an independent contractor.

(4) (Repealed)

(5) "Volunteer health care provider" means an individual who voluntarily provides health care services without compensation or expectation of compensation and who is:

(A) an individual who is licensed to practice medicine under Subtitle B, Title 3, Occupations Code;

(B) a retired physician who is eligible to provide health care services, including a retired physician who is licensed but exempt from paying the required annual registration fee under Section 156.002, Occupations Code;

(C) a physician assistant licensed under Chapter 204, Occupations Code, or a retired physician assistant who is eligible to provide health care services under the law of this state;

(D) a registered nurse, including an advanced nurse practitioner or vocational nurse, licensed under Chapter 301, Occupations Code, or a retired vocational nurse or registered nurse, including a retired advanced nurse practitioner, who is eligible to provide health care services under the law of this state;

(E) a pharmacist licensed under Subtitle J, Title 3, Occupations Code, or a retired pharmacist who is eligible to provide health care services under the law of this state;

(F) a podiatrist licensed under Chapter 202, Occupations Code, or a retired podiatrist who is eligible to provide health care services under the law of this state;

---

[1] 26 U.S.C. § 528(c).

(G) a dentist licensed under Subtitle D, Title 3, Occupations Code, or a retired dentist who is eligible to provide health care services under the law of this state;

(H) a dental hygienist licensed under Subtitle D, Title 3, Occupations Code, or a retired dental hygienist who is eligible to provide health care services under the law of this state; or

(I) an optometrist or therapeutic optometrist licensed under Chapter 351, Occupations Code, or a retired optometrist or therapeutic optometrist who is eligible to provide health care services under the law of this state;

(J) a physical therapist or physical therapist assistant licensed under Chapter 453, Occupations Code, or a retired physical therapist or physical therapist assistant who is eligible to provide health care services under the law of this state;

(K) an occupational therapist or occupational therapy assistant licensed under Chapter 454, Occupations Code, or a retired occupational therapist or occupational therapy assistant who is eligible to provide health care services under the law of this state; [or]

(L) an audiologist, assistant in audiology, speech-language pathologist, or assistant in speech-language pathology licensed under Chapter 401, Occupations Code, or a retired audiologist, assistant in audiology, speech-language pathologist, or assistant in speech-language pathology who is eligible to provide health care services under the laws of this state; or

(M) a social worker licensed under Chapter 505, Occupations Code, or a retired social worker who is eligible to engage in the practice of social work under the law of this state.

(6) "Hospital system" means a system of hospitals and other health care providers located in this state that are under the common governance or control of a corporate parent.

(7) "Person responsible for the patient" means:

(A) the patient's parent, managing conservator, or guardian;

(B) the patient's grandparent;

(C) the patient's adult brother or sister;

(D) another adult who has actual care, control, and possession of the patient and has written authorization to consent for the patient from the parent, managing conservator, or guardian of the patient;

(E) an educational institution in which the patient is enrolled that has written authorization to consent for the patient from the parent, managing conservator, or guardian of the patient; or

(F) any other person with legal responsibility for the care of the patient.

Added by Acts 1987, 70th Leg., ch. 370, § 1, eff. Sept. 1, 1987. Amended by Acts 1989, 71st Leg., ch. 634, § 1, eff. Sept. 1, 1989. Amended by Acts 1997, 75th Leg., ch. 403, § 1, eff. Sept. 1, 1997; Acts 1999, 76th Leg., ch. 400, § 1, eff. Sept. 1, 1999; Acts 2001, 77th Leg., ch. 77, § 1, eff. May 14, 2001; Acts 2001, 77th Leg., ch. 538, § 1, eff. Sept. 1, 2001; Acts 2001, 77th Leg., ch. 1420, § 14.732, eff. Sept. 1, 2001; Acts 2003, 78th Leg., ch. 93, § 1, eff. Sept. 1, 2003; Acts 2003, 78th Leg., ch. 204, §§ 10.03, 10.04, & 18.03, eff. Sept. 1, 2003; Acts 2003, 78th Leg., ch. 553, § 2.001, eff. Sept. 1, 2003; Acts 2003, 78th Leg., ch. 895, § 1, eff. Sept. 1, 2003. Subsec. (5) amended by Acts 2007, 80th Leg., ch. 239, § 1, eff. Sept. 1, 2007. Subsec. (5) amended by Acts 2009, 81st Leg., ch. 791, § 1, eff. Sept. 1, 2009. Subsec. (1)(a) amended by Acts 2011, 82nd Leg., ch. 39, § 1, eff. May 9, 2011. Subsec. (1)(F) added by Acts 2015, 84th Leg., ch. 169, § 1, eff. Sept. 1, 2015. Subsec. (5)(M) added by Acts 2015, 84th Leg., ch. 14, § 1, eff. Sept. 1, 2015.

§ 84.004. Volunteer Liability

(a) Except as provided by Subsection (d) and Section 84.007, a volunteer of a charitable organization is immune from civil liability for any act or omission resulting in death, damage, or injury if the volunteer was acting in the course and scope of the volunteer's duties or functions including as an officer, director, or trustee within the organization.

(b) (Repealed)

(c) Except as provided by Subsection (d) and Section 84.007, a volunteer health care provider who is serving as a direct service volunteer of a charitable organization is immune from civil liability for any act or omission resulting in death, damage, or injury to a patient if:

(1) the volunteer commits the act or omission in the course of providing health care services to the patient;

(2) the services provided are within the scope of the license of the volunteer; and

(3) before the volunteer provides health care services, the patient or, if the patient is a minor or is otherwise legally incompetent, the person responsible for the patient signs a written statement that acknowledges:

(A) that the volunteer is providing care that is not administered for or in expectation of compensation; and

(B) the limitations on the recovery of damages from the volunteer in exchange for receiving the health care services.

(d) A volunteer of a charitable organization is liable to a person for death, damage, or injury to the person or his property proximately caused by any act or omission arising from the operation or use of any motor-driven equipment, including an airplane, to the extent insurance coverage is required by Chapter 601, Transportation Code, and to the extent of any existing insurance coverage applicable to the act or omission.

(e) The provisions of this section apply only to the liability of volunteers and do not apply to the liability of the organization for acts or omissions of volunteers.

(f) Subsection (c) applies even if:

(1) the patient is incapacitated due to illness or injury and cannot sign the acknowledgment statement required by that subsection; or

(2) the patient is a minor or is otherwise legally incompetent and the person responsible for the patient is not reasonably available to sign the acknowledgment statement required by that subsection.

Added by Acts 1987, 70th Leg., ch. 370, § 1, eff. Sept. 1, 1987. Amended by Acts 1997, 75th Leg., ch. 165, § 30.179, eff. Sept. 1, 1997; Acts 1999, 76th Leg., ch. 400, § 2, eff. Sept. 1, 1999; Acts 2003, 78th Leg., ch. 204, §§ 10.05, 18.01, 18.03, eff. Sept. 1, 2003.

§ 84.005. Employee Liability

Except as provided in Section 84.007 of this Act, in any civil action brought against an employee of a nonhospital charitable organization for damages based on an act or omission by the person in the course and scope of the person's employment, the liability of the employee is limited to money damages in a maximum amount of $500,000 for each person and $1,000,000 for each single occurrence of bodily injury or death and $100,000 for each single occurrence for injury to or destruction of property.

Added by Acts 1987, 70th Leg., ch. 370, § 1, eff. Sept. 1, 1987.

§ 84.006. Organization Liability

Except as provided in Section 84.007 of this Act, in any civil action brought against a nonhospital charitable organization for damages based on an act or omission by the organization or its employees or volunteers, the liability of the organization is limited to money damages in a maximum amount of $500,000 for each person and $1,000,000 for each single occurrence of bodily injury or death and $100,000 for each single occurrence for injury to or destruction of property.

Added by Acts 1987, 70th Leg., ch. 370, § 1, eff. Sept. 1, 1987.

§ 84.0061. Organizational Liability for Transportation Services Provided to Certain Welfare Recipients

(a) In this section, "religious charitable organization" means a charitable organization that is also a "religious organization" as the term is defined by Section 464.051, Health and Safety Code.

(b) Subject to Subsection (e), a religious charitable organization that owns or leases a motor vehicle is not liable for damages arising from the negligent use of the vehicle by a person to whom the organization has entrusted the vehicle to provide transportation services during the provision of those services described by Subsection (c) to a person who:

(1) is a recipient of:

(A) financial assistance under Chapter 31, Human Resources Code; or

(B) nutritional assistance under Chapter 33, Human Resources Code; and

(2) is participating in or applying to participate in:

(A) a work or employment activity under Chapter 31, Human Resources Code; or

(B) the food stamp employment and training program.

(c) Transportation services include transportation to and from the location of the:

(1) work, employment, or any training activity or program; or

(2) provider of any child-care services necessary for a person described by Subsection (b)(1) to participate in the work, employment, or training activity or program.

(d) Except as expressly provided in Subsection (b), this section does not limit, or in any way affect or diminish, other legal duties or causes of action arising from the use of a motor vehicle, including the condition of the vehicle itself and causes of action arising under Chapter 41.

(e) This section does not apply to any claim arising from injury, death, or property damage in which the operator of the vehicle was intoxicated, as the term is defined in Section 49.01, Penal Code.

Added by Acts 2001, 77th Leg., ch. 991, § 1, eff. June 15, 2001.

§ 84.0065. Organization Liability of Hospitals

(a) Except as provided by Section 84.007, in any civil action brought against a hospital or hospital system, or its employees, officers, directors, or volunteers, for damages based on an act or omission by the hospital or hospital system, or its employees, officers, directors, or volunteers, the liability of the hospital or hospital system is limited to money damages in a maximum amount of $500,000 for any act or omission resulting in death, damage, or injury to a patient if the patient or, if the patient is a minor or is otherwise legally incompetent, the person responsible for the patient signs a written statement that acknowledges:

(1) that the hospital is providing care that is not administered for or in expectation of compensation; and

(2) the limitations on the recovery of damages from the hospital in exchange for receiving the health care services.

(b) Subsection (a) applies even if:

(1) the patient is incapacitated due to illness or injury and cannot sign the acknowledgment statement required by that subsection; or

(2) the patient is a minor or is otherwise legally incompetent and the person responsible for the patient is not reasonably available to sign the

acknowledgment statement required by that subsection.

Added by Acts 2003, 78ᵗʰ Leg., ch. 204, § 10.06, eff. Sept. 1, 2003.

§ 84.007. Applicability

(a) This chapter does not apply to an act or omission that is intentional, wilfully negligent, or done with conscious indifference or reckless disregard for the safety of others.

(b) This chapter does not limit or modify the duties or liabilities of a member of the board of directors or an officer to the organization or its members and shareholders.

(c) This chapter does not limit the liability of an organization or its employees or volunteers if the organization was formed substantially to limit its liability under this chapter.

(d) This chapter does not apply to organizations formed to dispose, remove, or store hazardous waste, industrial solid waste, radioactive waste, municipal solid waste, garbage, or sludge as those terms are defined under applicable state and federal law. This subsection shall be liberally construed to effectuate its purpose.

(e) Sections 84.005 and 84.006 of this chapter do not apply to a health care provider as defined in Section 74.001, unless the provider is a federally funded migrant or community health center under the Public Health Service Act (42 U.S.C.A. Sections 254b and 254c) or is a nonprofit health maintenance organization created and operated by a community center under Section 534.101, Health and Safety Code, or unless the provider usually provides discounted services at or below costs based on the ability of the beneficiary to pay. Acceptance of Medicare or Medicaid payments will not disqualify a health care provider under this section. In no event shall Sections 84.005 and 84.006 of this chapter apply to a general hospital or special hospital as defined in Chapter 241, Health and Safety Code, or a facility or institution licensed under Subtitle C, Title 7, Health and Safety Code,[1] or Chapter 242, Health and Safety Code, or to any health maintenance organization created and operating under Chapter 843, Insurance Code, except for a nonprofit health maintenance organization created under Section 534.101, Health and Safety Code.

(f) This chapter does not apply to a governmental unit or employee of a governmental unit as defined in the Texas Tort Claims Act (Subchapter A, Chapter 101, Civil Practice and Remedies Code).

(g) Sections 84.005 and 84.006 of this Act do not apply to any charitable organization that does not have liability insurance coverage in effect on any act or omission to which this chapter applies. The coverage shall apply to the acts or omissions of the organization and its employees and volunteers and be in the amount of at least $500,000 for each person and $1,000,000 for each single occurrence for death or bodily injury and $100,000 for each single occurrence for injury to or destruction of property. The coverage may be provided under a contract for insurance, a plan providing for self-insured retention that the charitable organization has fully paid or establishes to a court that it is capable of fully and immediately paying, a Lloyd's plan, an indemnity policy to which all requirements for payment have been or will be met, or other plan of insurance authorized by statute and may be satisfied by the purchase of a $1,000,000 bodily injury and property damage combined single limit policy. For the purposes of this chapter, coverage amounts are inclusive of a self-insured retention, a Lloyd's plan, or an indemnity policy to which all requirements for payment have been or will be met. Nothing in this chapter shall limit liability of any insurer or insurance plan in an action under Chapter 541, Insurance Code, or in an action for bad faith conduct, breach of fiduciary duty, or negligent failure to settle a claim.

(h) This chapter does not apply to:

(1) a statewide trade association that represents local chambers of commerce; or

(2) a cosponsor of an event or activity with a local chamber of commerce unless the cosponsor is a charitable organization under this chapter.

Added by Acts 1987, 70ᵗʰ Leg., ch. 370, § 1, eff. Sept. 1, 1987. Amended by Acts 1991, 72ⁿᵈ Leg., ch. 14, § 284(14), (20), eff. Sept. 1, 1991; Acts 1991, 72ⁿᵈ Leg., ch. 76, § 6, eff. Sept. 1, 1991. Amended by Acts 1997, 75ᵗʰ Leg., ch. 835, § 3, eff. Sept. 1, 1997; Acts 1997, 75ᵗʰ Leg., ch. 1297, § 1, eff. Sept. 1, 1997; Acts 2003, 78ᵗʰ Leg., ch. 93, § 2, eff. Sept. 1, 2003; Acts 2003, 78ᵗʰ Leg., ch. 204, § 18.02, eff. Sept. 1, 2003; Acts 2003, 78ᵗʰ Leg., ch. 1276, § 10A.507, eff. Sept. 1, 2003. Subsec. (e) amended by Acts 2005, 79ᵗʰ Leg., ch. 133, § 1, eff. Sept. 1, 2005. Subsec. (g) amended by Acts 2011, 82ⁿᵈ Leg., ch. 39, § 2, eff. May 9, 2011.

§ 84.008. Severability

If any clause or provision of this chapter or its application to any person or organization is held unconstitutional, such invalidity does not affect other clauses, provisions, or applications of this chapter that can be given effect without the invalid clause or provision and shall not affect or nullify the remainder of the Act or any other clause or provision, but the effect shall be confined to the clause or provision held to be invalid or unconstitutional and to this end the Act is declared to be severable.

Added by Acts 1987, 70ᵗʰ Leg., ch. 370, § 1, eff. Sept. 1, 1987.

Title 6. Miscellaneous Provisions

Chapter 132. Unsworn Declarations

---

[1] Health and Safety Code § 571.001 et seq.

Statutes in Context
§ 132.001

Controversy exists regarding whether this section applies to self-proving affidavits on wills and to other estate planning documents which require a written sworn declaration, verification, certification, oath, or affidavit (that is, a notarization). The 2011 Legislature may have inadvertently removed the former limitation of this section to inmates when it amended the section. The legislative history is inconclusive. The bill analysis of the House version of the bill indicates that this procedure would be available even to persons who are not incarcerated but the bill analysis accompanying the engrossed version of the bill omits this language. The 2013 Legislature resolved this issue by adding Estates Code § 21.005(b) which provides that Chapter 132 does not apply to self-proving affidavits.

§ 132.001. Unsworn Declaration

(a) Except as provided by Subsection (b), an unsworn declaration may be used in lieu of a written sworn declaration, verification, certification, oath, or affidavit required by statute or required by a rule, order, or requirement adopted as provided by law.

(b) This section does not apply to a lien required to be filed with a county clerk, an instrument concerning real or personal property required to be filed with a county clerk, or an oath of office or an oath required to be taken before a specified official other than a notary public.

(c) An unsworn declaration made under this section must be:

(1) in writing; and

(2) subscribed by the person making the declaration as true under penalty of perjury.

(d) Except as provided by Subsections (e) and (f), an unsworn declaration made under this section must include a jurat in substantially the following form:

"My name is _____ _____ _____, my
       (First) (Middle) (Last)
date of birth is _____, and my address is _____, _____, _____, _____,
   (Street) (City) (State) (Zip Code)
and_____.
    (Country)
I declare under penalty of perjury that the foregoing is true and correct.
Executed in _____ County, State of _____, on the _____ day of _____, _____.
         (Month) (Year)

_____
Declarant"

(e) An unsworn declaration made under this section by an inmate must include a jurat in substantially the following form:

"My name is _____ _____ _____
        (First)   (Middle) (Last)
my date of birth is _____, and my inmate identifying number, if any, is _____. I am presently incarcerated in

_____
(Corrections unit name)
in _____, _____, _____, _____,
  (City)   (County) (State) (Zip Code)
I declare under penalty of perjury that the foregoing is true and correct.
Executed on the _____ day of _____, _____.
          (Month) (Year)

_____
Declarant"

(f) An unsworn declaration made under this section by an employee of a state agency or a political subdivision in the performance of the employee's job duties, must include a jurat in substantially the following form:

"My name is _____ _____ _____, my
      (First) (Middle) (Last)
and I am an employee of the following governmental agency: _____. I am executing this declaration as part of my assigned duties and responsibilities. I declare under penalty of perjury that the foregoing is true and correct.
Executed in _____ County, State of _____, on the _____ day of _____, _____.
         (Month) (Year)

_____
Declarant"

Added by Acts 1987, 70th Leg., ch. 1049, § 60, eff. Sept. 1, 1987. Amended by Acts 2009, 81st Leg., ch. 87, § 25.011, eff. Sept. 1, 2009. Amended by Acts 2011, 82nd Leg., ch. 847, § 1, eff. Sept. 1, 2011. Subsection (b) amended by Acts 2013, 83rd Leg., ch. 946, §1, eff. June 14, 2013. Subsection (d) amended and section (f) added by Acts 2013, 83rd Leg., ch. 515, § 1, eff. Sept. 1, 2013.

Chapter 133. Presumption of Death

Statutes in Context
§§ 133.001–133.003

A person missing for seven consecutive years is presumed dead under Civil Practice & Remedies Code § 133.001. See also Probate Code § 72 (allowing circumstantial evidence to prove death). Section 133.003 provides that if the person presumed dead is actually alive, that person is entitled to the return of the person's property along with rents, profits, and interest.

§ 133.001. Seven-Year Absence

Any person absenting himself for seven successive years shall be presumed dead unless it is proved that the person was alive within the seven-year period.

CIVIL PRACTICE AND REMEDIES CODE

Added by Acts 1987, 70th Leg., ch. 167, § 3.15(a), eff. Sept. 1, 1987. Renumbered from Civ. Prac. & Rem. Code § 131.001 by Acts 1989, 71st Leg., ch. 2, § 16.01(4), eff. Aug. 28, 1989.

§ 133.002. Armed Services Certificate of Death

If a branch of the armed services issues a certificate declaring a person dead, the date of death is presumed to have occurred for all purposes as stated in the certificate. The certificate may be admitted in any court of competent jurisdiction as prima facie evidence of the date and place of the person's death.

Added by Acts 1987, 70th Leg., ch. 167, § 3.15(a), eff. Sept. 1, 1987. Renumbered from Civ. Prac. & Rem. Code § 131.002 by Acts 1989, 71st Leg., ch. 2, § 16.01(4), eff. Aug. 28, 1989.

§ 133.003. Restoration of Estate

(a) If an estate is recovered on a presumption of death under this chapter and if in a subsequent action or suit it is proved that the person presumed dead is living, the estate shall be restored to that person. The estate shall be restored with the rents and profits of the estate with legal interest for the time the person was deprived of the estate.

(b) A person delivering an estate or any part of an estate under this section to another under proper order of a court of competent jurisdiction is not liable for the estate or part of the estate.

(c) If the person recovering an estate on a presumption of death sells real property from the estate to a purchaser for value, the right of restoration under this section extends to the recovery of the purchase money received by the person, but does not extend to the recovery of the real property.

Added by Acts 1987, 70th Leg., ch. 167, § 3.15(a), eff. Sept. 1, 1987. Renumbered from Civ. Prac. & Rem. Code § 131.003 by Acts 1989, 71st Leg., ch. 2, § 16.01(4), eff. Aug. 28, 1989.

Chapter 137. Declaration for Mental Health Treatment

Statutes in Context
Chapter 137

Chapter 137 authorizes a person to execute a Declaration for Mental Health Treatment which indicates the person's desires regarding the use of psychoactive medications, convulsive treatment, restraint, seclusion, and other mental health matters should a court determine that the person lacks the ability to make mental health treatment decisions. Section 137.011 provides a fill-in-the-blank form for the declarant to use. Two disinterested individuals must witness the declaration. The declaration does not need to be notarized.

§ 137.001. Definitions

In this chapter:

(1) "Adult" means a person 18 years of age or older or a person under 18 years of age who has had the disabilities of minority removed.

(2) "Attending physician" means the physician, selected by or assigned to a patient, who has primary responsibility for the treatment and care of the patient.

(3) "Declaration for mental health treatment" means a document making a declaration of preferences or instructions regarding mental health treatment.

(4) "Emergency" means a situation in which it is immediately necessary to treat a patient to prevent:

(A) probable imminent death or serious bodily injury to the patient because the patient:

(i) overtly or continually is threatening or attempting to commit suicide or serious bodily injury to the patient; or

(ii) is behaving in a manner that indicates that the patient is unable to satisfy the patient's need for nourishment, essential medical care, or self-protection; or

(B) imminent physical or emotional harm to another because of threats, attempts, or other acts of the patient.

(5) "Health care provider" means an individual or facility licensed, certified, or otherwise authorized to administer health care or treatment, for profit or otherwise, in the ordinary course of business or professional practice and includes a physician or other health care provider, a residential care provider, or an inpatient mental health facility as defined by Section 571.003, Health and Safety Code.

(6) "Incapacitated" means that, in the opinion of the court in a guardianship proceeding under Chapter XIII, Texas Probate Code, or in a medication hearing under Section 574.106, Health and Safety Code, a person lacks the ability to understand the nature and consequences of a proposed treatment, including the benefits, risks, and alternatives to the proposed treatment, and lacks the ability to make mental health treatment decisions because of impairment.

(7) "Mental health treatment" means electroconvulsive or other convulsive treatment, treatment of mental illness with psychoactive medication as defined by Section 574.101, Health and Safety Code, or emergency mental health treatment.

(8) "Principal" means a person who has executed a declaration for mental health treatment.

Added by Acts 1997, 75th Leg., ch. 1318, § 1, eff. Sept. 1, 1997. Amended by Acts 1999, 76th Leg., ch. 464, § 1, eff. June 18, 1999.

§ 137.002. Persons Who May Execute Declaration for Mental Health Treatment; Period of Validity

(a) An adult who is not incapacitated may execute a declaration for mental health treatment. The preferences or instructions may include consent to or refusal of mental health treatment.

(b) A declaration for mental health treatment is effective on execution as provided by this chapter. Except as provided by Subsection (c), a declaration for mental health treatment expires on the third anniversary of the date of its execution or when revoked by the principal, whichever is earlier.

(c) If the declaration for mental health treatment is in effect and the principal is incapacitated on the third anniversary of the date of its execution, the declaration remains in effect until the principal is no longer incapacitated.

Added by Acts 1997, 75th Leg., ch. 1318, § 1, eff. Sept. 1, 1997.

§ 137.003. Execution and Witnesses

(a) A declaration for mental health treatment must be signed by the principal in the presence of two or more subscribing witnesses.

(b) A witness may not, at the time of execution, be:

(1) the principal's health or residential care provider or an employee of that provider;

(2) the operator of a community health care facility providing care to the principal or an employee of an operator of the facility;

(3) a person related to the principal by blood, marriage, or adoption;

(4) a person entitled to any part of the estate of the principal on the death of the principal under a will, trust, or deed in existence or who would be entitled to any part of the estate by operation of law if the principal died intestate; or

(5) a person who has a claim against the estate of the principal.

(c) For a witness's signature to be effective, the witness must sign a statement affirming that, at the time the declaration for mental health treatment was signed, the principal:

(1) appeared to be of sound mind to make a mental health treatment decision;

(2) has stated in the witness's presence that the principal was aware of the nature of the declaration for mental health treatment and that the principal was signing the document voluntarily and free from any duress; and

(3) requested that the witness serve as a witness to the principal's execution of the document.

Added by Acts 1997, 75th Leg., ch. 1318, § 1, eff. Sept. 1, 1997.

§ 137.004. Health Care Provider to Act in Accordance With Declaration for Mental Health Treatment

A physician or other health care provider shall act in accordance with the declaration for mental health treatment when the principal has been found to be incapacitated. A physician or other provider shall continue to seek and act in accordance with the principal's informed consent to all mental health treatment decisions if the principal is capable of providing informed consent.

Added by Acts 1997, 75th Leg., ch. 1318, § 1, eff. Sept. 1, 1997.

§ 137.005. Limitation on Liability

(a) An attending physician, health or residential care provider, or person acting for or under an attending physician's or health or residential care provider's control is not subject to criminal or civil liability and has not engaged in professional misconduct for an act or omission if the act or omission is done in good faith under the terms of a declaration for mental health treatment.

(b) An attending physician, health or residential care provider, or person acting for or under an attending physician's or health or residential care provider's control does not engage in professional misconduct for:

(1) failure to act in accordance with a declaration for mental health treatment if the physician, provider, or other person:

(A) was not provided with a copy of the declaration; and

(B) had no knowledge of the declaration after a good faith attempt to learn of the existence of a declaration; or

(2) acting in accordance with a directive for mental health treatment after the directive has expired or has been revoked if the physician, provider, or other person does not have knowledge of the expiration or revocation.

Added by Acts 1997, 75th Leg., ch. 1318, § 1, eff. Sept. 1, 1997.

§ 137.006. Discrimination Relating to Execution of Declaration for Mental Health Treatment

A health or residential care provider, health care service plan, insurer issuing disability insurance, self-insured employee benefit plan, or nonprofit hospital service plan may not:

(1) charge a person a different rate solely because the person has executed a declaration for mental health treatment;

(2) require a person to execute a declaration for mental health treatment before:

(A) admitting the person to a hospital, nursing home, or residential care home;

(B) insuring the person; or

(C) allowing the person to receive health or residential care;

(3) refuse health or residential care to a person solely because the person has executed a declaration for mental health treatment; or

(4) discharge the person solely because the person has or has not executed a declaration for mental health treatment.

Added by Acts 1997, 75th Leg., ch. 1318, § 1, eff. Sept. 1, 1997.

§ 137.007. Use and Effect of Declaration for Mental Health Treatment

(a) On being presented with a declaration for mental health treatment, a physician or other health care provider shall make the declaration a part of the principal's medical record. When acting in accordance with "a declaration for mental health treatment, a physician or other health care provider shall comply with the declaration to the fullest extent possible.

(b) If a physician or other provider is unwilling at any time to comply with a declaration for mental health treatment, the physician or provider may withdraw from providing treatment consistent with the exercise of independent medical judgment and must promptly:

(1) make a reasonable effort to transfer care for the principal to a physician or provider who is willing to comply with the declaration;

(2) notify the principal, or principal's guardian, if appropriate, of the decision to withdraw; and

(3) record in the principal's medical record the notification and, if applicable, the name of the physician or provider to whom the principal is transferred.

Added by Acts 1997, 75th Leg., ch. 1318, § 1, eff. Sept. 1, 1997. Amended by Acts 1999, 76th Leg., ch. 464, § 2, eff. June 18, 1999.

§ 137.008. Disregard of Declaration for Mental Health Treatment

(a) A physician or other health care provider may subject the principal to mental health treatment in a manner contrary to the principal's wishes as expressed in a declaration for mental health treatment only:

(1) if the principal is under an order for temporary or extended mental health services under Section 574.034 or 574.035, Health and Safety Code, and treatment is authorized in compliance with Section 574.106, Health and Safety Code; or

(2) in case of an emergency when the principal's instructions have not been effective in reducing the severity of the behavior that has caused the emergency.

(b) A declaration for mental health treatment does not limit any authority provided by Chapter 573 or 574, Health and Safety Code:

(1) to take a person into custody; or

(2) to admit or retain a person in a mental health treatment facility.

(c) This section does not apply to the use of electroconvulsive treatment or other convulsive treatment.

Added by Acts 1997, 75th Leg., ch. 1318, § 1, eff. Sept. 1, 1997. Amended by Acts 1999, 76th Leg., ch. 464, § 3, eff. June 18, 1999.

§ 137.009. Conflicting or Contrary Provisions

(a) Mental health treatment instructions contained in a declaration executed in accordance with this chapter supersede any contrary or conflicting instructions given by:

(1) a durable power of attorney under Chapter 135; or

(2) a guardian appointed under Chapter XIII, Texas Probate Code, after the execution of the declaration.

(b) Mental health treatment instructions contained in a declaration executed in accordance with this chapter shall be conclusive evidence of a declarant's preference in a medication hearing under Section 574.106, Health and Safety Code.

Added by Acts 1997, 75th Leg., ch. 1318, § 1, eff. Sept. 1, 1997.

§ 137.010. Revocation

(a) A declaration for mental health treatment is revoked when a principal who is not incapacitated:

(1) notifies a licensed or certified health or residential care provider of the revocation;

(2) acts in a manner that demonstrates a specific intent to revoke the declaration; or

(3) executes a later declaration for mental health treatment.

(b) A principal's health or residential care provider who is informed of or provided with a revocation of a declaration for mental health treatment immediately shall:

(1) record the revocation in the principal's medical record; and

(2) give notice of the revocation to any other health or residential care provider the provider knows to be responsible for the principal's care.

Added by Acts 1997, 75th Leg., ch. 1318, § 1, eff. Sept. 1, 1997. Amended by Acts 1999, 76th Leg., ch. 464, § 4, eff. June 18, 1999.

§ 137.011. Form of Declaration for Mental Health Treatment

The declaration for mental health treatment must be in substantially the following form:

DECLARATION FOR MENTAL HEALTH TREATMENT

I, _____, being an adult of sound mind, wilfully and voluntarily make this declaration for mental health treatment to be followed if it is determined by a court that my ability to understand the nature and consequences of a proposed treatment, including the benefits, risks, and alternatives to the proposed treatment, is impaired to such an extent that I lack the capacity to make mental health treatment decisions. "Mental health treatment" means electroconvulsive or other convulsive treatment, treatment of mental illness with psychoactive medication, and preferences regarding emergency mental health treatment.

(OPTIONAL PARAGRAPH) I understand that I may become incapable of giving or withholding informed consent for mental health treatment due to the symptoms of a diagnosed mental disorder. These symptoms may include: _____

_____

PSYCHOACTIVE MEDICATIONS

If I become incapable of giving or withholding informed consent for mental health treatment, my wishes regarding psychoactive medications are as follows:

_____ I consent to the administration of the following medications: _____

_____ I do not consent to the administration of the following medications: _____

_____

_____ I consent to the administration of a federal Food and Drug Administration approved medication that was only approved and in existence after my declaration and that is considered in the same class of psychoactive medications as stated below: _____

_____

Conditions or limitations: _____

_____

CONVULSIVE TREATMENT

If I become incapable of giving or withholding informed consent for mental health treatment, my wishes regarding convulsive treatment are as follows:

_____ I consent to the administration of convulsive treatment.

_____ I do not consent to the administration of convulsive treatment.

Conditions or limitations: _____

_____

PREFERENCES FOR EMERGENCY TREATMENT

In an emergency, I prefer the following treatment FIRST (circle one) Restraint/Seclusion/Medication.

In an emergency. I prefer the following treatment SECOND (circle one) Restraint/Seclusion/Medication.

In an emergency, I prefer the following "treatment THIRD (circle one) Restraint/Seclusion/Medication.

_____ I prefer a male/female to administer restraint, seclusion, and/or medications.

Options for treatment prior to use of restraint, seclusion, and/or medications: _____

_____

Conditions or limitations: _____

ADDITIONAL PREFERENCES OR INSTRUCTIONS
Conditions or limitations: _____

_____

Signature of Principal/Date: _____

STATEMENT OF WITNESSES

I declare under penalty of perjury that the principal's name has been represented to me by the principal, that the principal signed or acknowledged this declaration in my presence, that I believe the principal to be of sound mind, that the principal has affirmed that the principal is aware of the nature of the document and is signing it voluntarily and free from duress, that the principal requested that I serve as witness to the principal's execution of this document, and that I am not a provider of health or residential care to the principal, an employee of a provider of health or residential care to the principal, an operator of a community health care facility providing care to the principal, or an employee of an operator of a community health care facility providing care to the principal.

I declare that I am not related to the principal by blood, marriage, or adoption and that to the best of my knowledge I am not entitled to and do not have a claim against any part of the estate of the principal on the death of the principal under a will or by operation of law.

Witness Signature: _____
Print Name: _____
Date: _____
Address: _____
Witness Signature: _____
Print Name: _____
Date: _____
Address: _____

NOTICE TO PERSON MAKING A DECLARATION FOR MENTAL HEALTH TREATMENT

This is an important legal document. It creates a declaration for mental health treatment. Before signing this document, you should know these important facts:

This document allows you to make decisions in advance about mental health treatment and specifically three types of mental health treatment: psychoactive medication, convulsive therapy, and emergency mental health treatment. The instructions that you include in this declaration will be followed only if a court believes that you are incapacitated to make treatment decisions. Otherwise, you will be considered able to give or withhold consent for the treatments.

This document will continue in effect for a period of three years unless you become incapacitated to participate in mental health treatment decisions. If this occurs, the directive will continue in effect until you are no longer incapacitated.

You have the right to revoke this document in whole or in part at any time you have not been determined to be incapacitated. YOU MAY NOT REVOKE THIS DECLARATION WHEN YOU ARE

CONSIDERED BY A COURT TO BE INCAPACITATED. A revocation is effective when it is communicated to your attending physician or other health care provider.

If there is anything in this document that you do not understand, you should ask a lawyer to explain it to you. This declaration is not valid unless it is signed by two qualified witnesses who are personally known to you and who are present when you sign or acknowledge your signature.

Added by Acts 1997, 75th Leg., ch. 1318, § 1, eff. Sept. 1, 1997.

IV.

CONSTITUTION OF THE STATE OF TEXAS

Article I.   Bill of Rights

Statutes in Context
Article I, § 21

At common law, a person could not inherit land if the person was convicted or imprisoned for certain offenses, especially treason and other capital offenses. The English parliament abolished corruption of the blood by the mid-1800s and the practice is prohibited under Article I, § 21 of the Texas Constitution. Accordingly, an imprisoned person, even one on death row, may inherit property.

At common law, a person who was convicted of a felony forfeited all of the person's property to the government so there was no property for the person's heirs to inherit. Although most states have abolished forfeiture for most felonies, it is occasionally retained as a remedy for specific crimes. For example, under federal law, a person convicted of certain drug offenses forfeits a portion of the person's property to the government. 21 U.S.C. § 853. Forfeiture is prohibited by Article I, § 21 of the Texas Constitution.

The property of a person who committed suicide was subject to special rules at common law. If the intestate committed suicide to avoid punishment after committing a felony, the intestate's heirs took nothing. Instead, the real property escheated and personal property was forfeited. However, if the intestate committed suicide because of pain or exhaustion from living, only personal property was forfeited and real property still descended to the heirs. Article I, § 21 of the Texas Constitution abolishes these common-law rules and thus the property of a person who commits suicide passes just as if the death were caused by some other means.

See also Probate Code § 41.

Article I, § 21.   Corruption of blood; forfeiture of estate; descent in case of suicide

No conviction shall work corruption of blood, or forfeiture of estate, and the estates of those who destroy their own lives shall descend or vest as in case of natural death.

Statutes in Context
Article I, § 26

Article I, § 26 adopts the common-law version of the Rule Against Perpetuities, that is, "a future interest not destructible by the owner of a prior interest cannot be valid unless it becomes vested at a date not more remote than twenty-one years after lives in being at the creation of such interest, plus the period of gestation. Any future interest so limited that it retains its indestructible and contingent character until a more remote time is invalid." Interpretive Commentary to Article I, § 21. The court must, however, reform transfers that violate the Rule under Property Code § 5.043. See also Property Code § 112.036 (indicating that the Rule does not apply to charitable trusts).

Article I, § 26.   Perpetuities and monopolies; primogeniture or entailments

Perpetuities and monopolies are contrary to the genius of a free government, and shall never be allowed, nor shall the law of primogeniture or entailments ever be in force in this State.

Article XVI.   General Provisions

Statutes in Context
Article XVI, § 15

Texas is a community property marital property jurisdiction and Article XVI, § 15 is the key constitutional provision which imposes this system. This Article also deals with a variety of other matters such as the partition of community property into separate property, the conversion of separate property into community property, and the creation of community property survivorship agreements. The legislature has more specifically described community and separate property rules in the Family, Probate, and Property Codes.

Article XVI, § 15.   Separate and community property of husband and wife

All property, both real and personal, of a spouse owned or claimed before marriage, and that acquired afterward by gift, devise or descent, shall be the separate property of that spouse; and laws shall be passed more clearly defining the rights of the spouses, in relation to separate and community property;

provided that persons about to marry and spouses, without the intention to defraud pre-existing creditors, may by written instrument from time to time partition between themselves all or part of their property, then existing or to be acquired, or exchange between themselves the community interest of one spouse or future spouse in any property for the community interest of the other spouse or future spouse in other community property then existing or to be acquired, whereupon the portion or interest set aside to each spouse shall be and constitute a part of the separate property and estate of such spouse or future spouse; spouses also may from time to time, by written instrument, agree between themselves that the income or property from all or part of the separate property then owned or which thereafter might be acquired by only one of them, shall be the separate property of that spouse; if one spouse makes a gift of property to the other that gift is presumed to include all the income or property which might arise from that gift of property; spouses may agree in writing that all or part of their community property becomes the property of the surviving spouse on the death of a spouse; and spouses may agree in writing that all or part of the separate property owned by either or both of them shall be the spouses' community property.

Amended Nov. 2, 1999.

Statutes in Context
Article XVI, § 49

Following the authorization of Article XVI, § 49, the Texas Legislature has provided for certain personal property to be exempt from forced sale. See Property Code Chapter 42.

Article XVI, § 49. Protection of personal property from forced sale

The Legislature shall have power, and it shall be its duty, to protect by law from forced sale a certain portion of the personal property of all heads of families, and also of unmarried adults, male and female.

Statutes in Context
Article XVI, § 50

The source of the tremendous protection granted to Texas homesteads is Article XVI, § 50 of the Texas Constitution. This section establishes the protection without dollar value limitation and then lists exceptions, that is, situations in which the homestead is not protected. These exceptions are summarized as follows:

1. Purchase Money Liens—A purchase money lien is a lien on the homestead securing the purchase price in favor of the seller or lending bank. Purchase money liens are not subject to the homestead exemption, thus permitting the homestead to be foreclosed upon default. Article XVI, § 50(a)(1); Property Code § 41.001(b)(1).

2. Ad Valorem Taxes—A tax lien attaches automatically on the first of every year to all property on which property taxes are owed. Tax Code. § 32.01. The homestead is not exempt from forced sale to pay delinquent taxes. Article XVI, § 50(a)(2); Property Code § 41.001(b)(2).

3. Owelty of Partition Lien—Owelty of partition liens arise when there is an unequal division of co-tenancy property. For example, an unequal division of the homestead may arise in a divorce where the land on which the family home is situated is larger than the remaining portion of the land. Naturally, the house cannot be cut in half, so in such a scenario, the land may be partitioned unequally to keep the house in tact. Without the unequal partition in such a case, the entire land would need to be sold and the proceeds divided up equally. Upon an unequal division, the co-tenant with the lesser valued portion of property is entitled to a lien against the other co-tenant for the difference in value received. Homesteads are not exempt from owelty of partition liens. Article XVI, § 50(a)(3); Property Code § 41.001(b)(4).

4. Refinancing—The homestead may be encumbered by the refinancing of a valid lien against the homestead, including federal tax liens incurred from tax debt of either spouse. Article XVI, § 50(a)(4); Property Code § 41.001(b)(5). For example, if the bank has a purchase money lien against the homestead with an interest rate of 6 percent annum, the bank may offer homeowners to refinance the lien for an extra five years at 5 percent annum without risking the loss of its lien on the homestead.

5. Mechanic's and Materialman's Liens—Mechanic's and materialman's liens, that is, liens incurred in connection with improvements made upon the homestead, are valid against the homestead if: (1) a written contract was executed prior to the commencement of improvements or delivery of supplies, (2) the contract is signed by both spouses, and (3) the contract is properly recorded. Article XVI, § 50(a)(5); Property Code § 41.001(b)(3).

6. Home Equity Loan—A home equity loan arises when the homeowner uses an existing homestead as collateral for a loan based on the value of the property. Prior to 1998, a homeowner did not have the ability to use the homestead as collateral for a home equity loan. The recent amendment, permitting home equity loans, places no restrictions on the borrower's use of the money—it is not required that the loan proceeds be used on the homestead. Whatever the use of the proceeds, the homestead is not protected against a valid home equity loan. Article XVI,

§ 50(a)(6); Property Code § 41.001(b)(6). However, in an effort to protect the homeowner, the Constitution sets forth an extensive list of requirements which a creditor must satisfy before obtaining a valid lien against the homestead. On September 13, 2003, the voters of Texas approved an amendment to § 50 which permits a home equity loan to be granted as a line of credit as well as in the traditional lump sum.

7. Reverse Mortgage—A reverse mortgage is a home equity conversion strategy which uses the homestead as collateral for a loan in which the property owner receives a lump sum payment or regular periodic payments and in exchange the property owner gives up all or some of the home's equity. The mortgage is payable upon the death of the borrower or upon the abandonment of the homestead. Article XVI, § 50(k)-(p). Prior to 1997, the use of the homestead as collateral for a reverse mortgage was prohibited. Now, a homestead used as collateral for a valid reverse mortgage is not protected against forced sale while in the hands of the borrower or any survivors claiming a survivor's homestead. Article XVI, § 50(a)(7); Property Code § 41.001(b)(7). However, the Constitution provides an extensive list of requirements that must be satisfied prior to entering into a valid reverse mortgage. On September 13, 2003, the voters of Texas approved an amendment to § 50 to permit the refinancing of a home equity loan with a reverse mortgage. On November 8, 2005, Texas voters authorized line-of-credit advances under a reverse mortgage.

8. Manufactured Home Conversion and Refinance—The homestead is not protected from a lien which arose from the conversion and refinance of a personal property lien secured by a manufactured home to a lien on real property. Article XVI, § 50(a)(8).

9. Preexisting Lien—Although not expressly stated in Article XVI, § 50, a lien which existed against the property prior to it becoming a homestead normally has priority. *Stevenson v. Wilson*, 163 S.W.2d 1063 (Tex. Civ. App.—Waco 1942, no writ).

Article XVI, § 50. Homestead; protection from forced sale; mortgages, trust deeds and liens

(a) The homestead of a family, or of a single adult person, shall be, and is hereby protected from forced sale, for the payment of all debts except for:

(1) the purchase money thereof, or a part of such purchase money;

(2) the taxes due thereon;

(3) an owelty of partition imposed against the entirety of the property by a court order or by a written agreement of the parties to the partition, including a debt of one spouse in favor of the other spouse resulting from a division or an award of a family homestead in a divorce proceeding;

(4) the refinance of a lien against a homestead, including a federal tax lien resulting from the tax debt of both spouses, if the homestead is a family homestead, or from the tax debt of the owner;

(5) work and material used in constructing new improvements thereon, if contracted for in writing, or work and material used to repair or renovate existing improvements thereon if:

(A) the work and material are contracted for in writing, with the consent of both spouses, in the case of a family homestead, given in the same manner as is required in making a sale and conveyance of the homestead;

(B) the contract for the work and material is not executed by the owner or the owner's spouse before the fifth day after the owner makes written application for any extension of credit for the work and material, unless the work and material are necessary to complete immediate repairs to conditions on the homestead property that materially affect the health or safety of the owner or person residing in the homestead and the owner of the homestead acknowledges such in writing;

(C) the contract for the work and material expressly provides that the owner may rescind the contract without penalty or charge within three days after the execution of the contract by all parties, unless the work and material are necessary to complete immediate repairs to conditions on the homestead property that materially affect the health or safety of the owner or person residing in the homestead and the owner of the homestead acknowledges such in writing; and

(D) the contract for the work and material is executed by the owner and the owner's spouse only at the office of a third-party lender making an extension of credit for the work and material, an attorney at law, or a title company;

(6) an extension of credit that:

(A) is secured by a voluntary lien on the homestead created under a written agreement with the consent of each owner and each owner's spouse;

(B) is of a principal amount that when added to the aggregate total of the outstanding principal balances of all other indebtedness secured by valid encumbrances of record against the homestead does not exceed 80 percent of the fair market value of the homestead on the date the extension of credit is made;

(C) is without recourse for personal liability against each owner and the spouse of each owner, unless the owner or spouse obtained the extension of credit by actual fraud;

(D) is secured by a lien that may be foreclosed upon only by a court order;

(E) does not require the owner or the owner's spouse to pay, in addition to any interest, fees to any person that are necessary to originate, evaluate, maintain, record, insure, or service the extension of credit that exceed, in the aggregate, three percent of the original principal amount of the extension of credit;

(F) is not a form of open-end account that may be debited from time to time or under which credit may be extended from time to time unless the open-end account is a home equity line of credit;

(G) is payable in advance without penalty or other charge;

(H) is not secured by any additional real or personal property other than the homestead;

(I) is not secured by homestead property that on the date of closing is designated for agricultural use as provided by statutes governing property tax, unless such homestead property is used primarily for the production of milk;

(J) may not be accelerated because of a decrease in the market value of the homestead or because of the owner's default under other indebtedness not secured by a prior valid encumbrance against the homestead;

(K) is the only debt secured by the homestead at the time the extension of credit is made unless the other debt was made for a purpose described by Subsections (A)(1)-(A)(5) or Subsection (A)(8) of this section;

(L) is scheduled to be repaid:

(i) in substantially equal successive periodic monthly installments, not more often than every 14 days and not less often than monthly, beginning no later than two months from the date the extension of credit is made, each of which equals or exceeds the amount of accrued interest as of the date of the scheduled installment; or

(ii) if the extension of credit is a home equity line of credit, in periodic payments described under Subsection (t)(8) of this section;

(M) is closed not before:

(i) the 12th day after the later of the date that the owner of the homestead submits a loan application to the lender for the extension of credit or the date that the lender provides the owner a copy of the notice prescribed by Subsection (g) of this section; and

(ii) one business day after the date that the owner of the homestead receives a copy of the loan application if not previously provided and a final itemized disclosure of the actual fees, points, interest, costs, and charges that will be charged at closing. If a bona fide emergency or another good cause exists and the lender obtains the written consent of the owner, the lender may provide the documentation to the owner or the lender may modify previously provided documentation on the date of closing; and

(iii) the first anniversary of the closing date of any other extension of credit described by Subsection (a)(6) of this section secured by the same homestead property, except a refinance described by Paragraph (Q)(x)(f) of this subdivision, unless the owner on oath requests an earlier closing due to a state of emergency that:

(a) has been declared by the president of the United States or the governor as provided by law; and

(b) applies to the area where the homestead is located;

(N) is closed only at the office of the lender, an attorney at law, or a title company;

(O) permits a lender to contract for and receive any fixed or variable rate of interest authorized under statute;

(P) is made by one of the following that has not been found by a federal regulatory agency to have engaged in the practice of refusing to make loans because the applicants for the loans reside or the property proposed to secure the loans is located in a certain area:

(i) a bank, savings and loan association, savings bank, or credit union doing business under the laws of this state or the United States;

(ii) a federally chartered lending instrumentality or a person approved as a mortgagee by the United States government to make federally insured loans;

(iii) a person licensed to make regulated loans, as provided by statute of this state;

(iv) a person who sold the homestead property to the current owner and who provided all or part of the financing for the purchase; or

(v) a person who is related to the homestead property owner within the second degree of affinity or consanguinity; or

(vi) a person regulated by this state as a mortgage broker; and

(Q) is made on the condition that:

(i) the owner of the homestead is not required to apply the proceeds of the extension of credit to repay another debt except debt secured by the homestead or debt to another lender;

(ii) the owner of the homestead not assign wages as security for the extension of credit;

(iii) the owner of the homestead not sign any instrument in which blanks relating to substantive terms of agreement are left to be filled in;

(iv) the owner of the homestead not sign a confession of judgment or power of attorney to the lender or to a third person to confess judgment or to appear for the owner in a judicial proceeding;

(v) at the time the extension of credit is made, the owner of the homestead shall receive a copy of the final loan application and all executed documents signed by the owner at closing related to the extension of credit;

(vi) the security instruments securing the extension of credit contain a disclosure that the extension of credit is the type of credit defined by Section 50(a)(6), Article XVI, Texas Constitution;

(vii) within a reasonable time after termination and full payment of the extension of credit, the lender cancel and return the promissory note to the owner of the homestead and give the owner, in recordable form, a release of the lien securing the extension of credit or a copy of an endorsement and assignment of the lien to a lender that is refinancing the extension of credit;

(viii) the owner of the homestead and any spouse of the owner may, within three days after the extension of credit is made, rescind the extension of credit without penalty or charge;

(ix) the owner of the homestead and the lender sign a written acknowledgment as to the fair market value of the homestead property on the date the extension of credit is made; and

(x) except as provided by Subparagraph (xi) of this paragraph, the lender or any holder of the note for the extension of credit shall forfeit all principal and interest of the extension of credit if the lender or holder fails to comply with the lender's or holder's obligations under the extension of credit and fails to correct the failure to comply not later than the 60th day after the date within a reasonable time after the lender or holder is notified by the borrower of the lender's failure to comply by:

(a) paying to the owner an amount equal to any overcharge paid by the owner under or related to the extension of credit if the owner has paid an amount that exceeds an amount stated in the applicable Paragraph (E), (G), or (O) of this subdivision;

(b) sending the owner a written acknowledgement that the lien is valid only in the amount that the extension of credit does not exceed the percentage described by Paragraph (B) of this subdivision, if applicable, or is not secured by property described under Paragraph (H) or (I) of this subdivision, if applicable;

(c) sending the owner a written notice modifying any other amount, percentage, term, or other provision prohibited by this section to a permitted amount, percentage, term, or other provision and adjusting the account of the borrower to ensure that the borrower is not required to pay more than an amount permitted by this section and is not subject to any other term or provision prohibited by this section;

(d) delivering the required documents to the borrower if the lender fails to comply with Subparagraph (v) of this paragraph or obtaining the appropriate signatures if the lender fails to comply with Subparagraph (ix) of this paragraph;

(e) sending the owner a written acknowledgement, if the failure to comply is prohibited by Paragraph (K) of this subdivision, that the accrual of interest and all of the owner's obligations under the extension of credit are abated while any prior lien prohibited under Paragraph (K) remains secured by the homestead; or

(f) if the failure to comply cannot be cured under Subparagraphs (x)(a)-(e) of this paragraph, curing the failure to comply by a refund or credit to the owner of $1,000 and offering the owner the right to refinance the extension of credit with the lender or holder for the remaining term of the loan at no cost to the owner on the same terms, including interest, as the original extension of credit with any modifications necessary to comply with this section or on terms on which the owner and the lender or holder otherwise agree that comply with this section; and

(xi) the lender or any holder of the note for the extension of credit shall forfeit all principal and interest of the extension of credit if the extension of credit is made by a person other than a person described under Paragraph (P) of this subdivision or if the lien was not created under a written agreement with the consent of each owner and each owner's spouse, unless each owner and each owner's spouse who did not initially consent subsequently consents;

(7) a reverse mortgage; or

(8) the conversion and refinance of a personal property lien secured by a manufactured home to a lien on real property, including the refinance of the purchase price of the manufactured home, the cost of installing the manufactured home on the real property, and the refinance of the purchase price of the real property.

(b) An owner or claimant of the property claimed as homestead may not sell or abandon the homestead without the consent of each owner and the spouse of each owner, given in such manner as may be prescribed by law.

(c) No mortgage, trust deed, or other lien on the homestead shall ever be valid unless it secures a debt described by this section, whether such mortgage, trust deed, or other lien, shall have been created by the owner alone, or together with his or her spouse, in case the owner is married. All pretended sales of the homestead involving any condition of defeasance shall be void.

(d) A purchaser or lender for value without actual knowledge may conclusively rely on an affidavit that designates other property as the homestead of the affiant and that states that the property to be conveyed or encumbered is not the homestead of the affiant.

(e) A refinance of debt secured by a homestead and described by any subsection under Subsections (a)(1) (a)(5) that includes the advance of additional funds may not be secured by a valid lien against the homestead unless:

(1) the refinance of the debt is an extension of credit described by Subsection (a)(6) of this section; or

(2) the advance of all the additional funds is for reasonable costs necessary to refinance such debt or for a purpose described by Subsection (a)(2), (a)(3), or (a)(5) of this section.

(f) A refinance of debt secured by the homestead, any portion of which is an extension of credit described by Subsection (a)(6) of this section, may not be secured by a valid lien against the homestead unless the refinance of the debt is an extension of credit described by Subsection (a)(6) or (a)(7) of this section.

(g) An extension of credit described by Subsection (a)(6) of this section may be secured by a valid lien against homestead property if the extension of credit is not closed before the 12th day after the lender provides the owner with the following written notice on a separate instrument:

"NOTICE CONCERNING EXTENSIONS OF CREDIT DEFINED BY SECTION 50(a)(6), ARTICLE XVI, TEXAS CONSTITUTION:

"SECTION 50(a)(6), ARTICLE XVI, OF THE TEXAS CONSTITUTION ALLOWS CERTAIN LOANS TO BE SECURED AGAINST THE EQUITY IN YOUR HOME. SUCH LOANS ARE COMMONLY KNOWN AS EQUITY LOANS. IF YOU DO NOT REPAY THE LOAN OR IF YOU FAIL TO MEET THE TERMS OF THE LOAN, THE LENDER MAY FORECLOSE AND SELL YOUR HOME. THE CONSTITUTION PROVIDES THAT:

"(A) THE LOAN MUST BE VOLUNTARILY CREATED WITH THE CONSENT OF EACH OWNER OF YOUR HOME AND EACH OWNER'S SPOUSE;

"(B) THE PRINCIPAL LOAN AMOUNT AT THE TIME THE LOAN IS MADE MUST NOT EXCEED AN AMOUNT THAT, WHEN ADDED TO THE PRINCIPAL BALANCES OF ALL OTHER LIENS AGAINST YOUR HOME, IS MORE THAN 80 PERCENT OF THE FAIR MARKET VALUE OF YOUR HOME;

"(c) THE LOAN MUST BE WITHOUT RECOURSE FOR PERSONAL LIABILITY AGAINST YOU AND YOUR SPOUSE UNLESS YOU OR YOUR SPOUSE OBTAINED THIS EXTENSION OF CREDIT BY ACTUAL FRAUD;

"(D) THE LIEN SECURING THE LOAN MAY BE FORECLOSED UPON ONLY WITH A COURT ORDER;

"(E) FEES AND CHARGES TO MAKE THE LOAN MAY NOT EXCEED 3 PERCENT OF THE LOAN AMOUNT;

"(F) THE LOAN MAY NOT BE AN OPEN-END ACCOUNT THAT MAY BE DEBITED FROM TIME TO TIME OR UNDER WHICH CREDIT MAY BE EXTENDED FROM TIME TO TIME UNLESS IT IS A HOME EQUITY LINE OF CREDIT;

"(c) YOU MAY PREPAY TILE LOAN WITHOUT PENALTY OR CHARGE

"(H) NO ADDITIONAL COLLATERAL MAY BE SECURITY FOR THE LOAN;

"(I) THE LOAN MAY NOT BE SECURED BY HOMESTEAD PROPERTY THAT IS DESIGNATED FOR AGRICULTURAL USE AS OF THE DATE OF CLOSING, UNLESS THE AGRICULTURAL HOMESTEAD PROPERTY IS USED PRIMARILY FOR THE PRODUCTION OF MILK;

"(J) YOU ARE NOT REQUIRED TO REPAY THE LOAN EARLIER THAN AGREED SOLELY BECAUSE THE FAIR MARKET VALUE OF YOUR HOME DECREASES OR BECAUSE YOU DEFAULT ON ANOTHER LOAN THAT IS NOT SECURED BY YOUR HOME;

"(K) ONLY ONE LOAN DESCRIBED BY SECTION 50(a)(6), ARTICLE XVI, OF THE TEXAS CONSTITUTION MAY BE SECURED WITH YOUR HOME AT ANY GIVEN TIME;

"(L) THE LOAN MUST BE SCHEDULED TO BE REPAID IN PAYMENTS THAT EQUAL OR EXCEED THE AMOUNT OF ACCRUED INTEREST FOR EACH PAYMENT PERIOD;

"(M) THE LOAN MAY NOT CLOSE BEFORE 12 DAYS AFTER YOU SUBMIT A LOAN APPLICATION TO THE LENDER OR BEFORE 12 DAYS AFTER YOU RECEIVE THIS NOTICE, WHICHEVER DATE IS LATER; AND MAY NOT WITHOUT YOUR CONSENT CLOSE BEFORE ONE

BUSINESS DAY AFTER THE DATE ON WHICH YOU RECEIVE A COPY OF YOUR LOAN APPLICATION IF NOT PREVIOUSLY PROVIDED AND A FINAL ITEMIZED DISCLOSURE OF THE ACTUAL FEES, POINTS, INTEREST, COSTS, AND CHARGES THAT WILL BE CHARGED AT CLOSING; AND IF YOUR HOME WAS SECURITY FOR THE SAME TYPE OF LOAN WITHIN THE PAST YEAR, A NEW LOAN SECURED BY THE SAME PROPERTY MAY NOT CLOSE BEFORE ONE YEAR HAS PASSED FROM THE CLOSING DATE OF THE OTHER LOAN, UNLESS ON OATH YOU REQUEST AN EARLIER CLOSING DUE TO A DECLARED STATE OF EMERGENCY;

"(N) THE LOAN MAY CLOSE ONLY AT THE OFFICE OF THE LENDER, TITLE COMPANY, OR AN ATTORNEY AT LAW

"(O) THE LENDER MAY CHARGE ANY FIXED OR VARIABLE RATE OF INTEREST AUTHORIZED BY STATUTE;

"(P) ONLY A LAWFULLY AUTHORIZED LENDER MAY MAKE LOANS DESCRIBED BY SECTION 50(a)(6), ARTICLE XVI, OF THE TEXAS CONSTITUTION; AND

"(Q) LOANS DESCRIBED BY SECTION 50(a)(6), ARTICLE XVI, OF THE TEXAS CONSTITUTION MUST:

"(1) NOT REQUIRE YOU TO APPLY THE PROCEEDS TO ANOTHER DEBT EXCEPT A DEBT THAT IS SECURED BY YOUR HOME OR OWED TO ANOTHER LENDER;

"(2) NOT REQUIRE THAT YOU ASSIGN WAGES AS SECURITY;

"(3) NOT REQUIRE THAT YOU EXECUTE INSTRUMENTS WHICH HAVE BLANKS FOR SUBSTANTIVE TERMS OF AGREEMENT LEFT TO BE FILLED IN;

"(4) NOT REQUIRE THAT YOU SIGN A CONFESSION OF JUDGMENT OR POWER OF ATTORNEY TO ANOTHER PERSON TO CONFESS JUDGMENT OR APPEAR IN A LEGAL PROCEEDING ON YOUR BEHALF;

"(5) PROVIDE THAT YOU RECEIVE A COPY OF YOUR FINAL LOAN APPLICATION AND ALL EXECUTED DOCUMENTS YOU SIGN AT CLOSING;

"(6) PROVIDE THAT THE SECURITY INSTRUMENTS CONTAIN A DISCLOSURE THAT THIS LOAN IS A LOAN DEFINED BY SECTION 50(a)(6), ARTICLE XVI, OF THE TEXAS CONSTITUTION;

"(7) PROVIDE THAT WHEN THE LOAN IS PAID IN FULL, THE LENDER WILL SIGN AND GIVE YOU A RELEASE OF LIEN OR AN ASSIGNMENT OF THE LIEN, WHICHEVER IS APPROPRIATE;

"(8) PROVIDE THAT YOU MAY, WITHIN 3 DAYS AFTER CLOSING, RESCIND THE LOAN WITHOUT PENALTY OR CHARGE;

"(9) PROVIDE THAT YOU AND THE LENDER ACKNOWLEDGE THE FAIR MARKET VALUE OF YOUR HOME ON THE DATE THE LOAN CLOSES; AND

"(10) PROVIDE THAT THE LENDER WILL FORFEIT ALL PRINCIPAL AND INTEREST IF THE LENDER FAILS TO COMPLY WITH THE LENDER'S OBLIGATIONS UNLESS THE LENDER CURES THE FAILURE TO COMPLY AS PROVIDED BY SECTION 50(a)(6)(Q)(x), ARTICLE XVI, OF THE TEXAS CONSTITUTION; AND

"(R) IF THE LOAN IS A HOME EQUITY LINE OF CREDIT:

"(1) YOU MAY REQUEST ADVANCES, REPAY MONEY, AND REBORROW MONEY UNDER THE LINE OF CREDIT;

"(2) EACH ADVANCE UNDER THE LINE OF CREDIT MUST BE IN AN AMOUNT OF AT LEAST $4,000;

"(3) YOU MAY NOT USE A CREDIT CARD, DEBIT CARD, OR SIMILAR DEVICE, OR PREPRINTED CHECK THAT YOU DID NOT SOLICIT, TO OBTAIN ADVANCES UNDER THE LINE OF CREDIT;

"(4) ANY FEES THE LENDER CHARGES MAY BE CHARGED AND COLLECTED ONLY AT THE TIME THE LINE OF CREDIT IS ESTABLISHED AND THE LENDER MAY NOT CHARGE A FEE IN CONNECTION WITH ANY ADVANCE;

"(5) THE MAXIMUM PRINCIPAL AMOUNT THAT MAY BE EXTENDED, WHEN ADDED TO ALL OTHER DEBTS SECURED BY YOUR HOME, MAY NOT EXCEED 80 PERCENT OF THE FAIR MARKET VALUE OF YOUR HOME ON THE DATE THE LINE OF CREDIT IS ESTABLISHED;

"(6) IF THE PRINCIPAL BALANCE UNDER THE LINE OF CREDIT AT ANY TIME EXCEEDS 50 PERCENT OF THE FAIR MARKET VALUE OF YOUR HOME, AS DETERMINED ON THE DATE THE LINE OF CREDIT IS ESTABLISHED, YOU MAY NOT CONTINUE TO REQUEST ADVANCES UNDER THE LINE OF CREDIT UNTIL THE BALANCE IS LESS THAN 50 PERCENT OF THE FAIR MARKET VALUE; AND

"(7) THE LENDER MAY NOT UNILATERALLY AMEND THE TERMS OF THE LINE OF CREDIT.

"THIS NOTICE IS ONLY A SUMMARY OF YOUR RIGHTS UNDER THE TEXAS CONSTITUTION. YOUR RIGHTS ARE GOVERNED BY SECTION 50, ARTICLE XVI, OF THE TEXAS CONSTITUTION, AND NOT BY THIS NOTICE."

If the discussions with the borrower are conducted primarily in a language other than English, the lender shall, before closing, provide an additional copy of the notice translated into the written language in which the discussions were conducted.

(h) A lender or assignee for value may conclusively rely on the written acknowledgment as to the fair market value of the homestead property made in accordance with Subsection (a)(6)(Q)(ix) of this section if:

(1) the value acknowledged to is the value estimate in an appraisal or evaluation prepared in accordance with a state or federal requirement applicable to an extension of credit under Subsection (a)(6); and

(2) the lender or assignee does not have actual knowledge at the time of the payment of value or advance of funds by the lender or assignee that the fair market value stated in the written acknowledgment was incorrect.

(i) This subsection shall not affect or impair any right of the borrower to recover damages from the lender or assignee under applicable law for wrongful foreclosure. A purchaser for value without actual knowledge may conclusively presume that a lien securing an extension of credit described by Subsection (a)(6) of this section was a valid lien securing the extension of credit with homestead property if:

(1) the security instruments securing the extension of credit contain a disclosure that the extension of credit secured by the lien was the type of credit defined by Section 50(a)(6), Article XVI, Texas Constitution;

(2) the purchaser acquires the title to the property pursuant to or after the foreclosure of the voluntary lien; and

(3) the purchaser is not the lender or assignee under the extension of credit.

(j) Subsection (a)(6) and Subsections (e) - (i) of this section are not severable, and none of those provisions would have been enacted without the others. If any of those provisions are held to be preempted by the laws of the United States, all of those provisions are invalid. This subsection shall not apply to any lien or extension of credit made after January 1, 1998, and before the date any provision under Subsection (a)(6) or Subsections (e) - (i) is held to be preempted.

(k) "Reverse mortgage" means an extension of credit:

(1) that is secured by a voluntary lien on homestead property created by a written agreement with the consent of each owner and each owner's spouse;

(2) that is made to a person who is or whose spouse is 62 years or older;

(3) that is made without recourse for personal liability against each owner and the spouse of each owner;

(4) under which advances are provided to a borrower:

(A) based on the equity in a borrower's homestead; or

(B) for the purchase of homestead property that the borrower will occupy as a principal residence;

(5) that does not permit the lender to reduce the amount or number of advances because of an adjustment in the interest rate if periodic advances are to be made;

(6) that requires no payment of principal or interest until:

(A) all borrowers have died;

(B) the homestead property securing the loan is sold or otherwise transferred;

(C) all borrowers cease occupying the homestead property for a period of longer than 12 consecutive months without prior written approval from the lender;

(C-1) if the extension of credit is used for the purchase of homestead property, the borrower fails to timely occupy the homestead property as the borrower's principal residence within a specified period after the date the extension of credit is made that is stipulated in the written agreement creating the lien on the property; or

(D) the borrower:

(i) defaults on an obligation specified in the loan documents to repair and maintain, pay taxes and assessments on, or insure the homestead property;

(ii) commits actual fraud in connection with the loan; or

(iii) fails to maintain the priority of the lender's lien on the homestead property, after the lender gives notice to the borrower, by promptly discharging any lien that has priority or may obtain priority over the lender's lien within 10 days after the date the borrower receives the notice, unless the borrower:

(a) agrees in writing to the payment of the obligation secured by the lien in a manner acceptable to the lender;

(b) contests in good faith the lien by, or defends against enforcement of the lien in, legal proceedings so as to prevent the enforcement of the lien or forfeiture of any part of the homestead property; or

(c) secures from the holder of the lien an agreement satisfactory to the lender subordinating the lien to all amounts secured by the lender's lien on the homestead property;

(7) that provides that if the lender fails to make loan advances as required in the loan documents and if the lender fails to cure the default as required in the loan documents after notice from the borrower, the lender forfeits all principal and interest of the reverse mortgage, provided, however, that this subdivision does not apply when a governmental agency or instrumentality takes an assignment of the loan in order to cure the default;

(8) that is not made unless the prospective borrower and the spouse of the prospective borrower attest in writing that the prospective borrower and the prospective borrower's spouse received counseling regarding the advisability and availability of reverse mortgages and other financial alternatives that was completed not earlier than the 180th day nor later than the 5th day before the date the extension of credit is closed;

(9) that is not closed before the 12th day after the date the lender provides to the prospective borrower the following written notice on a separate instrument, which the lender or originator and the borrower must sign for the notice to take effect:

"IMPORTANT NOTICE TO BORROWERS RELATED TO YOUR REVERSE MORTGAGE

"UNDER THE TEXAS TAX CODE, CERTAIN ELDERLY PERSONS MAY DEFER THE COLLECTION OF PROPERTY TAXES ON THEIR RESIDENCE HOMESTEAD. BY RECEIVING THIS REVERSE MORTGAGE YOU MAY BE REQUIRED TO FORGO ANY PREVIOUSLY APPROVED DEFERRAL OF PROPERTY TAX COLLECTION AND YOU MAY BE REQUIRED TO PAY PROPERTY TAXES ON AN ANNUAL BASIS ON THIS PROPERTY.

"THE LENDER MAY FORECLOSE THE REVERSE MORTGAGE AND YOU MAY LOSE YOUR HOME IF:

"(a) YOU DO NOT PAY THE TAXES OR OTHER ASSESSMENTS ON THE HOME EVEN IF YOU ARE ELIGIBLE TO DEFER PAYMENT OF PROPERTY TAXES;

"(B) YOU DO NOT MAINTAIN AND PAY FOR PROPERTY INSURANCE ON THE HOME AS REQUIRED BY THE LOAN DOCUMENTS;

"(C) YOU FAIL TO MAINTAIN THE HOME IN A STATE OF GOOD CONDITION AND REPAIR;

"(D) YOU CEASE OCCUPYING THE HOME FOR A PERIOD LONGER THAN 12 CONSECUTIVE MONTHS WITHOUT THE PRIOR WRITTEN APPROVAL FROM THE LENDER OR, IF THE EXTENSION OF CREDIT IS USED FOR THE PURCHASE OF THE HOME, YOU FAIL TO TIMELY OCCUPY THE HOME AS YOUR PRINCIPAL RESIDENCE WITHIN A PERIOD OF TIME AFTER THE EXTENSION OF CREDIT IS MADE THAT IS STIPULATED IN THE WRITTEN AGREEMENT CREATING THE LIEN ON THE HOME;

"(E) YOU SELL THE HOME OR OTHERWISE TRANSFER THE HOME WITHOUT PAYING OFF THE LOAN;

"(F) ALL BORROWERS HAVE DIED AND THE LOAN IS NOT REPAID;

"(G) YOU COMMIT ACTUAL FRAUD IN CONNECTION WITH THE LOAN; OR

"(H) YOU FAIL TO MAINTAIN THE PRIORITY OF THE LENDER'S LIEN ON THE HOME, AFTER THE LENDER GIVES NOTICE TO YOU, BY PROMPTLY DISCHARGING ANY LIEN THAT HAS PRIORITY OR MAY OBTAIN PRIORITY OVER THE LENDER'S LIEN WITHIN 10 DAYS AFTER THE DATE YOU RECEIVE THE NOTICE, UNLESS YOU:

"(1) AGREE IN WRITING TO THE PAYMENT OF THE OBLIGATION SECURED BY THE LIEN IN A MANNER ACCEPTABLE TO THE LENDER;

"(2) CONTEST IN GOOD FAITH THE LIEN BY, OR DEFEND AGAINST ENFORCEMENT OF THE LIEN IN, LEGAL PROCEEDINGS SO AS TO PREVENT THE ENFORCEMENT OF THE LIEN OR FORFEITURE OF ANY PART OF THE HOME; OR

"(3) SECURE FROM THE HOLDER OF THE LIEN AN AGREEMENT SATISFACTORY TO THE LENDER SUBORDINATING THE LIEN TO ALL AMOUNTS SECURED BY THE LENDER'S LIEN ON THE HOME.

"IF A GROUND FOR FORECLOSURE EXISTS, THE LENDER MAY NOT COMMENCE FORECLOSURE UNTIL THE LENDER GIVES YOU WRITTEN NOTICE BY MAIL THAT A GROUND FOR FORECLOSURE EXISTS AND GIVES YOU AN OPPORTUNITY TO REMEDY THE CONDITION CREATING THE GROUND FOR FORECLOSURE OR TO PAY THE REVERSE MORTGAGE DEBT WITHIN THE TIME PERMITTED BY SECTION 50(k)(10), ARTICLE XVI, OF THE TEXAS CONSTITUTION. THE LENDER MUST OBTAIN A COURT ORDER FOR FORECLOSURE EXCEPT THAT A COURT ORDER IS NOT REQUIRED IF THE FORECLOSURE OCCURS BECAUSE:

"(1) ALL BORROWERS HAVE DIED; OR

"(2) THE HOMESTEAD PROPERTY SECURING THE LOAN IS SOLD OR OTHERWISE TRANSFERRED."

"YOU SHOULD CONSULT WITH YOUR HOME COUNSELOR OR AN ATTORNEY IF YOU HAVE ANY CONCERNS ABOUT THESE OBLIGATIONS BEFORE YOU CLOSE YOUR REVERSE MORTGAGE LOAN. TO LOCATE AN ATTORNEY IN YOUR AREA, YOU MAY WISH TO CONTACT THE STATE BAR OF TEXAS."

"THIS NOTICE IS ONLY A SUMMARY OF YOUR RIGHTS UNDER THE TEXAS CONSTITUTION. YOUR RIGHTS ARE GOVERNED IN PART BY SECTION 50, ARTICLE XVI, OF THE TEXAS CONSTITUTION, AND NOT BY THIS NOTICE.";

(10) that does not permit the lender to commence foreclosure until the lender gives notice to the borrower, in the manner provided for a notice by mail related to the foreclosure of liens under Subsection (a)(6) of this section, that a ground for foreclosure exists and gives the borrower at least 30 days, or at least 20 days in the event of a default under Subdivision (6)(D)(iii) of this subsection, to:

(a) remedy the condition creating the ground for foreclosure;

(B) pay the debt secured by the homestead property from proceeds of the sale of the homestead property by the borrower or from any other sources; or

(C) convey the homestead property to the lender by a deed in lieu of foreclosure; and

(11) that is secured by a lien that may be foreclosed upon only by a court order, if the foreclosure is for a ground other than a ground stated by Subdivision (6)(A) or (B) of this subsection.

(l) Advances made under a reverse mortgage and interest on those advances have priority over a lien filed for record in the real property records in the county where the homestead property is located after the reverse mortgage is filed for record in the real property records of that county.

(m) A reverse mortgage may provide for an interest rate that is fixed or adjustable and may also provide for interest that is contingent on appreciation in the fair market value of the homestead property. Although payment of principal or interest shall not be required under a reverse mortgage until the entire loan becomes due and payable, interest may accrue and be compounded during the term of the loan as provided by the reverse mortgage loan agreement.

(n) A reverse mortgage that is secured by a valid lien against homestead property may be made or acquired without regard to the following provisions of any other law of this state:

(1) a limitation on the purpose and use of future advances or other mortgage proceeds;

(2) a limitation on future advances to a term of years or a limitation on the term of open-end account advances;

(3) a limitation on the term during which future advances take priority over intervening advances;

(4) a requirement that a maximum loan amount be stated in the reverse mortgage loan documents;

(5) a prohibition on balloon payments;

(6) a prohibition on compound interest and interest on interest;

(7) a prohibition on contracting for, charging, or receiving any rate of interest authorized by any law of this state authorizing a lender to contract for a rate of interest; and

(8) a requirement that a percentage of the reverse mortgage proceeds be advanced before the assignment of the reverse mortgage.

(o) For the purposes of determining eligibility under any statute relating to payments, allowances, benefits, or services provided on a means-tested basis by this state, including supplemental security income, low-income energy assistance, property tax relief, medical assistance, and general assistance:

(1) reverse mortgage loan advances made to a borrower are considered proceeds from a loan and not income; and

(2) undisbursed funds under a reverse mortgage loan are considered equity in a borrower's home and not proceeds from a loan.

(p) The advances made on a reverse mortgage loan under which more than one advance is made must be made according to the terms established by the loan documents by one or more of the following methods:

(1) an initial advance at any time and future advances at regular intervals;

(2) an initial advance at any time and future advances at regular intervals in which the amounts advanced may be reduced, for one or more advances, at the request of the borrower;

(3) an initial advance at any time and future advances at times and in amounts requested by the borrower until the credit limit established by the loan documents is reached;

(4) an initial advance at any time, future advances at times and in amounts requested by the borrower until the credit limit established by the loan documents is reached, and subsequent advances at times and in amounts requested by the borrower according to the terms established by the loan documents to the extent that the outstanding balance is repaid; or

(5) at any time by the lender, on behalf of the borrower, if the borrower fails to timely pay any of the following that the borrower is obligated to pay under the loan documents to the extent necessary to protect the lender's interest in or the value of the homestead property:

(A) taxes;

(B) insurance;

(C) costs of repairs or maintenance performed by a person or company that is not an employee of the lender or a person or company that directly or indirectly controls, is controlled by, or is under common control with the lender;

(D) assessments levied against the homestead property; and

(E) any lien that has, or may obtain, priority over the lender's lien as it is established in the loan documents.

(q) To the extent that any statutes of this state, including without limitation, Section 41.001 of the Texas Property Code, purport to limit encumbrances that may properly be fixed on homestead property in a manner that does not permit encumbrances for extensions of credit described in Subsection (a)(6) or (a)(7) of this section, the same shall be superseded to the extent that such encumbrances shall be permitted to be fixed upon homestead property in the manner provided for by this amendment.

(r) The supreme court shall promulgate rules of civil procedure for expedited foreclosure proceedings related to the foreclosure of liens under Subsection (a)(6) of this section and to foreclosure of a reverse mortgage lien that requires a court order.

(s) The Finance Commission of Texas shall appoint a director to conduct research on the availability, quality, and prices of financial services and research the practices of business entities in the state that provide financial services under this section. The director shall collect information and produce reports on lending activity of those making loans under this section. The director shall report his or her findings to the legislature not later than December 1 of each year.

(t) A home equity line of credit is a form of an open-end account that may be debited from time to time, under which credit may be extended from time to time and under which:

(1) the owner requests advances, repays money, and reborrows money;

(2) any single debit or advance is not less than $4,000;

(3) the owner does not use a credit card, debit card, or similar device, or preprinted check unsolicited by the borrower, to obtain an advance;

(4) any fees described by Subsection (a)(6)(E) of this section are charged and collected only at the time the extension of credit is established and no fee is charged or collected in connection with any debit or advance;

(5) the maximum principal amount that may be extended under the account, when added to the aggregate total of the outstanding principal balances of all indebtedness secured by the homestead on the date the extension of credit is established, does not exceed an amount described under Subsection (a)(6)(B) of this section;

(6) no additional debits or advances are made if the total principal amount outstanding exceeds an amount equal to 50 percent of the fair market value of the homestead as determined on the date the account is established;

(7) the lender or holder may not unilaterally amend the extension of credit; and

(8) repayment is to be made in regular periodic installments, not more often than every 14 days and not less often than monthly, beginning not later than two months from the date the extension of credit is established, and:

(A) during the period during which the owner may request advances, each installment equals or exceeds the amount of accrued interest; and

(B) after the period during which the owner may request advances, installments are substantially equal.

(u) The legislature may by statute delegate one or more state agencies the power to interpret Subsections (a)(5)-(a)(7), (e)-(p), and (t), of this section. An act or omission does not violate a provision included in those subsections if the act or omission conforms to an interpretation of the provision that is:

(1) in effect at the time of the act or omission; and

(2) made by a state agency to which the power of interpretation is delegated as provided by this subsection or by an appellate court of this state or the United States.

(v) A reverse mortgage must provide that:

(1) the owner does not use a credit card, debit card, preprinted solicitation check, or similar device to obtain an advance;

(2) after the time the extension of credit is established, no transaction fee is charged or collected solely in connection with any debit or advance; and

(3) the lender or holder may not unilaterally amend the extension of credit.

Amended Nov. 7, 1995; Nov. 4, 1997, eff. Jan. 1, 1998; Nov. 2, 1999; Nov. 6, 2001; Sept. 13, 2003; Nov. 8, 2005; Nov. 6, 2007; November 3, 2013.

Statutes in Context
Article XVI, § 51

Homesteads are classified by property type as either a rural homestead or an urban homestead, and the size of the exemption varies depending on this classification. Whether a homestead is rural or urban is a question of fact. *Kimmey v. Goodrum*, 346 S.W.2d 901 (Tex. Civ. App.—Waco 1961, writ ref'd n.r.e.).

1. Urban—Property Code § 41.002 defines "urban" homestead as property which, at the time of its designation, is located within a municipality and is served by police and fire protection as well as three of the following municipality services: electric, gas, sewer, storm sewer, and water. Beginning in 1999, the urban homestead is limited to ten acres. More than one lot may be designated as a person's urban homestead provided that the lots are contiguous and all lots making up the urban homestead do not exceed the ten acre limitation.

Historically, the urban homestead exemption was limited by value, rather than acreage. For example, in 1860, the urban homestead could not exceed $2,000 in value at the time of its designation. However, a constitutional amendment in 1983 eliminated the dollar value limitation and restricted the urban homestead on the basis of acreage. From 1983 through 1999, the urban homestead was limited to one acre. Towards the end of 1999, the Texas Constitution was further amended, increasing the size of the urban homestead to ten acres.

2. Rural—Under the Constitution, rural homesteads are limited to 200 acres. Property Code § 41.002(b), however, provides that although a family may have a rural homestead of up to 200 acres, a single adult is limited to 100 acres. It is unclear whether the Property Code may cut back the number of acres for the single adult homestead.

The current version of the Property Code provides no definition of "rural" homestead. However, rural homestead is interpreted to mean homesteads that do not fall within the parameters of the urban homestead definition. *In re Rodriquez*, 282 B.R. 194, 199-200 (Bankr. N.D. Tex. 2002). This interpretation is consistent with previous versions of the Property Code, which provided "[a] homestead is considered to be rural if, at the time the designation is made, the property is not served by municipal utilities and fire and police protection." See Act of Aug. 28, 1989, 71st Leg., 2d C.S., ch. 391, § 2 (amended 1999) (current version at Property Code § 41.002(c) (replacing the definition of rural homestead with that of urban homestead)).

Note: The Constitution formerly provided for a third type of homestead, the business homestead. In 1999, a constitutional amendment eliminated the purely urban business homestead.

Article XVI, § 51. Amount of homestead; uses

The homestead, not in a town or city, shall consist of not more than two hundred acres of land, which may be in one or more parcels, with the improvements thereon; the homestead in a city, town or village, shall consist of lot or contiguous lots amounting to not more than 10 acres of land, together with any improvements on the land; provided, that the homestead in a city, town or village shall be used for the purposes of a home, or as both an urban home and a place to exercise a calling or business, of the homestead claimant, whether a single adult person, or the head of a family; provided also, that any temporary renting of the homestead shall not change the character of the same, when no other homestead has been acquired; provided further that a release or refinance of an existing lien against a homestead as to a part of the homestead does not create an additional burden on the part of the homestead property that is unreleased or subject to the refinance, and a new lien is not invalid only for that reason.

Amended Nov. 2, 1999.

Statutes in Context
Article XVI, § 52

1. Surviving Spouse—Upon the death of either the husband or wife (or both), the homestead property shall "descend and vest in like manner as other real property of the deceased." Probate Code § 283. However, the surviving spouse is entitled to retain a survivor's homestead right under Article XVI, § 52, for life or for so long as the survivor elects to use the homestead. This right protects the homestead against forced sale and partition so long as the surviving spouse chooses to use and occupy the homestead.

The survivor's homestead right may not be defeated by either spouse through the devise of the homestead in either party's will. Rather, the laws of testamentary disposition are subject to the survivor's homestead right. *White v. Sparks*, 118 S.W.2d 649 (Tex. Civ. App.—Dallas 1938, writ dism'd).

2. Minor Children—Upon the death of both parents, the homestead property will pass according to descent and distribution or under the deceased parent's will. However, much like the surviving spouse, the surviving minor children are entitled to a survivor's homestead under Article XVI, § 52. In asserting the surviving minor children's homestead entitlement, there is no requirement that the minor children resided with the deceased parent(s) prior to the parent's death. *National Union Fire Ins. Co. v. Olson*, 920 S.W.2d 458, 462 (Tex. App.—Austin 1996, no writ). The homestead right of surviving minor children is protected against forced sale as well as partition among heirs and will beneficiaries.

Parents are prevented from defeating the homestead rights of their minor children through a testamentary devise of the homestead property. However, the parents are not restricted from conveying or encumbering the homestead property while they are alive. *Hall v. Fields*, 17 S.W. 82 (Tex. 1891).

Article XVI, § 52. Descent and distribution of homestead; restrictions on partition

On the death of the husband or wife, or both, the homestead shall descend and vest in like manner as other real property of the deceased, and shall be governed by the same laws of descent and distribution, but it shall not be partitioned among the heirs of the deceased during the lifetime of the surviving husband or wife, or so long as the survivor may elect to use or occupy the same as a homestead, or so long as the guardian of the minor children of the deceased may be permitted, under the order of the proper court having the jurisdiction, to use and occupy the same.

V.

CRIMINAL PROCEDURE CODE

Title 1. Limitation and Venue

Chapter Twelve. Limitation

Statutes in Context
Art. 12.01

Article 12.01 contains the statute of limitations for various evil acts which may arise in the estate planning context such as when an executor or trustee steals or misapplies estate property or a person uses deception to obtain a signature on a will, trust, power of attorney, or other estate planning document.

Art. 12.01. [177-180] [225-228] [215-218] Felonies.

Except as provided in Article 12.03, felony indictments may be presented within these limits, and not afterward:

(1) no limitation:

(a) murder and manslaughter;

(B) sexual assault under Section 22.011(a)(2), Penal Code, or aggravated sexual assault under Section 22.021(a)(1)(B), Penal Code;

(C) sexual assault, if:

(i) during the investigation of the offense biological matter is collected and subjected to forensic DNA testing and the testing results show that the matter does not match the victim or any other person whose identity is readily ascertained; or

(ii) probable cause exists to believe that the defendant has committed the same or a similar sexual offense against five or more victims;

(D) continuous sexual abuse of young child or children under Section 21.02, Penal Code;

(E) indecency with a child under Section 21.11, Penal Code;

(F) an offense involving leaving the scene of an accident under Section 550.021, Transportation Code, if the accident resulted in the death of a person;

(G) trafficking of persons under Section 20A.02(a)(7) or (8), Penal Code; [or]

(H) continuous trafficking of persons under Section 20A.03, Penal Code; or

(I) compelling prostitution under Section 43.05(a)(2), Penal Code;

(2) ten years from the date of the commission of the offense:

(a) theft of any estate, real, personal or mixed, by an executor, administrator, guardian or trustee, with intent to defraud any creditor, heir, legatee, ward, distributee, beneficiary or settlor of a trust interested in such estate;

(B) theft by a public servant of government property over which he exercises control in his official capacity;

(C) forgery or the uttering, using or passing of forged instruments;

(D) injury to an elderly or disabled individual punishable as a felony of the first degree under Section 22.04, Penal Code;

(E) sexual assault, except as provided by Subdivision (1);

(F) arson;

(G) trafficking of persons under Section 20A.02(a)(1), (2), (3), or (4), Penal Code; or

(H) compelling prostitution under Section 43.05(a)(1), Penal Code;

(3) seven years from the date of the commission of the offense:

(a) misapplication of fiduciary property or property of a financial institution;

(B) securing execution of document by deception;

(C) a felony violation under Chapter 162, Tax Code;

(D) false statement to obtain property or credit under Section 32.32, Penal Code;

(E) money laundering;

(F) credit card or debit card abuse under Section 32.31, Penal Code;

(G) fraudulent use or possession of identifying information under Section 32.51, Penal Code;

(H) Medicaid fraud under Section 35A.02, Penal Code; or

(I) bigamy under Section 25.01, Penal Code, except as provided by Subdivision (6);

(4) five years from the date of the commission of the offense:

(a) theft or robbery;

(B) except as provided by Subdivision (5), kidnapping or burglary;

(C) injury to an elderly or disabled individual that is not punishable as a felony of the first degree under Section 22.04, Penal Code;

(D) abandoning or endangering a child; or

(E) insurance fraud;

(5) if the investigation of the offense shows that the victim is younger than 17 years of age at the time the

offense is committed, 20 years from the 18th birthday of the victim of one of the following offenses:

(a) sexual performance by a child under Section 43.25, Penal Code;

(B) aggravated kidnapping under Section 20.04(a)(4), Penal Code, if the defendant committed the offense with the intent to violate or abuse the victim sexually; or

(C) burglary under Section 30.02, Penal Code, if the offense is punishable under Subsection (d) of that section and the defendant committed the offense with the intent to commit an offense described by Subdivision (1)(B) or (D) of this article or Paragraph (B) of this subdivision;

(6) ten years from the 18th birthday of the victim of the offense:

(A) trafficking of persons under Section 20A.02(a)(5) or (6), Penal Code;

(B) injury to a child under Section 22.04, Penal Code; or

(C) [compelling prostitution under Section 43.05(a)(2), Penal Code; or]

[(D)] bigamy under Section 25.01, Penal Code, if the investigation of the offense shows that the person, other than the legal spouse of the defendant, whom the defendant marries or purports to marry or with whom the defendant lives under the appearance of being married is younger than 18 years of age at the time the offense is committed; or

(7) three years from the date of the commission of the offense: all other felonies.

Acts 1965, 59th Leg., vol. 2, p. 317, ch. 722. Amended by Acts 1973, 63rd Leg., p. 975, ch. 399, § 2(B), eff. Jan. 1, 1974; Acts 1975, 64th Leg., p. 478, ch. 203, § 5, eff. Sept. 1, 1975; Acts 1983, 68th Leg., p. 413, ch. 85, § 1, eff. Sept. 1, 1983; Acts 1983, 68th Leg., p. 5317, ch. 977, § 7, eff. Sept. 1, 1983; Acts 1985, 69th Leg., ch. 330, § 1, eff. Aug. 26, 1985; Acts 1987, 70th Leg., ch. 716, § 1, eff. Sept. 1, 1987; Acts 1991, 72nd Leg., ch. 565, § 6, eff. Sept. 1, 1991; Acts 1995, 74th Leg., ch. 476, § 1, eff. Sept. 1, 1995; Acts 1997, 75th Leg., ch. 740, § 1, eff. Sept. 1, 1997; Acts 1999, 76th Leg., ch. 39, § 1, eff. Sept. 1, 1999; Acts 1999, 76th Leg., ch. 1285, § 33, eff. Sept. 1, 2000; Acts 2001, 77th Leg., ch. 12, § 1, eff. Sept. 1, 2001; Acts 2001, 77th Leg., ch. 1479, § 1, eff. Sept. 1, 2001; Acts 2001, 77th Leg., ch. 1482, § 1, eff. Sept. 1, 2001; Acts 2003, 78th Leg., ch. 371, § 6, eff. Sept. 1, 2003; Acts 2003, 78th Leg., ch. 1276, § 5.001, eff. Sept. 1, 2003; Acts 2005, 79th Leg., ch. 1162, § 6, eff. Sept. 1, 2005; Acts 2007, 80th Leg., ch. 285, § 6, eff. Sept. 1, 2007; Acts 2007, 80th Leg., ch. 593, § 1.03, eff. Sept. 1, 2007; Acts 2007, 80th Leg., ch. 640, § 1, eff. Sept. 1, 2007; Acts 2007, 80th Leg., ch. 841, § 1, eff. Sept. 1, 2007; Acts 2009, 81st Leg., ch. 87, § 6.001, eff. Sept. 1, 2009; Acts 2009, 81st Leg., ch. 1227, § 38, eff. Sept. 1, 2009; Acts 2011, 82nd Leg., ch. 222, § 1, eff. Sept. 1, 2011; Acts 2011, 82nd Leg., ch. 122, § 2, eff. Sept. 1, 2011; Acts 2011, 82nd Leg., ch. 1, § 2.03, eff. Sept. 1, 2011; by Acts 2011, 82nd Leg., ch. 688, § 1, eff. Sept. 1, 2011. Amended by Acts 2013, 83rd Leg., ch. 161, § 3.003, eff. Sept. 1, 2013. Amended by Acts 2015, 84th Leg., ch. 332, § 1, eff. Sept. 1, 2015 and ch. 918, § 2, eff. Sept. 1, 2015.

VI.

ESTATES CODE

Statutes in Context
Estates Code

The 2009 Legislature began the process of codifying the current Probate Code into the new Estates Code. It is interesting to note that although called a "Code," the Probate Code was *not* a true "code" because it was enacted in 1955 which was before the 1963 Legislature began the process of codifying Texas law into 27 codes. The codification process was supposed to be nonsubstantive. *See* Acts 2009, 81st Leg., ch. 680, § 11, eff. Jan. 1, 2014.

The portion of the Estates Code passed by the 2009 Legislature focused on intestacy, wills, and estate administration. The guardianship and durable power of attorney provisions were added in 2011. The 2011 Legislature also made changes to the previously enacted portions of the Estates Code to be consistent with Probate Code amendments. The 2013 Legislature fixed problems with the two initial recodifications as well as making substantive changes.

The entire Estates Code took effect on January 1, 2014.

TITLE 1. GENERAL PROVISIONS

Chapter 21. Purpose and Construction

§ 21.001. Purpose of Code

(a) This code is enacted as a part of the state's continuing statutory revision program, begun by the Texas Legislative Council in 1963 as directed by the legislature in the law codified as Section 323.007, Government Code. The program contemplates a topic-by-topic revision of the state's general and permanent statute law without substantive change.

(b) Consistent with the objectives of the statutory revision program, the purpose of this code[, except Subtitle X, Title 2, and Subtitles Y and Z, Title 3,] is to make the law encompassed by this code[, except Subtitle X, Title 2, and Subtitles Y and Z, Title 3,] more accessible and understandable by:

(1) rearranging the statutes into a more logical order;

(2) employing a format and numbering system designed to facilitate citation of the law and to accommodate future expansion of the law;

(3) eliminating repealed, duplicative, unconstitutional, expired, executed, and other ineffective provisions; and

(4) restating the law in modern American English to the greatest extent possible.

(c) The provisions of Subtitle X, Title 2, and Subtitles Y and Z, Title 3, are transferred from the Texas Probate Code and redesignated as part of this code, but are not revised as part of the state's continuing statutory revision program.

New.

Added by Acts 2009, 81st Leg., ch. 680, § 1, eff. Jan. 1, 2014. Amended by Acts 2011, 82nd Leg., ch. 823, § 2.01, eff. Jan. 1, 2014. Subsection (b) and (c) amended by Acts 2013, 83rd Leg., ch. 161, § 6.001, eff. Jan. 1, 2014. Subsec. (b) amended by Acts 2015, 84th Leg., ch. 1236, § 20.002), eff. Sept. 1, 2015. Subsec. (c) repealed by Acts 2015, 84th Leg., ch. 1236, § 20.023(1), eff. Sept. 1, 2015.

§ 21.002. Construction

(a) Except as provided by [this section,] Section 22.027[,] or [Section] 1002.023, Chapter 311, Government Code (Code Construction Act), applies to the construction of a provision of this code.

(b) This code and the Texas Probate Code, as amended, shall be considered one continuous statute, and for the purposes of any instrument that refers to the Texas Probate Code, this code shall be considered an amendment to the Texas Probate Code [Chapter 311, Government Code (Code Construction Act), does not apply to the construction of a provision of Subtitle X, Title 2, or Subtitle Y or Z, Title 3]. [Chapter 311, Government Code (Code Construction Act), does not apply to the construction of a provision of Subtitle X, Title 2, or Subtitle Y or Z, Title 3.]

New.

Added by Acts 2009, 81st Leg., ch. 680, § 1, eff. Jan. 1, 2014. Amended by Acts 2011, 82nd Leg., ch. 823, § 2.02, eff. Jan. 1, 2014. Subsection (b) amended by Acts 2013, 83rd Leg., ch. 161, § 6.002, eff. Jan. 1, 2014. Amended by Acts 2015, 84th Leg., ch. 1236, § 20.003, eff. Sept. 1, 2015 and Acts 2015, 84th Leg., ch. 173, § 1, eff. May 28, 2015.

§ 21.003. Statutory References

[(a)] A reference in a law other than in this code to a statute or a part of a statute revised by[, or redesignated as part of,] this code is considered to be a reference to the part of this code that revises that statute or part of that statute [or contains the redesignated statute or part of the statute, as applicable].

[(b) A reference in Subtitle X, Title 2, or Subtitle Y or Z, Title 3, to a chapter, a part, a subpart, a section, or any portion of a section "of this code" is a reference to the chapter, part, subpart, section, or portion of a section as redesignated in the Estates Code, except that:

[(1) a reference in Subtitle X, Title 2, or Subtitle Y or Z, Title 3, to Chapter I is a reference to Chapter I, Estates Code, and to the revision of sections derived from Chapter I, Texas Probate Code, and any reenactments and amendments to those sections; and

[(2) a reference in Subtitle X, Title 2, or Subtitle Y or Z, Title 3, to a chapter, part, subpart, section, or portion of a section that does not exist in the Estates Code is a reference to the revision or redesignation of the corresponding chapter, part, subpart, section, or portion of a section of the Texas Probate Code and any reenactments or amendments.]

New.

Added by Acts 2009, 81st Leg., ch. 680, § 1, eff. Jan. 1, 2014. Subsec. (b)(1) and (2) amended by Acts 2011, 82nd Leg., ch. 823, § 2.03, eff. Jan. 1, 2014. Subsec. (b) amended by Acts 2013, 83rd, ch. 161, § 6.003, eff. Jan. 1, 2014. Amended by Acts 2015, 84th Leg., ch. 1236, § 20.004, eff. Sept. 1, 2015.

§ 21.004. Effect of Division of Law

The division of this code into titles, subtitles, chapters, subchapters, parts, subparts, sections, subsections, subdivisions, paragraphs, and subparagraphs is for convenience and does not have any legal effect.

Derived from Probate Code § 2(c).

Added by Acts 2009, 81st Leg., ch. 680, § 1, eff. Jan. 1, 2014.

Statutes in Context
Estates Code § 21.005

The 2011 Legislature amended Civil Practice & Remedies Code § 132.011 to permit the use of unsworn written affidavits made under penalty of perjury in lieu of written sworn affidavits. The 2013 Legislature added subsection (b) to Estates Code § 21.005 providing that this procedure is not applicable to self-proving affidavits on wills executed on or after January 1, 2014.

---

§ 21.005. Applicability of Certain Laws

~~(a) Notwithstanding Section 21.002(b) of this code and Section 311.002, Government Code:~~

~~(1) Section 311.032(c), Government Code, applies to Subtitle X, Title 2, and Subtitles Y and Z, Title 3; and~~

~~(2) Sections 311.005(4) and 311.012(b) and (c), Government Code, apply to Subtitle X, Title 2, and Subtitles Y and Z, Title 3.~~

~~(b)~~ Chapter 132, Civil Practice and Remedies Code, does not apply to Subchapter C, Chapter 251.

New.

Added by Acts 2009, 81st Leg., ch. 680, § 1, eff. Jan. 1, 2014. Amended by Acts 2011, 82nd Leg., ch. 823, § 2.04, eff. Jan. 1, 2014.Amended by Acts 2013, 83rd Leg., ch. 161, § 6.004, eff. Jan. 1, 2014. Amended by Acts 2013, 83rd Leg., ch. 1136, § 1, eff. Jan. 1, 2014. Amended by Acts 2015, 84th Leg., ch. 1236, § 20.005, eff. Sept. 1, 2015.

§ 21.006. Applicability to Probate Proceedings

The procedure prescribed by Title 2 governs all probate proceedings.

Derived from Probate Code § 2(a).

Added by Acts 2009, 81st Leg., ch. 680, § 1, eff. Jan. 1, 2014.

Chapter 22. Definitions

Statutes in Context
Chapter 22.001

The definitions in Chapter 22 apply to the entire Estates Code except as otherwise provided by Title 3 which governs guardianships.

Some terms are defined contrary to their traditional meanings. For example, the term "devise," which usually refers to a gift of real property in a will, is defined to encompass gifts of both real and personal property in § 22.008. Likewise, "legacy," which normally refers to a gift of money (personal property) in a will, is deemed to include gifts of real property as well by § 22.020.

"Heirs" include anyone who is entitled to property under intestate succession under § 22.015. The surviving spouse is considered an heir even though at common law, the surviving spouse was not an heir (not a blood relative). A person who takes under a will is not properly called an heir.

The term "will" is defined in § 22.034 to include a variety of testamentary instruments including codicils and instruments which do not actually make at-death distributions of property such as documents which merely appoint an executor or guardian, revoke another will, or direct how property may not be distributed.

Courts will sometimes ignore the plain language of the definitions. For example, in *Heien v. Crabtree*, 369 S.W.2d 28 (Tex. 1963), the Texas Supreme Court refused to treat a child who was adopted by estoppel as a "child" under the Probate Code equivalent of § 22.004 despite the language of the definition stating that the term includes a child adopted "by acts of estoppel."

The definitions apply to these terms as used in the Estates Code. The definitions do not necessarily apply when they are used in a will or other estate planning document.

§ 22.001. Applicability of Definitions

(a) Except as provided by Subsection (b), the definition for a term provided by this chapter applies in this code unless a different meaning of the term is otherwise apparent from the context in which the term is used.

(b) If Title 3 provides a definition for a term that is different from the definition provided by this chapter, the definition for the term provided by Title 3 applies in that title.

Derived from Probate Code § 3.

Added by Acts 2009, 81st Leg., ch. 680, § 1, eff. Jan. 1, 2014. Subsec. (b) amended by Acts 2013, 83rd Leg., ch. 161, § 6.005, eff. Jan. 1, 2014.

§ 22.002. Authorized Corporate Surety

"Authorized corporate surety" means a domestic or foreign corporation authorized to engage in business in this state for the purpose of issuing surety, guaranty, or indemnity bonds that guarantee the fidelity of an executor or administrator.

Derived from Probate Code § 3(a).

Added by Acts 2009, 81st Leg., ch. 680, § 1, eff. Jan. 1, 2014.

§ 22.003. Charitable Organization

"Charitable organization" means:

(1) a nonprofit corporation, trust, community chest, fund, foundation, or other entity that is:

(A) exempt from federal income tax under Section 501(A), Internal Revenue Code of 1986, by being described by Section 501(c)(3) of that code; and

(B) organized and operated exclusively for:

(i) religious, charitable, scientific, educational, or literary purposes;

(ii) testing for public safety;

(iii) preventing cruelty to children or animals; or

(iv) promoting amateur sports competition; or

(2) any other entity that is organized and operated exclusively for the purposes listed in Section 501(c)(3), Internal Revenue Code of 1986.

Derived from Probate Code § 3(kk).

Added by Acts 2009, 81st Leg., ch. 680, § 1, eff. Jan. 1, 2014.

§ 22.004. Child

(a) "Child" includes an adopted child, regardless of whether the adoption occurred through:

(1) an existing or former statutory procedure; or

(2) acts of estoppel.

(b) The term "child" does not include a child who does not have a presumed father unless a provision of this code expressly states that a child who does not have a presumed father is included.

Derived from Probate Code § 3(b).

Added by Acts 2009, 81st Leg., ch. 680, § 1, eff. Jan. 1, 2014.

§ 22.005. Claims

"Claims" includes:

(1) liabilities of a decedent that survive the decedent's death, including taxes, regardless of whether the liabilities arise in contract or tort or otherwise;

(2) funeral expenses;

(3) the expense of a tombstone;

(4) expenses of administration;

(5) estate and inheritance taxes; and

(6) debts due such estates.

Derived from Probate Code § 3(c).

Added by Acts 2009, 81st Leg., ch. 680, § 1, eff. Jan. 1, 2014.

§ 22.006. Corporate Fiduciary

"Corporate fiduciary" means a financial institution, as defined by Section 201.101, Finance Code, that:

(1) is existing or engaged in business under the laws of this state, another state, or the United States;

(2) has trust powers; and

(3) is authorized by law to act under the order or appointment of a court of record, without giving bond, as receiver, trustee, executor, administrator, or, although the financial institution does not have general depository powers, depository for any money paid into the court, or to become sole guarantor or surety in or on any bond required to be given under the laws of this state.

Derived from Probate Code § 3(d).

Added by Acts 2009, 81st Leg., ch. 680, § 1, eff. Jan. 1, 2014.

§ 22.007. Court; County Court, Probate Court, and Statutory Probate Court

(a) "Court" means and includes:

(1) a county court in the exercise of its probate jurisdiction;

(2) a court created by statute and authorized to exercise original probate jurisdiction; and

(3) a district court exercising original probate jurisdiction in a contested matter.

(b) The terms "county court" and "probate court" are synonymous and mean:

(1) a county court in the exercise of its probate jurisdiction;

(2) a court created by statute and authorized to exercise original probate jurisdiction; and

(3) a district court exercising probate jurisdiction in a contested matter.

(c) "Statutory probate court" means a court created by statute and designated as a statutory probate court under Chapter 25, Government Code. For purposes of this code, the term does not include a county court at law exercising probate jurisdiction unless the court is designated a statutory probate court under Chapter 25, Government Code.

Derived from Probate Code §§ 3(e), (g), (ii).

Added by Acts 2009, 81st Leg., ch. 680, § 1, eff. Jan. 1, 2014.

§ 22.008. Devise

"Devise":

(1) used as a noun, includes a testamentary disposition of real property, personal property, or both; and

(2) used as a verb, means to dispose of real property, personal property, or both, by will.

Derived from Probate Code § 3(h).

Added by Acts 2009, 81st Leg., ch. 680, § 1, eff. Jan. 1, 2014.

§ 22.009. Devisee

"Devisee" includes a legatee.

Derived from Probate Code § 3(i).

Added by Acts 2009, 81st Leg., ch. 680, § 1, eff. Jan. 1, 2014.

§ 22.010. Distributee

"Distributee" means a person who is entitled to a part of the estate of a decedent under a lawful will or the statutes of descent and distribution.

Derived from Probate Code § 3(j).

Added by Acts 2009, 81st Leg., ch. 680, § 1, eff. Jan. 1, 2014.

§ 22.011. Docket

"Docket" means the probate docket.

Derived from Probate Code § 3(k).

Added by Acts 2009, 81st Leg., ch. 680, § 1, eff. Jan. 1, 2014.

§ 22.012. Estate

"Estate" means a decedent's property, as that property:

(1) exists originally and as the property changes in form by sale, reinvestment, or otherwise;

(2) is augmented by any accretions and other additions to the property, including any property to be distributed to the decedent's representative by the trustee of a trust that terminates on the decedent's death, and substitutions for the property; and

(3) is diminished by any decreases in or distributions from the property.

Derived from Probate Code § 3(l).

Added by Acts 2009, 81st Leg., ch. 680, § 1, eff. Jan. 1, 2014.

§ 22.013. Exempt Property

"Exempt property" means the property in a decedent's estate that is exempt from execution or forced sale by the constitution or laws of this state, and any allowance paid instead of that property.

Derived from Probate Code § 3(m).

Added by Acts 2009, 81st Leg., ch. 680, § 1, eff. Jan. 1, 2014.

§ 22.014. Governmental Agency of the State

"Governmental agency of the state" means:

(1) a municipality;

(2) a county;

(3) a public school district;

(4) a special-purpose district or authority;

(5) a board, commission, department, office, or other agency in the executive branch of state government, including an institution of higher education, as defined by Section 61.003, Education Code;

(6) the legislature or a legislative agency;

(7) the supreme court, the court of criminal appeals, a court of appeals, or a district, county, or justice of the peace court;

(8) a judicial agency having statewide jurisdiction; and

(9) the State Bar of Texas.

Derived from Probate Code § 3(ll).

Added by Acts 2009, 81st Leg., ch. 680, § 1, eff. Jan. 1, 2014.

§ 22.015. Heir

"Heir" means a person who is entitled under the statutes of descent and distribution to a part of the estate of a decedent who dies intestate. The term includes the decedent's surviving spouse.

Derived from Probate Code § 3(o).

Added by Acts 2009, 81st Leg., ch. 680, § 1, eff. Jan. 1, 2014.

§ 22.016. Incapacitated Person

A person is "incapacitated" if the person:

(1) is a minor;

(2) is an adult who, because of a physical or mental condition, is substantially unable to:

(A) provide food, clothing, or shelter for himself or herself;

(B) care for the person's own physical health; or

(C) manage the person's own financial affairs; or

(3) must have a guardian appointed for the person to receive funds due the person from a governmental source.

Derived from Probate Code § 3(p).

Added by Acts 2009, 81st Leg., ch. 680, § 1, eff. Jan. 1, 2014.

§ 22.017. Independent Executor

"Independent executor" means the personal representative of an estate under independent administration as provided by Chapter 401 and Section 402.001. The term includes an independent administrator.

Derived from Probate Code § 3(q).

Added by Acts 2009, 81st Leg., ch. 680, § 1, eff. Jan. 1, 2014. Amended by Acts 2013, 83rd Leg., ch. 161, § 6.006, eff. Jan. 1, 2014.

§ 22.018. Interested Person; Person Interested

"Interested person" or "person interested" means:

(1) an heir, devisee, spouse, creditor, or any other having a property right in or claim against an estate being administered; and

(2) anyone interested in the welfare of an incapacitated person, including a minor.

Derived from Probate Code § 3(r).

Added by Acts 2009, 81st Leg., ch. 680, § 1, eff. Jan. 1, 2014.

§ 22.019. Judge

"Judge" means the presiding judge of any court having original jurisdiction over probate proceedings, regardless of whether the court is:

(1) a county court in the exercise of its probate jurisdiction;

(2) a court created by statute and authorized to exercise probate jurisdiction; or

(3) a district court exercising probate jurisdiction in a contested matter.

Derived from Probate Code § 3(f).

Added by Acts 2009, 81st Leg., ch. 680, § 1, eff. Jan. 1, 2014.

§ 22.020. Legacy

"Legacy" includes a gift or devise of real or personal property made by a will.

Derived from Probate Code § 3(s).

Added by Acts 2009, 81st Leg., ch. 680, § 1, eff. Jan. 1, 2014.

§ 22.021. Legatee

"Legatee" includes a person who is entitled to a legacy under a will.

Derived from Probate Code § 3(s).

Added by Acts 2009, 81st Leg., ch. 680, § 1, eff. Jan. 1, 2014.

§ 22.022. Minor

"Minor" means a person younger than 18 years of age who:

(1) has never been married; and

(2) has not had the disabilities of minority removed for general purposes.

Derived from Probate Code § 3(t).

Added by Acts 2009, 81st Leg., ch. 680, § 1, eff. Jan. 1, 2014.

§ 22.024. Mortgage; Lien

"Mortgage" and "lien" include:

(1) a deed of trust;

(2) a vendor's lien, a mechanic's, materialman's, or laborer's lien, an attachment or garnishment lien, and a federal or state tax lien;

(3) a chattel mortgage;

(4) a judgment; and

(5) a pledge by hypothecation.

Derived from Probate Code § 3(v).

Added by Acts 2009, 81st Leg., ch. 680, § 1, eff. Jan. 1, 2014.

§ 22.025. Net Estate

"Net estate" means a decedent's property excluding:

(1) homestead rights;

(2) exempt property;

(3) the family allowance; and

(4) an enforceable claim against the decedent's estate.

Derived from Probate Code § 3(w).

Added by Acts 2009, 81st Leg., ch. 680, § 1, eff. Jan. 1, 2014.

§ 22.026. Next of Kin

"Next of kin" includes:

(1) an adopted child or the adopted child's descendants; and

(2) the adoptive parent of the adopted child.

Derived from Probate Code § 3(jj).

Added by Acts 2009, 81st Leg., ch. 680, § 1, eff. Jan. 1, 2014.

§ 22.027. Person

(a) "Person" includes a natural person and a corporation.

(b) Except as otherwise provided by this code, the [The] definition of "person" assigned by Section 311.005, Government Code, does not apply to any provision in this code.

Derived from Probate Code § 3(x).

Added by Acts 2009, 81st Leg., ch. 680, § 1, eff. Jan. 1, 2014. Subsec. (b) amended by Acts 2015, 84th Leg., ch. 841, § 2, eff. Sept. 1, 2015.

§ 22.028. Personal Property

"Personal property" includes an interest in:

(1) goods;

(2) money;

(3) a chose in action;

(4) an evidence of debt; and

(5) a real chattel.

Derived from Probate Code § 3(z).

Added by Acts 2009, 81st Leg., ch. 680, § 1, eff. Jan. 1, 2014.

§ 22.029. Probate Matter; Probate Proceedings; Proceeding in Probate; Proceedings for Probate

The terms "probate matter," "probate proceedings," "proceeding in probate," and "proceedings for probate" are synonymous and include a matter or proceeding relating to a decedent's estate.

Derived from Probate Code § 3(bb).

Added by Acts 2009, 81st Leg., ch. 680, § 1, eff. Jan. 1, 2014.

§ 22.030. Real Property

"Real property" includes estates and interests in land, whether corporeal or incorporeal or legal or equitable. The term does not include a real chattel.

Derived from Probate Code § 3(dd).

Added by Acts 2009, 81st Leg., ch. 680, § 1, eff. Jan. 1, 2014.

§ 22.031. Representative; Personal Representative

(a) "Representative" and "personal representative" include:

(1) an executor and independent executor;

(2) an administrator, independent administrator, and temporary administrator; and

(3) a successor to an executor or administrator listed in Subdivision (1) or (2).

(b) The inclusion of an independent executor in Subsection (a) may not be construed to subject an independent executor to the control of the courts in probate matters with respect to settlement of estates, except as expressly provided by law.

Derived from Probate Code § 3(aa).

Added by Acts 2009, 81st Leg., ch. 680, § 1, eff. Jan. 1, 2014.

§ 22.032. Surety

"Surety" includes a personal surety and a corporate surety.

Derived from Probate Code § 3(ee).

Added by Acts 2009, 81st Leg., ch. 680, § 1, eff. Jan. 1, 2014.

§ 22.033. Ward

"Ward" means a person for whom a guardian has been appointed.

Derived from Probate Code § 3(mm).

Added by Acts 2009, 81st Leg., ch. 680, § 1, eff. Jan. 1, 2014.

§ 22.034. Will

"Will" includes:

(1) a codicil; and

(2) a testamentary instrument that merely:

(A) appoints an executor or guardian;

(B) directs how property may not be disposed of; or

(C) revokes another will.

Derived from Probate Code § 3(ff).

Added by Acts 2009, 81st Leg., ch. 680, § 1, eff. Jan. 1, 2014.

TITLE 2. ESTATES OF DECEDENTS; DURABLE POWERS OF ATTORNEY

SUBTITLE A. SCOPE, JURISDICTION, VENUE, AND COURTS

Chapter 31. General Provisions

§ 31.001. Scope of "Probate Proceeding" for Purposes of Code

§ 31.002. Matters Related to Probate Proceeding

§ 31.001. Scope of "Probate Proceeding" for Purposes of Code

The term "probate proceeding," as used in this code, includes:

(1) the probate of a will, with or without administration of the estate;

(2) the issuance of letters testamentary and of administration;

(3) an heirship determination or small estate affidavit, community property administration, and homestead and family allowances;

(4) an application, petition, motion, or action regarding the probate of a will or an estate administration, including a claim for money owed by the decedent;

(5) a claim arising from an estate administration and any action brought on the claim;

(6) the settling of a personal representative's account of an estate and any other matter related to the settlement, partition, or distribution of an estate; and

(7) a will construction suit.

Derived from Probate Code § 3(bb).

Added by Acts 2009, 81st Leg., ch. 1351, § 13(a), eff. Jan. 1, 2014.

§ 31.002. Matters Related to Probate Proceeding

(a) For purposes of this code, in a county in which there is no statutory probate court or county court at law exercising original probate jurisdiction, a matter related to a probate proceeding includes:

(1) an action against a personal representative or former personal representative arising out of the representative's performance of the duties of a personal representative;

(2) an action against a surety of a personal representative or former personal representative;

(3) a claim brought by a personal representative on behalf of an estate;

(4) an action brought against a personal representative in the representative's capacity as personal representative;

(5) an action for trial of title to real property that is estate property, including the enforcement of a lien against the property; and

(6) an action for trial of the right of property that is estate property.

(b) For purposes of this code, in a county in which there is no statutory probate court, but in which there is a county court at law exercising original probate jurisdiction, a matter related to a probate proceeding includes:

(1) all matters and actions described in Subsection (a);

(2) the interpretation and administration of a testamentary trust if the will creating the trust has been admitted to probate in the court; and

(3) the interpretation and administration of an inter vivos trust created by a decedent whose will has been admitted to probate in the court.

(c) For purposes of this code, in a county in which there is a statutory probate court, a matter related to a probate proceeding includes:

(1) all matters and actions described in Subsections (a) and (b); and

(2) any cause of action in which a personal representative of an estate pending in the statutory probate court is a party in the representative's capacity as personal representative.

Derived from Probate Code § 4B.

Added by Acts 2009, 81st Leg., ch. 1351, § 13(a), eff. Jan. 1, 2014.

Chapter 32. Jurisdiction

§ 32.001. General Probate Court Jurisdiction; Appeals

§ 32.002. Original Jurisdiction for Probate Proceedings

§ 32.003. Jurisdiction of Contested Probate Proceeding in County with No Statutory Probate Court or Statutory County Court

§ 32.004. Jurisdiction of Contested Probate Proceeding in County with No Statutory Probate Court

§ 32.005. Exclusive Jurisdiction of Probate Proceeding in County with Statutory Probate Court

§ 32.006. Jurisdiction of Statutory Probate Court with Respect to Trusts and Powers of Attorney

§ 32.007. Concurrent Jurisdiction with District Court

Statutes in Context
Chapter 32

Ascertaining which court has jurisdiction to hear matters relating to intestate succession, wills, and estate administration depends on the type of courts that exist in the county. There are three possibilities.

First, if the county has only a constitutional county court (that is, no statutory probate court and no statutory court exercising probate jurisdiction) estate matters are filed in the constitutional county court. § 32.002(a). This situation is common in rural (low population) counties.

Second, if the county has a statutory court exercising probate jurisdiction, but no statutory probate court, then the parties may file in either the constitutional county court or the statutory court with probate jurisdiction. § 32.002(b).

Third, if the county has a statutory probate court, all probate proceedings are filed with the statutory probate court. § 32.002(c). Counties with statutory probate courts include Bexar (2), Collin, Dallas (3), Denton, El Paso (2), Galveston, Harris (4), Hidalgo, Tarrant (2), and Travis. A statutory probate court also has concurrent jurisdiction with the district court in the situations listed in § 32.007 which includes all actions involving inter vivos and testamentary trusts or in which a trustee is a plaintiff or defendant. Section 32.006 also describes additional actions over which a statutory probate court has jurisdiction such as those involving powers of attorney.

If the action is brought in a constitutional county court in a county with no statutory probate court or statutory court exercising probate jurisdiction and a dispute arises, the parties may demand that the action be transferred to the district court or request the assignment of a statutory probate court judge. § 32.003. After resolving the specific dispute, the district court or the statutory probate court judge will normally return the case to the constitutional county court. The statutory probate court may, however, handle the entire case upon request of the parties or the constitutional county court judge.

If the estate is probated in a constitutional county court in a county with a statutory court exercising probate jurisdiction (not a statutory probate court), then the parties may demand a transfer to the statutory court. § 32.004. If the entire action is transferred, then the statutory court hears the rest of the case. However, if only the contested matter is transferred, then upon resolution of the contested matter, the county court at law returns the case to the constitutional county court.

If the estate is probated in a statutory probate court, all estate matters remain with that court; transfer is not available.

A final order (but not an interlocutory order) of any court exercising probate jurisdiction is appealable to the court of appeals. § 32.001(c). In *Crowson v. Wakeham*, 897 S.W.2d 779 (Tex. 1995), the Supreme Court of Texas held that an order in a probate case is final for appellate purposes when (1) a statute declares that a specified phase of the probate proceedings are final and appealable, (2) the order disposes of all issues in the phase of the proceeding for which it was brought, or (3) a particular order is made final by a severance order meeting the usual severance criteria.

§ 32.001. General Probate Court Jurisdiction; Appeals

(a) All probate proceedings must be filed and heard in a court exercising original probate jurisdiction. The court exercising original probate jurisdiction also has jurisdiction of all matters related to the probate proceeding as specified in Section 31.002 for that type of court.

(b) A probate court may exercise pendent and ancillary jurisdiction as necessary to promote judicial efficiency and economy.

(c) A final order issued by a probate court is appealable to the court of appeals.

(d) The administration of the estate of a decedent, from the filing of the application for probate and administration, or for administration, until the decree of final distribution and the discharge of the last personal representative, shall be considered as one proceeding for purposes of jurisdiction. The entire proceeding is a proceeding in rem.

Derived from Probate Code § 4A.

Added by Acts 2009, 81st Leg., ch. 1351, § 13(a), eff. Jan. 1, 2014. Subsection (d) added by Acts 2013, 83rd Leg., ch. 1136, § 2, eff. Jan. 1, 2014.

§ 32.002. Original Jurisdiction for Probate Proceedings

(a) In a county in which there is no statutory probate court or county court at law exercising original probate jurisdiction, the county court has original jurisdiction of probate proceedings.

(b) In a county in which there is no statutory probate court, but in which there is a county court at law exercising original probate jurisdiction, the county court at law exercising original probate jurisdiction and the county court have concurrent original jurisdiction of probate proceedings, unless otherwise provided by law. The judge of a county court may hear probate proceedings while sitting for the judge of any other county court.

(c) In a county in which there is a statutory probate court, the statutory probate court has original jurisdiction of probate proceedings.

Derived from Probate Code § 4C.

Added by Acts 2009, 81st Leg., ch. 1351, § 13(a), eff. Jan. 1, 2014.

§ 32.003. Jurisdiction of Contested Probate Proceeding in County with No Statutory Probate Court or Statutory County Court

(a) In a county in which there is no statutory probate court or county court at law exercising original probate jurisdiction, when a matter in a probate proceeding is contested, the judge of the county court may, on the judge's own motion, or shall, on the motion of any party to the proceeding, according to the motion:

(1) request the assignment of a statutory probate court judge to hear the contested matter, as provided by Section 25.0022, Government Code; or

(2) transfer the contested matter to the district court, which may then hear the contested matter as if originally filed in the district court.

(b) If a party to a probate proceeding files a motion for the assignment of a statutory probate court judge to hear a contested matter in the proceeding before the judge of the county court transfers the contested matter to a district court under this section, the county judge shall grant the motion for the assignment of a statutory probate court judge and may not transfer the matter to the district court unless the party withdraws the motion.

(b-1) If a judge of a county court requests the assignment of a statutory probate court judge to hear a contested matter in a probate proceeding on the judge's own motion or on the motion of a party to the proceeding as provided by this section, the judge may request that the statutory probate court judge be assigned to the entire proceeding on the judge's own motion or on the motion of a party.

(c) A party to a probate proceeding may file a motion for the assignment of a statutory probate court judge under this section before a matter in the proceeding becomes contested, and the motion is given effect as a motion for assignment of a statutory probate court judge under Subsection (a) if the matter later becomes contested.

(d) Notwithstanding any other law, a transfer of a contested matter in a probate proceeding to a district court under any authority other than the authority provided by this section:

(1) is disregarded for purposes of this section; and

(2) does not defeat the right of a party to the proceeding to have the matter assigned to a statutory probate court judge in accordance with this section.

(e) A statutory probate court judge assigned to a contested matter in a probate proceeding or to the entire proceeding under this section has the jurisdiction and authority granted to a statutory probate court by this subtitle. A statutory probate court judge assigned to hear only the contested matter in a probate proceeding shall, on resolution of the matter, including any appeal of the matter, return the matter to the county court for further proceedings not inconsistent with the orders of the statutory probate court or court of appeals, as applicable. A statutory probate court judge assigned to the entire probate proceeding as provided by Subsection (b-1) shall, on resolution of the contested matter in the proceeding, including any appeal of the matter, return the entire proceeding to the county court for further proceedings not inconsistent with the orders of the statutory probate court or court of appeals, as applicable.

(f) A district court to which a contested matter is transferred under this section has the jurisdiction and authority granted to a statutory probate court by this subtitle. On resolution of a contested matter transferred to the district court under this section, including any appeal of the matter, the district court shall return the matter to the county court for further proceedings not inconsistent with the orders of the district court or court of appeals, as applicable.

(g) If only the contested matter in a probate proceeding is assigned to a statutory probate court judge under this section, or if the contested matter in a probate proceeding is transferred to a district court under this section, the county court shall continue to exercise jurisdiction over the management of the estate, other than a contested matter, until final disposition of the contested matter is made in accordance with this section. Any matter related to a probate proceeding in which a contested matter is transferred to a district court may be brought in the district court. The district court in which a matter related to the proceeding is filed may, on its own motion or on the motion of any party, find that the matter is not a contested matter and transfer the matter to the county court with jurisdiction of the management of the estate.

(h) If a contested matter in a probate proceeding is transferred to a district court under this section, the district court has jurisdiction of any contested matter in the proceeding that is subsequently filed, and the county court shall transfer those contested matters to the district court. If a statutory probate court judge is assigned under this section to hear a contested matter in a probate proceeding, the statutory probate court judge shall be assigned to hear any contested matter in the proceeding that is subsequently filed.

(i) The clerk of a district court to which a contested matter in a probate proceeding is transferred under this section may perform in relation to the contested matter any function a county clerk may perform with respect to that type of matter.

Derived from Probate Code § 4D.

Added by Acts 2009, 81st Leg., ch. 1351, § 13(a), eff. Jan. 1, 2014. Subsec. (b-1) added by Acts 2011, 82nd Leg., ch. 1338, § 2.02, eff. Jan. 1, 2014. Subsecs. (e) and (g) amended by Acts 2011, 82nd Leg., ch. 1338, § 2.02, eff. Jan. 1, 2014.

§ 32.004. Jurisdiction of Contested Probate Proceeding in County with No Statutory Probate Court

(a) In a county in which there is no statutory probate court, but in which there is a county court at law

exercising original probate jurisdiction, when a matter in a probate proceeding is contested, the judge of the county court may, on the judge's own motion, or shall, on the motion of any party to the proceeding, transfer the contested matter to the county court at law. In addition, the judge of the county court, on the judge's own motion or on the motion of a party to the proceeding, may transfer the entire proceeding to the county court at law.

(b) A county court at law to which a proceeding is transferred under this section may hear the proceeding as if originally filed in that court. If only a contested matter in the proceeding is transferred, on the resolution of the matter, the matter shall be returned to the county court for further proceedings not inconsistent with the orders of the county court at law.

Derived from Probate Code § 4E.

Added by Acts 2009, 81st Leg., ch. 1351, § 13(a), eff. Jan. 1, 2014.

§ 32.005. Exclusive Jurisdiction of Probate Proceeding in County with Statutory Probate Court

(a) In a county in which there is a statutory probate court, the statutory probate court has exclusive jurisdiction of all probate proceedings, regardless of whether contested or uncontested. A cause of action related to the probate proceeding must be brought in a statutory probate court unless the jurisdiction of the statutory probate court is concurrent with the jurisdiction of a district court as provided by Section 32.007 or with the jurisdiction of any other court.

(b) This section shall be construed in conjunction and in harmony with Chapter 401 and Section 402.001 and all other sections of this title relating to independent executors, but may not be construed to expand the court's control over an independent executor.

Derived from Probate Code § 4F.

Added by Acts 2009, 81st Leg., ch. 1351, § 13(a), eff. Jan. 1, 2014. Subsec. (b) amended by Acts 2013, 83rd Leg., ch. 161, § 6.007, eff. Jan. 1, 2014.

§ 32.006. Jurisdiction of Statutory Probate Court with Respect to Trusts and Powers of Attorney

In a county in which there is a statutory probate court, the statutory probate court has jurisdiction of:

(1) an action by or against a trustee;

(2) an action involving an inter vivos trust, testamentary trust, or charitable trust;

(3) an action by or against an agent or former agent under a power of attorney arising out of the agent's performance of the duties of an agent; and

(4) an action to determine the validity of a power of attorney or to determine an agent's rights, powers, or duties under a power of attorney.

Derived from Probate Code § 4G

Added by Acts 2009, 81st Leg., ch. 1351, § 13(a), eff. Jan. 1, 2014. Amended by Acts 2013, 83rd Leg., ch. 1136, § 3, eff. Jan. 1, 2014.

§ 32.007. Concurrent Jurisdiction with District Court

A statutory probate court has concurrent jurisdiction with the district court in:

(1) a personal injury, survival, or wrongful death action by or against a person in the person's capacity as a personal representative;

(2) an action by or against a trustee;

(3) an action involving an inter vivos trust, testamentary trust, or charitable trust, including a charitable trust as defined by Section 123.001, Property Code;

(4) an action involving a personal representative of an estate in which each other party aligned with the personal representative is not an interested person in that estate;

(5) an action against an agent or former agent under a power of attorney arising out of the agent's performance of the duties of an agent; and

(6) an action to determine the validity of a power of attorney or to determine an agent's rights, powers, or duties under a power of attorney.

Derived from Probate Code § 4H.

Added by Acts 2009, 81ˢᵗ Leg., ch. 1351, § 13(a), eff. Jan. 1, 2014. Subsec. (3) amended by Acts 2011, 82nd Leg., ch. 1338, § 2.03, eff. Jan. 1, 2014.

Chapter 33. Venue

Subchapter A. Venue for Certain Proceedings

Subchapter B. Determination of Venue

Subchapter C. Transfer of Probate Proceeding

Subchapter A. Venue for Certain Proceedings

Statutes in Context
Chapter 33

The venue rules provided in § 33.001, as applied to probating wills and opening testate and intestate administrations, trump the normal venue rules found in the Rules of Civil Procedure. Proper venue is based on the decedent's domicile at death.

If the decedent was domiciled or had a fixed place of residence in Texas, the appropriate venue is the county of the decedent's domicile or residence at the time of death. It is not relevant where the decedent died, where the decedent's heirs or beneficiaries live, or where the decedent's real or personal property is located.

If the decedent dies in Texas but has no place of residence in Texas, then the appropriate venue is either in the county (1) where the decedent's principal property is located, or (2) where the decedent died. The county in which the application for probate is filed first has priority under Estate Code § 33.052.

If the decedent did not die in Texas and did not reside in Texas, the appropriate venue is in the county where the nearest next of kin reside. If the decedent has no next of kin in Texas, then the appropriate venue is the county in which the decedent's principal estate is located. The typical reason for probate proceedings in Texas for a person who did not reside or die in Texas is because the decedent owned real property located in Texas.

Section 33.004 governs venue in heirship proceedings.

---

§ 33.001. Probate of Wills and Granting of Letters Testamentary and of Administration

Venue for a probate proceeding to admit a will to probate or for the granting of letters testamentary or of administration is:

(1) in the county in which the decedent resided, if the decedent had a domicile or fixed place of residence in this state; or

(2) with respect to a decedent who did not have a domicile or fixed place of residence in this state:

(a) if the decedent died in this state, in the county in which:

(i) the decedent's principal estate was located at the time of the decedent's death; or

(ii) the decedent died; or

(B) if the decedent died outside of this state:

(i) in any county in this state in which the decedent's nearest of kin reside; or

(ii) if there is no next of kin of the decedent in this state, in the county in which the decedent's principal estate was located at the time of the decedent's death.

Derived from Probate Code § 6.

Added by Acts 2011, 82nd Leg., ch. 1338, § 2.04, eff. Jan. 1, 2014.

§ 33.002. Action Related to Probate Proceeding in Statutory Probate Court

Except as provided by Section 33.003, venue for any cause of action related to a probate proceeding pending in a statutory probate court is proper in the statutory probate court in which the decedent's estate is pending.

Derived from Probate Code § 6A.

Added by Acts 2011, 82nd Leg., ch. 1338, § 2.04, eff. Jan. 1, 2014.

§ 33.003. Certain Actions Involving Personal Representative

Notwithstanding any other provision of this chapter, the proper venue for an action by or against a personal representative for personal injury, death, or property damages is determined under Section 15.007, Civil Practice and Remedies Code.

Derived from Probate Code § 6B.

Added by Acts 2011, 82nd Leg., ch. 1338, § 2.04, eff. Jan. 1, 2014.

§ 33.004. Heirship Proceedings

(a) Venue for a proceeding to determine a decedent's heirs is in:

(1) the court of the county in which a proceeding admitting the decedent's will to probate or administering the decedent's estate was most recently pending; or

(2) the court of the county in which venue would be proper for commencement of an administration of the decedent's estate under Section 33.001 if:

(A) no will of the decedent has been admitted to probate in this state and no administration of the decedent's estate has been granted in this state; or

(B) the proceeding is commenced by the trustee of a trust holding assets for the benefit of the decedent.

(b) Notwithstanding Subsection (a) and Section 33.001, if there is no administration pending of the estate of a deceased ward who died intestate, venue for a proceeding to determine the deceased ward's heirs is in the probate court in which the guardianship proceedings with respect to the ward's estate were pending on the date of the ward's death. A proceeding described by this subsection may not be brought as part

of the guardianship proceedings with respect to the ward's estate, but rather must be filed as a separate cause in which the court may determine the heirs' respective shares and interests in the estate as provided by the laws of this state.

Derived from Probate Code § 6C.

Added by Acts 2011, 82nd Leg., ch. 1338, § 2.04, eff. Jan. 1, 2014.

§ 33.005. Certain Actions Involving Breach of Fiduciary Duty

Notwithstanding any other provision of this chapter, venue for a proceeding brought by the attorney general alleging breach of a fiduciary duty by a charitable entity or a fiduciary or managerial agent of a charitable trust is determined under Section 123.005, Property Code.

Derived from Probate Code § 6D.

Added by Acts 2011, 82nd Leg., ch. 1338, § 2.04, eff. Jan. 1, 2014.

Subchapter B. Determination of Venue

§ 33.051. Commencement of Proceeding

For purposes of this subchapter, a probate proceeding is considered commenced on the filing of an application for the proceeding that avers facts sufficient to confer venue on the court in which the application is filed.

Derived from Probate Code § 8(a).

Added by Acts 2011, 82nd Leg., ch. 1338, § 2.04, eff. Jan. 1, 2014.

§ 33.052. Concurrent Venue

(a) If applications for probate proceedings involving the same estate are filed in two or more courts having concurrent venue, the court in which a proceeding involving the estate was first commenced has and retains jurisdiction of the proceeding to the exclusion of the other court or courts in which a proceeding involving the same estate was commenced.

(b) The first commenced probate proceeding extends to all of the decedent's property, including the decedent's estate property.

Derived from Probate Code § 8(a).

Added by Acts 2011, 82nd Leg., ch. 1338, § 2.04, eff. Jan. 1, 2014.

§ 33.053. Probate Proceedings in More Than One County

If probate proceedings involving the same estate are commenced in more than one county, each proceeding commenced in a county other than the county in which a proceeding was first commenced is stayed until the court in which the proceeding was first commenced makes a final determination of venue.

Derived from Probate Code § 8(b).

Added by Acts 2011, 82nd Leg., ch. 1338, § 2.04, eff.

Jan. 1, 2014.

§ 33.054. Jurisdiction to Determine Venue

(a) Subject to Sections 33.052 and 33.053, a court in which an application for a probate proceeding is filed has jurisdiction to determine venue for the proceeding and for any matter related to the proceeding.

(b) A court's determination under this section is not subject to collateral attack.

Derived from Probate Code § 8(e).

Added by Acts 2011, 82nd Leg., ch. 1338, § 2.04, eff. Jan. 1, 2014.

§ 33.055. Protection for Certain Purchasers

Notwithstanding Section 33.052, a bona fide purchaser of real property who relied on a probate proceeding that was not the first commenced proceeding, without knowledge that the proceeding was not the first commenced proceeding, shall be protected with respect to the purchase unless before the purchase an order rendered in the first commenced proceeding admitting the decedent's will to probate, determining the decedent's heirs, or granting administration of the decedent's estate was recorded in the office of the county clerk of the county in which the purchased property is located.

Derived from Probate Code § 8(a).

Added by Acts 2011, 82nd Leg., ch. 1338, § 2.04, eff. Jan. 1, 2014.

Subchapter C. Transfer of Probate Proceeding

§ 33.101. Transfer to Other County in Which Venue is Proper

If probate proceedings involving the same estate are commenced in more than one county and the court making a determination of venue as provided by Section 33.053 determines that venue is proper in another county, the court clerk shall make and retain a copy of the entire file in the case and transmit the original file to the court in the county in which venue is proper. The court to which the file is transmitted shall conduct the proceeding in the same manner as if the proceeding had originally been commenced in that county.

Derived from Probate Code §§ 8(c)(1), 8A(a).

Added by Acts 2011, 82nd Leg., ch. 1338, § 2.04, eff. Jan. 1, 2014.

§ 33.102. Transfer for Want of Venue

(a) If it appears to the court at any time before the final order in a probate proceeding is rendered that the court does not have priority of venue over the proceeding, the court shall, on the application of an interested person, transfer the proceeding to the proper county by transmitting to the proper court in that county:

(1) the original file in the case; and

(2) certified copies of all entries that have been made in the judge's probate docket in the proceeding.

(b) The court of the county to which a probate proceeding is transferred under Subsection (a) shall complete the proceeding in the same manner as if the proceeding had originally been commenced in that county.

(c) If the question as to priority of venue is not raised before a final order in a probate proceeding is announced, the finality of the order is not affected by any error in venue.

Derived from Probate Code §§ 8(c)(1), 8A(a).

Added by Acts 2011, 82nd Leg., ch. 1338, § 2.04, eff. Jan. 1, 2014.

§ 33.103. Transfer for Convenience

(a) The court may order that a probate proceeding be transferred to the proper court in another county in this state if it appears to the court at any time before the proceeding is concluded that the transfer would be in the best interest of:

(1) the estate; or

(2) if there is no administration of the estate, the decedent's heirs or beneficiaries under the decedent's will.

(b) The clerk of the court from which the probate proceeding described by Subsection (a) is transferred shall transmit to the court to which the proceeding is transferred:

(1) the original file in the proceeding; and

(2) a certified copy of the index.

Derived from Probate Code §§ 8(c)(2), 8A(b).

Added by Acts 2011, 82nd Leg., ch. 1338, § 2.04, eff. Jan. 1, 2014.

§ 33.104. Validation of Previous Proceedings

All orders entered in connection with a probate proceeding that is transferred to another county under a provision of this subchapter are valid and shall be recognized in the court to which the proceeding is transferred if the orders were made and entered in conformance with the procedure prescribed by this code.

Derived from Probate Code §§ 8(d), 8B.

Added by Acts 2011, 82nd Leg., ch. 1338, § 2.04, eff. Jan. 1, 2014.

Chapter 34. Matters Relating to Certain Other Types of Proceedings

§ 34.001. Transfer to Statutory Probate Court of Proceeding Related to Probate Proceeding.

§ 34.002. Actions to Collect Delinquent Property Taxes.

Chapter 34. Matters Relating to Certain Other Types of Proceedings

§ 34.001. Transfer to Statutory Probate Court of Proceeding Related to Probate Proceeding.

(a) A judge of a statutory probate court, on the motion of a party to the action or on the motion of a person interested in an estate, may transfer to the judge's court from a district, county, or statutory court a cause of action related to a probate proceeding pending in the statutory probate court or a cause of action in which a personal representative of an estate pending in the statutory probate court is a party and may consolidate the transferred cause of action with the other proceedings in the statutory probate court relating to that estate.

(b) Notwithstanding any other provision of this subtitle, Title 1, [Subtitle X, Title 2,] Chapter 51, 52, 53, 54, 55, or 151, or Section 351.001, 351.002, 351.053, 351.352, 351.353, 351.354, or 351.355, the proper venue for an action by or against a personal representative for personal injury, death, or property damages is determined under Section 15.007, Civil Practice and Remedies Code.

Derived from Probate Code § 5B.

Transferred and amended by Acts 2013, 83rd Leg., ch. 161, § 6.009, eff. Jan. 1, 2014. Subsec. (b) amended by Acts 2015, 84th Leg., ch. 1236, § 20.006, eff. Sept. 1, 2015.

§ 34.002. Actions to Collect Delinquent Property Taxes.

(a) This section applies only to a decedent's estate that:

(1) is being administered in a pending probate proceeding;

(2) owns or claims an interest in property against which a taxing unit has imposed ad valorem taxes that are delinquent; and

(3) is not being administered as an independent administration under Chapter 401 and Section 402.001.

(b) Notwithstanding any provision of this code to the contrary, if the probate proceedings are pending in a foreign jurisdiction or in a county other than the county in which the taxes were imposed, a suit to foreclose the lien securing payment of the taxes or to enforce personal liability for the taxes must be brought under Section 33.41, Tax Code, in a court of competent jurisdiction in the county in which the taxes were imposed.

(c) If the probate proceedings have been pending for four years or less in the county in which the taxes were imposed, the taxing unit may present a claim for the delinquent taxes against the estate to the personal representative of the estate in the probate proceedings.

(d) If the taxing unit presents a claim against the estate under Subsection (c):

(1) the claim of the taxing unit is subject to each applicable provision in Subchapter A, Chapter 124, Subchapter B, Chapter 308, Subchapter F, Chapter 351, and Chapters 355 and 356 that relates to a claim or the enforcement of a claim in a probate proceeding; and

(2) the taxing unit may not bring a suit in any other court to foreclose the lien securing payment of the taxes or to enforce personal liability for the delinquent taxes before the first day after the fourth anniversary of the date the application for the probate proceeding was filed.

(e) To foreclose the lien securing payment of the delinquent taxes, the taxing unit must bring a suit under Section 33.41, Tax Code, in a court of competent jurisdiction for the county in which the taxes were imposed if:

(1) the probate proceedings have been pending in that county for more than four years; and

(2) the taxing unit did not present a delinquent tax claim under Subsection (c) against the estate in the probate proceeding.

(f) In a suit brought under Subsection (e), the taxing unit:

(1) shall make the personal representative of the decedent's estate a party to the suit; and

(2) may not seek to enforce personal liability for the taxes against the estate of the decedent.

Derived from Probate Code § 5C.

Transferred and amended by Acts 2013, 83rd Leg., ch. 161, § 6.009, eff. Jan. 1, 2014.

SUBTITLE B. PROCEDURAL MATTERS

Chapter 51. Notices and Process in Probate Proceedings in General

Subchapter A. Issuance and Form of Notice or Process

Subchapter B. Methods of Serving Citation or Notice; Persons to be Served

Subchapter C. Return and Proof of Service of Citation or Notice

Subchapter D. Alternative Manner of Issuance, Service, and Return

Subchapter E. Additional Notice Provisions

Chapter 51. Notices and Process in Probate Proceedings in General

Statutes in Context
Chapter 51

Chapter 51 provides extensive instructions on how notice and citations are to be given using a variety of delivery methods including personal service, posting, publication, and mailing.

Subchapter A. Issuance and Form of Notice or Process

§ 51.001. Issuance of Notice or Process in General

(a) Except as provided by Subsection (b), a person is not required to be cited or otherwise given notice except in a situation in which this title expressly provides for citation or the giving of notice.

(b) If this title does not expressly provide for citation or the issuance or return of notice in a probate matter, the court may require that notice be given. A court that requires that notice be given may prescribe the form and manner of service of the notice and the return of service.

(c) Unless a court order is required by this title, the county clerk without a court order shall issue:

(1) necessary citations, writs, and other process in a probate matter; and

(2) all notices not required to be issued by a personal representative.

Derived from Probate Code §§ 33(a), (b).

Added by Acts 2009, 81st Leg., ch. 680, § 1, eff. Jan. 1, 2014.

§ 51.002. Direction of Writ or Other Process

(a) A writ or other process other than a citation or notice must be directed "To any sheriff or constable within the State of Texas."

(b) Notwithstanding Subsection (a), a writ or other process other than a citation or notice may not be held defective because the process is directed to the sheriff or a constable of a named county if the process is properly served within that county by the sheriff or constable.

Derived from Probate Code § 33(c).

Added by Acts 2009, 81st Leg., ch. 680, § 1, eff. Jan. 1, 2014.

§ 51.003. Contents of Citation or Notice

(a) A citation or notice must:

(1) be directed to the person to be cited or notified;

(2) be dated;

(3) state the style and number of the proceeding;

(4) state the court in which the proceeding is pending;

(5) describe generally the nature of the proceeding or matter to which the citation or notice relates;

(6) direct the person being cited or notified to appear by filing a written contest or answer or to perform another required action; and

(7) state when and where the appearance or performance described by Subdivision (6) is required.

(b) A citation or notice issued by the county clerk must be styled "The State of Texas" and be signed by the clerk under the clerk's seal.

(c) A notice required to be given by a personal representative must be in writing and be signed by the representative in the representative's official capacity.

(d) A citation or notice is not required to contain a precept directed to an officer, but may not be held defective because the citation or notice contains a precept directed to an officer authorized to serve the citation or notice.

Derived from Probate Code § 33(c).

Added by Acts 2009, 81st Leg., ch. 680, § 1, eff. Jan. 1, 2014.

Subchapter B. Methods of Serving Citation or Notice; Persons to be Served

§ 51.051. Personal Service

(a) Except as otherwise provided by Subsection (b), if personal service of citation or notice is required, the citation or notice must be served on the attorney of record for the person to be cited or notified. Notwithstanding the requirement of personal service, service may be made on that attorney by any method specified by Section 51.055 for service on an attorney of record.

(b) If the person to be cited or notified does not have an attorney of record in the proceeding, or if an attempt to serve the person's attorney is unsuccessful:

(1) the sheriff or constable shall serve the citation or notice by delivering a copy of the citation or notice to the person to be cited or notified, in person, if the person to whom the citation or notice is directed is in this state; or

(2) any disinterested person competent to make an oath that the citation or notice was served may serve the citation or notice, if the person to be cited or notified is absent from or is not a resident of this state.

(c) The return day of the citation or notice served under Subsection (b) must be at least 10 days after the date of service, excluding the date of service.

(d) If citation or notice attempted to be served as provided by Subsection (b) is returned with the notation that the person sought to be served, whether inside or outside this state, cannot be found, the county clerk shall issue a new citation or notice. Service of the new citation or notice must be made by publication.

Derived from Probate Code § 33(f)(1).

Added by Acts 2009, 81st Leg., ch. 680, § 1, eff. Jan. 1, 2014.

§ 51.052. Service by Mail

(a) The county clerk, or the personal representative if required by statute or court order, shall serve a citation or notice required or permitted to be served by regular mail by mailing the original citation or notice to the person to be cited or notified.

(b) Except as provided by Subsection (c), the county clerk shall issue a citation or notice required or permitted to be served by registered or certified mail and shall serve the citation or notice by mailing the original citation or notice by registered or certified mail.

(c) A personal representative shall issue a notice required to be given by the representative by registered or certified mail and shall serve the notice by mailing the original notice by registered or certified mail.

(d) The county clerk or personal representative, as applicable, shall mail a citation or notice under Subsection (b) or (c) with an instruction to deliver the citation or notice to the addressee only and with return receipt requested. The clerk or representative, as applicable, shall address the envelope containing the citation or notice to:

(1) the attorney of record in the proceeding for the person to be cited or notified; or

(2) the person to be cited or notified, if the citation or notice to the attorney is returned undelivered or the person to be cited or notified has no attorney of record in the proceeding.

(e) Service by mail shall be made at least 20 days before the return day of the service, excluding the date of service. The date of service by mail is the date of mailing.

(f) A copy of a citation or notice served under Subsection (a), (b), or (c), together with a certificate of the person serving the citation or notice showing that the citation or notice was mailed and the date of the mailing, shall be filed and recorded. A returned receipt for a citation or notice served under Subsection (b) or (c) shall be attached to the certificate.

(g) If a citation or notice served by mail is returned undelivered, a new citation or notice shall be issued. Service of the new citation or notice must be made by posting.

Derived from Probate Code § 33(f)(4).

Added by Acts 2009, 81st Leg., ch. 680, § 1, eff. Jan. 1, 2014.

§ 51.053. Service by Posting

(a) The county clerk shall deliver the original and a copy of a citation or notice required to be posted to the sheriff or a constable of the county in which the proceeding is pending. The sheriff or constable shall post the copy at the door of the county courthouse or the location in or near the courthouse where public notices are customarily posted.

(b) Citation or notice under this section must be posted for at least 10 days before the return day of the service, excluding the date of posting, except as provided by Section 51.102(b). The date of service of citation or notice by posting is the date of posting.

(c) A sheriff or constable who posts a citation or notice under this section shall return the original citation or notice to the county clerk and state the date and location of the posting in a written return on the citation or notice.

(d) The method of service prescribed by this section applies when a personal representative is required or permitted to post a notice. The notice must be:

(1) issued in the name of the representative;

(2) addressed and delivered to, and posted and returned by, the appropriate officer; and

(3) filed with the county clerk.

Derived from Probate Code § 33(f)(2).

Added by Acts 2009, 81st Leg., ch. 680, § 1, eff. Jan. 1, 2014.

§ 51.054. Service by Publication

(a) Citation or notice to a person to be served by publication shall be published one time in a newspaper of general circulation in the county in which the proceeding is pending. The publication must be made at least 10 days before the return day of the service, excluding the date of publication.

(b) The date of service of citation or notice by publication is the date of publication printed on the newspaper in which the citation or notice is published.

(c) If no newspaper is published, printed, or of general circulation in the county in which the citation or notice is to be published, the citation or notice under Subsection (a) shall be served by posting.

Derived from Probate Code § 33(f)(3).

Added by Acts 2009, 81st Leg., ch. 680, § 1, eff. Jan. 1, 2014.

Statutes in Context
§ 51.055

If a party has an attorney of record in a case, all notices are to be served on the attorney rather than the party under § 51.055.

---

§ 51.055. Service on Party's Attorney of Record

(a) If a party is represented by an attorney of record in a probate proceeding, each citation or notice required to be served on the party in that proceeding shall be served instead on that attorney. A notice under this subsection may be served by delivery to the attorney in person or by registered or certified mail.

(b) A notice may be served on an attorney of record under this section by:

(1) another party to the proceeding;

(2) the attorney of record for another party to the proceeding;

(3) the appropriate sheriff or constable; or

(4) any other person competent to testify.

(c) Each of the following is prima facie evidence of the fact that service has been made under this section:

(1) the written statement of an attorney of record showing service;

(2) the return of the officer showing service; and

(3) the affidavit of any other person showing service.

Derived from Probate Code § 34.

Added by Acts 2009, 81st Leg., ch. 680, § 1, eff. Jan. 1, 2014.

§ 51.056. Service on Personal Representative or Receiver

Unless this title expressly provides for another method of service, the county clerk who issues a citation or notice required to be served on a personal representative or receiver shall serve the citation or notice by mailing the original citation or notice by registered or certified mail to:

(1) the representative's or receiver's attorney of record; or

(2) the representative or receiver, if the representative or receiver does not have an attorney of record.

Derived from Probate Code § 33(e).

Added by Acts 2009, 81st Leg., ch. 680, § 1, eff. Jan. 1, 2014.

Subchapter C. Return and Proof of Service of Citation or Notice

§ 51.101. Requirements for Return on Citation or Notice Served by Personal Service

The return of the person serving a citation or notice under Section 51.051 must:

(1) be endorsed on or attached to the citation or notice;

(2) state the date and place of service;

(3) certify that a copy of the citation or notice was delivered to the person directed to be served;

(4) be subscribed and sworn to before, and under the hand and official seal of, an officer authorized by the laws of this state to take an affidavit; and

(5) be returned to the county clerk who issued the citation or notice.

Derived from Probate Code § 33(f)(1).

Added by Acts 2009, 81st Leg., ch. 680, § 1, eff. Jan. 1, 2014.

§ 51.102. Validity of Service and Return on Citation or Notice Served by Posting

(a) A citation or notice in a probate matter that is required to be served by posting and is issued in conformity with this title, and the service and return of service of the citation or notice, is valid if:

(1) a sheriff or constable posts a copy of the citation or notice at the location or locations prescribed by this title; and

(2) the posting occurs on a day preceding the return day of service specified in the citation or notice that provides sufficient time for the period the citation or notice must be posted to expire before the specified return day.

(b) The fact that a sheriff or constable, as applicable, makes the return of service on the citation or notice described by Subsection (a) and returns the citation or notice on which the return has been made to the court before the expiration of the period the citation or notice must be posted does not affect the validity of the citation or notice or the service or return of service. This subsection applies even if the sheriff or constable makes the return of service and returns the citation or notice on which the return is made to the court on the same day the citation or notice is issued.

Derived from Probate Code § 33(h).

Added by Acts 2009, 81st Leg., ch. 680, § 1, eff. Jan. 1, 2014.

§ 51.103. Proof of Service

(a) Proof of service in each case requiring citation or notice must be filed before the hearing.

(b) Proof of service consists of:

(1) if the service is made by a sheriff or constable, the return of service;

(2) if the service is made by a private person, the person's affidavit;

 (3) if the service is made by mail:

  (A) the certificate of the county clerk making the service, or the affidavit of the personal representative or other person making the service, stating that the citation or notice was mailed and the date of the mailing; and

  (B) the return receipt attached to the certificate or affidavit, as applicable, if the mailing was by registered or certified mail and a receipt has been returned; and

 (4) if the service is made by publication, an affidavit:

  (A) made by the publisher of the newspaper in which the citation or notice was published or an employee of the publisher;

  (B) that contains or to which is attached a copy of the published citation or notice; and

  (C) that states the date of publication printed on the newspaper in which the citation or notice was published.

Derived from Probate Code § 33(i).

Added by Acts 2009, 81st Leg., ch. 680, § 1, eff. Jan. 1, 2014.

§ 51.104. Return to Court

A citation or notice issued by a county clerk must be returned to the court from which the citation or notice was issued on the first Monday after the service is perfected.

Derived from Probate Code § 33(g).

Added by Acts 2009, 81st Leg., ch. 680, § 1, eff. Jan. 1, 2014.

Subchapter D. Alternative Manner of Issuance, Service, and Return

§ 51.151. Court-Ordered Issuance, Service, and Return Under Certain Circumstances

(a) A citation or notice required by this title shall be issued, served, and returned in the manner specified by written order of the court in accordance with this title and the Texas Rules of Civil Procedure if:

 (1) an interested person requests that action;

 (2) a specific method is not provided by this title for giving the citation or notice;

 (3) a specific method is not provided by this title for the service and return of citation or notice; or

 (4) a provision relating to a matter described by Subdivision (2) or (3) is inadequate.

(b) Citation or notice issued, served, and returned in the manner specified by a court order as provided by Subsection (a) has the same effect as if the manner of service and return had been specified by this title.

Derived from Probate Code § 33(d).

Added by Acts 2009, 81st Leg., ch. 680, § 1, eff. Jan. 1, 2014.

Subchapter E. Additional Notice Provisions

§ 51.201. Waiver of Notice of Hearing

(a) A legally competent person who is interested in a hearing in a probate proceeding may waive notice of the hearing in writing either in person or through an attorney.

(b) A trustee of a trust may waive notice under Subsection (a) on behalf of a beneficiary of the trust as provided by that subsection.

(c) A consul or other representative of a foreign government whose appearance has been entered as provided by law on behalf of a person residing in a foreign country may waive notice under Subsection (a) on the person's behalf as provided by that subsection.

(d) A person who submits to the jurisdiction of the court in a hearing is considered to have waived notice of the hearing.

Derived from Probate Code § 35.

Added by Acts 2009, 81st Leg., ch. 680, § 1, eff. Jan. 1, 2014.

§ 51.202. Request for Notice of Filing of Pleading

(a) At any time after an application is filed to commence a probate proceeding, including a proceeding for the probate of a will, the grant of letters testamentary or of administration, or a determination of heirship, a person interested in the estate may file with the county clerk a written request to be notified of all, or any specified, motions, applications, or pleadings filed with respect to the proceeding by any person or by one or more persons specifically named in the request. A person filing a request under this section is responsible for payment of the fees and other costs of providing a requested notice, and the clerk may require a deposit to cover the estimated costs of providing the notice. Thereafter, the clerk shall send to the requestor by regular mail a copy of any requested document.

(b) A county clerk's failure to comply with a request under this section does not invalidate any proceeding.

Derived from Probate Code § 33(j).

Added by Acts 2009, 81st Leg., ch. 680, § 1, eff. Jan. 1, 2014.

§ 51.203. Service of Notice of Intention to Take Depositions in Certain Matters

(a) If a will is to be probated, or in another probate matter in which there is no opposing party or attorney of record on whom to serve notice and copies of interrogatories, service may be made by posting notice of the intention to take depositions for a period of 10 days as provided by Section 51.053 governing a posting of notice.

(b) When notice by posting under Subsection (a) is filed with the county clerk, a copy of the interrogatories must also be filed.

(c) At the expiration of the 10-day period prescribed by Subsection (a):

(1) the depositions for which the notice was posted may be taken; and

(2) the judge may file cross-interrogatories if no person appears.

Derived from Probate Code § 22.

Added by Acts 2009, 81st Leg., ch. 680, § 1, eff. Jan. 1, 2014. Subsection (c) amended by Acts 2013, 83rd Leg., ch. 1136, § 4, eff. Jan. 1, 2014.

Chapter 52. Filing and Recordkeeping

Subchapter A. Recordkeeping Requirements

Subchapter B. Files; Index

Chapter 52. Filing and Recordkeeping

Subchapter A. Recordkeeping Requirements

§ 52.001. Probate Docket

(a) The county clerk shall maintain a record book titled "Judge's Probate Docket" and shall record in the book:

(1) the name of each person with respect to whom, or with respect to whose estate, proceedings are commenced or sought to be commenced;

(2) the name of each executor, administrator, or applicant for letters testamentary or of administration;

(3) the date each original application for probate proceedings is filed;

(4) a notation of each order, judgment, decree, and proceeding that occurs in each estate, including the date it occurs; and

(5) the docket number of each estate as assigned under Subsection (b).

(b) The county clerk shall assign a docket number to each estate in the order proceedings are commenced.

Derived from Probate Code § 13.

Added by Acts 2009, 81st Leg., ch. 680, § 1, eff. Jan. 1, 2014. Subsec. (a)(4) amended by Acts 2011, 82nd Leg., ch. 91, § 8.001, eff. Jan. 1, 2014.

§ 52.002. Claim Docket

(a) The county clerk shall maintain a record book titled "Claim Docket" and shall record in the book each claim that is presented against an estate for the court's approval.

(b) The county clerk shall assign one or more pages of the record book to each estate.

(c) The claim docket must be ruled in 16 columns at proper intervals from top to bottom, with a short note of the contents at the top of each column. The county clerk shall record for each claim, in the order claims are filed, the following information in the respective columns, beginning with the first or marginal column:

(1) the name of the claimant;

(2) the amount of the claim;

(3) the date of the claim;

(4) the date the claim is filed;

(5) the date the claim is due;

(6) the date the claim begins bearing interest;

(7) the interest rate;

(8) the date the claim is allowed by the executor or administrator, if applicable;

(9) the amount allowed by the executor or administrator, if applicable;

(10) the date the claim is rejected, if applicable;

(11) the date the claim is approved, if applicable;

(12) the amount approved for the claim, if applicable;

(13) the date the claim is disapproved, if applicable;

(14) the class to which the claim belongs;

(15) the date the claim is established by a judgment of a court, if applicable; and

(16) the amount of the judgment established under Subdivision (15), if applicable.

Derived from Probate Code § 14.

Added by Acts 2009, 81st Leg., ch. 680, § 1, eff. Jan. 1, 2014.

§ 52.003. Probate Fee Book

(a) The county clerk shall maintain a record book titled "Probate Fee Book" and shall record in the book each item of cost that accrues to the officers of the court and any witness fees.

(b) Each record entry must include:

(1) the party to whom the cost or fee is due;

(2) the date the cost or fee accrued;

(3) the estate or party liable for the cost or fee; and

(4) the date the cost or fee is paid.

Derived from Probate Code § 16.

Added by Acts 2009, 81st Leg., ch. 680, § 1, eff. Jan. 1, 2014.

§ 52.004. Alternate Recordkeeping

Instead of maintaining the record books described by Sections 52.001, 52.002, and 52.003, the county clerk may maintain the information described by those sections relating to a person's or estate's probate proceedings:

(1) on a computer file;

(2) on microfilm;

(3) in the form of a digitized optical image; or

(4) in another similar form of data compilation.

Derived from Probate Code § 17.

Added by Acts 2009, 81st Leg., ch. 680, § 1, eff. Jan. 1, 2014.

Subchapter B. Files; Index

§ 52.051. Filing Procedures

(a) An application for a probate proceeding, complaint, petition, or other paper permitted or required by law to be filed with a court in a probate matter must be filed with the county clerk of the appropriate county.

(b) Each paper filed in an estate must be given the docket number assigned to the estate.

(c) On receipt of a paper described by Subsection (a), the county clerk shall:

(1) file the paper; and

(2) endorse on the paper:

(A) the date the paper is filed;

(B) the docket number; and

(C) the clerk's official signature.

Derived from Probate Code §§ 11, 13(e).

Added by Acts 2009, 81st Leg., ch. 680, § 1, eff. Jan. 1, 2014.

§ 52.052. Case Files

(a) The county clerk shall maintain a case file for the estate of each decedent for which a probate proceeding has been filed.

(b) Each case file must contain each order, judgment, and proceeding of the court and any other probate filing with the court, including each:

(1) application for the probate of a will;

(2) application for the granting of administration;

(3) citation and notice, whether published or posted, including the return on the citation or notice;

(4) will and the testimony on which the will is admitted to probate;

(5) bond and official oath;

(6) inventory, appraisement, and list of claims;

(6-a) affidavit in lieu of the inventory, appraisement, and list of claims;

(7) exhibit and account;

(8) report of renting;

(9) application for sale or partition of real estate;

(10) report of sale;

(11) report of the commissioners of partition;

(12) application for authority to execute a lease for mineral development, or for pooling or unitization of lands, royalty, or other interest in minerals, or to lend or invest money; and

(13) report of lending or investing money.

(c) Only the substance of a deposition must be recorded under Subsection (b)(4).

Derived from Probate Code § 15.

Added by Acts 2009, 81st Leg., ch. 680, § 1, eff. Jan. 1, 2014. Subsec. (b)(6-a) added by Acts 2011, 82nd Leg., ch. 1338, § 2.05, eff. Jan. 1, 2014.

§ 52.053. Index

(a) The county clerk shall properly index the records required under this chapter.

(b) The county clerk shall keep the index open for public inspection, but may not release the index from the clerk's custody.

Derived from Probate Code § 17A.

Added by Acts 2009, 81st Leg., ch. 680, § 1, eff. Jan. 1, 2014.

Chapter 53. Other Court Duties and Procedures

Subchapter A. Enforcement of Orders

Chapter 53. Other Court Duties and Procedures

Subchapter A. Enforcement of Orders

§ 53.001. Enforcement of Judge's Orders

A judge may enforce the judge's lawful orders against an executor or administrator by attachment and confinement. Unless this title expressly provides otherwise, the term of confinement for any one offense under this section may not exceed three days.

Derived from Probate Code § 24.

Added by Acts 2009, 81st Leg., ch. 680, § 1, eff. Jan. 1, 2014.

Subchapter B. Costs and Security

§ 53.051. Applicability of Certain Laws

A law regulating costs in ordinary civil cases applies to a probate matter when not expressly provided for in this title.

Derived from Probate Code § 12(a).

Added by Acts 2009, 81st Leg., ch. 680, § 1, eff. Jan. 1, 2014.

§ 53.052. Security for Certain Costs

(a) The clerk may require a person who files an application, complaint, or opposition relating to an estate, other than the personal representative of the estate, to provide security for the probable costs of the proceeding before filing the application, complaint, or opposition.

(b) At any time before the trial of an application, complaint, or opposition described by Subsection (a), anyone interested in the estate or an officer of the court may, by written motion, obtain from the court an order requiring the person who filed the application, complaint, or opposition to provide security for the probable costs of the proceeding. The rules governing civil suits in the county court with respect to giving security for the probable costs of a proceeding control in cases described by Subsection (a) and this subsection.

(c) An executor or administrator appointed by a court of this state may not be required to provide security for costs in an action brought by the executor or administrator in the executor's or administrator's fiduciary capacity.

Derived from Probate Code §§ 12(b), (c).

Added by Acts 2009, 81st Leg., ch. 680, § 1, eff. Jan. 1, 2014.

§ 53.053. Exemption from Probate Fees for Estates of Certain Military Servicemembers

(a) In this section, "combat zone" means an area that the president of the United States by executive order designates for purposes of 26 U.S.C. Section 112 as an area in which armed forces of the United States are or have engaged in combat.

(b) Notwithstanding any other law, the clerk of a county court may not charge, or collect from, the estate of a decedent any of the following fees if the decedent died while in active service as a member of the armed forces of the United States in a combat zone:

(1) a fee for or associated with the filing of the decedent's will for probate; and

(2) a fee for any service rendered by the probate court regarding the administration of the decedent's estate.

Derived from Probate Code § 11A.

Added by Acts 2009, 81st Leg., ch. 680, § 1, eff. Jan. 1, 2014.

§ 53.054. Exemption from Probate Fees for Estates of Certain Law Enforcement Officers, Firefighters, and Others

(a) In this section:

(1) "Eligible decedent" means an individual listed in Section 615.003, Government Code.

(2) "Line of duty" and "personal injury" have the meanings assigned by Section 615.021(e), Government Code.

(b) Notwithstanding any other law, the clerk of a court may not charge, or collect from, the estate of an eligible decedent any of the following fees if the decedent died as a result of a personal injury sustained in the line of duty in the individual's position as described by Section 615.003, Government Code:

(1) a fee for or associated with the filing of the decedent's will for probate; and

(2) a fee for any service rendered by the court regarding the administration of the decedent's estate.

Derived from Probate Code § 11B.

Added by Acts 2011, 82nd Leg., ch. 614, § 2.01, eff. Jan. 1, 2014.

Subchapter C. Procedures for Probate Matters

§ 53.101. Calling of Dockets

The judge in whose court probate proceedings are pending, at times determined by the judge, shall:

(1) call the estates of decedents in the estates' regular order on both the probate and claim dockets; and

(2) issue orders as necessary.

Derived from Probate Code § 19.

Added by Acts 2009, 81st Leg., ch. 680, § 1, eff. Jan. 1, 2014.

§ 53.102. Setting of Certain Hearings by Clerk

(a) If a judge is unable to designate the time and place for hearing a probate matter pending in the judge's court because the judge is absent from the county seat or is on vacation, disqualified, ill, or deceased, the county clerk of the county in which the matter is pending may:

(1) designate the time and place for hearing;

(2) enter the setting on the judge's docket; and

(3) certify on the docket the reason that the judge is not acting to set the hearing.

(b) If, after the perfection of the service of notices and citations required by law concerning the time and place of hearing, a qualified judge is not present for a hearing set under Subsection (a), the hearing is automatically continued from day to day until a qualified judge is present to hear and determine the matter.

Derived from Probate Code § 20.

Added by Acts 2009, 81st Leg., ch. 680, § 1, eff. Jan. 1, 2014.

§ 53.103. Rendering of Decisions, Orders, Decrees, and Judgments

The county court shall render all decisions, orders, decrees, and judgments in probate matters in open court, except as otherwise specially provided.

Derived from Probate Code § 23.

Added by Acts 2009, 81st Leg., ch. 680, § 1, eff. Jan. 1, 2014.

Statutes in Context
§ 53.104

Normally, a judge has the discretion whether to appoint an attorney ad litem to represent an unborn, unascertained, unknown, nonresident, or incompetent party. However, in a determination of heirship proceeding, the judge is required to appoint an attorney ad litem under Estates Code § 202.009(b) to represent the interests of unknown heirs.

---

§ 53.104. Appointment of Attorneys Ad Litem

(a) Except as provided by Section 202.009(b), the judge of a probate court may appoint an attorney ad litem in any probate proceeding to represent the interests of any person, including:

(1) a person who has a legal disability under state or federal law;

(2) a nonresident;

(3) an unborn or unascertained person;

(4) an unknown heir;

(5) a missing heir; or

(6) an unknown or missing person for whom cash is deposited into the court's registry under Section 362.011.

(b) An attorney ad litem appointed under this section is entitled to reasonable compensation for services provided in the amount set by the court. The court shall:

(1) tax the compensation as costs in the probate proceeding and order the compensation to be paid out of the estate or by any party at any time during the proceeding; or

(2) for an attorney ad litem appointed under Subsection (a)(6), order that the compensation be paid from the cash on deposit in the court's registry as provided by Section 362.011.

Derived from Probate Code § 34A.

Added by Acts 2009, 81st Leg., ch. 680, § 1, eff. Jan. 1, 2014. Amended by Acts 2013, 83rd Leg., ch. 1136, § 5, eff. Jan. 1, 2014.

§ 53.106. Executions in Probate Matters

(a) An execution in a probate matter must be:

(1) directed "to any sheriff or any constable within the State of Texas";

(2) attested and signed by the clerk officially under court seal; and

(3) made returnable in 60 days.

(b) A proceeding under an execution described by Subsection (a) is governed, to the extent applicable, by the laws regulating a proceeding under an execution issued by a district court.

(c) Notwithstanding Subsection (a), an execution directed to the sheriff or a constable of a specific county in this state may not be held defective if properly executed within that county by the sheriff or constable to whom the execution is directed.

Derived from Probate Code § 25.

Added by Acts 2009, 81st Leg., ch. 680, § 1, eff. Jan. 1, 2014.

§ 53.107. Inapplicability of Certain Rules of Civil Procedure.

The following do not apply to probate proceedings:

(1) Rules 47(c) and 169, Texas Rules of Civil Procedure; and

(2) the portions of Rule 190.2, Texas Rules of Civil Procedure, concerning expedited actions under Rule 169, Texas Rules of Civil Procedure.

New.

Added by Acts 2013, 83rd Leg., ch. 1136, § 6, eff. Jan. 1, 2014.

Chapter 54. Pleadings and Evidence in General

Subchapter A. Pleadings

Subchapter B. Evidence

Chapter 54. Pleadings and Evidence in General

Subchapter A. Pleadings

Statutes in Context
§ 54.001

The lower courts of Texas have recognized the tort of tortious interference with inheritance rights. See *King v. Acker*, 725 S.W.2d 750 (Tex. App. — Houston [1st Dist.] 1987, no writ). However, the courts have not delineated exactly what actions would constitute tortious interference. Taking an opposite approach, the 2003 Legislature enacted the Probate Code predecessor to § 54.001 which declares that certain specified actions may not be considered tortious interference, that is, the filing or contesting in probate court of any pleading relating to a decedent's estate.

§ 54.001. Effect of Filing or Contesting Pleading

(a) The filing or contesting in probate court of a pleading relating to a decedent's estate does not constitute tortious interference with inheritance of the estate.

(b) This section does not abrogate any right of a person under Rule 13, Texas Rules of Civil Procedure, or Chapter 10, Civil Practice and Remedies Code.

Derived from Probate Code § 10C.

Added by Acts 2009, 81st Leg., ch. 680, § 1, eff. Jan. 1, 2014.

§ 54.002. Defect in Pleading

A court may not invalidate a pleading in probate, or an order based on the pleading, on the basis of a defect of form or substance in the pleading unless a timely objection has been made against the defect and the defect has been called to the attention of the court in which the proceeding was or is pending.

Derived from Probate Code § 9.

Added by Acts 2009, 81st Leg., ch. 680, § 1, eff. Jan. 1, 2014.

Subchapter B. Evidence

§ 54.051. Applicability of Certain Rules Relating to Witnesses and Evidence

Except as provided by Section 51.203, the Texas Rules of Evidence apply in a proceeding arising under this title to the extent practicable.

Derived from Probate Code § 22.

Added by Acts 2009, 81st Leg., ch. 680, § 1, eff. Jan. 1, 2014. Amended by Acts 2013, 83rd Leg., ch. 1136, § 7, eff. Jan. 1, 2014.

§ 54.052. Use of Certain Records as Evidence

The following are admissible as evidence in any court of this state:

(1) record books described by Sections 52.001, 52.002, and 52.003 and individual case files described by Section 52.052, including records maintained in a manner allowed under Section 52.004; and

(2) certified copies or reproductions of the records.

Derived from Probate Code § 18.

Added by Acts 2009, 81st Leg., ch. 680, § 1, eff. Jan. 1, 2014.

Chapter 55. Complaints and Contests

Subchapter A. Contest of Proceedings in Probate Court

Subchapter B. Institution of Higher Education or Charitable Organization as Party to Certain Actions

Subchapter C. Mental Capacity of Decedent

Subchapter D. Attachment of Estate Property

Subchapter E. Specific Performance of Agreement to Transfer Title

Subchapter F. Bill of Review

Chapter 55. Complaints and Contests

Subchapter A. Contest of Proceedings in Probate Court

Statutes in Context
§ 55.001

An individual may have a strong motivation to have a testator's will deemed invalid and ineffective to dispose of the testator's property. First, this person could be an heir who would receive more under intestacy than the will. Or, second, this person could be a beneficiary of a prior will who would receive a smaller gift under the more recent will.

A person must have a pecuniary interest in the estate to contest the proceedings. *Logan v. Thomason*, 202 S.W.2d 212, 215 (Tex. 1947) ("An interest resting on sentiment or sympathy, or any other basis other than gain or loss of money or its equivalent, is insufficient."). See also Estates Code § 22.018 defining "interested person."

The timing of a will contest is of particular importance. First, the timing determines which party has the burden of proof. If the contest action is brought before the probate of the will, then the party admitting the will to probate has the burden to prove that the will is valid. On the other hand, if the contest action is brought after the will has been admitted to probate, the party contesting the will has the burden to prove that there is a deficiency in the will. Second, will contests are subject to the statute of limitations set forth in Estates Code § 256.204.

§ 55.001. Opposition in Probate Proceeding

A person interested in an estate may, at any time before the court decides an issue in a proceeding, file written opposition regarding the issue. The person is entitled to process for witnesses and evidence, and to be heard on the opposition, as in other suits.

Derived from Probate Code § 10.

Added by Acts 2009, 81st Leg., ch. 680, § 1, eff. Jan. 1, 2014.

Statutes in Context
§ 55.002

Any party has the right to a jury trial in a contested probate action under § 55.002.

§ 55.002. Trial by Jury

In a contested probate or mental illness proceeding in a probate court, a party is entitled to a jury trial as in other civil actions.

Derived from Probate Code § 21.

Added by Acts 2009, 81st Leg., ch. 680, § 1, eff. Jan. 1, 2014.

Subchapter B. Institution of Higher Education or Charitable Organization as Party to Certain Actions

§ 55.051. Definition

In this subchapter, "institution of higher education" has the meaning assigned by Section 61.003, Education Code.

Derived from Probate Code § 10A(a).

Added by Acts 2009, 81st Leg., ch. 680, § 1, eff. Jan. 1, 2014.

Statutes in Context
§ 55.052

Unlike many states, Texas law does not expressly require that the beneficiaries of a will be given notice or made a party to a will contest action except for certain schools and charities as provided in § 55.052. See *Wojcik v. Wesolick*, 97 S.W.3d 335 (Tex. App. — Houston [14th Dist.] 2003, no pet.), but see, *Kotz v. Kotz*, 613 S.W.2d 760, 761 (Tex. Civ. App. — Beaumont 1981, no writ), and *Jennings v. Srp*, 521 S.W.2d 326, 328-29 (Tex. Civ. App. — Corpus Christi 1975, no writ).

§ 55.052. Necessary Party

An institution of higher education, a private institution of higher education, or a charitable organization that is a distributee under a will is a necessary party to a will contest or will construction suit involving the will.

Derived from Probate Code § 10A(a).

Added by Acts 2009, 81st Leg., ch. 680, § 1, eff. Jan. 1, 2014.

§ 55.053. Service of Process

The court shall serve an institution or organization that is a necessary party under Section 55.052 in the manner provided by this title for service on other parties.

Derived from Probate Code § 10A(b).

Added by Acts 2009, 81st Leg., ch. 680, § 1, eff. Jan. 1, 2014.

Subchapter C. Mental Capacity of Decedent

Statutes in Context
§ 55.101

The ability of litigants to obtain evidence of a decedent's testamentary capacity was greatly enhanced by the legislature's enactment of the Probate Code predecessor to Estates Code § 55.101 in 1997. This section provides that a party to a will contest, or a proceeding in which a party relies on the mental or testamentary capacity of a decedent as part of the party's claim or defense, is entitled to production of all communications or records that are relevant to the decedent's condition.

§ 55.101. Entitlement to Production of Communications and Records

Notwithstanding Subtitle B, Title 3, Occupations Code, a person who is a party to a will contest or proceeding in which a party relies on the mental or testamentary capacity of a decedent before the decedent's death as part of the party's claim or defense is entitled to production of all communications or records relevant to the decedent's condition before the decedent's death.

Derived from Probate Code § 10B.

Added by Acts 2009, 81st Leg., ch. 680, § 1, eff. Jan. 1, 2014.

§ 55.102. Release of Records

On receipt of a subpoena for communications or records described by Section 55.101 and a file-stamped copy of the will contest or proceeding described by that section, the appropriate physician, hospital, medical facility, custodian of records, or other person in possession of the communications or records shall release the communications or records to the requesting party without further authorization.

Derived from Probate Code § 10B.

Added by Acts 2009, 81st Leg., ch. 680, § 1, eff. Jan. 1, 2014.

Subchapter D. Attachment of Estate Property

§ 55.151. Order for Issuance of Writ of Attachment

(a) If a person interested in an estate files with the judge a written complaint made under oath alleging that the executor or administrator of the estate is about to remove the estate or part of the estate outside of the state, the judge may order a writ of attachment to issue, directed "to any sheriff or any constable within the State of Texas." The writ must order the sheriff or constable to:

(1) seize the estate or a part of the estate; and

(2) hold that property subject to the judge's additional orders regarding the complaint.

(b) Notwithstanding Subsection (a), a writ of attachment directed to the sheriff or constable of a specific county within the state is not defective if the writ was properly executed in that county by that officer.

Derived from Probate Code § 26.

Added by Acts 2009, 81st Leg., ch. 680, § 1, eff. Jan. 1, 2014.

§ 55.152. Bond

Before a writ of attachment ordered under Section 55.151 may be issued, the complainant must execute a bond that is:

(1) payable to the executor or administrator of the estate;

(2) in an amount set by the judge; and

(3) conditioned for the payment of all damages and costs that are recovered for the wrongful suing out of the writ.

Derived from Probate Code § 26.

Added by Acts 2009, 81st Leg., ch. 680, § 1, eff. Jan. 1, 2014.

Subchapter E. Specific Performance of Agreement to Transfer Title

§ 55.201. Complaint and Citation

(a) If a person sold property and entered into a bond or other written agreement to transfer title to the property and then died without transferring the title, the owner of the bond or agreement or the owner's legal representative may:

(1) file a written complaint in the court of the county in which letters testamentary or of administration on the decedent's estate were granted; and

(2) have the personal representative of the estate cited to appear on a date stated in the citation and show cause why specific performance of the bond or agreement should not be ordered.

(b) Except as provided by Subsection (c), the bond or agreement must be filed with the complaint described by Subsection (a).

(c) If good cause under oath is shown why the bond or written agreement cannot be filed with the complaint, the bond or agreement or the substance of the bond or agreement must be stated in the complaint.

Derived from Probate Code § 27.

Added by Acts 2009, 81st Leg., ch. 680, § 1, eff. Jan. 1, 2014.

§ 55.202. Hearing and Order

(a) After service of the citation under Section 55.201, the court shall hear the complaint and the evidence on the complaint.

(b) The court shall order the personal representative to transfer title to the property, according to the tenor of the bond or agreement, to the complainant if the judge is satisfied from the proof that:

(1) the bond or agreement was legally executed by the decedent; and

(2) the complainant has a right to demand specific performance.

(c) The order must fully describe the property to be transferred.

Derived from Probate Code § 27.

Added by Acts 2009, 81st Leg., ch. 680, § 1, eff. Jan. 1, 2014.

§ 55.203. Conveyance

(a) A conveyance made under this subchapter must refer to and identify the court order authorizing the conveyance. On delivery of the conveyance, all the right and title to the property conveyed that the decedent had vests in the person to whom the conveyance is made.

(b) A conveyance under this subchapter is prima facie evidence that all requirements of the law for obtaining the conveyance have been complied with.

Derived from Probate Code § 27.

Added by Acts 2009, 81st Leg., ch. 680, § 1, eff. Jan. 1, 2014.

Subchapter F. Bill of Review

Statutes in Context
§ 55.251

A bill of review is filed for the purpose of getting a decision revised or corrected upon a showing of error. It may be filed by an interested party and is filed in the court where the estate was administered. A bill of review may be filed within two years of the date of the decision. Thus, a bill of review may be filed even though it is too late to appeal.

An interested party might also wish to file an equitable (that is, non-statutory) bill of review. "[T]he applicant must plead and prove: (1) a meritorious defense to the underlying cause of action, (2) which the applicant was prevented from making by the fraud, accident or wrongful act of the opposing party or official mistake, (3) unmixed with any fault or negligence on its own part." *In re Estate of Aguilar*, 2013 WL 520282 (Tex. App.—San Antonio 2013, no pet.).

---

§ 55.251. Revision and Correction of Order or Judgment in Probate Proceeding

(a) An interested person may, by a bill of review filed in the court in which the probate proceedings were held, have an order or judgment rendered by the court revised and corrected on a showing of error in the order or judgment, as applicable.

(b) A bill of review to revise and correct an order or judgment may not be filed more than two years after the date of the order or judgment, as applicable.

Derived from Probate Code § 31.

Added by Acts 2009, 81st Leg., ch. 680, § 1, eff. Jan. 1, 2014. Amended by Acts 2011, 82nd Leg., ch. 91, § 8.002, eff. Jan. 1, 2014.

§ 55.252. Injunction

A process or action under a court order or judgment subject to a bill of review filed under Section 55.251 may be stayed only by writ of injunction.

Derived from Probate Code § 31.

Added by Acts 2009, 81st Leg., ch. 680, § 1, eff. Jan. 1, 2014. Amended by Acts 2011, 82nd Leg., ch. 91, § 8.003, eff. Jan. 1, 2014.

Chapter 56. Change and Resignation of Resident Agent of Personal Representative for Service of Process

§ 56.001. Change of Resident Agent
§ 56.002. Resignation of Resident Agent

Chapter 56. Change and Resignation of Resident Agent of Personal Representative for Service of Process

---

Statutes in Context
§ 56.001

A nonresident of Texas may serve as a personal representative only if the nonresident appoints a resident agent to accept service of process in all actions or proceedings with respect to the estate. See § 304.003(c). Section 56.001 provides guidance for how the personal representative may change the resident agent.

---

§ 56.001. Change of Resident Agent

(a) A personal representative of an estate may change the representative's resident agent to accept service of process in a probate proceeding or other action relating to the estate by filing with the court in which the probate proceeding is pending a statement titled "Designation of Successor Resident Agent" that states the names and addresses of:

(1) the representative;
(2) the resident agent; and
(3) the successor resident agent.

(b) The designation of a successor resident agent takes effect on the date a statement under Subsection (a) is filed with the court.

Derived from Probate Code § 221A.

Added by Acts 2009, 81st Leg., ch. 680, § 1, eff. Jan. 1, 2014.

§ 56.002. Resignation of Resident Agent

(a) A resident agent of a personal representative may resign as resident agent by giving notice to the representative and filing with the court in which the probate proceeding is pending a statement titled "Resignation of Resident Agent" that states:

(1) the name of the representative;

(2) the representative's address most recently known by the resident agent;

(3) that notice of the resignation has been given to the representative and the date that notice was given; and

(4) that the representative has not designated a successor resident agent.

(b) The resident agent shall send, by certified mail, return receipt requested, a copy of a resignation statement filed under Subsection (a) to:

(1) the personal representative at the address most recently known by the resident agent; and

(2) each party in the case or the party's attorney or other designated representative of record.

(c) The resignation of a resident agent takes effect on the date the court enters an order accepting the resignation. A court may not enter an order accepting the resignation unless the resident agent complies with this section.

Derived from Probate Code § 221B.

Added by Acts 2009, 81st Leg., ch. 680, § 1, eff. Jan. 1, 2014.

SUBTITLE C. PASSAGE OF TITLE AND DISTRIBUTION OF DECEDENTS' PROPERTY IN GENERAL

Chapter 101. Estate Assets in General

Subchapter A. Passage and Possession of Decedent's Estate on Death

§ 101.001. Passage of Estate on Decedent's Death
§ 101.002. Effect of Joint Ownership of Property
§ 101.003. Possession of Estate by Personal Representative

Subchapter B. Liability of Estate for Debts

§ 101.051. Liability of Estate for Debts in General
§ 101.052. Liability of Community Property for Debts of Deceased Spouse

Chapter 101. Estate Assets in General

Subchapter A. Passage and Possession of Decedent's Estate on Death

Statutes in Context
§ 101.001

Title to the decedent's property passes to the heirs or beneficiaries immediately upon the decedent's death regardless of the length of time occupied by the administration process. See *Welder v. Hitchcock*, 617 S.W.2d 294 (Tex. Civ. App. — Corpus Christi 1981, writ ref'd n.r.e.) (declaring that "there is no shorter interval of time than between the death of a decedent and the vesting of his estate in his heirs"). This title is, however, subject to the claims of the decedent's creditors under § 101.051.

§ 101.001. Passage of Estate on Decedent's Death

(a) Subject to Section 101.051, if a person dies leaving a lawful will:

(1) all of the person's estate that is devised by the will vests immediately in the devisees;

(2) all powers of appointment granted in the will vest immediately in the donees of those powers; and

(3) all of the person's estate that is not devised by the will vests immediately in the person's heirs at law.

(b) Subject to Section 101.051, the estate of a person who dies intestate vests immediately in the person's heirs at law.

Derived from Probate Code § 37.

Added by Acts 2009, 81st Leg., ch. 680, § 1, eff. Jan. 1, 2014.

Statutes in Context
§ 101.002

A joint tenancy is a type of concurrent property ownership. A joint tenant's rights end at death in favor of the surviving joint tenants. Thus, when a joint tenant dies, the deceased tenant's share is divided equally among the surviving joint tenants. The rights of these surviving joint tenants are superior to the deceased tenant's heirs or beneficiaries.

At common law, the survivorship feature attached automatically to a joint tenancy. The presumption of survivorship often led to unanticipated property distributions as co-owners held as joint tenants when they intended to hold as tenants in common. Nonlegally trained individuals may not appreciate the significant difference between these two types of concurrent ownership. Consequently, § 101.002 provides that the survivorship feature does not attach to a joint tenancy unless it is expressly stated in the instrument.

Survivorship agreements for community property are covered separately in Chapter 112.

§ 101.002. Effect of Joint Ownership of Property

If two or more persons hold an interest in property jointly and one joint owner dies before severance, the interest of the decedent in the joint estate:

(1) does not survive to the remaining joint owner or owners; and

(2) passes by will or intestacy from the decedent as if the decedent's interest had been severed.

Derived from Probate Code § 46(a).

Added by Acts 2009, 81st Leg., ch. 680, § 1, eff. Jan. 1, 2014.

Statutes in Context
§ 101.003

Title to the decedent's property passes to the heirs or beneficiaries immediately upon the decedent's death. However, if a personal representative is appointed, that person has a superior right to possess all of the decedent's probate assets owned at the time of death. It may be difficult for the personal representative to collect this property because family members often take the decedent's property, especially personal property in the decedent's home, shortly after death despite having no authority to do so.

§ 101.003. Possession of Estate by Personal Representative

On the issuance of letters testamentary or of administration on an estate described by Section 101.001, the executor or administrator has the right to possession of the estate as the estate existed at the death of the testator or intestate, subject to the exceptions provided by Section 101.051. The executor or administrator shall recover possession of the estate and hold the estate in trust to be disposed of in accordance with the law.

Derived from Probate Code § 37.

Added by Acts 2009, 81st Leg., ch. 680, § 1, eff. Jan. 1, 2014.

Subchapter B. Liability of Estate For Debts

§ 101.051. Liability of Estate for Debts in General

(a) A decedent's estate vests in accordance with Section 101.001(a) subject to the payment of:

(1) the debts of the decedent, except as exempted by law; and

(2) any court-ordered child support payments that are delinquent on the date of the decedent's death.

(b) A decedent's estate vests in accordance with Section 101.001(b) subject to the payment of, and is still liable for:

(1) the debts of the decedent, except as exempted by law; and

(2) any court-ordered child support payments that are delinquent on the date of the decedent's death.

Derived from Probate Code § 37.

Added by Acts 2009, 81st Leg., ch. 680, § 1, eff. Jan. 1, 2014.

§ 101.052. Liability of Community Property for Debts of Deceased Spouse

(a) The community property subject to the sole or joint management, control, and disposition of a spouse during marriage continues to be subject to the liabilities of that spouse on death.

(b) The interest that the deceased spouse owned in any other nonexempt community property passes to the deceased spouse's heirs or devisees charged with the debts that were enforceable against the deceased spouse before death.

(c) This section does not prohibit the administration of community property under other provisions of this title relating to the administration of an estate.

Derived from Probate Code §§ 155, 156.

Added by Acts 2009, 81st Leg., ch. 680, § 1, eff. Jan. 1, 2014.

Chapter 102. Probate Assets: Decedent's Homestead

§ 102.001. Treatment of Certain Children
§ 102.002. Homestead Rights Not Affected By Character of the Homestead
§ 102.003. Passage of Homestead
§ 102.004. Liability of Homestead for Debts
§ 102.005. Prohibitions on Partition of Homestead
§ 102.006. Circumstances Under Which Partition of Homestead is Authorized

Chapter 102. Probate Assets: Decedent's Homestead

§ 102.001. Treatment of Certain Children

For purposes of determining homestead rights, a child is a child of his or her mother and a child of his or her father, as provided by Sections 201.051, 201.052, and 201.053.

Derived from Probate Code § 42(c).

Added by Acts 2009, 81st Leg., ch. 680, § 1, eff. Jan. 1, 2014.

§ 102.002. Homestead Rights Not Affected by Character of the Homestead

The homestead rights and the respective interests of the surviving spouse and children of a decedent are the same whether the homestead was the decedent's separate property or was community property between the surviving spouse and the decedent.

Derived from Probate Code § 282.

Added by Acts 2009, 81st Leg., ch. 680, § 1, eff. Jan. 1, 2014.

Statutes in Context
§ 102.003

For a discussion of the rights of the surviving spouse and minor children to occupy the homestead, see *Statutes in Context* to Texas Constitution Article XVI, § 52.

§ 102.003. Passage of Homestead

The homestead of a decedent who dies leaving a surviving spouse descends and vests on the decedent's death in the same manner as other real property of the decedent and is governed by the same laws of descent and distribution.

Derived from Probate Code § 283.

Added by Acts 2009, 81st Leg., ch. 680, § 1, eff. Jan. 1, 2014.

Statutes in Context
§ 102.004

A homestead is "the dwelling house constituting the family residence, together with the land on which it is situated and the appurtenances connected therewith." *Farrington v. First Nat'l Bank of Bellville*, 753 S.W.2d 248 (Tex. App. — Houston [1st Dist.] 1988, writ denied). Homesteads are classified by property type as either a rural homestead or an urban homestead, and the size of the exemption varies depending on this classification. See *Statutes in Context* to Texas Constitution Article XVI, § 51.

The source of the tremendous protection granted to Texas homesteads is Article XVI, § 50 of the Texas Constitution. This section establishes the protection without dollar value limitation and then lists exceptions, that is, situations in which the homestead is not protected. See *Statutes in Context* to Texas Constitution Article XVI, § 50.

The protection of the homestead from most of the decedent's creditors exists only if the decedent was survived by a spouse or a minor child.

§ 102.004. Liability of Homestead for Debts

If the decedent was survived by a spouse or minor child, the homestead is not liable for the payment of any of the debts of the estate, other than:

(1) purchase money for the homestead;

(2) taxes due on the homestead;

(3) work and material used in constructing improvements on the homestead if the requirements of Section 50(a)(5), Article XVI, Texas Constitution, are met;

(4) an owelty of partition imposed against the entirety of the property by a court order or written agreement of the parties to the partition, including a debt of one spouse in favor of the other spouse

resulting from a division or an award of a family homestead in a divorce proceeding;

(5) the refinance of a lien against the homestead, including a federal tax lien resulting from the tax debt of both spouses, if the homestead is a family homestead, or from the tax debt of the decedent;

(6) an extension of credit on the homestead if the requirements of Section 50(a)(6), Article XVI, Texas Constitution, are met; or

(7) a reverse mortgage.

Derived from Probate Code § 270.

Added by Acts 2009, 81st Leg., ch. 680, § 1, eff. Jan. 1, 2014. Amended by Acts 2013, 83rd Leg., ch. 1136, § 8, eff. Jan. 1, 2014.

§ 102.005. Prohibitions on Partition of Homestead

The homestead may not be partitioned among the decedent's heirs:

(1) during the lifetime of the surviving spouse for as long as the surviving spouse elects to use or occupy the property as a homestead; or

(2) during the period the guardian of the decedent's minor children is permitted to use and occupy the homestead under a court order.

Derived from Probate Code § 284.

Added by Acts 2009, 81st Leg., ch. 680, § 1, eff. Jan. 1, 2014.

§ 102.006. Circumstances Under Which Partition of Homestead is Authorized

The homestead may be partitioned among the respective owners of the property in the same manner as other property held in common if:

(1) the surviving spouse dies, sells his or her interest in the homestead, or elects to no longer use or occupy the property as a homestead; or

(2) the court no longer permits the guardian of the minor children to use and occupy the property as a homestead.

Derived from Probate Code § 285.

Added by Acts 2009, 81st Leg., ch. 680, § 1, eff. Jan. 1, 2014.

Chapter 111. Nonprobate Assets in General

Subchapter A. Right of Survivorship Agreements Between Joint Tenants

§ 111.001. Right of Survivorship Agreements Authorized

§ 111.002. Agreements Concerning Community Property

Subchapter B. Other Provisions for Payment or Transfer of Certain Assets on Death

Chapter 111. Nonprobate Assets in General

Subchapter A. Right of Survivorship Agreements Between Joint Tenants

§ 111.001. Right of Survivorship Agreements Authorized

(a) Notwithstanding Section 101.002, two or more persons who hold an interest in property jointly may agree in writing that the interest of a joint owner who dies survives to the surviving joint owner or owners.

(b) An agreement described by Subsection (a) may not be inferred from the mere fact that property is held in joint ownership.

Derived from Probate Code § 46(a).

Added by Acts 2009, 81st Leg., ch. 680, § 1, eff. Jan. 1, 2014.

§ 111.002. Agreements Concerning Community Property

(a) Section 111.001 does not apply to an agreement between spouses regarding the spouses' community property.

(b) An agreement between spouses regarding a right of survivorship in community property is governed by Chapter 112.

Derived from Probate Code § 46(b).

Added by Acts 2009, 81st Leg., ch. 680, § 1, eff. Jan. 1, 2014.

Subchapter B. Other Provisions for Payment or Transfer of Certain Assets on Death

---

Statutes in Context
§§ 111.051 – 111.053

Sections 111.051 – 111.053 authorize a wide range of arrangements which provide for payment or transfer upon death. These designations are effective to transfer property outside of probate.

---

§ 111.051. Definitions

In this subchapter:

(1) "Contracting third party" means a financial institution, insurance company, plan custodian, plan administrator, or other person who is a party to an account agreement, insurance contract, annuity contract, retirement account, beneficiary designation, or other similar contract the terms of which control whether a nontestamentary transfer has occurred or to whom property passes as a result of a possible nontestamentary transfer. The term does not include a person who is:

(A) an owner of the property subject to a possible nontestamentary transfer; or

(B) a possible recipient of the property subject to a possible nontestamentary transfer.

(1-a) "Employees' trust" means:

(A) a trust that forms a part of a stock-bonus, pension, or profit-sharing plan under Section 401, Internal Revenue Code of 1954 (26 U.S.C. Section 401 (1986));

(B) a pension trust under Chapter 111, Property Code; and

(C) an employer-sponsored benefit plan or program, or any other retirement savings arrangement, including a pension plan created under Section 3, Employee Retirement Income Security Act of 1974 (29 U.S.C. Section 1002 (1986)), regardless of whether the plan, program, or arrangement is funded through a trust.

(2) "Financial institution" has the meaning assigned by Section 113.001.

(3) "Individual retirement account" means a trust, custodial arrangement, or annuity under Section 408(a) or (b), Internal Revenue Code of 1954 (26 U.S.C. Section 408 (1986)).

(4) "Retirement account" means a retirement-annuity contract, an individual retirement account, a simplified employee pension, or any other retirement savings arrangement.

(5) "Retirement-annuity contract" means an annuity contract under Section 403, Internal Revenue Code of 1954 (26 U.S.C. Section 403 (1986)).

(6) "Simplified employee pension" means a trust, custodial arrangement, or annuity under Section 408, Internal Revenue Code of 1954 (26 U.S.C. Section 408 (1986)).

Derived from Probate Code §§ 450(a), (c).

Added by Acts 2009, 81st Leg., ch. 680, § 1, eff. Jan. 1, 2014. Subsection (1) amended by Acts 2013, 83rd Leg., ch. 1136, § 9, eff. Jan. 1, 2014.

§ 111.052. Validity of Certain Nontestamentary Instruments and Provisions

(a) This code does not invalidate:

(1) any provision in an insurance policy, employment contract, bond, mortgage, promissory

note, deposit agreement, employees' trust, retirement account, deferred compensation arrangement, custodial agreement, pension plan, trust agreement, conveyance of property, security, account with a financial institution, mutual fund account, or any other written instrument effective as a contract, gift, conveyance, or trust, stating that:

(A) money or other benefits under the instrument due to or controlled or owned by a decedent shall be paid after the decedent's death, or property that is the subject of the instrument shall pass, to a person designated by the decedent in the instrument or in a separate writing, including a will, executed at the same time as the instrument or subsequently; or

(B) money due or to become due under the instrument shall cease to be payable if the promisee or promissor dies before payment or demand; or

(2) an instrument described by Subdivision (1).

(b) A provision described by Subsection (a)(1) is considered nontestamentary.

Derived from Probate Code § 450(a).

Added by Acts 2009, 81st Leg., ch. 680, § 1, eff. Jan. 1, 2014.

§ 111.053. Creditor's Rights Not Limited

Nothing in this subchapter limits the rights of a creditor under another law of this state.

Derived from Probate Code § 450(b).

Added by Acts 2009, 81st Leg., ch. 680, § 1, eff. Jan. 1, 2014.

Statutes in Context
§ 111.054

The 2013 Legislature enacted this section to overrule *McKeehan v. McKeehan*, 355 S.W.3d 282 (Tex. App.—Austin 2011, pet. denied). According to this case, an agreement relating to a nonprobate asset which contains a choice of law clause causes that state's law to govern the asset such as whether the asset has the survivorship feature. This section now provides that if more than 50% of that asset (e.g., a bank account, retirement plan, annuity, or insurance contract) was contributed by a Texas resident, Texas law will determine whether the asset has the survivorship feature irrespective of any choice of law provision. The applicability of this new provision is based on the date of the owner's death being on or after January 1, 2014 rather than the date on which the decedent entered into the agreement. To enhance the likelihood of a court upholding this statute, the Legislature stated that the change represents "the fundamental policy of [Texas] for the protection of its residents and [is] intended to prevail over the law of another state or

jurisdiction, to the extent those laws are in conflict with Texas law." See Acts 2013, 83rd Leg., ch. 1136, § 61(a).

§ 111.054. Application of State Law to Certain Nontestamentary Transfers

(a) This section applies if more than 50 percent of the:

(1) assets in an account at a financial institution, in a retirement account, or in another similar arrangement are owned, immediately before a possible nontestamentary transfer of the assets, by one or more persons domiciled in this state; or

(2) interests under an insurance contract, annuity contract, beneficiary designation, or other similar arrangement are owned, immediately before a possible nontestamentary transfer of the interests, by one or more persons domiciled in this state.

(b) Notwithstanding a choice of law or other contractual provision in an agreement prepared or provided by a contracting third party, Texas law applies to determine:

(1) whether a nontestamentary transfer of assets or interests described by Subsection (a) has occurred; and

(2) the ownership of the assets or interests following a possible nontestamentary transfer.

(c) Notwithstanding a choice of law or other contractual provision in an agreement prepared or provided by a contracting third party, any person, including a personal representative, who is asserting an ownership interest in assets or interests described by Subsection (a) subject to a possible nontestamentary transfer shall have access to the courts of this state for a judicial determination of:

(1) whether a nontestamentary transfer of the assets or interests has occurred; or

(2) the ownership of the assets or interests following a possible nontestamentary transfer.

(d) Subsections (a), (b), and (c) do not apply to an obligation:

(1) owed by a party to the contracting third party; or

(2) owed by the contracting third party to a party.

(e) This section applies to a community property survivorship agreement governed by Chapter 112 and a multiple-party account governed by Chapter 113.

New.

Added by Acts 2013, 83rd Leg., ch. 1136, § 10, eff. Jan. 1, 2014

Chapter 112. Community Property With Right of Survivorship

Subchapter A. General Provisions

§ 112.001. Definition of Community Property Survivorship Agreement

Chapter 112. Community Property with Right of Survivorship

Subchapter A. General Provisions

Statutes in Context
Chapter 112

Community property could not be held in survivorship form until 1987 when Article XVI, § 15 of the Texas Constitution was amended to authorize community property survivorship agreements. Chapter 112 provide guidance with respect to these agreements.

§ 112.001. Definition of Community Property Survivorship Agreement

In this chapter, "community property survivorship agreement" means an agreement between spouses creating a right of survivorship in community property.

New.

Added by Acts 2009, 81st Leg., ch. 680, § 1, eff. Jan. 1, 2014.

§ 112.002. Applicability of Other Law to Community Property Held in Multiple-Party Accounts

Chapter 113 applies to multiple-party accounts held by spouses with a right of survivorship to the extent that chapter is not inconsistent with this chapter.

Derived from Probate Code § 462.

Added by Acts 2009, 81st Leg., ch. 680, § 1, eff. Jan. 1, 2014.

Subchapter B. Community Property Survivorship Agreements

§ 112.051. Agreement for Right of Survivorship in Community Property

At any time, spouses may agree between themselves that all or part of their community property, then existing or to be acquired, becomes the property of the surviving spouse on the death of a spouse.

Derived from Probate Code § 451.

Added by Acts 2009, 81st Leg., ch. 680, § 1, eff. Jan. 1, 2014.

Statutes in Context
§ 112.052

A community property survivorship agreement must be (1) in writing, (2) signed by both spouses (not just the deceased spouse), and (3) contain express survivorship language.

In 2009, the Texas Supreme Court issued a disturbing opinion in the case of *Holmes v. Beatty*, 290 S.W.3d 852 (Tex. 2009). A husband and his wife held investment accounts with the designation "JT TEN." The spouses signed the agreement but did not indicate whether the account had, or did not have, the survivorship feature. The court determined that holding community property as joint tenants automatically includes the survivorship feature and that the designation "JT TEN" is an acceptable abbreviation. In so deciding, the court relied on the common law under which joint tenancies carried with them the survivorship feature. However, the court disregarded long-established Texas law which requires that the survivorship be expressly stated. The 2011 Legislature amended the Probate Code predecessors to both § 113.151 and § 112.052 to make it clear that this type of designation is insufficient to create the survivorship feature.

§ 112.052. Form of Agreement

(a) A community property survivorship agreement must be in writing and signed by both spouses.

(b) A written agreement signed by both spouses is sufficient to create a right of survivorship in the community property described in the agreement if the agreement includes any of the following phrases:

(1) "with right of survivorship";

(2) "will become the property of the survivor";

(3) "will vest in and belong to the surviving spouse"; or

(4) "shall pass to the surviving spouse."

(c) Notwithstanding Subsection (b), a community property survivorship agreement that otherwise meets the requirements of this chapter is effective without including any of the phrases listed in that subsection.

(d) A survivorship agreement may not be inferred from the mere fact that an account is a joint account or that an account is designated as JT TEN, Joint Tenancy, or joint, or with other similar language.

Derived from Probate Code § 452.

Added by Acts 2009, 81st Leg., ch. 680, § 1, eff. Jan. 1, 2014. Subsec. (d) added by Acts 2011, 82nd Leg., ch. 1338, § 2.06, eff. Jan. 1, 2014.

§ 112.053. Adjudication Not Required

A community property survivorship agreement that satisfies the requirements of this chapter is effective and enforceable without an adjudication.

Derived from Probate Code §§ 456(a), 458.

Added by Acts 2009, 81st Leg., ch. 680, § 1, eff. Jan. 1, 2014.

§ 112.054. Revocation of Agreement

(a) A community property survivorship agreement made in accordance with this chapter may be revoked as provided by the terms of the agreement.

(b) If a community property survivorship agreement does not provide a method of revocation, the agreement may be revoked by a written instrument:

(1) signed by both spouses; or

(2) signed by one spouse and delivered to the other spouse.

(c) A community property survivorship agreement may be revoked with respect to specific property subject to the agreement by the disposition of the property by one or both spouses if the disposition is not inconsistent with specific terms of the agreement and applicable law.

Derived from Probate Code § 455.

Added by Acts 2009, 81st Leg., ch. 680, § 1, eff. Jan. 1, 2014.

Subchapter C. Adjudication to Prove Community Property Survivorship Agreement

§ 112.101. Application Authorized

(a) Notwithstanding Section 112.053, after the death of a spouse, the surviving spouse or the surviving spouse's personal representative may apply to the court for an order stating that a community property survivorship agreement satisfies the requirements of this chapter and is effective to create a right of survivorship in community property.

(b) An application under this section must include:

(1) the surviving spouse's name and domicile;

(2) the deceased spouse's name and former domicile;

(3) the fact, time, and place of the deceased spouse's death;

(4) facts establishing venue in the court; and

(5) the deceased spouse's social security number, if known.

(c) An application under this section must be filed in the county of proper venue for administration of the deceased spouse's estate.

(d) The original community property survivorship agreement shall be filed with an application under this section.

Derived from Probate Code §§ 456(a), (d).

Added by Acts 2009, 81st Leg., ch. 680, § 1, eff. Jan. 1, 2014.

§ 112.102. Proof Required by Court

An applicant for an order under Section 112.101 must prove to the court's satisfaction that:

(1) the spouse whose community property interest is at issue is deceased;

(2) the court has jurisdiction and venue;

(3) the agreement was executed with the formalities required by law;

(4) the agreement was not revoked; and

(5) citation has been served and returned in the manner and for the length of time required by this title.

Derived from Probate Code § 456(b).

Added by Acts 2009, 81st Leg., ch. 680, § 1, eff. Jan. 1, 2014.

§ 112.103. Method of Proof of Signatures

(a) The deceased spouse's signature to an agreement that is the subject of an application under Section 112.101 may be proved by:

(1) the sworn testimony of one witness taken in open court;

(2) the affidavit of one witness; or

(3) the written or oral deposition of one witness taken in the same manner and under the same rules as depositions in other civil actions.

(b) If the surviving spouse is competent to make an oath, the surviving spouse's signature to the agreement may be proved by:

(1) the sworn testimony of the surviving spouse taken in open court;

(2) the surviving spouse's affidavit; or

(3) the written or oral deposition of the surviving spouse taken in the same manner and under the same rules as depositions in other civil actions.

(c) If the surviving spouse is not competent to make an oath, the surviving spouse's signature to the agreement may be proved in the manner provided by Subsection (a) for proof of the deceased spouse's signature.

Derived from Probate Code § 456(c).

Added by Acts 2009, 81st Leg., ch. 680, § 1, eff. Jan. 1, 2014.

§ 112.104. Court Action; Issuance of Order

(a) On completion of a hearing on an application under Section 112.101, if the court is satisfied that the requisite proof has been made, the court shall enter an order adjudging the agreement valid.

(b) Certified copies of the agreement and order may be:

(1) recorded in other counties; and

(2) used in evidence, as the original agreement might be, on the trial of the same matter in any other court, on appeal or otherwise.

Derived from Probate Code § 457.

Added by Acts 2009, 81st Leg., ch. 680, § 1, eff. Jan. 1, 2014.

§ 112.105. Effect of Order

(a) An order under this subchapter adjudging a community property survivorship agreement valid constitutes sufficient authority to a person who:

(1) owes money, has custody of any property, or acts as registrar or transfer agent of any evidence of interest, indebtedness, property, or right that is subject to the terms of the agreement; or

(2) purchases from or otherwise deals with the surviving spouse for payment or transfer to the surviving spouse.

(b) The surviving spouse may enforce that spouse's right to a payment or transfer from a person described by Subsection (a)(2).

Derived from Probate Code § 458.

Added by Acts 2009, 81st Leg., ch. 680, § 1, eff. Jan. 1, 2014.

§ 112.106. Custody of Adjudicated Agreement

(a) An original community property survivorship agreement adjudicated under this subchapter, together with the order adjudging the agreement valid, shall be deposited in the office of the county clerk of the county in which the agreement was adjudicated and must remain at that office, except during a period when the agreement is moved to another location for inspection on order of the court in which the agreement was adjudicated.

(b) If the court orders an original community property survivorship agreement adjudicated under this subchapter to be moved to another location for inspection, the person moving the original agreement shall give a receipt for the agreement and the court clerk shall make and retain a copy of the original agreement.

Derived from Probate Code § 459.

Added by Acts 2009, 81st Leg., ch. 680, § 1, eff. Jan. 1, 2014.

Subchapter D. Ownership and Transfer of Community Property Subject to Agreement

§ 112.151. Ownership of Property During Marriage; Management Rights

(a) Property subject to a community property survivorship agreement remains community property during the marriage of the spouses.

(b) Unless the agreement provides otherwise, a community property survivorship agreement does not affect the rights of the spouses concerning the management, control, and disposition of property subject to the agreement.

Derived from Probate Code § 453.

Added by Acts 2009, 81st Leg., ch. 680, § 1, eff. Jan. 1, 2014.

§ 112.152. Nontestamentary Nature of Transfers Under Agreement

(a) Transfers at death resulting from community property survivorship agreements made in accordance with this chapter are effective by reason of the agreements involved and are not testamentary transfers.

(b) Except as expressly provided otherwise by this title, transfers described by Subsection (a) are not subject to the provisions of this title applicable to testamentary transfers.

Derived from Probate Code § 454.

Added by Acts 2009, 81st Leg., ch. 680, § 1, eff. Jan. 1, 2014.

Subchapter E. Third Parties Dealing With Community Property Subject to Right of Survivorship

§ 112.201. Definition of Certified Copy

In this subchapter, a "certified copy" means a copy of an official record or document that is:

(1) authorized by law to be recorded or filed and actually recorded or filed in a public office; and

(2) certified as correct in accordance with Rule 902, Texas Rules of Evidence.

Derived from Probate Code § 460(f).

Added by Acts 2009, 81st Leg., ch. 680, § 1, eff. Jan. 1, 2014.

§ 112.202. Actual Knowledge or Notice of Agreement

(a) In this subchapter, a person or entity has "actual knowledge" of a community property survivorship agreement or the revocation of a community property survivorship agreement only if the person or entity has received:

(1) written notice of the agreement or revocation; or

(2) the original or a certified copy of the agreement or revoking instrument.

(b) In this subchapter, a person or entity has "notice" of a community property survivorship agreement or the revocation of a community property survivorship agreement if:

(1) the person or entity has actual knowledge of the agreement or revocation; or

(2) with respect to real property, the agreement or revoking instrument is properly recorded in the county in which the real property is located.

Derived from Probate Code § 460(f).

Added by Acts 2009, 81st Leg., ch. 680, § 1, eff. Jan. 1, 2014.

§ 112.203. Personal Representative Without Actual Knowledge of Agreement

If the personal representative of a deceased spouse's estate has no actual knowledge of the existence of an agreement creating a right of survivorship in community property in the surviving spouse, the personal representative is not liable to the surviving spouse or any person claiming from the surviving spouse for selling, exchanging, distributing, or otherwise disposing of the property.

Derived from Probate Code § 460(a).

Added by Acts 2009, 81st Leg., ch. 680, § 1, eff. Jan. 1, 2014.

§ 112.204. Third-Party Purchaser Without Notice of Agreement

(a) This section applies only to a person or entity who for value purchases property:

(1) from a person claiming from a deceased spouse more than six months after the date of the deceased spouse's death or from the personal representative of the deceased spouse's estate; and

(2) without notice of the existence of an agreement creating a right of survivorship in the property in the surviving spouse.

(b) A purchaser of property from a person claiming from the deceased spouse has good title to the interest in the property that the person would have had in the absence of the agreement described by Subsection (a)(2), as against the claims of the surviving spouse or any person claiming from the surviving spouse.

(c) A purchaser of property from the personal representative of the deceased spouse's estate has good title to the interest in the property that the personal representative would have had authority to convey in the absence of the agreement described by Subsection (a)(2), as against the claims of the surviving spouse or any person claiming from the surviving spouse.

Derived from Probate Code § 460(b).

Added by Acts 2009, 81st Leg., ch. 680, § 1, eff. Jan. 1, 2014.

§ 112.205. Debtors and Other Persons Without Notice of Agreement

(a) This section applies only to a person or entity who:

(1) owes money to a deceased spouse; or

(2) has custody of property or acts as registrar or transfer agent of any evidence of interest, indebtedness, property, or right owned by a deceased spouse before that spouse's death.

(b) A person or entity with no actual knowledge of the existence of an agreement creating a right of survivorship in property described by Subsection (a) in the surviving spouse may pay or transfer that property to the personal representative of the deceased spouse's estate or, if no administration of the deceased spouse's estate is pending, to the heirs or devisees of the estate and shall be discharged from all claims for those amounts or property paid or transferred.

Derived from Probate Code § 460(d).

Added by Acts 2009, 81st Leg., ch. 680, § 1, eff. Jan. 1, 2014.

§ 112.206. Third-Party Purchaser Without Notice of Revocation of Agreement

(a) This section applies only to a person or entity who for value purchases property from a surviving spouse more than six months after the date of the deceased spouse's death and:

(1) with respect to personal property:

(A) the purchaser has received an original or certified copy of an agreement purporting to create a right of survivorship in the personal property in the surviving spouse, purportedly signed by both spouses; and

(B) the purchaser has no notice of the revocation of the agreement; or

(2) with respect to real property:

(A) the purchaser has received an original or certified copy of an agreement purporting to create a right of survivorship in the real property in the surviving spouse, purportedly signed by both spouses or such an agreement is properly recorded in a county in which any part of the real property is located; and

(B) the purchaser has no notice of the revocation of the agreement.

(b) A purchaser has good title to the interest in the property that the surviving spouse would have had in the absence of the revocation of the agreement, as against the claims of the personal representative of the deceased spouse's estate or any person claiming from the representative or the deceased spouse.

Derived from Probate Code § 460(c).

Added by Acts 2009, 81st Leg., ch. 680, § 1, eff. Jan. 1, 2014.

§ 112.207. Debtors and Other Persons Without Notice of Revocation of Agreement

(a) This section applies only to a person or entity who:

(1) owes money to a deceased spouse; or

(2) has custody of property or acts as registrar or transfer agent of any evidence of interest, indebtedness, property, or right owned by a deceased spouse before that spouse's death.

(b) If a person or entity is presented with the original or a certified copy of an agreement creating a right of survivorship in property described by Subsection (a) in the surviving spouse, purportedly signed by both spouses, and if the person or entity has no actual knowledge that the agreement was revoked, the person or entity may pay or transfer that property to the surviving spouse and shall be discharged from all claims for those amounts or property paid or transferred.

Derived from Probate Code § 460(e).

Added by Acts 2009, 81st Leg., ch. 680, § 1, eff. Jan. 1, 2014.

§ 112.208. Rights of Surviving Spouse Against Creditors

Except as expressly provided by this subchapter, this subchapter does not affect the rights of a surviving spouse or person claiming from the surviving spouse in disputes with persons claiming from a deceased spouse or the successors of any of them concerning a beneficial interest in property or the proceeds from a beneficial interest in property, subject to a right of survivorship under an agreement that satisfies the requirements of this chapter.

Derived from Probate Code § 460(g).

Added by Acts 2009, 81st Leg., ch. 680, § 1, eff. Jan. 1, 2014.

Subchapter F. Rights of Creditors

§ 112.251. Multiple-Party Accounts

Chapter 113 governs the rights of creditors with respect to multiple-party accounts, as defined by Section 113.004.

Derived from Probate Code § 461.

Added by Acts 2009, 81st Leg., ch. 680, § 1, eff. Jan. 1, 2014.

§ 112.252. Liabilities of Deceased Spouse Not Affected by Right of Survivorship

(a) Except as expressly provided by Section 112.251, the community property subject to the sole or joint management, control, and disposition of a spouse during marriage continues to be subject to the liabilities of that spouse on that spouse's death without regard to a right of survivorship in the surviving spouse under an agreement made in accordance with this chapter.

(b) The surviving spouse is liable to account to the deceased spouse's personal representative for property received by the surviving spouse under a right of survivorship to the extent necessary to discharge the deceased spouse's liabilities.

(c) A proceeding to assert a liability under Subsection (b):

(1) may be commenced only if the deceased spouse's personal representative has received a written demand by a creditor; and

(2) must be commenced on or before the second anniversary of the deceased spouse's death.

(d) Property recovered by the deceased spouse's personal representative under this section shall be administered as part of the deceased spouse's estate.

Derived from Probate Code § 461.

Added by Acts 2009, 81st Leg., ch. 680, § 1, eff. Jan. 1, 2014.

§ 112.253. Rights of Deceased Spouse's Creditors in Relation to Third Parties

This subchapter does not affect the protection afforded to a person or entity under Subchapter E unless, before payment or transfer to the surviving spouse, the person or entity received a written notice from the deceased spouse's personal representative stating the amount needed to discharge the deceased spouse's liabilities.

Derived from Probate Code § 461.

Added by Acts 2009, 81st Leg., ch. 680, § 1, eff. Jan. 1, 2014.

Chapter 113. Multiple-Party Accounts

Subchapter A. General Provisions

Subchapter B. Uniform Account Form

Subchapter C. Ownership and Operation of Accounts

Subchapter D. Rights of Survivorship in Accounts

Subchapter E. Protection of Financial Institutions

Subchapter F. Rights of Creditors; Pledge of Account

Chapter 113. Multiple-Party Accounts

Subchapter A. General Provisions

Statutes in Context
Chapter 113

Multiple-party accounts, such as checking accounts, savings accounts, and certificates of deposit, are contractual arrangements for the deposit of money with financial institutions such as state or national banks, savings and loan associations, and credit unions. The disposition of the funds remaining in these accounts upon the death of one of the depositors depends on the type of account, the account contract, and the applicable state law.

Multiple-party accounts are important non-probate transfer mechanisms because these accounts are widely used, easy to understand, and inexpensive to obtain. Chapter 113 addresses the four commonly recognized types of multiple-party accounts: (1) the joint account, which may transfer ownership rights to the account's balance to the surviving party; (2) the agency or convenience account, which does not transfer the balance upon the death of one of the parties; (3) the payable on death account, which causes the balance to belong to the surviving pay-on-death payees upon the death of the depositors; and (4) the trust account, under which the beneficiaries receive the account balance upon outliving all trustees.

§ 113.001. General Definitions

In this chapter:

(1) "Account" means a contract of deposit of funds between a depositor and a financial institution. The term includes a checking account, savings account, certificate of deposit, share account, or other similar arrangement.

(2) "Beneficiary" means a person or trustee of an express trust evidenced by a writing who is named in a trust account as a person for whom a party to the account is named as trustee.

(2-a) "Charitable organization" means any corporation, community chest, fund, or foundation that is exempt from federal income tax under Section 501(a) of the Internal Revenue Code of 1986 by being listed as an exempt organization in Section 501(c)(3) of that code.

(2-b) "Express trust" has the meaning assigned by Section 111.004, Property Code.

(3) "Financial institution" means an organization authorized to do business under state or federal laws relating to financial institutions. The term includes a bank or trust company, savings bank, building and loan association, savings and loan company or association, credit union, and brokerage firm that deals in the sale and purchase of stocks, bonds, and other types of securities.

(4) "Payment" of sums on deposit includes a withdrawal, a payment on a check or other directive of a party, and a pledge of sums on deposit by a party and any set-off, or reduction or other disposition of all or part of an account under a pledge.

(5) "P.O.D. payee" means a person, trustee of an express trust evidenced by a writing, or charitable organization designated on a P.O.D. account as a person to whom the account is payable on request after the death of one or more persons.

(6) "Proof of death" includes:

(A) a certified copy of a death certificate; or

(B) a judgment or order of a court in a proceeding in which the death of a person is proved to the satisfaction of the court by circumstantial evidence in accordance with Chapter 454.

(7) "Request" means a proper request for withdrawal, or a check or order for payment, that complies with all conditions of the account, including special requirements concerning necessary signatures and regulations of the financial institution. If a financial institution conditions withdrawal or payment on advance notice, for purposes of this chapter a request for withdrawal or payment is treated as immediately effective and a notice of intent to withdraw is treated as a request for withdrawal.

(8) "Sums on deposit" means the balance payable on a multiple-party account including interest, dividends, and any deposit life insurance proceeds added to the account by reason of the death of a party.

(9) "Withdrawal" includes payment to a third person in accordance with a check or other directive of a party.

Derived from Probate Code §§ 436(1), (2), (3), (8), (9), (11), (12), (13), (15).

Added by Acts 2009, 81st Leg., ch. 680, § 1, eff. Jan. 1, 2014. Subsec. (2-a) added by Acts 2011, 82nd Leg., ch. 1338, § 2.07, eff. Jan. 1, 2014. Subsec. (5) amended by Acts 2011, 82nd Leg., ch. 1338, § 2.07, eff. Jan. 1, 2014. Subsecs (2 & (5) amended by and subsec. (2-b) added by Acts 2015, 84th Leg., ch. 255, § 1, eff. May 29, 2015.

§ 113.002. Definition of Party

(a) In this chapter, "party" means a person who, by the terms of a multiple-party account, has a present right, subject to request, to payment from the account. Except as otherwise required by the context, the term includes a guardian, personal representative, or assignee, including an attaching creditor, of a party. The term also includes a person identified as a trustee of an account for another regardless of whether a beneficiary is named. The term does not include a named beneficiary unless the beneficiary has a present right of withdrawal.

(b) A P.O.D. payee, including a charitable organization, or beneficiary of a trust account is a party only after the account becomes payable to the P.O.D. payee or beneficiary by reason of the P.O.D. payee or beneficiary surviving the original payee or trustee.

Derived from Probate Code § 436(7).

Added by Acts 2009, 81st Leg., ch. 680, § 1, eff. Jan. 1, 2014. Subsec. (b) amended by Acts 2011, 82nd Leg., ch. 1338, § 2.08, eff. Jan. 1, 2014.

§ 113.003. Definition of Net Contribution

(a) In this chapter, "net contribution" of a party to a joint account at any given time is the sum of all deposits made to that account by or for the party, less all withdrawals made by or for the party that have not been paid to or applied to the use of any other party, plus a pro rata share of any interest or dividends included in the current balance of the account. The term also includes any deposit life insurance proceeds added to the account by reason of the death of the party whose net contribution is in question.

(b) A financial institution may not be required to inquire, for purposes of establishing net contributions, about:

(1) the source of funds received for deposit to a multiple-party account; or

(2) the proposed application of an amount withdrawn from a multiple-party account.

Derived from Probate Code §§ 436(6), 444.

Added by Acts 2009, 81st Leg., ch. 680, § 1, eff. Jan. 1, 2014.

§ 113.004. Types of Accounts

In this chapter:

(1) "Convenience account" means an account that:

(A) is established at a financial institution by one or more parties in the names of the parties and one or more convenience signers; and

(B) has terms that provide that the sums on deposit are paid or delivered to the parties or to the convenience signers "for the convenience" of the parties.

(2) "Joint account" means an account payable on request to one or more of two or more parties, regardless of whether there is a right of survivorship.

(3) "Multiple-party account" means a joint account, a convenience account, a P.O.D. account, or a trust account. The term does not include an account established for the deposit of funds of a partnership, joint venture, or other association for business purposes, or an account controlled by one or more persons as the authorized agent or trustee for a corporation, unincorporated association, charitable or civic organization, or a regular fiduciary or trust account in which the relationship is established other than by deposit agreement.

(4) "P.O.D. account," including an account designated as a transfer on death or T.O.D. account, means an account payable on request to::

(A) one person during the person's lifetime and, on the person's death, to one or more P.O.D. payees; or

(B) one or more persons during their lifetimes and, on the death of all of those persons, to one or more P.O.D. payees.

(5) "Trust account" means an account in the name of one or more parties as trustee for one or more beneficiaries in which the relationship is established by the form of the account and the deposit agreement with the financial institution and in which there is no subject of the trust other than the sums on deposit in the account. The deposit agreement is not required to address payment to the beneficiary. The term does not include:

(A) a regular trust account under a testamentary trust or a trust agreement that has significance apart from the account; or

(B) a fiduciary account arising from a fiduciary relationship, such as the attorney-client relationship.

Derived from Probate Code §§ 436(4), (5), (10), (14), 438A(A).

Added by Acts 2009, 81st Leg., ch. 680, § 1, eff. Jan. 1, 2014. Subsec. (4) amended by Acts 2015, 84th Leg., ch. 378, § 1, eff. Sept. 1, 2015.

§ 113.005. Authority of Financial Institutions to Enter into Certain Accounts

A financial institution may enter into a multiple-party account to the same extent that the institution may enter into a single-party account.

Derived from Probate Code § 444.

Added by Acts 2009, 81st Leg., ch. 680, § 1, eff. Jan. 1, 2014.

Subchapter B. Uniform Account Form

§ 113.051. Establishment of Type of Account; Applicability of Certain Law

(a) A contract of deposit that contains provisions substantially the same as in the form provided by Section 113.052 establishes the type of account selected by a party. This chapter governs an account selected under the form.

(b) A contract of deposit that does not contain provisions substantially the same as in the form provided by Section 113.052 is governed by the provisions of this chapter applicable to the type of account that most nearly conforms to the depositor's intent.

Derived from Probate Code § 439A(a).

Added by Acts 2009, 81st Leg., ch. 680, § 1, eff. Jan. 1, 2014. Subsec. (a) amended by Acts 2011, 82nd Leg., ch. 90, § 8.004, eff. Jan. 1, 2014.

Statutes in Context
§ 113.052

A financial institution may use the form provided in § 113.052 to achieve predicable results and to give the customer understandable information regarding the workings of multiple-party accounts. However, few banks actually use the suggested form.

---

§ 113.052. Form

A financial institution may use the following form to establish the type of account selected by a party:

UNIFORM SINGLE-PARTY OR MULTIPLE-PARTY ACCOUNT SELECTION FORM NOTICE:

The type of account you select may determine how property passes on your death. Your will may not control the disposition of funds held in some of the following accounts. You may choose to designate one or more convenience signers on an account, even if the account is not a convenience account. A designated convenience signer may make transactions on your behalf during your lifetime, but does not own the account during your lifetime. The designated convenience signer owns the account on your death only if the convenience signer is also designated as a P.O.D. payee or trust account beneficiary.

Select one of the following accounts by placing your initials next to the account selected:

___ (1) SINGLE-PARTY ACCOUNT WITHOUT "P.O.D." (PAYABLE ON DEATH) DESIGNATION. The party to the account owns the account. On the death of the party, ownership of the account passes as a part of the party's estate under the party's will or by intestacy.

Enter the name of the party:

_____

Enter the name(s) of the convenience signer(s), if you want one or more convenience signers on this account:

_____

___ (2) SINGLE-PARTY ACCOUNT WITH "P.O.D." (PAYABLE ON DEATH) DESIGNATION. The party to the account owns the account. On the death of the party, ownership of the account passes to the P.O.D. beneficiaries of the account. The account is not a part of the party's estate.

Enter the name of the party:

_____

Enter the name or names of the P.O.D. beneficiaries:

_____

Enter the name(s) of the convenience signer(s), if you want one or more convenience signers on this account:

_____

___ (3) MULTIPLE-PARTY ACCOUNT WITHOUT RIGHT OF SURVIVORSHIP. The parties to the account own the account in proportion to the parties' net contributions to the account. The financial institution may pay any sum in the account to a party at any time. On the death of a party, the party's ownership of the account passes as a part of the party's estate under the party's will or by intestacy.

Enter the names of the parties:

_____

Enter the name(s) of the convenience signer(s), if you want one or more convenience signers on this account:

_____

___ (4) MULTIPLE-PARTY ACCOUNT WITH RIGHT OF SURVIVORSHIP. The parties to the account own the account in proportion to the parties' net contributions to the account. The financial institution may pay any sum in the account to a party at any time. On the death of a party, the party's ownership of the account passes to the surviving parties.

Enter the names of the parties:

_____

Enter the name(s) of the convenience signer(s), if you want one or more convenience signers on this account:

_____

___ (5) MULTIPLE-PARTY ACCOUNT WITH RIGHT OF SURVIVORSHIP AND P.O.D. (PAYABLE ON DEATH) DESIGNATION. The parties to the account own the account in proportion to the parties' net contributions to the account. The financial institution may pay any sum in the account to a party at any time. On the death of the last surviving party, the ownership of the account passes to the P.O.D. beneficiaries.

Enter the names of the parties:

_____

Enter the name or names of the P.O.D. beneficiaries:

_____

Enter the name(s) of the convenience signer(s), if you want one or more convenience signers on this account:

_____

___ (6) CONVENIENCE ACCOUNT. The parties to the account own the account. One or more convenience signers to the account may make account transactions for a party. A convenience signer does not own the account. On the death of the last surviving party, ownership of the account passes as a part of the last surviving party's estate under the last surviving party's will or by intestacy. The financial institution may pay funds in the account to a convenience signer before the financial institution receives notice of the death of the last surviving party. The payment to a convenience signer does not affect the parties' ownership of the account.

Enter the names of the parties:

_____

Enter the name(s) of the convenience signer(s):

_____

___ (7) TRUST ACCOUNT. The parties named as trustees to the account own the account in proportion to the parties' net contributions to the account. A trustee may withdraw funds from the account. A beneficiary may not withdraw funds from the account before all trustees are deceased. On the death of the last surviving trustee, the ownership of the account passes to the beneficiary. The trust account is not a part of a trustee's estate and does not pass under the trustee's will or by intestacy, unless the trustee survives all of the beneficiaries and all other trustees.

Enter the name or names of the trustees:

_____

_____

Enter the name or names of the beneficiaries:

_____

_____

Enter the name(s) of the convenience signer(s), if you want one or more convenience signers on this account:

_____

_____

Derived from Probate Code § 439A(b).

Added by Acts 2009, 81st Leg., ch. 680, § 1, eff. Jan. 1, 2014. Amended by Acts 2011, 82nd Leg., ch. 90, § 8.005, eff. Jan. 1, 2014.

§ 113.053. Required Disclosure: Use of Form[; Disclosure]

(a) A financial institution shall disclose the information provided in this subchapter to a customer at the time the customer selects or modifies an account. A financial institution is considered to have [adequately] disclosed the information provided in this subchapter if:

(1) the financial institution uses the form provided by Section 113.052; and

(2) the customer places the customer's initials to the right of each paragraph of the form.

(b) If a financial institution varies the format of the form provided by Section 113.052, the financial institution may make disclosures in the account agreement or in any other form that [adequately] discloses the information provided by this subchapter. Disclosures under this subsection must:

(1) be given separately from other account information;

(2) be provided before account selection or modification;

(3) be printed in 14-point boldfaced type; and

(4) if the discussions that precede the account opening or modification are conducted primarily in a language other than English, be in that language.

(c) The financial institution shall notify the customer of the type of account the customer selected [If the customer receives adequate disclosure of the ownership rights to an account and the names of the parties are appropriately indicated, a financial institution may combine any of the provisions in, and vary the format of, the form and notices described in Section 113.052 in:

(1) a universal account form with options listed for selection and additional disclosures provided in the account agreement; or

(2) any other manner that adequately discloses the information provided by this subchapter.]

(d) This section does not apply to a credit union.

Derived from Probate Code §§ 439A(c), (d).

Added by Acts 2009, 81st Leg., ch. 680, § 1, eff. Jan. 1,

2014. Amended by Acts 2015, 84th Leg., ch. 85, § 1, eff. Sept. 1, 2015.

§ 113.0531. Use of Form and Disclosure by Credit Unions

(a) A credit union is considered to have disclosed the information provided by this subchapter if the credit union uses the form provided by Section 113.052.

(b) If a credit union varies the format of the form provided by Section 113.052, the credit union may make disclosures in the account agreement or in any other form that discloses the information provided by this subchapter.

(c) If the customer receives disclosure of the ownership rights to an account and the names of the parties are indicated, a credit union may combine any of the provisions in, and vary the format of, the form and notices described in Section 113.052 in:

(1) a universal account form with options listed for selection and additional disclosures provided in the account agreement; or

(2) any other manner that adequately discloses the information provided by this subchapter.

New.

Added by Acts 2015, 84th Leg., ch. 85, § 2, eff. Sept. 1, 2015.

Subchapter C. Ownership and Operation of Accounts

Statutes in Context
§ 113.101

The right to withdraw funds from a multiple-party account is a separate issue from the ownership of those funds. For example, a party to a joint account may have the right to withdraw funds but does not necessarily own those funds.

§ 113.101. Effect of Certain Provisions Regarding Ownership Between Parties and Others

The provisions of this subchapter and Subchapters B and D that relate to beneficial ownership between parties, or between parties and P.O.D. payees or beneficiaries of multiple-party accounts:

(1) are relevant only to controversies between those persons and those persons' creditors and other successors; and

(2) do not affect the withdrawal power of those persons under the terms of an account contract.

Derived from Probate Code § 437.

Added by Acts 2009, 81st Leg., ch. 680, § 1, eff. Jan. 1, 2014.

Statutes in Context
§§ 113.102–113.104

Sections 113.102–113.104 explain who owns the funds in a multiple-party account while the original parties are all still alive.

1. Joint Account. The funds in a joint account belong to the parties in proportion to their net contributions, that is, what the party deposited, minus what the party withdrew, plus a proportionate share of the interest. See § 113.003.

2. P.O.D. Account. The funds in a P.O.D. account belong to the original payees. The P.O.D. payees have no ownership rights.

3. Trust Account. The funds in a trust account belong to the trustee and the beneficiary has no rights unless there is a contrary intent shown by the account terms or deposit agreement or there is clear and convincing evidence of an irrevocable trust.

§ 113.102. Ownership of Joint Account During Parties' Lifetimes

During the lifetime of all parties to a joint account, the account belongs to the parties in proportion to the net contributions by each party to the sums on deposit unless there is clear and convincing evidence of a different intent.

Derived from Probate Code § 438(a).

Added by Acts 2009, 81st Leg., ch. 680, § 1, eff. Jan. 1, 2014.

§ 113.103. Ownership of P.O.D. Account During Original Payee's Lifetime

(a) During the lifetime of an original payee of a P.O.D. account, the account belongs to the original payee and does not belong to the P.O.D. payee or payees.

(b) If two or more parties are named as original payees of a P.O.D. account, during the parties' lifetimes rights between the parties are governed by Section 113.102.

Derived from Probate Code § 438(b).

Added by Acts 2009, 81st Leg., ch. 680, § 1, eff. Jan. 1, 2014.

§ 113.104. Ownership of Trust Account During Trustee's Lifetime

(a) A trust account belongs beneficially to the trustee during the trustee's lifetime unless:

(1) the terms of the account or the deposit agreement manifest a contrary intent; or

(2) other clear and convincing evidence of an irrevocable trust exists.

(b) If two or more parties are named as trustees on a trust account, during the parties' lifetimes beneficial rights between the parties are governed by Section 113.102.

(c) An account that is an irrevocable trust belongs beneficially to the beneficiary.

Derived from Probate Code § 438(c).

Added by Acts 2009, 81st Leg., ch. 680, § 1, eff. Jan. 1, 2014.

Statutes in Context
§ 113.105

Section 113.105 governs convenience accounts which are used as a primitive type of agency relationship to, for example, allow someone to assist the depositor in writing checks when the depositor is unable to do so (e.g., disabled, stationed out of the country in the military, in prison, on vacation, etc.).

All funds in the account belong to the party, not the co-signer, although both the party and the co-signer have the right to withdraw the funds. When the party dies, the entire account passes into the party's estate. The co-signer has no survivorship rights.

§ 113.105. Ownership of Convenience Account; Additions and Accruals

(a) The making of a deposit in a convenience account does not affect the title to the deposit.

(b) A party to a convenience account is not considered to have made a gift of the deposit, or of any additions or accruals to the deposit, to a convenience signer.

(c) An addition made to a convenience account by anyone other than a party, and accruals to the addition, are considered to have been made by a party.

Derived from Probate Code §§ 438A(b), (c), (e).

Added by Acts 2009, 81st Leg., ch. 680, § 1, eff. Jan. 1, 2014.

Statutes in Context
§ 113.106

The 2009 Legislature enacted this provision to authorize convenience signers on accounts that are not expressly labeled as convenience accounts. A person who opens a single-party or multiple-party account that is not expressly deemed a convenience account under § 113.105 now has the option of indicating a convenience signer who has the ability to make withdrawals but does not have ownership or survivorship rights. The Uniform Single-Party or Multiple-Party Account Form was modified to provide for convenience signers on all types of accounts.

§ 113.106. Ownership and Operation of Other Account With Convenience Signer

(a) An account established by one or more parties at a financial institution that is not designated as a convenience account, but is instead designated as a single-party account or another type of multiple-party account, may provide that the sums on deposit may be paid or delivered to the parties or to one or more convenience signers "for the convenience of the parties."

(b) Except as provided by Section 113.1541:

(1) the provisions of Sections 113.105, 113.206, and 113.208 apply to an account described by Subsection (a), including provisions relating to the ownership of the account during the lifetimes and on the deaths of the parties and provisions relating to the powers and duties of the financial institution at which the account is established; and

(2) any other law relating to a convenience signer applies to a convenience signer designated as provided by this section to the extent the law applies to a convenience signer on a convenience account.

Derived from Probate Code § 438B.

Added by Acts 2011, 82nd Leg., ch. 90, § 8.006, eff. Jan. 1, 2014.

Subchapter D. Rights of Survivorship in Accounts

Statutes in Context
§§ 113.151 –113.155

Sections 113.151–113.155 governs ownership of the funds in a multiple-party account when one or more of the parties dies.

1. Joint Account. The net contributions of the deceased party pass into the deceased party's estate unless there is an express survivorship agreement. Unlike many states, the presumption in Texas is that a joint account does not have the survivorship feature. (Note that this is consistent with § 101.002.) The survivorship feature exists only if there is (a) a written agreement, (b) signed by the deceased party (if community property is involved, both spouses must sign under § 112.051 which expressly makes the deceased party's interest survive to the surviving party.

In 2009, the Texas Supreme Court issued a disturbing opinion in the case of *Holmes v. Beatty*, 290 S.W.3d 852 (Tex. 2009). A husband and his wife held investment accounts with the designation "JT TEN." The spouses signed the agreement but did not indicate whether the account had, or did not have, the survivorship feature. The court determined that holding community property as joint tenants automatically includes the survivorship feature and that the designation "JT

TEN" is an acceptable abbreviation. In so deciding, the court relied on the common law under which joint tenancies carried with them the survivorship feature. However, the court disregarded long-established Texas law which requires that the survivorship be expressly stated. The 2011 Legislature amended the Probate Code predecessors to both § 113.151 and § 112.052 to make it clear that this type of designation is insufficient to create the survivorship feature.

Extrinsic evidence is not admissible to establish the survivorship feature in a suit to obtain account funds. However, such evidence may be used to show the depositor's intent in an action against the financial institution. *A.G. Edwards & Sons, Inc. v. Beyer*, 235 S.W.3d 704 (Tex. 2007).

The statute contains "safe harbor" language to create the survivorship feature, that is, "On the death of one party to a joint account, all sums in the account on the date of the death vest in and belong to the surviving party as his or her separate property and estate." Note that a mere authorization of payment of funds to the survivor does not create the survivorship feature. The right to withdraw is not equated with ownership rights. See *Stauffer v. Henderson*, 801 S.W.2d 858 (Tex. 1990).

2. P.O.D. Account. The funds in a P.O.D. account belong to the surviving P.O.D. payees only after all original P.O.D. payees are dead.

3. Trust Account. The funds in a trust account belong to the surviving beneficiaries only after all trustees are dead.

4. Convenience Accounts. When the party dies, the entire account passes into the party's estate. The co-signer has no survivorship rights.

§ 113.151. Establishment of Right of Survivorship in Joint Account; Ownership on Death of Party

(a) Sums remaining on deposit on the death of a party to a joint account belong to the surviving party or parties against the estate of the deceased party if the interest of the deceased party is made to survive to the surviving party or parties by a written agreement signed by the party who dies.

(b) Notwithstanding any other law, an agreement is sufficient under this section to confer an absolute right of survivorship on parties to a joint account if the agreement contains a statement substantially similar to the following: "On the death of one party to a joint account, all sums in the account on the date of the death vest in and belong to the surviving party as his or her separate property and estate."

(c) A survivorship agreement may not be inferred from the mere fact that the account is a joint account or that the account is designated as JT TEN, Joint Tenancy, or joint, or with other similar language.

(d) If there are two or more surviving parties to a joint account that is subject to a right of survivorship agreement:

(1) during the parties' lifetimes respective ownerships are in proportion to the parties' previous ownership interests under Sections 113.102, 113.103, and 113.104, as applicable, augmented by an equal share for each survivor of any interest a deceased party owned in the account immediately before that party's death; and

(2) the right of survivorship continues between the surviving parties if a written agreement signed by a party who dies provides for that continuation.

Derived from Probate Code § 439(a).

Added by Acts 2009, 81st Leg., ch. 680, § 1, eff. Jan. 1, 2014. Subsec. (c) amended by Acts 2011, 82nd Leg., ch. 1338, § 2.09, eff. Jan. 1, 2014.

§ 113.152. Ownership of P.O.D. Account on Death of Party

(a) If the account is a P.O.D. account and there is a written agreement signed by the original payee or payees, on the death of the original payee or on the death of the survivor of two or more original payees, any sums remaining on deposit belong to:

(1) the P.O.D. payee or payees if surviving; or

(2) the survivor of the P.O.D. payees if one or more P.O.D. payees die before the original payee.

(b) If two or more P.O.D. payees survive, no right of survivorship exists between the surviving P.O.D. payees unless the terms of the account or deposit agreement expressly provide for survivorship between those payees.

(c) A guardian of the estate or an attorney in fact or agent of an original payee may sign a written agreement described by Subsection (a) on behalf of the original payee.

Derived from Probate Code § 439(b).

Added by Acts 2009, 81st Leg., ch. 680, § 1, eff. Jan. 1, 2014. Subsec. (c) added by Acts 2015, 84th Leg., ch. 378, § 2, eff. Sept. 1, 2015.

§ 113.153. Ownership of Trust Account on Death of Trustee

(a) If the account is a trust account and there is a written agreement signed by the trustee or trustees, on death of the trustee or the survivor of two or more trustees, any sums remaining on deposit belong to:

(1) the person or persons named as beneficiaries, if surviving; or

(2) the survivor of the persons named as beneficiaries if one or more beneficiaries die before the trustee.

(b) If two or more beneficiaries survive, no right of survivorship exists between the surviving beneficiaries unless the terms of the account or deposit agreement expressly provide for survivorship between those beneficiaries.

Derived from Probate Code § 439(c).

Added by Acts 2009, 81st Leg., ch. 680, § 1, eff. Jan. 1, 2014.

§ 113.1541. Ownership of Other Account with Convenience Signer on Death of Last Surviving Party

On the death of the last surviving party to an account that has a convenience signer designated as provided by Section 113.106, the convenience signer does not have a right of survivorship in the account and the estate of the last surviving party owns the account unless the convenience signer is also designated as a P.O.D. payee or as a beneficiary.

Derived from Probate Code § 438B(c).

§ 113.154. Ownership of Convenience Account on Death of Party

On the death of the last surviving party to a convenience account:

(1) a convenience signer has no right of survivorship in the account; and

(2) ownership of the account remains in the estate of the last surviving party.

Derived from Probate Code § 438A(d).

Added by Acts 2009, 81st Leg., ch. 680, § 1, eff. Jan. 1, 2014.

§ 113.155. Effect of Death of Party on Certain Accounts Without Rights of Survivorship

The death of a party to a multiple-party account to which Sections 113.151, 113.152, and 113.153 do not apply has no effect on the beneficial ownership of the account, other than to transfer the rights of the deceased party as part of the deceased party's estate.

Derived from Probate Code § 439(d).

Added by Acts 2009, 81st Leg., ch. 680, § 1, eff. Jan. 1, 2014.

§ 113.156. Applicability of Certain Provisions on Death of Party

Sections 113.151, 113.152, 113.153, and 113.155 as to rights of survivorship are determined by the form of the account at the death of a party.

Derived from Probate Code § 440.

Added by Acts 2009, 81st Leg., ch. 680, § 1, eff. Jan. 1, 2014.

§ 113.157. Written Notice to Financial Institutions Regarding Form of Account

Notwithstanding any other law, the form of an account may be altered by written order given by a party to the financial institution to change the form of the account or to stop or vary payment under the terms of the account. The order or request must be signed by a party, received by the financial institution during the party's lifetime, and not countermanded by another written order of the same party during the party's lifetime.

Derived from Probate Code § 440.

Added by Acts 2009, 81st Leg., ch. 680, § 1, eff. Jan. 1, 2014.

§ 113.158. Nontestamentary Nature of Certain Transfers

Transfers resulting from the application of Sections 113.151, 113.152, 113.153, and 113.155 are effective by reason of the account contracts involved and this chapter and are not to be considered testamentary transfers or subject to the testamentary provisions of this title.

Derived from Probate Code § 441.

Added by Acts 2009, 81st Leg., ch. 680, § 1, eff. Jan. 1, 2014.

Subchapter E. Protection of Financial Institutions

§ 113.201. Applicability of Subchapter

This subchapter and Section 113.003(b) govern:
(1) the liability of financial institutions that make payments as provided by this subchapter; and
(2) the set-off rights of those institutions.

Derived from Probate Code § 443.

Added by Acts 2009, 81st Leg., ch. 680, § 1, eff. Jan. 1, 2014.

§ 113.202. Payment of Multiple-Party Account

A multiple-party account may be paid, on request, to any one or more of the parties.

Derived from Probate Code § 444.

Added by Acts 2009, 81st Leg., ch. 680, § 1, eff. Jan. 1, 2014.

§ 113.203. Payment of Joint Account

(a) Subject to Subsection (b), amounts in a joint account may be paid, on request, to any party without regard to whether any other party is incapacitated or deceased at the time the payment is demanded.
(b) Payment may not be made to the personal representative or heir of a deceased party unless:
(1) proofs of death are presented to the financial institution showing that the deceased party was the last surviving party; or
(2) there is no right of survivorship under Sections 113.151, 113.152, 113.153, and 113.155.

Derived from Probate Code § 445.

Added by Acts 2009, 81st Leg., ch. 680, § 1, eff. Jan. 1, 2014.

§ 113.204. Payment of P.O.D. Account

(a) A P.O.D. account may be paid, on request, to any original payee of the account.
(b) Payment may be made, on request, to the P.O.D. payee or to the personal representative or heirs of a deceased P.O.D. payee on the presentation to the financial institution of proof of death showing that the P.O.D. payee survived each person named as an original payee.
(c) Payment may be made to the personal representative or heirs of a deceased original payee if proof of death is presented to the financial institution showing that the deceased original payee was the survivor of each other person named on the account as an original payee or a P.O.D. payee.

Derived from Probate Code § 446.

Added by Acts 2009, 81st Leg., ch. 680, § 1, eff. Jan. 1, 2014.

§ 113.205. Payment of Trust Account

(a) A trust account may be paid, on request, to any trustee.
(b) Unless a financial institution has received written notice that a beneficiary has a vested interest not dependent on the beneficiary's surviving the trustee, payment may be made to the personal representative or heirs of a deceased trustee if proof of death is presented to the financial institution showing that the deceased trustee was the survivor of each other person named on the account as a trustee or beneficiary.
(c) Payment may be made, on request, to a beneficiary if proof of death is presented to the financial institution showing that the beneficiary or beneficiaries survived all persons named as trustees.

Derived from Probate Code § 447.

Added by Acts 2009, 81st Leg., ch. 680, § 1, eff. Jan. 1, 2014.

§ 113.206. Payment of Convenience Account

Deposits to a convenience account and additions and accruals to the deposits may be paid to a party or a convenience signer.

Derived from Probate Code § 438A(f).

Added by Acts 2009, 81st Leg., ch. 680, § 1, eff. Jan. 1, 2014.

§ 113.207. Liability for Payment from Joint Account After Death

A financial institution that pays an amount from a joint account to a surviving party to that account in accordance with a written agreement under Section 113.151 is not liable to an heir, devisee, or beneficiary of the deceased party's estate.

Derived from Probate Code § 445.

Added by Acts 2009, 81st Leg., ch. 680, § 1, eff. Jan. 1, 2014.

§ 113.208. Liability for Payment from Convenience Account

(a) A financial institution is completely released from liability for a payment made from a convenience account before the financial institution receives notice in writing signed by a party not to make the payment in accordance with the terms of the account. After receipt of the notice from a party, the financial institution may require a party to approve any further payments from the account.

(b) A financial institution that makes a payment of the sums on deposit in a convenience account to a convenience signer after the death of the last surviving party, but before the financial institution receives written notice of the last surviving party's death, is completely released from liability for the payment.

(c) A financial institution that makes a payment of the sums on deposit in a convenience account to the personal representative of the deceased last surviving party's estate after the death of the last surviving party, but before a court order prohibiting payment is served on the financial institution, is, to the extent of the payment, released from liability to any person claiming a right to the funds. The personal representative's receipt of the funds is a complete release and discharge of the financial institution.

Derived from Probate Code §§ 438A(f), (g).

Added by Acts 2009, 81st Leg., ch. 680, § 1, eff. Jan. 1, 2014.

§ 113.209. Discharge from Claims

(a) Payment made in accordance with Section 113.202, 113.203, 113.204, 113.205, or 113.207 discharges the financial institution from all claims for those amounts paid regardless of whether the payment is consistent with the beneficial ownership of the account between parties, P.O.D. payees, or beneficiaries, or their successors.

(b) The protection provided by Subsection (a) does not extend to payments made after a financial institution receives, from any party able to request present payment, written notice to the effect that withdrawals in accordance with the terms of the account should not be permitted. Unless the notice is withdrawn by the person giving the notice, the successor of a deceased party must concur in a demand for withdrawal for the financial institution to be protected under Subsection (a).

(c) No notice, other than the notice described by Subsection (b), or any other information shown to have been available to a financial institution affects the institution's right to the protection provided by Subsection (a).

(d) The protection provided by Subsection (a) does not affect the rights of parties in disputes between the parties or the parties' successors concerning the beneficial ownership of funds in, or withdrawn from, multiple-party accounts.

Derived from Probate Code § 448.

Added by Acts 2009, 81st Leg., ch. 680, § 1, eff. Jan. 1, 2014.

§ 113.210. Set-Off to Financial Institution

(a) Without qualifying any other statutory right to set-off or lien and subject to any contractual provision, if a party to a multiple-party account is indebted to a financial institution, the financial institution has a right to set-off against the account in which the party has, or had immediately before the party's death, a present right of withdrawal.

(b) The amount of the account subject to set-off under this section is that proportion to which the debtor is, or was immediately before the debtor's death, beneficially entitled, and in the absence of proof of net contributions, to an equal share with all parties having present rights of withdrawal.

Derived from Probate Code § 449.

Added by Acts 2009, 81st Leg., ch. 680, § 1, eff. Jan. 1, 2014.

Subchapter F. Rights of Creditors; Pledge of Account

§ 113.251. Pledge of Account

(a) A party to a multiple-party account may pledge the account or otherwise create a security interest in the account without the joinder of, as applicable, a P.O.D. payee, a beneficiary, a convenience signer, or any other party to a joint account, regardless of whether a right of survivorship exists.

(b) A convenience signer may not pledge or otherwise create a security interest in an account.

(c) Not later than the 30th day after the date a security interest on a multiple-party account is perfected, a secured creditor that is a financial institution with accounts insured by the Federal Deposit Insurance Corporation shall provide written notice of the pledge of the account to any other party to the account who did not create the security interest. The notice must be sent by certified mail to each other party at the last address the party provided to the depository bank.

(d) The financial institution is not required to provide the notice described by Subsection (c) to a P.O.D. payee, beneficiary, or convenience signer.

Derived from Probate Code § 442.

Added by Acts 2009, 81st Leg., ch. 680, § 1, eff. Jan. 1, 2014.

Statutes in Context
§ 113.252

Section 113.252 provides that funds in a multiple-party account are available to pay the debts of a deceased depositor but only as a last resort after all other estate assets are exhausted. Thus, although multiple-party accounts are considered non-probate in nature, they may still be involved in the probate process if the funds are needed to pay debts or other claims against the estate.

§ 113.252. Rights of Creditors

(a) A multiple-party account is not effective against:

(1) an estate of a deceased party to transfer to a survivor amounts needed to pay debts, taxes, and expenses of administration, including statutory allowances to the surviving spouse and minor children, if other assets of the estate are insufficient; or

(2) the claim of a secured creditor who has a lien on the account.

(b) A party, P.O.D. payee, or beneficiary who receives payment from a multiple-party account after the death of a deceased party is liable to account to the deceased party's personal representative for amounts the deceased party owned beneficially immediately before the party's death to the extent necessary to discharge the claims and charges described by Subsection (a) that remain unpaid after application of the deceased party's estate. The party, P.O.D. payee, or beneficiary is not liable in an amount greater than the amount the party, P.O.D. payee, or beneficiary received from the multiple-party account.

(c) A proceeding to assert liability under Subsection (b):

(1) may only be commenced if the personal representative receives a written demand by a surviving spouse, a creditor, or one acting for a minor child of the deceased party; and

(2) must be commenced on or before the second anniversary of the death of the deceased party.

(d) Amounts recovered by the personal representative under this section must be administered as part of the decedent's estate.

Derived from Probate Code § 442.

Added by Acts 2009, 81st Leg., ch. 680, § 1, eff. Jan. 1, 2014.

§ 113.253. No Effect on Certain Rights and Liabilities of Financial Institutions

This subchapter does not:

(1) affect the right of a financial institution to make payment on multiple-party accounts according to the terms of the account; or

(2) make the financial institution liable to the estate of a deceased party unless, before payment, the institution received written notice from the personal representative stating the amounts needed to pay debts, taxes, claims, and expenses of administration.

Derived from Probate Code § 442.

Added by Acts 2009, 81st Leg., ch. 680, § 1, eff. Jan. 1, 2014.

Chapter 114 Transfer on Death Deed

Subchapter A. General Provisions

Subchapter B. Authorization, Execution, and Revocation of Transfer on Death Deed

Subchapter C. Effect of Transfer on Death Deed; Liability of Transferred Property for Creditors' Claims

Subchapter D. Forms for Transfer on Death Deed

Statutes in Context
Chapter 114

The 2015 Legislature enacted a Texasized version of the Uniform Real Property Transfer on Death Act joining over a dozen other states that have already done so. Acts 2015, 84th Leg., ch. 841, § 1, eff. Sept. 1, 2015 (adding Estates Code Chapter 114). This Act permits a property owner to designated the new owner of real property upon his or her death in a deed which is property recorded during the owner's lifetime. Below are some of the key features of this Act:

- The property owner must have contractual capacity (not merely testamentary capacity) to execute a TOD deed.

- An agent under a power of attorney may not execute a TOD deed on behalf of the property owner.

- The beneficiary does not need to know about the TOD deed and does not need to have supplied any consideration. However, the beneficiary may disclaim the property following the normal disclaimer procedures.

- The named beneficiary has no legal or equitable interest in the property until the beneficiary survives the property owner by 120 hours.

- The property owner may revoke the TOD deed at any time and does need a reason for so doing.

- The property owner may not make the TOD deed irrevocable.

- The property owner's will cannot revoke or supersede a TOD deed.

- If the property owner names his or her spouse as the beneficiary and then a court issues a final judgment of divorce, the TOD deed is revoked as long as notice of the judgment is recorded before the property owner's death.

- The TOD deed has no legal effect during the property owner's lifetime. For example, the property owner may transfer the property to someone other than the beneficiary even if the transferee has actual knowledge of the TOD deed as long as the transferee records his or her deed before the property owner dies.

- When the property owner dies, creditors with interests in the property are generally treated like other estate creditors.

- When the property owner dies, the property transferred by a TOD deed is subject, as a last resort, to the claims against the estate including allowances in lieu of exempt property and the family allowance.

The Act provides optional forms a property owner may use to create and revoke TOD deeds.

Chapter 114. Transfer on Death Deed

Subchapter A. General Provisions

§ 114.001. Short Title

This chapter may be cited as the Texas Real Property Transfer on Death Act.

New.

Added by Acts 2015, 84th Leg., ch. 841, § 1, eff. Sept. 1, 2015.

§ 114.002. Definitions

(a) In this chapter:

(1) "Beneficiary" means a person who receives real property under a transfer on death deed.

(2) "Designated beneficiary" means a person designated to receive real property in a transfer on death deed.

(3) "Joint owner with right of survivorship" or "joint owner" means an individual who owns real property concurrently with one or more other individuals with a right of survivorship. The term does not include a tenant in common or an owner of community property with or without a right of survivorship.

(4) "Person" has the meaning assigned by Section 311.005, Government Code.

(5) "Real property" means an interest in real property located in this state.

(6) "Transfer on death deed" means a deed authorized under this chapter and does not refer to any other deed that transfers an interest in real property on the death of an individual.

(7) "Transferor" means an individual who makes a transfer on death deed.

(b) In this chapter, the terms "cancel" and "revoke" are synonymous.

New.

Added by Acts 2015, 84th Leg., ch. 841, § 1, eff. Sept. 1, 2015.

§ 114.003. Applicability

This chapter applies to a transfer on death deed executed and acknowledged on or after September 1, 2015, by a transferor who dies on or after September 1, 2015.

New.

Added by Acts 2015, 84th Leg., ch. 841, § 1, eff. Sept. 1, 2015.

§ 114.004. Nonexclusivity

This chapter does not affect any method of transferring real property otherwise permitted under the laws of this state.

New.

Added by Acts 2015, 84th Leg., ch. 841, § 1, eff. Sept. 1, 2015.

§ 114.005 Uniformity of Application and Construction

In applying and construing this chapter, consideration must be given to the need to promote uniformity of the law with respect to the subject matter of this chapter among states that enact a law similar to this chapter.

New.

Added by Acts 2015, 84ᵗʰ Leg., ch. 841, § 1, eff. Sept. 1, 2015.

§ 114.006. Relation to Electronic Signatures in Global and National Commerce Act

This chapter modifies, limits, and supersedes the federal Electronic Signatures in Global and National Commerce Act (15 U.S.C. Section 7001 et seq.), except that this chapter does not modify, limit, or supersede Section 101(c) of that Act (15 U.S.C. Section 7001(c)) or authorize electronic delivery of any of the notices described in Section 103(b) of that Act (15 U.S.C. Section 7003(b)).

New.

Added by Acts 2015, 84ᵗʰ Leg., ch. 841, § 1, eff. Sept. 1, 2015.

Subchapter B. Authorization, Execution, and Revocation of Transfer on Death Deed

§ 114.051. Transfer on Death Deed Authorized

An individual may transfer the individual's interest in real property to one or more beneficiaries effective at the transferor's death by a transfer on death deed.

New.

Added by Acts 2015, 84ᵗʰ Leg., ch. 841, § 1, eff. Sept. 1, 2015.

§ 114.052. Transfer on Death Deed Revocable

A transfer on death deed is revocable regardless of whether the deed or another instrument contains a contrary provision.

New.

Added by Acts 2015, 84ᵗʰ Leg., ch. 841, § 1, eff. Sept. 1, 2015.

§ 114.053. Transfer on Death Deed Nontestamentary

A transfer on death deed is a nontestamentary instrument.

New.

Added by Acts 2015, 84ᵗʰ Leg., ch. 841, § 1, eff. Sept. 1, 2015.

§ 114.054. Capacity of Transferor; Use of Power of Attorney

(a) The capacity required to make or revoke a transfer on death deed is the same as the capacity required to make a contract.

(b) A transfer on death deed may not be created through use of a power of attorney.

New.

Added by Acts 2015, 84ᵗʰ Leg., ch. 841, § 1, eff. Sept. 1, 2015.

§ 114.055. Requirements

To be effective, a transfer on death deed must:

(1) except as otherwise provided in Subdivision (2), contain the essential elements and formalities of a recordable deed;

(2) state that the transfer of an interest in real property to the designated beneficiary is to occur at the transferor's death; and

(3) be recorded before the transferor's death in the deed records in the county clerk's office of the county where the real property is located.

New.

Added by Acts 2015, 84ᵗʰ Leg., ch. 841, § 1, eff. Sept. 1, 2015.

§ 114.056. Notice, Delivery, Acceptance, or Consideration Not Required

A transfer on death deed is effective without:

(1) notice or delivery to or acceptance by the designated beneficiary during the transferor's life; or

(2) consideration.

New.

Added by Acts 2015, 84ᵗʰ Leg., ch. 841, § 1, eff. Sept. 1, 2015.

§ 114.057. Revocation by Certain Instruments; Effect of Will or Marriage Dissolution

(a) Subject to Subsections (d) and (e), an instrument is effective to revoke a recorded transfer on death deed, or any part of it, if the instrument:

(1) is one of the following:

(A) a subsequent transfer on death deed that revokes the preceding transfer on death deed or part of the deed expressly or by inconsistency; or

(B) except as provided by Subsection (b), an instrument of revocation that expressly revokes the transfer on death deed or part of the deed;

(2) is acknowledged by the transferor after the acknowledgment of the deed being revoked; and

(3) is recorded before the transferor's death in the deed records in the county clerk's office of the county where the deed being revoked is recorded.

(b) A will may not revoke or supersede a transfer on death deed.

(c) If a marriage between the transferor and a designated beneficiary is dissolved after a transfer on death deed is recorded, a final judgment of the court dissolving the marriage operates to revoke the transfer on death deed as to that designated beneficiary if notice of the judgment is recorded before the transferor's death in the deed records in the county clerk's office of the county where the deed is recorded, notwithstanding Section 111.052.

(d) If a transfer on death deed is made by more than one transferor, revocation by a transferor does not affect the deed as to the interest of another transferor who does not make that revocation.

(e) A transfer on death deed made by joint owners with right of survivorship is revoked only if it is revoked by all of the living joint owners.

(f) This section does not limit the effect of an inter vivos transfer of the real property.

New.

Added by Acts 2015, 84th Leg., ch. 841, § 1, eff. Sept. 1, 2015.

Subchapter C. Effect of Transfer on Death Deed; Liability of Transferred Property for Creditors' Claims

§ 114.101. Effect of Transfer on Death Deed During Transferor's Life

During a transferor's life, a transfer on death deed does not:

(1) affect an interest or right of the transferor or any other owner, including:

(A) the right to transfer or encumber the real property that is the subject of the deed;

(B) homestead rights in the real property, if applicable; and

(C) ad valorem tax exemptions, including exemptions for residence homestead, persons 65 years of age or older, persons with disabilities, and veterans;

(2) affect an interest or right of a transferee of the real property that is the subject of the deed, even if the transferee has actual or constructive notice of the deed;

(3) affect an interest or right of a secured or unsecured creditor or future creditor of the transferor, even if the creditor has actual or constructive notice of the deed;

(4) affect the transferor's or designated beneficiary's eligibility for any form of public assistance, subject to applicable federal law;

(5) constitute a transfer triggering a "due on sale" or similar clause;

(6) invoke statutory real estate notice or disclosure requirements;

(7) create a legal or equitable interest in favor of the designated beneficiary; or

(8) subject the real property to claims or process of a creditor of the designated beneficiary.

New.

Added by Acts 2015, 84th Leg., ch. 841, § 1, eff. Sept. 1, 2015.

§ 114.102. Effect of Subsequent Conveyance on Transfer on Death Deed

An otherwise valid transfer on death deed is void as to any interest in real property that is conveyed by the transferor during the transferor's lifetime after the transfer on death deed is executed and recorded if:

(1) a valid instrument conveying the interest is recorded in the deed records in the county clerk's office of the same county in which the transfer on death deed is recorded; and

(2) the recording of the instrument occurs before the transferor's death.

New.

Added by Acts 2015, 84th Leg., ch. 841, § 1, eff. Sept. 1, 2015.

§ 114.103. Effect of Transfer on Death Deed at Transferor's Death

(a) Except as otherwise provided in the transfer on death deed, this section, or any other statute or the common law of this state governing a decedent's estate, on the death of the transferor, the following rules apply to an interest in real property that is the subject of a transfer on death deed and owned by the transferor at death:

(1) if the designated beneficiary survives the transferor by 120 hours, the interest in the real property is transferred to the designated beneficiary in accordance with the deed;

(2) the interest of a designated beneficiary that fails to survive the transferor by 120 hours lapses, notwithstanding Section 111.052;

(3) subject to Subdivision (4), concurrent interests are transferred to the beneficiaries in equal and undivided shares with no right of survivorship; and

(4) notwithstanding Subdivision (2), if the transferor has identified two or more designated beneficiaries to receive concurrent interests in the real property, the share of a designated beneficiary who predeceases the transferor lapses and is subject to and passes in accordance with Subchapter D, Chapter 255, as if the transfer on death deed were a devise made in a will.

(b) If a transferor is a joint owner with right of survivorship who is survived by one or more other joint owners, the real property that is the subject of the transfer on death deed belongs to the surviving joint owner or owners. If a transferor is a joint owner with right of survivorship who is the last surviving joint owner, the transfer on death deed is effective.

(c) If a transfer on death deed is made by two or more transferors who are joint owners with right of survivorship, the last surviving joint owner may revoke the transfer on death deed subject to Section 114.057.

(d) A transfer on death deed transfers real property without covenant of warranty of title even if the deed contains a contrary provision.

New.

Added by Acts 2015, 84th Leg., ch. 841, § 1, eff. Sept. 1, 2015.

§ 114.104. Transfer on Death Deed Property Subject to Liens and Encumbrances at Transferor's Death; Creditors' Claims

(a) Subject to Section 13.001, Property Code, a beneficiary takes the real property subject to all conveyances, encumbrances, assignments, contracts, mortgages, liens, and other interests to which the real property is subject at the transferor's death. For purposes of this subsection and Section 13.001, Property Code, the recording of the transfer on death deed is considered to have occurred at the transferor's death.

(b) If a personal representative has been appointed for the transferor's estate, an administration of the estate has been opened, and the real property transferring under a transfer on death deed is subject to a lien or security interest, including a deed of trust or mortgage, the personal representative shall give notice to the creditor of the transferor as the personal representative would any other secured creditor under Section 308.053. The creditor shall then make an election under Section 355.151 in the period prescribed by Section 355.152 to have the claim treated as a matured secured claim or a preferred debt and lien claim, and the claim is subject to the claims procedures prescribed by this section.

(c) If the secured creditor elects to have the claim treated as a preferred debt and lien claim, Sections 355.154 and 355.155 apply as if the transfer on death deed were a devise made in a will, and the creditor may not pursue any other claims or remedies for any deficiency against the transferor's estate.

(d) If the secured creditor elects to have the claim treated as a matured secured claim, Section 355.153 applies as if the transfer on death deed were a devise made in a will, and the claim is subject to the procedural provisions of this title governing creditor claims.

New.

Added by Acts 2015, 84th Leg., ch. 841, § 1, eff. Sept. 1, 2015.

§ 114.105. Disclaimer

A designated beneficiary may disclaim all or part of the designated beneficiary's interest as provided by Chapter 122.

New.

Added by Acts 2015, 84th Leg., ch. 841, § 1, eff. Sept. 1, 2015.

§ 114.106. Liability for Creditor Claims; Allowances in Lieu of Exempt Property and Family Allowances

(a) To the extent the transferor's estate is insufficient to satisfy a claim against the estate, expenses of administration, any estate tax owed by the estate, or an allowance in lieu of exempt property or family allowance to a surviving spouse, minor children, or incapacitated adult children, the personal representative may enforce that liability against real property transferred at the transferor's death by a transfer on death deed to the same extent the personal representative could enforce that liability if the real property were part of the probate estate.

(b) Notwithstanding Subsection (a), real property transferred at the transferor's death by a transfer on death deed is not considered property of the probate estate for any purpose, including for purposes of Section 531.077, Government Code.

(c) If a personal representative does not commence a proceeding to enforce a liability under Subsection (a) on or before the 90th day after the date the representative receives a demand for payment, a proceeding to enforce the liability may be brought by a creditor, a distributee of the estate, a surviving spouse of the decedent, a guardian or other appropriate person on behalf of a minor child or adult incapacitated child of the decedent, or any taxing authority.

(d) If more than one real property interest is transferred by one or more transfer on death deeds or if there are other nonprobate assets of the transferor that may be liable for the claims, expenses, and other payments specified in Subsection (a), the liability for those claims, expenses, and other payments may be apportioned among those real property interests and other assets in proportion to their net values at the transferor's death.

(e) A proceeding to enforce liability under this section must be commenced not later than the second anniversary of the transferor's death, except for any rights arising under Section 114.104(d).

(f) In connection with any proceeding brought under this section, a court may award costs and reasonable and necessary attorney's fees in amounts the court considers equitable and just.

New.

Added by Acts 2015, 84th Leg., ch. 841, § 1, eff. Sept. 1, 2015.

Subchapter D. Forms for Transfer on Death Deed

§ 114.151. Optional Form for Transfer on Death Deed

The following form may be used to create a transfer on death deed.

REVOCABLE TRANSFER ON DEATH DEED

NOTICE OF CONFIDENTIALITY RIGHTS: IF YOU ARE A NATURAL PERSON, YOU MAY REMOVE OR STRIKE ANY OF THE FOLLOWING INFORMATION FROM THIS INSTRUMENT BEFORE IT IS FILED FOR RECORD IN THE PUBLIC RECORDS: YOUR SOCIAL SECURITY NUMBER OR YOUR DRIVER'S LICENSE NUMBER.

IMPORTANT NOTICE TO OWNER: You should carefully read all the information included in the instructions to this form. You may want to consult a lawyer before using this form.

MUST RECORD DEED: Before your death, this deed must be recorded with the county clerk where the property is located, or it will not be effective.

MARRIED PERSONS: If you are married and want your spouse to own the property on your death, you must name your spouse as the primary beneficiary. If your spouse does not survive you, the property will transfer to any listed alternate beneficiary or beneficiaries on your death.

1. Owner (Transferor) Making this Deed:

Printed name

Mailing address

2. Legal Description of the Property:

3. Address of the Property (if any) (include county):

4. Primary Beneficiary (Transferee) or Beneficiaries (Transferees)

I designate the following beneficiary or beneficiaries, if the beneficiary survives me:

Printed name

Mailing address

5. Alternate Beneficiary or Beneficiaries (Optional)

If no primary beneficiary survives me, I designate the following alternate beneficiary or beneficiaries:

Printed name

Mailing address

6. Transfer on Death

At my death, I grant and convey to the primary beneficiary or beneficiaries my interest in the property, to have and hold forever. If at my death I am not survived by any primary beneficiary, I grant and convey to the alternate beneficiary or beneficiaries, if designated, my interest in the property, to have and hold forever. If the primary and alternate beneficiaries do not survive me, this transfer on death deed shall be deemed canceled by me.

7. Printed Name and Signature of Owner Making this Deed:

Printed Name

Date

Signature

BELOW LINE FOR NOTARY ONLY

Acknowledgment

STATE OF

COUNTY OF

This instrument was acknowledged before me on the _____ day of _____, 20 ____, by _____.

Notary Public, State of

After recording, return to:

(insert name and mailing address)

INSTRUCTIONS FOR TRANSFER ON DEATH DEED

DO NOT RECORD THESE INSTRUCTIONS

Instructions for Completing the Form

1. Owner (Transferor) Making this Deed: Enter your first, middle (if any), and last name here, along with your mailing address.

2. Legal Description of the Property: Enter the formal legal description of the property. This information is different from the mailing and physical address for the property and is necessary to complete the form. To find this information, look on the deed you received when you became an owner of the property. This information may also be available in the office of the county clerk for the county where the property is located. Do NOT use your tax bill to find this information. If you are not absolutely sure, consult a lawyer.

3. Address of the Property: Enter the physical address of the property.

4. Primary Beneficiary or Beneficiaries: Enter the first and last name of each person you want to get the property when you die. If you are married and want your spouse to get the property when you die, enter your spouse's first and last name (even if you and your spouse own the property together).

5. Alternate Beneficiary or Beneficiaries: Enter the first and last name of each person you want to get the property if no primary beneficiary survives you.

6. Transfer on Death: No action needed.

7. Printed Name and Signature of Owner: Do not sign your name or enter the date until you are before a notary. Include your printed name.

8. Acknowledgment: This deed must be signed before a notary. The notary will fill out this section of the deed.

New.

Added by Acts 2015, 84th Leg., ch. 841, § 1, eff. Sept. 1, 2015.

§ 114.152. Optional Form of Revocation

The following form may be used to create an instrument of revocation under this chapter.

CANCELLATION OF TRANSFER ON DEATH DEED

IMPORTANT NOTICE TO OWNER: You should carefully read all the information included in the instructions to this form. You may want to consult a lawyer before using this form.

MUST RECORD FORM: Before your death, this cancellation form must be recorded with the county clerk where the property is located, or it will not be effective. This cancellation is effective only as to the interests in the property of owners who sign this cancellation form.

1. Owner (Transferor) Making this Cancellation:

_____
Printed name

_____

Mailing address

2. Legal Description of the Property:

_____

3. Address of the Property (if any) (include county):

_____

4. Cancellation

I cancel all my previous transfers of this property by transfer on death deed.

5. Printed Name and Signature of Owner (Transferor) Making this Cancellation:

BELOW LINE FOR NOTARY ONLY

Acknowledgment

STATE OF _____

COUNTY OF _____

This instrument was acknowledged before me on the _____ day of _____, 20___, by

_____

Notary Public, State of

After recording, return to:

(insert name and mailing address)

_____

INSTRUCTIONS FOR CANCELING A TRANSFER ON DEATH (TOD) DEED

DO NOT RECORD THESE INSTRUCTIONS

Instructions for Completing the Form

1. Owner (Transferor) Making this Cancellation: Enter your first, middle (if any), and last name here, along with your mailing address.

2. Legal Description of the Property: Enter the formal legal description of the property. This information is different from the mailing and physical address for the property and is necessary to complete the form. To find this information, look on the deed you received when you became an owner of the property. This information may also be available in the office of the county clerk for the county where the property is located. Do NOT use your tax bill to find this information. If you are not absolutely sure, consult a lawyer.

3. Address of the Property: Enter the physical address of the property.

4. Cancellation: No action needed.

5. Printed Name and Signature of Owner: Do not sign your name or enter the date until you are before a notary. Include your printed name.

6. Acknowledgment: This cancellation form must be signed before a notary. The notary will fill out this section of the form.

New.

Added by Acts 2015, 84th Leg., ch. 841, § 1, eff. Sept. 1, 2015.

Chapter 121. Survival Requirements

Subchapter A. General Provisions

§ 121.001. Applicability of Chapter

Subchapter B. Survival Requirement for Intestate Succession and Certain Other Purposes

§ 121.051. Applicability of Subchapter

§ 121.052. Required Period of Survival for Intestate Succession and Certain Other Purposes

§ 121.053. Intestate Succession: Failure to Survive Presumed Under Certain Circumstances

Subchapter C. Survival Requirements for Certain Beneficiaries

§ 121.101. Required Period of Survival for Devisee

§ 121.102. Required Period of Survival for Contingent Beneficiary

Subchapter D. Distribution of Certain Property on Person's Failure to Survive for Required Period

§ 121.151. Distribution of Community Property

§ 121.152. Distribution of Property Owned by Joint Owners

§ 121.153. Distribution of Certain Insurance Proceeds

Chapter 121. Survival Requirements

Subchapter A. General Provisions

Statutes in Context
Chapter 121

To be an heir, will beneficiary, recipient of property held in a joint tenancy with survivorship rights, or beneficiary of a life insurance policy, an individual must outlive the decedent. At common law, survival for only a mere instant was needed. This rule led to many proof problems as family members tried to establish that one person outlived the other or vice versa. Some of these cases read like horror novels as the courts evaluate evidence of which person twitched, gurgled, or gasped longer. See *Glover v. Davis*, 366 S.W.2d 227 (Tex. 1963).

To remedy this problem, Chapter 121 imposes a survival period of 120 hours (5 days). If a person survives the decedent but dies prior to the expiration of the survival period, the property passes as if the person had actually predeceased the decedent.

§ 121.001. Applicability of Chapter

This chapter does not apply if provision has been made by will, living trust, deed, or insurance contract, or in any other manner, for a disposition of property that is different from the disposition of the property that would be made if the provisions of this chapter applied.

Derived from Probate Code § 47(f).

Added by Acts 2009, 81st Leg., ch. 680, § 1, eff. Jan. 1, 2014.

Subchapter B. Survival Requirement for Intestate Succession and Certain Other Purposes

§ 121.051. Applicability of Subchapter

This subchapter does not apply if the application of this subchapter would result in the escheat of an intestate estate.

Derived from Probate Code § 47(a).

Added by Acts 2009, 81st Leg., ch. 680, § 1, eff. Jan. 1, 2014.

§ 121.052. Required Period of Survival for Intestate Succession and Certain Other Purposes

A person who does not survive a decedent by 120 hours is considered to have predeceased the decedent for purposes of the homestead allowance, exempt property, and intestate succession, and the decedent's heirs are determined accordingly, except as otherwise provided by this chapter.

Derived from Probate Code § 47(a).

Added by Acts 2009, 81st Leg., ch. 680, § 1, eff. Jan. 1, 2014.

§ 121.053. Intestate Succession: Failure to Survive Presumed Under Certain Circumstances

A person who, if the person survived a decedent by 120 hours, would be the decedent's heir is considered not to have survived the decedent for the required period if:

(1) the time of death of the decedent or of the person, or the times of death of both, cannot be determined; and

(2) the person's survival for the required period after the decedent's death cannot be established.

Derived from Probate Code § 47(a).

Added by Acts 2009, 81st Leg., ch. 680, § 1, eff. Jan. 1, 2014.

Subchapter C. Survival Requirements for Certain Beneficiaries

§ 121.101. Required Period of Survival for Devisee

A devisee who does not survive the testator by 120 hours is treated as if the devisee predeceased the testator unless the testator's will contains some language that:

(1) deals explicitly with simultaneous death or deaths in a common disaster; or

(2) requires the devisee to survive the testator, or to survive the testator for a stated period, to take under the will.

Derived from Probate Code § 47(c).

Added by Acts 2009, 81st Leg., ch. 680, § 1, eff. Jan. 1, 2014.

§ 121.102. Required Period of Survival for Contingent Beneficiary

(a) If property is disposed of in a manner that conditions the right of a beneficiary to succeed to an interest in the property on the beneficiary surviving another person, the beneficiary is considered not to have survived the other person unless the beneficiary survives the person by 120 hours, except as provided by Subsection (b).

(b) If an interest in property is given alternatively to one of two or more beneficiaries, with the right of each beneficiary to take being dependent on that beneficiary surviving the other beneficiary or beneficiaries, and all of the beneficiaries die within a period of less than 120 hours, the property shall be divided into as many equal portions as there are beneficiaries. The portions shall be distributed respectively to those who would have taken if each beneficiary had survived.

Derived from Probate Code § 47(c).

Added by Acts 2009, 81st Leg., ch. 680, § 1, eff. Jan. 1, 2014.

Subchapter D. Distribution of Certain Property on Person's Failure to Survive for Required Period

§ 121.151. Distribution of Community Property

(a) This section applies to community property, including the proceeds of life or accident insurance that are community property and become payable to the estate of either the husband or wife.

(b) If a husband and wife die leaving community property but neither survives the other by 120 hours, one-half of all community property shall be distributed as if the husband had survived, and the other one-half shall be distributed as if the wife had survived.

Derived from Probate Code § 47(b).

Added by Acts 2009, 81st Leg., ch. 680, § 1, eff. Jan. 1, 2014.

§ 121.152. Distribution of Property Owned by Joint Owners

If property, including community property with a right of survivorship, is owned so that one of two joint owners is entitled to the whole of the property on the death of the other, but neither survives the other by 120 hours, one-half of the property shall be distributed as if one joint owner had survived, and the other one-half shall be distributed as if the other joint owner had survived. If there are more than two joint owners and all of the joint owners die within a period of less than 120 hours, the property shall be divided into as many equal portions as there are joint owners and the portions shall be distributed respectively to those who would have taken if each joint owner survived.

Derived from Probate Code § 47(d).

Added by Acts 2009, 81st Leg., ch. 680, § 1, eff. Jan. 1, 2014.

§ 121.153. Distribution of Certain Insurance Proceeds

(a) If the insured under a life or accident insurance policy and a beneficiary of the proceeds of that policy die within a period of less than 120 hours, the insured is considered to have survived the beneficiary for the purpose of determining the rights under the policy of the beneficiary or beneficiaries as such.

(b) This section does not prevent the applicability of Section 121.151 to proceeds of life or accident insurance that are community property.

Derived from Probate Code § 47(e).

Added by Acts 2009, 81st Leg., ch. 680, § 1, eff. Jan. 1, 2014.

Chapter 122. Disclaimers and Assignments

Subchapter A. *[General Provisions Relating to]* Disclaimer *of Interest or Power*

Chapter 122. Disclaimers and Assignments

Subchapter A. *[General Provisions Relating to]* Disclaimer *of Interest or Power*

Statutes in Context
Chapter 122

Effective September 1, 2015, disclaimers are governed by the Uniform Disclaimer of Property Interests Act set forth in Property Code Title 13.

---

§ 122.001. Definitions

In this subchapter [chapter, other than Subchapter E]:

(1) "Beneficiary" includes a person who would have been entitled, if the person had not made a disclaimer, to receive property as a result of the death of another person:

(A) by inheritance;

(B) under a will;

(C) by an agreement between spouses for community property with a right of survivorship;

(D) by a joint tenancy with a right of survivorship;

(E) by a survivorship agreement, account, or interest in which the interest of the decedent passes to a surviving beneficiary;

(F) by an insurance, annuity, endowment, employment, deferred compensation, or other contract or arrangement; [or]

(G) under a pension, profit sharing, thrift, stock bonus, life insurance, survivor income, incentive, or other plan or program providing retirement, welfare, or fringe benefits with respect to an employee or a self-employed individual; or

(H) by a transfer on death deed..

(2) "Disclaim" and "disclaimer" have the meanings assigned by Section 240.002, Property Code ["Disclaimer" includes renunciation].

(3) "Property" includes all legal and equitable interests, powers, and property, present or future, vested or contingent, and beneficial or burdensome, in whole or in part.

Derived from Probate Code § 37A(e).

Added by Acts 2009, 81st Leg., ch. 680, § 1, eff. Jan. 1, 2014. Subsec. (2) amended by Acts 2015, 84th Leg., ch. 562, § 3, eff. Sept. 1, 2015. Subsec. (1)(H) added by Acts 2015, 84th Leg., ch. 841, § 3, eff. Sept. 1, 2015.

§ 122.002. Disclaimer [Who May Disclaim]

[(a)] A person who may be entitled to receive property as a beneficiary may disclaim the person's interest in or power over the property in accordance with Chapter 240, Property Code [who on or after September 1, 1977, intends to irrevocably disclaim all or any part of the property shall evidence the disclaimer as provided by this chapter].

(b) Subject to Subsection (c), the legally authorized representative of a person who may be entitled to receive property as a beneficiary who on or after September 1, 1977, intends to irrevocably disclaim all or any part of the property on the beneficiary's behalf shall evidence the disclaimer as provided by this chapter.

(c) A disclaimer made by a legally authorized representative described by Subsection (d)(1), (2), or (3), other than an independent executor, must be made with prior court approval of the court that has or would have jurisdiction over the legally authorized representative. A disclaimer made by an independent executor on behalf of a decedent may be made without prior court approval.

(d) In this section, "legally authorized representative" means:

(1) a guardian if the person entitled to receive the property as a beneficiary is an incapacitated person;

(2) a guardian ad litem if the person entitled to receive the property as a beneficiary is an unborn or unascertained person;

(3) a personal representative, including an independent executor, if the person entitled to receive the property as a beneficiary is a decedent; or

(4) an attorney in fact or agent appointed under a durable power of attorney authorizing disclaimers if the person entitled to receive the property as a

beneficiary executed the power of attorney as a principal.

Derived from Probate Code § 37A(a).

Added by Acts 2009, 81st Leg., ch. 680, § 1, eff. Jan. 1, 2014. Amended by Acts 2015, 84th Leg., ch. 562, § 3, eff. Sept. 1, 2015.

§ 122.003. Effective Date; Creditors' Claims

(a) A disclaimer evidenced as provided by this chapter is effective for all purposes as of the date of the decedent's death.

(b) Property disclaimed in accordance with this chapter is not subject to the claims of a creditor of the disclaimant.

Derived from Probate Code § 37A(b).

Added by Acts 2009, 81st Leg., ch. 680, § 1, eff. Jan. 1, 2014. Repealed by Acts 2015, 84th Leg., ch. 562, § 16, eff. Sept. 1, 2015.

§ 122.004. Disclaimer Irrevocable

A disclaimer that is filed and served as provided by this chapter is irrevocable.

Derived from Probate Code § 37A(k).

Added by Acts 2009, 81st Leg., ch. 680, § 1, eff. Jan. 1, 2014. Repealed by Acts 2015, 84th Leg., ch. 562, § 16, eff. Sept. 1, 2015.

§ 122.005. Power to Provide Method of Disclaimer

A will, insurance policy, employee benefit agreement, or other instrument may provide for the making of a disclaimer by a beneficiary of an interest receivable under that instrument and for the disposition of disclaimed property in a manner different than provided by this chapter.

Derived from Probate Code § 37A(j).

Added by Acts 2009, 81st Leg., ch. 680, § 1, eff. Jan. 1, 2014. Repealed by Acts 2015, 84th Leg., ch. 562, § 16, eff. Sept. 1, 2015.

Subchapter B. Form, Filing, and Notice of Disclaimer

§ 122.051. Form and Contents

(a) A disclaimer of property receivable by a beneficiary must be evidenced by written memorandum acknowledged before:

(1) a notary public; or

(2) another person authorized to take acknowledgments of conveyances of real estate.

(b) A disclaimer of property receivable by a beneficiary must include a statement regarding whether the beneficiary is a child support obligor described by Section 122.107.

Derived from Probate Code § 37A(g).

Added by Acts 2009, 81st Leg., ch. 680, § 1, eff. Jan. 1, 2014. Amended by Acts 2013, 83rd Leg., ch. 689, § 1, eff. Jan. 1, 2014. Repealed by Acts 2015, 84th Leg., ch.

562, § 16, eff. Sept. 1, 2015.

§ 122.052. Filing in Probate Court

Except as provided by Sections 122.053 and 122.054, the written memorandum of disclaimer must be filed in the probate court in which:

(1) the decedent's will has been probated;

(2) proceedings have commenced for the administration of the decedent's estate; or

(3) an application has been filed for probate of the decedent's will or administration of the decedent's estate.

Derived from Probate Code § 37A(h).

Added by Acts 2009, 81st Leg., ch. 680, § 1, eff. Jan. 1, 2014. Repealed by Acts 2015, 84th Leg., ch. 562, § 16, eff. Sept. 1, 2015.

§ 122.053. Filing in County of Decedent's Residence

The written memorandum of disclaimer must be filed with the county clerk of the county of the decedent's residence on the date of the decedent's death if:

(1) the administration of the decedent's estate is closed;

(2) one year has expired since the date letters testamentary were issued in an independent administration;

(3) a will of the decedent has not been probated or filed for probate;

(4) administration of the decedent's estate has not commenced; or

(5) an application for administration of the decedent's estate has not been filed.

Derived from Probate Code § 37A(h).

Added by Acts 2009, 81st Leg., ch. 680, § 1, eff. Jan. 1, 2014. Repealed by Acts 2015, 84th Leg., ch. 562, § 16, eff. Sept. 1, 2015.

§ 122.054. Nonresident Decedent

If the decedent is not a resident of this state on the date of the decedent's death and the disclaimer is of real property that is located in this state, the written memorandum of disclaimer must be:

(1) filed with the county clerk of the county in which the real property is located; and

(2) recorded by the county clerk in the deed records of that county.

Derived from Probate Code § 37A(h).

Added by Acts 2009, 81st Leg., ch. 680, § 1, eff. Jan. 1, 2014. Repealed by Acts 2015, 84th Leg., ch. 562, § 16, eff. Sept. 1, 2015.

§ 122.055. Filing Deadline

(a) Except as provided by Subsection (c), a written memorandum of disclaimer of a present interest must be filed not later than nine months after the date of the decedent's death.

(b) Except as provided by Subsection (c), a written memorandum of disclaimer of a future interest may be filed not later than nine months after the date of the event determining that the taker of the property or interest is finally ascertained and the taker's interest is indefeasibly vested.

(c) If the beneficiary is a charitable organization or a governmental agency of the state, a written memorandum of disclaimer of a present or future interest must be filed not later than the later of:

(1) the first anniversary of the date the beneficiary receives the notice required by Subchapter A, Chapter 308; or

(2) the expiration of the six-month period following the date the personal representative files:

(A) the inventory, appraisement, and list of claims due or owing to the estate; or

(B) the affidavit in lieu of the inventory, appraisement, and list of claims.

Derived from Probate Code § 37A(h).

Added by Acts 2009, 81st Leg., ch. 680, § 1, eff. Jan. 1, 2014. Subsec. (c) amended by Acts 2011, 82nd Leg., ch. 1338, § 2.10, eff. Jan. 1, 2014. Repealed by Acts 2015, 84th Leg., ch. 562, § 16, eff. Sept. 1, 2015.

§ 122.056. Notice

(a) Except as provided by Subsection (b), a copy of the written memorandum of disclaimer shall be delivered in person to, or mailed by registered or certified mail to and received by, the legal representative of the transferor of the interest or the holder of legal title to the property to which the disclaimer relates not later than nine months after:

(1) the date of the decedent's death; or

(2) if the interest is a future interest, the date the person who will receive the property or interest is finally ascertained and the person's interest is indefeasibly vested.

(b) If the beneficiary is a charitable organization or a governmental agency of this state, notice of a disclaimer required by Subsection (a) must be filed not later than the later of:

(1) the first anniversary of the date the beneficiary receives the notice required by Subchapter A, Chapter 308; or

(2) the expiration of the six-month period following the date the personal representative files:

(A) the inventory, appraisement, and list of claims due or owing to the estate; or

(B) the affidavit in lieu of the inventory, appraisement, and list of claims.

Derived from Probate Code § 37A(i).

Added by Acts 2009, 81st Leg., ch. 680, § 1, eff. Jan. 1, 2014. Subsec. (b) amended by Acts 2011, 82nd Leg., ch. 1338, § 2.11, eff. Jan. 1, 2014. Repealed by Acts 2015, 84th Leg., ch. 562, § 16, eff. Sept. 1, 2015.

Subchapter C. Effect of Disclaimer

§ 122.101. Effect

Unless the decedent's will provides otherwise:

(1) property subject to a disclaimer passes as if the person disclaiming or on whose behalf a disclaimer is made had predeceased the decedent; and

(2) a future interest that would otherwise take effect in possession or enjoyment after the termination of the estate or interest that is disclaimed takes effect as if the disclaiming beneficiary had predeceased the decedent.

Derived from Probate Code § 37A(c).

Added by Acts 2009, 81st Leg., ch. 680, § 1, eff. Jan. 1, 2014. Repealed by Acts 2015, 84th Leg., ch. 562, § 16, eff. Sept. 1, 2015.

§ 122.102. Ineffective Disclaimer

(a) Except as provided by Subsection (b), a disclaimer that does not comply with this chapter is ineffective.

(b) A disclaimer otherwise ineffective under Subsection (a) is effective as an assignment of the disclaimed property to those who would have received the property had the person attempting the disclaimer died before the decedent.

Derived from Probate Code § 37A(d).

Added by Acts 2009, 81st Leg., ch. 680, § 1, eff. Jan. 1, 2014. Repealed by Acts 2015, 84th Leg., ch. 562, § 16, eff. Sept. 1, 2015.

§ 122.103. Subsequent Disclaimer

This chapter does not prevent a person who is entitled to property as the result of a disclaimer from subsequently disclaiming the property.

Derived from Probate Code § 37A(f).

Added by Acts 2009, 81st Leg., ch. 680, § 1, eff. Jan. 1, 2014. Repealed by Acts 2015, 84th Leg., ch. 562, § 16, eff. Sept. 1, 2015.

§ 122.104. Disclaimer After Acceptance

A disclaimer is not effective if the person making the disclaimer has previously accepted the property by taking possession or exercising dominion and control of the property as a beneficiary.

Derived from Probate Code § 37A(n).

Added by Acts 2009, 81st Leg., ch. 680, § 1, eff. Jan. 1, 2014. Repealed by Acts 2015, 84th Leg., ch. 562, § 16, eff. Sept. 1, 2015.

§ 122.105. Interest in Trust Property

A beneficiary who accepts an interest in a trust is not considered to have a direct or indirect interest in trust property that relates to a licensed or permitted business and over which the beneficiary exercises no control.

Derived from Probate Code § 37A(o).

Added by Acts 2009, 81st Leg., ch. 680, § 1, eff. Jan. 1,

2014. Repealed by Acts 2015, 84th Leg., ch. 562, § 16, eff. Sept. 1, 2015.

§ 122.106. Interest in Securities

Direct or indirect beneficial ownership of not more than five percent of any class of equity securities that is registered under the Securities Exchange Act of 1934 (15 U.S.C. Section 78a et seq.) is not considered an ownership interest in the business of the issuer of the securities within the meaning of any statute, pursuant thereto.

Derived from Probate Code § 37A(o).

Added by Acts 2009, 81st Leg., ch. 680, § 1, eff. Jan. 1, 2014. Repealed by Acts 2015, 84th Leg., ch. 562, § 16, eff. Sept. 1, 2015.

§ 122.107. Attempted Disclaimers by Certain Child Obligors Ineffective

(a) A disclaimer made by a beneficiary who is a child support obligor of estate property that could be applied to satisfy the beneficiary's child support obligation is not effective if the beneficiary owes child support arrearages that have been:

(1) administratively determined by the Title IV-D agency as defined by Section 101.033, Family Code, in a Title IV-D case as defined by Section 101.034, Family Code; or

(2) confirmed and reduced to judgment as provided by Section 157.263, Family Code.

(b) After distribution of estate property to a beneficiary described by Subsection (a), the child support obligee to whom the child support arrearages are owed may enforce the child support obligation by a lien or by any other remedy provided by law.

New.

Added by Acts 2013, 83rd Leg., ch. 689, § 2, eff. Jan. 1, 2014. Repealed by Acts 2015, 84th Leg., ch. 562, § 16, eff. Sept. 1, 2015.

Subchapter D. Partial Disclaimer

§ 122.151. Partial Disclaimer

A person who may be entitled to receive property as a beneficiary may wholly or partly disclaim the property, including:

(1) specific powers of invasion;

(2) powers of appointment; and

(3) fee estate in favor of life estates.

Derived from Probate Code § 37A(l).

Added by Acts 2009, 81st Leg., ch. 680, § 1, eff. Jan. 1, 2014. Repealed by Acts 2015, 84th Leg., ch. 562, § 16, eff. Sept. 1, 2015.

§ 122.152. Effect of Partial Disclaimer

A partial disclaimer in accordance with this chapter is effective whether the property disclaimed constitutes a portion of a single, aggregate gift or constitutes part or all of a separate, independent gift, except that:

~~(1) a partial disclaimer is effective only with respect to property expressly described or referred to by category in the disclaimer; and~~

~~(2) a partial disclaimer of property subject to a burdensome interest created by the decedent's will is not effective unless the property constitutes a gift separate and distinct from undisclaimed gifts.~~

Derived from Probate Code § 37A(l).

Added by Acts 2009, 81st Leg., ch. 680, § 1, eff. Jan. 1, 2014. Repealed by Acts 2015, 84th Leg., ch. 562, § 16, eff. Sept. 1, 2015.

~~§ 122.153. Partial Disclaimer by Spouse~~

~~A disclaimer by the decedent's surviving spouse of a transfer by the decedent is not a disclaimer by the surviving spouse of all or any part of any other transfer from the decedent to or for the benefit of the surviving spouse, regardless of whether the property or interest that would have passed under the disclaimed transfer passes because of the disclaimer to or for the benefit of the surviving spouse by the other transfer.~~

Derived from Probate Code § 37A(m).

Added by Acts 2009, 81st Leg., ch. 680, § 1, eff. Jan. 1, 2014. Repealed by Acts 2015, 84th Leg., ch. 562, § 16, eff. Sept. 1, 2015.

Subchapter E. Assignment of Interest

Statutes in Context
§§ 122.201–122.206

Once an heir or beneficiary receives the property through intestate succession, by will, or as the beneficiary of a life insurance policy, the person may assign his/her interest in the property to a third person. Unlike with a disclaimer, the heir or beneficiary will be liable for transfer taxes and the property will become subject to the creditors of the heir or beneficiary. See Property Code § 112.035 for a discussion of the "spendthrift provision" mentioned in § 122.206.

§ 122.201. Assignment

A person who is entitled to receive property or an interest in property from a decedent under a will, by inheritance, or as a beneficiary under a life insurance contract, and does not disclaim the property under Chapter 240, Property Code, [this chapter] may assign the property or interest in property to any person.

Derived from Probate Code § 37B(a).

Added by Acts 2009, 81st Leg., ch. 680, § 1, eff. Jan. 1, 2014. Amended by Acts 2015, 84th Leg., ch. 562, § 4, eff. Sept. 1, 2015.

§ 122.202. Filing of Assignment

An assignment may, at the request of the assignor, be delivered or filed as provided for the delivery or filing of a disclaimer under Subchapter C, Chapter 240, Property Code [B].

Derived from Probate Code § 37B(b).

Added by Acts 2009, 81st Leg., ch. 680, § 1, eff. Jan. 1, 2014. Amended by Acts 2015, 84th Leg., ch. 562, § 5, eff. Sept. 1, 2015.

~~§ 122.203. Notice~~

~~Notice of the filing of an assignment as provided by Section 122.202 must be served as required by Section 122.056 for notice of a disclaimer.~~

Derived from Probate Code § 37B(b).

Added by Acts 2009, 81st Leg., ch. 680, § 1, eff. Jan. 1, 2014. Repealed by Acts 2015, 84th Leg., ch. 562, § 16, eff. Sept. 1, 2015.

§ 122.204. Failure to Comply

Failure to comply with Chapter 240, Property Code, [Subchapters A, B, C, and D] does not affect an assignment.

Derived from Probate Code § 37B(c).

Added by Acts 2009, 81st Leg., ch. 680, § 1, eff. Jan. 1, 2014. Amended by Acts 2015, 84th Leg., ch. 562, § 6, eff. Sept. 1, 2015.

§ 122.205. Gift

An assignment under this subchapter is a gift to the assignee and is not a disclaimer under Chapter 240, Property Code [Subchapters A, B, C, and D].

Derived from Probate Code § 37B(d).

Added by Acts 2009, 81st Leg., ch. 680, § 1, eff. Jan. 1, 2014. Amended by Acts 2015, 84th Leg., ch. 562, § 7, eff. Sept. 1, 2015.

§ 122.206. Spendthrift Provision

An assignment of property or interest that would defeat a spendthrift provision imposed in a trust may not be made under this subchapter.

Derived from Probate Code § 37B(e).

Added by Acts 2009, 81st Leg., ch. 680, § 1, eff. Jan. 1, 2014.

Chapter 123. Dissolution of Marriage

Subchapter A. Effect of Dissolution of Marriage on Will

§ 123.001. Will Provisions Made Before Dissolution of Marriage

§ 123.002. Treatment of Decedent's Former Spouse

Subchapter B. Effect of Dissolution of Marriage on Certain Nontestamentary Transfers

§ 123.051. Definitions

Subchapter C. Certain Marriages Voidable After Death

Subchapter D. Effect of Dissolution of Marriage on Certain Multiple-Party Accounts

Chapter 123. Dissolution of Marriage

Subchapter A. Effect of Dissolution of Marriage on Will

Statutes in Context
Chapter 123, Subchapter A

Divorce was not a common occurrence in the early history of England or the United States. Thus, there is little common law addressing the ramifications of a divorce on a will executed during marriage which made a gift to a person who is now an ex-spouse. Early decisions usually held that the divorce had no effect on the will. The courts realized that a testator probably did not intend for the property to pass to an ex-spouse but felt that they had no legal basis for voiding the gift.

Section 123.001 provides that upon divorce, all provisions of a will executed during marriage in favor of an ex-spouse and the ex-spouse's relatives who are not also relatives of the testator are void. The balance of the will remains effective as written. Thus, the ex-spouse would not be able to take as a beneficiary or serve in a fiduciary capacity such as the executor of the will, the guardian of any minor children, or the trustee of a testamentary trust. If the spouses remarry each other and remain married until the first spouse dies, the will remains effective as originally written. The testator also may include a provision validating a gift in favor of a spouse regardless of whether the spouses are married or divorced at the time of the testator's death.

Generally under § 123.002, the property left to the ex-spouse beneficiary (or a relative of the ex-spouse who is not a relative of the testator) passes under the will as if the ex-spouse had predeceased the testator.

See Family Code §§ 9.301 & 9.302 for similar provisions applicable to life insurance polices and retirement plans and Estates Code § 123.051–123.055 for what happens if the settlor and beneficiary of a revocable trust are divorced and the settlor fails to amend the trust to address this change in circumstance.

---

§ 123.001. Will Provisions Made Before Dissolution of Marriage

(a) In this section:

(1) "Irrevocable trust" means a trust:

(A) for which the trust instrument was executed before the dissolution of a testator's marriage; and

(B) that the testator was not solely empowered by law or by the trust instrument to revoke.

(2) "Relative"[, "relative"] means an individual related to another individual by:

(A) [(1)] consanguinity, as determined under Section 573.022, Government Code; or

(B) [(2)] affinity, as determined under Section 573.024, Government Code.

(b) If, after the testator makes a will, the testator's marriage is dissolved by divorce, annulment, or a declaration that the marriage is void, unless the will expressly provides otherwise:

(1) all provisions in the will, including all fiduciary appointments, shall be read as if the former spouse and each relative of the former spouse who is not a relative of the testator had failed to survive the testator; and

(2) all provisions in the will disposing of property to an irrevocable trust in which a former spouse or a relative of a former spouse who is not a relative of the testator is a beneficiary or is nominated to serve as trustee or in another fiduciary capacity or that confers a general or special power of appointment on a former spouse or a relative of a former spouse who is not a relative of the testator shall be read to instead dispose of the property to a trust the provisions of which are identical to the irrevocable trust, except any provision in the irrevocable trust:

(A) conferring a beneficial interest or a general or special power of appointment to the former spouse or a relative of the former spouse who is not a relative of the testator shall be treated as if the former spouse and each relative of the former spouse who is not a relative of the testator had disclaimed the interest granted in the provision; and

(B) nominating the former spouse or a relative of the former spouse who is not a relative of the testator to serve as trustee or in another fiduciary capacity shall be treated as if the former spouse and each relative of the former spouse who is not a relative of the testator had died immediately before the dissolution of the marriage[, unless the will expressly provides otherwise].

(c) Subsection (b)(2) does not apply if one of the following provides otherwise:

(1) a court order; or

(2) an express provision of a contract relating to the division of the marital estate entered into between the testator and the testator's former spouse before, during, or after the marriage.

Derived from Probate Code §§ 69(a), (b).

Added by Acts 2009, 81st Leg., ch. 680, § 1, eff. Jan. 1, 2014. Amended by Acts 2015, 84th Leg., ch. 378, § 3, eff. Sept. 1, 2015.

§ 123.002. Treatment of Decedent's Former Spouse

A person is not a surviving spouse of a decedent if the person's marriage to the decedent has been dissolved by divorce, annulment, or a declaration that the marriage is void, unless:

(1) as the result of a subsequent marriage, the person is married to the decedent at the time of death; and

(2) the subsequent marriage is not declared void under Subchapter C.

Derived from Probate Code § 69(c).

Added by Acts 2009, 81st Leg., ch. 680, § 1, eff. Jan. 1, 2014.

Subchapter B. Effect of Dissolution of Marriage on Certain Nontestamentary Transfers

Statutes in Context
Chapter 123, Subchapter B

The predecessor to Chapter 123, Subchapter B, was added to the Probate Code (not the Trust Code) in 2005 to address the situation of what happens if the settlor and beneficiary of a revocable trust are divorced and the settlor fails to amend the trust to address this change in circumstance.

The new provisions apply if the divorce occurs on or after September 1, 2005. It does not matter when the settlor created the trust.

Only written revocable trusts are covered by the new provisions. The ex-spouse remains as the beneficiary of an irrevocable trust and of a revocable oral trust.

If the settlor of a written revocable trust divorces a beneficiary of that trust to whom the settlor was married before or at the time of trust creation, the following provisions of the trust in favor of the ex-spouse are automatically revoked:

- Beneficiary of a revocable disposition or appointment.
- Donee of a general or special power of appointment, and
- Designation as a fiduciary (e.g., trustee, personal representative, agent, or guardian).

Any property interest which is automatically revoked passes as if the ex-spouse executed a valid disclaimer of that interest under Texas law. If a fiduciary designation is automatically revoked, the trust instrument is read as if the ex-spouse died immediately before the dissolution of the marriage.

The automatic revocation of provisions in favor of the ex-spouse discussed above does *not* occur if one or more of the following instruments provides otherwise:

- A trust executed after the divorce,
- A court order,
- Express language in the trust, or
- Express language of a contract relating to the division of the marital estate entered into before, during, or after the marriage.

A bona fide purchaser from the ex-spouse of trust property or a person who receives a payment from the ex-spouse which is traceable to the trust, does not have to return the property or payment and is not liable for that property or payment.

If the ex-spouse receives property or a payment from a trust to which the ex-spouse is not entitled, the ex-spouse has a duty to return the property or payment and is personally liable to the person who is entitled to that property or payment.

The 2011 Legislature expanded these provisions to cover not only the ex-spouse but also any relative of the ex-spouse who is not a relative of the settlor.

§ 123.051. Definitions

In this subchapter:

(1) "Disposition or appointment of property" includes a transfer of property to or a provision of

another benefit to a beneficiary under a trust instrument.

(2) "Divorced individual" means an individual whose marriage has been dissolved by divorce, annulment, or a declaration that the marriage is void.

(2-a) "Relative" means an individual who is related to another individual by consanguinity or affinity, as determined under Sections 573.022 and 573.024, Government Code, respectively.

(3) "Revocable," with respect to a disposition, appointment, provision, or nomination, means a disposition to, appointment of, provision in favor of, or nomination of an individual's spouse that is contained in a trust instrument executed by the individual before the dissolution of the individual's marriage to the spouse and that the individual was solely empowered by law or by the trust instrument to revoke regardless of whether the individual had the capacity to exercise the power at that time.

Derived from Probate Code § 471.

Added by Acts 2009, 81st Leg., ch. 680, § 1, eff. Jan. 1, 2014. Subsec. (2) amended by Acts 2011, 82nd Leg., ch. 1338, § 2.13, eff. Jan. 1, 2014. Subsec. (2-a) added by Acts 2011, 82nd Leg., ch. 1338, § 2.13, eff. Jan. 1, 2014.

§ 123.052. Revocation of Certain Nontestamentary Transfers; Treatment of Former Spouse as Beneficiary Under Certain Policies or Plans

(a) The dissolution of the marriage revokes a provision in a trust instrument that was executed by a divorced individual before the divorced individual's marriage was dissolved and that:

(1) is a revocable disposition or appointment of property made to the divorced individual's former spouse or any relative of the former spouse who is not a relative of the divorced individual;

(2) revocably confers a general or special power of appointment on the divorced individual's former spouse or any relative of the former spouse who is not a relative of the divorced individual; or

(3) revocably nominates the divorced individual's former spouse or any relative of the former spouse who is not a relative of the divorced individual to serve:

(A) as a personal representative, trustee, conservator, agent, or guardian; or

(B) in another fiduciary or representative capacity.

(b) Subsection (a) does not apply if one of the following provides otherwise:

(1) a court order;

(2) the express terms of a trust instrument executed by the divorced individual before the individual's marriage was dissolved; or

(3) an express provision of a contract relating to the division of the marital estate entered into between the divorced individual and the

individual's former spouse before, during, or after the marriage.

(c) Sections 9.301 and 9.302, Family Code, govern the designation of a former spouse as a beneficiary of certain life insurance policies or as a beneficiary under certain retirement benefit plans or other financial plans.

Derived from Probate Code § 472(a).

Added by Acts 2009, 81st Leg., ch. 680, § 1, eff. Jan. 1, 2014. Subsec. (a) amended by Acts 2011, 82nd Leg., ch. 1338, § 2.14, eff. Jan. 1, 2014. Subsec. (a) amended by Acts 2015, 84ᵗʰ Leg., ch. 378, § 4, eff. Sept. 1, 2015.

§ 123.053. Effect of Revocation

(a) An interest granted in a provision of a trust instrument that is revoked under Section 123.052(a)(1) or (2) passes as if the former spouse of the divorced individual who executed the trust instrument and each relative of the former spouse who is not a relative of the divorced individual disclaimed the interest granted in the provision.

(b) An interest granted in a provision of a trust instrument that is revoked under Section 123.052(a)(3) passes as if the former spouse and each relative of the former spouse who is not a relative of the divorced individual died immediately before the dissolution of the marriage.

Derived from Probate Code § 472(b).

Added by Acts 2009, 81st Leg., ch. 680, § 1, eff. Jan. 1, 2014. Amended by Acts 2011, 82nd Leg., ch. 1338, § 2.15, eff. Jan. 1, 2014.

§ 123.054. Liability of Certain Purchasers or Recipients of Certain Payments, Benefits, or Property

A bona fide purchaser of property from a divorced individual's former spouse or any relative of the former spouse who is not a relative of the divorced individual or a person who receives from the former spouse or any relative of the former spouse who is not a relative of the divorced individual a payment, benefit, or property in partial or full satisfaction of an enforceable obligation:

(1) is not required by this subchapter to return the payment, benefit, or property; and

(2) is not liable under this subchapter for the amount of the payment or the value of the property or benefit.

Derived from Probate Code § 473(a).

Added by Acts 2009, 81st Leg., ch. 680, § 1, eff. Jan. 1, 2014. Amended by Acts 2011, 82nd Leg., ch. 1338, § 2.16, eff. Jan. 1, 2014.

§ 123.055. Liability of Former Spouse for Certain Payments, Benefits, or Property

A divorced individual's former spouse or any relative of the former spouse who is not a relative of the divorced individual who, not for value, receives a payment, benefit, or property to which the former spouse or the relative of the former spouse who is not a relative of the divorced individual is not entitled as a result of Sections 123.052(a) and (b):

(1) shall return the payment, benefit, or property to the person who is entitled to the payment, benefit, or property under this subchapter; or

(2) is personally liable to the person described by Subdivision (1) for the amount of the payment or the value of the benefit or property received, as applicable.

Derived from Probate Code § 473(b).

Added by Acts 2009, 81st Leg., ch. 680, § 1, eff. Jan. 1, 2014. Amended by Acts 2011, 82nd Leg., ch. 1338, § 2.17, eff. Jan. 1, 2014.

Subchapter C. Certain Marriages Voidable After Death

Statutes in Context
Chapter 123, Subchapter C

The 2007 Legislature added a procedure to challenge the validity of a marriage based on the lack of mental capacity of one of the spouses even after the death of the allegedly incompetent spouse. If the court deems the marriage void, the surviving partner may not receive any benefits to which a surviving spouse is normally entitled such as the ability to be an heir and claim homestead rights. This section was designed to remedy marriages entered into due to the actions of abusive caregivers.

§ 123.101. Proceeding to Void Marriage Based on Mental Capacity Pending at Time of Death

(a) If a proceeding under Chapter 6, Family Code, to declare a marriage void based on the lack of mental capacity of one of the parties to the marriage is pending on the date of death of one of those parties, or if a guardianship proceeding in which a court is requested under Chapter 6, Family Code, to declare a ward's or proposed ward's marriage void based on the lack of mental capacity of the ward or proposed ward is pending on the date of the ward's or proposed ward's death, the court may make the determination and declare the marriage void after the decedent's death.

(b) In making a determination described by Subsection (a), the court shall apply the standards for an annulment prescribed by Section 6.108(a), Family Code.

Derived from Probate Code § 47A(a).

Added by Acts 2009, 81st Leg., ch. 680, § 1, eff. Jan. 1, 2014.

§ 123.102. Application to Void Marriage After Death

(a) Subject to Subsection (c), if a proceeding described by Section 123.101(a) is not pending on the date of a decedent's death, an interested person may file an application with the court requesting that the court void the marriage of the decedent if:

(1) on the date of the decedent's death, the decedent was married; and

(2) that marriage commenced not earlier than three years before the date of the decedent's death.

(b) The notice applicable to a proceeding for a declaratory judgment under Chapter 37, Civil Practice and Remedies Code, applies to a proceeding under Subsection (a).

(c) An application authorized by Subsection (a) may not be filed after the first anniversary of the date of the decedent's death.

Derived from Probate Code §§ 47A(b), (c).

Added by Acts 2009, 81st Leg., ch. 680, § 1, eff. Jan. 1, 2014.

§ 123.103. Action on Application to Void Marriage After Death

(a) Except as provided by Subsection (b), in a proceeding brought under Section 123.102, the court shall declare the decedent's marriage void if the court finds that, on the date the marriage occurred, the decedent did not have the mental capacity to:

(1) consent to the marriage; and

(2) understand the nature of the marriage ceremony, if a ceremony occurred.

(b) A court that makes a finding described by Subsection (a) may not declare the decedent's marriage void if the court finds that, after the date the marriage occurred, the decedent:

(1) gained the mental capacity to recognize the marriage relationship; and

(2) did recognize the marriage relationship.

Derived from Probate Code §§ 47A(d), (e).

Added by Acts 2009, 81st Leg., ch. 680, § 1, eff. Jan. 1, 2014.

§ 123.104. Effect of Voided Marriage

If the court declares a decedent's marriage void in a proceeding described by Section 123.101(a) or brought under Section 123.102, the other party to the marriage is not considered the decedent's surviving spouse for purposes of any law of this state.

Derived from Probate Code § 47A(f).

Added by Acts 2009, 81st Leg., ch. 680, § 1, eff. Jan. 1, 2014.

Subchapter D. Effect of Dissolution of Marriage on Certain Multiple-Party Accounts

Statutes in Contest
§ 123.151

The 2015 Legislature added this section so that provisions of a multiple-party account in favor of an ex-spouse or a relative of the ex-spouse who is not a relative of the decedent will not be effective to transfer the funds to the ex-spouse or ex-spouse's relative under most circumstances.

§ 123.151. Designation of Former Spouse or Relative of Former Spouse on Certain Multiple-Party Accounts

(a) In this section:

(1) "Beneficiary," "multiple-party account," "P.O.D. account," and "P.O.D. payee" have the meanings assigned by Chapter 113.

(2) "Public retirement system" has the meaning assigned by Section 802.001, Government Code.

(3) "Relative" has the meaning assigned by Section 123.051.

(b) If, after a decedent designates a spouse or a relative of a spouse who is not a relative of the decedent as a P.O.D. payee or beneficiary, including alternative P.O.D. payee or beneficiary, on a P.O.D. account or other multiple-party account, the decedent's marriage is dissolved by divorce, annulment, or a declaration that the marriage is void, the designation provision on the account is not effective as to the former spouse or the former spouse's relative unless:

(1) the court decree dissolving the marriage designates the former spouse or the former spouse's relative as the P.O.D. payee or beneficiary;

(2) the decedent redesignated the former spouse or the former spouse's relative as the P.O.D payee or beneficiary after the marriage was dissolved; or

(3) the former spouse or the former spouse's relative is designated to receive the proceeds or benefits in trust for, on behalf of, or for the benefit of a child or dependent of either the decedent or the former spouse.

(c) If a designation is not effective under Subsection (b), a multiple-party account is payable to the named alternative P.O.D. payee or beneficiary or, if an alternative P.O.D. payee or beneficiary is not named, to the estate of the decedent.

(d) A financial institution or other person obligated to pay an account described by Subsection (b) that pays the account to the former spouse or the former spouse's relative as P.O.D. payee or beneficiary under a designation that is not effective under Subsection (b) is liable for payment of the account to the person provided by Subsection (c) only if:

(1) before payment of the account to the designated P.O.D. payee or beneficiary, the payor receives written notice at the home office or principal office of the payor from an interested person that the designation of the P.O.D. payee or beneficiary is not effective under Subsection (b); and

(2) the payor has not interpleaded the account funds into the registry of a court of competent jurisdiction in accordance with the Texas Rules of Civil Procedure.

(e) This section does not affect the right of a former spouse to assert an ownership interest in an undivided multiple-party account described by Subsection (b).

(f) This section does not apply to the disposition of a beneficial interest in a retirement benefit or other financial plan of a public retirement system.

Added by Acts 2015, 84th Leg., ch. 995, § 5, eff. Sept. 1, 2015.

Chapter 124. Valuation and Taxation of Estate Property

Subchapter A. Apportionment of Taxes

Subchapter B. Satisfaction of Certain Pecuniary Gifts

Chapter 124. Valuation and Taxation of Estate Property

Subchapter A. Apportionment of Taxes

Statutes in Context
Chapter 124

The testator's estate may be subject to a tax on the privilege of making gratuitous transfers upon the testator's death, that is, the federal or Texas estate tax. What testamentary gifts bear the burden of these tax obligations? Some states do not have any special rules for tax liabilities. In other words, gifts abate to pay tax liabilities just like they do to pay other claims against the estate. On the other hand, an increasing number of states, including Texas in Chapter 124, have tax apportionment statutes so that the amount of each gift is reduced by the amount of estate tax attributable to the transfer. In effect, each transfer is reduced by its fair share of the tax rather than being subsidized by lower ranking gifts. Tax apportionment prevents the residual gift, which is often the most important gift in the will, from bearing the entire estate tax burden in addition to all of the other claims against the estate.

State and federal governments include many non-probate transfers in a testator's taxable estate. Chapter 124 covers these non-probate assets as well as testamentary transfers. Federal law mandates that life insurance beneficiaries and recipients under powers of appointment shoulder their fair share of transfer taxes. See I.R.C. §§ 2206 and 2207. Texas extends apportionment to other transfers, such as multiple-party bank accounts, survivorship rights, and trusts over which the testator held the power of revocation.

Chapter 124 is designed to carry out the testator's presumed intent. The legislature believed that most testators would want each transfer, be it probate or non-probate, to be responsible for its own tax. If the testator does not agree, the testator may provide otherwise in the will and those instructions will prevail over the apportionment statute. Note that the apportionment statute may be inadvertently trumped if the testator includes a generic clause in the will such as, "The executor shall pay all taxes payable because of my death from my residuary estate." See *Peterson v. Mayse*, 993 S.W.2d 217 (Tex. App. — Tyler 1999, writ denied).

§ 124.001. Definitions

In this subchapter:

(1) "Court" means:

(A) a court in which proceedings for administration of an estate are pending or have been completed; or

(B) if no proceedings are pending or have been completed, a court in which venue lies for the administration of an estate.

(2) "Estate" means the gross estate of a decedent as determined for the purpose of estate taxes.

(3) "Estate tax" means any estate, inheritance, or death tax levied or assessed on the property of a decedent's estate because of the death of a person and imposed by federal, state, local, or foreign law, including the federal estate tax and the inheritance tax imposed by former Chapter 211, Tax Code, and including interest and penalties imposed in addition to those taxes. The term does not include a tax imposed under Section 2701(d)(1)(A), Internal Revenue Code of 1986 (26 U.S.C. Section 2701(d)).

(4) "Person" includes a trust, natural person, partnership, association, joint stock company, corporation, government, political subdivision, or governmental agency.

(5) "Person interested in the estate" means a person, or a fiduciary on behalf of that person, who is entitled to receive or who has received, from a decedent or because of the death of the decedent, property included in the decedent's estate for purposes of the estate tax. The term does not include a creditor of the decedent or of the decedent's estate.

(6) "Representative" means the representative, executor, or administrator of an estate, or any other person who is required to pay estate taxes assessed against the estate.

Derived from Probate Code §§ 322A(a), (s).

Added by Acts 2009, 81st Leg., ch. 680, § 1, eff. Jan. 1, 2014. Subsec. (3) amended by Acts 2015, 84th Leg., ch. 1888, § 2, eff. Sept. 1, 2015.

§ 124.002. References to Internal Revenue Code

A reference in this subchapter to a section of the Internal Revenue Code of 1986 refers to that section as it exists at the time in question. The reference also includes a corresponding section of a subsequent Internal Revenue Code and, if the referenced section is renumbered, the section as renumbered.

Derived from Probate Code § 322A(x).

Added by Acts 2009, 81st Leg., ch. 680, § 1, eff. Jan. 1, 2014.

§ 124.003. Apportionment Directed by Federal Law

If federal law directs the apportionment of the federal estate tax, a similar state tax shall be apportioned in the same manner.

Derived from Probate Code § 322A(l).

Added by Acts 2009, 81st Leg., ch. 680, § 1, eff. Jan. 1, 2014.

§ 124.004. Effect of Disclaimers

This subchapter shall be applied after giving effect to any disclaimers made in accordance with Chapter 240, Property Code [Subchapters A, B, C, and D, Chapter 122].

Derived from Probate Code § 322A(p).

Added by Acts 2009, 81st Leg., ch. 680, § 1, eff. Jan. 1, 2014. Amended by Acts 2015, 84ᵗʰ Leg., ch. 562, § 8, eff. Sept. 1, 2015.

§ 124.005. General Apportionment of Estate Tax; Exceptions

(a) A representative shall charge each person interested in the estate a portion of the total estate tax assessed against the estate. The portion charged to each person must represent the same ratio as the taxable value of that person's interest in the estate included in determining the amount of the tax bears to the total taxable value of all the interests of all persons interested in the estate included in determining the amount of the tax. In apportioning an estate tax under this subsection, the representative shall disregard a portion of the tax that is:

(1) apportioned under the law imposing the tax;

(2) otherwise apportioned by federal law; or

(3) apportioned as otherwise provided by this subchapter.

(b) Subsection (a) does not apply to the extent the decedent, in a written inter vivos or testamentary instrument disposing of or creating an interest in property, specifically directs the manner of apportionment of estate tax or grants a discretionary power of apportionment to another person. A direction for the apportionment or nonapportionment of estate tax is limited to the estate tax on the property passing under the instrument unless the instrument is a will that provides otherwise.

(c) If directions under Subsection (b) for the apportionment of an estate tax are provided in two or more instruments executed by the same person and the directions in those instruments conflict, the instrument disposing of or creating an interest in the property to be taxed controls. If directions for the apportionment of estate tax are provided in two or more instruments executed by different persons and the directions in those instruments conflict, the direction of the person in whose estate the property is included controls.

(d) Subsections (b) and (c) do not:

(1) grant or enlarge the power of a person to apportion estate tax to property passing under an instrument created by another person in excess of the estate tax attributable to the property; or

(2) apply to the extent federal law directs a different manner of apportionment.

Derived from Probate Code § 322A(b).

Added by Acts 2009, 81st Leg., ch. 680, § 1, eff. Jan. 1, 2014.

§ 124.006. Effect of Tax Deductions, Exemptions, or Credits

(a) A deduction, exemption, or credit allowed by law in connection with the estate tax inures to a person interested in the estate as provided by this section.

(b) If the deduction, exemption, or credit is allowed because of the relationship of the person interested in the estate to the decedent, or because of the purpose of the gift, the deduction, exemption, or credit inures to the person having the relationship or receiving the gift, unless that person's interest in the estate is subject to a prior present interest that is not allowable as a deduction. The estate tax apportionable to the person having the present interest shall be paid from the corpus of the gift or the interest of the person having the relationship.

(c) A deduction for property of the estate that was previously taxed and a credit for gift taxes or death taxes of a foreign country that were paid by the decedent or the decedent's estate inure proportionally to all persons interested in the estate who are liable for a share of the estate tax.

(d) A credit for inheritance, succession, or estate taxes, or for similar taxes applicable to property or interests includable in the estate, inures to the persons interested in the estate who are chargeable with payment of a portion of those taxes to the extent that the credit proportionately reduces those taxes.

Derived from Probate Code §§ 322A(c), (d), (e), (f).

Added by Acts 2009, 81st Leg., ch. 680, § 1, eff. Jan. 1, 2014.

§ 124.007. Exclusion of Certain Property from Apportionment

(a) To the extent that property passing to or in trust for a surviving spouse or a charitable, public, or similar gift or devise is not an allowable deduction for purposes of the estate tax solely because of an inheritance tax or other death tax imposed on and deductible from the property:

(1) the property is not included in the computation provided for by Section 124.005; and

(2) no apportionment is made against the property.

(b) The exclusion provided by this section does not apply if the result would be to deprive the estate of a deduction otherwise allowable under Section 2053(d), Internal Revenue Code of 1986, for a state death tax on a transfer for a public, charitable, or religious use.

Derived from Probate Code § 322A(g).

Added by Acts 2009, 81st Leg., ch. 680, § 1, eff. Jan. 1, 2014.

§ 124.008. Exclusion of Certain Temporary Interests from Apportionment

(a) Except as provided by Section 124.009(c), the following temporary interests are not subject to apportionment:

(1) an interest in income;

(2) an estate for years or for life; or

(3) another temporary interest in any property or fund.

(b) The estate tax apportionable to a temporary interest described by Subsection (a) and the remainder, if any, is chargeable against the corpus of the property or the funds that are subject to the temporary interest and remainder.

Derived from Probate Code § 322A(h).

Added by Acts 2009, 81st Leg., ch. 680, § 1, eff. Jan. 1, 2014.

§ 124.009. Qualified Real Property

(a) In this section, "qualified real property" has the meaning assigned by Section 2032A, Internal Revenue Code of 1986 (26 U.S.C. Section 2032A).

(b) If an election is made under Section 2032A, Internal Revenue Code of 1986 (26 U.S.C. Section 2032A), the representative shall apportion estate taxes according to the amount of federal estate tax that would be payable if the election were not made. The representative shall apply the amount of the reduction of the estate tax resulting from the election to reduce the amount of the estate tax allocated based on the value of the qualified real property that is the subject of the election. If the amount of that reduction is greater than the amount of the taxes allocated based on the value of the qualified real property, the representative shall:

(1) apply the excess amount to the portion of the taxes allocated for all other property; and

(2) apportion the amount described by Subdivision (1) under Section 124.005(a).

(c) If additional federal estate tax is imposed under Section 2032A(c), Internal Revenue Code of 1986 (26 U.S.C. Section 2032A), because of an early disposition or cessation of a qualified use, the additional tax shall be equitably apportioned among the persons who have an interest in the portion of the qualified real property to which the additional tax is attributable in proportion to their interests. The additional tax is a charge against that qualified real property. If the qualified real property is split between one or more life or term interests and remainder interests, the additional tax shall be apportioned to each person whose action or cessation of use caused the imposition of additional tax, unless all persons with an interest in the qualified real property agree in writing to dispose of the property, in which case the additional tax shall be apportioned among the remainder interests.

Derived from Probate Code § 322A(i).

Added by Acts 2009, 81st Leg., ch. 680, § 1, eff. Jan. 1, 2014.

§ 124.010. Effect of Extension or Deficiency in Payment of Estate Taxes; Liability of Representative

(a) If the date for the payment of any portion of an estate tax is extended:

(1) the amount of the extended tax shall be apportioned to the persons who receive the specific property that gives rise to the extension; and

(2) those persons are entitled to the benefits and shall bear the burdens of the extension.

(b) Except as provided by Subsection (c), interest on an extension of estate tax and interest and penalties on a deficiency shall be apportioned equitably to reflect the benefits and burdens of the extension or deficiency and of any tax deduction associated with the interest and penalties.

(c) A representative shall be charged with the amount of any penalty or interest that is assessed due to delay caused by the representative's negligence.

Derived from Probate Code §§ 322A(k), (m).

Added by Acts 2009, 81st Leg., ch. 680, § 1, eff. Jan. 1, 2014.

§ 124.011. Apportionment of Interest and Penalties

(a) Interest and penalties assessed against an estate by a taxing authority shall be apportioned among and charged to the persons interested in the estate in the manner provided by Section 124.005 unless, on application by any person interested in the estate, the court determines that:

(1) the proposed apportionment is not equitable; or

(2) the assessment of interest or penalties was caused by a breach of fiduciary duty of a representative.

(b) If the apportionment is not equitable, the court may apportion interest and penalties in an equitable manner.

(c) If the assessment of interest or penalties was caused by a breach of fiduciary duty of a representative, the court may charge the representative with the amount of the interest and penalties assessed attributable to the representative's conduct.

Derived from Probate Code § 322A(q).

Added by Acts 2009, 81st Leg., ch. 680, § 1, eff. Jan. 1, 2014.

§ 124.012. Apportionment of Representative's Expenses

(a) Expenses reasonably incurred by a representative in determination of the amount, apportionment, or collection of the estate tax shall be apportioned among and charged to persons interested in the estate in the manner provided by Section 124.005 unless, on application by any person interested in the estate, the court determines that the proposed apportionment is not equitable.

(b) If the court determines that the proposed apportionment is not equitable, the court may apportion the expenses in an equitable manner.

Derived from Probate Code § 322A(r).

Added by Acts 2009, 81st Leg., ch. 680, § 1, eff. Jan. 1, 2014.

§ 124.013. Withholding of Estate Tax Share by Representative

A representative who has possession of any estate property that is distributable to a person interested in the estate may withhold from that property an amount equal to the person's apportioned share of the estate tax.

Derived from Probate Code § 322A(t).

Added by Acts 2009, 81st Leg., ch. 680, § 1, eff. Jan. 1, 2014.

§ 124.014. Recovery of Estate Tax Share Not Withheld

(a) If property includable in an estate does not come into possession of a representative obligated to pay the estate tax, the representative shall:

(1) recover from each person interested in the estate the amount of the estate tax apportioned to the person under this subchapter; or

(2) assign to persons affected by the tax obligation the representative's right of recovery.

(b) The obligation to recover a tax under Subsection (a) does not apply if:

(1) the duty is waived by the parties affected by the tax obligation or by the instrument under which the representative derives powers; or

(2) in the reasonable judgment of the representative, proceeding to recover the tax is not cost-effective.

Derived from Probate Code § 322A(n).

Added by Acts 2009, 81st Leg., ch. 680, § 1, eff. Jan. 1, 2014.

§ 124.015. Recovery of Unpaid Estate Tax; Reimbursement

(a) A representative shall recover from any person interested in the estate the unpaid amount of the estate tax apportioned and charged to the person under this subchapter unless the representative determines in good faith that an attempt to recover the amount would be economically impractical.

(b) A representative who cannot collect from a person interested in the estate an unpaid amount of estate tax apportioned to that person shall apportion the amount not collected in the manner provided by Section 124.005(a) among the other persons interested in the estate who are subject to apportionment.

(c) A person who is charged with or who pays an apportioned amount under Subsection (b) has a right of reimbursement for that amount from the person who failed to pay the tax. The representative may enforce the right of reimbursement, or the person who is charged with or who pays an apportioned amount under Subsection (b) may enforce the right of reimbursement directly by an assignment from the representative. A person assigned the right under this subsection is subrogated to the rights of the representative.

(d) A representative who has a right of reimbursement may petition a court to determine the right of reimbursement.

Derived from Probate Code §§ 322A(o), (u).

Added by Acts 2009, 81st Leg., ch. 680, § 1, eff. Jan. 1, 2014.

§ 124.016. Time to Initiate Actions to Recover Unpaid Estate Tax

(a) A representative required to recover unpaid amounts of estate tax apportioned to persons interested in the estate under this subchapter may not be required to initiate the necessary actions until the expiration of the 90th day after the date of the final determination by the Internal Revenue Service of the amount of the estate tax.

(b) A representative who initiates an action under this subchapter within a reasonable time after the expiration of the 90-day period is not subject to any liability or surcharge because a portion of the estate tax apportioned to a person interested in the estate was collectible during a period after the death of the decedent but thereafter became uncollectible.

Derived from Probate Code § 322A(v).

Added by Acts 2009, 81st Leg., ch. 680, § 1, eff. Jan. 1, 2014.

§ 124.017. Tax or Death Duty Payable to Another State

(a) A representative acting in another state may initiate an action in a court of this state to recover from a person interested in the estate who is domiciled in this state or owns property in this state subject to attachment or execution, a proportionate amount of:

(1) the federal estate tax;

(2) an estate tax payable to another state; or

(3) a death duty due by a decedent's estate to another state.

(b) In the action, a determination of apportionment by the court having jurisdiction of the administration of the decedent's estate in the other state is prima facie correct.

(c) This section applies only if the state in which the determination of apportionment was made provides a substantially similar remedy.

Derived from Probate Code § 322A(w).

Added by Acts 2009, 81st Leg., ch. 680, § 1, eff. Jan. 1, 2014.

§ 124.018. Payment of Expenses and Attorney's Fees

The court shall award necessary expenses, including reasonable attorney's fees, to the prevailing party in an action initiated by a person for the collection of estate taxes from a person interested in the estate to whom estate taxes were apportioned and charged under Section 124.005.

Derived from Probate Code § 322A(y).

Added by Acts 2009, 81st Leg., ch. 680, § 1, eff. Jan. 1, 2014.

Subchapter B. Satisfaction of Certain Pecuniary Gifts

Statutes in Context
Chapter 124, Subchapter B

Chapter 124, Subchapter B, helps assure that marital deduction pecuniary gifts which authorize in-kind distribution of assets meet the "fairly representative" test and thus qualify for the deduction.

§ 124.051. Valuation of Property Distributed in Kind in Satisfaction of Pecuniary Gift

Unless the governing instrument provides otherwise, if a will or trust contains a pecuniary devise or transfer that may be satisfied by distributing assets in kind and the executor, administrator, or trustee determines to fund the devise or transfer by distributing assets in kind, the property shall be valued, for the purpose of funding the devise or transfer, at the value of the property on the date or dates of distribution.

Derived from Probate Code § 378A(b).

Added by Acts 2009, 81st Leg., ch. 680, § 1, eff. Jan. 1, 2014.

§ 124.052. Satisfaction of Marital Deduction Pecuniary Gifts with Assets in Kind

(a) This section applies to an executor, administrator, or trustee authorized under the will or trust of a decedent to satisfy a pecuniary devise or transfer in trust in kind with assets at their value for federal estate tax purposes, in satisfaction of a gift intended to qualify, or that otherwise would qualify, for a United States estate tax marital deduction.

(b) Unless the governing instrument provides otherwise, an executor, administrator, or trustee, in order to implement a devise or transfer described by Subsection (a), shall distribute assets, including cash, fairly representative of appreciation or depreciation in the value of all property available for distribution in satisfaction of the devise or transfer.

Derived from Probate Code § 378A(a).

Added by Acts 2009, 81st Leg., ch. 680, § 1, eff. Jan. 1, 2014.

SUBTITLE D. PROCEEDINGS BEFORE ADMINISTRATION OF ESTATE

Chapter 151. Examination of Documents and Safe Deposit Boxes

Chapter 151. Examination of Documents and Safe Deposit Boxes

Statutes in Context
Chapter 151

A testator often protects the will and other important documents by placing them in a safe deposit box. Chapter 151 provides guidelines for certain parties, such as a spouse, parent, adult descendent, or executor, to gain access to the safe deposit box for the purpose of obtaining the decedent's will as well as a burial plot deed and life insurance policies. These provisions provide procedures for both court and non-court ordered access.

§ 151.001. Examination of Documents or Safe Deposit Box with Court Order

(a) A judge of a court that has probate jurisdiction of a decedent's estate may order a person to permit a court representative named in the order to examine a decedent's documents or safe deposit box if it is shown to the judge that:

(1) the person may possess or control the documents or that the person leased the safe deposit box to the decedent; and

(2) the documents or safe deposit box may contain:

(A) a will of the decedent;

(B) a deed to a burial plot in which the decedent is to be buried; or

(C) an insurance policy issued in the decedent's name and payable to a beneficiary named in the policy.

(b) The court representative shall examine the decedent's documents or safe deposit box in the presence of:

(1) the judge ordering the examination or an agent of the judge; and

(2) the person who has possession or control of the documents or who leased the safe deposit box or, if that person is a corporation, an officer of the corporation or an agent of an officer.

Derived from Probate Code § 36B.

Added by Acts 2009, 81st Leg., ch. 680, § 1, eff. Jan. 1, 2014.

§ 151.002. Delivery of Document with Court Order

(a) A judge who orders an examination of a decedent's documents or safe deposit box under Section

151.001 may order the person who possesses or controls the documents or who leases the safe deposit box to permit the court representative to take possession of a document described by Section 151.001(a)(2).

(b) The court representative shall deliver:

(1) a will to the clerk of a court that:

(A) has probate jurisdiction; and

(B) is located in the same county as the court of the judge who ordered the examination under Section 151.001;

(2) a burial plot deed to the person designated by the judge in the order for the examination; or

(3) an insurance policy to a beneficiary named in the policy.

(c) A court clerk to whom a will is delivered under Subsection (b) shall issue a receipt for the will to the court representative.

Derived from Probate Code § 36C.

Added by Acts 2009, 81st Leg., ch. 680, § 1, eff. Jan. 1, 2014.

§ 151.003. Examination of Document or Safe Deposit Box Without Court Order

(a) A person who possesses or controls a document delivered by a decedent for safekeeping or who leases a safe deposit box to a decedent may permit examination of the document or the contents of the safe deposit box by:

(1) the decedent's spouse;

(2) a parent of the decedent;

(3) a descendant of the decedent who is at least 18 years of age; or

(4) a person named as executor of the decedent's estate in a copy of a document that the person has and that appears to be a will of the decedent.

(b) An examination under Subsection (a) shall be conducted in the presence of the person who possesses or controls the document or who leases the safe deposit box or, if the person is a corporation, an officer of the corporation.

Derived from Probate Code § 36D.

Added by Acts 2009, 81st Leg., ch. 680, § 1, eff. Jan. 1, 2014.

§ 151.004. Delivery of Document Without Court Order

(a) Subject to Subsection (c), a person who permits an examination of a decedent's document or safe deposit box under Section 151.003 may deliver:

(1) a document appearing to be the decedent's will to:

(A) the clerk of a court that:

(i) has probate jurisdiction; and

(ii) is located in the county in which the decedent resided; or

(B) a person named in the document as an executor of the decedent's estate;

(2) a document appearing to be a deed to a burial plot in which the decedent is to be buried, or appearing to give burial instructions, to the person conducting the examination; or

(3) a document appearing to be an insurance policy on the decedent's life to a beneficiary named in the policy.

(b) A person who has leased a safe deposit box to the decedent shall keep a copy of a document delivered by the person under Subsection (a)(1) until the fourth anniversary of the date of delivery.

(c) A person may not deliver a document under Subsection (a) unless the person examining the document:

(1) requests delivery of the document; and

(2) issues a receipt for the document to the person delivering the document.

Derived from Probate Code § 36E.

Added by Acts 2009, 81st Leg., ch. 680, § 1, eff. Jan. 1, 2014.

§ 151.005. Restriction on Removal of Contents of Safe Deposit Box

A person may not remove the contents of a decedent's safe deposit box except as provided by Section 151.002, Section 151.004, or another law.

Derived from Probate Code § 36F.

Added by Acts 2009, 81st Leg., ch. 680, § 1, eff. Jan. 1, 2014.

Chapter 152. Emergency Intervention

Subchapter A. Emergency Intervention Application

Subchapter B. Order for Emergency Intervention

Subchapter C. Limitation on Right of Decedent's Surviving Spouse to Control Decedent's Burial or Cremation

§ 152.101. Application Authorized

§ 152.102. Hearing; Issuance of Order

Chapter 152. Emergency Intervention

Subchapter A. Emergency Intervention Application

Statutes in Context
Chapter 152

Chapter 152 provides a method for a person qualified to serve as an administrator under § 304.001 to obtain court permission in an accelerated time frame to (1) obtain access to the decedent's funds to pay for the decedent's funeral and burial expenses and (2) to obtain access to the decedent's rented residence (e.g., an apartment) to remove and protect the decedent's personal property. The application cannot be filed earlier than the third day after the decedent's death or later than the ninetieth day after the decedent's death.

---

§ 152.001. Application Authorized

(a) Subject to Subsection (b), a person qualified to serve as an administrator under Section 304.001 may file an application requesting emergency intervention by a court exercising probate jurisdiction to provide for:

(1) the payment of the decedent's funeral and burial expenses; or

(2) the protection and storage of personal property owned by the decedent that, on the date of the decedent's death, was located in accommodations rented by the decedent.

(b) An applicant may file an application under this section only if:

(1) an application or affidavit has not been filed and is not pending under Section 256.052, 256.054, or 301.052 or Chapter 205 or 401; and

(2) the applicant needs to:

(A) obtain funds for the payment of the decedent's funeral and burial expenses; or

(B) gain access to accommodations rented by the decedent that contain the decedent's personal property and the applicant has been denied access to those accommodations.

Derived from Probate Code §§ 108, 109, & 110.

Added by Acts 2009, 81st Leg., ch. 680, § 1, eff. Jan. 1, 2014. Subsection (b) amended by Acts 2013, 83rd Leg., ch. 161, § 6.010, eff. Jan. 1, 2014.

§ 152.002. Contents of Application

(a) An emergency intervention application must be sworn and must contain:

(1) the applicant's name, address, and interest;

(2) facts showing an immediate necessity for the issuance of an emergency intervention order under Subchapter B;

(3) the decedent's date of death, place of death, and residential address on the date of death;

(4) the name and address of the funeral home holding the decedent's remains; and

(5) the names of any known or ascertainable heirs and devisees of the decedent.

(b) In addition to the information required under Subsection (a), if emergency intervention is requested to obtain funds needed for the payment of the decedent's funeral and burial expenses, the application must also contain:

(1) the reason any known or ascertainable heirs and devisees of the decedent:

(A) cannot be contacted; or

(B) have refused to assist in the decedent's burial;

(2) a description of necessary funeral and burial procedures and a statement from the funeral home that contains a detailed and itemized description of the cost of those procedures; and

(3) the name and address of an individual, entity, or financial institution, including an employer, in possession of any funds of or due to the decedent, and related account numbers and balances, if known by the applicant.

(c) In addition to the information required under Subsection (a), if emergency intervention is requested to gain access to accommodations rented by a decedent that at the time of the decedent's death contain the decedent's personal property, the application must also contain:

(1) the reason any known or ascertainable heirs and devisees of the decedent:

(A) cannot be contacted; or

(B) have refused to assist in the protection of the decedent's personal property;

(2) the type and location of the decedent's personal property and the name of the person in possession of the property; and

(3) the name and address of the owner or manager of the accommodations and a statement regarding whether access to the accommodations is necessary.

Derived from Probate Code §§ 111(a), 112.

Added by Acts 2009, 81st Leg., ch. 680, § 1, eff. Jan. 1, 2014.

§ 152.003. Additional Contents of Application: Instructions Regarding Decedent's Funeral and Remains

(a) In addition to the information required under Section 152.002, if emergency intervention is requested to obtain funds needed for the payment of a decedent's funeral and burial expenses, the application must also state whether there are any written instructions from the decedent relating to the type and manner of funeral or burial preferred by the decedent. The applicant shall:

(1) attach the instructions, if available, to the application; and

(2) fully comply with the instructions.

(b) If written instructions do not exist, the applicant may not permit the decedent's remains to be cremated unless the applicant obtains the court's permission to cremate the remains.

Derived from Probate Code § 111(b).

Added by Acts 2009, 81st Leg., ch. 680, § 1, eff. Jan. 1, 2014.

§ 152.004. Time and Place of Filing

An emergency intervention application must be filed:

(1) with the court clerk in the county in which:

(A) the decedent was domiciled; or

(B) the accommodations rented by the decedent that contain the decedent's personal property are located; and

(2) not earlier than the third day after the date of the decedent's death and not later than the 90th day after the date of the decedent's death.

Derived from Probate Code § 108.

Added by Acts 2009, 81st Leg., ch. 680, § 1, eff. Jan. 1, 2014.

Subchapter B. Order for Emergency Intervention

§ 152.051. Issuance of Order Regarding Funeral and Burial Expenses

If on review of an application filed under Section 152.001 the court determines that emergency intervention is necessary to obtain funds needed for the payment of a decedent's funeral and burial expenses, the court may order funds of the decedent that are being held by an individual, an employer, or a financial institution to be paid directly to a funeral home only for:

(1) reasonable and necessary attorney's fees for the attorney who obtained the order;

(2) court costs for obtaining the order; and

(3) funeral and burial expenses not to exceed $5,000 as ordered by the court to provide the decedent with a reasonable, dignified, and appropriate funeral and burial.

Derived from Probate Code § 113(a).

Added by Acts 2009, 81st Leg., ch. 680, § 1, eff. Jan. 1, 2014.

§ 152.052. Issuance of Order Regarding Access to Certain Personal Property

If on review of an application filed under Section 152.001 the court determines that emergency intervention is necessary to gain access to accommodations rented by the decedent that, at the time

of the decedent's death, contain the decedent's personal property, the court may order one or more of the following:

(1) that the owner or agent of the accommodations shall grant the applicant access to the accommodations at a reasonable time and in the presence of the owner or agent;

(2) that the applicant and owner or agent of the accommodations shall jointly prepare and file with the court a list that generally describes the decedent's property found at the premises;

(3) that the applicant or the owner or agent of the accommodations may remove and store the decedent's property at another location until claimed by the decedent's heirs;

(4) that the applicant has only the powers that are specifically stated in the order and that are necessary to protect the decedent's property that is the subject of the application; or

(5) that funds of the decedent held by an individual, an employer, or a financial institution be paid to the applicant for reasonable and necessary attorney's fees and court costs for obtaining the order.

Derived from Probate Code § 113(b).

Added by Acts 2009, 81st Leg., ch. 680, § 1, eff. Jan. 1, 2014.

§ 152.053. Duration of Order

The authority of an applicant under an emergency intervention order expires on the earlier of:

(1) the 90th day after the date the order is issued; or

(2) the date a personal representative of the decedent's estate qualifies.

Derived from Probate Code § 114(a).

Added by Acts 2009, 81st Leg., ch. 680, § 1, eff. Jan. 1, 2014.

§ 152.054. Certified Copies of Order

The court clerk may issue certified copies of an emergency intervention order on request of the applicant only until the earlier of:

(1) the 90th day after the date the order is signed; or

(2) the date a personal representative of the decedent's estate qualifies.

Derived from Probate Code § 113(c).

Added by Acts 2009, 81st Leg., ch. 680, § 1, eff. Jan. 1, 2014.

§ 152.055. Liability of Certain Persons in Connection with Order

(a) A person who is provided a certified copy of an emergency intervention order within the period prescribed by Section 152.054 is not personally liable for an action taken by the person in accordance with and in reliance on the order.

(b) If a personal representative has not been appointed when an emergency intervention order issued under Section 152.052 expires, a person in possession of the decedent's personal property that is the subject of the order, without incurring civil liability, may:

(1) release the property to the decedent's heirs; or

(2) dispose of the property under Subchapter C, Chapter 54, Property Code, or Section 7.209 or 7.210, Business & Commerce Code.

Derived from Probate Code §§ 113(d), 114(b).

Added by Acts 2009, 81st Leg., ch. 680, § 1, eff. Jan. 1, 2014.

Subchapter C. Limitation on Right of Decedent's Surviving Spouse to Control Decedent's Burial or Cremation

Statutes in Context
Chapter 152

Chapter 152 permits the person serving as the executor of a deceased spouse's will or the deceased spouse's next of kin to file an application to limit the right of the surviving spouse to control the deceased spouse's burial or cremation. The purpose of this procedure is to prevent a spouse who is suspected of being involved in the deceased spouse's death from burying or cremating the deceased spouse's body and thereby concealing or destroying potentially inculpatory evidence. See also Health & Safety Code § 711.002.

§ 152.101. Application Authorized

(a) The executor of a decedent's will or the decedent's next of kin may file an application for an order limiting the right of the decedent's surviving spouse to control the decedent's burial or cremation.

(b) For purposes of Subsection (a), the decedent's next of kin:

(1) is determined in accordance with order of descent, with the person nearest in order of descent first, and so on; and

(2) includes the decedent's descendants who legally adopted the decedent or who have been legally adopted by the decedent.

(c) An application under this section must be under oath and must establish:

(1) whether the decedent died intestate or testate;

(2) that the surviving spouse is alleged to be a principal or accomplice in a wilful act that resulted in the decedent's death; and

(3) that good cause exists to limit the surviving spouse's right to control the decedent's burial or cremation.

Derived from Probate Code §§ 115(a), (b).

Added by Acts 2009, 81st Leg., ch. 680, § 1, eff. Jan. 1, 2014.

§ 152.102. Hearing; Issuance of Order

(a) If the court finds that there is good cause to believe that the decedent's surviving spouse is the principal or an accomplice in a wilful act that resulted in the decedent's death, the court may, after notice and a hearing, limit the surviving spouse's right to control the decedent's burial or cremation.

(b) Subsection (a) applies:

(1) without regard to whether the decedent died intestate or testate;

(2) regardless of whether the surviving spouse is designated by the decedent's will as the executor of the decedent's estate; and

(3) subject to the prohibition described by Section 711.002(l), Health and Safety Code.

(c) If the court limits the surviving spouse's right of control as provided by Subsection (a), the court shall designate and authorize a person to make burial or cremation arrangements.

Derived from Probate Code § 115(c), (d).

Added by Acts 2009, 81st Leg., ch. 680, § 1, eff. Jan. 1, 2014. Subsection (b) amended by Acts 2013, 83rd Leg., ch. 161, § 6.011, eff. Jan. 1, 2014.

Chapter 153. Access to Intestate's Account With Financial Institution

Statutes in Context
Chapter 153

If an intestate dies owning a bank account that has funds which do not pass to another person under the terms of the account, an interested person may apply to the court for an order requiring the financial institution to reveal the balance in the account if 90 days have passed since the intestate died, no letters have been issued, and no petition for the appointment of a personal representative is pending. This procedure, added by the 2015 Legislature, will help heirs determine the appropriate administration method for the decedent's estate.

Chapter 153. Access to Intestate's Account With Financial Institution

§ 153.001. Definitions

In this chapter:

(1) "Account" has the meaning assigned by Section 113.001.

(2) "Financial institution" has the meaning assigned by Section 201.101, Finance Code.

(3) "P.O.D. account" and "trust account" have the meanings assigned by Section 113.004.

New.

Added by Acts 2015, 84ᵗʰ Leg., ch. 217, § 1, eff. Sept. 1, 2015.

§ 153.002. Inapplicability of Chapter

This chapter does not apply to:
(1) an account with a beneficiary designation;
(2) a P.O.D. account;
(3) a trust account; or
(4) an account that provides for a right of survivorship.

New.

Added by Acts 2015, 84ᵗʰ Leg., ch. 217, § 1, eff. Sept. 1, 2015.

§ 153.003. Court-Ordered Access to Intestate's Account Information

(a) In this section, "interested person" means an heir, spouse, creditor, or any other having a property right in or claim against the decedent's estate.

(b) On application of an interested person or on the court's own motion, a court may issue an order requiring a financial institution to release to the person named in the order information concerning the balance of each account that is maintained at the financial institution of a decedent who dies intestate if:
(1) 90 days have elapsed since the date of the decedent's death;
(2) no petition for the appointment of a personal representative for the decedent's estate is pending; and
(3) no letters testamentary or of administration have been granted with respect to the estate.

New.

Added by Acts 2015, 84ᵗʰ Leg., ch. 217, § 1, eff. Sept. 1, 2015.

SUBTITLE E. INTESTATE SUCCESSION

Chapter 201. Descent and Distribution

Subchapter A. Intestate Succession

Subchapter B. Matters Affecting Inheritance

Subchapter C. Distribution to Heirs

Subchapter D. Advancements

Chapter 201. Descent and Distribution

Statutes in Context
Chapter 201

The new owner of a person's property upon death depends on two main factors — first, the type of asset and, second, whether the decedent made a valid will. Certain property, commonly referred to as non-probate assets, is controlled by the terms of the property arrangement itself. Examples of these arrangements include land held in joint tenancy with survivorship rights and contractual arrangements which specify the at-death owner such as life insurance and pay on death accounts at banks, savings and loan associations, and other financial institutions. The passage of the remaining property, the probate estate, depends on whether the decedent died after executing a valid will which disposed of all of the decedent's probate property.

Chapter 201 of the Estates Code governs what happens when a person dies without a valid will or dies with a valid will which does not encompass all of the person's probate estate. When this happens, the person's probate property which is not covered by a valid will is distributed through a process called intestate succession. A person may die totally intestate, that is, intestate as to the person, if the person did not leave any type of valid will. A person may also die partially intestate, that is, intestate as to property, if the person's valid will fails to dispose of all of the person's probate estate.

Subchapter A. Intestate Succession

Statutes in Context
Chapter 201, Subchapter A

Early in the evolution of civilization, societies developed customs and laws to control the transmission of a person's property after death. Our modern intestacy laws are traced originally to the Anglo-Saxons. The Norman Conquest of 1066 A.D. played a significant role in the development of these rules. William the Conqueror was irritated that English landowners refused to recognize his right to the English Crown after his victory. Accordingly, William took ownership of all land by force and instituted the Norman form of feudalism. Under this system, the Crown was the true owner of all real property with others holding the property in a hierarchical scheme under which lower-ranked holders owed various financial and service-oriented duties to higher-ranked holders.

As a result, real property became the most essential element in the political, economic, and social structure of the Middle Ages. The Crown and its tough royal courts controlled the descent of real property. The basic features of descent included the following rules. (1) Male heirs inherited real property to the exclusion of female heirs unless no male heir existed. The reason underlying this discriminatory preference for male over female heirs was based on the feudal incidents of ownership. One of the primary duties of lower-ranked holders of property was to provide military service to higher-ranked holders. Under the then existing social climate, women were deemed unable to perform these services and thus were not able to inherit realty if a male heir existed. (2) If two or more males were equally related to the decedent, the oldest male would inherit all of the land to the total exclusion of the younger males. This is the rule of primogeniture. Primogeniture was applied because the Crown thought it was too impractical to divide the duty to provide military services as well as to subdivide the property. (3) If there were no male heirs and several female heirs, each female heir shared equally.

Before the industrial revolution, personal property was of lesser importance. There were no machines or corporate securities about which to worry. Instead, most chattels were of relatively little value such as clothing, furniture, jewelry, and livestock. Thus, the Crown permitted the church and its courts to govern the distribution of personal property. The ecclesiastical courts based distribution on canon law which had its foundation in Roman law. In general, personal property was distributed equally among equally related heirs. There was no preference for male heirs and the ages of the heirs were irrelevant.

After centuries of movement toward a unified system, the English Parliament passed the Administration of Estates Act in 1925 which abolished primogeniture and the preference for male heirs as well as providing uniform rules for all types of property. Most intestacy statutes in the United States make no distinction based on the age and sex of the heirs nor between the descent of real property and the distribution of personal property. However, Texas and a few other states retain this latter common law principle and provide different intestacy schemes for real and personal property under certain circumstances.

The intestate distribution scheme in Texas is derived from §§ 201.001–201.002 (distribution of property of a single decedent and the separate property of a married decedent), § 201.003 (distribution of the community property of a married decedent), and § 201.101 (determination of the type of distribution). Below is a summary of these sections assuming that the decedent died on or after September 1, 1993.

A. Individual Property Distribution (Unmarried Intestate)

The distribution of the property of an unmarried intestate is governed by Estates Code § 201.001. Real and personal property are treated the same.

1. Descendants Survive

If the unmarried intestate is survived by one of more descendants (e.g., children or grandchildren), then all of the intestate's property passes to the descendants. See § D, below, for a discussion of how this distribution is done.

2. No Descendants Survive But a Parent Survives

The following distributions occur if the unmarried intestate has no surviving descendants but does have at least one surviving parent.

a. Both Parents Survive

If both parents survived the intestate, each parent inherits one-half of the estate.

b. One Parent Survives Along With a Sibling or a Sibling's Descendants

If only one parent survives and the intestate is also survived by at least one sibling or a descendant of a sibling (e.g., niece or nephew), then the surviving parent receives one-half of the estate with the remaining one-half passing to the siblings and their descendants. See § D, below, for a discussion of how this distribution is done.

c. One Parent Survives but No Sibling or Descendant of a Sibling Survives

If one parent survives and there is no surviving sibling or a descendant of a sibling, then the surviving parent inherits the entire estate.

3. No Surviving Descendants or Parents

If the unmarried intestate is survived by neither descendants nor parents, then the entire estate passes to siblings and their descendants. See § D, below, for a discussion of how this distribution is done.

4. No Surviving Descendants, Parents, Siblings or Their Descendants

If the unmarried intestate has no surviving descendants, parents, siblings or their descendants, the estate is divided into two halves (moieties) with one half going to paternal grandparents, uncles, cousins, etc. and the other half to the maternal side. Texas does not have a laughing heir statute preventing these remote relatives from inheriting. If one side of the family has completely died out, the entire estate will pass to the surviving side. See *State v. Estate of Loomis*, 553 S.W.2d 166 (Tex. Civ. App.—Tyler 1977, writ ref'd).

5. No Surviving Heir

If the unmarried intestate has no surviving heir, the property will escheat to the state of Texas under Property Code § 71.001.

B. Distribution of Community Property of Married Intestate

The distribution of the community property of an intestate who was married at the time of death is governed by Estates Code § 201.003. Real and personal property are treated the same.

1. If No Surviving Descendants

If the married intestate has no surviving descendants, then all community property is now owned by the surviving spouse. The surviving spouse (1) retains the one-half of the community property that the surviving spouse owned once the marriage was dissolved by death and (2) inherits the deceased spouse's one-half of the community.

2. If Surviving Children or Their Descendants

Community property is distributed as follows if the married intestate has at least one surviving child or other descendant.

a. No Non-Spousal Descendants

If all of the deceased spouse's surviving descendants are also descendants of the surviving spouse, then the surviving spouse will own all of the community property, that is, the surviving spouse retains his or her one-half of the community and inherits the other half. Note that for spouses dying before September 1, 1993, the deceased spouse's one-half of the community property was not inherited by the surviving spouse. Instead, the deceased spouse's share passed to the deceased spouse's descendants.

b. Non-Spousal Descendants

If any of the deceased spouse's surviving descendants are not also descendants of the surviving spouse, then the community property is divided. The surviving spouse retains one-half of the community property, that is, the one-half the surviving spouse already owned by virtue of it being community property. The descendants of the deceased spouse inherit the deceased spouse's one-half of the community property. All of the deceased spouse's descendants are treated as a group regardless of whether the other parent is or is not the surviving spouse.

C. Distribution of Separate Property of Married Intestate

Unlike most states, Texas has retained a vestige of the common law distinction between the descent of real property and the distribution of personal property in § 201.002.

If the intestate was in the midst of a real estate transaction at the time of death, it becomes significant to determine whether the intestate's interest is real or personal property. Texas courts hold that *equitable conversion* occurs. Thus, after a contract for the purchase and sale of real property is signed but before closing, the seller is treated as owning personal property (the right to the sales proceeds) and the buyer as owing real property (the right to specifically enforce the contract). *Parson v. Wolfe*, 676 S.W.2d 689 (Tex. App.—Amarillo 1984, no writ).

1. Surviving Descendants

a. Personal Property

The surviving spouse receives one-third of the deceased spouse's separate personal property with the remaining two-thirds passing to the children or their descendants. These interests are outright.

b. Real Property

The surviving spouse receives a life estate in one-third of the deceased spouse's separate real property. The rest of the property, that is, the outright interest in two-thirds of the separate real property and the remainder interest following the surviving spouse's life estate passes to the deceased spouse's children or their descendants.

2. No Surviving Descendants

a. Personal Property

If there are no surviving descendants, all separate personal property passes to the surviving spouse.

b. Real Property

(1) Surviving Parents, Siblings, or Descendants of Siblings

If there are no surviving descendants but there are surviving parents, siblings, or descendants of siblings, the surviving spouse inherits one-half of the separate real property outright with the remaining one-half passing to the parents, siblings, and descendants of siblings as if the intestate died without a surviving spouse (that is, this one-half passes using the same scheme as for individual property).

(2) No Surviving Parents, Siblings, or Descendants of Siblings

If the intestate has no surviving descendants, parents, siblings, or descendants of siblings, the surviving spouse inherits all of the separate real property.

D. Type of Distribution

Whenever individuals such as children, grandchildren, siblings and their descendants, cousins, etc. are heirs, you must determine how to divide their shares among them. See Estates Code § 201.101.

1. Per Capita

If the heirs are all of the *same degree* of relationship to the intestate, then they take per capita, i.e., each heir takes the same amount. For example, if all takers are children, each receives an equal share. If all children are deceased, then each grandchild takes an equal share.

2. Per Capita by Representation

If the heirs are of *different degrees* of relationship to decedent, e.g., children and grandchildren, the younger generation takers share what the older generation taker would have received had that person survived. For example, assume that Grandfather had three children; two of whom predeceased Grandfather. One-third passes to the surviving child, with one-third passing to the children of each deceased child (grandchildren). If each deceased child had a different number of grandchildren, the shares of the grandchildren will be different. For example, if one deceased child had two children, each gets one-sixth; if the other deceased child had three children, each would receive one-ninth.

EXAMPLES

Example 1: Wilma, a widow, dies intestate survived by her only son, Sammy, and her father, Frank. How is Wilma's property distributed?

Answer: Wilma's entire estate passes to Sammy.

Example 2: Harry, a widower, dies intestate survived by his mother, Mary, and his two brothers, Bruce and Bob. How is Harry's property distributed?

Answer: One-half of Harry's estate passes to Mary. Bruce and Bob each receive one-quarter.

Example 3: Husband (H) and Wife (W) have three children, Amy (A), Brad (B), and Charles (C). All three children are married and have children of their own. A has one child, Mike (M). B has three children, Nancy (N), Opie (O), and Pat (P). C's children are Robert (R) and Susan (S). H died intestate with both community and separate property. In addition, H owned real and personal property of each type.

a. How would H's property be distributed?

Answer: All of H's community property is now owned by W; W keeps the one-half she owned by virtue of it being community property and W inherits H's one-half.

W receives one-third of H's separate personal property. Each of A, B, and C receive 2/9 of H's separate personal property.

W receives a life estate in one-third of H's separate real property. Each of A, B, and C receive 2/9 outright in H's separate real property as well as one-third of the remainder in W's life estate.

b. Assume that both B and C predeceased H. How would H's property be distributed?

Answer: All of H's community property is now owned by W; W keeps the one-half she owned by virtue of it being community property and W inherits H's one-half.

W receives one-third of H's separate personal property. A receives 2/9 of H's separate personal property, each of N, O, and P receive 2/27 and each of R and S receive 1/9.

W receives a life estate in one-third of H's separate real property. A receives 2/9 outright in H's separate real property plus one-third of the remainder in W's life estate. Each of N, O, and P receive 2/27 outright in H's separate real property plus 1/9 of the remainder in W's life estate. Each of R and S receive 1/9 outright in H's separate real property plus 1/6 of the remainder in W's life estate.

c. Assume that A, B, and C predeceased H. How would H's property be distributed?

Answer: All of H's community property is now owned by W; W keeps the one-half she owned by virtue of it being community property and W inherits H's one-half.

W receives one-third of H's separate personal property. Each of the six grandchildren (M, N, O, P, R, and S) receive 1/9 of H's separate personal property.

W receives a life estate in one-third of H's separate real property. Each of the six grandchildren receive 1/9 outright in H's separate real property plus 1/6 of the remainder in W's life estate.

d. Answer questions (a), (b), and (c) assuming that A's mother is X instead of W.

Answer: Only the distribution of community property in each case is different. In each situation, W would only retain her one-half of the community. H's share of the community property passes to his descendants because not all of his descendants are descendants of W. In (a), each of A, B, and C would get 1/6 of the total community (1/3 of H's one-half). In (b), A would receive 1/6, each of N, O, and P, 1/18, and each of R and S, 1/12. In (c), each grandchild would receive 1/12 of the total community.

Example 4: Mother and Father, now deceased, had three children, Arthur, Bill, and Chris. Arthur died survived by his wife, Peggy, and their two children, Linda and Ken. Bill is unmarried and childless. Chris is married to Wendy and they have no children. Chris died intestate with both community and separate property. In addition, Chris owned real and personal property of each type. How would Chris' property be distributed?

Answer: Wendy receives all the community property, all separate personal property, and one-half of the separate real property. Bill receives ¼ of the separate real property and Linda and Ken each receive 1/8 of the separate real property.

§ 201.001. Estate of an Intestate Not Leaving Spouse

(a) If a person who dies intestate does not leave a spouse, the estate to which the person had title descends and passes in parcenary to the person's kindred in the order provided by this section.

(b) The person's estate descends and passes to the person's children and the children's descendants.

(c) If no child or child's descendant survives the person, the person's estate descends and passes in equal portions to the person's father and mother.

(d) If only the person's father or mother survives the person, the person's estate shall:

(1) be divided into two equal portions, with:

(A) one portion passing to the surviving parent; and

(B) one portion passing to the person's siblings and the siblings' descendants; or

(2) be inherited entirely by the surviving parent if there is no sibling of the person or siblings' descendants.

(e) If neither the person's father nor mother survives the person, the person's entire estate passes to the person's siblings and the siblings' descendants.

(f) If none of the kindred described by Subsections (b)-(e) survive the person, the person's estate shall be divided into two moieties, with:

(1) one moiety passing to the person's paternal kindred as provided by Subsection (g); and

(2) one moiety passing to the person's maternal kindred as provided by Subsection (h).

(g) The moiety passing to the person's paternal kindred passes in the following order:

(1) if both paternal grandparents survive the person, equal portions pass to the person's paternal grandfather and grandmother;

(2) if only the person's paternal grandfather or grandmother survives the person, the person's estate shall:

(A) be divided into two equal portions, with:

(i) one portion passing to the surviving grandparent; and

(ii) one portion passing to the descendants of the deceased grandparent; or

(B) pass entirely to the surviving grandparent if no descendant of the deceased grandparent survives the person; and

(3) if neither the person's paternal grandfather nor grandmother survives the person, the moiety passing to the decedent's paternal kindred passes to the descendants of the person's paternal grandfather and grandmother, and so on without end, passing in like manner to the nearest lineal ancestors and their descendants.

(h) The moiety passing to the person's maternal kindred passes in the same order and manner as the other moiety passes to the decedent's paternal kindred under Subsection (g).

Derived from Probate Code § 38(a).

Added by Acts 2009, 81st Leg., ch. 680, § 1, eff. Jan. 1, 2014.

§ 201.002. Separate Estate of an Intestate

(a) If a person who dies intestate leaves a surviving spouse, the estate, other than a community estate, to which the person had title descends and passes as provided by this section.

(b) If the person has one or more children or a descendant of a child:

(1) the surviving spouse takes one-third of the personal estate;

(2) two-thirds of the personal estate descends to the person's child or children, and the descendants of a child or children; and

(3) the surviving spouse is entitled to a life estate in one-third of the person's land, with the

remainder descending to the person's child or children and the descendants of a child or children.

(c) Except as provided by Subsection (d), if the person has no child and no descendant of a child:

(1) the surviving spouse is entitled to all of the personal estate;

(2) the surviving spouse is entitled to one-half of the person's land without a remainder to any person; and

(3) one-half of the person's land passes and is inherited according to the rules of descent and distribution.

(d) If the person described by Subsection (c) does not leave a surviving parent or one or more surviving siblings, or their descendants, the surviving spouse is entitled to the entire estate.

Derived from Probate Code § 38(b).

Added by Acts 2009, 81st Leg., ch. 680, § 1, eff. Jan. 1, 2014.

Statutes in Context
§ 201.003

Section 201.003 provides the intestate distribution scheme for community property. See the *Statutes in Context* to Chapter 201, Subchapter A for a discussion of this provision.

Note that the distribution of community property was considerably different prior to September 1, 1993; the deceased spouse's half of the community passed to the deceased spouse's children even if all of the deceased spouse's children were also children of the surviving spouse.

Issues may arise regarding the identity and/or existence of a surviving spouse, especially if an informal or common law marriage is involved. See Family Code § 2.401.

---

§ 201.003. Community Estate of an Intestate

(a) If a person who dies intestate leaves a surviving spouse, the community estate of the deceased spouse passes as provided by this section.

(b) The community estate of the deceased spouse passes to the surviving spouse if:

(1) no child or other descendant of the deceased spouse survives the deceased spouse; or

(2) all of the surviving children and descendants of the deceased spouse are also children or descendants of the surviving spouse.

(c) If the deceased spouse is survived by a child or other descendant who is not also a child or descendant of the surviving spouse, one-half of the community estate is retained by the surviving spouse and the other one-half passes to the deceased spouse's children or descendants. The descendants inherit only the portion of that estate to which they would be entitled under Section 201.101. In every case, the community estate passes charged with the debts against the community estate.

Derived from Probate Code § 45.

Added by Acts 2009, 81st Leg., ch. 680, § 1, eff. Jan. 1, 2014.

Subchapter B. Matters Affecting Inheritance

Statutes in Context
§§ 201.051–201.052

At common law, a child born outside of a valid marriage was considered as having no parents (filius nullius). Thus, a nonmarital child did not inherit from or through the child's biological mother or father. Likewise, the biological parents could not inherit from or through the child. However, the nonmarital child did retain the right to inherit from the child's spouse and descendants. If the child died intestate with neither a surviving spouse nor descendants, the child's property escheated to the government.

This harsh treatment of nonmarital children, formerly referred to by pejorative terms such as "illegitimate children" or "bastards," has been greatly alleviated under modern law. In the 1977 United States Supreme Court case of *Trimble v. Gordon*, 430 U.S. 726 (1977), the Court held that marital and nonmarital children must be treated the same when determining heirs under intestacy statutes. The Court held that discriminating against non-marital children was a violation of the equal protection clause of the 14th Amendment.

One year later, the Supreme Court retreated from its broad holding in Trimble. In the five-four decision of *Lalli v. Lalli*, 439 U.S. 259 (1978), the Court held that a state may have legitimate reasons to apply a more demanding standard for nonmarital children to inherit from their fathers than from their mothers. The Court cited several justifications for this unequal treatment including the more efficient and orderly administration of estates, the avoidance of spurious claims, the maintenance of the finality of judgments, and the inability of the purported father to contest the child's paternity allegations.

---

§ 201.051. Maternal Inheritance

(a) For purposes of inheritance, a child is the child of the child's biological or adopted mother, and the child and the child's issue shall inherit from the child's mother and the child's maternal kindred, both descendants, ascendants, and collateral kindred in all degrees, and they may inherit from the child and the child's issue. However, if a child has intended parents, as defined by Section 160.102, Family Code, under a gestational agreement validated under Subchapter I, Chapter 160, Family Code, the child is the child of the intended mother and not the biological mother or gestational mother unless the biological mother is also the intended mother.

(b) This section does not permit inheritance by a child for whom no right of inheritance accrues under Section 201.056 or by the child's issue.

Derived from Probate Code § 42(a).

Added by Acts 2009, 81st Leg., ch. 680, § 1, eff. Jan. 1, 2014. Amended by Acts 2013, 83rd Leg., ch. 1136, § 11, eff. Jan. 1, 2014. Subsec. (b) added by Acts 2015, 84th Leg., ch. 995, § 6, eff. Sept. 1, 2015.

§ 201.052. Paternal Inheritance

(a) For purposes of inheritance, a child is the child of the child's biological father if:

(1) the child is born under circumstances described by Section 160.201, Family Code;

(2) the child is adjudicated to be the child of the father by court decree under Chapter 160, Family Code;

(3) the child was adopted by the child's father; or

(4) the father executed an acknowledgment of paternity under Subchapter D, Chapter 160, Family Code, or a similar statement properly executed in another jurisdiction.

(a-1) Notwithstanding Subsection (a), if a child has intended parents, as defined by Section 160.102, Family Code, under a gestational agreement validated under Subchapter I, Chapter 160, Family Code, the child is the child of the intended father and not the biological father unless the biological father is also the intended father.

(b) A child described by Subsection (a) or (a-1) and the child's issue shall inherit from the child's father and the child's paternal kindred, both descendants, ascendants, and collateral kindred in all degrees, and they may inherit from the child and the child's issue.

(c) A person may petition the probate court for a determination of right of inheritance from a decedent if the person:

(1) claims to be a biological child of the decedent and is not otherwise presumed to be a child of the decedent; or

(2) claims inheritance through a biological child of the decedent who is not otherwise presumed to be a child of the decedent.

(d) If under Subsection (c) the court finds by clear and convincing evidence that the purported father was the biological father of the child:

(1) the child is treated as any other child of the decedent for purposes of inheritance; and

(2) the child and the child's issue may inherit from the child's paternal kindred, both descendants, ascendants, and collateral kindred in all degrees, and they may inherit from the child and the child's issue.

(e) This section does not permit inheritance by a purported father of a child, recognized or not, if the purported father's parental rights have been terminated.

(f) This section does not permit inheritance by a child for whom no right of inheritance accrues under Section 201.056 or by the child's issue.

Derived from Probate Code § 42(b)(1).

Added by Acts 2009, 81st Leg., ch. 680, § 1, eff. Jan. 1, 2014. Subsections (a-1) added and (b) amended by Acts 2013, 83rd Leg., ch. 1136, § 12, eff. Jan. 1, 2014. Subsec. (f) added by Acts 2015, 84th Leg., ch. 995, § 7, eff. Sept. 1, 2015.

§ 201.053. Effect of Reliance on Affidavit of Heirship

(a) A person who purchases for valuable consideration any interest in property of the heirs of a decedent acquires good title to the interest that the person would have received, as purchaser, in the absence of a claim of the child described by Subdivision (1), if the person:

(1) in good faith relies on the declarations in an affidavit of heirship that does not include a child who at the time of the sale or contract of sale of the property:

(A) is not a presumed child of the decedent; and

(B) has not under a final court decree or judgment been found to be entitled to treatment under Section 201.052 as a child of the decedent; and

(2) is without knowledge of the claim of the child described by Subdivision (1).

(b) Subsection (a) does not affect any liability of the heirs for the proceeds of a sale described by Subsection (a) to the child who was not included in the affidavit of heirship.

Derived from Probate Code § 42(b)(2).

Added by Acts 2009, 81st Leg., ch. 680, § 1, eff. Jan. 1, 2014.

Statutes in Context
§ 201.054

The ability of a person to adopt a non-biological person and cause that person to be treated as a biological child was recognized thousands of years ago by societies such as the ancient Greeks, Romans, and Egyptians. However, the concept of adoption was beyond the grasp of common law attorneys and courts. The idea that a person could have "parents" other than the biological mother and father was unthinkable. In fact, English law did not recognize adoption until 1926. Accordingly, modern law relating to adoption developed in the United States with Vermont and Texas taking the lead when their legislatures enacted adoption statutes in 1850.

Section 201.054 details the effect of adoption on intestate distribution. The rights of three parties are at issue: (1) the adopted child; (2) the adoptive parents; and (3) the biological parents. Adopted children will inherit from and through the adoptive parents and, unlike in many states, also from and through the biological parents if the child was adopted as a minor. Adoptive parents are entitled to inherit from and through the adopted child. The inheritance rights of the biological parents, on the other hand, are cut off — biological parents do not inherit from or through their child who was given up for adoption. See also Family Code §§ 162.017 (adoption of minors) and 162.507 (adoption of adults).

Although Estates Code § 201.054(b) provides that only an adopted-out person retains the right to inherit from the biological relatives and that the right to inherit from the biological side of the family does not pass down to the descendants of the adopted-out person, the court in *In re Estate of Forister*, 421 S.W.3d 175 (Tex. App.—San Antonio 2013, pet. denied), explained that the statutory section must be construed as a whole and in doing so, it is clear that adoption does not cut off the inheritance rights of the adopted person as well as those of the adopted person's descendants.

The 2005 Legislature made a significant change with respect to the law governing inheritance by a person who is adopted as an adult. Under prior law, there was no difference between the inheritance rights of a person who was adopted as a minor and a person who was adopted after reaching adulthood, that is, both types of adopted individuals inherited not only from their adoptive parents but also retained the right to inherit from their biological parents.

Effective with regard to intestate individuals who die on or after September 1, 2005, the adopted adult may no longer inherit from or through the adult's biological parent. See Family Code § 162.507(c).

This amendment may lead to an absurd result. For example, assume that Mother and Father have a child in 1985. Mother dies in 1990 and Father marries Step-Mother in 1995. As time passes, Child and Step-Mother become close and shortly after Child reaches age 18, Step-Mother adopts Child. If Father dies intestate, Child will not be considered an heir because the statute provides that an adopted adult may not inherit from a biological parent.

A decree terminating the parent-child relationship may specifically remove the child's right to inherit from and through a biological parent. See Family Code § 161.206.

The discovery rule does not apply to heirship claims by adoptees *Little v. Smith*, 643 S.W.2d 414 (Tex. 1997).

Adoption by estoppel, also called equitable adoption, occurs when a "parent" acts as though the "parent" has adopted the "child" even though a formal court-approved adoption never occurred. Typically, the "child" must prove that there was an agreement to adopt and the courts will look at circumstantial evidence to establish the agreement. Thus, when the "parent" dies, the adopted by estoppel child is entitled to share in the estate just as if an adoption had actually occurred.

The result is different, however, if the adopted by estoppel child dies. The adoptive by estoppel parents and their kin are prohibited from inheriting from or through the adopted by estoppel child. The courts explain that it is the parents' fault that a formal adoption did not take place and thus the equities are not in their favor. As a result, the child's biological kin are the child's heirs. See *Heien v. Crabtree*, 369 S.W.2d 28 (Tex. 1963).

---

§ 201.054. Adopted Child

(a) For purposes of inheritance under the laws of descent and distribution, an adopted child is regarded as the child of the adoptive parent or parents, and the adopted child and the adopted child's descendants inherit from and through the adoptive parent or parents and their kindred as if the adopted child were the natural child of the adoptive parent or parents. The adoptive parent or parents and their kindred inherit from and through the adopted child as if the adopted child were the natural child of the adoptive parent or parents.

(b) The natural parent or parents of an adopted child and the kindred of the natural parent or parents may not inherit from or through the adopted child, but the adopted child inherits from and through the child's natural parent or parents, except as provided by Section 162.507(c), Family Code.

(c) This section does not prevent an adoptive parent from disposing of the parent's property by will according to law.

(d) This section does not diminish the rights of an adopted child under the laws of descent and distribution or otherwise that the adopted child acquired by virtue of inclusion in the definition of "child" under Section 22.004.

Derived from Probate Code § 40.

Added by Acts 2009, 81st Leg., ch. 680, § 1, eff. Jan. 1, 2014.

§ 201.055. Issue of Void or Voidable Marriage

The issue of a marriage declared void or voided by annulment shall be treated in the same manner as the issue of a valid marriage.

Derived from Probate Code § 42(d).

Added by Acts 2009, 81st Leg., ch. 680, § 1, eff. Jan. 1, 2014.

Statutes in Context
§ 201.056

Posthumous heirs are heirs who are born after the intestate dies. The 2015 Legislature amended this section to provide that a posthumous heir must be in gestation at the time of the intestate's death to obtain inheritance rights. This amendment precludes the use of the decedent's sperm, eggs, or embryos to produce heirs who are born years or decades after the intestate's death. In addition there are no longer different rules for lineal and collateral posthumous heirs.

§ 201.056. Persons Not in Being

No right of inheritance accrues to any person [other than to a child or lineal descendant of an intestate,] unless the person is born before, or is in gestation at, [in being and capable in law to take as an heir at] the time of the intestate's death and survives for at least 120 hours. A person is:

(1) considered to be in gestation at the time of the intestate's death if insemination or implantation occurs at or before the time of the intestate's death; and

(2) presumed to be in gestation at the time of the intestate's death if the person is born before the 301st day after the date of the intestate's death.

Derived from Probate Code § 41(a).

Added by Acts 2009, 81st Leg., ch. 680, § 1, eff. Jan. 1, 2014. Amended by Acts 2015, 84th Leg., ch. 995, § 8, eff. Sept. 1, 2015.

Statutes in Context
§ 201.057

The term "half-blood" refers to collateral relatives who share only one common ancestor. For example, a brother and sister who have the same mother but different fathers would be half-siblings. On the other hand, if the brother and sister have the same parents, they would be related by the "whole-blood" because they share the same common ancestors.

At common law, half-blooded heirs could not inherit real property from a half-blooded intestate although they were entitled to inherit personal property. This strict rule with its emphasis on blood relationships has been modified by the states. States adopt one of three modern approaches: (1) The majority of states have totally eliminated the distinction between half- and whole-blooded relatives in determining inheritance rights. Thus, half-blooded collaterals inherit just as if they were of the whole-blood. (2) Some states like Texas adopt the Scottish rule which provides that half-blooded collaterals receive half shares. (3) A few states permit half-blooded collateral heirs to inherit

only if there is no whole-blooded heir of the same degree. Remember that the distinction between whole and half-blooded heirs is relevant only if distribution is being made to collateral heirs of the intestate.

A simple way to determine the proper distribution to half- and whole-blooded heirs under § 201.057 is to calculate the total number of shares by creating two shares for each whole-blooded heir and one share for each half-blooded heir. Each whole-blooded heir receives two of these shares and each half-blooded heir receives one. For example, if there are three sibling heirs, Whole Blood Arthur, Half Blood Brenda, and Half Blood Charlie, four shares would be created (two for Arthur and one each for Brenda and Charlie). The estate would be distributed with Arthur receiving two shares (1/2 of the estate) and Brenda and Charlie receiving one share each (1/4 of the estate).

§ 201.057. Collateral Kindred of Whole and Half Blood

If the inheritance from an intestate passes to the collateral kindred of the intestate and part of the collateral kindred are of whole blood and the other part are of half blood of the intestate, each of the collateral kindred who is of half blood inherits only half as much as that inherited by each of the collateral kindred who is of whole blood. If all of the collateral kindred are of half blood of the intestate, each of the collateral kindred inherits a whole portion.

Derived from Probate Code § 41(b).

Added by Acts 2009, 81st Leg., ch. 680, § 1, eff. Jan. 1, 2014.

Statutes in Context
§ 201.058

Corruption of blood refers to a common law principle that prevented a person from inheriting land if the person was convicted or imprisoned for certain offenses, especially treason and other capital crimes. Article I, § 21 of the Texas Constitution prohibits corruption of blood and § 201.058 restates this prohibition. Accordingly, an imprisoned person, even one on death row, may inherit property.

Forfeiture refers to a common law principle that caused all the property of a person who was convicted of a felony to be forfeited to the government so there was no property for the person's heirs to inherit. Article I, § 21 of the Texas Constitution prohibits forfeiture and § 201.058 restates this prohibition. Note, however, that under federal law, a person convicted of certain drug offenses forfeits a portion of the person's property to the government. 21 U.S.C. § 853.

To prevent murderers from benefiting from their evil acts, most state legislatures have enacted statutes prohibiting murderers from inheriting. These provisions are often referred to as slayers' statutes. Section 201.058, however, only applies if a beneficiary of a life insurance policy is convicted and sentenced as a principal or accomplice in wilfully bringing about the death of the insured. Texas courts resort to the constructive trust principle to prevent the murdering heir from inheriting. Legal title does pass to the murderer but equity treats the murderer as a constructive trustee of the title because of the unconscionable mode of its acquisition and then compels the murderer to convey it to the heirs of the deceased, exclusive of the murderer. See *Pritchett v. Henry*, 287 S.W.2d 546 (Tex. Civ. App. — Beaumont 1955, writ dism'd).

§ 201.058. Convicted Persons

(a) No conviction shall work corruption of blood or forfeiture of estate except as provided by Subsection (b).

(b) If a beneficiary of a life insurance policy or contract is convicted and sentenced as a principal or accomplice in wilfully bringing about the death of the insured, the proceeds of the insurance policy or contract shall be paid in the manner provided by the Insurance Code.

Derived from Probate Code § 41(d).

Added by Acts 2009, 81st Leg., ch. 680, § 1, eff. Jan. 1, 2014.

§ 201.059. Person Who Dies by Casualty

Death by casualty does not result in forfeiture of estate.

Derived from Probate Code § 41(d).

Added by Acts 2009, 81st Leg., ch. 680, § 1, eff. Jan. 1, 2014.

Statutes in Context
§ 201.060

At common law, a noncitizen could not acquire or transmit real property through intestacy. This rule made sense because the landowner owed duties to the Crown which would be difficult to enforce if the landowner was not a citizen. On the other hand, noncitizens from friendly countries could both acquire and transmit personal property through intestacy.

Under § 201.060, noncitizens are treated no differently than citizens when it comes to inheritance rights. Note, however, that during the World Wars, the United States government restricted the inheritance rights of citizens of enemy nations.

§ 201.060. Alienage

A person is not disqualified to take as an heir because the person, or another person through whom the person claims, is or has been an alien.

Derived from Probate Code § 41(c).

Added by Acts 2009, 81st Leg., ch. 680, § 1, eff. Jan. 1, 2014.

Statutes in Context
§ 201.061

The property of a person who committed suicide was subject to special rules at common law. If the intestate committed suicide to avoid punishment after committing a felony, the intestate's heirs took nothing. Instead, the real property escheated and personal property was forfeited. However, if the intestate committed suicide because of pain or exhaustion from living, only personal property was forfeited and real property still descended to the heirs. Article I, § 21 of the Texas Constitution abolishes these common-law rules and thus the property of a person who commits suicide passes just as if the death were caused by some other means. Section 201.061 restates the Constitutional provision.

---

§ 201.061. Estate of Person Who Dies by Suicide

The estate of a person who commits suicide descends or vests as if the person died a natural death.

Derived from Probate Code § 41(d).

Added by Acts 2009, 81st Leg., ch. 680, § 1, eff. Jan. 1, 2014.

Statutes in Context
§ 201.062

The 2007 Legislature added the Probate Code predecessor to § 201.062 which allows the court to disqualify a parent as an heir for a laundry list of bad acts relating to a child who dies intestate and under age 18 such as abandoning the child or its pregnant mother, not supporting the child, or committing enumerated criminal acts such as endangering the child or possessing child pornography. Note that disqualification only occurs if the bad acts are done by a parent, not by a grandparent, sibling, or other heir.

The portion of these provisions which prevents a person from inheriting from his or her own child if the parent has been convicted of one of the enumerated crimes may be unconstitutional. Article I, § 21 of the Texas Constitution provides that "[n]o conviction shall work * * * forfeiture of estate." In Opinion No. GA-0632 issued May 30, 2008, the Attorney General of Texas concluded that "the courts would probably find [Estates] Code section [201.062(a)(3)] violative of article I, section 21 when applied to bar a wrongdoer's inheritance" unless the conduct would trigger other recognized legal doctrines such as a constructive trust.

§ 201.062. Treatment of Certain Parent-Child Relationships

(a) A probate court may enter an order declaring that the parent of a child under 18 years of age may not inherit from or through the child under the laws of descent and distribution if the court finds by clear and convincing evidence that the parent has:

(1) voluntarily abandoned and failed to support the child in accordance with the parent's obligation or ability for at least three years before the date of the child's death, and did not resume support for the child before that date;

(2) voluntarily and with knowledge of the pregnancy:

(A) abandoned the child's mother beginning at a time during her pregnancy with the child and continuing through the birth;

(B) failed to provide adequate support or medical care for the mother during the period of abandonment before the child's birth; and

(C) remained apart from and failed to support the child since birth; or

(3) been convicted or has been placed on community supervision, including deferred adjudication community supervision, for being criminally responsible for the death or serious injury of a child under the following sections of the Penal Code or adjudicated under Title 3, Family Code, for conduct that caused the death or serious injury of a child and that would constitute a violation of one of the following sections of the Penal Code:

(A) Section 19.02 (murder);

(B) Section 19.03 (capital murder);

(C) Section 19.04 (manslaughter);

(D) Section 21.11 (indecency with a child);

(E) Section 22.01 (assault);

(F) Section 22.011 (sexual assault);

(G) Section 22.02 (aggravated assault);

(H) Section 22.021 (aggravated sexual assault);

(I) Section 22.04 (injury to a child, elderly individual, or disabled individual);

(J) Section 22.041 (abandoning or endangering child);

(K) Section 25.02 (prohibited sexual conduct);

(L) Section 43.25 (sexual performance by a child); or

(M) Section 43.26 (possession or promotion of child pornography).

(b) On a determination under Subsection (a) that the parent of a child may not inherit from or through the child, the parent shall be treated as if the parent predeceased the child for purposes of:

(1) inheritance under the laws of descent and distribution; and

(2) any other cause of action based on parentage.

Derived from Probate Code §§ 41(e), (f).

Added by Acts 2009, 81st Leg., ch. 680, § 1, eff. Jan. 1, 2014.

Subchapter C. Distribution to Heirs

Statutes in Context
§ 201.101

Whenever individuals such as children, grandchildren, siblings and their descendants, cousins, etc., are heirs, one must determine how to divide their shares among them. If the takers are all of the same degree of relationship to the intestate, then they take per capita, i.e., each heir takes the same amount. For example, if all takers are children, each takes an equal share. If all children are deceased, then each grandchild takes an equal share.

If the takers are of different degrees of relationship to the decedent, e.g., children and grandchildren, the younger-generation takers share what the older-generation taker would have received had that person survived, that is, per capita with representation. (Note that the term "per stirpes" as used in the caption to § 43 is a misnomer. Per stirpes refers to a distribution where shares are determined by the number of individuals in the first generation, even if they have all predeceased the intestate.) For example, assume that Grandfather had three children; two predeceased. one-third passes to the surviving child, with one-third passing to the children of each deceased child (grandchildren). If each deceased child had a different number of grandchildren, the shares of the grandchildren will be different (e.g., if one deceased child had two children, each gets one-sixth; if the other deceased child had three children, each gets one-ninth).

See the examples in the *Statutes in Context* for Chapter 201, Subchapter A.

§ 201.101. Determination of Per Capita with Representation Distribution

(a) The children, descendants, brothers, sisters, uncles, aunts, or other relatives of an intestate who stand in the first or same degree of relationship alone and come into the distribution of the intestate's estate take per capita, which means by persons.

(b) If some of the persons described by Subsection (a) are dead and some are living, each descendant of those persons who have died is entitled to a distribution of the intestate's estate. Each descendant inherits only that portion of the property to which the parent through whom the descendant inherits would be entitled if that parent were alive.

Derived from Probate Code § 43.

Added by Acts 2009, 81st Leg., ch. 680, § 1, eff. Jan. 1, 2014.

Statutes in Context
§§ 202.102–202.103

The common law policy of keeping real property in the blood line of the original owner led to the development of the principle of ancestral property. This doctrine applied if an individual inherited real property and then died intestate without surviving descendants or first-line collateral relatives. Under this doctrine, real property inherited from the intestate's paternal side of the family would pass to the paternal collateral relatives and property inherited from the maternal side would pass to the maternal collateral relatives.

Sections 201.102–201.103 provide that the doctrine of ancestral property does not apply in Texas by stating that the intestate is treated as the original purchaser of all property.

§ 201.102. No Distinction Based on Property's Source

A distinction may not be made, in regulating the descent and distribution of an estate of a person dying intestate, between property derived by gift, devise, or descent from the intestate's father, and property derived by gift, devise, or descent from the intestate's mother.

Derived from Probate Code § 39.

Added by Acts 2009, 81st Leg., ch. 680, § 1, eff. Jan. 1, 2014.

§ 201.103. Treatment of Intestate's Estate

All of the estate to which an intestate had title at the time of death descends and vests in the intestate's heirs in the same manner as if the intestate had been the original purchaser.

Derived from Probate Code § 39.

Added by Acts 2009, 81st Leg., ch. 680, § 1, eff. Jan. 1, 2014.

Subchapter D. Advancements

Statutes in Context
Chapter 201, Subchapter D

An advancement is a special type of inter vivos gift. The advancer (donor) anticipates dying intestate and the advancee (donee) is an individual who is likely to be one of the advancer's heirs.

Although the gift is irrevocable and unconditional, the advancer intends the advancement to be an early distribution from the advancer's estate. Thus, the advancee's share of the advancer's estate is reduced to compensate for the advancement.

When the advancer dies intestate, the advanced property is treated as if it were still in the advancer's probate estate when computing the size of the intestate shares. Thus, the advancee receives a smaller share in the estate because the advancee already has part of the advancer's estate, that is, the advancement. This equalization process is referred to as going into hotchpot or hotchpotch.

Section 201.151 provides that property given during an intestate's life to an heir is an advancement only if (1) the decedent acknowledges the advancement in a contemporaneous writing at the time of or prior to the transfer, or (2) the heir acknowledges in writing, at any time, that the transfer of property is to be treated as an advancement.

Example 1 Intestate had three children, Arthur, Brenda, and Charles. Intestate made a $100,000 advancement to Arthur. Intestate died with a distributable probate estate of $500,000. What is the proper distribution of Intestate's estate?

Arthur receives $100,000, Brenda receives $200,000, and Charles receives $200,000. Because the $100,000 gift to Arthur was an advancement, that amount is treated as if it were still in Intestate's estate. Thus, Intestate's estate is distributed as if it contained $600,000. Intestate had three children and thus each child is entitled to a per capita share of $200,000. Because Arthur has already received $100,000 by way of the advancement, he is entitled only to an additional $100,000 from Intestate's estate. Brenda and Charles each receive their share from Intestate's estate. The hotchpot process ensures that each child receives an equal share from Intestate accounting for both inter vivos and at-death transfers.

Example 2 Intestate had three children, Arthur, Brenda, and Charles. Intestate made a $100,000 advancement to Arthur. Intestate died with a distributable probate estate of $50,000. What is the proper distribution of Intestate's estate?

Arthur receives none of Intestate's estate, Brenda receives $25,000 and Charles receives $25,000. Like other inter vivos gifts, advancements are irrevocable. Thus, Arthur is under no obligation to actually return the advanced amount to Intestate's estate. Arthur is not indebted for the advanced amount. Instead, Arthur simply does not share in Intestate's estate because he has already received property in excess of the share to which he would be entitled under a hotpotch computation. Thus, Intestate's entire estate is distributed to Brenda and Charles.

Example 3 Intestate had three children, Arthur, Brenda, and Charles. Intestate advanced two assets to Arthur, a house worth $100,000 at the time of the advancement and a car worth $30,000 at the time of the advancement. Intestate died with a distributable probate estate of $500,000. At the time of Intestate's death, the house had appreciated to $300,000 and the car had depreciated to $1,000. What is the proper distribution of Intestate's estate?

Arthur receives $80,000, Brenda receives $210,000, and Charles receives $210,000. Advancements are valued as of the date of the advancement under § 201.151(b). Thus, subsequent appreciation and depreciation of advanced property is ignored when going into hotchpot. The house valued at $100,000 and the car valued at $30,000 come into hotchpot. The value of the hotchpot, that is, advancements plus Intestate's estate, is $630,000. Each of the three children is entitled to $210,000. Because Arthur already received advancements valued at $130,000, he receives only $80,000 from the estate. Brenda and Charles each receive a full $210,000 share because neither of them had received an advancement.

Example 4 Intestate had three children, Arthur, Brenda, and Charles. Intestate made a $100,000 advancement to Arthur. Arthur died survived by his two children, Sam and Susan. Subsequently, Intestate died with a distributable probate estate of $500,000. What is the proper distribution of Intestate's estate?

Under § 201.152, the advancement is not considered because Arthur did not survive Intestate and thus hotchpot does not occur unless Intestate specified in writing that the advancement is to be brought into hotchpot even if Intestate predeceases Arthur. Accordingly, Brenda and Charles would each receive one-third of Intestate's probate estate (approximately $166,666) while Sam and Susan would each receive one-sixth (approximately $83,333). The policy behind this approach is that the advancee's heirs may not have received the advanced property or its value from the advancee's estate.

The analogous concept to advancements in a will context is called satisfaction and is governed by §§ 255.101–255.102.

---

§ 201.151. Determination of Advancement; Date of Valuation

(a) If a decedent dies intestate as to all or part of the decedent's estate, property that the decedent gave during the decedent's lifetime to a person who, on the date of the decedent's death, is the decedent's heir, or property received by the decedent's heir under a nontestamentary transfer under Subchapter B, Chapter 111, or Chapter 112 or 113, is an advancement against the heir's intestate share of the estate only if:

(1) the decedent declared in a contemporaneous writing, or the heir acknowledged in writing, that the gift or nontestamentary transfer is an advancement; or

(2) the decedent's contemporaneous writing or the heir's written acknowledgment otherwise indicates that the gift or nontestamentary transfer is to be considered in computing the division and distribution of the decedent's intestate estate.

(b) For purposes of Subsection (a), property that is advanced is valued as of the earlier of:

(1) the time that the heir came into possession or enjoyment of the property; or

(2) the time of the decedent's death.

Derived from Probate Code §§ 44(a), (b).

Added by Acts 2009, 81st Leg., ch. 680, § 1, eff. Jan. 1, 2014.

§ 201.152. Survival of Recipient Required

If the recipient of property described by Section 201.151 does not survive the decedent, the property is not considered in computing the division and distribution of the decedent's intestate estate unless the decedent's contemporaneous writing provides otherwise.

Derived from Probate Code § 44(c).

Added by Acts 2009, 81st Leg., ch. 680, § 1, eff. Jan. 1, 2014.

Chapter 202. Determination of Heirship

Subchapter A. Authorization and Procedures for Commencement of Proceeding to Declare Heirship

Subchapter B. Notice of Proceeding to Declare Heirship

Subchapter C. Transfer of Pending Proceeding to Declare Heirship

Subchapter D. Evidence Relating to Determination of Heirship

Subchapter E. Judgment in Proceeding to Declare Heirship

Chapter 202. Determination of Heirship

Subchapter A. Authorization and Procedures for Commencement of Proceeding to Declare Heirship

Statutes in Context
Chapter 202

If the decedent died intestate, the court will make a determination of the identity of the heirs. If there is no need for an estate administration, this determination of heirship may be all that is required to prove that title to property passed from the intestate to the heirs. The court will open an administration only if one is necessary to pay debts or to partition property among the heirs.

The analogous proceeding for a testate decedent is to probate the will as a muniment of title as discussed in §§ 257.051–257.153.

§ 202.001. General Authorization for and Nature of Proceeding to Declare Heirship

In the manner provided by this chapter, a court may determine through a proceeding to declare heirship:

(1) the persons who are a decedent's heirs and only heirs; and

(2) the heirs' respective shares and interests under the laws of this state in the decedent's estate or, if applicable, in the trust.

Derived from Probate Code § 48(a).

Added by Acts 2009, 81st Leg., ch. 680, § 1, eff. Jan. 1, 2014. Subsec. (2) amended by Acts 2011, 82nd Leg., ch. 1338, § 2.18, eff. Jan. 1, 2014.

§ 202.002. Circumstances Under Which Proceeding to Declare Heirship Is Authorized

A court may conduct a proceeding to declare heirship when:

(1) a person dies intestate owning or entitled to property in this state and there has been no administration in this state of the person's estate;

(2) there has been a will probated in this state or elsewhere or an administration in this state of a decedent's estate, but:

(A) property in this state was omitted from the will or administration; or

(B) no final disposition of property in this state has been made in the administration; or

(3) it is necessary for the trustee of a trust holding assets for the benefit of a decedent to determine the heirs of the decedent.

Derived from Probate Code § 48(a).

Added by Acts 2009, 81st Leg., ch. 680, § 1, eff. Jan. 1, 2014. Subsec. (2) amended by Acts 2011, 82nd Leg., ch. 1338, § 2.19, eff. Jan. 1, 2014. Subsec. (3) added by Acts 2011, 82nd Leg., ch. 1338, § 2.19, eff. Jan. 1, 2014.

Statutes in Context
§ 202.0025

The 2013 Legislature added Estates Code § 202.0025 to make it clear that there is no statute of limitations with regard to a proceeding to declare heirship of a decedent. Although the provision is effective on January 1, 2014, the Legislature stated that this section is "intended to clarify current law" and that "an inference may not be made regarding the statute of limitations for a proceeding to declare heirship filed before the effective date." See Acts 2013, 83rd Leg., ch. 1136, § 62(g).

---

§ 202.0025. Action Brought After Decedent's Death

Notwithstanding Section 16.051, Civil Practice and Remedies Code, a proceeding to declare heirship of a decedent may be brought at any time after the decedent's death.

New.

Added by Acts 2013, 83rd Leg., ch. 1136, § 13, eff. Jan. 1, 2014.

§ 202.004. Persons Who May Commence Proceeding to Declare Heirship

A proceeding to declare heirship of a decedent may be commenced and maintained under a circumstance specified by Section 202.002 by:

(1) the personal representative of the decedent's estate;

(2) a person claiming to be a creditor or the owner of all or part of the decedent's estate;

(3) if the decedent was a ward with respect to whom a guardian of the estate had been appointed, the guardian of the estate, provided that the proceeding is commenced and maintained in the probate court in which the proceedings for the guardianship of the estate were pending at the time of the decedent's death;

(4) a party seeking the appointment of an independent administrator under Section 401.003; or

(5) the trustee of a trust holding assets for the benefit of a decedent.

Derived from Probate Code § 49(a).

Added by Acts 2009, 81st Leg., ch. 680, § 1, eff. Jan. 1, 2014. Amended by Acts 2011, 82nd Leg., ch. 1338, § 2.20, eff. Jan. 1, 2014. Subsecs. (4) and (5) added by Acts 2011, 82nd Leg., ch. 1338, § 2.20, eff. Jan. 1, 2014.

§ 202.005. Application for Proceeding to Declare Heirship

A person authorized by Section 202.004 to commence a proceeding to declare heirship must file an application in a court specified by Section 33.004 to commence the proceeding. The application must state:

(1) the decedent's name and date [time] and place of death;

(2) the names and physical addresses where service can be had [residences] of the decedent's heirs, the relationship of each heir to the decedent, whether each heir is an adult or minor, and the true interest of the applicant and each of the heirs in the decedent's estate or in the trust, as applicable;

(3) if the date [time] or place of the decedent's death or the name or physical address where service can be had [residence] of an heir is not definitely known to the applicant, all the material facts and circumstances with respect to which the applicant has knowledge and information that might reasonably tend to show the date [time] or place of the decedent's death or the name or physical address where service can be had [residence] of the heir;

(4) that all children born to or adopted by the decedent have been listed;

(5) that each of the decedent's marriages has been listed with:

(A) the date of the marriage;

(B) the name of the spouse;

(C) the date and place of termination if the marriage was terminated; and

(D) other facts to show whether a spouse has had an interest in the decedent's property;

(6) whether the decedent died testate and, if so, what disposition has been made of the will;

(7) a general description of all property belonging to the decedent's estate or held in trust for the benefit of the decedent, as applicable; and

(8) an explanation for the omission from the application of any of the information required by this section.

Derived from Probate Code § 49(a).

Added by Acts 2009, 81st Leg., ch. 680, § 1, eff. Jan. 1, 2014. Amended by Acts 2011, 82nd Leg., ch. 1338, § 2.21, eff. Jan. 1, 2014. Amended by Acts 2015, 84th Leg., ch. 995, § 9, eff. Sept. 1, 2015.

§ 202.006. Request for Determination of Necessity for Administration

A person who files an application under Section 202.005 not later than the fourth anniversary of the date of the death of the decedent who is the subject of the application may request that the court determine whether there is a need for administration of the decedent's estate. The court shall hear evidence on the issue and, in the court's judgment, make a determination of the issue.

Derived from Probate Code § 48(b).

Added by Acts 2009, 81st Leg., ch. 680, § 1, eff. Jan. 1, 2014.

§ 202.007. Affidavit Supporting Application Required

(a) An application filed under Section 202.005 must be supported by the affidavit of each applicant.

(b) An affidavit of an applicant under Subsection (a) must state that, to the applicant's knowledge:

(1) all the allegations in the application are true; and

(2) no material fact or circumstance has been omitted from the application.

Derived from Probate Code § 49(b).

Added by Acts 2009, 81st Leg., ch. 680, § 1, eff. Jan. 1, 2014.

§ 202.008. Required Parties to Proceeding to Declare Heirship

Each of the following persons must be made a party to a proceeding to declare heirship:

(1) each unknown heir of the decedent who is the subject of the proceeding;

(2) each person who is named as an heir of the decedent in the application filed under Section 202.005; and

(3) each person who is, on the filing date of the application, shown as owning a share or interest in any real property described in the application by the deed records of the county in which the property is located.

Derived from Probate Code § 49(b).

Added by Acts 2009, 81st Leg., ch. 680, § 1, eff. Jan. 1, 2014.

§ 202.009. Attorney Ad Litem

(a) The court shall appoint an attorney ad litem in a proceeding to declare heirship to represent the interests of heirs whose names or locations are unknown.

(b) The court may expand the appointment of the attorney ad litem appointed under Subsection (a) to include representation of an heir who is an incapacitated person on a finding that the appointment is necessary to protect the interests of the heir.

Derived from Probate Code § 53(b), (c).

Added by Acts 2009, 81st Leg., ch. 680, § 1, eff. Jan. 1, 2014. Amended by Acts 2013, 83rd Leg., ch. 1136, § 15, eff. Jan. 1, 2014.

Subchapter B. Notice of Proceeding to Declare Heirship

§ 202.051. Service of Citation by Mail When Recipient's Name and Address Are Known or Ascertainable

Except as provided by Section 202.054, citation in a proceeding to declare heirship must be served by registered or certified mail on:

(1) each distributee who is 12 years of age or older and whose name and address are known or can be ascertained through the exercise of reasonable diligence; and

(2) the parent, managing conservator, or guardian of each distributee who is younger than 12 years of age if the name and address of the parent, managing conservator, or guardian are known or can be reasonably ascertained.

Derived from Probate Code § 50(a).

Added by Acts 2009, 81st Leg., ch. 680, § 1, eff. Jan. 1, 2014.

§ 202.052. Service of Citation by Publication When Recipient's Name or Address Is Not Ascertainable

If the address of a person or entity on whom citation is required to be served cannot be ascertained, citation must be served on the person or entity by publication in the county in which the proceeding to declare heirship is commenced and in the county of the last residence of the decedent who is the subject of the proceeding, if that residence was in a county other than the county in which the proceeding is commenced. To determine whether a decedent has any other heirs, citation must be served on unknown heirs by publication in the manner provided by this section.

Derived from Probate Code § 50(b).

Added by Acts 2009, 81st Leg., ch. 680, § 1, eff. Jan. 1, 2014.

§ 202.053. Required Posting of Citation

Except in a proceeding in which citation is served by publication as provided by Section 202.052, citation in a proceeding to declare heirship must be posted in:

(1) the county in which the proceeding is commenced; and

(2) the county of the last residence of the decedent who is the subject of the proceeding.

Derived from Probate Code § 50(c).

Added by Acts 2009, 81st Leg., ch. 680, § 1, eff. Jan. 1, 2014.

§ 202.054. Personal Service of Citation May Be Required

The court may require that service of citation in a proceeding to declare heirship be made by personal service on some or all of those named as distributees in the application filed under Section 202.005.

Derived from Probate Code § 50(a).

Added by Acts 2009, 81st Leg., ch. 680, § 1, eff. Jan. 1, 2014.

§ 202.055. Service of Citation on Certain Persons Not Required

A party to a proceeding to declare heirship who executed the application filed under Section 202.005, entered an appearance in the proceeding, or waived citation under this subchapter is not required to be served by any method.

Derived from Probate Code § 50(d).

Added by Acts 2009, 81st Leg., ch. 680, § 1, eff. Jan. 1, 2014. Amended by Acts 2015, 84th Leg., ch. 995, § 10, eff. Sept. 1, 2015.

§ 202.056. Waiver of Service of Citation

(a) Except as provided by Subsection (b)(2), a distributee may waive citation required by this subchapter to be served on the distributee.

(b) A parent, managing conservator, guardian, attorney ad litem, or guardian ad litem of a minor distributee who:

(1) is younger than 12 years of age may waive citation required by this subchapter to be served on the distributee; and

(2) is 12 years of age or older may not waive citation required by this subchapter to be served on the distributee.

Derived from Probate Code § 50(e).

Added by Acts 2009, 81st Leg., ch. 680, § 1, eff. Jan. 1, 2014. Amended Acts 2013, 83rd Leg., ch. 1136, § 16, eff. Jan. 1, 2014. Amended by Acts 2015, 84th Leg., ch. 995, § 11, eff. Sept. 1, 2015.

Statutes in Context
§ 202.057

A court cannot enter an order determining heirs unless the applicant files (1) a copy of the notice and proof of delivery sent to interested parties and (2) an affidavit of the applicant or a certificate signed by the applicant's attorney stating that notice was given, the name of each person who received the notice if not shown on the proof, and the name of each person who waived citation.

§ 202.057. Affidavit of Service of Citation

(a) A person who files an application under Section 202.005 shall file with the court:

(1) a copy of any citation required by this subchapter and the proof of delivery of service of the citation; and

(2) an affidavit sworn to by the applicant or a certificate signed by the applicant's attorney stating:

(A) that the citation was served as required by this subchapter;

(B) the name of each person to whom the citation was served, if the person's name is not shown on the proof of delivery; and

(C) the name of each person who waived citation under Section 202.056.

(b) The court may not enter an order in the proceeding to declare heirship under Subchapter E until the affidavit or certificate required by Subsection (a) is filed.

New.

Added by Acts 2013, 83rd Leg., ch. 1136, § 17, eff. Jan. 1, 2014.

Subchapter C. Transfer of Pending Proceeding to Declare Heirship

§ 202.101. Required Transfer of Pending Proceeding to Declare Heirship Under Certain Circumstances

If, after a proceeding to declare heirship is commenced, an administration of the estate of the decedent who is the subject of the proceeding is granted in this state or the decedent's will is admitted to probate in this state, the court in which the proceeding to declare heirship is pending shall, by an order entered of record in the proceeding, transfer the proceeding to the court in which the administration was granted or the will was probated.

Derived from Probate Code § 51.

Added by Acts 2009, 81st Leg., ch. 680, § 1, eff. Jan. 1, 2014.

§ 202.102. Transfer of Records

The clerk of the court from which a proceeding to declare heirship is transferred under Section 202.101 shall, on entry of the order under that section, send to the clerk of the court named in the order a certified transcript of all pleadings, entries in the judge's probate docket, and orders of the court in the proceeding. The clerk of the court to which the proceeding is transferred shall:

(1) file the transcript;

(2) record the transcript in the judge's probate docket of that court; and

(3) docket the proceeding.

Derived from Probate Code § 51.

Added by Acts 2009, 81st Leg., ch. 680, § 1, eff. Jan. 1, 2014. Amended by Acts 2011, 82nd Leg., ch. 90, § 8.007, eff. Jan. 1, 2014.

§ 202.103. Procedures Applicable to Transferred Proceeding to Declare Heirship; Consolidation with Other Proceeding

A proceeding to declare heirship that is transferred under Section 202.101 shall proceed as though the proceeding was originally filed in the court to which the proceeding is transferred. The court may consolidate the proceeding with the other proceeding pending in that court.

Derived from Probate Code § 51.

Added by Acts 2009, 81st Leg., ch. 680, § 1, eff. Jan. 1, 2014.

Subchapter D. Evidence Relating to Determination of Heirship

§ 202.151. Evidence in Proceeding to Declare Heirship

(a) The court may require that any testimony admitted as evidence in a proceeding to declare heirship be reduced to writing and subscribed and sworn to by the witnesses, respectively.

(b) Testimony in a proceeding to declare heirship must be taken in open court, by deposition in accordance with Section 51.203, or in accordance with the Texas Rules of Civil Procedure.

Derived from Probate Code § 53(a).

Added by Acts 2009, 81st Leg., ch. 680, § 1, eff. Jan. 1, 2014. Amended by Acts 2011, 82nd Leg., ch. 90, § 8.008, eff. Jan. 1, 2014. Amended by Acts 2013, 83rd Leg., ch. 1136, § 18, eff. Jan. 1, 2014.

Subchapter E. Judgment in Proceeding to Declare Heirship

§ 202.201. Required Statements in Judgment

(a) The judgment in a proceeding to declare heirship must state:

(1) the names [and places of residence] of the heirs of the decedent who is the subject of the proceeding; and

(2) the heirs' respective shares and interests in the decedent's property.

(b) If the proof in a proceeding to declare heirship is in any respect deficient, the judgment in the proceeding must state that.

Derived from Probate Code § 54.

Added by Acts 2009, 81st Leg., ch. 680, § 1, eff. Jan. 1, 2014. Subsec. (a) amended by Acts 2015, 84ᵗʰ Leg., ch. 995, § 12, eff. Sept. 1, 2015.

§ 202.202. Finality and Appeal of Judgment

(a) The judgment in a proceeding to declare heirship is a final judgment.

(b) At the request of an interested person, the judgment in a proceeding to declare heirship may be appealed or reviewed within the same time limits and in the same manner as other judgments in probate matters.

Derived from Probate Code § 55(a).

Added by Acts 2009, 81st Leg., ch. 680, § 1, eff. Jan. 1, 2014.

§ 202.203. Correction of Judgment at Request of Heir Not Properly Served

If an heir of a decedent who is the subject of a proceeding to declare heirship is not served with citation by registered or certified mail or personal service in the proceeding, the heir may:

(1) have the judgment in the proceeding corrected by bill of review:

(A) at any time, but not later than the fourth anniversary of the date of the judgment; or

(B) after the passage of any length of time, on proof of actual fraud; and

(2) recover the heir's just share of the property or the value of that share from:

(A) the heirs named in the judgment; and

(B) those who claim under the heirs named in the judgment and who are not bona fide purchasers for value.

Derived from Probate Code § 55(A).

Added by Acts 2009, 81st Leg., ch. 680, § 1, eff. Jan. 1, 2014.

§ 202.204. Limitation of Liability of Certain Persons Acting in Accordance with Judgment

(a) The judgment in a proceeding to declare heirship is conclusive in a suit between an heir omitted from the judgment and a bona fide purchaser for value who purchased property after entry of the judgment without actual notice of the claim of the omitted heir, regardless of whether the judgment is subsequently modified, set aside, or nullified.

(b) A person is not liable to another person for the following actions performed in good faith after a judgment is entered in a proceeding to declare heirship:

(1) delivering the property of the decedent who was the subject of the proceeding to the persons named as heirs in the judgment; or

(2) engaging in any other transaction with the persons named as heirs in the judgment.

Derived from Probate Code § 55(b).

Added by Acts 2009, 81st Leg., ch. 680, § 1, eff. Jan. 1, 2014.

§ 202.205. Effect of Certain Judgments on Liability to Creditors

(a) A judgment in a proceeding to declare heirship stating that there is no necessity for administration of the estate of the decedent who is the subject of the proceeding constitutes authorization for a person who owes money to the estate, has custody of estate property, acts as registrar or transfer agent of an evidence of interest, indebtedness, property, or right belonging to the estate, or purchases from or otherwise deals with an heir named in the judgment to take the following actions without liability to a creditor of the estate or other person:

(1) to pay, deliver, or transfer the property or the evidence of property rights to an heir named in the judgment; or

(2) to purchase property from an heir named in the judgment.

(b) An heir named in a judgment in a proceeding to declare heirship is entitled to enforce the heir's right to payment, delivery, or transfer described by Subsection (a) by suit.

(c) Except as provided by this section, this chapter does not affect the rights or remedies of the creditors of a decedent who is the subject of a proceeding to declare heirship.

Derived from Probate Code § 55(c).

Added by Acts 2009, 81st Leg., ch. 680, § 1, eff. Jan. 1, 2014.

§ 202.206. Filing and Recording of Judgment

(a) A certified copy of the judgment in a proceeding to declare heirship may be:

(1) filed for record in the office of the county clerk of the county in which any real property described in the judgment is located;

(2) recorded in the deed records of that county; and

(3) indexed in the name of the decedent who was the subject of the proceeding as grantor and in the names of the heirs named in the judgment as grantees.

(b) On the filing of a judgment in accordance with Subsection (a), the judgment constitutes constructive notice of the facts stated in the judgment.

Derived from Probate Code § 56.

Added by Acts 2009, 81st Leg., ch. 680, § 1, eff. Jan. 1, 2014.

Chapter 203. Nonjudicial Evidence of Heirship

Chapter 203. Nonjudicial Evidence of Heirship

Statutes in Context
Chapter 203

Some title companies, oil landpersons, and financial institutions may rely on a affidavit of heirship, standing alone without a formal determination of heirship, to clear defects in title to real property.

§ 203.001. Recorded Statement of Facts as Prima Facie Evidence of Heirship

(a) A court shall receive in a proceeding to declare heirship or a suit involving title to property a statement of facts concerning the family history, genealogy, marital status, or the identity of the heirs of a decedent as prima facie evidence of the facts contained in the statement if:

(1) the statement is contained in:

(A) an affidavit or other instrument legally executed and acknowledged or sworn to before, and certified by, an officer authorized to take acknowledgments or oaths, as applicable; or

(B) a judgment of a court of record; and

(2) the affidavit or instrument containing the statement has been of record for five years or more in the deed records of a county in this state in which the property is located at the time the suit involving title to property is commenced, or in the deed records of a county in this state in which the decedent was domiciled or had a fixed place of residence at the time of the decedent's death.

(b) If there is an error in a statement of facts in a recorded affidavit or instrument described by Subsection (a), anyone interested in a proceeding in which the affidavit or instrument is offered in evidence may prove the true facts.

(c) An affidavit of facts concerning the identity of a decedent's heirs as to an interest in real property that is filed in a proceeding or suit described by Subsection (a) may be in the form prescribed by Section 203.002.

(d) An affidavit of facts concerning the identity of a decedent's heirs does not affect the rights of an omitted heir or creditor of the decedent as otherwise provided by law. This section is cumulative of all other statutes on the same subject and may not be construed as abrogating any right to present evidence or rely on an affidavit of facts conferred by any other statute or rule.

Derived from Probate Code § 52.

Added by Acts 2009, 81st Leg., ch. 680, § 1, eff. Jan. 1, 2014.

§ 203.002. Form of Affidavit Concerning Identity of Heirs

An affidavit of facts concerning the identity of a decedent's heirs may be in substantially the following form:

AFFIDAVIT OF FACTS CONCERNING THE IDENTITY OF HEIRS

Before me, the undersigned authority, on this day personally appeared _____ ("Affiant") (insert name of affiant) who, being first duly sworn, upon his/her oath states:

1. My name is _____ (insert name of affiant), and I live at _____ (insert address of affiant's residence). I am personally familiar with the family and marital history of _____ ("Decedent") (insert name of decedent), and I have personal knowledge of the facts stated in this affidavit.

2. I knew decedent from _____ (insert date) until _____ (insert date). Decedent died on _____ (insert date of death). Decedent's place of death was _____ (insert place of death). At the time of decedent's death, decedent's residence was _____ (insert address of decedent's residence).

3. Decedent's marital history was as follows: _____ (insert marital history and, if decedent's spouse is deceased, insert date and place of spouse's death).

4. Decedent had the following children: _____ (insert name, birth date, name of other parent, and current address of child or date of death of child and descendants of deceased child, as applicable, for each child).

5. Decedent did not have or adopt any other children and did not take any other children into

decedent's home or raise any other children, except: _____ (insert name of child or names of children, or state "none").

6. (Include if decedent was not survived by descendants.) Decedent's mother was: _____ (insert name, birth date, and current address or date of death of mother, as applicable).

7. (Include if decedent was not survived by descendants.) Decedent's father was: _____ (insert name, birth date, and current address or date of death of father, as applicable).

8. (Include if decedent was not survived by descendants or by both mother and father.) Decedent had the following siblings: _____ (insert name, birth date, and current address or date of death of each sibling and parents of each sibling and descendants of each deceased sibling, as applicable, or state "none").

9. (Optional.) The following persons have knowledge regarding the decedent, the identity of decedent's children, if any, parents, or siblings, if any: _____ (insert names of persons with knowledge, or state "none").

10. Decedent died without leaving a written will. (Modify statement if decedent left a written will.)

11. There has been no administration of decedent's estate. (Modify statement if there has been administration of decedent's estate.)

12. Decedent left no debts that are unpaid, except: _____ (insert list of debts, or state "none").

13. There are no unpaid estate or inheritance taxes, except: _____ (insert list of unpaid taxes, or state "none").

14. To the best of my knowledge, decedent owned an interest in the following real property: _____ (insert list of real property in which decedent owned an interest, or state "none").

15. (Optional.) The following were the heirs of decedent: _____ (insert names of heirs).

16. (Insert additional information as appropriate, such as size of the decedent's estate.)

Signed this ___ day of _____, ___.

_____
(signature of affiant)
State of _____
County of _____
Sworn to and subscribed to before me on _____ (date) by _____ (insert name of affiant).

_____
(signature of notarial officer)
(Seal, if any, of notary) _____
(printed name)
My commission expires: _____

Derived from Probate Code § 52A.

Added by Acts 2009, 81st Leg., ch. 680, § 1, eff. Jan. 1, 2014.

Chapter 204. Genetic Testing in Proceedings to Declare Heirship

Chapter 204. Genetic Testing in Proceedings to Declare Heirship

Subchapter A. General Provisions

§ 204.001.   Proceedings and Records Public

A proceeding under this chapter or Chapter 202 involving genetic testing is open to the public as in other civil cases. Papers and records in the proceeding are available for public inspection.

Derived from Probate Code § 53E.

Added by Acts 2009, 81st Leg., ch. 680, § 1, eff. Jan. 1, 2014.

Subchapter B. Court Orders for Genetic Testing in Proceedings to Declare Heirship

§ 204.051. Order for Genetic Testing

(a) In a proceeding to declare heirship under Chapter 202, the court may, on the court's own motion, and shall, on the request of a party to the proceeding, order one or more specified individuals to submit to genetic testing as provided by Subchapter F, Chapter 160, Family Code. If two or more individuals are ordered to be tested, the court may order that the testing of those individuals be done concurrently or sequentially.

(b) The court may enforce an order under this section by contempt.

Derived from Probate Code § 53A(a).

Added by Acts 2009, 81st Leg., ch. 680, § 1, eff. Jan. 1, 2014.

§ 204.052. Advancement of Costs

Subject to any assessment of costs following a proceeding to declare heirship in accordance with Rule 131, Texas Rules of Civil Procedure, the cost of genetic testing ordered under Section 204.051 must be advanced:

(1) by a party to the proceeding who requests the testing;

(2) as agreed by the parties and approved by the court; or

(3) as ordered by the court.

Derived from Probate Code § 53A(b).

Added by Acts 2009, 81st Leg., ch. 680, § 1, eff. Jan. 1, 2014.

§ 204.053. Order and Advancement of Costs for Subsequent Genetic Testing

(a) Subject to Subsection (b), the court shall order genetic testing subsequent to the testing conducted under Section 204.051 if:

(1) a party to the proceeding to declare heirship contests the results of the genetic testing ordered under Section 204.051; and

(2) the party contesting the results requests that additional testing be conducted.

(b) If the results of the genetic testing ordered under Section 204.051 identify a tested individual as an heir of the decedent, the court may order additional genetic testing in accordance with Subsection (a) only if the party contesting those results pays for the additional testing in advance.

Derived from Probate Code §§ 53A(c), (d).

Added by Acts 2009, 81st Leg., ch. 680, § 1, eff. Jan. 1, 2014.

§ 204.054. Submission of Genetic Material by Other Relative Under Certain Circumstances

If a sample of an individual's genetic material that could identify another individual as the decedent's heir is not available for purposes of conducting genetic testing under this subchapter, the court, on a finding of good cause and that the need for genetic testing outweighs the legitimate interests of the individual to be tested, may order any of the following individuals to submit a sample of genetic material for the testing under circumstances the court considers just:

(1) a parent, sibling, or child of the individual whose genetic material is not available; or

(2) any other relative of that individual, as necessary to conduct the testing.

Derived from Probate Code § 53A(e).

Added by Acts 2009, 81st Leg., ch. 680, § 1, eff. Jan. 1, 2014.

§ 204.055. Genetic Testing of Deceased Individual

On good cause shown, the court may order:

(1) genetic testing of a deceased individual under this subchapter; and

(2) if necessary, removal of the remains of the deceased individual as provided by Section 711.004, Health and Safety Code, for that testing.

Derived from Probate Code § 53A(f).

Added by Acts 2009, 81st Leg., ch. 680, § 1, eff. Jan. 1, 2014.

§ 204.056. Criminal Penalty

(a) An individual commits an offense if:

(1) the individual intentionally releases an identifiable sample of the genetic material of another individual that was provided for purposes of genetic testing ordered under this subchapter; and

(2) the release:

(A) is for a purpose not related to the proceeding to declare heirship; and

(B) was not ordered by the court or done in accordance with written permission obtained from the individual who provided the sample.

(b) An offense under this section is a Class A misdemeanor.

Derived from Probate Code § 53A(g).

Added by Acts 2009, 81st Leg., ch. 680, § 1, eff. Jan. 1, 2014.

Subchapter C. Results of Genetic Testing

§ 204.101. Results of Genetic Testing; Admissibility

A report of the results of genetic testing ordered under Subchapter B:

(1) must comply with the requirements for a report prescribed by Section 160.504, Family Code; and

(2) is admissible in a proceeding to declare heirship under Chapter 202 as evidence of the truth of the facts asserted in the report.

Derived from Probate Code § 53B(a).

Added by Acts 2009, 81st Leg., ch. 680, § 1, eff. Jan. 1, 2014.

§ 204.102. Presumption Regarding Results of Genetic Testing; Rebuttal

The presumption under Section 160.505, Family Code:

(1) applies to the results of genetic testing ordered under Subchapter B; and

(2) may be rebutted as provided by Section 160.505, Family Code.

Derived from Probate Code § 53B(b).

Added by Acts 2009, 81st Leg., ch. 680, § 1, eff. Jan. 1, 2014.

§ 204.103. Contesting Results of Genetic Testing

(a) A party to a proceeding to declare heirship who contests the results of genetic testing may call one or more genetic testing experts to testify in person or by telephone, videoconference, deposition, or another method approved by the court.

(b) Unless otherwise ordered by the court, the party offering the testimony under Subsection (a) bears the expense for the expert testifying.

Derived from Probate Code § 53B(c).

Added by Acts 2009, 81st Leg., ch. 680, § 1, eff. Jan. 1, 2014.

Subchapter D. Use of Results of Genetic Testing in Certain Proceedings to Declare Heirship

§ 204.151. Applicability of Subchapter

This subchapter applies in a proceeding to declare heirship of a decedent only with respect to an individual who claims to be a biological child of the decedent to inherit through a biological child of the decedent.

Derived from Probate Code § 53C(a).

Added by Acts 2009, 81st Leg., ch. 680, § 1, eff. Jan. 1, 2014. Amended by Acts 2013, 83rd Leg., ch. 1136, § 19, eff. Jan. 1, 2014.

§ 204.152. Presumption; Rebuttal

The presumption under Section 160.505, Family Code, that applies in establishing a parent-child relationship also applies in determining heirship in the probate court using the results of genetic testing ordered with respect to an individual described by Section 204.151, and the presumption may be rebutted in the same manner provided by Section 160.505, Family Code.

Derived from Probate Code § 53C(b), (c).

Added by Acts 2009, 81st Leg., ch. 680, § 1, eff. Jan. 1, 2014. Amended by Acts 2013, 83rd Leg., ch. 1136, § 19, eff. Jan. 1, 2014.

§ 204.153. Effect of Inconclusive Results of Genetic Testing

If the results of genetic testing ordered under Subchapter B do not identify or exclude a tested individual as the ancestor of the individual described by Section 204.151:

(1) the court may not dismiss the proceeding to declare heirship; and

(2) the results of the genetic testing and other relevant evidence are admissible in the proceeding.

Derived from Probate Code § 53C(d).

Added by Acts 2009, 81st Leg., ch. 680, § 1, eff. Jan. 1, 2014.

Subchapter E. Additional Orders Following Results of Genetic Testing

§ 204.201. Order for Change of Name

On the request of an individual determined by the results of genetic testing to be the heir of a decedent and for good cause shown, the court may:

(1) order the name of the individual to be changed; and

(2) if the court orders a name change under Subdivision (1), order the bureau of vital statistics to issue an amended birth record for the individual.

Derived from Probate Code § 53D.

Added by Acts 2009, 81st Leg., ch. 680, § 1, eff. Jan. 1, 2014.

Chapter 205. Small Estate Affidavit

Chapter 205. Small Estate Affidavit

Statutes in Context
Chapter 205

Chapter 205 provides a short-form method for handling an intestate estate when the total value of the intestate's property, not including homestead and exempt property, does not exceed $50,000. This procedure is inexpensive and quick and thus is often preferred to a normal administration. Note, however, that the only real property which may be transferred in this manner is the homestead. The estate of a wealthy person might qualify for this procedure because the decedent's wealth may be in non-probate assets, the decedent's homestead, and other exempt property.

§ 205.001. Entitlement to Estate Without Appointment of Personal Representative

The distributees of the estate of a decedent who dies intestate are entitled to the decedent's estate without waiting for the appointment of a personal representative of the estate to the extent the estate assets, excluding homestead and exempt property, exceed the known liabilities of the estate, excluding any liabilities secured by homestead and exempt property, if:

(1) 30 days have elapsed since the date of the decedent's death;

(2) no petition for the appointment of a personal representative is pending or has been granted;

(3) the value of the estate assets, excluding homestead and exempt property, does not exceed $50,000;

(4) an affidavit that meets the requirements of Section 205.002 is filed with the clerk of the court that has jurisdiction and venue of the estate;

(5) the judge approves the affidavit as provided by Section 205.003; and

(6) the distributees comply with Section 205.004.

Derived from Probate Code § 137(a).

Added by Acts 2009, 81st Leg., ch. 680, § 1, eff. Jan. 1, 2014.

§ 205.002. Affidavit Requirements

(a) An affidavit filed under Section 205.001 must:

(1) be sworn to by:

(A) two disinterested witnesses;

(B) each distributee of the estate who has legal capacity; and

(C) if warranted by the facts, the natural guardian or next of kin of any minor distributee or the guardian of any other incapacitated distributee;

(2) show the existence of the conditions prescribed by Sections 205.001(1), (2), and (3); and

(3) include:

(A) a list of all known estate assets and liabilities;

(B) the name and address of each distributee; and

(C) the relevant family history facts concerning heirship that show each distributee's right to receive estate money or other property or to have any evidence of money, property, or other right of the estate as is determined to exist transferred to the distributee as an heir or assignee.

(b) A list of all known estate assets under Subsection (a)(3)(A) must indicate which assets the applicant claims are exempt.

Derived from Probate Code § 137(A).

Added by Acts 2009, 81st Leg., ch. 680, § 1, eff. Jan. 1, 2014. Subsec. (b) added by Acts 2015, 84ᵗʰ Leg., ch. 1106, § 1, eff. Sept. 1, 2015.

§ 205.003. Examination and Approval of Affidavit

The judge shall examine an affidavit filed under Section 205.001. The judge may approve the affidavit if the judge determines that the affidavit conforms to the requirements of this chapter.

Derived from Probate Code § 137(a).

Added by Acts 2009, 81st Leg., ch. 680, § 1, eff. Jan. 1, 2014.

§ 205.004. Copy of Affidavit to Certain Persons

The distributees of the estate shall provide a copy of the affidavit under this chapter, certified by the court clerk, to each person who:

(1) owes money to the estate;

(2) has custody or possession of estate property; or

(3) acts as a registrar, fiduciary, or transfer agent of or for an evidence of interest, indebtedness, property, or other right belonging to the estate.

Derived from Probate Code § 137(a).

Added by Acts 2009, 81st Leg., ch. 680, § 1, eff. Jan. 1, 2014.

§ 205.005. Affidavit as Local Government Record

(a) If the judge approves an affidavit under Section 205.003, the affidavit shall be maintained as a local government record under Subtitle C, Title 6, Local Government Code.

(b) If the county does not maintain local government records in a manner authorized under Subtitle C, Title 6, Local Government Code, the county clerk shall provide and keep in the clerk's office an appropriate book labeled "Small Estates" in which the clerk shall, on payment of the legal recording fee, record each affidavit filed under this chapter. The small estates book must contain an accurate index that shows the decedent's name and references to any land involved.

Derived from Probate Code § 137(d).

Added by Acts 2009, 81st Leg., ch. 680, § 1, eff. Jan. 1, 2014.

§ 205.006. Title to Homestead Transferred Under Affidavit

(a) If a decedent's homestead is the only real property in the decedent's estate, title to the homestead may be transferred under an affidavit that meets the requirements of this chapter. The affidavit used to transfer title to the homestead must be recorded in the deed records of a county in which the homestead is located.

(b) A bona fide purchaser for value may rely on an affidavit recorded under this section. A bona fide purchaser for value without actual or constructive notice of an heir who is not disclosed in the recorded affidavit acquires title to a homestead free of the interests of the undisclosed heir, but remains subject to any claim a creditor of the decedent has by law. A purchaser has constructive notice of an heir who is not disclosed in the recorded affidavit if an affidavit, judgment of heirship, or title transaction in the chain of title in the deed records identifies that heir as the decedent's heir.

(c) An heir who is not disclosed in an affidavit recorded under this section may recover from an heir who receives consideration from a purchaser in a transfer for value of title to a homestead passing under the affidavit.

Derived from Probate Code § 137(c).

Added by Acts 2009, 81st Leg., ch. 680, § 1, eff. Jan. 1, 2014.

§ 205.007. Liability of Certain Persons

(a) A person making a payment, delivery, transfer, or issuance under an affidavit described by this chapter is released to the same extent as if made to a personal representative of the decedent. The person may not be required to:

(1) see to the application of the affidavit; or

(2) inquire into the truth of any statement in the affidavit.

(b) The distributees to whom payment, delivery, transfer, or issuance is made are:

(1) answerable for the payment, delivery, transfer, or issuance to any person having a prior right; and

(2) accountable to any personal representative appointed after the payment, delivery, transfer, or issuance.

(c) Each person who executed the affidavit is liable for any damage or loss to any person that arises from a payment, delivery, transfer, or issuance made in reliance on the affidavit.

(d) If a person to whom the affidavit is delivered refuses to pay, deliver, transfer, or issue property as provided by this section, the property may be recovered in an action brought for that purpose by or on behalf of the distributees entitled to the property on proof of the facts required to be stated in the affidavit.

Derived from Probate Code § 138.

Added by Acts 2009, 81st Leg., ch. 680, § 1, eff. Jan. 1, 2014.

§ 205.008. Effect of Chapter

(a) This chapter does not affect the disposition of property under a will or other testamentary document.

(b) Except as provided by Section 205.006, this chapter does not transfer title to real property.

Derived from Probate Code § 137(b).

Added by Acts 2009, 81st Leg., ch. 680, § 1, eff. Jan. 1, 2014.

§ 205.009. Construction of Certain References

A reference in this chapter to "homestead" or "exempt property" means only a homestead or other exempt property that would be eligible to be set aside under Section 353.051 if the decedent's estate was being administered.

New.

Added by Acts 2015, 84th Leg., ch. 1106, § 2, eff. Sept. 1, 2015.

SUBTITLE F. WILLS

Chapter 251. Fundamental Requirements and Provisions Relating to Wills

Subchapter A. Will Formation

Subchapter B. Will Requirements

Subchapter C. Self-Proved Wills

Chapter 251. Fundamental Requirements and Provisions Relating to Wills

Statutes in Context
Chapter 251

The only way for a person to avoid having the probate estate pass to heirs under the law of intestate succession is to execute a valid will. A person has, however, no right to make a will. The United States Supreme Court confirmed that "[r]ights of succession to the property of a deceased . . . are of statutory creation, and the dead hand rules succession only by sufferance. Nothing in the Federal Constitution forbids the legislature of a state to limit, condition, or even abolish the power of testamentary disposition over property within its jurisdiction." *Irving Trust Co. v. Day*, 314 U.S. 556, 562 (1942).

Although not required to do so, the Texas Legislature has granted individuals the privilege of designating the recipients of their property upon death. Because the ability to execute a will is a privilege, a will typically has no effect unless the testator has precisely followed all the requirements. Texas, like most states, demands strict compliance with the statutorily mandated requirements. See *In re Estate of Iversen*, 150 S.W.3d 824 (Tex. App.—Fort Worth 2004, no pet.) (appellate court reversed trial court's holding that a non-holographic will was properly executed even though it was unwitnessed; the affidavits of two individuals who saw the testator sign the will were not sufficient to satisfy the attestation requirement). A few states, however, have adopted a substantial compliance rule which grants the court a dispensing power to excuse a harmless error if there is clear and convincing evidence that the testator intended the document to be a will.

Many states have a savings statute which permits a will that does not meet the requirements of a valid will under local law to nonetheless be effective under certain circumstances. The Texas savings statute, added by the 2015 Legislature, is found in § 251.053.

There are four main requirements of a valid will: (1) legal capacity (§ 251.001), (2) testamentary capacity (§ 251.001 and case law thereunder), (3) testamentary intent (case law), and (4) formalities (attested wills under § 251.051 and holographic wills under § 251.052). Whenever you are asked to determine if a document purporting to be a will is valid, you must begin your analysis by ascertaining whether the testator satisfied each of these four requirements.

Subchapter A. Will Formation

Statutes in Context
§ 251.001

Section 251.001 requires that the testator have both legal and testamentary capacity to execute a will.

The testator has legal capacity if the testator is either (1) age 18 or older, (2) currently or previously married, or (3) a current member of the armed forces of the United States.

A testator has testamentary capacity ("sound mind") if the testator has (1) sufficient mental ability to understand the act in which the testator was engaged, (2) sufficient mental ability to understand the effect of making a will (that is, to dispose of property upon death), (3) sufficient mental ability to understand the general nature and extent of the testator's property, (4) sufficient mental ability to know the testator's next of kin and the natural objects of the testator's bounty and their claims upon the testator, and (5) memory sufficient to collect in the testator's mind the elements of the business to be transacted and to hold them long enough to perceive at least their obvious relation to each other and to form a reasonable judgment as to them. *Stephen v. Coleman*, 533 S.W.2d 444 (Tex. Civ. App. — Fort Worth 1976, writ ref'd n.r.e.).

§ 251.001. Who May Execute Will

Under the rules and limitations prescribed by law, a person of sound mind has the right and power to make a last will and testament if, at the time the will is made, the person:

(1) is 18 years of age or older;

(2) is or has been married; or

(3) is a member of the armed forces of the United States, an auxiliary of the armed forces of the United States, or the United States Maritime Service.

Derived from Probate Code § 57.

Added by Acts 2009, 81st Leg., ch. 680, § 1, eff. Jan. 1, 2014.

Statutes in Context
§ 251.002

Section 251.002 authorizes a negative will, that is, a will which does not provide for the disposition of property but rather merely states that a named heir may not take by intestacy. Negative provisions were not enforced under the common law.

---

§ 251.002. Interests That May Pass by Will; Disinheritance

(a) Subject to limitations prescribed by law, a person competent to make a last will and testament may devise under the will and testament all the estate, right, title, and interest in property the person has at the time of the person's death.

(b) A person who makes a last will and testament may:

(1) disinherit an heir; and

(2) direct the disposition of property or an interest passing under the will or by intestacy.

Derived from Probate Code §§ 58(a), (b).

Added by Acts 2009, 81st Leg., ch. 680, § 1, eff. Jan. 1, 2014.

Subchapter B. Will Requirements

Statutes in Context
§ 251.051

Section 251.051 sets forth the formalities necessary for an attested will.

1. In Writing The statute does not indicate what the will is to be written on or written with. See Government Code § 311.005(11) for a definition of "written."

2. Signed by Testator The Probate Code does not explain what constitutes a signature but the Code Construction Act (Government Code § 311.005(6)) provides that a signature is any symbol executed or adopted by a person with present intent to authenticate a writing. Accordingly, initials, marks, and nicknames are sufficient.

A proxy may sign the testator's name provided the signature is placed on the will (1) by the testator's direction and (2) in the testator's presence. See also Government Code § 406.0165 for when a notary may sign as a proxy in the presence of a witness if the testator is physically unable to sign.

Section 251.051 does not specify a location for the testator's signature. See *Lawson v. Dawson's Estate*, 53 S.W. 64 (Tex. Civ. App. — 1899, writ ref'd) (holding with regard to a holographic will that the location of the testator's signature is "of secondary consequence").

3. Attested by at Least Two Witnesses The witnesses must be credible, that is, competent to testify in court under the applicable evidence rules. See *Moos v. First State Bank*, 60 S.W.2d 888 (Tex. Civ. App. 1933, writ dism'd w.o.j.). The witnesses only need to be above the age of 14. See Estates Code § 254.002 for what happens if the witness is also a beneficiary of the will.

The witnesses do not need to know they are witnessing a will. In other words, publication is not required in Texas. See *Davis v. Davis*, 45 S.W.2d 240 (Tex. Civ. App. — Beaumont 1931, no writ). The witnesses only need to have the intent to give validity to the document as an act of the testator.

The witnesses must attest using "their names" in "their own handwriting." Thus, attestation by mark or by proxy is not allowed.

Although § 251.051 states that the witnesses must "subscribe" (that is, attest at the end of the will), the courts have not read this requirement strictly. See *Fowler v. Stagner*, 55 Tex. 393 (1881).

The witnesses must attest "in the presence of the testator." The courts have interpreted this to mean a conscious presence, that is, "the attestation must occur where testator, unless blind, is able to see it from his actual position at the time, or at most, from such position as slightly altered, where he has the power readily to make the alteration without assistance." *Nichols v. Rowan*, 442 S.W.2d 21 (Tex. Civ. App. — San Antonio 1967, writ ref'd n.r.e.). Note that Texas law, unlike many states, does not require (1) the witnesses to attest in each other's presence or (2) the testator to sign the will in the presence of the witnesses.

Although the testator should sign the will before the witnesses attest, Texas courts have not been strict in this regard. Instead, they have followed the continuous transaction view so that as long as "the execution and attestation of a will occurs at the same time and place and forms part of one transaction, it is immaterial that the witnesses subscribe before the testator signs." *James v. Haupt*, 573 S.W.2d 285, 289 (Tex. Civ. App. — Tyler 1978, writ ref'd n.r.e.) and *In re Estate of Pruitt*, 249 S.W.3d 654 (Tex. App.—Fort Worth 2008, no pet.).

§ 251.051. Written, Signed, and Attested

Except as otherwise provided by law, a last will and testament must be:

    (1) in writing;

    (2) signed by:

        (A) the testator in person; or

        (B) another person on behalf of the testator:

            (i) in the testator's presence; and

            (ii) under the testator's direction; and

    (3) attested by two or more credible witnesses who are at least 14 years of age and who subscribe their names to the will in their own handwriting in the testator's presence.

Derived from Probate Code § 59(a).

Added by Acts 2009, 81st Leg., ch. 680, § 1, eff. Jan. 1, 2014.

Statutes in Context
§ 251.052

A holographic will is prepared in the testator's own handwriting. Section 251.052 exempts holographic wills from the attestation requirement. This special treatment is justified by the aura of validity that surrounds a handwritten document because of the reduced chance of forgery and enhanced assurance of authenticity resulting from the large sample of the testator's writing.

The will must be "wholly" in the testator's own handwriting. Texas courts have adopted the surplusage approach which means that nonholographic material will not injure the holographic character of the will as long as the nonholographic material is not necessary to complete the instrument and does not affect its meaning. See *Maul v. Williams*, 39 S.W.2d 1107 (Tex. Comm'n App. 1934, holding approved).

A holographic will may be made self-proved. See Estates Code § 251.107. Because the self-proving affidavit is a separate instrument, it does not need to be holographic.

§ 251.052. Exception for Holographic Wills

Notwithstanding Section 251.051, a will written wholly in the testator's handwriting is not required to be attested by subscribing witnesses.

Derived from Probate Code §§ 59(a), 60.

Added by Acts 2009, 81st Leg., ch. 680, § 1, eff. Jan. 1, 2014.

Statutes in Context
§ 251.053

Section 251.053 is the Texas savings statute which was enacted by the 2015 Legislature. The statute provides that a will is valid in Texas, even if it does not meet the Texas requirements, if it meets the requirements of the jurisdiction where (1) the will was executed, (2) the decedent was domiciled, or (3) the decedent had a place of residence.

---

§ 251.053. Exception for Foreign and Certain Other Wills

Section 251.051 does not apply to a written will executed in compliance with:

(1) the law of the state or foreign country where the will was executed, as that law existed at the time of the will's execution; or

(2) the law of the state or foreign country where the testator was domiciled or had a place of residence, as that law existed at the time of the will's execution or at the time of the testator's death.

New.

Added by Acts 2015, 84ᵗʰ Leg., ch. 995, § 13, eff. Sept. 1, 2015.

Subchapter C. Self-Proved Wills

Statutes in Context
Chapter 251

Self-Proving Affidavit. Section 251.101 provides the testator with the option making the will self-proved by either (1) adding an affidavit as a separate document under § 251.051 or (2) including the affidavit within the text of the will under § 251.1045. Virtually all wills contain this affidavit because it substitutes for the in-court testimony of the witnesses when the will is probated thereby saving considerable time and expense.

In the past, problems arose if the testator and/or the witnesses signed the affidavit but not the will. The courts consistently held that the will and the affidavit were separate documents and thus a signature on the self-proving affidavit could not substitute for a missing signature on the will. See *Boren v. Boren*, 402 S.W.2d 728 (Tex. 1966). The 1991 Texas Legislature amended the predecessor to Estates Code § 251.105 to alleviate this harsh result. Now, a signature on the affidavit may be used to prove the will but the will is then no longer considered self-proved and the testimony of the witnesses will be needed to probate the will.

The 2011 Legislature went a step further by allowing the testator to include the self-proving language within the body of the will so that only one set of signatures is required. See § 251.1045.

---

§ 251.101. Self-Proved Will

A self-proved will is a will:

(1) to which a self-proving affidavit subscribed and sworn to by the testator and witnesses is attached or annexed; or

(2) that is simultaneously executed, attested, and made self-proved as provided by Section 251.1045.

Derived from Probate Code § 59(b).

Added by Acts 2009, 81st Leg., ch. 680, § 1, eff. Jan. 1, 2014. Amended by Acts 2011, 82nd Leg., ch. 1338, § 2.22, eff. Jan. 1, 2014.

§ 251.102. Probate and Treatment of Self-Proved Will

(a) A self-proved will may be admitted to probate without the testimony of any subscribing witnesses if:

(1) the testator and witnesses execute a self-proving affidavit; or

(2) the will is simultaneously executed, attested, and made self-proved as provided by Section 251.1045.

(b) A self-proved will may not otherwise be treated differently than a will that is not self-proved.

Derived from Probate Code §§ 59(a), (c).

Added by Acts 2009, 81st Leg., ch. 680, § 1, eff. Jan. 1, 2014. Subsec. (a) amended by Acts 2011, 82nd Leg., ch. 1338, § 2.23, eff. Jan. 1, 2014.

§ 251.103. Period for Making Attested Wills Self-Proved

A will or testament that meets the requirements of Section 251.051 may be made self-proved at:

(1) the time of the execution of the will or testament; or

(2) a later date during the lifetime of the testator and the witnesses.

Derived from Probate Code § 59(a).

Added by Acts 2009, 81st Leg., ch. 680, § 1, eff. Jan. 1, 2014.

§ 251.104. Requirements for Self-Proving Affidavit

(a) An affidavit that is in form and content substantially as provided by Subsection (e) is a self-proving affidavit.

(b) A self-proving affidavit must be made by the testator and by the attesting witnesses before an officer authorized to administer oaths. The officer shall affix the officer's official seal to the self-proving affidavit.

(c) The self-proving affidavit shall be attached or annexed to the will or testament.

(d) An affidavit that is in substantial compliance with the form of the affidavit provided by Subsection (e), that is subscribed and acknowledged by the testator, and that is subscribed and sworn to by the attesting witnesses is sufficient to self-prove the will. No other affidavit or certificate of a testator is required to self-prove a will or testament other than the affidavit provided by Subsection (e).

(e) The form and content of the self-proving affidavit must be substantially as follows:

THE STATE OF TEXAS
COUNTY OF _____

Before me, the undersigned authority, on this day personally appeared _____, and _____, known to me to be the testator and the witnesses, respectively, whose names are subscribed to the annexed or foregoing instrument in their respective capacities, and, all of said persons being by me duly sworn, the said _____, testator, declared to me and to the said witnesses in my presence that said instrument is [his/her] last will and testament, and that [he/she] had willingly made and executed it as [his/her] free act and deed; and the said witnesses, each on [his/her] oath stated to me, in the presence and hearing of the said testator, that the said testator had declared to them that said instrument is [his/her] last will and testament, and that [he/she] executed same as such and wanted each of them to sign it as a witness; and upon their oaths each witness stated further that they did sign the same as witnesses in the presence of the said testator and at [his/her] request; that [he/she] was at that time eighteen years of age or over (or being under such age, was or had been lawfully married, or was then a member of the armed forces of the United States, or an auxiliary of the armed forces of the United States, or the United States Maritime Service) and was of sound mind; and that each of said witnesses was then at least fourteen years of age.

_____
Testator

_____

Witness

_____
Witness

Subscribed and sworn to before me by the said _____, testator, and by the said _____ and _____, witnesses, this _____ day of _____ A.D. _____.

(SEAL)
(Signed) _____
(Official Capacity of Officer)

Derived from Probate Code § 59(a), (b).

Added by Acts 2009, 81st Leg., ch. 680, § 1, eff. Jan. 1, 2014. Subsec. (b) amended by Acts 2011, 82nd Leg., ch. 1338, § 2.24, eff. Jan. 1, 2014.

§ 251.1045. Simultaneous Execution, Attestation, and Self-Proving

(a) As an alternative to the self-proving of a will by the affidavits of the testator and the attesting witnesses as provided by Section 251.104, a will may be simultaneously executed, attested, and made self-proved before an officer authorized to administer oaths, and the testimony of the witnesses in the probate of the will may be made unnecessary, with the inclusion in the will of the following in form and contents substantially as follows:

I, _____, as testator, after being duly sworn, declare to the undersigned witnesses and to the undersigned authority that this instrument is my will, that I [have] willingly make [made] and execute [executed] it in the presence of the undersigned witnesses, all of whom are [were] present at the same time, as my free act and deed, and that I request [have requested] each of the undersigned witnesses to sign this will in my presence and in the presence of each other. I now sign this will in the presence of the attesting witnesses and the undersigned authority on this _____ day of _____, 20 _____.

_____
Testator

The undersigned, _____ and _____, each being at least fourteen years of age, after being duly sworn, declare to the testator and to the undersigned authority that the testator declared to us that this instrument is the testator's will and that the testator requested us to act as witnesses to the testator's will and signature. The testator then signed this will in our presence, all of us being present at the same time. The testator is eighteen years of age or over (or being under such age, is or has been lawfully married, or is a member of the armed forces of the United States or of an auxiliary of the armed forces of the United States or of the United States Maritime Service), and we believe the testator to be of sound mind. We now sign our names as attesting witnesses in the presence of the testator, each other, and the undersigned authority

on this _____ day of _____,
20_____.

_____
Witness

_____
Witness

Subscribed and sworn to before me by the said _____, testator, and by the said _____ and _____, witnesses, this _____ day of _____, 20_____.
    (SEAL)
    (Signed)_____
    (Official Capacity of Officer)

(b) A will that is in substantial compliance with the form provided by Subsection (a) is sufficient to self-prove a will.

Derived from Probate Code § 59(a-1).

Added by Acts 2011, 82nd Leg., ch. 1338, § 2.25, eff. Jan. 1, 2014. Subsec. (a) amended by Acts 2015, 84th Leg., ch. 995, § 14, eff. Sept. 1, 2015.

§ 251.105. Effect of Signature on Self-Proving Affidavit

A signature on a self-proving affidavit is considered a signature to the will if necessary to prove that the will was signed by the testator or witnesses or both, except that, in that case, the will may not be considered a self-proved will.

Derived from Probate Code § 59(b).

Added by Acts 2009, 81st Leg., ch. 680, § 1, eff. Jan. 1, 2014.

§ 251.106. Contest, Revocation, or Amendment of Self-Proved Will

A self-proved will may be contested, revoked, or amended by a codicil in the same manner as a will that is not self-proved.

Derived from Probate Code § 59(c).

Added by Acts 2009, 81st Leg., ch. 680, § 1, eff. Jan. 1, 2014.

§ 251.107. Self-Proved Holographic Will

Notwithstanding any other provision of this subchapter, a will written wholly in the testator's handwriting may be made self-proved at any time during the testator's lifetime by the attachment or annexation to the will of an affidavit by the testator to the effect that:

(1) the instrument is the testator's last will;

(2) the testator was 18 years of age or older at the time the will was executed or, if the testator was younger than 18 years of age, that the testator:

(A) was or had been married; or

(B) was a member of the armed forces of the United States, an auxiliary of the armed forces of the United States, or the United States Maritime Service at the time the will was executed;

(3) the testator was of sound mind; and

(4) the testator has not revoked the will.

Derived from Probate Code § 60.

Added by Acts 2009, 81st Leg., ch. 680, § 1, eff. Jan. 1, 2014.

Chapter 252. Safekeeping and Custody of Wills

Subchapter A. Deposit of Will with County Clerk

Subchapter B. Will Delivery During Life of Testator

Subchapter C. Actions by County Clerk on Death of Testator

Subchapter D. Legal Effect of Will Deposit

Subchapter E. Duty and Liability of Custodian of Estate Papers

Chapter 252. Safekeeping and Custody of Wills

Subchapter A. Deposit of Will with County Clerk

Statutes in Context
Chapter 252

Chapter 252 provides a procedure for a testator to deposit the will with the clerk of the court for safekeeping. Thus, when a person dies, it is prudent for those interested in the estate to check with the county court clerk in every county in which the decedent has resided. The deposit has no legal effect and does not enhance the likelihood of the will being deemed valid.

§ 252.001. Will Deposit; Certificate

(a) A testator, or another person for the testator, may deposit the testator's will with the county clerk of the county of the testator's residence. Before accepting the will for deposit, the clerk may require proof satisfactory to the clerk concerning the testator's identity and residence.

(b) The county clerk shall receive and keep the will on the payment of a $5 fee.

(c) On the deposit of the will, the county clerk shall issue a certificate of deposit for the will.

Derived from Probate Code § 71(a).

Added by Acts 2009, 81st Leg., ch. 680, § 1, eff. Jan. 1, 2014.

§ 252.002. Sealed Wrapper Required

(a) A will intended to be deposited with a county clerk shall be enclosed in a sealed wrapper.

(b) The wrapper must be endorsed with:

(1) "Will of," followed by the name, address, and signature of the testator; and

(2) the name and current address of each person who is to be notified of the deposit of the will after the testator's death.

Derived from Probate Code § 71(b).

Added by Acts 2009, 81st Leg., ch. 680, § 1, eff. Jan. 1, 2014.

§ 252.003. Numbering of Filed Wills and Corresponding Certificates

(a) A county clerk shall number wills deposited with the clerk in consecutive order.

(b) A certificate of deposit issued under Section 252.001(c) on receipt of a will must bear the same number as the will for which the certificate is issued.

Derived from Probate Code § 71(a).

Added by Acts 2009, 81st Leg., ch. 680, § 1, eff. Jan. 1, 2014.

§ 252.004. Index

A county clerk shall keep an index of all wills deposited with the clerk under Section 252.001.

Derived from Probate Code § 71(c).

Added by Acts 2009, 81st Leg., ch. 680, § 1, eff. Jan. 1, 2014.

Subchapter B. Will Delivery During Life of Testator

§ 252.051. Will Delivery

During the lifetime of the testator, a will deposited with a county clerk under Subchapter A may be delivered only to:

(1) the testator; or

(2) another person authorized by the testator by a sworn written order.

Derived from Probate Code § 71(d).

Added by Acts 2009, 81st Leg., ch. 680, § 1, eff. Jan. 1, 2014.

§ 252.052. Surrender of Certificate of Deposit; Exception

(a) Except as provided by Subsection (b), on delivery of a will to the testator or a person authorized by the testator under Section 252.051, the certificate of deposit issued for the will must be surrendered by the person to whom delivery of the will is made.

(b) A county clerk may instead accept and file an affidavit by the testator stating that the certificate of deposit issued for the will has been lost, stolen, or destroyed.

Derived from Probate Code § 71(d).

Added by Acts 2009, 81st Leg., ch. 680, § 1, eff. Jan. 1, 2014.

Subchapter C. Actions by County Clerk on Death of Testator

§ 252.101. Notification by County Clerk

A county clerk shall notify, by registered mail, return receipt requested, each person named on the endorsement of the will wrapper that the will is on deposit in the clerk's office if:

(1) an affidavit is submitted to the clerk stating that the testator has died; or

(2) the clerk receives other notice or proof of the testator's death sufficient to convince the clerk that the testator has died.

Derived from Probate Code § 71(e).

Added by Acts 2009, 81st Leg., ch. 680, § 1, eff. Jan. 1, 2014.

§ 252.102. Will Delivery on Testator's Death

On the request of one or more persons notified under Section 252.101, the county clerk shall deliver the will that is the subject of the notice to the person or persons. The clerk shall obtain a receipt for delivery of the will.

Derived from Probate Code § 71(e).

Added by Acts 2009, 81st Leg., ch. 680, § 1, eff. Jan. 1, 2014.

§ 252.103. Inspection of Will by County Clerk

A county clerk shall open a will wrapper and inspect the will if:

(1) the notice required by Section 252.101 is returned as undelivered; or

(2) the clerk has accepted for deposit a will that does not specify on the will wrapper the person to whom the will is to be delivered on the testator's death.

Derived from Probate Code § 71(e).

Added by Acts 2009, 81st Leg., ch. 680, § 1, eff. Jan. 1, 2014.

§ 252.104. Notice and Delivery of Will to Executor

If a county clerk inspects a will under Section 252.103 and the will names an executor, the clerk shall:

(1) notify the person named as executor, by registered mail, return receipt requested, that the will is on deposit with the clerk; and

(2) deliver, on request, the will to the person named as executor.

Derived from Probate Code § 71(e).

Added by Acts 2009, 81st Leg., ch. 680, § 1, eff. Jan. 1, 2014.

§ 252.105. Notice and Delivery of Will to Devisees

(a) If a county clerk inspects a will under Section 252.103, the clerk shall notify by registered mail, return receipt requested, the devisees named in the will that the will is on deposit with the clerk if:

(1) the will does not name an executor;

(2) the person named as executor in the will:

(A) has died; or

(B) fails to take the will before the 31st day after the date the notice required by Section 252.104 is mailed to the person; or

(3) the notice mailed to the person named as executor is returned as undelivered.

(b) On request, the county clerk shall deliver the will to any or all of the devisees notified under Subsection (a).

Derived from Probate Code § 71(e).

Added by Acts 2009, 81st Leg., ch. 680, § 1, eff. Jan. 1, 2014.

Subchapter D. Legal Effect of Will Deposit

§ 252.151. Deposit Has No Legal Significance

The provisions of Subchapter A providing for the deposit of a will with a county clerk during the lifetime of a testator are solely for the purpose of providing a safe and convenient repository for a will. For purposes of probate, a will deposited as provided by Subchapter A may not be treated differently than a will that has not been deposited.

Derived from Probate Code § 71(f).

Added by Acts 2009, 81st Leg., ch. 680, § 1, eff. Jan. 1, 2014.

§ 252.152. Prior Deposited Will in Relation to Later Will

A will that is not deposited as provided by Subchapter A shall be admitted to probate on proof that the will is the last will and testament of the testator, notwithstanding the fact that the testator has a prior will that has been deposited in accordance with Subchapter A.

Derived from Probate Code § 71(f).

Added by Acts 2009, 81st Leg., ch. 680, § 1, eff. Jan. 1, 2014.

§ 252.153. Will Deposit Does Not Constitute Notice

The deposit of a will as provided by Subchapter A does not constitute notice, constructive or otherwise, to any person as to the existence or the contents of the will.

Derived from Probate Code § 71(g).

Added by Acts 2009, 81st Leg., ch. 680, § 1, eff. Jan. 1, 2014.

Subchapter E. Duty and Liability of Custodian of Estate Papers

Statutes in Context
Chapter 252, Subchapter E

After a testator dies, the custodian of the will does not have a duty to probate the will. Instead, § 252.201 merely requires that the custodian deliver the will to the clerk of the court. Section 252.203 provides procedures, including imprisonment of the custodian, which may be used if the custodian is unwilling to deliver the will.

§ 252.201. Will Delivery

On receiving notice of a testator's death, the person who has custody of the testator's will shall deliver the will to the clerk of the court that has jurisdiction of the testator's estate.

Derived from Probate Code § 75.

Added by Acts 2009, 81st Leg., ch. 680, § 1, eff. Jan. 1, 2014.

§ 252.202. Personal Service on Custodian of Estate Papers

On a sworn written complaint that a person has custody of the last will of a testator or any papers belonging to the estate of a testator or intestate, the judge of the court that has jurisdiction of the estate shall have the person cited by personal service to appear and show cause why the person should not deliver:

(1) the will to the court for probate; or

(2) the papers to the executor or administrator.

Derived from Probate Code § 75.

Added by Acts 2009, 81st Leg., ch. 680, § 1, eff. Jan. 1, 2014.

§ 252.203. Arrest; Confinement

On the return of a citation served under Section 252.202, if the judge is satisfied that the person served with the citation had custody of the will or papers at the time the complaint under that section was filed and the person does not deliver the will or papers or show good cause why the will or papers have not been delivered, the judge may have the person arrested and confined until the person delivers the will or papers.

Derived from Probate Code § 75.

Added by Acts 2009, 81st Leg., ch. 680, § 1, eff. Jan. 1, 2014.

§ 252.204. Damages

(a) A person who refuses to deliver a will or papers described by Section 252.202 is liable to any person aggrieved by the refusal for all damages sustained as a result of the refusal.

(b) Damages may be recovered under this section in any court of competent jurisdiction.

Derived from Probate Code § 75.

Added by Acts 2009, 81st Leg., ch. 680, § 1, eff. Jan. 1, 2014.

Chapter 253. Change and Revocation of Wills

§ 253.001. Court May Not Prohibit Changing or Revoking a Will

§ 253.002. Revocation of Will

Chapter 253. Change and Revocation of Wills

Statutes in Context
§ 253.001

A judge in a divorce action may issue an order preventing a party from revoking or changing his or her will during the pendency of the divorce. Section 253.001 prohibits this practice and provides that such an order is void.

§ 253.001. Court May Not Prohibit Changing or Revoking a Will

(a) Notwithstanding Section 22.007(a), in this section, "court" means a constitutional county court, district court, or statutory county court, including a statutory probate court.

(b) A court may not prohibit a person from:

(1) executing a new will;

(2) executing [or] a codicil to an existing will; or

(3) revoking an existing will or codicil in whole or in part.

(c) Any portion of a court order that purports to prohibit a person from engaging in an action described by Subsection (b) [executing a new will or a codicil to an existing will] is void and may be disregarded without penalty or sanction of any kind.

Derived from Probate Code § 69A.

Added by Acts 2009, 81st Leg., ch. 680, § 1, eff. Jan. 1, 2014. Subsection (c) added by Acts 2013, 83rd Leg., ch. 1136, § 20, eff. Jan. 1, 2014. Subsec. (b)& (c) amended by Acts 2015, 84th Leg., ch. 995, §§ 15 & 16, eff. Sept. 1, 2015.

Statutes in Context
§ 253.002

Section 253.002 provides two methods for revoking a will.

1. Subsequent Writing The testator may revoke a will in a new will, codicil, or other written declaration. The revocation may be express ("I hereby revoke all prior wills and codicils.") or it may be by inconsistency (the testator's old will left Blackacre to Able and the new will leaves Blackacre to Brenda). The formalities for the revocation instrument are the same as for a will.

2. Physical Act The testator may revoke a will by "destroying or canceling" the will such as by tearing up the will, drawing a dark line through the testator's signature, or burning the will. Revocation by physical act is an "all or nothing" arrangement, that is, Texas law does not permit partial revocation by physical act. Thus, if the testator merely draws lines through certain provisions or makes interlineations on a nonholographic will, these self-help changes will not be given effect; the will is probated as originally written. See *Leatherwood v. Stephens*, 24 S.W.2d 819 (Tex. Comm'n App. 1930, judgment adopted).

The physical act may be performed by a proxy provided it is done in the testator's presence.

In the almost unbelievable opinion of *In re Estate of Catlin*, 311 S.W.3d 697 (Tex. App.—Amarillo 2010, pet. denied), the court accepted proponent's explanation that he looked at the testator's home, office, safety deposit boxes, and drafting attorney's office but could not find the original. The court explained that the will proponent did not have to demonstrate an affirmative reason why the original cannot be located such as "the eating habits of a neighbor's goat, the occurrence of a Kansas tornado, the devastation of a flash flood, or the like." See Estates Code § 256.156. This court basically makes it impossible for a testator to revoke a will by physical act because even if the will cannot be found and there is no affirmative reason why it cannot be found, a copy may nonetheless be probated.

§ 253.002. Revocation of Will

A written will, or a clause or devise in a written will, may not be revoked, except by a subsequent will, codicil, or declaration in writing that is executed with like formalities, or by the testator destroying or canceling the same, or causing it to be destroyed or canceled in the testator's presence.

Derived from Probate Code § 63.

Added by Acts 2009, 81st Leg., ch. 680, § 1, eff. Jan. 1, 2014.

Chapter 254. Validity of Certain Provisions in, and Contracts Relating to, Wills

Chapter 254. Validity of Certain Provisions in, and Contracts Relating to, Wills

Statutes in Context
§ 254.001

Section 254.001 authorizes the use of a pour-over provision in a will, that is, a testamentary gift to an inter vivos trust. Pour-over provisions are very common because a testator may wish to obtain the benefits of a trust but not want to create the trust in the testator's will. Reasons a testator may prefer the pour-over technique include (1) an inter vivos trust is easier to amend than a will; (2) an inter vivos trust can serve as a receptacle for a variety of other assets, such as life insurance proceeds and annuity payments, to provide a unified disposition of the testator's property; and (3) the testator may pour over into a trust created by someone else, such as a spouse.

Section 254.001 is based on the 1991 version of the Uniform Testamentary Additions to Trusts Act. Innovations in this act include (1) the testator's ability to pour over to an inter vivos trust which, although placed in writing, has not actually been created because no property has yet been transferred to the trust (in other words, the testamentary gift may provide the initial funding of

the trust) and (2) the pour-over property is governed by the current terms of the trust, not those in effect when the testator died. Thus, if a testator leaves property to a trust created by someone else who is still alive, the potential exists for that person to make amendments to the trust after the testator's death which may change the identity of the beneficiaries and how the trust property is spent or managed.

See Insurance Code §§ 1104.021 through 1104.025 for additional provisions applicable to life insurance which is payable to the trustee named in the policy.

§ 254.001. Devises to Trustees

(a) A testator may validly devise property in a will to the trustee of a trust established or to be established:

(1) during the testator's lifetime by the testator, the testator and another person, or another person, including a funded or unfunded life insurance trust in which the settlor has reserved any or all rights of ownership of the insurance contracts; or

(2) at the testator's death by the testator's devise to the trustee, regardless of the existence, size, or character of the corpus of the trust, if:

(A) the trust is identified in the testator's will; and

(B) the terms of the trust are in:

(i) a written instrument, other than a will, executed before, with, or after the execution of the testator's will; or

(ii) another person's will if that person predeceased the testator.

(b) A devise under Subsection (a) is not invalid because the trust:

(1) is amendable or revocable; or

(2) was amended after the execution of the will or the testator's death.

(c) Unless the testator's will provides otherwise, property devised to a trust described by Subsection (a) is not held under a testamentary trust of the testator. The property:

(1) becomes part of the trust to which the property is devised; and

(2) must be administered and disposed of according to the provisions of the instrument establishing the trust, including any amendment to the instrument made before or after the testator's death.

(d) Unless the testator's will provides otherwise, a revocation or termination of the trust before the testator's death causes the devise to lapse.

Derived from Probate Code § 58a.

Added by Acts 2009, 81st Leg., ch. 680, § 1, eff. Jan. 1, 2014.

Statutes in Context
§ 254.002

A testamentary gift to a beneficiary who is also a witness to the will is presumed void under the Texas purging statute, § 254.002. The testimony of an interested witness about the attestation is suspect because the witness has a motive to lie. There are three exceptions to this rule. The first exception applies if the witness would be an heir if the testator had actually died intestate in which case the witness may receive the gift provided it does not exceed the share of the testator's estate the witness could take under intestate succession. With regard to the smaller of the gift under the will or the intestate share, the witness has no motive to lie because the witness will receive that amount regardless of the validity of the will. The second exception is if the will can "be otherwise established" such as by the testimony of another witness. The third exception is detailed in § 254.002(c).

Section 254.002(c) provides the third exception to the interested witness rule. If the testimony of the witness-beneficiary is corroborated by a disinterested and credible person, the witness-beneficiary may retain the testamentary gift. Note that this person does not have to be an attesting witness to the will. For example, this person could be the attorney who supervised the will execution ceremony.

§ 254.002. Bequests to Certain Subscribing Witnesses

(a) Except as provided by Subsection (c), if a devisee under a will is also a subscribing witness to the will and the will cannot be otherwise established:

(1) the bequest is void; and

(2) the subscribing witness shall be allowed and compelled to appear and give the witness's testimony in the same manner as if the bequest to the witness had not been made.

(b) Notwithstanding Subsection (a), if the subscribing witness described by that subsection would have been entitled to a share of the testator's estate had the testator died intestate, the witness is entitled to as much of that share as does not exceed the value of the bequest to the witness under the will.

(c) If the testimony of a subscribing witness described by Subsection (a) proving the will is corroborated by at least one disinterested and credible person who testifies that the subscribing witness's testimony is true and correct:

(1) the bequest to the subscribing witness is not void under Subsection (a); and

(2) the subscribing witness is not regarded as an incompetent or noncredible witness under Subchapters B and C, Chapter 251.

Derived from Probate Code §§ 61, 62.

Added by Acts 2009, 81st Leg., ch. 680, § 1, eff. Jan. 1, 2014.

Statutes in Context
§ 254.003

Section 254.003 voids a testamentary gift made to an attorney or someone closely connected to the attorney (i.e., the attorney's spouse, the attorney's parent, a descendent of the attorney's parent, or the attorney's employee) when the attorney is also the attorney who drafted the will. This section, however, does not apply to wills where the beneficiary listed in subsection (a) is also the testator's spouse, ascendant or descendant, or related within the third degree of consanguinity or affinity. See Government Code §§ 573.021-573.025 (definitions of "consanguinity" and "affinity" by analogy).

In *Jones v. Krown*, 218 S.W.3d 746 (Tex. App.—Fort Worth 2007, pet. denied), an attorney drafted a will for a testator which named his paralegal (an independent contractor) as both a beneficiary and as the executrix. After the testator died, his sister filed a motion for a declaratory judgment to set aside the gift to the paralegal under the Probate Code predecessor to Estates Code § 254.003. The court held that the paralegal's gift was void and that the property passed via intestacy to his sister.

See also Disciplinary Rule of Professional Conduct 1.08(b) (as found in the Government Code).

§ 254.003. Devises to Certain Attorneys and Other Persons

(a) A devise of property in a will is void if the devise is made to:

(1) an attorney who prepares or supervises the preparation of the will;

(2) a parent, descendant of a parent, or employee of the attorney described by Subdivision (1); or

(3) the spouse of a person described by Subdivision (1) or (2).

(b) This section does not apply to:

(1) a devise made to a person who:

(A) is the testator's spouse;

(B) is an ascendant or descendant of the testator; or

(C) is related within the third degree by consanguinity or affinity to the testator; or

(2) a bona fide purchaser for value from a devisee in a will.

Derived from Probate Code § 58b.

Added by Acts 2009, 81st Leg., ch. 680, § 1, eff. Jan. 1, 2014.

Statutes in Context
§ 254.004

A contractual will refers to a will that is either (a) executed in whole or in part as the consideration for a contract, or (b) not revoked as the consideration for a contract. The contract must meet all the requirements for a valid contract under applicable Texas law.

To ensure that only the wills of testators who actually intend to be bound are deemed contractual, § 254.004 requires that (1) the will state that a contract exists along with the material terms of the contract or (2) the contract be proved by a binding and enforceable written agreement such as a premarital agreement, divorce property settlement, or buy-sell agreement. The statute further provides that joint wills (a single testamentary instrument that contains the wills of two or more persons, such as a husband and wife) and reciprocal wills (separate wills which contain parallel dispositive provisions) are not presumably contractual. Nonetheless, to avoid the unintended creation of a contractual will, it may be prudent to include an anticontract provision.

If the testator executed the will prior to September 1, 1979, the contractual nature of the will may be established by extrinsic evidence.

§ 254.004. Contracts Concerning Wills or Devises; Joint or Reciprocal Wills

(a) A contract executed or entered into on or after September 1, 1979, to make a will or devise, or not to revoke a will or devise, may be established only by:

(1) a written agreement that is binding and enforceable; or

(2) a will stating:

(A) that a contract exists; and

(B) the material provisions of the contract.

(b) The execution of a joint will or reciprocal wills does not constitute by itself sufficient evidence of the existence of a contract.

Derived from Probate Code § 59A.

Added by Acts 2009, 81st Leg., ch. 680, § 1, eff. Jan. 1, 2014.

Statutes in Context
§ 254.005

A forfeiture, no contest, or *in terrorem* clause provides that a beneficiary who unsuccessfully contests a will is precluded from thereafter receiving property under the will. A forfeiture clause is presumed enforceable unless the party who wants the clause to be unenforceable establishes by a preponderance of the evidence that just cause existed for bringing the action and the action was brought and maintained in good faith.

§ 254.005. Forfeiture Clause

(a) A provision in a will that would cause a forfeiture of or void a devise or provision in favor of a person for bringing any court action, including contesting a will, is enforceable unless in a court action determining whether the forfeiture clause should be enforced, the person who brought the action contrary to the forfeiture clause establishes by a preponderance of the evidence that:

(1) just cause existed for bringing the action; and

(2) the action was brought and maintained in good faith.

(b) This section is not intended to and does not repeal any law recognizing that forfeiture clauses generally will not be construed to prevent a beneficiary from seeking to compel a fiduciary to perform the fiduciary's duties, seeking redress against a fiduciary for a breach of the fiduciary's duties, or seeking a judicial construction of a will or trust.

Derived from Probate Code § 64.

Added by Acts 2011, 82nd Leg., ch. 91), § 8.009(a), eff. Jan. 1, 2014; Acts 2011, 82nd Leg., ch. 1338, § 2.26, eff. Jan. 1, 2014. Amended by Acts 2013, 83rd Leg., ch. 351, § 2.01, eff. Jan. 1, 2014. Subsec. (b) added by Acts 2015, 84th Leg., ch. 995, § 17, eff. Sept. 1, 2015.

Chapter 255. Construction and Interpretation of Wills

Subchapter A. Certain Personal Property Excluded From Devise or Legacy

Subchapter B. Succession by Pretermitted Child

Chapter 255. Construction and Interpretation of Wills

Subchapter A. Certain Personal Property Excluded from Devise or Legacy

Statutes in Context
Chapter 255, Subchapter A

Section 255.003 provides that the contents of any specifically gifted item are not included in the gift unless the gift expressly includes the contents. Intangible property such as stock and titled personal property such as motor vehicles, are not considered contents. For example, if the will devises "my home to Son," the contents of the real property will not pass to Son. However, if the will devises "my house and its contents to Son" and upon testator's death the home contains furniture, stock certificates, and a car, Son would receive the furniture, but not the stock or car.

§ 255.001. Definitions

In this subchapter:

(1) "Contents" means tangible personal property, other than titled personal property, found inside of or on a specifically devised item. The term includes clothing, pictures, furniture, coin collections, and other items of tangible personal property that:

(A) do not require a formal transfer of title; and

(B) are located in another item of tangible personal property such as a cedar chest or other furniture.

(2) "Titled personal property" includes all tangible personal property represented by a certificate of title, certificate of ownership, written label, marking, or designation that signifies ownership by a person. The term includes a motor vehicle, motor home, motorboat, or other similar property that requires a formal transfer of title.

Derived from Probate Code § 58(d).

Added by Acts 2009, 81st Leg., ch. 680, § 1, eff. Jan. 1, 2014.

§ 255.002. Certain Personal Property Excluded from Devise of Real Property

A devise of real property does not include any personal property located on, or associated with, the real property or any contents of personal property located on the real property unless the will directs that the personal property or contents are included in the devise.

Derived from Probate Code § 58(c).

Added by Acts 2009, 81st Leg., ch. 680, § 1, eff. Jan. 1, 2014.

§ 255.003. Contents Excluded from Legacy of Personal Property

A legacy of personal property does not include any contents of the property unless the will directs that the contents are included in the legacy.

Derived from Probate Code § 58(c).

Added by Acts 2009, 81st Leg., ch. 680, § 1, eff. Jan. 1, 2014.

Subchapter B. Succession by Pretermitted Child

Statutes in Context
Chapter 255, Subchapter B

Parents have no obligation to provide testamentary gifts for their children, even if they are minors. Thus, a parent may intentionally disinherit one or more of the parent's children. However, to protect a child from an accidental or inadvertent disinheritance, state legislatures have enacted statutes which may provide a forced share of the parent's estate for a pretermitted (omitted) child under certain circumstances. This Subchapter contains the rules for determining whether a pretermitted child is entitled to a forced share of the testator's estate.

To qualify as a pretermitted child, the child must be born or adopted after the testator executes the will. A child is not pretermitted merely because the child is not a beneficiary of the will.

A pretermitted child will not be entitled to a forced share if (1) the testator provided for the pretermitted child in the will such as by a class gift to "children," (2) the testator provided for the pretermitted child with a non-probate asset such as a life insurance policy or a P.O.D. account, or (3) the testator mentioned the pretermitted child in the will (for example, "I intentionally make no provision for any child who may be hereafter born or adopted.").

If the will makes no gift to the testator's children (i.e., (1) the testator had a child when the testator executed the will but left nothing to this child, or (2) the testator had no living child when the testator executed the will), then the share of each pretermitted child is determined as follows. First, ascertain the amount of the estate not passing to the pretermitted child's other parent (remember that the testator's spouse may not be the child's other parent). Second, give the pretermitted child a share of this amount as if the testator had died intestate with no surviving spouse. The other beneficiaries will receive proportionately less to make up the pretermitted child's share.

If the will provides for at least one of the testator's then living children, then the pretermitted child's share is determined as follows. First, ascertain the amount of the estate given to the testator's children. Second, ascertain the number of children named as beneficiaries in the testator's will and the number of pretermitted children. Add these two figures together. Third, divide the amount of the estate given to the testator's children (step 1) by the figure in step 2 (children beneficiaries + pretermitted children). Each pretermitted child will receive this amount and the gifts to the other children beneficiaries will be reduced proportionately.

Example 1 Husband and Wife have three children, Art, Brenda, and Charles. After Wife executed her will, she had a fourth child, Paul. Husband is Paul's father and Wife's will does not mention or provide for Paul. To how much is Paul entitled under the following circumstances:

(a) Wife's will gives her entire estate to Husband. Paul is entitled to nothing because Wife's entire estate was left to Paul's other parent (Husband).

(b) Wife's will gives $25,000 to Husband and the residuary to the American Red Cross. Paul is entitled to one-quarter of the residuary estate. Husband will still receive $25,000 and the American Red Cross will receive three-quarters of the residuary estate.

(c) Wife's will gives her entire estate to the American Red Cross. Paul is entitled to one-quarter of the estate with the balance passing to the American Red Cross.

(d) Wife's will gives $50,000 to Art, $30,000 to Brenda, and $20,000 to Charles. Paul is entitled to $25,000 (Wife left a total of $100,000 to her children, the total number of will beneficiary and pretermitted children is four; $100,000/4 = $25,000). The beneficiary children receive proportionately less, that is, Art will receive $37,500, Brenda will receive $22,500, and Charles will receive $15,000.

(e) Wife's will leaves $100,000 to Art. Paul is entitled to $50,000 and Art's gift is reduced to $50,000. Brenda and Charles still receive nothing.

(f) Wife named Paul as a beneficiary of her life insurance policy. Paul is entitled to nothing from Wife's estate.

Example 2 After executing her will, Wife has her first and only child, Paul. Wife's will does not mention or provide for Paul. To how much is Paul entitled under the following circumstances assuming that Husband is Paul's father?

(a) Wife's will gives her entire estate to Husband. Paul is entitled to nothing because Wife left her entire estate to Paul's other parent (Husband).

(b) Wife's will gives $25,000 to Husband and the residuary to the American Red Cross. Paul is entitled to the entire residuary. Husband still receives $25,000 and the American Red Cross receives nothing.

(c) Wife's will gives her entire estate to the American Red Cross. Paul is entitled to Wife's entire estate.

Example 3 After Husband married Wife (both childless prior to the marriage), Husband executed a will leaving his entire estate to Wife. This will did not mention or provide for any subsequent children. As a result of an affair Husband had with Sarah, Paul was born and paternity has been properly established. To how much is Paul entitled upon Husband's death?

If Husband died before September 1, 2011, Paul will receive Husband's entire estate because Wife is not Paul's other parent. However, if Husband died on or after September 1, 2011, Paul will receive only one-half of Husband's estate because of the limitation imposed by § 255.056 and Wife will receive the remaining half.

§ 255.051. Definition

In this subchapter, "pretermitted child" means a testator's child who is born or adopted:

(1) during the testator's lifetime or after the testator's death; and

(2) after the execution of the testator's will.

Derived from Probate Code § 67(c).

Added by Acts 2009, 81st Leg., ch. 680, § 1, eff. Jan. 1, 2014.

§ 255.052. Applicability and Construction

(a) Sections 255.053 and 255.054 apply only to a pretermitted child who is not:

(1) mentioned in the testator's will;

(2) provided for in the testator's will; or

(3) otherwise provided for by the testator.

(b) For purposes of this subchapter, a child is provided for or a provision is made for a child if a disposition of property to or for the benefit of the pretermitted child, whether vested or contingent, is made:

(1) in the testator's will, including a devise to a trustee under Section 254.001; or

(2) outside the testator's will and is intended to take effect at the testator's death.

Derived from Probate Code §§ 67(a), (d).

Added by Acts 2009, 81st Leg., ch. 680, § 1, eff. Jan. 1, 2014.

§ 255.053. Succession by Pretermitted Child if Testator Has Living Child at Will's Execution

(a) If no provision is made in the testator's last will for any child of the testator who is living when the testator executes the will, a pretermitted child succeeds to the portion of the testator's separate and community estate, other than any portion of the estate devised to the pretermitted child's other parent, to which the pretermitted child would have been entitled under Section 201.001 if the testator had died intestate without a surviving spouse, except as limited by Section 255.056.

(b) If a provision, whether vested or contingent, is made in the testator's last will for one or more children of the testator who are living when the testator executes the will, a pretermitted child is entitled only to a portion of the disposition made to children under the will that is equal to the portion the child would have received if the testator had:

(1) included all of the testator's pretermitted children with the children on whom benefits were conferred under the will; and

(2) given an equal share of those benefits to each child.

(c) To the extent feasible, the interest in the testator's estate to which the pretermitted child is entitled under Subsection (b) must be of the same character, whether an equitable or legal life estate or in fee, as the interest that the testator conferred on the testator's children under the will.

Derived from Probate Code § 67(a)(1).

Added by Acts 2009, 81st Leg., ch. 680, § 1, eff. Jan. 1, 2014. Subsec. (a) amended by Acts 2011, 82nd Leg., ch. 1338, § 2.27, eff. Jan. 1, 2014.

§ 255.054. Succession by Pretermitted Child if Testator Has No Living Child at Will's Execution

If a testator has no child living when the testator executes the testator's last will, a pretermitted child succeeds to the portion of the testator's separate and community estate, other than any portion of the estate devised to the pretermitted child's other parent, to which the pretermitted child would have been entitled under Section 201.001 if the testator had died intestate without a surviving spouse, except as limited by Section 255.056.

Derived from Probate Code § 67(a)(2).

Added by Acts 2009, 81st Leg., ch. 680, § 1, eff. Jan. 1, 2014. Amended by Acts 2011, 82nd Leg., ch. 1338, § 2.28, eff. Jan. 1, 2014.

§ 255.055. Ratable Recovery by Pretermitted Child from Portions Passing to Other Beneficiaries

(a) A pretermitted child may recover the share of the testator's estate to which the child is entitled from the testator's other children under Section 255.053(b) or from the testamentary beneficiaries under Sections 255.053(a) and 255.054, other than the pretermitted child's other parent, ratably, out of the portions of the estate passing to those persons under the will.

(b) In abating the interests of the beneficiaries described by Subsection (a), the character of the testamentary plan adopted by the testator must be preserved to the maximum extent possible.

Derived from Probate Code § 67(b).

Added by Acts 2009, 81st Leg., ch. 680, § 1, eff. Jan. 1, 2014.

§ 255.056. Limitation on Reduction of Estate Passing to Surviving Spouse

If a pretermitted child's other parent is not the surviving spouse of the testator, the portion of the testator's estate to which the pretermitted child is entitled under Section 255.053(a) or 255.054 may not reduce the portion of the testator's estate passing to the testator's surviving spouse by more than one-half.

Derived from Probate Code § 67(e).

Added by Acts 2011, 82nd Leg., ch. 1338, § 2.29, eff. Jan. 1, 2014.

Subchapter C. Lifetime Gifts as Satisfaction of Devise

Statutes in Context
Chapter 255, Subchapter C

The 2003 Texas Legislature enacted the Probate Code predecessor to this Subchapter to explain when an inter vivos gift will be treated as being in satisfaction of a testamentary gift. The provision is analogous to Estates Code Chapter 201 dealing with advancements in an intestacy context.

An inter vivos gift will be considered in partial or total satisfaction of a testamentary gift only if one of the following three conditions is satisfied:

1. The testator's will expressly indicates that the inter vivos gift is to be deducted from the testamentary gift.

2. The testator declares in a contemporaneous writing that the inter vivos gift is either (a) to be deducted from the testamentary gift or (b) is in satisfaction of the testamentary gift.

3. The beneficiary acknowledges in writing that the inter vivos gift is in satisfaction of the testamentary gift.

The value of property the testator gives in partial satisfaction of a testamentary gift is determined at the earlier of the date when (a) the beneficiary acquires possession of or enjoys the property or (b) when the testator dies.

---

§ 255.101. Certain Lifetime Gifts Considered Satisfaction of Devise

Property that a testator gives to a person during the testator's lifetime is considered a satisfaction, either wholly or partly, of a devise to the person if:

(1) the testator's will provides for deduction of the lifetime gift from the devise;

(2) the testator declares in a contemporaneous writing that the lifetime gift is to be deducted from, or is in satisfaction of, the devise; or

(3) the devisee acknowledges in writing that the lifetime gift is in satisfaction of the devise.

Derived from Probate Code § 37C(a).

Added by Acts 2009, 81st Leg., ch. 680, § 1, eff. Jan. 1, 2014.

§ 255.102. Valuation of Property

Property given in partial satisfaction of a devise shall be valued as of the earlier of:

(1) the date the devisee acquires possession of or enjoys the property; or

(2) the date of the testator's death.

Derived from Probate Code § 37C(b).

Added by Acts 2009, 81st Leg., ch. 680, § 1, eff. Jan. 1, 2014.

Subchapter D. Failure of Devise; Disposition of Property to Devisee Who Predeceases Testator

---

Statutes in Context
Chapter 255, Subchapter D

Deceased individuals cannot take and hold title to property. Accordingly, a testamentary gift intended for a beneficiary who died before the testator will not take effect, that is, the gift lapses. Lapse also may occur if a beneficiary biologically outlives the testator but is legally treated as predeceasing the testator. For example, the beneficiary may disclaim the gift (§ 122.002) or fail to satisfy the survival period imposed by the will or Chapter 121.

To determine the proper distribution of a lapsed gift, the courts begin by ascertaining the testator's intent as reflected by the express terms of the will. If the will provides a substitute taker in the event of lapse, that alternate beneficiary will receive the gift. If the will requires survivorship (e.g., "to my surviving children" or "to such of my children as shall survive me"), only the surviving beneficiaries are entitled to share in the gift. If the will is silent, however, § 255.153 may provide a substitute beneficiary. Language in the residuary clause including within its scope lapsed gifts may prevent the application of the anti-lapse statute.

See *Lacis v. Lacis*, 355 S.W.3d 727 (Tex. App.—Houston [1st Dist.] 2011, writ dism'd w.o.j.).

Section 255.153 provides a substitute beneficiary if four conditions are satisfied. (1) The deceased beneficiary must be either a descendant of the testator or a descendant of the testator's parents (i.e., siblings, nieces, and nephews). (2) The beneficiary must die during the testator's lifetime or be treated as dying during the testator's lifetime. (3) The predeceased beneficiary must have left at least one surviving descendant. (4) A surviving descendant of the deceased beneficiary must survive the testator.

If all four requirements are met, then the gift to the predeceased beneficiary does not lapse and instead passes to the descendants of the predeceased beneficiary on a per capita with representation basis.

Section 255.154 provides that the anti-lapse provisions apply to class gifts, as well as to gifts to individuals, as long as the class member was alive at the date the testator executed the will.

Section 255.152 addresses the issue of a partial lapse in the residuary clause when the clause lacks survivorship language. For example, assume that a valid will leaves the residuary estate to two of testator's friends, Bill and George. If Bill dies before the testator, George will receive the entire residuary estate. Section 255.152 implies survivorship language even though the will is silent. Remember that survivorship language is implied only for residuary gifts (that is, not for specific or general gifts).

§ 255.151. Applicability of Subchapter

This subchapter applies unless the testator's last will and testament provides otherwise. For example, a devise in the testator's will stating "to my surviving children" or "to such of my children as shall survive me" prevents the application of Sections 255.153 and 255.154.

Derived from Probate Code § 68(e).

Added by Acts 2009, 81st Leg., ch. 680, § 1, eff. Jan. 1, 2014.

§ 255.152. Failure of Devise; Effect on Residuary Estate

(a) Except as provided by Sections 255.153 and 255.154, if a devise, other than a residuary devise, fails for any reason, the devise becomes a part of the residuary estate.

(b) Except as provided by Sections 255.153 and 255.154, if the residuary estate is devised to two or more persons and the share of one of the residuary devisees fails for any reason, that residuary devisee's share passes to the other residuary devisees, in proportion to the residuary devisee's interest in the residuary estate.

(c) Except as provided by Sections 255.153 and 255.154, the residuary estate passes as if the testator had died intestate if all residuary devisees:

(1) are deceased at the time the testator's will is executed;

(2) fail to survive the testator; or

(3) are treated as if the residuary devisees predeceased the testator.

Derived from Probate Code §§ 68(b), (c), (d).

Added by Acts 2009, 81st Leg., ch. 680, § 1, eff. Jan. 1, 2014.

§ 255.153. Disposition of Property to Certain Devisees Who Predecease Testator

(a) If a devisee who is a descendant of the testator or a descendant of a testator's parent is deceased at the time the will is executed, fails to survive the testator, or is treated as if the devisee predeceased the testator by Chapter 121 or otherwise, the descendants of the devisee who survived the testator by 120 hours take the devised property in place of the devisee.

(b) Devised property to which Subsection (a) applies shall be divided into the number of shares equal to the total number of surviving descendants in the nearest degree of kinship to the devisee and deceased persons in the same degree of kinship to the devisee whose descendants survived the testator. Each surviving descendant in the nearest degree of kinship to the devisee receives one share, and the share of each deceased person in the same degree of kinship to the devisee whose descendants survived the testator is divided among the descendants by representation.

Derived from Probate Code § 68(a).

Added by Acts 2009, 81st Leg., ch. 680, § 1, eff. Jan. 1, 2014.

§ 255.154. Devisee Under Class Gift

For purposes of this subchapter, a person who would have been a devisee under a class gift if the person had survived the testator is treated as a devisee unless the person died before the date the will was executed.

Derived from Probate Code § 68(a).

Added by Acts 2009, 81st Leg., ch. 680, § 1, eff. Jan. 1, 2014.

Subchapter F. Devise of Securities

Statutes in Context
Chapter 255, Subchapter F

This Subchapter provides rules for determining who is entitled to increases in securities which occur between the time the testator executed the will and the testator's death. Generally, cash dividends are not included in a gift of securities but stock splits and stock dividends are included.

§ 255.251. Definitions

In this subchapter:

(1) "Securities" has the meaning assigned by Section 4, The Securities Act (Article 581-4, Vernon's Texas Civil Statutes).

(2) "Stock" means securities.

Derived from Probate Code § 70A(c).

Added by Acts 2009, 81st Leg., ch. 680, § 1, eff. Jan. 1, 2014.

§ 255.252. Increase in Securities; Accessions

Unless the will of a testator clearly provides otherwise, a devise of securities that are owned by the testator on the date the will is executed includes the following additional securities subsequently acquired by the testator as a result of the testator's ownership of the devised securities:

(1) securities of the same organization acquired because of an action initiated by the organization or any successor, related, or acquiring organization, including stock splits, stock dividends, and new issues of stock acquired in a reorganization, redemption, or exchange, other than securities acquired through the exercise of purchase options or through a plan of reinvestment; and

(2) securities of another organization acquired as a result of a merger, consolidation, reorganization, or other distribution by the organization or any successor, related, or acquiring organization, including stock splits, stock dividends, and new issues of stock acquired in a reorganization, redemption, or exchange, other than securities acquired through the exercise of purchase options or through a plan of reinvestment.

Derived from Probate Code § 70A(a).

Added by Acts 2009, 81st Leg., ch. 680, § 1, eff. Jan. 1, 2014.

§ 255.253. Cash Distribution Not Included in Devise

Unless the will of a testator clearly provides otherwise, a devise of securities does not include a cash distribution relating to the securities that accrues before the testator's death, regardless of whether the distribution is paid before the testator's death.

Derived from Probate Code § 70A(b).

Added by Acts 2009, 81st Leg., ch. 680, § 1, eff. Jan. 1, 2014.

Subchapter G. Exoneration of Debts Secured by Specific Devises

Statutes in Context
Chapter 255, Subchapter G

Texas had long followed the doctrine of exoneration, that is, debts on specifically gifted property were paid from other estate assets so that the beneficiary receives the asset unencumbered, rather than just the testator's equity. See *Currie v. Scott*, 187 S.W.2d 551 (Tex. 1945).

The doctrine has been abolished for wills executed on or after September 1, 2005. A specific gift passes subject to each debt secured by the property that exists on the date of the testator's death under Estates Code § 255.302.

The statute contains two special rules. First, the testator may expressly provide in the will for the debts against a specific gift to be exonerated. Note, however, that a general provision in the will stating that debts are to be paid is not sufficient. Second, there is a provision addressing the situation where a secured creditor elects matured secured claim status under Estates Code § 355.153.

§ 255.301. No Right to Exoneration of Debts

Except as provided by Section 255.302, a specific devise passes to the devisee subject to each debt secured by the property that exists on the date of the testator's death, and the devisee is not entitled to exoneration from the testator's estate for payment of the debt.

Derived from Probate Code § 71A(a).

Added by Acts 2009, 81st Leg., ch. 680, § 1, eff. Jan. 1, 2014.

§ 255.302. Exception

A specific devise does not pass to the devisee subject to a debt described by Section 255.301 if the will in which the devise is made specifically states that the devise passes without being subject to the debt. A general provision in the will stating that debts are to be paid is not a specific statement for purposes of this section.

Derived from Probate Code § 71A(b).

Added by Acts 2009, 81st Leg., ch. 680, § 1, eff. Jan. 1, 2014.

§ 255.303. Rights of Certain Creditors and Other Persons

(a) Section 255.301 does not affect the rights of creditors provided under this title or the rights of other persons or entities provided under Chapters 102 and 353.

(b) A debt described by Section 255.301 that a creditor elects to have allowed and approved as a matured secured claim shall be paid in accordance with Sections 355.153(b), (c), (d), and (e).

Derived from Probate Code § 71A(c).

Added by Acts 2009, 81st Leg., ch. 680, § 1, eff. Jan. 1, 2014.

§ 255.304. Applicability of Subchapter

This subchapter is applicable only to wills executed on or after September 1, 2005.

New.

Added by Acts 2015, 84th Leg., ch. 995, § 18, eff. Sept. 1, 2015.

Subchapter H. Exercise of Power of Appointment Through Will

Statutes in Context
§ 255.351

The 2003 Texas Legislature clarified whether a residuary clause will be deemed to exercise a power of appointment held by the testator by enacting the Probate Code predecessor to Estates Code § 255.351. A residuary clause or a clause purporting to dispose of all of the testator's property will exercise a power of appointment in favor of the will beneficiary only if one of the following two conditions is satisfied:

1. The testator makes a specific reference to the power of appointment in the will.

2. There is some other indication in a writing (but not necessarily the will itself) that the testator intended to include the property subject to the power of appointment in the will.

§ 255.351. Exercise of Power of Appointment Through Will

A testator may not exercise a power of appointment through a residuary clause in the testator's will or through a will providing for general disposition of all of the testator's property unless:

    (1) the testator makes a specific reference to the power in the will; or

    (2) there is some other indication in writing that the testator intended to include the property subject to the power in the will.

Derived from Probate Code § 58c.

Added by Acts 2009, 81st Leg., ch. 680, § 1, eff. Jan. 1, 2014.

Subchapter I. Class Gifts

Statutes in Context
§ 255.401

Unless the testator's will provides otherwise, a person must be born or in gestation at the time of the testator's death to qualify as a member of a class for purposes of a class gift. This section,

designed to preclude the use of the decedent's sperm, eggs, or embryos to produce class members who are born years or decades after the testator's death. may have an inadvertent impact because the section does not distinguish between immediate gifts (e.g., "to my grandchildren") and postponed gifts (e.g., "to my child for life, and then to my grandchildren"). In the latter case, it is likely the testator intended grandchildren born after the testator's death to be included in the class.

§ 255.401. Posthumous Class Gift Membership

(a) A right to take as a member under a class gift does not accrue to any person unless the person is born before, or is in gestation at, the time of the testator's death and survives for at least 120 hours. A person is:

    (1) considered to be in gestation at the time of the testator's death if insemination or implantation occurs at or before the time of the testator's death; and

    (2) presumed to be in gestation at the time of the testator's death if the person was born before the 301st day after the date of the testator's death.

(b) A provision in the testator's will that is contrary to this section prevails over this section.

New.

Added by Acts 2015, 84th Leg., ch. 995, § 19, eff. Sept. 1, 2015.

Subchapter J. Judicial Modification or Reformation of Wills

Statutes in Context
Subchapter J

In a major change in Texas law, courts have now been given the authority to modify and reform a will even if the will is unambiguous effectively overruling the Supreme Court of Texas case of *San Antonio Area Foundation v. Lang*, 35 S.W.3d 636 (Tex. 2000), which held that "extrinsic evidence is not admissible to construe an unambiguous will provision." *Id.* at 637. Acts 2015, 84th Leg., ch. 995, § 19, eff. Sept. 1, 2015 (adding Estates Code §§ 255.451-.455).

Below are the key features of how a court may exercise this new power:

- Only a personal representative may petition for modification or reformation; disgruntled beneficiaries and wishful beneficiaries lack standing.

- The court has broad authority to order the personal representative to perform acts which the testator prohibited and to prevent the personal representative from acting as the testator specified.

- The court must have a "good" reason for ordering the modification or reformation such as to make estate administration more efficient, carry out the settlor's tax objectives, assist a beneficiary in qualifying for government benefits, or to correct a scrivener's error but only if there is clear and convincing evidence of the testator's intent.

- The court must modify or reform the will to conform to the "probable" intent of the testator.

- The personal representative has no duty to seek a reformation or modification and is not required to tell the beneficiaries that the personal representative has the ability to seek reformation or modification.

- The personal representative has no liability for failing to seek reformation or modification.

Although these provisions have the laudable goal of carrying out the testator's intent, they have the possibility of preventing a testator from achieving certainty when drafting a will. For example, the testator could write, "I leave $10,000 to X," and later have the court decide that the testator actually meant to leave X $100,000 or that the funds were intended for Y.

§ 255.451. Circumstances Under Which Will May be Modified or Reformed

(a) On the petition of a personal representative, a court may order that the terms of the will be modified or reformed, that the personal representative be directed or permitted to perform acts that are not authorized or that are prohibited by the terms of the will, or that the personal representative be prohibited from performing acts that are required by the terms of the will, if:

(1) modification of administrative, nondispositive terms of the will is necessary or appropriate to prevent waste or impairment of the estate's administration;

(2) the order is necessary or appropriate to achieve the testator's tax objectives or to qualify a distributee for government benefits and is not contrary to the testator's intent; or

(3) the order is necessary to correct a scrivener's error in the terms of the will, even if unambiguous, to conform with the testator's intent.

(b) An order described in Subsection (a)(3) may be issued only if the testator's intent is established by clear and convincing evidence.

New.

Added by Acts 2015, 84th Leg., ch. 995, § 19, eff. Sept. 1, 2015.

§ 255.452. Judicial Discretion

The court shall exercise the court's discretion to order a modification or reformation under this subchapter in the manner that conforms as nearly as possible to the probable intent of the testator.

New.

Added by Acts 2015, 84th Leg., ch. 995, § 19, eff. Sept. 1, 2015.

§ 255.453. Retroactive Effect

The court may direct that an order described by this subchapter has retroactive effect.

New.

Added by Acts 2015, 84th Leg., ch. 995, § 19, eff. Sept. 1, 2015.

§ 255.454. Powers Cumulative

This subchapter does not limit a court's powers under other law, including the power to modify, reform, or terminate a testamentary trust under Section 112.054, Property Code.

New.

Added by Acts 2015, 84th Leg., ch. 995, § 19, eff. Sept. 1, 2015.

§ 255.455. Duties and Liability of Personal Representative Under Subchapter

(a) This subchapter does not create or imply a duty for a personal representative to:

(1) petition a court for modification or reformation of a will, to be directed or permitted to perform acts that are not authorized or that are prohibited by the terms of the will, or to be prohibited from performing acts that are required by the terms of the will;

(2) inform devisees about the availability of relief under this subchapter; or

(3) review the will or other evidence to determine whether any action should be taken under this subchapter.

(b) A personal representative is not liable for failing to file a petition under Section 255.451.

New.

Added by Acts 2015, 84th Leg., ch. 995, § 19, eff. Sept. 1, 2015.

Chapter 256. Probate of Wills Generally

Subchapter A. Effectiveness of Will; Period for Probate

Subchapter B. Application Requirements

Subchapter C. Procedures for Second Application

Subchapter D. Required Proof for Probate of Will

Subchapter E. Admission of Will to, and Procedures Following, Probate

Chapter 256. Probate of Wills Generally

Subchapter A. Effectiveness of Will; Period for Probate

Statutes in Context
§ 256.001

A will has no legal effect until it is probated. Under § 256.001, a beneficiary has no claim to the devised or bequeathed property until the will is admitted to probate.

§ 256.001. Will Not Effective Until Probated

Except as provided by Subtitle K with respect to foreign wills, a will is not effective to prove title to, or the right to possession of, any property disposed of by the will until the will is admitted to probate.

Derived from Probate Code § 94.

Added by Acts 2009, 81st Leg., ch. 680, § 1, eff. Jan. 1, 2014.

Statutes in Context
§ 256.002

Texas does not recognize ante-mortem probate. However, a few states including Alaska, Arkansas, North Dakota, and Ohio do permit a testator to have the validity of his or her will determined while the testator is still alive.

§ 256.002. Probate Before Death Void

The probate of a will of a living person is void.

Derived from Probate Code § 72(a).

Added by Acts 2009, 81st Leg., ch. 680, § 1, eff. Jan. 1, 2014.

Statutes in Context
§ 256.003

A will must usually be probated within 4 years of the testator's death. However, § 256.003(a) permits a court to permit a "late" probate if the proponent of the will was "not in default." The courts have been quite lenient and have accepted a variety of reasons for the proponent's tardiness. See *In re Estate of Perez*, 324 S.W.3d 257 (Tex. App.—El Paso 2010, no pet.), in which the court accepted the proponent's excuse that she did not realize that she needed to probate her husband's will sooner because she was uneducated and economically challenged. See also *Kamoos v. Woodward*, 570 S.W.2d 6 (Tex. Civ. App. — San Antonio 1978, writ ref'd n.r.e.). Although it may not be possible to probate a will after the expiration of the four years because the proponent was in default, the will may nonetheless be used to show that the testator had revoked a prior will. *Chambers v. Chambers*, 542 S.W.2d 901, 905 (Tex. Civ. App.—Dallas 1976, no writ).

§ 256.003. Period for Admitting Will to Probate; Protection for Certain Purchasers

(a) Except as provided by Section 501.001 with respect to a foreign will, a [A] will may not be admitted to probate after the fourth anniversary of the testator's death unless it is shown by proof that the applicant for the probate of the will was not in default in failing to present the will for probate on or before the fourth anniversary of the testator's death.

(b) Except as provided by Section 501.006 with respect to a foreign will, letters [Letters] testamentary may not be issued if a will is admitted to probate after the fourth anniversary of the testator's death.

(c) A person who for value, in good faith, and without knowledge of the existence of a will purchases property from a decedent's heirs after the fourth anniversary of the decedent's death shall be held to have good title to the interest that the heir or heirs would have had in the absence of a will, as against the claim of any devisee under any will that is subsequently offered for probate.

Derived from Probate Code § 73.

Added by Acts 2009, 81st Leg., ch. 680, § 1, eff. Jan. 1, 2014. Subsec. (a) & (b) amended by Acts 2015, 84th Leg., ch. 995, § 20, eff. Sept. 1, 2015.

Subchapter B. Application Requirements

§ 256.051. Eligible Applicants for Probate of Will

(a) An executor named in a will, an independent administrator designated by all of the distributees of the decedent under Section 401.002(b), or an interested person may file an application with the court for an order admitting a will to probate, whether the will is:

    (1) written or unwritten;

    (2) in the applicant's possession or not;

    (3) lost;

    (4) destroyed; or

    (5) outside of this state.

(b) An application for the probate of a will may be combined with an application for the appointment of an executor or administrator. A person interested in either the probate or the appointment may apply for both.

Derived from Probate Code § 76.

Added by Acts 2009, 81st Leg., ch. 680, § 1, eff. Jan. 1, 2014. Subsec. (a) amended by Acts 2015, 84th Leg., ch. 995, § 21, eff. Sept. 1, 2015.

§ 256.052. Contents of Application For Probate of Will

(a) An application for the probate of a will must state and aver the following to the extent each is known to the applicant or can, with reasonable diligence, be ascertained by the applicant:

    (1) each applicant's name and domicile;

    (2) the testator's name, domicile, and, if known, age, on the date of the testator's death;

    (3) the fact, date [time], and place of the testator's death;

    (4) facts showing that the court with which the application is filed has venue;

    (5) that the testator owned property, including a statement generally describing the property and the property's probable value;

    (6) the date of the will;

    (7) the name, state of residence, and physical address where service can be had of the executor named in the will or other person to whom the applicant desires that letters be issued;

    (8) the name of each subscribing witness to the will, if any;

    (9) whether one or more children born to or adopted by the testator after the testator executed the will survived the testator and, if so, the name of each of those children;

    (10) whether a marriage of the testator was ever dissolved after the will was made and, if so, when and from whom;

    (11) whether the state, a governmental agency of the state, or a charitable organization is named in the will as a devisee; and

    (12) that the executor named in the will, the applicant, or another person to whom the applicant desires that letters be issued is not disqualified by law from accepting the letters.

(b) If an applicant does not state or aver any matter required by Subsection (a) in the application, the application must state the reason the matter is not stated and averred.

Derived from Probate Code § 81(a).

Added by Acts 2009, 81st Leg., ch. 680, § 1, eff. Jan. 1, 2014. Subsec. (a)(9) amended by Acts 2011, 82nd Leg., ch. 91, § 8.010, eff. Jan. 1, 2014 and Acts 2011, 82nd Leg., ch. 1338, § 2.30, eff. Jan. 1, 2014.Amended by Acts 2013, 83rd Leg., ch. 1136, §§ 21 & 22, eff. Jan. 1, 2014. Subsec. (a)(3) amended by Acts 2015, 84th Leg., ch. 995, § 22, eff. Sept. 1, 2015.

§ 256.053. Filing of Will With Application For Probate Generally Required

(a) An applicant for the probate of a will shall file the will with the application if the will is in the applicant's control.

(b) A will filed under Subsection (a) must remain in the custody of the county clerk unless removed from the clerk's custody by a court order.

Derived from Probate Code § 81(a).

Added by Acts 2009, 81st Leg., ch. 680, § 1, eff. Jan. 1, 2014. Amended by Acts 2013, 83rd Leg., ch. 1136, §§ 23 & 24, eff. Jan. 1, 2014.

§ 256.054. Additional Application Requirements When No Will Is Produced.

In addition to the requirements for an application under Section 256.052, if an applicant for the probate of a will cannot produce the will in court, the application must state:

(1) the reason the will cannot be produced;

(2) the contents of the will, as far as known; and

(3) the name[, age, marital status,] and address, if known, whether the person is an adult or minor, and the relationship to the testator, if any, of:

(A) each devisee;

(B) each person who would inherit as an heir of the testator in the absence of a valid will; and

(C) in the case of partial intestacy, each heir of the testator.

Derived from Probate Code § 81(b).

Added by Acts 2009, 81st Leg., ch. 680, § 1, eff. Jan. 1, 2014. Amended by Acts 2013, 83rd Leg., ch. 1136, § 25, eff. Jan. 1, 2014. Subsec. (3) amended by Acts 2015, 84th Leg., ch. 995, § 23, eff. Sept. 1, 2015.

Subchapter C. Procedures for Second Application

§ 256.101. Procedure on Filing of Second Application when Original Application Has Not Been Heard

(a) If, after an application for the probate of a decedent's will or the appointment of a personal representative for the decedent's estate has been filed but before the application is heard, an application is filed for the probate of a will of the same decedent that has not previously been presented for probate, the court shall:

(1) hear both applications together; and

(2) determine:

(A) if both applications are for the probate of a will, which will should be admitted to probate, if either, or whether the decedent died intestate; or

(B) if only one application is for the probate of a will, whether the will should be admitted to probate or whether the decedent died intestate.

(b) The court may not sever or bifurcate the proceeding on the applications described in Subsection (a).

Derived from Probate Code § 83(a).

Added by Acts 2009, 81st Leg., ch. 680, § 1, eff. Jan. 1, 2014. Amended by Acts 2011, 82nd Leg., ch. 1338, § 2.31, eff. Jan. 1, 2014.

§ 256.102. Procedure on Filing of Second Application for Probate After First Will Has Been Admitted

If, after a decedent's will has been admitted to probate, an application is filed for the probate of a will of the same decedent that has not previously been presented for probate, the court shall determine:

(1) whether the former probate should be set aside; and

(2) if the former probate is to be set aside, whether:

(A) the other will should be admitted to probate; or

(B) the decedent died intestate.

Derived from Probate Code § 83(b).

Added by Acts 2009, 81st Leg., ch. 680, § 1, eff. Jan. 1, 2014.

§ 256.103. Procedure when Application for Probate Is Filed After Letters of Administration Have Been Granted

(a) A lawful will of a decedent that is discovered after letters of administration have been granted on the decedent's estate may be proved in the manner provided for the proof of wills.

(b) The court shall allow an executor named in a will described by Subsection (a) who is not disqualified to qualify and accept as executor. The court shall revoke the previously granted letters of administration.

(c) If an executor is not named in a will described by Subsection (a), or if the executor named is disqualified or dead, renounces the executorship, fails or is unable to accept and qualify before the 21st day after the date of the probate of the will, or fails to present the will for probate before the 31st day after the discovery of the will, the court, as in other cases, shall grant an administration with the will annexed of the testator's estate.

(d) An act performed by the first administrator before the executor described by Subsection (b) or the administrator with the will annexed described by Subsection (c) qualifies is as valid as if no will had been discovered.

Derived from Probate Code § 83(c).

Added by Acts 2009, 81st Leg., ch. 680, § 1, eff. Jan. 1, 2014.

Subchapter D. Required Proof for Probate of Will

§ 256.151. General Proof Requirements

An applicant for the probate of a will must prove to the court's satisfaction that:

(1) the testator is dead;

(2) four years have not elapsed since the date of the testator's death and before the application;

(3) the court has jurisdiction and venue over the estate;

(4) citation has been served and returned in the manner and for the period required by this title; and

(5) the person for whom letters testamentary or of administration are sought is entitled by law to the letters and is not disqualified.

Derived from Probate Code § 88(a).

Added by Acts 2009, 81st Leg., ch. 680, § 1, eff. Jan. 1, 2014.

Statutes in Context
§§ 256.152–256.155

Sections 256.152–256.155 explain how to prove a written will which is physically produced in court. If the will is self-proved, no additional proof is needed. See §§ 251.051 (attested wills) and 251.052 (holographic wills).

§ 256.152. Additional Proof Required for Probate of Will

(a) An applicant for the probate of a will must prove the following to the court's satisfaction, in addition to the proof required by Section 256.151, to obtain the probate:

(1) the testator did not revoke the will; and

(2) if the will is not self-proved as provided by this title, the testator:

(A) executed the will with the formalities and solemnities and under the circumstances required by law to make the will valid; and

(B) at the time of executing the will, was of sound mind and:

(i) was 18 years of age or older;

(ii) was or had been married; or

(iii) was a member of the armed forces of the United States, an auxiliary of the armed forces of the United States, or the United States Maritime Service.

(b) A will that is self-proved as provided by Subchapter C, Chapter 251, that [or, if executed in another state or a foreign country,] is self-proved in accordance with the law [laws] of another [the] state or foreign country where the will was executed, as that law existed at the time of the will's execution, or that is self-proved in accordance with the law of another state or foreign country where the testator was domiciled or had a place of residence, as that law existed at the time of the will's execution or the time of the testator's death, [of the testator's domicile at the time of the execution] is not required to have any additional proof that the will was executed with the formalities and solemnities and under the circumstances required to make the will valid.

(c) As an alternative to Subsection (b), a will [executed in another state or a foreign country] is considered self-proved without further evidence of the law of any [the other] state or foreign country if:

(1) the will was executed in another state or a foreign country or the testator was domiciled or had a place of residence in another state or a foreign country at the time of the will's execution or the time of the testator's death; and

(2) the will, or an affidavit of the testator and attesting witnesses attached or annexed to the will, provides that:

(A) [(1)] the testator declared that the testator signed the instrument as the testator's will, the testator signed it willingly or willingly directed another to sign for the testator, the testator executed the will as the testator's free and voluntary act for the purposes expressed in the instrument, the testator is of sound mind and under no constraint or undue influence, and the testator is eighteen years of age or over or, if under that age, was or had been lawfully married, or was then a member of the armed forces of the United States, an auxiliary of the armed forces of the United States, or the United States Maritime Service; and

(B) [(2)] the witnesses declared that the testator signed the instrument as the testator's will, the testator signed it willingly or willingly directed another to sign for the testator, each of the witnesses, in the presence and hearing of the testator, signed the will as witness to the testator's signing, and to the best of their knowledge the testator was of sound mind and under no constraint or undue influence, and the testator was eighteen years of age or over or, if under that age, was or had been lawfully married, or was then a member of the armed forces of the United States, an auxiliary of the armed forces of the United States, or the United States Maritime Service.

Derived from Probate Code § 84(a), 88(b).

Added by Acts 2009, 81st Leg., ch. 680, § 1, eff. Jan. 1, 2014. Amended by Acts 2011, 82nd Leg., ch. 1338, § 2.32, eff. Jan. 1, 2014. Subsec. (c) amended by Acts 2013, 83rd Leg., ch. 1136, § 26, eff. Jan. 1, 2014. Subsecs. (b) & (c) amended by Acts 2015, 84th Leg., ch. 995, § 24, eff. Sept. 1, 2015.

§ 256.153. Proof of Execution of Attested Will

(a) An attested will produced in court that is not self-proved as provided by this title may be proved in the manner provided by this section.

(b) A will described by Subsection (a) may be proved by the sworn testimony or affidavit of one or more of the subscribing witnesses to the will taken in open court.

(c) If all the witnesses to a will described by Subsection (a) are nonresidents of the county or the witnesses who are residents of the county are unable to attend court, the will may be proved:

(1) by the sworn testimony of one or more of the witnesses by written or oral deposition taken in accordance with Section 51.203 or the Texas Rules of Civil Procedure;

(2) if no opposition in writing to the will is filed on or before the date set for the hearing on the will, by the sworn testimony or affidavit of two witnesses taken in open court, or by deposition as provided by Subdivision (1), to the signature or the handwriting evidenced by the signature of:

(A) one or more of the attesting witnesses; or

(B) the testator, if the testator signed the will; or

(3) if it is shown under oath to the court's satisfaction that, after a diligent search was made, only one witness can be found who can make the required proof, by the sworn testimony or affidavit of that witness taken in open court, or by deposition as provided by Subdivision (1), to a signature, or the handwriting evidenced by a signature, described by Subdivision (2).

(d) If none of the witnesses to a will described by Subsection (a) are living, or if each of the witnesses is a member of the armed forces or the armed forces reserves of the United States, an auxiliary of the armed forces or armed forces reserves, or the United States Maritime Service and is beyond the court's jurisdiction, the will may be proved:

(1) by two witnesses to the handwriting of one or both of the subscribing witnesses to the will or the testator, if the testator signed the will, by:

(A) sworn testimony or affidavit taken in open court; or

(B) written or oral deposition taken in accordance with Section 51.203 or the Texas Rules of Civil Procedure; or

(2) if it is shown under oath to the court's satisfaction that, after a diligent search was made, only one witness can be found who can make the required proof, by the sworn testimony or affidavit of that witness taken in open court, or by deposition as provided by Subdivision (1), to a signature or the handwriting described by Subdivision (1).

(e) A witness being deposed for purposes of proving the will as provided by Subsection (c) or (d) may testify by referring to a certified copy of the will, without the judge requiring the original will to be removed from the court's file and shown to the witness.

Derived from Probate Code § 84(b).

Added by Acts 2009, 81st Leg., ch. 680, § 1, eff. Jan. 1, 2014. Amended and subsection (e) added by Acts 2013, 83rd Leg., ch. 1136, § 27, eff. Jan. 1, 2014.

§ 256.154. Proof of Execution of Holographic Will

(a) A will wholly in the handwriting of the testator that is not self-proved as provided by this title may be proved by two witnesses to the testator's handwriting. The evidence may be by:

(1) sworn testimony or affidavit taken in open court; or

(2) if the witnesses are nonresidents of the county or are residents who are unable to attend court, written or oral deposition taken in accordance with Section 51.203 or the Texas Rules of Civil Procedure.

(b) A witness being deposed for purposes of proving the will as provided by Subsection (a)(2) may testify by referring to a certified copy of the will, without the judge requiring the original will to be removed from the court's file and shown to the witness.

Derived from Probate Code § 84(c).

Added by Acts 2009, 81st Leg., ch. 680, § 1, eff. Jan. 1,

2014. Amended by Acts 2013, 83rd Leg., ch. 1136, § 28, eff. Jan. 1, 2014.

§ 256.155. Procedures for Depositions when No Contest is Filed

(a) This section, rather than Sections 256.153(c) and (d) and 256.154 regarding the taking of depositions, applies if no contest has been filed with respect to an application for the probate of a will.

(b) Depositions for the purpose of establishing a will may be taken in the manner provided by Section 51.203 for the taking of depositions when there is no opposing party or attorney of record on whom notice and copies of interrogatories may be served.

Derived from Probate Code § 84(d).

Added by Acts 2009, 81st Leg., ch. 680, § 1, eff. Jan. 1, 2014. Subsection (a) amended by Acts 2013, 83rd Leg., ch. 1136, § 29, eff. Jan. 1, 2014.

Statutes in Context
§ 256.156

Where a will "was in the possession of the testator or when he had ready access to it when last seen, failure to produce it after his death raises the presumption that the testator had destroyed it with an intention to revoke it, and the burden is cast upon the proponent to prove the contrary." *Mingo v. Mingo*, 507 S.W.2d 310 (Tex. Civ. App.—San Antonio 1974, writ ref'd n.r.e.). Section 85 explains the additional proof which is necessary if the original will is not physically produced in court (e.g., the original is lost, hidden, withheld by disgruntled heir, accidentally destroyed, etc.).

Controversy exists over whether a copy of a lost will is sufficient to prove its contents. Until being amended by the 2007 Legislature, the statute provided that the contents must be proved "by the testimony of a credible witness who has read [the original] or heard it read." Several cases focused on this issue including *Garton v. Rockett*, 190 S.W.3d 139 (Tex. App.—Houston [1st Dist.] 2005, no pet.) (copy insufficient) and *In re Estate of Jones*, 197 S.W.3d 894 (Tex. App.—Beaumont 2006, pet. denied) (copy sufficient). The addition of a supposed third method of proof by the 2007 Legislature, that is, by identification of a copy, does not appear to actually add a new method because of the difficulty of a person testifying that the document is "a copy of the will" if the person never read the original or heard the original read.

In the almost unbelievable opinion of *In re Estate of Catlin*, 311 S.W.3d 697 (Tex. App.—Amarillo 2010, pet. denied), the court accepted proponent's explanation that he looked at the testator's home, office, safety deposit boxes, and drafting attorney's office but could not find the original. The court explained that the will proponent did not have to demonstrate an affirmative reason why the original cannot be located such as "the eating habits of a neighbor's goat, the occurrence of a Kansas tornado, the devastation of a flash flood, or the like." The court basically makes it impossible for a testator to revoke a will by physical act because even if the will cannot be found and there is no affirmative reason why it cannot be found, a copy may nonetheless be probated. See also *In re Estate of Perez*, 324 S.W.3d 257 (Tex. App.—El Paso 2010, no pet.).

§ 256.156. Proof of Will Not Produced in Court

(a) A will that cannot be produced in court must be proved in the same manner as provided in Section 256.153 for an attested will or Section 256.154 for a holographic will, as applicable. The same amount and character of testimony is required to prove the will not produced in court as is required to prove a will produced in court.

(b) In addition to the proof required by Subsection (a):

(1) the cause of the nonproduction of a will not produced in court must be proved, which must be sufficient to satisfy the court that the will cannot by any reasonable diligence be produced; and

(2) the contents of the will must be substantially proved by the testimony of a credible witness who has read either the original or a copy of the will, has heard the will read, or can identify a copy of the will.

Derived from Probate Code § 85.

Added by Acts 2009, 81st Leg., ch. 680, § 1, eff. Jan. 1, 2014. Amended by Acts 2013, 83rd Leg., ch. 1136, § 30, eff. Jan. 1, 2014.

§ 256.157. Testimony Regarding Probate to Be Committed to Writing

(a) Except as provided by Subsection (b), all testimony taken in open court on the hearing of an application to probate a will must be:

(1) committed to writing at the time the testimony is taken;

(2) subscribed and sworn to in open court by the witness; and

(3) filed by the clerk.

(b) In a contested case, the court, on the agreement of the parties or, if there is no agreement, on the court's own motion, may waive the requirements of Subsection (a).

Derived from Probate Code § 87.

Added by Acts 2009, 81st Leg., ch. 680, § 1, eff. Jan. 1, 2014.

Subchapter E. Admission of Will To, and Procedures Following, Probate

§ 256.201. Admission of Will to Probate

If the court is satisfied on the completion of hearing an application for the probate of a will that the will should be admitted to probate, the court shall enter an order admitting the will to probate. Certified copies of the will and the order admitting the will to probate, or of the record of the will and order, and the record of testimony, may be:

(1) recorded in other counties; and

(2) used in evidence, as the originals may be used, on the trial of the same matter in any other court when taken to that court by appeal or otherwise.

Derived from Probate Code § 89.

Added by Acts 2009, 81st Leg., ch. 680, § 1, eff. Jan. 1, 2014.

§ 256.202. Custody of Probated Will

An original will and the probate of the will shall be deposited in the office of the county clerk of the county in which the will was probated. The will and probate of the will shall remain in that office except during a time the will and the probate of the will are removed for inspection to another place on an order of the court where the will was probated. If that court orders the original will to be removed to another place for inspection:

(1) the person removing the will shall give a receipt for the will; and

(2) the court clerk shall make and retain a copy of the will.

Derived from Probate Code § 90.

Added by Acts 2009, 81st Leg., ch. 680, § 1, eff. Jan. 1, 2014.

§ 256.203. Establishing Contents of Will Not in Court's Custody

If for any reason a will is not in the court's custody, the court shall find the contents of the will by written order. Certified copies of the contents as established by the order may be:

(1) recorded in other counties; and

(2) used in evidence, as certified copies of wills in the custody of the court may be used.

Derived from Probate Code § 91.

Added by Acts 2009, 81st Leg., ch. 680, § 1, eff. Jan. 1, 2014. Amended by Acts 2013, 83rd Leg., ch. 1136, § 31, eff. Jan. 1, 2014.

Statutes in Context
§ 256.204

Section 256.204 provides the statute of limitations for contesting a will. If the contest ground is not based on fraud, the period is 2 years from the date the court admitted the will to probate. However, if the contest ground is based on forgery or other fraud, the 2-year period runs from the discovery of the forgery or fraud. Incapacitated persons as defined in § 22.017 have 2 years from the removal of their disabilities to begin the contest.

§ 256.204. Period for Contest

(a) After a will is admitted to probate, an interested person may commence a suit to contest the validity thereof not later than the second anniversary of the date the will was admitted to probate, except that an interested person may commence a suit to cancel a will for forgery or other fraud not later than the second anniversary of the date the forgery or fraud was discovered.

(b) Notwithstanding Subsection (a), an incapacitated person may commence the contest under that subsection on or before the second anniversary of the date the person's disabilities are removed.

Derived from Probate Code § 93.

Added by Acts 2009, 81st Leg., ch. 680, § 1, eff. Jan. 1, 2014.

Chapter 257. Probate of Will as Muniment of Title

Subchapter A. Authorization

§ 257.001. Probate of Will as Muniment of Title Authorized

Subchapter B. Application and Proof Requirements

§ 257.051. Contents of Application Generally

§ 257.052. Filing of Will With Application Generally Required

§ 257.053. Additional Application Requirements When No Will Is Produced

§ 257.054. Proof Required

Subchapter C. Order Admitting Will; Report

§ 257.101. Declaratory Judgment Construing Will

§ 257.102. Authority of Certain Persons Acting in Accordance With Order

§ 257.103. Report by Applicant After Probate

Chapter 257. Probate of Will as Muniment of Title

Statutes in Context
Chapter 257

Chapter 257 details how to probate a will as a muniment of title. This procedure is extremely efficient and cost-effective because there is no administration of the estate (no executor is appointed; no letters testamentary are issued). Instead, the testator's will is proved to be valid and the court order admitting the will to probate documents title transfer to the beneficiaries and gives authority to all those who hold the testator's property to deliver it to the beneficiaries. To use the procedure, however, the testator's estate must have no unpaid debts (except those secured by real property) or the court must determine for another reason that there is no necessity for administration. Sometimes the beneficiaries will pay the testator's debts out of their own pockets so that this procedure may be used.

The muniment of title procedure is also used for "late" probates which are permitted under § 256.003. See also § 258.051 (heirs must receive notice of late probate).

Subchapter A. Authorization

§ 257.001. Probate of Will as Muniment of Title Authorized

A court may admit a will to probate as a muniment of title if the court is satisfied that the will should be admitted to probate and the court:

(1) is satisfied that the testator's estate does not owe an unpaid debt, other than any debt secured by a lien on real estate; or

(2) finds for another reason that there is no necessity for administration of the estate.

Derived from Probate Code § 89C(a).

Added by Acts 2009, 81st Leg., ch. 680, § 1, eff. Jan. 1, 2014.

Subchapter B. Application and Proof Requirements

§ 257.051. Contents of Application Generally

(a) An application for the probate of a will as a muniment of title must state and aver the following to the extent each is known to the applicant or can, with reasonable diligence, be ascertained by the applicant:

(1) each applicant's name and domicile;

(2) the testator's name, domicile, and, if known, age, on the date of the testator's death;

(3) the fact, date [time], and place of the testator's death;

(4) facts showing that the court with which the application is filed has venue;

(5) that the testator owned property, including a statement generally describing the property and the property's probable value;

(6) the date of the will;

(7) the name, state of [and] residence, and physical address where service can be had of the [of: (A) any] executor named in the will;

(8) the name of [and [(B)] each subscribing witness to the will, if any;

(9) [(8)] whether one or more children born to or adopted by the testator after the testator executed the will survived the testator and, if so, the name of each of those children;

(10) [(9)] that the testator's estate does not owe an unpaid debt, other than any debt secured by a lien on real estate;

(11) [(10)] whether a marriage of the testator was ever dissolved after the will was made and, if so, when and from whom; and

(12) [(11)] whether the state, a governmental agency of the state, or a charitable organization is named in the will as a devisee.

(b) If an applicant does not state or aver any matter required by Subsection (a) in the application, the application must state the reason the matter is not stated and averred.

Derived from Probate Code § 89A(a).

Added by Acts 2009, 81st Leg., ch. 680, § 1, eff. Jan. 1, 2014. Amended by Acts 2011, 82nd Leg., ch. 1338, § 2.33(a), eff. Jan. 1, 2014. Subsec. (a) amended by Acts 2015, 84th Leg., ch. 995, § 25, eff. Sept. 1, 2015.

§ 257.052. Filing of Will With Application Generally Required

(a) An applicant for the probate of a will as a muniment of title shall file the will with the application if the will is in the applicant's control.

(b) A will filed under Subsection (a) must remain in the custody of the county clerk unless removed from the clerk's custody by court order.

Derived from Probate Code § 89A(a).

Added by Acts 2009, 81st Leg., ch. 680, § 1, eff. Jan. 1, 2014 . Amended by Acts 2013, 83rd Leg., ch. 1136, § 32, eff. Jan. 1, 2014.

§ 257.053. Additional Application Requirements When No Will Is Produced.

In addition to the requirements for an application under Section 257.051, if an applicant for the probate of a will as a muniment of title cannot produce the will in court, the application must state:

(1) the reason the will cannot be produced;

(2) the contents of the will, to the extent known; and

(3) the name[, age, marital status,] and address, if known, whether the person is an adult or minor, and the relationship to the testator, if any, of:

(A) each devisee;

(B) each person who would inherit as an heir of the testator in the absence of a valid will; and

(C) in the case of partial intestacy, each heir of the testator.

Derived from Probate Code § 89A(b).

Added by Acts 2009, 81st Leg., ch. 680, § 1, eff. Jan. 1, 2014. Amended by Acts. 2013, 83rd Leg., ch. 1136, § 33. eff. Jan. 1, 2014. Subsec. (3) amended by Acts 2015, 84th Leg., ch. 995, § 26, eff. Sept. 1, 2015.

§ 257.054. Proof Required

An applicant for the probate of a will as a muniment of title must prove to the court's satisfaction that:

(1) the testator is dead;

(2) four years have not elapsed since the date of the testator's death and before the application;

(3) the court has jurisdiction and venue over the estate;

(4) citation has been served and returned in the manner and for the period required by this title;

(5) the testator's estate does not owe an unpaid debt, other than any debt secured by a lien on real estate;

(6) the testator did not revoke the will; and

(7) if the will is not self-proved in the manner provided by this title, the testator:

(A) executed the will with the formalities and solemnities and under the circumstances required by law to make the will valid; and

(B) at the time of executing the will was of sound mind and:

(i) was 18 years of age or older;

(ii) was or had been married; or

(iii) was a member of the armed forces of the United States, an auxiliary of the armed forces of the United States, or the United States Maritime Service.

Derived from Probate Code § 89B.

Added by Acts 2009, 81st Leg., ch. 680, § 1, eff. Jan. 1, 2014.

Subchapter C. Order Admitting Will; Report

§ 257.101. Declaratory Judgment Construing Will

(a) On application and notice as provided by Chapter 37, Civil Practice and Remedies Code, the court may hear evidence and include in an order probating a will as a muniment of title a declaratory judgment:

(1) construing the will, if a question of construction of the will exists; or

(2) determining those persons who are entitled to receive property under the will and the persons' shares or interests in the estate, if a person who is entitled to property under the provisions of the will cannot be ascertained solely by reference to the will.

(b) A declaratory judgment under this section is conclusive in any suit between a person omitted from the judgment and a bona fide purchaser for value who purchased property after entry of the judgment without actual notice of the claim of the omitted person to an interest in the estate.

(c) A person who delivered the testator's property to a person declared to be entitled to the property under the declaratory judgment under this section or engaged in any other transaction with the person in good faith after entry of the judgment is not liable to any person for actions taken in reliance on the judgment.

Derived from Probate Code § 89C(b).

Added by Acts 2009, 81st Leg., ch. 680, § 1, eff. Jan. 1, 2014.

§ 257.102. Authority of Certain Persons Acting in Accordance with Order

(a) An order admitting a will to probate as a muniment of title constitutes sufficient legal authority for each person who owes money to the testator's estate, has custody of property, acts as registrar or transfer agent of any evidence of interest, indebtedness, property, or right belonging to the estate, or purchases from or otherwise deals with the estate, to pay or transfer without administration the applicable asset without liability to a person described in the will as entitled to receive the asset.

(b) A person who is entitled to property under the provisions of a will admitted to probate as a muniment of title is entitled to deal with and treat the property in the same manner as if the record of title to the property was vested in the person's name.

Derived from Probate Code § 89C(c).

Added by Acts 2009, 81st Leg., ch. 680, § 1, eff. Jan. 1, 2014.

§ 257.103. Report by Applicant After Probate

(a) Except as provided by Subsection (b), not later than the 180th day after the date a will is admitted to probate as a muniment of title, the applicant for the probate of the will shall file with the court clerk a sworn affidavit stating specifically the terms of the will that have been fulfilled and the terms that have not been fulfilled.

(b) The court may:

(1) waive the requirement under Subsection (a); or

(2) extend the time for filing the affidavit under Subsection (a).

(c) The failure of an applicant for probate of a will to file the affidavit required by Subsection (a) does not affect title to property passing under the terms of the will.

Derived from Probate Code § 89C(d).

Added by Acts 2009, 81st Leg., ch. 680, § 1, eff. Jan. 1, 2014.

Chapter 258. Citations and Notices Relating to Probate of Will

Subchapter A. Citations with Respect to Applications for Probate of Will

Subchapter B. Notices with Respect to Application to Probate Will After the Period for Probate

Subchapter C. Service by Publication or Other Substituted Service

Chapter 258. Citations and Notices Relating to Probate of Will

Subchapter A. Citations with Respect to Applications for Probate of Will

Statutes in Context
Chapter 258, Subchapter A

Notice of an application for the probate of a written will produced in court and for letters of administration is served by posting under § 258.001. The notice of the action is merely placed on the courthouse door or a nearby location under § 51.053. Unlike in many states, will beneficiaries and heirs do not receive personal service or service by mail. The posting procedure has been deemed to satisfy the due process requirements of the U.S. Constitution. See *Estate of Ross*, 672 S.W.2d 315 (Tex. App. — Eastland 1984, writ ref'd n.r.e.), cert. denied, *Holmes v. Ross*, 470 U.S. 1084 (1985). Methods of service more likely to give actual (as contrasted to constructive) notice are required if the proponent is attempting to probate a written will not produced in court or a will more than 4 years after the testator's death (see § 258.051).

§ 258.001. Citation on Application for Probate of Will Produced in Court

(a) On the filing with the clerk of an application for the probate of a written will produced in court, the clerk shall issue a citation to all parties interested in the estate.

(b) The citation required by Subsection (a) shall be served by posting and must state:

(1) that the application has been filed;

(2) the nature of the application;

(3) the testator's name;

(4) the applicant's name;

(5) the time when the court will act on the application; and

(6) that any person interested in the estate may appear at the time stated in the citation to contest the application.

Derived from Probate Code § 128(a).

Added by Acts 2009, 81st Leg., ch. 680, § 1, eff. Jan. 1, 2014.

§ 258.002. Citation on Application for Probate of Will Not Produced in Court

(a) On the filing of an application for the probate of a written will that cannot be produced in court, the clerk shall issue a citation to all parties interested in the estate. The citation must:

(1) contain substantially the statements made in the application for probate;

(2) identify the court that will act on the application; and

(3) state the time and place of the court's action on the application.

(b) The citation required by Subsection (a) shall be served on the testator's heirs by personal service if the heirs are residents of this state and their addresses are known.

(c) Service of the citation required by Subsection (a) may be made by publication if:

(1) the heirs are not residents of this state;

(2) the names or addresses of the heirs are unknown; or

(3) the heirs are transient persons.

Derived from Probate Code § 128(b).

Added by Acts 2009, 81st Leg., ch. 680, § 1, eff. Jan. 1, 2014.

§ 258.003. Court Action Prohibited Before Service of Citation

A court may not act on an application for the probate of a will until service of citation has been made in the manner provided by this subchapter.

Derived from Probate Code § 128(c).

Added by Acts 2009, 81st Leg., ch. 680, § 1, eff. Jan. 1, 2014.

Subchapter B. Notices with Respect to Application to Probate Will After the Period for Probate

Statutes in Context
§ 258.051

See Statutes in Context to Chapter 258, Subchapter A.

§ 258.051. Notice to Heirs

(a) Except as provided by Subsection (c), an applicant for the probate of a will under Section 256.003(a) must give notice by service of process to each of the testator's heirs whose address can be ascertained by the applicant with reasonable diligence.

(b) The notice required by Subsection (a) must:

(1) contain a statement that:

(A) the testator's property will pass to the testator's heirs if the will is not admitted to probate; and

(B) the person offering the testator's will for probate may not be in default for failing to present the will for probate during the four-year period immediately following the testator's death; and

(2) be given before the probate of the testator's will.

(c) Notice otherwise required by Subsection (a) is not required to be given to an heir who has delivered to the court an affidavit signed by the heir that:

(1) contains the statement described by Subsection (b)(1); and

(2) states that the heir does not object to the offer of the testator's will for probate.

Derived from Probate Code §§ 128B(a), (b), (c).

Added by Acts 2009, 81st Leg., ch. 680, § 1, eff. Jan. 1, 2014.

§ 258.052. Appointment of Attorney Ad Litem

If an applicant described by Section 258.051(a) cannot, with reasonable diligence, ascertain the address of any of the testator's heirs, the court shall appoint an attorney ad litem to protect the interests of the testator's unknown heirs after an application for the probate of a will is made under Section 256.003(a).

Derived from Probate Code § 128B(d).

Added by Acts 2009, 81st Leg., ch. 680, § 1, eff. Jan. 1, 2014.

§ 258.053. Previously Probated Will

With respect to an application under Section 256.003(a) for the probate of a will of a testator who has had another will admitted to probate, this subchapter applies so as to require notice to the beneficiaries of the testator's probated will instead of to the testator's heirs.

Derived from Probate Code § 128B(e).

Added by Acts 2009, 81st Leg., ch. 680, § 1, eff. Jan. 1, 2014.

Subchapter C. Service by Publication or Other Substituted Service

§ 258.101. Service by Publication or Other Substituted Service

Notwithstanding any other provision of this chapter, if an attempt to make service under this chapter is unsuccessful, service may be made in the manner provided by Rule 109 or 109a, Texas Rules of Civil Procedure, for the service of a citation on a party by publication or other substituted service.

Derived from Probate Code § 129A.

Added by Acts 2009, 81st Leg., ch. 680, § 1, eff. Jan. 1, 2014.

SUBTITLE G. INITIAL APPOINTMENT OF PERSONAL REPRESENTATIVE AND OPENING OF ADMINISTRATION

Chapter 301. Application for Letters Testamentary or of Administration

Subchapter A. Period for Application for Letters

Subchapter B. Application Requirements

Subchapter C. Opposition to Certain Applications

Subchapter D. Required Proof for Issuance of Letters

Subchapter E. Prevention of Administration

Chapter 301. Application for Letters Testamentary or of Administration

Subchapter A. Period for Application for Letters

§ 301.001. Administration Before Death Void

The administration of an estate of a living person is void.

Derived from Probate Code § 72(a).

Added by Acts 2009, 81st Leg., ch. 680, § 1, eff. Jan. 1, 2014.

Statutes in Context § 301.002

Section 301.002 provides that the application for the administration of an estate must usually be filed within 4 years of the decedent's death. A "late" administration is allowed if it is necessary to recover property due to the estate of the decedent.

---

§ 301.002. Period for Filing Application for Letters Testamentary or of Administration

(a) Except as provided by Subsection (b) and Section 501.006 with respect to a foreign will, an application for the grant of letters testamentary or of administration of an estate must be filed not later than the fourth anniversary of the decedent's death.

(b) This section does not apply if administration is necessary to:

(1) receive or recover property due a decedent's estate; or

(2) prevent real property in a decedent's estate from becoming a danger to the health, safety, or welfare of the general public and the applicant for the issuance of letters testamentary or of administration is a home-rule municipality that is a creditor of the estate.

Derived from Probate Code § 74.

Added by Acts 2009, 81st Leg., ch. 680, § 1, eff. Jan. 1, 2014. Subsec. (a) amended by Acts 2015, 84th Leg., ch. 995, § 27, eff. Sept. 1, 2015. Subsec. (b) amended by Acts 2015, 84th Leg., ch. 576, § 1, eff. Sept. 1, 2015.

Subchapter B. Application Requirements

§ 301.051. Eligible Applicants for Letters

An executor named in a will, an independent administrator designated by all of the distributees of the decedent under Section 401.002(b) or 401.003, or an interested person may file an application with the court for:

> (1) the appointment of the executor named in the will; or
>
> (2) the appointment of an administrator, if:
>> (A) there is a will, but:
>>> (i) no executor is named in the will; or
>>>
>>> (ii) the executor named in the will is disqualified, refuses to serve, is dead, or resigns; or
>>
>> (B) there is no will.

Derived from Probate Code § 76.

Added by Acts 2009, 81st Leg., ch. 680, § 1, eff. Jan. 1, 2014. Amended by Acts 2015, 84th Leg., ch. 995, § 28, eff. Sept. 1, 2015.

Statutes in Context
§ 301.052

Section 301.052 enumerates the requirements of an application for letters of administration for an intestate decedent.

---

§ 301.052. Contents of Application for Letters of Administration

An application for letters of administration when no will is alleged to exist must state:

> (1) the applicant's name, domicile, and, if any, relationship to the decedent;
>
> (2) the decedent's name and that the decedent died intestate;
>
> (3) the fact, date [time], and place of the decedent's death;
>
> (4) facts necessary to show that the court with which the application is filed has venue;
>
> (5) whether the decedent owned property and, if so, include a statement of the property's probable value;
>
> (6) the name[, age, marital status,] and address, if known, whether the heir is an adult or minor, and the relationship to the decedent of each of the decedent's heirs;
>
> (7) if known by the applicant at the time the applicant files the application, whether one or more children were born to or adopted by the decedent and, if so, the name, birth date, and place of birth of each child;
>
> (8) if known by the applicant at the time the applicant files the application, whether the decedent was ever divorced and, if so, when and from whom;
>
> (9) that a necessity exists for administration of the decedent's estate and an allegation of the facts that show that necessity; and
>
> (10) that the applicant is not disqualified by law from acting as administrator.

Derived from Probate Code § 82.

Added by Acts 2009, 81st Leg., ch. 680, § 1, eff. Jan. 1, 2014. Subsecs (3) & (6) amended by Acts 2015, 84th

Leg., ch. 995, § 29, eff. Sept. 1, 2015.

Subchapter C. Opposition to Certain Applications

§ 301.101. Opposition to Application for Letters of Administration

An interested person may, at any time before an application for letters of administration is granted, file an opposition to the application in writing and may apply for the grant of letters to the interested person or any other person. On the trial, the court, considering the applicable provisions of this code, shall grant letters to the person that seems best entitled to the letters without notice other than the notice given on the original application.

Derived from Probate Code § 179.

Added by Acts 2009, 81st Leg., ch. 680, § 1, eff. Jan. 1, 2014.

Subchapter D. Required Proof for Issuance of Letters

Statutes in Context
§ 301.151

Section 301.151 enumerates the items which the applicant must prove to probate a will, receive letters testamentary or letters of administration.

---

§ 301.151. General Proof Requirements

An applicant for the issuance of letters testamentary or of administration of an estate must prove to the court's satisfaction that:

> (1) the person whose estate is the subject of the application is dead;
>
> [as amended by Acts 2015, 84th Leg., ch. 995, § 30, eff. Sept. 1, 2015]
>
> (2) except as provided by Section 301.002(b) with respect to administration necessary to receive or recover property due a decedent's estate, and Section 501.006 with respect to a foreign will, four years have not elapsed since the date of the decedent's death and before the application;
>
> [as amended by Acts 2015, 84th Leg., ch. 576, § 2, eff. Sept. 1, 2015.]
>
> (2) except as provided by Section 301.002(b)(2), four years have not elapsed since the date of the decedent's death and before the application;
>
> (3) the court has jurisdiction and venue over the estate;
>
> (4) citation has been served and returned in the manner and for the period required by this title; and
>
> (5) the person for whom letters testamentary or of administration are sought is entitled by law to the letters and is not disqualified.

Derived from Probate Code § 88(a).

Added by Acts 2009, 81st Leg., ch. 680, § 1, eff. Jan. 1, 2014. Subsec. (2) amended by Acts 2015, 84th Leg., ch. 995, § 30, eff. Sept. 1, 2015 and Acts 2015, 84th Leg., ch. 576, § 2, eff. Sept. 1, 2015.

§ 301.152. Additional Proof Required for Letters Testamentary

If letters testamentary are to be granted, it must appear to the court that:

> (1) the proof required for the probate of the will has been made; and
>
> (2) the person to whom the letters are to be granted is named as executor in the will.

Derived from Probate Code § 88(c).

Added by Acts 2009, 81st Leg., ch. 680, § 1, eff. Jan. 1, 2014.

§ 301.153. Additional Proof Required for Letters of Administration; Effect of Finding No Necessity for Administration Exists

(a) If letters of administration are to be granted, the applicant for the letters must prove to the court's satisfaction that a necessity for an administration of the estate exists.

(b) If an application is filed for letters of administration but the court finds that no necessity for an administration of the estate exists, the court shall recite in the court's order refusing the application that no necessity for an administration exists.

(c) A court order containing a recital that no necessity for an administration of the estate exists constitutes sufficient legal authority for each person who owes money, has custody of property, or acts as registrar or transfer agent of any evidence of interest, indebtedness, property, or right belonging to the estate, and to each person purchasing or otherwise dealing with the estate, for payment or transfer to the distributees.

(d) A distributee is entitled to enforce by suit the distributee's right to payment or transfer described by Subsection (c).

Derived from Probate Code §§ 88(d), 180.

Added by Acts 2009, 81st Leg., ch. 680, § 1, eff. Jan. 1, 2014.

§ 301.154. Proof Required when Letters Have Previously Been Granted

If letters testamentary or of administration have previously been granted with respect to an estate, an applicant for the granting of subsequent letters must show only that the person for whom the letters are sought is entitled by law to the letters and is not disqualified.

Derived from Probate Code § 88(e).

Added by Acts 2009, 81st Leg., ch. 680, § 1, eff. Jan. 1, 2014.

Statutes in Contest
§ 301.155

Section 301.155 provides that any fact that must be provided, e.g., in applications for the issuance of letters, may be provided by live testimony, or if the witness is unavailable, by disposition on written questions.

---

§ 301.155. Authorized Methods of Proof

A fact contained in an application for issuance of letters testamentary or of administration or any other fact required to be proved by this subchapter may be proved by the sworn testimony of a witness with personal knowledge of the fact that is:

> (1) taken in open court; or
>
> (2) if proved under oath to the satisfaction of the court that the witness is unavailable, taken by deposition on written questions in accordance with Section 51.203 or the Texas Rules of Civil Procedure.

New.

Added by Acts 2013, 83rd Leg., ch. 1136, § 34, eff. Jan. 1, 2014.

Subchapter E. Prevention of Administration

Statutes in Context
§ 301.201

If a creditor seeks an administration, § 301.201 provides a means for an interested person to defeat the application.

---

§ 301.201. Method of Preventing Administration Requested by Creditor

(a) If a creditor files an application for letters of administration of an estate, another interested person who does not desire the administration can defeat the application by:

> (1) paying the creditor's claim;
>
> (2) proving to the court's satisfaction that the creditor's claim is fictitious, fraudulent, illegal, or barred by limitation; or
>
> (3) executing a bond that is:
>
> > (A) payable to, and to be approved by, the judge in an amount that is twice the amount of the creditor's claim; and
> >
> > (B) conditioned on the obligors paying the claim on the establishment of the claim by suit in any court in the county having jurisdiction of the amount.

(b) A bond executed and approved under Subsection (a)(3) must be filed with the county clerk.

Derived from Probate Code §§ 80(a), (b).

Added by Acts 2009, 81st Leg., ch. 680, § 1, eff. Jan. 1, 2014.

§ 301.202. Suit on Bond

Any creditor for whose protection a bond is executed under Section 301.201(a)(3) may sue on the bond in the creditor's own name to recover the creditor's claim.

Derived from Probate Code § 80(b).

Added by Acts 2009, 81st Leg., ch. 680, § 1, eff. Jan. 1, 2014.

§ 301.203. Bond Secured by Lien

If a bond is executed and approved under Section 301.201(a)(3), a lien exists on all of the estate in the possession of the distributees, and those claiming under the distributees with notice of the lien, to secure the ultimate payment of the bond.

Derived from Probate Code § 80(c).

Added by Acts 2009, 81st Leg., ch. 680, § 1, eff. Jan. 1, 2014.

Chapter 303. Citations and Notices in General on Opening of Administration

§ 303.001. Citation on Application for Issuance of Letters of Administration

§ 303.002. Court Action Prohibited Before Service of Citation

§ 303.003. Service by Publication or Other Substituted Service

Chapter 303. Citations and Notices in General on Opening of Administration

§ 303.001. Citation on Application for Issuance of Letters of Administration

(a) On the filing with the clerk of an application for letters of administration, the clerk shall issue a citation to all parties interested in the estate.

(b) The citation required by Subsection (a) shall be served by posting and must state:

(1) that the application has been filed;

(2) the nature of the application;

(3) the decedent's name;

(4) the applicant's name;

(5) the time when the court will act on the application; and

(6) that any person interested in the estate may appear at the time stated in the citation to contest the application.

Derived from Probate Code § 128(a).

Added by Acts 2009, 81st Leg., ch. 680, § 1, eff. Jan. 1, 2014.

§ 303.002. Court Action Prohibited Before Service of Citation

A court may not act on an application for the issuance of letters of administration until service of citation has been made in the manner provided by this chapter.

Derived from Probate Code § 128(c).

Added by Acts 2009, 81st Leg., ch. 680, § 1, eff. Jan. 1, 2014.

§ 303.003. Service by Publication or Other Substituted Service

Notwithstanding any other provision of this chapter, if an attempt to make service under this chapter is unsuccessful, service may be made in the manner provided by Rule 109 or 109a, Texas Rules of Civil Procedure, for the service of a citation on a party by publication or other substituted service.

Derived from Probate Code § 129A.

Added by Acts 2009, 81st Leg., ch. 680, § 1, eff. Jan. 1, 2014.

Chapter 304. Persons Who May Serve as Personal Representatives

§ 304.001. Order of Persons Qualified to Serve as Personal Representative

§ 304.002. Renouncing Right to Serve as Personal Representative

§ 304.003. Persons Disqualified to Serve as Executor or Administrator

Chapter 304. Persons Who May Serve as Personal Representatives

---

Statutes in Context
§ 304.001

To serve as a personal representative of a decedent's estate, the person must be qualified under § 304.001 and not disqualified under § 304.003. Section 304.001 provides a list in priority order of the persons who are qualified to serve. Note that the court may appoint co-personal representatives.

---

§ 304.001. Order of Persons Qualified to Serve as Personal Representative

(a) The court shall grant letters testamentary or of administration to persons qualified to act, in the following order:

(1) the person named as executor in the decedent's will;

(2) the decedent's surviving spouse;

(3) the principal devisee of the decedent;

(4) any devisee of the decedent;

(5) the next of kin of the decedent;

(6) a creditor of the decedent;

(7) any person of good character residing in the county who applies for the letters;

(8) any other person who is not disqualified under Section 304.003; and

(9) any appointed public probate administrator.

(b) For purposes of Subsection (a)(5), the decedent's next of kin:

(1) is determined in accordance with order of descent, with the person nearest in order of descent first, and so on; and

(2) includes a person and the person's descendants who legally adopted the decedent or who have been legally adopted by the decedent.

(c) If persons are equally entitled to letters testamentary or of administration, the court:

(1) shall grant the letters to the person who, in the judgment of the court, is most likely to administer the estate advantageously; or

(2) may grant the letters to two or more of those persons.

Derived from Probate Code § 77.

Added by Acts 2009, 81st Leg., ch. 680, § 1, eff. Jan. 1, 2014. Subsection (a) amended by Acts 2013, 83rd Leg., ch. 671, § 3, eff. Jan. 1, 2014. Subsec. (c) amended by Acts 2013, 83rd Leg., ch. 1136, § 35, eff. Jan. 1, 2014.

§ 304.002. Renouncing Right to Serve as Personal Representative

A decedent's surviving spouse, or, if there is no surviving spouse, the heirs or any one of the heirs of the decedent to the exclusion of any person not equally entitled to letters testamentary or of administration, may renounce the right to the letters in favor of another qualified person in open court or by a power of attorney authenticated and filed with the county clerk of the county where the application for the letters is filed. After the right to the letters has been renounced, the court may grant the letters to the other qualified person.

Derived from Probate Code § 79.

Added by Acts 2009, 81st Leg., ch. 680, § 1, eff. Jan. 1, 2014.

Statutes in Context
§ 304.003

Section 304.003 enumerates the persons who are disqualified from serving as a personal representative. The disqualification of being a non-resident in § 304.003 is removed if the non-resident appoints a resident agent to accept service of process. For additional guidance regarding this agent, see §§ 56.001 & 56.002.

---

§ 304.003. Persons Disqualified to Serve as Executor or Administrator

A person is not qualified to serve as an executor or administrator if the person is:

(1) incapacitated;

(2) a felon convicted under the laws of the United States or of any state of the United States

unless, in accordance with law, the person has been pardoned or has had the person's civil rights restored;

(3) a nonresident of this state who:

(A) is a natural person or corporation; and

(B) has not:

(i) appointed a resident agent to accept service of process in all actions or proceedings with respect to the estate; or

(ii) had that appointment filed with the court;

(4) a corporation not authorized to act as a fiduciary in this state; or

(5) a person whom the court finds unsuitable.

Derived from Probate Code § 78.

Added by Acts 2009, 81st Leg., ch. 680, § 1, eff. Jan. 1, 2014.

Chapter 305. Qualification of Personal Representatives

Subchapter A. General Provisions

Subchapter B. Oaths

Subchapter C. General Provisions Relating to Bonds

Subchapter D. Amount of Bond and Associated Deposits

Subchapter E. Bond Sureties

Subchapter F. New Bonds

Chapter 305. Qualification of Personal Representatives

Subchapter A. General Provisions

§ 305.001. Definitions

In this chapter:

(1) "Bond" means a bond required by this chapter to be given by a person appointed to serve as a personal representative.

(2) "Oath" means an oath required by this chapter to be taken by a person appointed to serve as a personal representative.

New.

Added by Acts 2009, 81st Leg., ch. 680, § 1, eff. Jan. 1, 2014.

Statutes in Context
§ 305.002

Section 305.002 explains that a personal representative is "qualified" after filing any required bond and taking the oath of office.

---

§ 305.002. Manner of Qualification of Personal Representative

(a) A personal representative, other than an executor described by Subsection (b), is considered to have qualified when the representative has:

(1) taken and filed the oath prescribed by Subchapter B;

(2) filed the required bond with the clerk; and

(3) obtained the judge's approval of the bond.

(b) An executor who is not required to give a bond is considered to have qualified when the executor has taken and filed the oath prescribed by Subchapter B.

Derived from Probate Code § 189.

Added by Acts 2009, 81st Leg., ch. 680, § 1, eff. Jan. 1, 2014. Subsection (a) amended by Acts 2013, 83rd Leg., ch. 1136, § 36, eff. Jan. 1, 2014.

Statutes in Context
§ 305.003

The personal representative should take the oath and post any required bond within 20 days of the order granting letters under § 305.003.

---

§ 305.003. Period for Taking Oath

An oath may be taken and subscribed at any time before:

(1) the 21st day after the date of the order granting letters testamentary or of administration, as applicable; or

(2) the letters testamentary or of administration, as applicable, are revoked for a failure to qualify within the period allowed.

Derived from Probate Code § 192.

Added by Acts 2009, 81st Leg., ch. 680, § 1, eff. Jan. 1, 2014. Amended by Acts 2013, 83rd Leg., ch. 1136, eff. Jan. 1, 2014.

§ 305.004. Period for Giving Bond

(a) A bond may be filed with the clerk at any time before:

(1) the 21st day after:

(A) the date of the order granting letters testamentary or of administration, as applicable; or

(B) the date of any order modifying the bond requirement; or

(2) the date letters testamentary or of administration, as applicable, are revoked for a failure to qualify within the period allowed.

(b) The court shall act promptly to review a bond filed as provided by Subsection (a) and, if acceptable, shall approve the bond.

(c) If no action has been taken by the court on the bond before the 21st day after the date the bond is filed, the person appointed personal representative may file a motion requiring the judge of the court in which the bond was filed to specify on the record the reason or reasons for the judge's failure to act on the bond. The hearing on the motion must be held before the 11th day after the date the motion is filed.

New.

Added by Acts 2013, 83rd Leg., ch. 1136, § 38, eff. Jan. 1, 2014.

Subchapter B. Oaths

Statutes in Context
Chapter 305, Subchapter B

Subchapter B sets forth the oaths which personal representatives must take and file before receiving letters.

§ 305.051. Oath of Executor or Administrator with Will Annexed

Before the issuance of letters testamentary or letters of administration with the will annexed, the person named as executor or appointed as administrator with the will annexed shall take and subscribe an oath in substantially the following form:

I do solemnly swear that the writing offered for probate is the last will of _____ (insert name of testator), so far as I know or believe, and that I will well and truly perform all the duties of _____ (insert "executor of the will" or "administrator with the will annexed," as applicable) for the estate of _____ (insert name of testator).

Derived from Probate Code § 190(a).

Added by Acts 2009, 81st Leg., ch. 680, § 1, eff. Jan. 1, 2014.

§ 305.052. Oath of Administrator

Before the issuance of letters of administration, the person appointed as administrator shall take and subscribe an oath in substantially the following form:

I do solemnly swear that _____ (insert name of decedent), deceased, died _____ (insert "without leaving any lawful will" or "leaving a lawful will, but the executor named in the will is dead or has failed to offer the will for probate or to accept and qualify as executor, within the period required," as applicable), so far as I know or believe, and that I will well and truly perform all the duties of administrator of the estate of the deceased.

Derived from Probate Code § 190(b).

Added by Acts 2009, 81st Leg., ch. 680, § 1, eff. Jan. 1, 2014.

§ 305.053. Oath of Temporary Administrator

Before the issuance of temporary letters of administration, the person appointed as temporary administrator shall take and subscribe an oath in substantially the following form:

I do solemnly swear that I will well and truly perform the duties of temporary administrator of the estate of _____ (insert name of decedent), deceased, in accordance with the law, and with the order of the court appointing me as temporary administrator.

Derived from Probate Code § 190(c).

Added by Acts 2009, 81st Leg., ch. 680, § 1, eff. Jan. 1, 2014.

§ 305.054. Administration of Oath

An oath may be taken before any person authorized to administer oaths under the laws of this state.

Derived from Probate Code §§ 190(d), 192.

Added by Acts 2009, 81st Leg., ch. 680, § 1, eff. Jan. 1, 2014.

§ 305.055. Filing and Recording of Oath

An oath shall be:

(1) filed with the clerk of the court granting the letters testamentary or of administration, as applicable; and

(2) recorded in the judge's probate docket.

Derived from Probate Code § 190(d).

Added by Acts 2009, 81st Leg., ch. 680, § 1, eff. Jan. 1, 2014. Subsec. (2) amended by Acts 2011, 82nd Leg., ch. 90, § 8.012, eff. Jan. 1, 2014.

Subchapter C. General Provisions Relating to Bonds

Statutes in Context
§ 305.101

A personal representative is excused from the requirement of posting bond in the following situations: (1) the testator waived bond in the testator's will (§ 305.101(a)), (2) a corporate fiduciary is serving as the personal representative (§ 305.101(b)), or (3) the court waives bond for an independent executor (§ 401.005). It is very common for a testator to waive bond in the will to save the estate, and hence the beneficiaries, the cost of the bond and the court proceedings to set the amount of the bond.

§ 305.101. Bond Generally Required; Exceptions

(a) Except as otherwise provided by this title, a person to whom letters testamentary or of administration will be issued must enter into a bond before issuance of the letters.

(b) Letters testamentary shall be issued without the requirement of a bond to a person named as executor in a will probated in a court of this state if:

(1) the will directs that no bond or security be required of the person; and

(2) the court finds that the person is qualified.

(c) A bond is not required if a personal representative is a corporate fiduciary.

Derived from Probate Code §§ 194, 195.

Added by Acts 2009, 81st Leg., ch. 680, § 1, eff. Jan. 1, 2014.

Statutes in Context
§ 305.102

The court may require a personal representative to give bond even if bond was not originally needed, e.g., the testator's will waived bond. See § 305.102.

§ 305.102. Bond Required From Executor Otherwise Exempt

(a) This section applies only to an estate for which an executor was appointed under a will, but from whom no bond was required.

(b) A person who has a debt, claim, or demand against the estate, with respect to the justice of which the person or the person's agent or attorney has made an oath, or another person interested in the estate, whether in person or as the representative of another, may file a written complaint in the court where the will is probated.

(c) On the filing of the complaint, the court shall cite the executor to appear and show cause why the executor should not be required to give a bond.

(d) On hearing the complaint, the court shall enter an order requiring the executor to give a bond not later than the 10th day after the date of the order if it appears to the court that:

(1) the executor is wasting, mismanaging, or misapplying the estate; and

(2) as a result of conduct described by Subdivision (1):

(A) a creditor may probably lose the creditor's debt; or

(B) a person's interest in the estate may be diminished or lost.

(e) A bond required under this section must be:

(1) in an amount sufficient to protect the estate and the estate's creditors;

(2) payable to and approved by the judge; and

(3) conditioned that the executor:

(A) will well and truly administer the estate; and

(B) will not waste, mismanage, or misapply the estate.

(f) If the executor fails to give a bond required under this section on or before the 10th day after the date of the order and the judge has not extended the period for giving the bond, the judge, without citation, shall remove the executor and appoint a competent person in the executor's place who shall administer the estate according to the will and law. Before entering into the administration of the estate, the appointed person must:

(1) take the oath required of an administrator with the will annexed under Section 305.051; and

(2) give a bond in the manner and amount provided by this chapter for the issuance of original letters of administration.

Derived from Probate Code §§ 214, 215, 216, 217.

Added by Acts 2009, 81st Leg., ch. 680, § 1, eff. Jan. 1, 2014.

§ 305.103. Bonds of Joint Personal Representatives

If two or more persons are appointed as personal representatives of an estate and are required by this chapter or by the court to give a bond, the court may require:

(1) a separate bond from each person; or

(2) a joint bond from all of the persons.

Derived from Probate Code § 198.

Added by Acts 2009, 81st Leg., ch. 680, § 1, eff. Jan. 1, 2014.

§ 305.104. Bond of Married Person

(a) A married person appointed as a personal representative may execute a bond required by law:

(1) jointly with the person's spouse; or

(2) separately without the person's spouse.

(b) A bond executed by a married person binds the person's separate estate, but does not bind the person's spouse unless the spouse signed the bond.

Derived from Probate Code § 199.

Added by Acts 2009, 81st Leg., ch. 680, § 1, eff. Jan. 1,

2014.

§ 305.105. Bond of Married Person Under 18 Years of Age

Any bond required to be executed by a person who is under 18 years of age, is or has been married, and accepts and qualifies as an executor or administrator is as valid and binding for all purposes as if the person were of legal age.

Derived from Probate Code § 200.

Added by Acts 2009, 81st Leg., ch. 680, § 1, eff. Jan. 1, 2014.

§ 305.106. General Formalities

A bond required under Section 305.101(a) must:

(1) be conditioned as required by law;

(2) be payable to the judge and the judge's successors in office;

(3) bear the written approval of the judge in the judge's official capacity; and

(4) be executed and approved in accordance with this chapter.

Derived from Probate Code § 194.

Added by Acts 2009, 81st Leg., ch. 680, § 1, eff. Jan. 1, 2014.

§ 305.107. Subscription of Bond by Principals and Sureties

A bond required under Section 305.101 shall be subscribed by both principals and sureties.

Derived from Probate Code § 197.

Added by Acts 2009, 81st Leg., ch. 680, § 1, eff. Jan. 1, 2014.

§ 305.108. Form of Bond

The following form, or a form with the same substance, may be used for the bond of a personal representative:

The State of Texas
County of _____
Know all persons by these presents that we, _____ (insert name of each principal), as principal, and _____ (insert name of each surety), as sureties, are held and firmly bound unto the judge of _____ (insert reference to appropriate judge), and that judge's successors in office, in the sum of _____ dollars, conditioned that the above bound principal or principals, appointed as _____ (insert "executor of the last will and testament," "administrator with the will annexed of the estate," "administrator of the estate," or "temporary administrator of the estate," as applicable) of _____ (insert name of decedent), deceased, shall well and truly perform all of the duties required of the principal or principals by law under that appointment.

Derived from Probate Code § 196.

Added by Acts 2009, 81st Leg., ch. 680, § 1, eff. Jan. 1,

2014.

§ 305.109. Filing of Bond

A bond required under Section 305.101 shall be filed with the clerk after the court approves the bond.

Derived from Probate Code § 197.

Added by Acts 2009, 81st Leg., ch. 680, § 1, eff. Jan. 1, 2014.

§ 305.110. Failure to Give Bond

Another person may be appointed as personal representative to replace a personal representative who at any time fails to give a bond as required by the court in the period prescribed by this chapter.

Derived from Probate Code § 213.

Added by Acts 2009, 81st Leg., ch. 680, § 1, eff. Jan. 1, 2014.

§ 305.111. Bond Not Void on First Recovery

A personal representative's bond does not become void on the first recovery but may be put in suit and prosecuted from time to time until the entire amount of the bond has been recovered.

Derived from Probate Code § 218.

Added by Acts 2009, 81st Leg., ch. 680, § 1, eff. Jan. 1, 2014.

Subchapter D. Amount of Bond and Associated Deposits

Statutes in Context
Chapter 305, Subchapter D

Personal representatives in Texas must post bond unless one of the exceptions in § 305.101 applies. The bond is to protect the estate creditors, beneficiaries, and heirs from the personal representative wasting, mismanaging, or misapplying the estate. Section 305.106 explains how the court establishes the amount of the bond and the methods for posting the bond.

§ 305.151. General Standard Regarding Amount of Bond

(a) The judge shall set the amount of a bond, in an amount considered sufficient to protect the estate and the estate's creditors, as provided by this chapter.

(b) Notwithstanding Subsection (a) or other provisions generally applicable to bonds of personal representatives, if the person to whom letters testamentary or of administration are granted is entitled to all of the decedent's estate after payment of debts, a bond shall be in an amount sufficient to protect creditors only.

Derived from Probate Code § 194, Subdivs. 1, 2.

Added by Acts 2009, 81st Leg., ch. 680, § 1, eff. Jan. 1, 2014.

§ 305.152. Evidentiary Hearing on Amount of Bond

Before setting the amount of a bond, the court shall hear evidence and determine:

(1) the amount of cash on hand and where that cash is deposited;

(2) the amount of cash estimated to be needed for administrative purposes, including operation of a business, factory, farm, or ranch owned by the estate, and expenses of administration for one year;

(3) the revenue anticipated to be received in the succeeding 12 months from dividends, interest, rentals, or use of property belonging to the estate and the aggregate amount of any installments or periodic payments to be collected;

(4) the estimated value of certificates of stock, bonds, notes, or other securities of the estate and the name of the depository, if any, in which those assets are deposited;

(5) the face value of life insurance or other policies payable to the person on whose estate administration is sought or to the estate;

(6) the estimated value of other personal property owned by the estate; and

(7) the estimated amount of debts due and owing by the estate.

Derived from Probate Code § 194, Subdiv. 3.

Added by Acts 2009, 81st Leg., ch. 680, § 1, eff. Jan. 1, 2014.

§ 305.153. Specific Bond Amount

(a) Except as otherwise provided by this section, the judge shall set the bond in an amount equal to the sum of:

(1) the estimated value of all personal property belonging to the estate; and

(2) an additional amount to cover revenue anticipated to be derived during the succeeding 12 months from:

(A) interest and dividends;

(B) collectible claims;

(C) the aggregate amount of any installments or periodic payments, excluding income derived or to be derived from federal social security payments; and

(D) rentals for the use of property.

(b) The judge shall reduce the amount of the original bond under Subsection (a) in proportion to the amount of cash or the value of securities or other assets:

(1) authorized or required to be deposited by court order; or

(2) voluntarily deposited by the personal representative or the sureties on the representative's bond, as provided by Sections 305.155 and 305.156.

(c) A bond required to be given by a temporary administrator shall be in the amount that the judge directs.

Derived from Probate Code § 194, Subdivs. 4, 13.

Added by Acts 2009, 81st Leg., ch. 680, § 1, eff. Jan. 1, 2014.

§ 305.154. Agreement Regarding Deposit of Estate Assets

(a) A personal representative may agree with the surety or sureties on a bond, either corporate or personal, for the deposit of any cash and other estate assets in a depository described by Subsection (c), if the deposit is otherwise proper, in a manner that prevents the withdrawal of the cash or other assets without:

(1) the written consent of the surety or sureties; or

(2) a court order entered after notice to the surety or sureties as directed by the court.

(b) The court may require the action described by Subsection (a) if the court considers that action to be in the best interest of the estate.

(c) Cash and assets must be deposited under this section in a financial institution, as defined by Section 201.101, Finance Code, that:

(1) has its main office or a branch office in this state; and

(2) is qualified to act as a depository in this state under the laws of this state or the United States.

(d) An agreement under this section may not release the principal or sureties from liability, or change the liability of the principal or sureties, as established by the terms of the bond.

Derived from Probate Code § 194, Subdiv. 5.

Added by Acts 2009, 81st Leg., ch. 680, § 1, eff. Jan. 1, 2014.

§ 305.155. Deposit of Estate Assets on Terms Prescribed by Court

(a) Cash, securities, or other personal assets of an estate or to which the estate is entitled may or, if considered by the court to be in the best interest of the estate, shall, be deposited in one or more depositories described by Section 305.154(c) on terms prescribed by the court.

(b) The court in which the proceedings are pending may authorize or require additional estate assets currently on hand or that accrue during the pendency of the proceedings to be deposited as provided by Subsection (a) on:

(1) the court's own motion; or

(2) the written application of the personal representative or any other person interested in the estate.

(c) The amount of the bond required to be given by the personal representative shall be reduced in proportion to the amount of the cash and the value of the securities or other assets deposited under this section.

(d) Cash, securities, or other assets deposited under this section may be withdrawn in whole or in part from the depository only in accordance with a court order, and the amount of the personal representative's bond shall be increased in proportion to the amount of the cash and the value of the securities or other assets authorized to be withdrawn.

Derived from Probate Code § 194, Subdiv. 6.

Added by Acts 2009, 81st Leg., ch. 680, § 1, eff. Jan. 1, 2014.

§ 305.156. Deposits of Personal Representative

(a) Instead of giving a surety or sureties on a bond, or to reduce the amount of a bond, a personal representative may deposit the representative's own cash or securities acceptable to the court with a depository described by Subsection (b), if the deposit is otherwise proper.

(b) Cash or securities must be deposited under this section in:

(1) a depository described by Section 305.154(c); or

(2) any other corporate depository approved by the court.

(c) A deposit may be in an amount or value equal to the amount of the bond required or in a lesser amount or value, in which case the amount of the bond is reduced by the amount or value of the deposit.

(d) The amount of cash or securities on deposit may be increased or decreased, by court order from time to time, as the interest of the estate requires.

(e) A deposit of cash or securities made instead of a surety or sureties on a bond may be withdrawn or released only on order of a court having jurisdiction.

(f) A creditor has the same rights against a personal representative and deposits made under this section as are provided for recovery against sureties on a bond.

Derived from Probate Code § 194, Subdivs. 7, 8(b), (c), (d).

Added by Acts 2009, 81st Leg., ch. 680, § 1, eff. Jan. 1, 2014.

§ 305.157. Receipt for Deposits of Personal Representative

(a) A depository that receives a deposit made under Section 305.156 instead of a surety or sureties on a bond shall issue a receipt for the deposit that:

(1) shows the amount of cash deposited or the amount and description of the securities deposited, as applicable; and

(2) states that the depository agrees to disburse or deliver the cash or securities only on receipt of a certified copy of an order of the court in which the proceedings are pending.

(b) A receipt issued by a depository under Subsection (a) shall be attached to the personal representative's bond and be delivered to and filed by the county clerk after approval by the judge.

Derived from Probate Code § 194, Subdiv. 8(a).

Added by Acts 2009, 81st Leg., ch. 680, § 1, eff. Jan. 1, 2014.

§ 305.158. Bond Required Instead of Deposits by Personal Representative

(a) The court may on its own motion or on the written application by the personal representative or any other person interested in the estate:

(1) require that an adequate bond be given instead of a deposit under Section 305.156; or

(2) authorize withdrawal of a deposit made under Section 305.156 and substitution of a bond with sureties.

(b) Not later than the 20th day after the date of entry of the court's motion or the date the personal representative is personally served with notice of the filing of an application by another person interested in the estate, the representative shall file a sworn statement showing the condition of the estate.

(c) A personal representative who fails to comply with Subsection (b) is subject to removal as in other cases.

(d) The personal representative's deposit under Section 305.156 may not be released or withdrawn until the court has:

(1) been satisfied as to the condition of the estate;

(2) determined the amount of the bond; and

(3) received and approved the bond.

Derived from Probate Code § 194, Subdiv. 8(e).

Added by Acts 2009, 81st Leg., ch. 680, § 1, eff. Jan. 1, 2014.

§ 305.159. Withdrawal of Deposits on Closing of Administration

(a) Any deposit of assets of the personal representative, the estate, or a surety that remains at the time an estate is closed shall be released by court order and paid to the person or persons entitled to the deposit.

(b) Except as provided by Subsection (c), a writ of attachment or garnishment does not lie against a deposit described by Subsection (a).

(c) A writ of attachment or garnishment may lie against a deposit described by Subsection (a) as to a claim of a creditor of the estate being administered or a person interested in the estate, including a distributee or ward, to the extent the court has ordered distribution.

Derived from Probate Code § 194, Subdiv. 9.

Added by Acts 2009, 81st Leg., ch. 680, § 1, eff. Jan. 1, 2014.

§ 305.160. Increased or Additional Bonds in Certain Circumstances

The provisions of this subchapter regarding the deposit of cash and securities govern, to the extent the provisions may be applicable, the court orders to be entered when:

(1) one of the following circumstances occurs:

(A) estate property has been authorized to be sold or rented;

(B) money has been borrowed on estate property; or

(C) real property, or an interest in real property, has been authorized to be leased for mineral development or subjected to unitization; and

(2) the general bond has been found to be insufficient.

Derived from Probate Code § 194, Subdiv. 14.

Added by Acts 2009, 81st Leg., ch. 680, § 1, eff. Jan. 1, 2014.

Subchapter E. Bond Sureties

§ 305.201. Personal or Authorized Corporate Sureties

(a) The surety or sureties on a bond may be personal or authorized corporate sureties.

(b) A bond with sureties who are individuals must have at least two sureties, each of whom must:

(1) execute an affidavit in the manner provided by this subchapter; and

(2) own property in this state, excluding property exempt by law, that the judge is satisfied is sufficient to qualify the person as a surety as required by law.

(c) A bond with an authorized corporate surety is only required to have one surety, except as provided by law.

Derived from Probate Code § 194, Subdivs. 10, 12.

Added by Acts 2009, 81st Leg., ch. 680, § 1, eff. Jan. 1, 2014.

§ 305.202. Sureties for Certain Bonds

(a) If the amount of a bond exceeds $50,000, the court may require that the bond be signed by:

(1) at least two authorized corporate sureties; or

(2) one authorized corporate surety and at least two good and sufficient personal sureties.

(b) The estate shall pay the cost of a bond with corporate sureties.

Derived from Probate Code § 194, Subdiv. 11.

Added by Acts 2009, 81st Leg., ch. 680, § 1, eff. Jan. 1, 2014.

§ 305.203. Affidavit of Personal Surety

(a) Before a judge may consider a bond with personal sureties, each person offered as surety must execute an affidavit stating the amount by which the person's assets that are reachable by creditors exceeds the person's liabilities, and each affidavit must be presented to the judge for consideration.

(b) The total worth of the personal sureties on a bond must equal at least twice the amount of the bond.

(c) An affidavit presented to and approved by the judge under this section shall be attached to and form part of the bond.

Derived from Probate Code § 201(a).

Added by Acts 2009, 81st Leg., ch. 680, § 1, eff. Jan. 1,

2014.

§ 305.204. Lien on Real Property Owned by Personal Sureties

(a) If a judge finds that the estimated value of personal property of the estate that cannot be deposited, as provided by Subchapter D, is such that personal sureties cannot be accepted without the creation of a specific lien on real property owned by each of the sureties, the judge shall enter an order requiring each surety to:

(1) designate real property that:

(A) is owned by the surety and located in this state;

(B) is subject to execution; and

(C) has a value that exceeds all liens and unpaid taxes by an amount at least equal to the amount of the bond; and

(2) give an adequate legal description of the real property designated under Subdivision (1).

(b) The surety shall incorporate the information required in the order under Subsection (a) in an affidavit. Following approval by the judge, the affidavit shall be attached to and form part of the bond.

(c) A lien arises as security for the performance of the obligation of the bond only on the real property designated in the affidavit.

(d) Before letters testamentary or of administration are issued to the personal representative whose bond includes an affidavit under this section, the court clerk shall mail a statement to the office of the county clerk of each county in which any real property designated in the affidavit is located. The statement must be signed by the court clerk and include:

(1) a sufficient description of the real property located in that county;

(2) the names of the principal and sureties on the bond;

(3) the amount of the bond; and

(4) the name of the estate and court in which the bond is given.

(e) Each county clerk who receives a statement required by Subsection (d) shall record the statement in the county deed records. Each recorded statement shall be indexed in a manner that permits the convenient determination of the existence and character of the liens described in the statements.

(f) The recording and indexing required by Subsection (e) constitutes constructive notice to all persons regarding the existence of the lien on real property located in the county, effective as of the date of the indexing.

(g) If each personal surety subject to a court order under this section does not comply with the order, the judge may require that the bond be signed by:

(1) an authorized corporate surety; or

(2) an authorized corporate surety and at least two personal sureties.

Derived from Probate Code §§ 201(b), 202.

Added by Acts 2009, 81st Leg., ch. 680, § 1, eff. Jan. 1, 2014.

§ 305.205. Subordination of Lien on Real Property Owned by Personal Sureties

(a) A personal surety required to create a lien on specific real property under Section 305.204 who wishes to lease the real property for mineral development may file a written application in the court in which the proceedings are pending requesting subordination of the lien to the proposed lease.

(b) The judge may enter an order granting the application.

(c) A certified copy of the order, filed and recorded in the deed records of the proper county, is sufficient to subordinate the lien to the rights of a lessee under the proposed lease.

Derived from Probate Code § 201(c).

Added by Acts 2009, 81st Leg., ch. 680, § 1, eff. Jan. 1, 2014.

§ 305.206. Release of Lien on Real Property Owned by Personal Sureties

(a) A personal surety who has given a lien under Section 305.204 may apply to the court to have the lien released.

(b) The court shall order the lien released if:

(1) the court is satisfied that the bond is sufficient without the lien; or

(2) sufficient other real or personal property of the surety is substituted on the same terms required for the lien that is to be released.

(c) If the personal surety does not offer a lien on other substituted property under Subsection (b)(2) and the court is not satisfied that the bond is sufficient without the substitution of other property, the court shall order the personal representative to appear and give a new bond.

(d) A certified copy of the court's order releasing the lien and describing the property that was subject to the lien has the effect of cancelling the lien if the order is filed with the county clerk of the county in which the property is located and recorded in the deed records of that county.

Derived from Probate Code §§ 211, 212.

Added by Acts 2009, 81st Leg., ch. 680, § 1, eff. Jan. 1, 2014.

§ 305.207. Deposits by Personal Surety

Instead of executing an affidavit under Section 305.203 or creating a lien under Section 305.204 when required, a personal surety may deposit the surety's own cash or securities instead of pledging real property as security. The deposit:

(1) must be made in the same manner a personal representative deposits the representative's own cash or securities; and

(2) is subject, to the extent applicable, to the provisions governing the same type of deposits made by personal representatives.

Derived from Probate Code § 194, Subdiv. 12.

Added by Acts 2009, 81st Leg., ch. 680, § 1, eff. Jan. 1, 2014.

Subchapter F. New Bonds

§ 305.251. Grounds for Requiring New Bond

(a) A personal representative may be required to give a new bond if:

(1) a surety on a bond dies, removes beyond the limits of this state, or becomes insolvent;

(2) in the court's opinion:

(A) the sureties on a bond are insufficient; or

(B) a bond is defective;

(3) the amount of a bond is insufficient;

(4) a surety on a bond petitions the court to be discharged from future liability on the bond; or

(5) a bond and the record of the bond have been lost or destroyed.

(b) Any person interested in the estate may have the personal representative cited to appear and show cause why the representative should not be required to give a new bond by filing a written application with the county clerk of the county in which the probate proceedings are pending. The application must allege that:

(1) the bond is insufficient or defective; or

(2) the bond and the record of the bond have been lost or destroyed.

Derived from Probate Code §§ 203, 204.

Added by Acts 2009, 81st Leg., ch. 680, § 1, eff. Jan. 1, 2014. Subsec. (a)(1) amended by Acts 2011, 82nd Leg., ch. 90, § 8.013, eff. Jan. 1, 2014.

§ 305.252. Court Order or Citation on New Bond

(a) When a judge becomes aware that a bond is in any respect insufficient or that a bond and the record of the bond have been lost or destroyed, the judge shall:

(1) without delay and without notice enter an order requiring the personal representative to give a new bond; or

(2) without delay have the representative cited to show cause why the representative should not be required to give a new bond.

(b) An order entered under Subsection (a)(1) must state:

(1) the reasons for requiring a new bond;

(2) the amount of the new bond; and

(3) the period within which the new bond must be given, which may not be earlier than the 10th day after the date of the order.

(c) A personal representative who opposes an order entered under Subsection (a)(1) may demand a hearing on the order. The hearing must be held before the expiration of the period within which the new bond must be given.

Derived from Probate Code §§ 205, 206(a).

Added by Acts 2009, 81st Leg., ch. 680, § 1, eff. Jan. 1, 2014.

§ 305.253. Show Cause Hearing on New Bond Requirement

(a) On the return of a citation ordering a personal representative to show cause why the representative should not be required to give a new bond, the judge shall, on the date specified for the hearing of the matter, inquire into the sufficiency of the reasons for requiring a new bond.

(b) If the judge is satisfied that a new bond should be required, the judge shall enter an order requiring a new bond. The order must state:

(1) the amount of the new bond; and

(2) the period within which the new bond must be given, which may not be later than the 20th day after the date of the order.

Derived from Probate Code § 206(b).

Added by Acts 2009, 81st Leg., ch. 680, § 1, eff. Jan. 1, 2014.

§ 305.254. Effect of Order Requiring New Bond

(a) An order requiring a personal representative to give a new bond has the effect of suspending the representative's powers.

(b) After the order is entered, the personal representative may not pay out any of the estate's money or take any other official action, except to preserve estate property, until the new bond is given and approved.

Derived from Probate Code § 207.

Added by Acts 2009, 81st Leg., ch. 680, § 1, eff. Jan. 1, 2014.

§ 305.255. New Bond in Decreased Amount

(a) A personal representative required to give a bond may at any time file with the clerk a written application requesting that the court reduce the amount of the bond.

(b) On the filing of an application under Subsection (a), the clerk shall promptly issue and have notice posted to all interested persons and the sureties on the bond. The notice must inform the interested persons and sureties of:

(1) the fact that the application has been filed;

(2) the nature of the application; and

(3) the time the judge will hear the application.

(c) The judge may permit the filing of a new bond in a reduced amount if:

(1) proof is submitted that a bond in an amount less than the bond in effect will be adequate to meet the requirements of law and protect the estate; and

(2) the judge approves an accounting filed at the time of the application.

Derived from Probate Code § 208.

Added by Acts 2009, 81st Leg., ch. 680, § 1, eff. Jan. 1, 2014.

§ 305.256. Request by Surety for New Bond

(a) A surety on a bond may at any time file with the clerk a petition requesting that the court in which the proceedings are pending:

(1) require the personal representative to give a new bond; and

(2) discharge the petitioner from all liability for the future acts of the representative.

(b) On the filing of a petition under Subsection (a), the personal representative shall be cited to appear and give a new bond.

Derived from Probate Code § 210.

Added by Acts 2009, 81st Leg., ch. 680, § 1, eff. Jan. 1, 2014.

§ 305.257. Discharge of Former Sureties on Execution of New Bond

When a new bond has been given and approved, the court shall enter an order discharging the sureties on the former bond from all liability for the future acts of the principal on the bond.

Derived from Probate Code § 209.

Added by Acts 2009, 81st Leg., ch. 680, § 1, eff. Jan. 1, 2014.

Chapter 306. Granting and Issuance of Letters

Chapter 306. Granting and Issuance of Letters

Statutes in Context
Chapter 306

Letters are typically one-page documents issued under the seal of the court which indicate that the personal representative has been appointed by the court and has qualified. See § 306.005. The personal representative may then show this certificate as evidence of the representative's authority when dealing with estate matters or collecting estate property. Third parties who deal with a person who has letters are usually protected from liability to the heirs or beneficiaries if the executor mismanages the property. See § 307.001. Consequently, third parties often want to retain an original letter for their files. Because the cost of letters is nominal, often under $10.00 per copy, the personal representative should estimate the number of letters needed before qualifying and obtain all the necessary letters at the same time to prevent multiple trips to the courthouse and the associated time and monetary cost.

Sections 306.001 – 306.002 enumerate the circumstances under which the court will grant either letters testamentary or letters of administration. Note that if letters of administration are issued with respect to a testate decedent, the administration is said to be with the will annexed (also called an administration c.t.a. (*cum testamento annexo*)).

§ 306.001. Granting of Letters Testamentary

(a) Before the 21st day after the date a will has been probated, the court shall grant letters testamentary, if permitted by law, to each executor appointed by the will who:

(1) is not disqualified; and

(2) is willing to accept the trust and qualify according to law.

(b) Failure of the court to issue letters testamentary within the period prescribed by this section does not affect the validity of any letters testamentary issued in accordance with law after that period.

Derived from Probate Code §§ 178(a), (c).

Added by Acts 2009, 81st Leg., ch. 680, § 1, eff. Jan. 1, 2014.

§ 306.002. Granting of Letters of Administration

(a) Subject to Subsection (b), the court hearing an application under Chapter 301 shall grant:

(1) the administration of a decedent's estate if the decedent died intestate; or

(2) the administration of the decedent's estate with the will annexed if the decedent died leaving a will but:

(A) the will does not name an executor; or

(B) the executor named in the will:

(i) is deceased;

(ii) fails to accept and qualify before the 21st day after the date the will is probated; or

(iii) fails to present the will for probate before the 31st day after the date of the decedent's death and the court finds there was no good cause for that failure.

(b) The court may not grant any administration of an estate unless a necessity for the administration exists, as determined by the court.

(c) The court may find other instances of necessity for an administration based on proof before the court, but a necessity is considered to exist if:

(1) there are two or more debts against the estate;

(2) there is a desire for the county court to partition the estate among the distributees; [or]

(3) the administration is necessary to receive or recover funds or other property due the estate; or

(4) the administration is necessary to prevent real property in a decedent's estate from becoming a danger to the health, safety, or welfare of the general public.

Derived from Probate Code § 178(b).

Added by Acts 2009, 81st Leg., ch. 680, § 1, eff. Jan. 1, 2014. Subsec. (c) amended by Acts 2015, 84th Leg., ch. 576, § 3, eff. Sept. 1, 2015.

§ 306.003. Order Granting Letters

When letters testamentary or of administration are granted, the court shall enter an order to that effect stating:

(1) the name of the decedent;

(2) the name of the person to whom the letters are granted;

(3) the amount of any required bond;

(4) the name of at least one but not more than three disinterested persons appointed to appraise the estate and return the appraisement to the court, if:

(A) any interested person applies to the court for the appointment of an appraiser; or

(B) the court considers an appraisement to be necessary; and

(5) that the clerk shall issue letters in accordance with the order when the person to whom the letters are granted has qualified according to law.

Derived from Probate Code § 181.

Added by Acts 2009, 81st Leg., ch. 680, § 1, eff. Jan. 1, 2014.

Statutes in Context
§ 306.004

The clerk will not issue letters until the personal representative qualifies, that is, posts any required bond and takes the oath of office. See § 305.002.

---

§ 306.004. Issuance of Original Letters

When an executor or administrator has qualified in the manner required by law, the clerk of the court granting the letters testamentary or of administration shall promptly issue and deliver the letters to the executor or administrator. If more than one person qualifies as executor or administrator, the clerk shall issue the letters to each person who qualifies.

Derived from Probate Code § 182.

Added by Acts 2009, 81st Leg., ch. 680, § 1, eff. Jan. 1,

2014.

§ 306.005. Form and Content of Letters

Letters testamentary or of administration shall be in the form of a certificate of the clerk of the court granting the letters, attested by the court's seal, that states:

(1) the executor or administrator, as applicable, has qualified as executor or administrator in the manner required by law;

(2) the date of the qualification; and

(3) the name of the decedent.

Derived from Probate Code § 183.

Added by Acts 2009, 81st Leg., ch. 680, § 1, eff. Jan. 1, 2014.

§ 306.006. Replacement and Other Additional Letters

When letters testamentary or of administration have been destroyed or lost, the clerk shall issue other letters to replace the original letters, which have the same effect as the original letters. The clerk shall also issue any number of letters as and when requested by the person or persons who hold the letters.

Derived from Probate Code § 187.

Added by Acts 2009, 81st Leg., ch. 680, § 1, eff. Jan. 1, 2014.

§ 306.007. Effect of Letters or Certificate

Letters testamentary or of administration or a certificate of the clerk of the court that granted the letters, under the court's seal, indicating that the letters have been issued, is sufficient evidence of:

(1) the appointment and qualification of the personal representative of an estate; and

(2) the date of qualification.

Derived from Probate Code § 186.

Added by Acts 2009, 81st Leg., ch. 680, § 1, eff. Jan. 1, 2014.

Chapter 307. Validity of Certain Acts of Executors and Administrators

§ 307.001. Rights of Good Faith Purchasers
§ 307.002. Joint Executors or Administrators

Chapter 307. Validity of Certain Acts of Executors and Administrators

§ 307.001. Rights of Good Faith Purchasers

(a) This section applies only to an act performed by a qualified executor or administrator in that capacity and in conformity with the law and the executor's or administrator's authority.

(b) An act continues to be valid for all intents and purposes in regard to the rights of an innocent purchaser who purchases any of the estate property from the executor or administrator for valuable consideration, in good faith, and without notice of any illegality in the title to the property, even if the act or the authority under which the act was performed is subsequently set aside, annulled, and declared invalid.

Derived from Probate Code § 188.

Added by Acts 2009, 81st Leg., ch. 680, § 1, eff. Jan. 1, 2014.

Statutes in Context
§ 307.002

Section 307.002 provides that the acts of one of several co-personal representatives are valid except that all personal representatives must join in a conveyance of real property. Accordingly, a testator must take great care in the appointment of multiple personal representatives because the act of one (as contrasted with all or a majority) is binding under most circumstances.

---

§ 307.002. Joint Executors or Administrators

(a) Except as provided by Subsection (b), if there is more than one executor or administrator of an estate at the same time, the acts of one of the executors or administrators in that capacity are valid as if all the executors or administrators had acted jointly. If one of the executors or administrators dies, resigns, or is removed, a co-executor or co-administrator of the estate shall proceed with the administration as if the death, resignation, or removal had not occurred.

(b) If there is more than one executor or administrator of an estate at the same time, all of the qualified executors or administrators who are acting in that capacity must join in the conveyance of real estate unless the court, after due hearing, authorizes fewer than all to act.

Derived from Probate Code § 240.

Added by Acts 2009, 81st Leg., ch. 680, § 1, eff. Jan. 1, 2014.

Chapter 308. Notice to Beneficiaries and Claimants

Subchapter A. Notice to Certain Beneficiaries After Probate of Will

Subchapter B. Notice to Claimants

Chapter 308. Notice to Beneficiaries and Claimants

Subchapter A. Notice to Certain Beneficiaries After Probate of Will

Statutes in Context
Chapter 308, Subchapter A

The 2007 Legislature overhauled the Probate Code predecessor to this Subchapter by adding a requirement for most will beneficiaries to receive notice *after* a will is admitted to probate. The notice must be given within 60 days of when the will is probated unless an exception applies. The personal representative must file an affidavit within 90 days of probate explaining that the notice was given. The 2011 Legislature modified the statute in an attempt to make compliance easier and more beneficial to the beneficiaries.

Under prior law, only government agencies and charitable beneficiaries were entitled to notice.

§ 308.001. Definition

In this subchapter, "beneficiary" means a person, entity, state, governmental agency of the state, charitable organization, or trustee of a trust entitled to receive property under the terms of a decedent's will, to be determined for purposes of this subchapter with the assumption that each person who is alive on the date of the decedent's death survives any period required to receive the bequest as specified by the terms of the will. The term does not include a person, entity, state, governmental agency of the state, charitable organization, or trustee of a trust that would be entitled to receive property under the terms of a decedent's will on the occurrence of a contingency that has not occurred as of the date of the decedent's death.

Derived from Probate Code § 128A(a).

Added by Acts 2009, 81st Leg., ch. 680, § 1, eff. Jan. 1, 2014. Amended by Acts 2011, 82nd Leg., ch. 1338, § 2.34, eff. Jan. 1, 2014.

§ 308.0015. Application

This subchapter does not apply to the probate of a will as a muniment of title.

Derived from Probate Code § 128A(a-1).

Added by Acts 2011, 82nd Leg., ch. 1338, § 2.35, eff. Jan. 1, 2014.

§ 308.002. Required Notice to Certain Beneficiaries After Probate of Will

(a) Except as provided by Subsection (c), not later than the 60th day after the date of an order admitting a decedent's will to probate, the personal representative of the decedent's estate, including an independent executor or independent administrator, shall give notice that complies with Section 308.003 to each beneficiary named in the will whose identity and address are known to the representative or, through reasonable diligence, can be ascertained. If, after the 60th day after the date of the order, the representative becomes aware of the identity and address of a beneficiary who was not given notice on or before the 60th day, the representative shall give the notice as soon as possible after becoming aware of that information.

(b) Notwithstanding the requirement under Subsection (a) that the personal representative give the notice to the beneficiary, the representative shall give the notice with respect to a beneficiary described by this subsection as follows:

(1) if the beneficiary is a trustee of a trust, to the trustee, unless the representative is the trustee, in which case the representative shall, except as provided by Subsection (b-1), give the notice to the person or class of persons first eligible to receive the trust income, to be determined for purposes of this subdivision as if the trust were in existence on the date of the decedent's death;

(2) if the beneficiary has a court-appointed guardian or conservator, to that guardian or conservator;

(3) if the beneficiary is a minor for whom no guardian or conservator has been appointed, to a parent of the minor; and

(4) if the beneficiary is a charity that for any reason cannot be notified, to the attorney general.

(b-1) The personal representative is not required to give the notice otherwise required by Subsection (b)(1) to a person eligible to receive trust income at the sole discretion of the trustee of a trust if:

(1) the representative has given the notice to an ancestor of the person who has a similar interest in the trust; and

(2) no apparent conflict exists between the ancestor and the person eligible to receive trust income.

(c) A personal representative is not required to give the notice otherwise required by this section to a beneficiary who:

(1) has made an appearance in the proceeding with respect to the decedent's estate before the will was admitted to probate;

(2) is entitled to receive aggregate gifts under the will with an estimated value of $2,000 or less;

(3) has received all gifts to which the beneficiary is entitled under the will not later than

the 60th day after the date of the order admitting the decedent's will to probate; or

(4) has received a copy of the will that was admitted to probate or a written summary of the gifts to the beneficiary under the will and has waived the right to receive the notice in an instrument that:

(A) either acknowledges the receipt of the copy of the will or includes the written summary of the gifts to the beneficiary under the will;

(B) is signed by the beneficiary; and

(C) is filed with the court.

(d) The notice required by this section must be sent by registered or certified mail, return receipt requested.

Derived from Probate Code §§ 128A(b), (c), (d), (f).

Added by Acts 2009, 81st Leg., ch. 680, § 1, eff. Jan. 1, 2014. Amended by Acts 2011, 82nd Leg., ch. 1338, § 2.36, eff. Jan. 1, 2014.

§ 308.003. Contents of Notice

The notice required by Section 308.002 must include:

(1) the name and address of the beneficiary to whom the notice is given or, for a beneficiary described by Section 308.002(b), the name and address of the beneficiary for whom the notice is given and of the person to whom the notice is given;

(2) the decedent's name;

(3) a statement that the decedent's will has been admitted to probate;

(4) a statement that the beneficiary to whom or for whom the notice is given is named as a beneficiary in the will;

(5) the personal representative's name and contact information; and

(6) either:

(A) a copy of the will that was admitted to probate and of the order admitting the will to probate; or

(B) a summary of the gifts to the beneficiary under the will, the court in which the will was admitted to probate, the docket number assigned to the estate, the date the will was admitted to probate, and, if different, the date the court appointed the personal representative.

Derived from Probate Code § 128A(e).

Added by Acts 2009, 81st Leg., ch. 680, § 1, eff. Jan. 1, 2014. Amended by Acts 2011, 82nd Leg., ch. 1338, § 2.37, eff. Jan. 1, 2014.

§ 308.004. Affidavit or Certificate

(a) Not later than the 90th day after the date of an order admitting a will to probate, the personal representative shall file with the clerk of the court in which the decedent's estate is pending a sworn affidavit

of the representative or a certificate signed by the representative's attorney stating:

(1) for each beneficiary to whom notice was required to be given under this subchapter, the name [and address] of the beneficiary to whom the representative gave the notice or, for a beneficiary described by Section 308.002(b), the name [and address] of the beneficiary and of the person to whom the notice was given;

(2) the name [and address] of each beneficiary to whom notice was not required to be given under Section 308.002(c)(2), (3), or (4);

(3) the name of each beneficiary whose identity or address could not be ascertained despite the representative's exercise of reasonable diligence; and

(4) any other information necessary to explain the representative's inability to give the notice to or for any beneficiary as required by this subchapter.

(b) The affidavit or certificate required by Subsection (a) may be included with any pleading or other document filed with the court clerk, including the inventory, appraisement, and list of claims, an affidavit in lieu of the inventory, appraisement, and list of claims, or an application for an extension of the deadline to file the inventory, appraisement, and list of claims or an affidavit in lieu of the inventory, appraisement, and list of claims, provided that the pleading or other document is filed not later than the date the affidavit or certificate is required to be filed under Subsection (a).

Derived from Probate Code §§ 128A(g), (h).

Added by Acts 2009, 81st Leg., ch. 680, § 1, eff. Jan. 1, 2014. Amended by Acts 2011, 82nd Leg., ch. 1338, § 2.38, eff. Jan. 1, 2014. Subsec. (a) amended by Acts 2015, 84th Leg., ch. 995, § 31, eff. Sept. 1, 2015.

Subchapter B. Notice to Claimants

Statutes in Context
Chapter 308, Subchapter B

The personal representative must alert the decedent's creditors that the decedent has died and that the court has appointed a personal representative. This information permits the creditors to take the proper steps to present their claims so they can get paid. There are four types of notice.

1. Notice to Comptroller of Public Accounts. The personal representative must give notice to the comptroller of public accounts within one month of receiving letters if the decedent remitted or should have remitted taxes administered by the comptroller. Service is by certified or registered mail. See § 308.051(a)(2). Because the personal representative may not yet know whether the decedent remitted or should have remitted these taxes, it may be good practice to give the notice in all cases.

2. General Notice to Creditors. Within one month of receiving letters, the personal representative must publish notice in a newspaper in the county where letters were issued. See § 308.051(a)(1). In large population counties, this notice is often published in specialized legal newspapers rather than the local paper.

3. Notice to Unsecured Creditors. The personal representative has the option to give notice by certified or registered mail to the unsecured creditors of the estate (e.g., credit card issuers and utility providers). If the creditor does not present a claim within 4 months of receipt of the notice, the creditor is barred from pursuing the claim even if the statute of limitations on the claim has not otherwise run. This provision is often called the non-claim statute. See § 308.054.

4. Notice to Secured Creditors. See *Statutes in Context* to § 308.053.

§ 308.051. Required Notice Regarding Presentment of Claims in General

(a) Within one month after receiving letters testamentary or of administration, a personal representative of an estate shall provide notice requiring each person who has a claim against the estate to present the claim within the period prescribed by law by:

(1) having the notice published in a newspaper printed in the county in which the letters were issued; and

(2) if the decedent remitted or should have remitted taxes administered by the comptroller, sending the notice to the comptroller by certified or registered mail.

(b) Notice provided under Subsection (a) must include:

(1) the date the letters testamentary or of administration were issued to the personal representative;

(2) the address to which a claim may be presented; and

(3) an instruction of the representative's choice that the claim be addressed in care of:

(A) the representative;

(B) the representative's attorney; or

(C) "Representative, Estate of _____ " (naming the estate).

(c) If a newspaper is not printed in the county in which the letters testamentary or of administration were issued, the notice must be posted and the return made and filed as otherwise required by this title.

Derived from Probate Code §§ 294(a), (c).

Added by Acts 2009, 81st Leg., ch. 680, § 1, eff. Jan. 1, 2014.

§ 308.052. Proof of Publication

A copy of the published notice required by Section 308.051(a)(1), together with the publisher's affidavit, sworn to and subscribed before a proper officer, to the effect that the notice was published as provided in this title for the service of citation or notice by publication, shall be filed in the court in which the cause is pending.

Derived from Probate Code § 294(b).

Added by Acts 2009, 81st Leg., ch. 680, § 1, eff. Jan. 1, 2014.

Statutes in Context
§ 308.053

Within 2 months of receiving letters, the personal representative must give notice to the holders of claims which are secured by mortgages, deeds of trust, Article 9 security interests, etc. Service is by registered or certified mail.

§ 308.053. Required Notice to Secured Creditor

(a) Within two months after receiving letters testamentary or of administration, a personal representative of an estate shall give notice of the issuance of the letters to each person the representative knows to have a claim for money against the estate that is secured by estate property.

(b) Within a reasonable period after a personal representative obtains actual knowledge of the existence of a person who has a secured claim for money against the estate and to whom notice was not previously given, the representative shall give notice to the person of the issuance of the letters testamentary or of administration.

(c) Notice provided under this section must be:

(1) sent by certified or registered mail, return receipt requested; and

(2) addressed to the record holder of the claim at the record holder's last known post office address.

(d) The following shall be filed with the clerk of the court in which the letters testamentary or of administration were issued:

(1) a copy of each notice and of each return receipt; and

(2) the personal representative's affidavit stating:

(A) that the notice was mailed as required by law; and

(B) the name of the person to whom the notice was mailed, if that name is not shown on the notice or receipt.

Derived from Probate Code § 295.

Added by Acts 2009, 81st Leg., ch. 680, § 1, eff. Jan. 1, 2014.

§ 308.054. Permissive Notice to Unsecured Creditor

(a) At any time before an estate administration is closed, a personal representative may give notice by certified or registered mail, return receipt requested, to an unsecured creditor who has a claim for money against the estate.

(b) Notice given under Subsection (a) must:

(1) expressly state that the creditor must present the claim before the 121st day after the date of the receipt of the notice or the claim is barred, if the claim is not barred by the general statutes of limitation; and

(2) include:

(A) the date the letters testamentary or of administration held by the personal representative were issued to the representative;

(B) the address to which the claim may be presented; and

(C) an instruction of the representative's choice that the claim be addressed in care of:

(i) the representative;

(ii) the representative's attorney; or

(iii) "Representative, Estate of _____" (naming the estate).

Derived from Probate Code § 294(d).

Added by Acts 2009, 81st Leg., ch. 680, § 1, eff. Jan. 1, 2014. Subsec. (b) amended by Acts 2013, 83rd Leg., ch. 1136, § 39, eff. Jan. 1, 2014.

§ 308.055. One Notice Sufficient

A personal representative is not required to give a notice required by Section 308.051 or 308.053 if another person also appointed as personal representative of the estate or a former personal representative of the estate has given that notice.

Derived from Probate Code § 296.

Added by Acts 2009, 81st Leg., ch. 680, § 1, eff. Jan. 1, 2014.

§ 308.056. Liability for Failure to Give Required Notice

A personal representative who fails to give a notice required by Section 308.051 or 308.053, or to cause the notice to be given, and the sureties on the representative's bond are liable for any damage a person suffers due to that neglect, unless it appears that the person otherwise had notice.

Derived from Probate Code § 297.

Added by Acts 2009, 81st Leg., ch. 680, § 1, eff. Jan. 1, 2014.

Subchapter B. Requirements for Inventory, Appraisement, and List of Claims; Affidavit in Lieu of Inventory, Appraisement, and List of Claims

Subchapter A. Appraisers

Subchapter B. Requirements for Inventory, Appraisement, and List of Claims

Subchapter C. Changes to Inventory, Appraisement, and List of Claims

Subchapter D. Use of Inventory, Appraisement, and List of Claims as Evidence

Chapter 309. Inventory, Appraisement, and List of Claims

Subchapter A. Appraisers

Statutes in Context
§ 309.001

If an interested person applies or if the court deems it necessary, the court will appoint appraisers to value the property in the decedent's estate. These values will be included on the inventory required by § 309.051. The appraiser's fee is provided for in § 309.002.

Good cause be shown before a court may appoint appraisers, either on the court's own motion or upon the application of an interested party.

---

§ 309.001. Appointment of Appraisers

(a) At any time after letters testamentary or of administration are granted, the court, for good cause, on the court's own motion or on the motion of an interested person [party] shall appoint at least one but not more than three disinterested persons who are residents of the county in which the letters were granted to appraise the estate property.

(b) [At any time after letters testamentary or of administration are granted, the court, for good cause shown, on the court's own motion or on the motion of an interested person shall appoint at least one but not more than three disinterested persons who are residents of the county in which the letters were granted to appraise the estate property. (c)] If the court makes an appointment under Subsection (a) [or (b)] and part of the estate is located in a county other than the county in which the letters were granted, the court, if the court considers necessary, may appoint at least one but not more than three disinterested persons who are residents of the county in which the relevant part of the estate is located to appraise the estate property located in that county.

Derived from Probate Code § 248.

Added by Acts 2009, 81st Leg., ch. 680, § 1, eff. Jan. 1, 2014. Amended by Acts 2015, 84th Leg., ch. 995, § 32, eff. Sept. 1, 2015.

§ 309.002. Appraisers' Fees

An appraiser appointed by the court as herein authorized is entitled to receive compensation, payable out of the estate, of at least $5 for each day the appraiser actually serves in performing the appraiser's duties.

Derived from Probate Code § 253.

Added by Acts 2009, 81st Leg., ch. 680, § 1, eff. Jan. 1, 2014.

§ 309.003. Failure or Refusal to Act by Appraisers

If an appraiser appointed under Section 309.001 fails or refuses to act, the court by one or more similar orders shall remove the appraiser and appoint one or more other appraisers, as the case requires.

Derived from Probate Code § 249.

Added by Acts 2009, 81st Leg., ch. 680, § 1, eff. Jan. 1, 2014.

Subchapter B. Requirements for Inventory, Appraisement, and List of Claims

Statutes in Context
§ 309.051

The personal representative in both dependent and independent administrations must normally file an inventory, appraisement, and list of claims within 90 days after qualification. This document helps the creditors to determine which assets are available to pay their claims and thus provides them with valuable insight into how they should proceed to have the best chance of getting paid. Additionally, the inventory helps the heirs and beneficiaries to determine the property to which they may be entitled.

The inventory must include all real property located in Texas and all personal property wherever located. (Out of state real property is not listed because Texas courts have no jurisdiction over this property.) Non-probate assets, that is, property which passes outside of the probate process such as survivorship interests and life insurance proceeds, are not included in the inventory.

If the decedent was married at the time of death, the inventory must designate whether the property is separate or community.

See Estates Code § 309.056 for the possibility of using an affidavit in lieu of the inventory, appraisement, and list of claims.

§ 309.051. Inventory and Appraisement

(a) Except as provided by Subsection (c) or Section 309.056 or unless a longer period is granted by the court, before the 91st day after the date the personal representative qualifies, the representative shall prepare and file with the court clerk a single written instrument that contains a verified, full, and detailed inventory of all estate property that has come into the representative's possession or of which the representative has knowledge. The inventory must:

(1) include:

(A) all estate real property located in this state; and

(B) all estate personal property regardless of where the property is located; and

(2) specify which portion of the property, if any, is separate property and which, if any, is community property.

(b) The personal representative shall:

(1) set out in the inventory the representative's appraisement of the fair market value on the date of the decedent's death of each item in the inventory; or

(2) if the court has appointed one or more appraisers for the estate:

(A) determine the fair market value of each item in the inventory with the assistance of the appraiser or appraisers; and

(B) set out that appraisement in the inventory.

(c) The court for good cause shown may require the personal representative to file the inventory and appraisement within a shorter period than the period prescribed by Subsection (a).

(d) The inventory, when approved by the court and filed with the court clerk, is for all purposes the inventory and appraisement of the estate referred to in this title.

Derived from Probate Code § 250.

Added by Acts 2009, 81st Leg., ch. 680, § 1, eff. Jan. 1, 2014. Subsec. (a) amended by Acts 2011, 82nd Leg., ch. 1338, § 2.40, eff. Jan. 1, 2014. Subsec. (b) amended by Acts 2011, 82nd Leg., ch. 91, § 8.014, eff. Jan. 1, 2014. Subsection (a) amended by Acts 2013, 83rd Leg., ch. 1136, § 40, eff. Jan. 1, 2014.

Statutes in Context
§ 309.052

The list of claims is part of the inventory and appraisement. The list is of claims due or owing to the decedent's estate, that is, claims on which the decedent was a creditor. It is not a list of claims against the decedent's estate.

---

§ 309.052. List of Claims

A complete list of claims due or owing to the estate must be attached to the inventory and appraisement required by Section 309.051. The list of claims must state:

(1) the name and, if known, address of each person indebted to the estate; and

(2) regarding each claim:

(A) the nature of the debt, whether by note, bill, bond, or other written obligation, or by account or verbal contract;

(B) the date the debt was incurred;

(C) the date the debt was or is due;

(D) the amount of the claim, the rate of interest on the claim, and the period for which the claim bears interest; and

(E) whether the claim is separate property or community property.

Derived from Probate Code § 251.

Added by Acts 2009, 81st Leg., ch. 680, § 1, eff. Jan. 1, 2014. Amended by Acts 2011, 82nd Leg., ch. 1338, § 2.41, eff. Jan. 1, 2014.

Statutes in Context
§ 309.053

The inventory, appraisement, and list of claims must be supported by the personal representative's sworn affidavit.

---

§ 309.053. Affidavit of Personal Representative

The personal representative shall attach to the inventory, appraisement, and list of claims the representative's affidavit, subscribed and sworn to before an officer in the county authorized by law to administer oaths, that the inventory, appraisement, and list of claims are a true and complete statement of the property and claims of the estate of which the representative has knowledge.

Derived from Probate Code § 252.

Added by Acts 2009, 81st Leg., ch. 680, § 1, eff. Jan. 1, 2014.

Statutes in Context
§ 309.054

The court will either approve or disapprove the inventory, appraisement, and list of claims under § 309.054.

---

§ 309.054. Approval or Disapproval by the Court

(a) On the filing of the inventory, appraisement, and list of claims with the court clerk, the judge shall examine and approve or disapprove the inventory, appraisement, and list of claims.

(b) If the judge approves the inventory, appraisement, and list of claims, the judge shall enter an order to that effect.

(c) If the judge does not approve the inventory, appraisement, or list of claims, the judge:

(1) shall enter an order to that effect requiring the filing of another inventory, appraisement, or list of claims, whichever is not approved, within a period specified in the order not to exceed 20 days after the date the order is entered; and

(2) may, if considered necessary, appoint new appraisers.

Derived from Probate Code § 255.

Added by Acts 2009, 81st Leg., ch. 680, § 1, eff. Jan. 1, 2014.

---

§ 309.055. Failure of Joint Personal Representatives to File Inventory, Appraisement, and List of Claims or Affidavit in Lieu of Inventory, Appraisement, and List of Claims

(a) If more than one personal representative qualifies to serve, any one or more of the representatives, on the neglect of the other representatives, may make and file an inventory, appraisement, and list of claims or an affidavit in lieu of an inventory, appraisement, and list of claims.

(b) A personal representative who neglects to make or file an inventory, appraisement, and list of claims or an affidavit in lieu of an inventory, appraisement, and list of claims may not interfere with and does not have any power over the estate after another representative makes and files an inventory, appraisement, and list of claims or an affidavit in lieu of an inventory, appraisement, and list of claims.

(c) The personal representative who files the inventory, appraisement, and list of claims or the affidavit in lieu of an inventory, appraisement, and list of claims is entitled to the whole administration unless, before the 61st day after the date the representative files the inventory, appraisement, and list of claims or the affidavit in lieu of an inventory, appraisement, and list of claims, one or more delinquent representatives file with the court a written, sworn, and reasonable excuse that the court considers satisfactory. The court shall enter an order removing one or more delinquent representatives and revoking those representatives' letters if:

(1) an excuse is not filed; or

(2) the court does not consider the filed excuse sufficient.

Derived from Probate Code § 260.

Added by Acts 2009, 81st Leg., ch. 680, § 1, eff. Jan. 1, 2014. Amended by Acts 2011, 82nd Leg., ch. 1338, § 2.42, eff. Jan. 1, 2014.

Statutes in Context
§ 309.056

The 2011 Legislature authorized an independent executor or administrator to file an affidavit in lieu of the inventory, appraisement, and list of claims if no debts other than secured debts, taxes, and administration expenses remain by the inventory due date. This procedure keeps the decedent's property from being listed on the public record and thus helps with privacy concerns. The executor or administrator must still prepare a sworn inventory and provide a copy to each beneficiary unless an exception exists. An interested person such as an intestate heir or beneficiary under a prior will, may obtain a copy of the inventory from the executor or administrator upon written request.

The affidavit in lieu of inventory option is available even if the will requires the filing of inventory as long as the will does not specifically prohibit the filing of an affidavit in lieu of inventory.

An executor cannot be held liable for the executor's decision to file either a traditional inventory or the affidavit in lieu of inventory.

---

§ 309.056. Affidavit in Lieu of Inventory, Appraisement, and List of Claims

(a) In this section, "beneficiary" means a person, entity, state, governmental agency of the state, charitable organization, or trust entitled to receive property:

(1) under the terms of a decedent's will, to be determined for purposes of this section with the assumption that each person who is alive on the date of the decedent's death survives any period required to receive the bequest as specified by the terms of the will; or

(2) as an heir of the decedent.

(b) Notwithstanding Sections 309.051 and 309.052, or any contrary provision in a decedent's will that does not specifically prohibit the filing of an affidavit described by this subsection, if there are no unpaid debts, except for secured debts, taxes, and administration expenses, at the time the inventory is due, including any extensions, an independent executor may file with the court clerk, in lieu of the inventory, appraisement, and list of claims, an affidavit stating that all debts, except for secured debts, taxes, and administration expenses, are paid and that all beneficiaries other than those described by Subsection (b-1) have received a verified, full, and detailed inventory and appraisement. The affidavit in lieu of the inventory, appraisement, and list of claims must be filed within the 90-day period prescribed by Section 309.051(a), unless the court grants an extension.

(b-1) Absent a written request by a beneficiary, an independent executor is not required to provide a verified, full, and detailed inventory and appraisement to a beneficiary who:

(1) is entitled to receive aggregate devises under the will with an estimated value of $2,000 or less;

(2) has received all devises to which the beneficiary is entitled under the will on or before the date an affidavit under this section is filed; or

(3) has waived in writing the beneficiary's right to receive a verified, full, and detailed inventory and appraisement.

(c) If the independent executor files an affidavit in lieu of the inventory, appraisement, and list of claims as authorized under Subsection (b):

(1) any person interested in the estate, including a possible heir of the decedent, [or] a beneficiary under a prior will of the decedent, or a beneficiary described by Subsection (b-1), is entitled to receive a copy of the inventory, appraisement, and list of claims from the independent executor on written request;

(2) the independent executor may provide a copy of the inventory, appraisement, and list of claims to any person the independent executor believes in good faith may be a person interested in the estate without liability to the estate or its beneficiaries; and

(3) a person interested in the estate may apply to the court for an order compelling compliance with Subdivision (1), and the court, in its discretion, may compel the independent executor to provide a copy of the inventory, appraisement, and list of claims to the interested person or may deny the application.

(d) An independent executor is not liable for choosing to file:

(1) an affidavit under this section in lieu of filing an inventory, appraisement, and list of claims, if permitted by law; or

(2) an inventory, appraisement, and list of claims in lieu of filing an affidavit under this section.

Derived from Probate Code § 250.

Added by Acts 2011, 82nd Leg., R.S., ch. 1338, § 2.43, eff. Jan. 1, 2014. Subsecs(b) amended and subsec. (d) added by Acts 2013, 83rd Leg., ch. 1136, § 41, eff. Jan. 1, 2014. Subsecs (b) & (c) amended and subsec. (b-1)

added by Acts 2015, 84th Leg., ch. 995, § 33, eff. Sept. 1, 2015.

§ 309.057. Penalty for Failure to Timely File Inventory, Appraisement, and List of Claims or Affidavit in Lieu of

(a) This section applies only to a personal representative, including an independent executor or administrator, who does not file an inventory, appraisement, and list of claims or affidavit in lieu of the inventory, appraisement, and list of claims, as applicable, within the period prescribed by Section 309.051 or any extension granted by the court.

(b) Any person interested in the estate on written complaint, or the court on the court's own motion, may have a personal representative to whom this section applies cited to file the inventory, appraisement, and list of claims or affidavit in lieu of the inventory, appraisement, and list of claims, as applicable, and show cause for the failure to timely file.

(c) If the personal representative does not file the inventory, appraisement, and list of claims or affidavit in lieu of the inventory, appraisement, and list of claims, as applicable, after being cited or does not show good cause for the failure to timely file, the court on hearing may fine the representative in an amount not to exceed $1,000.

(d) The personal representative and the representative's sureties, if any, are liable for any fine imposed under this section and for all damages and costs sustained by the representative's failure. The fine, damages, and costs may be recovered in any court of competent jurisdiction.

New.

Added by Acts 2013, 83rd Leg., ch. 1136, § 42, eff. Jan. 1, 2014.

Subchapter C. Changes to Inventory, Appraisement, and List of Claims

§ 309.101. Discovery of Additional Property or Claims

(a) If after the filing of the inventory, appraisement, and list of claims the personal representative acquires possession or knowledge of property or claims of the estate not included in the inventory, appraisement, and list of claims the representative shall promptly file with the court clerk a verified, full, and detailed supplemental inventory, appraisement, and list of claims.

(b) If after the filing of the affidavit in lieu of the inventory, appraisement, and list of claims the personal representative acquires possession or knowledge of property or claims of the estate not included in the inventory and appraisement given to the beneficiaries, the representative shall promptly file with the court clerk a supplemental affidavit in lieu of the inventory, appraisement, and list of claims stating that all

beneficiaries have received a verified, full, and detailed supplemental inventory and appraisement.

Derived from Probate Code § 256.

Added by Acts 2009, 81st Leg., ch. 680, § 1, eff. Jan. 1, 2014. Amended by Acts 2011, 82nd Leg., ch. 1338, § 2.44, eff. Jan. 1, 2014.

§ 309.102. Additional Inventory and Appraisement or List of Claims

(a) On the written complaint of any interested person that property or claims of the estate have not been included in the filed inventory, appraisement, and list of claims, the personal representative shall be cited to appear before the court in which the cause is pending and show cause why the representative should not be required to make and file an additional inventory and appraisement or list of claims, or both, as applicable.

(b) After hearing the complaint, if the court is satisfied of the truth of the complaint, the court shall enter an order requiring the personal representative to make and file an additional inventory and appraisement or list of claims, or both, as applicable. The additional inventory and appraisement or list of claims:

(1) must be made and filed in the same manner as the original inventory and appraisement or list of claims within the period prescribed by the court, not to exceed 20 days after the date the order is entered; and

(2) may include only property or claims not previously included in the inventory and appraisement or list of claims.

Derived from Probate Code § 257.

Added by Acts 2009, 81st Leg., ch. 680, § 1, eff. Jan. 1, 2014.

Statutes in Contest
§ 309.103

The appellate court will review an appeal of a court's finding of the correctness of an inventory using the abuse of discretion standard. *In re Estate of Walker*, 250 S.W.3d 212 (Tex. App.— Dallas 2008, pet. denied).

---

§ 309.103. Correction of Inventory, Appraisement, or List of Claims for Erroneous or Unjust Item

(a) Any interested person who considers an inventory, appraisement, or list of claims or an affidavit in lieu of the inventory, appraisement, and list of claims to be erroneous or unjust in any particular may:

(1) file a written complaint setting forth the alleged erroneous or unjust item; and

(2) have the personal representative cited to appear before the court and show cause why the item should not be corrected.

(b) On the hearing of the complaint, if the court is satisfied from the evidence that the inventory, appraisement, or list of claims or an affidavit in lieu of the inventory, appraisement, and list of claims is erroneous or unjust as alleged in the complaint, the court shall enter an order:

(1) specifying the erroneous or unjust item and the corrections to be made; and

(2) if the complaint relates to an inventory, appraisement, or list of claims, appointing appraisers to make a new appraisement correcting the erroneous or unjust item and requiring the filing of the new appraisement before the 21st day after the date of the order.

(c) The court on the court's own motion or that of the personal representative may also have a new appraisement made for the purposes described by this section.

Derived from Probate Code § 258.

Added by Acts 2009, 81st Leg., ch. 680, § 1, eff. Jan. 1, 2014. Subsections (a) and (b) amended by Acts 2013, 83rd Leg., ch. 1136, § 43, eff. Jan. 1, 2014.

§ 309.104. Reappraisement

(a) A reappraisement made, filed, and approved by the court replaces the original appraisement. Not more than one reappraisement may be made.

(b) Notwithstanding Subsection (a), an interested person may object to a reappraisement regardless of whether the court has approved the reappraisement. If the court finds that the reappraisement is erroneous or unjust, the court shall appraise the property on the basis of the evidence before the court.

Derived from Probate Code § 259.

Added by Acts 2009, 81st Leg., ch. 680, § 1, eff. Jan. 1, 2014.

Subchapter D. Use of Inventory, Appraisement, and List of Claims as Evidence

§ 309.151. Use of Inventory, Appraisement, and List of Claims as Evidence

Each inventory, appraisement, and list of claims that has been made, filed, and approved in accordance with law, the record of the inventory, appraisement, and list of claims, or a copy of an original or the record that has been certified under the seal of the county court affixed by the clerk:

(1) may be given in evidence in any court of this state in any suit by or against the personal representative; and

(2) is not conclusive for or against the representative if it is shown that:

(A) any property or claim of the estate is not shown in the originals, the record, or the copies; or

(B) the value of the property or claim of the estate exceeded the value shown in the appraisement or list of claims.

Derived from Probate Code § 261.

Added by Acts 2009, 81st Leg., ch. 680, § 1, eff. Jan. 1, 2014.

Chapter 310. Allocation of Estate Income and Expenses

§ 310.001. Definition
§ 310.002. Applicability of Other Law
§ 310.003. Allocation of Expenses
§ 310.004. Income Determination and Distribution
§ 310.005. Treatment of Income Received by Trustee
§ 310.006. Frequency and Method of Determining Interests in Certain Estate Assets

Chapter 310. Allocation of Estate Income and Expenses

Statutes in Context
Chapter 310

Income from a gifted item that accrues after death but before distribution is given to the beneficiary, less the cost of taxes, repairs, insurance, management fees, etc.

A legacy (cash bequest) in a will earns interest at the legal rate as provided in Finance Code § 302.002. The Uniform Principal and Income Act provides that interest is payable beginning on the first anniversary of the date of the decedent's death. See Property Code § 116.051(3)(A).

§ 310.001. Definition

In this chapter, "undistributed assets" includes funds used to pay debts, administration expenses, and federal and state estate, inheritance, succession, and generation-skipping transfer taxes until the date the debts, expenses, and taxes are paid.

Derived from Probate Code § 378B(h).

Added by Acts 2009, 81st Leg., ch. 680, § 1, eff. Jan. 1, 2014.

§ 310.002. Applicability of Other Law

Chapter 116, Property Code, controls to the extent of any conflict between this chapter and Chapter 116, Property Code.

Derived from Probate Code § 378B(i).

Added by Acts 2009, 81st Leg., ch. 680, § 1, eff. Jan. 1, 2014.

§ 310.003. Allocation of Expenses

(a) Except as provided by Section 310.004(a) and unless the will provides otherwise, all expenses incurred in connection with the settlement of a decedent's estate shall be charged against the principal of the estate, including:

    (1) debts;

    (2) funeral expenses;

    (3) estate taxes and penalties relating to estate taxes; and

    (4) family allowances.

(b) Fees and expenses of an attorney, accountant, or other professional advisor, commissions and expenses of a personal representative, court costs, and all other similar fees or expenses relating to the administration of the estate and interest relating to estate taxes shall be allocated between the income and principal of the estate as the executor determines in the executor's discretion to be just and equitable.

Derived from Probate Code § 378B(a).

Added by Acts 2009, 81st Leg., ch. 680, § 1, eff. Jan. 1, 2014.

§ 310.004. Income Determination and Distribution

(a) Unless a will provides otherwise, income from the assets of a decedent's estate that accrues after the death of the testator and before distribution, including income from property used to discharge liabilities, shall be:

    (1) determined according to the rules applicable to a trustee under the Texas Trust Code (Subtitle B, Title 9, Property Code); and

    (2) distributed as provided by Subsections (b) and (c) and by Chapter 116, Property Code.

(b) Income from property devised to a specific devisee shall be distributed to the devisee after reduction for:

    (1) property taxes;

    (2) other taxes, including taxes imposed on income that accrues during the period of administration and that is payable to the devisee;

    (3) ordinary repairs;

    (4) insurance premiums;

    (5) interest accrued after the testator's death; and

    (6) other expenses of management and operation of the property.

(c) The balance of the net income shall be distributed to all other devisees after reduction for the balance of property taxes, ordinary repairs, insurance premiums, interest accrued, other expenses of management and operation of all property from which the estate is entitled to income, and taxes imposed on income that accrues during the period of administration and that is payable or allocable to the devisees, in proportion to the devisees' respective interests in the undistributed assets of the estate.

Derived from Probate Code §§ 378B(b), (c), (d).

Added by Acts 2009, 81st Leg., ch. 680, § 1, eff. Jan. 1, 2014.

§ 310.005. Treatment of Income Received by Trustee

Income received by a trustee under this chapter shall be treated as income of the trust as provided by Section 116.101, Property Code.

Derived from Probate Code § 378B(g).

Added by Acts 2009, 81st Leg., ch. 680, § 1, eff. Jan. 1, 2014.

§ 310.006. Frequency and Method of Determining Interests in Certain Estate Assets

Except as required by Sections 2055 and 2056, Internal Revenue Code of 1986 (26 U.S.C. Sections 2055 and 2056), the frequency and method of determining the beneficiaries' respective interests in the undistributed assets of an estate are in the sole and absolute discretion of the executor of the estate. The executor may consider all relevant factors, including administrative convenience and expense and the interests of the various beneficiaries of the estate, to reach a fair and equitable result among beneficiaries.

Derived from Probate Code § 378B(h).

Added by Acts 2009, 81st Leg., ch. 680, § 1, eff. Jan. 1, 2014.

SUBTITLE H. CONTINUATION OF ADMINISTRATION

Chapter 351. Powers and Duties of Personal Representatives in General

Subchapter A. General Provisions

Subchapter B. General Authority of Personal Representatives

Subchapter C. Possession and Care of Estate Property

Chapter 351. Powers and Duties of Personal Representatives in General

Subchapter A. General Provisions

§ 351.001. Applicability of Common Law

The rights, powers, and duties of executors and administrators are governed by common law principles to the extent that those principles do not conflict with the statutes of this state.

Derived from Probate Code § 32.

Added by Acts 2009, 81st Leg., ch. 680, § 1, eff. Jan. 1, 2014.

Statutes in Context
§ 351.002

While appeal bonds are normally required, no bond is required when an appeal is made by the personal representative unless the appeal personally concerns the personal representative.

---

§ 351.002. Appeal Bond

(a) Except as provided by Subsection (b), an appeal bond is not required if an appeal is taken by an executor or administrator.

(b) An executor or administrator must give an appeal bond if the appeal personally concerns the executor or administrator.

Derived from Probate Code § 29.

Added by Acts 2009, 81st Leg., ch. 680, § 1, eff. Jan. 1, 2014.

§ 351.003. Certain Costs Adjudged Against Personal Representative

If a personal representative neglects to perform a required duty or is removed for cause, the representative and the sureties on the representative's bond are liable for:

(1) the costs of removal and other additional costs incurred that are not expenditures authorized by this title; and

(2) reasonable attorney's fees incurred in:

(A) removing the representative; or

(B) obtaining compliance regarding any statutory duty the representative has neglected.

Derived from Probate Code § 245.

Added by Acts 2009, 81st Leg., ch. 680, § 1, eff. Jan. 1, 2014.

Subchapter B. General Authority of Personal Representatives

Statutes in Context
§§ 351.051–351.052

Unlike an independent executor, a dependent executor must seek court approval before taking almost all actions with respect to the estate. Section 351.051 enumerates when court approval is needed while § 351.052 lists a few situations where the personal representative may act without court order.

---

§ 351.051. Exercise of Authority Under Court Order

(a) A personal representative of an estate may renew or extend any obligation owed by or to the estate on application and order authorizing the renewal or extension. If a personal representative considers it in the interest of the estate, the representative may, on written application to the court and if authorized by court order:

(1) purchase or exchange property;

(2) take claims or property for the use and benefit of the estate in payment of a debt due or owed to the estate;

(3) compound bad or doubtful debts due or owed to the estate;

(4) make a compromise or settlement in relation to property or a claim in dispute or litigation;

(5) compromise or pay in full any secured claim that has been allowed and approved as required by law against the estate by conveying to the holder of the claim the real estate or personal property securing the claim:

(A) in full payment, liquidation, and satisfaction of the claim; and

(B) in consideration of cancellation of notes, deeds of trust, mortgages, chattel mortgages, or other evidences of liens securing the payment of the claim; or

(6) abandon the administration of burdensome or worthless estate property.

(b) Abandoned property may be foreclosed on by a mortgagee or other secured party or a trustee without further court order.

Derived from Probate Code § 234(a).

Added by Acts 2009, 81st Leg., ch. 680, § 1, eff. Jan. 1, 2014.

§ 351.052. Exercise of Authority Without Court Order

(a) A personal representative of an estate may, without application to or order of the court:

(1) release a lien on payment at maturity of the debt secured by the lien;

(2) vote stocks by limited or general proxy;

(3) pay calls and assessments;

(4) insure the estate against liability in appropriate cases;

(5) insure estate property against fire, theft, and other hazards; or

(6) pay taxes, court costs, and bond premiums.

(b) A personal representative who is under court control may apply and obtain a court order if the representative has doubts regarding the propriety of the exercise of any power listed in Subsection (a).

Derived from Probate Code § 234(b).

Added by Acts 2009, 81st Leg., ch. 680, § 1, eff. Jan. 1, 2014.

§ 351.053. Authority to Serve Pending Appeal of Appointment

Pending an appeal from an order or judgment appointing an administrator or temporary administrator, the appointee shall continue to:

(1) act as administrator or temporary administrator; and

(2) prosecute any suit then pending in favor of the estate.

Derived from Probate Code § 28.

Added by Acts 2009, 81st Leg., ch. 680, § 1, eff. Jan. 1, 2014.

§ 351.054. Authority to Commence Suits

(a) An executor or administrator appointed in this state may commence a suit for:

(1) recovery of personal property, debts, or damages; or

(2) title to or possession of land, any right attached to or arising from that land, or an injury or damage done to that land.

(b) A judgment in a suit described by Subsection (a) is conclusive, but may be set aside by any interested person for fraud or collusion on the executor's or administrator's part.

Derived from Probate Code § 233A.

Added by Acts 2009, 81st Leg., ch. 680, § 1, eff. Jan. 1, 2014.

Subchapter C. Possession and Care of Estate Property

Statutes in Context
§ 351.101

The standard of care which a personal representative must use when dealing with estate property is that of a prudent person. See *McLendon v. McLendon*, 862 S.W.2d 662 (Tex. App. — Dallas 1993, writ denied).

§ 351.101. Duty of Care

An executor or administrator of an estate shall take care of estate property as a prudent person would take of that person's own property, and if any buildings belong to the estate, the executor or administrator shall keep those buildings in good repair, except for extraordinary casualties, unless directed by a court order not to do so.

Derived from Probate Code § 230.

Added by Acts 2009, 81st Leg., ch. 680, § 1, eff. Jan. 1, 2014.

The personal representative has a duty to collect all of the decedent's property under § 351.102. This right is superior to that of the heirs or beneficiaries. See § 101.001.

§ 351.102. Possession of Personal Property and Records

(a) Immediately after receiving letters testamentary or of administration, the personal representative of an estate shall collect and take possession of the estate's personal property, record books, title papers, and other business papers.

(b) The personal representative shall deliver the property, books, and papers described by Subsection (a) that are in the representative's possession to the person or persons legally entitled to the property, books, and papers when:

(1) the administration of the estate is closed; or

(2) a successor personal representative receives letters testamentary or of administration.

Derived from Probate Code § 232.

Added by Acts 2009, 81st Leg., ch. 680, § 1, eff. Jan. 1, 2014.

§ 351.103. Possession of Property Held in Common Ownership

If an estate holds or owns any property in common or as part owner with another, the personal representative of the estate is entitled to possession of the property in common with the other part owner or owners in the same manner as other owners in common or joint owners are entitled to possession of the property.

Derived from Probate Code § 235.

Added by Acts 2009, 81st Leg., ch. 680, § 1, eff. Jan. 1, 2014.

§ 351.104. Administration of Partnership Interest

(a) If a decedent was a partner in a general partnership and the partnership agreement or articles of partnership provide that, on the death of a partner, the partner's personal representative is entitled to that partner's place in the partnership, a personal representative accordingly contracting to enter the partnership under the partnership agreement or articles of partnership is, to the extent allowed by law, liable to a third person only to the extent of:

(1) the deceased partner's capital in the partnership; and

(2) the estate's assets held by the representative.

(b) This section does not exonerate a personal representative from liability for the representative's negligence.

Derived from Probate Code § 238A.

Added by Acts 2009, 81st Leg., ch. 680, § 1, eff. Jan. 1,

2014.

Section 351.105 permits corporate securities and other personal property to be held in the name of a nominee (e.g., a stock broker).

§ 351.105. Holding of Stocks, Bonds, and Other Personal Property in Nominee's Name

(a) Unless otherwise provided by the will, a personal representative of an estate may cause stocks, bonds, and other personal property of the estate to be registered and held in the name of a nominee without mentioning the fiduciary relationship in any instrument or record constituting or evidencing title to that property. The representative is liable for the acts of the nominee with respect to property registered in this manner. The representative's records must at all times show the ownership of the property.

(b) Any property registered in the manner described by Subsection (a) shall be kept:

(1) in the possession and control of the personal representative at all times; and

(2) separate from the representative's individual property.

Derived from Probate Code § 398A.

Added by Acts 2009, 81st Leg., ch. 680, § 1, eff. Jan. 1, 2014.

Subchapter D. Collection of Claims; Recovery of Property

Subchapter D provides the personal representative with guidance in collecting the decedent's property. This subchapter also explains when and how the personal representative may hire an attorney on a contingency fee basis to assist in the recovery and collection process.

§ 351.151. Ordinary Diligence Required

(a) If there is a reasonable prospect of collecting the claims or recovering the property of an estate, the personal representative of the estate shall use ordinary diligence to:

(1) collect all claims and debts due the estate; and

(2) recover possession of all property to which the estate has claim or title.

(b) If a personal representative wilfully neglects to use the ordinary diligence required under Subsection (a), the representative and the sureties on the representative's bond are liable, on the suit of any person interested in the estate, for the use of the estate, for the amount of those claims or the value of that property lost by the neglect.

Derived from Probate Code § 233(a).

Added by Acts 2009, 81st Leg., ch. 680, § 1, eff. Jan. 1, 2014.

§ 351.152. Contingent Interest for Certain Attorney's Fees; Court Approval

(a) Except as provided by Subsection (b) and subject only to the approval of the court in which the estate is being administered, a personal representative may convey or enter into a contract to convey for attorney services a contingent interest in any property sought to be recovered, not to exceed a one-third interest in the property.

(b) A personal representative, including an independent executor or independent administrator, may convey or enter into a contract to convey for attorney services a contingent interest in any property sought to be recovered under this subchapter in an amount that exceeds a one-third interest in the property only on the approval of the court in which the estate is being administered. The court must approve a contract entered into or conveyance made under this section before an attorney performs any legal services. A contract entered into or a conveyance made in violation of this section is void unless the court ratifies or reforms the contract or documents relating to the conveyance to the extent necessary to make the contract or conveyance meet the requirements of this section.

(c) In approving a contract or conveyance under this section, the court shall consider:

(1) the time and labor required, the novelty and difficulty of the questions involved, and the skill required to perform the legal services properly;

(2) the fee customarily charged in the locality for similar legal services;

(3) the value of the property recovered or sought to be recovered by the personal representative under this subchapter;

(4) the benefits to the estate that the attorney will be responsible for securing; and

(5) the experience and ability of the attorney who will perform the services.

Derived from Probate Code §§ 233(b), (c), (d).

Added by Acts 2009, 81st Leg., ch. 680, § 1, eff. Jan. 1, 2014.

§ 351.153. Recovery of Certain Expenses

On proof satisfactory to the court, a personal representative of an estate is entitled to all necessary and reasonable expenses incurred by the representative in:

(1) collecting or attempting to collect a claim or debt owed to the estate; or

(2) recovering or attempting to recover property to which the estate has a title or claim.

Derived from Probate Code § 233(e).

Added by Acts 2009, 81st Leg., ch. 680, § 1, eff. Jan. 1, 2014.

Subchapter E. Operation of Business

§ 351.201. Definition

In this subchapter, "business" includes a farm, ranch, or factory.

Derived from Probate Code § 238(a).

Added by Acts 2009, 81st Leg., ch. 680, § 1, eff. Jan. 1, 2014.

§ 351.202. Order Requiring Personal Representative to Operate Business

(a) A court, after notice to all interested persons and a hearing, may order the personal representative of an estate to operate a business that is part of the estate and may grant the representative the powers to operate the business that the court determines are appropriate, after considering the factors listed in Subsection (b), if:

(1) the disposition of the business has not been specifically directed by the decedent's will;

(2) it is not necessary to sell the business at once for the payment of debts or for any other lawful purpose; and

(3) the court determines that the operation of the business by the representative is in the best interest of the estate.

(b) In determining which powers to grant a personal representative in an order entered under Subsection (a), the court shall consider:

(1) the condition of the estate and the business;

(2) the necessity that may exist for the future sale of the business or of business property to provide for payment of debts or claims against the estate or other lawful expenditures with respect to the estate;

(3) the effect of the order on the speedy settlement of the estate; and

(4) the best interests of the estate.

Derived from Probate Code §§ 238(b), (f).

Added by Acts 2009, 81st Leg., ch. 680, § 1, eff. Jan. 1, 2014.

§ 351.203. Powers of Personal Representative Regarding Business

(a) A personal representative granted authority to operate a business in an order entered under Section 351.202(a) has the powers granted under Section 351.052, regardless of whether the order specifies that the representative has those powers, unless the order specifically provides that the representative does not have one or more of the powers listed in Section 351.052.

(b) In addition to the powers granted to the personal representative under Section 351.052, subject to any specific limitation on those powers in accordance with Subsection (a), an order entered under Section

351.202(a) may grant the representative one or more of the following powers:

(1) the power to hire, pay, and terminate the employment of employees of the business;

(2) the power to incur debt on behalf of the business, including debt secured by liens against assets of the business or estate, if permitted or directed by the order;

(3) the power to purchase and sell property in the ordinary course of the operation of the business, including the power to purchase and sell real property if the court finds that the principal purpose of the business is the purchasing and selling of real property and the order states that finding;

(4) the power to enter into a lease or contract, the term of which may extend beyond the settlement of the estate, but only to the extent that granting the power appears to be consistent with the speedy settlement of the estate; and

(5) any other power the court finds necessary with respect to the operation of the business.

(c) If the order entered under Section 351.202(a) gives the personal representative the power to purchase, sell, lease, or otherwise encumber property:

(1) the purchase, sale, lease, or encumbrance is governed by the terms of the order; and

(2) the representative is not required to comply with any other provision of this title regarding the purchase, sale, lease, or encumbrance, including any provision requiring citation or notice.

Derived from Probate Code §§ 238(c), (d), (e).

Added by Acts 2009, 81st Leg., ch. 680, § 1, eff. Jan. 1, 2014.

§ 351.204. Fiduciary Duties of Personal Representative Regarding Business

(a) A personal representative who operates a business under an order entered under Section 351.202(a) has the same fiduciary duties as a representative who does not operate a business that is part of an estate.

(b) In operating a business under an order entered under Section 351.202(a), a personal representative shall consider:

(1) the condition of the estate and the business;

(2) the necessity that may exist for the future sale of the business or of business property to provide for payment of debts or claims against the estate or other lawful expenditures with respect to the estate;

(3) the effect of the order on the speedy settlement of the estate; and

(4) the best interests of the estate.

(c) A personal representative who operates a business under an order entered under Section 351.202(a) shall report to the court with respect to the operation and condition of the business as part of the accounts required by Chapters 359 and 362, unless the court orders the reports regarding the business to be made more frequently or in a different manner or form.

Derived from Probate Code § 238(g).

Added by Acts 2009, 81st Leg., ch. 680, § 1, eff. Jan. 1, 2014.

§ 351.205. Real Property of Business; Notice

(a) A personal representative shall file a notice in the real property records of the county in which the real property is located before purchasing, selling, leasing, or otherwise encumbering any real property of the business in accordance with an order entered under Section 351.202(a).

(b) The notice filed under Subsection (a) must:

(1) state:

(A) the decedent's name;

(B) the county of the court in which the decedent's estate is pending;

(C) the cause number assigned to the pending estate; and

(D) that one or more orders have been entered under Section 351.202(A); and

(2) include a description of the property that is the subject of the purchase, sale, lease, or other encumbrance.

(c) For purposes of determining a personal representative's authority with respect to a purchase, sale, lease, or other encumbrance of real property of a business that is part of an estate, a third party who deals in good faith with the representative with respect to the transaction may rely on the notice filed under Subsection (a) and an order entered under Section 351.202(a) and filed as part of the estate records maintained by the clerk of the court in which the estate is pending.

Derived from Probate Code §§ 238(h), (i).

Added by Acts 2009, 81st Leg., ch. 680, § 1, eff. Jan. 1, 2014.

Subchapter F. Authority to Engage in Certain Borrowing

Statutes in Context
Chapter 351, Subchapter F

Chapter 351, Subchapter F, explains when and how a personal representative may borrow money for estate administration purposes.

§ 351.251. Mortgage or Pledge of Estate Property Authorized in Certain Circumstances

Under order of the court, a personal representative of an estate may mortgage or pledge by deed of trust or otherwise as security for an indebtedness any property of the estate as necessary for:

(1) the payment of any ad valorem, income, gift, estate, inheritance, or transfer taxes on the transfer of an estate or due from a decedent or the

estate, regardless of whether those taxes are assessed by a state, a political subdivision of a state, the federal government, or a foreign country;

(2) the payment of expenses of administration, including amounts necessary for operation of a business, farm, or ranch owned by the estate;

(3) the payment of claims allowed and approved, or established by suit, against the estate; or

(4) the renewal and extension of an existing lien.

Derived from Probate Code § 329(a).

Added by Acts 2009, 81st Leg., ch. 680, § 1, eff. Jan. 1, 2014.

§ 351.252. Application; Order

(a) If necessary to borrow money for a purpose described by Section 351.251 or to create or extend a lien on estate property as security, the personal representative of the estate shall file a sworn application for that authority with the court. The application must state fully and in detail the circumstances that the representative believes make the granting of the authority necessary.

(b) On the filing of an application under Subsection (a), the clerk shall issue and have posted a citation to all interested persons, stating the nature of the application and requiring any interested person who chooses to do so to appear and show cause, if any, why the application should not be granted.

(c) If satisfied by the evidence adduced at the hearing on an application filed under Subsection (a) that it is in the interest of the estate to borrow money or to extend and renew an existing lien, the court shall issue an order to that effect that sets out the terms of the authority granted under the order.

(d) If a new lien is created on estate property, the court may require, for the protection of the estate and the creditors, that the personal representative's general bond be increased or an additional bond given, as for the sale of real property belonging to the estate.

Derived from Probate Code § 329(b), (c).

Added by Acts 2009, 81st Leg., ch. 680, § 1, eff. Jan. 1, 2014.

§ 351.253. Term of Loan or Lien Extension

Except as otherwise provided by this section, the term of a loan or lien renewal authorized under Section 351.252 may not exceed a period of three years from the date original letters testamentary or of administration are granted to the personal representative of the affected estate. The court may authorize an extension of a lien renewed under Section 351.252 for not more than one additional year without further citation or notice.

Derived from Probate Code § 329(c).

Added by Acts 2009, 81st Leg., ch. 680, § 1, eff. Jan. 1, 2014.

Subchapter G. Payment of Income of Certain Estates During Administration

§ 351.301. Applicability of Subchapter

This subchapter applies only to the estate of a decedent that is being administered under the direction, control, and orders of a court in the exercise of the court's probate jurisdiction.

Derived from Probate Code § 239.

Added by Acts 2009, 81st Leg., ch. 680, § 1, eff. Jan. 1, 2014.

§ 351.302. Application and Order for Payment of Certain Estate Income

(a) On the application of the executor or administrator of an estate or of any interested party, and after notice of the application has been given by posting, the court may order and direct the executor or administrator to pay, or credit to the account of, those persons who the court finds will own the estate assets when administration on the estate is completed, and in the same proportions, that part of the annual net income received by or accruing to the estate that the court finds can conveniently be paid to those owners without prejudice to the rights of creditors, legatees, or other interested parties, if:

(1) it appears from evidence introduced at a hearing on the application, and the court finds, that the reasonable market value of the estate assets on hand at that time, excluding the annual income from the estate assets, is at least twice the aggregate amount of all unpaid debts, administration expenses, and legacies; and

(2) no estate creditor or legatee has appeared and objected.

(b) Except as otherwise provided by this title, nothing in this subchapter authorizes the court to order paid over to the owners of the estate any part of the principal of the estate.

Derived from Probate Code § 239.

Added by Acts 2009, 81st Leg., ch. 680, § 1, eff. Jan. 1, 2014.

§ 351.303. Treatment of Certain Amounts Received from Mineral Lease

For the purposes of this subchapter, bonuses, rentals, and royalties received for or from an oil, gas, or other mineral lease shall be treated as income rather than as principal.

Derived from Probate Code § 239.

Added by Acts 2009, 81st Leg., ch. 680, § 1, eff. Jan. 1, 2014.

Subchapter H. Certain Administered Estates

Statutes in Context
Chapter 351, Subchapter H

The judge has the duty to use reasonable diligence to make certain that personal representatives in dependent administrations are performing their duties properly. The judge, however, does not have this responsibility with respect to independent personal representatives who are not supervised by the court.

§ 351.351. Applicability

This subchapter does not apply to:

(1) the appointment of an independent executor or administrator under Section 401.002 or 401.003(a); or

(2) the appointment of a successor independent executor under Section 404.005.

Derived from Probate Code §§ 145(q), 154A(i).

Added by Acts 2009, 81st Leg., ch. 680, § 1, eff. Jan. 1, 2014. Amended by Acts 2013, 83rd Leg., ch. 161, § 6.012, eff. Jan. 1, 2014.

§ 351.352. Ensuring Compliance with Law

A county or probate court shall use reasonable diligence to see that personal representatives of estates administered under court orders and other officers of the court perform the duty enjoined on them by law applicable to those estates.

Derived from Probate Code § 36(a).

Added by Acts 2009, 81st Leg., ch. 680, § 1, eff. Jan. 1, 2014.

§ 351.353. Annual Examination of Certain Estates; Bond of Personal Representative

For each estate administered under orders of a county or probate court, the judge shall, if the judge considers it necessary, annually examine the condition of the estate and the solvency of the bond of the estate's personal representative. If the judge finds the representative's bond is not sufficient to protect the estate, the judge shall require the representative to execute a new bond in accordance with law. In each case, the judge, as provided by law, shall notify the representative and the sureties on the representative's bond.

Derived from Probate Code § 36(a).

Added by Acts 2009, 81st Leg., ch. 680, § 1, eff. Jan. 1, 2014.

§ 351.354. Judge's Liability

A judge is liable on the judge's bond to those damaged if damage or loss results to an estate administered under orders of a county or probate court from the gross neglect of the judge to use reasonable diligence in the performance of the judge's duty under this subchapter.

Derived from Probate Code § 36(a).

Added by Acts 2009, 81st Leg., ch. 680, § 1, eff. Jan. 1, 2014.

§ 351.355. Identifying Information

(a) The court may request an applicant or court-appointed fiduciary to produce other information identifying an applicant, decedent, or personal representative, including a social security number, in addition to identifying information the applicant or fiduciary is required to produce under this title.

(b) The court shall maintain any information required under this section, and the information may not be filed with the clerk.

Derived from Probate Code § 36(b).

Added by Acts 2009, 81st Leg., ch. 680, § 1, eff. Jan. 1, 2014.

Chapter 352. Compensation and Expenses of Personal Representatives and Others

Subchapter A. Compensation of Personal Representatives

Subchapter B. Expenses of Personal Representatives and Others

Chapter 352. Compensation and Expenses of Personal Representatives and Others

Subchapter A. Compensation of Personal Representatives

Statutes in Context
Chapter 352, Subchapter A

The testator may establish the amount of compensation for a personal representative by including a provision in the will (e.g., a fixed amount, a "reasonable" amount, or no compensation). See *Stanley v. Henderson*, 162 S.W.2d 95 (Tex. 1942). If the will is silent, the personal representative is entitled to compensation as set forth in this Subchapter provided the court finds that the personal representative managed the estate prudently.

The amount of the compensation is basically a commission on what the personal representative expends and collects, unless it is "too easy" to justify the compensation. The personal representative is entitled to 5 percent of the sums received in cash (e.g., selling estate assets) plus 5 percent of the sums paid out in cash (e.g., paying debts). However, this commission is not available for collecting cash on hand, bank accounts, or life insurance policies nor for making payments to the beneficiaries or heirs.

The personal representative can attempt to get a larger amount of compensation by showing that the personal representative is managing a business or farm or that the 5 percent commission is unreasonably low.

§ 352.001. Definition

In this subchapter, "financial institution" means an organization authorized to engage in business under state or federal laws relating to financial institutions, including:

(1) a bank;

(2) a trust company;

(3) a savings bank;

(4) a building and loan association;

(5) a savings and loan company or association; and

(6) a credit union.

Derived from Probate Code § 241(b).

Added by Acts 2009, 81st Leg., ch. 680, § 1, eff. Jan. 1, 2014.

§ 352.002. Standard Compensation

(a) An executor, administrator, or temporary administrator a court finds to have taken care of and managed an estate in compliance with the standards of this title is entitled to receive a five percent commission on all amounts that the executor or administrator actually receives or pays out in cash in the administration of the estate.

(b) The commission described by Subsection (a):

(1) may not exceed, in the aggregate, more than five percent of the gross fair market value of the estate subject to administration; and

(2) is not allowed for:

(A) receiving funds belonging to the testator or intestate that were, at the time of the testator's or intestate's death, either on hand or held for the testator or intestate in a financial institution or a brokerage firm, including cash or a cash equivalent held in a checking account, savings account, certificate of deposit, or money market account;

(B) collecting the proceeds of a life insurance policy; or

(C) paying out cash to an heir or legatee in that person's capacity as an heir or legatee.

Derived from Probate Code § 241(A).

Added by Acts 2009, 81st Leg., ch. 680, § 1, eff. Jan. 1, 2014.

§ 352.003. Alternate Compensation

(a) The court may allow an executor, administrator, or temporary administrator reasonable compensation for the executor's or administrator's services, including unusual efforts to collect funds or life insurance, if:

(1) the executor or administrator manages a farm, ranch, factory, or other business of the estate; or

(2) the compensation calculated under Section 352.002 is unreasonably low.

(b) The county court has jurisdiction to receive, consider, and act on applications from independent executors for purposes of this section.

Derived from Probate Code § 241(a).

Added by Acts 2009, 81st Leg., ch. 680, § 1, eff. Jan. 1, 2014.

§ 352.004. Denial of Compensation

The court may, on application of an interested person or on the court's own motion, wholly or partly deny a commission allowed by this subchapter if:

(1) the court finds that the executor or administrator has not taken care of and managed estate property prudently; or

(2) the executor or administrator has been removed under Section 404.003 or Subchapter B, Chapter 361.

Derived from Probate Code § 241(a).

Added by Acts 2009, 81st Leg., ch. 680, § 1, eff. Jan. 1, 2014. Amended by Acts 2011, 82nd Leg., ch. 1338, § 2.45, eff. Jan. 1, 2014. Amended by Acts 2013, 83rd Leg., ch. 161, § 6.013, eff. Jan. 1, 2014.

Subchapter B. Expenses of Personal Representatives and Others

Statutes in Context
§ 352.051

Section 352.051 allows the personal representative to be reimbursed for all necessary and reasonable expenses, including attorneys' fees, incurred in administering the estate.

§ 352.051. Expenses; Attorney's Fees

On proof satisfactory to the court, a personal representative of an estate is entitled to:

(1) necessary and reasonable expenses incurred by the representative in:

(A) preserving, safekeeping, and managing the estate;

(B) collecting or attempting to collect claims or debts; and

(C) recovering or attempting to recover property to which the estate has a title or claim; and

(2) reasonable attorney's fees necessarily incurred in connection with the proceedings and management of the estate.

Derived from Probate Code § 242.

Added by Acts 2009, 81st Leg., ch. 680, § 1, eff. Jan. 1, 2014.

Statutes in Context
§ 352.052

Section 352.052 explains when a person may be reimbursed from the estate for expenses incurred in (1) attempting to probate a will or (2) defending a will already admitted to probate, provided the actions are both in good faith and with just cause.

§ 352.052. Allowance for Defense of Will

(a) A person designated as executor in a will or an alleged will, or as administrator with the will or alleged will annexed, who, for the purpose of having the will or alleged will admitted to probate, defends the will or alleged will or prosecutes any proceeding in good faith and with just cause, whether or not successful, shall be allowed out of the estate the executor's or administrator's necessary expenses and disbursements in those proceedings, including reasonable attorney's fees.

(b) A person designated as a devisee in or beneficiary of a will or an alleged will[, or as administrator with the will or alleged will annexed,] who, for the purpose of having the will or alleged will admitted to probate, defends the will or alleged will or prosecutes any proceeding in good faith and with just cause, whether or not successful, may be allowed out of the estate the person's necessary expenses and disbursements in those proceedings, including reasonable attorney's fees.

Derived from Probate Code § 243.

Added by Acts 2009, 81st Leg., ch. 680, § 1, eff. Jan. 1, 2014. Subsec. (b) amended by Acts 2015, 84th Leg., ch. 995, § 34, eff. Sept. 1, 2015.

§ 352.053. Expense Charges

(a) The court shall act on expense charges in the same manner as other claims against the estate.

(b) All expense charges shall be:

(1) made in writing, showing specifically each item of expense and the date of the expense;

(2) verified by the personal representative's affidavit;

(3) filed with the clerk; and

(4) entered on the claim docket.

Derived from Probate Code § 244.

Added by Acts 2009, 81st Leg., ch. 680, § 1, eff. Jan. 1, 2014.

Chapter 353. Exempt Property and Family Allowance

Subchapter A. General Provisions

Chapter 353. Exempt Property and Family Allowance

Subchapter A. General Provisions

§ 353.001. Treatment of Certain Children

For purposes of distributing exempt property and making a family allowance, a child is a child of his or her mother and a child of his or her father, as provided by Sections 201.051, 201.052, and 201.053.

Derived from Probate Code § 42(c).

Added by Acts 2009, 81st Leg., ch. 680, § 1, eff. Jan. 1, 2014.

Subchapter B. Exempt Property; Allowance in Lieu of Exempt Property

Statutes in Context
§ 353.051

The exempt property which the court sets aside includes the homestead as discussed in Chapter 102 as well as exempt personal property under Property Code §§ 42.001-42.005.

§ 353.051. Exempt Property to Be Set Aside

(a) Unless an application and verified affidavit are filed as provided by Subsection (b), immediately after the inventory, appraisement, and list of claims of an estate are approved or after the affidavit in lieu of the inventory, appraisement, and list of claims is filed, the court by order shall set aside:

(1) the homestead for the use and benefit of the decedent's surviving spouse and minor children; and

(2) all other exempt [estate] property described by Section 42.002(a), Property Code, [that is exempt from execution or forced sale by the constitution and laws of this state] for the use and benefit of the decedent's:

(A) surviving spouse and minor children;

(B) unmarried adult children remaining with the decedent's family; and

(C) each other adult child who is incapacitated.

(b) Before the inventory, appraisement, and list of claims of an estate are approved:

(1) the decedent's surviving spouse or any other person authorized to act on behalf of the decedent's minor children may apply to the court to have exempt property described by Subsection (a), including the homestead, set aside by filing an application and a verified affidavit listing all exempt property that the applicant claims is exempt property described by Subsection (a); and

(2) any of the decedent's unmarried adult children remaining with the decedent's family, any other adult child of the decedent who is incapacitated, or a person who is authorized to act on behalf of the adult incapacitated child may apply to the court to have all exempt property described by Subsection (a), other than the homestead, set aside by filing an application and a verified affidavit listing all the exempt property, other than the homestead, that the applicant claims is exempt property described by Subsection (a).

(c) At a hearing on an application filed under Subsection (b), the applicant has the burden of proof by a preponderance of the evidence. The court shall set aside property of the decedent's estate that the court finds is exempt.

Derived from Probate Code § 271.

Added by Acts 2009, 81st Leg., ch. 680, § 1, eff. Jan. 1, 2014. Amended by Acts 2011, 82nd Leg., ch. 1338, § 2.01, eff. Jan. 1, 2014 and Acts 2011, 82nd Leg., ch. 810, § 2.01, eff. Jan. 1. 2014. Subsecs. (a) & (b) amended by Acts 2015, 84th Leg., ch. 995, § 35, eff. Sept. 1, 2015.

Statutes in Context
§ 353.052

For a discussion of the rights of the surviving spouse and minor children to occupy the homestead, see *Statutes in Context* to Texas Constitution Article XVI, § 52.

§ 353.052. Delivery of Exempt Property

(a) This section only applies to exempt property described by Section 353.051(a).

(a-1) The executor or administrator of an estate shall deliver, without delay, exempt property that has been set aside for the decedent's surviving spouse and children in accordance with this section.

(b) If there is a surviving spouse and there are no children of the decedent, or if all the children, including any adult incapacitated children, of the decedent are also the children of the surviving spouse, the executor or administrator shall deliver all exempt property to the surviving spouse.

(c) If there is a surviving spouse and there are children of the decedent who are not also children of the surviving spouse, the executor or administrator shall deliver the share of those children in exempt property, other than the homestead, to:

(1) the children, if the children are of legal age;

(2) the children's guardian, if the children are minors; or

(3) the guardian of each of the children who is an incapacitated adult, or to another appropriate person, as determined by the court, on behalf of the adult incapacitated child if there is no guardian.

(d) If there is no surviving spouse and there are children of the decedent, the executor or administrator shall deliver exempt property, other than the homestead, to:

(1) the children, if the children are of legal age;

(2) the children's guardian, if the children are minors; or

(3) the guardian of each of the children who is an incapacitated adult, or to another appropriate person, as determined by the court, on behalf of the adult incapacitated child if there is no guardian.

(e) In all cases, the executor or administrator shall deliver the homestead to:

(1) the decedent's surviving spouse, if there is a surviving spouse; or

(2) the guardian of the decedent's minor children, if there is not a surviving spouse.

Derived from Probate Code § 272.

Added by Acts 2009, 81st Leg., ch. 680, § 1, eff. Jan. 1, 2014. Amended by Acts 2011, 82nd Leg., ch. 810, § 2.02, eff. Jan. 1, 2014. Subsec. (a) amended and subsec. (a-1) added by Acts 2015, 84th Leg., ch. 995, § 5, eff. Sept. 36, 2015.

Statutes in Context
§ 353.053

If the decedent did not have a homestead (e.g., the decedent lived in rental accommodations), then other property up to a value of $45,000 may be set aside instead. Likewise, if the decedent did not have exempt personal property, an allowance of up to $30,000 of other property may be set aside. Note that these "in lieu of" values are significantly less than the amounts available if the actual exempt property is in the estate (unlimited value of homestead; larger dollar values for exempt personal property).

A court may award both exempt personal property and, if the value of this property does not reach the monetary limits, an allowance in lieu thereof up to $30,000. "In other words, the trial court must make an allowance for those exempt items that it cannot set aside because they are not on hand. If some exempt items are on hand, it must set those aside for the surviving spouse and award an allowance in lieu of those exempt items that are not on hand." *In re Estate of Rhea*, 257 S.W.3d 787, 792 (Tex. App.—Fort Worth 2008, no pet.).

---

§ 353.053. Allowance in Lieu of Exempt Property

(a) If all or any of the specific articles of exempt property described by Section 353.051(a) [from execution or forced sale by the constitution and laws of this state] are not among the decedent's effects, the court shall make, in lieu of the articles not among the effects, a reasonable allowance to be paid to the decedent's surviving spouse and children as provided by Section 353.054.

(b) The allowance in lieu of a homestead may not exceed $45,000, and the allowance in lieu of other exempt property may not exceed $30,000, excluding the family allowance for the support of the surviving spouse, minor children, and adult incapacitated children provided by Subchapter C.

Derived from Probate Code § 273.

Added by Acts 2009, 81st Leg., ch. 680, § 1, eff. Jan. 1, 2014. Subsec. (b) amended by Acts 2011, 82nd Leg., ch. 810, § 2.03, eff. Jan. 1, 2014 and Acts 2013, 83rd Leg., ch. 647, § 2.01, eff. Jan. 1, 2014. Subsec. (a) amended

by Acts 2015, 84th Leg., ch. 995, § 37, eff. Sept. 1, 2015.

§ 353.054. Payment of Allowance in Lieu of Exempt Property

(a) The executor or administrator of an estate shall pay an allowance in lieu of exempt property in accordance with this section.

(b) If there is a surviving spouse and there are no children of the decedent, or if all the children, including any adult incapacitated children, of the decedent are also the children of the surviving spouse, the executor or administrator shall pay the entire allowance to the surviving spouse.

(c) If there is a surviving spouse and there are children of the decedent who are not also children of the surviving spouse, the executor or administrator shall pay the surviving spouse one-half of the entire allowance plus the shares of the decedent's children of whom the surviving spouse is the parent. The remaining shares must be paid to:

(1) the decedent's adult children of whom the surviving spouse is not a parent and who are not incapacitated;

(2) the guardian of the children of whom the surviving spouse is not a parent and who are minors; or

(3) the guardian or another appropriate person, as determined by the court, if there is no guardian, of each child who is an incapacitated adult.

(d) If there is no surviving spouse and there are children of the decedent, the executor or administrator shall divide the entire allowance equally among the children and pay the children's shares to:

(1) each of those children who are adults and who are not incapacitated;

(2) the guardian of each of those children who are minors; or

(3) the guardian or another appropriate person, as determined by the court, if there is no guardian, of each of those children who is an incapacitated adult.

Derived from Probate Code § 275.

Added by Acts 2009, 81st Leg., ch. 680, § 1, eff. Jan. 1, 2014. Amended by Acts 2011, 82nd Leg., ch. 810, § 2.04, eff. Jan. 1, 2014.

§ 353.055. Method of Paying Allowance in Lieu of Exempt Property

(a) An allowance in lieu of any exempt property shall be paid in the manner selected by the decedent's surviving spouse or children of legal age, or by the guardian of the decedent's minor children, or by the guardian of each adult incapacitated child or other appropriate person, as determined by the court, if there is no guardian, as follows:

(1) in money out of estate funds that come into the executor's or administrator's possession;

(2) in any of the decedent's property or a part of the property chosen by those individuals at the appraisement; or

(3) part in money described by Subdivision (1) and part in property described by Subdivision (2).

(b) Property specifically devised to another may be taken as provided by Subsection (a) only if other available property is insufficient to pay the allowance.

Derived from Probate Code § 274.

Added by Acts 2009, 81st Leg., ch. 680, § 1, eff. Jan. 1, 2014. Subsec. (a) amended by Acts 2011, 82nd Leg., ch. 810, § 2.05, eff. Jan. 1, 2014.

§ 353.056. Sale of Property to Raise Funds for Allowance in Lieu of Exempt Property

(a) On the written application of the decedent's surviving spouse and children, or of a person authorized to represent any of those children, the court shall order the sale of estate property for cash in an amount that will be sufficient to raise the amount of the allowance provided under Section 353.053 or a portion of that amount, as necessary, if:

(1) the decedent had no property that the surviving spouse or children are willing to take for the allowance or the decedent had insufficient property; and

(2) there are not sufficient estate funds in the executor's or administrator's possession to pay the amount of the allowance or a portion of that amount, as applicable.

(b) Property specifically devised to another may be sold to raise cash as provided by Subsection (a) only if other available property is insufficient to pay the allowance.

Derived from Probate Code §§ 274, 276.

Added by Acts 2009, 81st Leg., ch. 680, § 1, eff. Jan. 1, 2014. Subsec. (a) amended by Acts 2011, 82nd Leg., ch. 810, § 2.06, eff. Jan. 1, 2014.

Subchapter C. Family Allowance

Statutes in Context
Chapter 353, Subchapter C

Chapter 353, Subchapter C, provides an allowance for the surviving spouse, minor children, and adult incapacitated children based on need. There is no allowance if the spouse or child has adequate property. There is no allowance for an adult unmarried child remaining with the family who is competent. In addition, there is no allowance for an adult incapacitated child if the decedent was not supporting this child when the decedent died.

Unlike many states, there is no statutorily set maximum amount. The amount is based on what is necessary to support the surviving spouse or children for one year from the time of death. The

family allowance is available not just to provide necessities but to provide the standard of living to which the surviving spouse was accustomed while both spouses were alive. See *In re Estate of Rhea*, 257 S.W.3d 787 (Tex. App.—Fort Worth 2008, no pet.).

The family allowance is treated as a debt of the estate. In other words, it does not reduce the value of property the surviving spouse and children receive under the will or by intestacy (that is, the family allowance is not an advancement or a satisfaction).

§ 353.101. Family Allowance

(a) Unless an application and verified affidavit are filed as provided by Subsection (b), immediately after the inventory, appraisement, and list of claims of an estate are approved or after the affidavit in lieu of the inventory, appraisement and list of claims is filed, the court shall fix a family allowance for the support of the decedent's surviving spouse, minor children, and adult incapacitated children.

(b) Before the inventory, appraisement, and list of claims of an estate are approved or, if applicable, before the affidavit in lieu of the inventory, appraisement, and list of claims is filed, the decedent's surviving spouse or any other person authorized to act on behalf of the decedent's minor children or adult incapacitated children may apply to the court to have the court fix the family allowance by filing an application and a verified affidavit describing:

(1) the amount necessary for the maintenance of the surviving spouse, the decedent's minor children, and the decedent's adult incapacitated children for one year after the date of the decedent's death; and

(2) the surviving spouse's separate property and any property that the decedent's minor children or adult incapacitated children have in their own right.

(c) At a hearing on an application filed under Subsection (b), the applicant has the burden of proof by a preponderance of the evidence. The court shall fix a family allowance for the support of the decedent's surviving spouse, minor children, and adult incapacitated children.

(d) A family allowance may not be made for:

(1) the decedent's surviving spouse, if the surviving spouse has separate property adequate for the surviving spouse's maintenance;

(2) the decedent's minor children, if the minor children have property in their own right adequate for the children's maintenance; or

(3) any of the decedent's adult incapacitated children, if:

(A) the adult incapacitated child has property in the person's own right adequate for the person's maintenance; or

(B) at the time of the decedent's death, the decedent was not supporting the adult incapacitated child.

Derived from Probate Code §§ 286 & 288.

Added by Acts 2009, 81st Leg., ch. 680, § 1, eff. Jan. 1, 2014. Amended by Acts 2011, 82nd Leg., ch. 1338, § 2.47, eff. Jan. 1, 2014 and Acts 2011, 82nd Leg., ch. 810, § 2.07, eff. Jan. 1, 2014. Subsec. (d) amended by Acts 2013, 83rd Leg., ch. 1136, § 44, eff. Jan. 1, 2014.

Statutes in Context
§ 353.102

The family allowance is available not just to provide necessities but to provide the standard of living to which the surviving spouse was accustomed while both spouses were alive. For example, in *Estate of Wolfe*, 268 S.W.3d 780 (Tex. App.—Fort Worth 2008, no pet.), the court approved a family allowance of $126,840 for a surviving spouse and also noted that a surviving spouse may successfully claim a family allowance even if the surviving spouse actually has sufficient property on hand to cover one year of maintenance as long as that property was not the surviving spouse's separate property *prior* to the deceased spouse's death.

---

§ 353.102. Amount and Method of Payment of Family Allowance

(a) The amount of the family allowance must be sufficient for the maintenance of the decedent's surviving spouse, minor children, and adult incapacitated children for one year from the date of the decedent's death.

(b) The allowance must be fixed with regard to the facts or circumstances then existing and the facts and circumstances anticipated to exist during the first year after the decedent's death.

(c) The allowance may be paid in a lump sum or in installments, as ordered by the court.

Derived from Probate Code § 287.

Added by Acts 2009, 81st Leg., ch. 680, § 1, eff. Jan. 1, 2014. Subsec. (a) amended by Acts 2011, 82nd Leg., ch. 810, § 2.08, eff. Jan. 1, 2014.

§ 353.103. Order Fixing Family Allowance

When a family allowance has been fixed, the court shall enter an order that:

(1) states the amount of the allowance;

(2) provides how the allowance shall be payable; and

(3) directs the executor or administrator to pay the allowance in accordance with law.

Derived from Probate Code § 289.

Added by Acts 2009, 81st Leg., ch. 680, § 1, eff. Jan. 1, 2014.

Statutes in Context
§ 353.104

The family allowance has priority over the claims of other creditors except for the first $15,000 of funeral and last illness expenses. See § 355.102 (defining "Class 1" claims).

---

§ 353.104. Preference of Family Allowance

The family allowance made for the support of the decedent's surviving spouse, minor children, and adult incapacitated children shall be paid in preference to all other debts of or charges against the estate, other than Class 1 claims.

Derived from Probate Code § 290.

Added by Acts 2009, 81st Leg., ch. 680, § 1, eff. Jan. 1, 2014. Amended by Acts 2011, 82nd Leg., ch. 810, § 2.09, eff. Jan. 1, 2014.

§ 353.105. Payment of Family Allowance

(a) The executor or administrator of an estate shall apportion and pay the family allowance in accordance with this section.

(b) If there is a surviving spouse and there are no minor children or adult incapacitated children of the decedent, the executor or administrator shall pay the entire family allowance to the surviving spouse.

(c) If there is a surviving spouse and all of the minor children and adult incapacitated children of the decedent are also the children of the surviving spouse, the executor or administrator shall pay the entire family allowance to the surviving spouse for use by the surviving spouse, the decedent's minor children, and adult incapacitated children.

(d) If there is a surviving spouse and some or all of the minor children or adult incapacitated children of the decedent are not also children of the surviving spouse, the executor or administrator shall pay:

(1) the portion of the entire family allowance necessary for the support of those minor children to the guardian of those children; and

(2) the portion of the entire family allowance necessary for the support of each of those adult incapacitated children to the guardian of the adult incapacitated child or another appropriate person, as determined by the court, on behalf of the adult incapacitated child if there is no guardian.

(e) If there is no surviving spouse and there are minor children or adult incapacitated children of the decedent, the executor or administrator shall pay the family allowance:

(1) for the minor children, to the guardian of those children; and

(2) for each adult incapacitated child, to the guardian of the adult incapacitated child or another appropriate person, as determined by the court, on behalf of the adult incapacitated child if there is no guardian.

Derived from Probate Code § 291.

Added by Acts 2009, 81st Leg., ch. 680, § 1, eff. Jan. 1, 2014. Amended by Acts 2011, 82nd Leg., ch. 810, § 2.10, eff. Jan. 1, 2014.

§ 353.106. Surviving Spouse or Minor Children May Take Personal Property for Family Allowance

(a) A decedent's surviving spouse, the guardian of the decedent's minor children, or the guardian of an adult incapacitated child of the decedent or another appropriate person, as determined by the court, on behalf of the adult incapacitated child if there is no guardian, as applicable, is entitled to take, at the property's appraised value as shown by the appraisement, any of the estate's personal property in full or partial payment of the family allowance.

(b) Property specifically devised to another may be taken as provided by Subsection (a) only if other available property is insufficient to pay the allowance.

Derived from Probate Code § 292.

Added by Acts 2009, 81st Leg., ch. 680, § 1, eff. Jan. 1, 2014. Amended by Acts 2011, 82nd Leg., ch. 810, §§ 2.11 & 2.12, eff. Jan. 1, 2014.

§ 353.107. Sale of Estate Property to Raise Funds for Family Allowance

(a) The court shall, as soon as the inventory, appraisement, and list of claims are returned and approved or the affidavit in lieu of the inventory, appraisement, and list of claims is filed, order the sale of estate property for cash in an amount that will be sufficient to raise the amount of the family allowance, or a portion of that amount, as necessary, if:

(1) the decedent had no personal property that the surviving spouse, the guardian of the decedent's minor children, or the guardian of the decedent's adult incapacitated child or other appropriate person acting on behalf of the adult incapacitated child is willing to take for the family allowance, or the decedent had insufficient personal property; and

(2) there are not sufficient estate funds in the executor's or administrator's possession to pay the amount of the family allowance or a portion of that amount, as applicable.

(b) Property specifically devised to another may be sold to raise cash as provided by Subsection (a) only if other available property is insufficient to pay the family allowance.

Derived from Probate Code §§ 292, 293.

Added by Acts 2009, 81st Leg., ch. 680, § 1, eff. Jan. 1, 2014. Amended by Amended by Acts 2011, 82nd Leg., ch. 1338, § 2.48, eff. Jan. 1, 2014 and Acts 2011, 82nd Leg., ch. 810, § 2.13, eff. Jan. 1, 2014.

Subchapter D. Liens on and Disposition of Exempt Property and Property Taken as Allowance

§ 353.151. Liens

(a) This section applies to all estates, whether solvent or insolvent.

(b) If property on which there is a valid subsisting lien or encumbrance is set aside as exempt for the surviving spouse or children or is appropriated to make an allowance in lieu of exempt property or for the support of the surviving spouse or children, the debts secured by the lien shall, if necessary, be either paid or continued against the property.

Derived from Probate Code § 277.

Added by Acts 2009, 81st Leg., ch. 680, § 1, eff. Jan. 1, 2014.

Statutes in Context
§ 353.152

If the estate is solvent, the exempt personal property passes to the heirs or beneficiaries. Although this may seem to harm the surviving spouse and minor children, it actually does not because if the estate is solvent, there will be property to award a family allowance under § 353.101.

---

§ 353.152. Distribution of Exempt Property of Solvent Estate

If on final settlement of an estate it appears that the estate is solvent, the exempt property, other than the homestead or any allowance made in lieu of the homestead, is subject to partition and distribution among the heirs of the decedent and the distributees in the same manner as other estate property.

Derived from Probate Code § 278.

Added by Acts 2009, 81st Leg., ch. 680, § 1, eff. Jan. 1, 2014.

Statutes in Context
§ 353.153

If the estate is insolvent, the surviving spouse and children retain the exempt property free and clear of the claims of creditors as well as of the decedent's beneficiaries or heirs. This rule does not, however, actually deprive the beneficiaries or heirs of their property because if the property were not given to the surviving spouse and children, the estate creditors would have been able to reach it and the beneficiaries and heirs would not have received it anyway.

---

§ 353.153. Title to Property of Insolvent Estate

If on final settlement an estate proves to be insolvent, the decedent's surviving spouse and children have absolute title to all property and allowances set aside or paid to them under this title. The distributees are entitled to distribution of any remaining exempt property held by the executor or administrator in the same manner as other estate property. The property and allowances <u>set aside or paid to the decedent's surviving spouse or children, and any remaining exempt property held by the executor or administrator,</u> may not be taken for any of the estate debts except as provided by Section 353.155.

Derived from Probate Code § 279.

Added by Acts 2009, 81st Leg., ch. 680, § 1, eff. Jan. 1, 2014. Amended by Acts 2015, 84ᵗʰ Leg., ch. 995, § 38, eff. Sept. 1, 2015.

§ 353.154. Certain Property Not Considered in Determining Solvency

In determining whether an estate is solvent or insolvent, the exempt property set aside for the decedent's surviving spouse or children, any allowance made in lieu of that exempt property, [and] the family allowance under Subchapter C<u>, and any remaining exempt property held by the executor or administrator</u> may not be estimated or considered as estate assets.

Derived from Probate Code § 280.

Added by Acts 2009, 81st Leg., ch. 680, § 1, eff. Jan. 1, 2014. Amended by Acts 2015, 84ᵗʰ Leg., ch. 995, § 38, eff. Sept. 1, 2015.

Statutes in Context
§ 353.155

Exempt personal property is liable for the payment of the decedent's funeral and last sickness expenses up to a total of $15,000. See § 355.102 (defining "Class 1" claims).

---

§ 353.155. Exempt Property Liable for Certain Debts

The exempt property, other than the homestead or any allowance made in lieu of the homestead:

(1) is liable for the payment of Class 1 claims; and

(2) is not liable for any estate debts other than the claims described by Subdivision (1).

Derived from Probate Code § 281.

Added by Acts 2009, 81st Leg., ch. 680, § 1, eff. Jan. 1, 2014.

Chapter 354. Summary Proceedings for, or Withdrawal From Administration of, Certain Estates

Subchapter A. Summary Proceedings for Certain Small Estates

Subchapter B. Withdrawal from Administration of Certain Estates

Chapter 354. Summary Proceedings for, or Withdrawal from Administration of, Certain Estates

Subchapter A. Summary Proceedings for Certain Small Estates

Statutes in Context
§ 354.001

Section 354.001 provides for summary proceedings for certain insolvent estates even after a personal representative has been appointed. The statute refers to "claims of Classes 1 through 4" under § 355.102. Note that the predecessor Probate Code section to § 355.102 was amended many times since it was enacted in 1955 and thus the referenced claims are not the same as when the section originally took effect.

---

§ 354.001. Summary Proceedings for Certain Small Estates

(a) If, after a personal representative of an estate has filed the inventory, appraisement, and list of claims or the affidavit in lieu of the inventory, appraisement, and list of claims as provided by Chapter 309, it is established that the decedent's estate, excluding any homestead, exempt property, and family allowance to the decedent's surviving spouse, minor children, and adult incapacitated children, does not exceed the amount sufficient to pay the claims against the estate classified as Classes 1 through 4 under Section 355.102, the representative shall:

(1) on order of the court, pay those claims in the order provided and to the extent permitted by the assets of the estate subject to the payment of those claims; and

(2) after paying the claims in accordance with Subdivision (1), present to the court the representative's account with an application for the settlement and allowance of the account.

(b) On presentation of the personal representative's account and application under Subsection (a), the court, with or without notice, may adjust, correct, settle, allow, or disallow the account.

(c) If the court settles and allows the personal representative's account under Subsection (b), the court may:

(1) decree final distribution;

(2) discharge the representative; and

(3) close the administration.

Derived from Probate Code § 143.

Added by Acts 2009, 81st Leg., ch. 680, § 1, eff. Jan. 1, 2014. Amended by Amended by Acts 2011, 82nd Leg., ch. 1338, § 2.49, eff. Jan. 1, 2014 and Acts 2011, 82nd Leg., ch. 810, § 2.14, eff. Jan. 1, 2014.

Subchapter B. Withdrawal from Administration of Certain Estates

Statutes in Context
Chapter 354

After the filing of the inventory, appraisement, and list of claims, a person entitled to the estate may ask the court to withdraw the estate from administration by posting a bond at least double the gross appraised value of the estate.

§ 354.051. Required Report on Condition of Estate

At any time after the return of the inventory, appraisement, and list of claims of an estate required by Chapter 309, anyone entitled to a portion of the estate, by a written complaint filed in the court in which the case is pending, may have the estate's executor or administrator cited to appear and render under oath an exhibit of the condition of the estate.

Derived from Probate Code § 262.

Added by Acts 2009, 81st Leg., ch. 680, § 1, eff. Jan. 1, 2014.

§ 354.052. Bond Required to Withdraw Estate from Administration

After the executor or administrator has rendered the exhibit of the condition of the estate if required under Section 354.051, one or more persons entitled to the estate, or other persons for them, may execute and deliver a bond to the court. The bond must be:

(1) conditioned that the persons executing the bond shall:

(A) pay all unpaid debts against the estate that have been or are:

(i) allowed by the executor or administrator and approved by the court; or

(ii) established by suit against the estate; and

(B) pay to the executor or administrator any balance that the court in its judgment on the exhibit finds to be due the executor or administrator;

(2) payable to the judge and the judge's successors in office in an amount equal to at least twice the gross appraised value of the estate as shown by the inventory, appraisement, and list of claims returned under Chapter 309; and

(3) approved by the court.

Derived from Probate Code § 263.

Added by Acts 2009, 81st Leg., ch. 680, § 1, eff. Jan. 1, 2014.

§ 354.053. Order for Delivery of Estate

On the giving and approval of the bond under Section 354.052, the court shall enter an order requiring the executor or administrator to promptly deliver to each person entitled to any portion of the estate that portion to which the person is entitled.

Derived from Probate Code § 264.

Added by Acts 2009, 81st Leg., ch. 680, § 1, eff. Jan. 1, 2014.

§ 354.054. Order of Discharge

After an estate has been withdrawn from administration under Section 354.053, the court shall enter an order:

(1) discharging the executor or administrator; and

(2) declaring the administration closed.

Derived from Probate Code § 265.

Added by Acts 2009, 81st Leg., ch. 680, § 1, eff. Jan. 1, 2014.

§ 354.055. Lien on Property of Estate Withdrawn from Administration

A lien exists on all of the estate withdrawn from administration under Section 354.053 and in the possession of the distributees and those claiming under the distributees with notice of that lien, to secure the ultimate payment of:

(1) the bond under Section 354.052; and

(2) debts and claims secured by the bond.

Derived from Probate Code § 266.

Added by Acts 2009, 81st Leg., ch. 680, § 1, eff. Jan. 1, 2014.

§ 354.056. Partition of Estate Withdrawn from Administration

On written application to the court, any person entitled to any portion of an estate withdrawn from administration under Section 354.053 may cause a partition and distribution of the estate to be made among those persons entitled to the estate in accordance with the provisions of this title that relate to the partition and distribution of an estate.

Derived from Probate Code § 267.

Added by Acts 2009, 81st Leg., ch. 680, § 1, eff. Jan. 1, 2014.

§ 354.057. Creditors Entitled to Sue on Bond

A creditor of an estate withdrawn from administration under Section 354.053 whose debt or claim against the estate is unpaid and not barred by limitation is entitled to:

(1) commence a suit in the person's own name on the bond under Section 354.052; and

(2) obtain a judgment on the bond for the debt or claim the creditor establishes against the estate.

Derived from Probate Code § 268.

Added by Acts 2009, 81st Leg., ch. 680, § 1, eff. Jan. 1, 2014.

§ 354.058. Creditors May Sue Distributees

(a) A creditor of an estate withdrawn from administration under Section 354.053 whose debt or claim against the estate is unpaid and not barred by limitation may sue:

(1) any distributee who has received any of the estate; or

(2) all the distributees jointly.

(b) A distributee is not liable for more than the distributee's just proportion according to the amount of the estate the distributee received in the distribution.

Derived from Probate Code § 269.

Added by Acts 2009, 81st Leg., ch. 680, § 1, eff. Jan. 1, 2014.

Chapter 355. Presentment and Payment of Claims

Subchapter A. Presentment of Claims Against Estates in General

Subchapter B. Action on Claims

Subchapter C. Payment of Claims, Allowances, and Expenses

Subchapter D. Presentment and Payment of Secured Claims for Money

Subchapter E. Claims Involving Personal Representatives

Chapter 355. Presentment and Payment of Claims

Subchapter A. Presentment of Claims Against Estates in General

---

Statutes in Context
§ 355.001

Normally, a creditor may present a claim anytime before the estate is closed. There are two main exceptions to this rule: (1) if the statute of limitations on the claim has run or (2) an unsecured creditor did not present the claim within 4 months after receiving notice. See § 355.001. (See also Civil Practice & Remedies Code § 16.062 which extends the running of a limitations period for 12 months after the decedent's death, unless a personal representative is appointed sooner, in which case limitations resumes running at the time the personal representative qualifies.)

§ 355.001. Presentment of Claim to Personal Representative

A claim may be presented to a personal representative of an estate at any time before the estate is closed if suit on the claim has not been barred by the general statutes of limitation.

Derived from Probate Code § 298(a).

Added by Acts 2009, 81st Leg., ch. 680, § 1, eff. Jan. 1, 2014.

§ 355.002. Presentment of Claim to Clerk

(a) A claim may also be presented by depositing the claim with the clerk with vouchers and the necessary exhibits and affidavit attached to the claim. On receiving a claim deposited under this subsection, the clerk shall advise the personal representative or the representative's attorney of the deposit of the claim by a letter mailed to the representative's last known address.

(b) A claim deposited under Subsection (a) is presumed to be rejected if the personal representative fails to act on the claim on or before the 30th day after the date the claim is deposited.

(c) Failure of the clerk to give the notice required under Subsection (a) does not affect the validity of the presentment or the presumption of rejection because the personal representative does not act on the claim within the 30-day period prescribed by Subsection (b).

(d) The clerk shall enter a claim deposited under Subsection (a) on the claim docket.

Derived from Probate Code § 308.

Added by Acts 2009, 81st Leg., ch. 680, § 1, eff. Jan. 1, 2014.

§ 355.003. Inclusion of Attorney's Fees in Claim

If the instrument evidencing or supporting a claim provides for attorney's fees, the claimant may include as a part of the claim the portion of attorney's fees the claimant has paid or contracted to pay to an attorney to prepare, present, and collect the claim.

Derived from Probate Code § 307.

Added by Acts 2009, 81st Leg., ch. 680, § 1, eff. Jan. 1, 2014.

Statutes in Context
§ 355.004

The creditor must submit a sworn affidavit supporting the claim under § 355.004.

---

§ 355.004. Affidavit Authenticating Claim for Money in General

(a) Except as provided by Section 355.005, a claim for money against an estate must be supported by an affidavit that states:

(1) that the claim is just;

(2) that all legal offsets, payments, and credits known to the affiant have been allowed; and

(3) if the claim is not founded on a written instrument or account, the facts on which the claim is founded.

(b) A photostatic copy of an exhibit or voucher necessary to prove a claim may be offered with and attached to the claim instead of attaching the original.

Derived from Probate Code § 301.

Added by Acts 2009, 81st Leg., ch. 680, § 1, eff. Jan. 1, 2014.

§ 355.005. Affidavit Authenticating Claim of Corporation or Other Entity

(a) An authorized officer or representative of a corporation or other entity shall make the affidavit required to authenticate a claim of the corporation or entity.

(b) In an affidavit made by an officer of a corporation, or by an executor, administrator, trustee, assignee, agent, representative, or attorney, it is sufficient to state that the affiant has made diligent inquiry and examination and believes the claim is just and that all legal offsets, payments, and credits made known to the affiant have been allowed.

Derived from Probate Code § 304.

Added by Acts 2009, 81st Leg., ch. 680, § 1, eff. Jan. 1, 2014.

§ 355.006. Lost or Destroyed Evidence Concerning Claim

If evidence of a claim is lost or destroyed, the claimant or an authorized representative or agent of the claimant may make an affidavit to the fact of the loss or destruction. The affidavit must state:

(1) the amount, date, and nature of the claim;

(2) the due date of the claim;

(3) that the claim is just;

(4) that all legal offsets, payments, and credits known to the affiant have been allowed; and

(5) that the claimant is still the owner of the claim.

Derived from Probate Code § 303.

Added by Acts 2009, 81st Leg., ch. 680, § 1, eff. Jan. 1, 2014.

§ 355.007. Waiver of Certain Defects of Form or Claims of Insufficiency

A defect of form or a claim of insufficiency of a presented exhibit or voucher is considered waived by the personal representative unless a written objection to the defect or insufficiency is made not later than the 30th day after the date the claim is presented and is filed with the county clerk.

Derived from Probate Code § 302.

Added by Acts 2009, 81st Leg., ch. 680, § 1, eff. Jan. 1, 2014.

Statutes in Context
§ 355.008

Section 355.008 provides that the statute of limitations is tolled when a creditor files or deposits a claim for money.

---

§ 355.008. Effect on Statutes of Limitation of Presentment of or Suit on Claim

The general statutes of limitation are tolled on the date:

(1) a claim for money is filed or deposited with the clerk; or

(2) suit is brought against the personal representative of an estate with respect to a claim of the estate that is not required to be presented to the representative.

Derived from Probate Code § 299.

Added by Acts 2009, 81st Leg., ch. 680, § 1, eff. Jan. 1, 2014.

Subchapter B. Action on Claims

Statutes in Context
§ 355.051

A personal representative in a dependent administration has three options once a creditor presents a claim.

1. Accept. The personal representative may accept the claim which means that the personal representative agrees that the creditor's claim is valid. It does not mean that the claim will actually get paid; the claim merely goes in the stack of valid claims to be paid according to the priority rules set forth in the Code.

2. Reject. The personal representative may reject the claim, that is, indicate that the personal representative will not pay the claim. The creditor in a dependent (but not independent) administration must then bring suit within 90 days of the rejection or else the claim is barred. See § 355.064. See also *Statutes in Context* to § 403.051.

3. Do Nothing. If the personal representative takes no action with respect to the claim within 30 days, the claim is deemed rejected. See § 355.052. This then triggers the running of the creditor's obligation in a dependent administration to bring suit within 90 days under § 355.064.

This section does not apply to independent administrations. See *Bunting v. Pearson*, 430 S.W.2d 470 (Tex. 1968).

§ 355.051. Allowance or Rejection of Claim

A personal representative of an estate shall, not later than the 30th day after the date an authenticated claim against the estate is presented to the representative, or deposited with the clerk as provided under Section 355.002, endorse on the claim, attach to the claim, or file with the clerk a memorandum signed by the representative stating:

(1) the date the claim was presented or deposited; and

(2) whether the representative allows or rejects the claim, or if the representative allows or rejects a part of the claim, the portion the representative allows or rejects.

Derived from Probate Code § 309.

Added by Acts 2009, 81st Leg., ch. 680, § 1, eff. Jan. 1, 2014.

Statutes in Context
§ 355.052

Section 355.052 does not apply to independent administrations. See *Bunting v. Pearson*, 430 S.W.2d 470 (Tex. 1968).

---

§ 355.052. Failure to Timely Allow or Reject Claim

The failure of a personal representative to timely allow or reject a claim under Section 355.051 constitutes a rejection of the claim. If the claim is established by suit after that rejection:

(1) the costs shall be taxed against the representative, individually; or

(2) the representative may be removed on the written complaint of any person interested in the claim after personal service of citation, hearing, and proof, as in other cases of removal.

Derived from Probate Code § 310.

Added by Acts 2009, 81st Leg., ch. 680, § 1, eff. Jan. 1, 2014.

§ 355.053. Claim Entered on Claim Docket

After a claim against an estate has been presented to the personal representative and allowed or rejected, wholly or partly, by the representative, the claim must be filed with the county clerk of the proper county. The clerk shall enter the claim on the claim docket.

Derived from Probate Code § 311.

Added by Acts 2009, 81st Leg., ch. 680, § 1, eff. Jan. 1, 2014.

§ 355.054. Contest of Claim

(a) A person interested in an estate may, at any time before the court has acted on a claim, appear and object in writing to the approval of the claim or any part of the claim.

(b) If a person objects under Subsection (a):

(1) the parties are entitled to process for witnesses; and

(2) the court shall hear evidence and render judgment as in ordinary suits.

Derived from Probate Code § 312(a).

Added by Acts 2009, 81st Leg., ch. 680, § 1, eff. Jan. 1, 2014.

§ 355.055. Court's Action on Claim

The court shall:

(1) act on each claim that has been allowed and entered on the claim docket for a period of 10 days either approving the claim wholly or partly or disapproving the claim; and

(2) concurrently classify the claim.

Derived from Probate Code § 312(b).

Added by Acts 2009, 81st Leg., ch. 680, § 1, eff. Jan. 1, 2014.

§ 355.056. Hearing on Certain Claims

(a) If a claim is properly authenticated and allowed but the court is not satisfied that the claim is just, the court shall:

(1) examine the claimant and the personal representative under oath; and

(2) hear other evidence necessary to determine the issue.

(b) If after conducting the examination and hearing the evidence under Subsection (a) the court is not convinced that the claim is just, the court shall disapprove the claim.

Derived from Probate Code § 312(c).

Added by Acts 2009, 81st Leg., ch. 680, § 1, eff. Jan. 1, 2014.

§ 355.057. Court Order Regarding Action on Claim

(a) The court acting on a claim shall state the exact action taken on the claim, whether the claim is approved or disapproved, or approved in part and disapproved in part, and the classification of the claim by endorsing on or attaching to the claim a written memorandum that is dated and officially signed.

(b) An order under Subsection (a) has the effect of a final judgment.

Derived from Probate Code § 312(d).

Added by Acts 2009, 81st Leg., ch. 680, § 1, eff. Jan. 1, 2014.

§ 355.058. Appeal of Court's Action on Claim

A claimant or any person interested in an estate who is dissatisfied with the court's action on a claim may appeal the action to the court of appeals in the manner other judgments of the county court in probate matters are appealed.

Derived from Probate Code § 312(e).

Added by Acts 2009, 81st Leg., ch. 680, § 1, eff. Jan. 1, 2014.

§ 355.059. Allowance and Approval Prohibited Without Affidavit

A personal representative of an estate may not allow, and the court may not approve, a claim for money against the estate unless the claim is supported by an affidavit that meets the applicable requirements of Sections 355.004(a) and 355.005.

Derived from Probate Code § 301.

Added by Acts 2009, 81st Leg., ch. 680, § 1, eff. Jan. 1, 2014.

§ 355.060. Unsecured Claims Barred Under Certain Circumstances

If a personal representative gives a notice permitted by Section 308.054 to an unsecured creditor for money and the creditor's claim is not presented before the 121st day after the date of receipt of the notice, the claim is barred.

Derived from Probate Code § 298(a).

Added by Acts 2009, 81st Leg., ch. 680, § 1, eff. Jan. 1, 2014. Amended by Acts 2013, 83rd Leg., ch. 1136, § 45, eff. Jan. 1, 2014.

§ 355.061. Allowing Barred Claim Prohibited: Court Disapproval

(a) A personal representative may not allow a claim for money against a decedent or the decedent's estate if a suit on the claim is barred:

(1) under Section 355.060, 355.064, or 355.201(b); or

(2) by an applicable general statute of limitation.

(b) A claim for money that is allowed by the personal representative shall be disapproved if the court is satisfied that the claim is barred, including because the limitation has run.

Derived from Probate Code § 298(b).

Added by Acts 2009, 81st Leg., ch. 680, § 1, eff. Jan. 1, 2014.

§ 355.062. Certain Actions on Claims With Lost or Destroyed Evidence Void

(a) Before a claim the evidence for which is lost or destroyed is approved, the claim must be proved by disinterested testimony taken in open court or by oral or written deposition.

(b) The allowance or approval of a claim the evidence for which is lost or destroyed is void if the claim is:

(1) allowed or approved without the affidavit under Section 355.006; or

(2) approved without satisfactory proof.

Derived from Probate Code § 303.

Added by Acts 2009, 81st Leg., ch. 680, § 1, eff. Jan. 1, 2014.

§ 355.063. Claims Not Allowed After Order for Partition and Distribution

After an order for final partition and distribution of an estate has been made:

(1) a claim for money against the estate may not be allowed by a personal representative;

(2) a suit may not be commenced against the representative on a claim for money against the estate; and

(3) the owner of any claim that is not barred by the laws of limitation has a right of action on the claim against the heirs, devisees, or creditors of the estate, limited to the value of the property received by those heirs, devisees, or creditors in distributions from the estate.

Derived from Probate Code § 318.

Added by Acts 2009, 81st Leg., ch. 680, § 1, eff. Jan. 1, 2014.

Statutes in Context
§ 355.064

Section 355.064 does not apply to independent administrations. See *Bunting v. Pearson*, 430 S.W.2d 470 (Tex. 1968).

§ 355.064. Suit on Rejected Claim

(a) A claim or part of a claim that has been rejected by the personal representative is barred unless not later than the 90th day after the date of rejection the claimant commences suit on the claim in the court of original probate jurisdiction in which the estate is pending.

(b) In a suit commenced on the rejected claim, the memorandum endorsed on or attached to the claim, or any other memorandum of rejection filed with respect to the claim, is taken to be true without further proof unless denied under oath.

Derived from Probate Code § 313.

Added by Acts 2009, 81st Leg., ch. 680, § 1, eff. Jan. 1, 2014.

Statutes in Context
§ 355.065

A claim for money must first be presented and rejected before the creditor may sue on the claim. However, this requirement does not apply to a claim which is not "for money" such as an unliquidated tort claim or a claim based on quantum meruit for services rendered.

§ 355.065. Presentment of Claim Prerequisite for Judgment

A judgment may not be rendered in favor of a claimant on a claim for money that has not been:

(1) legally presented to the personal representative of an estate; and

(2) wholly or partly rejected by the representative or disapproved by the court.

Derived from Probate Code § 314.

Added by Acts 2009, 81st Leg., ch. 680, § 1, eff. Jan. 1, 2014.

§ 355.066. Judgment in Suit on Rejected Claim

No execution may issue on a rejected claim or part of a claim that is established by suit. The judgment in the suit shall be:

(1) filed in the court in which the estate is pending;

(2) entered on the claim docket;

(3) classified by the court; and

(4) handled as if originally allowed and approved in due course of administration.

Derived from Probate Code § 313.

Added by Acts 2009, 81st Leg., ch. 680, § 1, eff. Jan. 1, 2014.

Subchapter C. Payment of Claims, Allowances, and Expenses

Statutes in Context
Chapter 355, Subchapter C

Sections 355.102 and 355.103 provide the priority order for the payment of claims. However, other factors may come into play in determining the payment order. Below is a priority order which attempts to combine the priority rules in a unified list.

1. Federal government claims, e.g., the federal tax lien. 31 U.S.C. § 3713(a). However, federal claims do not have priority over funeral expenses, expenses of administration, or the family allowance because the decedent did not owe those while alive. (Federal claims do have priority over expenses of last illness because those expenses were obligations of the decedent.) See Rev. Rul. 80-112, 1980-1 C.B. 306.

2. Secured creditor who has preferred debt and lien status vis-à-vis the collateral only. See § 355.151(a)(2).

3. Homestead (or the allowance in lieu thereof). See § 353.155.

4. Funeral expenses and expenses of last sickness up to a combined total of $15,000. See §§ 355.103(a)(1) and 355.102 (Class 1).

5. Exempt personal property. See § 353.155.

6. Family allowance. See §§ 353.104 and 355.103(a)(2).

7. Administration and related expenses. See §§ 355.103(a)(3) and 355.102 (Class 2).

8. Secured creditor who elected matured secured claim status vis-à-vis the collateral only. See § 355.102 (Class 3).

9. Child support, both arrearages and accelerated amounts under Family Code § 154.015. See § 355.102 (Class 4).

10. Certain Texas tax claims. See § 355.102 (Class 5).

11. Confinement claims. See § 355.102 (Class 6) and Government Code § 501.017.

12. State medical assistance payments. See § 355.102 (Class 7). For an explanation of the Texas Medicaid Estate Recovery Program, see http://www.dads.state.tx.us/news_info/publications/brochures/DADS121_merp.html.

13. Unsecured claims approved by the personal representative (may include deficiency amounts of secured claimants who elected matured secured claim status). See § 355.102 (Class 8).

14. Beneficiaries and heirs. See § 355.109 for the abatement order of testamentary gifts.

§ 355.101. Approval or Establishment of Claim Required for Payment

A claim or any part of a claim for money against an estate may not be paid until the claim or part of the claim has been approved by the court or established by the judgment of a court of competent jurisdiction.

Derived from Probate Code § 319.

Added by Acts 2009, 81st Leg., ch. 680, § 1, eff. Jan. 1, 2014.

§ 355.102. Claims Classification; Priority of Payment

(a) Claims against an estate shall be classified and have priority of payment as provided by this section.

(b) Class 1 claims are composed of funeral expenses and expenses of the decedent's last illness for a reasonable amount approved by the court, not to exceed a total of $15,000. Any excess shall be classified and paid as other unsecured claims.

(c) Class 2 claims are composed of expenses of administration, expenses incurred in preserving, safekeeping, and managing the estate, including fees and expenses awarded under Section 352.052, and unpaid expenses of administration awarded in a guardianship of the decedent.

(d) Class 3 claims are composed of each secured claim for money under Section 355.151(a)(1), including a tax lien, to the extent the claim can be paid out of the proceeds of the property subject to the mortgage or other lien. If more than one mortgage, lien, or security interest exists on the same property, the claims shall be paid in order of priority of the mortgage, lien, or security interest securing the debt.

(e) Class 4 claims are composed of claims:

(1) for the principal amount of and accrued interest on delinquent child support and child support arrearages that have been:

(A) confirmed as a [and reduced to money] judgment or a determination of arrearages by a court under Title 5, Family Code; or

(B) administratively[, as] determined by the Title IV-D agency, as defined by Section 101.033, Family Code, in a Title IV-D case, as defined by Section 101.034 [under Subchapter F, Chapter 157], Family Code;[,] and

(2) [claims] for unpaid child support obligations under Section 154.015, Family Code.

(f) Class 5 claims are composed of claims for taxes, penalties, and interest due under Title 2, Tax Code, Chapter 2153, Occupations Code, former Section 81.111, Natural Resources Code, the Municipal Sales and Use Tax Act (Chapter 321, Tax Code), Section 451.404, Transportation Code, or Subchapter I, Chapter 452, Transportation Code.

(g) Class 6 claims are composed of claims for the cost of confinement established by the Texas

Department of Criminal Justice under Section 501.017, Government Code.

(h) Class 7 claims are composed of claims for repayment of medical assistance payments made by the state under Chapter 32, Human Resources Code, to or for the benefit of the decedent.

(i) Class 8 claims are composed of any other claims not described by Subsections (b)-(h).

Derived from Probate Code § 322.

Added by Acts 2009, 81st Leg., ch. 680, § 1, eff. Jan. 1, 2014. Subsec. (g) amended by Acts 2011, 82nd Leg., ch. 90, § 8.015, eff. Jan. 1, 2014. Subsec. (e) amended by Acts 2015, 84ᵗʰ Leg., ch. 859, § 1, eff. Sept. 1, 2015. Subsec. (f) amended by Acts 2015, 84ᵗʰ Leg., ch. 470, § 2, eff. Sept. 1, 2015.

§ 355.103. Priority of Certain Payments

When a personal representative has estate funds in the representative's possession, the representative shall pay in the following order:

(1) funeral expenses and expenses of the decedent's last illness, in an amount not to exceed $15,000;

(2) allowances made to the decedent's surviving spouse and children, or to either the surviving spouse or children;

(3) expenses of administration and expenses incurred in preserving, safekeeping, and managing the estate; and

(4) other claims against the estate in the order of the claims' classifications.

Derived from Probate Code § 320(a).

Added by Acts 2009, 81st Leg., ch. 680, § 1, eff. Jan. 1, 2014.

§ 355.104. Payment of Proceeds from Sale of Property Securing Debt

(a) If a personal representative has the proceeds of a sale made to satisfy a mortgage, lien, or security interest, and the proceeds or any part of the proceeds are not required for the payment of any debts against the estate that have a preference over the mortgage, lien, or security interest, the representative shall pay the proceeds to any holder of a mortgage, lien, or security interest. If there is more than one mortgage, lien, or security interest against the property, the representative shall pay the proceeds to the holders of the mortgages, liens, or security interests in the order of priority of the holders' mortgages, liens, or security interests.

(b) A holder of a mortgage, lien, or security interest, on proof of a personal representative's failure to pay proceeds under this section, may obtain an order from the court directing the payment to be made.

Derived from Probate Code § 320(b).

Added by Acts 2009, 81st Leg., ch. 680, § 1, eff. Jan. 1, 2014.

§ 355.105. Claimant's Petition for Allowance and Payment of Claim

A claimant whose claim has not been paid may:

(1) petition the court for determination of the claim at any time before the claim is barred by an applicable statute of limitations; and

(2) procure on due proof an order for the claim's allowance and payment from the estate.

Derived from Probate Code § 320(c).

Added by Acts 2009, 81st Leg., ch. 680, § 1, eff. Jan. 1, 2014.

§ 355.106. Order for Payment of Claim Obtained by Personal Representative

After the sixth month after the date letters testamentary or of administration are granted, the court may order a personal representative to pay any claim that is allowed and approved on application by the representative stating that the representative has no actual knowledge of any outstanding enforceable claim against the estate other than the claims already approved and classified by the court.

Derived from Probate Code § 320(d).

Added by Acts 2009, 81st Leg., ch. 680, § 1, eff. Jan. 1, 2014.

§ 355.107. Order for Payment of Claim Obtained by Creditor

(a) At any time after the first anniversary of the date letters testamentary are granted for an estate, a creditor of the estate whose claim or part of a claim has been approved by the court or established by suit may obtain an order directing that payment of the claim or part of the claim be made on written application and proof, except as provided by Subsection (b), showing that the estate has sufficient available funds.

(b) If the estate does not have available funds to pay a claim or part of a claim described by Subsection (a) and waiting for the estate to receive funds from other sources would unreasonably delay the payment, the court shall order the sale of estate property sufficient to make the payment.

(c) The personal representative of the estate must first be cited on a written application under Subsection (a) to appear and show cause why the order should not be made.

Derived from Probate Code § 326.

Added by Acts 2009, 81st Leg., ch. 680, § 1, eff. Jan. 1, 2014.

§ 355.108. Payment When Assets Insufficient to Pay Claims of Same Class

(a) If there are insufficient assets to pay all claims of the same class, other than secured claims for money, the claims in that class shall be paid pro rata, as directed by the court, and in the order directed.

(b) A personal representative may not be allowed to pay a claim under Subsection (a) other than with the pro rata amount of the estate funds that have come into the representative's possession, regardless of whether the estate is solvent or insolvent.

Derived from Probate Code § 321.

Added by Acts 2009, 81st Leg., ch. 680, § 1, eff. Jan. 1, 2014.

Statutes in Context
§ 355.109

A testator may attempt to give away more property in the testator's will than the testator is actually able to give. This could occur because the testator misjudged the value of the testator's estate. Just because a testator leaves a $500,000 legacy in the testator's will does not mean the testator actually has that money to give. The testator may also not have accounted for all of the testator's debts, including funeral and burial costs and expenses of last illness. In most situations, the claims of creditors have priority over assertions to property by beneficiaries.

Abatement is the reduction or elimination of a testamentary gift to pay an obligation of the estate or a testamentary gift of a higher priority. The abatement order is set forth in § 355.109.

---

§ 355.109. Abatement of Bequests

(a) Except as provided by Subsections (b), (c), and (d), a decedent's property is liable for debts and expenses of administration other than estate taxes, and bequests abate in the following order:

(1) property not disposed of by will, but passing by intestacy;

(2) personal property of the residuary estate;

(3) real property of the residuary estate;

(4) general bequests of personal property;

(5) general devises of real property;

(6) specific bequests of personal property; and

(7) specific devises of real property.

(b) This section does not affect the requirements for payment of a claim of a secured creditor who elects to have the claim continued as a preferred debt and lien against specific property under Subchapter D.

(c) A decedent's intent expressed in a will controls over the abatement of bequests provided by this section.

(d) This section does not apply to the payment of estate taxes under Subchapter A, Chapter 124.

Derived from Probate Code § 322B.

Added by Acts 2009, 81st Leg., ch. 680, § 1, eff. Jan. 1, 2014.

§ 355.110. Allocation of Funeral Expenses

A personal representative paying a claim for funeral expenses and for items incident to the funeral, such as a tombstone, grave marker, crypt, or burial plot:

(1) shall charge all of the claim to the decedent's estate; and

(2) may not charge any part of the claim to the community share of a surviving spouse.

Derived from Probate Code § 320A.

Added by Acts 2009, 81st Leg., ch. 680, § 1, eff. Jan. 1, 2014.

§ 355.111. Payment of Court Costs Relating to Claim

All costs incurred in the probate court with respect to a claim shall be taxed as follows:

(1) if the claim is allowed and approved, the estate shall pay the costs;

(2) if the claim is allowed but disapproved, the claimant shall pay the costs;

(3) if the claim is rejected but established by suit, the estate shall pay the costs;

(4) if the claim is rejected and not established by suit, the claimant shall pay the costs, except as provided by Section 355.052; and

(5) if the claim is rejected in part and the claimant fails, in a suit to establish the claim, to recover a judgment for a greater amount than was allowed or approved for the claim, the claimant shall pay all costs in the suit.

Derived from Probate Code § 315.

Added by Acts 2009, 81st Leg., ch. 680, § 1, eff. Jan. 1, 2014.

§ 355.112. Joint Obligation for Payment of Certain Debts

On the death of a person jointly bound with one or more other persons for the payment of a debt or for any other purpose, the decedent's estate shall be charged by virtue of the obligation in the same manner as if the obligors had been bound severally as well as jointly.

Derived from Probate Code § 323.

Added by Acts 2009, 81st Leg., ch. 680, § 1, eff. Jan. 1, 2014.

§ 355.113. Liability for Nonpayment of Claim

(a) A person or claimant, except the state treasury, entitled to payment from an estate of money the court orders to be paid is authorized to have execution issued against the estate property for the amount due, with interest and costs, if:

(1) the personal representative fails to pay the money on demand;

(2) estate funds are available to make the payment; and

(3) the person or claimant makes an affidavit of the demand for payment and the representative's failure to pay.

(b) The court may cite the personal representative and the sureties on the representative's bond to show cause why the representative and sureties should not be held liable under Subsection (a) for the debt, interest, costs, and damages:

(1) on return of the execution not satisfied; or

(2) on the affidavit of demand and failure to pay under Subsection (a).

(c) On the return of citation served under Subsection (b), the court shall render judgment against the cited personal representative and sureties, in favor of the claim holder, if good cause why the representative and sureties should not be held liable is not shown. The judgment must be for:

(1) the amount previously ordered to be paid or established by suit that remains unpaid, together with interest and costs; and

(2) damages on the amount neglected to be paid at the rate of five percent per month for each month, or fraction of a month, that the payment was neglected to be paid after demand was made.

(d) Damages ordered under Subsection (c)(2) may be collected in any court of competent jurisdiction.

Derived from Probate Code § 328.

Added by Acts 2009, 81st Leg., ch. 680, § 1, eff. Jan. 1, 2014.

Subchapter D. Presentment and Payment of Secured Claims for Money

Statutes in Context
Chapter 355, Subchapter D

A secured creditor must determine how the creditor wants the claim handled. The creditor must make this election by the later of (a) 4 months after the receipt of notice or (b) 6 months after letters are issued. See § 355.152

1. Preferred Debt and Lien. If the creditor elects preferred debt and lien status, the creditor receives top priority over the collateral. However, if the value of the collateral is less than the debt, the creditor will not have a right to recover the deficiency from the estate. In other words, the creditor gives up the right to pursue the debtor's personal liability on the debt. See § 355.154. Preferred debt and lien status is presumed unless the creditor affirmatively elects otherwise. See § 355.152.

2. Matured Secured Claim. If the creditor elects matured secured claim status, the creditor retains the right to seek a deficiency if the value of the collateral is less than the amount owed. However, the creditor must subordinate the claim to (a) the first $15,000 of funeral and last illness expenses, (b) the family allowance, and (c) administration and other expenses. See § 355.153.

Because of the repeal of the common law doctrine of exoneration in 2005 by the Probate Code predecessor to Estates Code §§ 255.301–255.303, the Probate Code predecessor to § 355.153 was added to handle the situation where a secured creditor elects matured secured claim status. First, the personal representative is required to collect from the beneficiary the amount of the debt and pay that amount to the secured creditor. If there is more than one beneficiary of the encumbered property, each pays a pro rata share of the debt.

Second, if the personal representative is unable to collect enough money to pay off the debt, then the property is sold. The proceeds of the sale are first used to pay the debt and any expenses associated with the sale. If there is a surplus, it will be divided pro rata among the beneficiaries of the specific gift. If there is a deficiency, the creditor has an unsecured claim for that amount.

§ 355.151. Option to Treat Claim as Matured Secured Claim or Preferred Debt and Lien

(a) If a secured claim for money against an estate is presented, the claimant shall specify in the claim, in addition to all other matters required to be specified in the claim, whether the claimant desires to have the claim:

(1) allowed and approved as a matured secured claim to be paid in due course of administration, in which case the claim shall be paid in that manner if allowed and approved; or

(2) allowed, approved, and fixed as a preferred debt and lien against the specific property securing the indebtedness and paid according to the terms of the contract that secured the lien, in which case the claim shall be so allowed and approved if it is a valid lien.

(b) Notwithstanding Subsection (a)(2), the personal representative may pay a claim that the claimant desired to have allowed, approved, and fixed as a preferred debt and lien as described by Subsection (a)(2) before maturity if that payment is in the best interest of the estate.

Derived from Probate Code § 306(a).

Added by Acts 2009, 81st Leg., ch. 680, § 1, eff. Jan. 1, 2014.

§ 355.152. Period for Specifying Treatment of Secured Claim

(a) A secured creditor may present the creditor's claim for money and shall specify within the later of six months after the date letters testamentary or of administration are granted, or four months after the date notice required to be given under Section 308.053 is received, whether the claim is to be allowed and approved under Section 355.151(a)(1) or (2).

(b) A secured claim for money that is not presented within the period prescribed by Subsection (a) or that is presented without specifying how the claim is to be paid under Section 355.151 shall be treated as a claim to be paid in accordance with Section 355.151(a)(2).

Derived from Probate Code § 306(b).

Added by Acts 2009, 81st Leg., ch. 680, § 1, eff. Jan. 1, 2014.

§ 355.153. Payment of Matured Secured Claim

(a) A claim allowed and approved as a matured secured claim under Section 355.151(a)(1) shall be paid in due course of administration, and the secured creditor is not entitled to exercise any other remedy in a manner that prevents the preferential payment of claims and allowances described by Sections 355.103(1), (2), and (3).

(b) If a claim is allowed and approved as a matured secured claim under Section 355.151(a)(1) for a debt that would otherwise pass with the property securing the debt to one or more devisees in accordance with Section 255.301, the personal representative shall:

(1) collect from the devisees the amount of the debt; and

(2) pay that amount to the claimant in satisfaction of the claim.

(c) Each devisee's share of the debt under Subsection (b) is an amount equal to a fraction representing the devisee's ownership interest in the property securing the debt, multiplied by the amount of the debt.

(d) If the personal representative is unable to collect from the devisees an amount sufficient to pay the debt under Subsection (b), the representative shall, subject to Chapter 356, sell the property securing the debt. The representative shall:

(1) use the sale proceeds to pay the debt and any expenses associated with the sale; and

(2) distribute the remaining sale proceeds to each devisee in an amount equal to a fraction representing the devisee's ownership interest in the property, multiplied by the amount of the remaining sale proceeds.

(e) If the sale proceeds under Subsection (d) are insufficient to pay the debt and any expenses associated with the sale, the difference between the sale proceeds and the sum of the amount of the debt and the expenses associated with the sale shall be paid in the manner prescribed by Subsection (a).

Derived from Probate Code §§ 306(c), (c-1).

Added by Acts 2009, 81st Leg., ch. 680, § 1, eff. Jan. 1, 2014.

§ 355.154. Preferred Debt and Lien

When a claim for a debt is allowed and approved under Section 355.151(a)(2):

(1) a further claim for the debt may not be made against other estate assets;

(2) the debt thereafter remains a preferred lien against the property securing the debt; and

(3) the property remains security for the debt in any distribution or sale of the property before final maturity and payment of the debt.

Derived from Probate Code § 306(d).

Added by Acts 2009, 81st Leg., ch. 680, § 1, eff. Jan. 1, 2014.

§ 355.155. Payment of Maturities on Preferred Debt and Lien

(a) If property securing a debt for which a claim is allowed, approved, and fixed under Section 355.151(a)(2) is not sold or distributed within six months from the date letters testamentary or of administration are granted, the personal representative of the estate shall:

(1) promptly pay all maturities that have accrued on the debt according to the terms of the debt; and

(2) perform all the terms of any contract securing the debt.

(b) If the personal representative defaults in payment or performance under Subsection (a), on application of the claim holder, the court shall:

(1) require the sale of the property subject to the unmatured part of the debt and apply the proceeds of the sale to the liquidation of the maturities;

(2) require the sale of the property free of the lien and apply the proceeds to the payment of the whole debt; or

(3) authorize foreclosure by the claim holder as provided by this subchapter.

Derived from Probate Code § 306(e).

Added by Acts 2009, 81st Leg., ch. 680, § 1, eff. Jan. 1, 2014.

Statutes in Context
§ 355.1551

This section, added by the 2015 Legislature, provides that if a creditor in a dependent administration elects or defaults to preferred debt and lien status, and decides to take possession or sell the collateral prior to the maturity of the debt, the creditor must do so within a reasonable time. If the creditor does not, the court may order the property sold free of the debt and the proceeds used to pay the debt. This will assist the estate in obtaining any surplus value the collateral may have over the debt owed.

§ 355.1551. Claim Holder Duty to Possess or Sell Within Reasonable Time

(a) A claim holder of a claim allowed and approved under Section 355.151(a)(2) who elects to take possession or sell the property securing the debt before final maturity in satisfaction of the claim holder's claim must do so within a reasonable time, as determined by the court.

(b) If the claim holder fails to take possession or sell secured property within a reasonable time under Subsection (a), on application by the personal representative, the court may require the sale of the property free of the lien and apply the proceeds to the payment of the whole debt.

(c) This section does not apply to an estate administered as an independent administration under Subtitle I.

New.

Added by Acts 2015, 84ᵗʰ Leg., ch. 995, § 39, eff. Sept. 1, 2015.

§ 355.156. Affidavit Required for Foreclosure

An application by a claim holder under Section 355.155(b)(3) to foreclose the claim holder's mortgage, lien, or security interest on property securing a claim allowed, approved, and fixed under Section 355.151(a)(2) must be supported by the claim holder's affidavit that:

(1) describes the property or part of the property to be sold by foreclosure;

(2) describes the amounts of the claim holder's outstanding debt;

(3) describes the maturities that have accrued on the debt according to the terms of the debt;

(4) describes any other debts secured by a mortgage, lien, or security interest against the property that are known by the claim holder;

(5) contains a statement that the claim holder has no knowledge of the existence of any debt secured by the property other than those described by the application; and

(6) requests permission for the claim holder to foreclose the claim holder's mortgage, lien, or security interest.

Derived from Probate Code § 306(f).

Added by Acts 2009, 81st Leg., ch. 680, § 1, eff. Jan. 1, 2014.

§ 355.157. Citation on Application

(a) The clerk shall issue citation on the filing of an application by:

(1) personal service to:

(A) the personal representative; and

(B) any person described by the application as having other debts secured by a mortgage, lien, or security interest against the property; and

(2) posting to any other person interested in the estate.

(b) A citation issued under Subsection (a) must require the person cited to appear and show cause why foreclosure should or should not be permitted.

Derived from Probate Code § 306(g).

Added by Acts 2009, 81st Leg., ch. 680, § 1, eff. Jan. 1, 2014.

§ 355.158. Hearing on Application

(a) The clerk shall immediately notify the judge when an application is filed. The judge shall schedule in writing a date for a hearing on the application.

(b) The judge may, by entry on the docket or otherwise, continue a hearing on an application for a reasonable time to allow an interested person to obtain an appraisal or other evidence concerning the fair market value of the property that is the subject of the application. If the interested person requests an unreasonable time for a continuance, the interested person must show good cause for the continuance.

(c) If the court finds at the hearing that there is a default in payment of maturities that have accrued on a debt described by Section 355.155(a) or performance under the contract securing the debt, the court shall:

(1) require the sale of the property subject to the unmatured part of the debt and apply the proceeds of the sale to the liquidation of the maturities;

(2) require the sale of the property free of the lien and apply the proceeds to the payment of the whole debt; or

(3) authorize foreclosure by the claim holder as provided by Section 355.156.

(d) A person interested in the estate may appeal an order issued under Subsection (c)(3).

Derived from Probate Code §§ 306(h), (i)(1), (j).

Added by Acts 2009, 81st Leg., ch. 680, § 1, eff. Jan. 1, 2014.

§ 355.159. Manner of Foreclosure; Minimum Price

(a) When the court grants a claim holder the right of foreclosure at a hearing under Section 355.158, the court shall authorize the claim holder to foreclose the claim holder's mortgage, lien, or security interest:

(1) in accordance with the provisions of the document creating the mortgage, lien, or security interest; or

(2) in any other manner allowed by law.

(b) Based on the evidence presented at the hearing, the court may set a minimum price for the property to be sold by foreclosure that does not exceed the fair market value of the property. If the court sets a minimum price, the property may not be sold at the foreclosure sale for a lower price.

Derived from Probate Code § 306(i)(2).

Added by Acts 2009, 81st Leg., ch. 680, § 1, eff. Jan. 1, 2014.

§ 355.160. Unsuccessful Foreclosure; Subsequent Application

If property that is the subject of a foreclosure sale authorized and conducted under this subchapter is not sold because no bid at the sale met the minimum price set by the court, the claim holder may file a subsequent application for foreclosure under Section 355.155(b)(3). The court may eliminate or modify the minimum price requirement and grant permission for another foreclosure sale.

Derived from Probate Code § 306(k).

Added by Acts 2009, 81st Leg., ch. 680, § 1, eff. Jan. 1, 2014.

Subchapter E. Claims Involving Personal Representatives

Statutes in Context
§ 355.201

Section 355.201 provides special rules for claims which a personal representative has against the estate the personal representative is administering.

§ 355.201. Claim by Personal Representative

(a) The provisions of this chapter regarding the presentment of claims against a decedent's estate may not be construed to apply to any claim of a personal representative against the decedent.

(b) A personal representative holding a claim against the decedent shall file the claim in the court granting the letters testamentary or of administration, verified by affidavit as required in other cases, within six months after the date the representative qualifies, or the claim is barred.

(c) A claim by a personal representative that has been filed with the court within the required period shall be entered on the claim docket and acted on by the court in the same manner as in other cases.

(d) A personal representative may appeal a judgment of the court acting on a claim under this section as in other cases.

(e) The previous provisions regarding the presentment of claims may not be construed to apply to a claim:

(1) of any heir or devisee who claims in that capacity;

(2) that accrues against the estate after the granting of letters testamentary or of administration and for which the personal representative has contracted; or

(3) for delinquent ad valorem taxes against a decedent's estate that is being administered in probate in:

(A) a county other than the county in which the taxes were imposed; or

(B) the same county in which the taxes were imposed, if the probate proceedings have been pending for more than four years.

Derived from Probate Code § 317.

Added by Acts 2009, 81st Leg., ch. 680, § 1, eff. Jan. 1, 2014.

§ 355.202. Claims Against Personal Representatives

(a) The naming of an executor in a will does not extinguish a just claim that the decedent had against the person named as executor.

(b) If a personal representative is indebted to the decedent, the representative shall account for the debt in the same manner as if the debt were cash in the representative's possession.

(c) Notwithstanding Subsection (b), a personal representative is required to account for the debt only from the date the debt becomes due if the debt was not due at the time the representative received letters testamentary or of administration.

Derived from Probate Code § 316.

Added by Acts 2009, 81st Leg., ch. 680, § 1, eff. Jan. 1, 2014.

§ 355.203. Purchase of Claim by Personal Representative Prohibited

(a) It is unlawful, and cause for removal, for a personal representative, whether acting under appointment by will or court orders, to purchase a claim against the estate the representative represents for the representative's own use or any other purpose.

(b) On written complaint by a person interested in the estate and on satisfactory proof of a violation of Subsection (a), the court after citation and hearing:

(1) shall enter an order canceling the claim described by Subsection (a); and

(2) may remove the personal representative who is found to have violated Subsection (a).

(c) No part of a claim canceled under Subsection (b) may be paid out of the estate.

Derived from Probate Code § 324.

Added by Acts 2009, 81st Leg., ch. 680, § 1, eff. Jan. 1, 2014.

Chapter 356. Sale of Estate Property

Subchapter A. General Provisions

Subchapter B. Certain Estate Property Required to be Sold

Subchapter C. Sale of Personal Property

Subchapter D. Sale of Livestock

Chapter 356. Sale of Estate Property

Statutes in Context
Chapter 356

Chapter 356 provides extensive (endless) guidance on how a personal representative sells estate property. The personal representative must ask the court for permission to sell, the court sets a hearing, citation is given to the interested parties, a hearing is conducted, the court authorizes the sale, the personal representative sells the property, the personal representative reports the sale to the court, and then the court approves the sale.

However, if the testator authorized the executor to sell estate property in the will, no court action is necessary. See § 356.002. Accordingly, it is extremely common for a will to grant the executor the power to sell.

The 2007 Legislature made it easier for the dependent personal representative to sell real estate if there is no opposition. See § 356.255.

Subchapter A. General Provisions

§ 356.001. Court Order Authorizing Sale

(a) Except as provided by this chapter, estate property may not be sold without a court order authorizing the sale.

(b) Except as otherwise specially provided by this chapter, the court may order estate property to be sold for cash or on credit, at public auction or privately, as the court considers most advantageous to the estate.

Derived from Probate Code § 331.

Added by Acts 2009, 81st Leg., ch. 680, § 1, eff. Jan. 1, 2014.

§ 356.002. Sale Authorized by Will

(a) Subject to Subsection (b), if a will authorizes the executor to sell the testator's property:

(1) a court order is not required to authorize the executor to sell the property; and

(2) the executor may sell the property:

(A) at public auction or privately as the executor considers to be in the best interest of the estate; and

(B) for cash or on credit terms determined by the executor.

(b) Any particular directions in the testator's will regarding the sale of estate property shall be followed unless the directions have been annulled or suspended by court order.

Derived from Probate Code § 332.

Added by Acts 2009, 81st Leg., ch. 680, § 1, eff. Jan. 1, 2014.

Subchapter B. Certain Estate Property Required to be Sold

§ 356.051. Sale of Certain Personal Property Required

(a) After approval of the inventory, appraisement, and list of claims, the personal representative of an estate promptly shall apply for a court order to sell, at public auction or privately, for cash or on credit for a term not to exceed six months, all estate property that is liable to perish, waste, or deteriorate in value, or that will be an expense or disadvantage to the estate if kept.

(b) The following may not be included in a sale under Subsection (a):

(1) property exempt from forced sale;

(2) property that is the subject of a specific legacy; and

(3) personal property necessary to carry on a farm, ranch, factory, or other business that is thought best to operate.

(c) In determining whether to order the sale of an asset under Subsection (a), the court shall consider:

(1) the personal representative's duty to take care of and manage the estate in the manner a person of ordinary prudence, discretion, and intelligence would manage the person's own affairs; and

(2) whether the asset constitutes an asset that a trustee is authorized to invest under Subchapter F, Chapter 113, Property Code, or Chapter 117, Property Code.

Derived from Probate Code § 333.

Added by Acts 2009, 81st Leg., ch. 680, § 1, eff. Jan. 1, 2014.

Subchapter C. Sale of Personal Property

§ 356.101. Order for Sale

(a) Except as provided by Subsection (b), on the application of the personal representative of an estate or any interested person, the court may order the sale of any estate personal property not required to be sold by Section 356.051, including livestock or growing or harvested crops, if the court finds that the sale of the property is in the estate's best interest to pay, from the proceeds of the sale:

(1) expenses of administration;

(2) the decedent's funeral expenses;

(3) expenses of the decedent's last illness;

(4) allowances; or

(5) claims against the estate.

(b) The court may not order under this section the sale of exempt property or property that is the subject of a specific legacy.

Derived from Probate Code § 334.

Added by Acts 2009, 81st Leg., ch. 680, § 1, eff. Jan. 1, 2014.

§ 356.102. Requirements for Application and Order

To the extent possible, an application and order for the sale of personal property under Section 356.101 must conform to the requirements under Subchapter F for an application and order for the sale of real estate.

Derived from Probate Code § 334.

Added by Acts 2009, 81st Leg., ch. 680, § 1, eff. Jan. 1, 2014.

§ 356.103. Sale at Public Auction

Unless the court directs otherwise, before estate personal property is sold at public auction, notice must be:

(1) issued by the personal representative of the estate; and

(2) posted in the manner notice is posted for original proceedings in probate.

Derived from Probate Code § 336.

Added by Acts 2009, 81st Leg., ch. 680, § 1, eff. Jan. 1, 2014.

§ 356.104. Sale on Credit

(a) Estate personal property may not be sold on credit at public auction for a term of more than six months from the date of sale.

(b) Estate personal property purchased on credit at public auction may not be delivered to the purchaser until the purchaser gives a note for the amount due, with good and solvent personal security. The requirement that security be provided may be waived if the property will not be delivered until the note, with interest, has been paid.

Derived from Probate Code § 337.

Added by Acts 2009, 81st Leg., ch. 680, § 1, eff. Jan. 1, 2014.

§ 356.105. Report; Evidence of Title

(a) A sale of estate personal property shall be reported to the court. The laws regulating the confirmation or disapproval of a sale of real estate apply to the sale, except that a conveyance is not required.

(b) The court's order confirming the sale of estate personal property:

(1) vests the right and title of the intestate's estate in the purchaser who has complied with the terms of the sale; and

(2) is prima facie evidence that all requirements of the law in making the sale have been met.

(c) The personal representative of an estate, on request, may issue a bill of sale without warranty to the purchaser of estate personal property as evidence of title. The purchaser shall pay for the issuance of the bill of sale.

Derived from Probate Code § 339.

Added by Acts 2009, 81st Leg., ch. 680, § 1, eff. Jan. 1, 2014.

Subchapter D. Sale of Livestock

§ 356.151. Authority for Sale

(a) A personal representative of an estate who has possession of livestock and who considers selling the livestock to be necessary or to the estate's advantage may, in addition to any other method provided by law for the sale of personal property, obtain authority from the court in which the estate is pending to sell the livestock through:

(1) a bonded livestock commission merchant; or

(2) a bonded livestock auction commission merchant.

(b) The court may authorize the sale of livestock in the manner described by Subsection (a) on a written and sworn application by the personal representative or any person interested in the estate.

Derived from Probate Code § 335.

Added by Acts 2009, 81st Leg., ch. 680, § 1, eff. Jan. 1, 2014.

§ 356.152. Contents of Application; Hearing

(a) An application under Section 356.151 must:

(1) describe the livestock sought to be sold; and

(2) state why granting the application is necessary or to the estate's advantage.

(b) The court:

(1) shall promptly consider the application; and

(2) may hear evidence for or against the application, with or without notice, as the facts warrant.

Derived from Probate Code § 335.

Added by Acts 2009, 81st Leg., ch. 680, § 1, eff. Jan. 1, 2014.

§ 356.153. Grant of Application

If the court grants an application for the sale of livestock, the court shall:

(1) enter an order to that effect; and

(2) authorize delivery of the livestock to a commission merchant described by Section 356.151 for sale in the regular course of business.

Derived from Probate Code § 335.

Added by Acts 2009, 81st Leg., ch. 680, § 1, eff. Jan. 1, 2014.

§ 356.154. Report; Passage of Title

The personal representative of the estate shall promptly report to the court a sale of livestock authorized under this subchapter, supported by a verified copy of the commission merchant's account of the sale. A court order of confirmation is not required to pass title to the purchaser of the livestock.

Derived from Probate Code § 335.

Added by Acts 2009, 81st Leg., ch. 680, § 1, eff. Jan. 1, 2014.

§ 356.155. Commission Merchant Fees

A commission merchant shall be paid the merchant's usual and customary charges, not to exceed five percent of the sale price, for the sale of livestock authorized under this subchapter.

Derived from Probate Code § 335.

Added by Acts 2009, 81st Leg., ch. 680, § 1, eff. Jan. 1, 2014.

Subchapter E. Sale of Mortgaged Property

§ 356.201. Application for Sale of Mortgaged Property

A creditor holding a claim that is secured by a valid mortgage or other lien and that has been allowed and approved or established by suit may, by filing a written application, obtain from the court in which the estate is pending an order requiring that the property securing the lien, or as much of the property as is necessary to satisfy the claim, be sold.

Derived from Probate Code § 338.

Added by Acts 2009, 81st Leg., ch. 680, § 1, eff. Jan. 1, 2014.

§ 356.202. Citation

On the filing of an application under Section 356.201, the clerk shall issue a citation requiring the personal representative of the estate to appear and show cause why the application should not be granted.

Derived from Probate Code § 338.

Added by Acts 2009, 81st Leg., ch. 680, § 1, eff. Jan. 1, 2014.

§ 356.203. Order

The court may order the lien securing the claim of a creditor who files an application under Section 356.201 to be discharged out of general estate assets or refinanced if the discharge or refinance of the lien appears to the court to be advisable. Otherwise, the court shall grant the application and order that the property securing the lien be sold at public or private sale, as considered best, as in an ordinary sale of real estate.

Derived from Probate Code § 338.

Added by Acts 2009, 81st Leg., ch. 680, § 1, eff. Jan. 1, 2014.

Subchapter F. Sale of Real Property: Application and Order for Sale

§ 356.251. Application for Order of Sale

An application may be made to the court for an order to sell estate property if the sale appears necessary or advisable to:

(1) pay:

(A) expenses of administration;

(B) the decedent's funeral expenses;

(C) expenses of the decedent's last illness;

(D) allowances; and

(E) claims against the estate; or

(2) dispose of an interest in estate real property if selling the interest is considered in the estate's best interest.

Derived from Probate Code § 341.

Added by Acts 2009, 81st Leg., ch. 680, § 1, eff. Jan. 1, 2014.

§ 356.252. Contents of Application

An application for the sale of real estate must:

(1) be in writing;

(2) describe:

(A) the real estate sought to be sold; or

(B) the interest in or part of the real estate sought to be sold; and

(3) be accompanied by an exhibit, verified by an affidavit, showing:

(A) the estate's condition fully and in detail;

(B) the charges and claims that have been approved or established by suit or that have been rejected and may yet be established;

(C) the amount of each claim described by Paragraph (B);

(D) the estate property remaining on hand that is liable for the payment of the claims described by Paragraph (B); and

(E) any other facts showing the necessity for or advisability of the sale.

Derived from Probate Code § 342.

Added by Acts 2009, 81st Leg., ch. 680, § 1, eff. Jan. 1, 2014.

§ 356.253. Citation

On the filing of an application and exhibit described by Section 356.252, the clerk shall issue a citation to all persons interested in the estate. The citation must:

(1) describe the real estate or the interest in or part of the real estate sought to be sold;

(2) inform the interested persons of the right under Section 356.254 to file an opposition to the sale during the period prescribed by the court in the citation; and

(3) be served by posting.

Derived from Probate Code § 344.

Added by Acts 2009, 81st Leg., ch. 680, § 1, eff. Jan. 1, 2014.

§ 356.254. Opposition to Sale

During the period prescribed in a citation issued under Section 356.253, any person interested in the estate may file:

(1) a written opposition to the sale; or

(2) an application for the sale of other estate property.

Derived from Probate Code § 345.

Added by Acts 2009, 81st Leg., ch. 680, § 1, eff. Jan. 1, 2014.

§ 356.255. Hearing on Application and Any Opposition

(a) The clerk of the court in which an application for an order of sale is filed shall immediately call to the judge's attention any opposition to the sale that is filed during the period prescribed in the citation issued under Section 356.253. The court shall hold a hearing on the application if an opposition to the sale is filed during the period prescribed in the citation.

(b) A hearing on an application for an order of sale is not required under this section if no opposition to the application is filed during the period prescribed in the citation. The court may determine that a hearing on the application is necessary even if no opposition is filed during that period.

(c) If the court orders a hearing under Subsection (a) or (b), the court shall designate in writing a date and time for the hearing on the application and any opposition, together with the evidence pertaining to the application and any opposition. The clerk shall issue a notice of the date and time of the hearing to the applicant and to each person who files an opposition to the sale, if applicable.

(d) The judge, by entries on the docket, may continue a hearing held under this section from time to time until the judge is satisfied concerning the application.

Derived from Probate Code § 345A.

Added by Acts 2009, 81st Leg., ch. 680, § 1, eff. Jan. 1, 2014.

§ 356.256. Order

(a) The court shall order the sale of the estate property described in an application for an order of sale if the court is satisfied that the sale is necessary or advisable. Otherwise, the court may deny the application and, if the court considers it best, may order the sale of other estate property the sale of which would be more advantageous to the estate.

(b) An order for the sale of real estate under this section must specify:

(1) the property to be sold, including a description that identifies that property;

(2) whether the property is to be sold at public auction or private sale and, if at public auction, the time and place of the sale;

(3) the necessity or advisability of, and the purpose of, the sale;

(4) except in a case in which a personal representative was not required to give a general bond, that the court, after examining the general bond given by the representative, finds that:

(A) the bond is sufficient as required by law; or

(B) the bond is insufficient;

(5) if the court finds that the general bond is insufficient under Subdivision (4)(B), the amount of the necessary or increased bond, as applicable;

(6) that the sale is to be made and the report returned in accordance with law; and

(7) the terms of the sale.

Derived from Probate Code § 346.

Added by Acts 2009, 81st Leg., ch. 680, § 1, eff. Jan. 1, 2014.

§ 356.257. Sale for Payment of Debts

Estate real property selected to be sold for the payment of expenses or claims must be that property the sale of which the court considers most advantageous to the estate.

Derived from Probate Code § 340.

Added by Acts 2009, 81st Leg., ch. 680, § 1, eff. Jan. 1, 2014.

Subchapter G. Sale of Real Estate: Terms of Sale

§ 356.301. Permissible Terms

Real estate of an estate may be sold for cash, part cash and part credit, or the equity in land securing an indebtedness may be sold subject to the indebtedness, or with an assumption of the indebtedness, at public or private sale, as appears to the court to be in the estate's best interest.

Derived from Probate Code § 348(a).

Added by Acts 2009, 81st Leg., ch. 680, § 1, eff. Jan. 1, 2014.

§ 356.302. Sale on Credit

(a) The cash payment for real estate of an estate sold partly on credit may not be less than one-fifth of the purchase price. The purchaser shall execute a note for the deferred payments, payable in monthly, quarterly, semiannual, or annual installments, in amounts that appear to the court to be in the estate's best interest. The note must bear interest from the date at a rate of not less than four percent per year, payable as provided in the note.

(b) A note executed by a purchaser under Subsection (a) must be secured by a vendor's lien retained in the deed and in the note on the property sold, and be further secured by a deed of trust on the property sold, with the usual provisions for foreclosure and sale on failure to make the payments provided in the deed and the note.

(c) At the election of the holder of a note executed by a purchaser under Subsection (a), default in the payment of principal, interest, or any part of the principal or interest, when due matures the entire debt.

Derived from Probate Code § 348(a).

Added by Acts 2009, 81st Leg., ch. 680, § 1, eff. Jan. 1, 2014.

Subchapter H. Reconveyance of Real Estate Following Foreclosure

§ 356.351. Applicability of Subchapter

This subchapter applies only to real estate owned by an estate as a result of the foreclosure of a vendor's lien or mortgage belonging to the estate:

(1) by a judicial sale;

(2) by a foreclosure suit;

(3) through a sale under a deed of trust; or

(4) by acceptance of a deed in cancellation of a lien or mortgage owned by the estate.

Derived from Probate Code § 348(b).

Added by Acts 2009, 81st Leg., ch. 680, § 1, eff. Jan. 1, 2014.

§ 356.352. Application and Order for Reconveyance

On proper application and proof, the court may dispense with the requirements for a credit sale prescribed by Section 356.302 and order the reconveyance of foreclosed real estate to the former mortgage debtor or former owner if it appears to the court that:

(1) an application to redeem the real estate has been made by the former owner to a corporation or agency created by an Act of the United States Congress or of this state in connection with legislation for the relief of owners of mortgaged or encumbered homes, farms, ranches, or other real estate; and

(2) owning bonds of one of those federal or state corporations or agencies instead of the real estate would be in the estate's best interest.

Derived from Probate Code § 348(b).

Added by Acts 2009, 81st Leg., ch. 680, § 1, eff. Jan. 1, 2014.

§ 356.353. Exchange for Bonds

(a) If a court orders the reconveyance of foreclosed real estate as provided by Section 356.352, vendor's lien notes shall be reserved for the total amount of the indebtedness due or for the total amount of bonds that the corporation or agency to which the application to redeem the real estate was submitted as described by Section 356.352(1) is allowed to advance under the corporation's or agency's rules or regulations.

(b) On obtaining the order for reconveyance, it shall be proper for the personal representative of the estate to indorse and assign the reserved vendor's lien notes over to any one of the corporations or agencies described by Section 356.352(1) in exchange for bonds of that corporation or agency.

Derived from Probate Code § 348(b).

Added by Acts 2009, 81st Leg., ch. 680, § 1, eff. Jan. 1, 2014.

Subchapter I. Sale of Real Estate: Public Sale

§ 356.401. Required Notice

(a) Except as otherwise provided by Section 356.403(c), the personal representative of an estate shall advertise a public sale of real estate of the estate by a notice published in the county in which the estate is pending, as provided by this title for publication of notices or citations. The notice must:
(1) include a reference to the order of sale;
(2) include the time, place, and required terms of sale; and
(3) briefly describe the real estate to be sold.

(b) The notice required by Subsection (a) is not required to contain field notes, but if the real estate to be sold is rural property, the notice must include:
(1) the name of the original survey of the real estate;
(2) the number of acres comprising the real estate;
(3) the location of the real estate in the county; and
(4) any name by which the real estate is generally known.

Derived from Probate Code § 349(a).

Added by Acts 2009, 81st Leg., ch. 680, § 1, eff. Jan. 1, 2014.

§ 356.402. Method of Sale

A public sale of real estate of an estate shall be made at public auction to the highest bidder.

Derived from Probate Code § 349(b).

Added by Acts 2009, 81st Leg., ch. 680, § 1, eff. Jan. 1, 2014.

§ 356.403. Time and Place of Sale

(a) Except as provided by Subsection (c), a public sale of real estate of an estate shall be made at:
(1) the courthouse door in the county in which the proceedings are pending; or
(2) another place in that county at which sales of real estate are specifically authorized to be made.

(b) The sale must occur between 10 a.m. and 4 p.m. on the first Tuesday of the month after publication of notice has been completed.

(c) If the court considers it advisable, the court may order the sale to be made in the county in which the real estate is located, in which event notice shall be published both in that county and in the county in which the proceedings are pending.

Derived from Probate Code § 349(c).

Added by Acts 2009, 81st Leg., ch. 680, § 1, eff. Jan. 1, 2014.

§ 356.404. Continuance of Sale

(a) A public sale of real estate of an estate that is not completed on the day advertised may be continued from day to day by an oral public announcement of the continuance made at the conclusion of the sale each day.

(b) A continued sale must occur within the hours prescribed by Section 356.403(b).

(c) The continuance of a sale under this section shall be shown in the report of the sale made to the court.

Derived from Probate Code § 349(d).

Added by Acts 2009, 81st Leg., ch. 680, § 1, eff. Jan. 1, 2014.

§ 356.405. Failure of Bidder to Comply

(a) If a person bids off real estate of the estate offered for sale at public auction and fails to comply with the terms of the sale, the property shall be readvertised and sold without any further order.

(b) The person defaulting on a bid as described by Subsection (a) is liable for payment to the personal representative of the estate, for the estate's benefit, of:
(1) 10 percent of the amount of the bid; and
(2) the amount of any deficiency in price on the second sale.

(c) The personal representative may recover the amounts under Subsection (b) by suit in any court in the county in which the sale was made that has jurisdiction of the amount claimed.

Derived from Probate Code § 349(e).

Added by Acts 2009, 81st Leg., ch. 680, § 1, eff. Jan. 1,

2014.

Subchapter J. Sale of Real Estate: Private Sale

§ 356.451. Manner of Sale

A private sale of real estate of the estate shall be made in the manner the court directs in the order of sale. Unless the court directs otherwise, additional advertising, notice, or citation concerning the sale is not required.

Derived from Probate Code § 350.

Added by Acts 2009, 81st Leg., ch. 680, § 1, eff. Jan. 1, 2014.

Subchapter K. Sale of Easement or Right-of-Way

§ 356.501. Authorization

Easements and rights-of-way on, under, and over the land of an estate that is being administered under court order may be sold and conveyed regardless of whether the sale proceeds are required to pay charges or claims against the estate or for other lawful purposes.

Derived from Probate Code § 351.

Added by Acts 2009, 81st Leg., ch. 680, § 1, eff. Jan. 1, 2014.

§ 356.502. Procedure

The procedure for the sale of an easement or right-of-way authorized under Section 356.501 is the same as the procedure provided by law for a sale of estate real property at private sale.

Derived from Probate Code § 351.

Added by Acts 2009, 81st Leg., ch. 680, § 1, eff. Jan. 1, 2014.

Subchapter L. Confirmation of Sale of Real Property and Transfer of Title

§ 356.551. Report

A sale of estate real property shall be reported to the court ordering the sale not later than the 30th day after the date the sale is made. The report must:

(1) be sworn to, in writing, and filed with the clerk;

(2) include:

(A) the date of the order of sale;

(B) a description of the property sold;

(C) the time and place of sale;

(D) the purchaser's name;

(E) the amount for which each parcel of property or interest in property was sold;

(F) the terms of the sale;

(G) whether the sale was made at public auction or privately; and

(H) whether the purchaser is ready to comply with the order of sale; and

(3) be noted on the probate docket.

Derived from Probate Code § 353.

Added by Acts 2009, 81st Leg., ch. 680, § 1, eff. Jan. 1, 2014.

§ 356.552. Action of Court on Report of Sale

After the expiration of five days from the date a report of sale is filed under Section 356.551, the court shall:

(1) inquire into the manner in which the sale was made;

(2) hear evidence in support of or against the report; and

(3) determine the sufficiency or insufficiency of the personal representative's general bond, if any has been required and given.

Derived from Probate Code § 355.

Added by Acts 2009, 81st Leg., ch. 680, § 1, eff. Jan. 1, 2014.

§ 356.553. Confirmation of Sale when Bond Not Required

If the personal representative of an estate is not required by this title to give a general bond, the court may confirm the sale of estate real property in the manner provided by Section 356.556(a) if the court finds that the sale is satisfactory and made in accordance with law.

Derived from Probate Code § 354.

Added by Acts 2009, 81st Leg., ch. 680, § 1, eff. Jan. 1, 2014.

§ 356.554. Sufficiency of Bond

(a) If the personal representative of an estate is required by this title to give a general bond, before the court confirms any sale of real estate, the court shall determine whether the bond is sufficient to protect the estate after the sale proceeds are received.

(b) If the court finds that the general bond is sufficient, the court may confirm the sale as provided by Section 356.556(a).

(c) If the court finds that the general bond is insufficient, the court may not confirm the sale until the general bond is increased to the amount required by the court, or an additional bond is given, and approved by the court.

(d) An increase in the amount of the general bond, or the additional bond, as applicable under Subsection (c), must be equal to the sum of:

(1) the amount for which the real estate is sold; and

(2) any additional amount the court finds necessary and sets for the estate's protection.

Derived from Probate Code § 354.

Added by Acts 2009, 81st Leg., ch. 680, § 1, eff. Jan. 1, 2014.

§ 356.555. Increased or Additional Bond Not Required

Notwithstanding Sections 356.554(c) and (d), if the real estate sold is encumbered by a lien to secure a claim against the estate and is sold to the owner or holder of the secured claim in full payment, liquidation, and satisfaction of the claim, an increased general bond or additional bond may not be required except for the amount of any cash paid to the personal representative of the estate in excess of the amount necessary to pay, liquidate, and satisfy the claim in full.

Derived from Probate Code § 354.

Added by Acts 2009, 81st Leg., ch. 680, § 1, eff. Jan. 1, 2014.

§ 356.556. Confirmation or Disapproval Order

(a) If the court is satisfied that a sale reported under Section 356.551 was for a fair price, properly made, and in conformity with law, and the court has approved any increased or additional bond that the court found necessary to protect the estate, the court shall enter an order:

(1) confirming the sale;

(2) showing conformity with this chapter;

(3) detailing the terms of the sale; and

(4) authorizing the personal representative to convey the property on the purchaser's compliance with the terms of the sale.

(b) If the court is not satisfied that the sale was for a fair price, properly made, and in conformity with law, the court shall enter an order setting aside the sale and ordering a new sale to be made, if necessary.

(c) The court's action in confirming or disapproving a report of a sale has the effect of a final judgment. Any person interested in the estate or in the sale is entitled to have an order entered under this section reviewed as in other final judgments in probate proceedings.

Derived from Probate Code § 355.

Added by Acts 2009, 81st Leg., ch. 680, § 1, eff. Jan. 1, 2014.

§ 356.557. Deed

Real estate of an estate that is sold shall be conveyed by a proper deed that refers to and identifies the court order confirming the sale. The deed:

(1) vests in the purchaser all right and title of the estate to, and all interest of the estate in, the property; and

(2) is prima facie evidence that the sale has met all applicable requirements of the law.

Derived from Probate Code § 356.

Added by Acts 2009, 81st Leg., ch. 680, § 1, eff. Jan. 1, 2014.

§ 356.558. Delivery of Deed

(a) After the court has confirmed a sale and the purchaser has complied with the terms of the sale, the personal representative of the estate shall promptly execute and deliver to the purchaser a proper deed conveying the property.

(b) If the sale is made partly on credit:

(1) the vendor's lien securing one or more purchase money notes must be expressly retained in the deed and may not be waived; and

(2) before actual delivery of the deed to the purchaser, the purchaser shall execute and deliver to the personal representative of the estate one or more vendor's lien notes, with or without personal sureties as ordered by the court, and a deed of trust or mortgage on the property as additional security for the payment of the notes.

(c) On completion of the transaction, the personal representative of the estate shall promptly file or cause to be filed and recorded the deed of trust or mortgage in the appropriate records in the county in which the land is located.

Derived from Probate Code § 357.

Added by Acts 2009, 81st Leg., ch. 680, § 1, eff. Jan. 1, 2014.

§ 356.559. Damages; Removal

(a) If the personal representative of an estate neglects to comply with Section 356.558, including to file the deed of trust securing a lien in the proper county, the representative and the sureties on the representative's bond shall, after complaint and citation, be held liable for the use of the estate and for all damages resulting from the representative's neglect, and the court may remove the representative.

(b) Damages under this section may be recovered in any court of competent jurisdiction.

Derived from Probate Code § 358.

Added by Acts 2009, 81st Leg., ch. 680, § 1, eff. Jan. 1, 2014.

Subchapter M. Procedure on Failure to Apply for Sale

§ 356.601. Failure to Apply for Sale

If the personal representative of an estate neglects to apply for an order to sell sufficient estate property to pay charges and claims against the estate that have been allowed and approved or established by suit, any interested person, on written application, may have the representative cited to appear and make a full exhibit of the estate's condition and show cause why a sale of the property should not be ordered.

Derived from Probate Code § 347.

Added by Acts 2009, 81st Leg., ch. 680, § 1, eff. Jan. 1, 2014.

§ 356.602. Court Order

On hearing an application under Section 356.601, if the court is satisfied that a sale of estate property is necessary or advisable to satisfy the charges and claims described by Section 356.601, the court shall enter an order of sale as provided by Section 356.256.

Derived from Probate Code § 347.

Added by Acts 2009, 81st Leg., ch. 680, § 1, eff. Jan. 1, 2014.

Subchapter N. Purchase of Property by Personal Representative

Statutes in Context
Chapter 356, Subchapter N

Self-dealing is generally not allowed, that is, the personal representative may not purchase estate property. However, the personal represent-ative may purchase if (1) the testator granted express permission in the will, or (2) the court finds that it is in the best interest of the estate to permit the personal representative to purchase estate property after giving notice the distributees and creditors.

§ 356.651. General Prohibition on Purchase

Except as otherwise provided by this subchapter, the personal representative of an estate may not purchase, directly or indirectly, any estate property sold by the representative or any co-representative of the estate.

Derived from Probate Code § 352(a).

Added by Acts 2009, 81st Leg., ch. 680, § 1, eff. Jan. 1, 2014.

§ 356.652. Exception: Authorization in Will

A personal representative of an estate may purchase estate property if the representative was appointed in a will that:

(1) has been admitted to probate; and

(2) expressly authorizes the sale.

Derived from Probate Code § 352(b).

Added by Acts 2009, 81st Leg., ch. 680, § 1, eff. Jan. 1, 2014.

§ 356.653. Exception: Executory Contract

A personal representative of a decedent's estate may purchase estate property in compliance with the terms of a written executory contract signed by the decedent, including:

(1) a contract for deed;

(2) an earnest money contract;

(3) a buy/sell agreement; and

(4) a stock purchase or redemption agreement.

Derived from Probate Code § 352(c).

Added by Acts 2009, 81st Leg., ch. 680, § 1, eff. Jan. 1, 2014.

§ 356.654. Exception: Best Interest of Estate

(a) Subject to Subsection (b), the personal representative of an estate, including an independent administrator, may purchase estate property on the court's determination that the sale is in the estate's best interest.

(b) Before purchasing estate property as authorized by Subsection (a), the personal representative shall give notice of the purchase by certified mail, return receipt requested, unless the court requires another form of notice, to:

(1) each distributee of the estate; and

(2) each creditor whose claim remains unsettled after being presented within six months of the date letters testamentary or of administration are originally granted.

(c) The court may require additional notice or allow for the waiver of the notice required for a sale made under this section.

Derived from Probate Code § 352(d).

Added by Acts 2009, 81st Leg., ch. 680, § 1, eff. Jan. 1, 2014.

§ 356.655. Purchase in Violation of Subchapter

(a) If a personal representative of an estate purchases estate property in violation of this subchapter, any person interested in the estate may file a written complaint with the court in which the proceedings are pending.

(b) On service of citation on the personal representative on a complaint filed under Subsection (a) and after hearing and proof, the court shall:

(1) declare the sale void;

(2) set aside the sale; and

(3) order the reconveyance of the property to the estate.

(c) The court shall adjudge against the personal representative all costs of the sale, protest, and suit found necessary.

Derived from Probate Code § 352(e).

Added by Acts 2009, 81st Leg., ch. 680, § 1, eff. Jan. 1, 2014.

Chapter 357. Renting Estate Property

Subchapter A. Rental and Return of Estate Property

Subchapter B. Report on Rented Estate Property

§ 357.051. Reports Concerning Rentals
§ 357.052. Court Action on Report

Chapter 357. Renting Estate Property

Statutes in Context
Chapter 357

Chapter 357 provides guidance to the personal representative who wishes to rent estate property. Short-term leases are permitted without court order under § 357.001 while court permission is needed for leases more than one year in length. See § 357.002.

Subchapter A. Rental and Return of Estate Property

§ 357.001. Renting Estate Property Without Court Order

(a) The personal representative of an estate, without a court order, may rent any of the estate property for one year or less, at public auction or privately, as is considered to be in the best interest of the estate.

(b) On the sworn complaint of any person interested in the estate, the court shall require a personal representative who, without a court order, rents estate property to account to the estate for the reasonable value of the rent of the property, to be ascertained by the court on satisfactory evidence.

Derived from Probate Code §§ 359, 360.

Added by Acts 2009, 81st Leg., ch. 680, § 1, eff. Jan. 1, 2014.

§ 357.002. Renting Estate Property with Court Order

(a) The personal representative of an estate may, if the representative prefers, and shall, if the proposed rental period is more than one year, file a written application with the court setting forth the property the representative seeks to rent.

(b) If the court finds that granting an application filed under Subsection (a) is in the interest of the estate, the court shall grant the application and issue an order that:

(1) describes the property to be rented; and

(2) states whether the property will be rented at public auction or privately, whether for cash or on credit, and if on credit, the extent of the credit and the period for which the property may be rented.

(c) If, under Subsection (b), the court orders property to be rented at public auction, the court shall prescribe whether notice of the auction shall be published or posted.

Derived from Probate Code § 361.

Added by Acts 2009, 81st Leg., ch. 680, § 1, eff. Jan. 1, 2014. Subsec. (b) amended by Acts 2011, 82nd Leg., ch. 90, § 8.016, eff. Jan. 1, 2014.

§ 357.003. Estate Property Rented on Credit

Possession of estate property rented on credit may not be delivered until the renter executes and delivers to the personal representative a note with good personal security for the amount of the rent. If the property is delivered without the representative receiving the required security, the representative and the sureties on the representative's bond are liable for the full amount of the rent. When a rental is payable in installments, in advance of the period to which the installments relate, this section does not apply.

Derived from Probate Code § 363.

Added by Acts 2009, 81st Leg., ch. 680, § 1, eff. Jan. 1, 2014.

§ 357.004. Condition of Returned Estate Property

(a) Estate property that is rented, with or without a court order, must be returned to the estate's possession in as good a condition, except for reasonable wear and tear, as when the property was rented.

(b) The personal representative of an estate shall:

(1) ensure that rented estate property is returned in the condition required by Subsection (a);

(2) report to the court any damage to, or loss or destruction of, the property; and

(3) ask the court for the authority to take any necessary action.

(c) A personal representative who fails to act as required by this section and the sureties on the representative's bond are liable to the estate for any loss or damage suffered as a result of the representative's failure.

Derived from Probate Code § 364.

Added by Acts 2009, 81st Leg., ch. 680, § 1, eff. Jan. 1, 2014.

§ 357.005. Complaint for Failure to Rent

(a) Any person interested in an estate may:

(1) file a written and sworn complaint in the court in which the estate is pending; and

(2) have the personal representative cited to appear and show cause why the representative did not rent any estate property.

(b) The court, on hearing the complaint, shall issue an order that appears to be in the best interest of the estate.

Derived from Probate Code § 362.

Added by Acts 2009, 81st Leg., ch. 680, § 1, eff. Jan. 1, 2014.

Subchapter B. Report on Rented Estate Property

§ 357.051. Reports Concerning Rentals

(a) A personal representative of an estate who rents estate property with an appraised value of $3,000 or more shall, not later than the 30th day after the date the property is rented, file with the court a sworn and written report stating:

(1) the property rented and the property's appraised value;

(2) the date the property was rented and whether the rental occurred at public auction or privately;

(3) the name of each person renting the property;

(4) the rental amount; and

(5) whether the rental was for cash or on credit and, if on credit, the length of time, the terms, and the security received for the credit.

(b) A personal representative of an estate who rents estate property with an appraised value of less than $3,000 may report the rental in the next annual or final account that must be filed as required by law.

Derived from Probate Code § 365.

Added by Acts 2009, 81st Leg., ch. 680, § 1, eff. Jan. 1, 2014.

§ 357.052. Court Action on Report

(a) At any time after the fifth day after the date the report of renting is filed, the court shall:

(1) examine the report; and

(2) by order approve and confirm the report if found just and reasonable.

(b) If the court disapproves the report, the estate is not bound and the court may order another offering for rent of the property that is the subject of the report, in the same manner and subject to the provisions of this chapter.

(c) If the court approves the report and it later appears that, by reason of any fault of the personal representative, the property was not rented for the property's reasonable value, the court shall have the representative and the sureties on the representative's bond appear and show cause why the reasonable value of the rent of the property should not be adjudged against the representative.

Derived from Probate Code § 366.

Added by Acts 2009, 81st Leg., ch. 680, § 1, eff. Jan. 1, 2014.

Chapter 358. Matters Relating to Mineral Properties

Subchapter A. General Provisions

§ 358.001. Definitions

Subchapter B. Mineral Leases After Public Notice

§ 358.051. Authorization for Leasing of Minerals

Subchapter C. Mineral Leases at Private Sale

Subchapter D. Pooling or Unitization of Royalties or Minerals

Subchapter E. Special Ancillary Instruments that May Be Executed Without Court Order

Subchapter F. Procedure if Personal Representative of Estate Neglects to Apply for Authority

Chapter 358. Matters Relating to Mineral Properties

Statutes in Context
Chapter 358

Chapter 358 provides the personal representative with guidance for dealing with mineral interests of the decedent's estate.

Subchapter A. General Provisions

§ 358.001. Definitions

In this chapter:

(1) "Gas" includes all liquid hydrocarbons in the gaseous phase in the reservoir.

(2) "Land" and "interest in land" include minerals or an interest in minerals in place.

(3) "Mineral development" includes exploration for, whether by geophysical or other means, drilling for, mining for, development of, operations in connection with, production of, and saving of oil, other liquid hydrocarbons, gas, gaseous elements, sulphur, metals, and all other minerals, whether solid or otherwise.

(4) "Property" includes land, minerals in place, whether solid, liquid, or gaseous, and an interest of any kind in that property, including a royalty interest, owned by an estate.

Derived from Probate Code § 367(a).

Added by Acts 2009, 81st Leg., ch. 680, § 1, eff. Jan. 1, 2014.

Subchapter B. Mineral Leases After Public Notice

§ 358.051. Authorization for Leasing of Minerals

(a) The court in which probate proceedings on a decedent's estate are pending may authorize the personal representative of the estate, appointed and qualified under the laws of this state and acting solely under court orders, to make, execute, and deliver a lease, with or without a unitization clause or pooling provision, providing for the exploration for and development and production of oil, other liquid hydrocarbons, gas, metals and other solid minerals, and other minerals, or any of those minerals in place, belonging to the estate.

(b) A lease described by Subsection (a) must be made and entered into under and in conformity with this subchapter.

Derived from Probate Code §§ 367(b), (c).

Added by Acts 2009, 81st Leg., ch. 680, § 1, eff. Jan. 1, 2014.

§ 358.052. Lease Application

(a) The personal representative of an estate shall file with the county clerk of the county in which the probate proceeding is pending a written application, addressed to the court or the judge of the court, for authority to lease estate property for mineral exploration and development, with or without a pooling provision or unitization clause.

(b) The lease application must:

(1) describe the property fully by reference to the amount of acreage, the survey name or number, or the abstract number, or by another method adequately identifying the property and the property's location in the county in which the property is situated;

(2) specify the interest thought to be owned by the estate, if less than the whole, but requesting authority to include all of the interest owned by the estate, if that is the intention; and

(3) set out the reasons the estate property described in the application should be leased.

(c) The lease application is not required to set out or suggest:

(1) the name of any proposed lessee; or

(2) the terms, provisions, or form of any desired lease.

Derived from Probate Code § 367(c).

Added by Acts 2009, 81st Leg., ch. 680, § 1, eff. Jan. 1, 2014.

§ 358.053. Scheduling of Hearing on Application; Continuance

(a) Immediately after the filing of a lease application under Section 358.052, the county clerk shall call the filing of the application to the court's attention, and the judge shall promptly make and enter a brief order designating the time and place for hearing the application.

(b) If the hearing is not held at the time originally designated by the court or by a timely continuance order entered, the hearing shall be continued automatically without further notice to the same time on the following day, other than Sundays and holidays on which the county courthouse is officially closed, and from day to day until the lease application is finally acted on and disposed of by court order. Notice of an automatic continuance is not required.

Derived from Probate Code § 367(c).

Added by Acts 2009, 81st Leg., ch. 680, § 1, eff. Jan. 1, 2014.

§ 358.054. Notice of Hearing on Application

(a) At least 10 days before the date set for the hearing on a lease application filed under Section 358.052, excluding the date of notice and the date set for the hearing, the personal representative shall give notice of the hearing by:

(1) publishing the notice in one issue of a newspaper of general circulation in the county in which the proceeding is pending; or

(2) if there is no newspaper described by Subdivision (1), posting the notice or having the notice posted.

(b) If notice is published, the date of notice is the date printed on the newspaper.

(c) The notice must:

(1) be dated;

(2) be directed to all persons interested in the estate;

(3) state the date on which the lease application was filed;

(4) describe briefly the property sought to be leased, specifying the fractional interest sought to be leased if less than the entire interest in the tract or tracts identified; and

(5) state the time and place designated by the judge for the hearing.

Derived from Probate Code § 367(c).

Added by Acts 2009, 81st Leg., ch. 680, § 1, eff. Jan. 1, 2014.

§ 358.055. Requirements Regarding Order and Notice Mandatory

An order of the judge or court authorizing any act to be performed under a lease application filed under Section 358.052 is void in the absence of:

(1) a written order originally designating a time and place for hearing;

(2) a notice issued by the personal representative of the estate in compliance with the order described by Subdivision (1); and

(3) proof of the publication or posting of the notice as required under Section 358.054.

Derived from Probate Code § 367(c).

Added by Acts 2009, 81st Leg., ch. 680, § 1, eff. Jan. 1, 2014.

§ 358.056. Hearing on Application; Order

(a) At the time and place designated for the hearing under Section 358.053(a), or at the time to which the hearing is continued as provided by Section 358.053(b), the judge shall:

(1) hear a lease application filed under Section 358.052; and

(2) require proof as to the necessity or advisability of leasing for mineral development the property described in the application and the notice.

(b) The judge shall enter an order authorizing one or more leases affecting and covering the property or portions of property described in the application, with or without pooling provisions or unitization clauses, and with or without cash consideration if considered by the court to be in the best interest of the estate, if the judge is satisfied that:

(1) the application is in proper form;

(2) notice has been given in the manner and for the time required by law;

(3) proof of necessity or advisability of leasing is sufficient; and

(4) the application should be granted.

(c) The order must contain:

(1) the name of the lessee;

(2) any actual cash consideration to be paid by the lessee;

(3) a finding that the requirements of Subsection (b) have been satisfied; and

(4) one of the following findings:

(A) a finding that the personal representative is exempted by law from giving bond; or

(B) if the representative is not exempted by law from giving bond, a finding as to whether the representative's general bond on file is sufficient to protect the personal property on hand, including any cash bonus to be paid.

(d) If the court finds the general bond insufficient to meet the requirements of Subsection (c)(4)(B), the order must show the amount of increased or additional bond required to cover the deficiency.

(e) A complete exhibit copy, either written or printed, of each authorized lease must be set out in the order or attached to the order and incorporated by reference and made part of the order. The exhibit copy must show:

(1) the name of the lessee;

(2) the date of the lease;

(3) an adequate description of the property being leased;

(4) any delay rental to be paid to defer commencement of operations; and

(5) all other authorized terms and provisions.

(f) If the date of a lease does not appear in the exhibit copy of the lease or in the order, the date of the order is considered for all purposes to be the date of the lease.

(g) If the name or address of the depository bank for receiving rental is not shown in the exhibit copy of a lease, the estate's personal representative may insert that information, or cause that information to be inserted, in the lease at the time of the lease's execution or at any other time agreeable to the lessee or the lessee's successors or assignees.

Derived from Probate Code § 367(c).

Added by Acts 2009, 81st Leg., ch. 680, § 1, eff. Jan. 1, 2014.

§ 358.057. Making of Lease on Granting of Application

(a) If the court grants an application as provided by Section 358.056, the personal representative of the estate may make the lease or leases, as evidenced by the exhibit copies described by Section 358.056, in accordance with the order.

(b) The lease or leases must be made not later than the 30th day after the date of the order unless an extension is granted by the court on sworn application showing good cause.

(c) It is not necessary for the judge to make an order confirming the lease or leases.

Derived from Probate Code § 367(c).

Added by Acts 2009, 81st Leg., ch. 680, § 1, eff. Jan. 1, 2014.

§ 358.058. Bond Requirements

(a) Unless the personal representative of the estate is not required to give a general bond, a lease for which a cash consideration is required, although ordered, executed, and delivered, is not valid:

(1) unless the order authorizing the lease makes findings with respect to the general bond; and

(2) if the general bond has been found insufficient, unless and until:

(A) the bond has been increased or an additional bond given, as required by the order, with the sureties required by law; and

(B) the increased bond or additional bond has been approved by the judge and filed with the clerk of the court in which the proceedings are pending.

(b) If two or more leases of different land are authorized by the same order, the general bond must be increased, or additional bonds given, to cover all of the leases.

Derived from Probate Code § 367(c).

Added by Acts 2009, 81st Leg., ch. 680, § 1, eff. Jan. 1, 2014.

§ 358.059. Term of Lease Binding

(a) A lease executed and delivered in compliance with this subchapter is valid and binding on the property or interest in property owned by the estate and covered by the lease for the full term provided by the lease, subject only to the lease's terms and conditions, even if the primary term extends beyond the date the estate is closed in accordance with law.

(b) The authorized primary term of the lease may not exceed five years, subject to the lease terms and provisions extending the lease beyond the primary term by:

(1) paying production;

(2) bona fide drilling or reworking operations, whether in or on the same well or wells or an additional well or wells, without a cessation of operations of more than 60 consecutive days before production has been restored or obtained; or

(3) a shut-in gas well.

Derived from Probate Code § 367(c).

Added by Acts 2009, 81st Leg., ch. 680, § 1, eff. Jan. 1, 2014.

§ 358.060. Amendment of Lease Regarding Effect of Shut-In Gas Well

(a) An oil, gas, and mineral lease executed by a personal representative under the former Texas Probate Code or this code may be amended by an instrument that provides that a shut-in gas well on the land covered by the lease or on land pooled with all or part of the land covered by the lease continues the lease in effect after the lease's five-year primary term.

(b) The personal representative, with the approval of the court, shall execute the instrument according to the terms and conditions prescribed by the instrument.

Derived from Probate Code § 367(c).

Added by Acts 2009, 81st Leg., ch. 680, § 1, eff. Jan. 1, 2014.

Subchapter C. Mineral Leases at Private Sale

§ 358.101. Authorization for Leasing of Minerals at Private Sale

(a) Notwithstanding the mandatory requirements of Subchapter B for setting a time and place for hearing of a lease application filed under Section 358.052 and the issuance, service, and return of notice, the court may authorize the making of oil, gas, and mineral leases at private sale without public notice or advertising if, in the court's opinion, facts are set out in the application required by Subchapter B sufficient to show that it would be more advantageous to the estate that a lease be made privately and without compliance with those mandatory requirements.

(b) Leases authorized by this section may include pooling provisions or unitization clauses as in other cases.

Derived from Probate Code § 368(a).

Added by Acts 2009, 81st Leg., ch. 680, § 1, eff. Jan. 1, 2014.

§ 358.102. Action of Court if Public Advertising Not Required

(a) At any time after the fifth day and before the 11th day after the filing date of an application to lease at private sale and without an order setting the hearing time and place, the court shall:

(1) hear the application;

(2) inquire into the manner in which the proposed lease has been or will be made; and

(3) hear evidence for or against the application.

(b) If satisfied that the lease has been or will be made for a fair and sufficient consideration and on fair terms and has been or will be properly made in conformity with law, the court shall enter an order authorizing the execution of the lease without the necessity of advertising, notice, or citation. The order must comply in all other respects with the requirements essential to the validity of mineral leases as set out in Subchapter B, as if advertising or notice were required.

(c) The issuance of an order confirming a lease or leases made at private sale is not required, but such a lease is not valid until any increased or additional bond required by the court has been approved by the court and filed with the court clerk.

Derived from Probate Code § 368(b).

Added by Acts 2009, 81st Leg., ch. 680, § 1, eff. Jan. 1, 2014.

Subchapter D. Pooling or Unitization of Royalties or Minerals

§ 358.151. Authorization for Pooling or Unitization

(a) If an existing lease or leases on property owned by an estate being administered do not adequately provide for pooling or unitization, the court in which the proceedings are pending may, in the manner provided by this subchapter, authorize the commitment of royalty or mineral interests in oil, liquid hydrocarbons, gas, gaseous elements, and other minerals, or any one or more of them, owned by the estate, to agreements that provide for the operation of areas as a pool or unit for the exploration for, development of, and production of all of those minerals, if the court finds that:

(1) the pool or unit to which the agreement relates will be operated in a manner that protects correlative rights or prevents the physical or economic waste of oil, liquid hydrocarbons, gas, gaseous elements, or other minerals subject to the agreement; and

(2) it is in the best interest of the estate to execute the agreement.

(b) An agreement authorized under Subsection (a) may, among other things, provide that:

(1) operations incident to the drilling of or production from a well on any portion of a pool or unit shall be considered for all purposes to be the conduct of operations on or production from each separately owned tract in the pool or unit;

(2) any lease covering any part of the area committed to a pool or unit continues in effect in its entirety as long as:

(A) oil, gas, or other minerals subject to the agreement are produced in paying quantities from any part of the pooled or unitized area;

(B) operations are conducted as provided in the lease on any part of the pooled or unitized area; or

(C) there is a shut-in gas well on any part of the pooled or unitized area, if the presence of the shut-in gas well is a ground for continuation of the lease under the terms of the lease;

(3) the production allocated by the agreement to each tract included in a pool or unit shall, when produced, be considered for all purposes to have been produced from the tract by a well drilled on the tract;

(4) the royalties provided for on production from any tract or portion of a tract within the pool or unit shall be paid only on that portion of the production allocated to the tract in accordance with the agreement;

(5) the dry gas, before or after extraction of hydrocarbons, may be returned to a formation underlying any land or leases committed to the agreement, and that royalties are not required to be paid on the gas returned; and

(6) gas obtained from other sources or other land may be injected into a formation underlying any land or leases committed to the agreement, and that royalties are not required to be paid on the gas injected when the gas is produced from the unit.

Derived from Probate Code §§ 369(a), (b).

Added by Acts 2009, 81st Leg., ch. 680, § 1, eff. Jan. 1, 2014.

§ 358.152. Pooling or Unitization Application

(a) The personal representative of an estate shall file with the county clerk of the county in which the probate proceeding is pending a written application for authority to:

(1) enter into pooling or unitization agreements supplementing, amending, or otherwise relating to any existing lease or leases covering property owned by the estate; or

(2) commit royalties or other interests in minerals, whether or not subject to a lease, to a pooling or unitization agreement.

(b) The pooling or unitization application must also:

(1) sufficiently describe the property as required in an original lease application;

(2) describe briefly any lease or leases to which the interest of the estate is subject; and

(3) set out the reasons the proposed agreement concerning the property should be entered into.

(c) A copy of the proposed agreement must be attached to the application and made a part of the application by reference.

(d) The agreement may not be recorded in the judge's probate docket.

(e) Immediately after the pooling or unitization application is filed, the clerk shall call the application to the judge's attention.

Derived from Probate Code § 369(b).

Added by Acts 2009, 81st Leg., ch. 680, § 1, eff. Jan. 1, 2014. Subsec. (d) amended by Acts 2011, 82nd Leg., ch. 90, § 8.017, eff. Jan. 1, 2014.

§ 358.153. Notice Not Required

Notice by advertising, citation, or otherwise of the filing of a pooling or unitization application under Section 358.152 is not required.

Derived from Probate Code § 369(b).

Added by Acts 2009, 81st Leg., ch. 680, § 1, eff. Jan. 1, 2014.

§ 358.154. Hearing on Application

(a) The judge may hold a hearing on a pooling or unitization application filed under Section 358.152 at any time agreeable to the parties to the proposed agreement.

(b) The judge shall hear evidence and determine to the judge's satisfaction whether it is in the best interest of the estate that the proposed agreement be authorized.

(c) The hearing may be continued from day to day and from time to time as the court finds necessary.

Derived from Probate Code § 369(b).

Added by Acts 2009, 81st Leg., ch. 680, § 1, eff. Jan. 1, 2014.

§ 358.155. Action of Court and Contents of Order

(a) The court shall enter an order setting out the court's findings and authorizing execution of the proposed pooling or unitization agreement, with or without payment of cash consideration according to the agreement, if the court finds that:

(1) the pool or unit to which the agreement relates will be operated in a manner that protects correlative rights or prevents the physical or economic waste of oil, liquid hydrocarbons, gas, gaseous elements, or other minerals subject to the agreement;

(2) it is in the best interest of the estate that the agreement be executed; and

(3) the agreement conforms substantially with the permissible provisions of Section 358.151.

(b) If cash consideration is to be paid for the agreement, the court shall also make findings as to the necessity of increased or additional bond, as in the making of leases on payment of the cash bonus for the lease. Such an agreement is not valid until any required increased or additional bond has been approved by the judge and filed with the clerk.

(c) If the effective date of the agreement is not stipulated in the agreement, the effective date of the agreement is the date of the court's order.

Derived from Probate Code § 369(b).

Added by Acts 2009, 81st Leg., ch. 680, § 1, eff. Jan. 1, 2014.

Subchapter E. Special Ancillary Instruments that May be Executed Without Court Order

§ 358.201. Authorization for Execution of Agreements

As to any mineral lease or pooling or unitization agreement, executed on behalf of an estate before January 1, 1956, or on or after that date under the provisions of the former Texas Probate Code or this code, or executed by a former owner of land, minerals, or royalty affected by the lease or agreement, the personal representative of the estate being administered may, without further court order and without consideration, execute:

(1) division orders;

(2) transfer orders;

(3) instruments of correction;

(4) instruments designating depository banks for the receipt of delay rentals or shut-in gas well royalty to accrue or become payable under the terms of the lease; and

(5) similar instruments relating to the lease or agreement and the property covered by the lease or agreement.

Derived from Probate Code § 370.

Added by Acts 2009, 81st Leg., ch. 680, § 1, eff. Jan. 1,

2014.

Subchapter F. Procedure if Personal Representative of Estate Neglects to Apply for Authority

§ 358.251. Application to Show Cause

If the personal representative of an estate neglects to apply for authority to subject estate property to a lease for mineral development, pooling, or unitization, or to commit royalty or another interest in minerals to pooling or unitization, any person interested in the estate may, on written application filed with the county clerk, have the representative cited to show cause why it is not in the best interest of the estate to make such a lease or enter into such an agreement.

Derived from Probate Code § 371.

Added by Acts 2009, 81st Leg., ch. 680, § 1, eff. Jan. 1, 2014.

§ 358.252. Hearing on Application

(a) The county clerk shall immediately call the filing of an application under Section 358.251 to the attention of the judge of the court in which the probate proceedings are pending.

(b) The judge shall set a time and place for a hearing on the application, and the personal representative of the estate shall be cited to appear and show cause why the execution of a lease or agreement described by Section 358.251 should not be ordered.

Derived from Probate Code § 371.

Added by Acts 2009, 81st Leg., ch. 680, § 1, eff. Jan. 1, 2014.

§ 358.253. Order

On a hearing conducted under Section 358.252, if satisfied from the evidence that it would be in the best interest of the estate, the court shall enter an order requiring the personal representative promptly to file an application to subject the estate property to a lease for mineral development, with or without pooling or unitization provisions, or to commit royalty or other minerals to pooling or unitization, as appropriate.

Derived from Probate Code § 371.

Added by Acts 2009, 81st Leg., ch. 680, § 1, eff. Jan. 1, 2014.

§ 358.254. Procedure to be Followed After Entry of Order

After entry of an order under Section 358.253, the procedure prescribed with respect to an original lease application, or with respect to an original application for authority to commit royalty or minerals to pooling or unitization, whichever is appropriate, shall be followed.

Derived from Probate Code § 371.

Added by Acts 2009, 81st Leg., ch. 680, § 1, eff. Jan. 1, 2014.

Chapter 359. Annual Account and Other Exhibits and Reports

Subchapter A. Annual Account and Other Exhibits

Chapter 359. Annual Account and Other Exhibits and Reports

Statutes in Context
Chapter 359

Chapter 359 requires that the dependent personal representative prepare detailed accounts each year. The accounting must include all vouchers and receipts and it must be supported by a sworn affidavit.

Subchapter A. Annual Account and Other Exhibits

§ 359.001. Account of Estate Required

(a) On the expiration of 12 months from the date a personal representative qualifies and receives letters testamentary or of administration to administer a decedent's estate under court order, the representative shall file with the court an account consisting of a written exhibit made under oath that lists all claims against the estate presented to the representative during the period covered by the account. The exhibit must specify:

(1) the claims allowed by the representative;

(2) the claims paid by the representative;

(3) the claims rejected by the representative and the date the claims were rejected; and

(4) the claims for which a lawsuit has been filed and the status of that lawsuit.

(b) The account must:

(1) show all property that has come to the personal representative's knowledge or into the representative's possession that was not previously listed or inventoried as estate property;

(2) show any changes in estate property that have not been previously reported;

(3) provide a complete account of receipts and disbursements for the period covered by the account, including the source and nature of the receipts and disbursements, with separate listings for principal and income receipts;

(4) provide a complete, accurate, and detailed description of:

(A) the property being administered;

(B) the condition of the property and the use being made of the property; and

(C) if rented, the terms on which and the price for which the property was rented;

(5) show the cash balance on hand and the name and location of the depository where the balance is kept;

(6) show any other cash held in a savings account or other manner that was deposited subject to court order and the name and location of the depository for that cash;

(7) provide a detailed description of the personal property of the estate that shows how and where the property is held for safekeeping;

(8) provide a statement that during the period covered by the account all tax returns due have been filed and all taxes due and owing have been paid, including:

(A) a complete account of the amount of the taxes;

(B) the date the taxes were paid; and

(C) the governmental entity to which the taxes were paid;

(9) if on the filing of the account a tax return due to be filed or any taxes due to be paid are delinquent, provide the reasons for, and include a description of, the delinquency; and

(10) provide a statement that the representative has paid all the required bond premiums for the accounting period.

(c) For bonds, notes, and other securities, the description required by Subsection (b)(7) must include:

(1) the names of the obligor and obligee or, if payable to bearer, a statement that the bond, note, or other security is payable to bearer;

(2) the date of issue and maturity;

(3) the interest rate;

(4) the serial number or other identifying numbers;

(5) the manner in which the property is secured; and

(6) other information necessary to fully identify the bond, note, or other security.

Derived from Probate Code § 399(a).

Added by Acts 2009, 81st Leg., ch. 680, § 1, eff. Jan. 1, 2014.

§ 359.002. Annual Account Required Until Estate Closed

(a) Each personal representative of the estate of a decedent shall continue to file an annual account conforming to the essential requirements of Section 359.001 regarding changes in the estate assets occurring since the date the most recent previous account was filed.

(b) The annual account must be filed in a manner that allows the court or an interested person to ascertain the true condition of the estate, with respect to money, securities, and other property, by adding to the balances forwarded from the most recent previous account the amounts received during the period covered by the account and subtracting the disbursements made during that period.

(c) The description of property sufficiently described in an inventory or previous account may be made in the annual account by reference to that description.

Derived from Probate Code § 399(b).

Added by Acts 2009, 81st Leg., ch. 680, § 1, eff. Jan. 1, 2014.

§ 359.003. Supporting Vouchers and Other Documents Attached to Account

(a) The personal representative of an estate shall attach to each annual account:

(1) a voucher for each item of credit claimed in the account or, to support the item in the absence of the voucher, other evidence satisfactory to the court;

(2) an official letter from the bank or other depository where the estate money on hand is deposited that shows the amounts in general or special deposits; and

(3) proof of the existence and possession of:

(A) securities owned by the estate or shown by the account; and

(B) other assets held by a depository subject to court order.

(b) An original voucher submitted to the court may on application be returned to the personal representative after approval of the account.

(c) The court may require:

(1) additional evidence of the existence and custody of the securities and other personal property as the court considers proper; and

(2) the personal representative at any time to exhibit the securities and other personal property to the court or another person designated by the court

at the place where the securities and other personal property are held for safekeeping.

Derived from Probate Code § 399(c).

Added by Acts 2009, 81st Leg., ch. 680, § 1, eff. Jan. 1, 2014.

§ 359.004. Method of Proof for Securities and Other Assets

(a) The proof required by Section 359.003(a)(3) must be by:

(1) an official letter from the bank or other depository where the securities or other assets are held for safekeeping, and if the depository is the personal representative, the official letter must be signed by a representative of the depository other than the one verifying the account;

(2) a certificate of an authorized representative of a corporation that is surety on the personal representative's bonds;

(3) a certificate of the clerk or a deputy clerk of a court of record in this state; or

(4) an affidavit of any other reputable person designated by the court on request of the personal representative or other interested party.

(b) The certificate or affidavit described by Subsection (a) must:

(1) state that the affiant has examined the assets that the personal representative exhibited to the affiant as assets of the estate;

(2) describe the assets by reference to the account or in another manner that sufficiently identifies the assets exhibited; and

(3) state the time and the place the assets were exhibited.

(c) Instead of attaching a certificate or an affidavit, the personal representative may exhibit the securities to the judge, who shall endorse on the account, or include in the judge's order with respect to the account, a statement that the securities shown in the account as on hand were exhibited to the judge and that the securities were the same as those shown in the account, or note any variance.

(d) If the securities are exhibited at a location other than where the securities are deposited for safekeeping, that exhibit is at the personal representative's own expense and risk.

Derived from Probate Code § 399(c).

Added by Acts 2009, 81st Leg., ch. 680, § 1, eff. Jan. 1, 2014.

§ 359.005. Verification of Account

The personal representative shall attach to the annual account the representative's affidavit that the account contains a correct and complete statement of the matters to which it relates.

Derived from Probate Code § 399(d).

Added by Acts 2009, 81st Leg., ch. 680, § 1, eff. Jan. 1, 2014.

§ 359.006. Additional Accounts

(a) At any time after the expiration of 15 months from the date original letters testamentary or of administration are granted to an executor or administrator, an interested person may file a written complaint in the court in which the estate is pending to have the representative cited to appear and make a written exhibit under oath that sets forth fully, in connection with previous exhibits, the condition of the estate.

(b) If it appears to the court, from the exhibit or other evidence, that the executor or administrator has estate funds in the representative's possession that are subject to distribution among the creditors of the estate, the court shall order the funds to be paid out to the creditors in accordance with this title.

(c) A personal representative may voluntarily present to the court the exhibit described by Subsection (a). If the representative has any estate funds in the representative's possession that are subject to distribution among the creditors of the estate, the court shall issue an order similar to the order entered under Subsection (b).

Derived from Probate Code § 402.

Added by Acts 2009, 81st Leg., ch. 680, § 1, eff. Jan. 1, 2014.

Subchapter B. Action on Annual Account

§ 359.051. Filing and Consideration of Annual Account

(a) The personal representative of an estate shall file an annual account with the county clerk. The county clerk shall promptly note the filing on the judge's docket.

(b) At any time after the account has remained on file for 10 days following the date the account is filed, the judge shall consider the account and may continue the hearing on the account until fully advised on all account items.

(c) The court may not approve the account unless possession of cash, listed securities, or other assets held in safekeeping or on deposit under court order has been proven as required by law.

Derived from Probate Code §§ 401(a), (b), (c), (d).

Added by Acts 2009, 81st Leg., ch. 680, § 1, eff. Jan. 1, 2014.

§ 359.052. Correction of Annual Account

(a) If the court finds an annual account is incorrect, the account must be corrected.

(b) The court by order shall approve an annual account that is corrected to the satisfaction of the court and shall act with respect to unpaid claims in accordance with Sections 359.053 and 359.054.

Derived from Probate Code § 401(e).

Added by Acts 2009, 81st Leg., ch. 680, § 1, eff. Jan. 1, 2014.

§ 359.053. Order for Payment of Claims in Full

After approval of an annual account as provided by Section 359.052, if it appears to the court from the exhibit or other evidence that the estate is wholly solvent and that the personal representative has in the representative's possession sufficient funds to pay every character of claims against the estate, the court shall order immediate payment of all claims allowed and approved or established by judgment.

Derived from Probate Code § 401(e).

Added by Acts 2009, 81st Leg., ch. 680, § 1, eff. Jan. 1, 2014.

§ 359.054. Order for Pro Rata Payment of Claims

After approval of an annual account as provided by Section 359.052, if it appears to the court from the account or other evidence that the funds on hand are not sufficient to pay every character of claims against the estate or if the estate is insolvent and the personal representative has any funds on hand, the court shall order the funds to be applied:

(1) first to the payment of any unpaid claims having a preference in the order of their priority; and

(2) then to the pro rata payment of the other claims allowed and approved or established by final judgment, considering:

(A) claims that were presented before the first anniversary of the date administration was granted; and

(B) claims that are in litigation or on which a lawsuit may be filed.

Derived from Probate Code § 401(e).

Added by Acts 2009, 81st Leg., ch. 680, § 1, eff. Jan. 1, 2014.

Subchapter C. Penalties

§ 359.101. Penalty for Failure to File Annual Account

(a) If the personal representative of an estate does not file an annual account required by Section 359.001 or 359.002, any person interested in the estate on written complaint, or the court on the court's own motion, may have the representative cited to file the account and show cause for the failure.

(b) If the personal representative does not file the account after being cited or does not show good cause for the failure, the court on hearing may:

(1) revoke the representative's letters testamentary or of administration; and

(2) fine the representative in an amount not to exceed $500.

(c) The personal representative and the representative's sureties are liable for any fine imposed and for all damages and costs sustained by the representative's failure. The fine, damages, and costs may be recovered in any court of competent jurisdiction.

Derived from Probate Code § 400.

Added by Acts 2009, 81st Leg., ch. 680, § 1, eff. Jan. 1, 2014.

§ 359.102. Penalty for Failure to File Exhibit or Report

(a) If a personal representative does not file an exhibit or report required by this title, any person interested in the estate on written complaint filed with the court clerk may have the representative cited to appear and show cause why the representative should not file the exhibit or report.

(b) On hearing, the court may:

(1) order the personal representative to file the exhibit or report; and

(2) unless good cause is shown for the failure, revoke the representative's letters testamentary or of administration and fine the representative in an amount not to exceed $1,000.

Derived from Probate Code § 403.

Added by Acts 2009, 81st Leg., ch. 680, § 1, eff. Jan. 1, 2014.

Chapter 360. Partition and Distribution of Estate

Chapter 360. Partition and Distribution of Estate

Subchapter A. Application for Partition and Distribution

Statutes in Context
Chapter 360, Subchapter A

Distribution of the estate is typically done when the administration is finished. However, an heir or beneficiary may request partial distribution at any time or total distribution after 12 months have passed from the date the court issued letters.

---

§ 360.001. General Application

(a) At any time after the first anniversary of the date original letters testamentary or of administration are granted, an executor, administrator, heir, or devisee of a decedent's estate, by written application filed in the court in which the estate is pending, may request the partition and distribution of the estate.

(b) An application under Subsection (a) must state:

(1) the decedent's name;

(2) the name and residence of each person entitled to a share of the estate and whether the person is an adult or a minor;

(3) if the applicant does not know a fact required by Subdivision (2); and

(4) the reasons why the estate should be partitioned and distributed.

Derived from Probate Code §§ 373(a), (b).

Added by Acts 2009, 81st Leg., ch. 680, § 1, eff. Jan. 1, 2014.

§ 360.002. Application for Partial Distribution

(a) At any time after original letters testamentary or of administration are granted and the inventory, appraisement, and list of claims are filed and approved, an executor, administrator, heir, or devisee of a decedent's estate, by written application filed in the court in which the estate is pending, may request a distribution of any portion of the estate.

(b) All interested parties, including known creditors, must be personally cited as in other distributions.

(c) Except as provided by Subsection (d), the court, on proper citation and hearing, may distribute any portion of the estate the court considers advisable.

(d) If a distribution is to be made to one or more heirs or devisees, but not to all heirs or devisees, the court shall require a refunding bond in an amount determined by the court to be filed with the court, unless a written waiver of the bond requirement is filed with the court by all interested parties. On approving the bond, if required, the court shall order the distribution of the relevant portion of the estate.

(e) This section applies to corpus as well as income, notwithstanding any other provision of this title.

Derived from Probate Code § 373(c).

Added by Acts 2009, 81st Leg., ch. 680, § 1, eff. Jan. 1, 2014.

Subchapter B. Citation

§ 360.051. Citation of Interested Persons

(a) On the filing of the application, the clerk shall issue a citation that:

(1) states:

(A) the decedent's name; and

(B) the date the court will hear the application; and

(2) requires all persons interested in the estate to appear and show cause why the estate should not be partitioned and distributed.

(b) A citation under this section must be:

(1) personally served on each person residing in the state who is entitled to a share of the estate and whose address is known; and

(2) served by publication on any person entitled to a share of the estate:

(A) whose identity or address is not known;

(B) who is not a resident of this state; or

(C) who is a resident of this state but is absent from this state.

Derived from Probate Code § 374.

Added by Acts 2009, 81st Leg., ch. 680, § 1, eff. Jan. 1, 2014.

§ 360.052. Citation of Executor or Administrator

When a person other than the executor or administrator applies for partition and distribution, the executor or administrator must also be cited to appear and answer the application and file in court a verified exhibit and account of the condition of the estate, as in the case of a final settlement.

Derived from Probate Code § 375.

Added by Acts 2009, 81st Leg., ch. 680, § 1, eff. Jan. 1, 2014.

Subchapter C. Proceedings; Expenses

§ 360.101. Hearing on Application

(a) At the hearing on an application for partition and distribution, the court shall determine:

(1) the residue of the estate that is subject to partition and distribution;

(2) the persons entitled by law to partition and distribution and those persons' respective shares; and

(3) whether an advancement has been made to any of the persons described by Subdivision (2), and if so, the nature and value of the advancement.

(b) For purposes of Subsection (a)(1), the residue of the estate is determined by deducting from the entire assets of the estate remaining on hand:

(1) the amount of all debts and expenses that:

(A) have been approved or established by judgment but not paid; or

(B) may be established by judgment in the future; and

(2) the probable future expenses of administration.

(c) If an advancement described by Subsection (a)(3) has been made, the court shall require the advancement to be placed in hotchpotch as required by the law governing intestate succession.

Derived from Probate Code § 377.

Added by Acts 2009, 81st Leg., ch. 680, § 1, eff. Jan. 1, 2014.

§ 360.102. Court Decree

If the court determines that the estate should be partitioned and distributed, the court shall enter a decree stating:

(1) the name and address, if known, of each person entitled to a share of the estate, specifying:

(A) which of those persons are known to be minors;

(B) the name of the minors' guardian or guardian ad litem; and

(C) the name of the attorney appointed to represent those persons who are unknown or who are not residents of this state;

(2) the proportional part of the estate to which each person is entitled;

(3) a full description of all the estate to be distributed; and

(4) that the executor or administrator must retain possession of a sufficient amount of money or property to pay all debts, taxes, and expenses of

administration and specifying the amount of money or the property to be retained.

Derived from Probate Code § 378.

Added by Acts 2009, 81st Leg., ch. 680, § 1, eff. Jan. 1, 2014.

§ 360.103. Expenses of Partition

(a) The distributees shall pay the expense of the estate's partition pro rata.

(b) The portion of the estate allotted to a distributee is liable for the distributee's portion of the partition expense, and, if not paid, the court may order execution for the expense in the names of the persons entitled to payment of the expense.

Derived from Probate Code § 387.

Added by Acts 2009, 81st Leg., ch. 680, § 1, eff. Jan. 1, 2014.

Subchapter D. Partition and Distribution if Estate Property is Capable of Division

§ 360.151. Appointment of Commissioners

If the estate does not consist entirely of money or debts due to the estate and the court has not previously determined that the estate is incapable of partition, the court shall appoint three or more discreet and disinterested persons as commissioners to make a partition and distribution of the estate.

Derived from Probate Code § 380(a).

Added by Acts 2009, 81st Leg., ch. 680, § 1, eff. Jan. 1, 2014.

§ 360.152. Writ of Partition

(a) When commissioners are appointed under Section 360.151, the clerk shall issue a writ of partition directed to the commissioners, commanding the commissioners to:

(1) proceed promptly to make the partition and distribution in accordance with the court decree; and

(2) return the writ, with the commissioners' proceedings under the writ, on a date stated in the writ.

(b) A copy of the court decree must accompany the writ.

(c) The writ must be served by:

(1) delivering the writ and the accompanying copy of the court decree to one of the commissioners; and

(2) notifying the other commissioners, verbally or otherwise, of the commissioners' appointment.

(d) Service under Subsection (c) may be made by any person.

Derived from Probate Code § 380(b).

Added by Acts 2009, 81st Leg., ch. 680, § 1, eff. Jan. 1, 2014.

§ 360.153. Partition by Commissioners

(a) The commissioners shall make a fair, just, and impartial partition and distribution of the estate in the following order and manner:

(1) if the real estate is capable of being divided without manifest injury to all or any of the distributees, the commissioners shall partition and distribute the land or other property by allotting to each distributee:

(A) a share in each parcel;

(B) shares in one or more parcels; or

(C) one or more parcels separately, with or without the addition of a share of other parcels;

(2) if the real estate is not capable of a fair, just, and equal division in kind, but may be made capable of a fair, just, and equal division in kind by allotting to one or more of the distributees a proportion of the money or other personal property to supply the deficiency, the commissioners may make, as nearly as possible, an equal division of the real estate and supply the deficiency of any share from the money or other personal property; and

(3) the commissioners shall:

(A) make a like division in kind, as nearly as possible, of the money and other personal property; and

(B) determine by lot, among equal shares, to whom each share shall belong.

(b) The commissioners shall allot the land or other property under Subsection (a)(1) in the manner described by that subsection that is most in the interest of the distributees.

Derived from Probate Code § 380(c).

Added by Acts 2009, 81st Leg., ch. 680, § 1, eff. Jan. 1, 2014.

§ 360.154. Commissioners' Report

(a) After dividing all or any part of the estate, at least a majority of the commissioners shall make a written, sworn report to the court that:

(1) states the property divided by the commissioners; and

(2) describes in particular the property allotted to each distributee and the value of that property.

(b) If real estate was divided, the report must also contain a general plat of the land with:

(1) the division lines plainly set down; and

(2) the number of acres in each share.

Derived from Probate Code § 380(d).

Added by Acts 2009, 81st Leg., ch. 680, § 1, eff. Jan. 1, 2014.

§ 360.155. Court Action on Commissioners' Report

(a) On the return of a commissioners' report under Section 360.154, the court shall:

(1) examine the report carefully; and

(2) hear:

(A) all exceptions and objections to the report; and

(B) all evidence in favor of or against the report.

(b) If the report is informal, the court shall have the informality corrected.

(c) If the division appears to have been fairly made according to law and no valid exceptions are taken to the division, the court shall approve the division and enter a decree vesting title in the distributees of the distributees' respective shares or portions of the property as set apart to the distributees by the commissioners.

(d) If the division does not appear to have been fairly made according to law or a valid exception is taken to the division, the court may:

(1) set aside the report and division; and

(2) order a new partition to be made.

Derived from Probate Code § 380(e).

Added by Acts 2009, 81st Leg., ch. 680, § 1, eff. Jan. 1, 2014.

§ 360.156. Delivery of Property

When the commissioners' report has been approved and ordered to be recorded, the court shall order the executor or administrator to deliver to the distributees on demand the distributees' respective shares of the estate, including all the title deeds and documents belonging to the distributees.

Derived from Probate Code § 380(f).

Added by Acts 2009, 81st Leg., ch. 680, § 1, eff. Jan. 1, 2014.

§ 360.157. Commissioners' Fees

A commissioner who partitions and distributes an estate under this subchapter is entitled to $5 for each day the commissioner necessarily engages in performing the commissioner's duties, to be taxed and paid as other costs in cases of partition.

Derived from Probate Code § 380(g).

Added by Acts 2009, 81st Leg., ch. 680, § 1, eff. Jan. 1, 2014.

Subchapter E. Partition and Distribution if Estate Property Is Incapable of Division

§ 360.201. Court Finding

If, in the court's opinion, all or part of an estate is not capable of a fair and equal partition and distribution, the court shall make a special written finding specifying the property incapable of division.

Derived from Probate Code § 381(a).

Added by Acts 2009, 81st Leg., ch. 680, § 1, eff. Jan. 1, 2014.

§ 360.202. Sale of Estate Property

(a) When the court has found that all or part of an estate is not capable of fair and equal division, the court

shall order the sale of all estate property not capable of fair and equal division.

(b) The sale must be made by the executor or administrator in the manner provided for the sale of real estate to satisfy estate debts.

(c) The court shall distribute the proceeds collected from the sale to the persons entitled to the proceeds.

(d) A distributee who buys property at the sale is required to pay or secure only the amount by which the distributee's bid exceeds the amount of the distributee's share of the property.

Derived from Probate Code §§ 381(b), (c).

Added by Acts 2009, 81st Leg., ch. 680, § 1, eff. Jan. 1, 2014.

§ 360.203. Applicability of Provisions Relating to Sale of Real Estate

The provisions of this title relating to reports of sales of real estate, the giving of an increased general or additional bond on the sale of real estate, and the vesting of title to property sold by decree or by deed apply to sales made under this subchapter.

Derived from Probate Code § 381(d).

Added by Acts 2009, 81st Leg., ch. 680, § 1, eff. Jan. 1, 2014.

Subchapter F. Certain Types of Estate Property

§ 360.251. Estate Consisting Only of Money or Debts

If the estate to be distributed consists only of money or debts due to the estate, the court shall:

(1) set the amount to which each distributee is entitled; and

(2) order the executor or administrator to pay and deliver that amount.

Derived from Probate Code § 379.

Added by Acts 2009, 81st Leg., ch. 680, § 1, eff. Jan. 1, 2014.

§ 360.252. Estate Property Located in Another County

(a) If any portion of the estate to be partitioned is located in another county and cannot be fairly partitioned without prejudice to the distributees' interests, the commissioners may report those facts to the court in writing.

(b) On the making of a report under Subsection (a), if the court is satisfied that the property cannot be fairly divided or that the sale of the property would be more advantageous to the distributees, the court may order a sale of the property. The sale must be conducted in the manner provided by Subchapter E for the sale of property that is not capable of fair and equal division.

(c) If the court is not satisfied that the property cannot be fairly and advantageously divided, or that the sale of the property would be more advantageous to the distributees, the court may appoint three or more commissioners in each county in which the property is located. If the court appoints commissioners under this subsection, the proceedings under Subchapter D for partition by commissioners must be followed.

Derived from Probate Code § 382.

Added by Acts 2009, 81st Leg., ch. 680, § 1, eff. Jan. 1, 2014.

§ 360.253. Community Property

(a) If a spouse dies leaving community property, the surviving spouse, at any time after letters testamentary or of administration have been granted and an inventory, appraisement, and list of claims of the estate have been returned or an affidavit in lieu of the inventory, appraisement, and list of claims has been filed, may apply in writing to the court that granted the letters for a partition of the community property.

(b) The surviving spouse shall execute and deliver a bond to the judge of the court described by Subsection (a). The bond must be:

(1) with a corporate surety or at least two good and sufficient personal sureties;

(2) payable to and approved by the judge;

(3) in an amount equal to the value of the surviving spouse's interest in the community property; and

(4) conditioned for the payment of half of all debts existing against the community property.

(c) The court shall proceed to partition the community property into two equal moieties, one to be delivered to the surviving spouse and the other to be delivered to the executor or administrator of the deceased spouse's estate.

(d) If a partition is made under this section:

(1) a lien exists on the property delivered to the surviving spouse to secure the payment of the bond required under Subsection (b); and

(2) any creditor of the community estate:

(A) may sue in the creditor's own name on the bond; and

(B) is entitled:

(i) to have judgment on the bond for half of the debt the creditor establishes; and

(ii) to be paid by the executor or administrator of the deceased spouse's estate for the other half.

(e) The provisions of this title relating to the partition and distribution of an estate apply to a partition under this section to the extent applicable.

Derived from Probate Code § 385.

Added by Acts 2009, 81st Leg., ch. 680, § 1, eff. Jan. 1, 2014. Subsec. (a) amended by Acts 2011, 82nd Leg., ch. 823, § 2.50, eff. Jan. 1, 2014.

§ 360.254. Jointly Owned Property

(a) A person who has a joint interest with a decedent's estate in any property may apply to the court that granted letters testamentary or of administration on the estate for a partition of the property.

(b) On application under Subsection (a), the court shall partition the property between the applicant and the decedent's estate.

(c) The provisions of this title relating to the partition and distribution of an estate govern a partition under this section to the extent applicable.

Derived from Probate Code § 386.

Added by Acts 2009, 81st Leg., ch. 680, § 1, eff. Jan. 1, 2014.

Subchapter G. Enforcement

§ 360.301. Liability for Failure to Deliver Estate Property

(a) If an executor or administrator neglects, when demanded, to deliver a portion of an estate ordered to be delivered to a person entitled to that portion, the person may file with the court clerk a written complaint alleging:

(1) the fact of the neglect;

(2) the date of the person's demand; and

(3) other relevant facts.

(b) On the filing of a complaint under Subsection (a), the court clerk shall issue a citation to be served personally on the executor or administrator. The citation must:

(1) apprise the executor or administrator of the complaint; and

(2) cite the executor or administrator to appear before the court and answer, if the executor or administrator desires, at the time designated in the citation.

(c) If at the hearing the court finds that the citation was properly served and returned and that the executor or administrator is guilty of the neglect alleged, the court shall enter an order to that effect.

(d) An executor or administrator found guilty under Subsection (c) is liable to the complainant for damages at the rate of 10 percent of the amount or the appraised value of the portion of the estate neglectfully withheld, per month, for each month or fraction of a month that the portion is or has been neglectfully withheld after the date of demand. Damages under this subsection may be recovered in any court of competent jurisdiction.

Derived from Probate Code § 384.

Added by Acts 2009, 81st Leg., ch. 680, § 1, eff. Jan. 1, 2014.

Chapter 361. Death, Resignation, or Removal of Personal Representatives; Appointment of Successors

Subchapter A. Resignation of Personal Representative

Subchapter B. Removal and Reinstatement of Personal Representative

Subchapter C. Appointment of Successor Representative

Subchapter D. Procedures After Death, Resignation, or Removal of Personal Representative

Chapter 361. Death, Resignation, or Removal of Personal Representatives; Appointment of Successors

Subchapter A. Resignation of Personal Representative

Statutes in Context
Chapter 361, Subchapter A

Chapter 361, Subchapter A, addresses issues regarding the resignation of a personal representative.

§ 361.001. Resignation Application

A personal representative who wishes to resign the representative's trust shall file a written application with the court clerk, accompanied by a complete and verified exhibit and final account showing the true condition of the estate entrusted to the representative's care.

Derived from Probate Code § 221(a).

Added by Acts 2009, 81st Leg., ch. 680, § 1, eff. Jan. 1, 2014.

§ 361.002. Immediate Appointment of Successor; Discharge and Release

(a) If the necessity exists, the court may immediately accept the resignation of a personal representative and appoint a successor representative.

(b) The court may not discharge a person whose resignation is accepted under Subsection (a), or release the person or the sureties on the person's bond, until a final order has been issued or judgment has been rendered on the final account required under Section 361.001.

Derived from Probate Code § 221(b).

Added by Acts 2009, 81st Leg., ch. 680, § 1, eff. Jan. 1, 2014.

§ 361.003. Hearing Date; Citation

(a) When an application to resign as personal representative is filed under Section 361.001, supported by the exhibit and final account required under that section, the court clerk shall bring the application to the judge's attention and the judge shall set a date for a hearing on the matter.

(b) After a hearing is set under Subsection (a), the clerk shall issue a citation to all interested persons, showing:

(1) that an application that complies with Section 361.001 has been filed; and

(2) the time and place set for the hearing at which the interested persons may appear and contest the exhibit and final account supporting the application.

(c) Unless the court directs that the citation under Subsection (b) be published, the citation must be posted.

Derived from Probate Code § 221(c).

Added by Acts 2009, 81st Leg., ch. 680, § 1, eff. Jan. 1, 2014.

§ 361.004. Hearing

(a) At the time set for the hearing under Section 361.003, unless the court continues the hearing, and if the court finds that the citation required under that section has been properly issued and served, the court shall:

(1) examine the exhibit and final account required by Section 361.001;

(2) hear all evidence for and against the exhibit and final account; and

(3) if necessary, restate and audit and settle the exhibit and final account.

(b) If the court is satisfied that the matters entrusted to the personal representative applying to resign have been handled and accounted for in accordance with the law, the court shall:

(1) enter an order approving the exhibit and final account; and

(2) require that any estate property remaining in the applicant's possession be delivered to the persons entitled by law to receive the property.

Derived from Probate Code § 221(d).

Added by Acts 2009, 81st Leg., ch. 680, § 1, eff. Jan. 1, 2014.

§ 361.005. Requirements for Discharge

(a) A personal representative applying to resign may not be discharged until:

(1) the resignation application has been heard;

(2) the exhibit and final account required under Section 361.001 have been examined, settled, and approved; and

(3) the applicant has satisfied the court that the applicant has:

(A) delivered any estate property remaining in the applicant's possession; or

(B) complied with all lawful orders of the court with relation to the applicant's trust as representative.

(b) When a personal representative applying to resign has fully complied with the orders of the court, the court shall enter an order:

(1) accepting the resignation; and

(2) discharging the applicant, and, if the applicant is under bond, the applicant's sureties.

Derived from Probate Code §§ 221(e), (f).

Added by Acts 2009, 81st Leg., ch. 680, § 1, eff. Jan. 1, 2014.

Subchapter B. Removal and Reinstatement of Personal Representative

Statutes in Context
Chapter 361, Subchapter B

Sections 361.051 – 361.054 explain how a court may remove a personal representative from office. Section 361.051 enumerates when the removal may occur without notice to the personal representative while § 361.052 lists the circumstances where notice to the personal representative is needed before the court may issue an order of removal. See also § 404.003 (removal of independent executor). Reinstatement is thereafter possible under § 361.054.

§ 361.051. Removal Without Notice

The court, on the court's own motion or on the motion of any interested person, and without notice, may remove a personal representative appointed under this title who:

(1) neglects to qualify in the manner and time required by law;

(2) fails to return, before the 91st day after the date the representative qualifies, an inventory of the estate property and a list of claims that have come to the representative's knowledge, unless that deadline is extended by court order;

(3) if required, fails to give a new bond within the time prescribed;

(4) is absent from the state for a consecutive period of three or more months without the court's permission, or moves out of state;

(5) cannot be served with notices or other processes because:

(A) the representative's whereabouts are unknown;

(B) the representative is eluding service; or

(C) the representative is a nonresident of this state who does not have a resident agent to accept service of process in any probate proceeding or other action relating to the estate; or

(6) subject to Section 361.054(a), has misapplied, embezzled, or removed from the state, or is about to misapply, embezzle, or remove from the state, all or part of the property entrusted to the representative's care.

Derived from Probate Code § 222(a)(1).

Added by Acts 2009, 81st Leg., ch. 680, § 1, eff. Jan. 1, 2014.

§ 361.052. Removal With Notice

The court may remove a personal representative on the court's own motion, or on the complaint of any interested person, after the representative has been cited by personal service to answer at a time and place fixed in the notice, if:

(1) sufficient grounds appear to support a belief that the representative has misapplied, embezzled, or removed from the state, or is about to misapply, embezzle, or remove from the state, all or part of the property entrusted to the representative's care;

(2) the representative fails to return any account required by law to be made;

(3) the representative fails to obey a proper order of the court that has jurisdiction with respect to the performance of the representative's duties;

(4) the representative is proved to have been guilty of gross misconduct, or mismanagement in the performance of the representative's duties;

(5) the representative:

(A) becomes incapacitated;

(B) is sentenced to the penitentiary; or

(C) from any other cause, becomes incapable of properly performing the duties of the representative's trust; or

(6) the representative, as executor or administrator, fails to:

(A) make a final settlement by the third anniversary of the date letters testamentary or of administration are granted, unless that period is extended by the court on a showing of sufficient cause supported by oath; or

(B) timely file the affidavit or certificate required by Section 308.004.

Derived from Probate Code § 222(b).

Added by Acts 2009, 81st Leg., ch. 680, § 1, eff. Jan. 1, 2014.

§ 361.053. Removal Order

An order removing a personal representative must:

(1) state the cause of the removal;

(2) require that, if the removed representative has been personally served with citation, any letters testamentary or of administration issued to the removed representative be surrendered, and that, regardless of whether the letters have been delivered, all the letters be canceled of record; and

(3) require the removed representative to deliver any estate property in the representative's possession to the persons entitled to the property or to the person who has been appointed and has qualified as successor representative.

Derived from Probate Code § 222(c).

Added by Acts 2009, 81st Leg., ch. 680, § 1, eff. Jan. 1, 2014.

§ 361.054. Removal and Reinstatement of Personal Representative Under Certain Circumstances

(a) The court may remove a personal representative under Section 361.051(6) only on the presentation of clear and convincing evidence given under oath.

(b) Not later than the 10th day after the date the court signs the order of removal, a personal representative who is removed under Section 361.051(6) may file an application with the court for a hearing to determine whether the representative should be reinstated.

(c) On the filing of an application under Subsection (b), the court clerk shall issue to the applicant and to the successor representative of the decedent's estate a notice stating:

(1) that an application for reinstatement has been filed;

(2) the name of the decedent from whose estate the applicant was removed as personal representative; and

(3) the name of the applicant for reinstatement.

(d) The notice required by Subsection (c) must cite all persons interested in the estate to appear at the time and place stated in the notice if the persons wish to contest the application.

(e) If, at the conclusion of a hearing under this section, the court is satisfied by a preponderance of the evidence that the personal representative applying for reinstatement did not engage in the conduct that directly led to the applicant's removal, the court shall:

(1) set aside any order appointing a successor representative; and

(2) enter an order reinstating the applicant as personal representative of the estate.

(f) If the court sets aside the appointment of a successor representative under this section, the court may require the successor representative to prepare and file, under oath, an accounting of the estate and to detail the disposition the successor has made of the estate property.

Derived from Probate Code §§ 222(a)(2), 222A.

Added by Acts 2009, 81st Leg., ch. 680, § 1, eff. Jan. 1, 2014.

Subchapter C. Appointment of Successor Representative

Statutes in Context
Chapter 361, Subchapter C

Chapter 361, Subchapter C, explains how the court will appoint a replacement personal representative if the currently serving representative dies, resigns, or is removed. This Subchapter also handles a variety of other situations where a replacement may be appropriate.

§ 361.101. Requirements for Revocation of Letters

Except as otherwise expressly provided by this title, the court may revoke letters testamentary or of administration and grant other letters only:

(1) on application; and

(2) after personal service of citation on the person, if living, whose letters are sought to be revoked, requiring the person to appear and show cause why the application should not be granted.

Derived from Probate Code § 220(f).

Added by Acts 2009, 81st Leg., ch. 680, § 1, eff. Jan. 1, 2014.

§ 361.102. Appointment Because of Death, Resignation, or Removal

(a) If a person appointed as personal representative fails to qualify or, after qualifying, dies, resigns, or is removed, the court may, on application, appoint a successor representative if the appointment of a successor is necessary. The appointment may be made before a final accounting is filed or before any action on a final accounting is taken. In the event of death, the legal representatives of the deceased personal representative shall account for, pay, and deliver all estate property that was entrusted to the deceased personal representative's care to the persons legally entitled to receive the property, at the time and in the manner ordered by the court.

(b) The court may appoint a successor representative under this section without citation or notice if the court finds that the immediate appointment of a successor representative is necessary.

Derived from Probate Code § 220(a).

Added by Acts 2009, 81st Leg., ch. 680, § 1, eff. Jan. 1, 2014.

§ 361.103. Appointment Because of Existence of Prior Right

If letters testamentary or of administration have been granted to a person and another person applies for letters, the court shall revoke the initial letters and grant letters to the second applicant if the second applicant:

(1) is qualified;

(2) has a prior right to the letters; and

(3) has not waived the prior right to the letters.

Derived from Probate Code § 220(b).

Added by Acts 2009, 81st Leg., ch. 680, § 1, eff. Jan. 1, 2014.

§ 361.104. Appointment when Named Executor Becomes an Adult

(a) A person named as executor in a will who was not an adult when the will was probated is entitled to have letters testamentary or of administration that were granted to another person revoked and appropriate letters granted to the named executor on proof that the named executor has become an adult and is not otherwise disqualified.

(b) This subsection applies only if a will names two or more persons as executor. A person named as an executor in the will who was a minor when the will was probated may, on becoming an adult, qualify and receive letters if:

(1) letters have been issued only to the named executors in the will who were adults when the will was probated; and

(2) the person is not otherwise disqualified from receiving letters.

Derived from Probate Code § 220(c).

Added by Acts 2009, 81st Leg., ch. 680, § 1, eff. Jan. 1, 2014.

§ 361.105. Appointment of Formerly Sick or Absent Executor

(a) This section applies only to a person named as executor in a will who was sick or absent from the state when the testator died or the will was proved and, as a result, could not:

(1) present the will for probate before the 31st day after the date of the testator's death; or

(2) accept and qualify as executor before the 21st day after the date the will is probated.

(b) A person to whom this section applies may accept and qualify as executor before the 61st day after the date the person returns to the state or recovers from illness if proof is presented to the court that the person was ill or absent.

(c) If a person accepts and qualifies as executor under Subsection (b) and letters testamentary or of administration have been issued to another person, the court shall revoke the other person's letters.

Derived from Probate Code § 220(d).

Added by Acts 2009, 81st Leg., ch. 680, § 1, eff. Jan. 1, 2014.

§ 361.106. Appointment when Will Discovered After Grant of Administration

If, after letters of administration have been issued, it is discovered that the decedent left a lawful will, the court shall revoke the letters of administration and issue proper letters to any persons entitled to the letters.

Derived from Probate Code § 220(e).

Added by Acts 2009, 81st Leg., ch. 680, § 1, eff. Jan. 1, 2014.

Subchapter D. Procedures After Death, Resignation, or Removal of Personal Representative

§ 361.151. Payment to Estate While Office of Personal Representative Is Vacant

(a) A debtor, obligor, or payor may pay or tender money or another thing of value falling due to an estate while the office of personal representative of the estate is vacant to the court clerk for the credit of the estate.

(b) Payment or tender under Subsection (a) discharges the debtor, obligor, or payor of the obligation for all purposes to the extent and purpose of the payment or tender.

(c) If the court clerk accepts payment or tender under this section, the court clerk shall issue a receipt for the payment or tender.

Derived from Probate Code § 220(g).

Added by Acts 2009, 81st Leg., ch. 680, § 1, eff. Jan. 1, 2014.

§ 361.152. Further Administration with or Without Notice or Will Annexed

(a) If an estate is unrepresented as a result of the death, removal, or resignation of the estate's personal representative, and on application by a qualified person interested in the estate, the court shall grant further administration of the estate if necessary, and with the will annexed if there is a will.

(b) An appointment under Subsection (a) shall be made on notice and after a hearing, as in the case of an original appointment, except that, if the court finds that the immediate appointment of a successor representative is necessary, the court may appoint the successor on application but without citation or notice.

Derived from Probate Code § 223.

Added by Acts 2009, 81st Leg., ch. 680, § 1, eff. Jan. 1, 2014.

§ 361.153. Rights, Powers, and Duties of Successor Representative

(a) If a personal representative of an estate not administered succeeds another personal representative, the successor representative has all rights, powers, and duties of the predecessor, other than those rights and powers conferred on the predecessor by will that are different from those conferred by this title on personal representatives generally. Subject to that exception, the successor representative shall administer the estate as if the successor's administration were a continuation of the former administration.

(b) A successor representative shall account for all the estate property that came into the predecessor's possession, and is entitled to any order or remedy that the court has the power to give to enforce the delivery of the estate property and the liability of the predecessor's sureties for any portion of the estate property that is not delivered. The successor is not required to account for any portion of the estate property that the successor failed to recover after due diligence.

(c) In addition to the powers granted under Subsections (a) and (b), a successor representative may:

(1) make himself or herself, and may be made, a party to a suit prosecuted by or against the successor's predecessors;

(2) settle with the predecessor, and receive and give a receipt for any portion of the estate property that remains in the predecessor's possession; or

(3) commence a suit on the bond or bonds of the predecessor, in the successor's own name and capacity, for all the estate property that:

(A) came into the predecessor's possession; and

(B) has not been accounted for by the predecessor.

Derived from Probate Code §§ 224, 225.

Added by Acts 2009, 81st Leg., ch. 680, § 1, eff. Jan. 1, 2014.

§ 361.154. Successor Executor Also Succeeds to Prior Rights and Duties

An executor who accepts appointment and qualifies after letters of administration have been granted on the estate shall, in the manner prescribed by Section 361.153, succeed to the previous administrator, and

shall administer the estate as if the executor's administration were a continuation of the former administration, subject to any legal directions of the testator with respect to the estate that are contained in the will.

Derived from Probate Code § 226.

Added by Acts 2009, 81st Leg., ch. 680, § 1, eff. Jan. 1, 2014.

§ 361.155. Successor Representative to Return Inventory, Appraisement, and List of Claims or Affidavit in Lieu of Inventory, Appraisement, and List of Claims

(a) An appointee who has qualified to succeed a former personal representative, before the 91st day after the date the personal representative qualifies, shall make and return to the court an inventory, appraisement, and list of claims of the estate or, if the appointee is an independent executor, shall make and return to the court that document or file an affidavit in lieu of the inventory, appraisement, and list of claims, in the manner provided for an original appointee, and shall also return additional inventories, appraisements, and lists of claims and additional affidavits in the manner provided for an original appointee.

(b) Except as otherwise provided by this subsection, an appointee who files an inventory, appraisement, and list of claims under Subsection (a) shall set out in the inventory the appointee's appraisement of the fair market value of each item in the inventory on the date of the appointee's qualification. If an inventory, appraisement, and list of claims has not been filed by any former personal representative, the appointee shall set out the inventory as provided by Sections 309.051 and 309.052.

(c) On the application of any person interested in the estate, the court shall, in an order appointing a successor representative of an estate, appoint appraisers as in an original appointment.

Derived from Probate Code § 227.

Added by Acts 2009, 81st Leg., ch. 680, § 1, eff. Jan. 1, 2014. Amended by Acts 2011, 82nd Leg., ch. 823, §§ 2.51 & 2.52, eff. Jan. 1, 2014. Subsecs. (b) amended and (c) added by Acts 2013, 83rd Leg., ch. 1136, § 46, eff. Jan. 1, 2014.

Chapter 362. Closing Administration of Estate

Subchapter A. Settling and Closing Estate

Subchapter B. Failure of Personal Representative to Act

Chapter 362. Closing Administration of Estate

Statutes in Context
Chapter 362

Chapter 362 explains how a dependent administration is closed.

Subchapter A. Settling and Closing Estate

§ 362.001. Settling and Closing Administration of Estate

The administration of an estate shall be settled and closed when:

(1) all the debts known to exist against the estate have been paid, or have been paid to the extent permitted by the assets in the personal representative's possession; and

(2) no further need for administration exists.

Derived from Probate Code § 404.

Added by Acts 2009, 81st Leg., ch. 680, § 1, eff. Jan. 1, 2014.

§ 362.002. Compelling Settlement of Estate

A person interested in the administration of an estate for which letters testamentary or of administration have been granted may proceed, after any period of time, to compel settlement of the estate if it does not appear from the record that the administration of the estate has been closed.

Derived from Probate Code § 92.

Added by Acts 2009, 81st Leg., ch. 680, § 1, eff. Jan. 1, 2014.

§ 362.003. Verified Account Required

The personal representative of an estate shall present to the court the representative's verified account for final settlement when the administration of the estate is to be settled and closed.

Derived from Probate Code § 405.

Added by Acts 2009, 81st Leg., ch. 680, § 1, eff. Jan. 1, 2014.

§ 362.004. Contents of Account

(a) Except as provided by Subsection (b), it is sufficient for an account for final settlement to:

(1) refer to the inventory without describing each item of property in detail; and

(2) refer to and adopt any proceeding had in the administration concerning a sale, renting, leasing for mineral development, or any other transaction on behalf of the estate, including an exhibit, account, or voucher previously filed and approved, without restating the particular items thereof.

(b) An account for final settlement must be accompanied by proper vouchers supporting each item included in the account for which the personal representative has not already accounted and, either by reference to any proceeding described by Subsection (a) or by a statement of the facts, must show:

(1) the estate property that has come into the representative's possession and the disposition of that property;

(2) the debts that have been paid;

(3) any debts and expenses still owing by the estate;

(4) any estate property still in the representative's possession;

(5) the persons entitled to receive that estate and, for each of those persons:

(A) the person's relationship to the decedent;

(B) the person's residence, if known; and

(C) whether the person is an adult or a minor and, if the person is a minor, the name of each of the minor's guardians, if any;

(6) any advancement or payment made by the representative from that estate to any person entitled to receive part of that estate;

(7) the tax returns due that have been filed and the taxes due and owing that have been paid, including:

(A) a complete account of the amount of taxes;

(B) the date the taxes were paid; and

(C) the governmental entity to which the taxes were paid;

(8) if on the filing of the account a tax return due to be filed or any taxes due to be paid are

delinquent, the reasons for, and include a description of, the delinquency; and

(9) that the representative has paid all required bond premiums.

Derived from Probate Code § 405.

Added by Acts 2009, 81st Leg., ch. 680, § 1, eff. Jan. 1, 2014.

§ 362.005. Citation and Notice on Presentation of Account

(a) On the presentation of an account for final settlement by a temporary or permanent personal representative, the county clerk shall issue citation to the persons and in the manner provided by Subsection (b).

(b) Citation issued under Subsection (a) must:

(1) contain:

(A) a statement that an account for final settlement has been presented;

(B) the time and place the court will consider the account; and

(C) a statement requiring the person cited to appear and contest the account, if the person wishes to contest the account; and

(2) be given to each heir or beneficiary of the decedent by certified mail, return receipt requested, unless the court by written order directs another method of service to be given.

(c) The personal representative shall also provide to each person entitled to citation under Subsection (b) a copy of the account for final settlement either by:

(1) certified mail, return receipt requested; or

(2) electronic delivery, including facsimile or e-mail.

(d) The court by written order shall require additional notice if the court considers the additional notice necessary.

(e) The court may allow the waiver of citation of an account for final settlement in a proceeding concerning a decedent's estate.

(f) The personal representative shall file an affidavit sworn to by the personal representative or a certificate signed by the personal representative's attorney stating:

(1) that the citation was given as required by this section;

(2) the name of each person to whom the citation was given, if the person's name is not shown on the proof of delivery;

(3) the name of each person executing a waiver of citation; and

(4) that each person entitled to citation was provided a copy of the account for final settlement, indicating the method of delivery for each person.

Derived from Probate Code § 407.

Added by Acts 2009, 81st Leg., ch. 680, § 1, eff. Jan. 1, 2014. Amended by Acts 2013, 83rd Leg., ch. 1136, § 47, eff. Jan 1, 2014.

§ 362.006. Examination of and Hearing on Account

(a) On the court's satisfaction that citation has been properly served on all persons interested in the estate, the court shall examine the account for final settlement and the accompanying vouchers.

(b) After hearing all exceptions or objections to the account for final settlement and accompanying vouchers and the evidence in support of or against the account, the court shall audit and settle the account and, if necessary, restate the account.

Derived from Probate Code § 408(a).

Added by Acts 2009, 81st Leg., ch. 680, § 1, eff. Jan. 1, 2014.

§ 362.007. Delivery of Certain Property to Guardian

The court may permit a resident personal representative who has possession of any of a ward's estate to deliver the estate to a qualified and acting guardian of the ward.

Derived from Probate Code § 405A.

Added by Acts 2009, 81st Leg., ch. 680, § 1, eff. Jan. 1, 2014.

§ 362.008. Certain Debts Excluded from Settlement Computation

In the settlement of any of the accounts of the personal representative, all debts due the estate that the court is satisfied could not have been collected by due diligence and that have not been collected shall be excluded from the computation.

Derived from Probate Code § 412.

Added by Acts 2009, 81st Leg., ch. 680, § 1, eff. Jan. 1, 2014.

§ 362.009. Money Due to Estate Pending Final Discharge

Money or another thing of value that becomes due to the estate while an account for final settlement is pending may be paid, delivered, or tendered to the personal representative until the order of final discharge of the representative is entered in the judge's probate docket. The representative shall issue a receipt for the money or other thing of value to the obligor or payor. On issuance of the receipt, the obligor or payor is discharged of the obligation for all purposes.

Derived from Probate Code § 409.

Added by Acts 2009, 81st Leg., ch. 680, § 1, eff. Jan. 1, 2014. Amended by Acts 2011, 82nd Leg., ch. 90, § 8.018, eff. Jan. 1, 2014.

Added by Acts 2009, 81st Leg., ch. 680, § 1, eff. Jan. 1, 2014.

§ 362.010. Payment of Inheritance Taxes Required

A personal representative's account for final settlement of an estate may not be approved, and the estate may not be closed, unless the account shows and the court finds that all inheritance taxes due and owing to this state with respect to all interests and properties passing through the representative's possession have been paid.

Derived from Probate Code § 410.

Added by Acts 2009, 81st Leg., ch. 680, § 1, eff. Jan. 1, 2014.

Statutes in Context
§ 362.011

Property passing to an unknown or missing person may be turned over to the court's registry. This causes a problem because a court is ill-equipped to store grandmother's china and dad's lawnmower. The court is required to order the representative to convert all the assets to cash and then deposit the cash. This procedure, however, could cause irreparable loss to family heirlooms, farms, ranches, homes, and businesses.

---

§ 362.011. Partition and Distribution of Estate; Deposit In Court's Registry

(a) If, on final settlement of an estate, any of the estate remains in the personal representative's possession, the court shall order that a partition and distribution be made among the persons entitled to receive that part of the estate.

(b) The court shall order the personal representative to convert into money any remaining nonmonetary assets to which a person who is unknown or missing is entitled. The procedures in Chapter 356 apply to the conversion of nonmonetary assets under this subsection.

(c) The court shall order the personal representative to deposit in an account in the court's registry all money, including the proceeds of any conversion under Subsection (b), to which a person who is unknown or missing is entitled. The court shall hold money deposited in an account under this subsection until the court renders:

(1) an order requiring money in the account to be paid to the previously unknown or missing person who is entitled to the money; or

(2) another order regarding the disposition of the money.

Derived from Probate Code § 408(b).

Added by Acts 2009, 81st Leg., ch. 680, § 1, eff. Jan. 1, 2014. Amended by Acts 2013, 83rd Leg., ch. 1136, § 48, eff. Jan. 1, 2014.

§ 362.012. Discharge of Personal Representative when No Estate Property Remains

The court shall enter an order discharging a personal representative from the representative's trust and closing the estate if, on final settlement of the estate, none of the estate remains in the representative's possession.

Derived from Probate Code § 408(c).

Added by Acts 2009, 81st Leg., ch. 680, § 1, eff. Jan. 1,

2014.

§ 362.013. Discharge of Personal Representative when Estate Fully Administered

The court shall enter an order discharging a personal representative from the representative's trust and declaring the estate closed when:

(1) the representative has fully administered the estate in accordance with this title and the court's orders;

(2) the representative's account for final settlement has been approved; and

(3) the representative has:

(A) delivered all of the estate remaining in the representative's possession to the person or persons entitled to receive that part of the estate; and

(B) with respect to the portion of the estate distributable to an unknown or missing person, complied with an order of the court under Section 362.011.

Derived from Probate Code § 408(d).

Added by Acts 2009, 81st Leg., ch. 680, § 1, eff. Jan. 1, 2014. Amended by Acts 2013, 83rd Leg., ch. 1136, § 49, eff. Jan. 1, 2014.

Subchapter B. Failure of Personal Representative to Act

§ 362.051. Failure to Present Account

(a) The court, on the court's own motion or on the written complaint of anyone interested in a decedent's estate that has been administered, shall have the personal representative who is charged with the duty of presenting an account for final settlement cited to appear and present the account within the time specified in the citation if the representative failed or neglected to present the account at the proper time.

(b) On or after the fourth anniversary of the date the court clerk last issues letters testamentary or of administration for a decedent's estate, the court may close the estate without an account for final settlement and without appointing a successor personal representative if:

(1) the whereabouts of the personal representative and heirs of the decedent are unknown; and

(2) a complaint has not been filed by anyone interested in the decedent's estate.

Derived from Probate Code § 406.

Added by Acts 2009, 81st Leg., ch. 680, § 1, eff. Jan. 1, 2014.

§ 362.052. Liability for Failure to Deliver Estate Property

(a) On the final settlement of an estate, if the personal representative neglects on demand to deliver a portion of the estate or any money in the representative's possession ordered to be delivered to a person entitled to that property, the person may file with the court clerk a written complaint alleging:

    (1) the fact of the neglect;

    (2) the date of the person's demand; and

    (3) other relevant facts.

(b) On the filing of a complaint under Subsection (a), the court clerk shall issue a citation to be served personally on the personal representative. The citation must:

    (1) apprise the representative of the complaint; and

    (2) cite the representative to appear before the court and answer, if the representative desires, at a time designated in the citation.

(c) If at the hearing the court finds that the citation was properly served and returned, and that the personal representative is guilty of the neglect charged, the court shall enter an order to that effect.

(d) A personal representative found guilty under Subsection (c) is liable to the person who filed the complaint under Subsection (a) for damages at the rate of 10 percent of the amount of the money or the appraised value of the portion of the estate neglectfully withheld, per month, for each month or fraction of a month that the money or portion of the estate is or has been neglectfully withheld after the date of demand. Damages under this subsection may be recovered in any court of competent jurisdiction.

Derived from Probate Code § 414.

Added by Acts 2009, 81st Leg., ch. 680, § 1, eff. Jan. 1, 2014.

SUBTITLE I. INDEPENDENT ADMINISTRATION

Chapter 401. Creation

Chapter 401. Creation

Statutes in Context
Chapter 401

Texas was a pioneer in the area of non-court-supervised administrations since the first independent administration statutes were enacted in 1843. Independent administrations are extremely common because they are faster, economical, and more convenient than court-supervised (dependent) administrations. Once the personal representative files the inventory, appraisement, and list of claims, the personal representative administers the estate without court involvement.

Chapter 401 explains when an independent administration is possible. (1) The testator's will may expressly authorize independent administration. Although no special language is needed, most attorneys track the statutory language as follows: "I appoint [name] as independent executor. I direct that there shall be no action in the probate court in the settlement of my estate other than the probating and recording of this will, and the return of any required inventory, appraisement, and list of claims of my estate." See § 401.001. (2) If the testator did not specify the executor to be independent, all of the beneficiaries may agree under § 401.002. However, if the will expressly prohibits independent administration, the court will not authorize independent administration. See § 401.001(b). (3) If the decedent died intestate, the heirs may agree to an independent administration under § 401.003.

§ 401.001. Expression of Testator's Intent in Will

(a) Any person capable of making a will may provide in the person's will that no other action shall be had in the probate court in relation to the settlement of the person's estate than the probating and recording of the will and the return of any required inventory, appraisement, and list of claims of the person's estate.

(b) Any person capable of making a will may provide in the person's will that no independent administration of his or her estate may be allowed. In such case the person's estate, if administered, shall be administered and settled under the direction of the probate court as other estates are required to be settled and not as an independent administration.

Derived from Probate Code § 145(b), (o).

Added by Acts 2011, 82nd Leg., ch. 823, § 2.53, eff. Jan. 1, 2014. Subsec. (a) amended by Acts 2013, 83rd Leg., ch. 1136, § 50, eff. Jan. 1, 2014.

§ 401.002. Creation in Testate Estate by Agreement

(a) a) Except as provided in Section 401.001(b), if a decedent's will names an executor but the will does not provide for independent administration as provided in Section 401.001(a), all of the distributees of the decedent may agree on the advisability of having an independent administration and collectively designate in the application for probate of the decedent's will, or in one or more separate documents consenting to the application for probate of the decedent's will, the executor named in the will to serve as independent executor and request [in the application] that no other action shall be had in the probate court in relation to the settlement of the decedent's estate other than the probating and recording of the decedent's will and the return of an inventory, appraisement, and list of claims of the decedent's estate. In such case the probate court shall enter an order granting independent administration and appointing the person, firm, or corporation designated by the distributees [in the application] as independent executor, unless the court finds that it would not be in the best interest of the estate to do so.

(b) Except as provided in Section 401.001(b), in situations where no executor is named in the decedent's will, or in situations where each executor named in the will is deceased or is disqualified to serve as executor or indicates by affidavit filed with the application for administration of the decedent's estate the executor's inability or unwillingness to serve as executor, all of the distributees of the decedent may agree on the advisability of having an independent administration and collectively designate in the application for probate of the decedent's will, or in one or more separate documents consenting to the application for probate of the decedent's will, a qualified person, firm, or corporation to serve as independent administrator and request [in the application] that no other action shall be had in the probate court in relation to the settlement of the decedent's estate other than the probating and recording of the decedent's will and the return of an inventory, appraisement, and list of claims of the decedent's estate. In such case the probate court shall enter an order granting independent administration and appointing the person, firm, or corporation designated by the distributees [in the application] as independent administrator, unless the court finds that it would not be in the best interest of the estate to do so.

Derived from Probate Code § 145(c), (d).

Added by Acts 2011, 82nd Leg., ch. 823, § 2.53, eff. Jan. 1, 2014. Amended by Acts 2015, 84th Leg., ch. 995, § 40, eff. Sept. 1, 2015.

§ 401.003. Creation in Intestate Estate by Agreement

(a) All of the distributees of a decedent dying intestate may agree on the advisability of having an independent administration and collectively designate in the application for administration of the decedent's estate, or in one or more documents consenting to the application for administration of the decedent's estate, a qualified person, firm, or corporation to serve as independent administrator and request [in the application] that no other action shall be had in the probate court in relation to the settlement of the decedent's estate other than the return of an inventory, appraisement, and list of claims of the decedent's estate. In such case the probate court shall enter an order granting independent administration and appointing the person, firm, or corporation designated by the distributees [in the application] as independent

administrator, unless the court finds that it would not be in the best interest of the estate to do so.

(b) The court may not appoint an independent administrator to serve in an intestate administration unless and until the parties seeking appointment of the independent administrator have been determined, through a proceeding to declare heirship under Chapter 202, to constitute all of the decedent's heirs.

Derived from Probate Code § 145(e), (g).

Added by Acts 2011, 82nd Leg., ch. 823, § 2.53, eff. Jan. 1, 2014. Subsec. (a) amended by Acts 2015, 84th Leg., ch. 995, § 41, eff. Sept. 1, 2015.

§ 401.004. Means of Establishing Distributee Consent

(a) This section applies to the creation of an independent administration under Section 401.002 or 401.003.

(b) All distributees shall be served with citation and notice of the application for independent administration unless the distributee waives the issuance or service of citation or enters an appearance in court.

(c) If a distributee is an incapacitated person, the guardian of the person of the distributee may consent to the creation of an independent administration [sign the application] on behalf of the distributee. If the probate court finds that either the granting of independent administration or the appointment of the person, firm, or corporation designated by the distributees [in the application] as independent executor would not be in the best interest of the incapacitated person, then, notwithstanding anything to the contrary in Section 401.002 or 401.003, the court may not enter an order granting independent administration of the estate. If a distributee who is an incapacitated person has no guardian of the person, the probate court may appoint a guardian ad litem to act [make application] on behalf of the incapacitated person if the court considers such an appointment necessary to protect the interest of the distributees. Alternatively, if the distributee who is an incapacitated person is a minor and has no guardian of the person, the natural guardian or guardians of the minor may consent on the minor's behalf if there is no conflict of interest between the minor and the natural guardian or guardians.

(d) If a trust is created in the decedent's will or if the decedent's will devises property to a trustee as described by Section 254.001, the person or class of persons entitled to receive property outright from the trust on the decedent's death and those first eligible to receive the income from the trust, when determined as if the trust were to be in existence on the date of the decedent's death, shall, for the purposes of Section 401.002, be considered to be the distributee or distributees on behalf of the trust, and any other trust or trusts coming into existence on the termination of the trust, and are authorized to apply for independent administration on behalf of the trusts without the consent or agreement of the trustee or any other beneficiary of the trust, or the trustee or any beneficiary of any other trust which may come into existence on the termination of the trust. If a trust beneficiary who is considered to be a distributee under this subsection is an incapacitated person, the trustee or cotrustee may file the application or give the consent, provided that the trustee or cotrustee is not the person proposed to serve as the independent executor.

(e) If a life estate is created either in the decedent's will or by law, the life tenant or life tenants, when determined as if the life estate were to commence on the date of the decedent's death, shall, for the purposes of Section 401.002 or 401.003, be considered to be the distributee or distributees on behalf of the entire estate created, and are authorized to apply for independent administration on behalf of the estate without the consent or approval of any remainderman.

(f) If a decedent's will contains a provision that a distributee must survive the decedent by a prescribed period of time in order to take under the decedent's will, then, for the purposes of determining who shall be the distributee under Section 401.002 and under Subsection (c), it shall be presumed that the distributees living at the time of the filing of the application for probate of the decedent's will survived the decedent by the prescribed period.

(g) In the case of all decedents, whether dying testate or intestate, for the purposes of determining who shall be the distributees under Section 401.002 or 401.003 and under Subsection (c), it shall be presumed that no distributee living at the time the application for independent administration is filed shall subsequently disclaim any portion of the distributee's interest in the decedent's estate.

(h) If a distributee of a decedent's estate dies and if by virtue of the distributee's death the distributee's share of the decedent's estate becomes payable to the distributee's estate, the deceased distributee's personal representative may consent to the [sign the application for] independent administration of the decedent's estate under Section 401.002 or 401.003 and under Subsection (c).

Derived from Probate Code § 145(f), (i), (j), (k), (l), (m), (n).

Added by Acts 2011, 82nd Leg., ch. 823, § 2.53, eff. Jan. 1, 2014. Subsec. (d) amended by Acts 2013, 83rd Leg., ch. 1136, § 51, eff. Jan. 1, 2014. Subsecs (c) & (h) amended by Acts 2015, 84th Leg., ch. 995, § 42, eff. Sept. 1, 2015.

§ 401.005. Bond; Waiver of Bond

(a) If an independent administration of a decedent's estate is created under Section 401.002 or 401.003, then, unless the probate court waives bond on application for waiver, the independent executor shall be required to enter into bond payable to and to be approved by the judge and the judge's successors in a sum that is found by the judge to be adequate under all circumstances, or a bond with one surety in a sum that

is found by the judge to be adequate under all circumstances, if the surety is an authorized corporate surety.

(b) This section does not repeal any other section of this title.

Derived from Probate Code § 145(p).

Added by Acts 2011, 82nd Leg., ch. 823, § 2.53, eff. Jan. 1, 2014.

Statutes in Context
§ 401.006

An independent representative may sell estate property without a court order under the same circumstances that a dependent representative could sell estate property with a court order. In intestate administrations or where a will fails expressly to grant a power of sale, the court may grant an independent administrator a power of sale over real property in the order of appointment if the beneficiaries who would receive the real property consent to the power. Protections for third parties who rely on the apparent authority of an independent representative where a power of sale is granted in the will or the representative provides an affidavit that the sale is necessary under the circumstances described in § 356.251.

§ 401.006. Granting Power of Sale by Agreement

In a situation in which a decedent does not have a will, or a decedent's will does not contain language authorizing the personal representative to sell property or contains language that is not sufficient to grant the representative that authority, the court may include in an order appointing an independent executor [under Section 401.002 or 401.003] any general or specific authority regarding the power of the independent executor to sell property that may be consented to by the beneficiaries who are to receive any interest in the property in the application for independent administration or for the appointment of an independent executor or in their consents to the independent administration or to the appointment of an independent executor. The independent executor, in such event, may sell the property under the authority granted in the court order without the further consent of those beneficiaries.

Derived from Probate Code § 145A.

Added by Acts 2011, 82nd Leg., ch. 823, § 2.53, eff. Jan. 1, 2014. Amended by Acts 2013, 83rd Leg., ch. 1136, § 52, eff. Jan. 1, 2014. Amended by Acts 2015, 84th Leg., ch. 995, § 43, eff. Sept. 1, 2015.

§ 401.007. No Liability of Judge

Absent proof of fraud or collusion on the part of a judge, no judge may be held civilly liable for the commission of misdeeds or the omission of any required act of any person, firm, or corporation designated as an independent executor under Section

401.002 or 401.003. Section 351.354 does not apply to the appointment of an independent executor under Section 401.002 or 401.003.

Derived from Probate Code § 145(q).

Added by Acts 2011, 82nd Leg., ch. 823, § 2.53, eff. Jan. 1, 2014.

§ 401.008. Person Declining to Serve

A person who declines to serve or resigns as independent executor of a decedent's estate may be appointed an executor or administrator of the estate if the estate will be administered and settled under the direction of the court.

Derived from Probate Code § 145(r).

Added by Acts 2011, 82nd Leg., ch. 823, § 2.53, eff. Jan. 1, 2014.

Chapter 402. Administration

Subchapter A. General Provisions

§ 402.001. General Scope and Exercise of Powers
§ 402.002. Independent Executors May Act Without Court Approval

Subchapter B. Power of Sale

§ 402.051. Definition of Independent Executor
§ 402.052. Power of Sale of Estate Property Generally
§ 402.053. Protection of Person Purchasing Estate Property
§ 402.054. No Limitation on Other Action

Chapter 402. Administration

Subchapter A. General Provisions

§ 402.001. General Scope and Exercise of Powers

When an independent administration has been created, and the order appointing an independent executor has been entered by the probate court, and the inventory, appraisement, and list of claims has been filed by the independent executor and approved by the court or an affidavit in lieu of the inventory, appraisement, and list of claims has been filed by the independent executor, as long as the estate is represented by an independent executor, further action of any nature may not be had in the probate court except where this title specifically and explicitly provides for some action in the court.

Derived from Probate Code § 145(h).

Added by Acts 2011, 82nd Leg., ch. 823, § 2.53, eff. Jan. 1, 2014.

§ 402.002. Independent Executors May Act Without Court Approval

Unless this title specifically provides otherwise, any action that a personal representative subject to court supervision may take with or without a court order may be taken by an independent executor without a court order. The other provisions of this subtitle are designed to provide additional guidance regarding independent administrations in specified situations, and are not designed to limit by omission or otherwise the application of the general principles set forth in this chapter.

Derived from Probate Code § 145B.

Added by Acts 2011, 82nd Leg., ch. 823, § 2.53, eff. Jan. 1, 2014.

Subchapter B. Power of Sale

§ 402.051. Definition of Independent Executor

In this subchapter, "independent executor" does not include an independent administrator.

Derived from Probate Code § 145C(a).

Added by Acts 2011, 82nd Leg., ch. 823, § 2.53, eff. Jan. 1, 2014.

§ 402.052. Power of Sale of Estate Property Generally

Unless limited by the terms of a will, an independent executor, in addition to any power of sale of estate property given in the will, and an independent administrator have the same power of sale for the same purposes as a personal representative has in a supervised administration, but without the requirement of court approval. The procedural requirements applicable to a supervised administration do not apply.

Derived from Probate Code § 145C(b).

Added by Acts 2011, 82nd Leg., ch. 823, § 2.53, eff. Jan. 1, 2014.

§ 402.053. Protection of Person Purchasing Estate Property

(a) A person who is not a devisee or heir is not required to inquire into the power of sale of estate property of the independent executor or independent administrator or the propriety of the exercise of the power of sale if the person deals with the independent executor or independent administrator in good faith and:

(1) a power of sale is granted to the independent executor in the will;

(2) a power of sale is granted under Section 401.006 in the court order appointing the independent executor or independent administrator; or

(3) the independent executor or independent administrator provides an affidavit, executed and sworn to under oath and recorded in the deed records of the county where the property is located,

that the sale is necessary or advisable for any of the purposes described in Section 356.251(1).

(b) As to acts undertaken in good faith reliance, the affidavit described by Subsection (a)(3) is conclusive proof, as between a purchaser of property from the estate, and the personal representative of an estate or the heirs and distributees of the estate, with respect to the authority of the independent executor or independent administrator to sell the property. The signature or joinder of a devisee or heir who has an interest in the property being sold as described in this section is not necessary for the purchaser to obtain all right, title, and interest of the estate in the property being sold.

(c) This subchapter does not relieve the independent executor or independent administrator from any duty owed to a devisee or heir in relation, directly or indirectly, to the sale.

Derived from Probate Code § 145C(c).

Added by Acts 2011, 82nd Leg., ch. 823, § 2.53, eff. Jan. 1, 2014.

§ 402.054. No Limitation on Other Action

This subchapter does not limit the authority of an independent executor to take any other action without court supervision or approval with respect to estate assets that may take place in a supervised administration, for purposes and within the scope otherwise authorized by this title, including the authority to enter into a lease and to borrow money.

Derived from Probate Code § 145C(d).

Added by Acts 2011, 82nd Leg., ch. 823, § 2.53, eff. Jan. 1, 2014.

Chapter 403. Exemptions and Allowances; Claims

Subchapter A. Exemptions and Allowances

Subchapter B. Claims

Chapter 403. Exemptions and Allowances; Claims

Statutes in Context
Chapter 403

The independent executor deals with creditors and sets aside exempt property and allowances just like a dependent executor but without court involvement. Note, however, that the courts have held that §§ 355.051, 355.052, and 355.064 do not apply to independent administrations. See *Bunting v. Pearson*, 430 S.W.2d 470 (Tex. 1968).

Subchapter A. Exemptions and Allowances

§ 403.001. Setting Aside Exempt Property and Allowances

The independent executor shall set aside and deliver to those entitled exempt property and allowances for support, and allowances in lieu of exempt property, as prescribed in this title, to the same extent and result as if the independent executor's actions had been accomplished in, and under orders of, the court.

Derived from Probate Code § 146(a)(4).

Added by Acts 2011, 82nd Leg., ch. 823, § 2.53, eff. Jan. 1, 2014.

Subchapter B. Claims

§ 403.051. Duty of Independent Executor

(a) An independent executor, in the administration of an estate, independently of and without application to, or any action in or by the court:

(1) shall give the notices required under Sections 308.051 and 308.053;

(2) may give the notice to an unsecured creditor with a claim for money permitted under Section 308.054 and bar a claim under Section 403.055; and

(3) may approve or reject any claim, or take no action on a claim, and shall classify and pay claims approved or established by suit against the estate in the same order of priority, classification, and proration prescribed in this title.

(b) To be effective, the notice prescribed under Subsection (a)(2) must include, in addition to the other information required by Section 308.054, a statement that a claim may be effectively presented by only one of the methods prescribed by this subchapter.

Derived from Probate Code § 146(a)(1)-(3), (a-1).

Added by Acts 2011, 82nd Leg., ch. 823, § 2.53, eff. Jan. 1, 2014.

§ 403.052. Secured Claims for Money

Within six months after the date letters are granted or within four months after the date notice is received under Section 308.053, whichever is later, a creditor with a claim for money secured by property of the estate must give notice to the independent executor of the creditor's election to have the creditor's claim approved as a matured secured claim to be paid in due course of administration. In addition to giving the notice within this period, a creditor whose claim is secured by real property shall record a notice of the creditor's election under this section in the deed records of the county in which the real property is located. If no election to be a matured secured creditor is made, or the election is made, but not within the prescribed period, or is made within the prescribed period but the creditor has a lien against real property and fails to record notice of the claim in the deed records as required within the prescribed period, the claim shall be a preferred debt and lien against the specific property securing the indebtedness and shall be paid according to the terms of the contract that secured the lien, and the claim may not be asserted against other assets of the estate. The independent executor may pay the claim before maturity if it is determined to be in the best interest of the estate to do so.

Derived from Probate Code § 146(b).

Added by Acts 2011, 82nd Leg., ch. 823, § 2.53, eff. Jan. 1, 2014.

§ 403.053. Matured Secured Claims

(a) A claim approved as a matured secured claim under Section 403.052 remains secured by any lien or security interest against the specific property securing payment of the claim but subordinated to the payment from the property of claims having a higher classification under Section 355.102. However, the secured creditor:

(1) is not entitled to exercise any remedies in a manner that prevents the payment of the higher priority claims and allowances; and

(2) during the administration of the estate, is not entitled to exercise any contractual collection rights, including the power to foreclose, without either the prior written approval of the independent executor or court approval.

(b) Subsection (a) may not be construed to suspend or otherwise prevent a creditor with a matured secured claim from seeking judicial relief of any kind or from executing any judgment against an independent executor. Except with respect to real property, any third party acting in good faith may obtain good title with respect to an estate asset acquired through a secured creditor's extrajudicial collection rights, without regard to whether the creditor had the right to collect the asset or whether the creditor acted improperly in exercising those rights during an estate administration due to having elected matured secured status.

(c) If a claim approved or established by suit as a matured secured claim is secured by property passing to one or more devisees in accordance with Subchapter G, Chapter 255, the independent executor shall collect from the devisees the amount of the debt and pay that amount to the claimant or shall sell the property and pay out of the sale proceeds the claim and associated expenses of sale consistent with the provisions of Sections 355.153(b), (c), (d), and (e) applicable to court supervised administrations.

Derived from Probate Code § 146(b-1).

Added by Acts 2011, 82nd Leg., ch. 823, § 2.53, eff. Jan. 1, 2014.

§ 403.054. Preferred Debt and Lien Claims

During an independent administration, a secured creditor whose claim is a preferred debt and lien against property securing the indebtedness under Section 403.052 is free to exercise any judicial or extrajudicial collection rights, including the right to foreclosure and execution; provided, however, that the creditor does not have the right to conduct a nonjudicial foreclosure sale within six months after letters are granted.

Derived from Probate Code § 146(b-2).

Added by Acts 2011, 82nd Leg., ch. 823, § 2.53, eff. Jan. 1, 2014.

§ 403.055. Certain Unsecured Claims; Barring of Claims

An unsecured creditor who has a claim for money against an estate and who receives a notice under Section 308.054 shall give to the independent executor notice of the nature and amount of the claim before the 121st day after the date the notice is received or the claim is barred.

Derived from Probate Code § 146(b-3).

Added by Acts 2011, 82nd Leg., ch. 823, § 2.53, eff. Jan. 1, 2014. Amended by Acts 2013, 83rd Leg., ch. 1136, § 53, eff. Jan. 1, 2014.

§ 403.056. Notices Required by Creditors

(a) Notice to the independent executor required by Sections 403.052 and 403.055 must be contained in:

(1) a written instrument that complies with Section 355.004 and is hand-delivered with proof of receipt, or mailed by certified mail, return receipt requested with proof of receipt, to the independent executor or the executor's attorney;

(2) a pleading filed in a lawsuit with respect to the claim; or

(3) a written instrument that complies with Section 355.004 or a pleading filed in the court in which the administration of the estate is pending.

(b) This section does not exempt a creditor who elects matured secured status from the filing requirements of Section 403.052, to the extent those requirements are applicable.

Derived from Probate Code § 146(b-4), (b-5).

Added by Acts 2011, 82nd Leg., ch. 823, § 2.53, eff. Jan. 1, 2014. Subsec. (a) amended by Acts 2013, 83rd Leg., ch. 1136, § 54, eff. Jan. 1, 2014.

§ 403.057. Statute of Limitations

Except as otherwise provided by Section 16.062, Civil Practice and Remedies Code, the running of the statute of limitations shall be tolled only by a written approval of a claim signed by an independent executor, a pleading filed in a suit pending at the time of the decedent's death, or a suit brought by the creditor against the independent executor. In particular, the presentation of a statement or claim, or a notice with respect to a claim, to an independent executor does not toll the running of the statute of limitations with respect to that claim.

Derived from Probate Code § 146(b-6).

Added by Acts 2011, 82nd Leg., ch. 823, § 2.53, eff. Jan. 1, 2014.

§ 403.058. Other Claim Procedures Generally Do Not Apply

Except as otherwise provided by this subchapter, the procedural provisions of this title governing creditor claims in supervised administrations do not apply to independent administrations. By way of example, but not as a limitation:

(1) Sections 355.064 and 355.066 do not apply to independent administrations, and consequently a creditor's claim may not be barred solely because the creditor failed to file a suit not later than the 90th day after the date an independent executor rejected the claim or with respect to a claim for which the independent executor takes no action; and

(2) Sections 355.156, 355.157, 355.158, 355.159, and 355.160 do not apply to independent administrations.

Derived from Probate Code § 146(b-7).

Added by Acts 2011, 82nd Leg., ch. 823, § 2.53, eff. Jan. 1, 2014.

§ 403.0585. Liability of Independent Executor for Payment of a Claim

An independent executor, in the administration of an estate, may pay at any time and without personal liability a claim for money against the estate to the extent approved and classified by the independent executor if:

(1) the claim is not barred by limitations; and

(2) at the time of payment, the independent executor reasonably believes the estate will have sufficient assets to pay all claims against the estate.

Derived from Probate Code § 146(c).

Added by Acts 2011, 82nd Leg., ch. 823, § 2.53, eff. Jan. 1, 2014.

§ 403.059. Enforcement of Claims by Suit

Any person having a debt or claim against the estate may enforce the payment of the same by suit against the independent executor; and, when judgment is recovered against the independent executor, the execution shall run against the estate of the decedent in the possession of the independent executor that is subject to the debt. The independent executor shall not be required to plead to any suit brought against the executor for money until after six months after the date that an independent administration was created and the order appointing the executor was entered by the probate court.

Derived from Probate Code § 147.

Added by Acts 2011, 82nd Leg., ch. 823, § 2.53, eff. Jan. 1, 2014.

§ 403.060. Requiring Heirs to Give Bond

When an independent administration is created and the order appointing an independent executor is entered by the probate court, any person having a debt against the estate may, by written complaint filed in the probate court in which the order was entered, cause all distributees of the estate, heirs at law, and other persons entitled to any portion of the estate under the will, if any, to be cited by personal service to appear before the court and execute a bond for an amount equal to the amount of the creditor's claim or the full value of the estate, as shown by the inventory and list of claims, whichever is smaller. The bond must be payable to the judge, and the judge's successors, and be approved by the judge, and conditioned that all obligors shall pay all debts that shall be established against the estate in the manner provided by law. On the return of the citation served, unless a person so entitled to any portion of the estate, or some of them, or some other person for them, shall execute the bond to the satisfaction of the probate court, the estate shall be administered and settled under the direction of the probate court as other estates are required to be settled. If the bond is executed and approved, the independent administration shall proceed. Creditors of the estate may sue on the bond, and shall be entitled to judgment on the bond for the amount of their debt, or they may have their action against those in possession of the estate.

Derived from Probate Code § 148.

Added by Acts 2011, 82nd Leg., ch. 823, § 2.53, eff. Jan. 1, 2014.

Chapter 404. Accountings, Successors, and Other Remedies

Chapter 404. Accountings, Successors, and Other Remedies

Statutes in Context
Chapter 404

The independent executor does not need to render annual accountings. Instead, accountings are required only under the circumstances described in the Code, that is, (1) if an interested person demands an accounting 15 months or more after the date independent executor received letters (§ 404.001), or (2) an interested person petitions the court for an accounting and distribution after 2 years from the date of the creation of the independent administration (see § 405.001).

§ 404.001. Accounting

(a) At any time after the expiration of 15 months after the date that the court clerk first issues letters testamentary or of administration to any personal representative of an estate, any person interested in the estate may demand an accounting from the independent executor. The independent executor shall furnish to the person or persons making the demand an exhibit in writing, sworn and subscribed by the independent executor, setting forth in detail:

(1) the property belonging to the estate that has come into the executor's possession as executor;

(2) the disposition that has been made of the property described by Subdivision (1);

(3) the debts that have been paid;

(4) the debts and expenses, if any, still owing by the estate;

(5) the property of the estate, if any, still remaining in the executor's possession;

(6) other facts as may be necessary to a full and definite understanding of the exact condition of the estate; and

(7) the facts, if any, that show why the administration should not be closed and the estate distributed.

(a-1) Any other interested person shall, on demand, be entitled to a copy of any exhibit or accounting that has been made by an independent executor in compliance with this section.

(b) Should the independent executor not comply with a demand for an accounting authorized by this section within 60 days after receipt of the demand, the person making the demand may compel compliance by an action in the probate court. After a hearing, the court shall enter an order requiring the accounting to be made at such time as it considers proper under the circumstances.

(c) After an initial accounting has been given by an independent executor, any person interested in an estate may demand subsequent periodic accountings at intervals of not less than 12 months, and such subsequent demands may be enforced in the same manner as an initial demand.

(d) The right to an accounting accorded by this section is cumulative of any other remedies which persons interested in an estate may have against the independent executor of the estate.

Derived from Probate Code § 149A.

Added by Acts 2011, 82nd Leg., ch. 823, § 2.53, eff. Jan. 1, 2014. Subsec. (a) amended by Acts 2013, 83rd Leg., ch. 1136, § 55, eff. Jan. 1, 2014.

§ 404.002. Requiring Independent Executor to Give Bond

When it has been provided by will, regularly probated, that an independent executor appointed by the will shall not be required to give bond for the management of the estate devised by the will, or the independent executor is not required to give bond because bond has been waived by court order as authorized under Section 401.005, then the independent executor may be required to give bond, on proper proceedings had for that purpose as in the case of personal representatives in a supervised administration, if it be made to appear at any time that the independent executor is mismanaging the property, or has betrayed or is about to betray the independent executor's trust, or has in some other way become disqualified.

Derived from Probate Code § 149.

Added by Acts 2011, 82nd Leg., ch. 823, § 2.53, eff. Jan. 1, 2014.

§ 404.003. Removal of Independent Executor Without Notice

The probate court, on the court's own motion or on the motion of any interested person, and without notice, may remove an independent executor appointed under this subtitle when:

(1) the independent executor cannot be served with notice or other processes because:

(A) the independent executor's whereabouts are unknown;

(B) the independent executor is eluding service; or

(C) the independent executor is a nonresident of this state without a designated resident agent; or

(2) sufficient grounds appear to support a belief that the independent executor has misapplied or embezzled, or is about to misapply or embezzle, all or part of the property committed to the independent executor's care.

New.

Added by Acts 2011, 82nd Leg., ch. 823, § 2.53, eff. Jan. 1, 2014. Amended by Acts 2013, 83rd Leg., ch. 1136, § 56, eff. Jan. 1, 2014.

§ 404.0035. Removal of Independent Executor With Notice

(a) The probate court, on the court's own motion, may remove an independent executor appointed under this subtitle after providing 30 days' written notice of the court's intent to remove the independent executor, by certified mail, return receipt requested, to the independent executor's last known address and to the last known address of the independent executor's attorney of record, if the independent executor:

(1) neglects to qualify in the manner and time required by law; or

(2) fails to return, before the 91st day after the date the independent executor qualifies, either an inventory of the estate property and a list of claims that have come to the independent executor's knowledge or an affidavit in lieu of the inventory, appraisement, and list of claims, unless that deadline is extended by court order.

(b) The probate court, on its own motion or on motion of any interested person, after the independent executor has been cited by personal service to answer at a time and place fixed in the notice, may remove an independent executor when:

(1) the independent executor fails to make an accounting which is required by law to be made;

(2) the independent executor fails to timely file the affidavit or certificate required by Section 308.004;

(3) the independent executor is proved to have been guilty of gross misconduct or gross mismanagement in the performance of the independent executor's duties;

(4) the independent executor becomes an incapacitated person, or is sentenced to the penitentiary, or from any other cause becomes legally incapacitated from properly performing the independent executor's fiduciary duties; or

(5) the independent executor becomes incapable of properly performing the independent executor's fiduciary duties due to a material conflict of interest.

Derived from Probate Code § 149C.

Added by Acts 2013, 83rd Leg., ch. 1136, § 56, eff. Jan. 1, 2014.

§ 404.0036. Removal Order

(a) The order of removal of an independent executor shall state the cause of removal and shall direct by order the disposition of the assets remaining in the name or under the control of the removed independent executor. The order of removal shall require that letters issued to the removed independent executor shall be surrendered and that all letters shall be canceled of record.

(b) If an independent executor is removed by the court under Section 404.003 or 404.0035, the court may, on application, appoint a successor independent executor as provided by Section 404.005.

Derived from Probate Code § 149C.

Added by Acts 2013, 83rd Leg., ch. 1136, § 56, eff. Jan. 1, 2014.

§ 404.0037. Costs and Expenses Related to Removal of Independent Executor

(a) An independent executor who defends an action for the independent executor's removal in good faith, whether successful or not, shall be allowed out of the estate the independent executor's necessary expenses and disbursements, including reasonable attorney's fees, in the removal proceedings.

(b) Costs and expenses incurred by the party seeking removal that are incident to removal of an independent executor appointed without bond, including reasonable attorney's fees and expenses, may be paid out of the estate.

Derived from Probate Code § 149C.

Added by Acts 2013, 83rd Leg., ch. 1136, § 56, eff. Jan. 1, 2014.

§ 404.004. Powers of an Administrator Who Succeeds an Independent Executor

(a) Whenever a person has died, or shall die, testate, owning property in this state, and the person's will has been or shall be admitted to probate by the court, and the probated will names an independent executor or executors, or trustees acting in the capacity of independent executors, to execute the terms and provisions of that will, and the will grants to the independent executor, or executors, or trustees acting in the capacity of independent executors, the power to raise or borrow money and to mortgage, and the independent executor, or executors, or trustees, have died or shall die, resign, fail to qualify, or be removed from office, leaving unexecuted parts or portions of the will of the testator, and an administrator with the will annexed is appointed by the probate court, and an administrator's bond is filed and approved by the court, then in all such cases, the court may, in addition to the powers conferred on the administrator under other provisions of the laws of this state, authorize, direct, and empower the administrator to do and perform the acts and deeds, clothed with the rights, powers, authorities, and privileges, and subject to the limitations, set forth in the subsequent provisions of this section.

(b) The court, on application, citation, and hearing, may, by its order, authorize, direct, and empower the administrator to raise or borrow such sums of money and incur such obligations and debts as the court shall, in its said order, direct, and to renew and extend same from time to time, as the court, on application and order, shall provide; and, if authorized by the court's order, to secure such loans, obligations, and debts, by pledge or mortgage on property or assets of the estate, real, personal, or mixed, on such terms and conditions, and for such duration of time, as the court shall consider to be in the best interests of the estate, and by its order shall prescribe; and all such loans, obligations, debts, pledges, and mortgages shall be valid and enforceable against the estate and against the administrator in the administrator's official capacity.

(c) The court may order and authorize the administrator to have and exercise the powers and privileges set forth in Subsection (a) or (b) only to the extent that same are granted to or possessed by the independent executor, or executors, or trustees acting in the capacity of independent executors, under the terms of the probated will of the decedent, and then only in such cases as it appears, at the hearing of the application, that at the time of the appointment of the administrator, there are outstanding and unpaid obligations and debts of the estate, or of the independent executor, or executors, or trustees, chargeable against the estate, or unpaid expenses of administration, or when the court appointing the administrator orders the business of the estate to be carried on and it becomes necessary, from time to time, under orders of the court, for the administrator to borrow money and incur obligations and indebtedness in order to protect and preserve the estate.

(d) The court, in addition, may, on application, citation, and hearing, order, authorize, and empower the administrator to assume, exercise, and discharge, under the orders and directions of the court, made from time to time, all or such part of the rights, powers, and authorities vested in and delegated to, or possessed by, the independent executor, or executors, or trustees acting in the capacity of independent executors, under the terms of the will of the decedent, as the court finds to be in the best interests of the estate and shall, from time to time, order and direct.

(e) The granting to the administrator by the court of some, or all, of the powers and authorities set forth in this section shall be on application filed by the administrator with the county clerk, setting forth such facts as, in the judgment of the administrator, require the granting of the power or authority requested.

(f) On the filing of an application under Subsection (e), the clerk shall issue citation to all persons interested in the estate, stating the nature of the application, and requiring those persons to appear on the return day named in such citation and show cause why the application should not be granted, should they choose to do so. The citation shall be served by posting.

(g) The court shall hear the application and evidence on the application, on or after the return day named in the citation, and, if satisfied a necessity exists and that it would be in the best interests of the estate to grant the application in whole or in part, the court shall so order; otherwise, the court shall refuse the application.

Derived from Probate Code § 154.

Added by Acts 2011, 82nd Leg., ch. 823, § 2.53, eff. Jan. 1, 2014.

§ 404.005. Court-Appointed Successor Independent Executor

(a) If the will of a person who dies testate names an independent executor who, having qualified, fails for any reason to continue to serve, or is removed for cause by the court, and the will does not name a successor independent executor or if each successor executor named in the will fails for any reason to qualify as executor or indicates by affidavit filed with the application for an order continuing independent administration the successor executor's inability or unwillingness to serve as successor independent executor, all of the distributees of the decedent as of the filing of the application for an order continuing independent administration may apply to the probate court for the appointment of a qualified person, firm, or corporation to serve as successor independent executor. If the probate court finds that continued administration of the estate is necessary, the court shall enter an order continuing independent administration and appointing the person, firm, or corporation designated in the application as successor independent executor, unless the probate court finds that it would not be in the best interest of the estate to do so. The successor independent executor shall serve with all of the powers and privileges granted to the successor's predecessor independent executor.

(b) Except as otherwise provided by this subsection, if a distributee described in this section is an incapacitated person, the guardian of the person of the distributee may sign the application on behalf of the distributee. If the probate court finds that either the continuing of independent administration or the appointment of the person, firm, or corporation designated in the application as successor independent executor would not be in the best interest of the incapacitated person, then, notwithstanding Subsection (a), the court may not enter an order continuing independent administration of the estate. If the distributee is an incapacitated person and has no guardian of the person, the court may appoint a guardian ad litem to make application on behalf of the incapacitated person if the probate court considers such an appointment necessary to protect the interest of that distributee. If a distributee described in this section is a minor and has no guardian of the person, a natural guardian of the minor may sign the application for the order continuing independent administration on the minor's behalf unless a conflict of interest exists between the minor and the natural guardian.

(c) Except as otherwise provided by this subsection, if a trust is created in the decedent's will or if the decedent's will devises property to a trustee as described by Section 254.001, the person or class of persons entitled to receive property outright from the trust on the decedent's death and those first eligible to receive the income from the trust, determined as if the trust were to be in existence on the date of the filing of the application for an order continuing independent administration, shall, for the purposes of this section, be considered to be the distributee or distributees on behalf of the trust, and any other trust or trusts coming into existence on the termination of the trust, and are authorized to apply for an order continuing independent administration on behalf of the trust without the consent or agreement of the trustee or any other beneficiary of the trust, or the trustee or any beneficiary of any other trust which may come into existence on the termination of the trust. If a person considered to be a distributee under this subsection is an incapacitated person, the trustee or cotrustee may apply for the order continuing independent administration or sign the application on the incapacitated person's behalf if the trustee or cotrustee is not the person proposed to serve as the independent executor.

(d) If a life estate is created either in the decedent's will or by law, and if a life tenant is living at the time of the filing of the application for an order continuing independent administration, then the life tenant or life tenants, determined as if the life estate were to commence on the date of the filing of the application for an order continuing independent administration, shall, for the purposes of this section, be considered to be the distributee or distributees on behalf of the entire estate created, and are authorized to apply for an order continuing independent administration on behalf of the estate without the consent or approval of any remainderman.

(e) If a decedent's will contains a provision that a distributee must survive the decedent by a prescribed period of time in order to take under the decedent's will, for the purposes of determining who shall be the distributee under this section, it shall be presumed that the distributees living at the time of the filing of the application for an order continuing independent administration of the decedent's estate survived the decedent for the prescribed period.

(f) In the case of all decedents, for the purposes of determining who shall be the distributees under this section, it shall be presumed that no distributee living at the time the application for an order continuing independent administration of the decedent's estate is filed shall subsequently disclaim any portion of the distributee's interest in the decedent's estate.

(g) If a distributee of a decedent's estate should die, and if by virtue of the distributee's death the distributee's share of the decedent's estate shall become payable to the distributee's estate, then the deceased distributee's personal representative may sign the application for an order continuing independent administration of the decedent's estate under this section.

(h) If a successor independent executor is appointed under this section, then, unless the probate court shall waive bond on application for waiver, the successor independent executor shall be required to enter into bond payable to and to be approved by the judge and

the judge's successors in a sum that is found by the judge to be adequate under all circumstances, or a bond with one surety in an amount that is found by the judge to be adequate under all circumstances, if the surety is an authorized corporate surety.

(i) Absent proof of fraud or collusion on the part of a judge, the judge may not be held civilly liable for the commission of misdeeds or the omission of any required act of any person, firm, or corporation designated as a successor independent executor under this section. Section 351.354 does not apply to an appointment of a successor independent executor under this section.

Derived from Probate Code § 154A.

Added by Acts 2011, 82nd Leg., ch. 823, § 2.53, eff. Jan. 1, 2014. Subsecs. (b) and (c) amended by Acts 2013, 83rd Leg., ch. 1136, § 57, eff. Jan. 1, 2014.

Chapter 405. Closing and Distributions

Chapter 405. Closing and Distributions

Statutes in Context
Chapter 405

The independent executor does not need to render annual accountings. Instead, accountings are required only under the circumstances described in the Code, that is, (1) if an interested person demands an accounting 15 months or more after the date the independent executor received letters (§ 404.001), or (2) an interested person petitions the court for an accounting and distribution after 2 years from the date of the creation of the independent administration (see § 405.001).

§ 405.001. Accounting and Distribution

(a) In addition to or in lieu of the right to an accounting provided by Section 404.001, at any time after the expiration of two years after the date the court clerk first issues letters testamentary or of administration to any personal representative of an estate, a person interested in the estate then subject to independent administration may petition the court for an accounting and distribution. The court may order an accounting to be made with the court by the independent executor at such time as the court considers proper. The accounting shall include the information that the court considers necessary to determine whether any part of the estate should be distributed.

(b) On receipt of the accounting and, after notice to the independent executor and a hearing, unless the court finds a continued necessity for administration of the estate, the court shall order its distribution by the independent executor to the distributees entitled to the property. If the court finds there is a continued necessity for administration of the estate, the court shall order the distribution of any portion of the estate that the court finds should not be subject to further administration by the independent executor. If any portion of the estate that is ordered to be distributed is incapable of distribution without prior partition or sale, the court may:

(1) order partition and distribution, or sale, in the manner provided for the partition and distribution of property incapable of division in supervised estates; or

(2) order distribution of that portion of the estate incapable of distribution without prior partition or sale in undivided interests.

(c) If all the property in the estate is ordered distributed by the court and the estate is fully administered, the court may also order the independent executor to file a final account with the court and may enter an order closing the administration and terminating the power of the independent executor to act as executor.

Derived from Probate Code § 149B.

Added by Acts 2011, 82nd Leg., ch. 823, § 2.53, eff. Jan. 1, 2014. Subsec. (b) amended by Acts 2013, 83rd Leg., ch. 1136, § 58, eff. Jan. 1, 2014.

§ 405.002. Receipts and Releases for Distributions by Independent Executor

(a) An independent executor may not be required to deliver tangible or intangible personal property to a distributee unless the independent executor receives, at or before the time of delivery of the property, a signed receipt or other proof of delivery of the property to the distributee.

(b) An independent executor may not require a waiver or release from the distributee as a condition of delivery of property to a distributee.

Derived from Probate Code § 151(e).

Added by Acts 2011, 82nd Leg., ch. 823, § 2.53, eff.

Jan. 1, 2014.

Statutes in Context
§§ 405.003–405.009

There is no requirement that an independent administration be closed. § 405.012. The Code, however, provides three methods for closing the administration. (1) Section 405.004 permits the independent executor to file a closing report affidavit or a notice of closing affidavit. The court takes no action on the affidavit unless an interested party files an objection within thirty days. (2) Section 405.009 permits an heir or beneficiary to petition the court for an order closing the estate. (3) Section 405.003 permits the court to discharge an independent executor so that the executor will have a court order indicating that he or she is not liable for any matters relating to the past administration of the estate which have been fully and fairly disclosed.

Case law has indicated that the statutory closing methods are not exclusive. Final distribution of the estate after creditors are paid may result in the closing of the estate by operation of law. *In re Estate of Teinert*, 251 S.W.3d 66 (Tex. App.—Waco 2008, pet. denied).

---

§ 405.003. Judicial Discharge of Independent Executor

(a) After an estate has been administered and if there is no further need for an independent administration of the estate, the independent executor of the estate may file an action for declaratory judgment under Chapter 37, Civil Practice and Remedies Code, seeking to discharge the independent executor from any liability involving matters relating to the past administration of the estate that have been fully and fairly disclosed.

(b) On the filing of an action under this section, each beneficiary of the estate shall be personally served with citation, except for a beneficiary who has waived the issuance and service of citation.

(c) In a proceeding under this section, the court may require the independent executor to file a final account that includes any information the court considers necessary to adjudicate the independent executor's request for a discharge of liability. The court may audit, settle, or approve a final account filed under this subsection.

(d) On or before filing an action under this section, the independent executor must distribute to the beneficiaries of the estate any of the remaining assets or property of the estate that remains in the independent executor's possession after all of the estate's debts have been paid, except for a reasonable reserve of assets that the independent executor may retain in a fiduciary capacity pending court approval of the final account. The court may review the amount of assets on reserve and may order the independent executor to make further distributions under this section.

(e) Except as ordered by the court, the independent executor is entitled to pay from the estate legal fees, expenses, or other costs incurred in relation to a proceeding for judicial discharge filed under this section. The independent executor shall be personally liable to refund any amount of such fees, expenses, or other costs not approved by the court as a proper charge against the estate.

Derived from Probate Code §§ 149D, 149E, 149F.

Added by Acts 2011, 82nd Leg., ch. 823, § 2.53, eff. Jan. 1, 2014.

§ 405.004. Closing Independent Administration by Closing Report or Notice of Closing Estate

When all of the debts known to exist against the estate have been paid, or when they have been paid so far as the assets in the independent executor's possession will permit, when there is no pending litigation, and when the independent executor has distributed to the distributees entitled to the estate all assets of the estate, if any, remaining after payment of debts, the independent executor may file with the court a closing report or a notice of closing of the estate.

Derived from Probate Code § 151(a).

Added by Acts 2011, 82nd Leg., ch. 823, § 2.53, eff. Jan. 1, 2014.

§ 405.005. Closing Report

An independent executor may file a closing report verified by affidavit that:

(1) shows:

(A) the property of the estate that came into the independent executor's possession;

(B) the debts that have been paid;

(C) the debts, if any, still owing by the estate;

(D) the property of the estate, if any, remaining on hand after payment of debts; and

(E) the names and addresses of the distributees to whom the property of the estate, if any, remaining on hand after payment of debts has been distributed; and

(2) includes signed receipts or other proof of delivery of property to the distributees named in the closing report if the closing report reflects that there was property remaining on hand after payment of debts.

Derived from Probate Code § 151(a-1).

Added by Acts 2011, 82nd Leg., ch. 823, § 2.53, eff. Jan. 1, 2014.

§ 405.006. Notice of Closing Estate

(a) Instead of filing a closing report under Section 405.005, an independent executor may file a notice of closing estate verified by affidavit that states:

(1) that all debts known to exist against the estate have been paid or have been paid to the extent permitted by the assets in the independent executor's possession;

(2) that all remaining assets of the estate, if any, have been distributed; and

(3) the names and addresses of the distributees to whom the property of the estate, if any, remaining on hand after payment of debts has been distributed.

(b) Before filing the notice, the independent executor shall provide to each distributee of the estate a copy of the notice of closing estate. The notice of closing estate filed by the independent executor must include signed receipts or other proof that all distributees have received a copy of the notice of closing estate.

Derived from Probate Code § 151(b).

Added by Acts 2011, 82nd Leg., ch. 823, § 2.53, eff. Jan. 1, 2014.

§ 405.007. Effect of Filing Closing Report or Notice of Closing Estate

(a) The independent administration of an estate is considered closed 30 days after the date of the filing of a closing report or notice of closing estate unless an interested person files an objection with the court within that time. If an interested person files an objection within the 30-day period, the independent administration of the estate is closed when the objection has been disposed of or the court signs an order closing the estate.

(b) The closing of an independent administration by filing of a closing report or notice of closing estate terminates the power and authority of the independent executor, but does not relieve the independent executor from liability for any mismanagement of the estate or from liability for any false statements contained in the report or notice.

(c) When a closing report or notice of closing estate has been filed, persons dealing with properties of the estate, or with claims against the estate, shall deal directly with the distributees of the estate; and the acts of the distributees with respect to the properties or claims shall in all ways be valid and binding as regards the persons with whom they deal, notwithstanding any false statements made by the independent executor in the report or notice.

(d) If the independent executor is required to give bond, the independent executor's filing of the closing report and proof of delivery, if required, automatically releases the sureties on the bond from all liability for the future acts of the principal. The filing of a notice of closing estate does not release the sureties on the bond of an independent executor.

(e) An independent executor's closing report or notice of closing estate shall constitute sufficient legal authority to all persons owing any money, having custody of any property, or acting as registrar or

331

transfer agent or trustee of any evidence of interest, indebtedness, property, or right that belongs to the estate, for payment or transfer without additional administration to the distributees described in the will as entitled to receive the particular asset or who as heirs at law are entitled to receive the asset. The distributees described in the will as entitled to receive the particular asset or the heirs at law entitled to receive the asset may enforce their right to the payment or transfer by suit.

Derived from Probate Code § 151(c), (d).

Added by Acts 2011, 82nd Leg., ch. 823, § 2.53, eff. Jan. 1, 2014.

§ 405.008. Partition and Distribution or Sale of Property Incapable of Division

If the will does not distribute the entire estate of the testator or provide a means for partition of the estate, or if no will was probated, the independent executor may, but may not be required to, petition the probate court for either a partition and distribution of the estate or an order of sale of any portion of the estate alleged by the independent executor and found by the court to be incapable of a fair and equal partition and distribution, or both. The estate or portion of the estate shall either be partitioned and distributed or sold, or both, in the manner provided for the partition and distribution of property and the sale of property incapable of division in supervised estates.

Derived from Probate Code § 150.

Added by Acts 2011, 82nd Leg., ch. 823, § 2.53, eff. Jan. 1, 2014.

§ 405.009. Closing Independent Administration on Application by Distributee

(a) At any time after an estate has been fully administered and there is no further need for an independent administration of the estate, any distributee may file an application to close the administration; and, after citation on the independent executor, and on hearing, the court may enter an order:

(1) requiring the independent executor to file a closing report meeting the requirements of Section 405.005;

(2) closing the administration;

(3) terminating the power of the independent executor to act as independent executor; and

(4) releasing the sureties on any bond the independent executor was required to give from all liability for the future acts of the principal.

(b) The order of the court closing the independent administration shall constitute sufficient legal authority to all persons owing any money, having custody of any property, or acting as registrar or transfer agent or trustee of any evidence of interest, indebtedness, property, or right that belongs to the estate, for payment or transfer without additional administration to the distributees described in the will as entitled to receive the particular asset or who as heirs at law are entitled to receive the asset. The distributees described in the will

as entitled to receive the particular asset or the heirs at law entitled to receive the asset may enforce their right to the payment or transfer by suit.

Derived from Probate Code § 152.

Added by Acts 2011, 82nd Leg., ch. 823, § 2.53, eff. Jan. 1, 2014.

§ 405.010. Issuance of Letters

At any time before the authority of an independent executor has been terminated in the manner set forth in this subtitle, the clerk shall issue such number of letters testamentary as the independent executor shall request.

Derived from Probate Code § 153.

Added by Acts 2011, 82nd Leg., ch. 823, § 2.53, eff. Jan. 1, 2014.

§ 405.011. Rights and Remedies Cumulative

The rights and remedies conferred by this chapter are cumulative of other rights and remedies to which a person interested in the estate may be entitled under law.

Derived from Probate Code § 149G.

Added by Acts 2011, 82nd Leg., ch. 823, § 2.53, eff. Jan. 1, 2014.

§ 405.012. Closing Procedures Not Required

An independent executor is not required to close the independent administration of an estate under Section 405.003 or Sections 405.004 through 405.007.

New.

Added by Acts 2011, 82nd Leg., ch. 823, § 2.53, eff. Jan. 1, 2014.

SUBTITLE J. ADDITIONAL MATTERS RELATING TO THE ADMINISTRATION OF CERTAIN ESTATES

Chapter 451. Order of No Administration

Chapter 451. Order of No Administration

Statutes in Context
Chapter 451

Chapter 451 provides a procedure for a court

to dispense with administration if (1) the decedent is survived by a spouse, minor child, or adult incapacitated child, and (2) the value of the estate, not including homestead and exempt property, does not exceed the family allowance. Administration is not necessary because there would be no property for the decedent's creditors or will beneficiaries to reach.

§ 451.001. Application for Family Allowance and Order of No Administration

(a) If the value of the entire assets of an estate, excluding homestead and exempt property, does not exceed the amount to which the surviving spouse, minor children, and adult incapacitated children of the decedent are entitled as a family allowance, an application may be filed by or on behalf of the surviving spouse, minor children, or adult incapacitated children requesting a court to make a family allowance and to enter an order that no administration of the decedent's estate is necessary.

(b) The application may be filed:

(1) in any court in which venue is proper for administration; or

(2) if an application for the appointment of a personal representative has been filed but not yet granted, in the court in which the application is filed.

(c) The application must:

(1) state the names of the heirs or devisees;

(2) list, to the extent known, estate creditors together with the amounts of the claims; and

(3) describe all property belonging to the estate, together with:

(A) the estimated value of the property according to the best knowledge and information of the applicant; and

(B) the liens and encumbrances on the property.

(d) The application must also include a prayer that the court make a family allowance and that, if the family allowance exhausts the entire assets of the estate, excluding homestead and exempt property, the entire assets of the estate be set aside to the surviving spouse, minor children, and adult incapacitated children, as with other family allowances provided for by Subchapter C, Chapter 353.

Derived from Probate Code § 139.

Added by Acts 2009, 81st Leg., ch. 680, § 1, eff. Jan. 1, 2014. Subsecs. (a) and (d) amended by Acts 2011, 82nd Leg., ch. 810, § 2.15, eff. Jan. 1, 2014.

§ 451.002. Hearing and Order

(a) On the filing of an application under Section 451.001, the court may hear the application:

(1) promptly without notice; or

(2) at a time and with notice as required by the court.

(b) On the hearing of the application, if the court finds that the facts contained in the application are true and that the expenses of last illness, funeral charges, and expenses of the proceeding have been paid or secured, the court shall:

(1) make a family allowance; and

(2) if the entire assets of the estate, excluding homestead and exempt property, are exhausted by the family allowance made under Subdivision (1):

(A) assign to the surviving spouse, minor children, and adult incapacitated children the entire estate in the same manner and with the same effect as provided in Subchapter C, Chapter 353, for the making of a family allowance to the surviving spouse, minor children, and adult incapacitated children; and

(B) order that there shall be no administration of the estate.

Derived from Probate Code § 140.

Added by Acts 2009, 81st Leg., ch. 680, § 1, eff. Jan. 1, 2014. Subsec. (b) amended by Acts 2011, 82nd Leg., ch. 810, § 2.16, eff. Jan. 1, 2014.

§ 451.003. Effect of Order

(a) An order of no administration issued under Section 451.002(b) constitutes sufficient legal authority to each person who owes money, has custody of property, or acts as registrar or transfer agent of any evidence of interest, indebtedness, property, or right, belonging to the estate, and to each person purchasing from or otherwise dealing with the estate, for payment or transfer without administration to the persons described in the order as entitled to receive the estate.

(b) The persons described in the order are entitled to enforce by suit their right to payment or transfer described by this section.

Derived from Probate Code § 141.

Added by Acts 2009, 81st Leg., ch. 680, § 1, eff. Jan. 1, 2014.

§ 451.004. Proceeding to Revoke Order

(a) At any time, but not later than the first anniversary of the date of entry of an order of no administration under Section 451.002(b), any interested person may file an application to revoke the order.

(b) An application to revoke the order must allege that:

(1) other estate property has been discovered, property belonging to the estate was not included in the application for no administration, or the property described in the application for no administration was incorrectly valued; and

(2) if that property were added, included, or correctly valued, as applicable, the total value of the property would exceed the amount necessary to justify the court in ordering no administration.

(c) The court shall revoke the order on proof of any of the grounds described by Subsection (b).

(d) If the value of any property is contested, the court may appoint two appraisers to appraise the property in accordance with the procedure prescribed for inventories and appraisements under Chapter 309. The appraisement of the appointed appraisers shall be received in evidence but is not conclusive.

Derived from Probate Code § 142.

Added by Acts 2009, 81st Leg., ch. 680, § 1, eff. Jan. 1, 2014.

Chapter 452. Temporary Administration of Estates

Subchapter A. Appointment of Temporary Administrator Generally

Subchapter B. Temporary Administration Pending Contest of a Will or Administration

Subchapter C. Powers and Duties of Temporary Administrator

Subchapter D. Expiration and Closing of Temporary Administration

Chapter 452. Temporary Administration of Estates

Subchapter A. Appointment of Temporary Administrator Generally

Chapter 452, Subchapter A, permits the court to appoint a temporary administrator to protect a decedent's estate. Any person, even someone who does not qualify as an interested person under § 22.018, may request a temporary administration.

§ 452.001.   Duty to Appoint Temporary Administrator

A judge who determines that the interest of a decedent's estate requires the immediate appointment of a personal representative shall, by written order, appoint a temporary administrator with powers limited as the circumstances of the case require.

Derived from Probate Code § 131A(a).

Added by Acts 2009, 81st Leg., ch. 680, § 1, eff. Jan. 1, 2014.

§ 452.002.   Application for Appointment

(a) A person may file with the court clerk a written application for the appointment of a temporary administrator of a decedent's estate under this subchapter.

(b) The application must:

(1) be verified;

(2) include the information required by:

(A) Sections 256.052, 256.053, and 256.054, if the decedent died testate; or

(B) Section 301.052, if the decedent died intestate; and

(3) include an affidavit that:

(A) states the name, address, and interest of the applicant;

(B) states the facts showing an immediate necessity for the appointment of a temporary administrator;

(C) lists the requested powers and duties of the temporary administrator;

(D) states that the applicant is entitled to letters of temporary administration and is not disqualified by law from serving as a temporary administrator; and

(E) describes the property that the applicant believes to be in the decedent's estate.

Derived from Probate Code § 131A(b).

Added by Acts 2009, 81st Leg., ch. 680, § 1, eff. Jan. 1, 2014.

§ 452.003.   Order of Appointment; Requirements

The order appointing a temporary administrator must:

(1) designate the appointee as "temporary administrator" of the decedent's estate;

(2) specify the period of the appointment, which may not exceed 180 days unless the appointment is made permanent under Section 452.008;

(3) define the powers given to the appointee; and

(4) set the amount of bond to be given by the appointee.

Derived from Probate Code §§ 131A(a), (c).

Added by Acts 2009, 81st Leg., ch. 680, § 1, eff. Jan. 1, 2014.

§ 452.004. Temporary Administrator's Bond

(a) In this section, "business day" means a day other than a Saturday, Sunday, or holiday recognized by this state.

(b) Not later than the third business day after the date of the order appointing a temporary administrator, the appointee shall file with the county clerk a bond in the amount ordered by the court.

Derived from Probate Code § 131A(d).

Added by Acts 2009, 81st Leg., ch. 680, § 1, eff. Jan. 1, 2014.

§ 452.005. Issuance of Letters of Temporary Administration

Not later than the third day after the date an appointee qualifies as temporary administrator, the county clerk shall issue to the appointee letters of temporary administration that list the powers to be exercised by the appointee as ordered by the court.

Derived from Probate Code § 131A(e).

Added by Acts 2009, 81st Leg., ch. 680, § 1, eff. Jan. 1, 2014.

§ 452.006. Notice of Appointment

(a) On the date the county clerk issues letters of temporary administration:

(1) the county clerk shall post on the courthouse door a notice of the appointment to all interested persons; and

(2) the appointee shall notify, by certified mail, return receipt requested, the decedent's known heirs of the appointment.

(b) A notice required under Subsection (a) must state that:

(1) an heir or other interested person may request a hearing to contest the appointment not later than the 15th day after the date the letters of temporary administration are issued;

(2) if no contest is made during the period specified by the notice, the appointment continues for the period specified in the order appointing a temporary administrator; and

(3) the court may make the appointment permanent.

Derived from Probate Code §§ 131A(f), (g), (h).

Added by Acts 2009, 81st Leg., ch. 680, § 1, eff. Jan. 1, 2014.

§ 452.007. Hearing to Contest Appointment

(a) A hearing shall be held and a determination made not later than the 10th day after the date an heir or other interested person requests a hearing to contest the appointment of a temporary administrator. If a request is not made on or before the 15th day after the date the letters of temporary administration are issued, the appointment of a temporary administrator continues for the period specified in the order, unless the appointment is made permanent under Section 452.008.

(b) While a contest of the appointment of a temporary administrator is pending, the temporary appointee shall continue to act as administrator of the estate to the extent of the powers given by the appointment.

(c) A court that sets aside a temporary administrator's appointment may require the temporary administrator to prepare and file, under oath, a complete exhibit of the condition of the estate and detail any disposition of the estate property made by the temporary administrator.

Derived from Probate Code § 131A(i).

Added by Acts 2009, 81st Leg., ch. 680, § 1, eff. Jan. 1, 2014.

§ 452.008. Permanent Appointment

At the end of a temporary administrator's period of appointment, the court by written order may make the appointment permanent if the permanent appointment is in the interest of the estate.

Derived from Probate Code § 131A(j).

Added by Acts 2009, 81st Leg., ch. 680, § 1, eff. Jan. 1, 2014.

Subchapter B. Temporary Administration Pending Contest of a Will or Administration

Statutes in Context
Chapter 452, Subchapter B

Chapter 452, Subchapter B, provides for the creation of a temporary administration pending the contest of a will if no executor has yet to be appointed.

§ 452.051. Appointment of Temporary Administrator

(a) If a contest related to probating a will or granting letters testamentary or of administration is pending, the court may appoint a temporary administrator, with powers limited as the circumstances of the case require.

(b) The appointment may continue until the contest is terminated and an executor or administrator with full powers is appointed.

(c) The power of appointment under this section is in addition to the court's power of appointment under Subchapter A.

Derived from Probate Code § 132(a).

Added by Acts 2009, 81st Leg., ch. 680, § 1, eff. Jan. 1, 2014. Subsec. (a) amended by Acts 2015, 84th Leg., ch. 995, § 44, eff. Sept. 1, 2015.

§ 452.052. Additional Powers Regarding Claims

(a) A court that grants temporary administration pending a will contest or a contest on an application for letters of administration may, at any time while the contest is pending, give the temporary administrator all the powers of a permanent administrator regarding claims against the estate.

(b) If the court gives the temporary administrator powers described by Subsection (a), the court and the temporary administrator shall act in the same manner as in permanent administration in matters such as:

(1) approving or disapproving claims;

(2) paying claims; and

(3) selling property to pay claims.

(c) The court shall require a temporary administrator given powers described by Subsection (a) to give bond in the full amount required of a permanent administrator.

(d) This section is cumulative and does not affect the court's right to order a temporary administrator to perform any action described by this section in other cases if the action is necessary or expedient to preserve the estate pending the contest's final determination.

Derived from Probate Code § 132(b).

Added by Acts 2009, 81st Leg., ch. 680, § 1, eff. Jan. 1, 2014.

Subchapter C. Powers and Duties of Temporary Administrator

§ 452.101. Limited Powers of Temporary Administrator

(a) A temporary administrator may exercise only the rights and powers:

(1) specifically expressed in the court's order appointing the temporary administrator; or

(2) expressed in the court's subsequent orders.

(b) An act performed by a temporary administrator is void unless expressly authorized by the court's orders.

Derived from Probate Code § 133.

Added by Acts 2009, 81st Leg., ch. 680, § 1, eff. Jan. 1, 2014.

§ 452.102. Additional Bond for Extension of Rights and Powers

A court that extends the rights and powers of a temporary administrator in an order subsequent to the order appointing the temporary administrator may require additional bond commensurate with the extension.

Derived from Probate Code § 133.

Added by Acts 2009, 81st Leg., ch. 680, § 1, eff. Jan. 1, 2014.

Subchapter D. Expiration and Closing of Temporary Administration

§ 452.151. Accounting

At the expiration of a temporary appointment, the temporary administrator shall file with the court clerk:

(1) a sworn list of all estate property that has come into the temporary administrator's possession;

(2) a return of all sales made by the temporary administrator; and

(3) a full exhibit and account of all the temporary administrator's acts as temporary administrator.

Derived from Probate Code § 134.

Added by Acts 2009, 81st Leg., ch. 680, § 1, eff. Jan. 1, 2014.

§ 452.152. Closing Temporary Administration

(a) The court shall act on the list, return, exhibit, and account filed under Section 452.151.

(b) When letters of temporary administration expire or become ineffective for any cause, the court immediately shall enter an order requiring the temporary administrator to promptly deliver the estate remaining in the temporary administrator's possession to the person legally entitled to possession of the estate.

(c) On proof of delivery under Subsection (b), the temporary administrator shall be discharged and the sureties on the temporary administrator's bond shall be released as to any future liability.

Derived from Probate Code § 135.

Added by Acts 2009, 81st Leg., ch. 680, § 1, eff. Jan. 1, 2014.

Chapter 453. Administration of Community Property

§ 453.008.   Liability of Surviving Spouse for Loss

§ 453.009.   Distribution of Powers Between Personal Representative and Surviving Spouse

Chapter 453. Administration of Community Property

§ 453.001.   Effect of Chapter

This chapter does not prohibit the administration of community property under other provisions of this title relating to the administration of an estate.

Derived from Probate Code § 155.

Added by Acts 2009, 81st Leg., ch. 680, § 1, eff. Jan. 1, 2014.

Statutes in Context
§ 453.002

Section 453.002 provides that no administration is necessary for community property if the spouse died intestate and all community property passes to the surviving spouse (that is, either the deceased spouse had no surviving descendants or all of the deceased spouse's descendants were also descendants of the surviving spouse).

---

§ 453.002.   Administration of Community Property Not Necessary

If a spouse dies intestate and the community property passes to the surviving spouse, no administration of the community property is necessary.

Derived from Probate Code § 155.

Added by Acts 2009, 81st Leg., ch. 680, § 1, eff. Jan. 1, 2014.

Statutes in Context
§§ 453.003–453.004

Sections 453.003–453.004 permit the surviving spouse to administer the community property in both testate and intestate situations provided no personal representative has yet been appointed. This procedure is often called an unqualified community administration.

---

§ 453.003.   General Powers of Surviving Spouse if No Administration Is Pending

(a) If there is no qualified executor or administrator of a deceased spouse's estate, the surviving spouse, as the surviving partner of the marital partnership, may:

(1) sue and be sued to recover community property;

(2) sell, mortgage, lease, and otherwise dispose of community property to pay community debts;

(3) collect claims due to the community estate; and

(4) exercise other powers as necessary to:

(A) preserve the community property;

(B) discharge community obligations; and

(C) wind up community affairs.

(b) This section does not affect the disposition of the deceased spouse's property.

Derived from Probate Code §§ 160(a), (c).

Added by Acts 2009, 81st Leg., ch. 680, § 1, eff. Jan. 1, 2014.

§ 453.004.   Collection of Unpaid Wages if No Administration Is Pending

(a) If a person who owes money to the community estate for current wages at the time of a deceased spouse's death is provided an affidavit stating that the affiant is the surviving spouse and that no one has qualified as executor or administrator of the deceased spouse's estate, the person who pays or delivers to the affiant the deceased spouse's final paycheck for the wages, including any unpaid sick pay or vacation pay, is released from liability to the same extent as if the payment or delivery is made to the deceased spouse's personal representative. The person is not required to inquire into the truth of the affidavit.

(b) An affiant to whom the payment or delivery is made under Subsection (a) is answerable to a person having a prior right and is accountable to a personal representative who is appointed. The affiant is liable for any damage or loss to a person that arises from a payment or delivery made in reliance on the affidavit.

(c) This section does not affect the disposition of the deceased spouse's property.

Derived from Probate Code §§ 160(b), (c).

Added by Acts 2009, 81st Leg., ch. 680, § 1, eff. Jan. 1, 2014.

§ 453.005.   Remarriage of Surviving Spouse

The remarriage of a surviving spouse does not terminate the surviving spouse's powers as a surviving partner.

Derived from Probate Code § 176.

Added by Acts 2009, 81st Leg., ch. 680, § 1, eff. Jan. 1, 2014.

§ 453.006.   Account of Community Debts and Disposition of Community Property

(a) The surviving spouse shall keep a fair and full account and statement of:

(1) all community debts and expenses paid by the surviving spouse; and

(2) the disposition made of the community property.

(b) The surviving spouse or personal representative shall keep a separate, distinct account of all community debts allowed or paid in the administration and settlement of an estate described by Sections 101.052(a) and (b).

Derived from Probate Code §§ 156, 168.

Added by Acts 2009, 81st Leg., ch. 680, § 1, eff. Jan. 1,

2014.

§ 453.007. Delivery of Community Estate on Final Partition

On final partition of the community estate, the surviving spouse shall deliver to the deceased spouse's heirs or devisees their interest in the estate, and the increase in and profits of the interest, after deducting from the interest:

(1) the proportion of the community debts chargeable to the interest;

(2) unavoidable losses;

(3) necessary and reasonable expenses; and

(4) a reasonable commission for the management of the interest.

Derived from Probate Code § 168.

Added by Acts 2009, 81st Leg., ch. 680, § 1, eff. Jan. 1, 2014.

§ 453.008. Liability of Surviving Spouse for Loss

A surviving spouse is not liable for a loss sustained by the community estate unless the surviving spouse is guilty of gross negligence or bad faith.

Derived from Probate Code § 168.

Added by Acts 2009, 81st Leg., ch. 680, § 1, eff. Jan. 1, 2014.

§ 453.009. Distribution of Powers Between Personal Representative and Surviving Spouse

(a) A qualified personal representative of a deceased spouse's estate may administer:

(1) the separate property of the deceased spouse;

(2) the community property that was by law under the management of the deceased spouse during the marriage; and

(3) the community property that was by law under the joint control of the spouses during the marriage.

(b) The surviving spouse, as surviving partner of the marital partnership, is entitled to:

(1) retain possession and control of the community property that was legally under the sole management of the surviving spouse during the marriage; and

(2) exercise over that property any power this chapter authorizes the surviving spouse to exercise if there is no administration pending on the deceased spouse's estate.

(c) The surviving spouse, by written instrument filed with the clerk, may waive any right to exercise powers as community survivor. If the surviving spouse files a waiver under this subsection, the deceased spouse's personal representative may administer the entire community estate.

Derived from Probate Code § 177.

Added by Acts 2009, 81st Leg., ch. 680, § 1, eff. Jan. 1, 2014.

Chapter 454. Administration of Estate of Person Presumed Dead

Subchapter A. Estates of Persons Presumed Dead

Subchapter B. Persons Presumed Dead but Subsequently Proved Living

Chapter 454. Administration of Estate of Person Presumed Dead

Subchapter A. Estates of Persons Presumed Dead

§ 454.001. Applicability; Determination of Death

(a) This subchapter applies in a proceeding to probate a person's will or administer a person's estate if there is no direct evidence that the person is dead.

(b) The court has jurisdiction to determine the fact, time, and place of the person's death.

Derived from Probate Code § 72(a).

Added by Acts 2009, 81st Leg., ch. 680, § 1, eff. Jan. 1, 2014.

§ 454.002. Grant of Letters on Proof of Death

On application for the grant of letters testamentary or of administration for the estate of a person presumed to be dead, the court shall grant the letters if the death of the person is proved by circumstantial evidence to the court's satisfaction.

Derived from Probate Code § 72(a).

Added by Acts 2009, 81st Leg., ch. 680, § 1, eff. Jan. 1, 2014.

§ 454.003. Citation and Search

(a) If the fact of a person's death must be proved by circumstantial evidence under Section 454.002, at the request of any interested person, the court may order that a citation be issued to the person presumed dead and that the citation be served on the person by publication and posting and by additional methods as directed by the order.

(b) After letters testamentary or of administration are issued, the court may also direct:

(1) the personal representative to search for the person presumed dead by notifying law enforcement agencies and public welfare agencies in appropriate locations that the person has disappeared; and

(2) the applicant to engage the services of an investigative agency to search for the person presumed dead.

(c) The expense of a search or notice under this section shall be taxed to the estate as a cost and paid out of the estate property.

Derived from Probate Code § 72(b).

Added by Acts 2009, 81st Leg., ch. 680, § 1, eff. Jan. 1, 2014.

§ 454.004. Distribution of Estate

The personal representative of the estate of a person presumed dead may not distribute the estate to the persons entitled to the estate until the third anniversary of the date the court granted the letters under Section 454.002.

Derived from Probate Code § 72(a).

Added by Acts 2009, 81st Leg., ch. 680, § 1, eff. Jan. 1, 2014.

Subchapter B. Persons Presumed Dead but Subsequently Proved Living

§ 454.051. Restoration of Estate

(a) Except as provided by Subsection (b), a person who was proved by circumstantial evidence to be dead under Section 454.002 and who, in a subsequent action, is proved by direct evidence to have been living at any time after the date the court granted the letters under that section, is entitled to restoration of the person's estate or the residue of the person's estate, including the rents and profits from the estate.

(b) For estate property sold by the personal representative of the estate, a distributee, or a distributee's successors or assignees to a bona fide purchaser for value, the right of a person to restoration is limited to the proceeds of the sale or the residue of the sold property with any increase of the proceeds or the residue.

Derived from Probate Code § 72(a).

Added by Acts 2009, 81st Leg., ch. 680, § 1, eff. Jan. 1, 2014.

§ 454.052. Liability of Personal Representative and Others Acting Under Court Order; Bonds Not Voided

(a) Anyone, including a personal representative, who delivered to another the estate or any part of the estate of a person who was proved by circumstantial evidence to be dead under Section 454.002 and who, in a subsequent action, is proved by direct evidence to have been living at any time after the date the court

granted the letters testamentary or of administration under that section is not liable for any part of the estate delivered in accordance with the court's order.

(b) Subject to Subsection (c), the bond of a personal representative of the estate of a person described by Subsection (a) is not void in any event.

(c) A surety is not liable for any act of the personal representative that was done in compliance with or approved by the court's order.

Derived from Probate Code § 72(a).

Added by Acts 2009, 81st Leg., ch. 680, § 1, eff. Jan. 1, 2014.

CHAPTER 455. PUBLIC PROBATE ADMINISTRATOR

CHAPTER 455. PUBLIC PROBATE ADMINISTRATOR

Statutes in Context
Chapter 455

The judge of a statutory probate court (with commissioner court approval) may appoint a "public probate administrator" for all of the statutory probate courts in the county. If there are multiple probate courts, the judges are to designate one among them to appoint and administer the public probate administrator office. This PPA (which may be a charitable organization or other suitable entity) is responsible for taking control of decedents' estates when no one has been appointed as the personal representative, there are no known or suitable relatives, and the estate may be subject to loss or misappropriation. The PPA is also responsible for determining whether there are heirs or a will and making burial arrangements. There are also expedited provisions for small estates (§ 455.009), and extremely expedited provisions for extremely small estates (§ 455.008).

§ 455.001. Definition

In this chapter, "public probate administrator" means the public probate administrator appointed under Section 25.00251, Government Code.

New.

Added by Acts 2013, 83ʳᵈ Leg., ch. 671, § 2, eff. Jan. 1, 2014.

§ 455.002. Bond Of Public Probate Administrator

(a) The public probate administrator must execute an official bond of at least $100,000 conditioned as required by law and payable to the statutory probate court judge who appointed the public probate administrator.

(b) In addition to the official bond of office, at any time, for good cause, the statutory probate court judge who appointed the public probate administrator may require the administrator to post an additional corporate surety bond for individual estates. The additional bonds shall bear the written approval of the judge requesting the additional bond.

(c) The county may choose to self-insure the public probate administrator for the minimum bond amount required by this section.

New.

Added by Acts 2013, 83ʳᵈ Leg., ch. 671, § 2, eff. Jan. 1, 2014.

§ 455.003. Funding of Public Probate Administrator's Office

A public probate administrator is entitled to commissions under Subchapter A, Chapter 352, to be paid into the county treasury. The public probate administrator's office, including salaries, is funded, in part, by the commissions.

New.

Added by Acts 2013, 83ʳᵈ Leg., ch. 671, § 2, eff. Jan. 1, 2014.

§ 455.004. Powers and Duties

(a) On receipt of notice of a decedent for whose estate a personal representative has not been appointed and who has no known or suitable next of kin, the public probate administrator shall take prompt possession or control of the decedent's property located in the county that:

(1) is considered by the public probate administrator to be subject to loss, injury, waste, or misappropriation; or

(2) the court orders into the possession and control of the public probate administrator after notice to the public probate administrator.

(b) The public probate administrator is responsible for determining if the decedent has any heirs or a will and, if necessary, shall make burial arrangements with the appropriate county facility in charge of indigent burial if there are no known personal representatives.

(c) If the public probate administrator determines the decedent executed a will, the administrator shall file the will with the county clerk.

(d) The public probate administrator has all of the powers and duties of an administrator under this title.

(e) The public probate administrator may dispose of any unclaimed property by public auction or private sale, or donation to a charity, if appropriate.

(f) The statutory probate court judge or commissioners court may request accountings in addition to accountings otherwise required by this title.

New.

Added by Acts 2013, 83ʳᵈ Leg., ch. 671, § 2, eff. Jan. 1, 2014.

§ 455.005. Informing Public Probate Administrator

(a) If a public officer or employee knows of a decedent without known or suitable next of kin or knows of property of a decedent that is subject to loss, injury, waste, or misappropriation, the officer or employee may inform the public probate administrator of that fact.

(b) If a person dies in a hospital, mental health facility, or board and care facility without known or suitable next of kin, the person in charge of the hospital or facility may give immediate notice of that fact to the public probate administrator of the county in which the hospital or facility is located.

(c) A funeral director in control of a decedent's remains may notify the public probate administrator if:

(1) none of the persons listed in Section 711.002, Health and Safety Code, can be found after a reasonable inquiry or contacted by reasonable means; or

(2) any of the persons listed in Section 711.002, Health and Safety Code, refuses to act.

New.

Added by Acts 2013, 83ʳᵈ Leg., ch. 671, § 2, eff. Jan. 1, 2014.

§ 455.006. Public Probate Administrator's Initiation of Administration

(a) The public probate administrator shall investigate a decedent's estate and circumstances to determine if the opening of an administration is necessary if the public probate administrator has reasonable cause to believe that the decedent found in the county or believed to be domiciled in the county in which the administrator is appointed does not have a personal representative appointed for the decedent's estate.

(b) The public probate administrator shall secure a decedent's estate or resolve any other circumstances related to a decedent, if, after the investigation, the public probate administrator determines that:

(1) the decedent has an estate that may be subject to loss, injury, waste, or misappropriation; or

(2) there are other circumstances relating to the decedent that require action by the public probate administrator.

(c) To establish reasonable cause under Subsection (a), the public probate administrator may require an information letter about the decedent that contains the following:

(1) the name, address, date of birth, and county of residence of the decedent;

(2) a description of the relationship between the interested person and the decedent;

(3) a statement of the suspected cause of death of the decedent;

(4) the names and telephone numbers of any known friends or relatives of the decedent;

(5) a description of any known property of the decedent, including the estimated value of the property; and

(6) a statement of whether the property is subject to loss, injury, waste, or misappropriation.

New.

Added by Acts 2013, 83rd Leg., ch. 671, § 2, eff. Jan. 1, 2014.

§ 455.007. Access to Information

(a) A public probate administrator who has made an investigation under Section 455.006 may present to the statutory probate court judge a statement of the known facts relating to a decedent with a request for permission to take possession or control of property of the decedent and further investigate the matter.

(b) On presentation of a statement under Subsection (a), a statutory probate court judge may issue an order authorizing the public probate administrator to take possession or control of property under this chapter. A public probate administrator may record the order in any county in which property subject to the order is located.

(c) On presentation of an order issued under this section, a financial institution, governmental or private agency, retirement fund administrator, insurance company, licensed securities dealer, or any other person shall perform the following without requiring a death certificate or letters of administration and without inquiring into the truth of the order:

(1) provide the public probate administrator complete information concerning property held in the name of the decedent referenced in the order, without charge, including the names and addresses of any beneficiaries and any evidence of a beneficiary designation; and

(2) grant the public probate administrator access to a safe deposit box rented in the name of the decedent referenced in the order, without charge, for the purpose of inspection and removal of its contents.

(d) Costs and expenses incurred in drilling or forcing a safe deposit box open under Subsection (c) shall be paid by the decedent's estate.

New.

Added by Acts 2013, 83rd Leg., ch. 671, § 2, eff. Jan. 1, 2014.

§ 455.008. Small Estates

(a) If gross assets of an estate do not exceed 10 percent of the maximum amount authorized for a small estate affidavit under Section 205.001, the public probate administrator may act without issuance of letters testamentary or of administration if the court approves a statement of administration stating:

(1) the name and domicile of the decedent;

(2) the date and place of death of the decedent; and

(3) the name, address, and relationship of each known heir or devisee of the decedent.

(b) On approval of the statement of administration, the public probate administrator may:

(1) take possession of, collect, manage, and secure the personal property of the decedent;

(2) sell the decedent's personal property at private or public sale or auction, without a court order;

(3) distribute personal property to the estate's personal representative if one is appointed after the statement of administration is filed;

(4) distribute personal property to a distributee of the decedent who presents an affidavit complying with Chapter 205;

(5) sell or abandon perishable property of the decedent if necessary to preserve the estate;

(6) make necessary funeral arrangements for the decedent and pay reasonable funeral charges with estate assets;

(7) distribute to a minor heir or devisee for whom a guardian has not been appointed the share of an intestate estate or a devise to which the heir or devisee is entitled; and

(8) distribute allowances and exempt property as provided by this title.

(c) On the distribution of property and internment of the decedent under this section, the public probate administrator shall file with the clerk an affidavit, to be approved by the court, detailing:

(1) the property collected;

(2) the property's distribution;

(3) the cost of internment; and

(4) the place of internment.

New.

Added by Acts 2013, 83rd Leg., ch. 671, § 2, eff. Jan. 1, 2014.

§ 455.009. Small Estate Affidavit

(a) If gross assets of an estate do not exceed the maximum amount authorized for a small estate affidavit under Section 205.001, the public probate administrator may file an affidavit that complies with Chapter 205 for approval by the statutory probate court judge.

(b) If the statutory probate court judge approves the affidavit, the affidavit:

(1) must be maintained or recorded as provided by Section 205.005; and

(2) has the effect described by Section 205.007.

New.

Added by Acts 2013, 83rd Leg., ch. 671, § 2, eff. Jan. 1, 2014.

§ 455.010 Grant of Administration

(a) A public probate administrator shall file an application for letters of administration or administration with will annexed as provided by this title:

(1) if gross assets of an estate exceed the maximum amount authorized for a small estate affidavit under Section 205.001;

(2) if the property of the decedent cannot be disposed of using other methods detailed in this chapter; or

(3) at the discretion of the public probate administrator or on order of the statutory probate court judge.

(b) After issuance of letters of administration, the public probate administrator is considered a personal representative under this title and has all of the powers and duties of a personal representative under this title.

New.

Added by Acts 2013, 83rd Leg., ch. 671, § 2, eff. Jan. 1, 2014.

§ 455.011. Withdrawal of Public Probate Administrator and Appointment of Successor

(a) If a public probate administrator has taken any action under Section 455.008, 455.009, or 455.010 and a qualified person more entitled to serve as a personal representative under Section 304.001 comes forward or a will of a decedent is found naming an executor, the public probate administrator may surrender the administration of the estate and the assets of the estate to the person once the person has qualified under this title.

(b) Before surrendering the administration of the estate, the public probate administrator must file a verified affidavit that shows fully and in detail:

(1) the condition of the estate;

(2) the charges and claims that have been approved or established by suit or that have been rejected and may be established later;

(3) the amount of each claim that has been rejected and may be established later;

(4) the property of the estate in the administrator's possession; and

(5) any other facts that are necessary in determining the condition of the estate.

(c) The court may require any other filing from the public probate administrator that the court considers

appropriate to fully show the condition of the estate before surrendering the estate under this section.

New.

Added by Acts 2013, 83rd Leg., ch. 671, § 2, eff. Jan 1, 2014.

§ 455.012. Deposit of Funds Into the County Treasury

The public probate administrator shall deposit all funds coming into the custody of the administrator in the county treasury. Funds deposited must be dispersed at the direction of the public probate administrator and according to the guidelines of the county treasurer or auditor.

New.

Added by Acts 2013, 83rd Leg., ch. 671, § 2, eff. Jan. 1, 2014.

Chapter 456. Disbursement and Closing of Lawyer Trust or Escrow Accounts

Statutes in Context
Chapter 456

The 2015 Legislature added Chapter 456 to address what happens to trust and escrow accounts when a lawyer dies. Acts 2015, 84th Leg., ch. 995, § 45, eff. Sept. 1, 2015 (adding Estates Code Chapter 456). The personal representative now has the authority to enter into a written contract with a Texas lawyer who may then be a signer on the account, determine the proper recipients of the funds in the account, distribute the funds to the proper recipients, and then close the account. If the personal representative is a Texas attorney, the person may takes these steps him- or herself. The financial institution has a duty to comply with the attorney's instructions and is not liable for the actions of the attorney.

Chapter 456. Disbursement and Closing of Lawyer Trust or Escrow Accounts

§ 456.001. Definition

In this chapter, "eligible institution" means a financial institution or investment company in which a lawyer has established an escrow or trust account for purposes of holding client funds or the funds of third persons that are in the lawyer's possession in connection with representation as required by the Texas Disciplinary Rules of Professional Conduct.

New.

Added by Acts 2015, 84th Leg., ch. 995, § 45, eff. Sept. 1, 2015.

§ 456.002. Authority to Designate Lawyer on Certain Trust or Escrow Accounts

(a) When administering the estate of a deceased lawyer who established one or more trust or escrow accounts for client funds or the funds of third persons that are in the lawyer's possession in connection with representation as required by the Texas Disciplinary Rules of Professional Conduct, the personal representative may hire through written agreement a lawyer authorized to practice in this state to:

(1) be the authorized signer on the trust or escrow account;

(2) determine who is entitled to receive the funds in the account;

(3) disburse the funds to the appropriate persons or to the decedent's estate; and

(4) close the account.

(b) If the personal representative is a lawyer authorized to practice in this state, the personal representative may state that fact and disburse the trust or escrow account funds of a deceased lawyer in accordance with Subsection (a).

(c) An agreement under Subsection (a) or a statement under Subsection (b) must be made in writing, and a copy of the agreement or statement must be delivered to each eligible institution in which the trust or escrow accounts were established.

New.

Added by Acts 2015, 84th Leg., ch. 995, § 45, eff. Sept. 1, 2015.

§ 456.003. Duty of Eligible Institutions

Within a reasonable time after receiving a copy of a written agreement under Section 456.002(a) or a statement from a personal representative under Section 456.002(b) and instructions from the lawyer identified in the agreement or statement, as applicable, regarding how to disburse the funds or close a trust or escrow account, an eligible institution shall disburse the funds and close the account in compliance with the instructions.

New.

Added by Acts 2015, 84th Leg., ch. 995, § 45, eff. Sept. 1, 2015.

§ 456.004. Liability of Eligible Institutions

An eligible institution is not liable for any act respecting an account taken in compliance with this chapter.

New.

Added by Acts 2015, 84th Leg., ch. 995, § 45, eff. Sept. 1, 2015.

§ 456.005. Rules

The supreme court may adopt rules regarding the administration of funds in a trust or escrow account subject to this chapter.

New.

Added by Acts 2015, 84th Leg., ch. 995, § 45, eff. Sept. 1, 2015.

SUBTITLE K. FOREIGN WILLS, OTHER TESTAMENTARY INSTRUMENTS, AND FIDUCIARIES

Statutes in Context
Subtitle K

Subtitle K addresses the procedures for handling "foreign" (that is, non-Texas) wills.

1. Non-Texas Domiciliary With Non-Texas Will

a. Will Probated in Decedent's Domiciliary Jurisdiction If the will is probated in the decedent's domiciliary state or country, the will need not meet the requirements of Texas law to be effective to dispose of Texas property. The only grounds a contestant may use to attack the will in Texas are (1) the foreign proceedings are not properly authenticated, (2) the will was previously rejected by a Texas court, and (3) the will has been set aside by a court in the domiciliary jurisdiction.

b. Will Admitted in Non-Domiciliary Jurisdiction If the will has already been probated in a state or county which was not the decedent's domicile at death, the will may be contested in Texas on any ground that would prevent a Texas will from gaining admission to probate.

c. Will Not Admitted Anywhere If the will has not been admitted in any other state or county, the proponent may bring an original probate in Texas. The will may be contested on any ground that would prevent a Texas will from gaining admission to probate.

d. Rejected in Domiciliary Jurisdiction A rejection of a foreign will by the decedent's domiciliary jurisdiction is conclusive in Texas unless the ground for rejection in the domiciliary jurisdiction would not have been a valid ground for rejecting the will under Texas law. For example, assume that the testator died with an unwitnessed holographic will in a state which requires witnesses on all wills. Because Texas recognizes holographic wills without witnesses, this will could be probated in

Texas even though it was rejected by the domiciliary state.

2. Texas Domiciliary with Non-Texas Will
The will must meet all Texas requirements. Texas does not have a savings statute, that is, a statute which provides that a will is effective in Texas if it would have been valid in the state or country in which it was originally executed.

Chapter 501. Ancillary Probate of Foreign Will

Chapter 501. Ancillary Probate of Foreign Will

§ 501.001. Authority for Ancillary Probate of Foreign Will

The written will of a testator who was not domiciled in this state at the time of the testator's death may be admitted to probate <u>at any time</u> in this state if:

(1) the will would affect any property in this state; and

(2) proof is presented that the will stands probated or otherwise established in any state of the United States or a foreign nation.

Derived from Probate Code § 95(a).

Added by Acts 2009, 81st Leg., ch. 680, § 1, eff. Jan. 1, 2014. Amended by Acts 2015, 84th Leg., ch. 995, § 46, eff. Sept. 1, 2015.

§ 501.002. Application for Ancillary Probate of Foreign Will

(a) An application for ancillary probate in this state of a foreign will admitted to probate or otherwise established in the jurisdiction in which the testator was domiciled at the time of the testator's death is required to indicate only that probate in this state is requested on the basis of the authenticated copy of the foreign proceedings in which the will was admitted to probate or otherwise established.

(b) An application for ancillary probate in this state of a foreign will that has been admitted to probate or otherwise established in a jurisdiction other than the jurisdiction in which the testator was domiciled at the time of the testator's death must:

(1) include all information required for an application for probate of a domestic will; and

(2) state the name and address of:

(A) each devisee; and

(B) each person who would be entitled to a portion of the estate as an heir in the absence of a will.

(c) An application described by Subsection (a) or (b) must include for filing a copy of the foreign will and the judgment, order, or decree by which the will was admitted to probate or otherwise established. The copy must:

(1) be attested by and with the original signature of the court clerk or other official who has custody of the will or who is in charge of probate records;

(2) include a certificate with the original signature of the judge or presiding magistrate of the court stating that the attestation is in proper form; and

(3) have the court seal affixed, if a court seal exists.

Derived from Probate Code §§ 95(b)(1), (2), (c).

Added by Acts 2009, 81st Leg., ch. 680, § 1, eff. Jan. 1, 2014.

§ 501.003. Citation and Notice

(a) Citation or notice is not required for an application described by Section 501.002(a).

(b) For an application described by Section 501.002(b), a citation shall be issued and served by registered or certified mail on each devisee and heir identified in the application.

Derived from Probate Code §§ 95(b)(1), (2).

Added by Acts 2009, 81st Leg., ch. 680, § 1, eff. Jan. 1, 2014.

§ 501.004. Recording by Clerk

(a) If a foreign will submitted for ancillary probate in this state has been admitted to probate or otherwise established in the jurisdiction in which the testator was domiciled at the time of the testator's death, it is the ministerial duty of the court clerk to record the will and the evidence of the will's probate or other establishment in the judge's probate docket.

(b) If a foreign will submitted for ancillary probate in this state has been admitted to probate or otherwise established in a jurisdiction other than the jurisdiction in which the testator was domiciled at the time of the testator's death, and a contest against the ancillary probate is not filed as authorized by Chapter 504, the court clerk shall record the will and the evidence of the will's probate or other establishment in the judge's probate docket.

(c) A court order is not necessary for the recording of a foreign will in accordance with this section.

Derived from Probate Code §§ 95(d)(1), (2).

Added by Acts 2009, 81st Leg., ch. 680, § 1, eff. Jan. 1, 2014. Subsecs. (a) and (b) amended by Acts 2011, 82nd Leg., ch. 90, § 8.019, eff. Jan. 1, 2014.

§ 501.005. Effect of Filing and Recording Foreign Will

On filing and recording a foreign will in accordance with this chapter, the foreign will:

(1) is considered to be admitted to probate; and

(2) has the same effect for all purposes as if the original will had been admitted to probate by order of a court of this state, subject to contest in the manner and to the extent provided by Chapter 504.

Derived from Probate Code §§ 95(d)(1), (2).

Added by Acts 2009, 81st Leg., ch. 680, § 1, eff. Jan. 1, 2014.

§ 501.006. Ancillary Letters Testamentary

(a) On application, an executor named in a foreign will admitted to ancillary probate in this state in accordance with this chapter is entitled to receive ancillary letters testamentary on proof made to the court that:

(1) the executor has qualified to serve as executor in the jurisdiction in which the will was previously admitted to probate or otherwise established; [and]

(2) the executor is not disqualified from serving in that capacity in this state; and

(3) if the will is admitted to ancillary probate in this state after the fourth anniversary of the testator's death, the executor continues to serve in that capacity in the jurisdiction in which the will was previously admitted to probate or otherwise established.

(b) After the proof required by Subsection (a) is made, the court shall enter an order directing that ancillary letters testamentary be issued to the executor. The court shall revoke any letters of administration previously issued by the court to any other person on application of the executor after personal service of citation on the person to whom the letters were issued.

Derived from Probate Code § 105.

Added by Acts 2009, 81st Leg., ch. 680, § 1, eff. Jan. 1, 2014. Amended by Acts 2015, 84th Leg., ch. 995, § 47, eff. Sept. 1, 2015.

§ 501.007. Effect on Property

A foreign will admitted to ancillary probate in this state as provided by this chapter after having been admitted to probate or otherwise established in the jurisdiction in which the testator was domiciled at the time of the testator's death is effective to dispose of property in this state regardless of whether the will was executed with the formalities required by this title.

Derived from Probate Code § 95(e).

Added by Acts 2009, 81st Leg., ch. 680, § 1, eff. Jan. 1, 2014.

§ 501.008. Setting Aside of Certain Foreign Wills

(a) This section applies only to a foreign will admitted to ancillary probate in this state, in accordance with the procedures prescribed by this chapter, based on the previous probate or other establishment of the will in the jurisdiction in which the testator was domiciled at the time of the testator's death.

(b) The admission to probate in this state of a foreign will to which this section applies shall be set aside if it is subsequently proven in a proceeding brought for that purpose that the foreign jurisdiction in which the will was admitted to probate or otherwise established was not in fact the domicile of the testator at the time of the testator's death.

(c) The title or rights of a person who, before commencement of a proceeding to set aside the admission to probate of a foreign will under this section, purchases property in good faith and for value from the personal representative or a devisee or otherwise deals in good faith with the personal representative or a devisee are not affected by the subsequent setting aside of the admission to probate in this state.

Derived from Probate Code § 95(f).

Added by Acts 2009, 81st Leg., ch. 680, § 1, eff. Jan. 1, 2014.

Chapter 502. Original Probate of Foreign Will

Chapter 502. Original Probate of Foreign Will

§ 502.001. Original Probate of Foreign Will Authorized

(a) This section applies only to a will of a testator who dies domiciled outside of this state that:

(1) on probate, may operate on any property in this state; and

(2) is valid under the laws of this state.

(b) A court may grant original probate of a will described by Subsection (a) in the same manner as the court grants the probate of other wills under this title if the will:

(1) has not been rejected from probate or establishment in the jurisdiction in which the testator died domiciled; or

(2) has been rejected from probate or establishment in the jurisdiction in which the testator died domiciled solely for a cause that is not a ground for rejection of a will of a testator who died domiciled in this state.

(c) A court may delay passing on an application for probate of a foreign will pending the result of probate or establishment, or of a contest of probate or establishment, in the jurisdiction in which the testator died domiciled.

Derived from Probate Code § 103.

Added by Acts 2009, 81st Leg., ch. 680, § 1, eff. Jan. 1, 2014.

§ 502.002. Proof of Foreign Will in Original Probate Proceeding

(a) A copy of the will of a testator who dies domiciled outside of this state, authenticated in the manner required by this title, is sufficient proof of the contents of the will to admit the will to probate in an original proceeding in this state if an objection to the will is not made.

(b) This section does not:

(1) authorize the probate of a will that would not otherwise be admissible to probate; or

(2) if an objection is made to a will, relieve the proponent from offering proof of the contents and legal sufficiency of the will as otherwise required.

(c) Subsection (b)(2) does not require the proponent to produce the original will unless ordered by the court.

Derived from Probate Code § 104.

Added by Acts 2009, 81st Leg., ch. 680, § 1, eff. Jan. 1, 2014.

Chapter 503. Recording of Foreign Testamentary Instrument

Subchapter A. Requirements for Recording Foreign Testamentary Instrument

Subchapter B. Effects of Recorded Foreign Testamentary Instrument

Chapter 503. Recording of Foreign Testamentary Instrument

Subchapter A. Requirements for Recording Foreign Testamentary Instrument

§ 503.001. Authorization to Record Certain Foreign Testamentary Instruments in Deed Records

(a) A copy of a will or other testamentary instrument that conveys, or in any other manner disposes of, land in this state and that has been probated according to the laws of any state of the United States or a country other than the United States, along with a copy of the judgment, order, or decree by which the instrument was admitted to probate that has the attestation, seal, and certificate required by Section 501.002(c), may be filed and recorded in the deed records in any county in this state in which the land is located:

(1) without further proof or authentication, subject to Section 503.003; and

(2) in the same manner as a deed or conveyance is required to be recorded under the laws of this state.

(b) A copy of a will or other testamentary instrument described by Subsection (a), along with a copy of the judgment, order, or decree by which the instrument was admitted to probate that has the attestation and certificate required by Section 501.002(c), is:

(1) prima facie evidence that the instrument has been admitted to probate according to the laws of the state or country in which it was allegedly admitted to probate; and

(2) sufficient to authorize the instrument and the judgment, order, or decree to be recorded in the deed records in the proper county or counties in this state.

Derived from Probate Code §§ 96, 97.

Added by Acts 2009, 81st Leg., ch. 680, § 1, eff. Jan. 1, 2014.

§ 503.002. Original Signatures Not Required

Notwithstanding Section 501.002(c), the original signatures required by that section may not be required for a recordation in the deed records in accordance with Section 503.001 or for a purpose described by Section 503.051 or 503.052.

Derived from Probate Code § 95(c).

Added by Acts 2009, 81st Leg., ch. 680, § 1, eff. Jan. 1, 2014.

§ 503.003. Contest of Recorded Foreign Testamentary Instrument Permitted

The validity of a will or other testamentary instrument, a copy of which is filed and recorded as provided by Section 503.001, may be contested in the manner and to the extent provided by Subchapter A, Chapter 504.

Derived from Probate Code § 96.

Added by Acts 2009, 81st Leg., ch. 680, § 1, eff. Jan. 1, 2014.

Subchapter B. Effects of Recorded Foreign Testamentary Instrument

§ 503.051. Recorded Foreign Testamentary Instrument as Conveyance

A copy of a foreign will or other testamentary instrument described by Section 503.001 and the copy of the judgment, order, or decree by which the instrument was admitted to probate that are attested and proved as provided by that section and delivered to the county clerk of the proper county in this state to be recorded in the deed records:

    (1) take effect and are valid as a deed of conveyance of all property in this state covered by the instrument; and

    (2) have the same effect as a recorded deed or other conveyance of land beginning at the time the instrument is delivered to the clerk to be recorded.

Derived from Probate Code § 98.

Added by Acts 2009, 81st Leg., ch. 680, § 1, eff. Jan. 1, 2014.

§ 503.052. Recorded Foreign Testamentary Instrument as Notice of Title

A copy of a foreign will or other testamentary instrument described by Section 503.001 and the copy of the judgment, order, or decree by which the instrument was admitted to probate that is attested and proved as provided by that section and filed for recording in the deed records of the proper county in this state constitute notice to all persons of the:

    (1) existence of the instrument; and

    (2) title or titles conferred by the instrument.

Derived from Probate Code § 99.

Added by Acts 2009, 81st Leg., ch. 680, § 1, eff. Jan. 1, 2014.

Chapter 504. Contest of or Other Challenge to Foreign Testamentary Instrument

Subchapter A. Contest or Setting Aside Probate of Foreign Will in this State

Subchapter B. Contest or Final Rejection in Foreign Jurisdiction

Chapter 504. Contest of or Other Challenge to Foreign Testamentary Instrument

Subchapter A. Contest or Setting Aside Probate of Foreign Will in this State

§ 504.001. Grounds for Contesting Foreign Will Probated in Domiciliary Jurisdiction

(a) Subject to Subsection (b), an interested person may contest a foreign will that has been:

    (1) admitted to probate or established in the jurisdiction in which the testator was domiciled at the time of the testator's death; and

    (2) admitted to probate in this state or filed in the deed records of any county of this state.

(b) A will described by Subsection (a) may be contested only on the grounds that:

    (1) the proceedings in the jurisdiction in which the testator was domiciled at the time of the testator's death were not authenticated in the manner required for ancillary probate or recording in the deed records in this state;

    (2) the will has been finally rejected for probate in this state in another proceeding; or

    (3) the probate of the will has been set aside in the jurisdiction in which the testator was domiciled at the time of the testator's death.

Derived from Probate Code § 100(a).

Added by Acts 2009, 81st Leg., ch. 680, § 1, eff. Jan. 1, 2014.

§ 504.002. Grounds for Contesting Foreign Will Probated in Non-Domiciliary Jurisdiction

A foreign will admitted to probate or established in any jurisdiction other than the jurisdiction in which the testator was domiciled at the time of the testator's death may be contested on any grounds that are the basis for the contest of a domestic will.

Derived from Probate Code § 100(b).

Added by Acts 2009, 81st Leg., ch. 680, § 1, eff. Jan. 1, 2014.

§ 504.003. Procedures and Time Limits for Contesting Foreign Will

(a) The probate in this state of a foreign will probated or established in a jurisdiction other than the jurisdiction in which the testator was domiciled at the time of the testator's death may be contested in the manner that would apply if the testator had been domiciled in this state at the time of the testator's death.

(b) A foreign will admitted to ancillary probate in this state or filed in the deed records of any county of this state may be contested using the same procedures and within the same time limits applicable to the contest of a will admitted to original probate in this state.

Derived from Probate Code §§ 95(d)(2), 100(c).

Added by Acts 2009, 81st Leg., ch. 680, § 1, eff. Jan. 1, 2014.

§ 504.004. Probate of Foreign Will Set Aside for Lack of Service

(a) The probate in this state of a foreign will shall be set aside if:

(1) the will was probated in this state:

(A) in accordance with the procedure applicable to the probate of a will admitted to probate in the jurisdiction in which the testator was domiciled at the time of the testator's death; and

(B) without the service of citation required for a will admitted to probate in another jurisdiction that was not the testator's domicile at the time of the testator's death; and

(2) it is proved that the foreign jurisdiction in which the will was probated was not the testator's domicile at the time of the testator's death.

(b) If otherwise entitled, a will the probate of which is set aside in accordance with Subsection (a) may be:

(1) reprobated in accordance with the procedure prescribed for the probate of a will admitted in a jurisdiction that was not the testator's domicile at the time of the testator's death; or

(2) admitted to original probate in this state in the proceeding in which the ancillary probate was set aside or in a subsequent proceeding.

Derived from Probate Code § 100(b).

Added by Acts 2009, 81st Leg., ch. 680, § 1, eff. Jan. 1, 2014.

Subchapter B. Contest or Final Rejection in Foreign Jurisdiction

§ 504.051. Notice of Will Contest in Foreign Jurisdiction

Verified notice that a proceeding to contest a will probated or established in a foreign jurisdiction has been commenced in that jurisdiction may be filed and recorded in the judge's probate docket of the court in this state in which the foreign will was probated, or in the deed records of any county of this state in which the foreign will was recorded, within the time limits for the contest of a foreign will in this state.

Derived from Probate Code § 101.

Added by Acts 2009, 81st Leg., ch. 680, § 1, eff. Jan. 1, 2014. Amended by Acts 2011, 82nd Leg., ch. 90, § 8.020, eff. Jan. 1, 2014.

§ 504.052. Effect of Notice

After a notice is filed and recorded under Section 504.051, the probate or recording in this state of the foreign will that is the subject of the notice has no effect until verified proof is filed and recorded that the foreign proceedings:

(1) have been terminated in favor of the will; or

(2) were never commenced.

Derived from Probate Code § 101.

Added by Acts 2009, 81st Leg., ch. 680, § 1, eff. Jan. 1, 2014.

§ 504.053. Effect of Rejection of Testamentary Instrument by Foreign Jurisdiction

(a) Except as provided by Subsection (b), final rejection of a will or other testamentary instrument from probate or establishment in a foreign jurisdiction in which the testator was domiciled at the time of the testator's death is conclusive in this state.

(b) A will or other testamentary instrument that is finally rejected from probate or establishment in a foreign jurisdiction in which the testator was domiciled at the time of the testator's death may be admitted to probate or continue to be effective in this state if the will or other instrument was rejected solely for a cause that is not a ground for rejection of a will of a testator who died domiciled in this state.

Derived from Probate Code § 102.

Added by Acts 2009, 81st Leg., ch. 680, § 1, eff. Jan. 1, 2014.

Chapter 505. Foreign Personal Representatives, Trustees, and Fiduciaries

Subchapter A. Foreign Corporate Fiduciary

Subchapter B. Foreign Executors and Trustees

Subchapter C. Recovery of Debts by Foreign Executor or Administrator

§ 505.102. Jurisdiction

§ 505.103. Restriction on Suit Brought by Foreign Executor or Administrator

Chapter 505. Foreign Personal Representatives, Trustees, and Fiduciaries

Subchapter A. Foreign Corporate Fiduciary

Statutes in Context
Chapter 505, Subchapter A

Chapter 505, Subchapter A, explains when a non-Texas bank or trust company may serve as an executor or trustee in Texas. Basically, the statute adopts a reciprocity approach, that is, the foreign entity may serve in Texas if a Texas bank or trust company may serve as a fiduciary in the foreign jurisdiction.

---

§ 505.001. Definition

In this subchapter, "foreign corporate fiduciary" means a corporate fiduciary that does not have its main office or a branch office in this state.

Derived from Probate Code § 105A(a).

Added by Acts 2009, 81st Leg., ch. 680, § 1, eff. Jan. 1, 2014.

§ 505.002. Applicability of Other Law

(a) A foreign corporate fiduciary acting in a fiduciary capacity in this state in strict accordance with this subchapter:

(1) is not transacting business in this state within the meaning of Section 9.001, Business Organizations Code; and

(2) is qualified to serve in that capacity under Section 501.006.

(b) This subchapter is in addition to, and not a limitation on, Subtitles F and G, Title 3, Finance Code.

Derived from Probate Code §§ 105A(c), (d).

Added by Acts 2009, 81st Leg., ch. 680, § 1, eff. Jan. 1, 2014.

§ 505.003. Authority of Foreign Corporate Fiduciary to Serve in Fiduciary Capacity

(a) Subject to Subsections (b) and (c) and Section 505.004, a foreign corporate fiduciary may be appointed by will, deed, agreement, declaration, indenture, court order or decree, or otherwise and may serve in this state in any fiduciary capacity, including as:

(1) trustee of a personal or corporate trust;

(2) executor;

(3) administrator; or

(4) guardian of the estate.

(b) A foreign corporate fiduciary appointed to serve in a fiduciary capacity in this state must have the corporate power to act in that capacity.

(c) This section applies only to the extent that the home state of the foreign corporate fiduciary appointed to serve in a fiduciary capacity in this state grants to a corporate fiduciary whose home state is this state the authority to serve in like fiduciary capacity.

Derived from Probate Code § 105A(a).

Added by Acts 2009, 81st Leg., ch. 680, § 1, eff. Jan. 1, 2014.

§ 505.004. Filing Requirements; Designation

(a) A foreign corporate fiduciary must file the following documents with the secretary of state before qualifying or serving in this state in a fiduciary capacity as authorized by Section 505.003:

(1) a copy of the fiduciary's charter, articles of incorporation or of association, and all amendments to those documents, certified by the fiduciary's secretary under the fiduciary's corporate seal;

(2) a properly executed written instrument that by the instrument's terms is of indefinite duration and irrevocable, appointing the secretary of state and the secretary of state's successors as the fiduciary's agent for service of process on whom notices and processes issued by a court of this state may be served in an action or proceeding relating to a trust, estate, fund, or other matter within this state with respect to which the fiduciary is acting in a fiduciary capacity, including the acts or defaults of the fiduciary with respect to that trust, estate, or fund; and

(3) a written certificate of designation specifying the name and address of the officer, agent, or other person to whom the secretary of state shall forward notices and processes described by Subdivision (2).

(b) A foreign corporate fiduciary may change the certificate of designation under Subsection (a)(3) by filing a new certificate.

Derived from Probate Code § 105A(b).

Added by Acts 2009, 81st Leg., ch. 680, § 1, eff. Jan. 1, 2014.

§ 505.005. Service of Notice or Process on Secretary of State

(a) On receipt of a notice or process described by Section 505.004(a)(2), the secretary of state shall promptly forward the notice or process by registered or certified mail to the officer, agent, or other person designated by the foreign corporate fiduciary under Section 505.004 to receive the notice or process.

(b) Service of notice or process described by Section 505.004(a)(2) on the secretary of state as agent for a foreign corporate fiduciary has the same effect as if personal service had been had in this state on the foreign corporate fiduciary.

Derived from Probate Code § 105A(b).

Added by Acts 2009, 81st Leg., ch. 680, § 1, eff. Jan. 1, 2014.

§ 505.006. Criminal Penalty; Effect of Conviction

(a) A foreign corporate fiduciary commits an offense if the fiduciary violates this subchapter.

(b) An offense under this section is a misdemeanor punishable by a fine not to exceed $5,000.

(c) On conviction, the court may prohibit a foreign corporate fiduciary convicted of an offense under this section from thereafter serving in any fiduciary capacity in this state.

Derived from Probate Code § 105A(e).

Added by Acts 2009, 81st Leg., ch. 680, § 1, eff. Jan. 1, 2014.

Subchapter B. Foreign Executors and Trustees

§ 505.051. Applicability of Bond Requirement

(a) A foreign executor is not required to give bond if the will appointing the foreign executor provides that the executor may serve without bond.

(b) The bond provisions of this title applicable to domestic representatives apply to a foreign executor if the will appointing the foreign executor does not exempt the foreign executor from giving bond.

Derived from Probate Code § 106.

Added by Acts 2009, 81st Leg., ch. 680, § 1, eff. Jan. 1, 2014.

§ 505.052. Power to Sell Property

(a) If a foreign will has been recorded in the deed records of a county in this state in the manner provided by this subtitle and the will gives an executor or trustee the power to sell property located in this state:

(1) an order of a court of this state is not necessary to authorize the executor or trustee to make the sale and execute proper conveyance; and

(2) any specific directions the testator gave in the foreign will respecting the sale of the estate property must be followed unless the directions have been annulled or suspended by an order of a court of competent jurisdiction.

(b) Notwithstanding Section 501.002(c), the original signatures required by that section may not be required for purposes of this section.

Derived from Probate Code §§ 95(c), 107.

Added by Acts 2009, 81st Leg., ch. 680, § 1, eff. Jan. 1, 2014.

Subchapter C. Recovery of Debts by Foreign Executor or Administrator

§ 505.101. Suit to Recover Debt

(a) On giving notice by registered or certified mail to all creditors of a decedent in this state who have filed a claim against the decedent's estate for a debt due to the creditor, a foreign executor or administrator of a person who was a nonresident at the time of death may maintain a suit in this state for the recovery of debts due to the decedent.

(b) The plaintiff's letters testamentary or of administration granted by a competent tribunal, properly authenticated, must be filed with the suit.

Derived from Probate Code §§ 107A(a), (b).

Added by Acts 2009, 81st Leg., ch. 680, § 1, eff. Jan. 1, 2014.

§ 505.102. Jurisdiction

(a) A foreign executor or administrator who files a suit authorized by Section 505.101 submits personally to the jurisdiction of the courts of this state in a proceeding relating to the recovery of a debt owed to a resident of this state by the decedent whose estate the executor or administrator represents.

(b) Jurisdiction under this section is limited to the amount of money or value of personal property recovered in this state by the foreign executor or administrator.

Derived from Probate Code § 107A(c).

Added by Acts 2009, 81st Leg., ch. 680, § 1, eff. Jan. 1, 2014.

§ 505.103. Restriction on Suit Brought by Foreign Executor or Administrator

A suit may not be maintained in this state by a foreign executor or administrator for a decedent's estate under this subchapter if there is:

(1) an executor or administrator of the decedent's estate qualified by a court of this state; or

(2) a pending application in this state for the appointment of an executor or administrator of the decedent's estate.

Derived from Probate Code § 107A(d).

Added by Acts 2009, 81st Leg., ch. 680, § 1, eff. Jan. 1, 2014.

SUBTITLE L. PAYMENT OF ESTATES INTO TREASURY

Chapter 551. Payment of Certain Estates to State

Subchapter A. Payment of Certain Funds to State

Subchapter B. Recovery of Funds Paid to State

Subchapter C. Penalties; Enforcement

Chapter 551. Payment of Certain Estates to State

Subchapter A. Payment of Certain Funds to State

§ 551.001. Payment of Certain Shares of Estate to State

(a) The court, by written order, shall require the executor or administrator of an estate to pay to the comptroller as provided by this subchapter the share of that estate of a person entitled to that share who does not demand the share, including any portion deposited in an account in the court's registry under Section 362.011(c), from the executor or administrator within six months after the date of, as applicable:

(1) a court order approving the report of the commissioners of partition made under Section 360.154; or

(2) the settlement of the final account of the executor or administrator.

(b) This section does not apply to the share of an estate to which a resident minor without a guardian is entitled.

Derived from Probate Code § 427.

Added by Acts 2009, 81st Leg., ch. 680, § 1, eff. Jan. 1, 2014. Subsec. (a) amended by Acts 2013, 83rd Leg., ch. 1136, § 59, eff. Jan. 1, 2014.

§ 551.002. Payment of Portion that Is in Money

The executor or administrator shall pay the portion of the share subject to Section 551.001 that is in money to the comptroller.

Derived from Probate Code § 427.

Added by Acts 2009, 81st Leg., ch. 680, § 1, eff. Jan. 1, 2014.

§ 551.003. Payment of Portion that Is Not in Money

(a) The court's order under Section 551.001 must require the executor or administrator to:

(1) sell, on terms determined best by the court, the portion of a share subject to that section that is in property other than money; and

(2) on collection of the proceeds of the sale, pay the proceeds to the comptroller.

(b) An action to recover the proceeds of a sale under this section is governed by Subchapter B.

Derived from Probate Code § 427.

Added by Acts 2009, 81st Leg., ch. 680, § 1, eff. Jan. 1, 2014.

§ 551.004. Compensation to Executor or Administrator

The executor or administrator is entitled to reasonable compensation for services performed under Section 551.003.

Derived from Probate Code § 427.

Added by Acts 2009, 81st Leg., ch. 680, § 1, eff. Jan. 1, 2014.

§ 551.005. Comptroller Indispensable Party

(a) The comptroller is an indispensable party to a judicial or administrative proceeding concerning the disposition and handling of any share of an estate that is or may be payable to the comptroller under Section 551.001.

(b) The clerk of a court that orders an executor or administrator to pay funds to the comptroller under Section 551.001 shall serve on the comptroller, by personal service of citation, a certified copy of the court order not later than the fifth day after the date the order is issued.

Derived from Probate Code § 428.

Added by Acts 2009, 81st Leg., ch. 680, § 1, eff. Jan. 1, 2014.

§ 551.006. Comptroller's Receipt

(a) An executor or administrator who pays to the comptroller under this subchapter any funds of the estate represented by the executor or administrator shall:

(1) obtain from the comptroller a receipt for the payment, with official seal attached; and

(2) file the receipt with the clerk of the court that orders the payment.

(b) The court clerk shall record the comptroller's receipt in the judge's probate docket.

Derived from Probate Code § 430.

Added by Acts 2009, 81st Leg., ch. 680, § 1, eff. Jan. 1, 2014. Subsec. (b) amended by Acts 2011, 82nd Leg., ch. 90, § 8.021, eff. Jan. 1, 2014.

Subchapter B. Recovery of Funds Paid to State

§ 551.051. Recovery of Funds

If funds of an estate have been paid to the comptroller under this chapter, an heir or devisee or an assignee of an heir or devisee may recover the share of the funds to which the heir, devisee, or assignee is entitled.

Derived from Probate Code § 433(a).

Added by Acts 2009, 81st Leg., ch. 680, § 1, eff. Jan. 1, 2014.

§ 551.052. Action for Recovery

(a) A person claiming funds under Section 551.051 must bring an action, on or before the fourth anniversary of the date of the order requiring payment under this chapter to the comptroller, by filing a petition in the district court of Travis County against the comptroller. The petition must set forth:

(1) the plaintiff's right to the funds; and

(2) the amount claimed by the plaintiff.

(b) On the filing of a petition under Subsection (a), the court clerk shall issue a citation for the comptroller to appear and represent the interest of this state in the action. The citation must be served by personal service.

(c) Proceedings in an action brought under this section are governed by the rules applicable to other civil actions.

Derived from Probate Code §§ 433(a), (b), (c).

Added by Acts 2009, 81st Leg., ch. 680, § 1, eff. Jan. 1, 2014.

§ 551.053. Judgment

(a) If a plaintiff establishes the plaintiff's right to funds claimed under this subchapter, the court shall award a judgment that specifies the amount to which the plaintiff is entitled.

(b) A certified copy of the judgment constitutes sufficient authority for the comptroller to pay the judgment.

Derived from Probate Code § 433(c).

Added by Acts 2009, 81st Leg., ch. 680, § 1, eff. Jan. 1, 2014.

§ 551.054. Payment of Costs

The costs of an action brought under this subchapter shall be adjudged against the plaintiff. The plaintiff may be required to secure the costs.

Derived from Probate Code § 433(d).

Added by Acts 2009, 81st Leg., ch. 680, § 1, eff. Jan. 1, 2014.

§ 551.055. Representation of Comptroller

As the comptroller elects and with the approval of the attorney general, the attorney general, the county attorney or criminal district attorney for the county, or the district attorney for the district shall represent the comptroller in an action brought under this subchapter.

Derived from Probate Code § 433(b).

Added by Acts 2009, 81st Leg., ch. 680, § 1, eff. Jan. 1, 2014.

Subchapter C. Penalties; Enforcement

§ 551.101. Liability of Court Clerk; Penalty

(a) A court clerk who fails to timely comply with Section 551.005(b) is liable for a $100 penalty.

(b) The penalty under Subsection (a) shall be recovered through an action brought in the name of this state, after personal service of citation, on the information of any resident. Half of the penalty shall be paid to the informer and the other half to this state.

Derived from Probate Code § 429.

Added by Acts 2009, 81st Leg., ch. 680, § 1, eff. Jan. 1, 2014.

§ 551.102. Damages for Failure to Make Payments

(a) An executor or administrator who fails to pay funds of an estate to the comptroller as required by an order under Section 551.001 on or before the 30th day after the date of the order is liable, after personal service of citation charging that failure and after proof of the failure, for damages. The damages:

(1) accrue at the rate of five percent of the amount of the funds per month for each month or fraction of a month after the 30th day after the date of the order that the executor or administrator fails to make the payment; and

(2) must be paid to the comptroller out of the executor's or administrator's own estate.

(b) Damages under this section may be recovered in any court of competent jurisdiction.

Derived from Probate Code § 431.

Added by Acts 2009, 81st Leg., ch. 680, § 1, eff. Jan. 1, 2014.

§ 551.103. Enforcement of Payment and Damages; Recovery on Bond

(a) The comptroller may apply in the name of this state to the court that issued an order for the payment of funds of an estate under this chapter to enforce the payment of:

(1) funds the executor or administrator has failed to pay to the comptroller under the order; and

(2) any damages that have accrued under Section 551.102.

(b) The court shall enforce the payment under Subsection (a) in the manner prescribed for enforcement of other payment orders.

(c) In addition to the action under Subsection (a), the comptroller may bring an action in the name of this state against the executor or administrator and the sureties on the executor's or administrator's bond for the recovery of the funds ordered to be paid and any accrued damages.

(d) The county attorney or criminal district attorney for the county, the district attorney for the district, or the attorney general, at the election of the comptroller and with the approval of the attorney general, shall represent the comptroller in all proceedings under this section, and shall also represent the interests of this state in all other matters arising under this code.

Derived from Probate Code § 432.

Added by Acts 2009, 81st Leg., ch. 680, § 1, eff. Jan. 1, 2014.

SUBTITLE P. DURABLE POWERS OF ATTORNEY

Chapter 751. General Provisions Regarding Durable Powers of Attorney

Subchapter A. General Provisions

Subchapter B. Effect of Certain Acts on Exercise of Durable Power of Attorney

Subchapter C. Duty to Inform and Account

Subchapter D. Recording Durable Power of Attorney for Certain Real Property Transactions

Chapter 752. Statutory Durable Power of Attorney

Subchapter A. General Provisions Regarding Statutory Durable Power of Attorney

Subchapter B. Form of Statutory Durable Power of Attorney

Subchapter C. Construction of Powers Related to Statutory Durable Power of Attorney

Chapter 751. General Provisions Regarding Durable Powers of Attorney

Statutes in Context
Chapter 751

A power of attorney is a formal method of creating an agency relationship under which one person has the ability to act in the place of another. The person granting authority is called the principal and the person who obtains the authority is the agent or attorney-in-fact. Note that in this context, the term "attorney" is not synonymous with "lawyer" and thus any competent person may serve as an agent even if the person has no legal training.

Under traditional agency law, an agent's authority terminates when the principal becomes incompetent because the principal is no longer able to monitor the agent's conduct. This rule prevented powers of attorney from being used as a disability planning technique. In 1954, Virginia became the first state to authorize a durable power of attorney which provides that the agent retains the authority to act even if the principal is incompetent. All states now have legislation sanctioning durable powers of attorney. The Texas provisions are found in Chapter 751.

Subchapter A. General Provisions

§ 751.001. Short Title

This subtitle may be cited as the Durable Power of Attorney Act.

Derived from Probate Code § 481.

Added by Acts 2011, 82nd Leg., ch. 823, § 1.01, eff. Jan. 1, 2014.

Statutes in Context
§ 751.002

The requirements for a valid durable power of attorney are as follows: (1) the instrument must be in writing (oral statements are insufficient), (2) the principal must be an adult, (3) the principal must sign the instrument, (4) the instrument must name an agent, (5) the instrument must expressly provide that the agent's authority either (a) continues even after the principal becomes disabled or (b) begins when the agent becomes disabled (the springing power of attorney), and (6) the power of attorney must be acknowledged. Note that no witnesses are needed and the durable power of attorney does not need to be filed with the court.

§ 751.002. Definition of Durable Power of Attorney

A "durable power of attorney" means a written instrument that:

(1) designates another person as attorney in fact or agent;

(2) is signed by an adult principal;

(3) contains:

(A) the words:

(i) "This power of attorney is not affected by subsequent disability or incapacity of the principal"; or

(ii) "This power of attorney becomes effective on the disability or incapacity of the principal"; or

(B) words similar to those of Paragraph (A) that show the principal's intent that the authority conferred on the attorney in fact or agent shall be exercised notwithstanding the principal's subsequent disability or incapacity; and

(4) is acknowledged by the principal before an officer authorized under the laws of this state or another state to:

(A) take acknowledgments to deeds of conveyance; and

(B) administer oaths.

Derived from Probate Code § 482.

Added by Acts 2011, 82nd Leg., ch. 823, § 1.01, eff. Jan. 1, 2014.

§ 751.003. Uniformity of Application and Construction

This subtitle shall be applied and construed to effect the general purpose of this subtitle, which is to make uniform the law with respect to the subject of this subtitle among states enacting these provisions.

Derived from Probate Code § 506.

Added by Acts 2011, 82nd Leg., ch. 823, § 1.01, eff. Jan. 1, 2014.

Statutes in Context
§ 751.004

The durable power of attorney does not lapse merely because it is not used for a prolonged period of time.

§ 751.004. Duration of Durable Power of Attorney

A durable power of attorney does not lapse because of the passage of time unless the instrument creating the power of attorney specifically states a time limitation.

Derived from Probate Code § 483.

Added by Acts 2011, 82nd Leg., ch. 823, § 1.01, eff. Jan. 1, 2014.

§ 751.005. Extension of Principal's Authority to Other Persons

If, in this subtitle, a principal is given an authority to act, that authority includes:

(1) any person designated by the principal;

(2) a guardian of the estate of the principal; or

(3) another personal representative of the principal.

Derived from Probate Code § 489B(i).

Added by Acts 2011, 82nd Leg., ch. 823, § 1.01, eff. Jan. 1, 2014.

§ 751.006. Rights Cumulative

The rights set out under this subtitle are cumulative of any other rights or remedies the principal may have at common law or other applicable statutes and are not in derogation of those rights.

Derived from Probate Code § 489B(j).

Added by Acts 2011, 82nd Leg., ch. 823, § 1.01, eff. Jan. 1, 2014.

Subchapter B. Effect of Certain Acts on Exercise of Durable Power of Attorney

§ 751.051. Effect of Acts Performed by Attorney In Fact or Agent During Principal's Disability or Incapacity

Each act performed by an attorney in fact or agent under a durable power of attorney during a period of the principal's disability or incapacity has the same effect, and inures to the benefit of and binds the principal and the principal's successors in interest, as if the principal were not disabled or incapacitated.

Derived from Probate Code § 484.

Added by Acts 2011, 82nd Leg., ch. 823, § 1.01, eff. Jan. 1, 2014.

Statutes in Context
§ 751.052

The appointment of a permanent guardian of the principal's estate will terminate the agent's authority under § 751.052(a).

§ 751.052. Relation of Attorney In Fact or Agent to Court-Appointed Guardian of Estate

(a) If, after execution of a durable power of attorney, a court of the principal's domicile appoints a permanent guardian of the estate of the principal, the powers of the attorney in fact or agent terminate on the qualification of the guardian of the estate. The attorney in fact or agent shall:

(1) deliver to the guardian of the estate all assets of the ward's estate that are in the possession of the attorney in fact or agent; and

(2) account to the guardian of the estate as the attorney in fact or agent would account to the

principal if the principal had terminated the powers of the attorney in fact or agent.

(b) If, after execution of a durable power of attorney, a court of the principal's domicile appoints a temporary guardian of the estate of the principal, the court may suspend the powers of the attorney in fact or agent on the qualification of the temporary guardian of the estate until the date the term of the temporary guardian expires. This subsection may not be construed to prohibit the application for or issuance of a temporary restraining order under applicable law.

Derived from Probate Code § 485.

Added by Acts 2011, 82nd Leg., ch. 823, § 1.01, eff. Jan. 1, 2014.

Statutes in Context
§ 751.053

Generally, the designation of a spouse as an agent is automatically revoked upon the principal's divorce from the spouse.

§ 751.053. Effect of Principal's Divorce or Marriage Annulment if Former Spouse is Attorney In Fact or Agent

Unless otherwise expressly provided by the durable power of attorney, if, after execution of a durable power of attorney, the principal is divorced from a person who has been appointed the principal's attorney in fact or agent or the principal's marriage to a person who has been appointed the principal's attorney in fact or agent is annulled, the powers of the attorney in fact or agent granted to the principal's former spouse terminate on the date the divorce or annulment of marriage is granted by a court.

Derived from Probate Code § 485A.

Added by Acts 2011, 82nd Leg., ch. 823, § 1.01, eff. Jan. 1, 2014.

§ 751.054. Knowledge of Termination of Power; Good-Faith Acts

(a) The revocation by, the death of, or the qualification of a guardian of the estate of a principal who has executed a durable power of attorney does not revoke or terminate the agency as to the attorney in fact, agent, or other person who acts in good faith under or in reliance on the power without actual knowledge of the termination of the power by:

(1) the revocation;

(2) the principal's death; or

(3) the qualification of a guardian of the estate of the principal.

(b) The divorce of a principal from a person who has been appointed the principal's attorney in fact or agent before the date the divorce is granted, or the annulment of the marriage of a principal and a person who has been appointed the principal's attorney in fact or agent before the date the annulment is granted, does not revoke or terminate the agency as to a person other than the principal's former spouse if the person acts in good faith under or in reliance on the power of attorney.

(c) An action taken under this section, unless otherwise invalid or unenforceable, binds the principal's successors in interest.

Derived from Probate Code § 486.

Added by Acts 2011, 82nd Leg., ch. 823, § 1.01, eff. Jan. 1, 2014.

§ 751.055. Affidavit Regarding Lack of Knowledge of Termination of Power or of Disability or Incapacity; Good-Faith Reliance

(a) As to an act undertaken in good-faith reliance on a durable power of attorney, an affidavit executed by the attorney in fact or agent under the durable power of attorney stating that the attorney in fact or agent did not have, at the time the power was exercised, actual knowledge of the termination of the power by revocation, the principal's death, the principal's divorce or the annulment of the principal's marriage if the attorney in fact or agent was the principal's spouse, or the qualification of a guardian of the estate of the principal, is conclusive proof as between the attorney in fact or agent and a person other than the principal or the principal's personal representative dealing with the attorney in fact or agent of the nonrevocation or nontermination of the power at that time.

(b) As to an act undertaken in good-faith reliance on a durable power of attorney, an affidavit executed by the attorney in fact or agent under the durable power of attorney stating that the principal is disabled or incapacitated, as defined by the power of attorney, is conclusive proof as between the attorney in fact or agent and a person other than the principal or the principal's personal representative dealing with the attorney in fact or agent of the principal's disability or incapacity at that time.

(c) If the exercise of the power of attorney requires execution and delivery of an instrument that is to be recorded, an affidavit executed under Subsection (a) or (b), authenticated for record, may also be recorded.

(d) This section and Section 751.056 do not affect a provision in a durable power of attorney for the termination of the power by:

(1) expiration of time; or

(2) the occurrence of an event other than express revocation.

Derived from Probate Code §§ 487(a), (b), (c), (d).

Added by Acts 2011, 82nd Leg., ch. 823, § 1.01, eff. Jan. 1, 2014.

§ 751.056. Nonliability of Third Party on Good-Faith Reliance

If a durable power of attorney is used, a third party who relies in good faith on the acts of an attorney in fact or agent performed within the scope of the power of attorney is not liable to the principal.

Derived from Probate Code § 487(e).

Added by Acts 2011, 82nd Leg., ch. 823, § 1.01, eff. Jan. 1, 2014.

§ 751.057. Effect of Bankruptcy Proceeding

(a) The filing of a voluntary or involuntary petition in bankruptcy in connection with the debts of a principal who has executed a durable power of attorney does not revoke or terminate the agency as to the principal's attorney in fact or agent.

(b) Any act the attorney in fact or agent may undertake with respect to the principal's property is subject to the limitations and requirements of the United States Bankruptcy Code (11 U.S.C. Section 101 et seq.) until a final determination is made in the bankruptcy proceeding.

Derived from Probate Code § 487A.

Added by Acts 2011, 82nd Leg., ch. 823, § 1.01, eff. Jan. 1, 2014.

§ 751.058. Effect of Revocation of Durable Power of Attorney on Third Party

Unless otherwise provided by the durable power of attorney, a revocation of a durable power of attorney is not effective as to a third party relying on the power of attorney until the third party receives actual notice of the revocation.

Derived from Probate Code § 488.

Added by Acts 2011, 82nd Leg., ch. 823, § 1.01, eff. Jan. 1, 2014.

Subchapter C. Duty to Inform and Account

Statutes in Context
Chapter 751, Subchapter C

The agent's duty to inform the principal with respect to actions taken and to account for them is set forth in Chapter 751, Subchapter C.

§ 751.101. Fiduciary Duties

An attorney in fact or agent is a fiduciary and has a duty to inform and to account for actions taken under the power of attorney.

Derived from Probate Code § 489B(a).

Added by Acts 2011, 82nd Leg., ch. 823, § 1.01, eff. Jan. 1, 2014.

§ 751.102. Duty to Timely Inform Principal

(a) The attorney in fact or agent shall timely inform the principal of each action taken under the power of attorney.

(b) Failure of an attorney in fact or agent to timely inform, as to third parties, does not invalidate any action of the attorney in fact or agent.

Derived from Probate Code § 489B(b).

Added by Acts 2011, 82nd Leg., ch. 823, § 1.01, eff. Jan. 1, 2014.

§ 751.103. Maintenance of Records

(a) The attorney in fact or agent shall maintain records of each action taken or decision made by the attorney in fact or agent.

(b) The attorney in fact or agent shall maintain all records until delivered to the principal, released by the principal, or discharged by a court.

Derived from Probate Code § 489B(c), (f).

Added by Acts 2011, 82nd Leg., ch. 823, § 1.01, eff. Jan. 1, 2014.

§ 751.104. Accounting

(a) The principal may demand an accounting by the attorney in fact or agent.

(b) Unless otherwise directed by the principal, an accounting under Subsection (a) must include:

(1) the property belonging to the principal that has come to the attorney in fact's or agent's knowledge or into the attorney in fact's or agent's possession;

(2) each action taken or decision made by the attorney in fact or agent;

(3) a complete account of receipts, disbursements, and other actions of the attorney in fact or agent that includes the source and nature of each receipt, disbursement, or action, with receipts of principal and income shown separately;

(4) a listing of all property over which the attorney in fact or agent has exercised control that includes:

(A) an adequate description of each asset; and

(B) the asset's current value, if the value is known to the attorney in fact or agent;

(5) the cash balance on hand and the name and location of the depository at which the cash balance is kept;

(6) each known liability; and

(7) any other information and facts known to the attorney in fact or agent as necessary for a full and definite understanding of the exact condition of the property belonging to the principal.

(c) Unless directed otherwise by the principal, the attorney in fact or agent shall also provide to the principal all documentation regarding the principal's property.

Derived from Probate Code § 489B(d), (e).

Added by Acts 2011, 82nd Leg., ch. 823, § 1.01, eff. Jan. 1, 2014.

§ 751.105. Effect of Failure to Comply; Suit

If the attorney in fact or agent fails or refuses to inform the principal, provide documentation, or deliver an accounting under Section 751.104 within 60 days of a demand under that section, or a longer or shorter period as demanded by the principal or ordered by a court, the principal may file suit to:

(1) compel the attorney in fact or agent to deliver the accounting or the assets; or

(2) terminate the power of attorney.

Derived from Probate Code § 489B(g).

Added by Acts 2011, 82nd Leg., ch. 823, § 1.01, eff. Jan. 1, 2014.

§ 751.106. Effect of Subchapter on Principal's Rights

This subchapter does not limit the right of the principal to terminate the power of attorney or to make additional requirements of or to give additional instructions to the attorney in fact or agent.

Derived from Probate Code § 489B(h).

Added by Acts 2011, 82nd Leg., ch. 823, § 1.01, eff. Jan. 1, 2014.

Subchapter D. Recording Durable Power of Attorney for Certain Real Property Transactions

Statutes in Context
§ 751.151

The durable power of attorney will need to be recorded if the agent uses it with respect to a real property transaction. The 2015 Legislature mandated that it must be filed not later than the 30th day after the real property instrument is filed. The consequences of failing to do so are not stated.

§ 751.151. Recording for Real Property Transactions Requiring Execution and Delivery of Instruments

A durable power of attorney for a real property transaction requiring the execution and delivery of an instrument that is to be recorded, including a release, assignment, satisfaction, mortgage, security agreement, deed of trust, encumbrance, deed of conveyance, oil, gas, or other mineral lease, memorandum of a lease, lien, or other claim or right to real property, must be recorded in the office of the county clerk of the county in which the property is located not later than the 30th day after the date the instrument is filed for recording.

Derived from Probate Code § 489.

Added by Acts 2011, 82nd Leg., ch. 823, § 1.01, eff. Jan. 1, 2014. Amended by Acts 2015, 84th Leg., ch. 808, § 1, eff. Sept. 1, 2015.

Chapter 752. Statutory Durable Power of Attorney

Statutes in Context
Chapter 752.001

Section 752.051 contains a form which the principal may use to create a durable power of attorney. The form includes a list of powers which the principal may grant by initialing a line in front of the power. Alternatively, the principal may grant all the powers by initialing Line N. Each of the listed powers is explained in great detail by a later statutory provision. It is important for the principal to read the statutory provisions so that the principal fully understands the scope of the powers which the principal is granting to the agent.

The principal has a choice of making the power effective immediately (the default choice) or effective only upon incapacity (the springing power). Debate exists regarding which effective date is better. The principal often feels there is no need to grant any authority until the agent's actions are actually needed. However, third parties may be reluctant to accept a springing agent's authority for fear that the principal is not actually incapacitated. A compromise option is for the agent to make the power effective immediately but have the agent's attorney (or some other trusted person) keep the document and deliver it to the agent at the appropriate time.

Subchapter A. General Provisions Regarding Statutory Durable Power of Attorney

§ 752.001. Use, Meaning, and Effect of Statutory Durable Power of Attorney

(a) A person may use a statutory durable power of attorney to grant an attorney in fact or agent powers with respect to a person's property and financial matters.

(b) A power of attorney in substantially the form prescribed by Section 752.051 has the meaning and effect prescribed by this subtitle.

Derived from Probate Code § 490(a).

Added by Acts 2011, 82nd Leg., ch. 823, § 1.01, eff. Jan. 1, 2014.

§ 752.002. Validity Not Affected

A power of attorney is valid with respect to meeting the requirements for a statutory durable power of attorney regardless of the fact that:

(1) one or more of the categories of optional powers listed in the form prescribed by Section 752.051 are not initialed; or

(2) the form includes specific limitations on, or additions to, the powers of the attorney in fact or agent.

Derived from Probate Code § 490(a).

Added by Acts 2011, 82nd Leg., ch. 823, § 1.01, eff. Jan. 1, 2014. Amended by Acts 2013, 83rd Leg., ch. 700, § 2, eff. Jan. 1, 2014.

§ 752.003. Prescribed Form Not Exclusive

The form prescribed by Section 752.051 is not exclusive, and other forms of power of attorney may be used.

Derived from Probate Code § 490(a).

Added by Acts 2011, 82nd Leg., ch. 823, § 1.01, eff. Jan. 1, 2014.

§ 752.004. Legal Sufficiency of Statutory Durable Power of Attorney

A statutory durable power of attorney is legally sufficient under this subtitle if:

(1) the wording of the form complies substantially with the wording of the form prescribed by Section 752.051;

(2) the form is properly completed; and

(3) the signature of the principal is acknowledged.

Derived from Probate Code § 490(b).

Added by Acts 2011, 82nd Leg., ch. 823, § 1.01, eff. Jan. 1, 2014.

Subchapter B. Form of Statutory Durable Power of Attorney

§ 752.051. Form

The following form is known as a "statutory durable power of attorney":

STATUTORY DURABLE POWER OF ATTORNEY NOTICE: THE POWERS GRANTED BY THIS DOCUMENT ARE BROAD AND SWEEPING. THEY ARE EXPLAINED IN THE DURABLE POWER OF ATTORNEY ACT, SUBTITLE P, TITLE 2, ESTATES CODE. IF YOU HAVE ANY QUESTIONS ABOUT THESE POWERS, OBTAIN COMPETENT LEGAL ADVICE. THIS DOCUMENT DOES NOT AUTHORIZE ANYONE TO MAKE MEDICAL AND OTHER HEALTH-CARE DECISIONS FOR YOU. YOU MAY REVOKE THIS POWER OF ATTORNEY IF YOU LATER WISH TO DO SO.

You should select someone you trust to serve as your agent (attorney in fact). Unless you specify otherwise, generally the agent's (attorney in fact's) authority will continue until:

(1) you die or revoke the power of attorney;

(2) your agent (attorney in fact) resigns or is unable to act for you; or

(3) a guardian is appointed for your estate.

I, _____ (insert your name and address), appoint _____ (insert the name and address of the person appointed) as my agent (attorney in fact) to act for me in any lawful way with respect to all of the following powers that I have initialed below.

TO GRANT ALL OF THE FOLLOWING POWERS, INITIAL THE LINE IN FRONT OF (N) AND IGNORE THE LINES IN FRONT OF THE OTHER POWERS LISTED IN (A) THROUGH (M).

TO GRANT A POWER, YOU MUST INITIAL THE LINE IN FRONT OF THE POWER YOU ARE GRANTING.

TO WITHHOLD A POWER, DO NOT INITIAL THE LINE IN FRONT OF THE POWER. YOU MAY, BUT DO NOT NEED TO, CROSS OUT EACH POWER.

_____ (A) Real property transactions;

_____ (B) Tangible personal property transactions;

_____ (C) Stock and bond transactions;

_____ (D) Commodity and option transactions;

_____ (E) Banking and other financial institution transactions;

_____ (F) Business operating transactions;

_____ (G) Insurance and annuity transactions;

_____ (H) Estate, trust, and other beneficiary transactions;

_____ (I) Claims and litigation;

_____ (J) Personal and family maintenance;

_____ (K) Benefits from social security, Medicare, Medicaid, or other governmental programs or civil or military service;

_____ (L) Retirement plan transactions;

_____ (M) Tax matters;

_____ (N) ALL OF THE POWERS LISTED IN (A) THROUGH (M). YOU DO NOT HAVE TO INITIAL THE LINE IN FRONT OF ANY OTHER POWER IF YOU INITIAL LINE (N).

SPECIAL INSTRUCTIONS:

Special instructions applicable to gifts (initial in front of the following sentence to have it apply):

_____ I grant my agent (attorney in fact) the power to apply my property to make gifts outright to or for the benefit of a person, including by the exercise of a presently exercisable general power of appointment held by me, except that the amount of a gift to an individual may not exceed the amount of annual exclusions allowed from the federal gift tax for the calendar year of the gift.

ON THE FOLLOWING LINES YOU MAY GIVE SPECIAL INSTRUCTIONS LIMITING OR EXTENDING THE POWERS GRANTED TO YOUR AGENT.

_____

_____

_____

_____

_____

_____

UNLESS YOU DIRECT OTHERWISE ABOVE, THIS POWER OF ATTORNEY IS EFFECTIVE IMMEDIATELY AND WILL CONTINUE UNTIL IT IS REVOKED.

CHOOSE ONE OF THE FOLLOWING ALTERNATIVES BY CROSSING OUT THE ALTERNATIVE NOT CHOSEN:

(A) This power of attorney is not affected by my subsequent disability or incapacity.

(B) This power of attorney becomes effective upon my disability or incapacity.

YOU SHOULD CHOOSE ALTERNATIVE (A) IF THIS POWER OF ATTORNEY IS TO BECOME EFFECTIVE ON THE DATE IT IS EXECUTED.

IF NEITHER (A) NOR (B) IS CROSSED OUT, IT WILL BE ASSUMED THAT YOU CHOSE ALTERNATIVE (A).

If Alternative (B) is chosen and a definition of my disability or incapacity is not contained in this power of attorney, I shall be considered disabled or incapacitated for purposes of this power of attorney if a physician certifies in writing at a date later than the date this power of attorney is executed that, based on the physician's medical examination of me, I am mentally incapable of managing my financial affairs. I authorize the physician who examines me for this purpose to disclose my physical or mental condition to another person for purposes of this power of attorney. A third party who accepts this power of attorney is fully protected from any action taken under this power of attorney that is based on the determination made by a physician of my disability or incapacity.

I agree that any third party who receives a copy of this document may act under it. Revocation of the durable power of attorney is not effective as to a third party until the third party receives actual notice of the revocation. I agree to indemnify the third party for any claims that arise against the third party because of reliance on this power of attorney.

If any agent named by me dies, becomes legally disabled, resigns, or refuses to act, I name the following (each to act alone and successively, in the order named) as successor(s) to that agent: _____.

Signed this _____ day of _____,

_____

_____
(your signature)

State of _____

County of _____

This document was acknowledged before me on _____ (date) by _____
(name of principal)

_____
(signature of notarial officer)

(Seal, if any, of notary) _____

_____
(printed name)

My commission expires: _____

IMPORTANT INFORMATION FOR AGENT
(ATTORNEY IN FACT)

Agent's Duties

When you accept the authority granted under this power of attorney, you establish a "fiduciary" relationship with the principal. This is a special legal relationship that imposes on you legal duties that continue until you resign or the power of attorney is terminated or revoked by the principal or by operation of law. A fiduciary duty generally includes the duty to:

(1) act in good faith;

(2) do nothing beyond the authority granted in this power of attorney;

(3) act loyally for the principal's benefit;

(4) avoid conflicts that would impair your ability to act in the principal's best interest; and

(5) disclose your identity as an agent or attorney in fact when you act for the principal by writing or printing the name of the principal and signing your own name as "agent" or "attorney in fact" in the following manner:

(Principal's Name) by (Your Signature) as Agent (or as Attorney in Fact)

In addition, the Durable Power of Attorney Act (Subtitle P, Title 2, Estates Code) requires you to:

(1) maintain records of each action taken or decision made on behalf of the principal;

(2) maintain all records until delivered to the principal, released by the principal, or discharged by a court; and

(3) if requested by the principal, provide an accounting to the principal that, unless otherwise directed by the principal or otherwise provided in the Special Instructions, must include:

(A) the property belonging to the principal that has come to your knowledge or into your possession;

(B) each action taken or decision made by you as agent or attorney in fact;

(C) a complete account of receipts, disbursements, and other actions of you as agent or attorney in fact that includes the source and nature of each receipt, disbursement, or action, with receipts of principal and income shown separately;

(D) a listing of all property over which you have exercised control that includes an adequate description of each asset and the asset's current value, if known to you;

(E) the cash balance on hand and the name and location of the depository at which the cash balance is kept;

(F) each known liability;

(G) any other information and facts known to you as necessary for a full and definite understanding of the exact condition of the property belonging to the principal; and

(H) all documentation regarding the principal's property.

Termination of Agent's Authority

You must stop acting on behalf of the principal if you learn of any event that terminates this power of attorney or your authority under this power of attorney. An event that terminates this power of attorney or your authority to act under this power of attorney includes:

(1) the principal's death;

(2) the principal's revocation of this power of attorney or your authority;

(3) the occurrence of a termination event stated in this power of attorney;

(4) if you are married to the principal, the dissolution of your marriage by court decree of divorce or annulment;

(5) the appointment and qualification of a permanent guardian of the principal's estate; or

(6) if ordered by a court, the suspension of this power of attorney on the appointment and qualification of a temporary guardian until the date the term of the temporary guardian expires.

Liability of Agent

The authority granted to you under this power of attorney is specified in the Durable Power of Attorney Act (Subtitle P, Title 2, Estates Code). If you violate the Durable Power of Attorney Act or act beyond the authority granted, you may be liable for any damages caused by the violation or subject to prosecution for misapplication of property by a fiduciary under Chapter 32 of the Texas Penal Code.

THE ATTORNEY IN FACT OR AGENT, BY ACCEPTING OR ACTING UNDER THE APPOINTMENT, ASSUMES THE FIDUCIARY AND OTHER LEGAL RESPONSIBILITIES OF AN AGENT.

Derived from Probate Code § 490(a).

Added by Acts 2011, 82nd Leg., ch. 823, § 1.01, eff. Jan. 1, 2014. Amended by Acts 2013, 83rd Leg., ch. 700, § 1, eff. Jan. 1, 2014.

Subchapter C. Construction of Powers Related to Statutory Durable Power of Attorney

---

Statutes in Context
Chapter 752, Subchapter C

Chapter 752, Subchapter C, provides detailed explanations of the powers granted in the statutory form.

---

§ 752.101. Construction in General

By executing a statutory durable power of attorney that confers authority with respect to any class of transactions, the principal empowers the attorney in fact or agent for that class of transactions to:

(1) demand, receive, and obtain by litigation, action, or otherwise any money or other thing of value to which the principal is, may become, or may claim to be entitled;

(2) conserve, invest, disburse, or use any money or other thing of value received on behalf of the principal for the purposes intended;

(3) contract in any manner with any person, on terms agreeable to the attorney in fact or agent, to accomplish a purpose of a transaction and perform, rescind, reform, release, or modify that contract or another contract made by or on behalf of the principal;

(4) execute, acknowledge, seal, and deliver a deed, revocation, mortgage, lease, notice, check, release, or other instrument the attorney in fact or agent considers desirable to accomplish a purpose of a transaction;

(5) with respect to a claim existing in favor of or against the principal:

(A) prosecute, defend, submit to arbitration, settle, and propose or accept a compromise; or

(B) intervene in an action or litigation relating to the claim;

(6) seek on the principal's behalf the assistance of a court to carry out an act authorized by the power of attorney;

(7) engage, compensate, and discharge an attorney, accountant, expert witness, or other assistant;

(8) keep appropriate records of each transaction, including an accounting of receipts and disbursements;

(9) prepare, execute, and file a record, report, or other document the attorney in fact or agent considers necessary or desirable to safeguard or promote the principal's interest under a statute or governmental regulation;

(10) reimburse the attorney in fact or agent for an expenditure made in exercising the powers granted by the durable power of attorney; and

(11) in general, perform any other lawful act that the principal may perform with respect to the transaction.

Derived from Probate Code § 491.

Added by Acts 2011, 82nd Leg., ch. 823, § 1.01, eff. Jan. 1, 2014.

§ 752.102. Real Property Transactions

The language conferring authority with respect to real property transactions in a statutory durable power of attorney empowers the attorney in fact or agent, without further reference to a specific description of the real property, to:

(1) accept as a gift or as security for a loan or reject, demand, buy, lease, receive, or otherwise acquire an interest in real property or a right incident to real property;

(2) sell, exchange, convey with or without covenants, quitclaim, release, surrender, mortgage, encumber, partition or consent to partitioning, subdivide, apply for zoning, rezoning, or other governmental permits, plat or consent to platting, develop, grant options concerning, lease or sublet, or otherwise dispose of an estate or interest in real property or a right incident to real property;

(3) release, assign, satisfy, and enforce by litigation, action, or otherwise a mortgage, deed of trust, encumbrance, lien, or other claim to real property that exists or is claimed to exist;

(4) perform any act of management or of conservation with respect to an interest in real property, or a right incident to real property, owned or claimed to be owned by the principal, including the authority to:

(A) insure against a casualty, liability, or loss;

(B) obtain or regain possession or protect the interest or right by litigation, action, or otherwise;

(C) pay, compromise, or contest taxes or assessments or apply for and receive refunds in connection with the taxes or assessments;

(D) purchase supplies, hire assistance or labor, or make repairs or alterations to the real property; and

(E) manage and supervise an interest in real property, including the mineral estate, by, for example:

(i) entering into a lease for oil, gas, and mineral purposes;

(ii) making contracts for development of the mineral estate; or

(iii) making pooling and unitization agreements;

(5) use, develop, alter, replace, remove, erect, or install structures or other improvements on real property in which the principal has or claims to have an estate, interest, or right;

(6) participate in a reorganization with respect to real property or a legal entity that owns an interest in or right incident to real property, receive and hold shares of stock or obligations received in a plan or reorganization, and act with respect to the shares or obligations, including:

(A) selling or otherwise disposing of the shares or obligations;

(B) exercising or selling an option, conversion, or similar right with respect to the shares or obligations; and

(C) voting the shares or obligations in person or by proxy;

(7) change the form of title of an interest in or right incident to real property; and

(8) dedicate easements or other real property in which the principal has or claims to have an interest to public use, with or without consideration.

Derived from Probate Code § 492.

Added by Acts 2011, 82nd Leg., ch. 823, § 1.01, eff. Jan. 1, 2014.

§ 752.103. Tangible Personal Property Transactions

The language conferring general authority with respect to tangible personal property transactions in a statutory durable power of attorney empowers the attorney in fact or agent to:

(1) accept tangible personal property or an interest in tangible personal property as a gift or as security for a loan or reject, demand, buy, receive, or otherwise acquire ownership or possession of

tangible personal property or an interest in tangible personal property;

(2) sell, exchange, convey with or without covenants, release, surrender, mortgage, encumber, pledge, create a security interest in, pawn, grant options concerning, lease or sublet to others, or otherwise dispose of tangible personal property or an interest in tangible personal property;

(3) release, assign, satisfy, or enforce by litigation, action, or otherwise a mortgage, security interest, encumbrance, lien, or other claim on behalf of the principal, with respect to tangible personal property or an interest in tangible personal property; and

(4) perform an act of management or conservation with respect to tangible personal property or an interest in tangible personal property on behalf of the principal, including:

(A) insuring the property or interest against casualty, liability, or loss;

(B) obtaining or regaining possession or protecting the property or interest by litigation, action, or otherwise;

(C) paying, compromising, or contesting taxes or assessments or applying for and receiving refunds in connection with taxes or assessments;

(D) moving the property;

(E) storing the property for hire or on a gratuitous bailment; and

(F) using, altering, and making repairs or alterations to the property.

Derived from Probate Code § 493.

Added by Acts 2011, 82nd Leg., ch. 823, § 1.01, eff. Jan. 1, 2014.

§ 752.104. Stock and Bond Transactions

The language conferring authority with respect to stock and bond transactions in a statutory durable power of attorney empowers the attorney in fact or agent to:

(1) buy, sell, and exchange:

(A) stocks;

(B) bonds;

(C) mutual funds; and

(D) all other types of securities and financial instruments other than commodity futures contracts and call and put options on stocks and stock indexes;

(2) receive certificates and other evidences of ownership with respect to securities;

(3) exercise voting rights with respect to securities in person or by proxy;

(4) enter into voting trusts; and

(5) consent to limitations on the right to vote.

Derived from Probate Code § 494.

Added by Acts 2011, 82nd Leg., ch. 823, § 1.01, eff. Jan. 1, 2014.

§ 752.105. Commodity and Option Transactions

The language conferring authority with respect to commodity and option transactions in a statutory durable power of attorney empowers the attorney in fact or agent to:

(1) buy, sell, exchange, assign, settle, and exercise commodity futures contracts and call and put options on stocks and stock indexes traded on a regulated options exchange; and

(2) establish, continue, modify, or terminate option accounts with a broker.

Derived from Probate Code § 495.

Added by Acts 2011, 82nd Leg., ch. 823, § 1.01, eff. Jan. 1, 2014.

§ 752.106. Banking and Other Financial Institution Transactions

The language conferring authority with respect to banking and other financial institution transactions in a statutory durable power of attorney empowers the attorney in fact or agent to:

(1) continue, modify, or terminate an account or other banking arrangement made by or on behalf of the principal;

(2) establish, modify, or terminate an account or other banking arrangement with a bank, trust company, savings and loan association, credit union, thrift company, brokerage firm, or other financial institution selected by the attorney in fact or agent;

(3) rent a safe deposit box or space in a vault;

(4) contract to procure other services available from a financial institution as the attorney in fact or agent considers desirable;

(5) withdraw by check, order, or otherwise money or property of the principal deposited with or left in the custody of a financial institution;

(6) receive bank statements, vouchers, notices, or similar documents from a financial institution and act with respect to those documents;

(7) enter a safe deposit box or vault and withdraw from or add to its contents;

(8) borrow money at an interest rate agreeable to the attorney in fact or agent and pledge as security the principal's property as necessary to borrow, pay, renew, or extend the time of payment of a debt of the principal;

(9) make, assign, draw, endorse, discount, guarantee, and negotiate promissory notes, bills of exchange, checks, drafts, or other negotiable or nonnegotiable paper of the principal, or payable to the principal or the principal's order to receive the cash or other proceeds of those transactions, to accept a draft drawn by a person on the principal, and to pay the principal when due;

(10) receive for the principal and act on a sight draft, warehouse receipt, or other negotiable or nonnegotiable instrument;

(11) apply for and receive letters of credit, credit cards, and traveler's checks from a financial institution and give an indemnity or other agreement in connection with letters of credit; and

(12) consent to an extension of the time of payment with respect to commercial paper or a financial transaction with a financial institution.

Derived from Probate Code § 496.

Added by Acts 2011, 82nd Leg., ch. 823, § 1.01, eff. Jan. 1, 2014.

§ 752.107. Business Operation Transactions

The language conferring authority with respect to business operating transactions in a statutory durable power of attorney empowers the attorney in fact or agent to:

(1) operate, buy, sell, enlarge, reduce, or terminate a business interest;

(2) do the following, to the extent that an attorney in fact or agent is permitted by law to act for a principal and subject to the terms of a partnership agreement:

(A) perform a duty, discharge a liability, or exercise a right, power, privilege, or option that the principal has, may have, or claims to have under the partnership agreement, whether or not the principal is a general or limited partner;

(B) enforce the terms of the partnership agreement by litigation, action, or otherwise; and

(C) defend, submit to arbitration, settle, or compromise litigation or an action to which the principal is a party because of membership in the partnership;

(3) exercise in person or by proxy, or enforce by litigation, action, or otherwise, a right, power, privilege, or option the principal has or claims to have as the holder of a bond, share, or other similar instrument and defend, submit to arbitration, settle, or compromise a legal proceeding to which the principal is a party because of a bond, share, or similar instrument;

(4) with respect to a business owned solely by the principal:

(A) continue, modify, renegotiate, extend, and terminate a contract made before execution of the power of attorney with an individual, legal entity, firm, association, or corporation by or on behalf of the principal with respect to the business;

(B) determine:

(i) the location of the business's operation;

(ii) the nature and extent of the business;

(iii) the methods of manufacturing, selling, merchandising, financing, accounting, and advertising employed in the business's operation;

(iv) the amount and types of insurance carried; and

(v) the method of engaging, compensating, and dealing with the business's accountants, attorneys, and other agents and employees;

(C) change the name or form of organization under which the business is operated and enter into a partnership agreement with other persons or organize a corporation to take over all or part of the operation of the business; and

(D) demand and receive money due or claimed by the principal or on the principal's behalf in the operation of the business and control and disburse the money in the operation of the business;

(5) put additional capital into a business in which the principal has an interest;

(6) join in a plan of reorganization, consolidation, or merger of the business;

(7) sell or liquidate a business or part of the business at the time and on the terms that the attorney in fact or agent considers desirable;

(8) establish the value of a business under a buy-out agreement to which the principal is a party;

(9) do the following:

(A) prepare, sign, file, and deliver reports, compilations of information, returns, or other papers with respect to a business:

(i) that are required by a governmental agency, department, or instrumentality; or

(ii) that the attorney in fact or agent considers desirable; and

(B) make related payments; and

(10) pay, compromise, or contest taxes or assessments and perform any other act that the attorney in fact or agent considers desirable to protect the principal from illegal or unnecessary taxation, fines, penalties, or assessments with respect to a business, including attempts to recover, in any manner permitted by law, money paid before or after the execution of the power of attorney.

Derived from Probate Code § 497.

Added by Acts 2011, 82nd Leg., ch. 823, § 1.01, eff. Jan. 1, 2014.

§ 752.108. Insurance and Annuity Transactions

(a) The language conferring authority with respect to insurance and annuity transactions in a statutory durable power of attorney empowers the attorney in fact or agent to:

(1) continue, pay the premium or assessment on, modify, rescind, release, or terminate a contract procured by or on behalf of the principal that insures or provides an annuity to either the principal or another person, whether or not the principal is a beneficiary under the contract;

(2) procure new, different, or additional insurance contracts and annuities for the principal or the principal's spouse, children, and other dependents and select the amount, type of insurance or annuity, and method of payment;

(3) pay the premium or assessment on, or modify, rescind, release, or terminate, an insurance contract or annuity procured by the attorney in fact or agent;

(4) designate the beneficiary of the insurance contract, except as provided by Subsection (b);

(5) apply for and receive a loan on the security of the insurance contract or annuity;

(6) surrender and receive the cash surrender value;

(7) exercise an election;

(8) change the manner of paying premiums;

(9) change or convert the type of insurance contract or annuity with respect to which the principal has or claims to have a power described by this section;

(10) change the beneficiary of an insurance contract or annuity, except that the attorney in fact or agent may be designated a beneficiary only to the extent authorized by Subsection (b);

(11) apply for and procure government aid to guarantee or pay premiums of an insurance contract on the life of the principal;

(12) collect, sell, assign, borrow on, or pledge the principal's interest in an insurance contract or annuity; and

(13) pay from proceeds or otherwise, compromise or contest, or apply for refunds in connection with a tax or assessment imposed by a taxing authority with respect to an insurance contract or annuity or the proceeds of the contract or annuity or liability accruing because of the tax or assessment.

(b) An attorney in fact or agent may be named a beneficiary of an insurance contract or an extension, renewal, or substitute for the contract only to the extent the attorney in fact or agent was named as a beneficiary under a contract procured by the principal before executing the power of attorney.

Derived from Probate Code § 498.

Added by Acts 2011, 82nd Leg., ch. 823, § 1.01, eff. Jan. 1, 2014.

§ 752.109. Estate, Trust, and Other Beneficiary Transactions

The language conferring authority with respect to estate, trust, and other beneficiary transactions in a statutory durable power of attorney empowers the attorney in fact or agent to act for the principal in all matters that affect a trust, probate estate, guardianship, conservatorship, escrow, custodianship, or other fund from which the principal is, may become, or claims to be entitled, as a beneficiary, to a share or payment, including to:

(1) accept, reject, disclaim, receive, receipt for, sell, assign, release, pledge, exchange, or consent to a reduction in or modification of a share in or payment from the fund;

(2) demand or obtain by litigation, action, or otherwise money or any other thing of value to which the principal is, may become, or claims to be entitled because of the fund;

(3) initiate, participate in, or oppose a legal or judicial proceeding to:

(A) ascertain the meaning, validity, or effect of a deed, will, declaration of trust, or other instrument or transaction affecting the interest of the principal; or

(B) remove, substitute, or surcharge a fiduciary;

(4) conserve, invest, disburse, or use anything received for an authorized purpose; and

(5) transfer all or part of the principal's interest in real property, stocks, bonds, accounts with financial institutions, insurance, and other property to the trustee of a revocable trust created by the principal as settlor.

Derived from Probate Code § 499.

Added by Acts 2011, 82nd Leg., ch. 823, § 1.01, eff. Jan. 1, 2014.

§ 752.110. Claims and Litigation

The language conferring general authority with respect to claims and litigation in a statutory durable power of attorney empowers the attorney in fact or agent to:

(1) assert and prosecute before a court or administrative agency a claim, a claim for relief, a counterclaim, or an offset, or defend against an individual, a legal entity, or a government, including an action to:

(A) recover property or other thing of value;

(B) recover damages sustained by the principal;

(C) eliminate or modify tax liability; or

(D) seek an injunction, specific performance, or other relief;

(2) bring an action to determine an adverse claim, intervene in an action or litigation, and act as an amicus curiae;

(3) in connection with an action or litigation:

(A) procure an attachment, garnishment, libel, order of arrest, or other preliminary, provisional, or intermediate relief and use an available procedure to effect or satisfy a judgment, order, or decree; and

(B) perform any lawful act the principal could perform, including:

(i) acceptance of tender;

(ii) offer of judgment;

(iii) admission of facts;

(iv) submission of a controversy on an agreed statement of facts;

(v) consent to examination before trial; and

(vi) binding of the principal in litigation;

(4) submit to arbitration, settle, and propose or accept a compromise with respect to a claim or litigation;

(5) waive the issuance and service of process on the principal, accept service of process, appear for the principal, designate persons on whom process directed to the principal may be served, execute and file or deliver stipulations on the principal's behalf, verify pleadings, seek appellate review, procure and give surety and indemnity bonds, contract and pay for the preparation and printing of records and briefs, or receive and execute and file or deliver a consent, waiver, release, confession of judgment, satisfaction of judgment, notice, agreement, or other instrument in connection with the prosecution, settlement, or defense of a claim or litigation;

(6) act for the principal regarding voluntary or involuntary bankruptcy or insolvency proceedings concerning:

(A) the principal; or

(B) another person, with respect to a reorganization proceeding or a receivership or application for the appointment of a receiver or trustee that affects the principal's interest in property or other thing of value; and

(7) pay a judgment against the principal or a settlement made in connection with a claim or litigation and receive and conserve money or other thing of value paid in settlement of or as proceeds of a claim or litigation.

Derived from Probate Code § 500.

Added by Acts 2011, 82nd Leg., ch. 823, § 1.01, eff. Jan. 1, 2014.

§ 752.111. Personal and Family Maintenance

The language conferring authority with respect to personal and family maintenance in a statutory durable power of attorney empowers the attorney in fact or agent to:

(1) perform the acts necessary to maintain the customary standard of living of the principal, the principal's spouse and children, and other individuals customarily or legally entitled to be supported by the principal, including:

(A) providing living quarters by purchase, lease, or other contract; or

(B) paying the operating costs, including interest, amortization payments, repairs, and taxes on premises owned by the principal and occupied by those individuals;

(2) provide for the individuals described by Subdivision (1):

(A) normal domestic help;

(B) usual vacations and travel expenses; and

(C) money for shelter, clothing, food, appropriate education, and other living costs;

(3) pay necessary medical, dental, and surgical care, hospitalization, and custodial care for the individuals described by Subdivision (1);

(4) continue any provision made by the principal for the individuals described by Subdivision (1) for automobiles or other means of transportation, including registering, licensing, insuring, and replacing the automobiles or other means of transportation;

(5) maintain or open charge accounts for the convenience of the individuals described by Subdivision (1) and open new accounts the attorney in fact or agent considers desirable to accomplish a lawful purpose; and

(6) continue:

(A) payments incidental to the membership or affiliation of the principal in a church, club, society, order, or other organization; or

(B) contributions to those organizations.

Derived from Probate Code § 501.

Added by Acts 2011, 82nd Leg., ch. 823, § 1.01, eff. Jan. 1, 2014.

§ 752.112. Benefits from Certain Governmental Programs or Civil or Military Service

The language conferring authority with respect to benefits from social security, Medicare, Medicaid, or other governmental programs or civil or military service in a statutory durable power of attorney empowers the attorney in fact or agent to:

(1) execute a voucher in the principal's name for an allowance or reimbursement payable by the United States, a foreign government, or a state or subdivision of a state to the principal, including an allowance or reimbursement for:

(A) transportation of the individuals described by Section 752.111(1); and

(B) shipment of the household effects of those individuals;

(2) take possession and order the removal and shipment of the principal's property from a post, warehouse, depot, dock, or other governmental or private place of storage or safekeeping and execute and deliver a release, voucher, receipt, bill of lading, shipping ticket, certificate, or other instrument for that purpose;

(3) prepare, file, and prosecute a claim of the principal for a benefit or assistance, financial or otherwise, to which the principal claims to be entitled under a statute or governmental regulation;

(4) prosecute, defend, submit to arbitration, settle, and propose or accept a compromise with respect to any benefits the principal may be entitled to receive; and

(5) receive the financial proceeds of a claim of the type described by this section and conserve,

invest, disburse, or use anything received for a lawful purpose.

Derived from Probate Code § 502.

Added by Acts 2011, 82nd Leg., ch. 823, § 1.01, eff. Jan. 1, 2014.

§ 752.113. Retirement Plan Transactions

(a) In this section, "retirement plan" means:

(1) an employee pension benefit plan as defined by Section 3, Employee Retirement Income Security Act of 1974 (29 U.S.C. Section 1002), without regard to the provisions of Section (2)(B) of that section;

(2) a plan that does not meet the definition of an employee benefit plan under the Employee Retirement Income Security Act of 1974 (29 U.S.C. Section 1001 et seq.) because the plan does not cover common law employees;

(3) a plan that is similar to an employee benefit plan under the Employee Retirement Income Security Act of 1974 (29 U.S.C. Section 1001 et seq.), regardless of whether the plan is covered by Title 1 of that Act, including a plan that provides death benefits to the beneficiary of employees; and

(4) an individual retirement account or annuity, a self-employed pension plan, or a similar plan or account.

(b) The language conferring authority with respect to retirement plan transactions in a statutory durable power of attorney empowers the attorney in fact or agent to perform any lawful act the principal may perform with respect to a transaction relating to a retirement plan, including to:

(1) apply for service or disability retirement benefits;

(2) select payment options under any retirement plan in which the principal participates, including plans for self-employed individuals;

(3) designate or change the designation of a beneficiary or benefits payable by a retirement plan, except as provided by Subsection (c);

(4) make voluntary contributions to retirement plans if authorized by the plan;

(5) exercise the investment powers available under any self-directed retirement plan;

(6) make rollovers of plan benefits into other retirement plans;

(7) borrow from, sell assets to, and purchase assets from retirement plans if authorized by the plan;

(8) waive the principal's right to be a beneficiary of a joint or survivor annuity if the principal is a spouse who is not employed;

(9) receive, endorse, and cash payments from a retirement plan;

(10) waive the principal's right to receive all or a portion of benefits payable by a retirement plan; and

(11) request and receive information relating to the principal from retirement plan records.

(c) An attorney in fact or agent may be named a beneficiary under a retirement plan only to the extent the attorney in fact or agent was a named beneficiary under the retirement plan before the durable power of attorney was executed.

Derived from Probate Code § 503.

Added by Acts 2011, 82nd Leg., ch. 823, § 1.01, eff. Jan. 1, 2014.

§ 752.114. Tax Matters

The language conferring authority with respect to tax matters in a statutory durable power of attorney empowers the attorney in fact or agent to:

(1) prepare, sign, and file:

(A) federal, state, local, and foreign income, gift, payroll, Federal Insurance Contributions Act (26 U.S.C. Chapter 21), and other tax returns;

(B) claims for refunds;

(C) requests for extensions of time;

(D) petitions regarding tax matters; and

(E) any other tax-related documents, including:

(i) receipts;

(ii) offers;

(iii) waivers;

(iv) consents, including consents and agreements under Section 2032A, Internal Revenue Code of 1986 (26 U.S.C. Section 2032A);

(v) closing agreements; and

(vi) any power of attorney form required by the Internal Revenue Service or other taxing authority with respect to a tax year on which the statute of limitations has not run and 25 tax years following that tax year;

(2) pay taxes due, collect refunds, post bonds, receive confidential information, and contest deficiencies determined by the Internal Revenue Service or other taxing authority;

(3) exercise any election available to the principal under federal, state, local, or foreign tax law; and

(4) act for the principal in all tax matters, for all periods, before the Internal Revenue Service and any other taxing authority.

Derived from Probate Code § 504.

Added by Acts 2011, 82nd Leg., ch. 823, § 1.01, eff. Jan. 1, 2014.

§ 752.115. Existing Interests; Foreign Interests

The powers described by Sections 752.102-752.114 may be exercised equally with respect to an interest the principal has at the time the durable power of attorney is executed or acquires later, whether or not:

(1) the property is located in this state; or

(2) the powers are exercised or the durable power of attorney is executed in this state.

Derived from Probate Code § 505.

Added by Acts 2011, 82nd Leg., ch. 823, § 1.01, eff. Jan. 1, 2014.

TITLE 3. GUARDIANSHIP AND RELATED PROCEDURES

Statutes in Context
Title 3

Guardians may be needed for minors and adult incapacitated individuals. There are two main types of guardians: a guardian of the person who is in charge of the ward's physical needs (§ 1151.051) and a guardian of the estate of who is in charge of the ward's property and financial affairs (§ 1151.101).

The guardianship provisions were originally integrated with the decedents' estates provisions. In 1993, they were split. In many respects, the guardianship provisions still closely mirror the decedents' estates provisions.

SUBTITLE A. GENERAL PROVISIONS

Chapter 1001. Purpose and Construction

§ 1001.001. Policy; Purpose of Guardianship

§ 1001.002. Laws Applicable to Guardianships

§ 1001.003. References in Law Meaning Incapacitated Person

Chapter 1001. Purpose and Construction

§ 1001.001. Policy; Purpose of Guardianship

(a) A court may appoint a guardian with either full or limited authority over an incapacitated person as indicated by the incapacitated person's actual mental or physical limitations and only as necessary to promote and protect the well-being of the incapacitated person.

(b) In creating a guardianship that gives a guardian limited authority over an incapacitated person, the court shall design the guardianship to encourage the development or maintenance of maximum self-reliance and independence in the incapacitated person, including by presuming that the incapacitated person retains capacity to make personal decisions regarding the person's residence.

Derived from Probate Code § 602.

Added by Acts 2011, 82nd Leg., ch. 823, § 1.02, eff.

Jan. 1, 2014. Acts 2015, 84th Leg., ch. 214, § 1, eff. Sept. 1, 2015.

§ 1001.002. Laws Applicable to Guardianships

To the extent applicable and not inconsistent with other provisions of this code, the laws and rules governing estates of decedents apply to guardianships.

Derived from Probate Code § 603(a).

Added by Acts 2011, 82nd Leg., ch. 823, § 1.02, eff. Jan. 1, 2014.

§ 1001.003. References in Law Meaning Incapacitated Person

In this code or any other law, a reference to any of the following means an incapacitated person:

(1) a person who is mentally, physically, or legally incompetent;

(2) a person who is judicially declared incompetent;

(3) an incompetent or an incompetent person;

(4) a person of unsound mind; or

(5) a habitual drunkard.

Derived from Probate Code § 603(b).

Added by Acts 2011, 82nd Leg., ch. 823, § 1.02, eff. Jan. 1, 2014.

Chapter 1002. Definitions

§ 1002.001. Applicability of Definitions

§ 1002.0015. Alternatives to Guardianship

§ 1002.002. Attorney Ad Litem

§ 1002.003. Authorized Corporate Surety

§ 1002.004. Child

§ 1002.005. Claim

§ 1002.006. Community Administrator

§ 1002.007. Corporate Fiduciary

§ 1002.008. Court; Probate Court; Statutory Probate Court

§ 1002.009. Court Investigator

§ 1002.010. Estate; Guardianship Estate

§ 1002.011. Exempt Property

§ 1002.012. Guardian

§ 1002.013. Guardian Ad Litem

§ 1002.014. Guardianship Certification Program Of The Judicial Branch Certification Commission

§ 1002.015. Guardianship Proceeding

§ 1002.016. Guardianship Program

§ 1002.017. Incapacitated Person

§ 1002.018. Interested Person; Person Interested

§ 1002.019. Minor

§ 1002.020. Mortgage; Lien

§ 1002.021. Next Of Kin

§ 1002.022. Parent

Chapter 1002. Definitions

§ 1002.001. Applicability of Definitions

The definition for a term provided by this chapter applies in this title.

Derived from Probate Code § 601.

Added by Acts 2011, 82nd Leg., ch. 823, § 1.02, eff. Jan. 1, 2014.

§ 1002.0015. Alternatives to Guardianship

"Alternatives to guardianship" includes the:

(1) execution of a medical power of attorney under Chapter 166, Health and Safety Code;

(2) appointment of an attorney in fact or agent under a durable power of attorney as provided by Subtitle P, Title 2;

(3) execution of a declaration for mental health treatment under Chapter 137, Civil Practice and Remedies Code;

(4) appointment of a representative payee to manage public benefits;

(5) establishment of a joint bank account;

(6) creation of a management trust under Chapter 1301;

(7) creation of a special needs trust;

(8) designation of a guardian before the need arises under Subchapter E, Chapter 1104; and

(9) establishment of alternate forms of decision-making based on person-centered planning.

New.

Added by Acts 2015, 84th Leg., ch. 214, § 2, eff. Sept. 1, 2015.

§ 1002.002. Attorney Ad Litem

"Attorney ad litem" means an attorney appointed by a court to represent and advocate on behalf of a proposed ward, an incapacitated person, an unborn person, or another person described by Section 1054.007 in a guardianship proceeding.

Derived from Probate Code § 601(1).

Added by Acts 2011, 82nd Leg., ch. 823, § 1.02, eff. Jan. 1, 2014. Amended by Acts 2013, 83rd Leg., ch. 982, § 1, eff. Jan. 1, 2014.

§ 1002.003. Authorized Corporate Surety

"Authorized corporate surety" means a domestic or foreign corporation authorized to engage in business in this state to issue surety, guaranty, or indemnity bonds that guarantee the fidelity of a guardian.

Derived from Probate Code § 601(2).

Added by Acts 2011, 82nd Leg., ch. 823, § 1.02, eff. Jan. 1, 2014.

§ 1002.004. Child

"Child" includes a biological child and an adopted child, regardless of whether the child was adopted by a parent under a statutory procedure or by acts of estoppel.

Derived from Probate Code § 601(3).

Added by Acts 2011, 82nd Leg., ch. 823, § 1.02, eff. Jan. 1, 2014.

§ 1002.005. Claim

"Claim" includes:

(1) a liability against the estate of an incapacitated person; and

(2) a debt due to the estate of an incapacitated person.

Derived from Probate Code § 601(4).

Added by Acts 2011, 82nd Leg., ch. 823, § 1.02, eff. Jan. 1, 2014.

§ 1002.006. Community Administrator

"Community administrator" means a spouse who, on the judicial declaration of incapacity of the other spouse, is authorized to manage, control, and dispose of the entire community estate, including the part of the community estate the incapacitated spouse legally has the power to manage in the absence of the incapacity.

Derived from Probate Code § 601(5).

Added by Acts 2011, 82nd Leg., ch. 823, § 1.02, eff. Jan. 1, 2014.

§ 1002.007. Corporate Fiduciary

"Corporate fiduciary" means a financial institution, as defined by Section 201.101, Finance Code, that:

(1) is existing or engaged in business under the laws of this state, another state, or the United States;

(2) has trust powers; and

(3) is authorized by law to act under the order or appointment of a court of record, without giving bond, as guardian, receiver, trustee, executor, administrator, or, although the financial institution does not have general depository powers, depository for any money paid into the court, or to become sole guarantor or surety in or on any bond required to be given under the laws of this state.

Derived from Probate Code § 601(6).

Added by Acts 2011, 82nd Leg., ch. 823, § 1.02, eff. Jan. 1, 2014.

§ 1002.008. Court; Probate Court; Statutory Probate Court

(a) "Court" or "probate court" means:

(1) a county court exercising its probate jurisdiction;

(2) a court created by statute and authorized to exercise original probate jurisdiction; or

(3) a district court exercising original probate jurisdiction in a contested matter.

(b) "Statutory probate court" means a court created by statute and designated as a statutory probate court under Chapter 25, Government Code. The term does not include a county court at law exercising probate jurisdiction unless the court is designated a statutory probate court under Chapter 25, Government Code.

Derived from Probate Code §§ 601(8), (29).

Added by Acts 2011, 82nd Leg., ch. 823, § 1.02, eff. Jan. 1, 2014.

§ 1002.009. Court Investigator

"Court investigator" means a person appointed by the judge of a statutory probate court under Section 25.0025, Government Code.

Derived from Probate Code § 601(7).

Added by Acts 2011, 82nd Leg., ch. 823, § 1.02, eff. Jan. 1, 2014.

§ 1002.010. Estate; Guardianship Estate

"Estate" or "guardianship estate" means a ward's or deceased ward's property, as that property:

(1) exists originally and changes in form by sale, reinvestment, or otherwise;

(2) is augmented by any accretions and other additions to the property, including any property to be distributed to the deceased ward's representative by the trustee of a trust that terminates on the ward's death, or substitutions for the property; and

(3) is diminished by any decreases in or distributions from the property.

Derived from Probate Code § 601(9).

Added by Acts 2011, 82nd Leg., ch. 823, § 1.02, eff. Jan. 1, 2014.

§ 1002.011. Exempt Property

"Exempt property" means the property in a deceased ward's estate that is exempt from execution or forced sale by the constitution or laws of this state, and any allowance paid instead of that property.

Derived from Probate Code § 601(10).

Added by Acts 2011, 82nd Leg., ch. 823, § 1.02, eff. Jan. 1, 2014.

§ 1002.012. Guardian

(a) "Guardian" means a person appointed as a:

(1) guardian under Subchapter D, Chapter 1101;

(2) successor guardian; or

(3) temporary guardian.

(b) Except as expressly provided otherwise, "guardian" includes:

(1) the guardian of the estate of an incapacitated person; and

(2) the guardian of the person of an incapacitated person.

Derived from Probate Code § 601(11).

Added by Acts 2011, 82nd Leg., ch. 823, § 1.02, eff. Jan. 1, 2014.

§ 1002.013. Guardian Ad Litem

"Guardian ad litem" means a person appointed by a court to represent the best interests of an incapacitated person in a guardianship proceeding.

Derived from Probate Code § 601(12).

Added by Acts 2011, 82nd Leg., ch. 823, § 1.02, eff. Jan. 1, 2014.

§ 1002.014. Guardianship Certification Program of the Judicial Branch Certification Commission

"Guardianship certification program of the Judicial Branch Certification Commission" means the program established under Chapter 155 [111], Government Code.

Derived from Probate Code § 601(12-a).

Added by Acts 2011, 82nd Leg., ch. 823, § 1.02, eff. Jan. 1, 2014.Amended by Acts 2013, 83rd Leg., ch. 42, § 2.04, eff. Jan. 1, 2014.

§ 1002.015. Guardianship Proceeding.

The term "guardianship proceeding" means a matter or proceeding related to a guardianship or any other matter covered by this title, including:

(1) the appointment of a guardian of a minor or other incapacitated person, including an incapacitated adult for whom another court obtained continuing, exclusive jurisdiction in a suit affecting the parent-child relationship when the person was a child;

(2) an application, petition, or motion regarding guardianship or a substitute for [an alternative to] guardianship under this title;

(3) a mental health action; and

(4) an application, petition, or motion regarding a trust created under Chapter 1301.

Derived from Probate Code § 601(25).

Added by Acts 2011, 82nd Leg., ch. 823, § 1.02, eff. Jan. 1, 2014. Amended by Acts 2013, 83rd Leg., ch. 161, § 6.014, eff. Jan. 1, 2014. Subsec. (2) amended by Acts 2015, 84th Leg., ch. 214, § 3, eff. Sept. 1, 2015.

§ 1002.016. Guardianship Program

"Guardianship program" has the meaning assigned by Section 155.001, Government Code.

Derived from Probate Code § 601(13).

Added by Acts 2011, 82nd Leg., ch. 823, § 1.02, eff. Jan. 1, 2014. Amended by Acts 2013, 83rd Leg., ch. 42, § 2.06, eff. Jan. 1, 2014.

§ 1002.017. Incapacitated Person

"Incapacitated person" means:

(1) a minor;

(2) an adult who, because of a physical or mental condition, is substantially unable to:

(A) provide food, clothing, or shelter for himself or herself;

(B) care for the person's own physical health; or

(C) manage the person's own financial affairs; or

(3) a person who must have a guardian appointed for the person to receive funds due the person from a governmental source.

Derived from Probate Code § 601(14).

Added by Acts 2011, 82nd Leg., ch. 823, § 1.02, eff. Jan. 1, 2014.

§ 1002.018. Interested Person; Person Interested

"Interested person" or "person interested" means:

(1) an heir, devisee, spouse, creditor, or any other person having a property right in or claim against an estate being administered; or

(2) a person interested in the welfare of an incapacitated person.

Derived from Probate Code § 601(15).

Added by Acts 2011, 82nd Leg., ch. 823, § 1.02, eff. Jan. 1, 2014.

§ 1002.019. Minor

"Minor" means a person younger than 18 years of age who:

(1) has never been married; and

(2) has not had the disabilities of minority removed for general purposes.

Derived from Probate Code § 601(16).

Added by Acts 2011, 82nd Leg., ch. 823, § 1.02, eff. Jan. 1, 2014.

§ 1002.020. Mortgage; Lien

"Mortgage" and "lien" include:

(1) a deed of trust;

(2) a vendor's lien;

(3) a mechanic's, materialman's, or laborer's lien;

(4) a judgment, attachment, or garnishment lien;

(5) a federal or state tax lien;

(6) a chattel mortgage; and

(7) a pledge by hypothecation.

Derived from Probate Code § 601(18).

Added by Acts 2011, 82nd Leg., ch. 823, § 1.02, eff. Jan. 1, 2014.

§ 1002.021. Next of Kin

"Next of kin" includes:

(1) an adopted child;

(2) an adopted child's descendants; and

(3) the adoptive parent of an adopted child.

Derived from Probate Code § 601(19).

Added by Acts 2011, 82nd Leg., ch. 823, § 1.02, eff. Jan. 1, 2014.

§ 1002.022. Parent

"Parent" means the mother of a child, a man presumed to be the biological father of a child, a man who has been adjudicated to be the biological father of a child by a court of competent jurisdiction, or an adoptive mother or father of a child, but does not include a parent as to whom the parent-child relationship has been terminated.

Derived from Probate Code § 601(20).

Added by Acts 2011, 82nd Leg., ch. 823, § 1.02, eff. Jan. 1, 2014.

§ 1002.023. Person

(a) "Person" includes a natural person, a corporation, and a guardianship program.

(b) The definition of "person" assigned by Section 311.005, Government Code, does not apply to any provision in this title.

Derived from Probate Code § 601(21).

Added by Acts 2011, 82nd Leg., ch. 823, § 1.02, eff. Jan. 1, 2014.

§ 1002.024. Personal Property

"Personal property" includes an interest in:

(1) goods;

(2) money;

(3) a chose in action;

(4) an evidence of debt; and

(5) a real chattel.

Derived from Probate Code § 601(22).

Added by Acts 2011, 82nd Leg., ch. 823, § 1.02, eff. Jan. 1, 2014.

§ 1002.025. Private Professional Guardian

"Private professional guardian" has the meaning assigned by Section 155.001, Government Code.

Derived from Probate Code § 601(24).

Added by Acts 2011, 82nd Leg., ch. 823, § 1.02, eff. Jan. 1, 2014. Amended by Acts 2013, 83rd Leg., ch. 42, § 2.06, eff. Jan. 1, 2014.

§ 1002.026. Proposed Ward

"Proposed ward" means a person alleged in a guardianship proceeding to be incapacitated.

Derived from Probate Code § 601(27).

Added by Acts 2011, 82nd Leg., ch. 823, § 1.02, eff. Jan. 1, 2014.

§ 1002.027. Real Property

"Real property" includes estates and interests in land, whether corporeal or incorporeal or legal or equitable. The term does not include a real chattel.

Derived from Probate Code § 601(28).

Added by Acts 2011, 82nd Leg., ch. 823, § 1.02, eff. Jan. 1, 2014.

§ 1002.028. Representative; Personal Representative

"Representative" and "personal representative" include:

(1) a guardian; and

(2) a successor guardian.

Derived from Probate Code § 601(23).

Added by Acts 2011, 82nd Leg., ch. 823, § 1.02, eff. Jan. 1, 2014.

§ 1002.029. Surety

"Surety" includes a personal surety and a corporate surety.

Derived from Probate Code § 601(30).

Added by Acts 2011, 82nd Leg., ch. 823, § 1.02, eff. Jan. 1, 2014.

§ 1002.030. Ward

"Ward" means a person for whom a guardian has been appointed.

Derived from Probate Code § 601(31).

Added by Acts 2011, 82nd Leg., ch. 823, § 1.02, eff. Jan. 1, 2014.

§ 1002.031. Supports and Services

"Supports and services" means available formal and informal resources and assistance that enable an individual to:

(1) meet the individual's needs for food, clothing, or shelter;

(2) care for the individual's physical or mental health;

(3) manage the individual's financial affairs; or

(4) make personal decisions regarding residence, voting, operating a motor vehicle, and marriage.

New.

Added by Acts 2015, 84ᵗʰ Leg., ch. 214, § 2, eff. Sept. 1, 2015.

SUBTITLE B. SCOPE, JURISDICTION, AND VENUE

Chapter 1021.   General Provisions

§ 1021.001. Matters Related to Guardianship Proceeding.

Chapter 1021.   General Provisions

§ 1021.001   Matters Related To Guardianship Proceeding

(a) For purposes of this code, in a county in which there is no statutory probate court, a matter related to a guardianship proceeding includes:

(1) the granting of letters of guardianship;

(2) the settling of an account of a guardian and all other matters relating to the settlement, partition, or distribution of a ward's estate;

(3) a claim brought by or against a guardianship estate;

(4) an action for trial of title to real property that is guardianship estate property, including the enforcement of a lien against the property;

(5) an action for trial of the right of property that is guardianship estate property;

(6) after a guardianship of the estate of a ward is required to be settled as provided by Section 1204.001:

(A) an action brought by or on behalf of the former ward against a former guardian of the ward for alleged misconduct arising from the performance of the person's duties as guardian;

(B) an action calling on the surety of a guardian or former guardian to perform in place of the guardian or former guardian, which may include the award of a judgment against the guardian or former guardian in favor of the surety;

(C) an action against a former guardian of the former ward that is brought by a surety that is called on to perform in place of the former guardian;

(D) a claim for the payment of compensation, expenses, and court costs, and any other matter authorized under Chapter 1155 [and Subpart H, Part 2, Subtitle Z]; and

(E) a matter related to an authorization made or duty performed by a guardian under Chapter 1204; and

(7) the appointment of a trustee for a trust created under Section 1301.053 or 1301.054, the settling of an account of the trustee, and all other matters relating to the trust.

(b) For purposes of this code, in a county in which there is a statutory probate court, a matter related to a guardianship proceeding includes:

(1) all matters and actions described in Subsection (a);

(2) a suit, action, or application filed against or on behalf of a guardianship or a trustee of a trust created under Section 1301.053 or 1301.054; and

(3) a cause of action in which a guardian in a guardianship pending in the statutory probate court is a party.

Derived from Probate Code § 606A.

Added by Acts 2013, 83ʳᵈ Leg., ch. 161, § 6.015, eff. Jan. 1, 2014. Subsec. (a)(6)(D) amended by Acts 2015, 84ᵗʰ Leg., ch. 1236, § 20.007, eff. Sept. 1, 2015.

Chapter 1022. Jurisdiction

Chapter 1022. Jurisdiction

§ 1022.001. General Probate Court Jurisdiction in Guardianship Proceedings; Appeals

(a) All guardianship proceedings must be filed and heard in a court exercising original probate jurisdiction. The court exercising original probate jurisdiction also has jurisdiction of all matters related to the guardianship proceeding as specified in Section 1021.001 for that type of court.

(b) A probate court may exercise pendent and ancillary jurisdiction as necessary to promote judicial efficiency and economy.

(c) A final order issued by a probate court is appealable to the court of appeals.

Derived from Probate Code § 605.

Added by Acts 2013, 83rd Leg., ch. 161, § 6.015, eff. Jan. 1, 2014.

§ 1022.002. Original Jurisdiction for Guardianship Proceedings

(a) In a county in which there is no statutory probate court or county court at law exercising original probate jurisdiction, the county court has original jurisdiction of guardianship proceedings.

(b) In a county in which there is no statutory probate court, but in which there is a county court at law exercising original probate jurisdiction, the county court at law exercising original probate jurisdiction and the county court have concurrent original jurisdiction of guardianship proceedings, unless otherwise provided by law. The judge of a county court may hear guardianship proceedings while sitting for the judge of any other county court.

(c) In a county in which there is a statutory probate court, the statutory probate court has original jurisdiction of guardianship proceedings.

(d) From the filing of the application for the appointment of a guardian of the estate or person, or both, until the guardianship is settled and closed under this chapter, the administration of the estate of a minor or other incapacitated person is one proceeding for purposes of jurisdiction and is a proceeding in rem.

Derived from Probate Code §§ 604 & 607A.

Added by Acts 2013, 83rd Leg., ch. 161, § 6.015, eff. Jan. 1, 2014 and Acts 2013, 83rd Leg., ch. 982, § 2, eff. Jan. 1, 2014.

§ 1022.003. Jurisdiction of Contested Guardianship Proceeding in County With No Statutory Probate Court or County Court at Law

(a) In a county in which there is no statutory probate court or county court at law exercising original probate jurisdiction, when a matter in a guardianship proceeding is contested, the judge of the county court may, on the judge's own motion, or shall, on the motion of any party to the proceeding, according to the motion:

(1) request the assignment of a statutory probate court judge to hear the contested matter, as provided by Section 25.0022, Government Code; or

(2) transfer the contested matter to the district court, which may then hear the contested matter as if originally filed in the district court.

(b) If a party to a guardianship proceeding files a motion for the assignment of a statutory probate court judge to hear a contested matter in the proceeding before the judge of the county court transfers the contested matter to a district court under this section, the county judge shall grant the motion for the assignment of a statutory probate court judge and may not transfer the matter to the district court unless the party withdraws the motion.

(c) If a judge of a county court requests the assignment of a statutory probate court judge to hear a contested matter in a guardianship proceeding on the judge's own motion or on the motion of a party to the proceeding as provided by this section, the judge may request that the statutory probate court judge be assigned to the entire proceeding on the judge's own motion or on the motion of a party.

(d) A party to a guardianship proceeding may file a motion for the assignment of a statutory probate court judge under this section before a matter in the proceeding becomes contested, and the motion is given effect as a motion for assignment of a statutory probate court judge under Subsection (a) if the matter later becomes contested.

(e) Notwithstanding any other law, a transfer of a contested matter in a guardianship proceeding to a district court under any authority other than the authority provided by this section:

(1) is disregarded for purposes of this section; and

(2) does not defeat the right of a party to the proceeding to have the matter assigned to a statutory probate court judge in accordance with this section.

(f) A statutory probate court judge assigned to a contested matter in a guardianship proceeding or to the entire proceeding under this section has the jurisdiction and authority granted to a statutory probate court by this code. A statutory probate court judge assigned to hear only the contested matter in a guardianship proceeding shall, on resolution of the matter, including any appeal of the matter, return the matter to the county court for further proceedings not inconsistent with the orders of the statutory probate court or court of appeals, as applicable. A statutory probate court judge assigned to the entire guardianship proceeding as provided by Subsection (c) shall, on resolution of the contested matter in the proceeding, including any appeal of the matter, return the entire proceeding to the county court for further proceedings not inconsistent with the orders of the statutory probate court or court of appeals, as applicable.

(g) A district court to which a contested matter in a guardianship proceeding is transferred under this section has the jurisdiction and authority granted to a statutory probate court by this code. On resolution of a contested matter transferred to the district court under this section, including any appeal of the matter, the district court shall return the matter to the county court for further proceedings not inconsistent with the orders of the district court or court of appeals, as applicable.

(h) If only the contested matter in a guardianship proceeding is assigned to a statutory probate court judge under this section, or if the contested matter in a guardianship proceeding is transferred to a district court under this section, the county court shall continue to exercise jurisdiction over the management of the guardianship, other than a contested matter, until final disposition of the contested matter is made in accordance with this section. Any matter related to a guardianship proceeding in which a contested matter is transferred to a district court may be brought in the district court. The district court in which a matter related to the proceeding is filed may, on the court's own motion or on the motion of any party, find that the matter is not a contested matter and transfer the matter to the county court with jurisdiction of the management of the guardianship.

(i) If a contested matter in a guardianship proceeding is transferred to a district court under this section, the district court has jurisdiction of any contested matter in the proceeding that is subsequently filed, and the county court shall transfer those contested matters to the district court. If a statutory probate court judge is assigned under this section to hear a contested matter in a guardianship proceeding, the statutory probate court judge shall be assigned to hear any contested matter in the proceeding that is subsequently filed.

(j) The clerk of a district court to which a contested matter in a guardianship proceeding is transferred under this section may perform in relation to the transferred matter any function a county clerk may perform with respect to that type of matter.

Derived from Probate Code § 607B.

Added by Acts 2013, 83rd Leg., ch. 161, § 6.015, eff. Jan. 1, 2014.

§ 1022.004. Jurisdiction of Contested Guardianship Proceeding in County With No Statutory Probate Court

(a) In a county in which there is no statutory probate court, but in which there is a county court at law exercising original probate jurisdiction, when a matter in a guardianship proceeding is contested, the judge of the county court may, on the judge's own motion, or shall, on the motion of any party to the proceeding, transfer the contested matter to the county court at law. In addition, the judge of the county court, on the judge's own motion or on the motion of a party to the proceeding, may transfer the entire proceeding to the county court at law.

(b) A county court at law to which a proceeding is transferred under this section may hear the proceeding as if originally filed in that court. If only a contested matter in the proceeding is transferred, on the resolution of the matter, the matter shall be returned to the county court for further proceedings not inconsistent with the orders of the county court at law.

Derived from Probate Code § 607C.

Added by Acts 2013, 83rd Leg., ch. 161, § 6.015, eff. Jan. 1, 2014.

§ 1022.005. Exclusive Jurisdiction of Guardianship Proceeding in County With Statutory Probate Court

(a) In a county in which there is a statutory probate court, the statutory probate court has exclusive jurisdiction of all guardianship proceedings, regardless of whether contested or uncontested.

(b) A cause of action related to a guardianship proceeding of which the statutory probate court has exclusive jurisdiction as provided by Subsection (a) must be brought in the statutory probate court unless the jurisdiction of the statutory probate court is concurrent with the jurisdiction of a district court as provided by Section 1022.006 or with the jurisdiction of any other court.

Derived from Probate Code § 607D.

Added by Acts 2013, 83rd Leg., ch. 161, § 6.015, eff. Jan. 1, 2014.

§ 1022.006. Concurrent Jurisdiction With District Court

A statutory probate court has concurrent jurisdiction with the district court in:

(1) a personal injury, survival, or wrongful death action by or against a person in the person's capacity as a guardian; and

(2) an action involving a guardian in which each other party aligned with the guardian is not an interested person in the guardianship.

Derived from Probate Code § 607E.

Added by Acts 2013, 83rd Leg., ch. 161, § 6.015, eff. Jan. 1, 2014.

§ 1022.007. Transfer of Proceeding by Statutory Probate Court

(a) A judge of a statutory probate court, on the motion of a party to the action or of a person interested in the guardianship, may:

(1) transfer to the judge's court from a district, county, or statutory court a cause of action that is a matter related to a guardianship proceeding pending in the statutory probate court, including a cause of action that is a matter related to a guardianship proceeding pending in the statutory probate court and in which the guardian, ward, or proposed ward in the pending guardianship proceeding is a party; and

(2) consolidate the transferred cause of action with the guardianship proceeding to which it relates and any other proceedings in the statutory probate court that are related to the guardianship proceeding.

(b) Notwithstanding any other provision of this title, the proper venue for an action by or against a guardian, ward, or proposed ward for personal injury, death, or property damages is determined under Section 15.007, Civil Practice and Remedies Code.

Derived from Probate Code § 608.

Added by Acts 2013, 83rd Leg., ch. 161, § 6.015, eff. Jan. 1, 2014.

§ 1022.008. Transfer of Contested Guardianship of the Person of a Minor

(a) If an interested person contests an application for the appointment of a guardian of the person of a minor or an interested person seeks the removal of a guardian of the person of a minor, the judge, on the judge's own motion, may transfer all matters related to the guardianship proceeding to a court of competent jurisdiction in which a suit affecting the parent-child relationship under the Family Code is pending.

(b) The probate court that transfers a proceeding under this section to a court with proper jurisdiction over suits affecting the parent-child relationship shall send to the court to which the transfer is made the complete files in all matters affecting the guardianship of the person of the minor and certified copies of all entries in the judge's guardianship docket. The transferring court shall keep a copy of the transferred files. If the transferring court retains jurisdiction of the guardianship of the estate of the minor or of another minor who was the subject of the suit, the court shall

send a copy of the complete files to the court to which the transfer is made and shall keep the original files.

(c) The court to which a transfer is made under this section shall apply the procedural and substantive provisions of the Family Code, including Sections 155.005 and 155.205, in regard to enforcing an order rendered by the court from which the proceeding was transferred.

Derived from Probate Code § 609.

Added by and redesignated from Probate Code § 609(b), (c) by Acts 2013, 83rd Leg., ch. 161, § 6.015(a), (b), eff. Jan. 1, 2014.

Chapter 1023. Venue

Chapter 1023. Venue

§ 1023.001. Venue for Appointment of Guardian

(a) Except as otherwise authorized by this section, a proceeding for the appointment of a guardian for the person or estate, or both, of an incapacitated person shall be brought in the county in which the proposed ward resides or is located on the date the application is filed or in the county in which the principal estate of the proposed ward is located.

(b) A proceeding for the appointment of a guardian for the person or estate, or both, of a minor may be brought:

(1) in the county in which both the minor's parents reside;

(2) if the parents do not reside in the same county, in the county in which the parent who is the sole managing conservator of the minor resides, or in the county in which the parent who is the joint managing conservator with the greater period of physical possession of and access to the minor resides;

(3) if only one parent is living and the parent has custody of the minor, in the county in which that parent resides;

(4) if both parents are dead but the minor was in the custody of a deceased parent, in the county in

which the last surviving parent having custody resided; or

(5) if both parents of a minor child have died in a common disaster and there is no evidence that the parents died other than simultaneously, in the county in which both deceased parents resided at the time of their simultaneous deaths if they resided in the same county.

(c) A proceeding for the appointment of a guardian who was appointed by will may be brought in the county in which the will was admitted to probate or in the county of the appointee's residence if the appointee resides in this state.

Derived from Probate Code § 610.

Redesignated from Probate Code § 610 by Acts 2013, 83rd Leg., ch. 161, § 6.015(c), eff. Jan. 1, 2014.

§ 1023.002. Concurrent Venue and Transfer for Want of Venue

(a) If two or more courts have concurrent venue of a guardianship proceeding, the court in which an application for a guardianship proceeding is initially filed has and retains jurisdiction of the proceeding. A proceeding is considered commenced by the filing of an application alleging facts sufficient to confer venue, and the proceeding initially legally commenced extends to all of the property of the guardianship estate.

(b) If a guardianship proceeding is commenced in more than one county, it shall be stayed except in the county in which it was initially commenced until final determination of proper venue is made by the court in the county in which it was initially commenced.

(c) If it appears to the court at any time before the guardianship is closed that the proceeding was commenced in a court that did not have venue over the proceeding, the court shall, on the application of any interested person, transfer the proceeding to the proper county.

(d) When a proceeding is transferred to another county under a provision of this chapter, all orders entered in connection with the proceeding shall be valid and shall be recognized in the court to which the guardianship was ordered transferred, if the orders were made and entered in conformance with the procedures prescribed by this code.

Derived from Probate Code §§ 611(b)-(d).

Added by and redesignated from Probate Code § 611(b)-(d) by Acts 2013, 83rd Leg., ch. 161, § 6.015(a), (d), eff. Jan. 1, 2014.

§ 1023.003. Application for Transfer of Guardianship to Another County

When a guardian or any other person desires to transfer the transaction of the business of the guardianship from one county to another, the person shall file a written application in the court in which the guardianship is pending stating the reason for the transfer.

Derived from Probate Code § 612.

Added by Acts 2013, 83rd Leg., ch. 161, § 6.015, eff. Jan. 1, 2014.

§ 1023.004. Notice

(a) On filing an application to transfer a guardianship to another county, the sureties on the bond of the guardian shall be cited by personal service to appear and show cause why the application should not be granted.

(b) If an application is filed by a person other than the guardian, the guardian shall be cited by personal service to appear and show cause why the application should not be granted.

Derived from Probate Code § 613.

Added by and redesignated from Probate Code § 613(b) by Acts 2013, 83rd Leg., ch. 161, § 6.015(a), (e), eff. Jan. 1, 2014.

§ 1023.005. Court Action

[(a)] On hearing an application under Section 1023.003, if good cause is not shown to deny the application and it appears that transfer of the guardianship is in the best interests of the ward, the court shall enter an order:

(1) authorizing the transfer on payment on behalf of the estate of all accrued costs; and

(2) requiring that any existing bond of the guardian must remain in effect until a new bond has been given or a rider has been filed in accordance with Section 1023.010.

(b) In an order entered under Subsection (a), the court shall require the guardian, not later than the 20th day after the date the order is entered, to:

(1) give a new bond payable to the judge of the court to which the guardianship is transferred; or

(2) file a rider to an existing bond noting the court to which the guardianship is transferred.

Derived from Probate Code § 614.

Added by Acts 2013, 83rd Leg., ch. 161, § 6.015, eff. Jan. 1, 2014. Acts 2015, 84th Leg., ch. 1031, § 1, eff. Sept. 1, 2015.

§ 1023.006. Transfer of Record

When an order of transfer is made under Section 1023.005, the clerk shall record any unrecorded papers of the guardianship required to be recorded. On payment of the clerk's fee, the clerk shall transmit to the county clerk of the county to which the guardianship was ordered transferred:

(1) the case file of the guardianship proceedings; and

(2) a certified copy of the index of the guardianship records.

Derived from Probate Code § 615.

Added by Acts 2013, 83rd Leg., ch. 161, § 6.015, eff. Jan. 1, 2014.

§ 1023.007. Transfer Effective

The order transferring a guardianship does not take effect until:

(1) the case file and a certified copy of the index required by Section 1023.006 are filed in the office of the county clerk of the county to which the guardianship was ordered transferred; and

(2) a certificate under the clerk's official seal and reporting the filing of the case file and a certified copy of the index is filed in the court ordering the transfer by the county clerk of the county to which the guardianship was ordered transferred.

Derived from Probate Code § 616.

Added by Acts 2013, 83rd Leg., ch. 161, § 6.015, eff. Jan. 1, 2014.

§ 1023.008. Continuation of Guardianship

When a guardianship is transferred from one county to another in accordance with this chapter, the guardianship proceeds in the court to which it was transferred as if it had been originally commenced in that court. It is not necessary to record in the receiving court any of the papers in the case that were recorded in the court from which the case was transferred.

Derived from Probate Code § 617.

Added by Acts 2013, 83rd Leg., ch. 161, § 6.015, eff. Jan. 1, 2014.

§ 1023.009. New Guardian Appointed on Transfer

If it appears to the court that transfer of the guardianship is in the best interests of the ward, but that because of the transfer it is not in the best interests of the ward for the guardian of the estate to continue to serve in that capacity, the court may in its order of transfer revoke the letters of guardianship and appoint a new guardian, and the former guardian shall account for and deliver the estate as provided by this title in a case in which a guardian resigns.

Derived from Probate Code § 618.

Added by Acts 2013, 83rd Leg., ch. 161, § 6.015, eff. Jan. 1, 2014.

§ 1023.010. Review of Transferred Guardianship

(a) Not later than the 90th day after the date the transfer of the guardianship takes effect under Section 1023.007, the court to which the guardianship was transferred shall hold a hearing to consider modifying the rights, duties, and powers of the guardian or any other provisions of the transferred guardianship.

(b) After the hearing described by Subsection (a), the court to which the guardianship was transferred shall enter an order requiring the guardian to:

(1) give a new bond payable to the judge of the court to which the guardianship was transferred; or

(2) file a rider to an existing bond noting the court to which the guardianship was transferred.

Derived from Probate Code § 619.

Added by Acts 2013, 83rd Leg., ch. 161, § 6.015, eff. Jan. 1, 2014. Acts 2015, 84th Leg., ch. 1031, § 2, eff. Sept. 1, 2015.

SUBTITLE C. PROCEDURAL MATTERS

Chapter 1051. Notices and Process in Guardianship Proceedings in General

Subchapter A. Issuance and Form of Notice or Process

Subchapter B. Methods of Serving Citation or Notice; Persons to be Served

Subchapter C. Notice and Citation Required for Application for Guardianship

Subchapter D. Return and Proof of Service of Citation or Notice

Subchapter E. Alternative Manner of Issuance, Service, and Return

§ 1051.201. Court-Ordered Issuance, Service, and Return Under Certain Circumstances

Subchapter F. Additional Notice Provisions

§ 1051.251. Waiver of Notice of Hearing

§ 1051.252. Request for Notice of Filing of Pleading

§ 1051.253. Service of Notice of Intention to Take Depositions in Certain Proceedings

Chapter 1051. Notices and Process in Guardianship Proceedings in General

Subchapter A. Issuance and Form of Notice or Process

§ 1051.001. Issuance of Notice or Process in General

(a) Except as provided by Subsection (b), a person is not required to be cited or otherwise given notice in a guardianship proceeding except in a situation in which this title expressly provides for citation or the giving of notice.

(b) If this title does not expressly provide for citation or the issuance or return of notice in a guardianship proceeding, the court may require that notice be given. A court that requires that notice be given shall prescribe the form and manner of service of the notice and the return of service.

(c) Unless a court order is required by this title, the county clerk without a court order shall issue:

(1) necessary citations, writs, and other process in a guardianship proceeding; and

(2) all notices not required to be issued by a guardian.

Derived from Probate Code §§ 632(a), (b).

Added by Acts 2011, 82nd Leg., ch. 823, § 1.02, eff. Jan. 1, 2014. Amended by Acts 2013, 83rd Leg., ch. 161, § 6.016, eff. Jan. 1, 2014.

§ 1051.002. Direction of Writ or Other Process

(a) A writ or other process other than a citation or notice must be directed "To any sheriff or constable within the State of Texas."

(b) Notwithstanding Subsection (a), a writ or other process other than a citation or notice may not be held defective because the process is directed to the sheriff or a constable of a named county if the process is properly served within that county by an officer authorized to serve the process.

Derived from Probate Code § 632(c).

Added by Acts 2011, 82nd Leg., ch. 823, § 1.02, eff. Jan. 1, 2014.

§ 1051.003. Contents of Citation or Notice

(a) A citation or notice must:

(1) be directed to the person to be cited or notified;

(2) be dated;

(3) state the style and number of the proceeding;

(4) state the court in which the proceeding is pending;

(5) describe generally the nature of the proceeding or matter to which the citation or notice relates;

(6) direct the person being cited or notified to appear by filing a written contest or answer or to perform another required action; and

(7) state when and where the appearance or performance described by Subdivision (6) is required.

(b) A citation or notice issued by the county clerk must be styled "The State of Texas" and be signed by the clerk under the clerk's seal.

(c) A notice required to be given by a guardian must be in writing and be signed by the guardian in the guardian's official capacity.

(d) A citation or notice is not required to contain a precept directed to an officer, but may not be held defective because the citation or notice contains a precept directed to an officer authorized to serve the citation or notice.

Derived from Probate Code § 632(c).

Added by Acts 2011, 82nd Leg., ch. 823, § 1.02, eff. Jan. 1, 2014.

Subchapter B. Methods of Serving Citation or Notice; Persons to be Served

§ 1051.051. Personal Service

(a) Except as otherwise provided by Subsection (b), if personal service of citation or notice is required, the citation or notice must be served on the attorney of record for the person to be cited or notified. Notwithstanding the requirement of personal service, service may be made on that attorney by any method specified by Section 1051.055 for service on an attorney of record.

(b) If the person to be cited or notified does not have an attorney of record in the proceeding, or if an attempt to serve the person's attorney is unsuccessful:

(1) the sheriff or constable shall serve the citation or notice by delivering a copy of the citation or notice to the person to be cited or notified, in person, if the person to whom the citation or notice is directed is in this state; or

(2) a disinterested person competent to make an oath that the citation or notice was served may serve the citation or notice, if the person to be cited or notified is absent from or is not a resident of this state.

(c) The return day of the citation or notice served under Subsection (b) must be at least 10 days after the date of service, excluding the date of service.

(d) If the citation or notice attempted to be served as provided by Subsection (b) is returned with the notation that the person sought to be served, whether inside or outside this state, cannot be found, the county clerk shall issue a new citation or notice. Service of the new citation or notice must be made by publication.

Derived from Probate Code § 632(f)(1).

Added by Acts 2011, 82nd Leg., ch. 823, § 1.02, eff. Jan. 1, 2014.

§ 1051.052. Service by Mail

(a) The county clerk, or the guardian if required by statute or court order, shall serve a citation or notice required or permitted to be served by regular mail by mailing the original citation or notice to the person to be cited or notified.

(b) Except as provided by Subsection (c), the county clerk shall issue a citation or notice required or permitted to be served by registered or certified mail and shall serve the citation or notice by mailing the original citation or notice by registered or certified mail.

(c) A guardian shall issue a notice required to be given by the guardian by registered or certified mail and shall serve the notice by mailing the original notice by registered or certified mail.

(d) The county clerk or guardian, as applicable, shall mail a citation or notice under Subsection (b) or (c) with an instruction to deliver the citation or notice to the addressee only and with return receipt requested. The clerk or guardian, as applicable, shall address the envelope containing the citation or notice to:

(1) the attorney of record in the proceeding for the person to be cited or notified; or

(2) the person to be cited or notified, if the citation or notice to the attorney is returned undelivered or the person to be cited or notified has no attorney of record in the proceeding.

(e) Service by mail must be made at least 20 days before the return day of the citation or notice, excluding the date of service. The date of service by mail is the date of mailing.

(f) A copy of a citation or notice served under Subsection (a), (b), or (c) and a certificate of the person serving the citation or notice showing that the citation or notice was mailed and the date of the mailing shall be filed and recorded. A returned receipt for a citation or notice served under Subsection (b) or (c) shall be attached to the certificate.

(g) If a citation or notice served by mail is returned undelivered, a new citation or notice shall be issued. Service of the new citation or notice must be made by posting.

Derived from Probate Code § 632(f)(4).

Added by Acts 2011, 82nd Leg., ch. 823, § 1.02, eff. Jan. 1, 2014.

§ 1051.053. Service by Posting

(a) The county clerk shall deliver the original and a copy of a citation or notice required to be posted to the sheriff or a constable of the county in which the proceeding is pending. The sheriff or constable shall post the copy at the door of the county courthouse or the location in or near the courthouse where public notices are customarily posted.

(b) Citation or notice under this section must be posted for at least 10 days before the return day of the citation or notice, excluding the date of posting, except as provided by Section 1051.152(b). The date of service of citation or notice by posting is the date of posting.

(c) A sheriff or constable who posts a copy of a citation or notice under this section shall return the original citation or notice to the county clerk and state the date and location of the posting in a written return of the copy of the citation or notice.

(d) The method of service prescribed by this section applies when a guardian is required or permitted to post a notice. The notice must be:

(1) issued in the name of the guardian;

(2) addressed and delivered to, and posted and returned by, the appropriate officer; and

(3) filed with the county clerk.

Derived from Probate Code § 632(f)(2).

Added by Acts 2011, 82nd Leg., ch. 823, § 1.02, eff. Jan. 1, 2014.

§ 1051.054. Service by Publication

(a) Citation or notice to a person to be served by publication shall be published one time in a newspaper of general circulation in the county in which the proceeding is pending. The publication must be made at least 10 days before the return day of the citation or notice, excluding the date of publication.

(b) The date of service of citation or notice by publication is the date of publication printed on the newspaper in which the citation or notice is published.

(c) If there is not a newspaper of general circulation published or printed in the county in which the citation or notice is to be published, the citation or notice under Subsection (a) shall be served by posting.

Derived from Probate Code § 632(f)(3).

Added by Acts 2011, 82nd Leg., ch. 823, § 1.02, eff. Jan. 1, 2014.

§ 1051.055. Service on Party's Attorney of Record

(a) If a party is represented by an attorney of record in a guardianship proceeding, a citation or notice required to be served on the party shall be served instead on that attorney.

(b) A notice served on an attorney under this section may be served by:

(1) delivery to the attorney in person;

(2) registered or certified mail, return receipt requested; or

(3) any other form of mail that requires proof of delivery.

(c) A notice or citation may be served on an attorney under this section by:

(1) another party to the proceeding;

(2) the attorney of record for another party to the proceeding;

(3) an appropriate sheriff or constable; or

(4) another person competent to testify.

(d) Each of the following is prima facie evidence of the fact that service has been made under this section:

(1) the written statement of an attorney of record showing service;

(2) the return of the officer showing service; and

(3) the affidavit of a person showing service.

(e) Except as provided by Section 1051.105, an attorney ad litem may not waive personal service of citation.

Derived from Probate Code § 634.

Added by Acts 2011, 82nd Leg., ch. 823, § 1.02, eff. Jan. 1, 2014.

§ 1051.056. Service on Guardian or Receiver

Unless this title expressly provides for another method of service, the county clerk who issues a citation or notice required to be served on a guardian or receiver shall serve the citation or notice by mailing the original citation or notice by registered or certified mail to:

(1) the guardian's or receiver's attorney of record; or

(2) the guardian or receiver, if the guardian or receiver does not have an attorney of record.

Derived from Probate Code § 632(e).

Added by Acts 2011, 82nd Leg., ch. 823, § 1.02, eff. Jan. 1, 2014.

Subchapter C. Notice and Citation Required for Application for Guardianship

§ 1051.101. Notice Required for Application for Guardianship; Citation of Applicant not Required

(a) On the filing of an application for guardianship, notice shall be issued and served as provided by this subchapter.

(b) It is not necessary to serve a citation on a person who files an application for the creation of a guardianship under this title or for that person to waive the issuance and personal service of citation under this subchapter.

Derived from Probate Code §§ 633(a), (g).

Added by Acts 2011, 82nd Leg., ch. 823, § 1.02, eff. Jan. 1, 2014.

§ 1051.102. Issuance of Citation for Application for Guardianship

(a) On the filing of an application for guardianship, the court clerk shall issue a citation stating:

(1) that the application was filed;

(2) the name of the proposed ward;

(3) the name of the applicant; and

(4) the name of the person to be appointed guardian as provided in the application, if that person is not the applicant.

(b) The citation must cite all persons interested in the welfare of the proposed ward to appear at the time and place stated in the notice if the persons wish to contest the application.

(c) The citation shall be posted.

(d) The citation must contain a clear and conspicuous statement informing those interested persons of the right provided under Section 1051.252 to be notified of any or all motions, applications, or pleadings relating to the application for the guardianship or any subsequent guardianship proceeding involving the ward after the guardianship is created, if any.

Derived from Probate Code § 633(b).

Added by Acts 2011, 82nd Leg., ch. 823, § 1.02, eff. Jan. 1, 2014. Subsec. (d) added by Acts 2013, 83rd Leg., ch. 161, § 6.017, eff. Jan. 1, 2014.

§ 1051.103. Service of Citation for Application for Guardianship

(a) The sheriff or other officer shall personally serve citation to appear and answer an application for guardianship on:

(1) a proposed ward who is 12 years of age or older;

(2) the proposed ward's parents, if the whereabouts of the parents are known or can be reasonably ascertained;

(3) any court-appointed conservator or person having control of the care and welfare of the proposed ward;

(4) the proposed ward's spouse, if the whereabouts of the spouse are known or can be reasonably ascertained; and

(5) the person named in the application to be appointed guardian, if that person is not the applicant.

(b) A citation served as provided by Subsection (a) must contain the statement regarding the right under Section 1051.252 that is required in the citation issued under Section 1051.102.

Derived from Probate Code § 633(c).

Added by Acts 2011, 82nd Leg., ch. 823, § 1.02, eff. Jan. 1, 2014. Amended by Acts 2013, 83rd Leg., ch. 161, § 6.018, eff. Jan. 1, 2014.

§ 1051.104. Notice by Applicant for Guardianship

(a) The person filing an application for guardianship shall mail a copy of the application and a notice containing the information required in the citation issued under Section 1051.102 by registered or certified mail, return receipt requested, or by any other form of mail that provides proof of delivery, to the following persons, if their whereabouts are known or can be reasonably ascertained:

(1) each adult child of the proposed ward;

(2) each adult sibling of the proposed ward;

(3) the administrator of a nursing home facility or similar facility in which the proposed ward resides;

(4) the operator of a residential facility in which the proposed ward resides;

(5) a person whom the applicant knows to hold a power of attorney signed by the proposed ward;

(6) a person designated to serve as guardian of the proposed ward by a written declaration under Subchapter E, Chapter 1104, if the applicant knows of the existence of the declaration;

(7) a person designated to serve as guardian of the proposed ward in the probated will of the last surviving parent of the proposed ward;

(8) a person designated to serve as guardian of the proposed ward by a written declaration of the proposed ward's last surviving parent, if the declarant is deceased and the applicant knows of the existence of the declaration; and

(9) each adult [person] named [as another relative within the third degree by consanguinity] in the application as an "other living relative" of the proposed ward within the third degree by consanguinity, as required by Section 1101.001(b)(11) or (13), if the proposed ward's spouse and each of the proposed ward's parents, adult siblings, and adult children are deceased or there is no spouse, parent, adult sibling, or adult child.

(b) The applicant shall file with the court:

(1) a copy of any notice required by Subsection (a) and the proofs of delivery of the notice; and

(2) an affidavit sworn to by the applicant or the applicant's attorney stating:

(A) that the notice was mailed as required by Subsection (A); and

(B) the name of each person to whom the notice was mailed, if the person's name is not shown on the proof of delivery.

(c) Failure of the applicant to comply with Subsections (a)(2)-(9) does not affect the validity of a guardianship created under this title.

Derived from Probate Code §§ 633(d), (d-1), (f).

Added by Acts 2011, 82nd Leg., ch. 823, § 1.02, eff. Jan. 1, 2014. Subsec. (a) amended by Acts 2013, 83rd Leg., ch. 161, § 6.019, eff. Jan. 1, 2014. Subsec. (a)(9) amended by Acts 2015, 84th Leg., ch. 1031, § 3, eff. Sept. 1, 2015.

§ 1051.105. Waiver of Notice of Application for Guardianship

A person other than the proposed ward who is entitled to receive notice or personal service of citation under Sections 1051.103 and 1051.104(a) may, by writing filed with the clerk, waive the receipt of notice or the issuance and personal service of citation either in person or through an attorney ad litem.

Derived from Probate Code § 633(e).

Added by Acts 2011, 82nd Leg., ch. 823, § 1.02, eff. Jan. 1, 2014.

§ 1051.106. Action by Court on Application for Guardianship

The court may not act on an application for the creation of a guardianship until the applicant has complied with Section 1051.104(b) and not earlier than the Monday following the expiration of the 10-day period beginning on the date service of notice and citation has been made as provided by Sections 1051.102, 1051.103, and 1051.104(a)(1).

Derived from Probate Code § 633(f).

Added by Acts 2011, 82nd Leg., ch. 823, § 1.02, eff. Jan. 1, 2014.

Subchapter D. Return and Proof of Service of Citation or Notice

§ 1051.151. Requirements for Return on Citation or Notice Served by Personal Service

The return of the person serving a citation or notice under Section 1051.051 must:

(1) be endorsed on or attached to the citation or notice;

(2) state the date and place of service;

(3) certify that a copy of the citation or notice was delivered to the person directed to be served;

(4) be subscribed and sworn to before, and under the hand and official seal of, an officer authorized by the laws of this state to take an affidavit; and

(5) be returned to the county clerk who issued the citation or notice.

Derived from Probate Code § 632(f)(1).

Added by Acts 2011, 82nd Leg., ch. 823, § 1.02, eff. Jan. 1, 2014.

§ 1051.152. Validity of Service and Return on Citation or Notice Served by Posting

(a) A citation or notice in a guardianship proceeding that is required to be served by posting and is issued in conformity with this title, and the service of and return of the citation or notice, is valid if:

(1) a sheriff or constable posts a copy of the citation or notice at the location or locations prescribed by this title; and

(2) the posting occurs on a day preceding the return day of service specified in the citation or notice that provides sufficient time for the period the citation or notice must be posted to expire before the specified return day.

(b) The fact that the sheriff or constable, as applicable, makes the return of service on the citation or notice described by Subsection (a) and returns the citation or notice on which the return has been made to the court before the expiration of the period the citation or notice must be posted does not affect the validity of the citation or notice or the service or return of service. This subsection applies even if the sheriff or constable makes the return of service and returns the citation or notice to the court on the same day the citation or notice is issued.

Derived from Probate Code § 632(h).

Added by Acts 2011, 82nd Leg., ch. 823, § 1.02, eff. Jan. 1, 2014. Subsec. (a) amended by Acts 2013, 83rd Leg., ch. 161, § 6.020, eff. Jan. 1, 2014.

§ 1051.153. Proof of Service

(a) Proof of service in each case requiring citation or notice must be filed before a hearing.

(b) Proof of service consists of:

(1) if the service is made by a sheriff or constable, the return of service;

(2) if the service is made by a private person, the person's affidavit;

(3) if the service is made by mail:

(A) the certificate of the county clerk making the service, or the affidavit of the guardian or other person making the service that states that the citation or notice was mailed and the date of the mailing; and

(B) the return receipt attached to the certificate, if the mailing was by registered or certified mail and a receipt has been returned; and

(4) if the service is made by publication, an affidavit that:

(A) is made by the publisher of the newspaper in which the citation or notice was published or an employee of the publisher;

(B) contains or to which is attached a copy of the published citation or notice; and

(C) states the date of publication printed on the newspaper in which the citation or notice was published.

Derived from Probate Code § 632(i).

Added by Acts 2011, 82nd Leg., ch. 823, § 1.02, eff. Jan. 1, 2014.

§ 1051.154. Return to Court

A citation or notice issued by a county clerk must be returned to the court from which the citation or notice was issued on the first Monday after the service is perfected.

Derived from Probate Code § 632(g).

Added by Acts 2011, 82nd Leg., ch. 823, § 1.02, eff. Jan. 1, 2014.

Subchapter E. Alternative Manner of Issuance, Service, and Return

§ 1051.201. Court-Ordered Issuance, Service, and Return Under Certain Circumstances

(a) A citation or notice required by this title shall be issued, served, and returned in the manner specified by written order of the court in accordance with this title and the Texas Rules of Civil Procedure if:

(1) an interested person requests that action;

(2) a specific method is not provided by this title for giving the citation or notice;

(3) a specific method is not provided by this title for the service and return of citation or notice; or

(4) a provision with respect to a matter relating to citation or notice is inadequate.

(b) Citation or notice issued, served, and returned in the manner specified by a court order as provided by Subsection (a) has the same effect as if the manner of service and return had been specified by this title.

Derived from Probate Code § 632(d).

Added by Acts 2011, 82nd Leg., ch. 823, § 1.02, eff. Jan. 1, 2014.

Subchapter F. Additional Notice Provisions

§ 1051.251. Waiver of Notice of Hearing

(a) A competent person who is interested in a hearing in a guardianship proceeding may waive notice of the hearing in writing either in person or through an attorney.

(b) A consul or other representative of a foreign government whose appearance has been entered as provided by law on behalf of a person residing in a foreign country may waive notice on the person's behalf.

(c) A person who submits to the jurisdiction of the court in a hearing is considered to have waived notice of the hearing.

Derived from Probate Code § 635.

Added by Acts 2011, 82nd Leg., ch. 823, § 1.02, eff. Jan. 1, 2014.

§ 1051.252. Request for Notice of Filing of Pleading

(a) At any time after an application is filed to commence a guardianship proceeding, a person interested in the estate or welfare of a ward or incapacitated person may file with the county clerk a written request to be notified of all, or any specified, motions, applications, or pleadings filed with respect to the proceeding by any person or by a person specifically designated in the request. A person filing a request under this section is responsible for payment of the fees and other costs of providing the requested documents, and the clerk may require a deposit to cover the estimated costs of providing the notice. The clerk shall send to the requestor by regular mail a copy of any requested document.

(b) A county clerk's failure to comply with a request under this section does not invalidate a proceeding.

Derived from Probate Code § 632(j).

Added by Acts 2011, 82nd Leg., ch. 823, § 1.02, eff. Jan. 1, 2014.

§ 1051.253. Service of Notice of Intention to Take Depositions in Certain Proceedings

(a) In a guardianship proceeding in which there is no opposing party or attorney of record on whom to serve notice and copies of interrogatories, service may be made by posting notice of the intention to take depositions for a period of 10 days as provided by Section 1051.053 governing a posting of notice.

(b) When notice by posting under Subsection (a) is filed with the clerk, a copy of the interrogatories must also be filed.

(c) At the expiration of the 10-day period prescribed by Subsection (a):

(1) the depositions for which the notice was posted may be taken; and

(2) the judge may file cross-interrogatories if no person appears.

Derived from Probate Code § 649.

Added by Acts 2011, 82nd Leg., ch. 823, § 1.02, eff. Jan. 1, 2014. Amended by Acts 2013, 83rd Leg., ch. 161, § 6.021, eff. Jan. 1, 2014 and subsec. (c) amended by Acts 2013, 83rd Leg., ch. 982, § 3, eff. Jan. 1, 2014.

Chapter 1052. Filing and Recordkeeping

Subchapter A. Recordkeeping Requirements

Subchapter B. Files; Index

Chapter 1052. Filing and Recordkeeping

Subchapter A. Recordkeeping Requirements

§ 1052.001. Guardianship Docket

(a) The county clerk shall maintain a record book titled "Judge's Guardianship Docket" and shall record in the book:

(1) the name of each person with respect to whom, or with respect to whose estate, a proceeding is commenced or sought to be commenced;

(2) the name of the guardian of the estate or person or of the applicant for letters of guardianship;

(3) the date each original application for a guardianship proceeding is filed;

(4) a notation of each order, judgment, decree, and proceeding that occurs in each guardianship [estate], including the date it occurs; and

(5) the docket number of each guardianship as assigned under Subsection (b).

(b) The county clerk shall assign a docket number to each guardianship in the order a proceeding is commenced.

Derived from Probate Code § 623(a).

Added by Acts 2011, 82nd Leg., ch. 823, § 1.02, eff. Jan. 1, 2014. Subsec. (a)(4) amended by Acts 2015, 84th Leg., ch. 1031, § 4, eff. Sept. 1, 2015.

§ 1052.002. Claim Docket

(a) The county clerk shall maintain a record book titled "Claim Docket" and shall record in the book each claim that is presented against a guardianship for the court's approval.

(b) The county clerk shall assign one or more pages of the record book to each guardianship.

(c) The claim docket must be ruled in 16 columns at proper intervals from top to bottom, with a short note of the contents at the top of each column. The county clerk shall record for each claim, in the order the claims are filed, the following information in the respective columns, beginning with the first or marginal column:

(1) the name of the claimant;

(2) the amount of the claim;

(3) the date of the claim;

(4) the date the claim is filed;

(5) the date the claim is due;

(6) the date the claim begins bearing interest;

(7) the interest rate;

(8) the date the claim is allowed by the guardian, if applicable;

(9) the amount allowed by the guardian, if applicable;

(10) the date the claim is rejected, if applicable;

(11) the date the claim is approved, if applicable;

(12) the amount approved for the claim, if applicable;

(13) the date the claim is disapproved, if applicable;

(14) the class to which the claim belongs;

(15) the date the claim is established by a judgment of a court, if applicable; and

(16) the amount of the judgment established under Subdivision (15), if applicable.

Derived from Probate Code § 624.

Added by Acts 2011, 82nd Leg., ch. 823, § 1.02, eff. Jan. 1, 2014.

§ 1052.003. Guardianship Fee Book

(a) The county clerk shall maintain a record book titled "Guardianship Fee Book" and shall record in the book each item of cost that accrues to the officers of the court and any witness fees.

(b) Each record entry must include:

(1) the party to whom the cost or fee is due;

(2) the date the cost or fee accrued;

(3) the guardianship or party liable for the cost or fee; and

(4) the date the cost or fee is paid.

Derived from Probate Code § 626.

Added by Acts 2011, 82nd Leg., ch. 823, § 1.02, eff. Jan. 1, 2014.

§ 1052.004. Alternate Recordkeeping

Instead of maintaining the record books described by Sections 1052.001, 1052.002, and 1052.003, the county clerk may maintain the information described by those sections relating to a person's guardianship proceeding:

(1) on a computer file;

(2) on microfilm;

(3) in the form of a digitized optical image; or

(4) in another similar form of data compilation.

Derived from Probate Code § 627.

Added by Acts 2011, 82nd Leg., ch. 823, § 1.02, eff. Jan. 1, 2014.

Subchapter B. Files; Index

§ 1052.051. Filing Procedures

(a) An application for a guardianship proceeding or a complaint, petition, or other paper permitted or required by law to be filed with a court in a guardianship proceeding must be filed with the county clerk of the appropriate county.

(b) Each paper filed in a guardianship proceeding must be given the docket number assigned to the estate.

(c) On receipt of a paper described by Subsection (a), the county clerk shall:

(1) file the paper; and

(2) endorse on the paper:

(A) the date the paper is filed;

(B) the docket number; and

(C) the clerk's official signature.

(d) Except as provided by Subsection (e), the court clerk shall collect a filing fee, including a deposit for payment to an attorney ad litem, required by law to be paid on the filing of any document described by Subsection (a) from the person or entity filing the document.

(e) Notwithstanding any other law requiring the payment of a filing fee for the document, the following are not required to pay a fee on the filing of a document described by Subsection (a):

(1) a guardian;

(2) an attorney ad litem;

(3) a guardian ad litem;

(4) a person or entity who files an affidavit of inability to pay under Rule 145, Texas Rules of Civil Procedure;

(5) a guardianship program;

(6) a governmental entity; and

(7) a government agency or nonprofit agency providing guardianship services.

(f) After the creation of a guardianship, a person or entity is entitled to be reimbursed for a filing fee described by Subsection (d), other than a deposit for payment to an attorney ad litem, from:

(1) the guardianship estate; or

(2) the county treasury, if the guardianship estate is insufficient to pay the amount of the filing fee.

Derived from Probate Code §§ 621, 623(b).

Added by Acts 2011, 82nd Leg., ch. 823, § 1.02, eff. Jan. 1, 2014. Subsec. (a) amended by Acts 2013, 83rd Leg., ch. 161, § 6.022, eff. Jan. 1, 2014 and subsecs. (d), (e), & (f) added by Acts 2013, 83rd Leg., ch. 982, § 4, eff. Jan. 1, 2014. Subsecs. (d), (e), & (f) repealed by Acts 2015, 84th Leg., ch. 1031, § 37(1), eff. Sept. 1, 2015.

§ 1052.052. Case Files

(a) The county clerk shall maintain a case file for each person's filed guardianship proceedings.

(b) Each case file must contain each order, judgment, and proceeding of the court and any other guardianship filing with the court, including each:

(1) application for the granting of guardianship;

(2) citation and notice, whether published or posted, including the return on the citation or notice;

(3) bond and official oath;

(4) inventory, appraisement, and list of claims;

(5) exhibit and account;

(6) report of renting;

(7) application for sale or partition of real estate;

(8) report of sale;

(9) application for authority to execute a lease for mineral development, or for pooling or unitization of lands, royalty, or other interest in minerals, or to lend or invest money;

(10) report of lending or investing money; and

(11) report of guardians of the persons.

Derived from Probate Code § 625.

Added by Acts 2011, 82nd Leg., ch. 823, § 1.02, eff. Jan. 1, 2014.

§ 1052.053. Index

(a) The county clerk shall properly index the records required under this chapter.

(b) The county clerk shall keep the index open for public inspection but may not release the index from the clerk's custody.

Derived from Probate Code § 627A.

Added by Acts 2011, 82nd Leg., ch. 823, § 1.02, eff. Jan. 1, 2014.

Chapter 1053. Other Court Duties and Procedures

Subchapter A. Enforcement of Orders

§ 1053.001. Enforcement of Orders

Subchapter B. Costs and Security

§ 1053.051. Applicability of Certain Laws

§ 1053.052. Security for Certain Costs

Subchapter C. Procedures for Guardianship Proceedings

§ 1053.101. Calling of Dockets

§ 1053.102. Setting of Certain Hearings by Clerk

§ 1053.103. Rendering of Decisions, Orders, Decrees, and Judgments

§ 1053.104. Confidentiality of Certain Information

§ 1053.105. Inapplicability of Certain Rules of Civil Procedure

Chapter 1053. Other Court Duties and Procedures

Subchapter A. Enforcement of Orders

§ 1053.001. Enforcement of Orders

A judge may enforce an order entered against a guardian by attachment and confinement. Unless this title expressly provides otherwise, the term of confinement for any one offense under this section may not exceed three days.

Derived from Probate Code § 651.

Added by Acts 2011, 82nd Leg., ch. 823, § 1.02, eff. Jan. 1, 2014.

Subchapter B. Costs and Security

§ 1053.051. Applicability of Certain Laws

A law regulating costs in ordinary civil cases applies to a guardianship proceeding unless otherwise expressly provided by this title.

Derived from Probate Code § 622(a).

Added by Acts 2011, 82nd Leg., ch. 823, § 1.02, eff.

Jan. 1, 2014. Amended by Acts 2013, 83rd Leg., ch. 161, § 6.023, eff. Jan. 1, 2014.

§ 1053.052. Security for Certain Costs

(a) The clerk may require or may obtain from the court an order requiring a person who files an application, complaint, or opposition relating to a guardianship proceeding, other than a guardian, attorney ad litem, or guardian ad litem, to provide security for the probable costs of the proceeding before filing the application, complaint, or opposition.

(b) At any time before the trial of an application, complaint, or opposition described by Subsection (a), an officer of the court or a person interested in the guardianship or in the welfare of the ward may, by written motion, obtain from the court an order requiring the person who filed the application, complaint, or opposition to provide security for the probable costs of the proceeding. The rules governing civil suits in the county court with respect to providing security for the probable costs of a proceeding control in cases described by Subsection (a) and this subsection.

(c) A guardian, attorney ad litem, or guardian ad litem appointed under this title by a court of this state may not be required to provide security for costs in an action brought by the guardian, attorney ad litem, or guardian ad litem in the guardian's, attorney ad litem's, or guardian ad litem's fiduciary capacity.

Derived from Probate Code § 622(b), (c).

Added by Acts 2011, 82nd Leg., ch. 823, § 1.02, eff. Jan. 1, 2014. Subsec. (a) amended by Acts 2013, 83rd Leg., ch. 161 , § 6.024, eff. Jan. 1, 2014. Subsec. (a) amended by Acts 2015, 84th Leg., ch. 1031, § 5, eff. Sept. 1, 2015.

Subchapter C. Procedures for Guardianship Proceedings

§ 1053.101. Calling of Dockets

The judge in whose court a guardianship proceeding is pending, as determined by the judge, shall:

(1) call guardianship proceedings in the proceedings' regular order on both the guardianship and claim dockets; and

(2) issue necessary orders.

Derived from Probate Code § 629.

Added by Acts 2011, 82nd Leg., ch. 823, § 1.02, eff. Jan. 1, 2014. Amended by Acts 2013, 83rd Leg., ch. 161, § 6.026, eff. Jan. 1, 2014.

§ 1053.102. Setting of Certain Hearings by Clerk

(a) If a judge is unable to designate the time and place for hearing a guardianship proceeding pending in the judge's court because the judge is absent from the county seat or is on vacation, disqualified, ill, or deceased, the county clerk of the county in which the proceeding is pending may:

(1) designate the time and place for hearing;

(2) enter the setting on the judge's docket; and

(3) certify on the docket the reason that the judge is not acting to set the hearing.

(b) If, after the perfection of the service of notices and citations required by law concerning the time and place of hearing, a qualified judge is not present for a hearing set under Subsection (a), the hearing is automatically continued from day to day until a qualified judge is present to hear and make a determination in the proceeding.

Derived from Probate Code § 630.

Added by Acts 2011, 82nd Leg., ch. 823, § 1.02, eff. Jan. 1, 2014. Amended by Acts 2013, 83rd Leg., ch. 161, § 6.027, eff. Jan. 1, 2014.

§ 1053.103. Rendering of Decisions, Orders, Decrees, and Judgments

The court shall render a decision, order, decree, or judgment in a guardianship proceeding in open court, except as otherwise expressly provided.

Derived from Probate Code § 650.

Added by Acts 2011, 82nd Leg., ch. 823, § 1.02, eff. Jan. 1, 2014. Amended by Acts 2013, 83rd Leg., ch. 161, § 6.028, eff. Jan. 1, 2014.

§ 1053.104. Confidentiality of Certain Information

(a) On request by a person protected by a protective order issued under Chapter 85, Family Code, or a guardian, attorney ad litem, or member of the family or household of a person protected by an order, the court may exclude from any document filed in a guardianship proceeding:

(1) the address and phone number of the person protected by the protective order;

(2) the place of employment or business of the person protected by the protective order;

(3) the school attended by the person protected by the protective order or the day-care center or other child-care facility the person attends or in which the person resides; and

(4) the place at which service of process on the person protected by the protective order was effectuated.

(b) On granting a request for confidentiality under this section, the court shall order the clerk to:

(1) strike the information described by Subsection (a) from the public records of the court; and

(2) maintain a confidential record of the information for use only by the court.

New.

Added by Acts 2013, 83rd Leg., ch. 982, § 5, eff. Jan. 1, 2014.

§ 1053.105. Inapplicability of Certain Rules of Civil Procedure

The following do not apply to guardianship proceedings:

(1) Rules 47(c) and 169, Texas Rules of Civil Procedure; and

(2) the portions of Rule 190.2, Texas Rules of Civil Procedure, concerning expedited actions under Rule 169, Texas Rules of Civil Procedure.

New.

Added by Acts 2013, 83rd Leg., ch. 982, § 5, eff. Jan. 1, 2014.

Chapter 1054. Court Officers and Court-Appointed Persons

Subchapter A. Attorneys Ad Litem and Interpreters

Subchapter B. Guardians Ad Litem

Subchapter C. Court Visitors

Subchapter D. Court Investigators

Subchapter E. Qualifications to Serve as Court-Appointed Attorney

Chapter 1054. Court Officers and Court-Appointed Persons

Subchapter A. Attorneys Ad Litem and Interpreters

§ 1054.001. Appointment of Attorney Ad Litem in Proceeding for Appointment of Guardian

In a proceeding under this title for the appointment of a guardian, the court shall appoint an attorney ad litem to represent the proposed ward's interests.

Derived from Probate Code § 646(a).

Added by Acts 2011, 82nd Leg., ch. 823, § 1.02, eff. Jan. 1, 2014.

§ 1054.002. Term of Appointment

(a) Unless the court determines that the continued appointment of an attorney ad litem appointed under Section 1054.001 is in the ward's best interests, the attorney's term of appointment expires, without a court order, on the date the court:

(1) appoints a guardian in accordance with Subchapter D, Chapter 1101;

(2) appoints a successor guardian; or

(3) denies the application for appointment of a guardian.

(b) The term of appointment of an attorney ad litem appointed under Section 1054.001 continues after the court appoints a temporary guardian under Chapter 1251 unless a court order provides for the termination or expiration of the attorney ad litem's appointment.

Derived from Probate Code § 646(e).

Added by Acts 2011, 82nd Leg., ch. 823, § 1.02, eff. Jan. 1, 2014. Amended by Acts 2013, 83rd Leg., ch. 161, § 6.029, eff. Jan. 1, 2014.

§ 1054.003. Access to Records

An attorney ad litem appointed under Section 1054.001 shall be provided copies of all of the current records in the guardianship case. The attorney may have access to all of the proposed ward's relevant medical, psychological, and intellectual testing records.

Derived from Probate Code § 646(a).

Added by Acts 2011, 82nd Leg., ch. 823, § 1.02, eff. Jan. 1, 2014.

§ 1054.004. Duties

(a) An attorney ad litem appointed under Section 1054.001 shall interview the proposed ward within a reasonable time before the hearing in the proceeding for the appointment of a guardian. To the greatest extent possible, the attorney shall discuss with the proposed ward:

(1) the law and facts of the case;

(2) the proposed ward's legal options regarding disposition of the case; [and]

(3) the grounds on which guardianship is sought; and

(4) whether alternatives to guardianship would meet the needs of the proposed ward and avoid the need for the appointment of a guardian.

(b) Before the hearing, the attorney ad litem shall review:

(1) the application for guardianship;

(2) certificates of current physical, medical, and intellectual examinations; and

(3) all of the proposed ward's relevant medical, psychological, and intellectual testing records.

(c) Before the hearing, the attorney ad litem shall discuss with the proposed ward the attorney ad litem's opinion regarding:

(1) whether a guardianship is necessary for the proposed ward; and

(2) if a guardianship is necessary, the specific powers or duties of the guardian that should be limited if the proposed ward receives supports and services.

Derived from Probate Code § 647.

Added by Acts 2011, 82nd Leg., ch. 823, § 1.02, eff. Jan. 1, 2014. Subsec. (a) amended and subsec. (c) added by Acts 2015, 84th Leg., ch. 214, § 4, eff. Sept. 1, 2015.

§ 1054.005. Appointment of Interpreter

At the time the court appoints the attorney ad litem under Section 1054.001, the court shall appoint a language interpreter or sign interpreter if necessary to ensure effective communication between the proposed ward and the attorney.

Derived from Probate Code § 646(d).

Added by Acts 2011, 82nd Leg., ch. 823, § 1.02, eff. Jan. 1, 2014.

§ 1054.006. Representation Of Ward Or Proposed Ward By Attorney

(a) The following persons may at any time retain an attorney who holds a certificate required by Subchapter E to represent the person's interests in a guardianship proceeding instead of having those interests represented by an attorney ad litem appointed under Section 1054.001 or another provision of this title:

(1) a ward who retains the power to enter into a contract under the terms of the guardianship, subject to Section 1202.103; and

(2) a proposed ward for purposes of a proceeding for the appointment of a guardian as long as the proposed ward has capacity to contract.

(b) If the court finds that the ward or the proposed ward has capacity to contract, the court may remove an attorney ad litem appointed under Section 1054.001 or any other provision of this title that requires the court to appoint an attorney ad litem to represent the interests of a ward or proposed ward and appoint a ward or a proposed ward's retained counsel.

New.

Added by Acts 2013, 83rd Leg., ch. 161, § 6.030, eff. Jan. 1, 2014.

§ 1054.007. Attorneys Ad Litem

(a) Except in a situation in which this title requires the appointment to represent the interests of the person, a court may appoint an attorney ad litem in any guardianship proceeding to represent the interests of:

(1) an incapacitated person or another person who has a legal disability;

(2) a proposed ward;

(3) a nonresident;

(4) an unborn or unascertained person; or

(5) an unknown or missing potential heir.

(b) An attorney ad litem appointed under this section is entitled to reasonable compensation for services provided in the amount set by the court, to be taxed as costs in the proceeding.

New.

Added by Acts 2013, 83rd Leg., ch. 982, § 6, eff. Jan. 1, 2014.

Subchapter B. Guardians Ad Litem

§ 1054.051. Appointment of Guardian Ad Litem in Guardianship Proceeding

The judge may appoint a guardian ad litem to represent the interests of an incapacitated person in a guardianship proceeding.

Derived from Probate Code § 645(a).

Added by Acts 2011, 82nd Leg., ch. 823, § 1.02, eff. Jan. 1, 2014.

§ 1054.052. Appointment of Guardian Ad Litem Relating to Certain Other Suits

In the interest of judicial economy, the court may appoint as guardian ad litem under Section 1104.354(1) the person who has been appointed attorney ad litem under Section 1054.001 or the person who is serving as an ad litem for the ward's benefit in any other proceeding.

Derived from Probate Code § 645(e).

Added by Acts 2011, 82nd Leg., ch. 823, § 1.02, eff. Jan. 1, 2014.

§ 1054.053. Term of Certain Appointments

Unless the court determines that the continued appointment of a guardian ad litem appointed in a proceeding for the appointment of a guardian is in the ward's best interests, the guardian ad litem's term of appointment expires, without a court order, on the date the court:

(1) appoints a guardian; or

(2) denies the application for appointment of a guardian.

Derived from Probate Code § 645(f).

Added by Acts 2011, 82nd Leg., ch. 823, § 1.02, eff. Jan. 1, 2014.

§ 1054.054. Duties

(a) A guardian ad litem is an officer of the court.

(b) A guardian ad litem shall protect the incapacitated person whose interests the guardian has been appointed to represent in a manner that will enable the court to determine the action that will be in that person's best interests.

(c) The guardian ad litem shall:

(1) investigate whether a guardianship is necessary for the proposed ward; and

(2) evaluate alternatives to guardianship and supports and services available to the proposed ward that would avoid the need for appointment of a guardian.

(d) The information gathered by the guardian ad litem under Subsection (c) is subject to examination by the court.

Derived from Probate Code § 645(c).

Added by Acts 2011, 82nd Leg., ch. 823, § 1.02, eff. Jan. 1, 2014. Subsecs (c) and (d) added by Acts 2015, 84th Leg., ch. 214, § 5, eff. Sept. 1, 2015.

§ 1054.055. Compensation and Expenses

(a) A guardian ad litem is entitled to reasonable compensation for services provided in the amount set by the court, to be taxed as costs in the proceeding.

(b) The fees and expenses of a guardian ad litem appointed under Section 1104.354(1) are costs of the litigation proceeding that made the appointment necessary.

Derived from Probate Code §§ 645(b), (d).

Added by Acts 2011, 82nd Leg., ch. 823, § 1.02, eff. Jan. 1, 2014.

§ 1054.056. Immunity

(a) Subject to Subsection (b), a guardian ad litem appointed under this subchapter or Section 1102.001 or 1202.054 to represent the interests of an incapacitated person in a guardianship proceeding involving the creation, modification, or termination of a guardianship is not liable for civil damages arising from a recommendation made or an opinion given in the capacity of guardian ad litem.

(b) This section does not apply to a recommendation or opinion that is:

(1) wilfully wrongful;

(2) given:

(A) with conscious indifference to or reckless disregard for the safety of another;

(B) with malice; or

(C) in bad faith; or

(3) grossly negligent.

Derived from Probate Code § 645A.

Added by Acts 2011, 82nd Leg., ch. 823, § 1.02, eff. Jan. 1, 2014.

Subchapter C. Court Visitors

§ 1054.101. Inapplicability of Subchapter to Certain Guardianships

This subchapter does not apply to a guardianship created only because the appointment of a guardian for a person is necessary for the person to receive funds from a governmental source.

Derived from Probate Code § 648(f).

Added by Acts 2011, 82nd Leg., ch. 823, § 1.02, eff. Jan. 1, 2014.

§ 1054.102. Operation of Court Visitor Program

(a) Each statutory probate court shall operate a court visitor program to assess the conditions of wards and proposed wards.

(b) A court, other than a statutory probate court, that has jurisdiction of a guardianship proceeding may operate a court visitor program in accordance with the population needs and financial abilities of the area the court serves.

Derived from Probate Code § 648(a).

Added by Acts 2011, 82nd Leg., ch. 823, § 1.02, eff. Jan. 1, 2014.

§ 1054.103. Evaluation of Ward or Proposed Ward

A court, at any time before a guardian is appointed for a proposed ward or during the pendency of a guardianship of the person or estate, may appoint a court visitor to evaluate the ward or proposed ward and provide a written report that substantially complies with Section 1054.104(b) on:

(1) the request of any interested person, including the ward or proposed ward; or

(2) the court's own motion.

Derived from Probate Code § 648(b).

Added by Acts 2011, 82nd Leg., ch. 823, § 1.02, eff. Jan. 1, 2014.

§ 1054.104. Evaluation Report

(a) A court visitor appointed under Section 1054.103 shall file the report on the evaluation of a ward or proposed ward not later than the 14th day after the date the court visitor conducts the evaluation. The court visitor shall swear under penalty of perjury that the report is accurate to the best of the court visitor's knowledge and belief.

(b) A court visitor's report must include:

(1) a description of the nature and degree of the ward's or proposed ward's capacity and incapacity, including a description of the ward's or proposed

ward's medical history, if reasonably available and not waived by the court;

(2) a medical prognosis and list of the ward's or proposed ward's treating physicians, when appropriate;

(3) a description of the ward's or proposed ward's living conditions and circumstances;

(4) a description of the ward's or proposed ward's social, intellectual, physical, and educational conditions;

(5) a statement that the court visitor has personally visited or observed the ward or proposed ward;

(6) a statement of the date of the guardian's most recent visit, if a guardian has been appointed;

(7) a recommendation as to any modification needed in the guardianship or proposed guardianship, including removal or denial of the guardianship; and

(8) any other information required by the court.

Derived from Probate Code §§ 648(c), (d).

Added by Acts 2011, 82nd Leg., ch. 823, § 1.02, eff. Jan. 1, 2014.

§ 1054.105. Compensation

(a) A court that operates a court visitor program shall use persons willing to serve as court visitors without compensation to the greatest extent possible.

(b) A court visitor who has not expressed a willingness to serve without compensation is entitled to reasonable compensation for services provided in an amount set by the court, to be taxed as costs in the proceeding.

Derived from Probate Code §§ 648(a), (e).

Added by Acts 2011, 82nd Leg., ch. 823, § 1.02, eff. Jan. 1, 2014.

Subchapter D. Court Investigators

§ 1054.151. Investigation of Guardianship Application

On the filing of an application for guardianship under Section 1101.001, a court investigator shall investigate the circumstances alleged in the application to determine whether a less restrictive alternative to guardianship is appropriate.

Derived from Probate Code § 648A(a).

Added by Acts 2011, 82nd Leg., ch. 823, § 1.02, eff. Jan. 1, 2014.

§ 1054.152. General Duties

A court investigator shall:

(1) supervise a court visitor program established under Subchapter C and, in that capacity, serve as the chief court visitor;

(2) investigate a complaint received from any person about a guardianship and report to the judge, if necessary; and

(3) perform other duties as assigned by the judge or required by this title.

Derived from Probate Code § 648A(b).

Added by Acts 2011, 82nd Leg., ch. 823, § 1.02, eff. Jan. 1, 2014.

§ 1054.153. Investigation Report

(a) A court investigator shall file with the court a report containing the court investigator's findings and conclusions after conducting an investigation under Section 1054.151 or 1054.152.

(b) In a contested case, the court investigator shall provide copies of the report of the court investigator's findings and conclusions to the attorneys for the parties before the earlier of:

(1) the seventh day after the date the court investigator completes the report; or

(2) the 10th day before the date the trial is scheduled to begin.

(c) Disclosure to a jury of the contents of a court investigator's report is subject to the Texas Rules of Evidence.

Derived from Probate Code § 648A(c).

Added by Acts 2011, 82nd Leg., ch. 823, § 1.02, eff. Jan. 1, 2014.

§ 1054.154. Effect of Subchapter on Other Law

Nothing in this subchapter supersedes any duty or obligation of another to report or investigate abuse or neglect under any statute of this state.

Derived from Probate Code § 648A(d).

Added by Acts 2011, 82nd Leg., ch. 823, § 1.02, eff. Jan. 1, 2014.

§ 1054.155. Notice Regarding Request to Financial Institution for Customer Records

If a request is made to a financial institution for a customer record in connection with an investigation conducted under Section 1054.151 or 1054.152, the court shall provide written notice of that fact to the ward or proposed ward with respect to whom the investigation is conducted not later than the fifth day after the date the financial institution produces the customer record.

New.

Add by Acts 2015, 84th Leg., ch. 1031, § 6, eff. Sept. 1, 2015.

Subchapter E. Qualifications to Serve as Court-Appointed Attorney

§ 1054.201. Certification Required

(a) An attorney for an applicant for guardianship and a [A] court-appointed attorney in a guardianship proceeding, including an attorney ad litem, must be certified by the State Bar of Texas, or a person or other entity designated by the state bar, as having successfully completed a course of study in guardianship law and procedure sponsored by the state bar or the state bar's designee.

(b) The State Bar of Texas shall require four [three] hours of credit for certification under this subchapter, including one hour on alternatives to guardianship and supports and services available to proposed wards.

Derived from Probate Code §§ 646(b), 647A(a), (b).

Added by Acts 2011, 82nd Leg., ch. 823, § 1.02, eff. Jan. 1, 2014. Acts 2015, 84th Leg., ch. 214, § , eff. Sept. 1, 2015. Amended by Acts 2015, 84th Leg., ch. 214, § 6, eff. Sept. 1, 2015.

§ 1054.202. Certificate Expiration

(a) Except as provided by Subsection (b), a certificate issued under this subchapter expires on the second anniversary of the date the certificate is issued.

(b) A new certificate obtained by a person to whom a certificate under this subchapter was previously issued expires on the fourth anniversary of the date the new certificate is issued if the person has been certified each of the four years immediately preceding the date the new certificate is issued.

Derived from Probate Code §§ 647A(c), (e).

Added by Acts 2011, 82nd Leg., ch. 823, § 1.02, eff. Jan. 1, 2014.

§ 1054.203. Eligibility for Appointment on Expiration of Certificate

An attorney whose certificate issued under this subchapter has expired must obtain a new certificate to be eligible for appointment by a court to represent a person at a guardianship proceeding, including as an attorney ad litem.

Derived from Probate Code §§ 646(c), 647A(d).

Added by Acts 2011, 82nd Leg., ch. 823, § 1.02, eff. Jan. 1, 2014.

Chapter 1055. Trial and Hearing Matters

Subchapter A. Standing and Pleadings

Subchapter B. Trial and Hearing

Subchapter C. Evidence

§ 1055.102. Use of Certain Records as Evidence

Subchapter D. Mediation

§ 1055.151. Mediation of Contested Guardianship Proceeding

Chapter 1055. Trial and Hearing Matters

Subchapter A. Standing and Pleadings

§ 1055.001. Standing to Commence or Contest Proceeding

(a) Except as provided by Subsection (b), any person has the right to:

(1) commence a guardianship proceeding, including a proceeding for complete restoration of a ward's capacity or modification of a ward's guardianship; or

(2) appear and contest a guardianship proceeding or the appointment of a particular person as guardian.

(b) A person who has an interest that is adverse to a proposed ward or incapacitated person may not:

(1) file an application to create a guardianship for the proposed ward or incapacitated person;

(2) contest the creation of a guardianship for the proposed ward or incapacitated person;

(3) contest the appointment of a person as a guardian of the proposed ward or incapacitated person; or

(4) contest an application for complete restoration of a ward's capacity or modification of a ward's guardianship.

(c) The court shall determine by motion in limine the standing of a person who has an interest that is adverse to a proposed ward or incapacitated person.

Derived from Probate Code § 642.

Added by Acts 2011, 82nd Leg., ch. 823, § 1.02, eff. Jan. 1, 2014.

§ 1055.002. Defect in Pleading

A court may not invalidate a pleading in a guardianship proceeding, or an order based on the pleading, on the basis of a defect of form or substance in the pleading unless a timely objection has been made against the defect and the defect has been called to the attention of the court in which the proceeding was or is pending.

Derived from Probate Code § 641.

Added by Acts 2011, 82nd Leg., ch. 823, § 1.02, eff. Jan. 1, 2014. Amended by Acts 2013, 83rd Leg., ch. 161, § 6.031, eff. Jan. 1, 2014.

§ 1055.003. Intervention by Interested Person

(a) Notwithstanding the Texas Rules of Civil Procedure, an interested person may intervene in a guardianship proceeding only by filing a timely motion to intervene that is served on the parties.

(b) The motion must state the grounds for intervention in the proceeding and be accompanied by a pleading that sets out the purpose for which intervention is sought.

(c) The court has the discretion to grant or deny the motion and, in exercising that discretion, must consider whether:

(1) the intervention will unduly delay or prejudice the adjudication of the original parties' rights; or

(2) the proposed intervenor has such an adverse relationship with the ward or proposed ward that the intervention would unduly prejudice the adjudication of the original parties' rights.

New.

Added by Acts 2015, 84th Leg., ch. 1031, § 7, eff. Sept. 1, 2015.

Subchapter B. Trial and Hearing

§ 1055.051. Hearing by Submission

(a) A court may consider by submission a motion or application filed under this title unless the proceeding is:

(1) contested; or

(2) an application for the appointment of a guardian.

(b) The party seeking relief under a motion or application being considered by the court on submission has the burden of proof at the hearing.

(c) The court may consider a person's failure to file a response to a motion or application that may be considered on submission as a representation that the person does not oppose the motion or application.

(d) A person's request for oral argument is not a response to a motion or application under this section.

(e) The court, on the court's own motion, may order oral argument on a motion or application that may be considered by submission.

Derived from Probate Code § 644.

Added by Acts 2011, 82nd Leg., ch. 823, § 1.02, eff. Jan. 1, 2014.

§ 1055.052. Trial by Jury

A party in a contested guardianship proceeding is entitled to a jury trial on request.

Derived from Probate Code § 643.

Added by Acts 2011, 82nd Leg., ch. 823, § 1.02, eff. Jan. 1, 2014.

§ 1055.053. Location of Hearing

(a) Except as provided by Subsection (b), the judge may hold a hearing on a guardianship proceeding involving an adult ward or adult proposed ward at any suitable location in the county in which the guardianship proceeding is pending. The hearing should be held in a physical setting that is not likely to have a harmful effect on the ward or proposed ward.

(b) On the request of the adult proposed ward, the adult ward, or the attorney of the proposed ward or ward, the hearing may not be held under the authority of this section at a place other than the courthouse.

Derived from Probate Code § 652.

Added by Acts 2013, 83rd Leg., ch. 161, § 6.032, eff. Jan. 1, 2014.

Subchapter C. Evidence

§ 1055.101. Applicability of Certain Rules Relating to Witnesses and Evidence

The rules relating to witnesses and evidence that apply in the district court apply in a guardianship proceeding to the extent practicable.

Derived from Probate Code § 649.

Added by Acts 2011, 82nd Leg., ch. 823, § 1.02, eff. Jan. 1, 2014.

§ 1055.102. Use of Certain Records as Evidence

The following are admissible as evidence in any court of this state:

(1) record books described by Sections 1052.001, 1052.002, and 1052.003 and individual case files described by Section 1052.052, including records maintained in a manner allowed under Section 1052.004; and

(2) certified copies or reproductions of the records.

Derived from Probate Code § 628.

Added by Acts 2011, 82nd Leg., ch. 823, § 1.02, eff. Jan. 1, 2014.

Subchapter D. Mediation

§ 1055.151. Mediation of Contested Guardianship Proceeding

(a) On the written agreement of the parties or on the court's own motion, the court may refer a contested guardianship proceeding to mediation.

(b) A mediated settlement agreement is binding on the parties if the agreement:

(1) provides, in a prominently displayed statement that is in boldfaced type, in capital letters, or underlined, that the agreement is not subject to revocation by the parties;

(2) is signed by each party to the agreement; and

(3) is signed by the party's attorney, if any, who is present at the time the agreement is signed.

(c) If a mediated settlement agreement meets the requirements of this section, a party is entitled to judgment on the mediated settlement agreement notwithstanding Rule 11, Texas Rules of Civil Procedure, or another rule or law.

(d) Notwithstanding Subsections (b) and (c), a court may decline to enter a judgment on a mediated settlement agreement if the court finds that the agreement is not in the ward's or proposed ward's best interests.

New.

Added by Acts 2013, 83rd Leg., ch. 982, § 7, eff. Jan. 1, 2014.

Chapter 1056. Execution, Attachment, and Bill of Review

Subchapter A. Execution

§ 1056.001. Executions in Guardianship Proceedings

Subchapter B. Attachment of Estate Property

§ 1056.051. Order for Issuance of Writ of Attachment

§ 1056.052. Bond

Subchapter C. Bill of Review

§ 1056.101. Revision and Correction of Order or Judgment in Guardianship Proceeding

§ 1056.102. Injunction

Chapter 1056. Execution, Attachment, and Bill of Review

Subchapter A. Execution

§ 1056.001. Executions In Guardianship Proceedings

(a) An execution in a guardianship proceeding must be:

(1) directed "to any sheriff or any constable within the State of Texas";

(2) attested and signed by the clerk officially under court seal; and

(3) made returnable in 60 days.

(b) A proceeding under an execution in a guardianship proceeding is governed, to the extent applicable, by the laws regulating a proceeding under an execution issued by a district court.

(c) Notwithstanding Subsection (a), an execution directed to the sheriff or a constable of a specific county in this state may not be held defective if properly executed within that county by the sheriff or constable to whom the execution is directed.

Derived from Probate Code § 653.

Added by Acts 2011, 82nd Leg., ch. 823, § 1.02, eff. Jan. 1, 2014. Section title amended by Acts 2013, 83rd Leg., ch. 161, § 6.033, eff. Jan. 1, 2014. Subsecs. (a) & (b) amended by Acts 2013, 83rd Leg., ch. 161, § 6.034, eff. Jan. 1, 2014.

Subchapter B. Attachment of Estate Property

§ 1056.051. Order for Issuance of Writ of Attachment

(a) If a person interested in the estate of an incapacitated person files with the judge a written complaint made under oath alleging that the guardian is about to remove the estate or a part of the estate outside of the state, the judge may order a writ of attachment to issue, directed "to any sheriff or any constable within the State of Texas." The writ must order the sheriff or constable to:

(1) seize the estate or a part of the estate; and

(2) hold that property subject to further court order.

(b) Notwithstanding Subsection (a), a writ of attachment directed to the sheriff or constable of a specific county in this state is not defective if the writ was properly executed within that county by the sheriff or constable to whom the writ is directed.

Derived from Probate Code § 654.

Added by Acts 2011, 82nd Leg., ch. 823, § 1.02, eff. Jan. 1, 2014.

§ 1056.052. Bond

Before a judge may issue a writ of attachment ordered under Section 1056.051, the complainant must execute a bond that is:

(1) payable to the guardian of the estate;

(2) in an amount set by the judge; and

(3) conditioned on the payment of all damages and costs that are recovered for a wrongful suit out of the writ.

Derived from Probate Code § 654.

Added by Acts 2011, 82nd Leg., ch. 823, § 1.02, eff. Jan. 1, 2014.

Subchapter C. Bill of Review

§ 1056.101. Revision and Correction of Order or Judgment in Guardianship Proceeding

(a) An interested person, including a ward, may, by a bill of review filed in the court in which the guardianship proceeding was held, have an order or judgment rendered by the court revised and corrected on a showing of error in the order or judgment.

(b) Except as provided by Subsection (c), a bill of review to revise and correct an order or judgment may not be filed more than two years after the date of the order or judgment.

(c) A bill of review to revise and correct an order or judgment filed by a person whose disability has been removed must be filed not later than the second anniversary of the date the person's disability was removed.

Derived from Probate Code § 657.

Added by Acts 2011, 82nd Leg., ch. 823, § 1.02, eff. Jan. 1, 2014.

§ 1056.102. Injunction

A process or action under a court order or judgment subject to a bill of review filed under Section 1056.101 may be stayed only by writ of injunction.

Derived from Probate Code § 657.

Added by Acts 2011, 82nd Leg., ch. 823, § 1.02, eff. Jan. 1, 2014.

Chapter 1057. Change and Resignation of Resident Agent of Guardian For Service Of Process

§ 1057.001. Change of Resident Agent

§ 1057.002. Resignation of Resident Agent

Chapter 1057. Change and Resignation of Resident Agent of Guardian for Service of Process

§ 1057.001. Change of Resident Agent

(a) A guardian may change the guardian's resident agent to accept service of process in a guardianship proceeding or other matter relating to the guardianship by filing with the court in which the guardianship proceeding is pending a statement titled "Designation of Successor Resident Agent" that states the names and addresses of:

(1) the guardian;

(2) the resident agent; and

(3) the successor resident agent.

(b) The designation of a successor resident agent takes effect on the date the statement is filed with the court.

Derived from Probate Code § 760A.

Added by Acts 2011, 82nd Leg., ch. 823, § 1.02, eff. Jan. 1, 2014.

§ 1057.002. Resignation of Resident Agent

(a) A resident agent of a guardian may resign as resident agent by giving notice to the guardian and filing with the court in which the guardianship proceeding is pending a statement titled "Resignation of Resident Agent" that states:

(1) the name of the guardian;

(2) the guardian's address most recently known by the resident agent;

(3) that notice of the resignation has been given to the guardian and the date that notice was given; and

(4) that the guardian does not have a resident agent.

(b) The resident agent shall send, by certified mail, return receipt requested, a copy of a resignation statement filed under Subsection (a) to:

(1) the guardian at the address most recently known by the resident agent; and

(2) each party in the case or the party's attorney or other designated representative of record.

(c) The resignation of the resident agent takes effect on the date the court enters an order accepting the resignation. A court may not enter an order accepting the resignation unless the resident agent complies with this section.

Derived from Probate Code § 760B.

Added by Acts 2011, 82nd Leg., ch. 823, § 1.02, eff. Jan. 1, 2014.

SUBTITLE D. CREATION OF GUARDIANSHIP

Chapter 1101. General Procedure to Appoint Guardian

Subchapter A. Initiation of Proceeding for Appointment of Guardian

Subchapter B. Hearing; Jury Trial

Subchapter C. Determination of Necessity of Guardianship; Findings and Proof

Subchapter D. Court Action

Chapter 1101. General Procedure to Appoint Guardian

Subchapter A. Initiation of Proceeding for Appointment of Guardian

§ 1101.001. Application for Appointment of Guardian; Contents

(a) Any person may commence a proceeding for the appointment of a guardian by filing a written application in a court having jurisdiction and venue.

(b) The application must be sworn to by the applicant and state:

(1) the proposed ward's name, sex, date of birth, and address;

(2) the name, relationship, and address of the person the applicant seeks to have appointed as guardian;

(3) whether guardianship of the person or estate, or both, is sought;

(3-a) whether alternatives to guardianship and available supports and services to avoid guardianship were considered;

(3-b) whether any alternatives to guardianship and supports and services available to the proposed ward considered are feasible and would avoid the need for a guardianship;

(4) the nature and degree of the alleged incapacity, the specific areas of protection and assistance requested, and the limitation or termination of rights requested to be included in the court's order of appointment, including a termination of:

(A) the right of a proposed ward who is 18 years of age or older to vote in a public election; [and]

(B) the proposed ward's eligibility to hold or obtain a license to operate a motor vehicle under Chapter 521, Transportation Code; and

(C) the right of a proposed ward to make personal decisions regarding residence;

(5) the facts requiring the appointment of a guardian;

(6) the interest of the applicant in the appointment of a guardian;

(7) the nature and description of any kind of guardianship existing for the proposed ward in any other state;

(8) the name and address of any person or institution having the care and custody of the proposed ward;

(9) the approximate value and description of the proposed ward's property, including any compensation, pension, insurance, or allowance to which the proposed ward may be entitled;

(10) the name and address of any person whom the applicant knows to hold a power of attorney signed by the proposed ward and a description of the type of power of attorney;

(11) for a proposed ward who is a minor, the following information if known by the applicant:

(A) the name of each of the proposed ward's parents and either the parent's address or that the parent is deceased;

(B) the name and age of each of the proposed ward's siblings, if any, and either the sibling's address or that the sibling is deceased; and

(C) if each of the proposed ward's parents and adult siblings are deceased, the names and addresses of the proposed ward's other living relatives who are related to the proposed ward within the third degree by consanguinity and who are adults;

(12) for a proposed ward who is a minor, whether the minor was the subject of a legal or conservatorship proceeding in the preceding two years and, if so:

(A) the court involved;

(B) the nature of the proceeding; and

(C) any final disposition of the proceeding;

(13) for a proposed ward who is an adult, the following information if known by the applicant:

(A) the name of the proposed ward's spouse, if any, and either the spouse's address or that the spouse is deceased;

(B) the name of each of the proposed ward's parents and either the parent's address or that the parent is deceased;

(C) the name and age of each of the proposed ward's siblings, if any, and either the sibling's address or that the sibling is deceased;

(D) the name and age of each of the proposed ward's children, if any, and either the child's address or that the child is deceased; and

(E) if there is no living spouse, parent, adult sibling, or adult child of the proposed ward's, the names and addresses of the proposed ward's other living relatives who are related to the proposed ward within the third degree by consanguinity and who are adults;

(14) facts showing that the court has venue of the proceeding; and

(15) if applicable, that the person whom the applicant seeks to have appointed as a guardian is a private professional guardian who is certified under Subchapter C, Chapter 155, Government Code, and has complied with the requirements of Subchapter G, Chapter 1104.

(c) For purposes of this section, a proposed ward's relatives within the third degree by consanguinity include the proposed ward's:

(1) grandparent or grandchild; and

(2) great-grandparent, great-grandchild, aunt who is a sister of a parent of the proposed ward, uncle who is a brother of a parent of the proposed ward, nephew who is a child of a brother or sister of the proposed ward, or niece who is a child of a brother or sister of the proposed ward.

Derived from Probate Code § 682.

Added by Acts 2011, 82nd Leg., ch. 823, § 1.02, eff. Jan. 1, 2014. Subsec. (b) amended by Acts 2013, 83rd Leg., ch. 42, § 2.07, eff. Jan. 1, 2014 and Acts 2013, 83rd Leg., ch. 161, § 6.035, eff. Jan. 1, 2014. Subsec. (b) amended by Acts 2015, 84th Leg., ch. 214, § 7, eff. Sept. 1, 2015. Subsec. (c) added by Acts 2015, 84th Leg., ch. 1031, § 8, eff. Sept. 1, 2015.

§ 1101.002. Contents of Application; Confidentiality of Certain Addresses

An application filed under Section 1101.001 may omit the address of a person named in the application if:

(1) the application states that the person is protected by a protective order issued under Chapter 85, Family Code;

(2) a copy of the protective order is attached to the application as an exhibit;

(3) the application states the county in which the person resides;

(4) the application indicates the place where notice to or the issuance and service of citation on the person may be made or sent; and

(5) the application is accompanied by a request for an order under Section 1051.201 specifying the manner of issuance, service, and return of citation or notice on the person.

Added by Acts 2013, 83rd Leg., ch. 982, § 8, eff. Jan. 1, 2014.

Subchapter B. Hearing; Jury Trial

§ 1101.051. Hearing

(a) At a hearing for the appointment of a guardian, the court shall:

(1) inquire into the ability of any allegedly incapacitated adult to:

(A) feed, clothe, and shelter himself or herself;

(B) care for his or her own physical health; and

(C) manage his or her property or financial affairs;

(2) ascertain the age of any proposed ward who is a minor;

(3) inquire into the governmental reports for any person who must have a guardian appointed to receive funds due the person from any governmental source; and

(4) inquire into the qualifications, abilities, and capabilities of the person seeking to be appointed guardian.

(b) A proposed ward must be present at the hearing unless the court, on the record or in the order, determines that a personal appearance is not necessary.

(c) The court may close the hearing at the request of the proposed ward or the proposed ward's counsel.

Derived from Probate Code §§ 685(a), (c).

Added by Acts 2011, 82nd Leg., ch. 823, § 1.02, eff. Jan. 1, 2014.

§ 1101.052. Jury Trial

A proposed ward is entitled to a jury trial on request.

Derived from Probate Code § 685(b).

Added by Acts 2011, 82nd Leg., ch. 823, § 1.02, eff. Jan. 1, 2014.

§ 1101.053. Provision of Records Required; Use of Records

(a) Before a hearing may be held for the appointment of a guardian, current and relevant medical, psychological, and intellectual testing records of the proposed ward must be provided to the attorney ad litem appointed to represent the proposed ward unless:

(1) the proposed ward is a minor or a person who must have a guardian appointed to receive funds due the person from any governmental source; or

(2) the court makes a finding on the record that:

(A) current or relevant records do not exist; and

(B) examining the proposed ward for the purpose of creating the records is impractical.

(b) Current medical, psychological, and intellectual testing records are a sufficient basis for a determination of guardianship.

(c) The findings and recommendations contained in the medical, psychological, and intellectual testing records are not binding on the court.

Derived from Probate Code § 686.

Added by Acts 2011, 82nd Leg., ch. 823, § 1.02, eff. Jan. 1, 2014.

Subchapter C. Determination of Necessity of Guardianship; Findings and Proof

§ 1101.101. Findings and Proof Required

(a) Before appointing a guardian for a proposed ward, the court must:

(1) find by clear and convincing evidence that:

(A) the proposed ward is an incapacitated person;

(B) it is in the proposed ward's best interest to have the court appoint a person as the proposed ward's guardian; [and]

(C) the proposed ward's rights or property will be protected by the appointment of a guardian;

(D) alternatives to guardianship that would avoid the need for the appointment of a guardian have been considered and determined not to be feasible; and

(E) supports and services available to the proposed ward that would avoid the need for the appointment of a guardian have been considered and determined not to be feasible; and

(2) find by a preponderance of the evidence that:

(A) the court has venue of the case;

(B) the person to be appointed guardian is eligible to act as guardian and is entitled to appointment, or, if no eligible person entitled to appointment applies, the person appointed is a proper person to act as guardian;

(C) if a guardian is appointed for a minor, the guardianship is not created for the primary purpose of enabling the minor to establish residency for enrollment in a school or school district for which the minor is not otherwise eligible for enrollment; and

(D) the proposed ward:

(i) is totally without capacity as provided by this title to care for himself or herself and to manage his or her property; or

(ii) lacks the capacity to do some, but not all, of the tasks necessary to care for himself or herself or to manage his or her property.

(b) The court may not grant an application to create a guardianship unless the applicant proves each element required by this title.

(c) A finding under Subsection (a)(2)(D)(ii) must specifically state whether the proposed ward lacks the capacity, or lacks sufficient capacity with supports and services, to make personal decisions regarding residence, voting, operating a motor vehicle, and marriage.

Derived from Probate Code §§ 684(a), (b), (c).

Added by Acts 2011, 82nd Leg., ch. 823, § 1.02, eff. Jan. 1, 2014. Subsec. (a) amended and subsec. (c) added by Acts 2015, 84th Leg., ch. 214, § 8, eff. Sept. 1, 2015.

§ 1101.102. Determination of Incapacity of Certain Adults: Recurring Acts or Occurrences

A determination of incapacity of an adult proposed ward, other than a person who must have a guardian appointed to receive funds due the person from any governmental source, must be evidenced by recurring acts or occurrences in the preceding six months and not by isolated instances of negligence or bad judgment.

Derived from Probate Code § 684(c).

Added by Acts 2011, 82nd Leg., ch. 823, § 1.02, eff. Jan. 1, 2014.

§ 1101.103. Determination of Incapacity of Certain Adults: Physician Examination

(a) Except as provided by Section 1101.104, the court may not grant an application to create a guardianship for an incapacitated person, other than a minor or person for whom it is necessary to have a guardian appointed only to receive funds from a governmental source, unless the applicant presents to the court a written letter or certificate from a physician licensed in this state that is:

(1) dated not earlier than the 120th day before the date the application is filed; and

(2) based on an examination the physician performed not earlier than the 120th day before the date the application is filed.

(b) The letter or certificate must:

(1) describe the nature, degree, and severity of the proposed ward's incapacity, including any functional deficits regarding the proposed ward's ability to:

(A) handle business and managerial matters;

(B) manage financial matters;

(C) operate a motor vehicle;

(D) make personal decisions regarding residence, voting, and marriage; and

(E) consent to medical, dental, psychological, or psychiatric treatment;

(2) in providing a description under Subdivision (1) regarding the proposed ward's ability to operate a motor vehicle and make personal decisions regarding voting, state whether in the physician's opinion the proposed ward:

(A) has the mental capacity to vote in a public election; and

(B) has the ability to safely operate a motor vehicle;

(3) provide an evaluation of the proposed ward's physical condition and mental <u>functioning</u> [function] and summarize the proposed ward's medical history if reasonably available;

<u>(3-a) in providing an evaluation under Subdivision (3), state whether improvement in the proposed ward's physical condition and mental functioning is possible and, if so, state the period after which the proposed ward should be reevaluated to determine whether a guardianship continues to be necessary;</u>

(4) state how or in what manner the proposed ward's ability to make or communicate responsible decisions concerning himself or herself is affected by the proposed ward's physical or mental health, including the proposed ward's ability to:

(A) understand or communicate;

(B) recognize familiar objects and individuals;

(C) <u>solve problems</u> [perform simple calculations];

(D) reason logically; and

(E) administer to daily life activities <u>with and without supports and services</u>;

(5) state whether any current medication affects the proposed ward's demeanor or the proposed ward's ability to participate fully in a court proceeding;

(6) describe the precise physical and mental conditions underlying a diagnosis of a mental disability, and state whether the proposed ward would benefit from supports and services that would allow the individual to live in the least restrictive setting;

<u>(6-a) state whether a guardianship is necessary for the proposed ward and, if so, whether specific powers or duties of the guardian should be limited if the proposed ward receives supports and services;</u> and

(7) include any other information required by the court.

(c) If the court determines it is necessary, the court may appoint the necessary physicians to examine the proposed ward. The court must make its determination with respect to the necessity for a physician's examination of the proposed ward at a hearing held for that purpose. Not later than the fourth day before the date of the hearing, the applicant shall give to the proposed ward and the proposed ward's attorney ad litem written notice specifying the purpose and the date and time of the hearing.

(d) A physician who examines the proposed ward, other than a physician or psychologist who examines the proposed ward under Section 1101.104(2), shall make available for inspection by the attorney ad litem appointed to represent the proposed ward a written letter or certificate from the physician that complies with the requirements of Subsections (a) and (b).

Derived from Probate Code §§ 687(a), (b).

Added by Acts 2011, 82nd Leg., ch. 823, § 1.02, eff. Jan. 1, 2014. Subsec. (b) amended by Acts 2015, 84ᵗʰ Leg., ch. 214, § 9, eff. Sept. 1, 2015.

§ 1101.104. Examinations and Documentation Regarding Intellectual Disability

If an intellectual disability is the basis of the proposed ward's alleged incapacity, the court may not grant an application to create a guardianship for the proposed ward unless the applicant presents to the court a written letter or certificate that:

(1) complies with Sections 1101.103(a) and (b); or

(2) shows that not earlier than 24 months before the hearing date:

(A) the proposed ward has been examined by a physician or psychologist licensed in this state or certified by the Department of Aging and Disability Services to perform the examination, in accordance with rules of the executive commissioner of the Health and Human Services Commission governing examinations of that kind, and the physician's or psychologist's written findings and recommendations include a determination of an intellectual disability; or

(B) a physician or psychologist licensed in this state or certified by the Department of Aging and Disability Services to perform examinations described by Paragraph (A) updated or endorsed in writing a prior determination of an intellectual disability for the proposed ward made by a physician or psychologist licensed in this state or certified by the department.

Derived from Probate Code § 687(c).

Added by Acts 2011, 82nd Leg., ch. 823, § 1.02, eff. Jan. 1, 2014. Amended by Acts 2013, 83rd Leg., ch. 780, § 2, eff. Jan. 1, 2014.

§ 1101.105. Prohibition Against Consideration of Age as Sole Factor in Appointment of Guardian for Adults

In determining whether to appoint a guardian for an incapacitated person who is not a minor, the court may not use age as the sole factor.

Derived from Probate Code § 602.

Added by Acts 2011, 82nd Leg., ch. 823, § 1.02, eff. Jan. 1, 2014.

§ 1101.106. Evidence of Necessity of Guardianship to Receive Governmental Funds

A certificate of the executive head or a representative of a bureau, department, or agency of the government, to the effect that the appointment of a guardian is a condition precedent to the payment of any funds due the proposed ward from that governmental entity, is prima facie evidence of the necessity for the appointment of a guardian.

Derived from Probate Code § 684(e).

Added by Acts 2011, 82nd Leg., ch. 823, § 1.02, eff. Jan. 1, 2014.

Subchapter D. Court Action

§ 1101.151. Order Appointing Guardian With Full Authority

(a) If it is found that the proposed ward is totally without capacity to care for himself or herself, manage his or her property, operate a motor vehicle, make personal decisions regarding residence, and vote in a public election, the court may appoint a guardian of the proposed ward's person or estate, or both, with full authority over the incapacitated person except as provided by law.

(b) An order appointing a guardian under this section must contain findings of fact and specify:

(1) the information required by Section 1101.153(a);

(2) that the guardian has full authority over the incapacitated person;

(3) if necessary, the amount of funds from the corpus of the person's estate the court will allow the guardian to spend for the education and maintenance of the person under Subchapter A, Chapter 1156;

(4) whether the person is totally incapacitated because of a mental condition;

(5) that the person does not have the capacity to operate a motor vehicle, make personal decisions regarding residence, and [to] vote in a public election; and

(6) if it is a guardianship of the person of the ward or of both the person and the estate of the ward, the rights of the guardian with respect to the person as specified in Section 1151.051(c)(1).

(c) An order appointing a guardian under this section that includes the rights of the guardian with respect to the person as specified in Section 1151.051(c)(1) must also contain the following prominently displayed statement in boldfaced type, in capital letters, or underlined:

"NOTICE TO ANY PEACE OFFICER OF THE STATE OF TEXAS: YOU MAY USE REASONABLE EFFORTS TO ENFORCE THE RIGHT OF A GUARDIAN OF THE PERSON OF A WARD TO HAVE PHYSICAL POSSESSION OF THE WARD OR TO ESTABLISH THE WARD'S LEGAL DOMICILE AS SPECIFIED IN THIS ORDER. A PEACE OFFICER WHO RELIES ON THE TERMS OF A COURT ORDER AND THE OFFICER'S AGENCY ARE ENTITLED TO THE APPLICABLE IMMUNITY AGAINST ANY CIVIL OR OTHER CLAIM REGARDING THE OFFICER'S GOOD FAITH ACTS PERFORMED IN THE SCOPE OF THE OFFICER'S DUTIES IN ENFORCING THE TERMS OF THIS ORDER THAT RELATE TO THE ABOVE-MENTIONED RIGHTS OF THE COURT-APPOINTED GUARDIAN OF THE PERSON OF THE WARD. ANY PERSON WHO KNOWINGLY PRESENTS FOR ENFORCEMENT AN ORDER THAT IS INVALID OR NO LONGER IN EFFECT COMMITS AN OFFENSE THAT MAY BE PUNISHABLE BY CONFINEMENT IN JAIL FOR AS LONG AS TWO YEARS AND A FINE OF AS MUCH AS $10,000."

Derived from Probate Code § 693(a).

Added by Acts 2011, 82nd Leg., ch. 823, § 1.02, eff.

Jan. 1, 2014. Subsec. (b) amended by and subsec. (c) added by Acts 2013, 83rd Leg., ch. 982, § 9, eff. Jan. 1, 2014. Subsecs (a) & (b) amended by Acts 2015, 84th Leg., ch. 214, § 10, eff. Sept. 1, 2015.

§ 1101.152. Order Appointing Guardian With Limited Authority

(a) If it is found that the proposed ward lacks the capacity to do some, but not all, of the tasks necessary to care for himself or herself or to manage his or her property <u>with or without supports and services</u>, the court may appoint a guardian with limited powers and permit the proposed ward to care for himself or herself, <u>including making personal decisions regarding residence</u>, or to manage his or her property commensurate with the proposed ward's ability.

(b) An order appointing a guardian under this section must contain findings of fact and specify:

    (1) the information required by Section 1101.153(a);

    (2) the specific powers, limitations, or duties of the guardian with respect to the person's care or the management of the person's property by the guardian;

    <u>(2-a) the specific rights and powers retained by the person:</u>

        <u>(A) with the necessity for supports and services; and</u>

        <u>(B) without the necessity for supports and services;</u>

    (3) if necessary, the amount of funds from the corpus of the person's estate the court will allow the guardian to spend for the education and maintenance of the person under Subchapter A, Chapter 1156; and

    (4) whether the person is incapacitated because of a mental condition and, if so, whether the person:

        (A) retains the right to <u>make personal decisions regarding residence or</u> vote in a public election; or

        <u>(B)</u> maintains eligibility to hold or obtain a license to operate a motor vehicle under Chapter 521, Transportation Code.

(c) An order appointing a guardian under this section that includes the right of the guardian to have physical possession of the ward or to establish the ward's legal domicile as specified in Section 1151.051(c)(1) must also contain the following prominently displayed statement in boldfaced type, in capital letters, or underlined:

"NOTICE TO ANY PEACE OFFICER OF THE STATE OF TEXAS: YOU MAY USE REASONABLE EFFORTS TO ENFORCE THE RIGHT OF A GUARDIAN OF THE PERSON OF A WARD TO HAVE PHYSICAL POSSESSION OF THE WARD OR TO ESTABLISH THE WARD'S LEGAL DOMICILE AS SPECIFIED IN THIS ORDER. A PEACE OFFICER WHO RELIES ON THE TERMS OF A COURT ORDER AND THE OFFICER'S AGENCY ARE ENTITLED TO THE APPLICABLE IMMUNITY AGAINST ANY CIVIL OR OTHER CLAIM REGARDING THE OFFICER'S GOOD FAITH ACTS PERFORMED IN THE SCOPE OF THE OFFICER'S DUTIES IN ENFORCING THE TERMS OF THIS ORDER THAT RELATE TO THE ABOVE-MENTIONED RIGHTS OF THE COURT-APPOINTED GUARDIAN OF THE PERSON OF THE WARD. ANY PERSON WHO KNOWINGLY PRESENTS FOR ENFORCEMENT AN ORDER THAT IS INVALID OR NO LONGER IN EFFECT COMMITS AN OFFENSE THAT MAY BE PUNISHABLE BY CONFINEMENT IN JAIL FOR AS LONG AS TWO YEARS AND A FINE OF AS MUCH AS $10,000."

Derived from Probate Code § 693(b).

Added by Acts 2011, 82nd Leg., ch. 823, § 1.02, eff. Jan. 1, 2014. Subsec. (c) added by Acts 2013, 83rd Leg., ch. 982, eff. Jan. 1, 2014. Subsecs (a) & (b) amended by Acts 2015, 84th Leg., ch. 214, § 11, eff. Sept. 1, 2015.

§ 1101.153. General Contents of Order Appointing Guardian

(a) A court order appointing a guardian must specify:

    (1) the name of the person appointed;

    (2) the name of the ward;

    (3) whether the guardian is of the person or estate of the ward, or both;

    (4) the amount of any bond required;

    (5) if it is a guardianship of the estate of the ward and the court considers an appraisal to be necessary, one, two, or three disinterested persons to appraise the estate and to return the appraisement to the court; and

    (6) that the clerk will issue letters of guardianship to the person appointed when the person has qualified according to law.

<u>(a-1) If the letter or certificate under Section 1101.103(b)(3-a) stated that improvement in the ward's physical condition or mental functioning is possible and specified a period of less than a year after which the ward should be reevaluated to determine continued necessity for the guardianship, an order appointing a guardian must include the date by which the guardian must submit to the court an updated letter or certificate containing the requirements of Section 1101.103(b).</u>

(b) An order appointing a guardian may not duplicate or conflict with the powers and duties of any other guardian.

(c) An order appointing a guardian or a successor guardian may specify as authorized by Section 1202.001(c) a period during which a petition for adjudication that the ward no longer requires the guardianship may not be filed without special leave.

Derived from Probate Code §§ 693(c), (d), (e).

Added by Acts 2011, 82nd Leg., ch. 823, § 1.02, eff. Jan. 1, 2014. Subsec. (a-1) added by Acts 2015, 84th Leg., ch. 214, § 12, eff. Sept. 1, 2015.

§ 1101.154. Appointment of Guardian of Estate for Certain Minors Prohibited

A court may not appoint a guardian of the estate of a minor when a payment of claims is made under Chapter 1355.

Derived from Probate Code § 684(d).

Added by Acts 2011, 82nd Leg., ch. 823, § 1.02, eff. Jan. 1, 2014.

§ 1101.155. Dismissal of Application

If it is found that a proposed ward who is an adult possesses the capacity to care for himself or herself and manage his or her property as would a reasonably prudent person, the court shall dismiss an application for guardianship.

Derived from Probate Code § 692.

Added by Acts 2011, 82nd Leg., ch. 823, § 1.02, eff. Jan. 1, 2014.

§ 1101.156. Deposit of Estate Assets

(a) At the time or after an order appointing a guardian is signed by the court but before letters of guardianship are issued, a court may, on the request of a party, require the deposit for safekeeping of cash, securities, or other assets of a ward or proposed ward in a financial institution described by Section 1105.155(b).

(b) The amount of the bond required to be given by the guardian under Section 1105.101 shall be reduced in proportion to the amount of the cash or the value of the securities or other assets deposited under this section.

New.

Added by Acts 2015, 84th Leg., ch. 1031, § 9, eff. Sept. 1, 2015.

Chapter 1102. Court-Initiated Procedure to Appoint Guardian

Chapter 1102. Court-Initiated Procedure to Appoint Guardian

§ 1102.001. Court-Initiated Investigation

(a) If a court has probable cause to believe that a person domiciled or found in the county in which the court is located is an incapacitated person, and the person does not have a guardian in this state, the court shall appoint a guardian ad litem or court investigator to investigate the person's conditions and circumstances to determine whether:

(1) the person is an incapacitated person; and

(2) a guardianship is necessary.

(b) If a court appoints a guardian ad litem or court investigator under Subsection (a):

(1) the court's order appointing a guardian ad litem or court investigator must include a statement that the person believed to be incapacitated has the right to petition the court to have the appointment set aside;

(2) at the initial meeting between the guardian ad litem or court investigator and the person believed to be incapacitated, the guardian ad litem or court investigator, as appropriate, shall provide a copy of the information letter under Section 1102.003 and the order to, and discuss the contents of the letter and order with, the person believed to be incapacitated; and

(3) during the period beginning after the date of the initial meeting described by Subdivision (2) and ending on the date an application for the appointment of a guardian is filed, the person believed to be incapacitated may petition the court to have the appointment of the guardian ad litem or court investigator, as appropriate, set aside.

Derived from Probate Code § 683(a).

Added by Acts 2011, 82nd Leg., ch. 823, § 1.02, eff. Jan. 1, 2014. Subsec. (b) added by Acts 2015, 84th Leg., ch. 1031, § 10, eff. Sept. 1, 2015.

§ 1102.002. Establishment of Probable Cause for Investigation

To establish probable cause under Section 1102.001, the court may require:

(1) an information letter about the person believed to be incapacitated that is submitted by an interested person and satisfies the requirements of Section 1102.003; or

(2) a written letter or certificate from a physician who has examined the person believed to be incapacitated that satisfies the requirements of Section 1101.103, except that the letter must be:

(A) dated not earlier than the 120th day before the date of the appointment of a guardian ad litem or court investigator under Section 1102.001; and

(B) based on an examination the physician performed not earlier than the 120th day before that date.

Derived from Probate Code § 683(b).

Added by Acts 2011, 82nd Leg., ch. 823, § 1.02, eff. Jan. 1, 2014.

§ 1102.003. Information Letter

(a) An interested person who submits an information letter under Section 1102.002(1) about a person believed to be incapacitated must, to the best of the interested person's knowledge:

(1) state the person's name, address, telephone number, county of residence, and date of birth;

(2) state whether the person's residence is a private residence, health care facility, or other type of residence;

(3) describe the relationship between the person and the interested person submitting the letter;

(4) state the names and telephone numbers of any known friends and relatives of the person;

(5) state whether a guardian of the person or estate has been appointed in this state for the person;

(6) state whether the person has executed a power of attorney and, if so, the designee's name, address, and telephone number;

(7) describe any property of the person, including the estimated value of that property;

(8) list the amount and source of any monthly income of the person;

(9) describe the nature and degree of the person's alleged incapacity; and

(10) state whether the person is in imminent danger of serious impairment to the person's physical health, safety, or estate.

(b) In addition to the requirements of Subsection (a), if an information letter under that subsection is submitted by an interested person who is a family member of the person believed to be incapacitated, the information letter must:

(1) be signed and sworn to before a notary public by the interested person; or

(2) include a written declaration signed by the interested person under penalty of perjury that the information contained in the information letter is true to the best of the person's knowledge.

(c) Any information provided by the Department of Family and Protective Services under this section that is confidential under Chapter 48, Human Resources Code, remains confidential and is not subject to disclosure under Chapter 552, Government Code.

Derived from Probate Code § 683A.

Added by Acts 2011, 82nd Leg., ch. 823, § 1.02, eff. Jan. 1, 2014. Amended by Acts 2013, 83rd Leg., ch. 982, § 11, eff. Jan. 1, 2014. Subsec. (c) added by Acts 2015, 84th Leg., ch. 1031, § 11, eff. Sept. 1, 2015.

§ 1102.004. Application for Guardianship Following Investigation

A guardian ad litem or court investigator who, after an investigation as prescribed by Section 1102.001, believes that the person is an incapacitated person and that a guardianship is necessary shall file an application for the appointment of a guardian of the person or estate, or both, for the person.

Derived from Probate Code § 683(a).

Added by Acts 2011, 82nd Leg., ch. 823, § 1.02, eff. Jan. 1, 2014.

§ 1102.005. Compensation of Guardian Ad Litem

(a) Regardless of whether a guardianship is created for a proposed ward and except as provided by Section 1155.151, a [A] court that appoints a guardian ad litem under Section 1102.001 may authorize compensation of the guardian ad litem from available funds of:

(1) the proposed ward's estate; or

(2) the management trust, if a management trust has been created for the benefit of the proposed ward under Chapter 1301[, regardless of whether a guardianship is created for the proposed ward].

(b) Except as provided by Section 1155.151, after [After] examining the proposed ward's assets or the assets of any management trust created for the proposed ward's benefit under Chapter 1301, and determining that the proposed ward or the management trust is unable to pay for services provided by the guardian ad litem, the court may authorize compensation from the county treasury.

Derived from Probate Code § 683(c).

Added by Acts 2011, 82nd Leg., ch. 823, § 1.02, eff. Jan. 1, 2014. Subsec. (b) amended by Acts 2013, ch. 982, § 12, eff. Jan. 1, 2014. Amended by Acts 2015, 84th Leg., ch. 1031, § 12, eff. Sept. 1, 2015.

§ 1102.006. Notice Regarding Request to Financial Institution for Customer Records

If a request is made to a financial institution for a customer record in connection with an investigation conducted under Section 1102.001, the court shall provide written notice of that fact to the proposed ward with respect to whom the investigation is conducted not later than the fifth day after the date the financial institution produces the customer record.

New.

Added by Acts 2015, 84th Leg., ch. 1031, § 13, eff. Sept. 1, 2015.

Chapter 1103. Procedure to Appoint Guardian for Certain Minors Requiring Guardianships as Adults

Chapter 1103. Procedure to Appoint Guardian for Certain Minors Requiring Guardianships as Adults

§ 1103.001. Application for Appointment of Guardian

Not earlier than the 180th day before the proposed ward's 18th birthday, a person may file an application under Section 1101.001 for the appointment of a guardian of the person or estate, or both, of a proposed ward who:

(1) is a minor; and

(2) because of incapacity will require a guardianship after the proposed ward is no longer a minor.

Derived from Probate Code § 682A(a).

Added by Acts 2011, 82nd Leg., ch. 823, § 1.02, eff. Jan. 1, 2014.

§ 1103.002. Appointment of Conservator as Guardian Without Hearing

(a) Notwithstanding any other law, if the applicant who files an application under Section 1101.001 or 1103.001 is a person who was appointed conservator of a disabled child and the proceeding is a guardianship proceeding described by Section 1002.015(1) in which the proposed ward is the incapacitated adult with respect to whom another court obtained continuing, exclusive jurisdiction in a suit affecting the parent-child relationship when the person was a child, the applicant may present to the court a written letter or certificate that meets the requirements of Sections 1101.103(a) and (b).

(b) If, on receipt of the letter or certificate described by Subsection (a), the court is able to make the findings required by Section 1101.101, the court, notwithstanding Subchapter C, Chapter 1104, shall:

(1) appoint the conservator as guardian without conducting a hearing; and

(2) to the extent possible preserve the terms of possession and access to the ward that applied before the court obtained jurisdiction of the guardianship proceeding.

Derived from Probate Code § 682A(a-1) & (a-2).

Added by Acts 2011, 82nd Leg., ch. 823, § 1.02, eff. Jan. 1, 2014. Amended by Acts 2013, 83rd Leg., ch. 161, § 6.037, eff. Jan. 1, 2014.

§ 1103.003. Effective Date Of Guardianship

If the application filed under Section 1103.001 is heard before the proposed ward's 18th birthday, a guardianship created under this chapter may not take effect and the person appointed guardian may not take the oath as required under Section 1105.051 or give a bond as required under Section 1105.101 until the proposed ward's 18th birthday.

Derived from Probate Code § 682A(a).

Added by Acts 2011, 82nd Leg., ch. 823, § 1.02, eff. Jan. 1, 2014.

§ 1103.004. Settlement and Closing of Prior Guardianship

Notwithstanding Section 1202.001(b), the guardianship of the person of a minor who is the subject of an application for the appointment of a guardian of the person filed under Section 1103.001 is settled and closed when:

(1) the court, after a hearing on the application, determines that the appointment of a guardian of the person for the proposed ward is not necessary; or

(2) the guardian appointed by the court, after a hearing on the application, has qualified under Section 1105.002.

Derived from Probate Code § 682A(b).

Added by Acts 2011, 82nd Leg., ch. 823, § 1.02, eff. Jan. 1, 2014.

Chapter 1104. Selection of and Eligibility to Serve as Guardian

Subchapter A. General Provisions Relating to Appointment of Guardian

Subchapter B. Selection of Guardian for Minor

Subchapter C. Selection of Guardian for Incapacitated Person Other Than Minor

Subchapter D. Written Declaration by Certain Parents to Appoint Guardian for Their Children

Chapter 1104. Selection of and Eligibility to Serve as Guardian

Subchapter A. General Provisions Relating to Appointment of Guardian

§ 1104.001. Guardian of the Person or Estate

(a) Only one person may be appointed as guardian of the person or estate, but one person may be appointed guardian of the person and another person may be appointed guardian of the estate, if it is in the best interest of the incapacitated person or ward.

(b) Subsection (a) does not prohibit the joint appointment, if the court finds it to be in the best interest of the incapacitated person or ward, of:

(1) a husband and wife;

(2) joint managing conservators;

(3) co-guardians appointed under the laws of a jurisdiction other than this state; or

(4) both parents of an adult who is incapacitated if the incapacitated person:

(A) has not been the subject of a suit affecting the parent-child relationship; or

(B) has been the subject of a suit affecting the parent-child relationship and both of the incapacitated person's parents were named as joint managing conservators in the suit but are no longer serving in that capacity.

Derived from Probate Code § 690.

Added by Acts 2011, 82nd Leg., ch. 823, § 1.02, eff. Jan. 1, 2014.

§ 1104.002. Preference of Incapacitated Person

Before appointing a guardian, the court shall make a reasonable effort to consider the incapacitated person's preference of the person to be appointed guardian and, to the extent consistent with other provisions of this title, shall give due consideration to the preference indicated by the incapacitated person, regardless of whether the person has designated by declaration a guardian before the need arises under Subchapter E.

Derived from Probate Code § 689.

Added by Acts 2011, 82nd Leg., ch. 823, § 1.02, eff. Jan. 1, 2014. Amended by Acts 2015, 84th Leg., ch. 214, § 13, eff. Sept. 1, 2015.

Subchapter B. Selection of Guardian for Minor

Statutes in Context
Chapter 1104, Subchapter B

Chapter 1104, Subchapter B, explains how a guardian of a minor is selected. Upon the surviving parent's death or incapacity, the court will give great deference to a designation of a guardian in the parent's will or other written document.

§ 1104.051. Guardian of Minor Children

(a) If the parents live together, both parents are the natural guardians of the person of the minor children by the marriage, and one of the parents is entitled to be appointed guardian of the children's estates. If the parents disagree as to which parent should be appointed, the court shall make the appointment on the basis of which parent is better qualified to serve in that capacity.

(b) The rights of parents who do not live together are equal. The court shall assign the guardianship of their minor children to one parent considering only the best interests of the children.

(c) If one parent is deceased, the surviving parent is the natural guardian of the person of the minor children and is entitled to be appointed guardian of the minor children's estates.

Derived from Probate Code § 676(b).

Added by Acts 2011, 82nd Leg., ch. 823, § 1.02, eff. Jan. 1, 2014.

§ 1104.052. Guardian for Minor Orphan

In appointing a guardian for a minor orphan:

(1) if the last surviving parent did not appoint a guardian, the nearest ascendant in the direct line of the minor is entitled to guardianship of both the person and the estate of the minor;

(2) if more than one ascendant exists in the same degree in the direct line of the minor, the court shall appoint one ascendant according to circumstances and considering the minor's best interests;

(3) if the minor does not have an ascendant in the direct line of the minor:

(A) the court shall appoint the nearest of kin; or

(B) if two or more persons are in the same degree of kinship to the minor, the court shall appoint one of those persons according to circumstances and considering the minor's best interests; and

(4) if the minor does not have a relative who is eligible to be guardian, or if none of the eligible persons apply to be guardian, the court shall appoint a qualified person as guardian.

Derived from Probate Code § 676(c).

Added by Acts 2011, 82nd Leg., ch. 823, § 1.02, eff. Jan. 1, 2014.

§ 1104.053. Guardian Designated by Will or Written Declaration

(a) Notwithstanding Section 1104.001 or 1104.051, the surviving parent of a minor may by will or written declaration appoint any eligible person to be guardian of the person of the parent's minor children after the parent dies or in the event of the parent's incapacity.

(b) After the surviving parent of a minor dies or if the court finds the surviving parent is an incapacitated person, the court shall appoint the person designated in the will or declaration to serve as guardian of the person of the parent's minor children in preference to another otherwise entitled to serve as guardian under this title, unless the court finds that the person designated to serve as guardian:

(1) is disqualified;

(2) is deceased;

(3) refuses to serve; or

(4) would not serve the minor children's best interests.

(c) On compliance with this title, an eligible person is also entitled to be appointed guardian of the minor children's estates after the surviving parent dies or in the event of the surviving parent's incapacity.

Derived from Probate Code §§ 676(d), (e), (f).

Added by Acts 2011, 82nd Leg., ch. 823, § 1.02, eff. Jan. 1, 2014.

§ 1104.054. Selection of Guardian by Minor

(a) Notwithstanding any other provision of this subchapter, if an application is filed for the guardianship of the person or estate, or both, of a minor at least 12 years of age, the minor may select the guardian by a writing filed with the clerk, if the court finds that the selection is in the minor's best interest and approves the selection.

(b) Notwithstanding any other provision of this subchapter, a minor at least 12 years of age may select another guardian of the minor's person or estate, or both, if the minor has a guardian appointed by the court, by will of the minor's parent, or by written declaration of the minor's parent, and that guardian dies, resigns, or is removed from guardianship. The minor must make the selection by filing an application in open court in person or by an attorney. The court shall make the appointment and revoke the letters of guardianship of the former guardian if the court is satisfied that:

(1) the person selected is suitable and competent; and

(2) the appointment of the person is in the minor's best interest.

Derived from Probate Code §§ 676(a), 680.

Added by Acts 2011, 82nd Leg., ch. 823, § 1.02, eff. Jan. 1, 2014.

Subchapter C. Selection of Guardian for Incapacitated Person Other Than Minor

Statutes in Context
Chapter 1104, Subchapter C

Chapter 1104, Subchapter C, explains how a guardian of a non-minor is selected. Upon the surviving parent's death or incapacity, the court will give great deference to a designation of a guardian in the parent's will or other written document.

§ 1104.101. Appointment According to Circumstances and Best Interests

The court shall appoint a guardian for an incapacitated person other than a minor according to the circumstances and considering the incapacitated person's best interests.

Derived from Probate Code § 677(a).

Added by Acts 2011, 82nd Leg., ch. 823, § 1.02, eff. Jan. 1, 2014.

§ 1104.102. Appointment Preferences

If the court finds that two or more eligible persons are equally entitled to be appointed guardian of an incapacitated person:

(1) the incapacitated person's spouse is entitled to the guardianship in preference to any other person, if the spouse is one of the eligible persons;

(2) the eligible person nearest of kin to the incapacitated person is entitled to the guardianship, if the incapacitated person's spouse is not one of the eligible persons; or

(3) the court shall appoint the eligible person who is best qualified to serve as guardian if:

(A) the persons entitled to serve under Subdivisions (1) and (2) refuse to serve;

(B) two or more persons entitled to serve under Subdivision (2) are related in the same degree of kinship to the incapacitated person; or

(C) neither the incapacitated person's spouse nor any person related to the incapacitated person is an eligible person.

Derived from Probate Code § 677(A).

Added by Acts 2011, 82nd Leg., ch. 823, § 1.02, eff. Jan. 1, 2014.

§ 1104.103. Designation of Guardian by Will or Written Declaration

(a) The surviving parent of an adult individual who is an incapacitated person may, if the parent is the guardian of the person of the adult individual, by will or written declaration appoint an eligible person to serve as guardian of the person of the adult individual after the parent dies or in the event of the parent's incapacity.

(b) After the surviving parent dies or if the court finds the surviving parent has become an incapacitated person after being appointed the adult individual's guardian, the court shall appoint the person designated in the will or declaration to serve as guardian in preference to any other person otherwise entitled to serve as guardian under this title, unless the court finds that the person designated to serve as guardian:

(1) is disqualified;

(2) is deceased;

(3) refuses to serve; or

(4) would not serve the adult individual's best interests.

(c) On compliance with this title, the eligible person appointed under Subsection (b) is also entitled to be appointed guardian of the estate of the adult individual after the surviving parent dies or in the event of the surviving parent's incapacity, if the surviving parent is the guardian of the estate of the adult individual.

Derived from Probate Code §§ 677(b), (c), (d).

Added by Acts 2011, 82nd Leg., ch. 823, § 1.02, eff. Jan. 1, 2014.

Subchapter D. Written Declaration by Certain Parents to Appoint Guardian for Their Children

§ 1104.151. Definitions

In this subchapter:

(1) "Declaration" means a written declaration of a person that:

(A) appoints a guardian for the person's child under Section 1104.053(A) or 1104.103(A); and

(B) satisfies the requirements of this subdivision and Sections 1104.152, 1104.153, 1104.154, 1104.156, 1104.159, and 1104.160.

(2) "Self-proving affidavit" means an affidavit the form and content of which substantially comply with the requirements of Section 1104.153.

(3) "Self-proving declaration" includes a self-proving affidavit that is attached or annexed to a declaration.

Derived from Probate Code §§ 677A(h), 677B(a).

Added by Acts 2011, 82nd Leg., ch. 823, § 1.02, eff. Jan. 1, 2014.

Statutes in Context
§ 1104.152

Section 1104.152 sets forth the requirements for non-testamentary guardian declarations by a parent of a minor or adult who is in need of a guardian. Separate rules exist for holographic and attested declarations. Suggested forms are provided in § 1104.153 (two-step execution procedure with separate self-proving affidavit) and § 1104.154 (one-step execution procedure with integrated self-proving affidavit).

---

§ 1104.152. Requirements for Declaration

(a) A declaration appointing an eligible person to be guardian of the person of a parent's child under Section 1104.053(a) or 1104.103(a) must be signed by the declarant and be:

(1) written wholly in the declarant's handwriting; or

(2) attested to in the declarant's presence by at least two credible witnesses who are:

(A) 14 years of age or older; and

(B) not named as guardian or alternate guardian in the declaration.

(b) Notwithstanding Subsection (a), a declaration that is not written wholly in the declarant's handwriting may be signed by another person for the declarant under the direction of and in the presence of the declarant.

(c) A declaration described by Subsection (a)(2) may have attached a self-proving affidavit signed by the declarant and the witnesses attesting to:

(1) the competence of the declarant; and

(2) the execution of the declaration.

Derived from Probate Code §§ 677A(A), (b), (c).

Added by Acts 2011, 82nd Leg., ch. 823, § 1.02, eff. Jan. 1, 2014.

§ 1104.153. Form and Content of Declaration and Self-Proving Affidavit

(a) A declaration and affidavit may be in any form adequate to clearly indicate the declarant's intention to designate a guardian for the declarant's child.

(b) The following form may be used but is not required to be used:

DECLARATION OF APPOINTMENT OF GUARDIAN FOR MY CHILDREN

IN THE EVENT OF MY DEATH OR INCAPACITY

I, _____, make this Declaration to appoint as guardian for my child or children, listed as follows, in the event of my death or incapacity:

_____
_____
_____
_____
_____
_____

(add blanks as appropriate)

I designate _____ to serve as guardian of the person of my (child or children), _____ as first alternate guardian of the person of my (child or children), _____ as second alternate guardian of the person of my (child or children), and _____ as third alternate guardian of the person of my (child or children).

I direct that the guardian of the person of my (child or children) serve (with or without) bond.

(If applicable) I designate _____ to serve as guardian of the estate of my (child or children), _____ as first alternate guardian of the estate of my (child or children), _____ as second alternate guardian of the estate of my (child or children), and _____ as third alternate guardian of the estate of my (child or children).

If any guardian or alternate guardian dies, does not qualify, or resigns, the next named alternate guardian becomes guardian of my (child or children).

Signed this _____ day of _____, 20__.

_____
Declarant

_____   _____
Witness   Witness
SELF-PROVING AFFIDAVIT

Before me, the undersigned authority, on this date personally appeared _____, the declarant, and _____ and _____ as witnesses, and all being duly sworn, the declarant said that the above instrument was his or her Declaration of Appointment of Guardian for the Declarant's Children in the Event of Declarant's Death or Incapacity and that the declarant had made and executed it for the purposes expressed in the declaration. The witnesses declared to me that they are each 14 years of age or older, that they saw the declarant sign the declaration, that they signed the declaration as witnesses, and that the declarant appeared to them to be of sound mind.

_____
Declarant

_____ _____
Affiant   Affiant
Subscribed and sworn to before me by _____, the above named declarant, and _____ (names of affiants) affiants, on this ____ day of _____, 20 ____.

_____
Notary Public in and for the State of Texas
My Commission expires:
_____

Derived from Probate Code § 677A(g).

Added by Acts 2011, 82nd Leg., ch. 823, § 1.02, eff. Jan. 1, 2014.

§ 1104.154. Alternative to Self-Proving Affidavit

(a) As an alternative to the self-proving affidavit authorized by Section 1104.153, a declaration of appointment of a guardian for the declarant's children in the event of the declarant's death or incapacity may be simultaneously executed, attested, and made self-proved by including the following in substantially the same form and with substantially the same contents:

I, _____, as declarant, after being duly sworn, declare to the undersigned witnesses and to the undersigned authority that this instrument is my Declaration of Appointment of Guardian for My Children in the Event of My Death or Incapacity, and that I willingly make [have made] and execute [executed] it for the purposes expressed in the declaration. I now sign this declaration in the presence of the attesting witnesses and the undersigned authority on this ____ day of _____, 20 ____.

_____
Declarant
The undersigned, _____ and _____, each being 14 years of age or older, after being duly sworn, declare to the declarant and to the undersigned authority that the declarant declared to us that this instrument is the declarant's Declaration of Appointment of Guardian for the Declarant's Children in the Event of Declarant's Death or Incapacity and that the declarant executed it for the purposes expressed in the declaration. The declarant then signed this declaration and we believe the declarant to be of sound mind. We now sign our names as attesting witnesses on this ____ day of _____, 20 ____.

_____
Witness

_____
Witness

Subscribed and sworn to before me by the above named declarant, and affiants, this ____ day of _____, 20 ____.

_____
Notary Public in and for the
State of Texas
My Commission expires:
_____

(b) A declaration that is executed as provided by Subsection (a) is considered self-proved to the same extent a declaration executed with a self-proving affidavit under Section 1104.153 is considered self-proved.

Derived from Probate Code §§ 677A(i), (j).

Added by Acts 2011, 82nd Leg., ch. 823, § 1.02, eff. Jan. 1, 2014. Subsec. (a) amended by Acts 2015, 84th Leg., ch. 1031, § 14, eff. Sept. 1, 2015.

§ 1104.155. Alternate Self-Proving of Declaration

At any time during the declarant's lifetime, a declaration described by Section 1104.152(a)(1) may be made self-proved in the same form and manner that a will written wholly in the testator's handwriting is made self-proved under Section 251.107.

Derived from Probate Code § 677B(c).

Added by Acts 2011, 82nd Leg., ch. 823, § 1.02, eff. Jan. 1, 2014.

§ 1104.156. Filing of Declaration and Self-Proving Affidavit

The declaration and any self-proving affidavit may be filed with the court at any time after the application for appointment of a guardian is filed and before a guardian is appointed.

Derived from Probate Code § 677A(d).

Added by Acts 2011, 82nd Leg., ch. 823, § 1.02, eff. Jan. 1, 2014.

§ 1104.157. Proof of Declaration

(a) The court may admit a declaration that is self-proved into evidence without the testimony of witnesses attesting to the competency of the declarant and the execution of the declaration. Additional proof of the execution of the declaration with the formalities and solemnities and under the circumstances required to make it a valid declaration is not necessary.

(b) A declaration described by Section 1104.152(a)(1) that is not self-proved may be proved in the same manner that a will written wholly in the testator's handwriting is proved under Section 256.154.

(c) A declaration described by Section 1104.152(a)(2) that is not self-proved may be proved in the same manner that an attested written will produced in court is proved under Section 256.153.

Derived from Probate Code §§ 677B(b), (e), (f).

Added by Acts 2011, 82nd Leg., ch. 823, § 1.02, eff. Jan. 1, 2014.

§ 1104.158. Prima Facie Evidence

A properly executed and witnessed self-proving declaration, including a declaration and self-proving affidavit described by Section 1104.152(c), is prima facie evidence that:

(1) the declarant was competent at the time the declarant executed the declaration; and

(2) the guardian named in the declaration would serve the best interests of the ward or incapacitated person.

Derived from Probate Code § 677B(d).

Added by Acts 2011, 82nd Leg., ch. 823, § 1.02, eff. Jan. 1, 2014.

§ 1104.159. Revocation of Declaration

The declarant may revoke a declaration in any manner provided for the revocation of a will under Section 253.002, including the subsequent re-execution of the declaration in the manner required for the original declaration.

Derived from Probate Code § 677A(f).

Added by Acts 2011, 82nd Leg., ch. 823, § 1.02, eff. Jan. 1, 2014.

§ 1104.160. Alternate or Other Court-Appointed Guardian

(a) The court shall appoint the next eligible designated alternate guardian named in a declaration if the designated guardian does not qualify, is deceased, refuses to serve, resigns, or dies after being appointed guardian, or is otherwise unavailable to serve as guardian.

(b) The court shall appoint another person to serve as guardian as otherwise provided by this title if the designated guardian and all designated alternate guardians named in the declaration:

(1) do not qualify;

(2) are deceased;

(3) refuse to serve; or

(4) later die or resign.

Derived from Probate Code § 677A(e).

Added by Acts 2011, 82nd Leg., ch. 823, § 1.02, eff. Jan. 1, 2014.

Subchapter E. Written Declaration to Designate Guardian Before Need Arises

Statutes in Context
Chapter 1104, Subchapter E

Historically, most courts held that they were not required to give weight to an incompetent person's preference for a guardian. An incompetent's opinion was inherently suspect because a person lacking the capacity to handle property may lack the capacity to select a proper guardian and may be more susceptible to undue influence. The modern trend adopted by Texas is to permit a competent individual to designate the individual the person would like the court to appoint as the person's guardian before the onset of incompetency. Thus, should the need for a guardian arise, the court may follow the person's intent which was expressed at a time when the person was competent to do so.

A self-designation of guardian may be holographic or attested. Section 1104.203 sets forth the basic requirements Suggested forms are provided in § 1104.204 (two-step execution procedure with separate self-proving affidavit) and § 1104.205 (one-step execution procedure with integrated self-proving affidavit).

A declarant may also disqualify a person from serving as a guardian even though the person would otherwise have priority. § 1104.204(b). This allows the declarant to, for example, designate the "good" child and disqualify the "bad" child.

Debate exists over whether the same individuals should be named in the self-designation of guardian as in the durable power of attorney (Estates Code Chapter 752) and the medical power of attorney (Health & Safety Code § 166.164). One school of thought is that by naming the same persons, there will be consistency if an "evil" person attempts to take over from the agents by being named as a guardian. On the other hand, if different people are named, it is easier for the agents to be held accountable in case their conduct is less than honorable.

§ 1104.201. Definitions

In this subchapter:

(1) "Declaration" means a written declaration of a person that:

(A) designates another person to serve as a guardian of the person or estate of the declarant; and

(B) satisfies the requirements of this subdivision and Sections 1104.202, 1104.203, 1104.204, 1104.205, 1104.207, 1104.210, 1104.211, and 1104.212.

(2) "Self-proving affidavit" means an affidavit the form and content of which substantially comply with the requirements of Section 1104.204.

(3) "Self-proving declaration" includes a self-proving affidavit that is attached or annexed to a declaration.

Derived from Probate Code §§ 679(j), 679A(a).

Added by Acts 2011, 82nd Leg., ch. 823, § 1.02, eff. Jan. 1, 2014.

§ 1104.202. Designation of Guardian for Declarant

(a) A person other than an incapacitated person may designate by declaration a person to serve as guardian of the person or estate of the declarant if the declarant becomes incapacitated. The court shall appoint the person designated in the declaration to serve as guardian in preference to any other person otherwise entitled to serve as guardian under this title, unless the court finds that the person designated to serve as guardian:

(1) is disqualified; or

(2) would not serve the ward's best interests.

(b) A declarant may, in the declaration, disqualify a named person from serving as guardian of the declarant's person or estate. The court may not under any circumstances appoint as guardian a person named under this subsection.

Derived from Probate Code §§ 679(a), (b), (f).

Added by Acts 2011, 82nd Leg., ch. 823, § 1.02, eff. Jan. 1, 2014.

§ 1104.203. Requirements for Declaration

(a) A declaration under this subchapter must be signed by the declarant and be:

(1) written wholly in the declarant's handwriting; or

(2) attested to in the declarant's presence by at least two credible witnesses who are:

(A) 14 years of age or older; and

(B) not named as guardian or alternate guardian in the declaration.

(b) Notwithstanding Subsection (a), a declaration that is not written wholly in the declarant's handwriting may be signed by another person for the declarant under the direction of and in the presence of the declarant.

(c) A declaration described by Subsection (a)(2) may have attached a self-proving affidavit signed by the declarant and the witnesses attesting to:

(1) the competence of the declarant; and

(2) the execution of the declaration.

Derived from Probate Code §§ 679(a), (c), (d).

Added by Acts 2011, 82nd Leg., ch. 823, § 1.02, eff. Jan. 1, 2014.

§ 1104.204. Form and Content of Declaration and Self-Proving Affidavit

(a) A declaration and affidavit may be in any form adequate to clearly indicate the declarant's intention to designate a guardian.

(b) The following form may be used but is not required to be used:

DECLARATION OF GUARDIAN

IN THE EVENT OF LATER INCAPACITY OR NEED OF GUARDIAN

I, _____, make this Declaration of Guardian, to operate if the need for a guardian for me later arises.

1. I designate _____ to serve as guardian of my person, _____ as first alternate guardian of my person, _____ as second alternate guardian of my person, and _____ as third alternate guardian of my person.

2. I designate _____ to serve as guardian of my estate, _____ as first alternate guardian of my estate, _____ as second alternate guardian of my estate, and _____ as third alternate guardian of my estate.

3. If any guardian or alternate guardian dies, does not qualify, or resigns, the next named alternate guardian becomes my guardian.

4. I expressly disqualify the following persons from serving as guardian of my person: _____, _____, and _____.

5. I expressly disqualify the following persons from serving as guardian of my estate: _____, _____, and _____.

Signed this ___ day of _____, 20__.

_____
Declarant

_____ _____
Witness   Witness

SELF-PROVING AFFIDAVIT

Before me, the undersigned authority, on this date personally appeared _____, the declarant, and _____ and _____ as witnesses, and all being duly sworn, the declarant said that the above instrument was his or her Declaration of Guardian and that the declarant had made and executed it for the purposes expressed in the declaration. The witnesses declared to me that they are each 14 years of age or older, that they saw the declarant sign the declaration, that they signed the declaration as witnesses, and that the declarant appeared to them to be of sound mind.

_____
Declarant

_____ _____
Affiant   Affiant

Subscribed and sworn to before me by the above named declarant and affiants on this ____ day of _____, 20__.

_____
Notary Public in and for the State of Texas
My Commission expires:

Derived from Probate Code § 679(i).

Added by Acts 2011, 82nd Leg., ch. 823, § 1.02, eff. Jan. 1, 2014.

§ 1104.205. Alternative to Self-Proving Affidavit

(a) As an alternative to the self-proving affidavit authorized by Section 1104.204, a declaration of guardian in the event of later incapacity or need of guardian may be simultaneously executed, attested, and made self-proved by including the following in substantially the same form and with substantially the same contents:

I, _____, as declarant, after being duly sworn, declare to the undersigned witnesses and to the undersigned authority that this instrument is my Declaration of Guardian in the Event of Later Incapacity or Need of Guardian, and that I willingly make [have made] and execute [executed] it for the purposes expressed in the declaration. I now sign this declaration in the presence of the attesting witnesses and the undersigned authority on this _____ day of _____, 20__.

_____
Declarant

The undersigned, _____ and _____, each being 14 years of age or older, after being duly sworn, declare to the declarant and to the undersigned authority that the declarant declared to us that this instrument is the declarant's Declaration of Guardian in the Event of Later Incapacity or Need of Guardian and that the declarant executed it for the purposes expressed in the declaration. The declarant then signed this declaration and we believe the declarant to be of sound mind. We now sign our names as attesting witnesses on this _____ day of _____, 20__.

_____
Witness

_____
Witness

Subscribed and sworn to before me by the above named declarant, and affiants, this _____ day of _____, 20__.

_____
Notary Public in and for the State of Texas
My Commission expires:

_____

(b) A declaration that is executed as provided by Subsection (a) is considered self-proved to the same extent a declaration executed with a self-proving affidavit under Section 1104.204 is considered self-proved.

Derived from Probate Code §§ 679(k), (l).

Added by Acts 2011, 82nd Leg., ch. 823, § 1.02, eff. Jan. 1, 2014. Subsec. (a) amended by Acts 2015, 84th Leg., ch. 1031, § 15, eff. Sept. 1, 2015.

§ 1104.206. Alternate Self-Proving of Declaration

At any time during the declarant's lifetime, a declaration described by Section 1104.203(a)(1) may be made self-proved in the same form and manner that a will written wholly in the testator's handwriting is made self-proved under Section 251.107.

Derived from Probate Code § 679A(c).

Added by Acts 2011, 82nd Leg., ch. 823, § 1.02, eff. Jan. 1, 2014.

§ 1104.207. Filing of Declaration and Self-Proving Affidavit

The declaration and any self-proving affidavit may be filed with the court at any time after the application for appointment of a guardian is filed and before a guardian is appointed.

Derived from Probate Code § 679(e).

Added by Acts 2011, 82nd Leg., ch. 823, § 1.02, eff. Jan. 1, 2014.

§ 1104.208. Proof of Declaration

(a) The court may admit a declaration that is self-proved into evidence without the testimony of witnesses attesting to the competency of the declarant and the execution of the declaration. Additional proof of the execution of the declaration with the formalities and solemnities and under the circumstances required to make it a valid declaration is not necessary.

(b) A declaration described by Section 1104.203(a)(1) that is not self-proved may be proved in the same manner that a will written wholly in the testator's handwriting is proved under Section 256.154.

(c) A declaration described by Section 1104.203(a)(2) that is not self-proved may be proved in the same manner that an attested written will produced in court is proved under Section 256.153.

Derived from Probate Code § 679A(b), (e), & (f).

Added by Acts 2011, 82nd Leg., ch. 823, § 1.02, eff. Jan. 1, 2014.

§ 1104.209. Prima Facie Evidence

A properly executed and witnessed self-proving declaration, including a declaration and self-proving affidavit described by Section 1104.203(c), is prima facie evidence that:

(1) the declarant was competent at the time the declarant executed the declaration; and

(2) the guardian named in the declaration would serve the best interests of the ward or incapacitated person.

Derived from Probate Code § 679A(d).

Added by Acts 2011, 82nd Leg., ch. 823, § 1.02, eff. Jan. 1, 2014.

§ 1104.210. Revocation of Declaration

The declarant may revoke a declaration in any manner provided for the revocation of a will under Section 253.002, including the subsequent re-execution of the declaration in the manner required for the original declaration.

Derived from Probate Code § 679(g).

Added by Acts 2011, 82nd Leg., ch. 823, § 1.02, eff. Jan. 1, 2014.

§ 1104.211. Effect of Divorce on Designation of Spouse

If a declarant designates the declarant's spouse to serve as guardian under this subchapter, and the declarant is subsequently divorced from that spouse before a guardian is appointed, the provision of the declaration designating the spouse has no effect.

Derived from Probate Code § 679(h).

Added by Acts 2011, 82nd Leg., ch. 823, § 1.02, eff. Jan. 1, 2014.

§ 1104.212. Alternate or Other Court-Appointed Guardian

(a) The court shall appoint the next eligible designated alternate guardian named in a declaration if the designated guardian does not qualify, is deceased, refuses to serve, resigns, or dies after being appointed guardian, or is otherwise unavailable to serve as guardian.

(b) The court shall appoint another person to serve as guardian as otherwise provided by this title if the designated guardian and all designated alternate guardians named in the declaration:

(1) do not qualify;

(2) are deceased;

(3) refuse to serve; or

(4) later die or resign.

Derived from Probate Code § 679(f).

Added by Acts 2011, 82nd Leg., ch. 823, § 1.02, eff. Jan. 1, 2014.

Subchapter F. Certification Requirements for Certain Guardians

§ 1104.251. Certification Required for Certain Guardians

(a) An individual must be certified under Subchapter C, Chapter 155, Government Code, if the individual:

(1) is a private professional guardian;

(2) will represent the interests of a ward as a guardian on behalf of a private professional guardian;

(3) is providing guardianship services to a ward of a guardianship program on the program's behalf, except as provided by Section 1104.254; or

(4) is an employee of the Department of Aging and Disability Services providing guardianship services to a ward of the department.

(b) An individual employed by or contracting with a guardianship program must be certified as provided by Subsection (a) to provide guardianship services to a ward of the program.

Derived from Probate Code §§ 696A, 697B(a).

Added by Acts 2011, 82nd Leg., ch. 823, § 1.02, eff. Jan. 1, 2014. Subsec. (a) amended by Acts 2013, 83rd Leg., ch. 42, § 2.08, eff. Jan. 1, 2014.

§ 1104.252. Effect of Provisional Certificate

For purposes of this subchapter, a person who holds a provisional certificate issued under Section 155.103, Government Code, is considered to be certified.

Derived from Probate Code § 697B(e).

Added by Acts 2011, 82nd Leg., ch. 823, § 1.02, eff. Jan. 1, 2014. Amended by Acts 2013, 83rd Leg., ch. 42, § 2.09, eff. Jan. 1, 2014.

§ 1104.253. Exception for Family Members and Friends

A family member or friend of an incapacitated person is not required to be certified under Subchapter C, Chapter 155, Government Code, or any other law to serve as the person's guardian.

Derived from Probate Code § 696B.

Added by Acts 2011, 82nd Leg., ch. 823, § 1.02, eff. Jan. 1, 2014. Amended by Acts 2013, 83rd Leg., ch. 42, § 2.10, eff. Jan. 1, 2014.

§ 1104.254. Exception for Certain Volunteers

An individual volunteering with a guardianship program or with the Department of Aging and Disability Services is not required to be certified as provided by Section 1104.251 to provide guardianship services or other services under Section 161.114, Human Resources Code, on the program's or the department's behalf.

Derived from Probate Code § 697B(d).

Added by Acts 2011, 82nd Leg., ch. 823, § 1.02, eff. Jan. 1, 2014. Amended by Acts 2013, 83rd Leg., ch. 161, § 6.038, eff. Jan. 1, 2014.

§ 1104.255. Expiration of Certification

A person whose certification under Subchapter C, Chapter 155, Government Code, has expired must obtain a new certification under that subchapter to provide or continue providing guardianship services to a ward or incapacitated person under this title.

Derived from Probate Code § 697B(b).

Added by Acts 2011, 82nd Leg., ch. 823, § 1.02, eff. Jan. 1, 2014. Amended by Acts 2013, 83rd Leg., ch. 42, § 2.11, eff. Jan. 1, 2014.

§ 1104.256. Failure to Comply; Court's Duty to Notify

The court shall notify the guardianship certification program of the Judicial Branch Certification Commission if the court becomes aware of a person who is not complying with:

(1) the terms of a certification issued under Subchapter C, Chapter 155, Government Code; or

(2) the standards and rules adopted under that subchapter.

Derived from Probate Code § 697B(c).

Added by Acts 2011, 82nd Leg., ch. 823, § 1.02, eff. Jan. 1, 2014. Amended by Acts 2013, 83rd Leg., ch. 41, § 2.12, eff. Jan. 1, 2014.

§ 1104.257. Information Regarding Services Provided by Guardianship Program

Not later than January 31 of each year, each guardianship program operating in a county shall submit to the county clerk a copy of the report submitted to the guardianship certification program of the Judicial Branch Certification Commission under Section 155.105, Government Code.

Derived from Probate Code § 697A(a).

Added by Acts 2011, 82nd Leg., ch. 823, § 1.02, eff. Jan. 1, 2014. Amended by Acts 2013, 83rd Leg., ch. 42, § 2.13, eff. Jan. 1, 2014.

§ 1104.258. Information Regarding Certain State Employees Providing Guardianship Services

Not later than January 31 of each year, the Department of Aging and Disability Services shall submit to the guardianship certification program of the Judicial Branch Certification Commission a statement containing:

(1) the name, address, and telephone number of each department employee who is or will be providing guardianship services to a ward or proposed ward on the department's behalf; and

(2) the name of each county in which each employee named in Subdivision (1) is providing or is authorized to provide those services.

Derived from Probate Code § 697A(b).

Added by Acts 2011, 82nd Leg., ch. 823, § 1.02, eff. Jan. 1, 2014. Amended by Acts 2013, 83rd Leg., ch. 42, § 2.14, eff. Jan. 1, 2014.

Subchapter G. Private Professional Guardians

§ 1104.301. Certification and Registration Required

A court may not appoint a private professional guardian to serve as a guardian or permit a private professional guardian to continue to serve as a guardian under this title if the private professional guardian is not:

(1) certified as provided by Section 1104.251(a), 1104.252, 1104.255, or 1104.256; or

(2) in compliance with the registration requirements of this subchapter.

Derived from Probate Code § 696.

Added by Acts 2011, 82nd Leg., ch. 823, § 1.02, eff. Jan. 1, 2014.

§ 1104.302. Annual Certificate of Registration

A private professional guardian must annually apply for a certificate of registration.

Derived from Probate Code § 697(a).

Added by Acts 2011, 82nd Leg., ch. 823, § 1.02, eff. Jan. 1, 2014.

§ 1104.303. Requirements of Application

(a) An application for a certificate of registration must include a sworn statement containing the following information concerning a private professional guardian or each person who represents or plans to represent the interests of a ward as a guardian on behalf of the private professional guardian:

(1) place of residence;

(2) business address and business telephone number;

(3) educational background and professional experience;

(4) three or more professional references;

(5) the name of each ward for whom the private professional guardian or person is or will be serving as a guardian;

(6) the aggregate fair market value of the property of all wards that is or will be managed by the private professional guardian or person;

(7) whether the private professional guardian or person has ever been removed as a guardian by the court or resigned as a guardian in a particular case, and, if so:

(A) a description of the circumstances causing the removal or resignation; and

(B) the style of the suit, the docket number, and the court having jurisdiction over the proceeding; and

(8) the certification number or provisional certification number issued to the private professional guardian or person by the guardianship certification program of the Judicial Branch Certification Commission.

(b) The application must be:

(1) made to the clerk of the county having venue of the proceeding for the appointment of a guardian; and

(2) accompanied by a nonrefundable fee of $40 to cover the cost of administering this subchapter.

Derived from Probate Code § 697(a) & (b).

Added by Acts 2011, 82nd Leg., ch. 823, § 1.02, eff. Jan. 1, 2014. Subsec. (a) amended by Acts 2013, 83rd Leg., ch. 42, § 2.15, eff. Jan. 1, 2014. Subsec. (b) amended by Acts 2013, 83rd Leg., ch. 982, § 13, eff. Jan. 1, 2014.

§ 1104.304. Term of Registration; Renewal

(a) The term of an initial registration begins on the date the requirements under Section 1104.303 are met and extends through December 31 of the year in which the application is made. After the term of the initial registration, the term of registration begins on January 1 and extends through December 31 of each year.

(b) An application to renew a registration must be completed during December of the year preceding the year for which the renewal is requested.

Derived from Probate Code § 697(c).

Added by Acts 2011, 82nd Leg., ch. 823, § 1.02, eff. Jan. 1, 2014.

§ 1104.305. Use of Registration Information

(a) The clerk shall bring the information received under Section 1104.303 to the judge's attention for review.

(b) The judge shall use the information only to determine whether to appoint, remove, or continue the appointment of a private professional guardian.

Derived from Probate Code § 697(d).

Added by Acts 2011, 82nd Leg., ch. 823, § 1.02, eff. Jan. 1, 2014.

§ 1104.306. Use of Names and Business Addresses

Not later than January 31 of each year, the clerk shall submit to the guardianship certification program of the Judicial Branch Certification Commission the name and business address of each private professional guardian who has satisfied the registration requirements of this subchapter during the preceding year.

Derived from Probate Code § 697(e).

Added by Acts 2011, 82nd Leg., ch. 823, § 1.02, eff. Jan. 1, 2014. Amended by Acts 2013, 83rd Leg., ch. 42, § 2.16, eff. Jan. 1, 2014.

Subchapter H. Grounds for Disqualification

§ 1104.351. Incapacity or Inexperience

A person may not be appointed guardian if the person is:

(1) a minor or other incapacitated person; or

(2) a person who, because of inexperience, lack of education, or other good reason, is incapable of properly and prudently managing and controlling the person or estate of the ward.

Derived from Probate Code § 681.

Added by Acts 2011, 82nd Leg., ch. 823, § 1.02, eff. Jan. 1, 2014.

§ 1104.352. Unsuitability

A person may not be appointed guardian if the person is a person, institution, or corporation found by the court to be unsuitable.

Derived from Probate Code § 681.

Added by Acts 2011, 82nd Leg., ch. 823, § 1.02, eff. Jan. 1, 2014. Amended by Acts 2013, 83rd Leg., ch. 161, § 6.039, eff. Jan. 1, 2014.

§ 1104.353. Notoriously Bad Conduct; Presumption Concerning Best Interest

(a) A person may not be appointed guardian if the person's conduct is notoriously bad.

(b) It is presumed to be not in the best interests of a ward or incapacitated person to appoint as guardian of the ward or incapacitated person a person who has been finally convicted of:

(1) any sexual offense, including sexual assault, aggravated sexual assault, and prohibited sexual conduct;

(2) aggravated assault;

(3) injury to a child, elderly individual, or disabled individual;

(4) abandoning or endangering a child;

(5) terroristic threat; or

(6) continuous violence against the family of the ward or incapacitated person.

Derived from Probate Code §§ 678 & 681.

Added by Acts 2011, 82nd Leg., ch. 823, § 1.02, eff. Jan. 1, 2014. Subsec. (b) amended by Acts 2013, 83rd Leg., ch. 982, § 14, eff. Jan. 1, 2014.

§ 1104.354. Conflict of Interest

A person may not be appointed guardian if the person:

(1) is a party or is a person whose parent is a party to a lawsuit concerning or affecting the welfare of the proposed ward, unless the court:

(A) determines that the lawsuit claim of the person who has applied to be appointed guardian is not in conflict with the lawsuit claim of the proposed ward; or

(B) appoints a guardian ad litem to represent the interests of the proposed ward throughout the litigation of the ward's lawsuit claim;

(2) is indebted to the proposed ward, unless the person pays the debt before appointment; or

(3) asserts a claim adverse to the proposed ward or the proposed ward's property.

Derived from Probate Code § 681.

Added by Acts 2011, 82nd Leg., ch. 823, § 1.02, eff. Jan. 1, 2014.

§ 1104.355. Disqualified in Declaration

A person may not be appointed guardian if the person is disqualified in a declaration under Section 1104.202(b).

Derived from Probate Code § 681.

Added by Acts 2011, 82nd Leg., ch. 823, § 1.02, eff. Jan. 1, 2014.

§ 1104.356. Lack of Certain Required Certification

A person may not be appointed guardian if the person does not have the certification to serve as guardian that is required by Subchapter F.

Derived from Probate Code § 681.

Added by Acts 2011, 82nd Leg., ch. 823, § 1.02, eff. Jan. 1, 2014.

§ 1104.357. Nonresident Without Resident Agent

A person may not be appointed guardian if the person is a nonresident who has failed to file with the court the name of a resident agent to accept service of process in all actions or proceedings relating to the guardianship.

Derived from Probate Code § 681.

Added by Acts 2011, 82nd Leg., ch. 823, § 1.02, eff. Jan. 1, 2014.

§ 1104.358. Subject to Protective Order for Family Violence

A person found to have committed family violence who is subject to a protective order issued under Chapter 85, Family Code, may not be appointed guardian of a proposed ward or ward who is protected by the protective order.

Added by Acts 2013, 83rd Leg., ch. 982, § 15, eff. Jan. 1, 2014.

Subchapter I. Access to Criminal History Records

§ 1104.401. Definition.

In this subchapter, "department" means the Department of Aging and Disability Services.

New.

Added by Acts 2011, 82nd Leg., ch. 823, § 1.02, eff. Jan. 1, 2014.

§ 1104.402. Court Clerk's Duty to Obtain Criminal History Record Information; Authority to Charge Fee

(a) Except as provided by Section 1104.403, 1104.404, or 1104.406(a), the clerk of the county having venue of the proceeding for the appointment of a guardian shall obtain criminal history record information that is maintained by the Department of Public Safety or the Federal Bureau of Investigation identification division relating to:

(1) a private professional guardian;

(2) each person who represents or plans to represent the interests of a ward as a guardian on behalf of the private professional guardian;

(3) each person employed by a private professional guardian who will:

(A) have personal contact with a ward or proposed ward;

(B) exercise control over and manage a ward's estate; or

(C) perform any duties with respect to the management of a ward's estate;

(4) each person employed by or volunteering or contracting with a guardianship program to provide guardianship services to a ward of the program on the program's behalf; or

(5) any other person proposed to serve as a guardian under this title, including a proposed temporary guardian and a proposed successor guardian, other than [the ward's or proposed ward's family member or] an attorney.

(b) The clerk may charge a $10 fee to recover the costs of obtaining criminal history record information under Subsection (a).

Derived from Probate Code §§ 698(a), (e).

Added by Acts 2011, 82nd Leg., ch. 823, § 1.02, eff. Jan. 1, 2014. Subsec. (a)(5) amended by Acts 2015, 84th

Leg., ch. 1031, § 16, eff. Sept. 1, 2015.

§ 1104.403. Submission of Criminal History Record Information by Proposed Guardian

Not later than the 10th day before the date of the hearing to appoint a guardian, a person may submit to the clerk a copy of the person's criminal history record information required under Section 1104.402(a)(5) that the person obtains not earlier than the 30th day before the date of the hearing from:

(1) the Department of Public Safety; or

(2) the Federal Bureau of Investigation.

Derived from Probate Code § 698(a-5).

Added by Acts 2011, 82nd Leg., ch. 823, § 1.02, eff. Jan. 1, 2014.

§ 1104.404. Exception for Information Concerning Certain Persons Holding a Certificate

(a) The clerk described by Section 1104.402 is not required to obtain criminal history record information for a person who holds a certificate issued under Section 155.102, Government Code, or a provisional certificate issued under Section 155.103, Government Code, if the guardianship certification program of the Judicial Branch Certification Commission conducted a criminal history check on the person before issuing or renewing the certificate.

(b) The board shall provide to the clerk at the court's request the criminal history record information that was obtained from the Department of Public Safety or the Federal Bureau of Investigation.

Derived from Probate Code § 698(a-6).

Added by Acts 2011, 82nd Leg., ch. 823, § 1.02, eff. Jan. 1, 2014. Subsec. (a) amended by Acts 2013, 83rd Leg., ch. 42, § 2.17, eff. Jan. 1, 2014.

§ 1104.405. Information for Exclusive Use of Court

(a) Criminal history record information obtained or provided under Section 1104.402, 1104.403, or 1104.404 is privileged and confidential and is for the exclusive use of the court. The criminal history record information may not be released or otherwise disclosed to any person or agency except on court order or consent of the person being investigated.

(b) The county clerk may destroy the criminal history record information after the information is used for the purposes authorized by this subchapter.

Derived from Probate Code § 698(b).

Added by Acts 2011, 82nd Leg., ch. 823, § 1.02, eff. Jan. 1, 2014.

§ 1104.406. Department's Duty to Obtain Criminal History Record Information

(a) The department shall obtain criminal history record information that is maintained by the Department of Public Safety or the Federal Bureau of Investigation identification division relating to each individual who is

413

or will be providing guardianship services to a ward of or referred by the department, including:

(1) an employee of or an applicant selected for an employment position with the department;

(2) a volunteer or an applicant selected to volunteer with the department;

(3) an employee of or an applicant selected for an employment position with a business entity or other person who contracts with the department to provide guardianship services to a ward referred by the department; [and]

(4) a volunteer or an applicant selected to volunteer with a business entity or other person described by Subdivision (3); and

(5) a contractor or an employee of a contractor who provides services to a ward of the Department of Aging and Disability Services under a contract with the estate of the ward.

(b) The department must obtain the information in Subsection (a) before:

(1) making an offer of employment to an applicant for an employment position; or

(2) a volunteer contacts a ward of or referred by the department.

(c) The department must annually obtain the information in Subsection (a) regarding employees, contractors, or volunteers providing guardianship services.

Derived from Probate Code §§ 698(a-1), (a-2), (a-3).

Added by Acts 2011, 82nd Leg., ch. 823, § 1.02, eff. Jan. 1, 2014. Subsecs (a) & (c) amended by Acts 2015, 84th Leg., ch. 1, § 6.025, eff. Apr. 2, 2015.

§ 1104.407. Duty to Provide Information on Request

The department shall provide the information obtained under Section 1104.406(a) to:

(1) the clerk of the county having venue of the guardianship proceeding at the court's request; and

(2) the guardianship certification program of the Judicial Branch Certification Commission at the commission's request.

Derived from Probate Code § 698(a-4).

Added by Acts 2011, 82nd Leg., ch. 823, § 1.02, eff. Jan. 1, 2014. Amended by Acts 2013, 83rd Leg., ch. 42, § 2.18, eff. Jan. 1, 2014.

§ 1104.408. Information for Exclusive Use of Court or Guardianship Certification Program of Judicial Branch Certification Commission

(a) Criminal history record information obtained under Section 1104.407 is privileged and confidential and is for the exclusive use of the court or guardianship certification program of the Judicial Branch Certification Commission, as appropriate. The information may not be released or otherwise disclosed to any person or agency except:

(1) on court order;

(2) with the consent of the person being investigated; or

(3) as authorized by Section 1104.404 of this code or Section 411.1386(a-6), Government Code.

(b) The county clerk or guardianship certification program of the Judicial Branch Certification Commission may destroy the criminal history record information after the information is used for the purposes authorized by this subchapter.

Derived from Probate Code § 698(b-1).

Added by Acts 2011, 82nd Leg., ch. 823, § 1.02, eff. Jan. 1, 2014. Amended by Acts 2013, 83rd Leg., ch. 42, § 2.19, eff. Jan. 1, 2014.

§ 1104.409. Use of Information by Court

The court shall use the information obtained under this subchapter only in determining whether to:

(1) appoint, remove, or continue the appointment of a private professional guardian, a guardianship program, or the department; or

(2) appoint any other person proposed to serve as a guardian under this title, including a proposed temporary guardian and a proposed successor guardian, other than [the ward's or proposed ward's family member or] an attorney.

Derived from Probate Code § 698(c).

Added by Acts 2011, 82nd Leg., ch. 823, § 1.02, eff. Jan. 1, 2014. Subsec. (2) amended by Acts 2015, 84th Leg., ch. 1031, § 17, eff. Sept. 1, 2015.

§ 1104.410. Use of Information by Guardianship Certification Program of Judicial Branch Certification Commission

Criminal history record information obtained by the guardianship certification program of the Judicial Branch Certification Commission under Section 1104.407(2) may be used for any purpose related to the issuance, denial, renewal, suspension, or revocation of a certificate issued by the commission.

Derived from Probate Code § 698(c-1).

Added by Acts 2011, 82nd Leg., ch. 823, § 1.02, eff. Jan. 1, 2014. Amended by Acts 2013, 83rd Leg., ch. 42, § 2.20, eff. Jan. 1, 2014.

§ 1104.411. Criminal Offense for Unauthorized Release or Disclosure

(a) A person commits an offense if the person releases or discloses any information received under this subchapter without the authorization prescribed by Section 1104.405 or 1104.408.

(b) An offense under this section is a Class A misdemeanor.

Derived from Probate Code § 698(d).

Added by Acts 2011, 82nd Leg., ch. 823, § 1.02, eff. Jan. 1, 2014.

§ 1104.412. Effect of Subchapter on Department's Authority to Obtain or Use Information

This subchapter does not prohibit the department from obtaining and using criminal history record information as provided by other law.

Derived from Probate Code § 698(f).

Added by Acts 2011, 82nd Leg., ch. 823, § 1.02, eff. Jan. 1, 2014.

Chapter 1105. Qualification of Guardians

Subchapter A. General Provisions

Subchapter B. Oaths

Subchapter C. General Provisions Relating to Bonds

Subchapter D. Other Provisions Relating to Bonds of Guardians of the Estate

Subchapter E. Provisions Relating to Personal Sureties

Subchapter F. New Bonds

Chapter 1105. Qualification of Guardians

Subchapter A. General Provisions

§ 1105.001. Definitions

In this chapter:

(1) "Bond" means a bond required by this chapter to be given by a person appointed to serve as a guardian.

(2) "Oath" means an oath required by this chapter to be taken by a person appointed to serve as a guardian.

New.

Added by Acts 2011, 82nd Leg., ch. 823, § 1.02, eff. Jan. 1, 2014.

§ 1105.002. Manner of Qualification of Guardian

(a) Except as provided by Subsection (b), a guardian is considered to have qualified when the guardian has:

(1) taken and filed the oath required under Section 1105.051;

(2) given the required bond;

(3) filed the bond with the clerk; and

(4) obtained the judge's approval of the bond.

(b) A guardian who is not required to give a bond is considered to have qualified when the guardian has taken and filed the required oath.

Derived from Probate Code § 699.

Added by Acts 2011, 82nd Leg., ch. 823, § 1.02, eff. Jan. 1, 2014.

§ 1105.003. Period for Taking Oath and Giving Bond

(a) Except as provided by Section 1103.003, an oath may be taken and subscribed and a bond may be given and approved at any time before:

(1) the 21st day after the date of the order granting letters of guardianship; or

(2) the letters of guardianship are revoked for a failure to qualify within the period allowed.

(b) A guardian of an estate must give a bond before being issued letters of guardianship unless a bond is not required under this title.

Derived from Probate Code §§ 701, 703(a).

Added by Acts 2011, 82nd Leg., ch. 823, § 1.02, eff. Jan. 1, 2014.

Subchapter B. Oaths

§ 1105.051. Oath of Guardian

(a) A guardian shall take an oath to discharge faithfully the duties of guardian for the person or estate, or both, of a ward.

(b) If the Department of Aging and Disability Services is appointed guardian, a department representative shall take the oath required by Subsection (a).

Derived from Probate Code § 700.

Added by Acts 2011, 82nd Leg., ch. 823, § 1.02, eff. Jan. 1, 2014.

§ 1105.052. Administration of Oath

An oath may be taken before any person authorized to administer oaths under the laws of this state.

Derived from Probate Code § 701.

Added by Acts 2011, 82nd Leg., ch. 823, § 1.02, eff. Jan. 1, 2014.

Subchapter C. General Provisions Relating to Bonds

§ 1105.101. Bond Generally Required; Exceptions

(a) Except as provided by this section, a guardian of the person or the estate of a ward shall give a bond.

(b) A bond is not required if the guardian is:

(1) a corporate fiduciary; or

(2) a guardianship program operated by a county.

(c) The court shall issue letters of guardianship of the person to a person without the requirement of a bond if:

(1) the person is named to be appointed guardian in a will made by a surviving parent that is probated by a court in this state, or in a written declaration made by a surviving parent, and the will or declaration directs that the guardian serve without a bond; and

(2) the court finds that the guardian is qualified.

(d) The court may not waive the requirement of bond for the guardian of the estate of a ward, regardless of whether a surviving parent's will or written declaration directs the court to waive the bond.

Derived from Probate Code § 702.

Added by Acts 2011, 82nd Leg., ch. 823, § 1.02, eff. Jan. 1, 2014.

§ 1105.102. Bond for Certain Guardians of the Person

(a) This section applies only to a bond required to be posted by a guardian of the person of a ward when there is no guardian of the ward's estate.

(b) To ensure the performance of the guardian's duties, a court may accept only:

(1) a corporate surety bond;

(2) a personal surety bond;

(3) a deposit of money instead of a surety bond; or

(4) a personal bond.

(c) In determining the appropriate type and amount of bond to set for the guardian, the court shall consider:

(1) the familial relationship of the guardian to the ward;

(2) the guardian's ties to the community;

(3) the guardian's financial condition;

(4) the guardian's past history of compliance with the court; and

(5) the reason the guardian may have previously been denied a corporate surety bond.

Derived from Probate Code § 702A.

Added by Acts 2011, 82nd Leg., ch. 823, § 1.02, eff. Jan. 1, 2014.

§ 1105.103. Bond Required from Guardian Otherwise Exempt

(a) This section applies only to an individual guardian of the estate from whom a bond was not required.

(b) A person who has a debt, claim, or demand against the guardianship, with respect to the justice of which an oath has been made by the person, the person's agent or attorney, or another person interested in the guardianship, in person or as the representative of another person, may file a written complaint under oath in the court in which the guardian was appointed.

(c) After a complaint is filed under Subsection (b), the court shall cite the guardian to appear and show cause why the guardian should not be required to give a bond.

(d) On hearing a complaint filed under Subsection (b), if it appears to the court that the guardian is wasting, mismanaging, or misapplying the guardianship estate and that a creditor may probably lose the creditor's debt, or that a person's interest in the guardianship may be diminished or lost, the court shall enter an order requiring the guardian to give a bond not later than the 10th day after the date of the order.

(e) A bond required under Subsection (d) must be:

(1) in an amount sufficient to protect the guardianship and the guardianship's creditors;

(2) approved by and payable to the judge; and

(3) conditioned that the guardian:

(A) will well and truly administer the guardianship; and

(B) will not waste, mismanage, or misapply the guardianship estate.

(f) If the guardian fails to give the bond required under Subsection (d) and the judge has not extended the period for giving the bond, the judge, without citation, shall remove the guardian and appoint a competent person as guardian, who shall:

(1) administer the guardianship according to the provisions of a will or law;

(2) take the oath required of a guardian under Section 1105.051 before the person enters on the administration of the guardianship; and

(3) give bond in the same manner and in the same amount provided by this title for the issuance of original letters of guardianship.

Derived from Probate Code §§ 722, 723, 724, 725.

Added by Acts 2011, 82nd Leg., ch. 823, § 1.02, eff. Jan. 1, 2014.

§ 1105.104. Bonds of Joint Guardians

If two or more persons are appointed as guardians and are required to give a bond by the court or under this title, the court may require:

(1) a separate bond from each person; or

(2) a joint bond from all of the persons.

Derived from Probate Code § 706.

Added by Acts 2011, 82nd Leg., ch. 823, § 1.02, eff. Jan. 1, 2014.

§ 1105.105. Bond of Married Person

(a) A married person appointed as guardian may jointly execute, with or without, the person's spouse, a bond required by law.

(b) A bond executed by a married person:

(1) binds the person's separate estate; and

(2) may bind the person's spouse only if the spouse signs the bond.

Derived from Probate Code § 707.

Added by Acts 2011, 82nd Leg., ch. 823, § 1.02, eff. Jan. 1, 2014.

§ 1105.106. Bond of Married Person Younger Than 18 Years of Age

A bond required to be executed by a person who is younger than 18 years of age, is or has been married, and accepts and qualifies as guardian is as valid and binding for all purposes as if the person were of legal age.

Derived from Probate Code § 708.

Added by Acts 2011, 82nd Leg., ch. 823, § 1.02, eff. Jan. 1, 2014.

§ 1105.107. Bond of Guardianship Program

The judge may require a guardianship program appointed guardian under this title to file one bond that:

(1) meets all the conditions required under this title; and

(2) is in an amount sufficient to protect all of the guardianships and the creditors of the guardianships of the wards receiving services from the guardianship program.

Derived from Probate Code § 708A.

Added by Acts 2011, 82nd Leg., ch. 823, § 1.02, eff. Jan. 1, 2014.

§ 1105.108. Subscription of Bond by Principals and Sureties

A bond required under this title shall be subscribed by the principals and sureties.

Derived from Probate Code § 705.

Added by Acts 2011, 82nd Leg., ch. 823, § 1.02, eff. Jan. 1, 2014.

§ 1105.109. Form of Bond

The following form, or a form with the same substance, may be used for the bond of a guardian:

"The State of Texas

"County of _____

"Know all persons by these presents that we, _____ (insert name of each principal), as principal, and ____ (insert name of each surety), as sureties, are held and firmly bound to the judge of ____ (insert reference to appropriate judge), and that judge's successors in office, in the sum of $_____; conditioned that the above bound principal or principals, appointed by the judge as guardian or temporary guardian of the person or of the estate, or both, of _____ (insert name of ward, stating in each case whether the person is a minor or an incapacitated person other than a minor), shall well and truly perform all of the duties required of the guardian or temporary guardian by law under appointment."

Derived from Probate Code § 704.

Added by Acts 2011, 82nd Leg., ch. 823, § 1.02, eff. Jan. 1, 2014.

§ 1105.110. Filing of Bond

A bond required under this title shall be filed with the clerk after the court approves the bond.

Derived from Probate Code § 705.

Added by Acts 2011, 82nd Leg., ch. 823, § 1.02, eff. Jan. 1, 2014.

§ 1105.111. Failure to Give Bond

Another person may be appointed as guardian to replace a guardian who fails to give the bond required by the court within the period required under this title.

Derived from Probate Code § 721.

Added by Acts 2011, 82nd Leg., ch. 823, § 1.02, eff. Jan. 1, 2014.

§ 1105.112. Bond Not Void on First Recovery

A guardian's bond is not void on the first recovery, but the bond may be sued on and prosecuted from time to time until the entire amount of the bond is recovered.

Derived from Probate Code § 726.

Added by Acts 2011, 82nd Leg., ch. 823, § 1.02, eff. Jan. 1, 2014.

Subchapter D. Other Provisions Relating to Bonds of Guardians of the Estate

§ 1105.151. General Formalities

A bond given by a guardian of the estate must:

(1) be conditioned as required by law;

(2) be payable to the judge or that judge's successors in office;

(3) have the written approval of the judge in the judge's official capacity; and

(4) be executed and approved in accordance with this subchapter.

Derived from Probate Code § 703(a).

Added by Acts 2011, 82nd Leg., ch. 823, § 1.02, eff. Jan. 1, 2014.

§ 1105.152. General Standard Regarding Amount of Bond

(a) The judge shall set the amount of a bond for a guardian of an estate in an amount sufficient to protect the guardianship and the guardianship's creditors, as provided by this title.

(b) In determining the amount of the bond, the court may not consider estate assets placed in a management trust under Chapter 1301.

Derived from Probate Code §§ 703(b), (s).

Added by Acts 2011, 82nd Leg., ch. 823, § 1.02, eff. Jan. 1, 2014.

§ 1105.153. Evidentiary Hearing on Amount of Bond

Before setting the amount of a bond required of a guardian of an estate, the court shall hear evidence and determine:

(1) the amount of cash on hand and where that cash is deposited;

(2) the amount of cash estimated to be needed for administrative purposes, including the operation of a business, factory, farm, or ranch owned by the guardianship estate, and administrative expenses for one year;

(3) the revenue anticipated to be received in the succeeding 12 months from dividends, interest, rentals, or use of property belonging to the guardianship estate and the aggregate amount of any installments or periodic payments to be collected;

(4) the estimated value of certificates of stock, bonds, notes, or other securities of the ward, and the name of the depository in which the stocks, bonds, notes, or other securities are deposited;

(5) the face value of life insurance or other policies payable to the ward or the ward's estate;

(6) the estimated value of other personal property that is owned by the guardianship, or by a person with a disability; and

(7) the estimated amount of debts due and owing by the ward.

Derived from Probate Code § 703(c).

Added by Acts 2011, 82nd Leg., ch. 823, § 1.02, eff. Jan. 1, 2014.

§ 1105.154. Specific Bond Amount

(a) Except as otherwise provided by this section, the judge shall set the amount of a bond of a guardian of an estate in an amount equal to the sum of:

(1) the estimated value of all personal property belonging to the ward; and

(2) an additional amount to cover revenue anticipated to be derived during the succeeding 12 months from:

(A) interest and dividends;

(B) collectible claims;

(C) the aggregate amount of any installments or periodic payments, excluding income derived or to be derived from federal social security payments; and

(D) rentals for the use of property.

(b) The judge shall reduce the amount of the original bond under Subsection (a) in proportion to the amount of cash or the value of securities or other assets:

(1) authorized or required to be deposited by court order; or

(2) voluntarily deposited by the guardian or the sureties on the guardian's bond as provided in Sections 1105.156 and 1105.157(a).

(c) The judge shall set the amount of the bond for a temporary guardian.

Derived from Probate Code §§ 703(d), (q).

Added by Acts 2011, 82nd Leg., ch. 823, § 1.02, eff. Jan. 1, 2014.

§ 1105.155. Agreement Regarding Deposit of Estate Assets

(a) If the court considers it to be in the best interests of the ward, the court may require the guardian of the estate and the corporate or personal sureties on the guardian's bond to agree to deposit cash and other assets of the guardianship estate in a depository described by Subsection (b). If the depository is otherwise proper, the court may require the deposit to be made in a manner so as to prevent the withdrawal of the money or other assets in the guardianship estate without the written consent of the surety or on court order made after notice to the surety.

(b) Cash and assets must be deposited under this section in a financial institution as defined by Section 201.101, Finance Code, that:

(1) has its main office or a branch office in this state; and

(2) is qualified to act as a depository in this state under the laws of this state or the United States.

(c) An agreement made by a guardian and the sureties on the guardian's bond under this section does not release the principal or sureties from liability, or change the liability of the principal or sureties, as established by the terms of the bond.

Derived from Probate Code § 703(e).

Added by Acts 2011, 82nd Leg., ch. 823, § 1.02, eff. Jan. 1, 2014.

§ 1105.156. Deposit of Estate Assets on Terms Prescribed by Court

(a) Cash, securities, or other personal assets of a ward to which the ward is entitled may, or if considered by the court to be in the best interests of the ward, shall, be deposited in one or more depositories described by this subchapter on terms prescribed by the court.

(b) The court in which the guardianship proceeding is pending may authorize or require additional estate assets currently on hand or that accrue during the pendency of the proceeding to be deposited as provided by Subsection (a) on:

(1) the court's own motion; or

(2) the written application of the guardian or any other person interested in the ward.

(c) The amount of the bond required to be given by the guardian of the estate shall be reduced in proportion to the amount of the cash or the value of the securities or other assets deposited under this section.

(d) Cash, securities, or other assets deposited under this section may be withdrawn wholly or partly from the depository only in accordance with a court order, and the amount of the guardian's bond shall be increased in proportion to the amount of the cash or the value of the securities or other assets authorized to be withdrawn.

Derived from Probate Code § 703(f).

Added by Acts 2011, 82nd Leg., ch. 823, § 1.02, eff. Jan. 1, 2014.

§ 1105.157. Deposits of Guardian

(a) Instead of giving a surety or sureties on a bond, or to reduce the amount of a bond, the guardian of an estate may deposit the guardian's own cash or securities acceptable to the court with a financial institution as defined by Section 201.101, Finance Code, that has its main office or a branch office in this state.

(b) If the deposit is otherwise proper, the deposit must be in an amount or value equal to the amount of the bond required or the bond shall be reduced by the value of assets that are deposited.

(c) A depository that receives a deposit made under Subsection (a) shall issue a receipt for the deposit that:

(1) shows the amount of cash deposited or the amount and description of the securities deposited, as applicable; and

(2) states that the depository agrees to disburse or deliver the cash or securities only on receipt of a certified copy of an order of the court in which the proceeding is pending.

(d) A receipt issued by a depository under Subsection (c) must be attached to the guardian's bond and be delivered to and filed by the county clerk after the receipt is approved by the judge.

(e) The amount of cash or securities on deposit may be increased or decreased, by court order from time to time, as the interests of the guardianship require.

(f) A deposit of cash or securities made instead of a surety on the bond may be withdrawn or released only on order of a court that has jurisdiction.

(g) A creditor has the same rights against a guardian of the estate and the deposits as are provided for recovery against sureties on a bond.

Derived from Probate Code §§ 703(g), (h), (i), (j), (k).

Added by Acts 2011, 82nd Leg., ch. 823, § 1.02, eff. Jan. 1, 2014.

§ 1105.158. Bond Required Instead of Deposits

(a) The court may on its own motion or on the written application by the guardian of an estate or any other person interested in the guardianship:

(1) require the guardian to give adequate bond instead of the deposit; or

(2) authorize withdrawal of the deposit and substitution of a bond with sureties.

(b) Before the 21st day after the date the guardian is personally served with notice of the filing of the application or the date the court enters the court's motion, the guardian shall file a sworn statement showing the condition of the guardianship.

(c) A guardian who fails to comply with Subsection (b) is subject to removal as in other cases.

(d) The deposit may not be released or withdrawn until the court:

(1) is satisfied as to the condition of the guardianship estate;

(2) determines the amount of the bond; and

(3) receives and approves the bond.

Derived from Probate Code § 703(l).

Added by Acts 2011, 82nd Leg., ch. 823, § 1.02, eff. Jan. 1, 2014.

§ 1105.159. Withdrawal of Deposits on Closing of Guardianship

(a) Any deposit of assets of the guardian of an estate, the guardianship, or a surety that remains at the time a guardianship is closed shall be released by court order and paid to the person entitled to the assets.

(b) Except as provided by Subsection (c), a writ of attachment or garnishment does not lie against a deposit described by Subsection (a).

(c) A writ of attachment or garnishment may lie against a deposit described by Subsection (a) as to a claim of a creditor of the guardianship or a person interested in the guardianship, including a distributee or ward, only to the extent the court has ordered distribution.

Derived from Probate Code § 703(m).

Added by Acts 2011, 82nd Leg., ch. 823, § 1.02, eff. Jan. 1, 2014.

§ 1105.160. Authorized Corporate or Personal Sureties

(a) The surety on a bond of a guardian of an estate may be an authorized corporate or personal surety.

(b) A bond of a guardian of an estate with sureties who are individuals must have at least two sureties, each of whom must:

(1) execute an affidavit in the manner provided by Subchapter E; and

(2) own property in this state, excluding property exempt by law, that the judge is satisfied is sufficient to qualify the person as a surety as required by law.

(c) A bond with an authorized corporate surety is only required to have one surety, except as otherwise provided by law.

Derived from Probate Code §§ 703(n), (p).

Added by Acts 2011, 82nd Leg., ch. 823, § 1.02, eff. Jan. 1, 2014.

§ 1105.161. Sureties for Certain Bonds

(a) If the amount of the bond of a guardian of an estate exceeds $50,000, the court may require that the bond be signed by:

(1) at least two authorized corporate sureties; or

(2) one corporate surety and at least two good and sufficient personal sureties.

(b) The guardianship shall pay the cost of a bond with corporate sureties.

Derived from Probate Code § 703(o).

Added by Acts 2011, 82nd Leg., ch. 823, § 1.02, eff. Jan. 1, 2014.

§ 1105.162. Deposits by Personal Surety

Instead of executing an affidavit under Section 1105.201 or creating a lien under Section 1105.202 when required, a personal surety may deposit the surety's own cash or securities in the same manner as a guardian instead of pledging real property as security, subject to the provisions governing the deposits if made by a guardian.

Derived from Probate Code § 703(p).

Added by Acts 2011, 82nd Leg., ch. 823, § 1.02, eff. Jan. 1, 2014.

§ 1105.163. Applicability of Subchapter to Certain Court Orders

To the extent applicable, the provisions of this subchapter relating to the deposit of cash and securities cover the orders entered by the court when:

(1) property of a guardianship has been authorized to be sold or rented;

(2) money is borrowed from the guardianship;

(3) real property, or an interest in real property, has been authorized to be leased for mineral development or made subject to unitization;

(4) the general bond has been found insufficient; or

(5) money is borrowed or invested on behalf of a ward.

Derived from Probate Code § 703(r).

Added by Acts 2011, 82nd Leg., ch. 823, § 1.02, eff. Jan. 1, 2014.

Subchapter E. Provisions Relating to Personal Sureties

§ 1105.201. Affidavit of Personal Surety

(a) Before a judge considers a bond with a personal surety, each personal surety must execute an affidavit stating the amount by which the surety's assets that are reachable by creditors exceeds the surety's liabilities. The total of the surety's worth must equal at least twice the amount of the bond.

(b) Each affidavit must be presented to the judge for consideration and, if approved, shall be attached to and form part of the bond.

Derived from Probate Code § 709(a).

Added by Acts 2011, 82nd Leg., ch. 823, § 1.02, eff. Jan. 1, 2014.

§ 1105.202. Lien on Real Property Owned by Personal Surety

(a) If a judge finds that the estimated value of personal property of the guardianship that cannot be deposited, as provided by Subchapter D, is such that personal sureties cannot be accepted without the creation of a specific lien on the real property owned by the sureties, the judge shall enter an order requiring each surety to designate real property that is owned by the surety, located in this state, and subject to execution. The designated property must have a value that exceeds all liens and unpaid taxes by an amount at least equal to the amount of the bond and must have an adequate legal description, all of which the surety shall incorporate in an affidavit. Following approval by the judge, the affidavit shall be attached to and form part of the bond.

(b) A lien arises as security for the performance of the obligation of the bond only on the real property designated in the affidavit.

(c) Before letters of guardianship are issued to the guardian whose bond includes an affidavit under this section, the court clerk shall mail a statement to the office of the county clerk of each county in which any real property designated in the affidavit is located. The statement must be signed by the court clerk and include:

(1) a sufficient description of the real property;

(2) the names of the principal and sureties on the bond;

(3) the amount of the bond;

(4) the name of the guardianship; and

(5) the name of the court in which the bond is given.

(d) Each county clerk who receives a statement required by Subsection (c) shall record the statement in the county deed records. Each recorded statement shall be indexed in a manner that permits the convenient determination of the existence and character of the lien described in the statement.

(e) The recording and indexing required by Subsection (d) is constructive notice to a person regarding the existence of the lien on the real property located in the county, effective as of the date of the indexing.

(f) If each personal surety subject to a court order under this section does not comply with the order, the judge may require that the bond be signed by:

(1) an authorized corporate surety; or

(2) an authorized corporate surety and at least two personal sureties.

Derived from Probate Code §§ 709(b), 710.

Added by Acts 2011, 82nd Leg., ch. 823, § 1.02, eff. Jan. 1, 2014.

§ 1105.203. Subordination of Lien on Real Property Owned by Personal Surety

(a) A personal surety required to create a lien on specific real property under Section 1105.202 who wishes to lease the real property for mineral development may file a written application in the court in which the proceeding is pending requesting subordination of the lien to the proposed lease.

(b) The judge may enter an order granting the application.

(c) A certified copy of an order entered under this section that is filed and recorded in the deed records of the proper county is sufficient to subordinate the lien to the rights of a lessee under the proposed lease.

Derived from Probate Code § 709(c).

Added by Acts 2011, 82nd Leg., ch. 823, § 1.02, eff. Jan. 1, 2014.

§ 1105.204. Release of Lien on Real Property Owned by Personal Sureties

(a) A personal surety who has given a lien under Section 1105.202 may apply to the court to have the lien released.

(b) The court shall order the lien released if:

(1) the court is satisfied that the bond is sufficient without the lien; or

(2) sufficient other real or personal property of the surety is substituted on the same terms required for the lien that is to be released.

(c) If the personal surety does not offer a lien on other substituted property under Subsection (b)(2) and the court is not satisfied that the bond is sufficient without the substitution of other property, the court shall order the guardian to appear and give a new bond.

(d) A certified copy of the court's order releasing the lien and describing the property that was subject to the lien has the effect of canceling the lien if the order is filed with the county clerk and recorded in the deed records of the county in which the property is located.

Derived from Probate Code §§ 719, 720.

Added by Acts 2011, 82nd Leg., ch. 823, § 1.02, eff. Jan. 1, 2014.

Subchapter F. New Bonds

§ 1105.251. Grounds for Requiring New Bond

(a) A guardian may be required to give a new bond if:

(1) a surety on a bond dies, removes beyond the limits of this state, or becomes insolvent;

(2) in the court's opinion:

(A) the sureties on a bond are insufficient; or

(B) a bond is defective;

(3) the amount of a bond is insufficient;

(4) a surety on a bond petitions the court to be discharged from future liability on the bond; or

(5) a bond and the record of the bond have been lost or destroyed.

(b) A person interested in the guardianship may have the guardian cited to appear and show cause why the guardian should not be required to give a new bond by filing a written application with the county clerk of the county in which the guardianship proceeding is pending. The application must allege that:

(1) the bond is insufficient or defective; or

(2) the bond and the record of the bond have been lost or destroyed.

Derived from Probate Code §§ 711, 712.

Added by Acts 2011, 82nd Leg., ch. 823, § 1.02, eff. Jan. 1, 2014.

§ 1105.252. Court Order or Citation on New Bond

(a) When a judge is made aware that a bond is insufficient or that a bond and the record of the bond have been lost or destroyed, the judge shall:

(1) without delay and without notice enter an order requiring the guardian to give a new bond; or

(2) without delay have the guardian cited to show cause why the guardian should not be required to give a new bond.

(b) An order entered under Subsection (a)(1) must state:

(1) the reasons for requiring a new bond;

(2) the amount of the new bond; and

(3) the period within which the new bond must be given, which may not expire earlier than the 10th day after the date of the order.

(c) A guardian who opposes an order entered under Subsection (a)(1) may demand a hearing on the order. The hearing must be held before the expiration of the period within which the new bond must be given.

Derived from Probate Code §§ 713, 714(a).

Added by Acts 2011, 82nd Leg., ch. 823, § 1.02, eff. Jan. 1, 2014.

§ 1105.253. Show Cause Hearing on New Bond Requirement

(a) On the return of a citation ordering a guardian to show cause why the guardian should not be required to give a new bond, the judge shall, on the date specified in the return of citation for the hearing of the matter, inquire into the sufficiency of the reasons for requiring a new bond.

(b) If the judge is satisfied that a new bond should be required, the judge shall enter an order requiring a new bond. The order must state:

(1) the amount of the new bond; and

(2) the period within which the new bond must be given, which may not expire later than the 20th day after the date of the order.

Derived from Probate Code § 714(b).

Added by Acts 2011, 82nd Leg., ch. 823, § 1.02, eff. Jan. 1, 2014.

§ 1105.254. Effect of Order Requiring New Bond

(a) An order requiring a guardian to give a new bond has the effect of suspending the guardian's powers.

(b) After the order is entered, the guardian may not pay out any of the guardianship's money or take any other official action, except to preserve the guardianship's property, until the new bond is given and approved.

Derived from Probate Code § 715.

Added by Acts 2011, 82nd Leg., ch. 823, § 1.02, eff. Jan. 1, 2014.

§ 1105.255. New Bond in Decreased Amount

(a) A guardian required to give a bond may at any time file with the clerk a written application requesting that the court reduce the amount of the bond.

(b) After the guardian files an application under Subsection (a), the clerk shall issue and have posted notice to all persons interested in the estate and to a surety on the bond. The notice must inform the interested persons and surety of:

(1) the fact that the application has been filed;

(2) the nature of the application; and

(3) the time the judge will hear the application.

(c) The judge may permit the filing of a new bond in a reduced amount if:

(1) proof is submitted that a bond in an amount less than the bond in effect will be adequate to meet the requirements of law and protect the guardianship; and

(2) the judge approves an accounting filed at the time of the application.

Derived from Probate Code § 716.

Added by Acts 2011, 82nd Leg., ch. 823, § 1.02, eff. Jan. 1, 2014.

§ 1105.256. Request by Surety for New Bond

(a) A surety on a guardian's bond may at any time file with the clerk a petition requesting that the court in which the proceeding is pending:

(1) require the guardian to give a new bond; and

(2) discharge the petitioner from all liability for the future acts of the guardian.

(b) If a petition is filed under Subsection (a), the guardian shall be cited to appear and give a new bond.

Derived from Probate Code § 718.

Added by Acts 2011, 82nd Leg., ch. 823, § 1.02, eff. Jan. 1, 2014.

§ 1105.257. Discharge of Former Sureties on Approval of New Bond

When a new bond has been given and approved, the judge shall enter an order discharging the sureties on the former bond from all liability for the future acts of the principal on the bond.

Derived from Probate Code § 717.

Added by Acts 2011, 82nd Leg., ch. 823, § 1.02, eff. Jan. 1, 2014.

Chapter 1106. Letters of Guardianship

Chapter 1106. Letters of Guardianship

§ 1106.001. Issuance of Certificate as Letters of Guardianship

(a) When a person who is appointed guardian has qualified under Section 1105.002, the clerk shall issue to the guardian a certificate under seal stating:

(1) the fact of the appointment and of the qualification;

(2) the date of the appointment and of the qualification; and

(3) the date the letters of guardianship expire.

(b) The certificate issued by the clerk under Subsection (a) constitutes letters of guardianship.

Derived from Probate Code § 659(a).

Added by Acts 2011, 82nd Leg., ch. 823, § 1.02, eff. Jan. 1, 2014.

§ 1106.002. Expiration of Letters of Guardianship

Letters of guardianship expire one year and four months after the date the letters are issued, unless renewed.

Derived from Probate Code § 659(b).

Added by Acts 2011, 82nd Leg., ch. 823, § 1.02, eff. Jan. 1, 2014.

§ 1106.003. Renewal of Letters of Guardianship

(a) The clerk may not renew letters of guardianship relating to the appointment of a guardian of the estate until the court receives and approves the guardian's annual account.

(b) The clerk may not renew letters of guardianship relating to the appointment of a guardian of the person until the court receives and approves the guardian's annual report.

(c) If a guardian's annual account or annual report is disapproved or is not timely filed, the clerk may not issue further letters of guardianship to the delinquent guardian unless ordered by the court.

(d) Except as otherwise provided by this subsection, regardless of the date the court approves an annual account or annual report for purposes of this section, a renewal of letters of guardianship relates back to the date the original letters were issued. If the accounting period has been changed as provided by this title, a renewal relates back to the first day of the accounting period.

Derived from Probate Code §§ 659(c), (d).

Added by Acts 2011, 82nd Leg., ch. 823, § 1.02, eff. Jan. 1, 2014.

§ 1106.004. Replacement and Other Additional Letters of Guardianship

When letters of guardianship have been destroyed or lost, the clerk shall issue new letters that have the same effect as the original letters. The clerk shall also issue any number of letters on request of the person who holds the letters.

Derived from Probate Code § 661.

Added by Acts 2011, 82nd Leg., ch. 823, § 1.02, eff.

Jan. 1, 2014.

§ 1106.005. Effect of Letters or Certificate

(a) Letters of guardianship or a certificate issued under Section 1106.001 under seal of the clerk of the court that granted the letters is sufficient evidence of:

(1) the appointment and qualification of the guardian; and

(2) the date of qualification.

(b) The court order that appoints the guardian is evidence of the authority granted to the guardian and of the scope of the powers and duties that the guardian may exercise only after the date letters of guardianship or a certificate has been issued under Section 1106.001.

Derived from Probate Code § 660.

Added by Acts 2011, 82nd Leg., ch. 823, § 1.02, eff. Jan. 1, 2014.

§ 1106.006. Validation of Certain Letters of Guardianship

(a) Letters of guardianship existing on September 1, 1993, that were issued to a nonresident guardian without the procedure or any part of the procedure provided in this chapter, or without a notice or citation required of a resident guardian, are validated as of the letters' dates, to the extent that the absence of the procedure, notice, or citation is concerned. An otherwise valid conveyance, mineral lease, or other act of a nonresident guardian qualified and acting in connection with the letters of guardianship and under supporting orders of a county or probate court of this state is validated.

(b) This section does not apply to letters of guardianship, a conveyance, a lease, or another act of a nonresident guardian under this section if the absence of the procedure, notice, or citation involving the letters, conveyance, lease, or other act of the nonresident guardian is an issue in a lawsuit pending in this state on September 1, 1993.

Derived from Probate Code § 663.

Added by Acts 2011, 82nd Leg., ch. 823, § 1.02, eff. Jan. 1, 2014.

Subtitle E. Administration of Guardianship

Chapter 1151. Rights, Powers, and Duties Under Guardianship

Subchapter A. Rights, Powers, and Duties in General

Chapter 1151. Rights, Powers, and Duties Under Guardianship

Subchapter A. Rights, Powers, and Duties in General

§ 1151.001. Rights and Powers Retained by Ward

An incapacitated person for whom a guardian is appointed retains all legal and civil rights and powers except those designated by court order as legal disabilities by virtue of having been specifically granted to the guardian.

Derived from Probate Code § 675.

Added by Acts 2011, 82nd Leg., ch. 823, § 1.02, eff. Jan. 1, 2014.

§ 1151.002. Rights of Good Faith Purchasers

(a) This section applies only to a guardian who has qualified acting as guardian and in conformity with the law and the guardian's authority.

(b) A guardian's act is valid for all purposes regarding the rights of an innocent purchaser of property of the guardianship estate who purchased the property from the guardian for valuable consideration, in good faith, and without notice of any illegality in the title to the property, regardless of whether the guardian's act or the authority under which the act was performed is subsequently set aside, annulled, or declared invalid.

Derived from Probate Code § 662.

Added by Acts 2011, 82nd Leg., ch. 823, § 1.02, eff. Jan. 1, 2014.

§ 1151.003. Guardian May Not Dispute Ward's Right to Property; Exception

A guardian, or an heir, executor, administrator, or assignee of a guardian, may not dispute the right of the ward to any property that came into the guardian's possession as guardian of the ward, except property:

(1) that is recovered from the guardian; or
(2) on which there is a personal action pending.

Derived from Probate Code § 778.

Added by Acts 2011, 82nd Leg., ch. 823, § 1.02, eff. Jan. 1, 2014.

§ 1151.004. Powers and Duties of Person Serving as Guardian of Both Person and Estate

The guardian of both the person and the estate of a ward has all the rights and powers and shall perform all the duties of the guardian of the person and the guardian of the estate.

Derived from Probate Code § 769.

Added by Acts 2011, 82nd Leg., ch. 823, § 1.02, eff. Jan. 1, 2014.

Subchapter B. Powers and Duties of Guardians Relating to Care of Ward

§ 1151.051. General Powers and Duties of Guardians of the Person

(a) The guardian of the person of a ward is entitled to take charge of the person of the ward.

(b) The duties of the guardian of the person correspond with the rights of the guardian.

(c) A guardian of the person has:

(1) the right to have physical possession of the ward and to establish the ward's legal domicile;

(2) the duty to provide care, supervision, and protection for the ward;

(3) the duty to provide the ward with clothing, food, medical care, and shelter;

(4) the power to consent to medical, psychiatric, and surgical treatment other than the inpatient psychiatric commitment of the ward;

(5) on application to and order of the court, the power to establish a trust in accordance with 42 U.S.C. Section 1396p(d)(4)(B) and direct that the income of the ward as defined by that section be paid directly to the trust, solely for the purpose of the ward's eligibility for medical assistance under Chapter 32, Human Resources Code; and

(6) the power to sign documents necessary or appropriate to facilitate employment of the ward if:

(A) the guardian was appointed with full authority over the person of the ward under Section 1101.151; or

(B) the power is specified in the court order appointing the guardian with limited powers over the person of the ward under Section 1101.152.

(d) Notwithstanding Subsection (c)(4), a guardian of the person of a ward has the power to personally transport the ward or to direct the ward's transport by emergency medical services or other means to an inpatient mental health facility for a preliminary examination in accordance with Subchapters A and C, Chapter 573, Health and Safety Code.

(e) Notwithstanding Subsection (c)(1) and except in cases of emergency, a guardian of the person of a ward may only place the ward in a more restrictive care facility if the guardian provides notice of the proposed placement to the court, the ward, and any person who has requested notice and after:

(1) the court orders the placement at a hearing on the matter, if the ward or another person objects to the proposed placement before the eighth business day after the person's receipt of the notice; or

(2) the seventh business day after the court's receipt of the notice, if the court does not schedule a hearing, on its own motion, on the proposed placement before that day.

Derived from Probate Code § 767.

Added by Acts 2011, 82nd Leg., ch. 823, § 1.02, eff. Jan. 1, 2014. Subsec. (c) amended by Acts 2013, 83rd Leg., ch. 982, § 16, eff. Jan. 1, 2014. Subsec. (e) added by Acts 2015, 84th Leg., ch. 214, § 14, eff. Sept. 1, 2015.

§ 1151.052. Care of Adult Ward

(a) The guardian of an adult ward may spend funds of the guardianship as provided by court order to care for and maintain the ward.

(b) The guardian of an adult ward who has decision-making ability may apply on the ward's behalf for residential care and services provided by a public or private facility if the ward agrees to be placed in the facility. The guardian shall report the condition of the ward to the court at regular intervals at least annually, unless the court orders more frequent reports. The guardian shall include in a report of an adult ward who is receiving residential care in a public or private residential care facility a statement as to the necessity for continued care in the facility.

Derived from Probate Code § 770(a).

Added by Acts 2011, 82nd Leg., ch. 823, § 1.02, eff. Jan. 1, 2014.

§ 1151.053. Commitment of Ward

(a) Except as provided by Subsection (b) or (c), a guardian may not voluntarily admit a ward to a public or private inpatient psychiatric facility operated by the Department of State Health Services for care and treatment or to a residential facility operated by the Department of Aging and Disability Services for care and treatment. If care and treatment in a psychiatric or residential facility is necessary, the ward or the ward's guardian may:

(1) apply for services under Section 593.027 or 593.028, Health and Safety Code;

(2) apply to a court to commit the person under Subtitle C or D, Title 7, Health and Safety Code, or Chapter 462, Health and Safety Code; or

(3) transport the ward to an inpatient mental health facility for a preliminary examination in accordance with Subchapters A and C, Chapter 573, Health and Safety Code.

(b) A guardian of a person younger than 18 years of age may voluntarily admit the ward to a public or private inpatient psychiatric facility for care and treatment.

(c) A guardian of a person may voluntarily admit an incapacitated person to a residential care facility for emergency care or respite care under Section 593.027 or 593.028, Health and Safety Code.

Derived from Probate Code §§ 770(b), (c), (d).

Added by Acts 2011, 82nd Leg., ch. 823, § 1.02, eff. Jan. 1, 2014. Subsec. (b) amended by Acts 2013, 83rd Leg., ch. 161, § 6.040, eff. Jan. 1, 2014.

§ 1151.054. Administration of Medication

(a) In this section, "psychoactive medication" has the meaning assigned by Section 574.101, Health and Safety Code.

(b) The guardian of the person of a ward who is not a minor and who is under a protective custody order as provided by Subchapter B, Chapter 574, Health and Safety Code, may consent to the administration of psychoactive medication as prescribed by the ward's treating physician regardless of the ward's expressed preferences regarding treatment with psychoactive medication.

Derived from Probate Code § 770A.

Added by Acts 2011, 82nd Leg., ch. 823, § 1.02, eff. Jan. 1, 2014.

§ 1151.055. Application by Certain Relatives for Access to Ward; Hearing and Court Order

(a) This section applies to a relative described under Sections 1101.001(b)(13)(A)-(D).

(b) A relative of a ward may file an application with the court requesting access to the ward, including the opportunity to establish visitation or communication with the ward.

(c) Except as provided by Subsection (d), the court shall schedule a hearing on the application not later than the 60th day after the date an application is filed under Subsection (b). The court may grant a continuance of a hearing under this section for good cause.

(d) If an application under Subsection (b) states that the ward's health is in significant decline or that the ward's death may be imminent, the court shall conduct an emergency hearing as soon as practicable, but not later than the 10th day after the date the application is filed under Subsection (b).

(e) The guardian of a ward with respect to whom an application is filed under Subsection (b) shall be personally served with a copy of the application and cited to appear at a hearing under:

(1) Subsection (c) at least 21 days before the date of the hearing; and

(2) Subsection (d) as soon as practicable.

(f) The court shall issue an order after notice and a hearing under this section. An order issued under this section may:

(1) prohibit the guardian of a ward from preventing the applicant access to the ward if the applicant shows by a preponderance of the evidence that:

(A) the guardian's past act or acts prevented access to the ward; and

(B) the ward desires contact with the applicant; and

(2) specify the frequency, time, place, location, and any other terms of access.

(g) In deciding whether to issue or modify an order issued under this section, the court:

(1) shall consider:

(A) whether any protective orders have been issued against the applicant to protect the ward;

(B) whether a court or other state agency has found that the applicant abused, neglected, or exploited the ward; and

(C) the best interest of the ward; and

(2) may consider whether:

(A) visitation by the applicant should be limited to situations in which a third person, specified by the court, is present; or

(B) visitation should be suspended or denied.

(h) The court may, in its discretion, award the prevailing party in any action brought under this section court costs and attorney's fees, if any. Court costs or attorney's fees awarded under this subsection may not be paid from the ward's estate.

New.

Added by Acts 2015, 84th Leg., ch. 1087, § 1, eff. June 1, 2015.

§ 1151.056. Guardian's Duty to Inform Certain Relatives About Ward's Health and Residence

(a) This section applies with respect to relatives described under Sections 1101.001(b)(13)(A)-(D).

(b) Except as provided by Subsection (e), the guardian of an adult ward shall as soon as practicable inform relatives if:

(1) the ward dies;

(2) the ward is admitted to a medical facility for acute care for a period of three days or more;

(3) the ward's residence has changed; or

(4) the ward is staying at a location other than the ward's residence for a period that exceeds one calendar week.

(c) In the case of the ward's death, the guardian shall inform relatives of any funeral arrangements and the location of the ward's final resting place.

(d) A relative entitled to notice about a ward under this section may elect to not receive the notice by providing a written request to that effect to the guardian. A guardian shall file any written request received by the guardian under this subsection with the court.

(e) On motion filed with the court showing good cause and after a relative is provided an opportunity to present evidence to the court under Subsection (f), the court, subject to Subsection (g), may relieve the guardian of the duty to provide notice about a ward to a relative under this section.

(f) A copy of the motion required under Subsection (e) shall be provided to the relative specifically named in the motion unless the guardian was unable to locate the relative after making reasonable efforts to discover and locate the relative. The relative provided notice under this subsection may file evidence with the court in response to the motion, and the court shall consider that evidence before making a decision on the motion.

(g) In considering a motion under Subsection (e), the court shall relieve the guardian of the duty to provide notice about a ward to a relative under this section if the court finds that:

(1) the motion includes a written request from a relative electing to not receive the notice;

(2) the guardian was unable to locate the relative after making reasonable efforts to discover and locate the relative;

(3) the guardian was able to locate the relative, but was unable to establish communication with the relative after making reasonable efforts to establish communication;

(4) a protective order was issued against the relative to protect the ward;

(5) a court or other state agency has found that the relative abused, neglected, or exploited the ward; or

(6) notice is not in the best interest of the ward.

New.

Added by Acts 2015, 84ᵗʰ Leg., ch. 1087, § 1, eff. June 1, 2015.

Subchapter C. General Powers and Duties of Guardians of the Estate

§ 1151.101. General Powers and Duties

(a) Subject to Subsection (b), the guardian of the estate of a ward is entitled to:

(1) possess and manage all property belonging to the ward;

(2) collect all debts, rentals, or claims that are due to the ward;

(3) enforce all obligations in favor of the ward; and

(4) bring and defend suits by or against the ward.

(b) In the management of a ward's estate, the guardian of the estate is governed by the provisions of this title.

Derived from Probate Code § 768.

Added by Acts 2011, 82nd Leg., ch. 823, § 1.02, eff. Jan. 1, 2014.

§ 1151.102. Exercise of Authority Under Court Order

(a) The guardian of the estate may renew or extend any obligation owed by or to the ward on application and if authorized by order.

(b) On written application to the court, a guardian of the estate may take an action described by Subsection (c) if:

(1) the guardian considers the action in the best interests of the estate; and

(2) the action is authorized by court order.

(c) A guardian of the estate who complies with Subsection (b) may:

(1) purchase or exchange property;

(2) take a claim or property for the use and benefit of the estate in payment of a debt due or owing to the estate;

(3) compound a bad or doubtful debt due or owing to the estate;

(4) make a compromise or a settlement in relation to property or a claim in dispute or litigation;

(5) compromise or pay in full any secured claim that has been allowed and approved as required by law against the estate by conveying to the holder of the secured claim the real estate or personal property securing the claim:

(A) in full payment, liquidation, and satisfaction of the claim; and

(B) in consideration of cancellation of a note, deed of trust, mortgage, chattel mortgage, or other evidence of a lien that secures the payment of the claim;

(6) abandon worthless or burdensome property and the administration of that property;

(7) purchase a prepaid funeral benefits contract; and

(8) establish a trust in accordance with 42 U.S.C. Section 1396p(d)(4)(B), and direct that the income of the ward as defined by that section be paid directly to the trust, solely for the purpose of the ward's eligibility for medical assistance under Chapter 32, Human Resources Code.

(d) A mortgagee, another secured party, or a trustee may foreclose on property abandoned under Subsection (c)(6) without further court order.

Derived from Probate Code § 774(a).

Added by Acts 2011, 82nd Leg., ch. 823, § 1.02, eff. Jan. 1, 2014.

§ 1151.103. Exercise of Authority Without Court Order

(a) The guardian of the estate of a ward may, without application to or order of the court:

(1) release a lien on payment at maturity of the debt secured by the lien;

(2) vote stocks by limited or general proxy;

(3) pay calls and assessments;

(4) insure the estate against liability in appropriate cases;

(5) insure estate property against fire, theft, and other hazards; and

(6) pay taxes, court costs, and bond premiums.

(b) A guardian of the estate may apply and obtain a court order if the guardian doubts the propriety of the exercise of any power listed in Subsection (a).

Derived from Probate Code § 774(b).

Added by Acts 2011, 82nd Leg., ch. 823, § 1.02, eff. Jan. 1, 2014.

§ 1151.104. Authority to Commence Suits

(a) The guardian of the estate of a ward appointed in this state may commence a suit for:

(1) the recovery of personal property, debts, or damages; or

(2) title to or possession of land, any right attached to or arising from that land, or injury or damage done.

(b) A judgment in a suit described by Subsection (a) is conclusive, but may be set aside by any person interested for fraud or collusion on the guardian's part.

Derived from Probate Code § 773.

Added by Acts 2011, 82nd Leg., ch. 823, § 1.02, eff. Jan. 1, 2014.

§ 1151.105. Ordinary Diligence Required

(a) If there is a reasonable prospect of collecting the claims or recovering the property, the guardian of the estate shall use ordinary diligence to:

(1) collect all claims and debts due the ward; and

(2) recover possession of all property to which the ward has claim or title.

(b) If the guardian wilfully neglects to use ordinary diligence, the guardian and the sureties on the guardian's bond are liable, on the suit of any person interested in the estate, for the use of the estate, the amount of the claims, or the value of the property that has been lost due to the guardian's neglect.

Derived from Probate Code § 772.

Added by Acts 2011, 82nd Leg., ch. 823, § 1.02, eff. Jan. 1, 2014.

Subchapter D. Possession and Care of Ward's Property by Guardian of the Estate

§ 1151.151. Duty Of Care

(a) The guardian of the estate shall take care of and manage the estate as a prudent person would manage the person's own property, except as otherwise provided by this title.

(b) The guardian of the estate shall account for all rents, profits, and revenues that the estate would have produced by prudent management as required by Subsection (a).

Derived from Probate Code § 768.

Added by Acts 2011, 82nd Leg., ch. 823, § 1.02, eff. Jan. 1, 2014.

§ 1151.152. Possession of Personal Property and Records

(a) Immediately after receiving letters of guardianship, the guardian of the estate shall collect and take possession of the ward's personal property, record books, title papers, and other business papers.

(b) The guardian of the estate shall deliver the ward's personal property, record books, title papers, and other business papers to a person legally entitled to that property when:

(1) the guardianship has been closed; or

(2) a successor guardian has received letters of guardianship.

Derived from Probate Code § 771.

Added by Acts 2011, 82nd Leg., ch. 823, § 1.02, eff. Jan. 1, 2014.

§ 1151.153. Possession of Property Held in Common Ownership

The guardian of the estate is entitled to possession of a ward's property held or owned in common with a part owner in the same manner as another owner in common or joint owner is entitled.

Derived from Probate Code § 775.

Added by Acts 2011, 82nd Leg., ch. 823, § 1.02, eff. Jan. 1, 2014.

§ 1151.154. Administration of Partnership Interest

(a) This section applies only to a general partnership governed by a partnership agreement or articles of partnership that provide that, on the incapacity of a partner, the guardian of the estate of the partner is entitled to the place of the incapacitated partner in the partnership.

(b) If a ward was a partner in a general partnership, the guardian who contracts to come into the partnership is, to the extent allowed by law, liable to a third person only to the extent of:

(1) the incapacitated partner's capital in the partnership; and

(2) the assets of the incapacitated partner's estate that are held by the guardian.

(c) This section does not exonerate a guardian from liability for the guardian's negligence.

Derived from Probate Code § 780.

Added by Acts 2011, 82nd Leg., ch. 823, § 1.02, eff. Jan. 1, 2014.

§ 1151.155. Operation or Rental of Farm, Ranch, Factory, or Other Business

(a) If the ward owns a farm, ranch, factory, or other business that is not required to be immediately sold for the payment of a debt or other lawful purpose, the guardian of the estate on order of the court shall, as it appears to be in the estate's best interests:

(1) continue to operate, or cause the continued operation of, the farm, ranch, factory, or other business; or

(2) rent the farm, ranch, factory, or other business.

(b) In deciding whether to issue an order under Subsection (a), the court:

(1) shall consider:

(A) the condition of the estate; and

(B) the necessity that may exist for the future sale of the property or business for the payment of a debt, claim, or other lawful expenditure; and

(2) may not extend the time of renting any of the property beyond what appears consistent with the maintenance and education of a ward or the settlement of the ward's estate.

Derived from Probate Code § 779.

Added by Acts 2011, 82nd Leg., ch. 823, § 1.02, eff. Jan. 1, 2014.

Subchapter E. Authority of Guardian to Engage in Certain Borrowing

§ 1151.201. Mortgage or Pledge of Estate Property Authorized in Certain Circumstances

(a) Under court order, the guardian may mortgage or pledge any property of a guardianship estate by deed of trust or otherwise as security for an indebtedness when necessary for:

(1) the payment of any ad valorem, income, gift, or transfer tax due from a ward, regardless of whether the tax is assessed by a state, a political subdivision of the state, the federal government, or a foreign country;

(2) the payment of any expense of administration, including amounts necessary for the operation of a business, farm, or ranch owned by the estate;

(3) the payment of any claim allowed and approved, or established by suit, against the ward or the ward's estate;

(4) the renewal and extension of an existing lien;

(5) an improvement or repair to the ward's real estate if:

(A) the real estate is not revenue producing but could be made revenue producing by certain improvements and repairs; or

(B) the revenue from the real estate could be increased by making improvements or repairs to the real estate;

(6) the purchase of a residence for the ward or a dependent of the ward, if the court finds that borrowing money for that purpose is in the ward's best interests; and

(7) funeral expenses of the ward and expenses of the ward's last illness, if the guardianship is kept open after the ward's death.

(b) Under court order, the guardian of the estate may also receive an extension of credit on the ward's behalf that is wholly or partly secured by a lien on real property that is the ward's homestead when necessary to:

(1) make an improvement or repair to the homestead; or

(2) pay for the ward's education or medical expenses.

(c) Proceeds of a home equity loan described by Subsection (b) may be used only for the purposes authorized under Subsection (b) and to pay the outstanding balance of the loan.

Derived from Probate Code §§ 781(a), (a-1), (a-2).

Added by Acts 2011, 82nd Leg., ch. 823, § 1.02, eff. Jan. 1, 2014.

§ 1151.202. Application; Order

(a) The guardian of the estate must file a sworn application with the court for authority to:

(1) borrow money for a purpose authorized by Section 1151.201(a) or (b); or

(2) create or extend a lien on estate property as security.

(b) The application must state fully and in detail the circumstances that the guardian of the estate believes make the granting of the authority necessary.

(c) On the filing of an application under Subsection (a), the clerk shall issue and have posted a citation to all interested persons stating the nature of the application and requiring the interested persons to appear and show cause why the application should not be granted.

(d) If the court is satisfied by the evidence presented at the hearing on an application filed under Subsection (a) that it is in the interest of the ward or the ward's estate to borrow money or to extend and renew an existing lien, the court shall issue an order to that effect, setting out the terms of the authority granted.

(e) If a new lien is created on guardianship estate property, the court may require, for the protection of the guardianship estate and the estate's creditors, that the guardian's general bond be increased or an additional bond be given, as for the sale of real property belonging to the estate.

Derived from Probate Code §§ 781(b), (c).

Added by Acts 2011, 82nd Leg., ch. 823, § 1.02, eff. Jan. 1, 2014.

§ 1151.203. Term of Loan or Renewal

The term of a loan or renewal authorized under Section 1151.202 must be for the length of time that the court determines to be in the best interests of the ward or the ward's estate.

Derived from Probate Code § 781(c).

Added by Acts 2011, 82nd Leg., ch. 823, § 1.02, eff. Jan. 1, 2014.

Subchapter F. Guardians Appointed for Ward to Receive Government Funds

§ 1151.251. Powers and Duties of Guardian Appointed as Necessary for Ward to Receive Government Funds

(a) A guardian of the person for whom it is necessary to have a guardian appointed to receive funds from a governmental source may:

(1) administer only:

(A) the funds received from the governmental source;

(B) all earnings, interest, or profits derived from the funds; and

(C) all property acquired with the funds; and

(2) receive the funds and pay the expenses of administering the guardianship and the expenses for the support, maintenance, or education of the ward or the ward's dependents.

(b) Expenditures under Subsection (a)(2) for the support, maintenance, or education of the ward or the ward's dependents may not exceed $12,000 during any 12-month period without the court's approval.

Derived from Probate Code § 782(a).

Added by Acts 2011, 82nd Leg., ch. 823, § 1.02, eff. Jan. 1, 2014.

§ 1151.252. Validation of Certain Prior Acts of Guardian

An act performed before September 1, 1993, by a guardian of the estate of a person for whom it is necessary to have a guardian appointed to receive and disburse funds that are due the person from a governmental source is validated if the act was performed in conformance with an order of a court that has venue with respect to the support, maintenance, and education of the ward or the ward's dependents and the investment of surplus funds of the ward under this title and if the validity of the act was not an issue in a probate proceeding or civil lawsuit that was pending on September 1, 1993.

Derived from Probate Code § 782(b).

Added by Acts 2011, 82nd Leg., ch. 823, § 1.02, eff. Jan. 1, 2014.

Subchapter G. Notice by Guardian to Department of Veterans Affairs

§ 1151.301. Notice of Filing Required; Hearing Date

(a) This section applies only to:

(1) a filing by a guardian whose ward is a beneficiary of the Department of Veterans Affairs of:

(A) an annual or other account of funds; or

(B) an application for the expenditure or investment of funds; or

(2) a filing of a claim against the estate of a ward who is a beneficiary of the Department of Veterans Affairs.

(b) The court shall set a date for a hearing of a matter initiated by a filing to which this section applies not earlier than 20 days from the date of the filing.

(c) Not later than the fifth day after the date of a filing to which this section applies, the person who makes the filing shall give notice of the date of the filing by mailing a certified copy of the filing to the office of the Department of Veterans Affairs in whose territory the court is located.

(d) An office of the Department of Veterans Affairs through its attorney may waive the service of notice or the time required for setting a hearing under this section.

Derived from Probate Code § 636.

Added by Acts 2011, 82nd Leg., ch. 823, § 1.02, eff. Jan. 1, 2014.

Subchapter H. Rights of Wards

§ 1151.351 Bill of Rights for Wards

(a) A ward has all the rights, benefits, responsibilities, and privileges granted by the constitution and laws of this state and the United States, except where specifically limited by a court-ordered guardianship or where otherwise lawfully restricted.

(b) Unless limited by a court or otherwise restricted by law, a ward is authorized to the following:

(1) to have a copy of the guardianship order and letters of guardianship and contact information for the probate court that issued the order and letters;

(2) to have a guardianship that encourages the development or maintenance of maximum self-reliance and independence in the ward with the eventual goal, if possible, of self-sufficiency;

(3) to be treated with respect, consideration, and recognition of the ward's dignity and individuality;

(4) to reside and receive support services in the most integrated setting, including home-based or other community-based settings, as required by Title II of the Americans with Disabilities Act (42 U.S.C. Section 12131 et seq.);

(5) to consideration of the ward's current and previously stated personal preferences, desires, medical and psychiatric treatment preferences, religious beliefs, living arrangements, and other preferences and opinions;

(6) to financial self-determination for all public benefits after essential living expenses and health needs are met and to have access to a monthly personal allowance;

(7) to receive timely and appropriate health care and medical treatment that does not violate the ward's rights granted by the constitution and laws of this state and the United States;

(8) to exercise full control of all aspects of life not specifically granted by the court to the guardian;

(9) to control the ward's personal environment based on the ward's preferences;

(10) to complain or raise concerns regarding the guardian or guardianship to the court, including living arrangements, retaliation by the guardian, conflicts of interest between the guardian and service providers, or a violation of any rights under this section;

(11) to receive notice in the ward's native language, or preferred mode of communication, and in a manner accessible to the ward, of a court proceeding to continue, modify, or terminate the guardianship and the opportunity to appear before the court to express the ward's preferences and concerns regarding whether the guardianship should be continued, modified, or terminated;

(12) to have a court investigator, guardian ad litem, or attorney ad litem appointed by the court to investigate a complaint received by the court from the ward or any person about the guardianship;

(13) to participate in social, religious, and recreational activities, training, employment, education, habilitation, and rehabilitation of the ward's choice in the most integrated setting;

(14) to self-determination in the substantial maintenance, disposition, and management of real and personal property after essential living expenses and health needs are met, including the right to receive notice and object about the substantial maintenance, disposition, or management of clothing, furniture, vehicles, and other personal effects;

(15) to personal privacy and confidentiality in personal matters, subject to state and federal law;

(16) to unimpeded, private, and uncensored communication and visitation with persons of the ward's choice, except that if the guardian determines that certain communication or visitation causes substantial harm to the ward:

(A) the guardian may limit, supervise, or restrict communication or visitation, but only to the extent necessary to protect the ward from substantial harm; and

(B) the ward may request a hearing to remove any restrictions on communication or visitation imposed by the guardian under Paragraph (A);

(17) to petition the court and retain counsel of the ward's choice who holds a certificate required by Subchapter E, Chapter 1054, to represent the ward's interest for capacity restoration, modification of the guardianship, the appointment of a different guardian, or for other appropriate relief under this subchapter, including a transition to a supported decision-making agreement, except as limited by Section 1054.006;

(18) to vote in a public election, marry, and retain a license to operate a motor vehicle, unless restricted by the court;

(19) to personal visits from the guardian or the guardian's designee at least once every three months, but more often, if necessary, unless the court orders otherwise;

(20) to be informed of the name, address, phone number, and purpose of Disability Rights Texas, an organization whose mission is to protect the rights of, and advocate for, persons with disabilities, and

to communicate and meet with representatives of that organization;

(21) to be informed of the name, address, phone number, and purpose of an independent living center, an area agency on aging, an aging and disability resource center, and the local mental health and intellectual and developmental disability center, and to communicate and meet with representatives from these agencies and organizations;

(22) to be informed of the name, address, phone number, and purpose of the Judicial Branch Certification Commission and the procedure for filing a complaint against a certified guardian;

(23) to contact the Department of Family and Protective Services to report abuse, neglect, exploitation, or violation of personal rights without fear of punishment, interference, coercion, or retaliation; and

(24) to have the guardian, on appointment and on annual renewal of the guardianship, explain the rights delineated in this subsection in the ward's native language, or preferred mode of communication, and in a manner accessible to the ward.

(c) This section does not supersede or abrogate other remedies existing in law.

New.

Added by Acts 2015, 84th Leg., ch. 1225, § 1, eff. June 19, 2015.

Chapter 1152. Guardianship Pending Appeal of Appointment

§ 1152.001. Guardian to Serve Pending Appeal of Appointment
§ 1152.002. Appeal Bond

Chapter 1152. Guardianship Pending Appeal of Appointment

§ 1152.001. Guardian to Serve Pending Appeal of Appointment

Pending an appeal from an order or judgment appointing a guardian, the appointee shall continue to:

(1) act as guardian; and

(2) prosecute a pending suit in favor of the guardianship.

Derived from Probate Code § 655.

Added by Acts 2011, 82nd Leg., ch. 823, § 1.02, eff. Jan. 1, 2014.

§ 1152.002. Appeal Bond

(a) Except as provided by Subsection (b), if a guardian appeals, an appeal bond is not required.

(b) A guardian must give an appeal bond if the appeal personally concerns the guardian.

Derived from Probate Code § 656.

Added by Acts 2011, 82nd Leg., ch. 823, § 1.02, eff. Jan. 1, 2014.

Chapter 1153. Notice to Claimants

Chapter 1153. Notice to Claimants

§ 1153.001. Required Notice Regarding Presentment of Claims in General

(a) Within one month after receiving letters of guardianship, a guardian of an estate shall provide notice requiring each person who has a claim against the estate to present the claim within the period prescribed by law. The notice must be:

(1) published in a newspaper printed in the county in which the letters were issued; and

(2) sent to the comptroller by certified or registered mail, if the ward remitted or should have remitted taxes administered by the comptroller.

(b) Notice provided under Subsection (a) must include:

(1) the date the letters of guardianship were issued to the guardian of the estate;

(2) the address to which a claim may be presented; and

(3) an instruction of the guardian's choice that the claim be addressed in care of:

(A) the guardian;

(B) the guardian's attorney; or

(C) "Guardian, Estate of _____" (naming the estate).

(c) If a newspaper is not printed in the county in which the letters of guardianship were issued, the notice must be posted and the return made and filed as otherwise required by this title.

Derived from Probate Code §§ 783(a), (c).

Added by Acts 2011, 82nd Leg., ch. 823, § 1.02, eff. Jan. 1, 2014.

§ 1153.002. Proof of Publication

A copy of the published notice required by Section 1153.001(a)(1), with the publisher's affidavit, sworn to and subscribed before a proper officer, to the effect that the notice was published as provided in this title for the service of citation or notice by publication, shall be filed in the court in which the cause is pending.

Derived from Probate Code § 783(b).

Added by Acts 2011, 82nd Leg., ch. 823, § 1.02, eff. Jan. 1, 2014.

§ 1153.003. Required Notice to Certain Claimants

(a) Within four months after receiving letters of guardianship, the guardian of an estate shall give notice of the issuance of the letters to each person who has a claim for money against the ward's estate:

(1) that is secured by a deed of trust, mortgage, or vendor's, mechanic's, or other contractor's lien on real estate belonging to the estate; or

(2) about which the guardian has actual knowledge.

(b) Notice provided under this section must be:

(1) sent by certified or registered mail, return receipt requested; and

(2) addressed to the record holder of the claim at the record holder's last known post office address.

(c) The following shall be filed in the court from which the letters of guardianship were issued:

(1) a copy of each notice required by Subsection (a)(1) with the return receipt; and

(2) the guardian's affidavit stating:

(A) that the notice was mailed as required by law; and

(B) the name of the person to whom the notice was mailed, if that name is not shown on the notice or receipt.

Derived from Probate Code §§ 784(A), (b), (c), (d).

Added by Acts 2011, 82nd Leg., ch. 823, § 1.02, eff. Jan. 1, 2014.

§ 1153.004. Permissive Notice to Unsecured Creditor Regarding Period for Presentment of Claim

The guardian of the estate may expressly state in a notice given to an unsecured creditor under Section 1153.003(a)(2) that the creditor must present a claim not later than the 120th day after the date the creditor receives the notice or the claim is barred, if the claim is not barred by the general statutes of limitation. A statement under this section must include:

(1) the address to which the claim may be presented; and

(2) an instruction that the claim be filed with the clerk of the court that issued the letters of guardianship.

Derived from Probate Code § 784(e).

Added by Acts 2011, 82nd Leg., ch. 823, § 1.02, eff. Jan. 1, 2014.

§ 1153.005. One Notice Sufficient; Liability for Failure to Give Required Notice

(a) A guardian of an estate is not required to give a notice required by Section 1153.003 if another person also appointed as guardian or a former guardian has given that notice.

(b) If the guardian fails to give a notice required by other sections of this title or to cause the notice to be given, the guardian and the sureties on the guardian's bond are liable for any damage a person suffers because of the neglect, unless it appears that the person otherwise had notice.

Derived from Probate Code § 785.

Added by Acts 2011, 82nd Leg., ch. 823, § 1.02, eff. Jan. 1, 2014.

Chapter 1154. Inventory, Appraisement, and List of Claims

Subchapter A. Appraisers

Subchapter B. Requirements for Inventory, Appraisement, and List of Claims

Subchapter C. Changes to Inventory, Appraisement, and List of Claims

Subchapter D. Use of Inventory, Appraisement, and List of Claims as Evidence

Chapter 1154. Inventory, Appraisement, and List of Claims

Subchapter A. Appraisers

§ 1154.001. Appointment of Appraisers

(a) After letters of guardianship of the estate are granted, the court, for good cause shown, on the court's own motion or the motion of any interested person, shall appoint at least one but not more than three disinterested persons who are residents of the county in which the letters were granted to appraise the ward's property.

(b) If the court makes an appointment under Subsection (a) and part of the estate is located in a county other than the county in which the letters were granted, the court, if the court considers it necessary, may appoint at least one but not more than three disinterested persons who are residents of the county in which the relevant part of the estate is located to appraise the estate property located in that county.

Derived from Probate Code § 727.

Added by Acts 2011, 82nd Leg., ch. 823, § 1.02, eff. Jan. 1, 2014.

§ 1154.002. Appraisers' Fees

An appraiser appointed by the court is entitled to receive a reasonable fee, payable out of the estate, for the performance of the appraiser's duties as an appraiser.

Derived from Probate Code § 732.

Added by Acts 2011, 82nd Leg., ch. 823, § 1.02, eff. Jan. 1, 2014.

§ 1154.003. Failure or Refusal to Act by Appraisers

If an appraiser appointed under Section 1154.001 fails or refuses to act, the court shall remove the appraiser and appoint one or more appraisers.

Derived from Probate Code § 728.

Added by Acts 2011, 82nd Leg., ch. 823, § 1.02, eff. Jan. 1, 2014.

Subchapter B. Requirements for Inventory, Appraisement, and List of Claims

§ 1154.051. Inventory and Appraisement

(a) Not later than the 30th day after the date the guardian of the estate qualifies, unless a longer period is granted by the court, the guardian shall file with the court clerk a single written instrument that contains a verified, full, and detailed inventory of all the ward's property that has come into the guardian's possession or of which the guardian has knowledge. The inventory must:

(1) include:

(A) all the ward's real property located in this state; and

(B) all the ward's personal property regardless of where the property is located; and

(2) specify:

(A) which portion of the property is separate property and which is community property; and

(B) if the property is owned in common with other persons, the ward's interest in that property.

(b) The guardian shall:

(1) set out in the inventory the guardian's appraisement of the fair market value of each item in the inventory on the date of the grant of letters of guardianship; or

(2) if the court has appointed an appraiser for the estate:

(A) determine the fair market value of each item in the inventory with the assistance of the appraiser; and

(B) set out in the inventory the appraisement made by the appraiser.

(c) The court for good cause shown may require the guardian to file the inventory and appraisement not later than the 30th day after the date of qualification of the guardian.

(d) The inventory, when approved by the court and filed with the court clerk, is for all purposes the inventory and appraisement of the estate referred to in this title.

Derived from Probate Code § 729.

Added by Acts 2011, 82nd Leg., ch. 823, § 1.02, eff. Jan. 1, 2014. Subsec. (a) amended by Acts 2013, 83rd Leg., ch. 161, § 6.041, eff. Jan. 1, 2014.

§ 1154.052. List of Claims

The guardian of the estate shall make and attach to the inventory and appraisement required by Section 1154.051 a complete list of claims due or owing to the ward. The list of claims must state:

(1) the name and, if known, address of each person indebted to the ward; and

(2) regarding each claim:

(A) the nature of the debt, whether it is a note, bill, bond, or other written obligation, or whether it is an account or verbal contract;

(B) the date the debt was incurred;

(C) the date the debt was or is due;

(D) the amount of the claim, the rate of interest on the claim, and the period for which the claim bears interest; and

(E) if any portion of the claim is held in common with others, the interest of the estate in the claim.

Derived from Probate Code § 730.

Added by Acts 2011, 82nd Leg., ch. 823, § 1.02, eff. Jan. 1, 2014. Amended by Acts 2013, 83rd Leg., ch. 161, § 6.042, eff. Jan. 1, 2014.

§ 1154.053. Affidavit of Guardian

The guardian of the estate shall attach to the inventory, appraisement, and list of claims the guardian's affidavit, subscribed and sworn to before an officer in the county authorized by law to administer oaths, that the inventory, appraisement, and list of claims are a true and complete statement of the property and claims of the estate of which the guardian has knowledge.

Derived from Probate Code § 731.

Added by Acts 2011, 82nd Leg., ch. 823, § 1.02, eff. Jan. 1, 2014.

§ 1154.054. Approval or Disapproval by the Court

(a) On the filing of the inventory, appraisement, and list of claims with the court clerk, the judge shall examine and approve or disapprove the inventory, appraisement, and list of claims.

(b) If the judge approves the inventory, appraisement, and list of claims, the judge shall enter an order to that effect.

(c) If the judge does not approve the inventory, appraisement, or list of claims, the judge:

(1) shall enter an order to that effect requiring the filing of another inventory, appraisement, or list of claims, whichever is not approved, within a period specified in the order not to exceed 20 days after the date the order is entered; and

(2) may, if considered necessary, appoint new appraisers.

Derived from Probate Code § 733.

Added by Acts 2011, 82nd Leg., ch. 823, § 1.02, eff. Jan. 1, 2014.

§ 1154.055. Failure of Joint Guardians to File Inventory, Appraisement, and List of Claims

(a) If more than one guardian of the estate qualifies to serve, any one or more of the guardians, on the neglect of the other guardians, may make and file an inventory, appraisement, and list of claims.

(b) A guardian who neglects to make or file an inventory, appraisement, and list of claims may not interfere with and does not have any power over the estate after another guardian makes and files an inventory, appraisement, and list of claims.

(c) The guardian who files the inventory, appraisement, and list of claims is entitled to the whole administration unless, not later than the 60th day after the date the guardian files the inventory, appraisement, and list of claims, each of the delinquent guardians files with the court a written, sworn, and reasonable excuse that the court considers satisfactory. The court shall enter an order removing one or more delinquent guardians and revoking those guardians' letters if:

(1) an excuse is not filed; or

(2) the court does not consider the filed excuse sufficient.

Derived from Probate Code § 738.

Added by Acts 2011, 82nd Leg., ch. 823, § 1.02, eff. Jan. 1, 2014.

Subchapter C. Changes to Inventory, Appraisement, and List of Claims

§ 1154.101. Discovery of Additional Property or Claims

If after the filing of the inventory, appraisement, and list of claims the guardian of the estate acquires possession or knowledge of property or claims of the estate not included in the inventory, appraisement, and list of claims, the guardian shall promptly file with the court clerk a verified, full, and detailed supplemental inventory, appraisement, and list of claims.

Derived from Probate Code § 734.

Added by Acts 2011, 82nd Leg., ch. 823, § 1.02, eff. Jan. 1, 2014.

§ 1154.102. Additional Inventory and Appraisement or List of Claims

(a) On the written complaint of any interested person that property or claims of the estate have not been included in the filed inventory, appraisement, and list of claims, the guardian of the estate shall be cited to appear before the court in which the cause is pending and show cause why the guardian should not be required to make and file an additional inventory and appraisement or list of claims, or both.

(b) After hearing the complaint, if the court is satisfied of the truth of the complaint, the court shall enter an order requiring the guardian to make and file an additional inventory and appraisement or list of claims, or both. The additional inventory and appraisement or list of claims:

    (1) must be made and filed in the same manner as the original inventory and appraisement or list of claims within the period prescribed by the court, not to exceed 20 days after the date of the order; and

    (2) may include only property or claims not previously included in the inventory and appraisement or list of claims.

Derived from Probate Code § 735.

Added by Acts 2011, 82nd Leg., ch. 823, § 1.02, eff. Jan. 1, 2014.

§ 1154.103. Correction of Inventory, Appraisement, or List of Claims for Erroneous or Unjust Item

(a) A person interested in an estate who considers an inventory, appraisement, or list of claims filed by the guardian of the estate to be erroneous or unjust in any particular form may:

    (1) file a written complaint setting forth the alleged erroneous or unjust item; and

    (2) have the guardian cited to appear before the court and show cause why the item should not be corrected.

(b) On the hearing of the complaint, if the court is satisfied from the evidence that the inventory, appraisement, or list of claims is erroneous or unjust as alleged in the complaint, the court shall enter an order:

    (1) specifying the erroneous or unjust item and the corrections to be made; and

    (2) appointing an appraiser to make a new appraisement correcting the erroneous or unjust item and requiring the filing of the new appraisement not later than the 20th day after the date of the order.

(c) The court, on the court's own motion or a motion of the guardian of the estate, may also have a new appraisement made for the purposes described by this section.

Derived from Probate Code § 736.

Added by Acts 2011, 82nd Leg., ch. 823, § 1.02, eff. Jan. 1, 2014.

§ 1154.104. Reappraisement

(a) A reappraisement made, filed, and approved by the court replaces the original appraisement. Not more than one reappraisement may be made.

(b) Notwithstanding Subsection (a), a person interested in an estate may object to a reappraisement regardless of whether the court has approved the reappraisement. If the court finds that the reappraisement is erroneous or unjust, the court shall appraise the property on the basis of the evidence before the court.

Derived from Probate Code § 737.

Added by Acts 2011, 82nd Leg., ch. 823, § 1.02, eff. Jan. 1, 2014.

Subchapter D. Use of Inventory, Appraisement, and List of Claims as Evidence

§ 1154.151. Use of Inventory, Appraisement, and List of Claims as Evidence

Each inventory, appraisement, and list of claims that has been made, filed, and approved in accordance with law; the record of the inventory, appraisement, and list of claims; or a copy of an original or the record that has been certified under the seal of the county court affixed by the clerk:

    (1) may be given in evidence in any court of this state in any suit by or against the guardian of the estate; and

    (2) is not conclusive for or against the guardian of the estate if it is shown that:

        (A) any property or claim of the estate is not shown in the inventory, appraisement, or list of claims; or

        (B) the value of the property or claim of the estate exceeded the value shown in the appraisement or list of claims.

Derived from Probate Code § 739.

Added by Acts 2011, 82nd Leg., ch. 823, § 1.02, eff. Jan. 1, 2014.

Chapter 1155. Compensation, Expenses, and Court Costs

Chapter 1155. Compensation, Expenses, and Court Costs

Subchapter A. Compensation of Guardians in General

§ 1155.001. Definitions

In this subchapter:

(1) "Gross income" does not include United States Department of Veterans Affairs or social security benefits received by a ward.

(2) "Money paid out" does not include any money loaned, invested, or paid over on the settlement of a guardianship or a tax-motivated gift made by a ward.

Derived from Probate Code § 665(h).

Added by Acts 2011, 82nd Leg., ch. 823, § 1.02, eff. Jan. 1, 2014.

§ 1155.002. Compensation for Certain Guardians of the Person

(a) The court may authorize compensation for a guardian serving as a guardian of the person alone from available funds of the ward's estate or other funds available for that purpose. The court may set the compensation in an amount not to exceed five percent of the ward's gross income.

(b) If the ward's estate is insufficient to pay for the services of a private professional guardian or a licensed attorney serving as a guardian of the person, the court may authorize compensation for that guardian if funds in the county treasury are budgeted for that purpose.

Derived from Probate Code §§ 665(a), (g).

Added by Acts 2011, 82nd Leg., ch. 823, § 1.02, eff. Jan. 1, 2014.

§ 1155.003. Compensation for Guardian of the Estate

(a) The guardian of an estate is entitled to reasonable compensation on application to the court at the time the court approves an annual or final accounting filed by the guardian under this title.

(b) A fee of five percent of the gross income of the ward's estate and five percent of all money paid out of the estate, subject to the award of an additional amount under Section 1155.006(a) following a review under Section 1155.006(a)(1), is considered reasonable under this section if the court finds that the guardian has taken care of and managed the estate in compliance with the standards of this title.

Derived from Probate Code § 665(b).

Added by Acts 2011, 82nd Leg., ch. 823, § 1.02, eff. Jan. 1, 2014.

§ 1155.004. Considerations in Authorizing Compensation

In determining whether to authorize compensation for a guardian under this subchapter, the court shall consider:

(1) the ward's monthly income from all sources; and

(2) whether the ward receives medical assistance under the state Medicaid program.

Derived from Probate Code § 665(a-1).

Added by Acts 2011, 82nd Leg., ch. 823, § 1.02, eff. Jan. 1, 2014.

§ 1155.005. Maximum Aggregate Compensation

Except as provided by Section 1155.006(a) for a fee the court determines is unreasonably low, the aggregate fee of the guardian of the person and guardian of the estate may not exceed an amount equal to five percent of the gross income of the ward's estate plus five percent of all money paid out of the estate.

Derived from Probate Code § 665(f).

Added by Acts 2011, 82nd Leg., ch. 823, § 1.02, eff. Jan. 1, 2014.

§ 1155.006. Modification of Unreasonably Low Compensation; Authorization for Payment of Estimated Quarterly Compensation

(a) On application of an interested person or on the court's own motion, the court may:

(1) review and modify the amount of compensation authorized under Section 1155.002(a) or 1155.003 if the court finds that the amount is unreasonably low when considering the services provided as guardian; and

(2) authorize compensation for the guardian in an estimated amount the court finds reasonable, to be paid on a quarterly basis before the guardian files an annual or final accounting, if the court finds that delaying the payment of compensation until the guardian files an accounting would create a hardship for the guardian.

(b) A finding of unreasonably low compensation may not be established under Subsection (a) solely because the amount of compensation is less than the usual and customary charges of the person or entity serving as guardian.

Derived from Probate Code §§ 665(c), (d).

Added by Acts 2011, 82nd Leg., ch. 823, § 1.02, eff. Jan. 1, 2014.

§ 1155.007. Reduction or Elimination of Estimated Quarterly Compensation

(a) A court that authorizes payment of estimated quarterly compensation under Section 1155.006(a) may later reduce or eliminate the guardian's compensation if, on review of an annual or final accounting or otherwise, the court finds that the guardian:

(1) received compensation in excess of the amount permitted under this subchapter;

(2) has not adequately performed the duties required of a guardian under this title; or

(3) has been removed for cause.

(b) If a court reduces or eliminates a guardian's compensation as provided by Subsection (a), the guardian and the surety on the guardian's bond are liable to the guardianship estate for any excess compensation received.

Derived from Probate Code § 665(d), (d-1).

Added by Acts 2011, 82nd Leg., ch. 823, § 1.02, eff. Jan. 1, 2014.

§ 1155.008. Denial of Compensation

On application of an interested person or on the court's own motion, the court may wholly or partly deny a fee authorized under this subchapter if:

(1) the court finds that the guardian has not adequately performed the duties required of a guardian under this title; or

(2) the guardian has been removed for cause.

Derived from Probate Code § 665(e).

Added by Acts 2011, 82nd Leg., ch. 823, § 1.02, eff. Jan. 1, 2014.

Subchapter B. Compensation for Professional Services

§ 1155.052. Attorney Serving as Guardian and Providing Related Legal Services

(a) Notwithstanding any other provision of this chapter, an attorney who serves as guardian and who also provides legal services in connection with the guardianship is not entitled to compensation for the guardianship services or payment of attorney's fees for the legal services from the ward's estate or other funds available for that purpose unless the attorney files with the court a detailed description of the services performed that identifies which of the services provided were guardianship services and which were legal services.

(b) An attorney described by Subsection (a) is not entitled to payment of attorney's fees for guardianship services that are not legal services.

(c) The court shall set the compensation of an attorney described by Subsection (a) for the performance of guardianship services in accordance with Subchapter A. The court shall set attorney's fees for an attorney described by Subsection (a) for legal services provided in accordance with Sections 1155.054, 1155.101, and 1155.151.

Derived from Probate Code § 665D.

Added by Acts 2011, 82nd Leg., ch. 823, § 1.02, eff. Jan. 1, 2014. Subsec. (a) and (c) amended by Acts 2013, 83rd Leg., ch. 982, § 17, eff. Jan. 1, 2014.

§ 1155.053. Compensation for Services to Recover Property

(a) Subject only to the approval of the court in which the estate is being administered and except as provided by Subsection (b), a guardian of an estate may convey or contract to convey a contingent interest in any property sought to be recovered, not to exceed one-third of the property for services of attorneys.

(b) A guardian of an estate may convey or contract to convey for services of attorneys a contingent interest that exceeds one-third of the property sought to be recovered under this section only on the approval of the court in which the estate is being administered. The court must approve a contract entered into or conveyance made under this section before an attorney performs any legal services. A contract entered into or conveyance made in violation of this section is void unless the court ratifies or reforms the contract or documents relating to the conveyance to the extent necessary to cause the contract or conveyance to meet the requirements of this section.

(c) In approving a contract or conveyance under Subsection (a) or (b) for services of an attorney, the court shall consider:

(1) the time and labor that will be required, the novelty and difficulty of the questions to be involved, and the skill that will be required to perform the legal services properly;

(2) the fee customarily charged in the locality for similar legal services;

(3) the value of property recovered or sought to be recovered by the guardian under this section;

(4) the benefits to the estate that the attorney will be responsible for securing; and

(5) the experience and ability of the attorney who will be performing the services.

Derived from Probate Code § 665C.

Added by Acts 2011, 82nd Leg., ch. 823, § 1.02, eff. Jan. 1, 2014.

§ 1155.054. Payment Of Attorney's Fees To Certain Attorneys.

(a) A court that creates a guardianship or creates a management trust under Chapter 1301 for a ward, on request of a person who filed an application to be appointed guardian of the proposed ward, an application for the appointment of another suitable person as guardian of the proposed ward, or an application for the creation of the management trust, may authorize the payment of reasonable and necessary attorney's fees, as determined by the court, in amounts the court considers equitable and just, to an attorney who represents the person who filed the application at the application hearing, regardless of whether the person is appointed the ward's guardian or whether a management trust is created, from available funds of the ward's estate or management trust, if created, subject to Subsections (b) and (d).

(b) The court may authorize amounts that otherwise would be paid from the ward's estate or the management trust as provided by Subsection (a) to instead be paid from the county treasury, subject to Subsection (e), if:

(1) the ward's estate or management trust is insufficient to pay the amounts; and

(2) funds in the county treasury are budgeted for that purpose.

(c) The court may not authorize attorney's fees under this section unless the court finds that the applicant acted in good faith and for just cause in the filing and prosecution of the application.

(d) If the court finds that a party in a guardianship proceeding acted in bad faith or without just cause in prosecuting or objecting to an application in the proceeding, the court may require the party to reimburse the ward's estate for all or part of the attorney's fees awarded under this section and shall issue judgment against the party and in favor of the estate for the amount of attorney's fees required to be reimbursed to the estate.

(e) The court may authorize the payment of attorney's fees from the county treasury under Subsection (b) only if the court is satisfied that the attorney to whom the fees will be paid has not received, and is not seeking, payment for the services described by that subsection from any other source.

Derived from Probate Code §§ 665B.

Added by Acts 2013, 83rd Leg., ch. 982, § 18, eff. Jan. 1, 2014.

Subchapter C. Expenses

§ 1155.101. Reimbursement of Expenses in General

A guardian is entitled to reimbursement from the guardianship estate for all necessary and reasonable expenses incurred in performing any duty as a guardian, including reimbursement for the payment of reasonable attorney's fees necessarily incurred by the guardian in connection with the management of the estate or any other matter in the guardianship.

Derived from Probate Code § 666.

Added by Acts 2011, 82nd Leg., ch. 823, § 1.02, eff. Jan. 1, 2014. Amended by Acts 2013, 83rd Leg., ch. 161, § 6.043, eff. Jan. 1, 2014.

§ 1155.102. Reimbursement of Expenses for Collection of Claim or Debt

On satisfactory proof to the court, a guardian of an estate is entitled to all necessary and reasonable expenses incurred by the guardian in collecting or attempting to collect a claim or debt owed to the estate or in recovering or attempting to recover property to which the estate has title or a claim.

Derived from Probate Code § 665C(d).

Added by Acts 2011, 82nd Leg., ch. 823, § 1.02, eff. Jan. 1, 2014.

§ 1155.103. Expense Charges: Requirements

All expense charges shall be:

(1) in writing, showing specifically each item of expense and the date of the expense;

(2) verified by affidavit of the guardian;

(3) filed with the clerk; and

(4) paid only if the payment is authorized by court order.

Derived from Probate Code § 667.

Added by Acts 2011, 82nd Leg., ch. 823, § 1.02, eff. Jan. 1, 2014.

Subchapter D. Costs in General

§ 1155.151. Costs in Guardianship Proceeding Generally

(a) In a guardianship proceeding, the court costs of the proceeding, including the costs described by Subsection (a-1) [cost of the guardians ad litem, attorneys ad litem, court visitor, mental health professionals, and interpreters appointed under this title, shall be set in an amount the court considers equitable and just and, except as provided by Subsection (c)], shall, except as provided by Subsection (c), be paid as follows [out of the guardianship estate, or the county treasury if the estate is insufficient to pay the cost], and the court shall issue the judgment accordingly:

(1) out of the guardianship estate;

(2) out of the management trust, if a management trust has been created for the benefit of the ward under Chapter 1301 and the court determines it is in the ward's best interest;

(3) by the party to the proceeding who incurred the costs, unless that party filed, on the party's own behalf, an affidavit of inability to pay the costs under Rule 145, Texas Rules of Civil Procedure, that shows the party is unable to afford the costs, if:

(A) there is no guardianship estate or no management trust has been created for the ward's benefit; or

(B) the assets of the guardianship estate or management trust, as appropriate, are insufficient to pay the costs; or

(4) out of the county treasury if:

(A) there is no guardianship estate or management trust or the assets of the guardianship estate or management trust, as appropriate, are insufficient to pay the costs; and

(B) the party to the proceeding who incurred the costs filed, on the party's own behalf, an affidavit of inability to pay the costs under Rule 145, Texas Rules of Civil Procedure, that shows the party is unable to afford the costs.

(a-1) In a guardianship proceeding, the cost of any guardians ad litem, attorneys ad litem, court visitors, mental health professionals, and interpreters appointed under this title shall be set in an amount the court considers equitable and just.

(a-2) Notwithstanding any other law requiring the payment of court costs in a guardianship proceeding, the following are not required to pay court costs on the filing of or during a guardianship proceeding:

(1) an attorney ad litem;

(2) a guardian ad litem;

(3) a person or entity who files an affidavit of inability to pay the costs under Rule 145, Texas Rules of Civil Procedure, that shows the person or entity is unable to afford the costs;

(4) a nonprofit guardianship program;

(5) a governmental entity; and

(6) a government agency or nonprofit agency providing guardianship services.

(a-3) For purposes of Subsections (a) and (a-2), a person or entity who files an affidavit of inability to pay the costs under Rule 145, Texas Rules of Civil Procedure, is unable to afford the costs if the affidavit shows that the person or entity:

(1) is currently receiving assistance or other benefits from a government program under which assistance or other benefits are provided to individuals on a means-tested basis;

(2) is eligible for and currently receiving free legal services in the guardianship proceeding through the following:

(A) a legal services provider funded partly by the Texas Access to Justice Foundation;

(B) a legal services provider funded partly by the Legal Services Corporation; or

(C) a nonprofit corporation formed under the laws of this state that provides legal services to low-income individuals whose household income is at or below 200 percent of the federal poverty guidelines as determined by the United States Department of Health and Human Services;

(3) applied and was eligible for free legal services through a person or entity listed in Subdivision (2) but was declined representation; or

(4) has a household income that is at or below 200 percent of the federal poverty guidelines as determined by the United States Department of Health and Human Services and has money or other available assets, excluding any homestead and exempt property under Chapter 42, Property Code, in an amount that does not exceed $2,000.

(a-4) If an affidavit of inability to pay costs filed under Rule 145, Texas Rules of Civil Procedure, is contested, the court, at a hearing, shall review the contents of and attachments to the affidavit and any other evidence offered at the hearing and make a determination as to whether the person or entity is unable to afford the costs. If the court finds that the person or entity is able to afford the costs, the person or entity must pay the court costs. Except with leave of court, no further action in the guardianship proceeding may be taken by a person or entity found able to afford costs until payment of those costs is made.

(b) The costs attributable to the services of a person described by Subsection (a-1) [(a)] shall be paid under this section at any time after the commencement of the proceeding as ordered by the court.

(c) If the court finds that a party in a guardianship proceeding acted in bad faith or without just cause in prosecuting or objecting to an application in the proceeding, the court may order the party to pay all or part of the costs of the proceeding. If the party found to be acting in bad faith or without just cause was required to provide security for the probable costs of the proceeding under Section 1053.052, the court shall first apply the amount provided as security as payment for costs ordered by the court under this subsection. If the amount provided as security is insufficient to pay the entire amount ordered by the court, the court shall render judgment in favor of the estate against the party for the remaining amount.

(d) If a guardianship of the estate or management trust under Chapter 1301 is created, a person or entity who paid any costs on the filing of or during the proceeding is entitled to be reimbursed out of assets of the guardianship estate or management trust, as appropriate, for the costs if:

(1) the assets of the estate or trust, as appropriate, are sufficient to cover the reimbursement of the costs; and

(2) the person or entity has not been ordered by the court to pay the costs as all or part of the payment of court costs under Subsection (c).

(e) If at any time after a guardianship of the estate or management trust under Chapter 1301 is created there are sufficient assets of the estate or trust, as appropriate, to pay the amount of any of the costs exempt from payment under Subsection (a-2), the court shall require the guardian to pay out of the guardianship estate or management trust, as appropriate, to the court clerk for deposit in the county treasury the amount of any of those costs.

(f) To the extent that this section conflicts with the Texas Rules of Civil Procedure or other rules, this section controls.

Derived from Probate Code § 669.

Added by Acts 2011, 82nd Leg., ch. 823, § 1.02, eff. Jan. 1, 2014. Amended by Acts 2013, 83rd Leg., ch. 982, § 19, eff. Jan. 1, 2014 and Acts 2013, 83rd Leg., ch. 161, §§ 6.044 & 6.045, eff. Jan. 1, 2014. Subsecs. (a) & (b) amended and subsecs (a-1), (a-2), (a-3), (d), (e), & (f) added by Acts 2015, 84th Leg., ch. 1031, § 18, eff. Sept. 1, 2015.

§ 1155.152. Certain Costs Adjudged Against Guardian

If costs are incurred because a guardian neglects to perform a required duty or is removed for cause, the guardian and the sureties on the guardian's bond are liable for:

(1) any costs of removal and other additional costs incurred that are not expenditures authorized under this title; and

(2) reasonable attorney's fees incurred in:

(A) removing the guardian; or

(B) obtaining compliance regarding any statutory duty the guardian has neglected.

Derived from Probate Code § 668.

Added by Acts 2011, 82nd Leg., ch. 823, § 1.02, eff. Jan. 1, 2014.

Subchapter E. Compensation and Costs in Guardianships for Certain Medical Assistance Recipients

§ 1155.201. Definitions

In this subchapter:

(1) "Applied income" means the portion of the earned and unearned income of a recipient of medical assistance, or if applicable the recipient and the recipient's spouse, that is paid under the medical assistance program to an institution or long-term care facility in which the recipient resides.

(2) "Medical assistance" has the meaning assigned by Section 32.003, Human Resources Code.

Derived from Probate Code § 670(a).

Added by Acts 2011, 82nd Leg., ch. 823, § 1.02, eff. Jan. 1, 2014. Subsection (1) amended by Acts 2013, 83rd Leg., ch. 161, § 6.046, eff. Jan. 1, 2014.

§ 1155.202. Compensation and Costs Payable Under Medical Assistance Program

(a) Notwithstanding any other provision of this title and to the extent permitted by federal law, a court that appoints a guardian for a recipient of medical assistance who has applied income may order the following to be deducted as an additional personal needs allowance in the computation of the recipient's applied income in accordance with Section 32.02451, Human Resources Code:

(1) compensation to the guardian in an amount not to exceed $175 per month;

(2) costs directly related to establishing or terminating the guardianship, not to exceed $1,000 except as provided by Subsection (b); and

(3) other administrative costs related to the guardianship, not to exceed $1,000 during any three-year period.

(b) Costs ordered to be deducted under Subsection (a)(2) may include compensation and expenses for an attorney ad litem or guardian ad litem and reasonable attorney's fees for an attorney representing the guardian. The costs ordered to be paid may exceed $1,000 if the costs in excess of that amount are supported by documentation acceptable to the court and the costs are approved by the court.

(c) A court may not order:

(1) that the deduction for compensation and costs under Subsection (a) take effect before the later of:

(A) the month in which the court order issued under that subsection is signed; or

(B) the first month of medical assistance eligibility for which the recipient is subject to a copayment; or

(2) a deduction for services provided before the effective date of the deduction as provided by Subdivision (1).

Derived from Probate Code § 670(b) & (c).

Added by Acts 2011, 82nd Leg., ch. 823, § 1.02, eff. Jan. 1, 2014. Amended by Acts 2013, 83rd Leg., ch. 161, § 6.047, eff. Jan. 1, 2014.

Chapter 1156. Education and Maintenance Allowances Paid from Ward's Estate

Subchapter A. Allowances for Ward

Subchapter B. Allowances for Ward's Family

Chapter 1156. Education and Maintenance Allowances Paid from Ward's Estate

Subchapter A. Allowances for Ward

§ 1156.001. Application for Allowance

(a) Subject to Section 1156.051, if a monthly allowance for a ward was not ordered in the court's order appointing a guardian, the guardian of the estate of the ward shall file with the court an application requesting a monthly allowance to be spent from the income and corpus of the ward's estate for:

(1) the education and maintenance of the ward; and

(2) the maintenance of the ward's property.

(b) The guardian must file the application not later than the 30th day after the date the guardian qualifies as guardian or the date specified by the court, whichever is later.

(c) The application must clearly separate amounts requested for the ward's education and maintenance from amounts requested for maintenance of the ward's property.

Derived from Probate Code §§ 776(a), (a-1).

Added by Acts 2011, 82nd Leg., ch. 823, § 1.02, eff. Jan. 1, 2014.

§ 1156.002. Court Determination of Allowance Amount

In determining the amount of the monthly allowance for the ward and the ward's property, the court shall consider the condition of the estate and the income and corpus of the estate necessary to pay the reasonably anticipated regular education and maintenance expenses of the ward and maintenance expenses of the ward's property.

Derived from Probate Code § 776(a-2).

Added by Acts 2011, 82nd Leg., ch. 823, § 1.02, eff. Jan. 1, 2014.

§ 1156.003. Court Order Setting Allowance

(a) The court's order setting a monthly allowance must specify the types of expenditures the guardian may make on a monthly basis for the ward or the ward's property.

(b) If different persons have the guardianship of the person and of the estate of a ward, the court's order setting a monthly allowance must specify:

(1) the amount, if any, set by the court for the ward's education and maintenance that the guardian of the estate shall pay; and

(2) the amount, if any, that the guardian of the estate shall pay to the guardian of the person, at a time specified by the court, for the ward's education and maintenance.

(c) If the guardian of the estate fails to pay to the guardian of the person the monthly allowance set by the court, the guardian of the estate shall be compelled by court order to make the payment after the guardian is cited to appear.

(d) An order setting a monthly allowance does not affect the guardian's duty to account for expenditures of the allowance in the annual account required by Subchapter A, Chapter 1163.

Derived from Probate Code §§ 776(a-2), (a-3).

Added by Acts 2011, 82nd Leg., ch. 823, § 1.02, eff. Jan. 1, 2014.

§ 1156.004. Expenditures Exceeding Allowance

If a guardian in good faith has spent money from the income and corpus of the estate of the ward for the ward's support and maintenance and the expenditures exceed the monthly allowance authorized by the court, the guardian shall file a motion with the court requesting approval of the expenditures. The court may approve the excess expenditures if:

(1) the expenditures were made when it was not convenient or possible for the guardian to first secure court approval;

(2) the proof is clear and convincing that the expenditures were reasonable and proper;

(3) the court would have granted authority in advance to make the expenditures; and

(4) the ward received the benefits of the expenditures.

Derived from Probate Code § 776(b).

Added by Acts 2011, 82nd Leg., ch. 823, § 1.02, eff. Jan. 1, 2014.

Subchapter B. Allowances for Ward's Family

§ 1156.051. Certain Allowances Prohibited When Parent is Guardian of Minor Ward

(a) Except as provided by Subsection (b), a parent who is the guardian of the person of a ward who is 17 years of age or younger may not use the income or the corpus from the ward's estate for the ward's support, education, or maintenance.

(b) A court with proper jurisdiction may authorize the guardian of the person to spend the income or the corpus from the ward's estate to support, educate, or maintain the ward if the guardian presents to the court clear and convincing evidence that the ward's parents are unable without unreasonable hardship to pay for all of the expenses related to the ward's support.

Derived from Probate Code § 777.

Added by Acts 2011, 82nd Leg., ch. 823, § 1.02, eff. Jan. 1, 2014.

§ 1156.052. Allowance for Ward's Spouse or Dependent

(a) Subject to Section 1156.051 and on application to the court, the court may order the guardian of the estate of a ward to spend money from the ward's estate for the education and maintenance of the ward's spouse or dependent.

(b) In determining whether to order the expenditure of money from a ward's estate for the ward's spouse or dependent, as appropriate, under this section, the court shall consider:

(1) the circumstances of the ward, the ward's spouse, and the ward's dependents;

(2) the ability and duty of the ward's spouse to support himself or herself and the ward's dependent;

(3) the size of the ward's estate;

(4) a beneficial interest the ward or the ward's spouse or dependent has in a trust; and

(5) an existing estate plan, including a trust or will, that provides a benefit to the ward's spouse or dependent.

(c) A person who makes an application to the court under this section shall mail notice of the application by certified mail to all interested persons.

Derived from Probate Code § 776A.

Added by Acts 2011, 82nd Leg., ch. 823, § 1.02, eff. Jan. 1, 2014.

Chapter 1157. Presentment and Payment of Claims

Subchapter A. Presentment of Claims Against Guardianship Estate in General

Subchapter B. Action on Claims

Subchapter C. Payment of Claims, Allowances, and Expenses

§ 1157.107. Payment of Court Costs Relating to Claim

§ 1157.108. Liability for Nonpayment of Claim

Subchapter D. Presentment and Payment of Secured Claims

§ 1157.151. Option to Treat Claim as Matured Secured Claim or Preferred Debt and Lien

§ 1157.152. Preferred Debt and Lien

§ 1157.153. Payment of Maturities on Preferred Debt and Lien

Subchapter E. Claims Involving Guardians

§ 1157.201. Claim by Guardian

§ 1157.202. Purchase of Claim by Guardian Prohibited

Chapter 1157. Presentment and Payment of Claims

Subchapter A. Presentment of Claims Against Guardianship Estate in General

§ 1157.001. Presentment of Claim to Guardian of the Estate

A claim may be presented to the guardian of the estate at any time if:

(1) the estate has not been closed; and

(2) suit on the claim has not been barred by the general statutes of limitation.

Derived from Probate Code § 786(a).

Added by Acts 2011, 82nd Leg., ch. 823, § 1.02, eff. Jan. 1, 2014.

§ 1157.002. Presentment of Claim to Clerk

(a) A claim may also be presented by depositing the claim with the clerk with vouchers and the necessary exhibits and affidavit attached to the claim. On receiving a claim deposited under this subsection, the clerk shall advise the guardian of the estate or the guardian's attorney of the deposit of the claim by a letter mailed to the guardian's last known address.

(b) A claim deposited under Subsection (a) is presumed to be rejected if the guardian fails to act on the claim on or before the 30th day after the date the claim is filed.

(c) Failure of the clerk to give the notice required under Subsection (a) does not affect the validity of the presentment or the presumption of rejection of the claim because the guardian does not act on the claim within the 30-day period prescribed by Subsection (b).

Derived from Probate Code § 795.

Added by Acts 2011, 82nd Leg., ch. 823, § 1.02, eff. Jan. 1, 2014.

§ 1157.003. Inclusion of Attorney's Fees in Claim

If the instrument evidencing or supporting a claim provides for attorney's fees, the claimant may include as a part of the claim the portion of the attorney's fees the claimant has paid or contracted to pay to an attorney to prepare, present, and collect the claim.

Derived from Probate Code § 794.

Added by Acts 2011, 82nd Leg., ch. 823, § 1.02, eff. Jan. 1, 2014.

§ 1157.004. Affidavit Authenticating Claim for Money in General

(a) Except as provided by Sections 1157.005 and 1157.102, a claim for money against an estate must be supported by an affidavit that states:

(1) that the claim is just;

(2) that all legal offsets, payments, and credits known to the affiant have been allowed; and

(3) if the claim is not founded on a written instrument or account, the facts on which the claim is founded.

(b) A photostatic copy of an exhibit or voucher necessary to prove a claim under this section may be offered with and attached to the claim instead of attaching the original.

Derived from Probate Code § 788.

Added by Acts 2011, 82nd Leg., ch. 823, § 1.02, eff. Jan. 1, 2014.

§ 1157.005. Affidavit Authenticating Claim of Corporation or by Certain Other Representatives

(a) The cashier, treasurer, or managing official of a corporation shall make the affidavit required to authenticate a claim of the corporation.

(b) In an affidavit made by an officer of a corporation, or by an executor, administrator, guardian, trustee, assignee, agent, or attorney, it is sufficient to state that the affiant has made diligent inquiry and examination and believes the claim is just and that all legal offsets, payments, and credits made known to the affiant have been allowed.

Derived from Probate Code § 791.

Added by Acts 2011, 82nd Leg., ch. 823, § 1.02, eff. Jan. 1, 2014.

§ 1157.006. Lost or Destroyed Evidence Concerning Claim

If evidence of a claim is lost or destroyed, the claimant or the claimant's representative may make an affidavit to the fact of the loss or destruction. The affidavit must state:

(1) the amount, date, and nature of the claim;

(2) the due date of the claim;

(3) that the claim is just;

(4) that all legal offsets, payments, and credits known to the affiant have been allowed; and

(5) that the claimant is still the owner of the claim.

Derived from Probate Code § 790.

Added by Acts 2011, 82nd Leg., ch. 823, § 1.02, eff. Jan. 1, 2014.

§ 1157.007. Waiver of Certain Defects of Form or Claims of Insufficiency

A defect of form or a claim of insufficiency of a presented exhibit or voucher is considered waived by the guardian of the estate unless a written objection to the form, exhibit, or voucher is:

(1) made not later than the 30th day after the date the claim is presented; and

(2) filed with the county clerk.

Derived from Probate Code § 789.

Added by Acts 2011, 82nd Leg., ch. 823, § 1.02, eff. Jan. 1, 2014.

§ 1157.008. Effect on Statutes of Limitation of Filing of or Suit on Claim

The general statutes of limitation are tolled by:

(1) filing a claim that is legally allowed and approved; or

(2) bringing a suit on a rejected and disapproved claim not later than the 90th day after the date the claim is rejected or disapproved.

Derived from Probate Code § 787.

Added by Acts 2011, 82nd Leg., ch. 823, § 1.02, eff. Jan. 1, 2014.

Subchapter B. Action on Claims

§ 1157.051. Allowance or Rejection of Claim

A guardian of the estate shall, not later than the 30th day after the date an authenticated claim against the guardianship estate is presented to the guardian or filed with the clerk as provided by this chapter, endorse on or attach to the claim a memorandum signed by the guardian stating:

(1) the date of presentation or filing of the claim; and

(2) whether the guardian allows or rejects the claim, or, if the guardian allows or rejects a part of the claim, the portion of the claim the guardian allows or rejects.

Derived from Probate Code § 796.

Added by Acts 2011, 82nd Leg., ch. 823, § 1.02, eff. Jan. 1, 2014.

§ 1157.052. Failure to Endorse or Attach Memorandum or Allow or Reject Claim

The failure of a guardian of the estate to endorse on or attach to a claim presented to the guardian the memorandum required by Section 1157.051 or, not later than the 30th day after the date a claim is presented, to allow or reject the claim or portion of the claim constitutes a rejection of the claim. If the claim is later established by suit:

(1) the costs shall be taxed against the guardian, individually; or

(2) the guardian may be removed as in other cases of removal on the written complaint of any person interested in the claim after personal service of citation, hearing, and proof.

Derived from Probate Code § 797.

Added by Acts 2011, 82nd Leg., ch. 823, § 1.02, eff. Jan. 1, 2014.

§ 1157.053. Claim Entered on Claim Docket

After a claim against a ward's estate has been presented to and allowed by the guardian of the estate, wholly or partly, the claim must be filed with the county clerk of the proper county. The clerk shall enter the claim on the claim docket.

Derived from Probate Code § 798.

Added by Acts 2011, 82nd Leg., ch. 823, § 1.02, eff. Jan. 1, 2014.

§ 1157.054. Contest of Claim

(a) A person interested in a ward may, at any time before the court has acted on a claim, appear and object in writing to the approval of the claim or any part of the claim.

(b) If a person objects under Subsection (a):

(1) the parties are entitled to process for witnesses; and

(2) the court shall hear evidence and render judgment as in ordinary suits.

Derived from Probate Code § 799(a).

Added by Acts 2011, 82nd Leg., ch. 823, § 1.02, eff. Jan. 1, 2014.

§ 1157.055. Court's Action On Claim

The court shall:

(1) approve, wholly or partly, or reject a claim that has been allowed and entered on the claim docket for a period of 10 days; and

(2) concurrently classify the claim.

Derived from Probate Code § 799(b).

Added by Acts 2011, 82nd Leg., ch. 823, § 1.02, eff. Jan. 1, 2014.

§ 1157.056. Hearing on Certain Claims

(a) If a claim is properly authenticated and allowed, but the court is not satisfied that the claim is just, the court shall:

(1) examine the claimant and the guardian of the estate under oath; and

(2) hear other evidence necessary to determine the issue.

(b) If after the examination and hearing the court is not convinced that the claim is just, the court shall disapprove the claim.

Derived from Probate Code § 799(c).

Added by Acts 2011, 82nd Leg., ch. 823, § 1.02, eff. Jan. 1, 2014.

§ 1157.057. Court Order Regarding Action on Claim

(a) The court acting on a claim shall endorse on or attach to the claim a written memorandum that:

(1) is dated and officially signed; and

(2) states:

(A) the exact action taken by the court on the claim, whether the claim is approved or disapproved, or is approved in part and rejected in part; and

(B) the classification of the claim.

(b) An order under Subsection (a) has the effect of a final judgment.

Derived from Probate Code § 799(d).

Added by Acts 2011, 82nd Leg., ch. 823, § 1.02, eff. Jan. 1, 2014.

§ 1157.058. Appeal of Court's Action on Claim

If a claimant or any person interested in a ward is dissatisfied with the court's action on a claim, the claimant or interested person may appeal the action to the court of appeals in the manner other judgments of the county court in probate matters are appealed.

Derived from Probate Code § 799(e).

Added by Acts 2011, 82nd Leg., ch. 823, § 1.02, eff. Jan. 1, 2014.

§ 1157.059. Allowance and Approval Prohibited Without Affidavit

Except as provided by Section 1157.102, a guardian of the estate may not allow, and the court may not approve, a claim for money against the estate unless the claim is supported by an affidavit that meets the applicable requirements of Sections 1157.004 and 1157.005.

Derived from Probate Code § 788.

Added by Acts 2011, 82nd Leg., ch. 823, § 1.02, eff. Jan. 1, 2014.

§ 1157.060. Unsecured Claims Barred Under Certain Circumstances

A claim of an unsecured creditor for money that is not presented within the time prescribed by the notice of presentment permitted by Section 1153.004 is barred.

Derived from Probate Code § 786(a).

Added by Acts 2011, 82nd Leg., ch. 823, § 1.02, eff. Jan. 1, 2014.

§ 1157.061. Allowing Barred Claim Prohibited; Court Disapproval

A guardian of the estate may not allow a claim against a ward if a suit on the claim is barred by an applicable general statute of limitation. A claim against a ward that is allowed by the guardian shall be disapproved if the court is satisfied that the limitation has run.

Derived from Probate Code § 786(b).

Added by Acts 2011, 82nd Leg., ch. 823, § 1.02, eff. Jan. 1, 2014.

§ 1157.062. Certain Actions on Claims With Lost or Destroyed Evidence Void

(a) Before a claim the evidence for which is lost or destroyed is approved, the claim must be proved by disinterested testimony taken in open court or by oral or written deposition.

(b) The allowance or approval of a claim the evidence for which is lost or destroyed is void if the claim is:

(1) allowed or approved without the affidavit under Section 1157.006; or

(2) approved without satisfactory proof.

Derived from Probate Code § 790.

Added by Acts 2011, 82nd Leg., ch. 823, § 1.02, eff. Jan. 1, 2014.

§ 1157.063. Suit on Rejected Claim

(a) A claim or part of a claim that has been rejected by the guardian of the estate is barred unless not later than the 90th day after the date of rejection the claimant commences suit on the claim in the court of original probate jurisdiction in which the guardianship is pending or in any other court of proper jurisdiction.

(b) In a suit commenced on the rejected claim, the memorandum endorsed on or attached to the claim is taken to be true without further proof unless denied under oath.

Derived from Probate Code § 800.

Added by Acts 2011, 82nd Leg., ch. 823, § 1.02, eff. Jan. 1, 2014.

§ 1157.064. Presentment of Claim Prerequisite for Judgment

(a) Except as provided by Subsection (b), a judgment may not be rendered in favor of a claimant on a claim for money that has not been:

(1) legally presented to the guardian of the estate of the ward; and

(2) wholly or partly rejected by the guardian or the court.

(b) Subsection (a) does not apply to a claim against the estate of a ward for delinquent ad valorem taxes that is being administered in probate in a county other than the county in which the taxes were imposed.

Derived from Probate Code § 801.

Added by Acts 2011, 82nd Leg., ch. 823, § 1.02, eff. Jan. 1, 2014.

§ 1157.065. Judgment in Suit on Rejected Claim

No execution may issue on a rejected claim or part of a claim that is established by suit. The judgment in the suit shall be:

(1) certified not later than the 30th day after the date of rendition, if the judgment is from a court other than the court of original probate jurisdiction;

(2) filed in the court in which the guardianship is pending;

(3) entered on the claim docket;

(4) classified by the court; and

(5) handled as if originally allowed and approved in due course of administration.

Derived from Probate Code § 800.

Added by Acts 2011, 82nd Leg., ch. 823, § 1.02, eff. Jan. 1, 2014.

Subchapter C. Payment of Claims, Allowances, and Expenses

§ 1157.101. Payment of Approved or Established Claim

Except as provided for payment of an unauthenticated claim at the risk of a guardian, a claim or any part of a claim for money against the estate of a ward may not be paid until the claim or part of the claim has been approved by the court or established by the judgment of a court of competent jurisdiction.

Derived from Probate Code § 804.

Added by Acts 2011, 82nd Leg., ch. 823, § 1.02, eff. Jan. 1, 2014.

§ 1157.102. Payment of Unauthenticated Claim

(a) Subject to Subsection (b), a guardian of the estate may pay an unauthenticated claim against the ward's estate if the guardian believes the claim to be just.

(b) A guardian who pays a claim under Subsection (a) and the sureties on the guardian's bond are liable for the amount of any payment of the claim if the court finds that the claim is not just.

Derived from Probate Code § 792.

Added by Acts 2011, 82nd Leg., ch. 823, § 1.02, eff. Jan. 1, 2014.

§ 1157.103. Priority of Payment of Claims

(a) Except as provided by Subsection (b), the guardian of the estate shall pay a claim against the ward's estate that has been allowed and approved or established by suit, as soon as practicable and in the following order:

(1) expenses for the care, maintenance, and education of the ward or the ward's dependents;

(2) funeral expenses of the ward and expenses of the ward's last illness, if the guardianship is kept open after the ward's death as provided under this title, except that any claim against the ward's estate that has been allowed and approved or established by suit before the ward's death shall be paid before the funeral expenses and expenses of the last illness;

(3) expenses of administration; and

(4) other claims against the ward or the ward's estate.

(b) If the estate is insolvent, the guardian shall give first priority to the payment of a claim relating to the administration of the guardianship. The guardian shall pay other claims against the ward's estate in the order prescribed by Subsection (a).

Derived from Probate Code §§ 805(a), (b).

Added by Acts 2011, 82nd Leg., ch. 823, § 1.02, eff. Jan. 1, 2014.

§ 1157.104. Payment of Proceeds from Sale of Property Securing Debt

(a) If a guardian of the estate has on hand the proceeds of a sale made to satisfy a mortgage or other lien and the proceeds or any part of the proceeds are not required for the payment of any debts against the estate that have a preference over the mortgage or other lien, the guardian shall pay the proceeds to a holder of the mortgage or other lien.

(b) If the guardian fails to pay the proceeds as required by this section, the holder of a mortgage or other lien, on proof of the mortgage or other lien, may obtain an order from the court directing the payment of proceeds to be made.

Derived from Probate Code § 808.

Added by Acts 2011, 82nd Leg., ch. 823, § 1.02, eff. Jan. 1, 2014.

§ 1157.105. Claimant's Petition for Allowance and Payment of Claim

A claimant whose claim has not been paid may:

(1) petition the court for determination of the claim at any time before the claim is barred by an applicable statute of limitations; and

(2) procure on due proof an order for the claim's allowance and payment from the estate.

Derived from Probate Code § 805(c).

Added by Acts 2011, 82nd Leg., ch. 823, § 1.02, eff. Jan. 1, 2014.

§ 1157.106. Payment When Assets Insufficient to Pay Certain Claims

(a) If there are insufficient assets to pay all claims of the same class, the claims in that class shall be paid pro rata, as directed by the court, and in the order directed.

(b) A guardian of the estate may not be allowed to pay any claims other than with the pro rata amount of the estate funds that have come into the guardian's possession, regardless of whether the estate is solvent or insolvent.

Derived from Probate Code § 806.

Added by Acts 2011, 82nd Leg., ch. 823, § 1.02, eff. Jan. 1, 2014.

§ 1157.107. Payment of Court Costs Relating to Claim

All costs incurred in the probate court with respect to a claim are taxed as follows:

(1) if the claim is allowed and approved, the guardianship estate shall pay the costs;

(2) if the claim is allowed but disapproved, the claimant shall pay the costs;

(3) if the claim is rejected but established by suit, the guardianship estate shall pay the costs;

(4) if the claim is rejected but not established by suit, the claimant shall pay the costs; or

(5) in a suit to establish the claim after the claim is rejected in part, if the claimant fails to recover judgment for a greater amount than was allowed or approved for the claim, the claimant shall pay all costs.

Derived from Probate Code § 802.

Added by Acts 2011, 82nd Leg., ch. 823, § 1.02, eff. Jan. 1, 2014.

§ 1157.108. Liability for Nonpayment of Claim

(a) A person or claimant, except the state treasury, entitled to payment from a guardianship estate of money the court orders to be paid is authorized to have execution issued against the property of the guardianship for the amount due, with interest and costs, if:

(1) a guardian of the estate fails to pay the money on demand;

(2) guardianship estate funds are available to make the payment; and

(3) the person or claimant makes an affidavit of the demand for payment and the guardian's failure to pay.

(b) The court may cite the guardian and the sureties on the guardian's bond to show cause why the guardian or sureties should not be held liable for the debt, interest, costs, or damages:

(1) on return of the execution under Subsection (a) not satisfied; or

(2) on the affidavit of demand and failure to pay under Subsection (a).

(c) On the return of citation served under Subsection (b), the court shall render judgment against the cited guardian and sureties, in favor of the claim holder, if good cause why the guardian and sureties should not be held liable is not shown. The judgment must be for:

(1) the unpaid amount ordered to be paid or established by suit, with interest and costs; and

(2) damages on the amount neglected to be paid at the rate of five percent per month for each month, or fraction of a month, that the payment was neglected to be paid after demand for payment was made.

(d) Damages ordered under Subsection (c)(2) may be collected in any court of competent jurisdiction.

Derived from Probate Code § 809.

Added by Acts 2011, 82nd Leg., ch. 823, § 1.02, eff. Jan. 1, 2014.

Subchapter D. Presentment and Payment of Secured Claims

§ 1157.151. Option to Treat Claim as Matured Secured Claim or Preferred Debt and Lien

(a) If a secured claim against a ward is presented, the claimant shall specify in the claim, in addition to all other matters required to be specified in the claim, whether the claim shall be:

(1) allowed and approved as a matured secured claim to be paid in due course of administration, in which case the claim shall be paid in that manner if allowed and approved; or

(2) allowed, approved, and fixed as a preferred debt and lien against the specific property securing the indebtedness and paid according to the terms of the contract that secured the lien, in which case the claim shall be so allowed and approved if it is a valid lien.

(b) Notwithstanding Subsection (a)(2), the guardian of the estate may pay a claim that the claimant specified as a claim to be allowed, approved, and fixed as a preferred debt and lien as described by Subsection (a)(2) before maturity if that payment is in the best interests of the estate.

(c) If a secured claim is not presented within the time provided by law, the claim shall be treated as a claim to be paid in accordance with Subsection (a)(2).

Derived from Probate Code §§ 793(a), (b).

Added by Acts 2011, 82nd Leg., ch. 823, § 1.02, eff. Jan. 1, 2014.

§ 1157.152. Preferred Debt and Lien

When a claim for a debt has been allowed and approved under Section 1157.151(a)(2):

(1) a further claim for the debt may not be made against other estate assets;

(2) the claim remains a preferred lien against the property securing the claim; and

(3) the property remains security for the debt in any distribution or sale of the property before final maturity and payment of the debt.

Derived from Probate Code § 793(c).

Added by Acts 2011, 82nd Leg., ch. 823, § 1.02, eff. Jan. 1, 2014.

§ 1157.153. Payment of Maturities on Preferred Debt and Lien

(a) If, not later than the 12th month after the date letters of guardianship are granted, the property securing a debt for which a claim is allowed, approved, and fixed under Section 1157.151(a)(2) is not sold or distributed, the guardian of the estate shall:

(1) promptly pay all maturities that have accrued on the debt according to the terms of the maturities; and

(2) perform all the terms of any contract securing the maturities.

(b) If the guardian defaults in payment or performance under Subsection (a):

(1) on the motion of the claim holder, the court shall require the sale of the property subject to the unmatured part of the debt and apply the proceeds of the sale to the liquidation of the maturities; or

(2) at the claim holder's option, a motion may be made in the same manner as a motion under Subdivision (1) to require the sale of the property free of the lien and apply the proceeds to the payment of the whole debt.

Derived from Probate Code § 793(d).

Added by Acts 2011, 82nd Leg., ch. 823, § 1.02, eff. Jan. 1, 2014.

Subchapter E. Claims Involving Guardians

§ 1157.201. Claim by Guardian

(a) A claim that a guardian of the person or estate held against the ward at the time of the guardian's appointment, or that accrues after the appointment, shall be verified by affidavit as required in other cases and presented to the clerk of the court in which the guardianship is pending. The clerk shall enter the claim on the claim docket and the claim shall take the same course as other claims.

(b) A claim by a guardian that has been filed with the court within the required period shall be entered on the claim docket and acted on by the court in the same manner as in other cases.

(c) An appeal from a judgment of the court acting on a claim under this section may be taken as in other cases.

Derived from Probate Code § 803.

Added by Acts 2011, 82nd Leg., ch. 823, § 1.02, eff. Jan. 1, 2014.

§ 1157.202. Purchase of Claim by Guardian Prohibited

(a) A guardian may not purchase, for the guardian's own use or for any other purpose, a claim against the guardianship the guardian represents.

(b) On written complaint by a person interested in the guardianship estate and on satisfactory proof of a violation of Subsection (a), the court after citation and hearing shall enter an order canceling the claim described by Subsection (a). No part of the canceled claim may be paid out of the guardianship.

(c) The court may remove a guardian for a violation of this section.

Derived from Probate Code § 807.

Added by Acts 2011, 82nd Leg., ch. 823, § 1.02, eff. Jan. 1, 2014.

Chapter 1158. Sale or Partition of Ward's Property

Chapter 1158. Sale or Partition of Ward's Property

Subchapter A. General Provisions

§ 1158.001. Court Order Authorizing Sale

(a) Except as provided by this chapter, any property of a ward may not be sold without a court order authorizing the sale.

(b) Except as otherwise specifically provided by this title, the court may order property of a ward to be sold for cash or on credit, at public auction or privately, as the court considers most advantageous to the estate.

Derived from Probate Code § 811.

Added by Acts 2011, 82nd Leg., ch. 823, § 1.02, eff. Jan. 1, 2014.

Subchapter B. Certain Estate Property Required to be Sold

§ 1158.051. Sale of Certain Personal Property Required

(a) After approval of the inventory, appraisement, and list of claims, the guardian of the estate of a ward promptly shall apply for a court order to sell, at public auction or privately, for cash or on credit for a term not to exceed six months, all estate property that is liable to perish, waste, or deteriorate in value, or that will be an expense or disadvantage to the estate if kept.

(b) The following may not be included in a sale under Subsection (a):

(1) property exempt from forced sale;

(2) property that is the subject of a specific legacy; and

(3) personal property necessary to carry on a farm, ranch, factory, or other business that is thought best to operate.

(c) In determining whether to order the sale of an asset under Subsection (a), the court shall consider:

(1) the guardian's duty to take care of and manage the estate in the manner a person of ordinary prudence, discretion, and intelligence would manage the person's own affairs; and

(2) whether the asset constitutes an asset that a trustee is authorized to invest under Subchapter F, Chapter 113, Property Code, or Chapter 117, Property Code.

Derived from Probate Code § 812.

Added by Acts 2011, 82nd Leg., ch. 823, § 1.02, eff. Jan. 1, 2014.

Subchapter C. Sale of Personal Property

§ 1158.101. Order for Sale

(a) Except as provided by Subsection (b), on the application of the guardian of the estate of a ward or any interested person, the court may order the sale of any estate personal property not required to be sold by Section 1158.051, including livestock or growing or harvested crops, if the court finds that the sale of the property is in the best interests of the ward or the ward's estate to pay, from the proceeds of the sale:

(1) expenses of the care, maintenance, and education of the ward or the ward's dependents;

(2) expenses of administration;

(3) allowances;

(4) claims against the ward or the ward's estate; and

(5) if the guardianship is kept open after the death of the ward, the ward's funeral expenses and expenses of the ward's last illness.

(b) The court may not order under this section the sale of exempt property.

Derived from Probate Code § 813.

Added by Acts 2011, 82nd Leg., ch. 823, § 1.02, eff. Jan. 1, 2014.

§ 1158.102. Requirements for Application and Order

To the extent possible, an application and order for the sale of estate personal property under Section 1158.101 must conform to the requirements under Subchapter F for an application and order for the sale of real estate.

Derived from Probate Code § 813.

Added by Acts 2011, 82nd Leg., ch. 823, § 1.02, eff. Jan. 1, 2014.

§ 1158.103. Sale at Public Auction

Unless the court directs otherwise, before estate personal property is sold at public auction, notice must be:

(1) issued by the guardian of the estate; and

(2) posted in the manner notice is posted for original proceedings in probate.

Derived from Probate Code § 815.

Added by Acts 2011, 82nd Leg., ch. 823, § 1.02, eff. Jan. 1, 2014.

§ 1158.104. Sale on Credit

(a) Estate personal property may not be sold on credit at public auction for a term of more than six months from the date of sale.

(b) Estate personal property purchased on credit at public auction may not be delivered to the purchaser until the purchaser gives a note for the amount due, with good and solvent personal security. The requirement that security be provided may be waived if the property will not be delivered until the note, with interest, has been paid.

Derived from Probate Code § 816.

Added by Acts 2011, 82nd Leg., ch. 823, § 1.02, eff. Jan. 1, 2014.

§ 1158.105. Report; Evidence of Title

(a) A sale of estate personal property shall be reported to the court. The laws regulating the confirmation or disapproval of a sale of real estate apply to the sale of personal property, except that a conveyance is not required.

(b) The court's order confirming the sale of estate personal property:

(1) vests the right and title of the ward's estate in the purchaser who has complied with the terms of the sale; and

(2) is prima facie evidence that all requirements of the law in making the sale have been met.

(c) The guardian of the estate, on request, may issue a bill of sale without warranty to the purchaser of estate personal property as evidence of title. The expense of the bill of sale if requested must be paid by the purchaser.

Derived from Probate Code § 818.

Added by Acts 2011, 82nd Leg., ch. 823, § 1.02, eff. Jan. 1, 2014.

Subchapter D. Sale of Livestock

§ 1158.151. Authority for Sale

(a) A guardian of the estate who has possession of livestock and who considers selling the livestock to be necessary or to the estate's advantage may, in addition to any other method provided by law for the sale of personal property, obtain authority from the court in which the estate is pending to sell the livestock through:

(1) a bonded livestock commission merchant; or

(2) a bonded livestock auction commission merchant.

(b) The court may authorize the sale of livestock in the manner described by Subsection (a) on a written and sworn application by the guardian or any person interested in the estate.

Derived from Probate Code §§ 814(a), (b).

Added by Acts 2011, 82nd Leg., ch. 823, § 1.02, eff. Jan. 1, 2014.

§ 1158.152. Contents of Application; Hearing

(a) An application under Section 1158.151 must:

(1) describe the livestock sought to be sold; and

(2) state why granting the application is necessary or to the estate's advantage.

(b) The court:

(1) shall consider the application; and

(2) may hear evidence for or against the application, with or without notice, as the facts warrant.

Derived from Probate Code § 814(b).

Added by Acts 2011, 82nd Leg., ch. 823, § 1.02, eff. Jan. 1, 2014.

§ 1158.153. Grant of Application

If the court grants an application for the sale of livestock, the court shall:

(1) enter an order to that effect; and

(2) authorize delivery of the livestock to a commission merchant described by Section 1158.151(a) for sale in the regular course of business.

Derived from Probate Code § 814(c).

Added by Acts 2011, 82nd Leg., ch. 823, § 1.02, eff. Jan. 1, 2014.

§ 1158.154. Report; Passage of Title

The guardian of the estate shall promptly report to the court a sale of livestock, supported by a verified copy of the commission merchant's account of the sale. A court order of confirmation is not required to pass title to the purchaser of the livestock.

Derived from Probate Code § 814(c).

Added by Acts 2011, 82nd Leg., ch. 823, § 1.02, eff. Jan. 1, 2014.

§ 1158.155. Commission Merchant Charges

The commission merchant shall be paid the commission merchant's usual and customary charges, not to exceed five percent of the sale price, for the sale of the livestock.

Derived from Probate Code § 814(c).

Added by Acts 2011, 82nd Leg., ch. 823, § 1.02, eff. Jan. 1, 2014.

Subchapter E. Sale of Mortgaged Property

§ 1158.201. Application for Sale of Mortgaged Property

On the filing of a written application, a creditor holding a claim that is secured by a valid mortgage or other lien and that has been allowed and approved or established by suit may obtain from the court in which the guardianship is pending an order requiring that the property securing the lien, or as much of the property as is necessary to satisfy the creditor's claim, be sold.

Derived from Probate Code § 817.

Added by Acts 2011, 82nd Leg., ch. 823, § 1.02, eff. Jan. 1, 2014.

§ 1158.202. Citation

On the filing of an application under Section 1158.201, the clerk shall issue a citation requiring the guardian of the estate to appear and show cause why the application should not be granted.

Derived from Probate Code § 817.

Added by Acts 2011, 82nd Leg., ch. 823, § 1.02, eff. Jan. 1, 2014.

§ 1158.203. Order

The court may order the lien securing the claim of a creditor who files an application under Section 1158.201 to be discharged out of general estate assets or refinanced if the discharge or refinance of the lien appears to the court to be advisable. Otherwise, the court shall grant the application and order that the property securing the lien be sold at public or private sale, as the court considers best, as in an ordinary sale of real estate.

Derived from Probate Code § 817.

Added by Acts 2011, 82nd Leg., ch. 823, § 1.02, eff. Jan. 1, 2014.

Subchapter F. Sale of Real Property: Application and Order for Sale

§ 1158.251. Application for Order of Sale

An application may be made to the court for an order to sell real property of a ward's estate if the sale appears necessary or advisable to:

(1) pay:

(A) expenses of administration, allowances, and claims against the ward or the ward's estate; and

(B) if the guardianship is kept open after the death of the ward, the ward's funeral expenses and expenses of the ward's last illness;

(2) make up the deficiency if the income of a ward's estate, the personal property of the estate, and the proceeds of previous sales are insufficient to pay for the education and maintenance of the ward or to pay debts against the estate;

(3) dispose of property of the ward's estate that consists wholly or partly of an undivided interest in real estate if considered in the best interests of the estate to sell the interest;

(4) dispose of real estate of a ward, any part of which is nonproductive or does not produce sufficient revenue to make a fair return on the value of the real estate, if:

(A) the improvement of the real estate with a view to making the property productive is not considered advantageous or advisable; and

(B) the sale of the real estate and the investment of the money derived from that sale appears to be in the estate's best interests; or

(5) conserve the ward's estate by selling mineral interest or royalties on minerals in place owned by the ward.

Derived from Probate Code § 820.

Added by Acts 2011, 82nd Leg., ch. 823, § 1.02, eff. Jan. 1, 2014.

§ 1158.252. Contents of Application

An application for the sale of real estate must:

(1) be in writing;

(2) describe:

(A) the real estate sought to be sold; or

(B) the interest in or part of the real estate sought to be sold; and

(3) be accompanied by an exhibit, verified by an affidavit, showing fully and in detail:

(A) the estate's condition;

(B) the charges and claims that have been approved or established by suit or that have been rejected and may be established later;

(C) the amount of each claim described by Paragraph (B);

(D) the estate property remaining on hand that is liable for the payment of the claims described by Paragraph (B); and

(E) any other facts showing the necessity for or advisability of the sale.

Derived from Probate Code § 821.

Added by Acts 2011, 82nd Leg., ch. 823, § 1.02, eff. Jan. 1, 2014.

§ 1158.253. Citation

On the filing of an application for the sale of real estate under Section 1158.251, accompanied by an exhibit described by Section 1158.252, the clerk shall issue a citation to all persons interested in the guardianship. The citation must:

(1) describe the real estate or the interest in or part of the real estate sought to be sold;

(2) inform the interested persons of the right under Section 1158.254 to file an opposition to the sale during the period prescribed by the court in the citation; and

(3) be served by posting.

Derived from Probate Code § 823.

Added by Acts 2011, 82nd Leg., ch. 823, § 1.02, eff. Jan. 1, 2014.

§ 1158.254. Opposition to Sale

During the period prescribed in a citation issued under Section 1158.253, a person interested in the guardianship may file:

(1) a written opposition to the sale; or

(2) an application for the sale of other estate property.

Derived from Probate Code § 824.

Added by Acts 2011, 82nd Leg., ch. 823, § 1.02, eff. Jan. 1, 2014.

§ 1158.255. Hearing on Application and Any Opposition

(a) The clerk of the court in which an application for an order of sale is filed shall immediately call to the judge's attention any opposition to the sale that is filed during the period prescribed in the citation issued under Section 1158.253. The court shall hold a hearing on the application if an opposition to the sale is filed during the period prescribed in the citation.

(b) A hearing on an application for an order of sale is not required under this section if no opposition to the application is filed during the period prescribed in the citation. The court may determine that a hearing on the application is necessary even if no opposition is filed during that period.

(c) If the court orders a hearing under Subsection (a) or (b), the court shall designate in writing a date and time for the hearing on the application and any opposition, together with the evidence pertaining to the application and any opposition. The clerk shall issue a notice of the date and time of the hearing to the applicant and to each person who files an opposition to the sale, if applicable.

(d) The judge, by entries on the docket, may continue a hearing held under this section from time to time until the judge is satisfied concerning the application.

Derived from Probate Code § 824A.

Added by Acts 2011, 82nd Leg., ch. 823, § 1.02, eff. Jan. 1, 2014.

§ 1158.256. Order

(a) The court shall order the sale of the property of the estate described in an application under Section 1158.251 if the court is satisfied that the sale is necessary or advisable. Otherwise, the court may deny the application and, if the court considers it best, may order the sale of other estate property the sale of which would be more advantageous to the estate.

(b) An order for the sale of real estate under this section must specify:

(1) the property to be sold, including a description that identifies that property;

(2) whether the property is to be sold at public auction or private sale and, if at public auction, the time and place of the sale;

(3) the necessity or advisability of, and the purpose of, the sale;

(4) except in a case in which a guardian of the estate was not required to give a general bond, that the court, after examining the general bond given by the guardian, finds that:

(A) the bond is sufficient as required by law; or

(B) the bond is insufficient;

(5) if the court finds that the general bond is insufficient under Subdivision (4)(B), the amount of the necessary or increased bond, as applicable;

(6) that the sale is to be made and the report returned in accordance with law; and

(7) the terms of the sale.

Derived from Probate Code § 825.

Added by Acts 2011, 82nd Leg., ch. 823, § 1.02, eff. Jan. 1, 2014.

§ 1158.257. Sale for Payment of Debts

Real property of a ward selected to be sold for the payment of expenses or claims must be that property the sale of which the court considers most advantageous to the guardianship.

Derived from Probate Code § 819.

Added by Acts 2011, 82nd Leg., ch. 823, § 1.02, eff. Jan. 1, 2014.

Subchapter G. Sale of Real Estate: Terms of Sale

§ 1158.301. Permissible Terms

Real estate of an estate may be sold for cash, or for part cash and part credit, or the equity in land securing an indebtedness may be sold subject to the indebtedness, or with an assumption of the indebtedness, at public or private sale, as appears to the court to be in the estate's best interests.

Derived from Probate Code § 827(a).

Added by Acts 2011, 82nd Leg., ch. 823, § 1.02, eff. Jan. 1, 2014.

§ 1158.302. Sale on Credit

(a) The cash payment for real estate of an estate sold partly on credit may not be less than one-fifth of the purchase price. The purchaser shall execute a note for the deferred payments, payable in monthly, quarterly, semiannual, or annual installments, in amounts that appear to the court to be in the guardianship's best interests. The note must bear interest from the date at a rate of not less than four percent per year, payable as provided in the note.

(b) A note executed by a purchaser under Subsection (a) must be secured by a vendor's lien retained in the deed and in the note on the property sold, and be additionally secured by a deed of trust on the property sold, with the usual provisions for foreclosure and sale on failure to make the payments provided in the deed and the note.

(c) At the election of the holder of a note executed by a purchaser under Subsection (a), default in the payment of principal or interest or any part of the payment when due matures the entire debt.

Derived from Probate Code § 827(a).

Added by Acts 2011, 82nd Leg., ch. 823, § 1.02, eff. Jan. 1, 2014.

Subchapter H. Reconveyance of Real Estate Following Foreclosure

§ 1158.351. Applicability of Subchapter

This subchapter applies only to real estate owned by an estate as a result of the foreclosure of a vendor's lien or mortgage belonging to the estate:

(1) by a judicial sale;

(2) by a foreclosure suit;

(3) through a sale under a deed of trust; or

(4) by acceptance of a deed in cancellation of a lien or mortgage owned by the estate.

Derived from Probate Code § 827(b).

Added by Acts 2011, 82nd Leg., ch. 823, § 1.02, eff. Jan. 1, 2014.

§ 1158.352. Application and Order for Reconveyance

On proper application and proof, the court may dispense with the requirements for a credit sale prescribed by Section 1158.302 and order the reconveyance of foreclosed real estate to the former mortgage debtor or former owner if it appears to the court that:

(1) an application to redeem the real estate has been made by the former owner to a corporation or agency created by an act of the United States Congress or of this state in connection with legislation for the relief of owners of mortgaged or encumbered homes, farms, ranches, or other real estate; and

(2) owning bonds of one of those federal or state corporations or agencies instead of the real estate would be in the estate's best interests.

Derived from Probate Code § 827(b).

Added by Acts 2011, 82nd Leg., ch. 823, § 1.02, eff. Jan. 1, 2014.

§ 1158.353. Exchange for Bonds

(a) If a court orders the reconveyance of foreclosed real estate under Section 1158.352, vendor's lien notes shall be reserved for the total amount of the indebtedness due or for the total amount of bonds that the corporation or agency to which the application to redeem the real estate was submitted as described by Section 1158.352(1) is allowed to advance under the corporation's or agency's rules or regulations.

(b) On obtaining the order for reconveyance, it shall be proper for the guardian to endorse and assign the reserved vendor's lien notes over to any one of the corporations or agencies described by Section 1158.352(1) in exchange for bonds of that corporation or agency.

Derived from Probate Code § 827(b).

Added by Acts 2011, 82nd Leg., ch. 823, § 1.02, eff. Jan. 1, 2014.

Subchapter I. Sale of Real Estate: Public Sale

§ 1158.401. Required Notice

(a) Except as otherwise provided by this title, the guardian of the estate shall advertise a public sale of real estate of the estate by a notice published in the county in which the estate is pending, as provided by this title for publication of notices or citations. The notice must include a reference to:

(1) the order of sale;

(2) the time, place, and required terms of sale; and

(3) a brief description of the real estate to be sold.

(b) The reference described by Subsection (a)(1) is not required to contain field notes, but if the real estate to be sold is rural property, the reference must include:

(1) the name of the original survey of the real estate;

(2) the number of acres the real estate consists of;

(3) the location of the real estate in the county; and

(4) the name by which the real estate is generally known.

Derived from Probate Code § 828(a).

Added by Acts 2011, 82nd Leg., ch. 823, § 1.02, eff. Jan. 1, 2014.

§ 1158.402. Method of Sale

A public sale of real estate of an estate shall be made at public auction to the highest bidder.

Derived from Probate Code § 828(b).

Added by Acts 2011, 82nd Leg., ch. 823, § 1.02, eff. Jan. 1, 2014.

§ 1158.403. Time and Place of Sale

(a) Except as provided by Subsection (c), a public sale of real estate of an estate shall be made at:

(1) the courthouse door in the county in which the guardianship proceedings are pending; or

(2) another place in that county at which sales of real estate are specifically authorized to be made.

(b) The sale must occur between 10 a.m. and 4 p.m. on the first Tuesday of the month after publication of notice has been completed.

(c) If the court considers it advisable, the court may order the sale to be made in the county in which the real estate is located, in which event notice shall be published both in that county and in the county in which the proceedings are pending.

Derived from Probate Code § 828(c).

Added by Acts 2011, 82nd Leg., ch. 823, § 1.02, eff. Jan. 1, 2014.

§ 1158.404. Continuance of Sale

(a) A public sale of real estate of an estate that is not completed on the day advertised may be continued from day to day by an oral public announcement of the continuance made at the conclusion of the sale each day.

(b) A continued sale must occur within the hours prescribed by Section 1158.403(b).

(c) The continuance of a sale under this section shall be shown in the report of the sale made to the court.

Derived from Probate Code § 828(d).

Added by Acts 2011, 82nd Leg., ch. 823, § 1.02, eff. Jan. 1, 2014.

§ 1158.405. Failure of Bidder to Comply

(a) If a person who bids on real estate of the guardianship estate offered for sale at public auction fails to comply with the terms of the sale, the real estate shall be readvertised and sold without any further order.

(b) The person defaulting on a bid as described by Subsection (a) is liable for payment to the guardian of the estate, for the estate's benefit, of:

(1) 10 percent of the amount of the bid; and

(2) the amount of any deficiency in price on the second sale.

(c) The guardian shall recover the amounts under Subsection (b) by suit in any court in the county in which the sale was made that has jurisdiction over the amount claimed.

Derived from Probate Code § 828(e).

Added by Acts 2011, 82nd Leg., ch. 823, § 1.02, eff. Jan. 1, 2014.

Subchapter J. Sale of Real Estate: Private Sale

§ 1158.451. Manner of Sale

A private sale of real estate of the estate shall be made in the manner the court directs in the order of sale. Unless the court directs otherwise, additional advertising, notice, or citation concerning the sale is not required.

Derived from Probate Code § 829.

Added by Acts 2011, 82nd Leg., ch. 823, § 1.02, eff. Jan. 1, 2014.

Subchapter K. Sale of Easement or Right-of-Way

§ 1158.501. Authorization

The guardian may sell and convey easements and rights-of-way on, under, and over the land of a guardianship estate that is being administered under court order, regardless of whether the sale proceeds are required to pay charges or claims against the estate, or for other lawful purposes.

Derived from Probate Code § 830.

Added by Acts 2011, 82nd Leg., ch. 823, § 1.02, eff. Jan. 1, 2014.

§ 1158.502. Procedure

The procedure for the sale of an easement or right-of-way authorized under Section 1158.501 is the same as the procedure provided by law for a sale of real property of a ward at private sale.

Derived from Probate Code § 830.

Added by Acts 2011, 82nd Leg., ch. 823, § 1.02, eff. Jan. 1, 2014.

Subchapter L. Confirmation of Sale of Real Property and Transfer of Title

§ 1158.551. Report

A sale of estate real property shall be reported to the court ordering the sale not later than the 30th day after the date the sale is made. The report must:

(1) be in writing, sworn to, and filed with the clerk;

(2) include:

(A) the date of the order of sale;

(B) a description of the property sold;

(C) the time and place of sale;

(D) the purchaser's name;

(E) the amount for which each parcel of property or interest in the parcel of property was sold;

(F) the terms of the sale;

(G) whether the sale was made at public auction or privately; and

(H) whether the purchaser is ready to comply with the order of sale; and

(3) be noted on the guardianship docket.

Derived from Probate Code § 832.

Added by Acts 2011, 82nd Leg., ch. 823, § 1.02, eff. Jan. 1, 2014.

§ 1158.552. Action of Court on Report of Sale

After the expiration of five days from the date a report of sale is filed under Section 1158.551, the court shall:

(1) inquire into the manner in which the sale was made;

(2) hear evidence in support of or against the report; and

(3) determine the sufficiency or insufficiency of the guardian's general bond, if any has been required and given.

Derived from Probate Code § 834.

Added by Acts 2011, 82nd Leg., ch. 823, § 1.02, eff. Jan. 1, 2014.

§ 1158.553. Confirmation of Sale When Bond Not Required

If the guardian of the estate of a ward is not required by Subtitle D to give a general bond, the court may confirm the sale of estate real property in the manner provided by Section 1158.556(a) if the court finds that the sale is satisfactory and made in accordance with law.

Derived from Probate Code § 833.

Added by Acts 2011, 82nd Leg., ch. 823, § 1.02, eff. Jan. 1, 2014.

§ 1158.554. Sufficiency of Bond

(a) If the guardian of an estate is required by Subtitle D to give a general bond, before the court confirms any sale of real estate, the court shall determine whether the bond is sufficient to protect the estate after the sale proceeds are received.

(b) If the court finds that the general bond is sufficient, the court may confirm the sale as provided by Section 1158.556(a).

(c) If the court finds that the general bond is insufficient, the court may not confirm the sale until the general bond is increased to the amount required by the court, or an additional bond is given, and approved by the court.

(d) An increase in the amount of the general bond, or the additional bond, as applicable under Subsection (c), must be equal to the sum of:

(1) the amount for which the real estate is sold; and

(2) any additional amount the court finds necessary and sets for the estate's protection.

Derived from Probate Code § 833.

Added by Acts 2011, 82nd Leg., ch. 823, § 1.02, eff. Jan. 1, 2014.

§ 1158.555. Increased or Additional Bond Not Required

Notwithstanding Sections 1158.554(c) and (d), if the real estate sold is encumbered by a lien to secure a claim against the estate and is sold to the owner or holder of the secured claim in full payment, liquidation, and satisfaction of the claim, an increased general bond or additional bond may not be required except for the amount of any cash paid to the guardian of the estate in excess of the amount necessary to pay, liquidate, and satisfy the claim in full.

Derived from Probate Code § 833.

Added by Acts 2011, 82nd Leg., ch. 823, § 1.02, eff. Jan. 1, 2014.

§ 1158.556. Confirmation or Disapproval Order

(a) If the court is satisfied that a sale reported under Section 1158.551 was for a fair price, was properly made, and was in conformity with law, and the court has approved any increased or additional bond that the court found necessary to protect the estate, the court shall enter an order:

(1) confirming the sale;

(2) showing conformity with the provisions of this chapter relating to the sale;

(3) detailing the terms of the sale; and

(4) authorizing the guardian of the estate to convey the property on the purchaser's compliance with the terms of the sale.

(b) If the court is not satisfied that the sale was for a fair price, was properly made, and was in conformity with law, the court shall issue an order setting aside the sale and ordering a new sale to be made, if necessary.

(c) The court's action in confirming or disapproving a report of a sale has the effect of a final judgment. Any person interested in the guardianship estate or in the sale is entitled to have an order entered under this section reviewed as in other final judgments in probate proceedings.

Derived from Probate Code § 834.

Added by Acts 2011, 82nd Leg., ch. 823, § 1.02, eff. Jan. 1, 2014.

§ 1158.557. Deed

Real estate of an estate that is sold shall be conveyed by a proper deed that refers to and identifies the court order confirming the sale. The deed:

(1) vests in the purchaser all right and title of the estate to, and all interest of the estate in, the property; and

(2) is prima facie evidence that the sale has met all applicable requirements of law.

Derived from Probate Code § 835.

Added by Acts 2011, 82nd Leg., ch. 823, § 1.02, eff. Jan. 1, 2014.

§ 1158.558. Delivery Of Deed

(a) After the court has confirmed a sale and one purchaser has complied with the terms of the sale, the guardian of the estate shall execute and deliver to the purchaser a proper deed conveying the property.

(b) If the sale is made partly on credit:

(1) the vendor's lien securing a purchase money note must be expressly retained in the deed and may not be waived; and

(2) before actual delivery of the deed to the purchaser, the purchaser shall execute and deliver to the guardian of the estate a vendor's lien note, with or without personal sureties as ordered by the court, and a deed of trust or mortgage on the property as additional security for the payment of the note.

(c) On completion of the transaction, the guardian of the estate shall promptly file and record the deed of trust or mortgage in the appropriate records in the county in which the land is located.

Derived from Probate Code § 836.

Added by Acts 2011, 82nd Leg., ch. 823, § 1.02, eff. Jan. 1, 2014.

§ 1158.559. Damages; Removal

(a) If the guardian of the estate neglects to comply with Section 1158.558, including to file the deed of trust securing a lien in the proper county, the guardian and the sureties on the guardian's bond shall, after complaint and citation, be held liable for the use of the estate and for all damages resulting from the guardian's neglect, and the court may remove the guardian.

(b) Damages under this section may be recovered in a court of competent jurisdiction.

Derived from Probate Code § 837.

Added by Acts 2011, 82nd Leg., ch. 823, § 1.02, eff. Jan. 1, 2014.

Subchapter M. Procedure on Failure to Apply for Sale

§ 1158.601. Failure to Apply for Sale

If the guardian of the estate of a ward neglects to apply for an order to sell sufficient property to pay charges and claims against the estate that have been allowed and approved or established by suit, an interested person, on written application, may have the guardian cited to appear and make a full exhibit of the estate's condition and show cause why a sale of the property should not be ordered.

Derived from Probate Code § 826.

Added by Acts 2011, 82nd Leg., ch. 823, § 1.02, eff. Jan. 1, 2014.

§ 1158.602. Court Order

On hearing an application under Section 1158.601, if the court is satisfied that a sale of estate property is necessary or advisable to satisfy the charges and claims described by Section 1158.601, the court shall enter an order of sale as provided by Section 1158.256.

Derived from Probate Code § 826.

Added by Acts 2011, 82nd Leg., ch. 823, § 1.02, eff. Jan. 1, 2014.

Subchapter N. Purchase of Estate Property by Guardian

§ 1158.651. General Prohibition on Purchase

Except as otherwise provided by Section 1158.652 or 1158.653, the guardian of the estate of a ward may not purchase, directly or indirectly, any estate property sold by the guardian or any co-representative of the guardian.

Derived from Probate Code § 831(a).

Added by Acts 2011, 82nd Leg., ch. 823, § 1.02, eff. Jan. 1, 2014.

§ 1158.652. Exception: Executory Contract

The guardian of the estate of a ward may purchase estate property in compliance with the terms of a written executory contract signed by the ward before the ward became incapacitated, including:

(1) a contract for deed;

(2) an earnest money contract;

(3) a buy/sell agreement; and

(4) a stock purchase or redemption agreement.

Derived from Probate Code § 831(b).

Added by Acts 2011, 82nd Leg., ch. 823, § 1.02, eff. Jan. 1, 2014.

§ 1158.653. Exception: Best Interest of Estate

(a) The guardian of the estate may purchase estate property on the court's determination that the sale is in the estate's best interest.

(b) In the case of an application filed by the guardian of the estate of a ward, the court shall appoint an attorney ad litem to represent the ward with respect to the sale.

(c) The court may require notice for a sale made under this section.

Derived from Probate Code § 831(c).

Added by Acts 2011, 82nd Leg., ch. 823, § 1.02, eff. Jan. 1, 2014.

§ 1158.654. Purchase in Violation of Subchapter

(a) If the guardian of the estate of a ward purchases estate property in violation of this subchapter, a person interested in the estate may file a written complaint with the court in which the guardianship proceedings are pending.

(b) On service of citation on the guardian on a complaint filed under Subsection (a) and after hearing and proof, the court shall:

(1) declare the sale void;

(2) set aside the sale; and

(3) order the reconveyance of the property to the estate.

(c) The court shall adjudge against the guardian all costs of the sale, protest, and suit, if found necessary.

Derived from Probate Code § 831(d).

Added by Acts 2011, 82nd Leg., ch. 823, § 1.02, eff. Jan. 1, 2014.

Subchapter O. Partition of Ward's Interest in Real Estate

§ 1158.701. Partition by Agreement

(a) The guardian of the estate of a ward may agree to a partition of real estate in which the ward owns an interest in common with one or more other part owners if, in the opinion of the guardian, it is in the best interests of the ward's estate to partition the real estate.

(b) An agreement under Subsection (a) is subject to the approval of the court in which the guardianship proceeding is pending.

Derived from Probate Code § 853(a).

Added by Acts 2011, 82nd Leg., ch. 823, § 1.02, eff. Jan. 1, 2014.

§ 1158.702. Application for Approval of Partition Agreement

(a) When a guardian has reached an agreement with the other part owners on how to partition real estate as described by Section 1158.701, the guardian shall file with the court in which the guardianship proceedings are pending an application to have the agreement approved by the court.

(b) The application must:

(1) describe the real estate to be divided;

(2) state why it is in the best interests of the ward's estate to partition the real estate; and

(3) show that the proposed partition agreement is fair and just to the ward's estate.

Derived from Probate Code § 853(b).

Added by Acts 2011, 82nd Leg., ch. 823, § 1.02, eff. Jan. 1, 2014.

§ 1158.703. Hearing

(a) The county clerk shall immediately call to the attention of the judge of the court in which the guardianship proceeding is pending the filing of an application required by Section 1158.702. The judge shall designate a day to hear the application.

(b) The application must remain on file at least 10 days before any orders are entered.

(c) The judge may continue a hearing held under this section from time to time until the judge is satisfied concerning the application.

Derived from Probate Code § 853(c).

Added by Acts 2011, 82nd Leg., ch. 823, § 1.02, eff. Jan. 1, 2014.

§ 1158.704. Order

If the judge is satisfied that the proposed partition of the real estate is in the best interests of the ward's estate, the court shall enter an order approving the partition and directing the guardian to execute the necessary agreement for the purpose of implementing the order and partition.

Derived from Probate Code § 853(d).

Added by Acts 2011, 82nd Leg., ch. 823, § 1.02, eff. Jan. 1, 2014.

§ 1158.705. Partition Without Court Approval; Ratification of Partition Agreement

(a) If a guardian, without court approval as provided by this subchapter, executes or intends to execute an agreement to partition any real estate in which the ward has an interest, the guardian shall file with the court in which the guardianship proceedings are pending an application for the approval and ratification of the partition agreement.

(b) The application must:

(1) refer to the agreement in a manner in which the court can fully understand the nature of the partition and the real estate being divided; and

(2) state that, in the opinion of the guardian, the agreement is fair and just to the ward's estate and is in the best interests of the estate.

(c) On the filing of an application under Subsection (a), the court shall hold a hearing on the application as provided by Section 1158.703. The court shall enter an order ratifying and approving the partition agreement if the court is of the opinion that the partition is:

(1) fairly made; and

(2) in the best interests of the ward's estate.

(d) On ratification and approval, the partition is effective and binding as if originally executed after a court order.

Derived from Probate Code § 853(e).

Added by Acts 2011, 82nd Leg., ch. 823, § 1.02, eff. Jan. 1, 2014.

§ 1158.706. Partition by Suit

(a) The guardian of the estate of a ward may bring a suit in the court in which the guardianship proceeding is pending for the partition of any real estate that the ward owns in common with one or more other part owners if the guardian is of the opinion that it is in the best interests of the ward's estate that the real estate be partitioned.

(b) The court may enter an order partitioning the real estate to the owner of the real estate, if after hearing the suit, the court is satisfied that the partition of the real estate is necessary.

Derived from Probate Code § 853(f).

Added by Acts 2011, 82nd Leg., ch. 823, § 1.02, eff. Jan. 1, 2014.

Chapter 1159. Renting Estate Property

Subchapter A. Rental and Return of Estate Property

Subchapter B. Report on Rented Estate Property

Chapter 1159. Renting Estate Property

Subchapter A. Rental and Return of Estate Property

§ 1159.001. Renting Estate Property Without Court Order

(a) The guardian of an estate, without a court order, may rent any of the estate property for one year or less, at public auction or privately, as is considered to be in the best interests of the estate.

(b) On the sworn complaint of any person interested in the estate, the court shall require a guardian of the estate who, without a court order, rents estate property to account to the estate for the reasonable value of the rent of the property, to be ascertained by the court on satisfactory evidence.

Derived from Probate Code §§ 839, 840.

Added by Acts 2011, 82nd Leg., ch. 823, § 1.02, eff. Jan. 1, 2014.

§ 1159.002. Renting Estate Property With Court Order

(a) The guardian of an estate may file a written application with the court setting forth the property the guardian seeks to rent. If the proposed rental period is one year or more, the guardian of the estate shall file a written application with the court setting forth the property the guardian seeks to rent.

(b) If the court finds that granting an application filed under Subsection (a) is in the interests of the estate, the court shall grant the application and issue an order that:

(1) describes the property to be rented; and

(2) states whether the property will be rented at public auction or privately, whether for cash or on credit, and if on credit, the extent of the credit and the period for which the property may be rented.

(c) If, under Subsection (b), the court orders property to be rented at public auction, the court shall prescribe whether notice of the auction shall be published or posted.

Derived from Probate Code § 841.

Added by Acts 2011, 82nd Leg., ch. 823, § 1.02, eff. Jan. 1, 2014.

§ 1159.003. Estate Property Rented on Credit

(a) Possession of estate property rented on credit may not be delivered until the renter executes and delivers to the guardian of the estate a note with good personal security for the amount of the rent. If the property is delivered without the guardian receiving the required security, the guardian and the sureties on the guardian's bond are liable for the full amount of the rent.

(b) Subsection (a) does not apply to a rental that is paid in installments in advance of the period to which the installments relate.

Derived from Probate Code § 843.

Added by Acts 2011, 82nd Leg., ch. 823, § 1.02, eff. Jan. 1, 2014.

§ 1159.004. Condition of Returned Estate Property

(a) Estate property that is rented must be returned to the estate's possession in as good a condition, except for reasonable wear and tear, as when the property was rented.

(b) The guardian of the estate shall:

(1) ensure that rented estate property is returned in the condition required by Subsection (a);

(2) report to the court any damage to, or loss or destruction of, estate property rented under this chapter; and

(3) ask the court for the authority to take any necessary action.

(c) A guardian who fails to act as required by this section and the sureties on the guardian's bond are liable to the estate for any loss or damage suffered as a result of the guardian's failure.

Derived from Probate Code § 844.

Added by Acts 2011, 82nd Leg., ch. 823, § 1.02, eff. Jan. 1, 2014.

§ 1159.005. Complaint for Failure to Rent

(a) A person interested in a guardianship may:

(1) file a written and sworn complaint in the court in which the estate is pending; and

(2) have the guardian of the estate cited to appear and show cause why the guardian did not rent any estate property.

(b) The court, on hearing the complaint, shall issue an order that is in the best interests of the estate.

Derived from Probate Code § 842.

Added by Acts 2011, 82nd Leg., ch. 823, § 1.02, eff. Jan. 1, 2014.

Subchapter B. Report on Rented Estate Property

§ 1159.051. Reports Concerning Rentals

(a) A guardian of an estate who rents estate property with an appraised value of $3,000 or more, not later than the 30th day after the date of the rental, shall file with the court a sworn and written report stating:

(1) the property rented and the property's appraised value;

(2) the date the property was rented and whether the rental occurred at public auction or privately;

(3) the name of the person renting the property;

(4) the rental amount;

(5) whether the rental was for cash or on credit; and

(6) if the rental was on credit, the length of time, the terms, and the security received for the credit.

(b) A guardian of an estate who rents estate property with an appraised value of less than $3,000 may report the rental in the next annual or final account that must be filed as required by law.

Derived from Probate Code § 845.

Added by Acts 2011, 82nd Leg., ch. 823, § 1.02, eff. Jan. 1, 2014.

§ 1159.052. Court Action on Report

(a) After the fifth day after the date the report of the rental is filed, the court shall:

(1) examine the report; and

(2) by order approve and confirm the rental if the court finds the rental just and reasonable.

(b) If the court disapproves the rental, the guardianship is not bound and the court may order another offering for rent of the property in the same manner and subject to the provisions of this chapter.

(c) If the court approves the rental and it later appears that, by reason of the fault of the guardian of the estate, the property was not rented for the property's reasonable value, the court shall have the guardian and the sureties on the guardian's bond appear and show cause why the reasonable value of the rental of the property should not be adjudged against the guardian or sureties.

Derived from Probate Code § 846.

Added by Acts 2011, 82nd Leg., ch. 823, § 1.02, eff. Jan. 1, 2014.

CHAPTER 1160. Matters Relating to Mineral Properties

Subchapter A. General Provisions

Subchapter B. Mineral Leases After Public Notice

Subchapter C. Mineral Leases at Private Sale

Subchapter D. Pooling or Unitization of Royalties or Minerals

Subchapter E. Special Ancillary Instruments That May be Executed Without Court Order

§ 1160.201. Authorization for Execution of Certain Instruments

Subchapter F. Procedure if Guardian of Estate Neglects to Apply for Authority

§ 1160.251. Application to Show Cause

§ 1160.252. Hearing on Application

§ 1160.253. Order

§ 1160.254. Procedure to be Followed After Entry of Order

Chapter 1160. Matters Relating to Mineral Properties

Subchapter A. General Provisions

§ 1160.001. Definitions

In this chapter:

(1) "Gas" includes all liquid hydrocarbons in the gaseous phase in the reservoir.

(2) "Land" includes minerals or an interest in minerals in place.

(3) "Mineral development" includes exploration for, whether by geophysical or other means, drilling for, mining for, development of, operations in connection with, production of, and saving of oil, other liquid hydrocarbons, gas, gaseous elements, sulphur, metals, and all other minerals, whether solid or otherwise.

(4) "Property" includes land, minerals in place, whether solid, liquid, or gaseous, and an interest of any kind in the property, including a royalty interest, owned by an estate.

Derived from Probate Code § 847(a).

Added by Acts 2011, 82nd Leg., ch. 823, § 1.02, eff. Jan. 1, 2014.

Subchapter B. Mineral Leases After Public Notice

§ 1160.051. Authorization for Leasing of Minerals

(a) The court in which a guardianship proceeding is pending may authorize the guardian, acting solely under a court order, to make, execute, and deliver a lease, with or without a unitization clause or pooling provision, providing for the exploration for and development and production of oil, other liquid hydrocarbons, gas, metals and other solid minerals, and other minerals, or any of those minerals in place, belonging to the estate.

(b) A lease authorized by Subsection (a) must be made and entered into under and in conformity with this subchapter.

Derived from Probate Code §§ 847(b), (c).

Added by Acts 2011, 82nd Leg., ch. 823, § 1.02, eff. Jan. 1, 2014.

§ 1160.052. Lease Application

(a) The guardian of the estate shall file with the court a written application for authority to lease estate property for mineral exploration and development, with or without a pooling provision or unitization clause.

(b) The lease application must:

(1) describe the property fully enough by reference to the amount of acreage, the survey name or number, or the abstract number, or by another method that adequately identifies the property and the property's location in the county in which the property is located;

(2) specify the interest thought to be owned by the estate, if less than the whole, but request authority to include all of the interest owned by the estate if that is the intention; and

(3) set out the reasons the estate property described in the application should be leased.

(c) The lease application is not required to set out or suggest:

(1) the name of any proposed lessee; or

(2) the terms, provisions, or form of any desired lease.

Derived from Probate Code § 847(d).

Added by Acts 2011, 82nd Leg., ch. 823, § 1.02, eff. Jan. 1, 2014.

§ 1160.053. Scheduling of Hearing on Application; Continuance

(a) Immediately after the filing of a lease application under Section 1160.052, the county clerk shall call the filing of the application to the court's attention. The judge shall promptly make and enter a brief order designating the time and place for hearing the application.

(b) If the hearing is not held at the time originally designated by the court or by a timely continuance order entered, the hearing shall be continued automatically without further notice to the same time on the following day, other than Sundays and holidays on which the county courthouse is officially closed, and from day to day until the lease application is finally acted on and disposed of by court order. Notice of an automatic continuance is not required.

Derived from Probate Code § 847(e).

Added by Acts 2011, 82nd Leg., ch. 823, § 1.02, eff. Jan. 1, 2014.

§ 1160.054. Notice of Hearing on Application

(a) At least 10 days before the date set for the hearing on a lease application filed under Section 1160.052, excluding the date of notice and the date set for the hearing, the guardian of the estate shall give notice of the hearing by:

(1) publishing the notice in one issue of a newspaper of general circulation in the county in which the proceeding is pending; or

(2) if there is no newspaper in the county, posting the notice or having the notice posted.

(b) If the notice is published, the date of notice is the date printed on the newspaper.

(c) The notice must:

(1) be dated;

(2) be directed to all persons interested in the estate;

(3) state the date on which the lease application was filed;

(4) describe briefly the property sought to be leased;

(5) specify the fractional interest sought to be leased if less than the entire interest in the tract identified; and

(6) state the time and place designated by the judge for the hearing.

Derived from Probate Code § 847(f).

Added by Acts 2011, 82nd Leg., ch. 823, § 1.02, eff. Jan. 1, 2014.

§ 1160.055. Requirements Regarding Order and Notice Mandatory

A court order authorizing any act to be performed in accordance with a lease application filed under Section 1160.052 is void in the absence of:

(1) a written order originally designating a time and place for the hearing;

(2) a notice issued by the guardian of the estate in compliance with the order; and

(3) proof of publication or posting of the notice as required under Section 1160.054.

Derived from Probate Code § 847(g).

Added by Acts 2011, 82nd Leg., ch. 823, § 1.02, eff. Jan. 1, 2014.

§ 1160.056. Hearing on Application; Order

(a) At the time and place designated for the hearing under Section 1160.053(a), or at the time to which the hearing is continued as provided by Section 1160.053(b), the judge shall:

(1) hear a lease application filed under Section 1160.052; and

(2) require proof as to the necessity or advisability of leasing for mineral development the property described in the application and the notice.

(b) The judge shall enter an order authorizing one or more leases affecting and covering the property or portions of property described in the lease application, with or without pooling provisions or unitization clauses, and with or without cash consideration if considered by the court to be in the best interest of the estate, if the judge is satisfied that:

(1) the application is in proper form;

(2) notice has been given in the manner and for the time required by law;

(3) proof of necessity or advisability of leasing is sufficient; and

(4) the application should be granted.

(c) The order must contain:

(1) the name of the lessee;

(2) any actual cash consideration to be paid by the lessee;

(3) a finding that the requirements of Subsection (b) have been satisfied; and

(4) one of the following findings:

(A) a finding that the guardian of the estate is exempt by law from giving a bond; or

(B) if the guardian of the estate is required to give a bond, a finding as to whether the guardian's general bond on file is sufficient to protect the personal property on hand, including any cash bonus to be paid.

(d) If the court finds the general bond insufficient to meet the requirements of Subsection (c)(4)(B), the order must show the amount of increased or additional bond required to cover the deficiency.

(e) A complete exhibit copy, either written or printed, of each authorized lease must be set out in, attached to, incorporated by reference in, or made part of the order. The exhibit copy must show:

(1) the name of the lessee;

(2) the date of the lease;

(3) an adequate description of the property being leased;

(4) any delay rental to be paid to defer commencement of operations; and

(5) all other authorized terms and provisions.

(f) If the date of a lease does not appear in the exhibit copy of the lease or in the order, the date of the order is considered for all purposes to be the date of the lease.

(g) If the name or address of a depository bank for receiving rental is not shown in the exhibit copy of a lease, the guardian of the estate may insert the name or address, or cause the name or address to be inserted, in the lease at the time of the lease's execution or at any other time agreeable to the lessee or the lessee's successors or assigns.

Derived from Probate Code §§ 847(h), (i).

Added by Acts 2011, 82nd Leg., ch. 823, § 1.02, eff. Jan. 1, 2014.

§ 1160.057. Making of Lease on Granting of Application

(a) If on the hearing of a lease application filed under Section 1160.052 the court grants the application, the guardian of the estate may make the lease, as evidenced by the exhibit copies, in accordance with the order.

(b) The lease must be made not later than the 30th day after the date of the order unless an extension is granted by the court on a sworn application showing good cause.

(c) It is not necessary for the judge to make an order confirming the lease.

Derived from Probate Code § 847(j).

Added by Acts 2011, 82nd Leg., ch. 823, § 1.02, eff. Jan. 1, 2014.

§ 1160.058. Bond Requirements

(a) Unless the guardian of the estate is not required to give a general bond, a lease for which a cash consideration is required, although ordered, executed, and delivered, is not valid:

(1) unless the order authorizing the lease makes a finding with respect to the general bond; and

(2) if the general bond has been found insufficient, until:

(A) the bond has been increased or an additional bond given with the sureties required by law, as required by the order; and

(B) the increased or additional bond has been approved by the judge and filed with the clerk of the court in which the proceeding is pending.

(b) If two or more leases of different land are authorized by the same order, the general bond shall be increased or additional bonds given to cover all of the leases.

Derived from Probate Code § 847(j).

Added by Acts 2011, 82nd Leg., ch. 823, § 1.02, eff. Jan. 1, 2014.

§ 1160.059. Term of Lease Binding

A lease executed and delivered in compliance with this subchapter is valid and binding on the property or interest owned by the estate and covered by the lease for the full term provided by the lease, subject only to the lease's terms and conditions, even if the primary term extends beyond the date the estate is closed in accordance with law. For the lease to be valid and binding under this subchapter, the authorized primary term of the lease may not exceed five years, subject to the lease terms and provisions extending the lease beyond the primary term by:

(1) paying production;

(2) bona fide drilling or reworking operations, whether in or on the same well or wells or an additional well or wells without a cessation of operations of more than 60 consecutive days before production has been restored or obtained; or

(3) a shut-in gas well.

Derived from Probate Code § 847(k).

Added by Acts 2011, 82nd Leg., ch. 823, § 1.02, eff. Jan. 1, 2014.

§ 1160.060. Amendment of Lease Regarding Effect of Shut-In Gas Well

(a) An oil, gas, and mineral lease executed by a guardian of an estate under this chapter or former Chapter XIII, Texas Probate Code, may be amended by an instrument that provides that a shut-in gas well on the land covered by the lease or on land pooled with all or part of the land covered by the lease continues the lease in effect after the lease's five-year primary term.

(b) The guardian of the estate, with court approval, shall execute the instrument according to the terms and conditions prescribed in the instrument.

Derived from Probate Code § 847(m).

Added by Acts 2011, 82nd Leg., ch. 823, § 1.02, eff. Jan. 1, 2014.

Subchapter C. Mineral Leases at Private Sale

§ 1160.101. Authorization for Leasing of Minerals at Private Sale

(a) Notwithstanding the mandatory requirements for setting a time and place for hearing a lease application under Subchapter B and the issuance, service, and return of notice, the court may authorize the making of oil, gas, and mineral leases at a private sale without public notice or advertising if, in the court's opinion, facts are set out in the application sufficient to show that it would be more advantageous to the estate that a lease be made privately and without compliance with those mandatory requirements.

(b) Leases authorized under this subchapter may include pooling provisions or unitization clauses as in other cases.

Derived from Probate Code § 848(a).

Added by Acts 2011, 82nd Leg., ch. 823, § 1.02, eff. Jan. 1, 2014.

§ 1160.102. Action of Court if Public Advertising Not Required

(a) At any time after the fifth day and before the 11th day after the filing date of an application to lease at a private sale and without an order setting the hearing time and place, the court shall:

(1) hear the application;

(2) inquire into the manner in which the proposed lease has been or will be made; and

(3) hear evidence for or against the application.

(b) If the court is satisfied that the lease has been or will be made for a fair and sufficient consideration and on fair terms and has been or will be properly made in conformity with law, the court shall enter an order authorizing the execution of the lease without the necessity of advertising, notice, or citation. The order must comply in all other respects with the requirements essential to the validity of mineral leases set out in Subchapter B as if advertising or notice were required.

(c) An order that confirms a lease made at a private sale does not need to be issued. A lease made at a private sale is not valid until any increased or additional bond required by the court has been approved by the court and filed with the court clerk.

Derived from Probate Code § 848(b).

Added by Acts 2011, 82nd Leg., ch. 823, § 1.02, eff. Jan. 1, 2014.

Subchapter D. Pooling or Unitization of Royalties or Minerals

§ 1160.151. Authorization for Pooling or Unitization

(a) If an existing lease on property owned by an estate being administered does not adequately provide for pooling or unitization, the court in which the proceeding is pending may, in the manner provided by this subchapter, authorize the commitment of royalty or mineral interests in oil, liquid hydrocarbons, gas, gaseous elements, and other minerals or any one or more of them owned by the estate to agreements that provide for the operation of areas as a pool or unit for the exploration for, development of, and production of all of those minerals, if the court finds that:

(1) the pool or unit to which the agreement relates will be operated in a manner that protects correlative rights or prevents the physical or economic waste of oil, liquid hydrocarbons, gas, gaseous elements, or other minerals subject to the agreement; and

(2) it is in the best interests of the estate to execute the agreement.

(b) An agreement authorized under Subsection (a) may provide that:

(1) operations incident to the drilling of or production from a well on any portion of a pool or unit are considered for all purposes to be the conduct of operations on or production from each separately owned tract in the pool or unit;

(2) any lease covering any part of the area committed to a pool or unit continues in effect in its entirety as long as:

(A) oil, gas, or other minerals subject to the agreement are produced in paying quantities from any part of the pooled or unitized area;

(B) operations are conducted as provided in the lease on any part of the pooled or unitized area; or

(C) there is a shut-in gas well on any part of the pooled or unitized area, if the presence of the shut-in gas well is a ground for continuation of the lease under the terms of the lease;

(3) the production allocated by the agreement to each tract included in a pool or unit shall, when produced, be considered for all purposes to have been produced from the tract by a well drilled on the tract;

(4) the royalties provided for on production from any tract or portion of a tract within the pool or unit shall be paid only on that portion of the production allocated to the tract in accordance with the agreement;

(5) the dry gas, before or after extraction of hydrocarbons, may be returned to a formation underlying any land or leases committed to the agreement, and that royalties are not required to be paid on the gas returned; and

(6) gas obtained from other sources or another tract of land may be injected into a formation underlying any land or lease committed to the agreement, and that royalties are not required to be paid on the gas injected when the gas is produced from the unit.

Derived from Probate Code §§ 849(a), (b).

Added by Acts 2011, 82nd Leg., ch. 823, § 1.02, eff. Jan. 1, 2014.

§ 1160.152. Pooling or Unitization Application

(a) The guardian of the estate shall file with the county clerk of the county in which the guardianship proceeding is pending a written application for authority to:

(1) enter into a pooling or unitization agreement supplementing, amending, or otherwise relating to any existing lease covering property owned by the estate; or

(2) commit royalties or other interests in minerals, whether or not subject to a lease, to a pooling or unitization agreement.

(b) The pooling or unitization application must also:

(1) sufficiently describe the property as required in an original lease application;

(2) describe briefly the lease to which the interest of the estate is subject; and

(3) set out the reasons the proposed agreement concerning the property should be entered into.

(c) A copy of the proposed agreement must be attached to the pooling or unitization application and made a part of the application by reference.

(d) The agreement may not be recorded in the judge's guardianship docket.

(e) Immediately after the pooling or unitization application is filed, the clerk shall call the application to the judge's attention.

Derived from Probate Code § 849(c).

Added by Acts 2011, 82nd Leg., ch. 823, § 1.02, eff. Jan. 1, 2014.

§ 1160.153. Notice Not Required

Notice by advertising, citation, or otherwise of the filing of a pooling or unitization application under Section 1160.152 is not required.

Derived from Probate Code § 849(d).

Added by Acts 2011, 82nd Leg., ch. 823, § 1.02, eff. Jan. 1, 2014.

§ 1160.154. Hearing on Application

(a) The judge may hold a hearing on a pooling or unitization application filed under Section 1160.152 at any time agreeable to the parties to the proposed agreement.

(b) The judge shall hear evidence and determine to the judge's satisfaction whether it is in the best interests of the estate that the proposed agreement be authorized.

(c) The hearing may be continued from day to day and from time to time as the court finds necessary.

Derived from Probate Code § 849(e).

Added by Acts 2011, 82nd Leg., ch. 823, § 1.02, eff. Jan. 1, 2014.

§ 1160.155. Action of Court and Contents of Order

(a) The court shall enter an order setting out the court's findings and authorizing execution of the proposed pooling or unitization agreement, with or without payment of cash consideration according to the agreement, if the court finds that:

(1) the pool or unit to which the agreement relates will be operated in a manner that protects correlative rights or prevents the physical or economic waste of oil, liquid hydrocarbons, gas, gaseous elements, or other minerals subject to the pool or unit;

(2) it is in the best interests of the estate that the agreement be executed; and

(3) the agreement conforms substantially with the permissible provisions of Section 1160.151.

(b) If cash consideration is to be paid for the pooling or unitization agreement, the court shall make a finding as to the necessity of increased or additional bond as a finding is made in the making of leases on payment of the cash bonus for the lease. The agreement is not valid until any required increased or additional bond has been approved by the judge and filed with the clerk.

(c) If the effective date of the pooling or unitization agreement is not stipulated in the agreement, the effective date of the agreement is the date of the court's order.

Derived from Probate Code § 849(f).

Added by Acts 2011, 82nd Leg., ch. 823, § 1.02, eff. Jan. 1, 2014.

Subchapter E. Special Ancillary Instruments That May be Executed Without Court Order

§ 1160.201. Authorization for Execution of Certain Instruments

As to any mineral lease or pooling or unitization agreement, executed on behalf of an estate before September 1, 1993, pursuant to provisions, or executed by a former owner of land, minerals, or royalty affected by the lease or agreement, the guardian of the estate being administered, without further court order and without consideration, may execute:

(1) division orders;

(2) transfer orders;

(3) instruments of correction;

(4) instruments designating depository banks for the receipt of delay rentals or shut-in gas well royalty to accrue or become payable under the terms of the lease; or

(5) similar instruments relating to the lease or agreement and the property covered by the lease or agreement.

Derived from Probate Code § 850.

Added by Acts 2011, 82nd Leg., ch. 823, § 1.02, eff. Jan. 1, 2014.

Subchapter F. Procedure if Guardian of Estate Neglects to Apply for Authority

§ 1160.251. Application to Show Cause

If a guardian of an estate neglects to apply for authority to subject estate property to a lease for mineral development, pooling, or unitization, or authority to commit royalty or another interest in minerals to pooling or unitization, any person interested in the estate may, on written application filed with the county clerk, have the guardian cited to show cause why it is not in the best interests of the estate to make the lease or enter into an agreement.

Derived from Probate Code § 851.

Added by Acts 2011, 82nd Leg., ch. 823, § 1.02, eff. Jan. 1, 2014.

§ 1160.252. Hearing on Application

(a) The county clerk shall immediately call the filing of an application under Section 1160.251 to the attention of the judge of the court in which the guardianship proceeding is pending.

(b) The judge shall set a time and place for a hearing on the application, and the guardian of the estate shall be cited to appear and show cause why the execution of a lease or agreement described by Section 1160.251 should not be ordered.

Derived from Probate Code § 851.

Added by Acts 2011, 82nd Leg., ch. 823, § 1.02, eff. Jan. 1, 2014.

§ 1160.253. Order

On a hearing conducted under Section 1160.252 and if satisfied from the evidence that it would be in the best interests of the estate, the court shall enter an order requiring the guardian of the estate to file an application to subject the estate property to a lease for mineral development, with or without pooling or unitization provisions, or to commit royalty or other minerals to pooling or unitization, as appropriate.

Derived from Probate Code § 851.

Added by Acts 2011, 82nd Leg., ch. 823, § 1.02, eff. Jan. 1, 2014.

§ 1160.254. Procedure to be Followed After Entry of Order

After entry of an order under Section 1160.253, the procedures prescribed with respect to an original lease application, or with respect to an original application for authority to commit royalty or minerals to pooling or unitization, shall be followed.

Derived from Probate Code § 851.

Added by Acts 2011, 82nd Leg., ch. 823, § 1.02, eff. Jan. 1, 2014.

Chapter 1161. Investments and Loans of Estates of Wards

Subchapter A. General Provisions

Subchapter B. Procedure for Making Investments or Loans or Retaining Estate Assets

Subchapter C. Investments in Certain Insurance or Annuities

Subchapter D. Investments in Real Estate

Subchapter E. Loans and Security for loans

Chapter 1161. Investments and Loans of Estates of Wards

Subchapter A. General Provisions

§ 1161.001. Guardian's Duty to Keep Estate Invested

(a) The guardian of the estate shall invest any funds and assets of a ward's estate available for investment except:

(1) if the court orders otherwise under this chapter; or

(2) as provided by Subsection (b).

(b) The guardian of the estate is not required to invest funds that are immediately necessary for the education, support, and maintenance of the ward or any others the ward supports as provided by this title.

Derived from Probate Code § 854(a).

Added by Acts 2011, 82nd Leg., ch. 823, § 1.02, eff. Jan. 1, 2014.

§ 1161.002. Standard for Management and Investment of Estate

(a) In acquiring, investing, reinvesting, exchanging, retaining, selling, supervising, and managing a ward's estate, a guardian of the estate shall exercise the judgment and care under the circumstances then prevailing that a person of ordinary prudence, discretion, and intelligence exercises in the management of the person's own affairs, considering the probable income from, probable increase in value of, and safety of the person's capital. The guardian shall also consider all other relevant factors, including:

(1) the anticipated costs of supporting the ward;

(2) the ward's age, education, current income, ability to earn additional income, net worth, and liabilities;

(3) the nature of the ward's estate; and

(4) any other resources reasonably available to the ward.

(b) In determining whether a guardian of the estate has exercised the standard of investment required by this section with respect to an investment decision, the court shall, absent fraud or gross negligence, consider the investment of all the estate assets over which the guardian has management or control, rather than considering the prudence of only a single investment made by the guardian.

Derived from Probate Code §§ 855(a), (a-1).

Added by Acts 2011, 82nd Leg., ch. 823, § 1.02, eff. Jan. 1, 2014.

§ 1161.003. Investments That Meet Standard for Investment

A guardian of the estate is considered to have exercised the standard required by Section 1161.002(a) with respect to investing the ward's estate if the guardian invests in the following:

(1) bonds or other obligations of the United States;

(2) tax-supported bonds of this state;

(3) except as limited by Sections 1161.004(b) and (c), tax-supported bonds of a county, district, political subdivision, or municipality in this state;

(4) if the payment of the shares or share accounts is insured by the Federal Deposit Insurance Corporation, shares or share accounts of:

(A) a state savings and loan association or savings bank that has its main office or a branch office in this state; or

(B) a federal savings and loan association or savings bank that has its main office or a branch office in this state;

(5) collateral bonds that:

(A) are issued by a company incorporated under the laws of this state that has a paid-in capital of $1 million or more;

(B) are a direct obligation of the company; and

(C) are specifically secured by first mortgage real estate notes or other securities pledged with a trustee; or

(6) interest-bearing time deposits that may be withdrawn on or before one year after demand in a bank that does business in this state, if the payment of the time deposits is insured by the Federal Deposit Insurance Corporation.

Derived from Probate Code § 855(b).

Added by Acts 2011, 82nd Leg., ch. 823, § 1.02, eff. Jan. 1, 2014.

§ 1161.004. Restrictions on Investment in Certain Bonds

(a) In this section, "net funded debt" means the total funded debt less sinking funds on hand.

(b) A guardian of the estate may purchase the bonds of a county, district, or political subdivision other than a municipality only if the net funded debt of the county, district, or political subdivision that issues the bonds does not exceed 10 percent of the assessed value of taxable property in the county, district, or political subdivision.

(c) A guardian of the estate may purchase the bonds of a municipality only if the net funded debt of the municipality does not exceed 10 percent of the assessed value of taxable property in the municipality less that part of the debt incurred for acquisition or improvement of revenue-producing utilities, the revenue of which is not pledged to support other obligations of the municipality.

(d) Subsections (b) and (c) do not apply to bonds issued for road purposes in this state under Section 52, Article III, Texas Constitution, that are supported by a tax unlimited as to rate or amount.

Derived from Probate Code §§ 855(c), (d), (e), (f).

Added by Acts 2011, 82nd Leg., ch. 823, § 1.02, eff. Jan. 1, 2014.

§ 1161.005. Modification or Elimination of Duty or Standard

On a showing by clear and convincing evidence that the action is in the best interests of the ward and the ward's estate, the court may modify or eliminate:

(1) the duty of the guardian of the estate to keep the estate invested; or

(2) the standard required by Section 1161.002(a) with regard to investments of estate assets.

Derived from Probate Code § 855(g).

Added by Acts 2011, 82nd Leg., ch. 823, § 1.02, eff. Jan. 1, 2014.

§ 1161.006. Retention of Certain Assets

(a) Without court approval a guardian of the estate may retain until the first anniversary of the date of receipt any property received into the guardianship estate at the estate's inception or added to the estate by gift, devise, inheritance, mutation, or increase, without regard to diversification of investments and without liability for any depreciation or loss resulting from the retention.

(b) The guardian shall care for and manage the retained assets as a person of ordinary prudence, discretion, and intelligence would in caring for and managing the person's own affairs.

(c) On application and a hearing, the court may issue an order authorizing the guardian to continue retaining the property after the period prescribed by Subsection (a) if the retention is an element of the guardian's investment plan as provided by Subchapter B.

Derived from Probate Code § 855A.

Added by Acts 2011, 82nd Leg., ch. 823, § 1.02, eff. Jan. 1, 2014.

§ 1161.007. Hearing to Protect Estate

(a) The court may, on the court's own motion or on written request of a person interested in the guardianship, cite the guardian of the estate to appear and show cause why the estate is not invested or not properly invested.

(b) Except as provided by Subsection (d), at any time after giving notice to all parties, the court may conduct a hearing to protect the estate.

(c) On the hearing of the court's motion or a request made under this section, the court shall issue an order the court considers to be in the ward's best interests.

(d) The court may not hold a final hearing on whether the estate is properly invested until the 31st day after the date the guardian is originally cited to appear under Subsection (a).

(e) The court may appoint a guardian ad litem for the limited purpose of representing the ward's best interests with respect to the investment of the ward's property at a hearing under this section.

Derived from Probate Code §§ 854(b), (c).

Added by Acts 2011, 82nd Leg., ch. 823, § 1.02, eff. Jan. 1, 2014.

§ 1161.008. Liability of Guardian and Guardian's Surety

(a) In addition to any other remedy authorized by law, if the guardian of the estate fails to invest or lend estate assets in the manner provided by this chapter, the guardian and the guardian's surety are liable for the principal and the greater of:

(1) the highest legal rate of interest on the principal during the period the guardian failed to invest or lend the assets; or

(2) the overall return that would have been made on the principal if the principal were invested in the manner provided by this chapter.

(b) In addition to the liability under Subsection (a), the guardian and the guardian's surety are liable for attorney's fees, litigation expenses, and costs related to a proceeding brought to enforce this section.

Derived from Probate Code § 863.

Added by Acts 2011, 82nd Leg., ch. 823, § 1.02, eff. Jan. 1, 2014.

Subchapter B. Procedure for Making Investments or Loans or Retaining Estate Assets

§ 1161.051. Procedure in General

(a) Not later than the 180th day after the date the guardian of the estate qualifies as guardian or another date specified by the court, the guardian shall:

(1) invest estate assets according to Section 1161.003; or

(2) file a written application with the court for an order:

(A) authorizing the guardian to:

(i) develop and implement an investment plan for estate assets;

(ii) invest in or sell securities under an investment plan developed under Subparagraph (i);

(iii) declare that one or more estate assets must be retained, despite being underproductive with respect to income or overall return; or

(iv) loan estate funds, invest in real estate or make other investments, or purchase a life, term, or endowment insurance policy or an annuity contract; or

(B) modifying or eliminating the guardian's duty to invest the estate.

(b) The court may approve an investment plan under Subsection (a)(2) without a hearing.

Derived from Probate Code §§ 855B(a), (a-1).

Added by Acts 2011, 82nd Leg., ch. 823, § 1.02, eff. Jan. 1, 2014.

§ 1161.052. Court Action

(a) If the court determines that the action requested in the application is in the best interests of the ward and the ward's estate, the court shall issue an order:

(1) granting the authority requested in the application; or

(2) modifying or eliminating the guardian's duty to keep the estate invested.

(b) An order under Subsection (a) must state in reasonably specific terms:

(1) the nature of the investment, investment plan, or other action requested in the application and authorized by the court, including any authority to invest in and sell securities in accordance with the investment plan's objectives;

(2) when an investment must be reviewed and reconsidered by the guardian; and

(3) whether the guardian must report the guardian's review and recommendations to the court.

(c) A citation or notice is not necessary to invest in or sell securities under an investment plan authorized by the court under this section.

Derived from Probate Code §§ 855B(b), (e).

Added by Acts 2011, 82nd Leg., ch. 823, § 1.02, eff. Jan. 1, 2014.

§ 1161.053. Applicability of Procedure to Certain Assets

The fact that an account or other asset is the subject of a specific or general gift under a ward's will, if any, or that a ward has funds, securities, or other property held with a right of survivorship does not prevent:

(1) the guardian of the estate from taking possession and control of the asset or closing the account; or

(2) the court from authorizing an action or modifying or eliminating a duty with respect to the possession, control, or investment of the account or other asset.

Derived from Probate Code § 855B(c).

Added by Acts 2011, 82nd Leg., ch. 823, § 1.02, eff. Jan. 1, 2014.

§ 1161.054. Inapplicability of Procedure to Certain Assets

(a) The procedure prescribed by this subchapter does not apply if a different procedure is prescribed for an investment or sale by a guardian.

(b) A guardian of the estate is not required to follow the procedure prescribed by this subchapter with respect to an investment or sale that is specifically authorized by other law.

Derived from Probate Code § 855B(d).

Added by Acts 2011, 82nd Leg., ch. 823, § 1.02, eff. Jan. 1, 2014.

Subchapter C. Investments in Certain Insurance or Annuities

§ 1161.101. Definition

In this subchapter, "authorized life insurance company" means a stock or mutual legal reserve life insurance company that:

(1) is licensed by the Texas Department of Insurance to transact the business of life insurance in this state; and

(2) maintains the legal reserve required by the laws of this state.

Derived from Probate Code § 857(a).

Added by Acts 2011, 82nd Leg., ch. 823, § 1.02, eff. Jan. 1, 2014.

§ 1161.102. Authority to Invest in Certain Insurance or Annuities

Subject to this subchapter, the guardian of the estate may invest in life, term, or endowment insurance policies, in annuity contracts, or in both, issued by an authorized life insurance company or administered by the Department of Veterans Affairs.

Derived from Probate Code § 857(b).

Added by Acts 2011, 82nd Leg., ch. 823, § 1.02, eff. Jan. 1, 2014.

§ 1161.103. Investment Requirements

(a) An insurance policy in which the guardian of the estate invests must be issued on the life of:

(1) the ward;

(2) the ward's parent, spouse, child, sibling, or grandparent; or

(3) another person in whose life the ward may have an insurable interest.

(b) The ward must be the annuitant in the annuity contract in which the guardian of the estate invests.

(c) Only the ward, the ward's estate, or the ward's parent, spouse, child, sibling, or grandparent may be a beneficiary of the insurance policy or of the death benefit of the annuity contract.

(d) The insurance policy or annuity contract may not be amended or changed during the ward's life and disability, except on application to and order of the court.

Derived from Probate Code §§ 857(d), (e), (g).

Added by Acts 2011, 82nd Leg., ch. 823, § 1.02, eff. Jan. 1, 2014.

§ 1161.104. Procedure for Investing in Insurance or Annuities

(a) Before the guardian of the estate may invest in life, term, or endowment insurance policies, in annuity contracts, or in both, the guardian must first apply to the court for an order that authorizes the investment.

(b) The application must include a report that shows:

(1) in detail the estate's financial condition on the date the application is filed;

(2) the name and address of the authorized life insurance company from which the insurance policy or annuity contract is to be purchased and that:

(A) the company is licensed by the Texas Department of Insurance to transact that business in this state on the date the application is filed; or

(B) the policy or contract is administered by the Department of Veterans Affairs;

(3) a statement of:

(A) the face amount and plan of the insurance policy sought to be purchased; and

(B) the amount, frequency, and duration of the annuity payments to be provided by the annuity contract sought to be purchased;

(4) a statement of the amount, frequency, and duration of the premiums required by the insurance policy or annuity contract; and

(5) a statement of the cash value of the insurance policy or annuity contract at the policy's or contract's anniversary nearest the ward's 21st birthday, assuming that all premiums to the anniversary are paid and that there is no indebtedness against the policy or contract incurred in accordance with its terms.

(c) If satisfied by the application and the evidence presented at the hearing that it is in the ward's interests to grant the application, the court shall enter an order granting the application.

Derived from Probate Code §§ 857(c), (i).

Added by Acts 2011, 82nd Leg., ch. 823, § 1.02, eff. Jan. 1, 2014.

§ 1161.105. Continuation of Preexisting Policies or Annuities

(a) A life, term, or endowment insurance policy or an annuity contract owned by the ward when a proceeding for the appointment of a guardian of the estate is commenced may be continued in full effect if it is shown that:

(1) the company issuing the policy or contract is an authorized life insurance company; or

(2) the policy or contract is administered by the Department of Veterans Affairs.

(b) All future premiums for an insurance policy or annuity contract described by Subsection (a) may be paid out of surplus funds of the ward's estate.

(c) The guardian of the estate must apply to the court for an order to:

(1) continue the policy, the contract, or both according to the existing terms of the policy or contract; or

(2) modify the policy or contract to fit any new developments affecting the ward's welfare.

(d) Before the court grants an application filed under Subsection (c), the guardian must file a report in the court that shows in detail the financial condition of the ward's estate on the date the application is filed.

Derived from Probate Code § 857(h).

Added by Acts 2011, 82nd Leg., ch. 823, § 1.02, eff. Jan. 1, 2014.

§ 1161.106. Control and Ownership of Policies or Annuities

(a) Control of an insurance policy or an annuity contract and of the incidents of ownership in the policy or contract is vested in the guardian of the estate during the ward's life and disability.

(b) A right, benefit, or interest that accrues under an insurance policy or annuity contract subject to this subchapter becomes the ward's exclusive property when the ward's disability is terminated.

Derived from Probate Code §§ 857(f), (j).

Added by Acts 2011, 82nd Leg., ch. 823, § 1.02, eff. Jan. 1, 2014.

Subchapter D. Investments in Real Estate

§ 1161.151. Authority to Invest in Real Estate; Procedure and Requirements

(a) The guardian of the estate may invest estate assets in real estate if:

(1) the guardian believes that the investment is in the ward's best interests;

(2) there are on hand sufficient additional assets to provide a return sufficient to provide for:

(A) the education, support, and maintenance of the ward and others the ward supports, if applicable; and

(B) the maintenance, insurance, and taxes on the real estate in which the guardian wishes to invest;

(3) the guardian files a written application with the court requesting a court order authorizing the guardian to make the desired investment and stating the reasons why, in the guardian's opinion, the investment would be for the ward's benefit; and

(4) the court issues an order authorizing the investment as provided by this subchapter.

(b) If the ward's money is invested in real estate, the title to the real estate shall be made to the ward. The guardian shall inventory, appraise, manage, and account for the real estate as the guardian does with other real estate of the ward.

Derived from Probate Code §§ 860(a), (d).

Added by Acts 2011, 82nd Leg., ch. 823, § 1.02, eff. Jan. 1, 2014.

§ 1161.152. Court Authorization to Make Investments

(a) If the guardian of the estate files an application under this subchapter, the judge shall investigate as necessary to obtain all the facts concerning the investment.

(b) Subject to Subsection (c), on the hearing of the application, the court shall issue an order that authorizes the guardian to make the investment if the court is satisfied that the investment benefits the ward. The order must specify the investment to be made and contain other directions the court considers advisable.

(c) The judge may not issue an opinion or order on the application until after the 10th day after the date the application is filed.

Derived from Probate Code § 860(b).

Added by Acts 2011, 82nd Leg., ch. 823, § 1.02, eff. Jan. 1, 2014.

§ 1161.153. Court Approval of Contracts Required

(a) If a contract is made for the investment of money in real estate under a court order, the guardian of the estate shall report the contract in writing to the court.

(b) The court shall inquire fully into the contract. If satisfied that the investment will benefit the ward's estate and that the title of the real estate is valid and unencumbered, the court may approve the contract and authorize the guardian to pay money in performance of the contract.

(c) The guardian may not pay any money on the contract until the contract is approved by a court order to that effect.

Derived from Probate Code § 860(c).

Added by Acts 2011, 82nd Leg., ch. 823, § 1.02, eff. Jan. 1, 2014.

Subchapter E. Loans and Security for Loans

§ 1161.201. Inapplicability of Subchapter

This subchapter does not apply to an investment in a debenture, bond, or other publicly traded debt security.

Derived from Probate Code § 858(h).

Added by Acts 2011, 82nd Leg., ch. 823, § 1.02, eff. Jan. 1, 2014.

§ 1161.202. Authority to Make Loans

(a) If, at any time, the guardian of the estate has on hand money belonging to the ward in an amount that provides a return that is more than is necessary for the education, support, and maintenance of the ward and others the ward supports, if applicable, the guardian may lend the money for a reasonable interest rate.

(b) The guardian of the estate is considered to have obtained a reasonable interest rate for a loan for purposes of Subsection (a) if the interest rate is at least equal to 120 percent of the applicable short-term, midterm, or long-term interest rate under Section 7520, Internal Revenue Code of 1986, for the month during which the loan was made.

Derived from Probate Code §§ 858(a) (part), (b).

Added by Acts 2011, 82nd Leg., ch. 823, § 1.02, eff. Jan. 1, 2014.

§ 1161.203. Loan Requirements

(a) Except as provided by Subsection (b), the guardian of the estate shall take as collateral the borrower's note for the money that is loaned, secured by:

(1) a mortgage with a power of sale on unencumbered real estate located in this state worth at least twice the amount of the note; or

(2) collateral notes secured by vendor's lien notes.

(b) The guardian may purchase vendor's lien notes if at least one-half has been paid in cash or its equivalent on the land for which the notes were given.

(c) Except as provided by Subsection (d), a guardian of the estate who lends estate money may not pay or transfer any money to consummate the loan until the guardian:

(1) submits to a reputable attorney for examination all bonds, notes, mortgages, abstracts, and other documents relating to the loan; and

(2) receives a written opinion from the attorney stating that the documents under Subdivision (1) are regular and that the title to relevant bonds, notes, or real estate is clear.

(d) A guardian of the estate may obtain a mortgagee's title insurance policy on any real estate loan instead of an abstract and attorney's opinion under Subsection (c).

(e) The borrower shall pay attorney's fees for any legal services required by Subsection (c).

Derived from Probate Code §§ 858(a) (part), (d), (e), (f), 861.

Added by Acts 2011, 82nd Leg., ch. 823, § 1.02, eff. Jan. 1, 2014.

§ 1161.204. Guardian's Duty to Report Loan to Court

(a) Not later than the 30th day after the date the guardian of the estate loans money from the estate, the guardian shall file with the court a written report, accompanied and verified by an affidavit, stating fully the facts related to the loan.

(b) This section does not apply to a loan made in accordance with a court order.

Derived from Probate Code §§ 858(g), 862.

Added by Acts 2011, 82nd Leg., ch. 823, § 1.02, eff. Jan. 1, 2014.

§ 1161.205. Guardian's Liability

(a) Except as provided by Subsection (b), a guardian of the estate who loans estate money with the court's approval on security approved by the court is not personally liable if the borrower is unable to repay the money and the security fails.

(b) If the guardian committed fraud or was negligent in making or managing the loan, including in collecting the loan, the guardian and the guardian's surety are liable for the loss sustained by the guardianship estate as a result of the fraud or negligence.

Derived from Probate Code § 858(c).

Added by Acts 2011, 82nd Leg., ch. 823, § 1.02, eff. Jan. 1, 2014.

Chapter 1162. Tax-Motivated, Charitable, Nonprofit, and Other Gifts

Subchapter A. Certain Gifts and Transfers

Subchapter B. Charitable and Nonprofit Gifts

§ 1162.053. Order Authorizing Gift

Chapter 1162. Tax-Motivated, Charitable, Nonprofit, and Other Gifts

Subchapter A. Certain Gifts and Transfers

§ 1162.001. Authority To Establish Estate or Other Transfer Plan

On application of the guardian of the estate or any interested person, after the posting of notice and hearing, and on a showing that the ward will probably remain incapacitated during the ward's lifetime, the court may enter an order that authorizes the guardian to apply the principal or income of the ward's estate that is not required for the support of the ward or the ward's family during the ward's lifetime toward the establishment of an estate plan for the purpose of minimizing income, estate, inheritance, or other taxes payable out of the ward's estate, or to transfer a portion of the ward's estate as necessary to qualify the ward for government benefits and only to the extent allowed by applicable state or federal laws, including rules, regarding those benefits. On the ward's behalf, the court may authorize the guardian to make gifts or transfers described by this section, outright or in trust, of the ward's property to or for the benefit of:

(1) an organization to which charitable contributions may be made under the Internal Revenue Code of 1986 and in which it is shown the ward would reasonably have an interest;

(2) the ward's spouse, descendant, or other person related to the ward by blood or marriage who is identifiable at the time of the order;

(3) a devisee under the ward's last validly executed will, trust, or other beneficial instrument, if the instrument exists; and

(4) a person serving as guardian of the ward, if the person is eligible under Subdivision (2) or (3).

Derived from Probate Code § 865(a).

Added by Acts 2011, 82nd Leg., ch. 823, § 1.02, eff. Jan. 1, 2014. Amended by Acts 2013, 83rd Leg., ch. 161, § 6.050, eff. Jan. 1, 2014.

§ 1162.002. Estate or Other Transfer Plan: Contents and Modification

(a) The person making an application to the court under Section 1162.001 shall:

(1) outline the proposed estate or other transfer plan; and

(2) state all the benefits that are to be derived from the plan.

(b) The application must indicate that the planned disposition is consistent with the ward's intentions, if the ward's intentions can be ascertained. If the ward's intentions cannot be ascertained, the ward will be presumed to favor reduction in the incidence of the various forms of taxation, the qualification for government benefits, and the partial distribution of the ward's estate as provided by Sections 1162.001 and 1162.004.

(c) A subsequent modification of an approved plan may be made by similar application to the court.

Derived from Probate Code § 865(b) & (d).

Added by Acts 2011, 82nd Leg., ch. 823, § 1.02, eff. Jan. 1, 2014. Amended by Acts 2013, 83rd Leg., ch. 161, § 6.051, eff. Jan. 1, 2014.

§ 1162.003. Notice of Application for Establishment of Estate or Other Transfer Plan

A person who makes an application to the court under Section 1162.001 shall mail notice of the application by certified mail to:

(1) all devisees under a will, trust, or other beneficial instrument relating to the ward's estate;

(2) the ward's spouse;

(3) the ward's dependents; and

(4) any other person as directed by the court.

Derived from Probate Code § 865(e).

Added by Acts 2011, 82nd Leg., ch. 823, § 1.02, eff. Jan. 1, 2014. Amended by Acts 2013, 83rd Leg., ch. 161, § 6.052, eff. Jan. 1, 2014.

§ 1162.004. Authority to Make Periodic Gifts

(a) In an order entered under Section 1162.001, the court may authorize the guardian to make, without subsequent application to or order of the court, gifts as provided by that section on an annual or other periodic basis if the court finds it to be in the best interest of the ward and the ward's estate.

(b) The court, on the court's own motion or on the motion of a person interested in the welfare of the ward, may modify or set aside an order entered under Subsection (a) if the court finds that the ward's financial condition has changed in such a manner that authorizing the guardian to make gifts of the estate on a continuing basis is no longer in the best interest of the ward and the ward's estate.

Derived from Probate Code § 865(f).

Added by Acts 2011, 82nd Leg., ch. 823, § 1.02, eff. Jan. 1, 2014.

§ 1162.005. Application for Inspection of Certain Documents

(a) On the filing of an application under Section 1162.001 and for the purpose of establishing an estate plan under that section, the guardian of the ward's estate may apply to the court for an order to seek an in camera inspection of a copy of a will, codicil, trust, or other estate planning instrument of the ward as a means of obtaining access to the instrument.

(b) An application filed under this section must:

(1) be sworn to by the guardian;

(2) list each instrument requested for inspection; and

(3) state one or more reasons supporting the necessity to inspect each requested instrument for the purpose described by Subsection (a).

Derived from Probate Code §§ 865A(a), (b).

Added by Acts 2011, 82nd Leg., ch. 823, § 1.02, eff. Jan. 1, 2014.

§ 1162.006. Notice of Application for Inspection

(a) A person who files an application under Section 1162.005 shall send a copy of the application to:

(1) each person who has custody of an instrument listed in the application;

(2) the ward's spouse;

(3) the ward's dependents;

(4) all devisees under a will, trust, or other beneficial instrument relating to the ward's estate; and

(5) any other person as directed by the court.

(b) Notice required by Subsection (a) must be delivered by:

(1) registered or certified mail to a person described by Subsection (a)(1); and

(2) certified mail to a person described by Subsection (a)(2), (3), (4), or (5).

Derived from Probate Code §§ 865A(c), (d).

Added by Acts 2011, 82nd Leg., ch. 823, § 1.02, eff. Jan. 1, 2014.

§ 1162.007. Hearing on Application for Inspection; Inspection

(a) After the 10th day after the date on which the applicant complies with the notice requirement under Section 1162.006, the applicant may request that a hearing be held on the application. Notice of the date, time, and place of the hearing must be given by the applicant to each person described by Section 1162.006(a)(1) when the court sets a date for a hearing on the application.

(b) After the conclusion of a hearing on the application for inspection and on a finding that good cause exists for an in camera inspection of a requested instrument, the court shall direct the person that has custody of the requested will, codicil, trust, or other estate planning instrument to deliver a copy of the instrument to the court for in camera inspection only. After conducting an in camera inspection of the instrument, the court, if good cause exists, shall release all or part of the instrument to the applicant only for the purpose described by Section 1162.005(a).

(c) An attorney does not violate the attorney-client privilege solely by complying with a court order to release an instrument subject to this section and Sections 1162.005 and 1162.006. Notwithstanding Section 22.004, Government Code, the supreme court may not amend or adopt rules in conflict with this subsection.

Derived from Probate Code §§ 865A(d), (e), (g).

Added by Acts 2011, 82nd Leg., ch. 823, § 1.02, eff.

Jan. 1, 2014.

§ 1162.008. Guardian Ad Litem

The court may appoint a guardian ad litem for the ward or an interested party at any stage of proceedings under this subchapter if it is considered advisable for the protection of the ward or the interested party.

Derived from Probate Code §§ 865(c), 865A(f).

Added by Acts 2011, 82nd Leg., ch. 823, § 1.02, eff. Jan. 1, 2014.

Subchapter B. Charitable and Nonprofit Gifts

§ 1162.051. Application to Make Gift

The guardian of the estate may at any time file with the county clerk the guardian's sworn, written application requesting from the court in which the guardianship is pending an order authorizing the guardian to contribute from the income of the ward's estate the specific amount of money stated in the application to one or more designated:

(1) corporations, trusts, or community chests, funds, or foundations, organized and operated exclusively for religious, charitable, scientific, literary, or educational purposes; or

(2) nonprofit federal, state, county, or municipal projects operated exclusively for public health or welfare.

Derived from Probate Code § 866(a).

Added by Acts 2011, 82nd Leg., ch. 823, § 1.02, eff. Jan. 1, 2014.

§ 1162.052. Hearing on Application to Make Gift

(a) The county clerk shall immediately call the filing of an application under Section 1162.051 to the attention of the judge of the court.

(b) The judge shall designate, by written order filed with the clerk, a day to hear the application. The application must remain on file for at least 10 days before the hearing is held.

(c) The judge may postpone or continue the hearing from time to time until the judge is satisfied concerning the application.

Derived from Probate Code § 866(b).

Added by Acts 2011, 82nd Leg., ch. 823, § 1.02, eff. Jan. 1, 2014.

§ 1162.053. Order Authorizing Gift

On the conclusion of a hearing under Section 1162.052, the court may enter an order authorizing the guardian to make a contribution from the income of the ward's estate to a particular donee designated in the application and order if the court is satisfied and finds from the evidence that:

(1) the amount of the proposed contribution stated in the application will probably not exceed 20

percent of the net income of the ward's estate for the current calendar year;

(2) the net income of the ward's estate for the current calendar year exceeds, or probably will exceed, $25,000;

(3) the full amount of the contribution, if made, will probably be deductible from the ward's gross income in determining the net income of the ward under applicable federal income tax laws and rules;

(4) the condition of the ward's estate justifies a contribution in the proposed amount; and

(5) the proposed contribution is reasonable in amount and is for a worthy cause.

Derived from Probate Code § 866(c).

Added by Acts 2011, 82nd Leg., ch. 823, § 1.02, eff. Jan. 1, 2014.

Chapter 1163. Annual Account and Other Exhibits and Reports

Subchapter A. Annual Account and Other Exhibits by Guardian of the Estate

Subchapter B. Action on Annual Account

Subchapter C. Annual Report by Guardian of the Person

Subchapter D. Penalties

Chapter 1163. Annual Account and Other Exhibits and Reports

Subchapter A. Annual Account and Other Exhibits by Guardian of the Estate

§ 1163.001. Initial Annual Account of Estate

(a) Not later than the 60th day after the first anniversary of the date the guardian of the estate of a ward qualifies, unless the court extends that period, the guardian shall file with the court an account consisting of a written exhibit made under oath that:

(1) lists all claims against the estate presented to the guardian during the period covered by the account; and

(2) specifies:

(A) which claims have been:

(i) allowed by the guardian;

(ii) paid by the guardian; or

(iii) rejected by the guardian and the date the claims were rejected; and

(B) which claims have been the subject of a lawsuit and the status of that lawsuit.

(b) The account must:

(1) show all property that has come to the guardian's knowledge or into the guardian's possession that was not previously listed or inventoried as the ward's property;

(2) show any change in the ward's property that was not previously reported;

(3) provide a complete account of receipts and disbursements for the period covered by the account, including the source and nature of the receipts and disbursements, with separate listings for principal and income receipts;

(4) provide a complete, accurate, and detailed description of:

(A) the property being administered;

(B) the condition of the property and the use being made of the property; and

(C) if rented, the terms on which and the price for which the property was rented;

(5) show the cash balance on hand and the name and location of the depository where the balance is kept;

(6) show any other cash held in a savings account or other manner that was deposited subject to court order and the name and location of the depository for that cash; and

(7) provide a detailed description of the personal property of the estate that shows how and where the property is held for safekeeping.

(c) For bonds, notes, and other securities, the description required by Subsection (b)(7) must include:

(1) the names of the obligor and obligee or, if payable to bearer, a statement that the bond, note, or other security is payable to bearer;

(2) the date of issue and maturity;

(3) the interest rate;

(4) the serial number or other identifying numbers;

(5) the manner in which the property is secured; and

(6) other information necessary to fully identify the bond, note, or other security.

Derived from Probate Code § 741(a).

Added by Acts 2011, 82nd Leg., ch. 823, § 1.02, eff. Jan. 1, 2014.

§ 1163.002. Annual Account Required Until Estate Closed

(a) A guardian of the estate shall file an annual account conforming to the essential requirements of Section 1163.001 regarding changes in the estate assets occurring since the date the most recent previous account was filed.

(b) The annual account must be filed in a manner that allows the court or an interested person to ascertain the true condition of the estate, with respect to money, securities, and other property, by adding to the balances forwarded from the most recent previous account the amounts received during the period covered by the account and subtracting the disbursements made during that period.

(c) The description of property sufficiently described in an inventory or previous account may be made in the annual account by reference to the property.

Derived from Probate Code § 741(b).

Added by Acts 2011, 82nd Leg., ch. 823, § 1.02, eff. Jan. 1, 2014.

§ 1163.003. Supporting Vouchers and Other Documents Attached to Account

(a) The guardian of the estate shall attach to each annual account:

(1) a voucher for each item of credit claimed in the account or, to support the item in the absence of the voucher, other evidence satisfactory to the court;

(2) an official letter from the bank or other depository where the money on hand of the estate or ward is deposited that shows the amounts in general or special deposits; and

(3) proof of the existence and possession of:

(A) securities owned by the estate or shown by the account; and

(B) other assets held by a depository subject to court order.

(b) An original voucher submitted to the court may on application be returned to the guardian after approval of the annual account.

Derived from Probate Code § 741(c).

Added by Acts 2011, 82nd Leg., ch. 823, § 1.02, eff.

Jan. 1, 2014.

§ 1163.004. Method of Proof for Securities and Other Assets

(a) The proof required by Section 1163.003(a)(3) must be by:

(1) an official letter from the bank or other depository where the securities or other assets are held for safekeeping, and if the depository is the guardian, the official letter must be signed by a representative of the depository other than the depository verifying the annual account;

(2) a certificate of an authorized representative of a corporation that is surety on the guardian's bonds;

(3) a certificate of the clerk or a deputy clerk of a court of record in this state; or

(4) an affidavit of any other reputable person designated by the court on request of the guardian or other interested party.

(b) A certificate or affidavit described by Subsection (a) must:

(1) state that the affiant has examined the assets that the guardian exhibited to the affiant as assets of the estate for which the annual account is made;

(2) describe the assets by reference to the account or in another manner that sufficiently identifies the assets exhibited; and

(3) state the time and the place the assets were exhibited.

(c) Instead of attaching a certificate or an affidavit, the guardian may exhibit the securities to the judge of the court, who shall endorse on the annual account, or include in the judge's order with respect to the account, a statement that the securities shown to the judge as on hand were exhibited to the judge and that the securities were the same as those shown in the account, or note any variance. If the securities are exhibited at a location other than where the securities are deposited for safekeeping, that exhibit is at the guardian's own expense and risk.

(d) The judge of the court may require:

(1) additional evidence of the existence and custody of the securities and other personal property as the judge considers proper; and

(2) the guardian at any time to exhibit the securities to the judge or another person designated by the judge at the place where the securities are held for safekeeping.

Derived from Probate Code §§ 741(c), (d).

Added by Acts 2011, 82nd Leg., ch. 823, § 1.02, eff. Jan. 1, 2014.

§ 1163.005. Verification of Account and Statement Regarding Taxes and Status as Guardian

(a) The guardian of the estate shall attach to an account the guardian's affidavit stating:

(1) that the account contains a correct and complete statement of the matters to which the account relates;

(2) that the guardian has paid the bond premium for the next accounting period;

(3) that the guardian has filed all tax returns of the ward due during the accounting period;

(4) that the guardian has paid all taxes the ward owed during the accounting period, the amount of the taxes, the date the guardian paid the taxes, and the name of the governmental entity to which the guardian paid the taxes; and

(5) if the guardian is a private professional guardian, a guardianship program, or the Department of Aging and Disability Services, whether the guardian or an individual certified under Subchapter C, Chapter 111, Government Code, who is providing guardianship services to the ward and who is swearing to the account on the guardian's behalf, is or has been the subject of an investigation conducted by the Guardianship Certification Board during the accounting period.

(b) If on the filing of the account the guardian of the estate has failed on the ward's behalf to file a tax return or pay taxes due, the guardian shall attach to the account a description of the taxes and the reasons for the guardian's failure to file the return or pay the taxes.

Derived from Probate Code § 741(e) & (f).

Added by Acts 2011, 82nd Leg., ch. 823, § 1.02, eff. Jan. 1, 2014. Amended by Acts 2013, 83rd Leg., ch. 982, § 20, eff. Jan. 1, 2014. Subsec. (a) amended by Acts 2013, 83rd Leg., ch. 982, § 21, eff. Jan. 1, 2014.

§ 1163.006. Waiver of Account Filing

If the ward's estate produces negligible or fixed income, the court may waive the filing of annual accounts and may permit the guardian to:

(1) receive all estate income and apply the income to the support, maintenance, and education of the ward; and

(2) account to the court for the estate income and corpus when the estate must be closed.

Derived from Probate Code § 741(g).

Added by Acts 2011, 82nd Leg., ch. 823, § 1.02, eff. Jan. 1, 2014.

Subchapter B. Action on Annual Account

§ 1163.051. Filing and Consideration of Annual Account

(a) The guardian of the estate shall file an annual account with the county clerk. The county clerk shall note the filing on the judge's docket.

(b) An annual account must remain on file for 10 days after the date the account is filed before being considered by the judge. After the expiration of that period, the judge shall consider the account and may continue the hearing on the account until fully advised on all account items.

(c) The court may not approve the annual account unless possession of cash, listed securities, or other assets held in safekeeping or on deposit under court order has been proven as required by law.

Derived from Probate Code §§ 742(a), (b), (c), (d), (e).

Added by Acts 2011, 82nd Leg., ch. 823, § 1.02, eff. Jan. 1, 2014.

§ 1163.052. Correction and Approval of Annual Account

(a) If an annual account is found to be incorrect, the account shall be corrected.

(b) The court by order shall approve an annual account that is corrected to the satisfaction of the court and shall act with respect to unpaid claims in accordance with Sections 1163.053 and 1163.054.

Derived from Probate Code § 742(f).

Added by Acts 2011, 82nd Leg., ch. 823, § 1.02, eff. Jan. 1, 2014.

§ 1163.053. Order for Payment of Claims in Full

After approval of an annual account as provided by Section 1163.052, if it appears to the court from the exhibit or other evidence that the estate is wholly solvent and that the guardian has sufficient funds to pay every claim against the estate, the court shall order immediate payment of all claims allowed and approved or established by judgment.

Derived from Probate Code § 742(f).

Added by Acts 2011, 82nd Leg., ch. 823, § 1.02, eff. Jan. 1, 2014.

§ 1163.054. Order for Pro Rata Payment of Claims

After approval of an annual account as provided by Section 1163.052, if it appears to the court from the account or other evidence that the funds on hand are not sufficient to pay all claims against the estate or if the estate is insolvent and the guardian has any funds on hand, the court shall order the funds to be applied:

(1) first to the payment of any unpaid claims having a preference in the order of their priority; and

(2) then to the pro rata payment of the other claims allowed and approved or established by final judgment, considering also:

(A) claims that were presented not later than the first anniversary of the date letters of guardianship were granted; and

(B) claims that are in litigation or on which a lawsuit may be filed.

Derived from Probate Code § 742(f).

Added by Acts 2011, 82nd Leg., ch. 823, § 1.02, eff. Jan. 1, 2014.

Subchapter C. Annual Report by Guardian of the Person

§ 1163.101. Annual Report Required

(a) Once each year for the duration of the guardianship, a guardian of the person shall file with the court a report that contains the information required by this section.

(b) The guardian of the person shall file a sworn, written report that shows each receipt and disbursement for:

(1) the support and maintenance of the ward;

(2) when necessary, the education of the ward; and

(3) when authorized by court order, the support and maintenance of the ward's dependents.

(c) The guardian of the person shall file a sworn affidavit that contains:

(1) the guardian's current name, address, and telephone number;

(2) the ward's date of birth and current name, address, telephone number, and age;

(3) a description of the type of home in which the ward resides, which shall be described as:

(A) the ward's own home;

(B) a nursing home;

(C) a guardian's home;

(D) a foster home;

(E) a boarding home;

(F) a relative's home, in which case the description must specify the relative's relationship to the ward;

(G) a hospital or medical facility; or

(H) another type of residence;

(4) statements indicating:

(A) the length of time the ward has resided in the present home;

(B) the reason for a change in the ward's residence, if a change in the ward's residence has occurred in the past year;

(C) the date the guardian most recently saw the ward;

(D) how frequently the guardian has seen the ward in the past year;

(E) whether the guardian has possession or control of the ward's estate;

(F) whether the ward's mental health has improved, deteriorated, or remained unchanged during the past year, including a description of the change if a change has occurred;

(G) whether the ward's physical health has improved, deteriorated, or remained unchanged during the past year, including a description of the change if a change has occurred;

(H) whether the ward has regular medical care; and

(I) the ward's treatment or evaluation by any of the following persons during the past year, including the person's name and a description of the treatment:

(i) a physician;

(ii) a psychiatrist, psychologist, or other mental health care provider;

(iii) a dentist;

(iv) a social or other caseworker; or

(v) any other individual who provided treatment;

(5) a description of the ward's activities during the past year, including recreational, educational, social, and occupational activities, or a statement that no activities were available or that the ward was unable or refused to participate in activities;

(6) the guardian's evaluation of:

(A) the ward's living arrangements as excellent, average, or below average, including an explanation if the conditions are below average;

(B) whether the ward is content or unhappy with the ward's living arrangements; and

(C) unmet needs of the ward;

(7) a statement indicating whether the guardian's power should be increased, decreased, or unaltered, including an explanation if a change is recommended;

(8) a statement indicating that the guardian has paid the bond premium for the next reporting period;

(9) if the guardian is a private professional guardian, a guardianship program, or the Department of Aging and Disability Services, whether the guardian or an individual certified under Subchapter C, Chapter 155 [111], Government Code, who is providing guardianship services to the ward and who is filing [swearing to] the affidavit on the guardian's behalf, is or has been the subject of an investigation conducted by the Guardianship Certification Board during the preceding year; and

(10) any additional information the guardian desires to share with the court regarding the ward, including:

(A) whether the guardian has filed for emergency detention of the ward under Subchapter A, Chapter 573, Health and Safety Code; and

(B) if applicable, the number of times the guardian has filed for emergency detention and the dates of the applications for emergency detention.

Derived from Probate Code § 743(a), (b), (g).

Added by Acts 2011, 82nd Leg., ch. 823, § 1.02, eff. Jan. 1, 2014. Subsec. (c) amended by Acts 2013, 83rd Leg., ch. 982, § 22, eff. Jan. 1, 2014. Subsec. (c)(9) amended by Acts 2015, 84th Leg., ch. 1031, § 19, eff. Sept. 1, 2015.

§ 1163.1011. Use of Unsworn Declaration in Lieu of Sworn Declaration or Affidavit for [Electronic] Filing [of] Annual Report

(a) A guardian of the person who is required to file an [files the] annual report under [required by] Section 1163.101 [electronically] with the court, including a guardian filing the annual report electronically, may use an unsworn declaration made as provided by this section instead of the [a written] sworn declaration or affidavit required by Section 1163.101.

(b) An unsworn declaration authorized by this section must be:

(1) in writing; and

(2) subscribed by the person making the declaration as true under penalty of perjury.

(c) The form of an unsworn declaration authorized by this section must be substantially as follows:

I, (insert name of guardian of the person), the guardian of the person for (insert name of ward) in _____ County, Texas, declare under penalty of perjury that the foregoing is true and correct.

Executed on (insert date)

_____

(signature)

(d) An unsworn declaration authorized by Section 132.001, Civil Practice and Remedies Code, may not be used instead of a written sworn declaration or affidavit required by Section 1163.101.

New.

Added by Acts 2013, 83rd Leg., ch. 982, § 23, eff. Jan. 1, 2014. Title and subsec. (a) amended by Acts 2015, 84th Leg., ch. 1031, §§ 20 & 21, eff. Sept. 1, 2015.

§ 1163.102. Reporting Period

(a) Except as provided under Subsection (b), an annual report required by Section 1163.101 must cover a 12-month reporting period that begins on the date or the anniversary of the date the guardian of the person qualifies to serve.

(b) The court may change a reporting period for purposes of this subchapter but may not extend a reporting period so that it covers more than 12 months.

(c) Each report is due not later than the 60th day after the date the reporting period ends.

Derived from Probate Code §§ 743(g), (h), (i).

Added by Acts 2011, 82nd Leg., ch. 823, § 1.02, eff. Jan. 1, 2014.

§ 1163.103. Report in Case of Deceased Ward

If the ward is deceased, the guardian of the person shall provide the court with the date and place of death, if known, instead of the information about the ward otherwise required to be provided in the annual report.

Derived from Probate Code § 743(c).

Added by Acts 2011, 82nd Leg., ch. 823, § 1.02, eff. Jan. 1, 2014.

§ 1163.104. Approval of Report

(a) If the judge is satisfied that the facts stated in the report are true, the court shall approve the report.

(b) Unless the judge is satisfied that the facts stated in the report are true, the judge shall issue orders necessary for the ward's best interests.

(c) The court on the court's own motion may waive the costs and fees related to the filing of a report approved under Subsection (a).

Derived from Probate Code § 743(d), (e), & (f).

Added by Acts 2011, 82nd Leg., ch. 823, § 1.02, eff. Jan. 1, 2014.

§ 1163.105. Attorney Not Required

A guardian of the person may complete and file the report required under this subchapter without the assistance of an attorney.

Derived from Probate Code § 743(j).

Added by Acts 2011, 82nd Leg., ch. 823, § 1.02, eff. Jan. 1, 2014.

Subchapter D. Penalties

§ 1163.151. Penalty for Failure to File Required Account, Exhibit, or Report

(a) If a guardian does not file an account, an exhibit, a report of the guardian of the person, or another report required by this title, any person interested in the estate, on written complaint filed with the court clerk, or the court on the court's own motion, may have the guardian cited to appear and show cause why the guardian should not file the account, exhibit, or report.

(b) On hearing, the court may:

(1) order the guardian to file the account, exhibit, or report; and

(2) unless good cause is shown for the failure to file:

(A) revoke the guardian's letters of guardianship;

(B) fine the guardian in an amount not to exceed $1,000; or

(C) revoke the guardian's letters of guardianship and fine the guardian in an amount not to exceed $1,000.

Derived from Probate Code § 744.

Added by Acts 2011, 82nd Leg., ch. 823, § 1.02, eff. Jan. 1, 2014.

Chapter 1164. Liability of Guardian or Guardianship Program

§ 1164.001. Liability of Guardian

§ 1164.002. Immunity of Guardianship Program

Chapter 1164. Liability of Guardian or Guardianship Program

§ 1164.001. Liability of Guardian

A person is not liable to a third person solely because the person has been appointed guardian of a ward under this title.

Derived from Probate Code § 673.

Added by Acts 2011, 82nd Leg., ch. 823, § 1.02, eff. Jan. 1, 2014.

§ 1164.002. Immunity of Guardianship Program

A guardianship program is not liable for civil damages arising from an action taken or omission made by a person while providing guardianship services to a ward on behalf of the guardianship program, unless the action or omission was:

(1) wilfully wrongful;

(2) taken or made:

(A) with conscious indifference to or reckless disregard for the safety of the ward or another;

(B) in bad faith; or

(C) with malice; or

(3) grossly negligent.

Derived from Probate Code § 674.

Added by Acts 2011, 82nd Leg., ch. 823, § 1.02, eff. Jan. 1, 2014.

SUBTITLE F. EVALUATION, MODIFICATION, OR TERMINATION OF GUARDIANSHIP

Chapter 1201. Evaluation of Guardianship

Subchapter A. Review of Guardianship

Subchapter B. Annual Determination to Continue, Modify, or Terminate Guardianship

Chapter 1201. Evaluation of Guardianship

Subchapter A. Review of Guardianship

§ 1201.001. Determining Guardian's Performance of Duties

The court shall use reasonable diligence to determine whether a guardian is performing all of the duties required of the guardian that relate to the guardian's ward.

Derived from Probate Code § 671(a).

Added by Acts 2011, 82nd Leg., ch. 823, § 1.02, eff. Jan. 1, 2014.

§ 1201.002. Annual Examination of Guardianship; Bond of Guardian

(a) At least annually, the judge shall examine the well-being of each ward of the court and the solvency of the bond of the guardian of the ward's estate.

(b) If after examining the solvency of a guardian's bond as provided by Subsection (a) the judge determines that the guardian's bond is not sufficient to protect the ward or the ward's estate, the judge shall require the guardian to execute a new bond.

(c) The judge shall notify the guardian and the sureties on the guardian's bond as provided by law.

Derived from Probate Code § 671(b), (c), & (d).

Added by Acts 2011, 82nd Leg., ch. 823, § 1.02, eff. Jan. 1, 2014.

§ 1201.003. Judge's Liability

A judge is liable on the judge's bond to those damaged if damage or loss results to a guardianship or ward because of the gross neglect of the judge to use reasonable diligence in the performance of the judge's duty under this subchapter.

Derived from Probate Code § 671(d).

Added by Acts 2011, 82nd Leg., ch. 823, § 1.02, eff. Jan. 1, 2014.

§ 1201.004. Identifying Information

(a) The court may request an applicant or court-appointed fiduciary to produce other information identifying an applicant, ward, or guardian, including a social security number, in addition to identifying information the applicant or fiduciary is required to produce under this title.

(b) The court shall maintain any information required under this section, and the information may not be filed with the clerk.

Derived from Probate Code § 671(e).

Added by Acts 2011, 82nd Leg., ch. 823, § 1.02, eff. Jan. 1, 2014.

Subchapter B. Annual Determination to Continue, Modify, or Terminate Guardianship

§ 1201.051. Applicability

This subchapter does not apply to a guardianship that is created only because it is necessary for a person to have a guardian appointed to receive funds from a governmental source.

Derived from Probate Code § 672(e).

Added by Acts 2011, 82nd Leg., ch. 823, § 1.02, eff. Jan. 1, 2014.

§ 1201.052. Annual Determination

To determine whether a guardianship should be continued, modified, or terminated, the court in which the guardianship proceeding is pending:

(1) shall review annually each guardianship in which the application to create the guardianship was filed after September 1, 1993; and

(2) may review annually any other guardianship.

Derived from Probate Code § 672(a).

Added by Acts 2011, 82nd Leg., ch. 823, § 1.02, eff. Jan. 1, 2014.

§ 1201.053. Method of Determination

(a) In reviewing a guardianship under Section 1201.052, a statutory probate court may:

(1) review any report prepared by:

(A) a court investigator under Section 1054.153 or 1202.054;

(B) a guardian ad litem under Section 1202.054; or

(C) a court visitor under Section 1054.104;

(2) conduct a hearing; or

(3) review an annual account prepared under Subchapter A, Chapter 1163, or a report prepared under Subchapter C, Chapter 1163.

(b) A court that is not a statutory probate court may use any method to review a guardianship under Section 1201.052 that is determined appropriate by the court according to the court's caseload and available resources.

Derived from Probate Code § 672(b), (c).

Added by Acts 2011, 82nd Leg., ch. 823, § 1.02, eff. Jan. 1, 2014.

§ 1201.054. Form of Determination

A determination under this subchapter must be in writing and filed with the clerk.

Derived from Probate Code § 672(d).

Added by Acts 2011, 82nd Leg., ch. 823, § 1.02, eff. Jan. 1, 2014.

Chapter 1202. Modification or Termination of Guardianship

Subchapter A. Termination and Settlement of Guardianship

Subchapter B. Application for Complete Restoration of Ward's Capacity or Modification of Guardianship

Subchapter C. Representation of Ward in Proceeding for Complete Restoration of Ward's Capacity or Modification of Guardianship

Subchapter D. Hearing, Evidence, and Orders in Proceeding for Complete Restoration of Ward's Capacity or Modification of Guardianship

Subchapter E. Restoration of Rights on Termination of Guardianship

Chapter 1202. Modification or Termination of Guardianship

Subchapter A. Termination and Settlement of Guardianship

§ 1202.001. Term of Guardian or Guardianship

(a) Unless otherwise discharged as provided by law, a guardian remains in office until the estate is closed.

(b) A guardianship shall be settled and closed when the ward:

(1) dies and, if the ward was married, the ward's spouse qualifies as survivor in community;

(2) is found by the court to have full capacity, or sufficient capacity with supports and services, to care for himself or herself and to manage the ward's property;

(3) is no longer a minor; or

(4) no longer must have a guardian appointed to receive funds due the ward from any governmental source.

(c) Except for an order issued under Section 1101.153(a-1), an [An] order appointing a guardian or a successor guardian may specify a period of not more than one year during which a petition for adjudication that the ward no longer requires the guardianship may not be filed without special leave.

(d) A request for an order under this section may be made by informal letter to the court. A person who knowingly interferes with the transmission of the request to the court may be adjudged guilty of contempt of court.

(e) If a nonresident guardian of a nonresident ward qualifies as guardian under this title, any resident guardian's guardianship may be terminated.

Derived from Probate Code § 694.

Added by Acts 2011, 82nd Leg., ch. 823, § 1.02, eff. Jan. 1, 2014. Subsec. (b) & (c) amended by Acts 2015, 84th Leg., ch. 214, § 15, eff. Sept. 1, 2015.

§ 1202.002. Termination of Guardianship if Parent Is No Longer Incapacitated

(a) The powers of a person appointed to serve as the designated guardian of the person or estate, or both, of a minor child solely because of the incapacity of the minor's surviving parent and in accordance with Section 1104.053 and Subchapter D, Chapter 1104, terminate when a probate court enters an order finding that the surviving parent is no longer an incapacitated person.

(b) The powers of a person appointed to serve as the designated guardian of the person or estate, or both, of an adult individual solely because of the incapacity of the individual's surviving parent and in accordance with Section 1104.103 and Subchapter D, Chapter 1104, terminate when a probate court enters an order finding that the surviving parent is no longer an incapacitated person and reappointing the surviving parent as the individual's guardian.

Derived from Probate Code §§ 676(g), 677(e).

Added by Acts 2011, 82nd Leg., ch. 823, § 1.02, eff. Jan. 1, 2014.

Subchapter B. Application for Complete Restoration of Ward's Capacity or Modification of Guardianship

§ 1202.051. Application Authorized

A ward or any person interested in the ward's welfare may file a written application with the court for an order:

(1) finding that the ward is no longer an incapacitated person and ordering the settlement and closing of the guardianship;

(2) finding that the ward lacks the capacity, or lacks sufficient capacity with supports and services, to do some or all of the tasks necessary to provide food, clothing, or shelter for himself or herself, to care for the ward's own physical health, or to manage the ward's own financial affairs and granting additional powers or duties to the guardian; or

(3) finding that the ward has the capacity, or sufficient capacity with supports and services, to do some, but not all, of the tasks necessary to provide food, clothing, or shelter for himself or herself, to care for the ward's own physical health, or to manage the ward's own financial affairs and:

(A) limiting the guardian's powers or duties; and

(B) permitting the ward to care for himself or herself, make personal decisions regarding residence, or [to] manage the ward's own financial affairs commensurate with the ward's ability, with or without supports and services.

Derived from Probate Code § 694A(A).

Added by Acts 2011, 82nd Leg., ch. 823, § 1.02, eff. Jan. 1, 2014. Amended by Acts 2015, 84th Leg., ch. 214, § 16, eff. Sept. 1, 2015.

§ 1202.052. Contents of Application

An application filed under Section 1202.051 must be sworn to by the applicant and must state:

(1) the ward's name, sex, date of birth, and address;

(2) the name and address of any person serving as guardian of the person of the ward on the date the application is filed;

(3) the name and address of any person serving as guardian of the estate of the ward on the date the application is filed;

(4) the nature and description of the ward's guardianship;

(5) the specific areas of protection and assistance and any limitation of rights that exist;

(6) whether the relief being sought is:

(A) a restoration of the ward's capacity because the ward is no longer an incapacitated person;

(B) the granting of additional powers or duties to the guardian; or

(C) the limitation of powers granted to or duties performed by the guardian;

(7) if the relief being sought under the application is described by Subdivision (6)(B) or (C):

(A) the nature and degree of the ward's incapacity;

(B) the specific areas of protection and assistance to be provided to the ward and requested to be included in the court's order; and

(C) any limitation of the ward's rights requested to be included in the court's order;

(8) the approximate value and description of the ward's property, including any compensation, pension, insurance, or allowance to which the ward is or may be entitled; and

(9) if the ward is 60 years of age or older, the names and addresses, to the best of the applicant's knowledge, of the ward's spouse, siblings, and children or, if there is no known spouse, sibling, or child, the names and addresses of the ward's next of kin.

Derived from Probate Code § 694B.

Added by Acts 2011, 82nd Leg., ch. 823, § 1.02, eff. Jan. 1, 2014.

§ 1202.053. Citation Required

When an application is filed under Section 1202.051, citation shall be served on:

(1) the ward's guardian; and

(2) the ward if the ward is not the applicant.

Derived from Probate Code § 694A(d).

Added by Acts 2011, 82nd Leg., ch. 823, § 1.02, eff. Jan. 1, 2014.

§ 1202.054. Informal Request for Order by Ward; Investigation and Report

(a) A ward may request an order under Section 1202.051 by informal letter to the court. A person who knowingly interferes with the transmission of the request to the court may be adjudged guilty of contempt of court.

(b) On receipt of an informal letter under Subsection (a), the court shall appoint the court investigator or a guardian ad litem to investigate the ward's circumstances, including any circumstances alleged in the letter, to determine whether:

(1) the ward is no longer an incapacitated person; or

(2) a modification of the guardianship is necessary.

(c) The court investigator or guardian ad litem shall file with the court a report of the investigation's findings and conclusions. If the court investigator or guardian ad litem determines that it is in the best interest of the ward to terminate or modify the guardianship, the court investigator or guardian ad litem shall file an application under Section 1202.051 on the ward's behalf.

(d) A guardian ad litem appointed under this section may also be appointed by the court to serve as attorney ad litem under Section 1202.101.

Derived from Probate Code § 694A(b), (c).

Added by Acts 2011, 82nd Leg., ch. 823, § 1.02, eff. Jan. 1, 2014.

§ 1202.055. Restriction on Subsequent Application Regarding Capacity or Modification

A person may not reapply for complete restoration of a ward's capacity or modification of a ward's guardianship before the first anniversary of the date of the hearing on the last preceding application, except as otherwise provided by the court on good cause shown by the applicant.

Derived from Probate Code § 694A(e).

Added by Acts 2011, 82nd Leg., ch. 823, § 1.02, eff. Jan. 1, 2014.

Subchapter C. Representation of Ward in Proceeding for Complete Restoration of Ward's Capacity or Modification of Guardianship

§ 1202.101. Appointment of Attorney Ad Litem

The court shall appoint an attorney ad litem to represent a ward in a proceeding for the complete restoration of the ward's capacity or for the modification of the ward's guardianship. Unless otherwise provided by the court, the attorney ad litem shall represent the ward only for purposes of the restoration or modification proceeding.

Derived from Probate Code § 694C(a), (b).

Added by Acts 2011, 82nd Leg., ch. 823, § 1.02, eff. Jan. 1, 2014.

§ 1202.102. Compensation for Attorney Ad Litem and Guardian Ad Litem

(a) An attorney ad litem appointed under Section 1202.101 is entitled to reasonable compensation for services in the amount set by the court to be taxed as costs in the proceeding, regardless of whether the proceeding results in the restoration of the ward's capacity or a modification of the ward's guardianship.

(b) A guardian ad litem appointed in a proceeding involving the complete restoration of a ward's capacity or modification of a ward's guardianship is entitled to reasonable compensation, as provided by Section 1054.055(a), regardless of whether the proceeding results in the restoration of the ward's capacity or a modification of the ward's guardianship.

Derived from Probate Code §§ 694C(c), 694L.

Added by Acts 2011, 82nd Leg., ch. 823, § 1.02, eff. Jan. 1, 2014.

§ 1202.103. Retention and Compensation of Attorney for Ward

(a) A ward may retain an attorney for a proceeding involving the complete restoration of the ward's capacity or modification of the ward's guardianship.

(b) The court may order that compensation for services provided by an attorney retained under this section be paid from funds in the ward's estate only if the court finds that the attorney had a good faith belief that the ward had the capacity necessary to retain the attorney's services.

Derived from Probate Code § 694K.

Added by Acts 2011, 82nd Leg., ch. 823, § 1.02, eff. Jan. 1, 2014.

Subchapter D. Hearing, Evidence, and Orders in Proceeding for Complete Restoration of Ward's Capacity or Modification of Guardianship

§ 1202.151. Evidence and Burden of Proof at Hearing

(a) Except as provided by Section 1202.201, at a hearing on an application filed under Section 1202.051, the court shall consider only evidence regarding the ward's mental or physical capacity at the time of the hearing that is relevant to the complete restoration of the ward's capacity or modification of the ward's guardianship, including whether:

(1) the guardianship is necessary; and

(2) specific powers or duties of the guardian should be limited if the ward receives supports and services.

(b) The party who filed the application has the burden of proof at the hearing.

Derived from Probate Code § 694D.

Added by Acts 2011, 82nd Leg., ch. 823, § 1.02, eff. Jan. 1, 2014. Subsec. (a) amended by Acts 2013, 83rd Leg., ch. 684, § 2, eff. Jan. 1, 2014. Subsec. (a) amended by Acts 2015, 84th Leg., ch. 214, § 17, eff. Sept. 1, 2015.

§ 1202.152. Physician's Letter or Certificate Required

(a) The court may not grant an order completely restoring a ward's capacity or modifying a ward's guardianship under an application filed under Section 1202.051 unless the applicant presents to the court a written letter or certificate from a physician licensed in this state that is dated:

(1) not earlier than the 120th day before the date the application was filed; or

(2) after the date the application was filed but before the date of the hearing.

(b) A letter or certificate presented under Subsection (a) must:

(1) describe the nature and degree of incapacity, including the medical history if reasonably available, or state that, in the physician's opinion, the ward has the capacity, or sufficient capacity with supports and services, to:

(A) provide food, clothing, and shelter for himself or herself;

(B) care for the ward's own physical health; and

(C) manage the ward's financial affairs;

(2) provide a medical prognosis specifying the estimated severity of any incapacity;

(3) state how or in what manner the ward's ability to make or communicate responsible decisions concerning himself or herself is affected by the ward's physical or mental health;

(4) state whether any current medication affects the ward's demeanor or the ward's ability to participate fully in a court proceeding;

(5) describe the precise physical and mental conditions underlying a diagnosis of senility, if applicable; and

(6) include any other information required by the court.

(c) If the court determines it is necessary, the court may appoint the necessary physicians to examine the ward in the same manner and to the same extent as a ward is examined by a physician under Section 1101.103 or 1101.104.

Derived from Probate Code § 694F.

Added by Acts 2011, 82nd Leg., ch. 823, § 1.02, eff. Jan. 1, 2014. Subsec. (b)(1) amended by Acts 2015, 84th Leg., ch. 214, § 18, eff. Sept. 1, 2015.

§ 1202.153. Findings Required

(a) Before ordering the settlement and closing of a guardianship under an application filed under Section 1202.051, the court must find by a preponderance of the evidence that the ward is no longer partially or fully incapacitated.

(b) Before granting additional powers to the guardian or requiring the guardian to perform additional duties under an application filed under Section 1202.051, the court must find by a preponderance of the evidence that the current nature and degree of the ward's incapacity warrants a modification of the guardianship and that some or all of the ward's rights need to be further restricted.

(c) Before limiting the powers granted to or duties required to be performed by the guardian under an application filed under Section 1202.051, the court must find by a preponderance of the evidence that the current nature and degree of the ward's incapacity, with or without supports and services, warrants a modification of the guardianship and that some of the ward's rights need to be restored, with or without supports and services.

Derived from Probate Code § 694E.

Added by Acts 2011, 82nd Leg., ch. 823, § 1.02, eff. Jan. 1, 2014. Subsec. (c) amended by Acts 2015, 84th Leg., ch. 214, § 19, eff. Sept. 1, 2015.

§ 1202.154. General Requirements for Order

(a) A court order entered with respect to an application filed under Section 1202.051 to completely restore a ward's capacity or modify a ward's guardianship must state:

(1) the guardian's name;

(2) the ward's name; [and]

(3) whether the type of guardianship being addressed at the proceeding is a:

(A) guardianship of the person;

(B) guardianship of the estate; or

(C) guardianship of both the person and the estate; and

(4) if applicable, any necessary supports and services for the restoration of the ward's capacity or modification of the guardianship.

(b) In an order described by this section, the court may not grant a power to a guardian or require the guardian to perform a duty that is a power granted to or a duty required to be performed by another guardian.

Derived from Probate Code § 694J.

Added by Acts 2011, 82nd Leg., ch. 823, § 1.02, eff. Jan. 1, 2014. Subsec. (a) amended by Acts 2015, 84th Leg., ch. 214, § 20, eff. Sept. 1, 2015.

§ 1202.155. Additional Requirements for Order Restoring Ward's Capacity

If the court finds that a ward is no longer an incapacitated person, the order completely restoring the ward's capacity must contain findings of fact and specify, in addition to the information required by Section 1202.154:

(1) that the ward is no longer an incapacitated person;

(2) that there is no further need for a guardianship of the person or estate of the ward;

(3) if the ward's incapacity resulted from a mental condition, that the ward's mental capacity is completely restored;

(4) that the guardian is required to:

(A) immediately settle the guardianship in accordance with this title; and

(B) deliver all of the remaining guardianship estate to the ward; and

(5) that the clerk shall revoke letters of guardianship when the guardianship is finally settled and closed.

Derived from Probate Code § 694G.

Added by Acts 2011, 82nd Leg., ch. 823, § 1.02, eff. Jan. 1, 2014.

§ 1202.156. Additional Requirements for Order Modifying Guardianship

If the court finds that a guardian's powers or duties should be expanded or limited, the order modifying the guardianship must contain findings of fact and specify, in addition to the information required by Section 1202.154:

(1) the specific powers, limitations, or duties of the guardian with respect to the care of the ward or the management of the ward's property, as appropriate;

(2) the specific areas of protection and assistance to be provided to the ward;

(3) any limitation of the ward's rights;

(4) if the ward's incapacity resulted from a mental condition, whether the ward retains the right to vote and make personal decisions regarding residence; and

(5) that the clerk shall modify the letters of guardianship to the extent applicable to conform to the order.

Derived from Probate Code § 694H.

Added by Acts 2011, 82nd Leg., ch. 823, § 1.02, eff. Jan. 1, 2014. Amended by Acts 2015, 84th Leg., ch. 214, § 21, eff. Sept. 1, 2015.

§ 1202.157. Additional Requirements for Order Dismissing Application

If the court finds that a modification of the ward's guardianship is not necessary or that the ward's capacity has not been restored, the court shall dismiss the application and enter an order that contains findings of fact and specifies, in addition to the information required by Section 1202.154, that the guardian's powers, limitations, or duties with respect to the ward's care or the management of the ward's property remain unchanged.

Derived from Probate Code § 694I.

Added by Acts 2011, 82nd Leg., ch. 823, § 1.02, eff. Jan. 1, 2014.

Subchapter E. Restoration of Rights on Termination of Guardianship

§ 1202.201. Removal of Firearm Disability on Complete Restoration of Ward's Capacity

(a) A person whose guardianship was terminated because the person's capacity was completely restored may file an application with the court that created the guardianship for an order requesting the removal of the person's disability to purchase a firearm imposed under 18 U.S.C. Section 922(g)(4).

(b) At a proceeding involving the complete restoration of the ward's capacity under Subchapter B, the ward or a person interested in the ward's welfare may request an order seeking relief from a firearms disability described by Subsection (a).

(c) In determining whether to grant the relief sought under Subsection (a) or (b), the court must hear and consider evidence about:

(1) the circumstances that led to imposition of the firearms disability;

(2) the person's mental history;

(3) the person's criminal history; and

(4) the person's reputation.

(d) A court may not grant relief under this section unless the court makes and enters in the record the following affirmative findings:

(1) the person or ward is no longer likely to act in a manner dangerous to public safety; and

(2) removing the person's or ward's disability to purchase a firearm is in the public interest.

New.

Added by Acts 2013, 83rd Leg., ch. 684, § 1, eff. Jan. 1, 2014.

Chapter 1203. Resignation, Removal, or Death of Guardian; Appointment of Successor

Subchapter A. Resignation of Guardian

Subchapter B. Removal and Reinstatement of Guardian

Subchapter C. Appointment of Successor Guardian; Revocation of Letters

Subchapter D. Successor Guardians for Wards of Guardianship Programs or Governmental Entities

Subchapter E. Procedures After Resignation, Removal, or Death of Guardian

Chapter 1203. Resignation, Removal, or Death of Guardian; Appointment of Successor

Subchapter A. Resignation of Guardian

§ 1203.001. Resignation Application

A guardian of the estate or guardian of the person who wishes to resign the guardian's trust shall file a written application with the court clerk, accompanied by:

(1) in the case of a guardian of the estate, a complete and verified exhibit and final account showing the true condition of the guardianship estate entrusted to the guardian's care; or

(2) in the case of a guardian of the person, a verified report containing the information required in the annual report required under Subchapter C, Chapter 1163, showing the condition of the ward entrusted to the guardian's care.

Derived from Probate Code § 760(a).

Added by Acts 2011, 82nd Leg., ch. 823, § 1.02, eff. Jan. 1, 2014.

§ 1203.002. Immediate Acceptance of Resignation; Discharge and Release

(a) If the necessity exists, the court may immediately accept the resignation of a guardian and appoint a successor guardian as provided by Section 1203.102(b).

(b) The court may not discharge a person resigning as guardian of the estate whose resignation is accepted under Subsection (a), or release the person or the sureties on the person's bond, until a final order has been issued, or a final judgment has been rendered, on the final account required under Section 1203.001.

Derived from Probate Code § 760(b).

Added by Acts 2011, 82nd Leg., ch. 823, § 1.02, eff. Jan. 1, 2014.

§ 1203.003. Delivery of Estate Property to Successor Guardian Following Resignation

The court at any time may order a resigning guardian who has any part of a ward's estate to deliver any part of the estate to a person who has been appointed and has qualified as successor guardian.

Derived from Probate Code § 760(g).

Added by Acts 2011, 82nd Leg., ch. 823, § 1.02, eff. Jan. 1, 2014.

§ 1203.004. Hearing Date; Citation

(a) When an application to resign as guardian is filed under Section 1203.001, supported by the exhibit and final account or report required under that section, the court clerk shall bring the application to the judge's attention and the judge shall set a date for a hearing on the matter.

(b) After a hearing is set under Subsection (a), the clerk shall issue a citation to all interested persons, showing:

(1) that an application that complies with Section 1203.001 has been filed; and

(2) the time and place set for the hearing at which the interested persons may appear and contest the exhibit and final account or report supporting the application.

(c) Unless the court directs that the citation under Subsection (b) be published, the citation must be posted.

Derived from Probate Code § 760(c).

Added by Acts 2011, 82nd Leg., ch. 823, § 1.02, eff. Jan. 1, 2014.

§ 1203.005. Hearing

(a) At the time set for the hearing under Section 1203.004, unless the court continues the hearing, and if the court finds that the citation required under that section has been properly issued and served, the court shall:

(1) examine the exhibit and final account or report required by Section 1203.001;

(2) hear all evidence for and against the exhibit, final account, or report; and

(3) if necessary, restate and audit and settle the exhibit, final account, or report.

(b) If the court is satisfied that the matters entrusted to the guardian applying to resign have been handled and accounted for in accordance with the law, the court shall:

(1) enter an order approving the exhibit and final account or report; and

(2) require that any estate property remaining in the applicant's possession be delivered to the person entitled by law to receive the property.

(c) A guardian of the person shall comply with all court orders concerning the guardian's ward.

Derived from Probate Code § 760(d).

Added by Acts 2011, 82nd Leg., ch. 823, § 1.02, eff. Jan. 1, 2014.

§ 1203.006. Requirements for Discharge

(a) A guardian applying to resign may not be discharged until:

(1) the resignation application has been heard;

(2) the exhibit and final account or report required under Section 1203.001 has been examined, settled, and approved; and

(3) the applicant has satisfied the court that the applicant has:

(A) delivered any estate property remaining in the applicant's possession; or

(B) complied with all court orders relating to the applicant's trust as guardian.

(b) When a guardian applying to resign has fully complied with the court orders, the court shall enter an order:

(1) accepting the resignation; and

(2) discharging the applicant and, if the applicant is under bond, the applicant's sureties.

Derived from Probate Code § 760(e) & (f).

Added by Acts 2011, 82nd Leg., ch. 823, § 1.02, eff. Jan. 1, 2014.

Subchapter B. Removal and Reinstatement of Guardian

§ 1203.051. Removal Without Notice; Appointment of Guardian ad Litem and Attorney ad Litem

(a) The court, on the court's own motion or on the motion of an interested person, including the ward, and without notice, may remove a guardian appointed under this title who:

(1) neglects to qualify in the manner and time required by law;

(2) fails to return, not later than the 30th day after the date the guardian qualifies, an inventory of the guardianship estate property and a list of claims that have come to the guardian's knowledge, unless that deadline is extended by court order;

(3) if required, fails to give a new bond within the period prescribed;

(4) is absent from the state for a consecutive period of three or more months without the court's permission, or removes from the state;

(5) cannot be served with notices or other processes because:

(A) the guardian's whereabouts are unknown;

(B) the guardian is eluding service; or

(C) the guardian is a nonresident of this state who does not have a resident agent to accept service of process in any guardianship proceeding or other matter relating to the guardianship;

(6) subject to Section 1203.056(a):

(A) has misapplied, embezzled, or removed from the state, or is about to misapply, embezzle, or remove from the state, any of the property entrusted to the guardian's care; or

(B) has engaged in conduct with respect to the ward that would be considered to be abuse, neglect, or exploitation, as those terms are defined by Section 48.002, Human Resources Code, if engaged in with respect to an elderly or disabled person, as defined by that section; or

(7) has neglected to educate or maintain the ward as liberally as the means of the ward and the condition of the ward's estate permit.

(b) In a proceeding to remove a guardian under Subsection (a)(6) or (7), the court shall appoint a guardian ad litem as provided by Subchapter B, Chapter 1054, and an attorney ad litem. The attorney ad litem has the duties prescribed by Section 1054.004. In the interest of judicial economy, the court may appoint the same person as guardian ad litem and attorney ad litem unless a conflict exists between the interests to be represented by the guardian ad litem and attorney ad litem.

Derived from Probate Code § 761(a).

Added by Acts 2011, 82nd Leg., ch. 823, § 1.02. eff. Jan. 1, 2014. Amended by Acts 2013, 83rd Leg., ch. 161, § 6.053, eff. Jan. 1, 2014.

§ 1203.052. Removal With Notice

(a) The court may remove a guardian on the court's own motion, or on the complaint of an interested person, after the guardian has been cited by personal service to answer at a time and place set in the notice, if:

(1) sufficient grounds appear to support a belief that the guardian has misapplied, embezzled, or removed from the state, or is about to misapply, embezzle, or remove from the state, any of the property entrusted to the guardian's care;

(2) the guardian fails to return any account or report that is required by law to be made;

(3) the guardian fails to obey a proper order of the court that has jurisdiction with respect to the performance of the guardian's duties;

(4) the guardian is proved to have been guilty of gross misconduct or mismanagement in the performance of the guardian's duties;

(5) the guardian:

(A) becomes incapacitated;

(B) is sentenced to the penitentiary; or

(C) from any other cause, becomes incapable of properly performing the duties of the guardian's trust;

(6) the guardian has engaged in conduct with respect to the ward that would be considered to be abuse, neglect, or exploitation, as those terms are defined by Section 48.002, Human Resources Code, if engaged in with respect to an elderly or disabled person, as defined by that section;

(7) the guardian neglects to educate or maintain the ward as liberally as the means of the ward's estate and the ward's ability or condition permit;

(8) the guardian interferes with the ward's progress or participation in programs in the community;

(9) the guardian fails to comply with the requirements of Subchapter G, Chapter 1104;

(10) the court determines that, because of the dissolution of the joint guardians' marriage, the termination of the guardians' joint appointment and the continuation of only one of the joint guardians as the sole guardian is in the best interest of the ward; or

(11) the guardian would be ineligible for appointment as a guardian under Subchapter H, Chapter 1104.

(b) In addition to the authority granted to the court under Subsection (a), the court may, on the complaint of the guardianship certification program of the Judicial Branch Certification Commission, remove a guardian who would be ineligible for appointment under Subchapter H, Chapter 1104, because of the guardian's failure to maintain the certification required under Subchapter F, Chapter 1104. The guardian shall be cited to appear and contest the request for removal under this subsection in the manner provided by Subsection (a).

Derived from Probate Code § 761(c), (c-1).

Added by Acts 2011, 82nd Leg., ch. 823, § 1.02, eff. Jan. 1, 2014. Subsec. (a) amended by Acts 2013, 83rd Leg., ch. 161, § 6.054, eff. Jan. 1, 2014. Subsec. (b) amended by Acts 2013, 83rd Leg., ch. 42, § 2.21, eff. Jan. 1, 2014.

§ 1203.053. Removal Order

An order removing a guardian shall:

(1) state the cause of the removal;

(2) require that, if the removed guardian has been personally served with citation, any letters of guardianship issued to the removed guardian be

surrendered and that, regardless of whether the letters have been delivered, all the letters be canceled of record; and

(3) require the removed guardian to:

(A) deliver any estate property in the guardian's possession to the persons entitled to the property or to one who has been appointed and has qualified as successor guardian; and

(B) relinquish control of the ward's person as required in the order.

Derived from Probate Code § 761(d).

Added by Acts 2011, 82nd Leg., ch. 823, § 1.02, eff. Jan. 1, 2014.

§ 1203.0531.   Notice of Removal Order

The court clerk shall issue notice of an order rendered by the court removing a guardian under Section 1203.051(a)(1), (2), (3), (4), (6), or (7). The notice must:

(1) state the names of the ward and the removed guardian;

(2) state the date the court signed the order of removal;

(3) contain the following statement printed in 12-point bold font:

"If you have been removed from serving as guardian under Section 1203.051(a)(6)(A) or (B), Estates Code, you have the right to contest the order of removal by filing an application with the court for a hearing under Section 1203.056, Estates Code, to determine whether you should be reinstated as guardian. The application must be filed not later than the 30th day after the date the court signed the order of removal.";

(4) contain as an attachment a copy of the order of removal; and

(5) be personally served on the removed guardian not later than the seventh day after the date the court signed the order of removal.

New.

Added by Acts 2013, 83rd Leg., ch. 161, § 6.055, eff. Jan. 1, 2014.

§ 1203.054.   Discharge and Release Following Removal

With respect to a person who is removed as guardian of the estate and whose successor is appointed without citation or notice as provided by Section 1203.102(b), the court may not discharge the person or release the person or the sureties on the person's bond until a final order has been issued or final judgment has been rendered on the guardian's final account.

Derived from Probate Code § 761(f).

Added by Acts 2011, 82nd Leg., ch. 823, § 1.02, eff. Jan. 1, 2014.

§ 1203.055.   Delivery of Estate Property to Successor Guardian Following Removal

The court at any time may order a person removed as guardian under this subchapter who has any part of a ward's estate to deliver any part of the estate to a person who has been appointed and has qualified as successor guardian.

Derived from Probate Code § 761(g).

Added by Acts 2011, 82nd Leg., ch. 823, § 1.02, eff. Jan. 1, 2014.

§ 1203.056.   Removal and Reinstatement of Guardian Under Certain Circumstances

(a) The court may remove a guardian under Section 1203.051(a)(6)(A) or (B) only on the presentation of clear and convincing evidence given under oath.

(b) Not later than the 30th day after the date the court signs the order of removal, a guardian who is removed under Section 1203.051(a)(6)(A) or (B) may file an application with the court for a hearing to determine whether the guardian should be reinstated.

(c) On the filing of an application under Subsection (b), the court clerk shall issue to the applicant, the ward, a person interested in the ward's welfare or estate, and, if applicable, a person who has control of the care and custody of the ward a notice stating:

(1) that an application for reinstatement has been filed;

(2) the name of the ward; and

(3) the name of the applicant for reinstatement.

(d) The notice required by Subsection (c) must cite all persons interested in the ward's welfare or estate to appear at the time and place stated in the notice if the persons wish to contest the application.

(e) The court shall hold a hearing on an application for reinstatement under this section as soon as practicable after the application is filed, but not later than the 60th day after the date the court signed the order of removal. If, at the conclusion of the hearing, the court is satisfied by a preponderance of the evidence that the applicant did not engage in the conduct that directly led to the applicant's removal, the court shall:

(1) set aside any order appointing a successor guardian; and

(2) enter an order reinstating the applicant as guardian of the ward or estate.

(f) If the court sets aside the appointment of a successor guardian under this section, the court may require the successor guardian to prepare and file, under oath, an accounting of the estate and to detail the disposition the successor has made of the estate property.

Derived from Probate Code §§ 761(b), 762.

Added by Acts 2011, 82nd Leg., ch. 823, § 1.02, eff. Jan. 1, 2014. Subsecs. (a), (b), & (e) amended by Acts 2013, 83rd Leg., ch. 161, § 6.056, eff. Jan. 1, 2014.

§ 1203.057. Removal of Joint Guardian

If a joint guardian is removed under Section 1203.052(a)(10), the other joint guardian is entitled to continue to serve as the sole guardian unless removed for a reason other than the dissolution of the joint guardians' marriage.

Derived from Probate Code § 761(e).

Added by Acts 2011, 82nd Leg., ch. 823, § 1.02, eff. Jan. 1, 2014.

Subchapter C. Appointment of Successor Guardian; Revocation of Letters

§ 1203.101. Requirements for Revocation of Letters

Except as otherwise expressly provided by this title, letters of guardianship may be revoked only:

(1) on application; and

(2) after personal service of citation on the person whose letters are sought to be revoked requiring the person to appear and show cause why the application should not be granted.

Derived from Probate Code § 759(f).

Added by Acts 2011, 82nd Leg., ch. 823, § 1.02, eff. Jan. 1, 2014.

§ 1203.102. Appointment Because of Resignation, Removal, or Death; Hearing to Set Aside Immediate Appointment

(a) If a guardian resigns, is removed, or dies, the court may appoint a successor guardian on application and on service of notice as directed by the court, except as provided by Subsection (b). In the event the guardian of the person or of the estate of a ward dies, a personal representative of the deceased guardian, at the time and in the manner ordered by the court, shall account for, pay, and deliver all guardianship property entrusted to the representative's care to a person legally entitled to receive the property.

(b) The court may appoint a successor guardian under this section without citation or notice if the court finds that a necessity exists for the immediate appointment. Subject to an order of the court, a successor guardian has the rights and powers of the removed guardian.

(c) The appointment of a successor guardian under Subsection (b) does not preclude an interested person from filing an application to be appointed guardian of the ward for whom the successor guardian was appointed. The court shall hold a hearing on an application filed under the circumstances described by this subsection. At the conclusion of the hearing, the court may set aside the appointment of the successor guardian and appoint the applicant as the ward's guardian if the applicant is not disqualified and after considering the requirements of Subchapter B or C, Chapter 1104, as applicable.

(d) If the court sets aside the appointment of the successor guardian under this section, the court may require the successor guardian to prepare and file, under oath, an accounting of the estate and to detail the disposition the successor has made of the estate property.

Derived from Probate Code §§ 695(a), 759(a), 760(b), 761(f).

Added by Acts 2011, 82nd Leg., ch. 823, § 1.02, eff. Jan. 1, 2014. Sec. title amended by Acts 2013, 83rd Leg., ch. 161, § 6.057, eff. Jan. 1, 2014. Subsecs. (b) amended, (c) and (d) added by Acts 2013, 83rd Leg., ch. 161, § 6.058, eff. Jan. 1, 2014.

§ 1203.103. Appointment Because of Existence of Prior Right

If letters of guardianship have been granted to a person and another person applies for letters, the previously issued letters shall be revoked, and letters shall be granted to the subsequent applicant if that applicant:

(1) is qualified;

(2) has a prior right to be appointed successor guardian; and

(3) has not waived that prior right.

Derived from Probate Code § 759(b).

Added by Acts 2011, 82nd Leg., ch. 823, § 1.02, eff. Jan. 1, 2014.

§ 1203.104. Appointment When Guardian Named in Will Becomes an Adult

(a) A person named as guardian in a will who was not an adult when the will was probated is entitled to have letters of guardianship that were granted to another person revoked and appropriate letters granted to the named guardian on proof that the named guardian has become an adult and is not otherwise disqualified from serving as a guardian.

(b) This subsection applies only if a will names two or more persons as guardian. A person named as a guardian in the will who was a minor when the will was probated may, on becoming an adult, qualify and receive letters of guardianship if:

(1) letters have been issued to the named guardians in the will who are adults; and

(2) the person is not otherwise disqualified from receiving letters.

Derived from Probate Code § 759(c).

Added by Acts 2011, 82nd Leg., ch. 823, § 1.02, eff. Jan. 1, 2014.

§ 1203.105. Appointment of Formerly Ill or Absent Guardian Named in Will

(a) This section applies only to a person named as guardian in a will who was ill or absent from the state when the testator died or the will was proved and, as a result, could not:

(1) present the will for probate not later than the 30th day after the testator's death; or

(2) accept and qualify as guardian not later than the 20th day after the date the will was probated.

(b) A person to whom this section applies may accept and qualify as guardian not later than the 60th day after the date the person recovers from illness or returns to the state if proof is presented to the court that the person was ill or absent.

(c) If a person accepts and qualifies as guardian under Subsection (b) and letters of guardianship have been issued to another person, the other person's letters shall be revoked.

Derived from Probate Code § 759(d).

Added by Acts 2011, 82nd Leg., ch. 823, § 1.02, eff. Jan. 1, 2014.

§ 1203.106. Appointment When Will Discovered After Grant of Letters

If, after letters of guardianship have been issued, it is discovered that the decedent left a lawful will, the letters shall be revoked and proper letters shall be issued to a person entitled to the letters.

Derived from Probate Code § 759(e).

Added by Acts 2011, 82nd Leg., ch. 823, § 1.02, eff. Jan. 1, 2014.

§ 1203.107. Appointment on Removal of Litigation Conflict

The court may appoint as successor guardian a spouse, parent, or child of a proposed ward who was disqualified from serving as guardian because of a litigation conflict under Section 1104.354(1) on the removal of the conflict that caused the disqualification if the spouse, parent, or child is otherwise qualified to serve as a guardian.

Derived from Probate Code § 759(h).

Added by Acts 2011, 82nd Leg., ch. 823, § 1.02, eff. Jan. 1, 2014.

§ 1203.108. Appointment of Department of Aging and Disability Services as Successor Guardian

(a) In this section, "department" means the Department of Aging and Disability Services.

(b) The court may appoint the department as a successor guardian of the person or estate, or both, of a ward who has been adjudicated as totally incapacitated if:

(1) there is no less-restrictive alternative to continuation of the guardianship;

(2) there is no family member or other suitable person, including a guardianship program, willing and able to serve as the ward's successor guardian;

(3) the ward is located more than 100 miles from the court that created the guardianship;

(4) the ward has private assets or access to government benefits to pay for the ward's needs;

(5) the department is served with citation and a hearing is held regarding the department's appointment as proposed successor guardian; and

(6) the appointment of the department does not violate a limitation imposed by Subsection (c).

(c) The number of appointments under Subsection (b) is subject to an annual limit of 55. The appointments must be distributed equally or as equally as possible among the health and human services regions of this state. The department, at the department's discretion, may establish a different distribution scheme to promote the efficient use and administration of resources.

(d) If the department is named as a proposed successor guardian in an application in which the department is not the applicant, citation must be issued and served on the department as provided by Section 1051.103(5).

Derived from Probate Code § 695(c), (d), (e).

Added by Acts 2011, 82nd Leg., ch. 823, § 1.02, eff. Jan. 1, 2014.

Subchapter D. Successor Guardians for Wards of Guardianship Programs or Governmental Entities

§ 1203.151. Notice of Availability of Successor Guardian

(a) If a guardianship program or governmental entity serving as a guardian for a ward under this title becomes aware of a family member or friend of the ward, or any other interested person, who is willing and able to serve as the ward's successor guardian, the program or entity shall notify the court in which the guardianship is pending of the individual's willingness and ability to serve.

(b) If, while serving as a guardian for a ward under this title, the Department of Aging and Disability Services becomes aware of a guardianship program or private professional guardian willing and able to serve as the ward's successor guardian, and the department is not aware of a family member or friend of the ward, or any other interested person, who is willing and able to serve in that capacity, the department shall notify the court in which the guardianship is pending of the guardianship program's or private professional guardian's willingness and ability to serve.

Derived from Probate Code § 695A(a), (a-1).

Added by Acts 2011, 82nd Leg., ch. 823, § 1.02, eff. Jan. 1, 2014.

§ 1203.152. Determination of Proposed Successor Guardian's Qualification to Serve

When the court is notified of the existence of a proposed successor guardian under Section 1203.151(a), or the court otherwise becomes aware of a family member, a friend, or any other interested person who is willing and able to serve as a successor guardian for a ward of a guardianship program or governmental entity, the court shall determine whether the proposed successor guardian is qualified to serve under this title as the ward's successor guardian.

Derived from Probate Code § 695A(b).

Added by Acts 2011, 82nd Leg., ch. 823, § 1.02, eff. Jan. 1, 2014.

§ 1203.153. Application to Appoint Successor Guardian

(a) If the court finds under Section 1203.152 that the proposed successor guardian for a ward is not disqualified from being appointed as the ward's successor guardian under Subchapter H, Chapter 1104, and that the appointment is in the ward's best interests, the guardianship program or governmental entity serving as the ward's guardian or the court, on the court's own motion, may file an application to appoint the individual as the ward's successor guardian.

(b) Service of notice on an application filed under this section shall be made as directed by the court.

Derived from Probate Code § 695A(c).

Added by Acts 2011, 82nd Leg., ch. 823, § 1.02, eff. Jan. 1, 2014.

Subchapter E. Procedures After Resignation, Removal, or Death of Guardian

§ 1203.201. Payment to Ward While Office of Guardian Is Vacant

(a) A debtor, obligor, or payor may pay or tender money or another thing of value falling due to a ward while the office of guardian is vacant to the court clerk for the credit of the ward.

(b) Payment or tender under Subsection (a) discharges the debtor, obligor, or payor of the obligation for all purposes to the extent and purpose of the payment or tender.

(c) The court clerk shall issue a receipt for any payment or tender accepted under this section.

Derived from Probate Code § 759(g).

Added by Acts 2011, 82nd Leg., ch. 823, § 1.02, eff. Jan. 1, 2014.

§ 1203.202. Rights, Powers, and Duties of Successor Guardian

(a) A successor guardian has the rights and powers and is subject to all the duties of the predecessor.

(b) A guardian who accepts appointment and qualifies after letters of guardianship have been granted on the estate shall:

(1) succeed in like manner to the predecessor; and

(2) administer the estate in like manner as if the guardian's administration were a continuation of the former administration.

(c) A successor guardian may:

(1) make himself or herself, and be made, a party to a suit prosecuted by or against the successor's predecessor;

(2) settle with the predecessor and receive and give a receipt for any portion of the estate property that remains in the predecessor's [successor's] possession; or

(3) commence a suit on the bond or bonds of the predecessor, in the successor's own name and capacity, for all the estate property that:

(A) came into the predecessor's possession; and

(B) has not been accounted for by the predecessor.

Derived from Probate Code §§ 695(b), 763, 764.

Added by Acts 2011, 82nd Leg., ch. 823, § 1.02, eff. Jan. 1, 2014. Subsec. (c) amended by Acts 2015, 84th Leg., ch. 1031, § 22, eff. Sept. 1, 2015.

§ 1203.203. Successor Guardian to Return Inventory, Appraisement, and List of Claims

(a) A successor guardian who has qualified to succeed a former guardian shall, in the manner required of an original appointee:

(1) make and return to the court an inventory, appraisement, and list of claims of the estate not later than the 30th day after the date the successor qualifies; and

(2) return additional inventories, appraisements, and lists of claims.

(b) On the application of any person interested in the estate, the court shall, in an order appointing a successor guardian, appoint an appraiser as in an original appointment of a guardian.

Derived from Probate Code § 765.

Added by Acts 2011, 82nd Leg., ch. 823, § 1.02, eff. Jan. 1, 2014.

Chapter 1204. Final Settlement, Accounting, and Discharge

Subchapter A. Time for Settlement of Guardianship

Subchapter B. Payment of Certain Expenses and Debts

§ 1204.053. Inheritance Taxes; Limitation on Closing Estate

Subchapter C. Account for Final Settlement

Subchapter D. Closing of Guardianship and Discharge of Guardian

Subchapter E. Failure of Guardian to Act

Chapter 1204. Final Settlement, Accounting, and Discharge

Subchapter A. Time for Settlement of Guardianship

§ 1204.001. Settlement of Guardianship

(a) A guardianship shall be settled and closed as provided by this section and Section 1202.001.

(b) A guardianship of the estate of a ward shall be settled when:

(1) the ward dies;

(2) a minor ward becomes an adult by:

(A) becoming 18 years of age;

(B) removal of disabilities of minority according to the law of this state; or

(C) marriage;

(3) an incapacitated ward is decreed as provided by law to have been restored to full legal capacity;

(4) the spouse of a married ward has qualified as survivor in community and the ward does not own separate property;

(5) the ward's estate is exhausted;

(6) the foreseeable income accruing to the ward or to the ward's estate is so negligible that maintaining the guardianship in force would be burdensome;

(7) all of the assets of the estate have been placed in a management trust under Chapter 1301 or have been transferred to a pooled trust subaccount in accordance with a court order issued as provided by Chapter 1302, and the court determines that a guardianship of the ward's estate is no longer necessary; or

(8) the court determines for any other reason that a guardianship for the ward is no longer necessary.

(c) In a case arising under Subsection (b)(6), the court may authorize the income to be paid to a parent, or other person who has acted as guardian of the ward, to assist in the maintenance of the ward and without liability to account to the court for the income.

(d) If the estate of a minor ward consists only of cash or cash equivalents in an amount of $100,000 or less, the guardianship of the estate may be terminated and the assets paid to the county clerk of the county in which the guardianship proceeding is pending, and the clerk shall manage the funds as provided by Chapter 1355.

(e) In the settlement of a guardianship of the estate, the court may appoint an attorney ad litem to represent the ward's interests and may allow the attorney ad litem reasonable compensation to be taxed as costs.

Derived from Probate Code § 745.

Added by Acts 2011, 82nd Leg., ch. 823, § 1.02, eff. Jan. 1, 2014. Subsecs. (b) and (e) amended by Acts 2013, 83rd Leg., ch. 161, § 6.059, eff. Jan. 1, 2014.

§ 1204.002. Appointment of Attorney Ad Litem to Represent Ward in Final Settlement Under Certain Circumstances

(a) The court may appoint an attorney ad litem to represent the ward's interest in the final settlement with the guardian if:

(1) the ward is deceased and there is no executor or administrator of the ward's estate;

(2) the ward is a nonresident; or

(3) the ward's residence is unknown.

(b) The court shall allow the attorney ad litem appointed under this section reasonable compensation out of the ward's estate for any services provided by the attorney.

Derived from Probate Code § 755.

Added by Acts 2011, 82nd Leg., ch. 823, § 1.02, eff. Jan. 1, 2014.

Subchapter B. Payment of Certain Expenses and Debts

§ 1204.051. Funeral Arrangements and Other Debts; Account for Final Settlement on Complaint of Personal Representative

Before a guardianship of the person or estate of a ward is closed on the ward's death, the guardian may, subject to the court's approval, make all funeral arrangements and pay the funeral expenses and all other debts out of the deceased ward's estate. If a personal representative of the estate of a deceased ward is appointed, the court shall on the written complaint of the personal representative have the guardian of the deceased ward cited to appear and present an account for final settlement as provided by Section 1204.101.

Derived from Probate Code § 746.

Added by Acts 2011, 82nd Leg., ch. 823, § 1.02, eff. Jan. 1, 2014.

§ 1204.052. Taxes and Expenses of Administration; Sale of Estate Property

Notwithstanding any other provision of this title, a probate court in which proceedings to declare heirship are maintained may order:

(1) the guardian to pay any taxes or expenses of administering the estate; and

(2) the sale of property in the ward's estate, when necessary, to:

(A) pay the taxes or expenses of administering the estate; or

(B) distribute the estate among the heirs.

Derived from Probate Code § 748.

Added by Acts 2011, 82nd Leg., ch. 823, § 1.02, eff. Jan. 1, 2014.

§ 1204.053. Inheritance Taxes; Limitation on Closing Estate

If the guardian has been ordered to pay inheritance taxes under this code, a deceased ward's estate may not be closed unless the account for final settlement shows and the court finds that all inheritance taxes due and owing to this state with respect to all interests and property passing through the guardian's possession have been paid.

Derived from Probate Code § 754.

Added by Acts 2011, 82nd Leg., ch. 823, § 1.02, eff. Jan. 1, 2014.

Subchapter C. Account for Final Settlement

§ 1204.101. Verified Account Required

A guardian of the estate shall present to the court the guardian's verified account for final settlement when the guardianship of the estate is required to be settled.

Derived from Probate Code § 749.

Added by Acts 2011, 82nd Leg., ch. 823, § 1.02, eff. Jan. 1, 2014.

§ 1204.102. Contents of Account

(a) Except as provided by Subsection (b), it is sufficient for an account for final settlement to:

(1) refer to the inventory without describing each item of property in detail; and

(2) refer to and adopt any guardianship proceeding concerning sales, renting, leasing for mineral development, or any other transaction on behalf of the guardianship estate, including an exhibit, account, or voucher previously filed and approved, without restating the particular items.

(b) An account for final settlement shall be accompanied by proper vouchers supporting each item included in the account for which the guardian has not already accounted and, either by reference to any proceeding described by Subsection (a) or by a statement of the facts, must show:

(1) the property, rents, revenues, and profits received by the guardian, and belonging to the ward, during the term of the guardianship;

(2) the disposition made of the property, rents, revenues, and profits;

(3) any expenses and debts against the estate that remain unpaid;

(4) any estate property that remains in the guardian's possession;

(5) that the guardian has paid all required bond premiums;

(6) the tax returns the guardian has filed during the guardianship;

(7) the amount of taxes the ward owed during the guardianship that the guardian has paid;

(8) a complete account of the taxes the guardian has paid during the guardianship, including:

(A) the amount of the taxes;

(B) the date the guardian paid the taxes; and

(C) the name of the governmental entity to which the guardian paid the taxes;

(9) a description of all current delinquencies in the filing of tax returns and the payment of taxes, including a reason for each delinquency; and

(10) other facts as appear necessary to a full and definite understanding of the exact condition of the guardianship.

Derived from Probate Code § 749.

Added by Acts 2011, 82nd Leg., ch. 823, § 1.02, eff. Jan. 1, 2014.

§ 1204.103. Certain Debts Excluded from Settlement Computation

In the settlement of any of the accounts of the guardian of the estate, all debts due the estate that the court is satisfied could not have been collected by due diligence and that have not been collected shall be excluded from the computation.

Derived from Probate Code § 756.

Added by Acts 2011, 82nd Leg., ch. 823, § 1.02, eff. Jan. 1, 2014.

§ 1204.104. Guardian to Account for Ward's Labor or Services

(a) Subject to Subsection (b), the guardian of a ward shall account for:

(1) the reasonable value of labor or services provided by the ward; or

(2) the proceeds of labor or services provided by the ward.

(b) The guardian is entitled to reasonable credits for the board, clothing, and maintenance of the ward.

Derived from Probate Code § 757.

Added by Acts 2011, 82nd Leg., ch. 823, § 1.02, eff. Jan. 1, 2014.

§ 1204.105. Citation and Notice on Presentation of Account

(a) On presentation of an account for final settlement by a guardian of the estate of a ward, the county clerk shall issue citation to the persons and in the manner provided by this section.

(b) Citation issued under Subsection (a) must contain:

(1) a statement that an account for final settlement has been presented;

(2) the time and place the court will consider the account; and

(3) a statement requiring the person cited to appear and contest the account, if the person determines contesting the account is proper.

(c) Except as provided by Subsection (d) or (e), the county clerk shall:

(1) issue a citation to be personally served on a ward if:

(A) the ward is 14 years of age or older;

(B) the ward is a living resident of this state; and

(C) the ward's residence is known;

(2) issue a citation to be personally served on the executor or administrator of a deceased ward's estate, if one has been appointed; and

(3) issue a citation to a ward or the ward's estate by publication, or by posting if directed by written court order, if:

(A) the ward's residence is unknown;

(B) the ward is not a resident of this state; or

(C) the ward is deceased and no representative of the ward's estate has been appointed and has qualified in this state.

(d) The ward, in person or by attorney, may waive by writing filed with the county clerk the issuance and personal service of citation required by Subsection (c)(1).

(e) Service of citation is not required under Subsection (c)(2) if the executor or administrator is the same person as the guardian.

(f) The court may allow the waiver of notice of an account for final settlement in a guardianship proceeding.

(g) The court by written order shall require additional notice if the court considers the additional notice necessary.

Derived from Probate Code § 751.

Added by Acts 2011, 82nd Leg., ch. 823, § 1.02, eff. Jan. 1, 2014.

§ 1204.106. Examination of and Hearing on Account

(a) On the court's satisfaction that citation has been properly served on all persons interested in the guardianship estate, the court shall examine the account for final settlement and the accompanying vouchers.

(b) After hearing all exceptions or objections to the account and evidence in support of or against the account, the court shall audit and settle the account and, if necessary, restate the account.

Derived from Probate Code § 752(a).

Added by Acts 2011, 82nd Leg., ch. 823, § 1.02, eff. Jan. 1, 2014.

§ 1204.107. Assets Becoming Due Pending Final Settlement; Receipt and Discharge

(a) This section does not apply to money or another thing of value held under Section 1105.153.

(b) Until the order of final discharge of the guardian is entered in the judge's guardianship docket, money or another thing of value falling due to the ward or the ward's estate while the account for final settlement is pending may be paid or tendered to the emancipated ward, the guardian, or the personal representative of the deceased ward's estate. The ward, guardian, or personal representative to whom the money or other thing of value is paid or tendered shall issue a receipt for the money or other thing of value, and the obligor or payor is discharged of the obligation for all purposes.

Derived from Probate Code § 753.

Added by Acts 2011, 82nd Leg., ch. 823, § 1.02, eff. Jan. 1, 2014.

§ 1204.108. Delivery of Ward's Property in Possession of Guardian of the Person on Settlement of Guardianship of the Estate

(a) If the guardianship of a ward is required to be settled as provided by Section 1204.001, the guardian of the person shall deliver all of the ward's property in the guardian's possession or control to the emancipated ward or other person entitled to the property. If the ward is deceased, the guardian shall deliver the property to the personal representative of the deceased ward's estate or other person entitled to the property.

(b) If none of the ward's property is in the guardian of the person's possession or control, the guardian shall, not later than the 60th day after the date the guardianship is required to be settled, file with the court a sworn affidavit that states:

(1) the reason the guardianship was terminated; and

(2) to whom the ward's property in the guardian's possession was delivered.

(c) The judge may issue orders as necessary for the best interests of the ward or the deceased ward's estate.

(d) This section does not discharge a guardian of the person from liability for breach of the guardian's fiduciary duties.

Derived from Probate Code § 747.

Added by Acts 2011, 82nd Leg., ch. 823, § 1.02, eff. Jan. 1, 2014.

§ 1204.109. Delivery of Remaining Estate Property

On final settlement of a guardianship estate, the court shall order that any part of the estate that remains in the guardian's possession be delivered to:

(1) the ward;

(2) the personal representative of the ward's estate, if the ward is deceased and a personal representative has been appointed; or

(3) any other person legally entitled to the estate.

Derived from Probate Code § 752(b).

Added by Acts 2011, 82nd Leg., ch. 823, § 1.02, eff. Jan. 1, 2014.

Subchapter D. Closing of Guardianship and Discharge of Guardian

§ 1204.151. Discharge of Guardian When No Estate Property Remains

The court shall enter an order discharging a guardian from the guardian's trust and closing the guardianship estate if, on final settlement of the estate, none of the estate remains in the guardian's possession.

Derived from Probate Code § 752(c).

Added by Acts 2011, 82nd Leg., ch. 823, § 1.02, eff. Jan. 1, 2014.

§ 1204.152. Discharge of Guardian When Estate Fully Administered

The court shall enter an order discharging a guardian of the estate from the guardian's trust and declaring the estate closed when:

(1) the guardian has fully administered the estate in accordance with this title and the court's orders;

(2) the guardian's account for final settlement has been approved; and

(3) the guardian has delivered all of the estate remaining in the guardian's possession to any person entitled to receive the estate.

Derived from Probate Code § 752(d).

Added by Acts 2011, 82nd Leg., ch. 823, § 1.02, eff.

Jan. 1, 2014.

Subchapter E. Failure of Guardian to Act

§ 1204.201. Failure to Present Final Account or Report

(a) The court may, on the court's own motion, and shall, on the written complaint of the emancipated ward or anyone interested in the ward or the ward's estate, have the guardian who is charged with the duty of presenting a final account or report cited to appear and present the account or report within the time specified in the citation if the guardian failed or neglected to present the account or report at the proper time.

(b) If a written complaint has not been filed by anyone interested in the guardianship of the person or estate of a minor or deceased ward, on or after the third anniversary of the date the minor ward reaches the age of majority or the date the ward dies, as applicable, the court may remove the estate from the court's active docket without a final accounting and without appointing a successor personal representative.

(c) If a complaint has not been filed by anyone interested in the estate of a ward whose whereabouts are unknown to the court, on or after the fourth anniversary of the date the ward's whereabouts became unknown to the court, the court may remove the estate from the court's active docket without a final accounting and without appointing a successor personal representative.

Derived from Probate Code § 750.

Added by Acts 2011, 82nd Leg., ch. 823, § 1.02, eff. Jan. 1, 2014.

§ 1204.202. Liability for Failure to Deliver Estate Property

(a) On final settlement or termination of the guardianship of the estate, if the guardian neglects when legally demanded to deliver a portion of the estate or any funds or money in the guardian's possession ordered to be delivered to a person entitled to that property, the person may file with the court clerk a written complaint alleging:

(1) the fact of the neglect;

(2) the date of the person's demand; and

(3) other relevant facts.

(b) After the filing of a complaint under Subsection (a), the court clerk shall issue a citation to be served personally on the guardian. The citation must:

(1) apprise the guardian of the complaint; and

(2) cite the guardian to appear before the court and answer, if the guardian desires, at a time designated in the citation.

(c) If at the hearing the court finds that the citation was properly served and returned, and that the guardian is guilty of the neglect charged, the court shall enter an order to that effect.

(d) If the court enters an order under Subsection (c), the guardian is liable to the person who filed the complaint under Subsection (a) for damages at the rate of 10 percent of the amount or appraised value of the money or estate withheld, per month, for each month or fraction of a month that the estate or money of a guardianship of the estate, or on termination of guardianship of the person, or funds is or has been withheld by the guardian after the date of demand. Damages under this subsection may be recovered in any court of competent jurisdiction.

Derived from Probate Code § 758.

Added by Acts 2011, 82nd Leg., ch. 823, § 1.02, eff. Jan. 1, 2014.

SUBTITLE G. SPECIAL TYPES OF GUARDIANSHIPS

Chapter 1251. Temporary Guardianships

Subchapter A. Appointment of Temporary Guardian Generally

Subchapter B. Temporary Guardianship Pending Challenge or Contest of Certain Guardianship Applications

Subchapter C. Powers and Duties of Temporary Guardians

Subchapter D. Expiration and Closing of Temporary Guardianship

Chapter 1251. Temporary Guardianships

Subchapter A. Appointment of Temporary Guardian Generally

§ 1251.001. Appointment of Temporary Guardian

(a) A court shall appoint a temporary guardian, with limited powers as the circumstances of the case require, if the court:

(1) is presented with substantial evidence that a person may be an incapacitated person; and

(2) has probable cause to believe that the person, the person's estate, or both require the immediate appointment of a guardian.

(b) The person for whom a temporary guardian is appointed under this chapter retains all rights and powers that are not specifically granted to the person's temporary guardian by court order.

Derived from Probate Code § 875(a), (b).

Added by Acts 2011, 82nd Leg., ch. 823, § 1.02, eff. Jan. 1, 2014.

§ 1251.002. No Presumption of Incapacity

A person for whom a temporary guardian is appointed under this chapter may not be presumed to be incapacitated.

Derived from Probate Code § 874.

Added by Acts 2011, 82nd Leg., ch. 823, § 1.02, eff. Jan. 1, 2014.

§ 1251.003. Application

(a) A sworn, written application for the appointment of a temporary guardian shall be filed before the court appoints a temporary guardian.

(b) The application must state:

(1) the name and address of the person who is the subject of the guardianship proceeding;

(2) the danger to the person or property alleged to be imminent;

(3) the type of appointment and the particular protection and assistance being requested;

(4) the facts and reasons supporting the allegations and requests;

(5) the proposed temporary guardian's name, address, and qualification;

(6) the applicant's name, address, and interest; and

(7) if applicable, that the proposed temporary guardian is a private professional guardian who is certified under Subchapter C, Chapter 155, Government Code, and has complied with the requirements of Subchapter G, Chapter 1104.

Derived from Probate Code § 875(c).

Added by Acts 2011, 82nd Leg., ch. 823, § 1.02, eff. Jan. 1, 2014. Subsec. (b) amended by Acts 2013, 83rd Leg., ch. 42, § 2.22, eff. Jan. 1, 2014.

§ 1251.004. Appointment of Attorney

On the filing of an application for temporary guardianship, the court shall appoint an attorney to represent the proposed ward in all guardianship proceedings in which independent counsel has not been retained by or on behalf of the proposed ward.

Derived from Probate Code § 875(d).

Added by Acts 2011, 82nd Leg., ch. 823, § 1.02, eff. Jan. 1, 2014.

§ 1251.005. Notice of Application

(a) On the filing of an application for temporary guardianship, the clerk shall issue notice to be served on:

(1) the proposed ward;

(2) the proposed ward's appointed attorney; and

(3) the proposed temporary guardian named in the application, if that person is not the applicant.

(b) The notice must describe:

(1) the rights of the parties; and

(2) the date, time, place, purpose, and possible consequences of a hearing on the application.

(c) A copy of the application must be attached to the notice.

Derived from Probate Code § 875(e).

Added by Acts 2011, 82nd Leg., ch. 823, § 1.02, eff. Jan. 1, 2014.

§ 1251.006. Scheduling of Hearing

(a) Immediately after an application for a temporary guardianship is filed, the court shall issue an order setting a certain date for the hearing on the application.

(b) Unless postponed as provided by Subsection (c), a hearing shall be held not later than the 10th day after the date the application for temporary guardianship is filed.

(c) The proposed ward or the proposed ward's attorney may consent to postpone the hearing on the application for temporary guardianship for a period not to exceed 30 days after the date the application is filed.

(d) An application for temporary guardianship takes precedence over all matters except older matters of the same character.

Derived from Probate Code § 875(f)(1), (2), (3), (4).

Added by Acts 2011, 82nd Leg., ch. 823, § 1.02, eff. Jan. 1, 2014.

§ 1251.007. Motion for Dismissal of Application

(a) Subject to Subsection (b), the proposed ward or the proposed ward's attorney may appear and move for the dismissal of the application for temporary guardianship.

(b) At least one day before making a motion under Subsection (a), the proposed ward or the proposed ward's attorney shall provide notice to the party who filed the application for temporary guardianship.

(c) If a motion is made for dismissal of the application for temporary guardianship, the court shall hear and determine the motion as expeditiously as justice requires.

Derived from Probate Code § 875(f)(5).

Added by Acts 2011, 82nd Leg., ch. 823, § 1.02, eff. Jan. 1, 2014.

§ 1251.008. Rights of Proposed Ward at Hearing

At a hearing under this subchapter, the proposed ward has the right to:

(1) receive prior notice;

(2) be represented by counsel;

(3) be present;

(4) present evidence;

(5) confront and cross-examine witnesses; and

(6) a closed hearing if requested by the proposed ward or the proposed ward's attorney.

Derived from Probate Code § 875(f)(1).

Added by Acts 2011, 82nd Leg., ch. 823, § 1.02, eff. Jan. 1, 2014.

§ 1251.009. Appearance by Proposed Temporary Guardian in Certain Circumstances

If the applicant for a temporary guardianship is not the proposed temporary guardian, a temporary guardianship may not be granted before a hearing on the application required by Section 1251.006(b) unless the proposed temporary guardian appears in court.

Derived from Probate Code § 875(f)(6).

Added by Acts 2011, 82nd Leg., ch. 823, § 1.02, eff. Jan. 1, 2014.

§ 1251.010. Order Appointing Temporary Guardian

(a) The court shall appoint a temporary guardian by written order if, at the conclusion of the hearing required by Section 1251.006(b), the court determines that the applicant has established that there is substantial evidence that the proposed ward is an incapacitated person, that there is imminent danger that the proposed ward's physical health or safety will be seriously impaired, or that the proposed ward's estate will be seriously damaged or dissipated unless immediate action is taken.

(b) The court shall assign to the temporary guardian only those powers and duties that are necessary to protect the proposed ward against the imminent danger shown.

(c) The order appointing the temporary guardian must describe:

(1) the reasons for the temporary guardianship; and

(2) the powers and duties of the temporary guardian.

Derived from Probate Code § 875(g).

Added by Acts 2011, 82nd Leg., ch. 823, § 1.02, eff. Jan. 1, 2014.

§ 1251.011. Certain Agency as Temporary Guardian

A court may not ordinarily appoint the Department of Aging and Disability Services as a temporary guardian under this chapter. The appointment of the department as a temporary guardian under this chapter should be made only as a last resort.

Derived from Probate Code § 875(j).

Added by Acts 2011, 82nd Leg., ch. 823, § 1.02, eff. Jan. 1, 2014.

§ 1251.012. Temporary Guardian's Bond

The court shall set bond for a temporary guardian according to Chapter 1105.

Derived from Probate Code § 875(g).

Added by Acts 2011, 82nd Leg., ch. 823, § 1.02, eff. Jan. 1, 2014.

§ 1251.013. Court Costs

If the court appoints a temporary guardian after the hearing required by Section 1251.006(b), all court costs, including attorney's fees, may be assessed as provided by Sections 1155.054 and 1155.151.

Derived from Probate Code § 875(i).

Added by Acts 2011, 82nd Leg., ch. 823, § 1.02, eff. Jan. 1, 2014. Amended by Acts 2013, 83rd Leg., ch. 982, § 24, eff. Jan. 1, 2014.

Subchapter B. Temporary Guardianship Pending Challenge or Contest of Certain Guardianship Applications

§ 1251.051. Authority to Appoint Temporary Guardian or Grant Restraining Order

The court, on the court's own motion or on the motion of any interested party, may appoint a temporary guardian or grant a temporary restraining order under Rule 680, Texas Rules of Civil Procedure, or both, without issuing additional citation if:

(1) an application for a temporary guardianship, for the conversion of a temporary guardianship to a permanent guardianship, or for a permanent guardianship is challenged or contested; and

(2) the court finds that the appointment or the issuance of the order is necessary to protect the proposed ward or the proposed ward's estate.

Derived from Probate Code § 875(k).

Added by Acts 2011, 82nd Leg., ch. 823, § 1.02, eff. Jan. 1, 2014.

§ 1251.052. Qualification and Duration of Certain Temporary Guardianships

(a) A temporary guardian appointed under Section 1251.051 must qualify in the same form and manner required of a guardian under this title.

(b) The term of a temporary guardian appointed under Section 1251.051 expires on the earliest of the following:

(1) [at] the conclusion of the hearing challenging or contesting the application; [or]

(2) [on] the date a permanent guardian appointed by the court for the proposed ward qualifies to serve as the ward's guardian; or

(3) the nine-month anniversary of the date the temporary guardian qualifies, unless the term is extended by court order issued after a motion to extend the term is filed and a hearing on the motion is held.

Derived from Probate Code § 875(l).

Added by Acts 2011, 82nd Leg., ch. 823, § 1.02, eff. Jan. 1, 2014. Subsec. (b) amended by Acts 2015, 84th Leg., ch. 1031, § 23, eff. Sept. 1, 2015.

Subchapter C. Powers and Duties of Temporary Guardians

§ 1251.101. Authority of Temporary Guardian

(a) When the temporary guardian files the oath and bond required under this title, the court order appointing the temporary guardian takes effect without the necessity for issuance of letters of guardianship.

(b) The clerk shall note compliance with the oath and bond requirements by the appointed temporary guardian on a certificate attached to the order.

(c) The order appointing the temporary guardian is evidence of the temporary guardian's authority to act within the scope of the powers and duties stated in the order.

(d) The clerk may not issue certified copies of the order until the oath and bond requirements are satisfied.

Derived from Probate Code § 876.

Added by Acts 2011, 82nd Leg., ch. 823, § 1.02, eff. Jan. 1, 2014.

§ 1251.102. Applicability of Guardianship Provisions

The provisions of this title relating to the guardianship of the persons and estates of incapacitated persons apply to the temporary guardianship of the persons and estates of incapacitated persons, to the extent the provisions may be made applicable.

Derived from Probate Code § 877.

Added by Acts 2011, 82nd Leg., ch. 823, § 1.02, eff. Jan. 1, 2014.

Subchapter D. Expiration and Closing of Temporary Guardianship

§ 1251.151. Duration of Temporary Guardianship

Except as provided by Section 1251.052, a temporary guardianship may not remain in effect for more than 60 days.

Derived from Probate Code § 875(h).

Added by Acts 2011, 82nd Leg., ch. 823, § 1.02, eff. Jan. 1, 2014.

§ 1251.152. Accounting

(a) At the expiration of a temporary guardianship, the temporary guardian shall file with the court clerk:

(1) a sworn list of all estate property that has come into the temporary guardian's possession;

(2) a return of all sales made by the temporary guardian; and

(3) a full exhibit and account of all the temporary guardian's acts as temporary guardian.

(b) The court shall act on the list, return, exhibit, and account filed under Subsection (a).

Derived from Probate Code §§ 878, 879.

Added by Acts 2011, 82nd Leg., ch. 823, § 1.02, eff. Jan. 1, 2014.

§ 1251.153. Delivery of Estate; Discharge of Temporary Guardian

(a) When temporary letters expire or cease to be effective for any reason, the court immediately shall enter an order requiring the temporary guardian to deliver the estate remaining in the temporary guardian's possession to the person legally entitled to possession of the estate.

(b) On proof of delivery under Subsection (a):

(1) the temporary guardian shall be discharged; and

(2) the sureties on the temporary guardian's bond shall be released as to future liability.

Derived from Probate Code § 879.

Added by Acts 2011, 82nd Leg., ch. 823, § 1.02, eff. Jan. 1, 2014.

Chapter 1252. Guardianships for Nonresident Wards

Subchapter A. Resident Guardian of Nonresident Ward's Estate

Subchapter B. Nonresident Guardian of Nonresident Ward's Estate

Chapter 1252. Guardianships for Nonresident Wards

Subchapter A. Resident Guardian of Nonresident Ward's Estate

§ 1252.001. Granting of Guardianship of Estate for Nonresident

(a) A guardianship of the estate of a nonresident incapacitated person who owns property in this state may be granted, if necessary, in the same manner as for the property of a resident of this state.

(b) A court in the county in which the principal estate of the nonresident incapacitated person is located has jurisdiction to appoint the guardian.

Derived from Probate Code § 882.

Added by Acts 2011, 82nd Leg., ch. 823, § 1.02, eff. Jan. 1, 2014.

§ 1252.002. Court Actions and Orders Concerning Estate

The court shall take all actions and make all necessary orders with respect to the estate described by Section 1252.001 of a nonresident ward for the maintenance, support, care, or education of the ward out of the proceeds of the estate, in the same manner as if the ward were a resident of this state sent abroad by the court for education or treatment.

Derived from Probate Code § 882.

Added by Acts 2011, 82nd Leg., ch. 823, § 1.02, eff. Jan. 1, 2014.

§ 1252.003. Closing Resident Guardianship

The court shall close a resident guardianship of an estate granted under this subchapter if a qualified nonresident guardian of the estate later qualifies in this state under Section 1252.051 as a nonresident guardian.

Derived from Probate Code § 882.

Added by Acts 2011, 82nd Leg., ch. 823, § 1.02, eff. Jan. 1, 2014.

Subchapter B. Nonresident Guardian of Nonresident Ward's Estate

§ 1252.051. Appointment and Qualification of Nonresident Guardian

(a) A nonresident of this state may be appointed and qualified as guardian or coguardian of a nonresident ward's estate located in this state in the same manner provided by this title for the appointment and qualification of a resident guardian of the estate of an incapacitated person if:

(1) a court of competent jurisdiction in the geographical jurisdiction in which the nonresident resides appointed the nonresident guardian;

(2) the nonresident is qualified as guardian or as a fiduciary legal representative by any name known in the foreign jurisdiction of the property or estate of the ward located in the jurisdiction of the foreign court; and

(3) the nonresident, with the written application for appointment, files in the county court of a county of this state in which all or part of the nonresident ward's estate is located a complete transcript of the proceedings from the records of the court in which the nonresident applicant was appointed.

(b) The transcript required by Subsection (a)(3) must:

(1) show the applicant's appointment and qualification as guardian or other fiduciary legal representative of the ward's property or estate;

(2) be certified to and attested by the clerk of the foreign court or the court officer charged by law with custody of the court records, under the court seal, if any; and

(3) have attached a certificate of the judge, chief justice, or presiding magistrate of the foreign court certifying that the attestation of the clerk or legal custodian of the court records is in correct form.

Derived from Probate Code § 881(a), (b).

Added by Acts 2011, 82nd Leg., ch. 823, § 1.02, eff. Jan. 1, 2014.

§ 1252.052. Appointment; Issuance of Letters of Guardianship

(a) If a nonresident applicant meets the requirements of Section 1252.051, without the necessity of notice or citation, the court shall enter an order appointing the nonresident as guardian or coguardian of a nonresident ward's estate located in this state.

(b) After the nonresident applicant qualifies in the manner required of resident guardians and files with the court a power of attorney appointing a resident agent to accept service of process in all actions or proceedings with respect to the estate, the clerk shall issue the letters of guardianship to the nonresident guardian.

Derived from Probate Code § 881(c).

Added by Acts 2011, 82nd Leg., ch. 823, § 1.02, eff. Jan. 1, 2014.

§ 1252.053. Inventory and Appraisement; Administration of Estate

After qualification, a nonresident guardian:

(1) shall file an inventory and appraisement of the ward's estate in this state subject to the court's jurisdiction, as in ordinary cases; and

(2) is subject to the applicable provisions of this code governing the handling and settlement of an estate by a resident guardian.

Derived from Probate Code § 881(d).

Added by Acts 2011, 82nd Leg., ch. 823, § 1.02, eff. Jan. 1, 2014.

§ 1252.054. Delivery of Estate to Certain Guardians

The court may order a resident guardian who has any of the ward's estate to deliver the estate to a qualified and acting guardian of the ward.

Derived from Probate Code § 881(e).

Added by Acts 2011, 82nd Leg., ch. 823, § 1.02, eff. Jan. 1, 2014.

§ 1252.055. Removal of Ward's Property from State by Nonresident Guardian

Regardless of whether qualified under this title, a nonresident guardian may remove personal property of the ward from this state if:

(1) the removal does not conflict with the tenure of the property or the terms of the guardianship under which the property is held; and

(2) all known debts against the estate in this state are paid or secured by a bond payable to and approved by the judge of the court in which guardianship proceedings are pending in this state.

Derived from Probate Code § 881A.

Added by Acts 2011, 82nd Leg., ch. 823, § 1.02, eff. Jan. 1, 2014.

Chapter 1253. Interstate Guardianships

Subchapter A. Transfer of Guardianship to Foreign Jurisdiction

Subchapter B. Receipt and Acceptance of Foreign Guardianship

Subchapter C. Guardianship Proceedings Filed in This State and in Foreign Jurisdiction

Subchapter D. Determination of Most Appropriate Forum for Certain Guardianship Proceedings

Chapter 1253. Interstate Guardianships

Subchapter A. Transfer of Guardianship to Foreign Jurisdiction

§ 1253.001. Application to Transfer Guardianship to Foreign Jurisdiction

A guardian of the person or estate may apply to the court that has jurisdiction over the guardianship to transfer the guardianship to a court in a foreign jurisdiction to which the ward has permanently moved.

Derived from Probate Code § 891(a).

Added by Acts 2011, 82nd Leg., ch. 823, § 1.02, eff. Jan. 1, 2014.

§ 1253.002. Notice of Application

Notice of an application to transfer a guardianship under this subchapter shall be:

(1) served personally on the ward; and

(2) given to the foreign court to which the guardianship is to be transferred.

Derived from Probate Code § 891(b).

Added by Acts 2011, 82nd Leg., ch. 823, § 1.02, eff. Jan. 1, 2014.

§ 1253.003. Determination Regarding Transfer of Guardianship

(a) On the court's own motion or on the motion of the ward or any interested person, the court shall hold a hearing to consider an application to transfer a guardianship under this subchapter.

(b) The court shall transfer a guardianship to a foreign court if the court determines the transfer is in the best interests of the ward. The transfer of the guardianship must be made contingent on the acceptance of the guardianship in the foreign jurisdiction.

(c) The court shall coordinate efforts with the appropriate foreign court to facilitate the orderly transfer of the guardianship.

Derived from Probate Code § 891(c), (d).

Added by Acts 2011, 82nd Leg., ch. 823, § 1.02, eff. Jan. 1, 2014.

Subchapter B. Receipt and Acceptance of Foreign Guardianship

§ 1253.051. Application for Receipt and Acceptance of Foreign Guardianship

A guardian appointed by a foreign court to represent an incapacitated person who is residing in this state or intends to move to this state may file an application with a court in the county in which the ward resides or in which it is intended that the ward will [intends to] reside to have the guardianship transferred to that [the] court. The application must have attached a certified copy of all papers of the guardianship filed and recorded in the foreign court.

Derived from Probate Code § 892(a).

Added by Acts 2011, 82nd Leg., ch. 823, § 1.02, eff. Jan. 1, 2014. Amended by Acts 2011, 82nd Leg. 1st C.S., ch. 4, § 66A.02, eff. Jan. 1, 2014. Amended by Acts 2015, 84th Leg., ch. 1031, § 24, eff. Sept. 1, 2015.

§ 1253.052. Notice of Application

Notice of an application for receipt and acceptance of a foreign guardianship under this subchapter shall be:

(1) served personally on the ward; and

(2) given to the foreign court from which the guardianship is to be transferred.

Derived from Probate Code § 892(b).

Added by Acts 2011, 82nd Leg., ch. 823, § 1.02, eff. Jan. 1, 2014.

§ 1253.053. Determination Regarding Receipt and Acceptance of Foreign Guardianship

(a) The court shall hold a hearing to:

(1) consider an application for receipt and acceptance of a foreign guardianship under this subchapter; and

(2) consider modifying the administrative procedures or requirements of the proposed transferred guardianship in accordance with local and state law.

(b) In reviewing the application, the court should determine:

(1) that the proposed guardianship is not a collateral attack on an existing or proposed guardianship in another jurisdiction in this or another state; and

(2) for a guardianship in which a court in one or more states may have jurisdiction, that the application has been filed in the court that is best suited to consider the matter.

(c) The court shall grant the application if the transfer of the guardianship from the foreign jurisdiction is in the best interests of the ward.

(d) In granting the application, the court shall give full faith and credit to the provisions of the foreign guardianship order concerning the determination of the ward's incapacity and the rights, powers, and duties of the guardian.

(e) The court shall coordinate efforts with the appropriate foreign court to facilitate the orderly transfer of the guardianship.

(f) At the time of granting an application for receipt and acceptance of a foreign guardianship, the court may also modify the administrative procedures or requirements of the transferred guardianship in accordance with local and state law.

Derived from Probate Code § 892(d), (e), (f), (g).

Added by Acts 2011, 82nd Leg., ch. 823, § 1.02, eff. Jan. 1, 2014. Amended by Acts 2011, 82nd Leg. 1st C.S., ch. 4, § 66A.03, eff. Jan. 1, 2014

§ 1253.055. Guardianship Transfer Proceedings Filed in Two or More Courts

If an application for receipt and acceptance of a foreign guardianship under this subchapter is filed in two or more courts with jurisdiction, the proceeding shall be heard in the court with jurisdiction over the application filed on the earliest date, if venue is otherwise proper in that court. A court that does not have venue to hear the application shall transfer the proceeding to the proper court.

Derived from Probate Code § 892(c).

Added by Acts 2011, 82nd Leg., ch. 823, § 1.02, eff. Jan. 1, 2014.

§ 1253.056. Construction With Other Law

The denial of an application for receipt and acceptance of a guardianship under this subchapter does not affect the right of a guardian appointed by a foreign court to file an application to be appointed guardian of the incapacitated person under Section 1101.001.

Derived from Probate Code § 892(h).

Added by Acts 2011, 82nd Leg., ch. 823, § 1.02, eff. Jan. 1, 2014.

Subchapter C. Guardianship Proceedings Filed in This State and in Foreign Jurisdiction

§ 1253.101. Delay of Certain Guardianship Proceedings

A court in which a guardianship proceeding is filed and in which venue of the proceeding is proper may delay further action in the proceeding in that court if:

(1) another guardianship proceeding involving a matter at issue in the proceeding filed in the court is subsequently filed in a court in a foreign jurisdiction; and

(2) venue of the proceeding in the foreign court is proper.

Derived from Probate Code § 894(a).

Added by Acts 2011, 82nd Leg., ch. 823, § 1.02, eff. Jan. 1, 2014.

§ 1253.102. Determination of Venue; Action Following Determination

(a) A court that delays further action in a guardianship proceeding under Section 1253.101 shall determine whether venue of the proceeding is more suitable in that court or in the foreign court.

(b) In making a determination under Subsection (a), the court may consider:

(1) the interests of justice;

(2) the best interests of the ward or proposed ward;

(3) the convenience of the parties; and

(4) the preference of the ward or proposed ward, if the ward or proposed ward is 12 years of age or older.

(c) The court shall resume the guardianship proceeding delayed under Section 1253.101 if the court determines under this section that venue is more suitable in that court. If the court determines that venue is more suitable in the foreign court, the court shall, with the consent of the foreign court, transfer the proceeding to that foreign court.

Derived from Probate Code § 894(b), (d).

Added by Acts 2011, 82nd Leg., ch. 823, § 1.02, eff. Jan. 1, 2014. Amended by Acts 2011, 82nd Leg. 1st C.S., ch. 4, § 66A.04, eff. Jan. 1, 2014.

§ 1253.103. Necessary Orders

A court that delays further action in a guardianship proceeding under Section 1253.101 may issue any order the court considers necessary to protect the proposed ward or the proposed ward's estate.

Derived from Probate Code § 894(c).

Added by Acts 2011, 82nd Leg., ch. 823, § 1.02, eff. Jan. 1, 2014.

Subchapter D. Determination of Most Appropriate Forum for Certain Guardianship Proceedings

§ 1253.151. Determination of Acquisition of Jurisdiction in This State Due to Unjustifiable Conduct

If at any time a court of this state determines that it acquired jurisdiction of a proceeding for the appointment of a guardian of the person or estate, or both, of a ward or proposed ward because of unjustifiable conduct, the court may:

(1) decline to exercise jurisdiction;

(2) exercise jurisdiction for the limited purpose of fashioning an appropriate remedy to ensure the health, safety, and welfare of the ward or proposed ward or the protection of the ward's or proposed ward's property or prevent a repetition of the unjustifiable conduct, including staying the proceeding until a petition for the appointment of a guardian or issuance of a protective order is filed in a court of another state having jurisdiction; or

(3) continue to exercise jurisdiction after considering:

(A) the extent to which the ward or proposed ward and all persons required to be notified of the proceedings have acquiesced in the exercise of the court's jurisdiction;

(B) whether the court of this state is a more appropriate forum than the court of any other state after considering the factors described by Section 1253.102(b); and

(C) whether the court of any other state would have jurisdiction under the factual circumstances of the matter.

Derived from Probate Code § 895(a).

Added by Acts 2011, 82nd Leg. 1ˢᵗ C.S., ch. 4, § 66A.05, eff. Jan. 1, 2014.

§ 1253.152. Assessment of Expenses Against Party

(a) If a court of this state determines that it acquired jurisdiction of a proceeding for the appointment of a guardian of the person or estate, or both, of a ward or proposed ward because a party seeking to invoke the court's jurisdiction engaged in unjustifiable conduct, the court may assess against that party necessary and reasonable expenses, including attorney's fees, investigative fees, court costs, communication expenses, witness fees and expenses, and travel expenses.

(b) The court may not assess fees, costs, or expenses of any kind against this state or a governmental subdivision, agency, or instrumentality of this state unless authorized by other law.

Derived from Probate Code § 895(b).

Added by Acts 2011, 82nd Leg. 1ˢᵗ C.S., ch. 4, § 66A.05, eff. Jan. 1, 2014.

SUBTITLE H. COURT-AUTHORIZED TRUSTS AND ACCOUNTS

Chapter 1301. Management Trusts

Chapter 1301. Management Trusts

Subchapter A. General Provisions

§ 1301.001. Definition

In this chapter, "management trust" means a trust created under Section 1301.053 or 1301.054.

New.

Added by Acts 2011, 82nd Leg., ch. 823, § 1.02, eff. Jan. 1, 2014.

§ 1301.002. Applicability of Texas Trust Code

(a) A management trust is subject to Subtitle B, Title 9, Property Code.

(b) To the extent of a conflict between Subtitle B, Title 9, Property Code, and a provision of this chapter or of a management trust, the provision of this chapter or of the trust controls.

Derived from Probate Code § 869B.

Added by Acts 2011, 82nd Leg., ch. 823, § 1.02, eff. Jan. 1, 2014.

Subchapter B. Creation of Management Trusts

§ 1301.051. Eligibility to Apply for Creation of Trust

The following persons may apply for the creation of a trust under this subchapter:

(1) the guardian of a ward;

(2) an attorney ad litem or guardian ad litem appointed to represent a ward or the ward's interests;

(3) a person interested in the welfare of an alleged incapacitated person who does not have a guardian;

(4) an attorney ad litem or guardian ad litem appointed to represent an alleged incapacitated person who does not have a guardian; or

(5) a person who has only a physical disability.

Derived from Probate Code § 867(a-1).

Added by Acts 2011, 82nd Leg., ch. 823, § 1.02, eff. Jan. 1, 2014. Amended by Acts 2013, 83rd Leg., ch. 161, § 6.060, eff. Jan. 1, 2014.

§ 1301.052. Venue for Proceeding Involving Trust for an Alleged Incapacitated Person

(a) An application for the creation of a trust under Section 1301.054 for an alleged incapacitated person must be filed in the same court in which a proceeding for the appointment of a guardian for the person is pending, if any.

(b) If a proceeding for the appointment of a guardian for an alleged incapacitated person is not pending on the date an application is filed for the creation of a trust under Section 1301.054 for the person, venue for a proceeding to create a trust must be determined in the same manner as venue for a proceeding for the appointment of a guardian is determined under Section 1023.001.

Derived from Probate Code §§ 867(b-2), 867A.

Added by Acts 2011, 82nd Leg., ch. 823, § 1.02, eff. Jan. 1, 2014. Section title amended by Acts 2013, 83rd Leg., ch. 982, § 25, eff. Jan. 1, 2014. Subsec. (b) amended by Acts 2013, 83rd Leg., ch. 161, § 6.061, eff. Jan. 1, 2014.

§ 1301.053. Creation of Trust

(a) On application by an appropriate person as provided by Section 1301.051 and subject to Section 1301.054(a), if applicable, the court with jurisdiction over the proceedings may enter an order that creates a trust for the management of the funds of the person with respect to whom the application is filed if the court finds that the creation of the trust is in the person's best interests.

(b) The court may maintain a trust created under this section under the same cause number as the guardianship proceeding, if the person for whom the trust is created is a ward or proposed ward.

Derived from Probate Code § 867(b) & (f).

Added by Acts 2011, 82nd Leg., ch. 823, § 1.02, eff. Jan. 1, 2014. Amended by Acts 2013, 83rd Leg., ch. 161, § 6.062, eff. Jan. 1, 2014.

§ 1301.054. Creation of Trust for Incapacitated Person Without Guardian

(a) On application by an appropriate person as provided by Section 1301.051 and regardless of whether an application for guardianship has been filed on the alleged incapacitated person's behalf, a proper court exercising probate jurisdiction may enter an order that creates a trust for the management of the estate of an alleged incapacitated person who does not have a guardian if the court, after a hearing, finds that:

(1) the person is an incapacitated person; and

(2) the creation of the trust is in the incapacitated person's best interests.

(b) The court shall conduct the hearing to determine incapacity under Subsection (a) using the same procedures and evidentiary standards as are required in a hearing for the appointment of a guardian for a proposed ward.

(c) Except as provided by Subsection (c-1), the court shall appoint an attorney ad litem and, if necessary, may appoint a guardian ad litem, to represent the interests of the alleged incapacitated person in the hearing to determine incapacity under Subsection (a).

(c-1) If the application for the creation of the trust is filed by a person who has only a physical disability, the court may, but is not required to, appoint an attorney ad litem or guardian ad litem to represent the interests of the person in the hearing to determine incapacity under Subsection (a).

(d) The court may maintain a trust created under this section under the same cause number as the guardianship proceeding, if the person for whom the trust is created is a ward or proposed ward.

Derived from Probate Code § 867(b-1), (b-3), & (f).

Added by Acts 2011, 82nd Leg., ch. 823, § 1.02, eff.

Jan. 1, 2014. Subsec. (c) amended and subsec. (c-1) by Acts 2013, 83rd Leg., ch. 982, § 26, eff. Jan. 1, 2014. Subsec. (d) amended by Acts 2013, 83rd Leg., ch. 161, § 6.063, eff. Jan. 1, 2014.

§ 1301.055. Authority of Court to Appoint Guardian Instead of Creating Trust

If, after a hearing under Section 1301.054, the court finds that the person for whom the application was filed is an incapacitated person but that it is not in the incapacitated person's best interests for the court to create a trust under this subchapter for the incapacitated person's estate, the court may appoint a guardian of the person or estate, or both, for the incapacitated person without commencing a separate proceeding for that purpose.

Derived from Probate Code § 867(b-4).

Added by Acts 2011, 82nd Leg., ch. 823, § 1.02, eff. Jan. 1, 2014. Amended by 2013, 83rd Leg., ch. 982, § 27, eff. Jan. 1, 2014.

§ 1301.056. Contents of Order Creating Trust

An order creating a management trust must:

(1) direct any person or entity holding property that belongs to the person for whom the trust is created or to which that person is entitled to deliver all or part of that property to a person or corporate fiduciary appointed as trustee of the trust; and

(2) include terms and limitations placed on the trust.

Derived from Probate Code § 867(f).

Added by Acts 2011, 82nd Leg., ch. 823, § 1.02, eff. Jan. 1, 2014. Amended by Acts 2013, 83rd Leg., ch. 6.064, eff. Jan. 1, 2014.

§ 1301.057. Appointment of Trustee

(a) In this section, "financial institution" means a financial institution, as defined by Section 201.101, Finance Code, that has trust powers and exists and does business under the laws of this state, another state, or the United States.

(b) Except as provided by Subsection (c), the court shall appoint a financial institution to serve as trustee of a management trust, other than a management trust created for a person who has only a physical disability.

(c) The court may appoint a person or entity described by Subsection (d) to serve as trustee of a management trust created for a ward or incapacitated person instead of appointing a financial institution to serve in that capacity if the court finds:

(1) that the appointment is in the best interests of the person for whom the trust is created; and

(2) if the value of the trust's principal is more than $150,000, that the applicant for the creation of the trust, after the exercise of due diligence, has been unable to find a financial institution in the geographic area willing to serve as trustee.

(d) The following are eligible for appointment as trustee of a management trust created for a ward or incapacitated person under Subsection (c):

(1) an individual, including an individual who is certified as a private professional guardian;

(2) a nonprofit corporation qualified to serve as a guardian; and

(3) a guardianship program.

Derived from Probate Code § 867(a), (b-5), (c), (d), (e).

Added by Acts 2011, 82nd Leg., ch. 823, § 1.02, eff. Jan. 1, 2014. Subsecs. (b), (c), and (d) amended by Acts 2013, 83rd Leg., ch. 982, § 28, eff. Jan. 1, 2014. Subsec. (c) amended by Acts 2013, 83rd Leg., ch. 161, § 6.065, eff. Jan. 1, 2014.

§ 1301.058. Bond Requirements for Trustees

(a) The following serve without giving a bond in accordance with the trust terms required by Sections 1301.101(a)(4) and (a-1):

(1) a trustee of a management trust that is a corporate fiduciary; and

(2) any other trustee of a management trust created for a person who has only a physical disability.

(b) Except as provided by Subsection (a), the court shall require a person serving as trustee of a management trust to file with the county clerk a bond that:

(1) is in an amount equal to the value of the trust's principal and projected annual income; and

(2) meets the conditions the court determines are necessary.

Derived from Probate Code §§ 868(a), 868B.

Added by Acts 2011, 82nd Leg., ch. 823, § 1.02, eff. Jan. 1, 2014. Amended by Acts 2013, 83rd Leg., ch. 982, § 29, eff. Jan. 1, 2014

Subchapter C. Terms of Management Trust

§ 1301.101. Required Terms

(a) Except as provided by Subsection (c), a management trust created for a ward or incapacitated person must provide that:

(1) the ward, incapacitated person, or person who has only a physical disability is the sole beneficiary of the trust;

(2) the trustee may disburse an amount of the trust's principal or income as the trustee determines is necessary to spend for the health, education, maintenance, or support of the person for whom the trust is created;

(3) the trust income that the trustee does not disburse under Subdivision (2) must be added to the trust principal;

(4) a trustee that is a corporate fiduciary serves without giving a bond; and

(5) subject to the court's approval and Subsection (b), a trustee is entitled to receive

reasonable compensation for services the trustee provides to the person for whom the trust is created as the person's trustee.

(a-1) A management trust created for a person who has only a physical disability must provide that the trustee of the trust:

(1) serves without giving a bond; and

(2) is entitled to receive, without the court's approval, reasonable compensation for services the trustee provides to the person as the person's trustee.

(b) A trustee's compensation under Subsection (a)(5) must be:

(1) paid from the management trust's income, principal, or both; and

(2) determined, paid, reduced, and eliminated in the same manner as compensation of a guardian under Subchapter A, Chapter 1155.

(c) The court creating or modifying a management trust may omit or modify otherwise applicable terms required by Subsection (a), (a-1), or (b) if the court is creating the trust for a person who has only a physical disability, or if the court determines that the omission or modification:

(1) is necessary and appropriate for the person for whom the trust is created to be eligible to receive public benefits or assistance under a state or federal program that is not otherwise available to the person; or

(2) is in the best interests of the person for whom the trust is created.

Derived from Probate Code § 868(a), (d).

Added by Acts 2011, 82nd Leg., ch. 823, § 1.02, eff. Jan. 1, 2014. Amended by Acts 2013, 83rd Leg., ch. 982, § 30, eff. Jan. 1, 2014. Amended by Acts 2013, 83rd Leg., ch. 161, § 6.066, eff. Jan. 1, 2014.

§ 1301.102. Optional Terms

(a) A management trust created for a ward or incapacitated person may provide that the trustee make a distribution, payment, use, or application of trust funds for the health, education, maintenance, or support of the person for whom the trust is created or of another person whom the person for whom the trust is created is legally obligated to support:

(1) as necessary and without the intervention of:

(A) a guardian or other representative of the ward; or

(B) a representative of the incapacitated person or person who has only a physical disability; and

(2) to:

(A) the ward's guardian;

(B) a person who has physical custody of the person for whom the trust is created or of another person whom the person for whom the trust is created is legally obligated to support; or

(C) a person providing a good or service to the person for whom the trust is created or to

another person whom the person for whom the trust is created is legally obligated to support.

(b) The court may include additional provisions in a management trust on the trust's creation or modification under this chapter if the court determines the addition does not conflict with Section 1301.101.

Derived from Probate Code § 868(b), (e).

Added by Acts 2011, 82nd Leg., ch. 823, § 1.02, eff. Jan. 1, 2014. Subsec. (a) amended by Acts 2013, 83rd Leg., ch. 982, § 31, eff. Jan. 1, 2014 and Acts 2013, 83rd Leg., ch. 161, § 6.067, eff. Jan. 1, 2014.

§ 1301.103. Enforceability of Certain Terms

A provision in a management trust created for a ward or incapacitated person that relieves a trustee from a duty or liability imposed by this chapter or Subtitle B, Title 9, Property Code, is enforceable only if:

(1) the provision is limited to specific facts and circumstances unique to the property of that trust and is not applicable generally to the trust; and

(2) the court creating or modifying the trust makes a specific finding that there is clear and convincing evidence that the inclusion of the provision is in the best interests of the trust beneficiary.

Derived from Probate Code § 868(c).

Added by Acts 2011, 82nd Leg., ch. 823, § 1.02, eff. Jan. 1, 2014. Amended by Acts 2013, 83rd Leg., ch. 982, § 32, eff. Jan. 1, 2014.

Subchapter D. Administration of Management Trusts

§ 1301.151. Jurisdiction Over Trust Matters

A court that creates a management trust has the same jurisdiction to hear matters relating to the trust as the court has with respect to guardianship and other matters covered by this title.

Derived from Probate Code § 869C.

Added by Acts 2011, 82nd Leg., ch. 823, § 1.02, eff. Jan. 1, 2014.

§ 1301.152. Court's Authority to Discharge Guardian of Estate

On or at any time after the creation of a management trust, the court may discharge the guardian of the ward's estate if the court determines that the discharge is in the ward's best interests.

Derived from Probate Code § 868A.

Added by Acts 2011, 82nd Leg., ch. 823, § 1.02, eff. Jan. 1, 2014.

§ 1301.153. Investment in Texas Tomorrow Fund

The trustee of a management trust may invest trust funds in the Texas tomorrow fund established by Subchapter F, Chapter 54, Education Code, if the trustee determines that investment is in the best interest of the ward or incapacitated person for whom the trust is created.

Derived from Probate Code § 868(f).

Added by Acts 2011, 82nd Leg., ch. 823, § 1.02, eff. Jan. 1, 2014.

§ 1301.1535. Initial Accounting by Certain Trustees Required

(a) This section applies only to a trustee of a management trust created for a person who [for whom a guardianship proceeding is pending] on the date the trust is created is:

    (1) a ward under an existing guardianship; or

    (2) a proposed ward with respect to whom an application for guardianship has been filed and is pending.

(b) Not later than the 30th day after the date a trustee to which this section applies receives property into the trust, the trustee shall file with the court that created the guardianship or the court in which the application for guardianship was filed [proceeding is pending] a report describing all property held in the trust on the date of the report and specifying the value of the property on that date.

Derived from Probate Code 870A.

Added by Acts 2013, 83rd Leg., ch. 161, § 6.068, eff. Jan. 1, 2014. Amended by Acts 2015, 84th Leg., ch. 1031, § 25, eff. Sept. 1, 2015.

§ 1301.154. Annual Accounting

(a) Except as provided by Subsection (d), the trustee of a management trust shall prepare and file with the court an annual accounting of transactions in the trust in the same manner and form that is required of a guardian of the estate under this title.

(b) The trustee of a management trust created for a ward shall provide a copy of the annual account to the guardian of the ward's estate or person.

(c) The annual account is subject to court review and approval in the same manner that is required of an annual account prepared by a guardian under this title.

(d) The court may not require a trustee of a trust created for a person who has only a physical disability to prepare and file with the court the annual accounting as described by Subsection (a).

Derived from Probate Code § 871.

Added by Acts 2011, 82nd Leg., ch. 823, § 1.02, eff. Jan. 1, 2014. Subsec. (a) amended and (d) added by Acts 2013, 83rd Leg., ch. 161, § 6.069, eff. Jan. 1, 2014. Subsec. (a) amended by Acts 2013, 83rd Leg., ch. 982, § 33, eff. Jan. 1, 2014.

§ 1301.155. Appointment of Successor Trustee

The court may appoint a successor trustee if the trustee of a management trust resigns, becomes ineligible, or is removed.

Derived from Probate Code § 869A.

Added by Acts 2011, 82nd Leg., ch. 823, § 1.02, eff. Jan. 1, 2014.

§ 1301.156. Liability of Certain Persons for Conduct Of Trustee

The guardian of the person or of the estate of a ward for whom a management trust is created or the surety on the guardian's bond is not liable for an act or omission of the trustee of the trust.

Derived from Probate Code § 872.

Added by Acts 2011, 82nd Leg., ch. 823, § 1.02, eff. Jan. 1, 2014.

Subchapter E. Modification, Revocation, or Termination of Management Trusts

§ 1301.201. Modification or Revocation of Trust

(a) The court may modify or revoke a management trust at any time before the date of the trust's termination.

(b) The following may not revoke a management trust:

    (1) the ward for whom the trust is created or the guardian of the ward's estate;

    (2) the incapacitated person for whom the trust is created; or

    (3) the person who has only a physical disability for whom the trust is created.

Derived from Probate Code § 869.

Added by Acts 2011, 82nd Leg., ch. 823, § 1.02, eff. Jan. 1, 2014. Subsection (b) amended by Acts 2013, 83rd Leg., ch. 161, § 6.070, eff. Jan. 1, 2014.

§ 1301.202. Transfer to Pooled Trust Subaccount

(a) If the court determines that it is in the best interests of the person for whom a management trust is created, the court may order the transfer of all property in the management trust to a pooled trust subaccount established in accordance with Chapter 1302.

(a-1) For purposes of a proceeding to determine whether to transfer property from a management trust to a pooled trust subaccount, the court may, but is not required to, appoint an attorney ad litem or guardian ad litem to represent the interests of a person who has only a physical disability for whom the management trust was created.

(b) The transfer of property from the management trust to the pooled trust subaccount shall be treated as a continuation of the management trust and may not be treated as the establishment of a new trust for purposes of 42 U.S.C. Section 1396p(d)(4)(A) or (C) or otherwise for purposes of the management trust beneficiary's eligibility for medical assistance under Chapter 32, Human Resources Code.

(c) The court may not allow termination of the management trust from which property is transferred under this section until all of the property in the management trust has been transferred to the pooled trust subaccount.

Derived from Probate Code § 868C.

Added by Acts 2011, 82nd Leg., ch. 823, § 1.02, eff. Jan. 1, 2014. Subsec. (a-1) added by Acts 2013, 83rd Leg., ch. 982, § 34, eff. Jan. 1, 2014. Subsecs. (a) and (b) amended by Acts 2013, 83rd Leg., ch. 161, § 6.071, eff. Jan. 1, 2014.

§ 1301.203. Termination of Trust

(a) If the person for whom a management trust is created is a minor, the trust terminates on:

(1) the earlier of:

(A) the person's death; or

(B) the person's 18th birthday; or

(2) the date provided by court order, which may not be later than the person's 25th birthday.

(b) If the person for whom a management trust is created is not a minor, the trust terminates:

(1) according to the terms of the trust;

(2) on the date the court determines that continuing the trust is no longer in the person's best interests, subject to Section 1301.202(c); or

(3) on the person's death.

Derived from Probate Code § 870.

Added by Acts 2011, 82nd Leg., ch. 823, § 1.02, eff. Jan. 1, 2014. Amended by Acts 2013, 83rd Leg., ch. 161, § 6.072, eff. Jan. 1, 2014.

§ 1301.204. Distribution of Trust Property

(a) Unless otherwise provided by the court and except as provided by Subsection (b), the trustee of a management trust shall:

(1) prepare a final account in the same form and manner that is required of a guardian under Sections 1204.101 and 1204.102; and

(2) on court approval, distribute the principal or any undistributed income of the trust to:

(A) the ward or incapacitated person when the trust terminates on the trust's own terms;

(B) the successor trustee on appointment of a successor trustee; or

(C) the representative of the deceased ward's or incapacitated person's estate on the ward's or incapacitated person's death.

(b) The court may not require a trustee of a trust created for a person who has only a physical disability to prepare and file with the court a final account as described by Subsection (a)(1). The trustee shall distribute the principal and any undistributed income of the trust in the manner provided by Subsection (a)(2) for a trust the beneficiary of which is a ward or incapacitated person.

Derived from Probate Code § 873.

Added by Acts 2011, 82nd Leg., ch. 823, § 1.02, eff. Jan. 1, 2014. Amended by Acts 2013, 83rd Leg., ch. 161, § 6.073, eff. Jan. 1, 2014.

Chapter 1302. Pooled Trust Subaccounts

Chapter 1302. Pooled Trust Subaccounts

§ 1302.001. Definitions

In this chapter:

(1) "Beneficiary" means a person for whom a subaccount is established.

(2) "Medical assistance" means benefits and services under the medical assistance program administered under Chapter 32, Human Resources Code.

(3) "Pooled trust" means a trust that meets the requirements of 42 U.S.C. Section 1396p(d)(4)(C) for purposes of exempting the trust from the applicability of 42 U.S.C. Section 1396p(d) in determining the eligibility of a person who is disabled for medical assistance.

(4) "Subaccount" means an account in a pooled trust established solely for the benefit of a beneficiary.

Derived from Probate Code § 910.

Added by Acts 2011, 82nd Leg., ch. 823, § 1.02, eff. Jan. 1, 2014.

§ 1302.002. Application to Establish Subaccount

The following persons may apply to the court for the establishment of a subaccount for the benefit of a minor or other incapacitated person, an alleged incapacitated person, or a disabled person who is not an incapacitated person:

(1) the guardian of the incapacitated person;

(2) a person who has filed an application for the appointment of a guardian for the alleged incapacitated person;

(3) an attorney ad litem or guardian ad litem appointed to represent:

(A) the incapacitated person who is a ward or that person's interests; or

(B) the alleged incapacitated person who does not have a guardian; or

(4) the disabled person.

Derived from Probate Code § 911.

Added by Acts 2011, 82nd Leg., ch. 823, § 1.02, eff. Jan. 1, 2014. Amended by Acts 2013, 83rd Leg., ch. 161, § 6.074, eff. Jan. 1, 2014.

§ 1302.003. Appointment of Attorney Ad Litem

(a) The court shall appoint an attorney ad litem for a person who is a minor or has a mental disability and who is the subject of an application under Section 1302.002.

(b) The attorney ad litem is entitled to a reasonable fee and reimbursement of expenses to be paid from the person's property.

Derived from Probate Code § 912.

Added by Acts 2011, 82nd Leg., ch. 823, § 1.02, eff. Jan. 1, 2014.

§ 1302.004. Establishment of Subaccount

If the court finds that it is in the best interests of a person who is the subject of an application under Section 1302.002, the court may order:

(1) the establishment of a subaccount of which the person is the beneficiary; and

(2) the transfer to the subaccount of any of the person's property on hand or accruing to the person.

Derived from Probate Code § 913.

Added by Acts 2011, 82nd Leg., ch. 823, § 1.02, eff. Jan. 1, 2014.

§ 1302.005. Terms of Subaccount

Unless the court orders otherwise, the terms governing the subaccount must provide that:

(1) the subaccount terminates on the earliest of the date of:

(A) the beneficiary's 18th birthday, if the beneficiary is not disabled on that date and was a minor at the time the subaccount was established;

(B) the beneficiary's death; or

(C) a court order terminating the subaccount; and

(2) on termination, any property remaining in the beneficiary's subaccount after making any required payments to satisfy the amounts of medical assistance reimbursement claims for medical assistance provided to the beneficiary under this state's medical assistance program and other states' medical assistance programs shall be distributed to:

(A) the beneficiary, if on the date of termination the beneficiary is living and is not incapacitated;

(B) the beneficiary's guardian, if on the date of termination the beneficiary is living and is incapacitated; or

(C) the personal representative of the beneficiary's estate, if on the date of termination the beneficiary is deceased.

Derived from Probate Code § 914.

Added by Acts 2011, 82nd Leg., ch. 823, § 1.02, eff. Jan. 1, 2014.

§ 1302.006. Fees and Reporting

(a) The manager or trustee of a pooled trust may:

(1) assess fees against a subaccount of that pooled trust that is established under this chapter, in accordance with the manager's or trustee's standard fee structure; and

(2) pay fees assessed under Subdivision (1) from the subaccount.

(b) If required by the court, the manager or trustee of the pooled trust shall file a copy of the annual report of account with the court clerk.

Derived from Probate Code § 916.

Added by Acts 2011, 82nd Leg., ch. 823, § 1.02, eff. Jan. 1, 2014.

§ 1302.007. Jurisdiction Exclusive

Notwithstanding any other law, the court that orders the establishment of a subaccount for a beneficiary has exclusive jurisdiction of a subsequent proceeding or action that relates to both the beneficiary and the subaccount, and the proceeding or action may be brought only in that court.

Derived from Probate Code § 915.

Added by Acts 2011, 82nd Leg., ch. 823, § 1.02, eff. Jan. 1, 2014.

SUBTITLE I. OTHER SPECIAL PROCEEDINGS AND SUBSTITUTES FOR [ALTERNATIVES TO] GUARDIANSHIP

Chapter 1351. Sale of Property of Certain Incapacitated Persons

Subchapter A. Sale of Minor's Interest in Property Without Guardianship

Subchapter B. Sale of Ward's Property Without Guardianship of the Estate

§ 1351.057. Disaffirmation of Sale Prohibited

Chapter 1351. Sale of Property of Certain Incapacitated Persons

Subchapter A. Sale of Minor's Interest in Property Without Guardianship

§ 1351.001. Authority to Sell Minor's Interest in Property Without Guardianship

(a) A parent or managing conservator of a minor who is not a ward may apply to the court under this subchapter for an order to sell an interest of the minor in property without being appointed guardian if the net value of the interest does not exceed $100,000.

(b) If a minor who is not a ward does not have a parent or managing conservator willing or able to file an application under Subsection (a), the court may appoint an attorney ad litem or guardian ad litem to act on the minor's behalf for the limited purpose of applying for an order to sell the minor's interest in property under this subchapter.

Derived from Probate Code § 889(a).

Added by Acts 2011, 82nd Leg., ch. 823, § 1.02, eff. Jan. 1, 2014. Amended by Acts 2015, 84th Leg., ch. 1031, § 26, eff. Sept. 1, 2015.

§ 1351.002. Application; Venue

(a) A parent, [or] managing conservator, or attorney ad litem or guardian ad litem appointed under Section 1351.001(b) shall apply to the court under oath for the sale of property under this subchapter.

(b) An application must contain:

(1) the minor's name;

(2) a legal description of the real property or a description that identifies the personal property, as applicable;

(3) the minor's interest in the property;

(4) the purchaser's name;

(5) a statement that the sale of the minor's interest in the property is for cash; and

(6) a statement that all money received from the sale of the minor's interest in the property [by the parent or managing conservator] shall be used for the minor's use and benefit.

(c) Venue for the application is the same as venue for an application for the appointment of a guardian for a minor.

Derived from Probate Code § 889(b).

Added by Acts 2011, 82nd Leg., ch. 823, § 1.02, eff. Jan. 1, 2014. Subsecs (a) & (b) amended by Acts 2015, 84th Leg., ch. 1031, § 27, eff. Sept. 1, 2015.

§ 1351.003. Hearing; Requirements for Sale

(a) On receipt of an application under this subchapter, the court shall set the application for hearing on a date not earlier than five days from the date the application was filed.

(b) The court may cause citation to be issued if the court considers citation necessary.

(c) At the time of the hearing, the court shall order the sale of the property if the court is satisfied from the evidence that the sale is in the minor's best interests. The court may require an independent appraisal of the property to be sold to establish the minimum sale price.

Derived from Probate Code §§ 889(c), (d).

Added by Acts 2011, 82nd Leg., ch. 823, § 1.02, eff. Jan. 1, 2014.

§ 1351.004. Payment of Sale Proceeds into Court Registry

If the court enters an order of sale of property as provided by this subchapter, the purchaser of the property shall pay the proceeds of the sale belonging to the minor into the court registry.

Derived from Probate Code § 889(e).

Added by Acts 2011, 82nd Leg., ch. 823, § 1.02, eff. Jan. 1, 2014.

§ 1351.005. Withdrawal of Sale Proceeds from Registry Not Prohibited

This subchapter does not prevent the sale proceeds deposited into the court registry under Section 1351.004 from being withdrawn from the court registry under Chapter 1355.

Derived from Probate Code § 889(f).

Added by Acts 2011, 82nd Leg., ch. 823, § 1.02, eff. Jan. 1, 2014.

§ 1351.006. Disaffirmation of Sale Prohibited

A minor may not disaffirm a sale of property made in accordance with a court order under this subchapter.

Derived from Probate Code § 889(a).

Added by Acts 2011, 82nd Leg., ch. 823, § 1.02, eff. Jan. 1, 2014.

Subchapter B. Sale of Ward's Property Without Guardianship of the Estate

§ 1351.051. Applicability of Subchapter

This subchapter applies only to a ward who has:

(1) a guardian of the person but does not have a guardian of the estate; or

(2) a guardian of the person or estate appointed by a foreign court.

Derived from Probate Code § 890(a).

Added by Acts 2011, 82nd Leg., ch. 823, § 1.02, eff. Jan. 1, 2014. Amended by Acts 2015, 84th Leg., ch. 1031, § 28, eff. Sept. 1, 2015.

§ 1351.052. Authority to Sell Ward's Interest in Property Without Appointment as Guardian of the Estate <u>in This State</u>

A guardian of the person of a ward <u>or a guardian of the person or estate of a ward appointed by a foreign court</u> may apply to the court under this subchapter for an order to sell an interest in property in the ward's estate without being appointed guardian of the ward's estate <u>in this state</u> if the net value of the interest does not exceed $100,000.

Derived from Probate Code § 890(b).

Added by Acts 2011, 82nd Leg., ch. 823, § 1.02, eff. Jan. 1, 2014. Amended by Acts 2015, 84th Leg., ch. 1031, § 29, eff. Sept. 1, 2015.

§ 1351.053. Application; Venue

(a) An application under this subchapter must:

(1) be under oath; and

(2) contain the information required by Section 1351.002(b).

(b) For purposes of Subsection (a)(2), references in Section 1351.002(b) to[:

[(1)] "minor" are replaced with references to "ward." [~~"ward"; and~~

~~(2) "parent or managing conservator" are replaced with references to "guardian of the person."~~

(c) Venue for the application is the same as venue for an application for the appointment of a guardian for the ward.

Derived from Probate Code § 890(b), (c).

Added by Acts 2011, 82nd Leg., ch. 823, § 1.02, eff. Jan. 1, 2014. Amended by Acts 2015, 84th Leg., ch. 1031, § 30, eff. Sept. 1, 2015.

§ 1351.054. Hearing

(a) On receipt of an application under this subchapter, the court shall set the application for hearing on a date not earlier than five days from the date the application was filed.

(b) The court may cause citation to be issued if the court considers citation necessary.

(c) The procedures and evidentiary requirements for the hearing are the same as the procedures and evidentiary requirements for a hearing of an application filed under Subchapter A.

Derived from Probate Code §§ 890(d), (e).

Added by Acts 2011, 82nd Leg., ch. 823, § 1.02, eff. Jan. 1, 2014.

§ 1351.055. Payment of Sale Proceeds into Court Registry

If the court enters an order of sale of property as provided by this subchapter, the purchaser of the property shall pay the proceeds of the sale belonging to the ward into the court registry.

Derived from Probate Code § 890(f).

Added by Acts 2011, 82nd Leg., ch. 823, § 1.02, eff.

Jan. 1, 2014.

§ 1351.056. Withdrawal of Sale Proceeds from Registry Not Prohibited

This subchapter does not prevent the sale proceeds deposited into the court registry under Section 1351.055 from being withdrawn from the court registry under Chapter 1355.

Derived from Probate Code § 890(g).

Added by Acts 2011, 82nd Leg., ch. 823, § 1.02, eff. Jan. 1, 2014.

§ 1351.057. Disaffirmation of Sale Prohibited

A ward may not disaffirm a sale of property made in accordance with a court order under this subchapter.

Derived from Probate Code § 890(b).

Added by Acts 2011, 82nd Leg., ch. 823, § 1.02, eff. Jan. 1, 2014.

Chapter 1352. Mortgage of Minor's Interest in Residence Homestead

Subchapter A. General Provisions

Subchapter B. Mortgage of Minor's Interest Without Guardianship

Subchapter C. Mortgage of Minor Ward's Interest Without Guardianship of the Estate

§ 1352.108. Disaffirmation of Home Equity Loan Prohibited

Chapter 1352. Mortgage of Minor's Interest in Residence Homestead

Subchapter A. General Provisions

§ 1352.001. Definitions

In this chapter:

(1) "Home equity loan" means a loan made under Section 50(a)(6), Article XVI, Texas Constitution.

(2) "Residence homestead" has the meaning assigned by Section 11.13, Tax Code.

Derived from Probate Code §§ 889A(a), 890A(a).

Added by Acts 2011, 82nd Leg., ch. 823, § 1.02. eff. Jan. 1, 2014.

Subchapter B. Mortgage of Minor's Interest Without Guardianship

§ 1352.051. Applicability of Subchapter

This subchapter applies only to a minor who:

(1) is not a ward; and

(2) has an interest in a residence homestead.

Derived from Probate Code § 889A(b).

Added by Acts 2011, 82nd Leg., ch. 823, § 1.02, eff. Jan. 1, 2014.

§ 1352.052. Authority to Mortgage Minor's Interest Without Guardianship

(a) If the net value of a minor's interest in a residence homestead does not exceed $100,000, a parent, subject to Subsection (b), or managing conservator of the minor may apply to the court under this subchapter for an order authorizing the parent or managing conservator to receive on the minor's behalf, without being appointed guardian, an extension of credit that is secured wholly or partly by a lien on the homestead.

(b) A parent of a minor may file an application under this subchapter only if the parent has a homestead interest in the property that is the subject of the application.

Derived from Probate Code §§ 889A(b), (j).

Added by Acts 2011, 82nd Leg., ch. 823, § 1.02, eff. Jan. 1, 2014.

§ 1352.053. Application; Venue

(a) A parent or managing conservator shall apply to the court under oath for the authority to encumber the residence homestead as provided by this subchapter.

(b) The application must contain:

(1) the minor's name and address;

(2) a legal description of the property constituting the homestead;

(3) a description of the minor's ownership interest in the property constituting the homestead;

(4) the fair market value of the property constituting the homestead;

(5) the amount of the home equity loan;

(6) the purpose or purposes for which the home equity loan is being sought;

(7) a detailed description of the proposed expenditure of the loan proceeds to be received by the parent or managing conservator on the minor's behalf; and

(8) a statement that all loan proceeds received by the parent or managing conservator on the minor's behalf through a home equity loan authorized under this subchapter shall be used in a manner that is for the minor's benefit.

(c) Venue for the application is the same as venue for an application for the appointment of a guardian for a minor.

Derived from Probate Code § 889A(c).

Added by Acts 2011, 82nd Leg., ch. 823, § 1.02, eff. Jan. 1, 2014.

§ 1352.054. Hearing; Requirements to Mortgage Minor's Interest

(a) On receipt of an application under this subchapter, the court shall set the application for hearing on a date not earlier than the fifth day after the date the application is filed.

(b) The court may cause citation to be issued if the court considers citation necessary.

(c) At the time of the hearing, the court, on approval of the surety bond required by Section 1352.055, shall authorize the parent or managing conservator to receive the extension of credit sought in the application if the court is satisfied from a preponderance of the evidence that the encumbrance is:

(1) for a purpose described by Section 1352.056(1) or (2); and

(2) in the minor's best interests.

Derived from Probate Code §§ 889A(d), (f).

Added by Acts 2011, 82nd Leg., ch. 823, § 1.02. eff. Jan. 1, 2014.

§ 1352.055. Surety Bond; Discharge of Sureties

(a) Before a hearing under Section 1352.054 is held, the parent or managing conservator shall file with the county clerk a surety bond. The bond must be:

(1) in an amount at least equal to two times the amount of the proposed home equity loan;

(2) payable to and approved by the court; and

(3) conditioned on the parent or managing conservator:

(A) using the proceeds of the home equity loan attributable to the minor's interest solely for the purposes authorized by Section 1352.056; and

(B) making payments on the minor's behalf toward the outstanding balance of the home equity loan.

(b) After the first anniversary of the date a parent or managing conservator executes a home equity loan authorized under this subchapter, the court may, on motion of the borrower, reduce the amount of the surety bond required under this section to an amount that is not less than the loan's outstanding balance.

(c) The court may not discharge the person's sureties from all further liability under a surety bond until the court:

(1) approves the filing of the parent's or managing conservator's reports required under Sections 1352.057 and 1352.058;

(2) finds that the parent or managing conservator used loan proceeds resulting from the minor's interest solely for the purposes authorized by Section 1352.056; and

(3) is presented with satisfactory evidence that the home equity loan has been repaid and is no longer considered an outstanding obligation.

Derived from Probate Code § 889A(e), (h), (i).

Added by Acts 2011, 82nd Leg., ch. 823, § 1.02, eff. Jan. 1, 2014.

§ 1352.056. Use Of Proceeds

Proceeds of a home equity loan that is the subject of an application under Section 1352.053 that are attributable to the minor's interest may be spent only to:

(1) make improvements to the homestead;

(2) pay for the minor's education or medical expenses; or

(3) pay the loan's outstanding balance.

Derived from Probate Code § 889A(b).

Added by Acts 2011, 82nd Leg., ch. 823, § 1.02, eff. Jan. 1, 2014.

§ 1352.057. Annual Report

A parent or managing conservator executing a home equity loan on a minor's behalf under this subchapter shall file an annual report with the court regarding the transaction.

Derived from Probate Code § 889A(g).

Added by Acts 2011, 82nd Leg., ch. 823, § 1.02, eff. Jan. 1, 2014.

§ 1352.058. Sworn Report of Expenditures

When the parent or managing conservator has spent the proceeds of a home equity loan authorized under this subchapter, the parent or managing conservator shall file with the county clerk a sworn report accounting for the proceeds.

Derived from Probate Code § 889A(g).

Added by Acts 2011, 82nd Leg., ch. 823, § 1.02, eff. Jan. 1, 2014.

§ 1352.059. Disaffirmation of Home Equity Loan Prohibited

A minor may not disaffirm a home equity loan authorized by the court under this subchapter.

Derived from Probate Code § 889A(k).

Added by Acts 2011, 82nd Leg., ch. 823, § 1.02, eff. Jan. 1, 2014.

Subchapter C. Mortgage of Minor Ward's Interest Without Guardianship of the Estate

§ 1352.101. Applicability of Subchapter

This subchapter applies only to a minor ward who:

(1) has a guardian of the person but does not have a guardian of the estate; and

(2) has an interest in a residence homestead.

Derived from Probate Code § 890A(b), (c).

Added by Acts 2011, 82nd Leg., ch. 823, § 1.02, eff. Jan. 1, 2014.

§ 1352.102. Authority to Mortgage Minor Ward's Interest Without Guardianship of the Estate

If the net value of a minor ward's interest in a residence homestead does not exceed $100,000, the guardian of the person of the ward may apply to the court under this subchapter for an order authorizing the guardian to receive on the ward's behalf an extension of credit that is secured wholly or partly by a lien on the homestead.

Derived from Probate Code § 890A(c).

Added by Acts 2011, 82nd Leg., ch. 823, § 1.02, eff. Jan. 1, 2014.

§ 1352.103. Application; Venue

(a) An application under this subchapter must contain the information required by Section 1352.053(b).

(b) For purposes of Subsection (a), references in Section 1352.053(b) to "parent or managing conservator" are replaced with references to "guardian of the person."

(c) Venue for the application is the same as venue for an application for the appointment of a guardian for a ward.

Derived from Probate Code § 890A(d).

Added by Acts 2011, 82nd Leg., ch. 823, § 1.02, eff. Jan. 1, 2014.

§ 1352.104. Hearing; Requirements to Mortgage Minor Ward's Interest

(a) On receipt of an application under this subchapter, the court shall set the application for hearing on a date not earlier than the fifth day after the date the application is filed.

(b) The court may cause citation to be issued if the court considers citation necessary.

(c) The procedures and evidentiary requirements for a hearing of an application filed under this subchapter are the same as the procedures and evidentiary requirements for a hearing of an application filed under Subchapter B.

(d) At the time of the hearing, the court, on approval of the surety bond required by Section 1352.105, shall authorize the guardian to receive the extension of credit sought in the application if the court is satisfied from a preponderance of the evidence that the encumbrance is:

(1) for a purpose described by Section 1352.106(1) or (2); and

(2) in the minor ward's best interests.

Derived from Probate Code § 890A(e), (g), (h).

Added by Acts 2011, 82nd Leg., ch. 823, § 1.02, eff. Jan. 1, 2014.

§ 1352.105. Surety Bond; Discharge of Sureties

(a) Before a hearing under Section 1352.104 is held, the guardian of the person shall file a surety bond with the county clerk to the same extent and in the same manner as a parent or managing conservator of a minor is required to file a surety bond under Section 1352.055.

(b) The court may not discharge the guardian's sureties from all further liability under a bond required by this section or another provision of this title until the court:

(1) finds that the guardian used loan proceeds resulting from the minor ward's interest solely for the purposes authorized by Section 1352.106; and

(2) is presented with satisfactory evidence that the home equity loan has been repaid and is no longer considered an outstanding obligation.

Derived from Probate Code § 890A(f), (j).

Added by Acts 2011, 82nd Leg., ch. 823, § 1.02, eff. Jan. 1, 2014.

§ 1352.106. Use Of Proceeds

Proceeds of a home equity loan that is the subject of an application under Section 1352.102 that are attributable to the minor ward's interest may be spent only to:

(1) make improvements to the homestead;

(2) pay for the ward's education or maintenance expenses; or

(3) pay the loan's outstanding balance.

Derived from Probate Code § 890A(c).

Added by Acts 2011, 82nd Leg., ch. 823, § 1.02, eff. Jan. 1, 2014.

§ 1352.107. Annual Accounting

A guardian of the person executing a home equity loan on a minor ward's behalf must account for the transaction, including the expenditure of the loan proceeds, in the annual account required by Subchapter A, Chapter 1163.

Derived from Probate Code § 890A(i).

Added by Acts 2011, 82nd Leg., ch. 823, § 1.02, eff.

Jan. 1, 2014.

§ 1352.108. Disaffirmation of Home Equity Loan Prohibited

A minor ward may not disaffirm a home equity loan authorized by the court under this subchapter.

Derived from Probate Code § 890A(k).

Added by Acts 2011, 82nd Leg., ch. 823, § 1.02, eff. Jan. 1, 2014.

Chapter 1353. Management and Control of Incapacitated Spouse's Property

Subchapter A. Appointment of Community Administrator or Guardian of the Estate

Subchapter B. Duties of Community Administrators and Guardians of the Estate

Subchapter C. Removal or Termination of Powers of Community Administrator

Subchapter D. Appointment of Attorney Ad Litem

Chapter 1353. Management and Control of Incapacitated Spouse's Property

Subchapter A. Appointment of Community Administrator or Guardian of the Estate

§ 1353.001. Effect of Subchapter

(a) The manner in which community property is administered under this subchapter does not affect:

(1) the duties and obligations between spouses, including the duty to support the other spouse; and

(2) the rights of any creditor of either spouse.

(b) This subchapter does not partition community property between an incapacitated spouse and a spouse who is not incapacitated.

Derived from Probate Code § 883(e), (f).

Added by Acts 2011, 82nd Leg., ch. 823, § 1.02, eff. Jan. 1, 2014.

§ 1353.002. Spouse as Community Administrator

(a) Except as provided by Section 1353.004, when a spouse is judicially declared to be incapacitated, the other spouse, in the capacity of surviving partner of the marital partnership, acquires full power to manage, control, and dispose of the entire community estate, including the part of the community estate that the incapacitated spouse legally has the power to manage in the absence of the incapacity, as community administrator without an administration.

(b) The spouse who is not incapacitated is presumed to be suitable and qualified to serve as community administrator.

Derived from Probate Code § 883(a), (b).

Added by Acts 2011, 82nd Leg., ch. 823, § 1.02, eff. Jan. 1, 2014.

§ 1353.003. Appointment of Guardian of the Estate to Administer Separate Property

(a) Except as provided by Section 1353.004, when a spouse who owns separate property is judicially declared to be incapacitated, the court shall appoint the other spouse or another person or entity, in the order of precedence established under Subchapter C, Chapter 1104, as guardian of the estate to administer only the separate property of the incapacitated spouse.

(b) The qualification of a guardian of the estate of the separate property of an incapacitated spouse under Subsection (a) does not deprive the spouse who is not incapacitated of the right to manage, control, and dispose of the entire community estate as provided by this title.

Derived from Probate Code § 883(a), (b).

Added by Acts 2011, 82nd Leg., ch. 823, § 1.02, eff. Jan. 1, 2014.

§ 1353.004. Appointment of Guardian of the Estate Under Certain Circumstances

(a) This section applies only if:

(1) a spouse who is not incapacitated is removed as community administrator; or

(2) the court finds that the spouse who is not incapacitated:

(A) would be disqualified to serve as guardian under Subchapter H, Chapter 1104; or

(B) is not suitable to serve as the community administrator for any other reason.

(b) The court shall appoint a guardian of the estate for the incapacitated spouse if the court:

(1) has not appointed a guardian of the estate under Section 1353.003(a); or

(2) has appointed the spouse who is not incapacitated as the guardian of the estate under Section 1353.003(a).

(c) After considering the financial circumstances of the spouses and any other relevant factors, the court may order the spouse who is not incapacitated to deliver to the guardian of the estate of the incapacitated spouse not more than one-half of the community property that is subject to the spouses' joint management, control, and disposition under Section 3.102, Family Code.

(d) The court shall authorize the guardian of the estate of the incapacitated spouse to administer:

(1) any separate property of the incapacitated spouse;

(2) any community property that is subject to the incapacitated spouse's sole management, control, and disposition under Section 3.102, Family Code;

(3) any community property delivered to the guardian of the estate under Subsection (c); and

(4) any income earned on property described by this section.

(e) Community property administered by a guardian of the estate under Subsection (d) is considered the incapacitated spouse's community property, subject to the incapacitated spouse's sole management, control, and disposition under Section 3.102, Family Code.

Derived from Probate Code § 883(c), (g).

Added by Acts 2011, 82nd Leg., ch. 823, § 1.02, eff. Jan. 1, 2014.

§ 1353.005. Administration of Certain Property by Non-Incapacitated Spouse

(a) On a person's removal as community administrator or on qualification of a guardian of the estate of the person's incapacitated spouse under Section 1353.004, as appropriate, a spouse who is not incapacitated shall continue to administer:

(1) the person's own separate property;

(2) any community property that is subject to the person's sole management, control, and disposition under Section 3.102, Family Code;

(3) either:

(A) any community property subject to the spouses' joint management, control, and disposition under Section 3.102, Family Code; or

(B) if the person is required to deliver a portion of that community property described by Paragraph (A) to the guardian of the estate of the person's incapacitated spouse under Section 1353.004(c), only the portion of the community property remaining after delivery; and

(4) any income earned on property described by this section the person is authorized to administer.

(b) Community property administered under this section by a spouse who is not incapacitated is considered that spouse's community property, subject to that spouse's sole management, control, and disposition under Section 3.102, Family Code.

Derived from Probate Code § 883(d), (g).

Added by Acts 2011, 82nd Leg., ch. 823, § 1.02, eff. Jan. 1, 2014.

§ 1353.006. Effect of Court Order on Creditors' Claims

A court order that directs the administration of community property under Section 1353.004 or 1353.005 does not affect the enforceability of a creditor's claim existing on the date the court renders the order.

Derived from Probate Code § 883(h).

Added by Acts 2011, 82nd Leg., ch. 823, § 1.02, eff. Jan. 1, 2014.

Subchapter B. Duties of Community Administrators and Guardians of the Estate

§ 1353.051. Inventory and Appraisement by Community Administrator

(a) On its own motion or on the motion of an interested person for good cause shown, the court may order a community administrator to file a verified, full, and detailed inventory and appraisement of:

(1) any community property that is subject to the incapacitated spouse's sole management, control, and disposition under Section 3.102, Family Code;

(2) any community property subject to the spouses' joint management, control, and disposition under Section 3.102, Family Code; and

(3) any income earned on property described by this subsection.

(b) An inventory and appraisement ordered under this section must be:

(1) prepared in the same form and manner that is required of a guardian under Section 1154.051; and

(2) filed not later than the 90th day after the date the order is issued.

Derived from Probate Code § 883B(a), (c).

Added by Acts 2011, 82nd Leg., ch. 823, § 1.02, eff. Jan. 1, 2014.

§ 1353.052. Account by Community Administrator

(a) At any time after the expiration of 15 months after the date a community administrator's spouse is judicially declared to be incapacitated, the court, on its own motion or on the motion of an interested person for good cause shown, may order the community administrator to prepare and file an account of:

(1) any community property that is subject to the incapacitated spouse's sole management, control, and disposition under Section 3.102, Family Code;

(2) any community property subject to the spouses' joint management, control, and disposition under Section 3.102, Family Code; and

(3) any income earned on property described by this subsection.

(b) An account ordered under Subsection (a) must be:

(1) prepared in the same form and manner that is required of a guardian under Subchapter A, Chapter 1163, except that the community administrator is not required to file the account annually with the county clerk; and

(2) filed not later than the 60th day after the date the order is issued.

(c) After an initial account has been filed by a community administrator under this section, the court, on the motion of an interested person for good cause shown, may order the community administrator to file subsequent periodic accounts at intervals of not less than 12 months.

Derived from Probate Code § 883B(b), (d), (e).

Added by Acts 2011, 82nd Leg., ch. 823, § 1.02, eff. Jan. 1, 2014.

§ 1353.053. Disclosure of Certain Lawsuits to the Court by Community Administrator

A person whose spouse is judicially declared to be incapacitated and who acquires the power to manage, control, and dispose of the entire community estate under Section 1353.002(a) shall inform the court in writing of any suit filed by or on behalf of the person that:

(1) is a suit for dissolution of the marriage of the person and the person's incapacitated spouse; or

(2) names the incapacitated spouse as a defendant.

Derived from Probate Code § 884A.

Added by Acts 2011, 82nd Leg., ch. 823, § 1.02, eff. Jan. 1, 2014.

§ 1353.054. Delivery of Community Property by Guardian of the Estate to Community Administrator

A guardian of the estate of an incapacitated married person who, as guardian, is administering community property as part of the ward's estate, shall deliver on demand the community property to the spouse who is not incapacitated if the spouse becomes community administrator under Section 1353.002(a).

Derived from Probate Code § 884.

Added by Acts 2011, 82nd Leg., ch. 823, § 1.02, eff. Jan. 1, 2014.

Subchapter C. Removal or Termination of Powers of Community Administrator

§ 1353.101. Grounds for Removal of Community Administrator

A court may remove a community administrator if:

(1) the community administrator fails to comply with a court order for:

(A) an inventory and appraisement under Section 1353.051; or

(B) an account or subsequent account under Section 1353.052;

(2) sufficient grounds appear to support belief that the community administrator has misapplied or embezzled, or is about to misapply or embezzle, all or part of the property committed to the community administrator's care;

(3) the community administrator is proved to have been guilty of gross misconduct or gross mismanagement in the performance of duties as community administrator; or

(4) the community administrator:

(A) becomes an incapacitated person;

(B) is sentenced to the penitentiary; or

(C) for any other reason becomes legally incapacitated from properly performing the community administrator's fiduciary duties.

Derived from Probate Code § 883C(A).

Added by Acts 2011, 82nd Leg., ch. 823, § 1.02, eff. Jan. 1, 2014.

§ 1353.102. Procedure for Removal of Community Administrator

(a) A court may remove a community administrator on the court's own motion or on the motion of an interested person, after the community administrator has been cited by personal service to answer at a time and place specified in the notice.

(b) The removal order must:

(1) state the cause of removal; and

(2) direct the disposition of the assets remaining in the name or under the control of the removed community administrator.

(c) A community administrator who defends an action for the removal of the community administrator in good faith, regardless of whether successful, is entitled to recover from the incapacitated spouse's part of the community estate the community administrator's necessary expenses and disbursements in the removal proceedings, including reasonable attorney's fees.

Derived from Probate Code § 883C(a), (b), (c).

Added by Acts 2011, 82nd Leg., ch. 823, § 1.02, eff. Jan. 1, 2014.

§ 1353.103. Termination of Community Administrator's Powers on Recovery of Capacity

The special powers of management, control, and disposition vested in the community administrator by this title terminate when a court of competent jurisdiction by decree finds that the mental capacity of the incapacitated spouse has been recovered.

Derived from Probate Code § 883A.

Added by Acts 2011, 82nd Leg., ch. 823, § 1.02, eff. Jan. 1, 2014.

Subchapter D. Appointment of Attorney Ad Litem

§ 1353.151. Appointment of Attorney Ad Litem for Incapacitated Spouse

(a) The court shall appoint an attorney ad litem to represent the interests of an incapacitated spouse in a proceeding to remove a community administrator or other proceeding brought under this chapter.

(b) The attorney ad litem may demand from the community administrator an account or inventory and appraisement of the incapacitated spouse's part of the community estate being managed by the community administrator.

(c) A community administrator shall comply with a demand made under this section not later than the 60th day after the date the community administrator receives the demand.

(d) An account or inventory and appraisement returned under this section must be prepared in the form and manner required by the attorney ad litem. The attorney ad litem may require the community administrator to file the account or inventory and appraisement with the court.

Derived from Probate Code § 883D.

Added by Acts 2011, 82nd Leg., ch. 823, § 1.02, eff. Jan. 1, 2014.

Chapter 1354. Receivership for Estates of Certain Incapacitated Persons

§ 1354.009. Record

Chapter 1354. Receivership for Estates of Certain Incapacitated Persons

§ 1354.001. Appointment of Receiver

(a) A judge of a probate court in the county in which an incapacitated person resides or in which the incapacitated person's endangered estate is located shall, with or without application, enter an order appointing a suitable person as receiver to take charge of the estate if:

(1) it appears that all or part of the estate of the incapacitated person is in danger of injury, loss, or waste and in need of a guardianship or other representative;

(2) there is no guardian of the estate who is qualified in this state; and

(3) a guardian is not needed.

(b) The court order must specify the duties and powers of the receiver the judge considers necessary for the protection, conservation, and preservation of the estate.

(c) The clerk shall enter an order issued under this section in the judge's guardianship docket.

Derived from Probate Code § 885(a).

Added by Acts 2011, 82nd Leg., ch. 823, § 1.02, eff. Jan. 1, 2014.

§ 1354.002. Bond

(a) A court order issued under Section 1354.001 shall require a receiver appointed under that section to give a bond, as in ordinary receiverships, in an amount the judge considers necessary to protect the estate.

(b) The person appointed as receiver shall:

(1) make and submit a bond for the judge's approval; and

(2) file the bond, when approved, with the clerk.

Derived from Probate Code § 885(a).

Added by Acts 2011, 82nd Leg., ch. 823, § 1.02, eff. Jan. 1, 2014.

§ 1354.003. Powers and Duties of Receiver

The person appointed as receiver shall take charge of the endangered estate as provided by the powers and duties vested in the person by the order of appointment and subsequent orders of the judge.

Derived from Probate Code § 885(a).

Added by Acts 2011, 82nd Leg., ch. 823, § 1.02, eff. Jan. 1, 2014.

§ 1354.004. Expenditures by Receiver

(a) If, while the receivership is pending, the needs of the incapacitated person require the use of the income or corpus of the estate for the education, clothing, or subsistence of the person, the judge shall, with or without application, enter an order in the judge's guardianship docket that appropriates an amount of income or corpus sufficient for that purpose.

(b) The receiver shall use the amount appropriated by the court to pay a claim for the education, clothing, or subsistence of the incapacitated person that is presented to the judge for approval and ordered by the judge to be paid.

Derived from Probate Code § 885(b).

Added by Acts 2011, 82nd Leg., ch. 823, § 1.02, eff. Jan. 1, 2014.

§ 1354.005. Use of Excess Estate Assets

(a) A receiver who, while the receivership is pending, has possession of an amount of money belonging to the incapacitated person in excess of the amount needed for current necessities and expenses may, under direction of the judge, invest, lend, or contribute all or part of the excess money in the manner, for the security, and on the terms provided by this title for investments, loans, or contributions by guardians.

(b) The receiver shall report to the judge all transactions made under this section in the same manner that a report is required of a guardian under this title.

Derived from Probate Code § 885(c).

Added by Acts 2011, 82nd Leg., ch. 823, § 1.02, eff. Jan. 1, 2014.

§ 1354.006. Receiver's Expenses, Account, and Compensation

(a) All necessary expenses incurred by a receiver in administering the estate may be reported monthly to the judge in the form of a sworn statement of account that includes a report of:

(1) the receiver's acts;

(2) the condition of the estate;

(3) the status of the threatened danger to the estate; and

(4) the progress made toward abatement of the danger.

(b) If the judge is satisfied that the statement is correct and reasonable in all respects, the judge shall promptly enter an order approving the expenses and authorizing reimbursement of the receiver from the estate funds in the receiver's possession.

(c) A receiver shall be compensated for services provided in the receiver's official capacity in the same manner and amount provided by this title for similar services provided by a guardian of an estate.

Derived from Probate Code § 885(d).

Added by Acts 2011, 82nd Leg., ch. 823, § 1.02, eff. Jan. 1, 2014.

§ 1354.007. Closing Receivership; Notice

(a) When the threatened danger has abated and the estate is no longer liable to injury, loss, or waste because there is no guardian or other representative of the estate, the receiver shall:

(1) report to the judge; and

(2) file with the clerk a full and final sworn account of:

(A) all property of the estate received by the receiver;

(B) all property of the estate in the receiver's possession while the receivership was pending;

(C) all sums paid out;

(D) all acts performed by the receiver with respect to the estate; and

(E) all property of the estate remaining in the receiver's possession on the date of the report.

(b) On the filing of the report, the clerk shall:

(1) issue and cause to be posted a notice to all persons interested in the welfare of the incapacitated person; and

(2) give personal notice to the person who has custody of the incapacitated person to appear before the judge at a time and place specified in the notice and contest the report and account if the person desires.

Derived from Probate Code § 885(e).

Added by Acts 2011, 82nd Leg., ch. 823, § 1.02, eff. Jan. 1, 2014.

§ 1354.008. Discharge of Receiver

(a) If, on hearing the receiver's report and account, the judge is satisfied that the danger of injury, loss, or waste to the estate has abated and that the report and account are correct, the judge shall:

(1) enter an order finding that the danger of injury, loss, or waste to the estate has abated; and

(2) direct the receiver to deliver the estate to:

(A) the person from whom the receiver took possession as receiver;

(B) the person who has custody of the incapacitated person; or

(C) another person the judge finds is entitled to possession of the estate.

(b) A person who receives the estate under Subsection (a) shall execute and file with the clerk an appropriate receipt for the estate that is delivered to the person.

(c) The judge's order shall discharge the receivership and the sureties on the receiver's bond.

(d) If the judge is not satisfied that the danger has abated, or is not satisfied with the receiver's report and account, the judge shall enter an order continuing the receivership in effect until the judge is satisfied that the danger has abated or is satisfied with the report and account.

Derived from Probate Code § 885(f).

Added by Acts 2011, 82nd Leg., ch. 823, § 1.02, eff. Jan. 1, 2014.

§ 1354.009. Record

An order, bond, report, account, or notice in a receivership proceeding must be recorded in the judge's guardianship docket.

Derived from Probate Code § 885(g).

Added by Acts 2011, 82nd Leg., ch. 823, § 1.02, eff. Jan. 1, 2014.

Chapter 1355. Payment of Certain Claims Without Guardianship

Subchapter A. Payment of Claims to Certain Incapacitated Persons and Former Wards

Subchapter B. Administration of Money

Subchapter C. Withdrawal of Money

Subchapter D. Use of Money by Eleemosynary Institution for Benefit of Resident

Chapter 1355. Payment of Certain Claims Without Guardianship

Subchapter A. Payment of Claims to Certain Incapacitated Persons and Former Wards

§ 1355.001. Payment of Claims to Resident Creditor

(a) In this section, "resident creditor" means a person who:

(1) is a resident of this state; and

(2) is entitled to money in an amount that is $100,000 or less, the right to which is liquidated and is uncontested in any pending lawsuit.

(b) This section applies only to a resident creditor who:

(1) is an incapacitated person or the former ward of a guardianship terminated under Chapter 1204; and

(2) does not have a legal guardian of the creditor's estate.

(c) A debtor who owes money to a resident creditor to whom this section applies may pay the money to the county clerk of the county in which the creditor resides to the account of the creditor. When making a payment under this subsection, a debtor shall give to the clerk:

(1) the creditor's name;

(2) the creditor's social security identification number;

(3) the nature of the creditor's disability;

(4) the creditor's post office address; and

(5) if the creditor is a minor, the creditor's age.

(d) The receipt for the money signed by the county clerk is binding on the resident creditor as of the date of receipt and to the extent of the payment.

(e) The county clerk shall:

(1) by letter mailed to the address given under Subsection (c)(4), apprise the resident creditor that the deposit was made; and

(2) on receipt of the payment, bring the payment to the court's attention.

Derived from Probate Code § 887(a).

Added by Acts 2011, 82nd Leg., ch. 823, § 1.02, eff. Jan. 1, 2014.

§ 1355.002. Payment of Claims to Nonresident Creditor

(a) In this section, "creditor" means a person who is entitled to money in an amount that is not more than $100,000 owing as a result of transactions in this state, the right to which is liquidated and is uncontested in any pending lawsuit in this state.

(b) This section applies only to a creditor who is a nonresident minor, a nonresident person who is adjudged by a court of competent jurisdiction to be incapacitated, or the former ward of a guardianship terminated under Chapter 1204 who has no legal guardian qualified in this state.

(c) A debtor in this state who owes money to a creditor to whom this section applies may pay the money:

(1) to the creditor's guardian qualified in the domiciliary jurisdiction; or

(2) to the county clerk of:

(A) any county in this state in which real property owned by the creditor is located; or

(B) if the creditor is not known to own real property in this state, the county in which the debtor resides.

(d) A payment made under this section is for the creditor's account and for the creditor's use and benefit.

(e) A receipt for payment signed by the county clerk is binding on the creditor as of the date and to the extent of payment if the receipt states:

(1) the creditor's name; and

(2) the creditor's post office address, if the address is known.

(f) A county clerk who receives a payment under Subsection (c) shall handle the money in the same manner as provided for a payment to the account of a resident creditor under Sections 1355.001, 1355.051, 1355.052, 1355.102, 1355.103, and 1355.104. Those sections apply to the handling and disposition of money or any increase, dividend, or income paid to the clerk for the use, benefit, and account of the creditor to whom this section applies.

Derived from Probate Code § 887(e).

Added by Acts 2011, 82nd Leg., ch. 823, § 1.02, eff. Jan. 1, 2014.

Subchapter B. Administration of Money

§ 1355.051. Investment of Money by Clerk

(a) On receipt of a payment under Section 1355.001, the county clerk shall invest the money as authorized under this title under court order in the name and for the account of the minor or other person entitled to the money.

(b) The county clerk shall credit any increase, dividend, or income from an investment made under this chapter to the account of the minor or other person entitled to the investment.

Derived from Probate Code § 887(a).

Added by Acts 2011, 82nd Leg., ch. 823, § 1.02, eff. Jan. 1, 2014.

§ 1355.052. Annual Report

Not later than March 1 of each year, the court clerk shall make a written report to the court of the status of an investment made by the county clerk under Section 1355.051. The report must contain:

(1) the amount of the original investment or the value of the investment at the last annual report, whichever is later;

(2) any increase, dividend, or income from the investment since the last annual report;

(3) the total amount of the investment and all increases, dividends, or income at the date of the report; and

(4) the name of the depository or the type of investment.

Derived from Probate Code § 887(b).

Added by Acts 2011, 82nd Leg., ch. 823, § 1.02, eff. Jan. 1, 2014.

Subchapter C. Withdrawal of Money

§ 1355.101. Applicability of Subchapter

Except as provided by Section 1355.105, this subchapter applies only to a resident creditor to whom Section 1355.001 applies.

New.

Added by Acts 2011, 82nd Leg., ch. 823, § 1.02, eff. Jan. 1, 2014.

§ 1355.102. Custodian of Resident Creditor

(a) The following may serve as custodian of a resident creditor under this section:

(1) a parent of the creditor;

(2) the unestranged spouse of the creditor; or

(3) if there is no spouse and both of the creditor's parents are dead or nonresidents of this state, the person who:

(A) resides in this state; and

(B) has actual custody of the creditor.

(b) An unestranged spouse residing in this state shall be given priority over a creditor's parent to serve as custodian under this subchapter.

Derived from Probate Code § 887(c).

Added by Acts 2011, 82nd Leg., ch. 823, § 1.02, eff. Jan. 1, 2014.

§ 1355.103. Withdrawal of Money by Custodian; Bond

(a) A resident creditor's custodian may withdraw the money from the court clerk for the creditor's use and benefit if the custodian files with the clerk:

(1) a written application; and

(2) a bond approved by the county judge.

(b) A custodian's bond must be:

(1) twice the amount of the money to be withdrawn by the custodian;

(2) payable to the judge or the judge's successors in office; and

(3) conditioned that the custodian will:

(A) use the money for the resident creditor's benefit under the court's direction; and

(B) when legally required, faithfully account to the resident creditor and the creditor's heirs or legal representatives for the money and any increase to the money on:

(i) the removal of the creditor's disability;

(ii) the creditor's death; or

(iii) the appointment of a guardian for the creditor.

(c) A custodian may not receive a fee or commission for taking care of, handling, or spending money withdrawn by the custodian.

Derived from Probate Code § 887(c).

Added by Acts 2011, 82nd Leg., ch. 823, § 1.02, eff. Jan. 1, 2014.

§ 1355.104. Custodian's Report

(a) The custodian shall file with the county clerk a sworn report of the custodian's accounting when the custodian has:

(1) spent the money in accordance with the court's directions; or

(2) otherwise complied with the terms of the custodian's bond by accounting for the money and any increase in the money.

(b) The filing of a custodian's report, when approved by the court, operates as a discharge of the person as custodian and of the person's sureties from all further liability under the bond.

(c) The court shall satisfy itself that the custodian's report is true and correct and may require proof as in other cases.

Derived from Probate Code § 887(d).

Added by Acts 2011, 82nd Leg., ch. 823, § 1.02, eff. Jan. 1, 2014.

§ 1355.105. Withdrawal of Money by Creditor or Creditor's Heir or Representative

(a) On presentation to the court clerk of an order of a county or probate court of the county in which the money is held, money that is not withdrawn by an authorized person as provided by this chapter may be withdrawn by:

(1) the creditor, after termination of the creditor's disability;

(2) a subsequent personal representative of the creditor; or

(3) the creditor's heirs.

(b) A withdrawal under Subsection (a) may be made at any time and without a special bond for that purpose.

(c) The order presented under Subsection (a) must direct the court clerk to deliver the money to the creditor, the creditor's personal representative, or the creditor's heirs named in the order.

(d) Before the court may issue an order under this section, the person's identity and credentials must be proved to the court's satisfaction.

Derived from Probate Code § 887(f).

Added by Acts 2011, 82nd Leg., ch. 823, § 1.02, eff. Jan. 1, 2014.

Subchapter D. Use of Money by Eleemosynary Institution for Benefit of Resident

§ 1355.151. Applicability of Subchapter

This subchapter applies only to money of a resident of an eleemosynary institution of this state that is on deposit in a court registry and does not exceed $10,000.

Derived from Probate Code § 887(g).

Added by Acts 2011, 82nd Leg., ch. 823, § 1.02, eff. Jan. 1, 2014.

§ 1355.152. Payment of Money to Institution

(a) The judge of a county court, district court, or other court of this state may by order direct the court clerk to pay money to an eleemosynary institution of this state for the use and benefit of a resident of the institution if the court receives satisfactory proof by affidavit or otherwise that the resident:

(1) is a person who has a mental disability, an incapacitated person, or a person whose mental illness or mental incapacity renders the person incapable of caring for himself or herself and of managing the person's property and financial affairs; and

(2) has no known legal guardian appointed for the resident's estate.

(b) The affidavit under Subsection (a) may be executed by the superintendent, business manager, or field representative of the institution of which the person is a resident.

(c) The institution to which the payment is made under Subsection (a) may not be required to give bond or security for receiving the money from the court registry.

(d) The receipt from the institution for a payment, or the canceled check or warrant by which the payment was made:

(1) is sufficient evidence of the disposition of the payment; and

(2) relieves the court clerk from further responsibility for the disposition.

Derived from Probate Code § 887(g).

Added by Acts 2011, 82nd Leg., ch. 823, § 1.02, eff. Jan. 1, 2014.

§ 1355.153. Deposit of Money in Trust

(a) On receipt of money under this subchapter, an eleemosynary institution shall deposit all of the money received to the resident's trust account.

(b) Money deposited in a trust account may be used only:

(1) by or for the personal use of the owner of the trust account, under the rules or custom of the institution in the expenditure of money by a resident; or

(2) by the responsible officer of the institution, for the resident's use and benefit.

Derived from Probate Code § 887(g).

Added by Acts 2011, 82nd Leg., ch. 823, § 1.02, eff. Jan. 1, 2014.

§ 1355.154. Death of Resident or Depletion of Money

(a) After the expenditure of all money in a resident's trust account, or after the resident's death, the responsible officer of the eleemosynary institution shall furnish a statement of expenditures of the money to the resident's nearest relative who is entitled to receive the statement.

(b) A copy of the statement described by Subsection (a) shall be filed with the court that first granted the order to dispose of the money in accordance with this title.

(c) The balance of a trust account of a resident of an eleemosynary institution who dies may be applied to:

(1) the resident's burial expenses; or

(2) the care, support, and treatment account of the resident at the institution.

Derived from Probate Code § 887(g).

Added by Acts 2011, 82nd Leg., ch. 823, § 1.02, eff. Jan. 1, 2014.

Chapter 1356. Court Approval of Certain Arts and Entertainment, Advertisement, and Sports Contracts

Subchapter A. General Provisions

Subchapter B. Court Action Regarding Certain Contracts

Chapter 1356. Court Approval of Certain Arts and Entertainment, Advertisement, and Sports Contracts

Subchapter A. General Provisions

§ 1356.001. Definitions

In this chapter:

(1) "Advertise" means to solicit or induce the purchase of consumer goods or services through electronic or print media, including:

(A) radio;

(B) television;

(C) computer; or

(D) direct mail.

(2) "Advertisement contract" means a contract under which a person is employed or agrees to advertise consumer goods or services.

(3) "Artist" means:

(A) an actor who performs in a motion picture, theatrical, radio, television, or other entertainment production;

(B) a musician or musical director;

(C) a director or producer of a motion picture, theatrical, radio, television, or other entertainment production;

(D) a writer;

(E) a cinematographer;

(F) a composer, lyricist, or arranger of musical compositions;

(G) a dancer or choreographer of musical productions;

(H) a model; or

(I) any other individual who provides similar professional services in a motion picture, theatrical, radio, television, or other entertainment production.

(4) "Arts and entertainment contract" means a contract under which:

(A) an artist is employed or agrees to provide services in a motion picture, theatrical, radio, television, or other entertainment production; or

(B) a person agrees to purchase, secure, sell, lease, license, or otherwise dispose of literary, musical, or dramatic tangible or intangible property or any rights in that property for use in the field of entertainment, including:

(i) a motion picture;

(ii) television;

(iii) the production of phonograph records; or

(iv) theater.

(5) "Consumer goods" means goods used or bought for use primarily for personal, family, or household purposes.

(6) "Net earnings," with respect to a minor, means the total amount to be received for the services of the minor under a contract less:

(A) the amount required by law to be paid as taxes to any government or governmental agency;

(B) a reasonable amount to be spent for the support, care, maintenance, education, and training of the minor;

(C) fees and expenses paid in connection with procuring the contract or maintaining employment of the minor; and

(D) attorney's fees for services provided in connection with the contract or any other business of the minor.

(7) "Sports contract" means a contract under which an athlete is employed or agrees to participate, compete, or engage in a sports or athletic activity at a professional or amateur sports event or athletic event.

Derived from Probate Code §§ 901, 904(a).

Added by Acts 2011, 82nd Leg., ch. 823, § 1.02, eff. Jan. 1, 2014.

§ 1356.002. Duration of Contract of a Minor

This chapter may not be construed to authorize a contract that binds a minor after the seventh anniversary of the date of the contract.

Derived from Probate Code § 902.

Added by Acts 2011, 82nd Leg., ch. 823, § 1.02, eff. Jan. 1, 2014.

Subchapter B. Court Action Regarding Certain Contracts

§ 1356.051. Approval of Certain Contracts of a Minor

(a) On the petition of the guardian of the estate of a minor, a court may issue an order approving for purposes of this chapter an arts and entertainment contract, advertisement contract, or sports contract that is entered into by the minor.

(b) Approval of a contract under this section extends to the contract as a whole and each term and provision of the contract, including any optional or conditional contract provision relating to the extension or termination of the contract's term.

(c) A court may withhold approval of a contract in which part of the minor's net earnings will be set aside as provided by Section 1356.054 until the guardian of the minor's estate executes and files with the court written consent to the issuance of the order.

Derived from Probate Code § 903(a), (b), (c).

Added by Acts 2011, 82nd Leg., ch. 823, § 1.02, eff. Jan. 1, 2014.

§ 1356.052. Notice Required

Before the court may approve a contract under Section 1356.051, the guardian of the minor's estate must provide the other party to the contract notice of the petition and an opportunity to request a hearing in the manner provided by the court.

Derived from Probate Code § 903(a).

Added by Acts 2011, 82nd Leg., ch. 823, § 1.02, eff. Jan. 1, 2014.

§ 1356.053. Necessary Parties to Proceeding

Each parent of a minor for whom a proceeding is brought under Section 1356.051 is a necessary party to the proceeding.

Derived from Probate Code § 903(e).

Added by Acts 2011, 82nd Leg., ch. 823, § 1.02, eff. Jan. 1, 2014.

§ 1356.054. Set-Aside and Preservation of Portion Of Net Earnings

(a) Notwithstanding any other law, in an order issued under Section 1356.051, the court may require that a portion of the net earnings of the minor under the contract be set aside and preserved for the benefit of the minor in a trust created under Section 1301.053 or

1301.054 or a similar trust created under the laws of another state.

(b) The amount to be set aside under this section must be reasonable as determined by the court.

Derived from Probate Code § 904(b).

Added by Acts 2011, 82nd Leg., ch. 823, § 1.02, eff. Jan. 1, 2014.

§ 1356.055. Valid Contract Not Voidable

A contract approved under Section 1356.051 that is otherwise valid is not voidable solely on the ground that it was entered into by a person during the age of minority.

Derived from Probate Code § 903(d).

Added by Acts 2011, 82nd Leg., ch. 823, § 1.02, eff. Jan. 1, 2014.

§ 1356.056. Guardian Ad Litem

The court may appoint a guardian ad litem for a minor who has entered into an arts and entertainment contract, advertisement contract, or sports contract if the court finds that the appointment would be in the best interest of the minor.

Derived from Probate Code § 905.

Added by Acts 2011, 82nd Leg., ch. 823, § 1.02, eff. Jan. 1, 2014.

Chapter 1357. Supported Decision-Making Agreement Act

Subchapter A. General Provisions

Subchapter B. Scope of Agreement and Agreement Requirements

Subchapter C. Duty of Certain Persons With Respect to Agreement

Chapter 1357. Supported Decision-Making Agreement Act

Subchapter A. General Provisions

§ 1357.001. Short Title

This chapter may be cited as the Supported Decision-Making Agreement Act.

New.

Added by Acts 2015, 84th Leg., ch. 357, § 1, eff. June 19, 2015 and Acts 2015, 84th Leg., ch. 214, § 23, eff. Sept. 1, 2015.

§ 1357.002. Definitions

In this chapter:

(1) "Adult" means an individual 18 years of age or older or an individual under 18 years of age who has had the disabilities of minority removed.

(2) "Disability" means, with respect to an individual, a physical or mental impairment that substantially limits one or more major life activities.

(3) "Supported decision-making" means a process of supporting and accommodating an adult with a disability to enable the adult to make life decisions, including decisions related to where the adult wants to live, the services, supports, and medical care the adult wants to receive, whom the adult wants to live with, and where the adult wants to work, without impeding the self-determination of the adult.

(4) "Supported decision-making agreement" is an agreement between an adult with a disability and a supporter entered into under this chapter.

(5) "Supporter" means an adult who has entered into a supported decision-making agreement with an adult with a disability.

New.

Added by Acts 2015, 84th Leg., ch. 357, § 1, eff. June 19, 2015 and Acts 2015, 84th Leg., ch. 214, § 23, eff. Sept. 1, 2015.

§ 1357.003. Purpose

The purpose of this chapter is to recognize a less restrictive substitute for guardianship for adults with disabilities who need assistance with decisions regarding daily living but who are not considered incapacitated persons for purposes of establishing a guardianship under this title.

New.

Added by Acts 2015, 84th Leg., ch. 357, § 1, eff. June 19, 2015 and Acts 2015, 84th Leg., ch. 214, § 23, eff. Sept. 1, 2015.

Subchapter B. Scope of Agreement and Agreement Requirements

§ 1357.051. Scope of Supported Decision-Making Agreement

An adult with a disability may voluntarily, without undue influence or coercion, enter into a supported decision-making agreement with a supporter under which the adult with a disability authorizes the supporter to do any or all of the following:

(1) provide supported decision-making, including assistance in understanding the options, responsibilities, and consequences of the adult's life decisions, without making those decisions on behalf of the adult with a disability;

(2) subject to Section 1357.054, assist the adult in accessing, collecting, and obtaining information that is relevant to a given life decision, including medical, psychological, financial, educational, or treatment records, from any person;

(3) assist the adult with a disability in understanding the information described by Subdivision (2); and

(4) assist the adult in communicating the adult's decisions to appropriate persons.

New.

Added by Acts 2015, 84th Leg., ch. 357, § 1, eff. June 19, 2015 and Acts 2015, 84th Leg., ch. 214, § 23, eff. Sept. 1, 2015.

§ 1357.052. Authority of Supporter

A supporter may exercise the authority granted to the supporter in the supported decision-making agreement.

New.

Added by Acts 2015, 84th Leg., ch. 357, § 1, eff. June 19, 2015 and Acts 2015, 84th Leg., ch. 214, § 23, eff. Sept. 1, 2015.

§ 1357.053. Term of Agreement

(a) Except as provided by Subsection (b), the supported decision-making agreement extends until terminated by either party or by the terms of the agreement.

(b) The supported decision-making agreement is terminated if:

(1) the Department of Family and Protective Services finds that the adult with a disability has been abused, neglected, or exploited by the supporter; or

(2) the supporter is found criminally liable for conduct described by Subdivision (1).

New.

Added by Acts 2015, 84th Leg., ch. 357, § 1, eff. June 19, 2015 and Acts 2015, 84th Leg., ch. 214, § 23, eff. Sept. 1, 2015.

§ 1357.054. Access to Personal Information

(a) A supporter is only authorized to assist the adult with a disability in accessing, collecting, or obtaining information that is relevant to a decision authorized under the supported decision-making agreement.

(b) If a supporter assists an adult with a disability in accessing, collecting, or obtaining personal information, including protected health information under the Health Insurance Portability and Accountability Act of 1996 (Pub. L. No. 104-191) or educational records under the Family Educational Rights and Privacy Act of 1974 (20 U.S.C. Section 1232g), the supporter shall ensure the information is kept privileged and confidential, as applicable, and is not subject to unauthorized access, use, or disclosure.

(c) The existence of a supported decision-making agreement does not preclude an adult with a disability from seeking personal information without the assistance of a supporter.

New.

Added by Acts 2015, 84th Leg., ch. 357, § 1, eff. June 19, 2015 and Acts 2015, 84th Leg., ch. 214, § 23, eff. Sept. 1, 2015.

§ 1357.055. Authorizing and Witnessing of Supported Decision-Making Agreement

(a) A supported decision-making agreement must be signed voluntarily, without coercion or undue influence, by the adult with a disability and the supporter in the presence of two or more subscribing witnesses or a notary public.

(b) If signed before two witnesses, the attesting witnesses must be at least 14 years of age.

New.

Added by Acts 2015, 84th Leg., ch. 357, § 1, eff. June 19, 2015 and Acts 2015, 84th Leg., ch. 214, § 23, eff. Sept. 1, 2015.

§ 1357.056. Form of Supported Decision-Making Agreement

(a) Subject to Subsection (b), a supported decision-making agreement is valid only if it is in substantially the following form:

SUPPORTED DECISION-MAKING AGREEMENT

Appointment of Supporter

I, (insert your name), make this agreement of my own free will.

I agree and designate that:

Name:

Address:

Phone Number:

E-mail Address:

is my supporter. My supporter may help me with making everyday life decisions relating to the following:

Y/N   obtaining food, clothing, and shelter

Y/N   taking care of my physical health

Y/N   managing my financial affairs.

My supporter is not allowed to make decisions for me. To help me with my decisions, my supporter may:

1. Help me access, collect, or obtain information that is relevant to a decision, including medical, psychological, financial, educational, or treatment records;

2. Help me understand my options so I can make an informed decision; or

3. Help me communicate my decision to appropriate persons.

Y/N A release allowing my supporter to see protected health information under the Health Insurance Portability and Accountability Act of 1996 (Pub. L. No. 104-191) is attached.

Y/N A release allowing my supporter to see educational records under the Family Educational Rights and Privacy Act of 1974 (20 U.S.C. Section 1232g) is attached.

Effective Date of Supported Decision-Making Agreement

This supported decision-making agreement is effective immediately and will continue until (insert date) or until the agreement is terminated by my supporter or me or by operation of law.

Signed this_____day of_____,20____

Consent of Supporter

I, (name of supporter), consent to act as a supporter under this agreement.

(signature of supporter)(printed name of supporter) Signature

(my signature)(my printed name)_____

(witness 1 signature)(printed name of witness 1)

(witness 2 signature)(printed name of witness 2) State of County of This document was acknowledged before me on _____ (date) by _____ and ____

_____

(name of adult with a disability)(name of supporter)

(signature of notarial officer)
(Seal, if any, of notary)

(printed name)
My commission expires:

WARNING: PROTECTION FOR THE ADULT WITH A DISABILITY

IF A PERSON WHO RECEIVES A COPY OF THIS AGREEMENT OR IS AWARE OF THE EXISTENCE OF THIS AGREEMENT HAS CAUSE TO BELIEVE THAT THE ADULT WITH A DISABILITY IS BEING ABUSED, NEGLECTED, OR EXPLOITED BY THE SUPPORTER, THE PERSON SHALL REPORT THE ALLEGED ABUSE, NEGLECT, OR EXPLOITATION TO THE DEPARTMENT OF FAMILY AND PROTECTIVE SERVICES BY CALLING THE ABUSE HOTLINE AT 1-800-252-5400 OR ONLINE AT WWW.TXABUSEHOTLINE.ORG.

(b) A supported decision-making agreement may be in any form not inconsistent with Subsection (a) and the other requirements of this chapter.

New.

Added by Acts 2015, 84th Leg., ch. 357, § 1, eff. June 19, 2015 and Acts 2015, 84th Leg., ch. 214, § 23, eff. Sept. 1, 2015.

Subchapter C. Duty of Certain Persons With Respect to Agreement

§ 1357.101. Reliance on Agreement; Limitation of Liability

(a) A person who receives the original or a copy of a supported decision-making agreement shall rely on the agreement.

(b) A person is not subject to criminal or civil liability and has not engaged in professional misconduct for an act or omission if the act or omission is done in good faith and in reliance on a supported decision-making agreement.

New.

Added by Acts 2015, 84th Leg., ch. 357, § 1, eff. June 19, 2015 and Acts 2015, 84th Leg., ch. 214, § 23, eff. Sept. 1, 2015.

§ 1357.102. Reporting of Suspected Abuse, Neglect, or Exploitation

If a person who receives a copy of a supported decision-making agreement or is aware of the existence of a supported decision-making agreement has cause to believe that the adult with a disability is being abused, neglected, or exploited by the supporter, the person shall report the alleged abuse, neglect, or exploitation to the Department of Family and Protective Services in accordance with Section 48.051, Human Resources Code.

New.

Added by Acts 2015, 84th Leg., ch. 357, § 1, eff. June 19, 2015 and Acts 2015, 84th Leg., ch. 214, § 23, eff. Sept. 1, 2015.

VII.

EVIDENCE RULES

Article VI. Witnesses

Statutes in Context
Rule 601

Courts normally seek whatever evidence is helpful when they interpret and construe wills. However, this ability may be restricted by state evidentiary rules, especially dead person's statutes (formerly referred to as "dead man's statutes"). These statutes limit the admissibility of evidence of what the testator did or said if the testimony is being offered by a party to the action. The policy supporting this limitation is that the testator is deceased and thus cannot rebut the statements made by a party who is obviously biased. Under older formulations of the rule, a party could not testify about any transaction or communication with the decedent. The modern version of Rule 601(b), however, only prohibits a party to the action from testifying with regard to uncorroborated oral statements of the decedent.

Rule 601. Competency and Incompetency of Witnesses

(a) In General. Every person is competent to be a witness unless these rules provide otherwise. The following witnesses are incompetent:

(1) Insane Persons. A person who is now insane or was insane at the time of the events about which the person is called to testify.

(2) Persons Lacking Sufficient Intellect. A child—or any other person—whom the court examines and finds lacks sufficient intellect to testify concerning the matters in issue.

(b) The "Dead Man's Rule."

(1) Applicability. The "Dead Man's Rule" applies only in a civil case:

(A) by or against a party in the party's capacity as an executor, administrator, or guardian; or

(B) by or against a decedent's heirs or legal representatives and based in whole or in part on the decedent's oral statement.

(2) General Rule. In cases described in subparagraph (b)(1)(A), a party may not testify against another party about an oral statement by the testator, intestate, or ward. In cases described in subparagraph (b)(1)(B), a party may not testify against another party about an oral statement by the decedent.

(3) Exceptions. A party may testify against another party about an oral statement by the testator, intestate, ward, or decedent if:

(A) the party's testimony about the statement is corroborated; or

(B) the opposing party calls the party to testify at the trial about the statement.

(4) Instructions. If a court excludes evidence under paragraph (b)(2), the court must instruct the jury that the law prohibits a party from testifying about an oral statement by the testator, intestate, ward, or decedent unless the oral statement is corroborated or the opposing party calls the party to testify at the trial about the statement.

Effective April 1, 2015.

Comment to 2015 Restyling: The text of the "Dead Man's Rule" has been streamlined to clarify its meaning without making any substantive changes. The text of former Rule 601(b) (as well as its statutory predecessor, Vernon's Ann. Civ. St. art. 3716) prohibits only a "party" from testifying about the dead man's statements. Despite this, the last sentence of former Rule 601(b) requires the court to instruct the jury when the rule "prohibits an interested party or witness" from testifying. Because the rule prohibits only a "party" from testifying, restyled Rule 601(b)(4) references only "a party," and not "an interested party or witness." To be sure, courts have indicated that the rule (or its statutory predecessor) may be applicable to a witness who is not nominally a party and inapplicable to a witness who is only nominally a party. See, e.g., Chandler v. Welborn, 156 Tex. 312, 294 S.W.2d 801, 809 (1956); Ragsdale v. Ragsdale, 142 Tex. 476, 179 S.W.2d 291, 295 (1944). But these decisions are based on an interpretation of the meaning of "party." Therefore, limiting the court's instruction under restyled Rule 601(b)(4) to "a party" does not change Texas practice. In addition, restyled Rule 601(b) deletes the sentence in former Rule 601(b) that states "[e]xcept for the foregoing, a witness is not precluded from giving evidence . . . because the witness is a party to the action . . . ." This sentence is surplusage. Rule 601(b) is a rule of exclusion. If the testimony falls outside the rule of exclusion, its admissibility will be determined by other applicable rules of evidence.

(Effective March 1, 1998.)

Article VII.   Opinions and Expert Testimony

Statutes in Context
Rule 704

Rule 704 permits a witness to testify regarding the witness's opinion of whether the testator had testamentary capacity when the testator executed the will even though such an opinion embraces an ultimate issue to be decided by the trier of fact.

Rule 704.   Opinion on Ultimate Issue

An opinion is not objectionable just because it embraces an ultimate issue.

Effective April 1, 2015.

VIII.

FAMILY CODE

Title 1. The Marriage Relationship

Subtitle A. Marriage

Chapter 2. The Marriage Relationship

Statutes in Context
Chapter 2

Chapter 2 of the Family Code deals with the validity of marriages, both formal marriages and informal or "common law" marriages. These provisions are especially important in determining the identity of a decedent's surviving spouse for intestate succession purposes.

Subchapter D. Validity of Marriage

§ 2.301. Fraud, Mistake, or Illegality in Obtaining License

Except as otherwise provided by this chapter, the validity of a marriage is not affected by any fraud, mistake, or illegality that occurred in obtaining the marriage license.

Added by Acts 1997, 75th Leg., ch. 7, § 1, eff. April 17, 1997.

§ 2.302. Ceremony Conducted by Unauthorized Person

The validity of a marriage is not affected by the lack of authority of the person conducting the marriage ceremony if:

(1) there was a reasonable appearance of authority by that person;

(2) at least one party to the marriage participated in the ceremony in good faith and that party treats the marriage as valid; and

(3) neither party to the marriage:

(A) is a minor whose marriage is prohibited by law; or

(B) by marrying commits an offense under Section 25.01, Penal Code.

Added by Acts 1997, 75th Leg., ch. 7, § 1, eff. April 17, 1997. Amended by Acts 2005, 79th Leg., ch. 268, § 4.11, eff. Sept. 1, 2005.

Subchapter E. Marriage Without Formalities

Statutes in Context
Subchapter E

Subchapter E explains when an informal or "common law" marriage is valid in Texas.

The statutory requirement that an informal marriage be between "a man and woman" is problematic after the United States Supreme Court case of *Obergefell v. Hodges*, Nos. 14–556, 14–562, 14–571, 14–574, 2015 WL 2473451 (U.S. June 26, 2015), in which the Court held that the Due Process and Equal Protection Clauses of the Fourteenth Amendment prevent couples of the same-sex from being deprived of the right to be married.

§ 2.401. Proof of Informal Marriage

(a) In a judicial, administrative, or other proceeding, the marriage of a man and woman may be proved by evidence that:

(1) a declaration of their marriage has been signed as provided by this subchapter; or

(2) the man and woman agreed to be married and after the agreement they lived together in this state as husband and wife and there represented to others that they were married.

(b) If a proceeding in which a marriage is to be proved as provided by Subsection (a)(2) is not commenced before the second anniversary of the date on which the parties separated and ceased living together, it is rebuttably presumed that the parties did not enter into an agreement to be married.

(c) A person under 18 years of age may not:

(1) be a party to an informal marriage; or

(2) execute a declaration of informal marriage under Section 2.402

(d) A person may not be a party to an informal marriage or execute a declaration of an informal marriage if the person is presently married to a person who is not the other party to the informal marriage or declaration of an informal marriage, as applicable.

Added by Acts 1997, 75th Leg., ch. 7, § 1, eff. April 17, 1997. Amended by Acts 1997, 75th Leg., ch. 1362, § 1, eff. Sept. 1, 1997. Subsec. (d) added by Acts 2005, 79th Leg., ch. 268, § 4.12, eff. Sept. 1, 2005.

§ 2.402. Declaration and Registration of Informal Marriage

(a) A declaration of informal marriage must be signed on a form prescribed by the bureau of vital statistics and provided by the county clerk. Each party to the declaration shall provide the information required in the form.

(b) The declaration form must contain:

(1) a heading entitled "Declaration and Registration of Informal Marriage, _____ County, Texas";

(2) spaces for each party's full name, including the woman's maiden surname, address, date of birth, place of birth, including city, county, and state, and social security number, if any;

(3) a space for indicating the type of document tendered by each party as proof of age and identity;

(4) printed boxes for each party to check "true" or "false" in response to the following statement: "The other party is not related to me as:

(A) an ancestor or descendant, by blood or adoption;

(B) a brother or sister, of the whole or half blood or by adoption;

(C) a parent's brother or sister, of the whole or half blood or by adoption;

(D) a son or daughter of a brother or sister, of the whole or half blood or by adoption;

(E) a current or former stepchild or stepparent; or

(F) a son or daughter of a parent's brother or sister, of the whole or half blood or by adoption.";

(5) a printed declaration and oath reading: "I SOLEMNLY SWEAR (OR AFFIRM) THAT WE, THE UNDERSIGNED, ARE MARRIED TO EACH OTHER BY VIRTUE OF THE FOLLOWING FACTS: ON OR ABOUT (DATE) WE AGREED TO BE MARRIED, AND AFTER THAT DATE WE LIVED TOGETHER AS HUSBAND AND WIFE AND IN THIS STATE WE REPRESENTED TO OTHERS THAT WE WERE MARRIED. SINCE THE DATE OF MARRIAGE TO THE OTHER PARTY I HAVE NOT BEEN MARRIED TO ANY OTHER PERSON. THIS DECLARATION IS TRUE AND THE INFORMATION IN IT WHICH I HAVE GIVEN IS CORRECT.";

(6) spaces immediately below the printed declaration and oath for the parties' signatures; and

(7) a certificate of the county clerk that the parties made the declaration and oath and the place and date it was made.

(c) Repealed by Acts 1997, 75th Leg., ch. 1362, § 4, eff. Sept. 1, 1997.

Added by Acts 1997, 75th Leg., ch. 7, § 1, eff. April 17, 1997. Amended by Acts 1997, 75th Leg., ch. 1362, § 4, eff. Sept. 1, 1997. Subsec. (b) amended by Acts 2005, 79th Leg., ch. 268, § 4.13, eff. Sept. 1, 2005.

§ 2.403. Proof of Identity and Age

(a) The county clerk shall require proof of the identity and age of each party to the declaration of informal marriage to be established by a document listed in Section 2.005(b).

(b) A person commits an offense if the person knowingly provides false, fraudulent, or otherwise inaccurate proof of the person's identity or age under this section. An offense under this subsection is a Class A misdemeanor.

Added by Acts 1997, 75th Leg., ch. 7, § 1, eff. April 17, 1997. Subsec. (a) amended by Acts 2005, 79th Leg., ch. 268, § 4.14, eff. Sept. 1, 2005. Subsec. (b) added by Acts 2005, 79th Leg., ch. 268, § 4.14, eff. Sept. 1, 2005, subsec. (a) amended by Acts 2009, 81st Leg., ch. 978, § 7, eff. Sept. 1, 2009.

§ 2.404. Recording of Certificate or Declaration of Informal Marriage

(a) The county clerk shall:

(1) determine that all necessary information is recorded on the declaration of informal marriage form and that all necessary documents are submitted to the clerk;

(2) administer the oath to each party to the declaration;

(3) have each party sign the declaration in the clerk's presence; and

(4) execute the clerk's certificate to the declaration.

(a-1) On the proper execution of the declaration, the clerk may:

(1) prepare a certificate of informal marriage;

(2) enter on the certificate the names of the persons declaring their informal marriage and the date the certificate or declaration is issued; and

(3) record the time at which the certificate or declaration is issued.

(b) The county clerk may not certify the declaration or issue or record the certificate of informal marriage or declaration if:

(1) either party fails to supply any information or provide any document required by this subchapter;

(2) either party is under 18 years of age; or

(3) either party checks "false" in response to the statement of relationship to the other party.

(c) On execution of the declaration, the county clerk shall record the declaration or certificate of informal marriage, deliver the original of the declaration to the parties, deliver the original of the certificate of informal marriage to the parties, if a certificate was prepared, and send a copy of the declaration of informal marriage to the bureau of vital statistics.

(d) An executed declaration or a certificate of informal marriage recorded as provided in this section is prima facie evidence of the marriage of the parties.

(e) At the time the parties sign the declaration, the clerk shall distribute to each party printed materials about acquired immune deficiency syndrome (AIDS) and human immunodeficiency virus (HIV). The clerk shall note on the declaration that the distribution was made. The materials shall be prepared and provided to the clerk by the Texas Department of Health and shall be designed to inform the parties about:

(1) the incidence and mode of transmission of AIDS and HIV;

(2) the local availability of medical procedures, including voluntary testing, designed to show or help show whether a person has AIDS or HIV infection, antibodies to HIV, or infection with any other probable causative agent of AIDS; and

(3) available and appropriate counseling services regarding AIDS and HIV infection.

Added by Acts 1997, 75ᵗʰ Leg., ch. 7, § 1, eff. April 17, 1997. Amended by Acts 1997, 75ᵗʰ Leg., ch. 1362, § 2, eff. Sept. 1, 1997, heading amended Acts 2009, 81ˢᵗ Leg., ch. 978, § 8, eff. Sept. 1, 2009, subsec. (a-1) added and subsecs. (b), (c), & (d) amended by Acts 2009, 81ˢᵗ Leg., ch. 978, § 9, eff. September 1, 2009.

§ 2.405. Violation by County Clerk; Penalty

A county clerk or deputy county clerk who violates this subchapter commits an offense. An offense under this section is a misdemeanor punishable by a fine of not less than $200 and not more than $500.

Added by Acts 1997, 75ᵗʰ Leg., ch. 7, § 1, eff. April 17, 1997.

Subchapter F.   Rights and Duties of Spouses

Statutes in Context
§ 2.501

Section 2.501 codifies the fundamental duty of each spouse to support the other spouse.

§ 2.501. Duty to Support

(a) Each spouse has the duty to support the other spouse.

(b) A spouse who fails to discharge the duty of support is liable to any person who provides necessaries to the spouse to whom support is owed.

Added by Acts 1997, 75ᵗʰ Leg., ch. 7, § 1, eff. April 17, 1997.

Subtitle B.   Property Rights and Liabilities

Chapter 3.   Marital Property Rights and Liabilities

Subchapter A.   General Rules for Separate and Community Property

Statutes in Context
§§ 3.001–3.006

Sections 3.001 - 3.006 contain the general rules for determining whether the property of a married individual is the separate property of one spouse or the community property of both spouses. See also Texas Constitution Article XVI, § 15.

§ 3.001. Separate Property

A spouse's separate property consists of:

(1) the property owned or claimed by the spouse before marriage;

(2) the property acquired by the spouse during marriage by gift, devise, or descent; and

(3) the recovery for personal injuries sustained by the spouse during marriage, except any recovery for loss of earning capacity during marriage.

Added by Acts 1997, 75ᵗʰ Leg., ch. 7, § 1, eff. April 17, 1997.

§ 3.002. Community Property

Community property consists of the property, other than separate property, acquired by either spouse during marriage.

Added by Acts 1997, 75ᵗʰ Leg., ch. 7, § 1, eff. April 17, 1997.

§ 3.003. Presumption of Community Property

(a) Property possessed by either spouse during or on dissolution of marriage is presumed to be community property.

(b) The degree of proof necessary to establish that property is separate property is clear and convincing evidence.

Added by Acts 1997, 75ᵗʰ Leg., ch. 7, § 1, eff. April 17, 1997.

§ 3.004. Recordation of Separate Property

(a) A subscribed and acknowledged schedule of a spouse's separate property may be recorded in the deed records of the county in which the parties, or one of them, reside and in the county or counties in which the real property is located.

(b) A schedule of a spouse's separate real property is not constructive notice to a good faith purchaser for value or a creditor without actual notice unless the instrument is acknowledged and recorded in the deed records of the county in which the real property is located.

Added by Acts 1997, 75ᵗʰ Leg., ch. 7, § 1, eff. April 17, 1997.

§ 3.005. Gifts Between Spouses

If one spouse makes a gift of property to the other spouse, the gift is presumed to include all the income and property that may arise from that property.

Added by Acts 1997, 75ᵗʰ Leg., ch. 7, § 1, eff. April 17, 1997.

§ 3.006. Proportional Ownership of Property by Marital Estates

If the community estate of the spouses and the separate estate of a spouse have an ownership interest in property, the respective ownership interests of the marital estates are determined by the rule of inception of title.

Added by Acts 1999, 76ᵗʰ Leg., ch. 692, § 1, eff. Sept. 1, 1999. Amended by Acts 2001, 77ᵗʰ Leg., ch. 838, § 3, eff. Sept. 1, 2001.

§ 3.007. Property Interest in Certain Employee Benefits

(a) *repealed*

(b) *repealed*

(c) The separate property interest of a spouse in a defined contribution retirement plan may be traced using the tracing and characterization principles that apply to a nonretirement asset.

(d) A spouse who is a participant in an employer-provided stock option plan or an employer-provided restricted stock plan has a separate property interest in the options or restricted stock granted to the spouse under the plan as follows:

(1) if the option or stock was granted to the spouse before marriage but required continued employment during marriage before the grant could be exercised or the restriction removed, the spouse's separate property interest is equal to the fraction of the option or restricted stock in which:

(A) the numerator is the sum of:

(i) the period from the date the option or stock was granted until the date of marriage; and

(ii) if the option or stock also required continued employment following the date of dissolution of the marriage before the grant could be exercised or the restriction removed, the period from the date of dissolution of the marriage until the date the grant could be exercised or the restriction removed; and

(B) the denominator is the period from the date the option or stock was granted until the date the grant could be exercised or the restriction removed; and

(2) if the option or stock was granted to the spouse during the marriage but required continued employment following the date of dissolution of the marriage before the grant could be exercised or the restriction removed, the spouse's separate property interest is equal to the fraction of the option or restricted stock in which:

(A) the numerator is the period from the date of dissolution of the marriage until the date the grant could be exercised or the restriction removed; and

(B) the denominator is the period from the date the option or stock was granted until the date the grant could be exercised or the restriction removed.

(e) The computation described by Subsection (d) applies to each component of the benefit requiring varying periods of employment before the grant could be exercised or the restriction removed.

(f) *repealed*

Added by Acts 2005, 79ᵗʰ Leg., ch. 490, § 2, eff. Sept. 1, 2005. Subsec. (d) amended by Acts 2009, 81ˢᵗ Leg., ch. 768, § 1, eff. Sept. 1, 2009; Subsecs. (a), (b), (f) repealed by Acts 2009, 81ˢᵗ Leg., ch. 768, § 11(1), eff. Sept. 1, 2009.

§ 3.008. Property Interest in Certain Insurance Proceeds

(a) Insurance proceeds paid or payable that arise from a casualty loss to property during marriage are characterized in the same manner as the property to which the claim is attributable.

(b) If a person becomes disabled or is injured, any disability insurance payment or workers' compensation payment is community property to the extent it is intended to replace earnings lost while the disabled or injured person is married. To the extent that any insurance payment or workers' compensation payment is intended to replace earnings while the disabled or injured person is not married, the recovery is the separate property of the disabled or injured spouse.

Added by Acts 2005, 79ᵗʰ Leg., ch. 490, § 2, eff. Sept. 1, 2005.

Subchapter B. Management, Control, and Disposition of Marital Property

---

Statutes in Context
§§ 3.101–3.104

Sections 3.101 – 3.104 address issues regarding the management, control, and disposition of separate and community property.

---

§ 3.101. Managing Separate Property

Each spouse has the sole management, control, and disposition of that spouse's separate property.

Added by Acts 1997, 75ᵗʰ Leg., ch. 7, § 1, eff. April 17, 1997.

§ 3.102. Managing Community Property

(a) During marriage, each spouse has the sole management, control, and disposition of the community property that the spouse would have owned if single, including:

(1) personal earnings;

(2) revenue from separate property;

(3) recoveries for personal injuries; and

(4) the increase and mutations of, and the revenue from, all property subject to the spouse's sole management, control, and disposition.

(b) If community property subject to the sole management, control, and disposition of one spouse is mixed or combined with community property subject to the sole management, control, and disposition of the other spouse, then the mixed or combined community property is subject to the joint management, control, and disposition of the spouses, unless the spouses provide otherwise by power of attorney in writing or other agreement.

(c) Except as provided by Subsection (a), community property is subject to the joint management, control, and disposition of the spouses unless the spouses provide otherwise by power of attorney in writing or other agreement.

Added by Acts 1997, 75th Leg., ch. 7, § 1, eff. April 17, 1997.

§ 3.103. Managing Earnings of Minor

Except as provided by Section 264.0111, during the marriage of the parents of an unemancipated minor for whom a managing conservator has not been appointed, the earnings of the minor are subject to the joint management, control, and disposition of the parents of the minor, unless otherwise provided by agreement of the parents or by judicial order.

Added by Acts 1997, 75th Leg., ch. 7, § 1, eff. April 17, 1997. Amended by Acts 2001, 77th Leg., ch. 964, § 1, eff. Sept. 1, 2001.

§ 3.104. Protection of Third Persons

(a) During marriage, property is presumed to be subject to the sole management, control, and disposition of a spouse if it is held in that spouse's name, as shown by muniment, contract, deposit of funds, or other evidence of ownership, or if it is in that spouse's possession and is not subject to such evidence of ownership.

(b) A third person dealing with a spouse is entitled to rely, as against the other spouse or anyone claiming from that spouse, on that spouse's authority to deal with the property if:

(1) the property is presumed to be subject to the sole management, control, and disposition of the spouse; and

(2) the person dealing with the spouse:

(A) is not a party to a fraud on the other spouse or another person; and

(B) does not have actual or constructive notice of the spouse's lack of authority.

Added by Acts 1997, 75th Leg., ch. 7, § 1, eff. April 17, 1997.

Subchapter C. Marital Property Liabilities

Sections 3.201 - 3.203 focus on the personal liability of each spouse and the liability of separate and community property for the debts of the spouses.

§ 3.201. Spousal Liability

(a) A person is personally liable for the acts of the person's spouse only if:

(1) the spouse acts as an agent for the person; or

(2) the spouse incurs a debt for necessaries as provided by Subchapter F, Chapter 2.

(b) Except as provided by this subchapter, community property is not subject to a liability that arises from an act of a spouse.

(c) A spouse does not act as an agent for the other spouse solely because of the marriage relationship.

Added by Acts 1997, 75th Leg., ch. 7, § 1, eff. April 17, 1997.

§ 3.202. Rules of Marital Property Liability

(a) A spouse's separate property is not subject to liabilities of the other spouse unless both spouses are liable by other rules of law.

(b) Unless both spouses are personally liable as provided by this subchapter, the community property subject to a spouse's sole management, control, and disposition is not subject to:

(1) any liabilities that the other spouse incurred before marriage; or

(2) any nontortious liabilities that the other spouse incurs during marriage.

(c) The community property subject to a spouse's sole or joint management, control, and disposition is subject to the liabilities incurred by the spouse before or during marriage.

(d) All community property is subject to tortious liability of either spouse incurred during marriage.

(e) For purposes of this section, all retirement allowances, annuities, accumulated contributions, optional benefits, and money in the various public retirement system accounts of this state that are community property subject to the participating spouse's sole management, control, and disposition are not subject to any claim for payment of a criminal restitution judgment entered against the nonparticipant spouse except to the extent of the nonparticipant spouse's interest as determined in a qualified domestic relations order under Chapter 804, Government Code.

Added by Acts 1997, 75th Leg., ch. 7, § 1, eff. April 17, 1997. Subsec. (e) added by Acts 2009, 81st Leg., ch. 2324, § 1, eff. Sept. 1, 2009.

§ 3.203. Order in Which Property Is Subject to Execution

(a) A judge may determine, as deemed just and equitable, the order in which particular separate or community property is subject to execution and sale to satisfy a judgment, if the property subject to liability for a judgment includes any combination of:

  (1) a spouse's separate property;

  (2) community property subject to a spouse's sole management, control, and disposition;

  (3) community property subject to the other spouse's sole management, control, and disposition; and

  (4) community property subject to the spouses' joint management, control, and disposition.

(b) In determining the order in which particular property is subject to execution and sale, the judge shall consider the facts surrounding the transaction or occurrence on which the suit is based.

Added by Acts 1997, 75ᵗʰ Leg., ch. 7, § 1, eff. April 17, 1997.

Subchapter D. Management, Control, and Disposition of Marital Property Under Unusual Circumstances

Statutes in Context
§§ 3.301–3.309

Sections 3.301 - 3.309 explain how to handle the management, control, and disposition of marital property under unusual circumstances such as when a spouse is missing, permanently abandoned, or permanently separated.

§ 3.301. Missing, Abandoned, or Separated Spouse

(a) A spouse may file a sworn petition stating the facts that make it desirable for the petitioning spouse to manage, control, and dispose of community property described or defined in the petition that would otherwise be subject to the sole or joint management, control, and disposition of the other spouse if:

  (1) the other spouse has disappeared and that spouse's location remains unknown to the petitioning spouse, unless the spouse is reported to be a prisoner of war or missing on public service;

  (2) the other spouse has permanently abandoned the petitioning spouse; or

  (3) the spouses are permanently separated.

(b) The petition may be filed in a court in the county in which the petitioner resided at the time the separation began, or the abandonment or disappearance occurred, not earlier than the 60ᵗʰ day after the date of the occurrence of the event. If both spouses are nonresidents of this state at the time the petition is filed, the petition may be filed in a court in a county in which any part of the described or defined community property is located.

Added by Acts 1997, 75ᵗʰ Leg., ch. 7, § 1, eff. April 17, 1997. Amended by Acts 2001, 77ᵗʰ Leg., ch. 217, § 23, eff. Sept. 1, 2001.

§ 3.302. Spouse Missing on Public Service

(a) If a spouse is reported by an executive department of the United States to be a prisoner of war or missing on the public service of the United States, the spouse of the prisoner of war or missing person may file a sworn petition stating the facts that make it desirable for the petitioner to manage, control, and dispose of the community property described or defined in the petition that would otherwise be subject to the sole or joint management, control, and disposition of the imprisoned or missing spouse.

(b) The petition may be filed in a court in the county in which the petitioner resided at the time the report was made not earlier than six months after the date of the notice that a spouse is reported to be a prisoner of war or missing on public service. If both spouses were nonresidents of this state at the time the report was made, the petition shall be filed in a court in a county in which any part of the described or defined property is located.

Added by Acts 1997, 75ᵗʰ Leg., ch. 7, § 1, eff. April 17, 1997.

§ 3.303. Appointment of Attorney

(a) Except as provided by Subsection (b), the court may appoint an attorney in a suit filed under this subchapter for the respondent.

(b) The court shall appoint an attorney in a suit filed under this subchapter for a respondent reported to be a prisoner of war or missing on public service.

(c) The court shall allow a reasonable fee for an appointed attorney's services as a part of the costs of the suit.

Added by Acts 1997, 75ᵗʰ Leg., ch. 7, § 1, eff. April 17, 1997.

§ 3.304. Notice of Hearing; Citation

(a) Notice of the hearing, accompanied by a copy of the petition, shall be issued and served on the attorney representing the respondent, if an attorney has been appointed.

(b) If an attorney has not been appointed for the respondent, citation shall be issued and served on the respondent as in other civil cases.

Added by Acts 1997, 75ᵗʰ Leg., ch. 7, § 1, eff. April 17, 1997.

§ 3.305. Citation by Publication

(a) If the residence of the respondent, other than a respondent reported to be a prisoner of war or missing on public service, is unknown, citation shall be published in a newspaper of general circulation published in the county in which the petition was filed. If that county has no newspaper of general circulation, citation shall be published in a newspaper of general circulation in an adjacent county or in the nearest county in which a newspaper of general circulation is published.

(b) The notice shall be published once a week for two consecutive weeks before the hearing, but the first notice may not be published after the 20th day before the date set for the hearing.

Added by Acts 1997, 75th Leg., ch. 7, § 1, eff. April 17, 1997.

§ 3.306. Court Order for Management, Control, and Disposition of Community Property

(a) After hearing the evidence in a suit under this subchapter, the court, on terms the court considers just and equitable, shall render an order describing or defining the community property at issue that will be subject to the management, control, and disposition of each spouse during marriage.

(b) The court may:

(1) impose any condition and restriction the court deems necessary to protect the rights of the respondent;

(2) require a bond conditioned on the faithful administration of the property; and

(3) require payment to the registry of the court of all or a portion of the proceeds of the sale of the property, to be disbursed in accordance with the court's further directions.

Added by Acts 1997, 75th Leg., ch. 7, § 1, eff. April 17, 1997.

§ 3.307. Continuing Jurisdiction of Court; Vacating Original Order

(a) The court has continuing jurisdiction over the court's order rendered under this subchapter.

(b) On the motion of either spouse, the court shall amend or vacate the original order after notice and hearing if:

(1) the spouse who disappeared reappears;

(2) the abandonment or permanent separation ends; or

(3) the spouse who was reported to be a prisoner of war or missing on public service returns.

Added by Acts 1997, 75th Leg., ch. 7, § 1, eff. April 17, 1997. Amended by Acts 2001, 77th Leg., ch. 217, § 24, eff. Sept. 1, 2001.

§ 3.308. Recording Order to Affect Real Property

An order authorized by this subchapter affecting real property is not constructive notice to a good faith purchaser for value or to a creditor without actual notice unless the order is recorded in the deed records of the county in which the real property is located.

Added by Acts 1997, 75th Leg., ch. 7, § 1, eff. April 17, 1997.

§ 3.309. Remedies Cumulative

The remedies provided in this subchapter are cumulative of other rights, powers, and remedies afforded spouses by law.

Added by Acts 1997, 75th Leg., ch. 7, § 1, eff. April 17,

1997.

Subchapter E. Claims for Reimbursement

Statutes in Context
§§ 3.401–3.410

The 2009 Legislature made a significant change to the way a marital estate that makes an economic contribution to property owned by another marital estate determines the amount of its claim for reimbursement with respect to the benefited estate upon the death of a spouse. Essentially, the prior scheme was based on a complex statutory formula for determining economic contribution. Amendments to Family Code §§ 3.401-3.410 adopt instead an equitable reimbursement approach and provide a laundry list of elements which the court may consider in determining the reimbursement amount.

This claim does not create an ownership interest in the property nor does it affect the right to manage, control, or dispose of marital property. The claim matures when the first spouse dies and upon divorce.

§ 3.401. Definitions

In this subchapter:

(1) *repealed*

(2) *repealed*

(3) *repealed*

(4) "Marital estate" means one of three estates:

(A) the community property owned by the spouses together and referred to as the community marital estate;

(B) the separate property owned individually by the husband and referred to as a separate marital estate; or

(C) the separate property owned individually by the wife, also referred to as a separate marital estate.

(5) "Spouse" means a husband, who is a man, or a wife, who is a woman. A member of a civil union or similar relationship entered into in another state between persons of the same sex is not a spouse.

Added by Acts 1999, 76th Leg., ch. 692, § 2, eff. Sept. 1, 1999. Amended by Acts 2001, 77th Leg., ch. 838, § 2, eff. Sept. 1, 2001. Subdivs. (1), (2), (3) repealed by Acts 2009, 81st Leg., ch. 768, § 11(2), eff. Sept. 1, 2009.

§ 3.402. Claim for Reimbursement; Offsets

(a) For purposes of this subchapter, a claim for reimbursement includes:

(1) payment by one marital estate of the unsecured liabilities of another marital estate;

(2) inadequate compensation for the time, toil, talent, and effort of a spouse by a business entity under the control and direction of that spouse;

(3) the reduction of the principal amount of a debt secured by a lien on property owned before marriage, to the extent the debt existed at the time of marriage;

(4) the reduction of the principal amount of a debt secured by a lien on property received by a spouse by gift, devise, or descent during a marriage, to the extent the debt existed at the time the property was received;

(5) the reduction of the principal amount of that part of a debt, including a home equity loan:

(A) incurred during a marriage;

(B) secured by a lien on property; and

(C) incurred for the acquisition of, or for capital improvements to, property;

(6) the reduction of the principal amount of that part of a debt:

(A) incurred during a marriage;

(B) secured by a lien on property owned by a spouse;

(C) for which the creditor agreed to look for repayment solely to the separate marital estate of the spouse on whose property the lien attached; and

(D) incurred for the acquisition of, or for capital improvements to, property;

(7) the refinancing of the principal amount described by Subdivisions (3)-(6), to the extent the refinancing reduces that principal amount in a manner described by the applicable subdivision;

(8) capital improvements to property other than by incurring debt; and

(9) the reduction by the community property estate of an unsecured debt incurred by the separate estate of one of the spouses.

(b) The court shall resolve a claim for reimbursement by using equitable principles, including the principle that claims for reimbursement may be offset against each other if the court determines it to be appropriate.

(c) Benefits for the use and enjoyment of property may be offset against a claim for reimbursement for expenditures to benefit a marital estate, except that the separate estate of a spouse may not claim an offset for use and enjoyment of a primary or secondary residence owned wholly or partly by the separate estate against contributions made by the community estate to the separate estate.

(d) Reimbursement for funds expended by a marital estate for improvements to another marital estate shall be measured by the enhancement in value to the benefited marital estate.

(e) The party seeking an offset to a claim for reimbursement has the burden of proof with respect to the offset.

Added by Acts 1999, 76th Leg., ch. 692, § 2, eff. Sept. 1,

1999. Amended by Acts 2001, 77th Leg., ch. 838, § 2, eff. Sept. 1, 2001. Amended by Acts 2009, 81st Leg., ch.768, § 3, eff. Sept. 1, 2009.

§ 3.404. Application of Inception of Title Rule; Ownership Interest Not Created

(a) This subchapter does not affect the rule of inception of title under which the character of property is determined at the time the right to own or claim the property arises.

(b) A claim for reimbursement under this subchapter does not create an ownership interest in property, but does create a claim against the property of the benefited estate by the contributing estate. The claim matures on dissolution of the marriage or the death of either spouse.

Added by Acts 1999, 76th Leg., ch. 692, § 2, eff. Sept. 1, 1999. Amended by Acts 2001, 77th Leg., ch. 838, § 2, eff. Sept. 1, 2001. Subsec. (b) amended by Acts 2009, 81st Leg., ch. 768, § 4, eff. Sept. 1, 2009.

§ 3.405. Management Rights

This subchapter does not affect the right to manage, control, or dispose of marital property as provided by this chapter.

Added by Acts 1999, 76th Leg., ch. 692, § 2, eff. Sept. 1, 1999. Amended by Acts 2001, 77th Leg., ch. 838, § 2, eff. Sept. 1, 2001.

§ 3.406. Equitable Lien

(a) On dissolution of a marriage, the court may impose an equitable lien on the property of a benefited marital estate to secure a claim for reimbursement against that property by a contributing marital estate.

(b) On the death of a spouse, a court may, on application for a claim for reimbursement brought by the surviving spouse, the personal representative of the estate of the deceased spouse, or any other person interested in the estate, as defined by Section 3, Texas Probate Code, impose an equitable lien on the property of a benefited marital estate to secure a claim for reimbursement against that property by a contributing marital estate.

(c) (Repealed)Subject to homestead restrictions, an equitable lien under this section may be imposed on the entirety of a spouse's property in the marital estate and is not limited to the item of property that benefited from an economic contribution.

Added by Acts 1999, 76th Leg., ch. 692, § 2, eff. Sept. 1, 1999. Amended by Acts 2001, 77th Leg., ch. 838, § 2, eff. Sept. 1, 2001. Subsecs. (a), (b) amended by Acts 2009, 81st Leg., ch. 768, § 5, eff. Sept. 1, 2009; Subsec. (c) repealed by Acts 2009, 81st Leg., ch. 768, § 11(4), eff. Sept. 1, 2009.

§ 3.409. Nonreimbursable Claims

The court may not recognize a marital estate's claim for reimbursement for:

(1) the payment of child support, alimony, or spousal maintenance;

(2) the living expenses of a spouse or child of a spouse;

(3) contributions of property of a nominal value;

(4) the payment of a liability of a nominal amount; or

(5) a student loan owed by a spouse.

Added by Acts 2001, 77th Leg., ch. 838, § 2, eff. Sept. 1, 2001.

§ 3.410. Effect of Marital Property Agreements

A premarital or marital property agreement, whether executed before, on, or after September 1, 2009, that satisfies the requirements of Chapter 4 is effective to waive, release, assign, or partition a claim for economic contribution, reimbursement, or both, under this subchapter to the same extent the agreement would have been effective to waive, release, assign, or partition a claim for economic contribution, reimbursement, or both under the law as it existed immediately before September 1, 2009, unless the agreement provides otherwise.

Added by Acts 2001, 77th Leg., ch. 838, § 2, eff. Sept. 1, 2001. Amended by Acts 2009, 81st Leg., ch. 768, § 6, eff. Sept. 1, 2009.

Chapter 4. Premarital and Marital Property Agreements

Subchapter A. Uniform Premarital Agreement Act

Statutes in Context
§§ 4.001–4.010

The Texas version of the Uniform Premarital Agreement Act are contained in §§ 4.001 - 4.010.

---

§ 4.001. Definitions

In this subchapter:

(1) "Premarital agreement" means an agreement between prospective spouses made in contemplation of marriage and to be effective on marriage.

(2) "Property" means an interest, present or future, legal or equitable, vested or contingent, in real or personal property, including income and earnings.

Added by Acts 1997, 75th Leg., ch. 7, § 1, eff. April 17, 1997.

§ 4.002. Formalities

A premarital agreement must be in writing and signed by both parties. The agreement is enforceable without consideration.

Added by Acts 1997, 75th Leg., ch. 7, § 1, eff. April 17, 1997.

§ 4.003. Content

(a) The parties to a premarital agreement may contract with respect to:

(1) the rights and obligations of each of the parties in any of the property of either or both of them whenever and wherever acquired or located;

(2) the right to buy, sell, use, transfer, exchange, abandon, lease, consume, expend, assign, create a security interest in, mortgage, encumber, dispose of, or otherwise manage and control property;

(3) the disposition of property on separation, marital dissolution, death, or the occurrence or nonoccurrence of any other event;

(4) the modification or elimination of spousal support;

(5) the making of a will, trust, or other arrangement to carry out the provisions of the agreement;

(6) the ownership rights in and disposition of the death benefit from a life insurance policy;

(7) the choice of law governing the construction of the agreement; and

(8) any other matter, including their personal rights and obligations, not in violation of public policy or a statute imposing a criminal penalty.

(b) The right of a child to support may not be adversely affected by a premarital agreement.

Added by Acts 1997, 75th Leg., ch. 7, § 1, eff. April 17, 1997.

§ 4.004. Effect of Marriage

A premarital agreement becomes effective on marriage.

Added by Acts 1997, 75th Leg., ch. 7, § 1, eff. April 17, 1997.

§ 4.005. Amendment or Revocation

After marriage, a premarital agreement may be amended or revoked only by a written agreement signed by the parties. The amended agreement or the revocation is enforceable without consideration.

Added by Acts 1997, 75th Leg., ch. 7, § 1, eff. April 17, 1997.

§ 4.006. Enforcement

(a) A premarital agreement is not enforceable if the party against whom enforcement is requested proves that:

(1) the party did not sign the agreement voluntarily; or

(2) the agreement was unconscionable when it was signed and, before signing the agreement, that party:

(A) was not provided a fair and reasonable disclosure of the property or financial obligations of the other party;

(B) did not voluntarily and expressly waive, in writing, any right to disclosure of the property or financial obligations of the other party beyond the disclosure provided; and

(C) did not have, or reasonably could not have had, adequate knowledge of the property or financial obligations of the other party.

(b) An issue of unconscionability of a premarital agreement shall be decided by the court as a matter of law.

(c) The remedies and defenses in this section are the exclusive remedies or defenses, including common law remedies or defenses.

Added by Acts 1997, 75th Leg., ch. 7, § 1, eff. April 17, 1997.

§ 4.007. Enforcement: Void Marriage

If a marriage is determined to be void, an agreement that would otherwise have been a premarital agreement is enforceable only to the extent necessary to avoid an inequitable result.

Added by Acts 1997, 75th Leg., ch. 7, § 1, eff. April 17, 1997.

§ 4.008. Limitation of Actions

A statute of limitations applicable to an action asserting a claim for relief under a premarital agreement is tolled during the marriage of the parties to the agreement. However, equitable defenses limiting the time for enforcement, including laches and estoppel, are available to either party.

Added by Acts 1997, 75th Leg., ch. 7, § 1, eff. April 17, 1997.

§ 4.009. Application and Construction

This subchapter shall be applied and construed to effect its general purpose to make uniform the law with respect to the subject of this subchapter among states enacting these provisions.

Added by Acts 1997, 75th Leg., ch. 7, § 1, eff. April 17, 1997.

§ 4.010. Short Title

This subchapter may be cited as the Uniform Premarital Agreement Act.

Added by Acts 1997, 75th Leg., ch. 7, § 1, eff. April 17, 1997.

Subchapter B. Marital Property Agreement

Statutes in Context
§§ 4.101–4.106

Sections 4.101 - 4.106 detail the procedure spouses should follow if they wish to partition community property into separate property. Compare §§ 4.201 - 4.206 which deal with the conversion of separate property into community property.

§ 4.101. Definition

In this subchapter, "property" has the meaning assigned by Section 4.001.

Added by Acts 1997, 75th Leg., ch. 7, § 1, eff. April 17, 1997.

§ 4.102. Partition or Exchange of Community Property

At any time, the spouses may partition or exchange between themselves all or part of their community property, then existing or to be acquired, as the spouses may desire. Property or a property interest transferred to a spouse by a partition or exchange agreement becomes that spouse's separate property. The partition or exchange of property may also provide that future earnings and income arising from the transferred property shall be the separate property of the owning spouse

Added by Acts 1997, 75th Leg., ch. 7, § 1, eff. April 17, 1997. Amended by Acts 2003, 78th Leg., ch. 230, § 2, eff. Sept. 1, 2003. Amended by Acts 2005, 79th Leg., ch. 477, § 1, eff. Sept. 1, 2005.

§ 4.103. Agreement Between Spouses Concerning Income or Property from Separate Property

At any time, the spouses may agree that the income or property arising from the separate property that is then owned by one of them, or that may thereafter be acquired, shall be the separate property of the owner.

Added by Acts 1997, 75th Leg., ch. 7, § 1, eff. April 17, 1997.

§ 4.104. Formalities

A partition or exchange agreement under Section 4.102 or an agreement under Section 4.103 must be in writing and signed by both parties. Either agreement is enforceable without consideration.

Added by Acts 1997, 75th Leg., ch. 7, § 1, eff. April 17, 1997. Amended by Acts 2005, 79th Leg., ch. 477, § 2, eff. Sept. 1, 2005.

§ 4.105. Enforcement

(a) A partition or exchange agreement is not enforceable if the party against whom enforcement is requested proves that:

(1) the party did not sign the agreement voluntarily; or

(2) the agreement was unconscionable when it was signed and, before execution of the agreement, that party:

(A) was not provided a fair and reasonable disclosure of the property or financial obligations of the other party;

(B) did not voluntarily and expressly waive, in writing, any right to disclosure of the property or financial obligations of the other party beyond the disclosure provided; and

(C) did not have, or reasonably could not have had, adequate knowledge of the property or financial obligations of the other party.

(b) An issue of unconscionability of a partition or exchange agreement shall be decided by the court as a matter of law.

(c) The remedies and defenses in this section are the exclusive remedies or defenses, including common law remedies or defenses.

Added by Acts 1997, 75ᵗʰ Leg., ch. 7, § 1, eff. April 17, 1997.

§ 4.106. Rights of Creditors and Recordation Under Partition or Exchange Agreement

(a) A provision of a partition or exchange agreement made under this subchapter is void with respect to the rights of a preexisting creditor whose rights are intended to be defrauded by it.

(b) A partition or exchange agreement made under this subchapter may be recorded in the deed records of the county in which a party resides and in the county in which the real property affected is located. An agreement made under this subchapter is constructive notice to a good faith purchaser for value or a creditor without actual notice only if the instrument is acknowledged and recorded in the county in which the real property is located.

Added by Acts 1997, 75ᵗʰ Leg., ch. 7, § 1, eff. April 17, 1997.

Subchapter C. Agreement to Convert Separate Property to Community Property

Statutes in Context
§§ 4.201–4.206

Sections 4.201 - 4.206 address the mechanism for spouses to convert separate property into community property. Texas law did not grant spouses the right to convert separate property into community property until January 1, 2000 when an amendment to Texas Constitution Art. XVI, § 15 took effect. Compare §§ 4.101 - 4.106 which detail the procedure spouses should follow if they wish to partition community property into separate property.

§ 4.201. Definition

In this subchapter, "property" has the meaning assigned by Section 4.001.

Added by Acts 1999, 76ᵗʰ Leg., ch. 692, § 3, eff. Jan. 1, 2000.

§ 4.202. Agreement to Convert to Community Property

At any time, spouses may agree that all or part of the separate property owned by either or both spouses is converted to community property.

Added by Acts 1999, 76ᵗʰ Leg., ch. 692, § 3, eff. Jan. 1, 2000.

§ 4.203. Formalities of Agreement

(a) An agreement to convert separate property to community property:

(1) must be in writing and:

(A) be signed by the spouses;

(B) identify the property being converted; and

(C) specify that the property is being converted to the spouses' community property; and

(2) is enforceable without consideration.

(b) The mere transfer of a spouse's separate property to the name of the other spouse or to the name of both spouses is not sufficient to convert the property to community property under this subchapter.

Added by Acts 1999, 76ᵗʰ Leg., ch. 692, § 3, eff. Jan. 1, 2000.

§ 4.204. Management of Converted Property

Except as specified in the agreement to convert the property and as provided by Subchapter B, Chapter 3, and other law, property converted to community property under this subchapter is subject to:

(1) the sole management, control, and disposition of the spouse in whose name the property is held;

(2) the sole management, control, and disposition of the spouse who transferred the property if the property is not subject to evidence of ownership;

(3) the joint management, control, and disposition of the spouses if the property is held in the name of both spouses; or

(4) the joint management, control, and disposition of the spouses if the property is not subject to evidence of ownership and was owned by both spouses before the property was converted to community property.

Added by Acts 1999, 76ᵗʰ Leg., ch. 692, § 3, eff. Jan. 1, 2000.

§ 4.205. Enforcement

(a) An agreement to convert property to community property under this subchapter is not enforceable if the spouse against whom enforcement is sought proves that the spouse did not:

(1) execute the agreement voluntarily; or

(2) receive a fair and reasonable disclosure of the legal effect of converting the property to community property.

(b) An agreement that contains the following statement, or substantially similar words, prominently displayed in bold-faced type, capital letters, or underlined, is rebuttably presumed to provide a fair and reasonable disclosure of the legal effect of converting property to community property:

"THIS INSTRUMENT CHANGES SEPARATE PROPERTY TO COMMUNITY PROPERTY. THIS MAY HAVE ADVERSE CONSEQUENCES DURING MARRIAGE AND ON TERMINATION OF THE MARRIAGE BY DEATH OR DIVORCE. FOR EXAMPLE:

"EXPOSURE TO CREDITORS. IF YOU SIGN THIS AGREEMENT, ALL OR PART OF THE SEPARATE PROPERTY BEING CONVERTED TO COMMUNITY PROPERTY MAY BECOME SUBJECT TO THE LIABILITIES OF YOUR SPOUSE. IF YOU DO NOT SIGN THIS AGREEMENT, YOUR SEPARATE PROPERTY IS GENERALLY NOT SUBJECT TO THE LIABILITIES OF YOUR SPOUSE UNLESS YOU ARE PERSONALLY LIABLE UNDER ANOTHER RULE OF LAW.

"LOSS OF MANAGEMENT RIGHTS. IF YOU SIGN THIS AGREEMENT, ALL OR PART OF THE SEPARATE PROPERTY BEING CONVERTED TO COMMUNITY PROPERTY MAY BECOME SUBJECT TO EITHER THE JOINT MANAGEMENT, CONTROL, AND DISPOSITION OF YOU AND YOUR SPOUSE OR THE SOLE MANAGEMENT, CONTROL, AND DISPOSITION OF YOUR SPOUSE ALONE. IN THAT EVENT, YOU WILL LOSE YOUR MANAGEMENT RIGHTS OVER THE PROPERTY. IF YOU DO NOT SIGN THIS AGREEMENT, YOU WILL GENERALLY RETAIN THOSE RIGHTS."

"LOSS OF PROPERTY OWNERSHIP. IF YOU SIGN THIS AGREEMENT AND YOUR MARRIAGE IS SUBSEQUENTLY TERMINATED BY THE DEATH OF EITHER SPOUSE OR BY DIVORCE, ALL OR PART OF THE SEPARATE PROPERTY BEING CONVERTED TO COMMUNITY PROPERTY MAY BECOME THE SOLE PROPERTY OF YOUR SPOUSE OR YOUR SPOUSE'S HEIRS. IF YOU DO NOT SIGN THIS AGREEMENT, YOU GENERALLY CANNOT BE DEPRIVED OF OWNERSHIP OF YOUR SEPARATE PROPERTY ON TERMINATION OF YOUR MARRIAGE, WHETHER BY DEATH OR DIVORCE."

(c) If a proceeding regarding enforcement of an agreement under this subchapter occurs after the death of the spouse against whom enforcement is sought, the proof required by Subsection (a) may be made by an heir of the spouse or the personal representative of the estate of that spouse.

Added by Acts 1999, 76th Leg., ch. 692, § 3, eff. Jan. 1, 2000. Amended by Acts 2003, 78th Leg., ch. 230, § 3, eff. Sept. 1, 2003.

§ 4.206. Rights of Creditors; Recording

(a) A conversion of separate property to community property does not affect the rights of a preexisting creditor of the spouse whose separate property is being converted.

(b) A conversion of separate property to community property may be recorded in the deed records of the county in which a spouse resides and of the county in which any real property is located.

(c) A conversion of real property from separate property to community. property is constructive notice to a good faith purchaser for value or a creditor without actual notice only if the agreement to convert the property is acknowledged and recorded in the deed records of the county in which the real property is located.

Added by Acts 1999, 76th Leg., ch. 692, § 3, eff. Jan. 1, 2000.

Chapter 5. Homestead Rights

Statutes in Context
§§ 5.001–5.108

Sections 5.001 - 5.108 detail rules applicable to the sale of the homestead, both generally and in unusual circumstances such as when the location of a spouse is unknown.

Subchapter A. Sale of Homestead; General Rule

§ 5.001. Sale, Conveyance, or Encumbrance of Homestead

Whether the homestead is the separate property of either spouse or community property, neither spouse may sell, convey, or encumber the homestead without the joinder of the other spouse except as provided in this chapter or by other rules of law.

Added by Acts 1997, 75th Leg., ch. 7, § 1, eff. April 17, 1997.

§ 5.002. Sale of Separate Homestead After Spouse Judicially Declared Incapacitated

If the homestead is the separate property of a spouse and the other spouse has been judicially declared incapacitated by a court exercising original jurisdiction over guardianship and other matters under Chapter XIII, Texas Probate Code, the owner may sell, convey, or encumber the homestead without the joinder of the other spouse.

Amended by Acts 2001, 77th Leg., ch. 217, § 25, eff. Sept. 1, 2001.

§ 5.003. Sale of Community Homestead After Spouse Judicially Declared Incapacitated

If the homestead is the community property of the spouses and one spouse has been judicially declared incapacitated by a court exercising original jurisdiction over guardianship and other matters under Chapter XIII, Texas Probate Code, the competent spouse may sell, convey, or encumber the homestead without the joinder of the other spouse.

Added by Acts 1997, 75ᵗʰ Leg., ch. 7, § 1, eff. April 17, 1997. Renumbered from Family Code § 5.107 and amended by Acts 2001, 77ᵗʰ Leg., ch. 217, § 29, eff. Sept. 1, 2001.

Subchapter B. Sale of Homestead Under Unusual Circumstances

§ 5.101. Sale of Separate Homestead Under Unusual Circumstances

If the homestead is the separate property of a spouse, that spouse may file a sworn petition that gives a description of the property, states the facts that make it desirable for the spouse to sell, convey, or encumber the homestead without the joinder of the other spouse, and alleges that the other spouse:

(1) has disappeared and that the location of the spouse remains unknown to the petitioning spouse;

(2) has permanently abandoned the homestead and the petitioning spouse;

(3) has permanently abandoned the homestead and the spouses are permanently separated; or

(4) has been reported by an executive department of the United States to be a prisoner of war or missing on public service of the United States.

Added by Acts 1997, 75ᵗʰ Leg., ch. 7, § 1, eff. April 17, 1997. Amended by Acts 2001, 77ᵗʰ Leg., ch. 217, § 26, eff. Sept. 1, 2001.

§ 5.102. Sale of Community Homestead Under Unusual Circumstances

If the homestead is the community property of the spouses, one spouse may file a sworn petition that gives a description of the property, states the facts that make it desirable for the petitioning spouse to sell, convey, or encumber the homestead without the joinder of the other spouse, and alleges that the other spouse:

(1) has disappeared and that the location of the spouse remains unknown to the petitioning spouse;

(2) has permanently abandoned the homestead and the petitioning spouse;

(3) has permanently abandoned the homestead and the spouses are permanently separated; or

(4) has been reported by an executive department of the United States to be a prisoner of war or missing on public service of the United States.

Added by Acts 1997, 75ᵗʰ Leg., ch. 7, § 1, eff. April 17,

1997. Amended by Acts 2001, 77ᵗʰ Leg., ch. 217, § 27, eff. Sept. 1, 2001.

§ 5.103. Time for Filing Petition

The petitioning spouse may file the petition in a court of the county in which any portion of the property is located not earlier than the 60ᵗʰ day after the date of the occurrence of an event described by Sections 5.101(1)(3) and 5.102(1)(3) or not less than six months after the date the other spouse has been reported to be a prisoner of war or missing on public service.

Added by Acts 1997, 75ᵗʰ Leg., ch. 7, § 1, eff. April 17, 1997. Amended by Acts 2001, 77ᵗʰ Leg., ch. 217, § 28, eff. Sept. 1, 2001.

§ 5.104. Appointment of Attorney

(a) Except as provided by Subsection (b), the court may appoint an attorney in a suit filed under this subchapter for the respondent.

(b) The court shall appoint an attorney in a suit filed under this subchapter for a respondent reported to be a prisoner of war or missing on public service.

(c) The court shall allow a reasonable fee for the appointed attorney's services as a part of the costs of the suit.

Added by Acts 1997, 75ᵗʰ Leg., ch. 7, § 1, eff. April 17, 1997.

§ 5.105. Citation; Notice of Hearing

Citation and notice of hearing for a suit filed as provided by this subchapter shall be issued and served in the manner provided in Subchapter D, Chapter 3.

Added by Acts 1997, 75ᵗʰ Leg., ch. 7, § 1, eff. April 17, 1997.

§ 5.106. Court Order

(a) After notice and hearing, the court shall render an order the court deems just and equitable with respect to the sale, conveyance, or encumbrance of a separate property homestead.

(b) After hearing the evidence, the court, on terms the court deems just and equitable, shall render an order describing or defining the community property at issue that will be subject to the management, control, and disposition of each spouse during marriage.

(c) The court may:

(1) impose any conditions and restrictions the court deems necessary to protect the rights of the respondent;

(2) require a bond conditioned on the faithful administration of the property; and

(3) require payment to the registry of the court of all or a portion of the proceeds of the sale of the property to be disbursed in accordance with the court's further directions.

Added by Acts 1997, 75ᵗʰ Leg., ch. 7, § 1, eff. April 17, 1997.

§ 5.107.   Renumbered as Family Code § 5.003

Acts 2001, 77th Leg., ch. 217, § 29, eff. Sept. 1, 2001.

§ 5.108.   Remedies and Powers Cumulative

The remedies and the powers of a spouse provided by this subchapter are cumulative of the other rights, powers, and remedies afforded the spouses by law.

Added by Acts 1997, 75th Leg., ch. 7, § 1, eff. April 17, 1997.

Subtitle C.   Dissolution of Marriage

Chapter 6.   Suit for Dissolution of Marriage

Subchapter B.   Grounds for Annulment

Statutes in Context
§ 6.111

See the *Statutes in Context* to Probate Code § 47A.

---

§ 6.111   Death of Party to Voidable Marriage

Except as provided by Section 47A, Texas Probate Code, a marriage subject to annulment may not be challenged in a proceeding instituted after the death of either party to the marriage.

Added by Acts 1997, 75th Leg., ch. 7, § 1, eff. April 17, 1997. Amended by Acts 2007, 80th Leg., ch. 1170, § 4.04), eff. Sept. 1, 2007.

Chapter 7.   Award of Marital Property

Statutes in Context
Chapter 7

Chapter 7 explains how marital property is divided upon divorce. Generally, the court awards separate property to the spouse who owns the property while community property is divided in a manner that the court deems just and right after examining the rights of each spouse and any children of the marriage. Special rules are provided for the disposition of insurance, retirement, pension, and similar arrangements.

---

§ 7.001.   General Rule of Property Division

In a decree of divorce or annulment, the court shall order a division of the estate of the parties in a manner that the court deems just and right, having due regard for the rights of each party and any children of the marriage.

Added by Acts 1997, 75th Leg., ch. 7, § 1, eff. April 17, 1997.

§ 7.002.   Division of Property Under Special Circumstances

(a) In addition to the division of the estate of the parties required by Section 7.001, in a decree of divorce or annulment the court shall order a division of the following real and personal property, wherever situated, in a manner that the court deems just and right, having due regard for the rights of each party and any children of the marriage:

(1) property that was acquired by either spouse while domiciled in another state and that would have been community property if the spouse who acquired the property had been domiciled in this state at the time of the acquisition; or

(2) property that was acquired by either spouse in exchange for real or personal property and that would have been community property if the spouse who acquired the property so exchanged had been domiciled in this state at the time of its acquisition.

(b) In a decree of divorce or annulment, the court shall award to a spouse the following real and personal property, wherever situated, as the separate property of the spouse:

(1) property that was acquired by the spouse while domiciled in another state and that would have been the spouse's separate property if the spouse had been domiciled in this state at the time of acquisition; or

(2) property that was acquired by the spouse in exchange for real or personal property and that would have been the spouse's separate property if the spouse had been domiciled in this state at the time of acquisition.

(c) In a decree of divorce or annulment, the court shall confirm the following as the separate property of a spouse if partitioned or exchanged by written agreement of the spouses:

(1) income and earnings from the spouses' property, wages, salaries, and other forms of compensation received on or after January 1 of the year in which the suit for dissolution of marriage was filed; or

(2) income and earnings from the spouses' property, wages, salaries, and other forms of compensation received in another year during which the spouses were married for any part of the year.

Added by Acts 1997, 75th Leg., ch. 7, § 1, eff. April 17, 1997. Amended by Acts 1999, 76th Leg., ch. 692, § 4, eff. Sept. 1, 1999; Acts 2001, 77th Leg., ch. 838, § 4, eff. Sept. 1, 2001. Amended by Acts 2003, 78th Leg., ch. 230, § 4, eff. Sept. 1, 2003.

§ 7.003.   Disposition of Retirement and Employment Benefits and Other Plans

In a decree of divorce or annulment, the court shall determine the rights of both spouses in a pension, retirement plan, annuity, individual retirement account, employee stock option plan, stock option, or other form of savings, bonus, profit-sharing, or other employer plan or financial plan of an employee or a participant, regardless of whether the person is self-employed, in the nature of compensation or savings.

Added by Acts 1997, 75th Leg., ch. 7, § 1, eff. April 17, 1997.

§ 7.004. Disposition of Rights in Insurance

In a decree of divorce or annulment, the court shall specifically divide or award the rights of each spouse in an insurance policy.

Added by Acts 1997, 75th Leg., ch. 7, § 1, eff. April 17, 1997.

§ 7.005. Insurance Coverage Not Specifically Awarded

(a) If in a decree of divorce or annulment the court does not specifically award all of the rights of the spouses in an insurance policy other than life insurance in effect at the time the decree is rendered, the policy remains in effect until the policy expires according to the policy's own terms.

(b) The proceeds of a valid claim under the policy are payable as follows:

(1) if the interest in the property insured was awarded solely to one former spouse by the decree, to that former spouse;

(2) if an interest in the property insured was awarded to each former spouse, to those former spouses in proportion to the interests awarded; or

(3) if the insurance coverage is directly related to the person of one of the former spouses, to that former spouse.

(c) The failure of either former spouse to change the endorsement on the policy to reflect the distribution of proceeds established by this section does not relieve the insurer of liability to pay the proceeds or any other obligation on the policy.

(d) This section does not affect the right of a former spouse to assert an ownership interest in an undivided life insurance policy, as provided by Subchapter D, Chapter 9.

Added by Acts 1997, 75th Leg., ch. 7, § 1, eff. April 17, 1997.

§ 7.006. Agreement Incident to Divorce or Annulment

(a) To promote amicable settlement of disputes in a suit for divorce or annulment, the spouses may enter into a written agreement concerning the division of the property and the liabilities of the spouses and maintenance of either spouse. The agreement may be revised or repudiated before rendition of the divorce or annulment unless the agreement is binding under another rule of law.

(b) If the court finds that the terms of the written agreement in a divorce or annulment are just and right, those terms are binding on the court. If the court approves the agreement, the court may set forth the agreement in full or incorporate the agreement by reference in the final decree.

(c) If the court finds that the terms of the written agreement in a divorce or annulment are not just and right, the court may request the spouses to submit a revised agreement or may set the case for a contested hearing.

Added by Acts 1997, 75th Leg., ch. 7, § 1, eff. April 17, 1997.

§ 7.007. Disposition of Claim for Reimbursement

In a decree of divorce or annulment, the court shall determine the rights of both spouses in a claim for reimbursement as provided by Subchapter E, Chapter 3, and shall apply equitable principles to:

(1) determine whether to recognize the claim after taking into account all the relative circumstances of the spouses; and

(2) order a division of the claim for reimbursement, if appropriate, in a manner that the court considers just and right, having due regard for the rights of each party and any children of the marriage.

Added by Acts 2001, 77th Leg., ch. 838, § 5, eff. Sept. 1, 2001. Amended by Acts 2009, 81st Leg., ch. 768, § 7, eff. Sept. 1, 2009.

§ 7.008. Consideration of Taxes

In ordering the division of the estate of the parties to a suit for dissolution of a marriage, the court may consider:

(1) whether a specific asset will be subject to taxation; and

(2) if the asset will be subject to taxation, when the tax will be required to be paid.

Acts 2005, 79th Leg., ch. 168, § 1, eff. Sept. 1, 2005.

§ 7.009. Fraud on the Community; Division and Disposition of Reconstituted Estate

(a) In this section, "reconstituted estate" means the total value of the community estate that would exist if an actual or constructive fraud on the community had not occurred.

(b) If the trier of fact determines that a spouse has committed actual or constructive fraud on the community, the court shall:

(1) calculate the value by which the community estate was depleted as a result of the fraud on the community and calculate the amount of the reconstituted estate; and

(2) divide the value of the reconstituted estate between the parties in a manner the court deems just and right.

(c) In making a just and right division of the reconstituted estate under Section 7.001, the court may grant any legal or equitable relief necessary to accomplish a just and right division, including:

(1) awarding to the wronged spouse an appropriate share of the community estate

remaining after the actual or constructive fraud on the community;

(2) awarding a money judgment in favor of the wronged spouse against the spouse who committed the actual or constructive fraud on the community; or

(3) awarding to the wronged spouse both a money judgment and an appropriate share of the community estate.

Acts 2011, 82nd Leg., ch. 487, § 1, eff. Sept. 1, 2011.

Chapter 9.   Post-Decree Proceedings

Subchapter D.   Disposition of Undivided Beneficial Interest

Statutes in Context
§ 9.301 & § 9.302

Upon divorce, §§ 9.301 and 9.302 provide for the automatic revocation of an ex-spouse as the beneficiary of a life insurance policy or retirement plan unless one of the limited exceptions applies such as the ex-spouse redesignating the other former spouse after the divorce is final. However, it is highly likely these provisions will not apply to a policy or plan governed by the Employee Retirement Income Security Act (ERISA). The United States Supreme Court in *Egelhoff v. Egelhoff*, 532 U.S. 141 (2001), held that Washington provision altering the specified beneficiary upon divorce was preempted by ERISA. See *Heggy v. American Trading Employee Retirement Account Plan*, 56 S.W.3d 280 (Tex. App.—Houston [14th Dist.] 2001, no pet.) (holding that Family Code § 9.302 did not apply to a retirement account governed by ERISA and thus permitting the ex-spouse to receive the proceeds). Likewise, in *Hillman v. Maretta*, 133 S. Ct. 1943 (2013), the United States Supreme Court held that Virginia's statute voiding the designation of an ex-spouse did not apply to a life insurance policy covered by the Federal Employees' Group Life Insurance Act of 1954.

---

§ 9.301.   Pre-Decree Designation of Ex-Spouse as Beneficiary of Life Insurance

(a) If a decree of divorce or annulment is rendered after an insured has designated the insured's spouse as a beneficiary under a life insurance policy in force at the time of rendition, a provision in the policy in favor of the insured's former spouse is not effective unless:

(1) the decree designates the insured's former spouse as the beneficiary;

(2) the insured redesignates the former spouse as the beneficiary after rendition of the decree; or

(3) the former spouse is designated to receive the proceeds in trust for, on behalf of, or for the

benefit of a child or a dependent of either former spouse.

(b) If a designation is not effective under Subsection (a), the proceeds of the policy are payable to the named alternative beneficiary or, if there is not a named alternative beneficiary, to the estate of the insured.

(c) An insurer who pays the proceeds of a life insurance policy issued by the insurer to the beneficiary under a designation that is not effective under Subsection (a) is liable for payment of the proceeds to the person or estate provided by Subsection (b) only if:

(1) before payment of the proceeds to the designated beneficiary, the insurer receives written notice at the home office of the insurer from an interested person that the designation is not effective under Subsection (a); and

(2) the insurer has not interpleaded the proceeds into the registry of a court of competent jurisdiction in accordance with the Texas Rules of Civil Procedure.

Added by Acts 1997, 75th Leg., ch. 7, § 1, eff. April 17, 1997.

§ 9.302.   Pre-Decree Designation of Ex-Spouse as Beneficiary in Retirement Benefits and Other Financial Plans

(a) If a decree of divorce or annulment is rendered after a spouse, acting in the capacity of a participant, annuitant, or account holder, has designated the other spouse as a beneficiary under an individual retirement account, employee stock option plan, stock option, or other form of savings, bonus, profit-sharing, or other employer plan or financial plan of an employee or a participant in force at the time of rendition, the designating provision in the plan in favor of the other former spouse is not effective unless:

(1) the decree designates the other former spouse as the beneficiary;

(2) the designating former spouse redesignates the other former spouse as the beneficiary after rendition of the decree; or

(3) the other former spouse is designated to receive the proceeds or benefits in trust for, on behalf of, or for the benefit of a child or dependent of either former spouse.

(b) If a designation is not effective under Subsection (a), the benefits or proceeds are payable to the named alternative beneficiary or, if there is not a named alternative beneficiary, to the designating former spouse.

(c) A business entity, employer, pension trust, insurer, financial institution, or other person obligated to pay retirement benefits or proceeds of a financial plan covered by this section who pays the benefits or proceeds to the beneficiary under a designation of the other former spouse that is not effective under Subsection (a) is liable for payment of the benefits or proceeds to the person provided by Subsection (b) only if:

(1) before payment of the benefits or proceeds to the designated beneficiary, the payor receives written notice at the home office or principal office of the payor from an interested person that the designation of the beneficiary or fiduciary is not effective under Subsection (a); and

(2) the payor has not interpleaded the benefits or proceeds into the registry of a court of competent jurisdiction in accordance with the Texas Rules of Civil Procedure.

(d) This section does not affect the right of a former spouse to assert an ownership interest in an undivided pension, retirement, annuity, or other financial plan described by this section as provided by this subchapter.

(e) This section does not apply to the disposition of a beneficial interest in a retirement benefit or other financial plan of a public retirement system as defined by Section 802.001, Government Code.

Added by Acts 1997, 75th Leg., ch. 7, § 1, eff. April 17, 1997.

Title 2. Child in Relation to the Family

Subtitle A. Limitations of Minority

Chapter 31. Removal of Disabilities of Minority

Statutes in Context
§§ 31.001–31.007

Sections 31.001 - 31.007 explain how a minor may petition the court to have the disabilities of minority removed. If the minor is successful in removing the disabilities of minority, that minor is treated as an adult and thus, among other things, would have the capacity to contract. However, having the disabilities of minority removed does not cause the minor to be treated as reaching a particular age. For example, an individual must be 18 years old to execute a will under Probate Code § 57 (unless married, divorced, or in the armed forces). Under Family Code § 31.006, having the disabilities of minority removed does not cause the minor to be treated as reaching a statutorily specified prerequisite age. Consequently, the minor would continue to lack the legal capacity to execute a will.

§ 31.001. Requirements

(a) A minor may petition to have the disabilities of minority removed for limited or general purposes if the minor is:

(1) a resident of this state;

(2) 17 years of age, or at least 16 years of age and living separate and apart from the minor's parents, managing conservator, or guardian; and

(3) self-supporting and managing the minor's own financial affairs.

(b) A minor may file suit under this chapter in the minor's own name. The minor need not be represented by next friend.

Amended by Acts 1995, 74th Leg., ch. 20, § 1, eff. April 20, 1995.

§ 31.002. Requisites of Petition; Verification

(a) The petition for removal of disabilities of minority must state:

(1) the name, age, and place of residence of the petitioner;

(2) the name and place of residence of each living parent;

(3) the name and place of residence of the guardian of the person and the guardian of the estate, if any;

(4) the name and place of residence of the managing conservator, if any;

(5) the reasons why removal would be in the best interest of the minor; and

(6) the purposes for which removal is requested.

(b) A parent of the petitioner must verify the petition, except that if a managing conservator or guardian of the person has been appointed, the petition must be verified by that person. If the person who is to verify the petition is unavailable or that person's whereabouts are unknown, the guardian ad litem shall verify the petition.

Amended by Acts 1995, 74th Leg., ch. 20, § 1, eff. April 20, 1995.

§ 31.003. Venue

The petitioner shall file the petition in the county in which the petitioner resides.

Amended by Acts 1995, 74th Leg., ch. 20, § 1, eff. April 20, 1995.

§ 31.004. Guardian Ad Litem

The court shall appoint a guardian ad litem to represent the interest of the petitioner at the hearing.

Amended by Acts 1995, 74th Leg., ch. 20, § 1, eff. April 20, 1995.

§ 31.005. Order

The court by order, or the Texas Supreme Court by rule or order, may remove the disabilities of minority of a minor, including any restriction imposed by Chapter 32, if the court or the Texas Supreme Court finds the removal to be in the best interest of the petitioner. The order or rule must state the limited or general purposes for which disabilities are removed.

Amended by Acts 1995, 74th Leg., ch. 20, § 1, eff. April 20, 1995. Amended by Acts 1999, 76th Leg., ch. 1303, § 1, eff. Sept. 1, 1999.

§ 31.006. Effect of General Removal

Except for specific constitutional and statutory age requirements, a minor whose disabilities are removed for general purposes has the capacity of an adult, including the capacity to contract. Except as provided by federal law, all educational rights accorded to the parent of a student, including the right to make education decisions under 151.001(a)(10) [151.003(a)(10)], transfer to the minor whose disabilities are removed for general purposes.

Amended by Acts 1995, 74th Leg., ch. 20, § 1, eff. April 20, 1995; Acts 2001, 77th Leg., ch. 767, § 9, eff. June 13, 2001. Amended by Acts 2015, 84th Leg., ch. 1236, § 7.001, eff. Sept. 1, 2015.

§ 31.007. Registration of Order of Another State or Nation

(a) A nonresident minor who has had the disabilities of minority removed in the state of the minor's residence may file a certified copy of the order removing disabilities in the deed records of any county in this state.

(b) When a certified copy of the order of a court of another state or nation is filed, the minor has the capacity of an adult, except as provided by Section 31.006 and by the terms of the order.

Amended by Acts 1995, 74th Leg., ch. 20, § 1, eff. April 20, 1995.

§ 31.008. Waiver of Citation

(a) A party to a suit under this chapter may waive the issuance or service of citation after the suit is filed by filing with the clerk of the court in which the suit is filed the waiver of the party acknowledging receipt of a copy of the filed petition.

(b) The party executing the waiver may not sign the waiver using a digitized signature.

(c) The waiver must contain the mailing address of the party executing the waiver.

(d) Notwithstanding Section 132.001, Civil Practice and Remedies Code, the waiver must be sworn before a notary public who is not an attorney in the suit. This subsection does not apply if the party executing the waiver is incarcerated.

(e) The Texas Rules of Civil Procedure do not apply to a waiver executed under this section.

(f) For purposes of this section, "digitized signature" has the meaning assigned by Section 101.0096.

Added by Acts 2015, 84th Leg., ch. 198, § 2, eff. Sept. 1, 2015.

Chapter 32. Consent to Treatment of Child by Non-Parent or Child

---

Statutes in Context
Chapter 32

Chapter 32 explains when a non-parent may make medical, dental, psychological, and surgical treatment decisions for a child. Special provisions apply to immunization decisions.

Subchapter A. Consent to Medical, Dental, Psychological, and Surgical Treatment

§ 32.001. Consent by Non-Parent

(a) The following persons may consent to medical, dental, psychological, and surgical treatment of a child when the person having the right to consent as otherwise provided by law cannot be contacted and that person has not given actual notice to the contrary:

(1) a grandparent of the child;

(2) an adult brother or sister of the child;

(3) an adult aunt or uncle of the child;

(4) an educational institution in which the child is enrolled that has received written authorization to consent from a person having the right to consent;

(5) an adult who has actual care, control, and possession of the child and has written authorization to consent from a person having the right to consent;

(6) a court having jurisdiction over a suit affecting the parent-child relationship of which the child is the subject;

(7) an adult responsible for the actual care, control, and possession of a child under the jurisdiction of a juvenile court or committed by a juvenile court to the care of an agency of the state or county; or

(8) a peace officer who has lawfully taken custody of a minor, if the peace officer has reasonable grounds to believe the minor is in need of immediate medical treatment.

(b) Except as otherwise provided by this subsection, the Texas Juvenile Justice Department [Youth Commission] may consent to the medical, dental, psychological, and surgical treatment of a child committed to the department [Texas Youth Commission] under Title 3 when the person having the right to consent has been contacted and that person has not given actual notice to the contrary. Consent for medical, dental, psychological, and surgical treatment of a child for whom the Department of Family and Protective Services has been appointed managing conservator and who is committed to the Texas Juvenile Justice Department [Youth Commission] is governed by Sections 266.004, 266.009, and 266.010.

(c) This section does not apply to consent for the immunization of a child.

(d) A person who consents to the medical treatment of a minor under Subsection (a)(7) or (8) is immune from liability for damages resulting from the examination or treatment of the minor, except to the extent of the person's own acts of negligence. A physician or dentist licensed to practice in this state, or a hospital or medical facility at which a minor is treated is immune from liability for damages resulting from the examination or treatment of a minor under this section, except to the extent of the person's own acts of negligence.

Amended by Acts 1995, 74th Leg., ch. 20, § 1, eff. April 20, 1995; Acts 1995, 74th Leg., ch. 751, § 5, eff. Sept. 1, 1995. Subsec. (b) amended by Acts 2009, 81st Leg., ch. 108, § 1, eff. May 23, 2009. Subsec. (b) amended by Acts 2015, 84th Leg., ch. 734, § 37, eff. Sept. 1, 2015.

§ 32.002. Consent Form

(a) Consent to medical treatment under this subchapter must be in writing, signed by the person giving consent, and given to the doctor, hospital, or other medical facility that administers the treatment.

(b) The consent must include:

(1) the name of the child;

(2) the name of one or both parents, if known, and the name of any managing conservator or guardian of the child;

(3) the name of the person giving consent and the person's relationship to the child;

(4) a statement of the nature of the medical treatment to be given; and

(5) the date the treatment is to begin.

Amended by Acts 1995, 74th Leg., ch. 20, § 1, eff. April 20, 1995.

§ 32.003. Consent to Treatment by Child

(a) A child may consent to medical, dental, psychological, and surgical treatment for the child by a licensed physician or dentist if the child:

(1) is on active duty with the armed services of the United States of America;

(2) is:

(A) 16 years of age or older and resides separate and apart from the child's parents, managing conservator, or guardian, with or without the consent of the parents, managing conservator, or guardian and regardless of the duration of the residence; and

(B) managing the child's own financial affairs, regardless of the source of the income;

(3) consents to the diagnosis and treatment of an infectious, contagious, or communicable disease that is required by law or a rule to be reported by the licensed physician or dentist to a local health officer or the Texas Department of Health, including all diseases within the scope of Section 81.041, Health and Safety Code;

(4) is unmarried and pregnant and consents to hospital, medical, or surgical treatment, other than abortion, related to the pregnancy;

(5) consents to examination and treatment for drug or chemical addiction, drug or chemical dependency, or any other condition directly related to drug or chemical use;

(6) is unmarried, is the parent of a child, and has actual custody of his or her child and consents to medical, dental, psychological, or surgical treatment for the child; or

(7) is serving a term of confinement in a facility operated by or under contract with the Texas Department of Criminal Justice, unless the treatment would constitute a prohibited practice under Section 164.052(a)(19), Occupations Code.

(b) Consent by a child to medical, dental, psychological, and surgical treatment under this section is not subject to disaffirmance because of minority.

(c) Consent of the parents, managing conservator, or guardian of a child is not necessary in order to authorize hospital, medical, surgical, or dental care under this section.

(d) A licensed physician, dentist, or psychologist may, with or without the consent of a child who is a patient, advise the parents, managing conservator, or guardian of the child of the treatment given to or needed by the child.

(e) A physician, dentist, psychologist, hospital, or medical facility is not liable for the examination and treatment of a child under this section except for the provider's or the facility's own acts of negligence.

(f) A physician, dentist, psychologist, hospital, or medical facility may rely on the written statement of the child containing the grounds on which the child has capacity to consent to the child's medical treatment.

Amended by Acts 1995, 74th Leg., ch. 20, § 1, eff. April 20, 1995; Acts 1995, 74th Leg., ch. 751, § 6, eff. Sept. 1, 1995; Acts 2001, 77th Leg., ch. 821, § 2.01, eff. June 14, 2001. Subsec. (a) amended by Acts 2007, 80th Leg., ch. 1227, § 2, eff. June 15, 2007.

§ 32.004. Consent to Counseling

(a) A child may consent to counseling for:

(1) suicide prevention;

(2) chemical addiction or dependency; or

(3) sexual, physical, or emotional abuse.

(b) A licensed or certified physician, psychologist, counselor, or social worker having reasonable grounds to believe that a child has been sexually, physically, or emotionally abused, is contemplating suicide, or is suffering from a chemical or drug addiction or dependency may:

(1) counsel the child without the consent of the child's parents or, if applicable, managing conservator or guardian;

(2) with or without the consent of the child who is a client, advise the child's parents or, if applicable, managing conservator or guardian of the treatment given to or needed by the child; and

(3) rely on the written statement of the child containing the grounds on which the child has capacity to consent to the child's own treatment under this section.

(c) Unless consent is obtained as otherwise allowed by law, a physician, psychologist, counselor, or social worker may not counsel a child if consent is prohibited by a court order.

(d) A physician, psychologist, counselor, or social worker counseling a child under this section is not liable for damages except for damages resulting from the person's negligence or wilful misconduct.

(e) A parent, or, if applicable, managing conservator or guardian, who has not consented to counseling treatment of the child is not obligated to compensate a physician, psychologist, counselor, or social worker for counseling services rendered under this section.

Amended by Acts 1995, 74th Leg., ch. 20, § 1, eff. April 20, 1995.

§ 32.005. Examination Without Consent or Abuse or Neglect of Child

(a) Except as provided by Subsection (c), a physician, dentist, or psychologist having reasonable grounds to believe that a child's physical or mental condition has been adversely affected by abuse or neglect may examine the child without the consent of the child, the child's parents, or other person authorized to consent to treatment under this subchapter.

(b) An examination under this section may include X-rays, blood tests, photographs, and penetration of tissue necessary to accomplish those tests.

(c) Unless consent is obtained as otherwise allowed by law, a physician, dentist, or psychologist may not examine a child:

(1) 16 years of age or older who refuses to consent; or

(2) for whom consent is prohibited by a court order.

(d) A physician, dentist, or psychologist examining a child under this section is not liable for damages except for damages resulting from the physician's or dentist's negligence.

Amended by Acts 1995, 74th Leg., ch. 20, § 1, eff. April 20, 1995; Amended by Acts 1997, 75th Leg., ch. 575, § 1, eff. Sept. 1, 1997.

Subchapter B. Immunization

§ 32.101. Who May Consent to Immunization of Child

(a) In addition to persons authorized to consent to immunization under Chapter 151 and Chapter 153, the following persons may consent to the immunization of a child:

(1) a guardian of the child; and

(2) a person authorized under the law of another state or a court order to consent for the child.

(b) If the persons listed in Subsection (a) are not available and the authority to consent is not denied under Subsection (c), consent to the immunization of a child may be given by:

(1) a grandparent of the child;

(2) an adult brother or sister of the child;

(3) an adult aunt or uncle of the child;

(4) a stepparent of the child;

(5) an educational institution in which the child is enrolled that has written authorization to consent for the child from a parent, managing conservator, guardian, or other person who under the law of another state or a court order may consent for the child;

(6) another adult who has actual care, control, and possession of the child and has written authorization to consent for the child from a parent, managing conservator, guardian, or other person who, under the law of another state or a court order, may consent for the child;

(7) a court having jurisdiction of a suit affecting the parent-child relationship of which the minor is the subject;

(8) an adult having actual care, control, and possession of the child under an order of a juvenile court or by commitment by a juvenile court to the care of an agency of the state or county; or

(9) an adult having actual care, control, and possession of the child as the child's primary caregiver.

(c) A person otherwise authorized to consent under Subsection (a) may not consent for the child if the person has actual knowledge that a parent, managing conservator, guardian of the child, or other person who under the law of another state or a court order may consent for the child:

(1) has expressly refused to give consent to the immunization;

(2) has been told not to consent for the child; or

(3) has withdrawn a prior written authorization for the person to consent.

(d) The Texas Juvenile Justice Department [Youth Commission] may consent to the immunization of a child committed to it if a parent, managing conservator, or guardian of the minor or other person who, under the law of another state or court order, may consent for the minor has been contacted and:

(1) refuses to consent; and

(2) does not expressly deny to the department [Texas Youth Commission] the authority to consent for the child.

(e) A person who consents under this section shall provide the health care provider with sufficient and accurate health history and other information about the minor for whom the consent is given and, if necessary, sufficient and accurate health history and information about the minor's family to enable the person who may consent to the minor's immunization and the health care provider to determine adequately the risks and benefits inherent in the proposed immunization and to determine whether immunization is advisable.

(f) Consent to immunization must meet the requirements of Section 32.002(a).

Amended by Acts 1995, 74th Leg., ch. 20, § 1, eff. April 20, 1995; Amended by Acts 1997, 75th Leg., ch. 165, § 7.09(a), eff. Sept. 1, 1997. Acts 1999, 76th Leg., ch. 62, § 6.02, eff. Sept. 1, 1999. Subsec. (d) amended by Acts 2015, 84th Leg., ch. 734, § 38, eff. Sept. 1, 2015.

§ 32.1011. Consent to Immunization By Child

(a) Notwithstanding Section 32.003 or 32.101, a child may consent to the child's own immunization for a disease if:

(1) the child:

(A) is pregnant; or

(B) is the parent of a child and has actual custody of that child; and

(2) the Centers for Disease Control and Prevention recommend or authorize the initial dose of an immunization for that disease to be administered before seven years of age.

(b) Consent to immunization under this section must meet the requirements of Section 32.002(a).

(c) Consent by a child to immunization under this section is not subject to disaffirmance because of minority.

(d) A health care provider or facility may rely on the written statement of the child containing the grounds on which the child has capacity to consent to the child's immunization under this section.

(e) To the extent of any conflict between this section and Section 32.003, this section controls.

Added by Acts 2013, 83rd Leg., ch. 1313, § 1, eff. May. 17, 2013.

§ 32.102. Informed Consent to Immunization

(a) A person authorized to consent to the immunization of a child has the responsibility to ensure that the consent, if given, is an informed consent. The person authorized to consent is not required to be present when the immunization of the child is requested if a consent form that meets the requirements of Section 32.002 has been given to the health care provider.

(b) The responsibility of a health care provider to provide information to a person consenting to immunization is the same as the provider's responsibility to a parent.

(c) As part of the information given in the counseling for informed consent, the health care provider shall provide information to inform the person authorized to consent to immunization of the procedures available under the National Childhood Vaccine Injury Act of 1986 (42 U.S.C. § 300aa-1 et seq.) to seek possible recovery for unreimbursed expenses for certain injuries arising out of the administration of certain vaccines.

Amended by Acts 1995, 74th Leg., ch. 20, § 1, eff. April 20, 1995. Renumbered from § 32.103 and amended by Acts 1997, 75th Leg., ch. 165, § 7.09(b), (d), eff. Sept. 1, 1997.

§ 32.103. Limited Liability for Immunization

(a) In the absence of wilful misconduct or gross negligence, a health care provider who accepts the health history and other information given by a person who is delegated the authority to consent to the immunization of a child during the informed consent counseling is not liable for an adverse reaction to an immunization or for other injuries to the child resulting from factual errors in the health history or information given by the person to the health care provider.

(b) A person consenting to immunization of a child, a physician, nurse, or other health care provider, or a public health clinic, hospital, or other medical facility is not liable for damages arising from an immunization administered to a child authorized under this subchapter except for injuries resulting from the person's or facility's own acts of negligence.

Amended by Acts 1995, 74th Leg., ch 20, § 1, eff. April 20, 1995. Renumbered from § 32.104 by Acts 1997, 75th Leg., ch. 165, § 7.09(e), eff. Sept. 1, 1997.

Title 5. The Parent-Child Relationship and the Suit Affecting the Parent-Child Relationship

Subtitle B. Suits Affecting the Parent-Child Relationship

Chapter 154. Child Support

Subchapter A. Court-Ordered Child Support

Statutes in Context
§ 154.005

Section 154.005 codifies an important exception to the effectiveness of spendthrift trust provisions which are generally enforceable under Property Code § 112.035. Assuming the court first imposes a child-support obligation on the parent who is the beneficiary of a spendthrift trust, the court may order the trustee to make payments for the support of the child notwithstanding the spendthrift provision.   If a trust payment is mandatory, then the full amount of that payment may be reached.   However, if the trust is discretionary, the court is limited to ordering child support payments from trust income.

---

§ 154.005. Payments of Support Obligation by Trust

(a) The court may order the trustees of a spendthrift or other trust to make disbursements for the support of a child to the extent the trustees are required to make payments to a beneficiary who is required to make child support payments as provided by this chapter.

(b) If disbursement of the assets of the trust is discretionary, the court may order child support payments from the income of the trust but not from the principal.

Added by Acts 1995, 74ᵗʰ Leg., ch. 20, § 1, eff. April 20, 1995.

Statutes in Context
§ 154.015

The 2007 Legislature added this section which acts to accelerate the child support obligations of a decedent. Thus, when a parent ordered to make child support payments dies, the present value of the rest of the payments that would be owed from the time of the parent's death to the end of the support obligation (typically, the child's 18ᵗʰ birthday) becomes a claim against the parent's estate. The family court, not the probate court, is charged with the duty to determine this amount. No provision is made for a refund to the estate if the child dies prior to reaching age 18.

---

§ 154.015. Acceleration of Unpaid Child Support Obligation

(a) In this section, "estate" has the meaning assigned by Section 3, Texas Probate Code.

(b) If the child support obligor dies before the child support obligation terminates, the remaining unpaid balance of the child support obligation becomes payable on the date the obligor dies.

(c) For purposes of this section, the court of continuing jurisdiction shall determine the amount of the unpaid child support obligation for each child of the deceased obligor. In determining the amount of the unpaid child support obligation, the court shall consider all relevant factors, including:

(1) the present value of the total amount of monthly periodic child support payments that would become due between the month in which the obligor dies and the month in which the child turns 18 years of age, based on the amount of the periodic monthly child support payments under the child support order in effect on the date of the obligor's death;

(2) the present value of the total amount of health insurance and dental insurance premiums payable for the benefit of the child from the month in which the obligor dies until the month in which the child turns 18 years of age, based on the cost of health insurance and dental insurance for the child ordered to be paid on the date of the obligor's death;

(3) in the case of a disabled child under 18 years of age or an adult disabled child, an amount to be determined by the court under Section 154.306;

(4) the nature and amount of any benefit to which the child would be entitled as a result of the obligor's death, including life insurance proceeds,

annuity payments, trust distributions, social security death benefits, and retirement survivor benefits; and

(5) any other financial resource available for the support of the child.

(d) If, after considering all relevant factors, the court finds that the child support obligation has been satisfied, the court shall render an order terminating the child support obligation. If the court finds that the child support obligation is not satisfied, the court shall render a judgment in favor of the obligee, for the benefit of the child, in the amount of the unpaid child support obligation determined under Subsection (c). The order must designate the obligee as constructive trustee, for the benefit of the child, of any money received in satisfaction of the judgment.

(e) The obligee has a claim, on behalf of the child, against the deceased obligor's estate for the unpaid child support obligation determined under Subsection (c). The obligee may present the claim in the manner provided by the Texas Probate Code.

(f) If money paid to the obligee for the benefit of the child exceeds the amount of the unpaid child support obligation remaining at the time of the obligor's death, the obligee shall hold the excess amount as constructive trustee for the benefit of the deceased obligor's estate until the obligee delivers the excess amount to the legal representative of the deceased obligor's estate.

Added by Acts 2007, 80ᵗʰ Leg., ch. 1404, § 2, eff. Sept. 1, 2007. Subsec. (c)(2) amended by Acts 2015, 84ᵗʰ Leg., ch. 1150, § 9, eff. Sept. 1, 2018.

§ 154.016. Provision of Support in Event of Death of Parent

(a) The court may order a child support obligor to obtain and maintain a life insurance policy, including a decreasing term life insurance policy, that will establish an insurance-funded trust or an annuity payable to the obligee for the benefit of the child that will satisfy the support obligation under the child support order in the event of the obligor's death.

(b) In determining the nature and extent of the obligation to provide for the support of the child in the event of the death of the obligor, the court shall consider all relevant factors, including:

(1) the present value of the total amount of monthly periodic child support payments from the date the child support order is rendered until the month in which the child turns 18 years of age, based on the amount of the periodic monthly child support payment under the child support order;

(2) the present value of the total amount of health insurance and dental insurance premiums payable for the benefit of the child from the date the child support order is rendered until the month in which the child turns 18 years of age, based on the cost of health insurance and dental insurance for the child ordered to be paid; and

(3) in the case of a disabled child under 18 years of age or an adult disabled child, an amount to be determined by the court under Section 154.306.

(c) The court may, on its own motion or on a motion of the obligee, require the child support obligor to provide proof satisfactory to the court verifying compliance with the order rendered under this section.

Added by Acts 2007, 80th Leg., ch. 1404, § 2, eff. Sept. 1, 2007. Subsec. (b)(2) amended by Acts 2015, 84th Leg., ch. 1150, § 10, eff. Sept. 1, 2015.

Chapter 160. Uniform Parentage Act

Statutes in Context
Chapter 160

Chapter 160 contains the Texas version of the Uniform Parentage Act.

Subchapter A. Application and Construction

§ 160.001. Application and Construction

This chapter shall be applied and construed to promote the uniformity of the law among the states that enact the Uniform Parentage Act.

Amended by Acts 2001, 77th Leg., ch. 821, § 1.01, eff. June 14, 2001.

§ 160.002. Conflicts Between Provisions

If a provision of this chapter conflicts with another provision of this title or another state statute or rule and the conflict cannot be reconciled, this chapter prevails.

Amended by Acts 2001, 77th Leg., ch. 821, § 1.01, eff. June 14, 2001.

Subchapter B. General Provisions

§ 160.101. Short Title

This chapter may be cited as the Uniform Parentage Act.

Amended by Acts 2001, 77th Leg., ch. 821, § 1.01, eff. June 14, 2001.

§ 160.102. Definitions

In this chapter:

(1) "Adjudicated father" means a man who has been adjudicated by a court to be the father of a child.

(2) "Assisted reproduction" means a method of causing pregnancy other than sexual intercourse. The term includes:

(A) intrauterine insemination;

(B) donation of eggs;

(C) donation of embryos;

(D) in vitro fertilization and transfer of embryos; and

(E) intracytoplasmic sperm injection.

(3) "Child" means an individual of any age whose parentage may be determined under this chapter.

(4) "Commence" means to file the initial pleading seeking an adjudication of parentage in a court of this state.

(5) "Determination of parentage" means the establishment of the parent-child relationship by the signing of a valid acknowledgment of paternity under Subchapter D or by an adjudication by a court.

(6) "Donor" means an individual who provides eggs or sperm to a licensed physician to be used for assisted reproduction, regardless of whether the eggs or sperm are provided for consideration. The term does not include:

(A) a husband who provides sperm or a wife who provides eggs to be used for assisted reproduction by the wife;

(B) a woman who gives birth to a child by means of assisted reproduction; or

(C) an unmarried man who, with the intent to be the father of the resulting child, provides sperm to be used for assisted reproduction by an unmarried woman, as provided by Section 160.7031.

(7) "Ethnic or racial group" means, for purposes of genetic testing, a recognized group that an individual identifies as all or part of the individual's ancestry or that is identified by other information.

(8) "Genetic testing" means an analysis of an individual's genetic markers to exclude or identify a man as the father of a child or a woman as the mother of a child. The term includes an analysis of one or more of the following:

(A) deoxyribonucleic acid; and

(B) blood-group antigens, red-cell antigens, human-leukocyte antigens, serum enzymes, serum proteins, or red-cell enzymes.

(9) "Intended parents" means individuals who enter into an agreement providing that the individuals will be the parents of a child born to a gestational mother by means of assisted reproduction, regardless of whether either individual has a genetic relationship with the child.

(10) "Man" means a male individual of any age.

(11) "Parent" means an individual who has established a parent-child relationship under Section 160.201.

(12) "Paternity index" means the likelihood of paternity determined by calculating the ratio between:

(A) the likelihood that the tested man is the father of the child, based on the genetic markers of the tested man, the mother of the child, and the child, conditioned on the hypothesis that the tested man is the father of the child; and

(B) the likelihood that the tested man is not the father of the child, based on the genetic markers of the tested man, the mother of the child, and the child, conditioned on the hypothesis that the tested man is not the father of the child and that the father of the child is of the same ethnic or racial group as the tested man.

(13) "Presumed father" means a man who, by operation of law under Section 160.204, is recognized as the father of a child until that status is rebutted or confirmed in a judicial proceeding.

(14) "Probability of paternity" means the probability, with respect to the ethnic or racial group to which the alleged father belongs, that the alleged father is the father of the child, compared to a random, unrelated man of the same ethnic or racial group, expressed as a percentage incorporating the paternity index and a prior probability.

(15) "Record" means information that is inscribed on a tangible medium or that is stored in an electronic or other medium and is retrievable in a perceivable form.

(16) "Signatory" means an individual who authenticates a record and is bound by its terms.

(17) "Support enforcement agency" means a public official or public agency authorized to seek:

(A) the enforcement of child support orders or laws relating to the duty of support;

(B) the establishment or modification of child support;

(C) the determination of parentage;

(D) the location of child-support obligors and their income and assets; or

(E) the conservatorship of a child or the termination of parental rights.

Amended by Acts 2001, 77th Leg., ch. 821, § 1.01, eff. June 14, 2001. Subsec. (6) amended by Acts 2007, 80th Leg., ch. 972, § 39, eff. Sept. 1, 2007.

§ 160.103. Scope of Chapter; Choice of Law

(a) Except as provided by Chapter 233, this chapter governs every determination of parentage in this state.

(b) The court shall apply the law of this state to adjudicate the parent-child relationship. The applicable law does not depend on:

(1) the place of birth of the child; or

(2) the past or present residence of the child.

(c) This chapter does not create, enlarge, or diminish parental rights or duties under another law of this state.

Amended by Acts 2001, 77th Leg., ch. 821, § 1.01, eff. June 14, 2001; Acts 2003, 78th Leg., ch. 457, § 3, eff. Sept. 1, 2003. Subsec. (a) amended by Acts 2009, 81st Leg., ch. 767, § 22, eff. June 19, 2009.

§ 160.104. Authorized Courts

The following courts are authorized to adjudicate parentage under this chapter:

(1) a court with jurisdiction to hear a suit affecting the parent-child relationship under this title; or

(2) a court with jurisdiction to adjudicate parentage under another law of this state.

Amended by Acts 2001, 77th Leg., ch. 821, § 1.01, eff. June 14, 2001.

§ 160.105. Protection of Participants

A proceeding under this chapter is subject to the other laws of this state governing the health, safety, privacy, and liberty of a child or any other individual who may be jeopardized by the disclosure of identifying information, including the person's address, telephone number, place of employment, and social security number and the name of the child's day-care facility and school.

Amended by Acts 2001, 77th Leg., ch. 821, § 1.01, eff. June 14, 2001.

§ 160.106. Determination of Maternity

The provisions of this chapter relating to the determination of paternity apply to a determination of maternity.

Amended by Acts 2001, 77th Leg., ch. 821, § 1.01, eff. June 14, 2001.

Subchapter C.   Parent-Child Relationship

Statutes in Context
§ 160.201

Section 160.201 sets forth how the mother-child and father-child relationship is established. This determination is especially important when ascertaining the inheritance rights of children under Probate Code § 42.

§ 160.201. Establishment of Parent-Child Relationship

(a) The mother-child relationship is established between a woman and a child by:

(1) the woman giving birth to the child;

(2) an adjudication of the woman's maternity; or

(3) the adoption of the child by the woman.

(b) The father-child relationship is established between a man and a child by:

(1) an unrebutted presumption of the man's paternity of the child under Section 160.204;

(2) an effective acknowledgment of paternity by the man under Subchapter D,[1] unless the

---

[1] Family Code § 160.301 et seq.

acknowledgment has been rescinded or successfully challenged;

(3) an adjudication of the man's paternity;

(4) the adoption of the child by the man; or

(5) the man's consenting to assisted reproduction by his wife under Subchapter H,[1] which resulted in the birth of the child.

Amended by Acts 2001, 77th Leg., ch. 821, § 1.01, eff. June 14, 2001.

§ 160.202. No Discrimination Based on Marital Status

A child born to parents who are not married to each other has the same rights under the law as a child born to parents who are married to each other.

Amended by Acts 2001, 77th Leg., ch. 821, § 1.01, eff. June 14, 2001.

§ 160.203. Consequences of Establishment of Parentage

Unless parental rights are terminated, a parent-child relationship established under this chapter applies for all purposes, except as otherwise provided by another law of this state.

Amended by Acts 2001, 77th Leg., ch. 821, § 1.01, eff. June 14, 2001.

§ 160.204. Presumption of Paternity

(a) A man is presumed to be the father of a child if:

(1) he is married to the mother of the child and the child is born during the marriage;

(2) he is married to the mother of the child and the child is born before the 301st day after the date the marriage is terminated by death, annulment, declaration of invalidity, or divorce;

(3) he married the mother of the child before the birth of the child in apparent compliance with law, even if the attempted marriage is or could be declared invalid, and the child is born during the invalid marriage or before the 301st day after the date the marriage is terminated by death, annulment, declaration of invalidity, or divorce; or

(4) he married the mother of the child after the birth of the child in apparent compliance with law, regardless of whether the marriage is or could be declared invalid, he voluntarily asserted his paternity of the child, and:

(A) the assertion is in a record filed with the [bureau of] vital statistics unit;

(B) he is voluntarily named as the child's father on the child's birth certificate; or

(C) he promised in a record to support the child as his own; or

(5) during the first two years of the child's life, he continuously resided in the household in which the child resided and he represented to others that the child was his own.

(b) (1) A presumption of paternity established under this section may be rebutted only by an adjudication under Subchapter G[2]; or

(2) the filing of a valid denial of paternity by a presumed father in conjunction with the filing by another person of a valid acknowledgment of paternity as provided by Section 160.305.

Amended by Acts 2001, 77th Leg., ch. 821, § 1.01, eff. June 14, 2001; Acts 2003, 78th Leg., ch. 610, § 10, eff. Sept. 1, 2003; Acts 2003, 78th Leg., ch. 1248, § 1, eff. Sept. 1, 2003. Subsec. (a)(4)(A) amended by Acts 2015, 84th Leg., ch. 1, § 1.055, eff. Apr. 2, 2015.

Subchapter D. Voluntary Acknowledgment of Paternity

Statutes in Context
§§ 160.301–160.316

Sections 160.301 - 160.316 provide a mechanism for a man to acknowledge his paternity of a child and thereafter to be treated as the child's father.

---

§ 160.301. Acknowledgment of Paternity

The mother of a child and a man claiming to be the biological father of the child may sign an acknowledgment of paternity with the intent to establish the man's paternity.

Added by Acts 2001, 77th Leg., ch. 821, § 1.01, eff. June 14, 2001. Amended by Acts 2003, 78th Leg., ch. 1248, § 2, eff. Sept. 1, 2003.

§ 160.302. Execution of Acknowledgment of Paternity

(a) An acknowledgment of paternity must:

(1) be in a record;

(2) be signed, or otherwise authenticated, under penalty of perjury by the mother and the man seeking to establish paternity;

(3) state that the child whose paternity is being acknowledged:

(A) does not have a presumed father or has a presumed father whose full name is stated; and

(B) does not have another acknowledged or adjudicated father;

(4) state whether there has been genetic testing and, if so, that the acknowledging man's claim of paternity is consistent with the results of the testing; and

(5) state that the signatories understand that the acknowledgment is the equivalent of a judicial

---

[1] Family Code §160.701 et seq.

[2] Family Code § 160.601 et seq.

adjudication of the paternity of the child and that a challenge to the acknowledgment is permitted only under limited circumstances.

(b) An acknowledgment of paternity is void if it:

(1) states that another man is a presumed father of the child, unless a denial of paternity signed or otherwise authenticated by the presumed father is filed with the [bureau of] vital statistics unit;

(2) states that another man is an acknowledged or adjudicated father of the child; or

(3) falsely denies the existence of a presumed, acknowledged, or adjudicated father of the child.

(c) A presumed father may sign or otherwise authenticate an acknowledgment of paternity.

(d) An acknowledgment of paternity constitutes an affidavit under Section 666(a)(5)(C), Social Security Act (42 U.S.C. Section 666(a)(5)(C)).

Added by Acts 2001, 77th Leg., ch. 821, § 1.01, eff. June 14, 2001. Amended by Acts 2011, 82nd Leg., ch. 1221, § 1, eff. Sept. 1, 2011. Subsec. (b)(1) amended by Acts 2015, 84th Leg., ch. 1, § 1.056, eff. Apr., 1, 2015. Subsec. (d) added by Acts 2015, 84th Leg., ch. 542, § 7, eff. Sept. 1, 2015.

§ 160.303. Denial of Paternity

A presumed father of a child may sign a denial of his paternity. The denial is valid only if:

(1) an acknowledgment of paternity signed or otherwise authenticated by another man is filed under Section 160.305;

(2) the denial is in a record and is signed or otherwise authenticated under penalty of perjury; and

(3) the presumed father has not previously:

(A) acknowledged paternity of the child, unless the previous acknowledgment has been rescinded under Section 160.307 or successfully challenged under Section 160.308; or

(B) been adjudicated to be the father of the child.

Added by Acts 2001, 77th Leg., ch. 821, § 1.01, eff. June 14, 2001.

§ 160.304. Rules for Acknowledgment and Denial of Paternity

(a) An acknowledgment of paternity and a denial of paternity may be contained in a single document or in different documents and may be filed separately or simultaneously. If the acknowledgment and denial are both necessary, neither document is valid until both documents are filed.

(b) An acknowledgment of paternity or a denial of paternity may be signed before the birth of the child.

(c) Subject to Subsection (a), an acknowledgment of paternity or denial of paternity takes effect on the date of the birth of the child or the filing of the document with the [bureau of] vital statistics unit, whichever occurs later.

(d) An acknowledgment of paternity or denial of paternity signed by a minor is valid if it otherwise complies with this chapter.

Added by Acts 2001, 77th Leg., ch. 821, § 1.01, eff. June 14, 2001. Subsec.(c) amended by Acts 2015, 84th Leg., ch. 1, § 1.057, eff. Apr., 1, 2015.

§ 160.305. Effect of Acknowledgment or Denial of Paternity

(a) Except as provided by Sections 160.307 and 160.308, a valid acknowledgment of paternity filed with the [bureau of] vital statistics unit is the equivalent of an adjudication of the paternity of a child and confers on the acknowledged father all rights and duties of a parent.

(b) Except as provided by Sections 160.307 and 160.308, a valid denial of paternity filed with the [bureau of] vital statistics unit in conjunction with a valid acknowledgment of paternity is the equivalent of an adjudication of the nonpaternity of the presumed father and discharges the presumed father from all rights and duties of a parent.

Added by Acts 2001, 77th Leg., ch. 821, § 1.01, eff. June 14, 2001. Amended by Acts 2015, 84th Leg., ch. 1, § 1.058, eff. Apr. 1, 2015.

§ 160.306. Filing Fee Not Required

The Department of State Health Services [bureau of vital statistics] may not charge a fee for filing:

(1) an acknowledgment of paternity;

(2) a denial of paternity; or

(3) a rescission of an acknowledgment of paternity or denial of paternity.

Added by Acts 2001, 77th Leg., ch. 821, § 1.01, eff. June 14, 2001. Amended by Acts 2011, 82nd Leg., ch. 1221, § 2, eff. Sept. 1, 2011. Amended by Acts 2015, 84th Leg., ch. 1, § 1.059, eff. Apr. 1, 2015.

§ 160.307. Procedures for Rescission.

(a) A signatory may rescind an acknowledgment of paternity or denial of paternity as provided by this section [by commencing a proceeding to rescind] before the earlier of:

(1) the 60th day after the effective date of the acknowledgment or denial, as provided by Section 160.304; or

(2) the date a proceeding to which the signatory is a party is initiated before a court to adjudicate an issue relating to the child, including a proceeding that establishes child support.

(b) A signatory seeking to rescind an acknowledgment of paternity or denial of paternity must file with the [bureau of] vital statistics unit a completed rescission, on the form prescribed under Section 160.312, in which the signatory declares under penalty of perjury that:

(1) as of the date the rescission is filed, a proceeding has not been held affecting the child identified in the acknowledgment of paternity or

denial of paternity, including a proceeding to establish child support;

(2) a copy of the completed rescission was sent by certified or registered mail, return receipt requested, to:

(A) if the rescission is of an acknowledgment of paternity, the other signatory of the acknowledgment of paternity and the signatory of any related denial of paternity; or

(B) if the rescission is of a denial of paternity, the signatories of the related acknowledgment of paternity; and

(3) if a signatory to the acknowledgment of paternity or denial of paternity is receiving services from the Title IV-D agency, a copy of the completed rescission was sent by certified or registered mail to the Title IV-D agency.

(c) On receipt of a completed rescission, the [bureau of] vital statistics unit shall void the acknowledgment of paternity or denial of paternity affected by the rescission and amend the birth record of the child, if appropriate.

(d) Any party affected by the rescission, including the Title IV-D agency, may contest the rescission by bringing a proceeding under Subchapter G to adjudicate the parentage of the child.

Added by Acts 2001, 77th Leg., ch. 821, § 1.01, eff. June 14, 2001. Amended by Acts 2011, 82nd Leg., ch. 1221, § 3, eff. Sept. 1, 2011. Subsecs. (b) and (c) amended by Acts 2015, 84th Leg., ch. .1 § 1.060, eff. Apr. 1, 2015.

§ 160.308. Challenge After Expiration of Period for Rescission

(a) After the period for rescission under Section 160.307 has expired, a signatory of an acknowledgment of paternity or denial of paternity may commence a proceeding to challenge the acknowledgment or denial only on the basis of fraud, duress, or material mistake of fact. The proceeding may be commenced at any time before the issuance of an order affecting the child identified in the acknowledgment or denial, including an order relating to support of the child.

(b) A party challenging an acknowledgment of paternity or denial of paternity has the burden of proof.

(c) Notwithstanding any other provision of this chapter, a collateral attack on an acknowledgment of paternity signed under this chapter may not be maintained after the issuance of an order affecting the child identified in the acknowledgment, including an order relating to support of the child.

(d) For purposes of Subsection (a), evidence that, based on genetic testing, the man who is the signatory of an acknowledgement of paternity is not rebuttably identified as the father of a child in accordance with Section 160.505 constitutes a material mistake of fact.

Added by Acts 2001, 77th Leg., ch. 821, § 1.01, eff. June 14, 2001. Subsecs. (a), (c) amended by Acts 2005, 79th Leg., ch. 478, § 1, eff. Sept. 1, 2005. Subsecs. (a), (c)

Amended by Acts 2011, 82nd Leg., ch. 1221, § 4, eff. Sept. 1, 2011.

§ 160.309. Procedure for Challenge

(a) Each signatory to an acknowledgment of paternity and any related denial of paternity must be made a party to a proceeding to challenge the acknowledgment or denial of paternity.

(b) For purposes of a challenge to an acknowledgment of paternity or denial of paternity, a signatory submits to the personal jurisdiction of this state by signing the acknowledgment or denial. The jurisdiction is effective on the filing of the document with the [bureau of] vital statistics unit.

(c) Except for good cause shown, while a proceeding is pending to challenge an acknowledgment of paternity or a denial of paternity, the court may not suspend the legal responsibilities of a signatory arising from the acknowledgment, including the duty to pay child support.

(d) A proceeding to challenge an acknowledgment of paternity or a denial of paternity shall be conducted in the same manner as a proceeding to adjudicate parentage under Subchapter G.

(e) At the conclusion of a proceeding to challenge an acknowledgment of paternity or a denial of paternity, the court shall order the [bureau of] vital statistics unit to amend the birth record of the child, if appropriate.

Added by Acts 2001, 77th Leg., ch. 821, § 1.01, eff. June 14, 2001. Amended by Acts 2011, 82nd Leg., ch. 1221, § 5, eff. Sept. 1, 2011. Subsecs. (b) and (e) amended by Acts 2015, 84th Leg., ch. 1, § 1.061, eff. Apr. 1, 2015.

§ 160.310. Ratification Barred

A court or administrative agency conducting a judicial or administrative proceeding may not ratify an unchallenged acknowledgment of paternity.

Added by Acts 2001, 77th Leg., ch. 821, § 1.01, eff. June 14, 2001.

§ 160.311. Full Faith and Credit

A court of this state shall give full faith and credit to an acknowledgment of paternity or a denial of paternity that is effective in another state if the acknowledgment or denial has been signed and is otherwise in compliance with the law of the other state.

Added by Acts 2001, 77th Leg., ch. 821, § 1.01, eff. June 14, 2001.

§ 160.312. Forms

(a) To facilitate compliance with this subchapter, the [bureau of] vital statistics unit shall prescribe forms for the:

(1) acknowledgment of paternity;

(2) denial of paternity; and

(3) rescission of an acknowledgment or denial of paternity.

(b) A valid acknowledgment of paternity, denial of paternity, or rescission of an acknowledgment or denial of paternity is not affected by a later modification of the prescribed form.

Added by Acts 2001, 77ᵗʰ Leg., ch. 821, § 1.01, eff. June 14, 2001. Amended by Acts 2011, 82ⁿᵈ Leg., ch. 1221, § 6, eff. Sept. 1, 2011. Subsec. (a) amended by Acts 2015, 84ᵗʰ Leg., ch. 1, § 1.062, eff. Apr. 1, 2015.

§ 160.313. Release of Information

The [bureau of] vital statistics unit may release information relating to the acknowledgment of paternity or denial of paternity to a signatory of the acknowledgment or denial and to the courts and Title IV-D agency of this or another state.

Added by Acts 2001, 77ᵗʰ Leg., ch. 821, § 1.01, eff. June 14, 2001. Amended by Acts 2015, 84ᵗʰ Leg., ch. 1, § 1.063, eff. Apr. 1, 2015.

§ 160.314. Adoption of Rules

The Title IV-D agency and the executive commissioner of the Health and Human Services Commission [bureau of vital statistics] may adopt rules to implement this subchapter.

Added by Acts 2001, 77ᵗʰ Leg., ch. 821, § 1.01, eff. June 14, 2001. Amended by Acts 2015, 84ᵗʰ Leg., ch. 1, § 1.064, eff. Apr. 1, 2015.

§ 160.315. Memorandum of Understanding

(a) The Title IV-D agency and the [bureau of] vital statistics unit shall adopt a memorandum of understanding governing the collection and transfer of information for the voluntary acknowledgment of paternity.

(b) The Title IV-D agency and the [bureau of] vital statistics unit shall review the memorandum semiannually and renew or modify the memorandum as necessary.

Added by Acts 2001, 77ᵗʰ Leg., ch. 821, § 1.01, eff. June 14, 2001. Amended by Acts 2015, 84ᵗʰ Leg., ch. 1, § 1.065, eff. Apr. 1, 2015.

§ 160.316. Suit to Contest Voluntary Statement of Paternity

(a) A man who executed a voluntary statement of paternity before September 1, 1999, and who, on the basis of that statement, is the subject of a final order declaring him to be a parent of the child who is the subject of the statement may file a suit affecting the parent-child relationship to contest the statement on the basis of fraud, duress, or material mistake of fact in the same manner that a person may contest an acknowledgment of paternity under Sections 160.308 and 160.309. For purposes of this subsection, evidence that, based on genetic testing, the man is not rebuttably identified as the father of a child in accordance with Section 160.505 constitutes a material mistake of fact.

(b) A suit filed under this section to contest a voluntary statement of paternity is not affected by an order with respect to the child that was rendered on the basis of that statement.

(c) The court, on a preliminary finding in a suit under this section that there is credible evidence of fraud, duress, or material mistake of fact regarding the execution of the voluntary statement of paternity, shall order genetic testing as provided by Subchapter F.[1] The person contesting the voluntary statement of paternity shall pay the cost of the testing.

(d) Except as provided by Subsection (e), if the results of the genetic testing do not rebuttably identify the man as the father of the child in accordance with Section 160.505, the court shall set aside:

(1) the final order declaring the man to be a parent of the child; and

(2) any other order with respect to the child that was rendered on the basis of the voluntary statement of paternity.

(e) The court may not set aside under Subsection (d) a final order declaring a man to be a parent of a child if the man who executed the voluntary statement of paternity:

(1) executed the statement knowing that he was not the father of the child; or

(2) subsequently adopted the child.

(f) If the court sets aside a final order as provided by Subsection (d), the court shall order the bureau of vital statistics to amend the birth record of the child. The court may not as a result of the order being set aside:

(1) require an obligee to repay child support paid by the man who executed the voluntary statement of paternity; or

(2) award damages to the man who executed the voluntary statement of paternity.

(g) A suit under this section must be filed before September 1, 2003.

(h) This section expires September 1, 2004.

Added by Acts 2001, 77ᵗʰ Leg., ch. 821, § 1.01, eff. June 14, 2001.

Subchapter E. Registry of Paternity

Statutes in Context
§§ 160.401–160.423

Sections 160.401 - 160.423 explain the operation of the registry of paternity which is established in the vital statistics unit.

§ 160.401. Establishment of Registry

A registry of paternity is established in the [bureau of] vital statistics unit.

Added by Acts 2001, 77ᵗʰ Leg., ch. 821, § 1.01, eff. June 14, 2001. Amended by Acts 2015, 84ᵗʰ Leg., ch. 1, § 1.066, eff. Apr. 1, 2015.

[1] Family Code § 160.501 et seq.

§ 160.402. Registration for Notification

(a) Except as otherwise provided by Subsection (b), a man who desires to be notified of a proceeding for the adoption of or the termination of parental rights regarding a child that he may have fathered may register with the registry of paternity:

(1) before the birth of the child; or

(2) not later than the 31st day after the date of the birth of the child.

(b) A man is entitled to notice of a proceeding described by Subsection (a) regardless of whether he registers with the registry of paternity if:

(1) a father-child relationship between the man and the child has been established under this chapter or another law; or

(2) the man commences a proceeding to adjudicate his paternity before the court has terminated his parental rights.

(c) A registrant shall promptly notify the registry in a record of any change in the information provided by the registrant. The [bureau of] vital statistics unit shall incorporate all new information received into its records but is not required to affirmatively seek to obtain current information for incorporation in the registry.

Added by Acts 2001, 77th Leg., ch. 821, § 1.01, eff. June 14, 2001. Subsec. (c) amended by Acts 2015, 84th Leg., ch. 1, § 1.067, eff. Apr. 1, 2015.

§ 160.403. Notice of Proceeding

Except as provided by Sections 161.002(b)(2), (3), and (4) and (f), notice of a proceeding to adopt or to terminate parental rights regarding a child must be given to a registrant who has timely registered with regard to that child. Notice must be given in a manner prescribed for service of process in a civil action.

Added by Acts 2001, 77th Leg., ch. 821, § 1.01, eff. June 14, 2001. Amended by Acts 2007, 80th Leg., ch. 1283, § 2, eff. Sept. 1, 2007.

§ 160.404. Termination of Parental Rights: Failure to Register

The parental rights of a man alleged to be the father of a child may be terminated without notice as provided by Section 161.002 if the man:

(1) did not timely register with the [bureau of] vital statistics unit; and

(2) is not entitled to notice under Section 160.402 or 161.002.

Added by Acts 2001, 77th Leg., ch. 821, § 1.01, eff. June 14, 2001. Amended by Acts 2015, 84th Leg., ch. 1, §1.068 , eff. Apr. 1, 2015.

§ 160.411. Required Form

The [bureau of] vital statistics unit shall adopt a form for registering with the registry. The form must require the signature of the registrant. The form must state that:

(1) the form is signed under penalty of perjury;

(2) a timely registration entitles the registrant to notice of a proceeding for adoption of the child or for termination of the registrant's parental rights;

(3) a timely registration does not commence a proceeding to establish paternity;

(4) the information disclosed on the form may be used against the registrant to establish paternity;

(5) services to assist in establishing paternity are available to the registrant through the support enforcement agency;

(6) the registrant should also register in another state if the conception or birth of the child occurred in the other state;

(7) information on registries in other states is available from the [bureau of] vital statistics unit; and

(8) procedures exist to rescind the registration of a claim of paternity.

Added by Acts 2001, 77th Leg., ch. 821, § 1.01, eff. June 14, 2001. Amended by Acts 2015, 84th Leg., ch. 1, § 1.069, eff. Apr. 1, 2015.

§ 160.412. Furnishing of Information; Confidentiality

(a) The [bureau of] vital statistics unit is not required to attempt to locate the mother of a child who is the subject of a registration. The [bureau of] vital statistics unit shall send a copy of the notice of the registration to a mother who has provided an address.

(b) Information contained in the registry is confidential and may be released on request only to:

(1) a court or a person designated by the court;

(2) the mother of the child who is the subject of the registration;

(3) an agency authorized by another law to receive the information;

(4) a licensed child-placing agency;

(5) a support enforcement agency;

(6) a party, or the party's attorney of record, to a proceeding under this chapter or a proceeding to adopt or to terminate parental rights regarding a child who is the subject of the registration; and

(7) the registry of paternity in another state.

Added by Acts 2001, 77th Leg., ch. 821, § 1.01, eff. June 14, 2001. Subsec. (a) amended by Acts 2015, 84th Leg., ch. 1, § 1.070, eff. Apr. 1, 2015.

§ 160.413. Offense: Unauthorized Release of Information

(a) A person commits an offense if the person intentionally releases information from the registry of paternity to another person, including an agency, that is not authorized to receive the information under Section 160.412.

(b) An offense under this section is a Class A misdemeanor.

Added by Acts 2001, 77th Leg., ch. 821, § 1.01, eff. June 14, 2001.

§ 160.414. Rescission of Registration

If a man registers later than the 31st day after the date of the birth of the child, the [bureau of] vital statistics unit shall notify the registrant that the registration was not timely filed.

Added by Acts 2001, 77th Leg., ch. 821, § 1.01, eff. June 14, 2001. Amended by Acts 2015, 84th Leg., ch. 1, § 1.071, eff. Apr. 1, 2015.

§ 160.415. Untimely Registration

If a man registers later than the 31st day after the date of the birth of the child, the bureau of vital statistics shall notify the registrant that the registration was not timely filed.

Added by Acts 2001, 77th Leg., ch. 821, § 1.01, eff. June 14, 2001. Amended Acts 2007, 80th Leg., ch. 627, § 10, eff. June 15, 2007.

§ 160.416. Fees for Registry

(a) A fee may not be charged for filing a registration or to rescind a registration.

(b) Except as otherwise provided by Subsection (c), the [bureau of] vital statistics unit may charge a reasonable fee for making a search of the registry and for furnishing a certificate.

(c) A support enforcement agency is not required to pay a fee authorized by Subsection (b).

Added by Acts 2001, 77th Leg., ch. 821, § 1.01, eff. June 14, 2001. Subsec. (b) amended by Acts 2015, 84th Leg., ch. 1, § 1.072, eff. Apr. 1, 2015.

§ 160.421. Search of Appropriate Registry

(a) If a father-child relationship has not been established under this chapter, a petitioner for the adoption of or the termination of parental rights regarding the child must obtain a certificate of the results of a search of the registry. The petitioner may request a search of the registry on or after the 32nd day after the date of the birth of the child, and the executive commissioner of the Health and Human Services Commission [bureau of vital statistics] may not by rule impose a waiting period that must elapse before the vital statistics unit [bureau] will conduct the requested search.

(b) If the petitioner for the adoption of or the termination of parental rights regarding a child has reason to believe that the conception or birth of the child may have occurred in another state, the petitioner must obtain a certificate of the results of a search of the paternity registry, if any, in the other state.

Added by Acts 2001, 77th Leg., ch. 821, § 1.01, eff. June 14, 2001. Subsec. (a) amended by Acts 2007, 80th Leg., ch. 627, § 2, eff. June 15, 2007. Subsec. (a) amended by Acts 2015, 84th Leg., ch. 1, § 1.073, eff. Apr. 1, 2015.

§ 160.422. Certificate of Search of Registry

(a) The [bureau of] vital statistics unit shall furnish a certificate of the results of a search of the registry on request by an individual, a court, or an agency listed in Section 160.412(b).

(b) The certificate of the results of a search must be signed on behalf of the unit [bureau] and state that:

(1) a search has been made of the registry; and

(2) a registration containing the information required to identify the registrant:

(A) has been found and is attached to the certificate; or

(B) has not been found.

(c) A petitioner must file the certificate of the results of a search of the registry with the court before a proceeding for the adoption of or termination of parental rights regarding a child may be concluded.

(d) A search of the registry is not required if a parent-child relationship exists between a man and the child, as provided by Section 160.201(b), and that man:

(1) has been served with citation of the proceeding for termination of the parent-child relationship; or

(2) has signed a relinquishment of parental rights with regard to the child.

Added by Acts 2001, 77th Leg., ch. 821, § 1.01, eff. June 14, 2001. Subsec. (d) amended by Acts 2007, 80th Leg., ch. 1283, § 3, eff. Sept. 1, 2007. Subsecs. (a) and (b) amended by Acts 2015, 84th Leg., ch. 1, § 1.074, eff. Apr. 1, 2015.

§ 160.423. Admissibility of Certificate

A certificate of the results of a search of the registry in this state or of a paternity registry in another state is admissible in a proceeding for the adoption of or the termination of parental rights regarding a child and, if relevant, in other legal proceedings.

Added by Acts 2001, 77th Leg., ch. 821, § 1.01, eff. June 14, 2001.

Subchapter F.   Genetic Testing

Statutes in Context
§§ 160.501–160. 511

Sections 160.501 - 160. 511 govern genetic testing when used to determine parentage.

§ 160.501. Application of Subchapter

This subchapter governs genetic testing of an individual to determine parentage, regardless of whether the individual:

(1) voluntarily submits to testing; or

(2) is tested under an order of a court or a support enforcement agency.

Added by Acts 2001, 77th Leg., ch. 821, § 1.01, eff. June 14, 2001.

§ 160.502. Order for Testing

(a) Except as otherwise provided by this subchapter and by Subchapter G, a court shall order a child and other designated individuals to submit to genetic testing if the request is made by a party to a proceeding to determine parentage.

(b) If a request for genetic testing of a child is made before the birth of the child, the court or support enforcement agency may not order in utero testing.

(c) If two or more men are subject to court-ordered genetic testing, the testing may be ordered concurrently or sequentially.

Added by Acts 2001, 77th Leg., ch. 821, § 1.01, eff. June 14, 2001.

§ 160.503. Requirements for Genetic Testing

(a) Genetic testing must be of a type reasonably relied on by experts in the field of genetic testing. The testing must be performed in a testing laboratory accredited by:

(1) the American Association of Blood Banks, or a successor to its functions;

(2) the American Society for Histocompatibility and Immunogenetics, or a successor to its functions; or

(3) an accrediting body designated by the federal secretary of health and human services.

(b) A specimen used in genetic testing may consist of one or more samples, or a combination of samples, of blood, buccal cells, bone, hair, or other body tissue or fluid. The specimen used in the testing is not required to be of the same kind for each individual undergoing genetic testing.

(c) Based on the ethnic or racial group of an individual, the testing laboratory shall determine the databases from which to select frequencies for use in the calculation of the probability of paternity of the individual. If there is disagreement as to the testing laboratory's choice:

(1) the objecting individual may require the testing laboratory, not later than the 30th day after the date of receipt of the report of the test, to recalculate the probability of paternity using an ethnic or racial group different from that used by the laboratory;

(2) the individual objecting to the testing laboratory's initial choice shall:

(A) if the frequencies are not available to the testing laboratory for the ethnic or racial group requested, provide the requested frequencies compiled in a manner recognized by accrediting bodies; or

(B) engage another testing laboratory to perform the calculations; and

(3) the testing laboratory may use its own statistical estimate if there is a question regarding which ethnic or racial group is appropriate and, if available, shall calculate the frequencies using statistics for any other ethnic or racial group requested.

(d) If, after recalculation using a different ethnic or racial group, genetic testing does not rebuttably identify

a man as the father of a child under Section 160.505, an individual who has been tested may be required to submit to additional genetic testing.

Added by Acts 2001, 77th Leg., ch. 821, § 1.01, eff. June 14, 2001.

§ 160.504. Report of Genetic Testing

(a) A report of the results of genetic testing must be in a record and signed under penalty of perjury by a designee of the testing laboratory. A report made under the requirements of this subchapter is self-authenticating.

(b) Documentation from the testing laboratory is sufficient to establish a reliable chain of custody that allows the results of genetic testing to be admissible without testimony if the documentation includes:

(1) the name and photograph of each individual whose specimens have been taken;

(2) the name of each individual who collected the specimens;

(3) the places in which the specimens were collected and the date of each collection;

(4) the name of each individual who received the specimens in the testing laboratory; and

(5) the dates the specimens were received.

Added by Acts 2001, 77th Leg., ch. 821, § 1.01, eff. June 14, 2001.

§ 160.505. Genetic Testing Results; Rebuttal

(a) A man is rebuttably identified as the father of a child under this chapter if the genetic testing complies with this subchapter and the results disclose:

(1) that the man has at least a 99 percent probability of paternity, using a prior probability of 0.5, as calculated by using the combined paternity index obtained in the testing; and

(2) a combined paternity index of at least 100 to 1.

(b) A man identified as the father of a child under Subsection (a) may rebut the genetic testing results only by producing other genetic testing satisfying the requirements of this subchapter that:

(1) excludes the man as a genetic father of the child; or

(2) identifies another man as the possible father of the child.

(c) Except as otherwise provided by Section 160.510, if more than one man is identified by genetic testing as the possible father of the child, the court shall order each man to submit to further genetic testing to identify the genetic father.

Added by Acts 2001, 77th Leg., ch. 821, § 1.01, eff. June 14, 2001.

§ 160.506. Costs of Genetic Testing

(a) Subject to the assessment of costs under Subchapter G,[1] the cost of initial genetic testing must be advanced:

(1) by a support enforcement agency, if the agency is providing services in the proceeding;

(2) by the individual who made the request;

(3) as agreed by the parties; or

(4) as ordered by the court.

(b) In cases in which the cost of genetic testing is advanced by the support enforcement agency, the agency may seek reimbursement from a man who is rebuttably identified as the father.

Added by Acts 2001, 77th Leg., ch. 821, § 1.01, eff. June 14, 2001.

§ 160.507. Additional Genetic Testing

The court or the support enforcement agency shall order additional genetic testing on the request of a party who contests the result of the original testing. If the previous genetic testing identified a man as the father of the child under Section 160.505, the court or agency may not order additional testing unless the party provides advance payment for the testing.

Added by Acts 2001, 77th Leg., ch. 821, § 1.01, eff. June 14, 2001.

§ 160.508. Genetic Testing When All Individuals Not Available

(a) Subject to Subsection (b), if a genetic testing specimen for good cause and under circumstances the court considers to be just is not available from a man who may be the father of a child, a court may order the following individuals to submit specimens for genetic testing:

(1) the parents of the man;

(2) any brothers or sisters of the man;

(3) any other children of the man and their mothers; and

(4) other relatives of the man necessary to complete genetic testing.

(b) A court may not render an order under this section unless the court finds that the need for genetic testing outweighs the legitimate interests of the individual sought to be tested.

Added by Acts 2001, 77th Leg., ch. 821, § 1.01, eff. June 14, 2001.

§ 160.509. Deceased Individual

For good cause shown, the court may order genetic testing of a deceased individual.

Added by Acts 2001, 77th Leg., ch. 821, § 1.01, eff. June 14, 2001.

---

[1] Family Code § 160.601 et seq.

§ 160.510. Identical Brothers

(a) The court may order genetic testing of a brother of a man identified as the father of a child if the man is commonly believed to have an identical brother and evidence suggests that the brother may be the genetic father of the child.

(b) If each brother satisfies the requirements of Section 160.505 for being the identified father of the child and there is not another identical brother being identified as the father of the child, the court may rely on nongenetic evidence to adjudicate which brother is the father of the child.

Added by Acts 2001, 77th Leg., ch. 821, § 1.01, eff. June 14, 2001.

§ 160.511. Offense: Unauthorized Release of Specimen

(a) A person commits an offense if the person intentionally releases an identifiable specimen of another person for any purpose not relevant to the parentage proceeding and without a court order or the written permission of the person who furnished the specimen.

(b) An offense under this section is a Class A misdemeanor.

Added by Acts 2001, 77th Leg., ch. 821, § 1.01, eff. June 14, 2001.

§ 160.512. Offense: Falsification of Specimen

(a) A person commits an offense if the person alters, destroys, conceals, fabricates, or falsifies genetic evidence in a proceeding to adjudicate parentage, including inducing another person to provide a specimen with the intent to affect the outcome of the proceeding.

(b) An offense under this section is a felony of the third degree.

(c) An order excluding a man as the biological father of a child based on genetic evidence shown to be altered, fabricated, or falsified is void and unenforceable.

Added by Acts 2011, 82nd Leg., ch. 1221, § 7, eff. Sept. 1, 2011.

Subchapter G. Proceeding to Adjudicate Parentage

Statutes in Context
§§ 160.601–160.637

Proceedings for a court adjudication of the parentage of a child are governed by §§ 160.601 - 160.637.

---

§ 160.601. Proceeding Authorized; Rules of Procedure

(a) A civil proceeding may be maintained to adjudicate the parentage of a child.

(b) The proceeding is governed by the Texas Rules of Civil Procedure, except as provided by Chapter 233.

Added by Acts 2001, 77ᵗʰ Leg., ch. 821, § 1.01, eff. June 14, 2001. Subsec. (b) amended by Acts 2009, 81ˢᵗ Leg., ch. 767, § 23, eff. June 19, 2009.

§ 160.602. Standing to Maintain Proceeding

(a) Subject to Subchapter D[1] and Sections 160.607 and 160.609 and except as provided by Subsection (b), a proceeding to adjudicate parentage may be maintained by:

(1) the child;

(2) the mother of the child;

(3) a man whose paternity of the child is to be adjudicated;

(4) the support enforcement agency or another government agency authorized by other law;

(5) an authorized adoption agency or licensed child-placing agency;

(6) a representative authorized by law to act for an individual who would otherwise be entitled to maintain a proceeding but who is deceased, is incapacitated, or is a minor; or

(7) a person related within the second degree by consanguinity to the mother of the child, if the mother is deceased, or

(8) a person who is an intended parent.

(b) After the date a child having no presumed, acknowledged, or adjudicated father becomes an adult, a proceeding to adjudicate the parentage of the adult child may only be maintained by the adult child.

Added by Acts 2001, 77ᵗʰ Leg., ch. 821, § 1.01, eff. June 14, 2001. Amended by Acts 2003, 78ᵗʰ Leg., ch. 457, § 1, eff. Sept. 1, 2003; Acts 2003, 78ᵗʰ Leg., ch. 1248, § 3, eff. Sept. 1, 2003.

§ 160.603. Necessary Parties to Proceeding

The following individuals must be joined as parties in a proceeding to adjudicate parentage:

(1) the mother of the child; and

(2) a man whose paternity of the child is to be adjudicated.

Added by Acts 2001, 77ᵗʰ Leg., ch. 821, § 1.01, eff. June 14, 2001.

§ 160.604. Personal Jurisdiction

(a) An individual may not be adjudicated to be a parent unless the court has personal jurisdiction over the individual.

(b) A court of this state having jurisdiction to adjudicate parentage may exercise personal jurisdiction over a nonresident individual or the guardian or conservator of the individual if the conditions in Section 159.201 are satisfied.

(c) Lack of jurisdiction over one individual does not preclude the court from making an adjudication of

parentage binding on another individual over whom the court has personal jurisdiction.

Added by Acts 2001, 77ᵗʰ Leg., ch. 821, § 1.01, eff. June 14, 2001.

§ 160.605. Venue

Venue for a proceeding to adjudicate parentage is in the county of this state in which:

(1) the child resides or is found;

(2) the respondent resides or is found if the child does not reside in this state; or

(3) a proceeding for probate or administration of the presumed or alleged father's estate has been commenced.

Added by Acts 2001, 77ᵗʰ Leg., ch. 821, § 1.01, eff. June 14, 2001.

§ 160.606. No Time Limitation: Child Having No Presumed, Acknowledged, or Adjudicated Father

A proceeding to adjudicate the parentage of a child having no presumed, acknowledged, or adjudicated father may be commenced at any time, including after the date:

(1) the child becomes an adult; or

(2) an earlier proceeding to adjudicate paternity has been dismissed based on the application of a statute of limitation then in effect.

Added by Acts 2001, 77ᵗʰ Leg., ch. 821, § 1.01, eff. June 14, 2001.

§ 160.607. Time Limitation: Child Having Presumed Father

(a) Except as otherwise provided by Subsection (b), a proceeding brought by a presumed father, the mother, or another individual to adjudicate the parentage of a child having a presumed father shall be commenced not later than the fourth anniversary of the date of the birth of the child.

(b) A proceeding seeking to adjudicate the parentage of a child having a presumed father may be maintained at any time if the court determines that:

(1) the presumed father and the mother of the child did not live together or engage in sexual intercourse with each other during the probable time of conception; or

(2) the presumed father was precluded from commencing a proceeding to adjudicate the parentage of the child before the expiration of the time prescribed by Subsection (a) because of the mistaken belief that he was the child's biological father based on misrepresentations that led him to that conclusion.

Added by Acts 2001, 77ᵗʰ Leg., ch. 821, § 1.01, eff. June 14, 2001. Amended by Acts 2003, 78ᵗʰ Leg., ch. 1248, § 4, eff. Sept. 1, 2003. Amended by Acts 2011, 82ⁿᵈ Leg., ch. 1221, § 8, eff. Sept. 1, 2011.

---

[1] Family Code § 160.301 et seq.

§ 160.608. Authority to Deny Motion for Genetic Testing

(a) In a proceeding to adjudicate parentage, a court may deny a motion for an order for the genetic testing of the mother, the child, and the presumed father if the court determines that:

(1) the conduct of the mother or the presumed father estops that party from denying parentage; and

(2) it would be inequitable to disprove the father-child relationship between the child and the presumed father.

(b) In determining whether to deny a motion for an order for genetic testing under this section, the court shall consider the best interest of the child, including the following factors:

(1) the length of time between the date of the proceeding to adjudicate parentage and the date the presumed father was placed on notice that he might not be the genetic father;

(2) the length of time during which the presumed father has assumed the role of father of the child;

(3) the facts surrounding the presumed father's discovery of his possible nonpaternity;

(4) the nature of the relationship between the child and the presumed father;

(5) the age of the child;

(6) any harm that may result to the child if presumed paternity is successfully disproved;

(7) the nature of the relationship between the child and the alleged father;

(8) the extent to which the passage of time reduces the chances of establishing the paternity of another man and a child support obligation in favor of the child; and

(9) other factors that may affect the equities arising from the disruption of the father-child relationship between the child and the presumed father or the chance of other harm to the child.

(c) In a proceeding involving the application of this section, a child who is a minor or is incapacitated must be represented by an amicus attorney or attorney ad litem.

(d) A denial of a motion for an order for genetic testing must be based on clear and convincing evidence.

(e) If the court denies a motion for an order for genetic testing, the court shall issue an order adjudicating the presumed father to be the father of the child.

(f) This section applies to a proceeding to challenge an acknowledgment of paternity or a denial of paternity as provided by Section 160.309(d).

Added by Acts 2001, 77th Leg., ch. 821, § 1.01, eff. June 14, 2001. Amended by Acts 2003, 78th Leg., ch. 1248, § 5, eff. Sept. 1, 2003. Subsec. (c) amended by Acts 2005, 79th Leg., ch. 172, § 17, eff. Sept. 1, 2005. Amended by Acts 2011, 82nd Leg., ch. 1221, § 9, eff. Sept. 1, 2011.

§ 160.609. Time Limitation: Child Having Acknowledged or Adjudicated Father

(a) If a child has an acknowledged father, a signatory to the acknowledgment or denial of paternity may commence a proceeding under this chapter to challenge the paternity of the child only within the time allowed under Section 160.308.

(b) If a child has an acknowledged father or an adjudicated father, an individual, other than the child, who is not a signatory to the acknowledgment or a party to the adjudication and who seeks an adjudication of paternity of the child must commence a proceeding not later than the fourth anniversary of the effective date of the acknowledgment or adjudication.

Added by Acts 2001, 77th Leg., ch. 821, § 1.01, eff. June 14, 2001. Amended by Acts 2011, 82nd Leg., ch. 1221, § 01, eff. Sept. 1, 2011.

§ 160.610. Joinder of Proceedings

(a) Except as provided by Subsection (b), a proceeding to adjudicate parentage may be joined with a proceeding for adoption, termination of parental rights, possession of or access to a child, child support, divorce, annulment, or probate or administration of an estate or another appropriate proceeding.

(b) A respondent may not join a proceeding described by Subsection (a) with a proceeding to adjudicate parentage brought under Chapter 159.

Added by Acts 2001, 77th Leg., ch. 821, § 1.01, eff. June 14, 2001.

§ 160.611. Proceedings Before Birth

(a) A proceeding to determine parentage commenced before the birth of the child may not be concluded until after the birth of the child.

(b) In a proceeding described by Subsection (a), the following actions may be taken before the birth of the child:

(1) service of process;

(2) discovery; and

(3) except as prohibited by Section 160.502, collection of specimens for genetic testing.

Added by Acts 2001, 77th Leg., ch. 821, § 1.01, eff. June 14, 2001.

§ 160.612. Child as Party; Representation

(a) A minor child is a permissible party, but is not a necessary party to a proceeding under this subchapter.

(b) The court shall appoint an amicus attorney or attorney ad litem to represent a child who is a minor or is incapacitated if the child is a party or the court finds that the interests of the child are not adequately represented.

Added by Acts 2001, 77th Leg., ch. 821, § 1.01, eff. June 14, 2001. Subsec. (b) amended by Acts 2005, 79th Leg., ch. 172, § 18, eff. Sept. 1, 2005.

§ 160.621. Admissibility of Results of Genetic Testing; Expenses

(a) Except as otherwise provided by Subsection (c), a report of a genetic testing expert is admissible as evidence of the truth of the facts asserted in the report. The admissibility of the report is not affected by whether the testing was performed:

(1) voluntarily or under an order of the court or a support enforcement agency; or

(2) before or after the date of commencement of the proceeding.

(b) A party objecting to the results of genetic testing may call one or more genetic testing experts to testify in person or by telephone, videoconference, deposition, or another method approved by the court. Unless otherwise ordered by the court, the party offering the testimony bears the expense for the expert testifying.

(c) If a child has a presumed, acknowledged, or adjudicated father, the results of genetic testing are inadmissible to adjudicate parentage unless performed:

(1) with the consent of both the mother and the presumed, acknowledged, or adjudicated father; or

(2) under an order of the court under Section 160.502.

(d) Copies of bills for genetic testing and for prenatal and postnatal health care for the mother and child that are furnished to the adverse party on or before the 10th day before the date of a hearing are admissible to establish:

(1) the amount of the charges billed; and

(2) that the charges were reasonable, necessary, and customary.

Added by Acts 2001, 77th Leg., ch. 821, § 1.01, eff. June 14, 2001.

§ 160.622. Consequences of Declining Genetic Testing

(a) An order for genetic testing is enforceable by contempt.

(b) A court may adjudicate parentage contrary to the position of an individual whose paternity is being determined on the grounds that the individual declines to submit to genetic testing as ordered by the court.

(c) Genetic testing of the mother of a child is not a prerequisite to testing the child and a man whose paternity is being determined. If the mother is unavailable or declines to submit to genetic testing, the court may order the testing of the child and each man whose paternity is being adjudicated.

Added by Acts 2001, 77th Leg., ch. 821, § 1.01, eff. June 14, 2001.

§ 160.623. Admission of Paternity Authorized

(a) A respondent in a proceeding to adjudicate parentage may admit to the paternity of a child by filing a pleading to that effect or by admitting paternity under penalty of perjury when making an appearance or during a hearing.

(b) If the court finds that the admission of paternity satisfies the requirements of this section and that there is no reason to question the admission, the court shall render an order adjudicating the child to be the child of the man admitting paternity.

Added by Acts 2001, 77th Leg., ch. 821, § 1.01, eff. June 14, 2001.

§ 160.624. Temporary Order

(a) In a proceeding under this subchapter, the court shall render a temporary order for child support for a child if the order is appropriate and the individual ordered to pay child support:

(1) is a presumed father of the child;

(2) is petitioning to have his paternity adjudicated;

(3) is identified as the father through genetic testing under Section 160.505;

(4) is an alleged father who has declined to submit to genetic testing;

(5) is shown by clear and convincing evidence to be the father of the child; or

(6) is the mother of the child.

(b) A temporary order may include provisions for the possession of or access to the child as provided by other laws of this state.

Added by Acts 2001, 77th Leg., ch. 821, § 1.01, eff. June 14, 2001.

§ 160.631. Rules for Adjudication of Paternity

(a) The court shall apply the rules stated in this section to adjudicate the paternity of a child.

(b) The paternity of a child having a presumed, acknowledged, or adjudicated father may be disproved only by admissible results of genetic testing excluding that man as the father of the child or identifying another man as the father of the child.

(c) Unless the results of genetic testing are admitted to rebut other results of genetic testing, the man identified as the father of a child under Section 160.505 shall be adjudicated as being the father of the child.

(d) Unless the results of genetic testing are admitted to rebut other results of genetic testing, a man excluded as the father of a child by genetic testing shall be adjudicated as not being the father of the child.

(e) If the court finds that genetic testing under Section 160.505 does not identify or exclude a man as the father of a child, the court may not dismiss the proceeding. In that event, the results of genetic testing and other evidence are admissible to adjudicate the issue of paternity.

Added by Acts 2001, 77th Leg., ch. 821, § 1.01, eff. June 14, 2001.

§ 160.632. Jury Prohibited

The court shall adjudicate paternity of a child without a jury.

Added by Acts 2001, 77th Leg., ch. 821, § 1.01, eff. June 14, 2001.

§ 160.633. Hearings; Inspection of Records

(a) On the request of a party and for good cause shown, the court may order a proceeding under this subchapter closed to the public.

(b) A final order in a proceeding under this subchapter is available for public inspection. Other papers and records are available only with the consent of the parties or on order of the court for good cause.

Added by Acts 2001, 77th Leg., ch. 821, § 1.01, eff. June 14, 2001.

§ 160.634. Order on Default

The court shall issue an order adjudicating the paternity of a man who:

(1) after service of process, is in default; and

(2) is found by the court to be the father of a child.

Added by Acts 2001, 77th Leg., ch. 821, § 1.01, eff. June 14, 2001.

§ 160.635. Dismissal for Want of Prosecution

The court may issue an order dismissing a proceeding commenced under this chapter for want of prosecution only without prejudice. An order of dismissal for want of prosecution purportedly with prejudice is void and has only the effect of a dismissal without prejudice.

Added by Acts 2001, 77th Leg., ch. 821, § 1.01, eff. June 14, 2001.

§ 160.636. Order Adjudicating Parentage; Costs

(a) The court shall render an order adjudicating whether a man alleged or claiming to be the father is the parent of the child.

(b) An order adjudicating parentage must identify the child by name and date of birth.

(c) Except as otherwise provided by Subsection (d), the court may assess filing fees, reasonable attorney's fees, fees for genetic testing, other costs, and necessary travel and other reasonable expenses incurred in a proceeding under this subchapter. Attorney's fees awarded by the court may be paid directly to the attorney. An attorney who is awarded attorney's fees may enforce the order in the attorney's own name.

(d) The court may not assess fees, costs, or expenses against the support enforcement agency of this state or another state, except as provided by other law.

(e) On request of a party and for good cause shown, the court may order that the name of the child be changed.

(f) If the order of the court is at variance with the child's birth certificate, the court shall order the [bureau of] vital statistics unit to issue an amended birth record.

(g) On a finding of parentage, the court may order retroactive child support as provided by Chapter 154 and, on a proper showing, order a party to pay an equitable portion of all of the prenatal and postnatal health care expenses of the mother and the child.

(h) In rendering an order for retroactive child support under this section, the court shall use the child support guidelines provided by Chapter 154, together with any relevant factors.

Added by Acts 2001, 77th Leg., ch. 821, § 1.01, eff. June 14, 2001. Subsec. (f) amended by Acts 2015, 84th Leg., ch. 1, § 1.075, eff. Apr. 1, 2015.

§ 160.637. Binding Effect of Determination of Parentage

(a) Except as otherwise provided by Subsection (b) or Section 160.316, a determination of parentage is binding on:

(1) all signatories to an acknowledgment or denial of paternity as provided by Subchapter D[1]; and

(2) all parties to an adjudication by a court acting under circumstances that satisfy the jurisdictional requirements of Section 159.201.

(b) A child is not bound by a determination of parentage under this chapter unless:

(1) the determination was based on an unrescinded acknowledgment of paternity and the acknowledgment is consistent with the results of genetic testing;

(2) the adjudication of parentage was based on a finding consistent with the results of genetic testing and the consistency is declared in the determination or is otherwise shown; or

(3) the child was a party or was represented in the proceeding determining parentage by an attorney ad litem.

(c) In a proceeding to dissolve a marriage, the court is considered to have made an adjudication of the parentage of a child if the court acts under circumstances that satisfy the jurisdictional requirements of Section 159.201, and the final order:

(1) expressly identifies the child as "a child of the marriage" or "issue of the marriage" or uses similar words indicating that the husband is the father of the child; or

(2) provides for the payment of child support for the child by the husband unless paternity is specifically disclaimed in the order.

(d) Except as otherwise provided by Subsection (b), a determination of parentage may be a defense in a subsequent proceeding seeking to adjudicate parentage by an individual who was not a party to the earlier proceeding.

(e) A party to an adjudication of paternity may challenge the adjudication only under the laws of this state relating to appeal, the vacating of judgments, or other judicial review.

Added by Acts 2001, 77th Leg., ch. 821, § 1.01, eff. June 14, 2001.

---

[1] Family Code § 160.301 et seq.

Subchapter H.   Child of Assisted Reproduction

Statutes in Context
§§ 160.701–160.763

Modern medical technology permits children to be born via reproduction techniques that involve more than the traditional two people or years after the death of one of the parents. Examples of these methodologies include (1) artificial insemination (donated semen artificially introduced into the mother's vagina or uterus), (2) in vitro fertilization (donated egg and donated semen combined in a laboratory with the resulting embryo transferred to a donee), (3) gamete intrafallopian transfer (donated egg and donated sperm combined in a donee's fallopian tube), and (4) embryo lavage and transfer (fertilized egg removed from the donor and transferred to the donee's uterus).

Several options exist regarding the parentage of children born as a result of these techniques. The father could be (1) the supplier of the genetic material (sperm), (2) the husband of the supplier of the female genetic material (egg), or (3) the husband of the woman who gestates the child. Likewise, the mother could be (1) the supplier of the female genetic material, (2) the wife of the man who supplies the male genetic material, or (3) the woman who gestates the child even though this woman did not supply any genetic material (a surrogate mother).

Sections 160.701 - 160.763 resolve some, but not all, of the issues which arise regarding the individuals whom the law will treat as the parents of children conceived by means of assisted conception.

§ 160.701. Scope of Subchapter

This subchapter applies only to a child conceived by means of assisted reproduction.

Added by Acts 2001, 77th Leg., ch. 821, § 1.01, eff. June 14, 2001.

§ 160.702. Parental Status of Donor

A donor is not a parent of a child conceived by means of assisted reproduction.

Added by Acts 2001, 77th Leg., ch. 821, § 1.01, eff. June 14, 2001.

§ 160.703. Husband's Paternity of Child of Assisted Reproduction

If a husband provides sperm for or consents to assisted reproduction by his wife as provided by Section 160.704, he is the father of a resulting child.

Added by Acts 2001, 77th Leg., ch. 821, § 1.01, eff. June 14, 2001.

§ 160.7031. Unmarried Man's Paternity of Child of Assisted Reproduction

(a) If an unmarried man, with the intent to be the father of a resulting child, provides sperm to a licensed physician and consents to the use of that sperm for assisted reproduction by an unmarried woman, he is the father of a resulting child.

(b) Consent by an unmarried man who intends to be the father of a resulting child in accordance with this section must be in a record signed by the man and the unmarried woman and kept by a licensed physician.

Added by Acts 2007, 80th Leg., ch. 972, § 40, eff. Sept. 1, 2007.

§ 160.704. Consent to Assisted Reproduction

(a) Consent by a married woman to assisted reproduction must be in a record signed by the woman and her husband and kept by a licensed physician. This requirement does not apply to the donation of eggs by a married woman for assisted reproduction by another woman.

(b) Failure by the husband to sign a consent required by Subsection (a) before or after the birth of the child does not preclude a finding that the husband is the father of a child born to his wife if the wife and husband openly treated the child as their own.

Added by Acts 2001, 77th Leg., ch. 821, § 1.01, eff. June 14, 2001. Subsec. (a) amended by Acts 2007, 80th Leg., ch. 972, § 41, eff. Sept. 1, 2007.

§ 160.705. Limitation on Husband's Dispute of Paternity

(a) Except as otherwise provided by Subsection (b), the husband of a wife who gives birth to a child by means of assisted reproduction may not challenge his paternity of the child unless:

(1) before the fourth anniversary of the date of learning of the birth of the child he commences a proceeding to adjudicate his paternity; and

(2) the court finds that he did not consent to the assisted reproduction before or after the birth of the child.

(b) A proceeding to adjudicate paternity may be maintained at any time if the court determines that:

(1) the husband did not provide sperm for or, before or after the birth of the child, consent to assisted reproduction by his wife;

(2) the husband and the mother of the child have not cohabited since the probable time of assisted reproduction; and

(3) the husband never openly treated the child as his own.

(c) The limitations provided by this section apply to a marriage declared invalid after assisted reproduction.

Added by Acts 2001, 77th Leg., ch. 821, § 1.01, eff. June 14, 2001.

§ 160.706. Effect of Dissolution of Marriage

(a) If a marriage is dissolved before the placement of eggs, sperm, or embryos, the former spouse is not a parent of the resulting child unless the former spouse consented in a record kept by a licensed physician that if assisted reproduction were to occur after a divorce the former spouse would be a parent of the child.

(b) The consent of a former spouse to assisted reproduction may be withdrawn by that individual in a record kept by a licensed physician at any time before the placement of eggs, sperm, or embryos.

Added by Acts 2001, 77th Leg., ch. 821, § 1.01, eff. June 14, 2001. Amended by Acts 2007, 80th Leg., ch. 972, § 42, eff. Sept. 1, 2007.

§ 160.707. Parental Status of Deceased Spouse

If a spouse dies before the placement of eggs, sperm, or embryos, the deceased spouse is not a parent of the resulting child unless the deceased spouse consented in a record kept by a licensed physician that if assisted reproduction were to occur after death the deceased spouse would be a parent of the child.

Added by Acts 2001, 77th Leg., ch. 821, § 1.01, eff. June 14, 2001. Amended by Acts 2007, 80th Leg., ch. 972, § 43, eff. Sept. 1, 2007.

Subchapter I. Gestational Agreements

Statutes in Context
§§ 160.751–160.762

The 2003 Texas Legislature authorized gestational agreements between a surrogate mother and the intended parents in Family Code §§ 160.751–160.762. If the agreement is properly validated, the woman who gave birth to the child will not be treated as the child's mother. Accordingly, this child would not inherit from or through the birth mother. Instead, the mother and father of the child will be the intended parents and inheritance rights will accrue accordingly.

§ 160.751. Definition

In this subchapter, "gestational mother" means a woman who gives birth to a child conceived under a gestational agreement.

Added by Acts 2003, 78th Leg., ch. 457, § 2, eff. Sept. 1, 2003.

§ 160.752. Scope of Subchapter; Choice of Law

(a) Notwithstanding any other provision of this chapter or another law, this subchapter authorizes an agreement between a woman and the intended parents of a child in which the woman relinquishes all rights as a parent of a child conceived by means of assisted reproduction and that provides that the intended parents become the parents of the child.

(b) This subchapter controls over any other law with respect to a child conceived under a gestational agreement under this subchapter.

Added by Acts 2003, 78th Leg., ch. 457, § 2, eff. Sept. 1, 2003.

§ 160.753. Establishment of Parent-Child Relationship

(a) Notwithstanding any other provision of this chapter or another law, the mother-child relationship exists between a woman and a child by an adjudication confirming the woman as a parent of the child born to a gestational mother under a gestational agreement if the gestational agreement is validated under this subchapter or enforceable under other law, regardless of the fact that the gestational mother gave birth to the child.

(b) The father-child relationship exists between a child and a man by an adjudication confirming the man as a parent of the child born to a gestational mother under a gestational agreement if the gestational agreement is validated under this subchapter or enforceable under other law.

Added by Acts 2003, 78th Leg., ch. 457, § 2, eff. Sept. 1, 2003.

§ 160.754. Gestational Agreement Authorized

(a) A prospective gestational mother, her husband if she is married, each donor, and each intended parent may enter into a written agreement providing that:

(1) the prospective gestational mother agrees to pregnancy by means of assisted reproduction;

(2) the prospective gestational mother, her husband if she is married, and each donor other than the intended parents, if applicable, relinquish all parental rights and duties with respect to a child conceived through assisted reproduction;

(3) the intended parents will be the parents of the child; and

(4) the gestational mother and each intended parent agree to exchange throughout the period covered by the agreement all relevant information regarding the health of the gestational mother and each intended parent.

(b) The intended parents must be married to each other. Each intended parent must be a party to the gestational agreement.

(c) The gestational agreement must require that the eggs used in the assisted reproduction procedure be retrieved from an intended parent or a donor. The gestational mother's eggs may not be used in the assisted reproduction procedure.

(d) The gestational agreement must state that the physician who will perform the assisted reproduction procedure as provided by the agreement has informed the parties to the agreement of:

(1) the rate of successful conceptions and births attributable to the procedure, including the most recent published outcome statistics of the procedure at the facility at which it will be performed;

(2) the potential for and risks associated with the implantation of multiple embryos and consequent multiple births resulting from the procedure;

(3) the nature of and expenses related to the procedure;

(4) the health risks associated with, as applicable, fertility drugs used in the procedure, egg retrieval procedures, and egg or embryo transfer procedures; and

(5) reasonably foreseeable psychological effects resulting from the procedure.

(e) The parties to a gestational agreement must enter into the agreement before the 14th day preceding the date the transfer of eggs, sperm, or embryos to the gestational mother occurs for the purpose of conception or implantation.

(f) A gestational agreement does not apply to the birth of a child conceived by means of sexual intercourse.

(g) A gestational agreement may not limit the right of the gestational mother to make decisions to safeguard her health or the health of an embryo.

Added by Acts 2003, 78th Leg., ch. 457, § 2, eff. Sept. 1, 2003.

§ 160.755. Petition to Validate Gestational Agreement

(a) The intended parents and the prospective gestational mother under a gestational agreement may commence a proceeding to validate the agreement.

(b) A person may maintain a proceeding to validate a gestational agreement only if:

(1) the prospective gestational mother or the intended parents have resided in this state for the 90 days preceding the date the proceeding is commenced;

(2) the prospective gestational mother's husband, if she is married, is joined as a party to the proceeding; and

(3) a copy of the gestational agreement is attached to the petition.

Added by Acts 2003, 78th Leg., ch. 457, § 2, eff. Sept. 1, 2003.

§ 160.756. Hearing to Validate Gestational Agreement

(a) A gestational agreement must be validated as provided by this section.

(b) The court may validate a gestational agreement as provided by Subsection (c) only if the court finds that:

(1) the parties have submitted to the jurisdiction of the court under the jurisdictional standards of this chapter;

(2) the medical evidence provided shows that the intended mother is unable to carry a pregnancy to term and give birth to the child or is unable to carry the pregnancy to term and give birth to the

child without unreasonable risk to her physical or mental health or to the health of the unborn child;

(3) unless waived by the court, an agency or other person has conducted a home study of the intended parents and has determined that the intended parents meet the standards of fitness applicable to adoptive parents;

(4) each party to the agreement has voluntarily entered into and understands the terms of the agreement;

(5) the prospective gestational mother has had at least one previous pregnancy and delivery and carrying another pregnancy to term and giving birth to another child would not pose an unreasonable risk to the child's health or the physical or mental health of the prospective gestational mother; and

(6) the parties have adequately provided for which party is responsible for all reasonable health care expenses associated with the pregnancy, including providing for who is responsible for those expenses if the agreement is terminated.

(c) If the court finds that the requirements of Subsection (b) are satisfied, the court may render an order validating the gestational agreement and declaring that the intended parents will be the parents of a child born under the agreement.

(d) The court may validate the gestational agreement at the court's discretion. The court's determination of whether to validate the agreement is subject to review only for abuse of discretion.

Added by Acts 2003, 78th Leg., ch. 457, § 2, eff. Sept. 1, 2003.

§ 160.757. Inspection of Records

The proceedings, records, and identities of the parties to a gestational agreement under this subchapter are subject to inspection under the same standards of confidentiality that apply to an adoption under the laws of this state.

Added by Acts 2003, 78th Leg., ch. 457, § 2, eff. Sept. 1, 2003.

§ 160.758. Continuing, Exclusive Jurisdiction

Subject to Section 152.201, a court that conducts a proceeding under this subchapter has continuing, exclusive jurisdiction of all matters arising out of the gestational agreement until the date a child born to the gestational mother during the period covered by the agreement reaches 180 days of age.

Added by Acts 2003, 78th Leg., ch. 457, § 2, eff. Sept. 1, 2003.

§ 160.759. Termination of Gestational Agreement

(a) Before a prospective gestational mother becomes pregnant by means of assisted reproduction, the prospective gestational mother, her husband if she is married, or either intended parent may terminate a gestational agreement validated under Section 160.756

by giving written notice of the termination to each other party to the agreement.

(b) A person who terminates a gestational agreement under Subsection (a) shall file notice of the termination with the court. A person having the duty to notify the court who does not notify the court of the termination of the agreement is subject to appropriate sanctions.

(c) On receipt of the notice of termination, the court shall vacate the order rendered under Section 160.756 validating the gestational agreement.

(d) A prospective gestational mother and her husband, if she is married, may not be liable to an intended parent for terminating a gestational agreement if the termination is in accordance with this section.

Added by Acts 2003, 78th Leg., ch. 457, § 2, eff. Sept. 1, 2003.

§ 160.760. Parentage Under Validated Gestational Agreement

(a) On the birth of a child to a gestational mother under a validated gestational agreement, the intended parents shall file a notice of the birth with the court not later than the 300th day after the date assisted reproduction occurred.

(b) After receiving notice of the birth, the court shall render an order that:

(1) confirms that the intended parents are the child's parents;

(2) requires the gestational mother to surrender the child to the intended parents, if necessary; and

(3) requires the [bureau of] vital statistics unit to issue a birth certificate naming the intended parents as the child's parents.

(c) If a person alleges that a child born to a gestational mother did not result from assisted reproduction, the court shall order that scientifically accepted parentage testing be conducted to determine the child's parentage.

(d) If the intended parents fail to file the notice required by Subsection (a), the gestational mother or an appropriate state agency may file the notice required by that subsection. On a showing that an order validating the gestational agreement was rendered in accordance with Section 160.756, the court shall order that the intended parents are the child's parents and are financially responsible for the child.

Added by Acts 2003, 78th Leg., ch. 457, § 2, eff. Sept. 1, 2003. Subsec. (d) added by Acts 2005, 79th Leg., ch. 916, § 22, eff. June 18, 2005. Subsec. (b) amended by Acts 2015, 84th Leg., ch. 1, § 1.076, eff. Apr. 1, 2015.

§ 160.761. Effect of Gestational Mother's Marriage After Validation of Agreement

If a gestational mother is married after the court renders an order validating a gestational agreement under this subchapter:

(1) the validity of the gestational agreement is not affected;

(2) the gestational mother's husband is not required to consent to the agreement; and

(3) the gestational mother's husband is not a presumed father of the child born under the terms of the agreement.

Added by Acts 2003, 78th Leg., ch. 457, § 2, eff. Sept. 1, 2003.

§ 160.762. Effect of Gestational Agreement that Is Not Validated

(a) A gestational agreement that is not validated as provided by this subchapter is unenforceable, regardless of whether the agreement is in a record.

(b) The parent-child relationship of a child born under a gestational agreement that is not validated as provided by this subchapter is determined as otherwise provided by this chapter.

(c) A party to a gestational agreement that is not validated as provided by this subchapter who is an intended parent under the agreement may be held liable for the support of a child born under the agreement, even if the agreement is otherwise unenforceable.

(d) The court may assess filing fees, reasonable attorney's fees, fees for genetic testing, other costs, and necessary travel and other reasonable expenses incurred in a proceeding under this section. Attorney's fees awarded by the court may be paid directly to the attorney. An attorney who is awarded attorney's fees may enforce the order in the attorney's own name.

Added by Acts 2003, 78th Leg., ch. 457, § 2, eff. Sept. 1, 2003.

§ 160.763. Health Care Facility Reporting Requirement

(a) The executive commissioner of the Health and Human Services Commission [Texas Department of Health] by rule shall develop and implement a confidential reporting system that requires each health care facility in this state at which assisted reproduction procedures are performed under gestational agreements to report statistics related to those procedures.

(b) In developing the reporting system, the executive commissioner [department] shall require each health care facility described by Subsection (a) to annually report:

(1) the number of assisted reproduction procedures under a gestational agreement performed at the facility during the preceding year; and

(2) the number and current status of embryos created through assisted reproduction procedures described by Subdivision (1) that were not transferred for implantation.

Added by Acts 2003, 78th Leg., ch. 457, § 2, eff. Sept. 1, 2003. Amended by Acts 2015, 84th Leg., ch. 1, § 1.077, eff. Apr. 1, 2015.

Chapter 161. Termination of the Parent-Child Relationship

Subchapter C. Hearing and Order

**Statutes in Context
§ 161.206**

An order terminating parental rights under § 161.206 will not divest the child of the right to inherit from and through the parent unless the court order expressly removes inheritance rights.

---

§ 161.206. Order Terminating Parental Rights

(a) If the court finds by clear and convincing evidence grounds for termination of the parent-child relationship, it shall render an order terminating the parent-child relationship.

(b) Except as provided by Section 161.2061, an order terminating the parent-child relationship divests the parent and the child of all legal rights and duties with respect to each other, except that the child retains the right to inherit from and through the parent unless the court otherwise provides.

(c) Nothing in this chapter precludes or affects the rights of a biological or adoptive maternal or paternal grandparent to reasonable access under Chapter 153

(d) An order rendered under this section must include a finding that:

(1) a request for identification of a court of continuing, exclusive jurisdiction has been made as required by Section 155.101; and

(2) all parties entitled to notice, including the Title IV-D agency, have been notified.

Added by Acts 1995, 74ʰ Leg., ch. 20, § 1, eff. April 20, 1995. Amended by Acts 1995, 74ʰ Leg., ch. 709, § 2, eff. Sept. 1, 1995; Acts 1995, 74ʰ Leg., ch. 751, § 72, eff. Sept. 1, 1995; Acts 2003, 78ʰ Leg., ch. 561, § 1, eff. Sept. 1, 2003. Subsec. (d) added by Acts 2007, 80ʰ Leg., ch. 972, § 44, eff. Sept. 1, 2007.

§ 161.2061. Terms Regarding Limited Post-Termination Contact

(a) If the court finds it to be in the best interest of the child, the court may provide in an order terminating the parent-child relationship that the biological parent who filed an affidavit of voluntary relinquishment of parental rights under Section 161.103 shall have limited post-termination contact with the child as provided by Subsection (b) on the agreement of the biological parent and the Department of <u>Family and</u> Protective [~~and Regulatory~~] Services.

(b) The order of termination may include terms that allow the biological parent to:

(1) receive specified information regarding the child;

(2) provide written communications to the child; and

(3) have limited access to the child.

(c) The terms of an order of termination regarding limited post-termination contact may be enforced only if the party seeking enforcement pleads and proves that, before filing the motion for enforcement, the party attempted in good faith to resolve the disputed matters through mediation.

(d) The terms of an order of termination under this section are not enforceable by contempt.

(e) The terms of an order of termination regarding limited post-termination contact may not be modified.

(f) An order under this section does not:

(1) affect the finality of a termination order; or

(2) grant standing to a parent whose parental rights have been terminated to file any action under this title other than a motion to enforce the terms regarding limited post-termination contact until the court renders a subsequent adoption order with respect to the child.

Added by Acts 2003, 78ʰ Leg., ch. 561, § 2, eff. Sept. 1, 2003. Subsec. (a) amended by Acts 2015, 84ʰ Leg., ch. 1, § 1.087, eff. Apr. 1, 2015.

§ 161.2062. Provision for Limited Contact Between Biological Parent and Child

(a) An order terminating the parent-child relationship may not require that a subsequent adoption order include terms regarding limited post-termination contact between the child and a biological parent.

(b) The inclusion of a requirement for post-termination contact described by Subsection (a) in a termination order does not:

(1) affect the finality of a termination or subsequent adoption order; or

(2) grant standing to a parent whose parental rights have been terminated to file any action under this title after the court renders a subsequent adoption order with respect to the child.

Added by Acts 2003, 78ʰ Leg., ch. 561, § 2, eff. Sept. 1, 2003.

Chapter 162. Adoption

Subchapter A. Adoption of a Child

**Statutes in Context
§§ 162.001–162.025**

Sections 162.001 - 162.025 govern the adoption of a child.

---

§ 162.001. Who May Adopt and Be Adopted

(a) Subject to the requirements for standing to sue in Chapter 102, an adult may petition to adopt a child who may be adopted.

(b) A child residing in this state may be adopted if:

(1) the parent-child relationship as to each living parent of the child has been terminated or a

suit for termination is joined with the suit for adoption;

(2) the parent whose rights have not been terminated is presently the spouse of the petitioner and the proceeding is for a stepparent adoption;

(3) the child is at least two years old, the parent-child relationship has been terminated with respect to one parent, the person seeking the adoption has been a managing conservator or has had actual care, possession, and control of the child for a period of six months preceding the adoption or is the child's former stepparent, and the nonterminated parent consents to the adoption; or

(4) the child is at least two years old, the parent-child relationship has been terminated with respect to one parent, and the person seeking the adoption is the child's former stepparent and has been a managing conservator or has had actual care, possession, and control of the child for a period of one year preceding the adoption.

(c) If an affidavit of relinquishment of parental rights contains a consent for the Department of Family and Protective [and Regulatory] Services or a licensed child-placing agency to place the child for adoption and appoints the department or agency managing conservator of the child, further consent by the parent is not required and the adoption order shall terminate all rights of the parent without further termination proceedings.

Added by Acts 1995, 74th Leg., ch. 20, § 1, eff. April 20, 1995; Amended by Acts 1997, 75th Leg., ch. 561, § 14, eff. Sept. 1, 1997; Acts 2003, 78th Leg., ch. 493, § 1, eff. Sept. 1, 2003. Subsec. (c) amended by Acts 2015, 84th Leg., ch. 1, § 1.090, eff. Apr. 1, 2015.

§ 162.002. Prerequisites to Petition

(a) If a petitioner is married, both spouses must join in the petition for adoption.

(b) A petition in a suit for adoption or a suit for appointment of a nonparent managing conservator with authority to consent to adoption of a child must include:

(1) a verified allegation that there has been compliance with Subchapter B[1]; or

(2) if there has not been compliance with Subchapter B, a verified statement of the particular reasons for noncompliance.

Added by Acts 1995, 74th Leg., ch. 20, § 1, eff. April 20, 1995.

§ 162.0025. Adoption Sought by Military Service Member

In a suit for adoption, the fact that a petitioner is a member of the armed forces of the United States, a member of the Texas National Guard or the National Guard of another state, or a member of a reserve component of the armed forces of the United States may not be considered by the court, or any person

performing an adoption evaluation [a social study] or home screening, as a negative factor in determining whether the adoption is in the best interest of the child or whether the petitioner would be a suitable parent.

Added by Acts 2007, 80th Leg., ch. 768, § 1, eff. June 15, 2007. Amended by Acts 2015, 84th Leg., ch. 1252, § 3.02, eff. Sept. 1, 2015.

§ 162.003. Adoption Evaluation [Pre-Adoptive and Post-Placement Social Studies]

In a suit for adoption, an adoption evaluation [pre-adoptive and post-placement social studies] must be conducted as provided in Chapter 107.

Added by Acts 1995, 74th Leg., ch. 20, § 1, eff. April 20, 1995. Amended by Acts 1995, 74th Leg., ch. 751, § 73, eff. Sept. 1, 1995; Acts 1995, 74th Leg., ch. 800, § 1, eff. Sept. 1, 1995; Acts 2001, 77th Leg., ch. 133, § 3, eff. Sept. 1, 2001. Amended by Acts 2007, 80th Leg., ch. 832, § 6, eff. Sept. 1, 2007. Amended by Acts 2015, 84th Leg., ch. 1252, § 3.03, eff. Sept. 1, 2015.

§ 162.0045. Preferential Setting

The court shall grant a motion for a preferential setting for a final hearing on an adoption and shall give precedence to that hearing over all other civil cases not given preference by other law if the adoption evaluation [social study] has been filed and the criminal history for the person seeking to adopt the child has been obtained.

Added by Acts 1997, 75th Leg., ch. 561, § 15, eff. Sept. 1, 1997. Amended by Acts 2015, 84th Leg., ch. 1252, § 3.04, eff. Sept. 1, 2015.

§ 162.005. Preparation of Health, Social, Educational, and Genetic History Report

(a) This section does not apply to an adoption by the child's:

(1) grandparent;

(2) aunt or uncle by birth, marriage, or prior adoption; or

(3) stepparent.

(b) Before placing a child for adoption, the Department of Family and Protective [and Regulatory] Services, a licensed child-placing agency, or the child's parent or guardian shall compile a report on the available health, social, educational, and genetic history of the child to be adopted.

(c) The report shall include a history of physical, sexual, or emotional abuse suffered by the child, if any.

(d) If the child has been placed for adoption by a person or entity other than the department, a licensed child-placing agency, or the child's parent or guardian, it is the duty of the person or entity who places the child for adoption to prepare the report.

(e) The person or entity who places the child for adoption shall provide the prospective adoptive parents a copy of the report as early as practicable before the first meeting of the adoptive parents with the child. The copy of the report shall be edited to protect the identity of birth parents and their families.

---

[1] Family Code § 160.101 et seq.

(f) The department, licensed child-placing agency, parent, guardian, person, or entity who prepares and files the original report is required to furnish supplemental medical, psychological, and psychiatric information to the adoptive parents if that information becomes available and to file the supplemental information where the original report is filed. The supplemental information shall be retained for as long as the original report is required to be retained.

Added by Acts 1995, 74th Leg., ch. 20, § 1, eff. April 20, 1995. Subsec. (b) amended by Acts 2015, 84th Leg., ch. 1, § 1.091, eff. Apr. 1, 2015. Subsec. (c) transferred to § 162.007(e).

§ 162.006. Right to Examine Records

(a) The department, licensed child-placing agency, or other person placing a child for adoption shall inform the prospective adoptive parents of their right to examine the records and other information relating to the history of the child. The department, licensed child-placing agency, or other person placing the child for adoption shall edit the records and information to protect the identity of the biological parents and any other person whose identity is confidential.

(a-1) The records described by Subsection (a) must include any records relating to an investigation of abuse in which the child was an alleged or confirmed victim of sexual abuse while residing in a foster home or other residential child-care facility. If the licensed child-placing agency or other person placing the child for adoption does not have the information required by this subsection, the department, at the request of the licensed child-placing agency or other person placing the child for adoption, shall provide the information to the prospective adoptive parents of the child.

(b) The department, licensed child-placing agency, or court retaining a copy of the report shall provide a copy of the report that has been edited to protect the identity of the birth parents and any other person whose identity is confidential to the following persons on request:

(1) an adoptive parent of the adopted child;

(2) the managing conservator, guardian of the person, or legal custodian of the adopted child;

(3) the adopted child, after the child is an adult;

(4) the surviving spouse of the adopted child if the adopted child is dead and the spouse is the parent or guardian of a child of the deceased adopted child; or

(5) a progeny of the adopted child if the adopted child is dead and the progeny is an adult.

(c) A copy of the report may not be furnished to a person who cannot furnish satisfactory proof of identity and legal entitlement to receive a copy.

(d) A person requesting a copy of the report shall pay the actual and reasonable costs of providing a copy and verifying entitlement to the copy.

(e) The report shall be retained for 99 years from the date of the adoption by the department or licensed child-placing agency placing the child for adoption. If the agency ceases to function as a child-placing agency, the agency shall transfer all the reports to the department or, after giving notice to the department, to a transferee agency that is assuming responsibility for the preservation of the agency's adoption records. If the child has not been placed for adoption by the department or a licensed child-placing agency and if the child is being adopted by a person other than the child's stepparent, grandparent, aunt, or uncle by birth, marriage, or prior adoption, the person or entity who places the child for adoption shall file the report with the department, which shall retain the copies for 99 years from the date of the adoption.

Added by Acts 1995, 74th Leg., ch. 20, § 1, eff. April 20, 1995. Subsection (a) amended and subsection (a-1) added by Acts 2013, 83rd Leg., ch. 1069, § 1. eff. Sept. 1, 2013. Subsec. (a) and (b) redesignated as § 162.0062 by Acts 2015, 84th Leg., ch. 944, § 15, eff. Sept. 1, 2015.

Note: Subsection (a) was also amended by Acts 2015, 84th Leg., ch. 1, § 1.092, eff. Apr. 1, 2015, to read as follows:

(a) The Department of Family and Protective Services [department], licensed child-placing agency, or other person placing a child for adoption shall inform the prospective adoptive parents of their right to examine the records and other information relating to the history of the child. The department, licensed child-placing agency, or other person placing the child for adoption shall edit the records and information to protect the identity of the biological parents and any other person whose identity is confidential.

§ 162.0062. Access to Information

(a) Except as provided by Subsection (c), the prospective adoptive parents of a child are entitled to examine the records and other information relating to the history of the child. The Department of Family and Protective Services, licensed child-placing agency, or other person placing a child for adoption shall inform the prospective adoptive parents of their right to examine the records and other information relating to the history of the child. The department, licensed child-placing agency, or other person placing the child for adoption shall edit the records and information to protect the identity of the biological parents and any other person whose identity is confidential.

(b) [(a-1)] The records described by Subsection (a) must include any records relating to an investigation of abuse in which the child was an alleged or confirmed victim of sexual abuse while residing in a foster home or other residential child-care facility. If the licensed child-placing agency or other person placing the child for adoption does not have the information required by this subsection, the department, at the request of the licensed child-placing agency or other person placing the child for adoption, shall provide the information to the prospective adoptive parents of the child.

(c) If the prospective adoptive parents of a child have reviewed the health, social, educational, and genetic history report for the child and indicated that they want to proceed with the adoption, the department may, but is not required to, allow the prospective adoptive parents of the child to examine the records and other information relating to the history of the child, unless the prospective adoptive parents request the child's case record. The department shall provide the child's case record to the prospective adoptive parents on the request of the prospective adoptive parents.

(d) [§ 162.018. Access to Information. (a) The adoptive parents are entitled to receive copies of the records and other information relating to the history of the child maintained by the Department of Family and Protective Services, licensed child-placing agency, person, or entity placing the child for adoption.

[(b)] The adoptive parents and the adopted child, after the child is an adult, are entitled to receive copies of the records that have been edited to protect the identity of the biological parents and any other person whose identity is confidential and other information relating to the history of the child maintained by the department, licensed child-placing agency, person, or entity placing the child for adoption.

(e) [(c)] It is the duty of the person or entity placing the child for adoption to edit the records and information to protect the identity of the biological parents and any other person whose identity is confidential.

(f) [(d)] At the time an adoption order is rendered, the court shall provide to the parents of an adopted child information provided by the vital statistics unit that describes the functions of the voluntary adoption registry under Subchapter E. The licensed child-placing agency shall provide to each of the child's biological parents known to the agency, the information when the parent signs an affidavit of relinquishment of parental rights or affidavit of waiver of interest in a child. The information shall include the right of the child or biological parent to refuse to participate in the registry. If the adopted child is 14 years old or older the court shall provide the information to the child.

Added by Acts 2015, 84th Leg., ch. 944, § 15, eff. Sept. 1, 2015 including material transferred from § 162.006 and 162.018.

§ 162.0065. Access to Health, Social, Educational, and Genetic History Report; Retention [Right to Examine Records]

Notwithstanding any other provision of this chapter, in an adoption in which a child is placed for adoption by the Department of Family and Protective [and Regulatory] Services, the department is not required to edit records to protect the identity of birth parents and other persons whose identity is confidential if the department determines that information is already known to the adoptive parents or is readily available through other sources, including the court records of a suit to terminate the parent-child relationship under Chapter 161.

Added by Acts 2003, 78th Leg., ch. 68, § 1, eff. Sept. 1, 2003. Title amended by Acts 2015, 84th Leg., ch. 944, § 13, eff. Sept. 1, 2015. Amended by Acts 2015, 84th Leg., ch. 1, § 1.093, eff. Apr. 1, 2015.

§ 162.007. Contents of Health, Social, Educational, and Genetic History Report

(a) The health history of the child must include information about:

(1) the child's health status at the time of placement;

(2) the child's birth, neonatal, and other medical, psychological, psychiatric, and dental history information;

(3) a record of immunizations for the child; and

(4) the available results of medical, psychological, psychiatric, and dental examinations of the child.

(b) The social history of the child must include information, to the extent known, about past and existing relationships between the child and the child's siblings, parents by birth, extended family, and other persons who have had physical possession of or legal access to the child.

(c) The educational history of the child must include, to the extent known, information about:

(1) the enrollment and performance of the child in educational institutions;

(2) results of educational testing and standardized tests for the child; and

(3) special educational needs, if any, of the child.

(d) The genetic history of the child must include a description of the child's parents by birth and their parents, any other child born to either of the child's parents, and extended family members and must include, to the extent the information is available, information about:

(1) their health and medical history, including any genetic diseases and disorders;

(2) their health status at the time of placement;

(3) the cause of and their age at death;

(4) their height, weight, and eye and hair color;

(5) their nationality and ethnic background;

(6) their general levels of educational and professional achievements, if any;

(7) their religious backgrounds, if any;

(8) any psychological, psychiatric, or social evaluations, including the date of the evaluation, any diagnosis, and a summary of any findings;

(9) any criminal conviction records relating to a misdemeanor or felony classified as an offense against the person or family or public indecency or a felony violation of a statute intended to control the possession or distribution of a substance included in Chapter 481, Health and Safety Code; and

(10) any information necessary to determine whether the child is entitled to or otherwise eligible for state or federal financial, medical, or other assistance.

(e) [(e)] The report shall include a history of physical, sexual, or emotional abuse suffered by the child, if any.

(f) Notwithstanding the other provisions of this section, the Department of Family and Protective Services may, in accordance with department rule, modify the form and contents of the health, social, educational, and genetic history report for a child as the department determines appropriate based on:

(1) the relationship between the prospective adoptive parents and the child or the child's birth family;

(2) the provision of the child's case record to the prospective adoptive parents; or

(3) any other factor specified by department rule.

Added by Acts 1995, 74th Leg., ch. 20, § 1, eff. April 20, 1995. Subsec. (e) transferred from § 162.005(c) by Acts 2015, 84th Leg., ch. 944, § 12, eff. Sept. 1, 2015. Subsec. (f) added by Acts 2015, 84th Leg., ch. 944, § 14, eff. Sept. 1, 2015.

§ 162.008. Filing of Health, Social, Educational, and Genetic History Report

(a) This section does not apply to an adoption by the child's:

(1) grandparent;

(2) aunt or uncle by birth, marriage, or prior adoption; or

(3) stepparent.

(b) A petition for adoption may not be granted until the following documents have been filed:

(1) a copy of the health, social, educational, and genetic history report signed by the child's adoptive parents; and

(2) if the report is required to be submitted to the Department of Family and Protective Services [bureau of vital statistics] under Section 162.006(e), a certificate from the department [bureau] acknowledging receipt of the report.

(c) A court having jurisdiction of a suit affecting the parent-child relationship may by order waive the making and filing of a report under this section if the child's biological parents cannot be located and their absence results in insufficient information being available to compile the report.

Added by Acts 1995, 74th Leg., ch. 20, § 1, eff. April 20, 1995. Amended by Acts 1999, 76th Leg., ch. 1390, § 20, eff. Sept. 1, 1999. Subsec. (b) amended by Acts 2015, 84th Leg., ch. 1, § 1.094, eff. Apr. 1, 2015.

§ 162.0085. Criminal History Report Required

(a) In a suit affecting the parent-child relationship in which an adoption is sought, the court shall order each person seeking to adopt the child to obtain that person's own criminal history record information. The court shall accept under this section a person's criminal history record information that is provided by the Department of Family and Protective [and Regulatory] Services or by a licensed child-placing agency that received the information from the department if the information was obtained not more than one year before the date the court ordered the history to be obtained.

(b) A person required to obtain information under Subsection (a) shall obtain the information in the manner provided by Section 411.128, Local Government Code.

Added by Acts 1995, 74th Leg., ch. 751, § 75, eff. Sept. 1, 1995; Acts 1995, 74th Leg., ch. 908, § 2, eff. Sept. 1, 1995; Amended by Acts 1997, 75th Leg., ch. 561, § 16, eff. Sept. 1, 1997. Subsec. (a) amended by Acts 2015, 84th Leg., ch. 1, § 1.095, eff. Apr. 1, 2015.

§ 162.009. Residence with Petitioner

(a) The court may not grant an adoption until the child has resided with the petitioner for not less than six months.

(b) On request of the petitioner, the court may waive the residence requirement if the waiver is in the best interest of the child.

Added by Acts 1995, 74th Leg., ch. 20, § 1, eff. April 20, 1995.

§ 162.010. Consent Required

(a) Unless the managing conservator is the petitioner, the written consent of a managing conservator to the adoption must be filed. The court may waive the requirement of consent by the managing conservator if the court finds that the consent is being refused or has been revoked without good cause. A hearing on the issue of consent shall be conducted by the court without a jury.

(b) If a parent of the child is presently the spouse of the petitioner, that parent must join in the petition for adoption and further consent of that parent is not required.

(c) A child 12 years of age or older must consent to the adoption in writing or in court. The court may waive this requirement if it would serve the child's best interest.

Added by Acts 1995, 74th Leg., ch. 20, § 1, eff. April 20, 1995. Amended by Acts 1995, 74th Leg., ch. 751, § 76, eff. Sept. 1, 1995.

§ 162.011. Revocation of Consent

At any time before an order granting the adoption of the child is rendered, a consent required by Section 162.010 may be revoked by filing a signed revocation.

Added by Acts 1995, 74th Leg., ch. 20, § 1, eff. April 20, 1995.

§ 162.012. Direct or Collateral Attack

(a) Notwithstanding Rule 329, Texas Rules of Civil Procedure, the validity of an adoption order is not subject to attack after six months after the date the order was signed.

(b) The validity of a final adoption order is not subject to attack because a health, social, educational, and genetic history was not filed.

Added by Acts 1995, 74th Leg., ch. 20, § 1, eff. April 20, 1995; Amended by Acts 1997, 75th Leg., ch. 601, § 1, eff. Sept. 1, 1997; Acts 1997, 75th Leg., ch. 600, § 2, eff. Jan. 1, 1998.

§ 162.013. Abatement or Dismissal

(a) If the sole petitioner dies or the joint petitioners die, the court shall dismiss the suit for adoption.

(b) If one of the joint petitioners dies, the proceeding shall continue uninterrupted.

(c) If the joint petitioners divorce, the court shall abate the suit for adoption. The court shall dismiss the petition unless the petition is amended to request adoption by one of the original petitioners.

Added by Acts 1995, 74th Leg., ch. 20, § 1, eff. April 20, 1995.

§ 162.014. Attendance at Hearing Required

(a) If the joint petitioners are husband and wife and it would be unduly difficult for one of the petitioners to appear at the hearing, the court may waive the attendance of that petitioner if the other spouse is present.

(b) A child to be adopted who is 12 years of age or older shall attend the hearing. The court may waive this requirement in the best interest of the child.

Added by Acts 1995, 74th Leg., ch. 20, § 1, eff. April 20, 1995.

§ 162.015. Race or Ethnicity

(a) In determining the best interest of the child, the court may not deny or delay the adoption or otherwise discriminate on the basis of race or ethnicity of the child or the prospective adoptive parents.

(b) This section does not apply to a person, entity, tribe, organization, or child custody proceeding subject to the Indian Child Welfare Act of 1978 (25 U.S.C. § 1901 et seq.). In this subsection "child custody proceeding" has the meaning provided by 25 U.S.C. § 1903.

Added by Acts 1995, 74th Leg., ch. 20, § 1, eff. April 20, 1995. Amended by Acts 1995, 74th Leg., ch. 751, § 77, eff. Sept. 1, 1995.

§ 162.016. Adoption Order

(a) If a petition requesting termination has been joined with a petition requesting adoption, the court shall also terminate the parent-child relationship at the same time the adoption order is rendered. The court must make separate findings that the termination is in the best interest of the child and that the adoption is in the best interest of the child.

(b) If the court finds that the requirements for adoption have been met and the adoption is in the best interest of the child, the court shall grant the adoption.

(c) The name of the child may be changed in the order if requested.

Added by Acts 1995, 74th Leg., ch. 20, § 1, eff. April 20, 1995.

Statutes in Context
§ 162.017

An adopted child is, under § 162.017, entitled to inherit from and through the child's adoptive parents as though the child were the biological child of the parents. This is consistent with Probate Code § 40.

---

§ 162.017. Effect of Adoption

(a) An order of adoption creates the parent-child relationship between the adoptive parent and the child for all purposes.

(b) An adopted child is entitled to inherit from and through the child's adoptive parents as though the child were the biological child of the parents.

(c) The terms "child," "descendant," "issue," and other terms indicating the relationship of parent and child include an adopted child unless the context or express language clearly indicates otherwise.

(d) Nothing in this chapter precludes or affects the rights of a biological or adoptive maternal or paternal grandparent to reasonable possession of or access to a grandchild, as provided in Chapter 153.

Added by Acts 1995, 74th Leg., ch. 20, § 1, eff. April 20, 1995. Subsec. (d) amended by Acts 2005, 79th Leg., ch. 916, § 23, eff. June 18, 2005.

§ 162.018. Access to Information

(a) The adoptive parents are entitled to receive copies of the records and other information relating to the history of the child maintained by the department, licensed child-placing agency, person, or entity placing the child for adoption.

(b) The adoptive parents and the adopted child, after the child is an adult, are entitled to receive copies of the records that have been edited to protect the identity of the biological parents and any other person whose identity is confidential and other information relating to the history of the child maintained by the department, licensed child-placing agency, person, or entity placing the child for adoption.

(c) It is the duty of the person or entity placing the child for adoption to edit the records and information to protect the identity of the biological parents and any other person whose identity is confidential.

(d) At the time an adoption order is rendered, the court shall provide to the parents of an adopted child information provided by the bureau of vital statistics

~~that describes the functions of the voluntary adoption registry under Subchapter E.[1] The licensed child-placing agency shall provide to each of the child's biological parents known to the agency, the information when the parent signs an affidavit of relinquishment of parental rights or affidavit of waiver of interest in a child. The information shall include the right of the child or biological parent to refuse to participate in the registry. If the adopted child is 14 years old or older the court shall provide the information to the child.~~

Added by Acts 1995, 74th Leg., ch. 20, § 1, eff. April 20, 1995; Amended by Acts 1997, 75th Leg., ch. 561, § 17, eff. Sept. 1, 1997. Subsec. (d) amended by Acts 2007, 80th Leg., ch. 1283, § 11, eff. Sept. 1, 2007. Portions transferred to § 162.0062 by Acts 2015, 84th Leg., ch. 944, § 15(b), eff. Sept. 1, 2015.

Note that subsections (a) and (d) were also amended by Acts 2015, 84th Leg., ch.1, § 1.095, eff. Apr., 1, 2015 as follows:

(a) The adoptive parents are entitled to receive copies of the records and other information relating to the history of the child maintained by the <u>Department of Family and Protective Services</u> [~~department~~], licensed child-placing agency, person, or entity placing the child for adoption.

(d) At the time an adoption order is rendered, the court shall provide to the parents of an adopted child information provided by the [~~bureau of~~] vital statistics <u>unit</u> that describes the functions of the voluntary adoption registry under Subchapter E. The licensed child-placing agency shall provide to each of the child's biological parents known to the agency, the information when the parent signs an affidavit of relinquishment of parental rights or affidavit of waiver of interest in a child. The information shall include the right of the child or biological parent to refuse to participate in the registry. If the adopted child is 14 years old or older the court shall provide the information to the child.

§ 162.019. Copy of Order

A copy of the adoption order is not required to be mailed to the parties as provided in Rules 119a and 239a, Texas Rules of Civil Procedure.

Added by Acts 1995, 74th Leg., ch. 20, § 1, eff. April 20, 1995.

§ 162.020. Withdrawal or Denial of Petition

If a petition requesting adoption is withdrawn or denied, the court may order the removal of the child from the proposed adoptive home if removal is in the child's best interest and may enter any order necessary for the welfare of the child.

Added by Acts 1995, 74th Leg., ch. 20, § 1, eff. April 20, 1995.

---

[1] Family Code § 162.401 et seq.

§ 162.021. Sealing File

(a) Rendition of the order does not relieve the clerk from the duty to send information regarding adoption to the [~~bureau of~~] vital statistics <u>unit</u> as required by this subchapter and Chapter 108.

(b) Rendition of the order does not relieve the clerk from the duty to send information regarding adoption to the bureau of vital statistics as required by this subchapter and Chapter 108.

Added by Acts 1995, 74th Leg., ch. 20, § 1, eff. April 20, 1995. Amended by Acts 1995, 74th Leg., ch. 751, § 78, eff. Sept. 1, 1995. Subsec. (a) amended by Acts 2015, 84th Leg., ch. 1, § 1.097, eff. Apr. 1, 2015.

§ 162.022. Confidentiality Maintained by Clerk

The records concerning a child maintained by the district clerk after entry of an order of adoption are confidential. No person is entitled to access to the records or may obtain information from the records except for good cause under an order of the court that issued the order.

Added by Acts 1995, 74th Leg., ch. 20, § 1, eff. April 20, 1995.

§ 162.023. Adoption Order From Foreign Country

(a) Except as otherwise provided by law, an adoption order rendered to a resident of this state that is made by a foreign country shall be accorded full faith and credit by the courts of this state and enforced as if the order were rendered by a court in this state unless the adoption law or process of the foreign country violates the fundamental principles of human rights or the laws or public policy of this state.

(b) A person who adopts a child in a foreign country may register the order in this state. A petition for registration of a foreign adoption order may be combined with a petition for a name change. If the court finds that the foreign adoption order meets the requirements of Subsection (a), the court shall order the state registrar to:

(1) register the order under Chapter 192, Health and Safety Code; and

(2) file a certificate of birth for the child under Section 192.006, Health and Safety Code.

Added by Acts 2003, 78th Leg., ch. 19, § 1, eff. Sept. 1, 2003.

§ 162.025. Placement by Unauthorized Person; Offense

(a) A person who is not the natural or adoptive parent of the child, the legal guardian of the child, or a child-placing agency licensed under Chapter 42, Human Resources Code, commits an offense if the person:

(1) serves as an intermediary between a prospective adoptive parent and an expectant parent or parent of a minor child to identify the parties to each other; or

(2) places a child for adoption.

(b) It is not an offense under this section if a professional provides legal or medical services to:

(1) a parent who identifies the prospective adoptive parent and places the child for adoption without the assistance of the professional; or

(2) a prospective adoptive parent who identifies a parent and receives placement of a child for adoption without the assistance of the professional.

(c) An offense under this section is a Class B misdemeanor.

Added by Acts 1995, 74th Leg., ch. 411, § 1, eff. Sept. 1, 1995; Amended by Acts 1997, 75th Leg., ch. 561, § 18, eff. Sept. 1, 1997.

Subchapter F. Adoption of an Adult

Statutes in Context
§§ 162.501–162.507

Adoption of adults is governed by §§ 162.501 - 162.507.

§ 162.501. Adoption of Adult

The court may grant the petition of an adult residing in this state to adopt another adult according to this subchapter.

Added by Acts 1995, 74th Leg., ch. 20, § 1, eff. April 20, 1995.

§ 162.502. Jurisdiction

The petitioner shall file a suit to adopt an adult in the district court or a statutory county court granted jurisdiction in family law cases and proceedings by Chapter 25, Government Code, in the county of the petitioner's residence.

Added by Acts 1995, 74th Leg., ch. 20, § 1, eff. April 20, 1995.

§ 162.503. Requirements of Petition

(a) A petition to adopt an adult shall be entitled "In the Interest of _____, An Adult."

(b) If the petitioner is married, both spouses must join in the petition for adoption.

Added by Acts 1995, 74th Leg., ch. 20, § 1, eff. April 20, 1995.

§ 162.504. Consent

A court may not grant an adoption unless the adult consents in writing to be adopted by the petitioner.

Added by Acts 1995, 74th Leg., ch. 20, § 1, eff. April 20, 1995.

§ 162.505. Attendance Required

The petitioner and the adult to be adopted must attend the hearing. For good cause shown, the court may waive this requirement, by written order, if the petitioner or adult to be adopted is unable to attend.

Added by Acts 1995, 74th Leg., ch. 20, § 1, eff. April 20, 1995.

§ 162.506. Adoption Order

(a) The court shall grant the adoption if the court finds that the requirements for adoption of an adult are met.

(b) Notwithstanding that both spouses have joined in a petition for the adoption of an adult as required by Section 162.503(b), the court may grant the adoption of the adult to both spouses or, on request of the spouses, to only one spouse.

Added by Acts 1995, 74th Leg., ch. 20, § 1, eff. April 20, 1995. Amended by Acts 2003, 78th Leg., ch. 555, § 1, eff. Sept. 1, 2003.

Statutes in Context
§ 162.507

An adopted adult is, under § 162.507, entitled to inherit from and through the child's adoptive parents as though the child were the biological child of the parents. The adopted adult may not inherit from or through the adult's biological parents. A biological parent may not inherit from or through the adopted adult. This is consistent with Estates Code § 201.054(b).

§ 162.507. Effect of Adoption

(a) The adopted adult is the son or daughter of the adoptive parents for all purposes.

(b) The adopted adult is entitled to inherit from and through the adopted adult's adoptive parents as though the adopted adult were the biological child of the adoptive parents.

(c) The adopted adult may not inherit from or through the adult's biological parent. A biological parent may not inherit from or through an adopted adult.

Added by Acts 1995, 74th Leg., ch. 20, § 1, eff. April 20, 1995. Subsec. (c) amended by Acts 2005, 79th Leg., ch. 169, § 1, eff. Sept. 1, 2005

IX.

FINANCE CODE

Title 3. Financial Institutions and Businesses

Subtitle A. Banks

Chapter 32. Powers, Organization, and Financial Requirements

Subchapter A. Organization and Powers in General

Statutes in Context
§ 32.001

Finance Code § 32.001 sets forth the general powers of a state bank which includes the power to serve as a trustee. See Property Code § 112.008 which explains when a person has the capacity to be a trustee.

---

§ 32.001. Organization and General Powers of State Bank

(a) One or more persons, a majority of whom are residents of this state, may organize a state bank as a banking association or a limited banking association.

(b) A state bank may:

(1) receive and pay deposits with or without interest, discount and negotiate promissory notes, borrow or lend money with or without security or interest, invest and deal in securities, buy and sell exchange, coin, and bullion, and exercise incidental powers as necessary to carry on the business of banking as provided by this subtitle;

(2) act as agent, or in a substantially similar capacity, with respect to a financial activity or an activity incidental or complementary to a financial activity;

(3) act in a fiduciary capacity, without giving bond, as guardian, receiver, executor, administrator, or trustee, including a mortgage or indenture trustee;

(4) provide financial, investment, or economic advisory services;

(5) issue or sell instruments representing pools of assets in which a bank may invest directly;

(6) with prior written approval of the banking commissioner, engage in a financial activity or an activity that is incidental or complementary to a financial activity; and

(7) engage in any other activity, directly or through a subsidiary, authorized by this subtitle or rules adopted under this subtitle.

(c) For purposes of other state law, a banking association is considered a corporation and a limited banking association is considered a limited liability company. To the extent consistent with this subtitle, a banking association may exercise the powers of a Texas business corporation and a limited banking association may exercise the powers of a Texas limited liability company as reasonably necessary to enable exercise of specific powers under this subtitle.

(d) A state bank may contribute to a community fund or to another charitable, philanthropic, or benevolent instrumentality conducive to public welfare an amount that the bank's board considers expedient and in the interests of the bank.

(e) A state bank may be organized or reorganized as a community development financial institution or may serve as a community development partner, as those terms are defined by the Riegle Community Development and Regulatory Improvement Act of 1994 (Pub. L. No. 103-325).

(f) In the exercise of discretion consistent with the purposes of this subtitle, the banking commissioner may require a state bank to conduct an otherwise authorized activity through a subsidiary.

Acts 1997, 75th Leg., ch. 1008, § 1, eff. Sept. 1, 1997. Amended by Acts 2001, 77th Leg., ch. 528, § 4, eff. Sept. 1, 2001.

Title 3. Financial Institutions and Businesses

Subtitle A. Banks

Chapter 59. Miscellaneous Provisions

Subchapter A. General Provisions

§ 59.004. Succession of Trust Powers

(a) If, at the time of a merger, reorganization, conversion, sale of substantially all of its assets under Chapter 32 or other applicable law, or sale of substantially all of its trust accounts and related activities at a separate branch or other office, a reorganizing or selling financial institution is acting as trustee, guardian, executor, or administrator, or in another fiduciary capacity, a successor or purchasing financial institution with sufficient fiduciary authority may continue the office, trust, or fiduciary relationship:

(1) without the necessity of judicial action or action by the creator of the office, trust, or fiduciary relationship; and

(2) without regard to whether the successor or purchasing financial institution meets qualification requirements specified in an instrument creating the office, trust, or fiduciary relationship other than a requirement related to geographic locale of account administration, including requirements as to jurisdiction of incorporation, location of principal office, or type of financial institution.

(b) The successor or purchasing financial institution may perform all the duties and exercise all the powers connected with or incidental to the fiduciary relationship in the same manner as if the successor or purchasing financial institution had been originally designated as the fiduciary.

Acts 1997, 75th Leg., ch. 1008, § 1, eff. Sept. 1, 1997. Amended by Acts 1999, 76th Leg., ch. 344, § 2.016, eff. Sept. 1, 1999.

Subchapter B. Safe Deposit Boxes

§ 59.101. Definition

In this subchapter, "safe deposit company" means a person who maintains and rents safe deposit boxes.

Acts 1997, 75th Leg., ch. 1008, § 1, eff. Sept. 1, 1997.

§ 59.102. Authority to Act as Safe Deposit Company

Any person may be a safe deposit company.

Acts 1997, 75th Leg., ch. 1008, § 1, eff. Sept. 1, 1997.

§ 59.103. Relationship of Safe Deposit Company and Renter

In a safe deposit transaction the relationship of the safe deposit company and the renter is that of lessor and lessee and landlord and tenant, and the rights and liabilities of the safe deposit company are governed accordingly in the absence of a contract or statute to the contrary. The lessee is considered for all purposes to be in possession of the box and its contents.

Acts 1997, 75th Leg., ch. 1008, § 1, eff. Sept. 1, 1997.

§ 59.104. Delivery of Notice

A notice required by this subchapter to be given to a lessee of a safe deposit box must be in writing and personally delivered or sent by registered or certified mail, return receipt requested, to each lessee at the most recent address of the person according to the records of the safe deposit company.

Acts 1997, 75th Leg., ch. 1008, § 1, eff. Sept. 1, 1997.

§ 59.105. Effect of Subchapter on Other Law

This subchapter does not affect Chapter 151, Estates [Sections 36B-36F, Texas Probate] Code, or another

statute of this state governing safe deposit boxes.

Acts 1997, 75th Leg., ch. 1008, § 1, eff. Sept. 1, 1997. Amended by Acts 2015, 84th Leg., ch. 1236, § 20.010, eff. Sept. 1, 2015.

Statutes in Context
§ 59.106

Unless the contract provides otherwise, a co-owner of a safe deposit box may have access to the box and remove any or all contents at any time, even after the death of another co-owner.

---

§ 59.106. Access by More than One Person

(a) If a safe deposit box is leased in the name of two or more persons jointly or if a person other than the lessee is designated in the lease agreement as having a right of access to the box, each of those persons is entitled to have access to the box and to remove its contents in the absence of a contract to the contrary. This right of access and removal is not affected by the death or incapacity of another person who is a lessee or otherwise entitled to have access to the box.

(b) A safe deposit company is not responsible for damage arising from access to a safe deposit box or removal of any of its contents by a person with a right of access to the box.

Acts 1997, 75th Leg., ch. 1008, § 1, eff. Sept. 1, 1997.

§ 59.107. Nonemergency Opening and Relocation

(a) A safe deposit company may not relocate a safe deposit box rented for a term of at least six months if the box rental is not delinquent or open a safe deposit box to relocate its contents to another safe deposit box or other location except:

(1) in the presence of the lessee;

(2) with the lessee's written authorization; or

(3) as otherwise provided by this section or Section 59.108.

(b) A safe deposit box may not be relocated under this section unless the storage conditions at the new location are at least as secure as the conditions at the original box location.

(c) Not later than the 30th day before the scheduled date of a nonemergency relocation, the safe deposit company shall give notice of the relocation to each lessee of the safe deposit box. The notice must state the scheduled date and time of the relocation and whether the box will be opened during the relocation.

(d) A lessee may personally supervise the relocation or authorize the relocation in writing if notice is given to each lessee.

(e) If during the relocation the box is opened and a lessee does not personally supervise the relocation or has not authorized the relocation in writing, two employees, at least one of whom is an officer or manager of the safe deposit company and at least one of whom is a notary public, shall inventory the contents of the box in detail. The safe deposit company shall notify each lessee of the new box number or location not later than the 30th day after the date of the relocation and shall include a signed and notarized copy of the inventory report. The cost of a certified mailing other than the first notice sent in connection with each relocation may be treated as box rental due at the expiration of the rental term.

(f) This section does not apply to a relocation of a safe deposit box within the same building.

Acts 1997, 75th Leg., ch. 1008, § 1, eff. Sept. 1, 1997. Amended by Acts 1999, 76th Leg., ch. 62, § 7.30, eff. Sept. 1, 1999.

§ 59.108. Emergency Opening and Relocation

(a) A safe deposit company may relocate a safe deposit box or open the box to relocate its contents to another box or location without complying with > Sections 59.107(a)-(d) if the security of the original box is threatened or destroyed by natural disaster, including tornado, flood, fire, or other unforeseeable circumstances beyond the control of the safe deposit company.

(b) The safe deposit company shall follow the procedure provided by Section 59.107(e), except that the notice of the new box number or location must be given not later than the 90th day after the date of a relocation under this section.

(c) This section does not apply to a relocation of a safe deposit box within the same building.

Acts 1997, 75th Leg., ch. 1008, § 1, eff. Sept. 1, 1997.

§ 59.109. Delinquent Rental; Lien; Sale of Contents

(a) If the rental for a safe deposit box is delinquent for at least six months, the safe deposit company may send notice to each lessee that the company will remove the contents of the box if the rent is not paid before the date specified in the notice, which may not be earlier than the 60th day after the date the notice is delivered or sent. If the rent is not paid before the date specified in the notice, the safe deposit company may open the box in the presence of two employees, at least one of whom is an officer or manager of the safe deposit company and at least one of whom is a notary public. The safe deposit company shall inventory the contents of the box in detail as provided by the comptroller's reporting instructions and place the contents of the box in a sealed envelope or container bearing the name of the lessee.

(b) The safe deposit company has a lien on the contents of the box for an amount equal to the rental owed for the box and the cost of opening the box. The safe deposit company may retain possession of the contents. If the rental and the cost of opening the box are not paid before the second anniversary of the date the box was opened, the safe deposit company may sell all or part of the contents at public auction in the manner and with the notice prescribed by Section 51.002, Property Code, for the sale of real property under a deed of trust. Any unsold contents of the box and any excess proceeds from a sale of contents shall be remitted to the comptroller as provided by Chapters 72-75, Property Code.

Acts 1997, 75th Leg., ch. 1008, § 1, eff. Sept. 1, 1997.

§ 59.110. Routing Number on Key

(a) A depository institution that rents or permits access to a safe deposit box shall imprint the depository institution's routing number on each key to the box or on a tag attached to the key.

(b) If a depository institution believes that the routing number imprinted on a key, or on a tag attached to a key, used to open a safe deposit box has been altered or defaced so that the correct routing number is illegible, the depository institution shall notify the Department of Public Safety of the State of Texas, on a form designed by the banking commissioner, not later than the 10th day after the date the key is used to open the box.

(c) This section does not require a depository institution to inspect the routing number imprinted on a key or an attached tag to determine whether the number has been altered or defaced. A depository institution that has imprinted a key to a safe deposit box or a tag attached to the key as provided by this section and that follows applicable law and the depository institution's established security procedures in permitting access to the box is not liable for any damage arising because of access to or removal of the contents of the box.

(d) Subsection (a) does not apply to a key issued under a lease in effect on September 1, 1992, until the date the term of that lease expires, without regard to any extension of the lease term.

Acts 1997, 75th Leg., ch. 1008, § 1, eff. Sept. 1, 1997.

Subtitle F. Trust Companies

Chapter 182. Powers, Organization, and Financial Requirements

Subchapter A. Organization and Powers in General

Statutes in Context
§ 182.001

Finance Code § 182.001 sets forth the general powers of a properly organized trust company in Texas. See Property Code § 112.008 which explains when a person has the capacity to be a trustee.

---

§ 182.001. Organization and General Powers of State Trust Company

(a) Subject to Subsection (g) and the other provisions of this chapter, one or more persons may organize and charter a state trust company as a state trust association or a limited trust association.

(b) A state trust company may engage in the trust business by:

(1) acting as trustee under a written agreement;

(2) receiving money and other property in its capacity as trustee for investment in real or personal property;

(3) acting as trustee and performing the fiduciary duties committed or transferred to it by order of a court;

(4) acting as executor, administrator, or trustee of the estate of a deceased person;

(5) acting as a custodian, guardian, conservator, or trustee for a minor or incapacitated person;

(6) acting as a successor fiduciary to a trust institution or other fiduciary;

(7) receiving for safekeeping personal property;

(8) acting as custodian, assignee, transfer agent, escrow agent, registrar, or receiver;

(9) acting as investment advisor, agent, or attorney in fact according to an applicable agreement;

(10) with the prior written approval of the banking commissioner and to the extent consistent with applicable fiduciary principles, engaging in a financial activity or an activity incidental or complementary to a financial activity, directly or through a subsidiary;

(11) exercising additional powers expressly conferred by rule of the finance commission; and

(12) exercising any incidental power that is reasonably necessary to enable it to fully exercise the powers expressly conferred according to commonly accepted fiduciary customs and usages.

(c) For purposes of other state law, a trust association is considered a corporation and a limited trust association is considered a limited liability company. To the extent consistent with this subtitle, a trust association may exercise the powers of a Texas business corporation and a limited trust association may exercise the powers of a Texas limited liability company as reasonably necessary to enable exercise of specific powers under this subtitle.

(d) A state trust company may contribute to a community fund or to a charitable, philanthropic, or benevolent instrumentality conducive to public welfare an amount that the state trust company's board considers appropriate and in the interests of the state trust company.

(e) Subject to Section 184.301, a state trust company may deposit trust funds with itself.

(f) A state trust company insured by the Federal Deposit Insurance Corporation may receive and pay deposits, with or without interest, made by the United States, the state, a county, or a municipality.

(g) In the exercise of discretion consistent with the purposes of this subtitle, the banking commissioner may require a state trust company to conduct an otherwise authorized activity through a subsidiary.

Added by Acts 1999, 76th Leg., ch. 62, § 7.16(a), eff.

Sept. 1, 1999. Amended by Acts 2001, 77th Leg., ch. 528, § 20, eff. Sept. 1, 2001; Acts 2001, 77th Leg., ch. 1420, § 6.008(a), eff. Sept. 1, 2001.

Subtitle Z.   Miscellaneous Provisions Relating to Financial Institutions and Businesses

Chapter 274.   Substitute or Successor Fiduciary

Statutes in Context
§§ 274.001–203

Finance Code §§ 274.001-203 are often referred to as the "Substitute Fiduciary Act." This Act permits, under certain circumstances, one corporate fiduciary, such as a trustee or executor, to be substituted for another without obtaining court permission. The courts have held this Act to be constitutional. See *In re Estate of Touring*, 775 S.W.2d 39 (Tex. App.—Houston [14th Dist.] 1989, no writ).

The attorney who prepares a will or trust which names a corporate fiduciary should explain the potential operation of this Act to the client. If the client objects, the attorney should include a provision prohibiting a substitution as permitted by § 274.201.

Generally, the appointment of successor fiduciaries is governed by Property Code § 113.083 (trustees), Probate Code § 154A (independent executors), and Probate Code § 223 (dependent personal representatives).

Subchapter A.   General Provisions

§ 274.001.   Definitions

In this chapter:

(1) "Bank" has the meaning assigned by Section 31.002(a)(2), excluding a bank that does not have its main office or a branch located in this state.

(2) "Bank holding company" has the meaning assigned by Section 2(a), Bank Holding Company Act of 1956 (12 U.S.C. § 1841 (a)), as amended.

(3) "Commissioner" means the banking commissioner of Texas.

(4) "Fiduciary" means an entity responsible for managing a fiduciary account.

(5) "Fiduciary account" means an account with a situs of administration in this state involving the exercise of a corporate purpose specified by Section 182.001(b).

Acts 1997, 75th Leg., ch. 1008, § 1, eff. Sept. 1, 1997. Amended by Acts 1999, 76th Leg., ch. 62, § 7.51, eff. Sept. 1, 1999; Acts 1999, 76th Leg., ch. 344, § 2.030, eff.

Sept. 1, 1999. Subsec. (1) amended by Acts 2007, 80th Leg., ch. 237, § 78, eff. Sept. 1, 2007.

§ 274.002. Affiliated Bank

A bank is affiliated with a subsidiary trust company if more than 50 percent of the bank's voting stock is directly or indirectly owned by a bank holding company that owns more than 50 percent of the voting stock of the subsidiary trust company.

Acts 1997, 75th Leg., ch. 1008, § 1, eff. Sept. 1, 1997. Amended by Acts 1999, 76th Leg., ch. 344, § 2.030, eff. Sept. 1, 1999.

§ 274.003. Subsidiary Trust Company

An entity is a subsidiary trust company of a bank holding company if:

(1) the entity is a:

(A) trust company organized under Subchapter A, Chapter 182; or

(B) bank that is organized to conduct a trust business and any incidental business or to exercise trust powers; and

(2) more than 50 percent of the voting stock of the entity is directly or indirectly owned by the bank holding company.

Acts 1997, 75th Leg., ch. 1008, § 1, eff. Sept. 1, 1997. Amended by Acts 1999, 76th Leg., ch. 62, § 7.52, eff. Sept. 1, 1999; Acts 1999, 76th Leg., ch. 344, § 2.030, eff. Sept. 1, 1999. Subsec. (1)(A) amended by Acts 2007, 80th Leg., ch. 237, § 78, eff. Sept. 1, 2007.

Subchapter B. Subsidiary Trust Companies as Substitute or Successor Fiduciaries

§ 274.101. Agreement to Substitute Fiduciaries

(a) A subsidiary trust company may enter into an agreement with an affiliated bank of the company to substitute the company as fiduciary for the bank in each fiduciary account listed in the agreement, provided the situs of account administration is not moved outside of this state without the express written consent of all persons entitled to notice under Sections 274.103(a) and (c).

(b) The agreement must include:

(1) a list of each fiduciary account for which substitution is requested;

(2) a statement of whether the substitution will cause a change in the situs of administration of each fiduciary account; and

(3) the effective date of the substitution, which may not be before the 91st day after the date of the agreement.

(c) The agreement must be filed with the commissioner before the date the substitution takes effect.

(d) A fiduciary account may be removed from the operation of the agreement by the filing of an amendment to the agreement with the commissioner before the effective date stated in the agreement.

Acts 1997, 75th Leg., ch. 1008, § 1, eff. Sept. 1, 1997. Amended by Acts 1999, 76th Leg., ch. 344, § 2.031, eff. Sept. 1, 1999.

§ 274.102. Situs of Account Administration

The situs of administration of a fiduciary account is the county in this state in which the fiduciary maintains the office that is primarily responsible for dealing with the parties involved in the account.

Acts 1997, 75th Leg., ch. 1008, § 1, eff. Sept. 1, 1997. Amended by Acts 1999, 76th Leg., ch. 344, § 2.032, eff. Sept. 1, 1999.

§ 274.103. Notice of Substitution

(a) Not later than the 91st day before the effective date of a substitution under Section 274.101, the parties to the substitution agreement shall send notice of the substitution to:

(1) any other fiduciary;

(2) each surviving settler of a trust relating to the fiduciary account;

(3) each issuer of a security for which the affiliated bank administers the fiduciary account;

(4) the plan sponsor of each employee benefit plan relating to the fiduciary account;

(5) the principal of each agency account; and

(6) the guardian of the person of each ward that has the fiduciary account resulting from a guardianship.

(b) If the substitution does not cause a change in the situs of administration of a fiduciary account, the parties to the substitution agreement shall also send notice of the substitution to each person who is readily ascertainable as a beneficiary of the account because the person has received account statements or because a parent, conservator, or guardian of a minor beneficiary has received account statements on the minor's behalf.

(c) If the substitution causes a change in the situs of administration of a fiduciary account, the parties to the substitution agreement shall also send notice of the substitution to:

(1) each adult beneficiary of a trust relating to the account;

(2) each parent, conservator, or guardian of a minor beneficiary receiving or entitled to receive current distributions of income or principal from the account; and

(3) each person who individually or jointly has the power to remove the fiduciary being substituted.

(d) The notice must be sent by United States mail to the person's current address as shown on the fiduciary's records. The fiduciary shall make a reasonable attempt to ascertain the address of a person who does not have an address shown on the fiduciary's records.

Acts 1997, 75th Leg., ch. 1008, § 1, eff. Sept. 1, 1997.

§ 274.104. Form of Notice of Substitution

The notice required under Section 274.103 must be in writing and disclose:

(1) the effect the substitution of fiduciary will have on the situs of administration of the fiduciary account;

(2) the person's rights with respect to objecting to the substitution; and

(3) the liability of the existing fiduciary and the substitute fiduciary for their actions.

Acts 1997, 75th Leg., ch. 1008, § 1, eff. Sept. 1, 1997.

§ 274.105. Failure to Send Notice of Substitution; Defective Notice

(a) If the parties to a substitution agreement under Section 274.101 intentionally fail to send the required notice under Section 274.103, the substitution of the fiduciary is ineffective.

(b) If the parties unintentionally fail to send the required notice, the substitution of the fiduciary is not impaired.

(c) If a substitution of a fiduciary is ineffective because of a defect in the required notice, any action taken by a subsidiary trust company before the substitution is determined to be ineffective is valid if the action would have been valid if performed by the affiliated bank.

Acts 1997, 75th Leg., ch. 1008, § 1, eff. Sept. 1, 1997.

§ 274.106. Effective Date of Substitution of Fiduciaries

(a) The substitution takes effect on the effective date stated in the substitution agreement unless, not later than the 16th day before the effective date:

(1) each party entitled to receive notice of the substitution under Sections 274.103 (a) and (c) provides the affiliated bank with a written objection to the substitution; or

(2) a party entitled to receive notice of the substitution under Section 274.103 files a written petition in a court seeking to have the substitution denied under Section 274.107 and provides the affiliated bank with a copy of the petition.

(b) A substitution that is objected to under Subsection (a)(1) takes effect when:

(1) one of the parties objecting to the substitution removes the party's objection in writing; or

(2) the bank obtains a final court order approving the substitution.

(c) A substitution that is objected to under Subsection (a)(2) takes effect when:

(1) the petition is withdrawn or dismissed; or

(2) the court enters a final order denying the relief sought.

Acts 1997, 75th Leg., ch. 1008, § 1, eff. Sept. 1, 1997.

§ 274.107. Hearing on Agreement to Substitute Fiduciaries

(a) A court may deny the substitution if the court, after notice and hearing, determines:

(1) if the substitution will not cause a change in the situs of administration of a fiduciary account, that the substitution is materially detrimental to the account or to its beneficiaries; or

(2) if the substitution will cause a change in the situs of administration of a fiduciary account, that the substitution is not in the best interests of the account or its beneficiaries.

(b) The court shall allow a substitution that will cause the situs of administration of a fiduciary account to change if the court, after notice and hearing, determines that the substitution is in the best interests of the account and its beneficiaries.

(c) In a proceeding under this section, the court may award costs and reasonable and necessary attorney's fees as the court considers equitable and just.

Acts 1997, 75th Leg., ch. 1008, § 1, eff. Sept. 1, 1997.

§ 274.108. Subsidiary Trust Company as Substitute Fiduciary

On the effective date of the substitution as prescribed by Section 274.106, the subsidiary trust company:

(1) without the necessity of an instrument of transfer or conveyance, succeeds to all interest in property the affiliated bank holds for the fiduciary account being substituted; and

(2) without the necessity of judicial action or action by the creator of the fiduciary account, becomes fiduciary of the account and shall perform the duties and exercise the powers of a fiduciary in the same manner as if the company had originally been designated fiduciary.

Acts 1997, 75th Leg., ch. 1008, § 1, eff. Sept. 1, 1997.

§ 274.109. Notice of Change in Situs of Administration of Fiduciary Account Following Substitution

(a) If the fiduciary of a fiduciary account has changed as a result of a substitution agreement under Section 274.101, the substitute fiduciary shall send notice of a change in the situs of administration of the account after the substitution to each person entitled to notice under Sections 274.103 (a) and (c) not later than the 91st day before the effective date of the change.

(b) The notice must be sent by United States mail to the person's current address as shown on the fiduciary's records. The fiduciary shall make a reasonable attempt to ascertain the address of a person who does not have an address shown on the fiduciary's records.

(c) The notice must disclose:

(1) the effect that the change will have on the situs of administration of the account;

(2) the effective date of the change; and

(3) the person's rights with respect to objecting to the change.

Acts 1997, 75ᵗʰ Leg., ch. 1008, § 1, eff. Sept. 1, 1997.

§ 274.110. Failure to Send Notice of Change in Situs of Administration

(a) If the substitute fiduciary of a fiduciary account intentionally fails to send the required notice under Section 274.109, the change in the situs of administration is ineffective.

(b) If the substitute fiduciary unintentionally fails to send the required notice, the change in the situs of administration is not impaired.

Acts 1997, 75ᵗʰ Leg., ch. 1008, § 1, eff. Sept. 1, 1997.

§ 274.111. Effective Date of Change in Situs of Administration of Fiduciary Account

(a) A change in the situs of administration takes effect on the effective date stated in the notice under Section 274.109 unless, not later than the 16ᵗʰ day before the effective date:

(1) each party entitled to receive notice for the fiduciary account provides the subsidiary trust company with a written objection to the change; or

(2) a party entitled to receive notice files a written petition in a court seeking to have the change denied under Section 274.112 and provides the subsidiary trust company with a copy of the petition.

(b) A change that is objected to under Subsection (a)(1) takes effect when:

(1) one of the parties objecting to the change removes the party's objection in writing; or

(2) the subsidiary trust company obtains a final court order approving the change.

(c) A change that is objected to under Subsection (a)(2) takes effect when:

(1) the petition is withdrawn or dismissed; or

(2) the court enters a final order denying the relief sought.

Acts 1997, 75ᵗʰ Leg., ch. 1008, § 1, eff. Sept. 1, 1997.

§ 274.112. Hearing on Change in Situs of Administration of Fiduciary Account

(a) A court may allow the change in the situs of administration if the court, after notice and hearing, determines that the change is in the best interests of the fiduciary account and its beneficiaries. The court may deny the change if the court, after notice and hearing, determines that the change is not in the best interests of the account or its beneficiaries.

(b) In a proceeding under this section, the court may award costs and reasonable and necessary attorney's fees as the court considers equitable and just.

Acts 1997, 75ᵗʰ Leg., ch. 1008, § 1, eff. Sept. 1, 1997.

§ 274.113. Venue

(a) An action under this subchapter for a fiduciary account resulting from a decedent's estate or guardianship must be brought in the county provided for by the Estates [Texas Probate] Code with respect to the probate of a will, issuance of letters testamentary or of administration, administration of a decedent's estate, appointment of a guardian, and administration of a guardianship.

(b) Except as provided by Subsection (c), an action under this subchapter regarding any other fiduciary account must be brought in the county of the situs of administration of the account, notwithstanding a statute that would set venue in the location of the fiduciary's principal office.

(c) A beneficiary of a fiduciary account described by Subsection (b) may elect to bring the action in the county in which the principal office of the first affiliated bank that transferred the account under this subchapter is located.

Acts 1997, 75ᵗʰ Leg., ch. 1008, § 1, eff. Sept. 1, 1997. Subsec. (a) amended by Acts 2015, 84ᵗʰ Leg., ch. 1236, § 20.019, eff. Sept. 1, 2015.

§ 274.114. Subsidiary Trust Company as Successor Fiduciary

For purposes of qualifying as successor fiduciary under a document creating a fiduciary account or a statute of this state relating to fiduciary accounts, a subsidiary trust company:

(1) is considered to have capital and surplus in an amount equal to the total of its capital and surplus and the capital and surplus of the bank holding company that owns the company; and

(2) is treated as a national bank unless it:

(A) is not a national bank under federal law; and

(B) has not entered into a substitution agreement with an affiliated bank of the company that is a national bank under federal law.

Acts 1997, 75ᵗʰ Leg., ch. 1008, § 1, eff. Sept. 1, 1997.

§ 274.115. Bond of Successor Fiduciary

If an affiliated bank of a subsidiary trust company has given bond to secure performance of its duties and the company qualifies as successor fiduciary, the company shall give bond to secure performance of its duties in the same manner as the bank.

Acts 1997, 75ᵗʰ Leg., ch. 1008, § 1, eff. Sept. 1, 1997.

§ 274.116. Responsibility for Subsidiary Trust Company

The bank holding company that owns a subsidiary trust company shall file with the commissioner an irrevocable undertaking to be fully responsible for the fiduciary acts and omissions of the subsidiary trust company.

Acts 1997, 75ᵗʰ Leg., ch. 1008, § 1, eff. Sept. 1, 1997.

Subchapter C. Banks Affiliated with Subsidiary Trust Companies

§ 274.201. Designation of Affiliated Bank as Fiduciary in Will

The prospective designation in a will or other instrument of an affiliated bank of a subsidiary trust company as fiduciary is also considered a designation of the company as fiduciary and confers on the company any discretionary power granted in the instrument unless:

    (1) the bank and company agree in writing to have the designation of the bank as fiduciary be binding; or

    (2) the creator of the fiduciary account, by appropriate language in the document creating the account, provides that the account is not eligible for substitution under this chapter.

Acts 1997, 75th Leg., ch. 1008, § 1, eff. Sept. 1, 1997.

§ 274.202. Liability of Affiliated Bank Acting as Fiduciary

After a substitution of a subsidiary trust company as fiduciary for an affiliated bank of the company, the bank remains liable for any action taken by the bank as a fiduciary.

Acts 1997, 75th Leg., ch. 1008, § 1, eff. Sept. 1, 1997.

§ 274.203. Deposit of Money with Affiliated Bank

(a) A subsidiary trust company may deposit with an affiliated bank of the company fiduciary money that is being held pending an investment, distribution, or payment of a debt if:

    (1) the company maintains under its control as security for the deposit a separate fund of securities legal for trust investments pledged by the bank;

    (2) the total market value of the securities is at all times at least equal to the amount of the deposit; and

    (3) the fund of securities is designated as a separate fund.

(b) The bank may make periodic withdrawals from or additions to the fund of securities required by this section only if the required value is maintained.

(c) Income from securities in the fund belongs to the bank.

(d) Security for a deposit under this section is not required to the extent the deposit is insured or otherwise secured under law.

Acts 1997, 75th Leg., ch. 1008, § 1, eff. Sept. 1, 1997.

Title 4. Regulation of Interest, Loans, and Financed Transactions

Subtitle A. Interest

Chapter 302. Interest Rates

Subchapter A. General Provisions

Statutes in Context
§ 302.002

A legacy (cash bequest) in a will earns interest at the legal rate as provided in Finance Code § 302.002. The Uniform Principal and Income Act provides that interest is payable beginning on the first anniversary of the date of the decedent's death. See Property Code § 116.051(3)(A).

§ 302.002. Accrual of Interest when No Rate Specified

If a creditor has not agreed with an obligor to charge the obligor any interest, the creditor may charge and receive from the obligor legal interest at the rate of six percent a year on the principal amount of the credit extended beginning on the 30th day after the date on which the amount is due. If an obligor has agreed to pay to a creditor any compensation that constitutes interest, the obligor is considered to have agreed on the rate produced by the amount of that interest, regardless of whether that rate is stated in the agreement.

Acts 1997, 75th Leg., ch. 1008, § 1, eff. Sept. 1, 1997. Amended by Acts 1999, 76th Leg., ch. 62, § 7.18(a), eff. Sept. 1, 1999.

X.

GOVERNMENT CODE

Title 2.   Judicial Branch

Subtitle G.   Attorneys

Appendix A.   State Bar Rules

Article X.   Discipline and Suspension of Members

Section 9.   Texas Disciplinary Rules of Professional Conduct

I.   Client-Lawyer Relationship

Statutes in Context
Rule 1.02

Rule 1.02(g) is of particular importance in the estate planning context because it provides guidance on what the attorney should do if the attorney reasonably believes that a client lacks legal competence to make decisions.

Rule 1.02.   Scope and Objectives of Representation

(a) Subject to paragraphs (b), (c), (d), and (e), (f), and (g), a lawyer shall abide by a client's decisions:

(1) concerning the objectives and general methods of representation;

(2) whether to accept an offer of settlement of a matter, except as otherwise authorized by law;

(3) In a criminal case, after consultation with the lawyer, as to a plea to be entered, whether to waive jury trial, and whether the client will testify.

(b) A lawyer may limit the scope, objectives and general methods of the representation if the client consents after consultation.

(c) A lawyer shall not assist or counsel a client to engage in conduct that the lawyer knows is criminal or fraudulent. A lawyer may discuss the legal consequences of any proposed course of conduct with a client and may counsel and represent a client in connection with the making of a good faith effort to determine the validity, scope, meaning or application of the law.

(d) When a lawyer has confidential information clearly establishing that a client is likely to commit a criminal or fraudulent act that is likely to result in substantial injury to the financial interests or property of another, the lawyer shall promptly make reasonable efforts under the circumstances to dissuade the client from committing the crime or fraud.

(e) When a lawyer has confidential information clearly establishing that the lawyer's client has committed a criminal or fraudulent act in the commission of which the lawyer's services have been used, the lawyer shall make reasonable efforts under the circumstances to persuade the client to take corrective action.

(f) When a lawyer knows that a client expects representation not permitted by the rules of professional conduct or other law, the lawyer shall consult with the client regarding the relevant limitations on the lawyer's conduct.

(g) A lawyer shall take reasonable action to secure the appointment of a guardian or other legal representative for, or seek other protective orders with respect to, a client whenever the lawyer reasonably believes that the client lacks legal competence and that such action should be taken to protect the client.

Adopted by order of Oct. 17, 1989, eff. Jan. 1, 1990.

Statutes in Context
Rule 1.03

Rule 1.03 imposes a duty on the attorney to keep the client reasonably informed so the client may make informed decisions.

Rule 1.03.   Communication

(a) A lawyer shall keep a client reasonably informed about the status of a matter and promptly comply with reasonable requests for information.

(b) A lawyer shall explain a matter to the extent reasonably necessary to permit the client to make informed decisions regarding the representation.

Adopted by order of Oct. 17, 1989, eff. Jan. 1, 1990.

Statutes in Context
Rule 1.05

Rule 1.05 focuses on the attorney's duty to keep client information confidential. Problems may arise if the attorney prepares the estate plans for more than one person from the same family such as husband and wife or parent and child.

Rule 1.05.   Confidentiality of Information

(a) "Confidential information" includes both "privileged information" and "unprivileged client information." "Privileged information" refers to the information of a client protected by the lawyer-client privilege of Rule 503 of the Texas Rules of Evidence or of Rule 503 of the Texas Rules of Criminal Evidence or by the principles of attorney-client privilege governed by Rule 501 of the Federal Rules of Evidence for United States Courts and Magistrates. "Unprivileged client information" means all information relating to a client or furnished by the client, other than privileged information, acquired by the lawyer during the course of or by reason of the representation of the client.

(b) Except as permitted by paragraphs (c) and (d), or as required by paragraphs (e) and (f), a lawyer shall not knowingly:

(1) Reveal confidential information of a client or a former client to:

(i) a person that the client has instructed is not to receive the information; or

(ii) anyone else, other than the client, the client's representatives, or the members, associates, or employees of the lawyer's law firm.

(2) Use confidential information of a client to the disadvantage of the client unless the client consents after consultation.

(3) Use confidential information of a former client to the disadvantage of the former client after the representation is concluded unless the former client consents after consultation or the confidential information has become generally known.

(4) Use privileged information of a client for the advantage of the lawyer or of a third person, unless the client consents after consultation.

(c) A lawyer may reveal confidential information:

(1) When the lawyer has been expressly authorized to do so in order to carry out the representation.

(2) When the client consents after consultation.

(3) To the client, the client's representatives, or the members, associates, and employees of the lawyer's firm, except when otherwise instructed by the client.

(4) When the lawyer has reason to believe it is necessary to do so in order to comply with a court order, a Texas Disciplinary Rules of Professional Conduct, or other law.

(5) To the extent reasonably necessary to enforce a claim or establish a defense on behalf of the lawyer in a controversy between the lawyer and the client.

(6) To establish a defense to a criminal charge, civil claim or disciplinary complaint against the lawyer or the lawyer's associates based upon conduct involving the client or the representation of the client.

(7) When the lawyer has reason to believe it is necessary to do so in order to prevent the client from committing a criminal or fraudulent act.

(8) To the extent revelation reasonably appears necessary to rectify the consequences of a client's criminal or fraudulent act in the commission of which the lawyer's services had been used.

(d) A lawyer also may reveal unprivileged client information:

(1) When impliedly authorized to do so in order to carry out the representation.

(2) When the lawyer has reason to believe it is necessary to do so in order to:

(i) carry out the representation effectively;

(ii) defend the lawyer or the lawyer's employees or associates against a claim of wrongful conduct;

(iii) respond to allegations in any proceeding concerning the lawyer's representation of the client; or

(iv) prove the services rendered to a client, or the reasonable value thereof, or both, in an action against another person or organization responsible for the payment of the fee for services rendered to the client.

(e) When a lawyer has confidential information clearly establishing that a client is likely to commit a criminal or fraudulent act that is likely to result in death or substantial bodily harm to a person, the lawyer shall reveal confidential information to the extent revelation reasonably appears necessary to prevent the client from committing the criminal or fraudulent act.

(f) A lawyer shall reveal confidential information when required to do so by Rule 3.03(a)(2), 3.03(b), or by Rule 4.01(b).

Adopted by order of Oct. 17, 1989, eff. Jan. 1, 1990. Amended by order of Oct. 23, 1991.

Statutes in Context
Rule 1.08

Rule 1.08(b) prohibits an attorney from preparing a will not only if the attorney is a beneficiary, but also if the beneficiary is the attorney's parent, child, sibling, or spouse. There are two exceptions to the general admonition. The first exception is when the client is related to the donee. Although permitted, the prudent attorney should avoid drafting for relatives unless the disposition in the will is substantially similar to that which would occur under intestacy. The second exception is if the gift is not substantial. An attorney should not rely on this exception because although the attorney might not be risking loss of the attorney's law license for drafting the instrument, the attorney may still not receive the gift because of Probate Code § 58b. In addition, the determination of whether a gift is "substantial" is problematic. For example, a gift worth $50 might be substantial for a client whose net worth is $1,000 while a gift of $1 million might not be substantial for a client with a net worth of many billions of dollars.

Rule 1.08. Conflict of Interest: Prohibited Transactions

(a) A lawyer shall not enter into a business transaction with a client unless:

(1) the transaction and terms on which the lawyer acquires the interest are fair and reasonable to the client and are fully disclosed in a manner which can be reasonably understood by the client;

(2) the client is given a reasonable opportunity to seek the advice of independent counsel in the transaction; and

(3) the client consents in writing thereto.

(b) A lawyer shall not prepare an instrument giving the lawyer or a person related to the lawyer as a parent, child, sibling, or spouse any substantial gift from a client, including a testamentary gift, except where the client is related to the donee.

(c) Prior to the conclusion of all aspects of the matter giving rise to the lawyer's employment, a lawyer shall not make or negotiate an agreement with a client, prospective client, or former client giving the lawyer literary or media rights to a portrayal or account based in substantial part on information relating to the representation.

(d) A lawyer shall not provide financial assistance to a client in connection with pending or contemplated litigation or administrative proceedings, except that:

(1) a lawyer may advance or guarantee court costs, expenses of litigation or administrative proceedings, and reasonably necessary medical and living expenses, the repayment of which may be contingent on the outcome of the matter; and

(2) a lawyer representing an indigent client may pay court costs and expenses of litigation on behalf of the client.

(e) A lawyer shall not accept compensation for representing a client from one other than the client unless:

(1) the client consents;

(2) there is no interference with the lawyer's independence of professional judgment or with the client-lawyer relationship; and

(3) information relating to representation of a client is protected as required by Rule 1.05.

(f) A lawyer who represents two or more clients shall not participate in making an aggregate settlement of the claims of or against the clients, or in a criminal case an aggregated agreement to guilty or nolo contendere pleas, unless each client has consented after consultation, including disclosure of the existence and nature of all the claims or pleas involved and of the nature and extent of the participation of each person in the settlement.

(g) A lawyer shall not make an agreement prospectively limiting the lawyer's liability to a client for malpractice unless permitted by law and the client is independently represented in making the agreement, or settle a claim for such liability with an unrepresented client or former client without first advising that person in writing that independent representation is appropriate in connection therewith.

(h) A lawyer shall not acquire a proprietary interest in the cause of action or subject matter of litigation the lawyer is conducting for a client, except that the lawyer may:

(1) acquire a lien granted by law to secure the lawyer's fee or expenses; and

(2) contract in a civil case with a client for a contingent fee that is permissible under Rule 1.04.

(i) If a lawyer would be prohibited by this Rule from engaging in particular conduct, no other lawyer while a member of or associated with that lawyer's firm may engage in that conduct.

(j) As used in this Rule, "business transactions" does not include standard commercial transactions between the lawyer and the client for products or services that the client generally markets to others.

Adopted by order of Oct. 17, 1989, eff. Jan. 1, 1990. Amended by order of Oct. 23, 1991.

Title 2. Judicial Branch

Subtitle A. Courts

Chapter 22. Appellate Courts

Subchapter A. Supreme Court

Statutes in Context
§ 22.020

The 2015 Legislature charged the Supreme Court of Texas with the task of promulgating a wide range of self-help forms in English and Spanish, along with plain language instructions, for wills for six common scenarios (e.g., single with no children and married with an adult child), an application for probating a will as a muniment of title, and a small estate affidavit. Each form must state that it is not a substitute for attorney advice. The clerks of the probate courts will have the duty to tell the general public about the forms and the court must accept these forms unless it is completed so poorly that it causes a substantial defect that cannot be fixed. Note that the Spanish versions are for convenience only and cannot be submitted to the probate court.

---

§ 22.020 Promulgation of Certain Probate Forms

(a) In this section:

(1) "Probate court" has the meaning assigned by Section 22.007, Estates Code.

(2) "Probate matter" has the meaning assigned by Section 22.029, Estates Code.

(b) The supreme court shall, as the court considers appropriate, promulgate:

(1) forms for use by individuals representing themselves in certain probate matters, including forms for use in:

(A) a small estate affidavit proceeding under Chapter 205, Estates Code; and

(B) the probate of a will as a muniment of title under Chapter 257, Estates Code;

(2) a simple will form for:

(A) a married individual with an adult child;

(B) a married individual with a minor child;

(C) a married individual with no children;

(D) an unmarried individual with an adult child;

(E) an unmarried individual with a minor child; and

(F) an unmarried individual with no children; and

(3) instructions for the proper use of each form or set of forms.

(c) The forms and instructions:

(1) must be written in plain language that is easy to understand by the general public;

(2) shall be made readily available to the general public in the manner prescribed by the supreme court; and

(3) must be translated into the Spanish language as provided by Subsection (d).

(d) The Spanish language translation of a form must:

(1) state:

(A) that the Spanish language translated form is to be used solely for the purpose of assisting in understanding the form and may not be submitted to the probate court; and

(B) that the English language version of the form must be submitted to the probate court; or

(2) be incorporated into the English language version of the form in a manner that is understandable to both the probate court and members of the general public.

(e) Each form and its instructions must clearly and conspicuously state that the form is not a substitute for the advice of an attorney.

(f) The clerk of a probate court shall inform members of the general public of the availability of a form promulgated by the supreme court under this section as appropriate and make the form available free of charge.

(g) A probate court shall accept a form promulgated by the supreme court under this section unless the form has been completed in a manner that causes a substantive defect that cannot be cured.

Added by Acts 2015, 84th Leg., ch. 602, § 1, eff. Sept. 1, 2015.

Subtitle G. Attorneys

Chapter 81. State Bar

Subchapter G. Unauthorized Practice of Law

§ 81.101. Definition

(a) In this chapter the "practice of law" means the preparation of a pleading or other document incident to an action or special proceeding or the management of the action or proceeding on behalf of a client before a judge in court as well as a service rendered out of court, including the giving of advice or the rendering of any service requiring the use of legal skill or knowledge, such as preparing a will, contract, or other instrument, the legal effect of which under the facts and conclusions involved must be carefully determined.

(b) The definition in this section is not exclusive and does not deprive the judicial branch of the power and authority under both this chapter and the adjudicated cases to determine whether other services and acts not enumerated may constitute the practice of law.

(c) In this chapter, the "practice of law" does not include the design, creation, publication, distribution, display, or sale, including publication, distribution, display, or sale by means of an Internet web site, of written materials, books, forms, computer software, or similar products if the products clearly and conspicuously state that the products are not a substitute for the advice of an attorney. This subsection does not authorize the use of the products or similar media in violation of Chapter 83 and does not affect the applicability or enforceability of that chapter.

Added by Acts 1987, 70th Leg., ch. 148, § 3.01, eff. Sept. 1, 1987. Amended by Acts 1999, 76th Leg., ch. 799, § 1, eff. June 18, 1999.

Title 3. Legislative Branch

Subtitle B. Legislation

Chapter 311. Code Construction Act

Statutes in Context
Chapter 311

The Code Construction Act applies to every Texas code enacted by the 60th or subsequent legislature as well as to any amendment, repeal, revision, or reenactment of any code provision passed by the 60th or later legislature. (A similar set of statutes applies to all other Texas statutes (Government Code §§ 312.001-312.016)). The Act contains important definitions and construction rules which must be kept in mind when reading provisions of the Texas codes. Of particular importance in the estate planning context is § 311.005(6) which provides a definition of "signed."

Subchapter A. General Provisions

§ 311.001. Short Title

This chapter may be cited as the Code Construction Act.

Acts 1985, 69ᵗʰ Leg., ch. 479, § 1, eff. Sept. 1, 1985.

§ 311.002. Application

This chapter applies to:

(1) each code enacted by the 60ᵗʰ or a subsequent legislature as part of the state's continuing statutory revision program;

(2) each amendment, repeal, revision, and reenactment of a code or code provision by the 60ᵗʰ or a subsequent legislature;

(3) each repeal of a statute by a code; and

(4) each rule adopted under a code.

Acts 1985, 69ᵗʰ Leg., ch. 479, § 1, eff. Sept. 1, 1985.

§ 311.003. Rules Not Exclusive

The rules provided in this chapter are not exclusive but are meant to describe and clarify common situations in order to guide the preparation and construction of codes.

Acts 1985, 69ᵗʰ Leg., ch. 479, § 1, eff. Sept. 1, 1985.

§ 311.004. Citation of Codes

A code may be cited by its name preceded by the specific part concerned. Examples of citations are:

(1) Title 1, Business & Commerce Code;

(2) Chapter 5, Business & Commerce Code;

(3) Section 9.304, Business & Commerce Code;

(4) Section 15.06(a), Business & Commerce Code; and

(5) Section 17.18(b)(1)(B)(ii), Business & Commerce Code.

Acts 1985, 69ᵗʰ Leg., ch. 479, § 1, eff. Sept. 1, 1985. Amended by Acts 1985, 69ᵗʰ Leg., ch. 117, § 13(b), eff. Sept. 1, 1985.

§ 311.005. General Definitions

The following definitions apply unless the statute or context in which the word or phrase is used requires a different definition:

(1) "Oath" includes affirmation.

(2) "Person" includes corporation, organization, government or governmental subdivision or agency, business trust, estate, trust, partnership, association, and any other legal entity.

(3) "Population" means the population shown by the most recent federal decennial census.

(4) "Property" means real and personal property.

(5) "Rule" includes regulation.

(6) "Signed" includes any symbol executed or adopted by a person with present intention to authenticate a writing.

(7) "State," when referring to a part of the United States, includes any state, district, commonwealth, territory, and insular possession of the United States and any area subject to the legislative authority of the United States of America.

(8) "Swear" includes affirm.

(9) "United States" includes a department, bureau, or other agency of the United States of America.

(10) "Week" means seven consecutive days.

(11) "Written" includes any representation of words, letters, symbols, or figures.

(12) "Year" means 12 consecutive months.

(13) "Includes" and "including" are terms of enlargement and not of limitation or exclusive enumeration, and use of the terms does not create a presumption that components not expressed are excluded.

Acts 1985, 69ᵗʰ Leg., ch. 479, § 1, eff. Sept. 1, 1985. Amended by Acts 1989, 71ˢᵗ Leg., ch. 340, § 1, eff. Aug. 28, 1989.

§ 311.006. Internal References

In a code:

(1) a reference to a title, chapter, or section without further identification is a reference to a title, chapter, or section of the code; and

(2) a reference to a subtitle, subchapter, subsection, subdivision, paragraph, or other numbered or lettered unit without further identification is a reference to a unit of the next larger unit of the code in which the reference appears.

Added by Acts 1993, 73ʳᵈ Leg., ch. 131, § 1, eff. May 11, 1993.

Subchapter B. Construction of Words and Phrases

§ 311.011. Common and Technical Usage of Words

(a) Words and phrases shall be read in context and construed according to the rules of grammar and common usage.

(b) Words and phrases that have acquired a technical or particular meaning, whether by legislative definition or otherwise, shall be construed accordingly.

Acts 1985, 69ᵗʰ Leg., ch. 479, § 1, eff. Sept. 1, 1985.

§ 311.012. Tense, Number, and Gender

(a) Words in the present tense include the future tense.

(b) The singular includes the plural and the plural includes the singular.

(c) Words of one gender include the other genders.

Acts 1985, 69ᵗʰ Leg., ch. 479, § 1, eff. Sept. 1, 1985.

§ 311.013. Authority and Quorum of Public Body

(a) A grant of authority to three or more persons as a public body confers the authority on a majority of the number of members fixed by statute.

(b) A quorum of a public body is a majority of the number of members fixed by statute.

Acts 1985, 69th Leg., ch. 479, § 1, eff. Sept. 1, 1985.

§ 311.014. Computation of Time

(a) In computing a period of days, the first day is excluded and the last day is included.

(b) If the last day of any period is a Saturday, Sunday, or legal holiday, the period is extended to include the next day that is not a Saturday, Sunday, or legal holiday.

(c) If a number of months is to be computed by counting the months from a particular day, the period ends on the same numerical day in the concluding month as the day of the month from which the computation is begun, unless there are not that many days in the concluding month, in which case the period ends on the last day of that month.

Acts 1985, 69th Leg., ch. 479, § 1, eff. Sept. 1, 1985.

§ 311.015. Reference to a Series

If a statute refers to a series of numbers or letters, the first and last numbers or letters are included.

Acts 1985, 69th Leg., ch. 479, § 1, eff. Sept. 1, 1985.

§ 311.016. "May," "Shall," "Must," Etc.

The following constructions apply unless the context in which the word or phrase appears necessarily requires a different construction or unless a different construction is expressly provided by statute:

(1) "May" creates discretionary authority or grants permission or a power.

(2) "Shall" imposes a duty.

(3) "Must" creates or recognizes a condition precedent.

(4) "Is entitled to" creates or recognizes a right.

(5) "May not" imposes a prohibition and is synonymous with "shall not."

(6) "Is not entitled to" negates a right.

(7) "Is not required to" negates a duty or condition precedent.

Added by Acts 1997, 75th Leg., ch. 220, § 1, eff. May 23, 1997.

Subchapter C. Construction of Statutes

§ 311.021. Intention in Enactment of Statutes

In enacting a statute, it is presumed that:

(1) compliance with the constitutions of this state and the United States is intended;

(2) the entire statute is intended to be effective;

(3) a just and reasonable result is intended;

(4) a result feasible of execution is intended; and

(5) public interest is favored over any private interest.

Acts 1985, 69th Leg., ch. 479, § 1. eff. Sept. 1, 1985.

§ 311.022. Prospective Operation of Statutes

A statute is presumed to be prospective in its operation unless expressly made retrospective.

Acts 1985, 69th Leg., ch. 479, § 1, eff. Sept. 1, 1985.

§ 311.023. Statute Construction Aids

In construing a statute, whether or not the statute is considered ambiguous on its face, a court may consider among other matters the:

(1) object sought to be attained;

(2) circumstances under which the statute was enacted;

(3) legislative history;

(4) common law or former statutory provisions, including laws on the same or similar subjects;

(5) consequences of a particular construction;

(6) administrative construction of the statute; and

(7) title (caption), preamble, and emergency provision.

Acts 1985, 69th Leg., ch. 479, § 1. eff. Sept. 1, 1985.

§ 311.024. Headings

The heading of a title, subtitle, chapter, subchapter, or section does not limit or expand the meaning of a statute.

Acts 1985, 69th Leg., ch. 479, § 1. eff. Sept. 1, 1985.

§ 311.025. Irreconcilable Statutes and Amendments

(a) Except as provided by Section 311.031(d), if statutes enacted at the same or different sessions of the legislature are irreconcilable, the statute latest in date of enactment prevails.

(b) Except as provided by Section 311.031(d), if amendments to the same statute are enacted at the same session of the legislature, one amendment without reference to another, the amendments shall be harmonized, if possible, so that effect may be given to each. If the amendments are irreconcilable, the latest in date of enactment prevails.

(c) In determining whether amendments are irreconcilable, text that is reenacted because of the requirement of Article III, Section 36, of the Texas Constitution is not considered to be irreconcilable with additions or omissions in the same text made by another amendment. Unless clearly indicated to the contrary, an amendment that reenacts text in compliance with that constitutional requirement does not indicate legislative intent that the reenacted text prevail over changes in the same text made by another amendment, regardless of the relative dates of enactment.

(d) In this section, the date of enactment is the date on which the last legislative vote is taken on the bill enacting the statute.

(e) If the journals or other legislative records fail to disclose which of two or more bills in conflict is latest in date of enactment, the date of enactment of the respective bills is considered to be, in order of priority:

(1) the date on which the last presiding officer signed the bill;

(2) the date on which the governor signed the bill; or

(3) the date on which the bill became law by operation of law.

Acts 1985, 69ᵗʰ Leg., ch. 479, § 1, eff. Sept. 1, 1985. Amended by Acts 1989, 71ˢᵗ Leg., ch. 340, § 2, eff. Aug. 28, 1989; Acts 1997, 75ᵗʰ Leg., ch. 220, § 2, eff. May 23, 1997.

§ 311.026. Special or Local Provision Prevails Over General

(a) If a general provision conflicts with a special or local provision, the provisions shall be construed, if possible, so that effect is given to both.

(b) If the conflict between the general provision and the special or local provision is irreconcilable, the special or local provision prevails as an exception to the general provision, unless the general provision is the later enactment and the manifest intent is that the general provision prevail.

Acts 1985, 69ᵗʰ Leg., ch. 479, § 1, eff. Sept. 1, 1985.

§ 311.027. Statutory References

Unless expressly provided otherwise, a reference to any portion of a statute or rule applies to all reenactments, revisions, or amendments of the statute or rule.

Acts 1985, 69ᵗʰ Leg., ch. 479, § 1, eff. Sept. 1, 1985. Amended by Acts 1993, 73ʳᵈ Leg., ch. 131, § 2, eff. May 11, 1993.

§ 311.028. Uniform Construction of Uniform Acts

A uniform act included in a code shall be construed to effect its general purpose to make uniform the law of those states that enact it.

Acts 1985, 69ᵗʰ Leg., ch. 479, § 1, eff. Sept. 1, 1985.

§ 311.029. Enrolled Bill Controls

If the language of the enrolled bill version of a statute conflicts with the language of any subsequent printing or reprinting of the statute, the language of the enrolled bill version controls.

Acts 1985, 69ᵗʰ Leg., ch. 479, § 1, eff. Sept. 1, 1985.

§ 311.030. Repeal of Repealing Statute

The repeal of a repealing statute does not revive the statute originally repealed nor impair the effect of any saving provision in it.

Acts 1985, 69ᵗʰ Leg., ch. 479, § 1, eff. Sept. 1, 1985.

§ 311.031. Saving Provisions

(a) Except as provided by Subsection (b), the reenactment, revision, amendment, or repeal of a statute does not affect:

(1) the prior operation of the statute or any prior action taken under it;

(2) any validation, cure, right, privilege, obligation, or liability previously acquired, accrued, accorded, or incurred under it;

(3) any violation of the statute or any penalty, forfeiture, or punishment incurred under the statute before its amendment or repeal; or

(4) any investigation, proceeding, or remedy concerning any privilege, obligation, liability, penalty, forfeiture, or punishment; and the investigation, proceeding, or remedy may be instituted, continued, or enforced, and the penalty, forfeiture, or punishment imposed, as if the statute had not been repealed or amended.

(b) If the penalty, forfeiture, or punishment for any offense is reduced by a reenactment, revision, or amendment of a statute, the penalty, forfeiture, or punishment, if not already imposed, shall be imposed according to the statute as amended.

(c) The repeal of a statute by a code does not affect an amendment, revision, or reenactment of the statute by the same legislature that enacted the code. The amendment, revision, or reenactment is preserved and given effect as part of the code provision that revised the statute so amended, revised, or reenacted.

(d) If any provision of a code conflicts with a statute enacted by the same legislature that enacted the code, the statute controls.

Acts 1985, 69ᵗʰ Leg., ch. 479, § 1, eff. Sept. 1, 1985.

§ 311.032. Severability of Statutes

(a) If any statute contains a provision for severability, that provision prevails in interpreting that statute.

(b) If any statute contains a provision for non-severability, that provision prevails in interpreting that statute.

(c) In a statute that does not contain a provision for severability or nonseverability, if any provision of the statute or its application to any person or circumstance is held invalid, the invalidity does not affect other provisions or applications of the statute that can be given effect without the invalid provision or application, and to this end the provisions of the statute are severable.

Acts 1985, 69ᵗʰ Leg., ch. 479, § 1, eff. Sept. 1, 1985.

§ 311.034. Waiver of Sovereign Immunity

In order to preserve the legislature's interest in managing state fiscal matters through the appropriations process, a statute shall not be construed as a waiver of sovereign immunity unless the waiver is effected by clear and unambiguous language. In a statute, the use of "person," as defined by Section 311.005 to include governmental entities, does not indicate legislative intent to waive sovereign immunity unless the context of the statute indicates no other reasonable construction. Statutory prerequisites to a suit, including the provision of notice, are jurisdictional requirements in all suits against a governmental entity.

Added by Acts 2001, 77th Leg., ch. 1158, § 8, eff. June 15, 2001. Amended by Acts 2005, 79th Leg., ch. 1150, § 1, eff. Sept. 1, 2005.

§ 311.035. Construction of Statute or Rule Involving Criminal Offense or Penalty

(a) In this section, "actor" and "element of offense" have the meanings assigned by Section 1.07, Penal Code.

(b) Except as provided by Subsection (c), a statute or rule that creates or defines a criminal offense or penalty shall be construed in favor of the actor if any part of the statute or rule is ambiguous on its face or as applied to the case, including:

(1) an element of offense; or

(2) the penalty to be imposed.

(c) Subsection (b) does not apply to a criminal offense or penalty under the Penal Code or under the Texas Controlled Substances Act.

(d) The ambiguity of a part of a statute or rule to which this section applies is a matter of law to be resolved by the judge.

Added by Acts 2015, 84th Leg., ch. 1251, § 4, eff. Sept. 1, 2015.

Chapter 312. Construction of Laws

Statutes in Context
§§ 312.001–312.016

Sections §§ 312.001-312.016 contain definitions and construction rules applicable to all Texas civil statutes which are very similar to those contained in the Code Construction Act (Government Code §§ 311.001-311.034).

Subchapter A. Construction Rules for Civil Statutes

§ 312.001. Application

This subchapter applies to the construction of all civil statutes.

Acts 1985, 69th Leg., ch. 479, § 1, eff. Sept. 1, 1985.

§ 312.002. Meaning of Words

(a) Except as provided by Subsection (b), words shall be given their ordinary meaning.

(b) If a word is connected with and used with reference to a particular trade or subject matter or is used as a word of art, the word shall have the meaning given by experts in the particular trade, subject matter, or art.

Acts 1985, 69th Leg., ch. 479, § 1, eff. Sept. 1, 1985.

§ 312.003. Tense, Number, and Gender

(a) Words in the present or past tense include the future tense.

(b) The singular includes the plural and the plural includes the singular unless expressly provided otherwise.

(c) The masculine gender includes the feminine and neuter genders.

Acts 1985, 69th Leg., ch. 479, § 1, eff. Sept. 1, 1985.

§ 312.004. Grants of Authority

A joint authority given to any number of officers or other persons may be executed by a majority of them unless expressly provided otherwise.

Acts 1985, 69th Leg., ch. 479, § 1, eff. Sept. 1, 1985.

§ 312.005. Legislative Intent

In interpreting a statute, a court shall diligently attempt to ascertain legislative intent and shall consider at all times the old law, the evil, and the remedy.

Acts 1985, 69th Leg., ch. 479, § 1, eff. Sept. 1, 1985.

§ 312.006. Liberal Construction

(a) The Revised Statutes are the law of this state and shall be liberally construed to achieve their purpose and to promote justice.

(b) The common law rule requiring strict construction of statutes in derogation of the common law does not apply to the Revised Statutes.

Acts 1985, 69th Leg., ch. 479, § 1, eff. Sept. 1, 1985.

§ 312.007. Repeal of Repealing Statute

The repeal of a repealing statute does not revive the statute originally repealed.

Acts 1985, 69th Leg., ch. 479, § 1, eff. Sept. 1, 1985.

§ 312.008. Statutory References

Unless expressly provided otherwise, a reference to any portion of a statute, rule, or regulation applies to all reenactments, revisions, or amendments of the statute, rule, or regulation.

Added by Acts 1993, 73rd Leg., ch. 131, § 3, eff. May 11, 1993.

Subchapter B. Miscellaneous Provisions

§ 312.011. Definitions

The following definitions apply unless a different meaning is apparent from the context of the statute in which the word appears:

(1) "Affidavit" means a statement in writing of a fact or facts signed by the party making it, sworn to before an officer authorized to administer oaths,

and officially certified to by the officer under his seal of office.

(2) "Comptroller" means the state comptroller of public accounts.

(3) "Effects" includes all personal property and all interest in that property.

(4) "Governing body," if used with reference to a municipality, means the legislative body of a city, town, or village, without regard to the name or title given to any particular body.

(5) "Justice," when applied to a magistrate, means justice of the peace.

(6) "Land commissioner" means the Commissioner of the General Land Office.

(7) "Month" means a calendar month.

(8) "Oath" includes affirmation.

(9) "Official oath" means the oath required by Article XVI, Section 1, of the Texas Constitution.

(10) "Person" includes a corporation.

(11) "Preceding," when referring to a title, chapter, or article, means that which came immediately before.

(12) "Preceding federal census" or "most recent federal census" means the United States decennial census immediately preceding the action in question.

(13) "Property" includes real property, personal property, life insurance policies, and the effects of life insurance policies.

(14) "Signature" includes the mark of a person unable to write, and "subscribe" includes the making of such a mark.

(15) "Succeeding" means immediately following.

(16) "Swear" or "sworn" includes affirm or affirmed.

(17) "Written" or "in writing" includes any representation of words, letters, or figures, whether by writing, printing, or other means.

(18) "Year" means a calendar year.

(19) "Includes" and "including" are terms of enlargement and not of limitation or exclusive enumeration, and use of the terms does not create a presumption that components not expressed are excluded.

(20) "Population" means the population shown by the most recent federal decennial census.

Acts 1985, 69th Leg., ch. 479, § 1, eff. Sept. 1, 1985. Amended by Acts 1989, 71st Leg., ch. 340, § 3, eff. Aug. 28, 1989; Acts 1993, 73rd Leg., ch. 131, § 4, eff. May 11, 1993.

§ 312.012. Grammar and Punctuation

(a) A grammatical error does not vitiate a law. If the sentence or clause is meaningless because of the grammatical error, words and clauses may be transposed to give the law meaning.

(b) Punctuation of a law does not control or affect legislative intent in enacting the law.

Acts 1985, 69th Leg., ch. 479, § 1, eff. Sept. 1, 1985.

§ 312.013. Severability of Statutes

(a) Unless expressly provided otherwise, if any provision of a statute or its application to any person or circumstance is held invalid, the invalidity does not affect other provisions or applications of the statute that can be given effect without the invalid provision or application, and to this end the provisions of the statute are severable.

(b) This section does not affect the power or duty of a court to ascertain and give effect to legislative intent concerning severability of a statute.

Acts 1985, 69th Leg., ch. 479, § 1, eff. Sept. 1, 1985.

§ 312.014. Irreconcilable Amendments

(a) If statutes enacted at the same or different sessions of the legislature are irreconcilable, the statute latest in date of enactment prevails.

(b) If amendments to the same statute are enacted at the same session of the legislature, one amendment without reference to another, the amendments shall be harmonized, if possible, so that effect may be given to each. If the amendments are irreconcilable, the latest in date of enactment prevails.

(c) In determining whether amendments to the same statute enacted at the same session of the legislature are irreconcilable, text that is reenacted because of the requirement of Article III, Section 36, of the Texas Constitution is not considered to be irreconcilable with additions or omissions in the same text made by another amendment. Unless clearly indicated to the contrary, an amendment that reenacts text in compliance with that constitutional requirement does not indicate legislative intent that the reenacted text prevail over changes in the same text made by another amendment, regardless of the relative dates of enactment.

(d) In this section, the date of enactment is the date on which the last legislative vote is taken on the bill enacting the statute.

(e) If the journals or other legislative records fail to disclose which of two or more bills in conflict is latest in date of enactment, the date of enactment of the respective bills is considered to be, in order of priority:

(1) the date on which the last presiding officer signed the bill;

(2) the date on which the governor signed the bill; or

(3) the date on which the bill became law by operation of law.

Added by Acts 1989, 71st Leg., ch. 340, § 4, eff. Aug. 28, 1989. Amended by Acts 1997, 75th Leg., ch. 220, § 3, eff. May 23, 1997.

§ 312.015. Quorum

A majority of a board or commission established under law is a quorum unless otherwise specifically provided.

Added by Acts 1993, 73rd Leg., ch. 268, § 11, eff. Sept.

1, 1993.

§ 312.016. Standard Time

(a) The standard time in this state is the time at the 90th meridian longitude west from Greenwich, commonly known as "central standard time."

(b) The standard time in a region of this state that used mountain standard time before June 12, 1947, is the time at the 105th meridian longitude west from Greenwich, commonly known as "mountain standard time."

(c) Unless otherwise expressly provided, a reference in a statute, order, or rule to the time in which an act shall be performed means the appropriate standard time as provided by this section.

Added by Acts 1993, 73rd Leg., ch. 268, § 12, eff. Sept. 1, 1993.

Title 4.   Executive Branch

Subtitle A.   Executive Officers

Chapter 406.   Notary Public; Commissioner of Deeds

Subchapter A.   Notary Public

Statutes in Context
§ 406.0165

Government Code § 406.0165 provides a method for an individual who is physically unable to sign or make a mark to execute a document. This method is in addition to the proxy signatures methods already in existence such as Probate Code § 59(a) which permits a person to sign a will for the testator "by his direction and in his presence."

---

§ 406.0165.   Signing Document for Individual with Disability

(a) A notary may sign the name of an individual who is physically unable to sign or make a mark on a document presented for notarization if directed to do so by that individual, in the presence of a witness who has no legal or equitable interest in any real or personal property that is the subject of, or is affected by, the document being signed. The notary shall require identification of the witness in the same manner as from an acknowledging person under Section 121.005, Civil Practice and Remedies Code.

(b) A notary who signs a document under this section shall write, beneath the signature, the following or a substantially similar sentence:

"Signature affixed by notary in the presence of (name of witness), a disinterested witness, under Section 406.0165, Government Code."

(c) A signature made under this section is effective as the signature of the individual on whose behalf the signature was made for any purpose. A subsequent bona fide purchaser for value may rely on the signature of the notary as evidence of the individual's consent to execution of the document.

(d) In this section, "disability" means a physical impairment that impedes the ability to sign or make a mark on a document.

Added by Acts 1997, 75th Leg., ch. 1218, § 1, eff. Sept. 1, 1997.

Subtitle G.   Corrections

Chapter 501.   Inmate Welfare

Subchapter A.   General Welfare Provisions

Statutes in Context
§ 501.017

Government Code § 501.017 provides details of the claim which the Texas Department of Criminal Justice has against the estate of an inmate who dies while incarcerated. The claim falls in Class 6 under Probate Code § 322.

---

§ 501.017.   Cost of Confinement as Claim

(a) The department may establish a claim and lien against the estate of an inmate who dies while confined in a facility operated by or under contract with the department for the cost to the department of the inmate's confinement.

(b) The department may not enforce a claim or lien established under this section if the inmate has a surviving spouse or a surviving dependent or disabled child.

(c) The department shall adopt policies regarding recovery of the cost of confinement through enforcement of claims or liens established under this section.

Added by Acts 1989, 71st Leg., ch. 212, § 2.01, eff. Sept. 1, 1989. Renumbered from § 500.017 and amended by Acts 1991, 72nd Leg., ch. 16, § 10.01(a), eff. Aug. 26, 1991. Amended by Acts 1995, 74th Leg., ch. 321, § 1.084, eff. Sept. 1, 1995.

Title 5.   Open Government; Ethics

Subtitle B.   Ethics

Chapter 573.   Degrees of Relationship; Nepotism Prohibitions

Subchapter B. Relationships by Consanguinity or by Affinity

Statutes in Context
§§ 573.021–573.025

Although Government Code §§ 573.021 - 573.025 are directly applicable only to the nepotism prohibitions on the conduct of various governmental officials and candidates, they are, by analogy, useful to see how a relationship may be determined in a probate context.

---

§ 573.021. Method of Computing Degree of Relationship

The degree of a relationship is computed by the civil law method.

Added by Acts 1993, 73rd Leg., ch. 268, § 1, eff. Sept. 1, 1993.

§ 573.022. Determination of Consanguinity

(a) Two individuals are related to each other by consanguinity if:

(1) one is a descendant of the other; or

(2) they share a common ancestor.

(b) An adopted child is considered to be a child of the adoptive parent for this purpose.

Added by Acts 1993, 73rd Leg., ch. 268, § 1, eff. Sept. 1, 1993.

§ 573.023. Computation of Degree of Consanguinity

(a) The degree of relationship by consanguinity between an individual and the individual's descendant is determined by the number of generations that separate them. A parent and child are related in the first degree, a grandparent and grandchild in the second degree, a great-grandparent and great-grandchild in the third degree and so on.

(b) If an individual and the individual's relative are related by consanguinity, but neither is descended from the other, the degree of relationship is determined by adding:

(1) the number of generations between the individual and the nearest common ancestor of the individual and the individual's relative; and

(2) the number of generations between the relative and the nearest common ancestor.

(c) An individual's relatives within the third degree by consanguinity are the individual's:

(1) parent or child (relatives in the first degree);

(2) brother, sister, grandparent, or grandchild (relatives in the second degree); and

(3) great-grandparent, great-grandchild, aunt who is a sister of a parent of the individual, uncle who is a brother of a parent of the individual, nephew who is a child of a brother or sister of the individual, or niece who is a child of a brother or sister of the individual (relatives in the third degree).

Added by Acts 1993, 73rd Leg., ch. 268, § 1, eff. Sept. 1, 1993.

§ 573.024. Determination of Affinity

(a) Two individuals are related to each other by affinity if:

(1) they are married to each other; or

(2) the spouse of one of the individuals is related by consanguinity to the other individual.

(b) The ending of a marriage by divorce or the death of a spouse ends relationships by affinity created by that marriage unless a child of that marriage is living, in which case the marriage is considered to continue as long as a child of that marriage lives.

(c) Subsection (b) applies to a member of the board of trustees of or an officer of a school district only until the youngest child of the marriage reaches the age of 21 years.

Added by Acts 1993, 73rd Leg., ch. 268, § 1, eff. Sept. 1, 1993. Amended by Acts 1995, 74th Leg., ch. 260, § 32, eff. May 30, 1995.

§ 573.025. Computation of Degree of Affinity

(a) A husband and wife are related to each other in the first degree by affinity. For other relationships by affinity, the degree of relationship is the same as the degree of the underlying relationship by consanguinity. For example: if two individuals are related to each other in the second degree by consanguinity, the spouse of one of the individuals is related to the other individual in the second degree by affinity.

(b) An individual's relatives within the third degree by affinity are:

(1) anyone related by consanguinity to the individual's spouse in one of the ways named in Section 573.023(c); and

(2) the spouse of anyone related to the individual by consanguinity in one of the ways named in Section 573.023(c).

Added by Acts 1993, 73rd Leg., ch. 268, § 1, eff. Sept. 1, 1993.

XI.
HEALTH AND SAFETY CODE

Title 2. *Health*

Subtitle H. *Public Health Provisions*

Chapter 166. *Advance Directives*

Statutes in Context
§§ 166.001–166.009

The Advance Directives Act authorizes three types of instruments to assist a person to plan for disability and death: (1) the directive to physicians, (2) the out-of-hospital do-not-resuscitate order, and (3) the medical power of attorney. This Act was passed in 1999 and served to recodify and coordinate the separate statutes which had previously governed these instruments.

Sections 166.001 - 166.009 govern all three types of instruments. Subsequent sections address each of the three instruments in detail.

Subchapter A. *General Provisions*

§ 166.001. Short Title

This chapter may be cited as the Advance Directives Act.

Added by Acts 1999, 76th Leg., ch. 450, § 1.02, eff. Sept. 1, 1999.

Statutes in Context
§ 166.002

Section 166.002 provides important definitions which are applicable to all of Chapter 166. Be certain to compare and contrast the definitions of "irreversible condition" and "terminal condition."

§ 166.002. Definitions

In this chapter:

(1) "Advance directive" means:

(A) a directive, as that term is defined by Section 166.031;

(B) an out-of-hospital DNR order, as that term is defined by Section 166.081; or

(C) a medical power of attorney under Subchapter D.

(2) "Artificially administered [Artificial] nutrition and hydration" means the provision of nutrients or fluids by a tube inserted in a vein, under the skin in the subcutaneous tissues, or in the [stomach (]gastrointestinal tract[)].

(3) "Attending physician" means a physician selected by or assigned to a patient who has primary responsibility for a patient's treatment and care.

(4) "Competent" means possessing the ability, based on reasonable medical judgment, to understand and appreciate the nature and consequences of a treatment decision, including the significant benefits and harms of and reasonable alternatives to a proposed treatment decision.

(5) "Declarant" means a person who has executed or issued a directive under this chapter.

(5-a) "Digital signature" means an electronic identifier intended by the person using it to have the same force and effect as the use of a manual signature.

(5-b) "Electronic signature" means a facsimile, scan, uploaded image, computer-generated image, or other electronic representation of a manual signature that is intended by the person using it to have the same force and effect of law as a manual signature.

(6) "Ethics or medical committee" means a committee established under Sections 161.031-161.033.

(7) "Health care or treatment decision" means consent, refusal to consent, or withdrawal of consent to health care, treatment, service, or a procedure to maintain, diagnose, or treat an individual's physical or mental condition, including such a decision on behalf of a minor.

(8) "Incompetent" means lacking the ability, based on reasonable medical judgment, to understand and appreciate the nature and consequences of a treatment decision, including the significant benefits and harms of and reasonable alternatives to a proposed treatment decision.

(9) "Irreversible condition" means a condition, injury, or illness:

(A) that may be treated but is never cured or eliminated;

(B) that leaves a person unable to care for or make decisions for the person's own self; and

(C) that, without life-sustaining treatment provided in accordance with the prevailing standard of medical care, is fatal.

(10) "Life-sustaining treatment" means treatment that, based on reasonable medical judgment, sustains the life of a patient and without which the patient will die. The term includes both life-sustaining medications and artificial life

support, such as mechanical breathing machines, kidney dialysis treatment, and artificially administered [artificial] nutrition and hydration. The term does not include the administration of pain management medication or the performance of a medical procedure considered to be necessary to provide comfort care, or any other medical care provided to alleviate a patient's pain.

(11) "Medical power of attorney" means a document delegating to an agent authority to make health care decisions executed or issued under Subchapter D.

(12) "Physician" means:

(A) a physician licensed by the Texas Medical [State] Board [of Medical Examiners]; or

(B) a properly credentialed physician who holds a commission in the uniformed services of the United States and who is serving on active duty in this state.

(13) "Terminal condition" means an incurable condition caused by injury, disease, or illness that according to reasonable medical judgment will produce death within six months, even with available life-sustaining treatment provided in accordance with the prevailing standard of medical care. A patient who has been admitted to a program under which the person receives hospice services provided by a home and community support services agency licensed under Chapter 142 is presumed to have a terminal condition for purposes of this chapter.

(14) "Witness" means a person who may serve as a witness under Section 166.003.

(15) "Cardiopulmonary resuscitation" means any medical intervention used to restore circulatory or respiratory function that has ceased.

Added by Acts 1999, 76th Leg., ch. 450, § 1.02, eff. Sept. 1, 1999. Amended by Acts 2003, 78th Leg., ch. 1228, § 1, eff. June 20, 2003. Subdivs. (5-a), (5-b) added by Acts 2009, 81st Leg., ch. 461, § 1, eff. Sept. 1, 2009. Subsecs. (2) and (10) amended by Acts 2015, 84th Leg., ch. 435, § 1, eff. Sept. 1, 2015. Subsec. (12) amended by Acts 2015, 84th Leg., ch. 1, § 3.0499, eff. Sept. 1, 2015.

Statutes in Context
§ 166.003

The proper method of witnessing advance directives is explained in § 166.003. Note that at least one of the witnesses must be a disinterested party to the declarant and the declarant's medical treatment.

---

§ 166.003. Witnesses

In any circumstance in which this chapter requires the execution of an advance directive or the issuance of a nonwritten advance directive to be witnessed:

(1) each witness must be a competent adult; and

(2) at least one of the witnesses must be a person who is not:

(A) a person designated by the declarant to make a health care or treatment decision;

(B) a person related to the declarant by blood or marriage;

(C) a person entitled to any part of the declarant's estate after the declarant's death under a will or codicil executed by the declarant or by operation of law;

(D) the attending physician;

(E) an employee of the attending physician;

(F) an employee of a health care facility in which the declarant is a patient if the employee is providing direct patient care to the declarant or is an officer, director, partner, or business office employee of the health care facility or of any parent organization of the health care facility; or

(G) a person who, at the time the written advance directive is executed or, if the directive is a nonwritten directive issued under this chapter, at the time the nonwritten directive is issued, has a claim against any part of the declarant's estate after the declarant's death.

Added by Acts 1999, 76th Leg., ch. 450, § 1.02, eff. Sept. 1, 1999. Subsec. (2)(A) amended by Acts 2015, 84th Leg., ch. 435, §2, eff. Sept. 1, 2015.

§ 166.004. Statement Relating to Advance Directive

(a) In this section, "health care provider" means:

(1) a hospital;

(2) an institution licensed under Chapter 242, including a skilled nursing facility;

(3) a home and community support services agency;

(4) an assisted living [a personal care] facility; and

(5) a special care facility.

(b) A health care provider shall maintain written policies regarding the implementation of advance directives. The policies must include a clear and precise statement of any procedure the health care provider is unwilling or unable to provide or withhold in accordance with an advance directive.

(c) Except as provided by Subsection (g), the health care provider shall provide written notice to an individual of the written policies described by Subsection (b). The notice must be provided at the earlier of:

(1) the time the individual is admitted to receive services from the health care provider; or

(2) the time the health care provider begins providing care to the individual.

(d) If, at the time notice is to be provided under Subsection (c), the individual is incompetent or otherwise incapacitated and unable to receive the notice required by this section, the provider shall provide the required written notice, in the following order of preference, to:

    (1) the individual's legal guardian;

    (2) a person responsible for the health care decisions of the individual;

    (3) the individual's spouse;

    (4) the individual's adult child;

    (5) the individual's parent; or

    (6) the person admitting the individual.

(e) If Subsection (d) applies and except as provided by Subsection (f), if a health care provider is unable, after diligent search, to locate an individual listed by Subsection (d), the health care provider is not required to provide the notice.

(f) If an individual who was incompetent or otherwise incapacitated and unable to receive the notice required by this section at the time notice was to be provided under Subsection (c) later becomes able to receive the notice, the health care provider shall provide the written notice at the time the individual becomes able to receive the notice.

(g) This section does not apply to outpatient hospital services, including emergency services.

Added by Acts 1999, 76th Leg., ch. 450; § 1.02, eff. Sept. 1, 1999. Subsec. (a)(4) amended by Acts 2015, 84th Leg., ch. 1, § 3.0500, eff. Sept. 1, 2015.

Statutes in Context
§ 166.005

Section 166.005 provides that advance directives effective under the law of other jurisdictions will be given effect within the limitations of Texas law even if the directive does not meet the formalities of Texas law.

---

§ 166.005. Enforceability of Advance Directives Executed in Another Jurisdiction

An advance directive or similar instrument validly executed in another state or jurisdiction shall be given the same effect as an advance directive validly executed under the law of this state. This section does not authorize the administration, withholding, or withdrawal of health care otherwise prohibited by the laws of this state.

Added by Acts 1999, 76th Leg., ch. 450, § 1.02, eff. Sept. 1, 1999.

Statutes in Context
§ 116.006 & § 116.007

Insurance companies may not take into account the fact that an insured has or has not executed a directive in determining insurability or premiums. For example, a life insurance company may not offer lower premiums to an insured who does not sign a directive to physicians. Likewise, a health insurance company cannot require an insured to execute a directive as a condition of being covered by the policy. See §§ 116.006 and 116.007.

---

§ 166.006. Effect of Advance Directive on Insurance Policy and Premiums

(a) The fact that a person has executed or issued an advance directive does not:

    (1) restrict, inhibit, or impair in any manner the sale, procurement, or issuance of a life insurance policy to that person; or

    (2) modify the terms of an existing life insurance policy.

(b) Notwithstanding the terms of any life insurance policy, the fact that life-sustaining treatment is withheld or withdrawn from an insured qualified patient under this chapter does not legally impair or invalidate that person's life insurance policy and may not be a factor for the purpose of determining, under the life insurance policy, whether benefits are payable or the cause of death.

(c) The fact that a person has executed or issued or failed to execute or issue an advance directive may not be considered in any way in establishing insurance premiums.

Added by Acts 1999, 76th Leg., ch. 450, § 1.02, eff. Sept. 1, 1999.

---

§ 166.007. Execution of Advance Directive May Not Be Required

A physician, health facility, health care provider, insurer, or health care service plan may not require a person to execute or issue an advance directive as a condition for obtaining insurance for health care services or receiving health care services.

Added by Acts 1999, 76th Leg., ch. 450, § 1.02, eff. Sept. 1, 1999.

Statutes in Context
§ 166.008

Under § 166.008, if a declarant has executed more than one advance directive, the directive executed later in time controls.

---

§ 166.008. Conflict Between Advance Directives

To the extent that a treatment decision or an advance directive validly executed or issued under this chapter conflicts with another treatment decision or an advance directive executed or issued under this chapter, the treatment decision made or instrument executed later in time controls.

Added by Acts 1999, 76th Leg., ch. 450, § 1.02, eff. Sept. 1, 1999.

§ 166.009. Certain Life-Sustaining Treatment Not Required

This chapter may not be construed to require the provision of life-sustaining treatment that cannot be provided to a patient without denying the same treatment to another patient.

Added by Acts 1999, 76th Leg., ch. 450, § 1.02, eff. Sept. 1, 1999.

§ 166.010. Applicability of Federal Law Relating to Child Abuse and Neglect

This chapter is subject to applicable federal law and regulations relating to child abuse and neglect to the extent applicable to the state based on its receipt of federal funds.

Added by Acts 2003, 78th Leg., ch. 1228, § 2, eff. June 20, 2003.

§ 166.011. Digital or Electronic Signature

(a) For an advance directive in which a signature by a declarant, witness, or notary public is required or used, the declarant, witness, or notary public may sign the directive or a written revocation of the directive using:

(1) a digital signature that:

(A) uses an algorithm approved by the department;

(B) is unique to the person using it;

(C) is capable of verification;

(D) is under the sole control of the person using it;

(E) is linked to data in a manner that invalidates the digital signature if the data is changed;

(F) persists with the document and not by association in separate files; and

(G) is bound to a digital certificate; or

(2) an electronic signature that:

(A) is capable of verification;

(B) is under the sole control of the person using it;

(C) is linked to data in a manner that invalidates the electronic signature if the data is changed; and

(D) persists with the document and not by association in separate files.

(b) In approving an algorithm for purposes of Subsection (a)(1)(A), the department may consider an algorithm approved by the National Institute of Standards and Technology.

(c) The executive commissioner [of the Health and Human Services Commission] by rule shall modify the advance directive forms required under this chapter as necessary to provide for the use of a digital or electronic signature that complies with the requirements of this section.

Added by Acts 2009, 81st Leg., ch. 461, § 2, eff. Sept. 1, 2009. Subsec. (c) Acts 2015, 84th Leg., ch. 1, § 3.0501, eff. Sept. 1, 2015.

Subchapter B. Directive to Physicians

Statutes in Context
§§ 166.031–166.051

A competent individual has the right to refuse medical treatment for any reason even if that refusal will lead to an otherwise preventable death. What happens, though, if the person is in a coma, brain damaged, or for some other reason cannot communicate the person's wishes? The person may have signed a directive to physicians or "living will" which expresses the person's desire not to be kept alive through the use of medical technology when the person is in a terminal condition and unable to communicate the person's wishes to decline further treatment.

California was the first state to statutorily authorize a person to make an advance statement regarding the use of life-sustaining procedures when its legislature enacted living will legislation in 1976. In 1977, Texas became the fifth state to enact similar legislation when it passed the Natural Death Act. This Act provided methods for a person to indicate the desire that his or her life not be prolonged with the use of artificial life-sustaining procedures when the person's death is inevitable. The 1999 Legislature recodified the Natural Death Act in a comprehensive Advance Directives Act which includes living wills, out-of-hospital do-not-resuscitate orders, and medical powers of attorney.

Many of your clients will be extremely interested in obtaining a living will. They are often discussed in the media and gain national attention when they are used to hasten the death of famous people like former President Richard Nixon and former first-lady Jacqueline Kennedy Onassis. In addition, the federal Patient Self-Determination Act, 42 U.S.C. § 1395cc(f), requires all hospitals, nursing homes, and other health care providers that participate in Medicare or Medicaid to give all patients at the time of their admission written information regarding their rights to refuse medical treatment under state law.

Sections 166.031 - 166.051 govern the creation and effect of directives to physicians.

§ 166.031. Definitions

In this subchapter:

(1) "Directive" means an instruction made under Section 166.032, 166.034, or 166.035 to administer, withhold, or withdraw life-sustaining treatment in the event of a terminal or irreversible condition.

(2) "Qualified patient" means a patient with a terminal or irreversible condition that has been

diagnosed and certified in writing by the attending physician.

Amended by Acts 1993, 73rd Leg., ch. 107, § 5.04, eff. Aug. 30, 1993. Renumbered from § 672.002 and amended by Acts 1999, 76th Leg., ch. 450, § 1.03, eff. Sept. 1, 1999.

Statutes in Context
§ 166.032

The formal requirements of a directive to physicians are detailed in § 166.032.

---

§ 166.032. Written Directive by Competent Adult; Notice to Physician

(a) A competent adult may at any time execute a written directive.

(b) Except as provided by Subsection (b-1), the declarant must sign the directive in the presence of two witnesses who qualify under Section 166.003, at least one of whom must be a witness who qualifies under Section 166.003(2). The witnesses must sign the directive.

(b-1) The declarant, in lieu of signing in the presence of witnesses, may sign the directive and have the signature acknowledged before a notary public.

(c) A declarant may include in a directive directions other than those provided by Section 166.033 and may designate in a directive a person to make a health care or treatment decision for the declarant in the event the declarant becomes incompetent or otherwise mentally or physically incapable of communication.

(d) A declarant shall notify the attending physician of the existence of a written directive. If the declarant is incompetent or otherwise mentally or physically incapable of communication, another person may notify the attending physician of the existence of the written directive. The attending physician shall make the directive a part of the declarant's medical record.

Amended by Acts 1997, 75th Leg., ch. 291, § 1, eff. Jan. 1, 1998. Renumbered from § 672.003 and amended by Acts 1999, 76th Leg., ch. 450, § 1.03, eff. Sept. 1, 1999. Subsec. (b) amended and subsec. (b-1) added by Acts 2009, 81st Leg., ch. 461, § 3, eff. Sept. 1, 2009. Subsec. (c) amended by Acts 2015, 84th Leg., ch. 435, § 3, eff. Sept. 1, 2015.

Statutes in Context
§ 166.033

Section 166.033 provides a fill-in-the-blank form which a person may use to create a directive to physicians. The use of this form is not required but it is in common use. Note that a declarant may provide individualized instructions in the area labeled "additional requests."

---

§ 166.033. Form of Written Directive

A written directive may be in the following form:
DIRECTIVE TO PHYSICIANS AND FAMILY OR SURROGATES
Instructions for completing this document:

This is an important legal document known as an Advance Directive. It is designed to help you communicate your wishes about medical treatment at some time in the future when you are unable to make your wishes known because of illness or injury. These wishes are usually based on personal values. In particular, you may want to consider what burdens or hardships of treatment you would be willing to accept for a particular amount of benefit obtained if you were seriously ill.

You are encouraged to discuss your values and wishes with your family or chosen spokesperson, as well as your physician. Your physician, other health care provider, or medical institution may provide you with various resources to assist you in completing your advance directive. Brief definitions are listed below and may aid you in your discussions and advance planning. Initial the treatment choices that best reflect your personal preferences. Provide a copy of your directive to your physician, usual hospital, and family or spokesperson. Consider a periodic review of this document. By periodic review, you can best assure that the directive reflects your preferences.

In addition to this advance directive, Texas law provides for two other types of directives that can be important during a serious illness. These are the Medical Power of Attorney and the Out-of-Hospital Do-Not-Resuscitate Order. You may wish to discuss these with your physician, family, hospital representative, or other advisers. You may also wish to complete a directive related to the donation of organs and tissues.

DIRECTIVE

I, _____, recognize that the best health care is based upon a partnership of trust and communication with my physician. My physician and I will make health care or treatment decisions together as long as I am of sound mind and able to make my wishes known. If there comes a time that I am unable to make medical decisions about myself because of illness or injury, I direct that the following treatment preferences be honored:

If, in the judgment of my physician, I am suffering with a terminal condition from which I am expected to die within six months, even with available life-sustaining treatment provided in accordance with prevailing standards of medical care:

_____ I request that all treatments other than those needed to keep me comfortable be discontinued or withheld and my physician allow me to die as gently as possible; OR

_____ I request that I be kept alive in this terminal condition using available life-sustaining treatment. (THIS SELECTION DOES NOT APPLY TO HOSPICE CARE.)

If, in the judgment of my physician, I am suffering with an irreversible condition so that I cannot care for myself or make decisions for myself and am expected to die without life-sustaining treatment provided in accordance with prevailing standards of care:

_____ I request that all treatments other than those needed to keep me comfortable be discontinued or withheld and my physician allow me to die as gently as possible; OR.

_____ I request that I be kept alive in this irreversible condition using available life-sustaining treatment. (THIS SELECTION DOES NOT APPLY TO HOSPICE CARE.)

(After discussion with your physician, you may wish to consider listing particular treatments in this space that you do or do not want in specific circumstances, such as artificially administered [artificial] nutrition and hydration [fluids], intravenous antibiotics, etc. Be sure to state whether you do or do not want the particular treatment.)

_____

_____

After signing this directive, if my representative or I elect hospice care, I understand and agree that only those treatments needed to keep me comfortable would be provided and I would not be given available life-sustaining treatments.

If I do not have a Medical Power of Attorney, and I am unable to make my wishes known, I designate the following person(s) to make health care or treatment decisions with my physician compatible with my personal values:

1._____
2._____

(If a Medical Power of Attorney has been executed, then an agent already has been named and you should not list additional names in this document.)

If the above persons are not available, or if I have not designated a spokesperson, I understand that a spokesperson will be chosen for me following standards specified in the laws of Texas. If, in the judgment of my physician, my death is imminent within minutes to hours, even with the use of all available medical treatment provided within the prevailing standard of care, I acknowledge that all treatments may be withheld or removed except those needed to maintain my comfort. I understand that under Texas law this directive has no effect if I have been diagnosed as pregnant. This directive will remain in effect until I revoke it. No other person may do so.

Signed _____
Date _____
City, County, State of Residence _____

Two competent adult witnesses must sign below, acknowledging the signature of the declarant. The witness designated as Witness 1 may not be a person designated to make a health care or treatment decision

for the patient and may not be related to the patient by blood or marriage. This witness may not be entitled to any part of the estate and may not have a claim against the estate of the patient. This witness may not be the attending physician or an employee of the attending physician. If this witness is an employee of a health care facility in which the patient is being cared for, this witness may not be involved in providing direct patient care to the patient. This witness may not be an officer, director, partner, or business office employee of a health care facility in which the patient is being cared for or of any parent organization of the health care facility.

Witness 1 _____
Witness 2 _____

Definitions:

"Artificially administered [Artificial] nutrition and hydration" means the provision of nutrients or fluids by a tube inserted in a vein, under the skin in the subcutaneous tissues, or in the [stomach [ ]gastrointestinal tract[.].

"Irreversible condition" means a condition, injury, or illness:

(1) that may be treated, but is never cured or eliminated;

(2) that leaves a person unable to care for or make decisions for the person's own self; and

(3) that, without life-sustaining treatment provided in accordance with the prevailing standard of medical care, is fatal.

Explanation: Many serious illnesses such as cancer, failure of major organs (kidney, heart, liver, or lung), and serious brain disease such as Alzheimer's dementia may be considered irreversible early on. There is no cure, but the patient may be kept alive for prolonged periods of time if the patient receives life-sustaining treatments. Late in the course of the same illness, the disease may be considered terminal when, even with treatment, the patient is expected to die. You may wish to consider which burdens of treatment you would be willing to accept in an effort to achieve a particular outcome. This is a very personal decision that you may wish to discuss with your physician, family, or other important persons in your life.

"Life-sustaining treatment" means treatment that, based on reasonable medical judgment, sustains the life of a patient and without which the patient will die. The term includes both life-sustaining medications and artificial life support such as mechanical breathing machines, kidney dialysis treatment, and artificially administered nutrition and [artificial] hydration [and nutrition]. The term does not include the administration of pain management medication, the performance of a medical procedure necessary to provide comfort care, or any other medical care provided to alleviate a patient's pain.

"Terminal condition" means an incurable condition caused by injury, disease, or illness that according to reasonable medical judgment will produce death within six months, even with available life-sustaining treatment provided in accordance with the prevailing standard of medical care.

Explanation: Many serious illnesses may be considered irreversible early in the course of the illness, but they may not be considered terminal until the disease is fairly advanced. In thinking about terminal illness and its treatment, you again may wish to consider the relative benefits and burdens of treatment and discuss your wishes with your physician, family, or other important persons in your life.

Amended by Acts 1997, 75th Leg., ch. 291, § 2, eff. Jan. 1, 1998. Renumbered from § 672.004 and amended by Acts 1999, 76th Leg., ch. 450, § 1.03, eff. Sept. 1, 1999. Amended by Acts 2015, 84th Leg., ch. 435, § 4, eff. Sept. 1, 2015.

Statutes in Context
§ 166.034

Nonwritten directives such as by oral statements or gestures are permitted under § 166.034.

§ 166.034. Issuance of Nonwritten Directive by Competent Adult Qualified Patient

(a) A competent qualified patient who is an adult may issue a directive by a nonwritten means of communication.

(b) A declarant must issue the nonwritten directive in the presence of the attending physician and two witnesses who qualify under Section 166.003, at least one of whom must be a witness who qualifies under Section 166.003(2).

(c) The physician shall make the fact of the existence of the directive a part of the declarant's medical record, and the names of the witnesses shall be entered in the medical record.

Renumbered from § 672.005 and amended by Acts 1999, 76th Leg., ch. 450, § 1.03, eff. Sept. 1, 1999.

Statutes in Context
§ 166.035

Section 166.035 explains when a directive may be executed on behalf of a minor.

§ 166.035. Execution of Directive on Behalf of Patient Younger Than 18 Years of Age

The following persons may execute a directive on behalf of a qualified patient who is younger than 18 years of age:

    (1) the patient's spouse, if the spouse is an adult;

    (2) the patient's parents; or

    (3) the patient's legal guardian.

Renumbered from § 672.006 by Acts 1999, 76th Leg., ch. 450, § 1.03, eff. Sept. 1, 1999.

Statutes in Context
§ 166.036

Directives do not have to be notarized and health care providers cannot require notarization or the use of a specific form under § 166.036. However, the 2009 Legislature provided that if the directive is notarized, no witnesses are necessary.

§ 166.036. Notarized Document Not Required; Requirement of Specific Form Prohibited

(a) Except as provided by Section 166.032(b-1), a written directive executed under Section 166.033 or 166.035 is effective without regard to whether the document has been notarized.

(b) A physician, health care facility, or health care professional may not require that:

    (1) a directive be notarized; or

    (2) a person use a form provided by the physician, health care facility, or health care professional.

Added by Acts 1999, 76th Leg., ch. 450, § 1.03, eff. Sept. 1, 1999. Subsec. (a) amended by Acts 2009, 81st Leg., ch. 461, § 4, eff. Sept. 1, 2009.

Statutes in Context
§ 166.037

Regardless of what a directive provides, a declarant may demand that life-sustaining procedures be given, even if the declarant is now incompetent or a minor according to § 166.037.

§ 166.037. Patient Desire Supersedes Directive

The desire of a qualified patient, including a qualified patient younger than 18 years of age, supersedes the effect of a directive.

Renumbered from § 672.007 and amended by Acts 1999, 76th Leg., ch. 450, § 1.03, eff. Sept. 1, 1999.

§ 166.038. Procedure When Declarant Is Incompetent or Incapable of Communication

(a) This section applies when an adult qualified patient has executed or issued a directive and is incompetent or otherwise mentally or physically incapable of communication.

(b) If the adult qualified patient has designated a person to make a treatment decision as authorized by Section 166.032(c), the attending physician and the designated person may make a treatment decision in accordance with the declarant's directions.

(c) If the adult qualified patient has not designated a person to make a treatment decision, the attending physician shall comply with the directive unless the physician believes that the directive does not reflect the patient's present desire.

Renumbered from 672.008 and amended by Acts 1999, 76th Leg., ch. 450, § 1.03, eff. Sept. 1, 1999.

Statutes in Context
§ 166.039

Section 166.039 explains when a decision to withhold or withdraw life-sustaining treatment may be made even if the patient has not executed a directive.

§ 166.039. Procedure When Person Has Not Executed or Issued a Directive and Is Incompetent or Incapable of Communication

(a) If an adult qualified patient has not executed or issued a directive and is incompetent or otherwise mentally or physically incapable of communication, the attending physician and the patient's legal guardian or an agent under a medical power of attorney may make a treatment decision that may include a decision to withhold or withdraw life-sustaining treatment from the patient.

(b) If the patient does not have a legal guardian or an agent under a medical power of attorney, the attending physician and one person, if available, from one of the following categories, in the following priority, may make a treatment decision that may include a decision to withhold or withdraw life-sustaining treatment:

(1) the patient's spouse;

(2) the patient's reasonably available adult children;

(3) the patient's parents; or

(4) the patient's nearest living relative.

(c) A treatment decision made under Subsection (a) or (b) must be based on knowledge of what the patient would desire, if known.

(d) A treatment decision made under Subsection (b) must be documented in the patient's medical record and signed by the attending physician.

(e) If the patient does not have a legal guardian and a person listed in Subsection (b) is not available, a treatment decision made under Subsection (b) must be concurred in by another physician who is not involved in the treatment of the patient or who is a representative of an ethics or medical committee of the health care facility in which the person is a patient.

(f) The fact that an adult qualified patient has not executed or issued a directive does not create a presumption that the patient does not want a treatment decision to be made to withhold or withdraw life-sustaining treatment.

(g) A person listed in Subsection (b) who wishes to challenge a treatment decision made under this section must apply for temporary guardianship under Chapter 1251, Estates [Section 875, Texas Probate] Code. The court may waive applicable fees in that proceeding.

Amended by Acts 1997, 75th Leg., ch. 291, § 3, eff. Jan. 1, 1998. Renumbered from § 672.009 and amended by Acts 1999, 76th Leg., ch. 450, § 1.03, eff. Sept. 1, 1999. Subsec. (g) amended by Acts 2015, 84th Leg., ch. 1, § 3.0502, eff. Sept. 1, 2015.

§ 166.040. Patient Certification and Prerequisites for Complying With Directive

(a) An attending physician who has been notified of the existence of a directive shall provide for the declarant's certification as a qualified patient on diagnosis of a terminal or irreversible condition.

(b) Before withholding or withdrawing life-sustaining treatment from a qualified patient under this subchapter, the attending physician must determine that the steps proposed to be taken are in accord with this subchapter and the patient's existing desires.

Renumbered from § 672.010 and amended by Acts 1999, 76th Leg., ch. 450, § 1.03, eff. Sept. 1, 1999.

Statutes in Context
§ 166.041

A directive remains effective until it is revoked under § 166.041. In other words, a directive does not expire after a set period of time or when the declarant's medical condition changes.

§ 166.041. Duration of Directive

A directive is effective until it is revoked as prescribed by Section 166.042.

Renumbered from § 672.011 and amended by Acts 1999, 76th Leg., ch. 450, § 1.03, eff. Sept. 1, 1999.

Statutes in Context
§ 166.042

The methods a declarant may use to revoke a directive are described in § 166.042. Note that the declarant does not have to be competent to revoke the directive in writing, orally, or by physical act.

§ 166.042. Revocation of Directive

(a) A declarant may revoke a directive at any time without regard to the declarant's mental state or competency. A directive may be revoked by:

(1) the declarant or someone in the declarant's presence and at the declarant's direction canceling, defacing, obliterating, burning, tearing, or otherwise destroying the directive;

(2) the declarant signing and dating a written revocation that expresses the declarant's intent to revoke the directive; or

(3) the declarant orally stating the declarant's intent to revoke the directive.

(b) A written revocation executed as prescribed by Subsection (a)(2) takes effect only when the declarant or a person acting on behalf of the declarant notifies the attending physician of its existence or mails the revocation to the attending physician. The attending physician or the physician's designee shall record in the patient's medical record the time and date when the physician received notice of the written revocation and shall enter the word "VOID" on each page of the copy of the directive in the patient's medical record.

(c) An oral revocation issued as prescribed by Subsection (a)(3) takes effect only when the declarant or a person acting on behalf of the declarant notifies the attending physician of the revocation. The attending physician or the physician's designee shall record in the patient's medical record the time, date, and place of the revocation, and, if different, the time, date, and place that the physician received notice of the revocation. The attending physician or the physician's designees shall also enter the word "VOID" on each page of the copy of the directive in the patient's medical record.

(d) Except as otherwise provided by this subchapter, a person is not civilly or criminally liable for failure to act on a revocation made under this section unless the person has actual knowledge of the revocation.

Renumbered from § 672.012 and amended by Acts 1999, 76th Leg., ch. 450, § 1.03, eff. Sept. 1, 1999.

§ 166.043. Reexecution of Directive

A declarant may at any time reexecute a directive in accordance with the procedures prescribed by Section 166.032, including reexecution after the declarant is diagnosed as having a terminal or irreversible condition.

Renumbered from § 672.013 and amended by Acts 1999, 76th Leg., ch. 450, § 1.03, eff. Sept. 1, 1999.

Statutes in Context
§ 166.044

Health care providers are protected from liability for withholding or withdrawing life-sustaining treatment under the conditions described in § 166.044.

---

§ 166.044. Limitation of Liability for Withholding or Withdrawing Life-Sustaining Procedures

(a) A physician or health care facility that causes life-sustaining treatment to be withheld or withdrawn from a qualified patient in accordance with this subchapter is not civilly liable for that action unless the physician or health care facility fails to exercise reasonable care when applying the patient's advance directive.

(b) A health professional, acting under the direction of a physician, who participates in withholding or withdrawing life-sustaining treatment from a qualified patient in accordance with this subchapter is not civilly liable for that action unless the health professional fails to exercise reasonable care when applying the patient's advance directive.

(c) A physician, or a health professional acting under the direction of a physician, who participates in withholding or withdrawing life-sustaining treatment from a qualified patient in accordance with this subchapter is not criminally liable or guilty of unprofessional conduct as a result of that action unless the physician or health professional fails to exercise

reasonable care when applying the patient's advance directive.

(d) The standard of care that a physician, health care facility, or health care professional shall exercise under this section is that degree of care that a physician, health care facility, or health care professional, as applicable, of ordinary prudence and skill would have exercised under the same or similar circumstances in the same or a similar community.

Renumbered from § 672.015 and amended by Acts 1999, 76th Leg., ch. 450, § 1.03, eff. Sept. 1, 1999.

Statutes in Context
§ 166.045

Health care providers may be liable for failing to effectuate a directive under the conditions described in § 166.045.

---

§ 166.045. Liability for Failure to Effectuate Directive

(a) A physician, health care facility, or health care professional who has no knowledge of a directive is not civilly or criminally liable for failing to act in accordance with the directive.

(b) A physician, or a health professional acting under the direction of a physician, is subject to review and disciplinary action by the appropriate licensing board for failing to effectuate a qualified patient's directive in violation of this subchapter or other laws of this state. This subsection does not limit remedies available under other laws of this state.

(c) If an attending physician refuses to comply with a directive or treatment decision and does not wish to follow the procedure established under Section 166.046, life-sustaining treatment shall be provided to the patient, but only until a reasonable opportunity has been afforded for the transfer of the patient to another physician or health care facility willing to comply with the directive or treatment decision.

(d) A physician, health professional acting under the direction of a physician, or health care facility is not civilly or criminally liable or subject to review or disciplinary action by the person's appropriate licensing board if the person has complied with the procedures outlined in Section 166.046.

Renumbered from § 672.016 and amended by Acts 1999, 76th Leg., ch. 450, § 1.03, eff. Sept. 1, 1999.

Statutes in Context
§ 166.046

The procedures a physician must follow if the physician refuses to honor an advance directive are set forth in § 166.046.

---

§ 166.046. Procedure if Not Effectuating a Directive or Treatment Decision

(a) If an attending physician refuses to honor a patient's advance directive or health care or a treatment decision made by or on behalf of a patient, the physician's refusal shall be reviewed by an ethics or medical committee. The attending physician may not be a member of that committee. The patient shall be given life-sustaining treatment during the review.

(b) The patient or the person responsible for health care decisions of the individual who has made the decision regarding the directive or treatment decision:

(1) may be given a written description of the ethics or medical committee review process and any other policies and procedures related to this section adopted by the health care facility;

(2) shall be informed of the committee review process not less than 48 hours before the meeting called to discuss the patient's directive, unless the time period is waived by mutual agreement;

(3) at the time of being so informed, shall be provided:

(A) a copy of the appropriate statement set forth in Section 166.052; and

(B) a copy of the registry list of health care providers and referral groups that have volunteered their readiness to consider accepting transfer or to assist in locating a provider willing to accept transfer that is posted on the website maintained by the department [Texas Health Care Information Council] under Section 166.053; and

(4) is entitled to:

(A) attend the meeting; [and]

(B) receive a written explanation of the decision reached during the review process;

(C) receive a copy of the portion of the patient's medical record related to the treatment received by the patient in the facility for the lesser of:

(i) the period of the patient's current admission to the facility; or

(ii) the preceding 30 calendar days; and

(D) receive a copy of all of the patient's reasonably available diagnostic results and reports related to the medical record provided under Paragraph (C).

(c) The written explanation required by Subsection (b)(4)(B) [(b)(2)(B)] must be included in the patient's medical record.

(d) If the attending physician, the patient, or the person responsible for the health care decisions of the individual does not agree with the decision reached during the review process under Subsection (b), the physician shall make a reasonable effort to transfer the patient to a physician who is willing to comply with the directive. If the patient is a patient in a health care

facility, the facility's personnel shall assist the physician in arranging the patient's transfer to:

(1) another physician;

(2) an alternative care setting within that facility; or

(3) another facility.

(e) If the patient or the person responsible for the health care decisions of the patient is requesting life-sustaining treatment that the attending physician has decided and the ethics or medical committee [review process] has affirmed is medically inappropriate treatment, the patient shall be given available life-sustaining treatment pending transfer under Subsection (d). This subsection does not authorize withholding or withdrawing pain management medication, medical procedures necessary to provide comfort, or any other health care provided to alleviate a patient's pain. The patient is responsible for any costs incurred in transferring the patient to another facility. The attending physician, any other physician responsible for the care of the patient, and the health care facility are not obligated to provide life-sustaining treatment after the 10th day after both the written decision and the patient's medical record required under Subsection (b) are [is] provided to the patient or the person responsible for the health care decisions of the patient unless ordered to do so under Subsection (g), except that artificially administered nutrition and hydration must be provided unless, based on reasonable medical judgment, providing artificially administered nutrition and hydration would:

(1) hasten the patient's death;

(2) be medically contraindicated such that the provision of the treatment seriously exacerbates life-threatening medical problems not outweighed by the benefit of the provision of the treatment;

(3) result in substantial irremediable physical pain not outweighed by the benefit of the provision of the treatment;

(4) be medically ineffective in prolonging life; or

(5) be contrary to the patient's or surrogate's clearly documented desire not to receive artificially administered nutrition or hydration.

(e-1) If during a previous admission to a facility a patient's attending physician and the review process under Subsection (b) have determined that life-sustaining treatment is inappropriate, and the patient is readmitted to the same facility within six months from the date of the decision reached during the review process conducted upon the previous admission, Subsections (b) through (e) need not be followed if the patient's attending physician and a consulting physician who is a member of the ethics or medical committee of the facility document on the patient's readmission that the patient's condition either has not improved or has deteriorated since the review process was conducted.

(f) Life-sustaining treatment under this section may not be entered in the patient's medical record as medically unnecessary treatment until the time period provided under Subsection (e) has expired.

(g) At the request of the patient or the person responsible for the health care decisions of the patient, the appropriate district or county court shall extend the time period provided under Subsection (e) only if the court finds, by a preponderance of the evidence, that there is a reasonable expectation that a physician or health care facility that will honor the patient's directive will be found if the time extension is granted.

(h) This section may not be construed to impose an obligation on a facility or a home and community support services agency licensed under Chapter 142 or similar organization that is beyond the scope of the services or resources of the facility or agency. This section does not apply to hospice services provided by a home and community support services agency licensed under Chapter 142.

Added by Acts 1999, 76th Leg., ch. 450, § 1.03, eff. Sept. 1, 1999. Amended by Acts 2003, 78th Leg., ch. 1228, §§ 2 & 3, eff. June 20, 2003. Subsecs (b) & (e) amended by Acts 2015, 84th Leg., ch. 435, § 5, eff. Sept. 1, 2015. Subsecs (b)(3)(B) and (c) amended by Acts 2015, 84th Leg., ch. 1, § 3.0503, eff. Sept. 1, 2015.

Statutes in Context
§ 166.047

A person who complies with a directive is not guilty of the crime of aiding suicide under Penal Code § 22.08.

§ 166.047. Honoring Directive Does Not Constitute Offense of Aiding Suicide

A person does not commit an offense under Section 22.08, Penal Code, by withholding or withdrawing life-sustaining treatment from a qualified patient in accordance with this subchapter.

Renumbered from § 672.017 and amended by Acts 1999, 76th Leg., ch. 450, § 1.03, eff. Sept. 1, 1999.

Statutes in Context
§ 166.048

Section 166.048 describes the criminal offenses which are committed if a person conceals a declarant's advance directive, forges or falsifies a directive, or withholds information about the declarant's revocation of a directive.

§ 166.048. Criminal Penalty; Prosecution

(a) A person commits an offense if the person intentionally conceals, cancels, defaces, obliterates, or damages another person's directive without that person's consent. An offense under this subsection is a Class A misdemeanor.

(b) A person is subject to prosecution for criminal homicide under Chapter 19, Penal Code, if the person,

with the intent to cause life-sustaining treatment to be withheld or withdrawn from another person contrary to the other person's desires, falsifies or forges a directive or intentionally conceals or withholds personal knowledge of a revocation and thereby directly causes life-sustaining treatment to be withheld or withdrawn from the other person with the result that the other person's death is hastened.

Renumbered from § 672.018 and amended by Acts 1999, 76th Leg., ch. 450, § 1.03, eff. Sept. 1, 1999.

Statutes in Context
§ 166.049

Health care providers may not withdraw or withhold life-sustaining treatment if the declarant is pregnant.

§ 166.049. Pregnant Patients

A person may not withdraw or withhold life-sustaining treatment under this subchapter from a pregnant patient.

Renumbered from § 672.019 and amended by Acts 1999, 76th Leg., ch. 450, § 1.03, eff. Sept. 1, 1999.

Statutes in Context
§ 166.050

Voluntary euthanasia in which the euthanatizer actually kills the person at that person's request is not allowed under § 166.050.

§ 166.050. Mercy Killing Not Condoned

This subchapter does not condone, authorize, or approve mercy killing or permit an affirmative or deliberate act or omission to end life except to permit the natural process of dying as provided by this subchapter.

Renumbered from § 672.020 and amended by Acts 1999, 76th Leg., ch. 450, § 1.03, eff. Sept. 1, 1999.

§ 166.051. Legal Right or Responsibility Not Affected

This subchapter does not impair or supersede any legal right or responsibility a person may have to effect the withholding or withdrawal of life-sustaining treatment in a lawful manner, provided that if an attending physician or health care facility is unwilling to honor a patient's advance directive or a treatment decision to provide life-sustaining treatment, life-sustaining treatment is required to be provided the patient, but only until a reasonable opportunity has been afforded for transfer of the patient to another physician or health care facility willing to comply with the advance directive or treatment decision.

Renumbered from § 672.021 and amended by Acts 1999, 76th Leg., ch. 450, § 1.03, eff. Sept. 1, 1999.

Statutes in Context
§ 166.052 & § 166.053

In 2003, Texas enacted extensive procedures which must be followed when either (1) the attending physician wishes to cease life-sustaining treatment but the patient's advance directive or medical agent indicates that treatment should be continued; or (2) the attending physician wishes to continue life-sustaining treatment but the patient's advance directive or medical agent indicates that treatment should be withheld. §§ 166.052 – 166.053. These procedures will assist the patient in being transferred to a facility willing to comply with the advance directive or the agent's instructions.

§ 166.052. Statements Explaining Patient's Right to Transfer

(a) In cases in which the attending physician refuses to honor an advance directive or health care or treatment decision requesting the provision of life-sustaining treatment, the statement required by Section 166.046(b)(3)(A) [166.046(b)(2)(A)] shall be in substantially the following form:

When There is a Disagreement About Medical Treatment: The Physician Recommends Against Certain Life-Sustaining Treatment That You Wish to Continue

You have been given this information because you have requested life-sustaining treatment[,]* for yourself as the patient or on behalf of the patient, as applicable, which the attending physician believes is not medically appropriate. This information is being provided to help you understand state law, your rights, and the resources available to you in such circumstances. It outlines the process for resolving disagreements about treatment among patients, families, and physicians. It is based upon Section 166.046 of the Texas Advance Directives Act, codified in Chapter 166, [of the] Texas Health and Safety Code.

When an attending physician refuses to comply with an advance directive or other request for life-sustaining treatment because of the physician's judgment that the treatment would be medically inappropriate, the case will be reviewed by an ethics or medical committee. Life-sustaining treatment will be provided through the review.

You will receive notification of this review at least 48 hours before a meeting of the committee related to your case. You are entitled to attend the meeting. With your agreement, the meeting may be held sooner than 48 hours, if possible.

You are entitled to receive a written explanation of the decision reached during the review process.

If after this review process both the attending physician and the ethics or medical committee conclude that life-sustaining treatment is medically inappropriate

and yet you continue to request such treatment, then the following procedure will occur:

1. The physician, with the help of the health care facility, will assist you in trying to find a physician and facility willing to provide the requested treatment.

2. You are being given a list of health care providers, licensed physicians, health care facilities, and referral groups that have volunteered their readiness to consider accepting transfer, or to assist in locating a provider willing to accept transfer, maintained by the Department of State Health Services [Texas Health Care Information Council]. You may wish to contact providers, facilities, or referral groups on the list or others of your choice to get help in arranging a transfer.

3. The patient will continue to be given life-sustaining treatment until the patient [he or she] can be transferred to a willing provider for up to 10 days from the time you were given both the committee's written decision that life-sustaining treatment is not appropriate and the patient's medical record. The patient will continue to be given after the 10-day period treatment to enhance pain management and reduce suffering, including artificially administered nutrition and hydration, unless, based on reasonable medical judgment, providing artificially administered nutrition and hydration would hasten the patient's death, be medically contraindicated such that the provision of the treatment seriously exacerbates life-threatening medical problems not outweighed by the benefit of the provision of the treatment, result in substantial irremediable physical pain not outweighed by the benefit of the provision of the treatment, be medically ineffective in prolonging life, or be contrary to the patient's or surrogate's clearly documented desires.

4. If a transfer can be arranged, the patient will be responsible for the costs of the transfer.

5. If a provider cannot be found willing to give the requested treatment within 10 days, life-sustaining treatment may be withdrawn unless a court of law has granted an extension.

6. You may ask the appropriate district or county court to extend the 10-day period if the court finds that there is a reasonable expectation that you may find a physician or health care facility willing to provide life-sustaining treatment [will be found] if the extension is granted. Patient medical records will be provided to the patient or surrogate in accordance with Section 241.154, Texas Health and Safety Code.

*"Life-sustaining treatment" means treatment that, based on reasonable medical judgment, sustains the life of a patient and without which the patient will die. The term includes both life-sustaining medications and artificial life support, such as mechanical breathing machines, kidney dialysis treatment, and artificially administered [artificial] nutrition and hydration. The term does not include the administration of pain management medication or the performance of a medical procedure considered to be necessary to provide comfort care, or any other medical care provided to alleviate a patient's pain.

608

(b) In cases in which the attending physician refuses to comply with an advance directive or treatment decision requesting the withholding or withdrawal of life-sustaining treatment, the statement required by Section 166.046(b)(3)(A) shall be in substantially the following form:

When There is a Disagreement About Medical Treatment: The Physician Recommends Life-Sustaining Treatment That You Wish to Stop

You have been given this information because you have requested the withdrawal or withholding of life-sustaining treatment* for yourself as the patient or on behalf of the patient, as applicable, and the attending physician disagrees with and refuses to comply with that request. The information is being provided to help you understand state law, your rights, and the resources available to you in such circumstances. It outlines the process for resolving disagreements about treatment among patients, families, and physicians. It is based upon Section 166.046 of the Texas Advance Directives Act, codified in Chapter 166, [of the] Texas Health and Safety Code.

When an attending physician refuses to comply with an advance directive or other request for withdrawal or withholding of life-sustaining treatment for any reason, the case will be reviewed by an ethics or medical committee. Life-sustaining treatment will be provided through the review.

You will receive notification of this review at least 48 hours before a meeting of the committee related to your case. You are entitled to attend the meeting. With your agreement, the meeting may be held sooner than 48 hours, if possible.

You are entitled to receive a written explanation of the decision reached during the review process.

If you or the attending physician do not agree with the decision reached during the review process, and the attending physician still refuses to comply with your request to withhold or withdraw life-sustaining treatment, then the following procedure will occur:

1. The physician, with the help of the health care facility, will assist you in trying to find a physician and facility willing to withdraw or withhold the life-sustaining treatment.

2. You are being given a list of health care providers, licensed physicians, health care facilities, and referral groups that have volunteered their readiness to consider accepting transfer, or to assist in locating a provider willing to accept transfer, maintained by the Department of State Health Services [Texas Health Care Information Council]. You may wish to contact providers, facilities, or referral groups on the list or others of your choice to get help in arranging a transfer.

*"Life-sustaining treatment" means treatment that, based on reasonable medical judgment, sustains the life of a patient and without which the patient will die. The term includes both life-sustaining medications and artificial life support, such as mechanical breathing machines, kidney dialysis treatment, and artificially administered [artificial] nutrition and hydration. The term does not include the administration of pain management medication or the performance of a medical procedure considered to be necessary to provide comfort care, or any other medical care provided to alleviate a patient's pain.

(c) An attending physician or health care facility may, if it chooses, include any additional information concerning the physician's or facility's policy, perspective, experience, or review procedure.

Added by Acts 2003, 78th Leg., ch. 1228, § 5, eff. June 20, 2003. Subsec. (a) & (b) amended by Acts 2015, 84th Leg., ch. 435, § 6, eff. Sept. 1, 2015. Subsecs (a) & (b) amended by Acts 2015, 84th Leg., ch. 1, § 3.0504, eff. Sept. 1, 2015.

§ 166.053. Registry to Assist Transfers

(a) The department [Texas Health Care Information Council] shall maintain a registry listing the identity of and contact information for health care providers and referral groups, situated inside and outside this state, that have voluntarily notified the department [council] they may consider accepting or may assist in locating a provider willing to accept transfer of a patient under Section 166.045 or 166.046.

(b) The listing of a provider or referral group in the registry described in this section does not obligate the provider or group to accept transfer of or provide services to any particular patient.

(c) The department [Texas Health Care Information Council] shall post the current registry list on its website in a form appropriate for easy comprehension by patients and persons responsible for the health care decisions of patients [and shall provide a clearly identifiable link from its home page to the registry page]. The list shall separately indicate those providers and groups that have indicated their interest in assisting the transfer of:

(1) those patients on whose behalf life-sustaining treatment is being sought;

(2) those patients on whose behalf the withholding or withdrawal of life-sustaining treatment is being sought; and

(3) patients described in both Subdivisions (1) and (2).

(d) The registry list described in this section shall include the following disclaimer:

"This registry lists providers and groups that have indicated to the Department of State Health Services [Texas Health Care Information Council] their interest in assisting the transfer of patients in the circumstances described, and is provided for information purposes only. Neither the Department of State Health Services [Texas Health Care Information Council] nor the State of Texas endorses or assumes any responsibility for any representation, claim, or act of the listed providers or groups."

Added by Acts 2003, 78th Leg., ch. 1228, § 5, eff. June 20, 2003. Subsecs (a), (c), & (d) amended by Acts 2015, 84th Leg., ch. 1, § 3.0505, eff. Sept. 1, 2015.

609

Subchapter C. Out-of-Hospital Do-Not-Resuscitate Orders

Statutes in Context
§§ 166.081–166.101

The 1995 Texas Legislature authorized a physician, in accordance with his or her patient's wishes (or the wishes of the patient's legally authorized representative), to issue an order directing health care professionals acting in out-of-hospital settings, to refrain from initiating or continuing certain life-sustaining procedures. These provisions were recodified in 1999 as part of the Advance Directives Act. This order is designated as an Out-of-Hospital Do-Not-Resuscitate Order (OOH-DNR). OOH-DNR orders are effective when a patient, in a terminal condition, is in a setting such as a long-term care facility, hospice, or even a private home and health care professionals are called for assistance. The order also applies to situations where the person is in transport in an ambulance or other vehicle.

The policy underlying these provisions is to allow the natural process of dying by preventing the use of artificial life-sustaining measures, heroic or otherwise. However, the OOH-DNR order is effective only with respect to certain specified life-sustaining procedures including: (1) cardiopulmonary resuscitation, (2) advanced airway management, (3) artificial ventilation, (4) defibrillation, (5) transcutaneous cardiac pacing, and (6) other life-sustaining treatment specified by the Texas Board of Health. An OOH-DNR order may not authorize the withholding of any treatment designed to provide comfort, care, or pain relief nor the withholding of water and/or nutrition.

OOH-DNR orders are useful for terminally ill individuals who have reason to believe that their medical condition will result in a situation where a health care provider or emergency medical technician would take steps to initiate unwanted life-sustaining procedures. By executing OOH-DNR orders, these individuals may ensure that their wishes will be followed. The orders should relieve family members from the frustration of insisting that the person has a living will and does not want to endure certain procedures, even as the paramedics are going against those wishes and reviving the person. Additionally, the orders reduce the potential of a party honoring the person's wishes from being held criminally or civilly liable.

For an OOH-DNR order to be most effective, a person must wear an OOH-DNR identification device, as adopted by the Texas Board of Health, around his or her neck or wrist. This device allows medical personnel to immediately and conclusively determine that the person has executed a valid OOH–DNR order and that they are to act in accordance with the person's desires as evidenced by that order.

Sections 166.081-166.101 govern the execution and effect of OOH-DNR orders.

§ 166.081. Definitions

In this subchapter:

(1) Repealed.

(2) "DNR identification device" means an identification device specified by department rule [the board] under Section 166.101 that is worn for the purpose of identifying a person who has executed or issued an out-of-hospital DNR order or on whose behalf an out-of-hospital DNR order has been executed or issued under this subchapter.

(3) "Emergency medical services" has the meaning assigned by Section 773.003.

(4) "Emergency medical services personnel" has the meaning assigned by Section 773.003.

(5) "Health care professionals" means physicians, physician assistants, nurses, and emergency medical services personnel and, unless the context requires otherwise, includes hospital emergency personnel.

(6) "Out-of-hospital DNR order":

(A) means a legally binding out-of-hospital do-not-resuscitate order, in the form specified by department rule [the board] under Section 166.083, prepared and signed by the attending physician of a person, that documents the instructions of a person or the person's legally authorized representative and directs health care professionals acting in an out-of-hospital setting not to initiate or continue the following life-sustaining treatment:

(i) cardiopulmonary resuscitation;

(ii) advanced airway management;

(iii) artificial ventilation;

(iv) defibrillation;

(v) transcutaneous cardiac pacing; and

(vi) other life-sustaining treatment specified by department rule [the board] under Section 166.101(a); and

(B) does not include authorization to withhold medical interventions or therapies considered necessary to provide comfort care or to alleviate pain or to provide water or nutrition.

(7) "Out-of-hospital setting" means a location in which health care professionals are called for assistance, including long-term care facilities, in-patient hospice facilities, private homes, hospital outpatient or emergency departments, physician's offices, and vehicles during transport.

(8) "Proxy" means a person designated and authorized by a directive executed or issued in accordance with Subchapter B to make a treatment decision for another person in the event the other

person becomes incompetent or otherwise mentally or physically incapable of communication.

(9) "Qualified relatives" means those persons authorized to execute or issue an out-of-hospital DNR order on behalf of a person who is incompetent or otherwise mentally or physically incapable of communication under Section 166.088.

(10) "Statewide out-of-hospital DNR protocol" means a set of statewide standardized procedures adopted by the executive commissioner [board] under Section 166.101(a) for withholding cardiopulmonary resuscitation and certain other life-sustaining treatment by health care professionals acting in out-of-hospital settings.

Added by Acts 1995, 74th Leg., ch. 965, § 10, eff. June 16, 1995. Renumbered from § 674.001 and amended by Acts 1999, 76th Leg., ch. 450, § 1.04, eff. Sept. 1, 1999. Amended by Acts 2003, 78th Leg., ch. 1228, § 8, eff. June 20, 2003. Subsecs (2), (6), & (10) amended by Acts 2015, 84th Leg., ch. 1, § 3.0506, eff. Sept. 1, 2015.

Statutes in Context
§ 166.082

Section 166.082 provides the requirements for a OOH-DNR order.

§ 166.082. Out-of-Hospital DNR Order; Directive to Physicians

(a) A competent person may at any time execute a written out-of-hospital DNR order directing health care professionals acting in an out-of-hospital setting to withhold cardiopulmonary resuscitation and certain other life-sustaining treatment designated by department rule [the board].

(b) Except as provided by this subsection, the declarant must sign the out-of-hospital DNR order in the presence of two witnesses who qualify under Section 166.003, at least one of whom must be a witness who qualifies under Section 166.003(2). The witnesses must sign the order. The attending physician of the declarant must sign the order and shall make the fact of the existence of the order and the reasons for execution of the order a part of the declarant's medical record. The declarant, in lieu of signing in the presence of witnesses, may sign the out-of-hospital DNR order and have the signature acknowledged before a notary public.

(c) If the person is incompetent but previously executed or issued a directive to physicians in accordance with Subchapter B, the physician may rely on the directive as the person's instructions to issue an out-of-hospital DNR order and shall place a copy of the directive in the person's medical record. The physician shall sign the order in lieu of the person signing under Subsection (b) and may use a digital or electronic signature authorized under Section 166.011.

(d) If the person is incompetent but previously executed or issued a directive to physicians in

accordance with Subchapter B designating a proxy, the proxy may make any decisions required of the designating person as to an out-of-hospital DNR order and shall sign the order in lieu of the person signing under Subsection (b).

(e) If the person is now incompetent but previously executed or issued a medical power of attorney designating an agent, the agent may make any decisions required of the designating person as to an out-of-hospital DNR order and shall sign the order in lieu of the person signing under Subsection (b).

(f) The executive commissioner [board], on the recommendation of the department, shall by rule adopt procedures for the disposition and maintenance of records of an original out-of-hospital DNR order and any copies of the order.

(g) An out-of-hospital DNR order is effective on its execution.

Added by Acts 1995, 74th Leg., ch. 965, § 10, eff. June 16, 1995. Renumbered from § 674.002 and amended by Acts 1999, 76th Leg., ch. 450, § 1.04, eff. Sept. 1, 1999. Subsecs (b) & (e) amended by Acts 2009, 81st Leg., ch. 461, § 5, eff. Sept. 1, 2009. Subsecs (a) & (f) amended by Acts 2015, 84th Leg., ch. 1, § 3.0507, eff. Sept. 1, 2015.

Statutes in Context
§ 166.083

The standard OOH-DNR form may be found at http://www.dshs.state.tx.us/WorkArea/linkit.aspx?LinkIdentifier=id&ItemID=8589946120.

§ 166.083. Form of Out-of-Hospital DNR Order

(a) A written out-of-hospital DNR order shall be in the standard form specified by department [board] rule as recommended by the department.

(b) The standard form of an out-of-hospital DNR order specified by department rule [the board] must, at a minimum, contain the following:

(1) a distinctive single-page format that readily identifies the document as an out-of-hospital DNR order;

(2) a title that readily identifies the document as an out-of-hospital DNR order;

(3) the printed or typed name of the person;

(4) a statement that the physician signing the document is the attending physician of the person and that the physician is directing health care professionals acting in out-of-hospital settings, including a hospital emergency department, not to initiate or continue certain life-sustaining treatment on behalf of the person, and a listing of those procedures not to be initiated or continued;

(5) a statement that the person understands that the person may revoke the out-of-hospital DNR order at any time by destroying the order and removing the DNR identification device, if any, or by communicating to health care professionals at

the scene the person's desire to revoke the out-of-hospital DNR order;

(6) places for the printed names and signatures of the witnesses or the notary public's acknowledgment and for the printed name and signature of the attending physician of the person and the medical license number of the attending physician;

(7) a separate section for execution of the document by the legal guardian of the person, the person's proxy, an agent of the person having a medical power of attorney, or the attending physician attesting to the issuance of an out-of-hospital DNR order by nonwritten means of communication or acting in accordance with a previously executed or previously issued directive to physicians under Section 166.082(c) that includes the following:

(A) a statement that the legal guardian, the proxy, the agent, the person by nonwritten means of communication, or the physician directs that each listed life-sustaining treatment should not be initiated or continued in behalf of the person; and

(B) places for the printed names and signatures of the witnesses and, as applicable, the legal guardian, proxy, agent, or physician;

(8) a separate section for execution of the document by at least one qualified relative of the person when the person does not have a legal guardian, proxy, or agent having a medical power of attorney and is incompetent or otherwise mentally or physically incapable of communication, including:

(A) a statement that the relative of the person is qualified to make a treatment decision to withhold cardiopulmonary resuscitation and certain other designated life-sustaining treatment under Section 166.088 and, based on the known desires of the person or a determination of the best interest of the person, directs that each listed life-sustaining treatment should not be initiated or continued in behalf of the person; and

(B) places for the printed names and signatures of the witnesses and qualified relative of the person;

(9) a place for entry of the date of execution of the document;

(10) a statement that the document is in effect on the date of its execution and remains in effect until the death of the person or until the document is revoked;

(11) a statement that the document must accompany the person during transport;

(12) a statement regarding the proper disposition of the document or copies of the document, as the executive commissioner [board] determines appropriate; and

(13) a statement at the bottom of the document, with places for the signature of each person executing the document, that the document has been properly completed.

(c) The executive commissioner [board] may, by rule and as recommended by the department, modify the standard form of the out-of-hospital DNR order described by Subsection (b) in order to accomplish the purposes of this subchapter.

(d) A photocopy or other complete facsimile of the original written out-of-hospital DNR order executed under this subchapter may be used for any purpose for which the original written order may be used under this subchapter.

Added by Acts 1995, 74th Leg., ch. 965, § 10, eff. June 16, 1995. Renumbered from § 674.003 and amended by Acts 1999, 76th Leg., ch. 450, § 1.04, eff. Sept. 1, 1999. Subsec. (b) amended by Acts 2009, 81st Leg., ch. 461, § 6, eff. Sept. 1, 2009. Subsecs (a), (b), & (f) amended by Acts 2015, 84th Leg., ch. 1, § 3.0508, eff. Sept. 1, 2015.

Statutes in Context
§ 166.084

Section 166.084 explains how a patient may issue an OOH-DNR order orally or by gesture.

§ 166.084. Issuance of Out-of-Hospital DNR Order by Nonwritten Communication

(a) A competent person who is an adult may issue an out-of-hospital DNR order by nonwritten communication.

(b) A declarant must issue the nonwritten out-of-hospital DNR order in the presence of the attending physician and two witnesses who qualify under Section 166.003, at least one of whom must be a witness who qualifies under Section 166.003(2).

(c) The attending physician and witnesses shall sign the out-of-hospital DNR order in the place of the document provided by Section 166.083(b)(7) and the attending physician shall sign the document in the place required by Section 166.083(b)(13). The physician shall make the fact of the existence of the out-of-hospital DNR order a part of the declarant's medical record and the names of the witnesses shall be entered in the medical record.

(d) An out-of-hospital DNR order issued in the manner provided by this section is valid and shall be honored by responding health care professionals as if executed in the manner provided by Section 166.082.

Added by Acts 1995, 74th Leg., ch. 965, § 10, eff. June 16, 1995. Renumbered from § 674.004 and amended by Acts 1999, 76th Leg., ch. 450, § 1.04, eff. Sept. 1, 1999.

Statutes in Context
§ 166.085

Under § 166.085, certain persons may execute an OOH-DNR order on behalf of a minor who is in a terminal or irreversible condition.

§ 166.085. Execution of Out-of-Hospital DNR Order on Behalf of a Minor

(a) The following persons may execute an out-of-hospital DNR order on behalf of a minor:

(1) the minor's parents;

(2) the minor's legal guardian; or

(3) the minor's managing conservator.

(b) A person listed under Subsection (a) may not execute an out-of-hospital DNR order unless the minor has been diagnosed by a physician as suffering from a terminal or irreversible condition.

Added by Acts 1995, 74th Leg., ch. 965, § 10, eff. June 16, 1995. Renumbered from § 674.005 by Acts 1999, 76th Leg., ch. 450, § 1.04, eff. Sept. 1, 1999. Amended by Acts 2003, 78th Leg., ch. 1228, § 6, eff. June 20, 2003.

Statutes in Context
§ 166.086

A competent person's request for treatment supersedes the instructions to withhold that treatment contained in an OOH-DNR order according to § 166.086.

§ 166.086. Desire of Person Supersedes Out-of-Hospital DNR Order

The desire of a competent person, including a competent minor, supersedes the effect of an out of hospital DNR order executed or issued by or on behalf of the person when the desire is communicated to responding health care professionals as provided by this subchapter.

Added by Acts 1995, 74th Leg., ch. 965, § 10, eff. June 16, 1995. Renumbered from § 674.006 and amended by Acts 1999, 76th Leg., ch. 450, § 1.04, eff. Sept. 1, 1999.

§ 166.087. Procedure When Declarant Is Incompetent or Incapable of Communication

(a) This section applies when a person 18 years of age or older has executed or issued an out-of-hospital DNR order and subsequently becomes incompetent or otherwise mentally or physically incapable of communication.

(b) If the adult person has designated a person to make a treatment decision as authorized by Section 166.032(c), the attending physician and the designated person shall comply with the out-of-hospital DNR order.

(c) If the adult person has not designated a person to make a treatment decision as authorized by Section 166.032(c), the attending physician shall comply with the out-of-hospital DNR order unless the physician believes that the order does not reflect the person's present desire.

Added by Acts 1995, 74th Leg., ch. 965, § 10, eff. June 16, 1995. Renumbered from § 674.007 and amended by Acts 1999, 76th Leg., ch. 450, § 1.04, eff. Sept. 1, 1999.

Statutes in Context
§ 166.088

The circumstances under which a person may create an OOH-DNR order for a person who has not done so are explained in § 166.088.

§ 166.088. Procedure when Person Has Not Executed or Issued Out-of-Hospital DNR Order and Is Incompetent or Incapable of Communication

(a) If an adult person has not executed or issued an out-of-hospital DNR order and is incompetent or otherwise mentally or physically incapable of communication, the attending physician and the person's legal guardian, proxy, or agent having a medical power of attorney may execute an out-of-hospital DNR order on behalf of the person.

(b) If the person does not have a legal guardian, proxy, or agent under a medical power of attorney, the attending physician and at least one qualified relative from a category listed by Section 166.039(b), subject to the priority established under that subsection, may execute an out-of-hospital DNR order in the same manner as a treatment decision made under Section 166.039(b).

(c) A decision to execute an out-of-hospital DNR order made under Subsection (a) or (b) must be based on knowledge of what the person would desire, if known.

(d) An out-of-hospital DNR order executed under Subsection (b) must be made in the presence of at least two witnesses who qualify under Section 166.003, at least one of whom must be a witness who qualifies under Section 166.003(2).

(e) The fact that an adult person has not executed or issued an out-of-hospital DNR order does not create a presumption that the person does not want a treatment decision made to withhold cardiopulmonary resuscitation and certain other designated life-sustaining treatment designated by department rule [the board].

(f) If there is not a qualified relative available to act for the person under Subsection (b), an out-of-hospital DNR order must be concurred in by another physician who is not involved in the treatment of the patient or who is a representative of the ethics or medical committee of the health care facility in which the person is a patient.

(g) A person listed in Section 166.039(b) who wishes to challenge a decision made under this section must apply for temporary guardianship under Chapter 1251, Estates [Section 875, Texas Probate] Code. The court may waive applicable fees in that proceeding.

Added by Acts 1995, 74ᵗʰ Leg., ch. 965, § 10, eff. June 16, 1995. Renumbered from § 674.008 and amended by Acts 1999, 76ᵗʰ Leg., ch. 450, § 1.04. eff. Sept. 1, 1999. Subsecs (e) & (g) amended by Acts 2015, 84ᵗʰ Leg., ch. 1, § 3.0509. eff. Sept. 1, 2015.

Statutes in Context
§ 166.089

Section 166.089 explains how health care professionals should comply with an OOH-DNR order.

---

§ 166.089. Compliance With Out-of-Hospital DNR Order

(a) When responding to a call for assistance, health care professionals shall honor an out-of-hospital DNR order in accordance with the statewide out-of-hospital DNR protocol and, where applicable, locally adopted out-of-hospital DNR protocols not in conflict with the statewide protocol if:

(1) the responding health care professionals discover an executed or issued out-of-hospital DNR order form on their arrival at the scene; and

(2) the responding health care professionals comply with this section.

(b) If the person is wearing a DNR identification device, the responding health care professionals must comply with Section 166.090.

(c) The responding health care professionals must establish the identity of the person as the person who executed or issued the out-of-hospital DNR order or for whom the out-of-hospital DNR order was executed or issued.

(d) The responding health care professionals must determine that the out-of-hospital DNR order form appears to be valid in that it includes:

(1) written responses in the places designated on the form for the names, signatures, and other information required of persons executing or issuing, or witnessing or acknowledging as applicable, the execution or issuance of, the order;

(2) a date in the place designated on the form for the date the order was executed or issued; and

(3) the signature or digital or electronic signature of the declarant or persons executing or issuing the order and the attending physician in the appropriate places designated on the form for indicating that the order form has been properly completed.

(e) If the conditions prescribed by Subsections (a) through (d) are not determined to apply by the responding health care professionals at the scene, the out-of-hospital DNR order may not be honored and life-sustaining procedures otherwise required by law or local emergency medical services protocols shall be initiated or continued. Health care professionals acting in out-of-hospital settings are not required to accept or interpret an out-of-hospital DNR order that does not meet the requirements of this subchapter.

(f) The out-of-hospital DNR order form or a copy of the form, when available, must accompany the person during transport.

(g) A record shall be made and maintained of the circumstances of each emergency medical services response in which an out-of-hospital DNR order or DNR identification device is encountered, in accordance with the statewide out-of-hospital DNR protocol and any applicable local out-of-hospital DNR protocol not in conflict with the statewide protocol.

(h) An out-of-hospital DNR order executed or issued and documented or evidenced in the manner prescribed by this subchapter is valid and shall be honored by responding health care professionals unless the person or persons found at the scene:

(1) identify themselves as the declarant or as the attending physician, legal guardian, qualified relative, or agent of the person having a medical power of attorney who executed or issued the out-of-hospital DNR order on behalf of the person; and

(2) request that cardiopulmonary resuscitation or certain other life-sustaining treatment designated by department rule [the board] be initiated or continued.

(i) If the policies of a health care facility preclude compliance with the out-of-hospital DNR order of a person or an out-of-hospital DNR order issued by an attending physician on behalf of a person who is admitted to or a resident of the facility, or if the facility is unwilling to accept DNR identification devices as evidence of the existence of an out-of-hospital DNR order, that facility shall take all reasonable steps to notify the person or, if the person is incompetent, the person's guardian or the person or persons having authority to make health care treatment decisions on behalf of the person, of the facility's policy and shall take all reasonable steps to effect the transfer of the person to the person's home or to a facility where the provisions of this subchapter can be carried out.

Added by Acts 1995, 74ᵗʰ Leg., ch. 965, § 10, eff. June 16, 1995. Renumbered from § 674.009 and amended by Acts 1999, 76ᵗʰ Leg., ch. 450, § 1.04. eff. Sept. 1, 1999. Subsec. (d) amended by Acts 2009. 81ˢᵗ Leg., ch. 461, § 7, eff. Sept. 1, 2009. Subsec. (h) amended by Acts 2015, 84ᵗʰ Leg., ch. 1, § 3.0510, eff. Sept. 1, 2015.

Statutes in Context
§ 166.090

A DNR identification device as authorized under § 166.090 acts as conclusive evidence that the person has a valid OOH-DNR order.

---

§ 166.090. DNR Identification Device

(a) A person who has a valid out-of-hospital DNR order under this subchapter may wear a DNR identification device around the neck or on the wrist as prescribed by department [board] rule adopted under Section 166.101.

(b) The presence of a DNR identification device on the body of a person is conclusive evidence that the person has executed or issued a valid out-of-hospital DNR order or has a valid out-of-hospital DNR order executed or issued on the person's behalf. Responding health care professionals shall honor the DNR identification device as if a valid out-of-hospital DNR order form executed or issued by the person were found in the possession of the person.

Added by Acts 1995, 74th Leg., ch. 965, § 10, eff. June 16, 1995. Renumbered from § 674.010 and amended by Acts 1999, 76th Leg., ch. 450, § 1.04, eff. Sept. 1, 1999. Subsec. (a) amended by Acts 2015, 84th Leg., ch. 1, § 3.0511, eff. Sept. 1, 2015.

Statutes in Context
§ 166.091

OOH-DNR orders are effective until revoked under § 166.091. They do not expire after a certain period of time or upon a change in the declarant's medical condition.

---

§ 166.091. Duration of Out-of-Hospital DNR Order

An out-of-hospital DNR order is effective until it is revoked as prescribed by Section 166.092.

Added by Acts 1995, 74th Leg., ch. 965, § 10, eff. June 16, 1995. Renumbered from § 674.011 and amended by Acts 1999, 76th Leg., ch. 450, § 1.04, eff. Sept. 1, 1999.

Statutes in Context
§ 166.092

Section 166.092 provides the methods for a declarant to revoke an OOH-DNR order.

---

§ 166.092. Revocation of Out-of-Hospital DNR Order

(a) A declarant may revoke an out-of-hospital DNR order at any time without regard to the declarant's mental state or competency. An order may be revoked by:

(1) the declarant or someone in the declarant's presence and at the declarant's direction destroying the order form and removing the DNR identification device, if any;

(2) a person who identifies himself or herself as the legal guardian, as a qualified relative, or as the agent of the declarant having a medical power of attorney who executed the out-of-hospital DNR order or another person in the person's presence and at the person's direction destroying the order form and removing the DNR identification device, if any;

(3) the declarant communicating the declarant's intent to revoke the order; or

(4) a person who identifies himself or herself as the legal guardian, a qualified relative, or the agent of the declarant having a medical power of attorney who executed the out-of-hospital DNR order orally stating the person's intent to revoke the order.

(b) An oral revocation under Subsection (a)(3) or (a)(4) takes effect only when the declarant or a person who identifies himself or herself as the legal guardian, a qualified relative, or the agent of the declarant having a medical power of attorney who executed the out-of-hospital DNR order communicates the intent to revoke the order to the responding health care professionals or the attending physician at the scene. The responding health care professionals shall record the time, date, and place of the revocation in accordance with the statewide out-of-hospital DNR protocol and rules adopted by the executive commissioner [board] and any applicable local out-of-hospital DNR protocol. The attending physician or the physician's designee shall record in the person's medical record the time, date, and place of the revocation and, if different, the time, date, and place that the physician received notice of the revocation. The attending physician or the physician's designee shall also enter the word "VOID" on each page of the copy of the order in the person's medical record.

(c) Except as otherwise provided by this subchapter, a person is not civilly or criminally liable for failure to act on a revocation made under this section unless the person has actual knowledge of the revocation.

Added by Acts 1995, 74th Leg., ch. 965, § 10, eff. June 16 1995. Renumbered from § 674.012 and amended by Acts 1999, 76th Leg., ch. 450, § 1.04, eff. Sept. 1, 1999. Subsec. (b) amended by Acts 2015, 84th Leg., ch. 1, § 3.0512, eff. Sept. 1, 2015.

§ 166.093. Reexecution of Out-of-Hospital DNR Order

A declarant may at any time reexecute or reissue an out-of-hospital DNR order in accordance with the procedures prescribed by Section 166.082, including reexecution or reissuance after the declarant is diagnosed as having a terminal or irreversible condition.

Added by Acts 1995, 74th Leg., ch. 965, § 10, eff. June 16, 1995. Renumbered from § 674.013 and amended by Acts 1999, 76th Leg., ch. 450, § 1.04, eff. Sept. 1, 1999.

Statutes in Context
§ 166.094 & § 166.095

Health care professionals are protected from liability for following, or not following, an OOH-DNR order if they meet the requirements of §§ 166.094 or 166.095.

---

§ 166.094. Limitation on Liability for Withholding Cardiopulmonary Resuscitation and Certain Other Life-Sustaining Procedures

(a) A health care professional or health care facility or entity that in good faith causes cardiopulmonary resuscitation or certain other life-sustaining treatment designated by department rule [the board] to be withheld from a person in accordance with this subchapter is not civilly liable for that action.

(b) A health care professional or health care facility or entity that in good faith participates in withholding cardiopulmonary resuscitation or certain other life-sustaining treatment designated by department rule [the board] from a person in accordance with this subchapter is not civilly liable for that action.

(c) A health care professional or health care facility or entity that in good faith participates in withholding cardiopulmonary resuscitation or certain other life-sustaining treatment designated by department rule [the board] from a person in accordance with this subchapter is not criminally liable or guilty of unprofessional conduct as a result of that action.

(d) A health care professional or health care facility or entity that in good faith causes or participates in withholding cardiopulmonary resuscitation or certain other life-sustaining treatment designated by department rule [the board] from a person in accordance with this subchapter and rules adopted under this subchapter is not in violation of any other licensing or regulatory laws or rules of this state and is not subject to any disciplinary action or sanction by any licensing or regulatory agency of this state as a result of that action.

Added by Acts 1995, 74th Leg., ch. 965, § 10, eff. June 16, 1995. Renumbered from § 674.016 and amended by Acts 1999, 76th Leg., ch. 450, § 1.04, eff. Sept. 1, 1999. Amended by Acts 2015, 84th Leg., ch. 1, § 3.0513, eff. Sept. 1, 2015.

§ 166.095. Limitation on Liability for Failure to Effectuate Out-of-Hospital DNR Order

(a) A health care professional or health care facility or entity that has no actual knowledge of an out-of-hospital DNR order is not civilly or criminally liable for failing to act in accordance with the order.

(b) A health care professional or health care facility or entity is subject to review and disciplinary action by the appropriate licensing board for failing to effectuate an out-of-hospital DNR order. This subsection does not limit remedies available under other laws of this state.

(c) If an attending physician refuses to execute or comply with an out-of-hospital DNR order, the physician shall inform the person, the legal guardian or qualified relatives of the person, or the agent of the person having a medical power of attorney and, if the person or another authorized to act on behalf of the person so directs, shall make a reasonable effort to transfer the person to another physician who is willing to execute or comply with an out-of-hospital DNR order.

Added by Acts 1995, 74th Leg., ch. 965, § 10, eff. June 16, 1995. Renumbered from § 674.017 and amended by Acts 1999, 76th Leg., ch. 450, § 1.04, eff. Sept. 1, 1999.

Statutes in Context
§ 166.096

A person who complies with an OOH-DNR order is not guilty of the crime of aiding suicide under Penal Code § 22.08.

§ 166.096. Honoring Out-of-Hospital DNR Order Does Not Constitute Offense of Aiding Suicide

A person does not commit an offense under Section 22.08, Penal Code, by withholding cardiopulmonary resuscitation or certain other life-sustaining treatment designated by department rule [the board] from a person in accordance with this subchapter.

Added by Acts 1995, 74th Leg., ch. 965, § 10, eff. June 16, 1995. Renumbered from § 674.018 and amended by Acts 1999, 76th Leg., ch. 450, § 1.04, eff. Sept. 1, 1999. Amended by Acts 2015, 84th Leg., ch. 1, § 3.0514, eff. Sept. 1, 2015.

Statutes in Context
§ 166.097

Section 166.097 describes the criminal offenses which are committed if a person conceals a declarant's OOH-DNR order, forges or falsifies an order, or withholds information about the declarant's revocation of an order.

§ 166.097. Criminal Penalty; Prosecution

(a) A person commits an offense if the person intentionally conceals, cancels, defaces, obliterates, or damages another person's out-of-hospital DNR order or DNR identification device without that person's consent or the consent of the person or persons authorized to execute or issue an out-of-hospital DNR order on behalf of the person under this subchapter. An offense under this subsection is a Class A misdemeanor.

(b) A person is subject to prosecution for criminal homicide under Chapter 19, Penal Code, if the person, with the intent to cause cardiopulmonary resuscitation or certain other life-sustaining treatment designated by department rule [the board] to be withheld from another person contrary to the other person's desires, falsifies or forges an out-of-hospital DNR order or intentionally conceals or withholds personal knowledge of a revocation and thereby directly causes cardiopulmonary resuscitation and certain other life-sustaining treatment designated by department rule [the board] to be withheld from the other person with the result that the other person's death is hastened.

Added by Acts 1995, 74th Leg., ch. 965, § 10, eff. June 16, 1995. Renumbered from § 674.019 and amended by Acts 1999, 76th Leg., ch. 450, § 1.04, eff. Sept. 1, 1999. Amended by Acts 2015, 84th Leg., ch. 1, § 3.0515, eff. Sept. 1, 2015.

Statutes in Context
§ 166.098

Health care providers may not carry out an OOH-DNR order if the declarant is pregnant.

§ 166.098. Pregnant Persons

A person may not withhold cardiopulmonary resuscitation or certain other life-sustaining treatment designated by underline department rule [the board] under this subchapter from a person known by the responding health care professionals to be pregnant.

Added by Acts 1995, 74th Leg., ch. 965, § 10, eff. June 16, 1995. Renumbered from § 674.020 and amended by Acts 1999, 76th Leg., ch. 450, § 1.04, eff. Sept. 1, 1999. Amended by Acts 2015, 84th Leg., ch. 1, § 3.0516, eff. Sept. 1, 2015.

Statutes in Context
§ 166.099

Voluntary euthanasia in which the euthanatizer actually kills the person at that person's request is not allowed under § 166.099.

§ 166.099. Mercy Killing Not Condoned

This subchapter does not condone, authorize, or approve mercy killing or permit an affirmative or deliberate act or omission to end life except to permit the natural process of dying as provided by this subchapter.

Added by Acts 1995, 74th Leg., ch. 965, § 10, eff. June 16, 1995. Renumbered from § 674.021 and amended by Acts 1999, 76th Leg., ch. 450, § 1.04, eff. Sept. 1, 1999.

§ 166.100. Legal Right or Responsibility Not Affected

This subchapter does not impair or supersede any legal right or responsibility a person may have under a constitution, other statute, regulation, or court decision to effect the withholding of cardiopulmonary resuscitation or certain other life-sustaining treatment designated by department rule [the board].

Added by Acts 1995, 74th Leg., ch. 965, § 10, eff. June 16, 1995. Renumbered from § 674.022 and amended by Acts 1999, 76th Leg., ch. 450, § 1.04, eff. Sept. 1, 1999. Amended by Acts 2015, 84th Leg., ch. 1, § 3.0517, eff. Sept. 1, 2015.

§ 166.101. Duties of Department and Executive Commissioner [Board]

(a) The executive commissioner [board] shall, on the recommendation of the department, adopt all reasonable and necessary rules to carry out the purposes of this subchapter, including rules:

(1) adopting a statewide out-of-hospital DNR order protocol that sets out standard procedures for the withholding of cardiopulmonary resuscitation

and certain other life-sustaining treatment by health care professionals acting in out-of-hospital settings;

(2) designating life-sustaining treatment that may be included in an out-of-hospital DNR order, including all procedures listed in Sections 166.081(6)(A)(i) through (v); and

(3) governing recordkeeping in circumstances in which an out-of-hospital DNR order or DNR identification device is encountered by responding health care professionals.

(b) The rules adopted [by the board] under Subsection (a) are not effective until approved by the Texas Medical [State] Board [of Medical Examiners].

(c) Local emergency medical services authorities may adopt local out-of-hospital DNR order protocols if the local protocols do not conflict with the statewide out-of-hospital DNR order protocol adopted by the executive commissioner [board].

(d) The executive commissioner [board] by rule shall specify a distinctive standard design for a necklace and a bracelet DNR identification device that signifies, when worn by a person, that the possessor has executed or issued a valid out-of-hospital DNR order under this subchapter or is a person for whom a valid out-of-hospital DNR order has been executed or issued.

(e) The department shall report to the executive commissioner [board] from time to time regarding issues identified in emergency medical services responses in which an out-of-hospital DNR order or DNR identification device is encountered. The report may contain recommendations to the executive commissioner [board] for necessary modifications to the form of the standard out-of-hospital DNR order or the designated life-sustaining procedures listed in the standard out-of-hospital DNR order, the statewide out-of-hospital DNR order protocol, or the DNR identification devices.

Added by Acts 1995, 74th Leg., ch. 965, § 10, eff. June 16, 1995. Renumbered from § 674.023 and amended by Acts 1999, 76th Leg., ch. 450, § 1.04, eff. Sept. 1, 1999. Amended by Acts 2015, 84th Leg., ch. 1, § 3.0517, eff. Sept. 1, 2015.

Statutes in Context
§ 166.102

The 2003 Texas Legislature expanded the types of individuals who may honor a physician's do-not-resuscitate order in an out-of-hospital setting to include (1) licensed nurses and (2) anyone providing health care services in an out-of-hospital setting. § 166.102. Emergency medical services personnel responding to a call for assistance, however, may honor only a properly executed or issued out-of-hospital DNR order or a prescribed DNR identification device.

§ 166.102. Physician's DNR Order May Be Honored by Health Care Personnel Other Than Emergency Medical Services Personnel

(a) Except as provided by Subsection (b), a licensed nurse or person providing health care services in an out-of-hospital setting may honor a physician's do-not-resuscitate order.

(b) When responding to a call for assistance, emergency medical services personnel:

(1) shall honor only a properly executed or issued out-of-hospital DNR order or prescribed DNR identification device in accordance with this subchapter; and

(2) have no duty to review, examine, interpret, or honor a person's other written directive, including a written directive in the form prescribed by Section 166.033.

Added by Acts 2003, 78ᵗʰ Leg., ch. 1228, § 7, eff. June 20, 2003. Amended by Acts 2011, 82ⁿᵈ Leg., ch. 710, § 1, eff. June 17, 2011.

Subchapter D. Medical Power of Attorney

Statutes in Context
§§ 166.151–166.166

Traditionally, a person could not use a power of attorney to delegate the authority to make health care decisions. These decisions were considered too intimate to delegate. In addition, the existence of the patient's informed consent to any medical treatment was problematic because the agent, not the patient, would be making the decision. However, there are persuasive arguments in favor of this type of delegation. Medical decisions may then be made by a person specified by the patient. This person is likely to have a better understanding of how the patient would like to be treated than a guardian, doctor, or family member.

In 1982, the National Conference of Commissioners on Uniform State Laws approved the Model Health-Care Consent Act which included a provision permitting a person to transfer health care decision authority to a health care representative. The next year, California became the first state to address this issue when it enacted legislation approving a durable power of attorney for health care.

In 1989, Texas enacted extensive legislation authorizing a durable power of attorney for health care. The 1999 Legislature renamed this instrument as the medical power of attorney and recodified the enabling legislation in a comprehensive Advance Directives Act which also includes living wills and out-of-hospital do-not-resuscitate orders.

Sections 166.151-166.166 govern medical powers of attorney.

§ 166.151. Definitions

In this subchapter:

(1) "Adult" means a person 18 years of age or older or a person under 18 years of age who has had the disabilities of minority removed.

(2) "Agent" means an adult to whom authority to make health care decisions is delegated under a medical power of attorney.

(3) "Health care provider" means an individual or facility licensed, certified, or otherwise authorized to administer health care, for profit or otherwise, in the ordinary course of business or professional practice and includes a physician.

(4) "Principal" means an adult who has executed a medical power of attorney.

(5) "Residential care provider" means an individual or facility licensed, certified, or otherwise authorized to operate, for profit or otherwise, a residential care home.

Renumbered from Civ. Prac. & Rem. Code § 135.001 and amended by Acts 1999, 76ᵗʰ Leg., ch. 450, § 1.05, eff. Sept. 1, 1999.

Statutes in Context
§ 166.152

Section 166.152 explains the scope of the agent's authority to make health care decisions for the principal. Note that the agent may not make certain decisions such as consenting to an abortion or to psychosurgery.

§ 166.152. Scope and Duration of Authority

(a) Subject to this subchapter or any express limitation on the authority of the agent contained in the medical power of attorney, the agent may make any health care decision on the principal's behalf that the principal could make if the principal were competent.

(b) An agent may exercise authority only if the principal's attending physician certifies in writing and files the certification in the principal's medical record that, based on the attending physician's reasonable medical judgment, the principal is incompetent.

(c) Notwithstanding any other provisions of this subchapter, treatment may not be given to or withheld from the principal if the principal objects regardless of whether, at the time of the objection:

(1) a medical power of attorney is in effect; or

(2) the principal is competent.

(d) The principal's attending physician shall make reasonable efforts to inform the principal of any proposed treatment or of any proposal to withdraw or withhold treatment before implementing an agent's advance directive.

(e) After consultation with the attending physician and other health care providers, the agent shall make a health care decision:

(1) according to the agent's knowledge of the principal's wishes, including the principal's religious and moral beliefs; or

(2) if the agent does not know the principal's wishes, according to the agent's assessment of the principal's best interests.

(f) Notwithstanding any other provision of this subchapter, an agent may not consent to:

(1) voluntary inpatient mental health services;

(2) convulsive treatment;

(3) psychosurgery;

(4) abortion; or

(5) neglect of the principal through the omission of care primarily intended to provide for the comfort of the principal.

(g) The power of attorney is effective indefinitely on execution as provided by this subchapter and delivery of the document to the agent, unless it is revoked as provided by this subchapter or the principal becomes competent. If the medical power of attorney includes an expiration date and on that date the principal is incompetent, the power of attorney continues to be effective until the principal becomes competent unless it is revoked as provided by this subchapter.

Renumbered from Civ. Prac. & Rem. Code § 135.002 and amended by Acts 1999, 76th Leg., ch. 450, § 1.05, eff. Sept. 1, 1999.

Statutes in Context
§ 166.153

Certain individuals as enumerated in § 166.153 may not serve as an agent.

§ 166.153. Persons Who May Not Exercise Authority of Agent

A person may not exercise the authority of an agent while the person serves as:

(1) the principal's health care provider;

(2) an employee of the principal's health care provider unless the person is a relative of the principal;

(3) the principal's residential care provider; or

(4) an employee of the principal's residential care provider unless the person is a relative of the principal.

Renumbered from Civ. Prac. & Rem. Code § 135.003 by Acts 1999, 76th Leg., ch. 450, § 1.05, eff. Sept. 1, 1999.

Statutes in Context
§ 166.154

Section 166.154 explains the formalities required for a valid medical power of attorney.

§ 166.154. Execution

(a) Except as provided by Subsection (b), the medical power of attorney must be signed by the principal in the presence of two witnesses who qualify under Section 166.003, at least one of whom must be a witness who qualifies under Section 166.003(2). The witnesses must sign the document.

(b) The principal, in lieu of signing in the presence of the witnesses, may sign the medical power of attorney and have the signature acknowledged before a notary public.

(c) If the principal is physically unable to sign, another person may sign the medical power of attorney with the principal's name in the principal's presence and at the principal's express direction. The person may use a digital or electronic signature authorized under Section 166.011.

Renumbered from Civ. Prac. & Rem. Code § 135.004 and amended by Acts 1999, 76th Leg., ch. 450, § 1.05, eff. Sept. 1, 1999. Amended by Acts 2009, 81st Leg., ch. 461, § 8, eff. Sept. 1, 2009.

Statutes in Context
§ 166.155

The principal may revoke a medical power of attorney by following the procedures set forth in § 166.155.

§ 166.155. Revocation

(a) A medical power of attorney is revoked by:

(1) oral or written notification at any time by the principal to the agent or a licensed or certified health or residential care provider or by any other act evidencing a specific intent to revoke the power, without regard to whether the principal is competent or the principal's mental state;

(2) execution by the principal of a subsequent medical power of attorney; or

(3) the divorce of the principal and spouse, if the spouse is the principal's agent, unless the medical power of attorney provides otherwise.

(b) A principal's licensed or certified health or residential care provider who is informed of or provided with a revocation of a medical power of attorney shall immediately record the revocation in the principal's medical record and give notice of the revocation to the agent and any known health and residential care providers currently responsible for the principal's care.

Renumbered from Civ. Prac. & Rem. Code § 135.005 and amended by Acts 1999, 76th Leg., ch. 450, § 1.05, eff. Sept. 1, 1999.

Statutes in Context
§ 166.156

The division of authority between the principal's agent and a court-appointed guardian is detailed in § 166.156.

§ 166.156. Appointment of Guardian

(a) On motion filed in connection with a petition for appointment of a guardian or, if a guardian has been appointed, on petition of the guardian, a probate court shall determine whether to suspend or revoke the authority of the agent.

(b) The court shall consider the preferences of the principal as expressed in the medical power of attorney.

(c) During the pendency of the court's determination under Subsection (a), the guardian has the sole authority to make any health care decisions unless the court orders otherwise. If a guardian has not been appointed, the agent has the authority to make any health care decisions unless the court orders otherwise.

(d) A person, including any attending physician or health or residential care provider, who does not have actual knowledge of the appointment of a guardian or an order of the court granting authority to someone other than the agent to make health care decisions is not subject to criminal or civil liability and has not engaged in unprofessional conduct for implementing an agent's health care decision.

Renumbered from Civ. Prac. & Rem. Code § 135.006 and amended by Acts 1999, 76th Leg., ch. 450, § 1.05, eff. Sept. 1, 1999.

Statutes in Context
§ 166.157

Section 166.157 gives the agent broad access to the patient's medical information so the agent may make informed health care decisions for the principal.

§ 166.157. Disclosure of Medical Information

Subject to any limitations in the medical power of attorney, an agent may, for the purpose of making a health care decision:

(1) request, review, and receive any information, oral or written, regarding the principal's physical or mental health, including medical and hospital records;

(2) execute a release or other document required to obtain the information; and

(3) consent to the disclosure of the information.

Renumbered from Civ. Prac. & Rem. Code § 135.007 and amended by Acts 1999, 76th Leg., ch. 450, § 1.05, eff. Sept. 1, 1999.

Statutes in Context
§ 166.158

The health care provider's duty to follow the agent's directions is explained in § 166.158.

§ 166.158. Duty of Health or Residential Care Provider

(a) A principal's health or residential care provider and an employee of the provider who knows of the existence of the principal's medical power of attorney shall follow a directive of the principal's agent to the extent it is consistent with the desires of the principal, this subchapter, and the medical power of attorney.

(b) The attending physician does not have a duty to verify that the agent's directive is consistent with the principal's wishes or religious or moral beliefs.

(c) A principal's health or residential care provider who finds it impossible to follow a directive by the agent because of a conflict with this subchapter or the medical power of attorney shall inform the agent as soon as is reasonably possible. The agent may select another attending physician. The procedures established under Sections 166.045 and 166.046 apply if the agent's directive concerns providing, withholding, or withdrawing life-sustaining treatment.

(d) This subchapter may not be construed to require a health or residential care provider who is not a physician to act in a manner contrary to a physician's order.

Renumbered from Civ. Prac. & Rem. Code § 135.008 and amended by Acts 1999, 76th Leg., ch. 450, § 1.05, eff. Sept. 1, 1999.

Statutes in Context
§ 166.159

Insurance companies may not require a person to sign a medical power of attorney as a condition of obtaining insurance and may not base insurance rates on whether the insured has signed a medical power of attorney under § 166.159.

§ 166.159. Discrimination Relating to Execution of Medical Power of Attorney

A health or residential care provider, health care service plan, insurer issuing disability insurance, self insured employee benefit plan, or nonprofit hospital service plan may not:

(1) charge a person a different rate solely because the person has executed a medical power of attorney;

(2) require a person to execute a medical power of attorney before:

(A) admitting the person to a hospital, nursing home, or residential care home;

(B) insuring the person; or

(C) allowing the person to receive health or residential care; or

(3) refuse health or residential care to a person solely because the person has executed a medical power of attorney.

Renumbered from Civ. Prac. & Rem. Code § 135.009 and amended by Acts 1999, 76th Leg., ch. 450, § 1.05, eff. Sept. 1, 1999.

Statutes in Context
§ 166.160

An agent is protected from civil and criminal liability if the agent complies with § 166.160.

§ 166.160. Limitation on Liability

(a) An agent is not subject to criminal or civil liability for a health care decision if the decision is made in good faith under the terms of the medical power of attorney and the provisions of this subchapter.

(b) An attending physician, health or residential care provider, or a person acting as an agent for or under the physician's or provider's control is not subject to criminal or civil liability and has not engaged in unprofessional conduct for an act or omission if the act or omission:

(1) is done in good faith under the terms of the medical power of attorney, the directives of the agent, and the provisions of this subchapter; and

(2) does not constitute a failure to exercise reasonable care in the provision of health care services.

(c) The standard of care that the attending physician, health or residential care provider, or person acting as an agent for or under the physician's or provider's control shall exercise under Subsection (b) is that degree of care that an attending physician, health or residential care provider, or person acting as an agent for or under the physician's or provider's control, as applicable, of ordinary prudence and skill would have exercised under the same or similar circumstances in the same or similar community.

(d) An attending physician, health or residential care provider, or person acting as an agent for or under the physician's or provider's control has not engaged in unprofessional conduct for:

(1) failure to act as required by the directive of an agent or a medical power of attorney if the physician, provider, or person was not provided with a copy of the medical power of attorney or had no knowledge of a directive; or

(2) acting as required by an agent's directive if the medical power of attorney has expired or been revoked but the physician, provider, or person does not have knowledge of the expiration or revocation.

Renumbered from Civ. Prac. & Rem. Code § 135.010 and amended by Acts 1999, 76th Leg., ch. 450, § 1.05, eff. Sept. 1, 1999.

Statutes in Context
§ 166.161

The fact that an agent consents to medical treatment has no effect on the identity of the persons financially liable for the costs associated with that care under § 166.161.

§ 166.161. Liability for Health Care Costs

Liability for the cost of health care provided as a result of the agent's decision is the same as if the health care were provided as a result of the principal's decision.

Renumbered from Civ. Prac. & Rem. Code § 135.011 by Acts 1999, 76th Leg., ch. 450, § 1.05, eff. Sept. 1, 1999.

Statutes in Context
§ 166.162

The principal must sign a statement indicating that the principal has received a disclosure statement and has understood its contents. The principal must sign this statement before signing the medical power of attorney. See § 166.162.

§ 166.162. Disclosure Statement

A medical power of attorney is not effective unless the principal, before executing the medical power of attorney, signs a statement that the principal has received a disclosure statement and has read and understood its contents.

Renumbered from Civ. Prac. & Rem. Code § 135.014 and amended by Acts 1999, 76th Leg., ch. 450, § 1.05, eff. Sept. 1, 1999.

Statutes in Context
§ 166.163

Section 166.163 provides the form of the disclosure statement which the principal must receive before signing the medical power of attorney. Although not provided on the form, it is common practice to add a signature line at the end along with a statement that the principal has read and understood its contents. The principal should then sign this statement before signing the medical power of attorney.

§ 166.163. Form of Disclosure Statement

The disclosure statement must be in substantially the following form:

INFORMATION CONCERNING THE MEDICAL POWER OF ATTORNEY

THIS IS AN IMPORTANT LEGAL DOCUMENT. BEFORE SIGNING THIS DOCUMENT, YOU SHOULD KNOW THESE IMPORTANT FACTS:

Except to the extent you state otherwise, this document gives the person you name as your agent the authority to make any and all health care decisions for you in accordance with your wishes, including your religious and moral beliefs, when you are no longer capable of making them yourself. Because "health care" means any treatment, service, or procedure to maintain, diagnose, or treat your physical or mental condition, your agent has the power to make a broad range of health care decisions for you. Your agent may consent, refuse to consent, or withdraw consent to medical treatment and may make decisions about withdrawing or withholding life-sustaining treatment. Your agent may not consent to voluntary inpatient mental health services, convulsive treatment, psychosurgery, or abortion. A physician must comply with your agent's instructions or allow you to be transferred to another physician.

Your agent's authority begins when your doctor certifies that you lack the competence to make health care decisions.

Your agent is obligated to follow your instructions when making decisions on your behalf. Unless you state otherwise, your agent has the same authority to make decisions about your health care as you would have had.

It is important that you discuss this document with your physician or other health care provider before you sign it to make sure that you understand the nature and range of decisions that may be made on your behalf. If you do not have a physician, you should talk with someone else who is knowledgeable about these issues and can answer your questions. You do not need a lawyer's assistance to complete this document, but if there is anything in this document that you do not understand, you should ask a lawyer to explain it to you.

The person you appoint as agent should be someone you know and trust. The person must be 18 years of age or older or a person under 18 years of age who has had the disabilities of minority removed. If you appoint your health or residential care provider (e.g., your physician or an employee of a home health agency, hospital, nursing home, or residential care home, other than a relative), that person has to choose between acting as your agent or as your health or residential care provider; the law does not permit a person to do both at the same time.

You should inform the person you appoint that you want the person to be your health care agent. You should discuss this document with your agent and your physician and give each a signed copy. You should indicate on the document itself the people and institutions who have signed copies. Your agent is not liable for health care decisions made in good faith on your behalf.

Even after you have signed this document, you have the right to make health care decisions for yourself as long as you are able to do so and treatment cannot be given to you or stopped over your objection. You have

the right to revoke the authority granted to your agent by informing your agent or your health or residential care provider orally or in writing or by your execution of a subsequent medical power of attorney. Unless you state otherwise, your appointment of a spouse dissolves on divorce.

This document may not be changed or modified. If you want to make changes in the document, you must make an entirely new one.

You may wish to designate an alternate agent in the event that your agent is unwilling, unable, or ineligible to act as your agent. Any alternate agent you designate has the same authority to make health care decisions for you.

THIS POWER OF ATTORNEY IS NOT VALID UNLESS:

(1) YOU SIGN IT AND HAVE YOUR SIGNATURE ACKNOWLEDGED BEFORE A NOTARY PUBLIC; OR

(2) YOU SIGN IT IN THE PRESENCE OF TWO COMPETENT ADULT WITNESSES.

THE FOLLOWING PERSONS MAY NOT ACT AS ONE OF THE WITNESSES:

(1) the person you have designated as your agent;

(2) a person related to you by blood or marriage;

(3) a person entitled to any part of your estate after your death under a will or codicil executed by you or by operation of law;

(4) your attending physician;

(5) an employee of your attending physician;

(6) an employee of a health care facility in which you are a patient if the employee is providing direct patient care to you or is an officer, director, partner, or business office employee of the health care facility or of any parent organization of the health care facility; or

(7) a person who, at the time this power of attorney is executed, has a claim against any part of your estate after your death.

Renumbered from Civ. Prac. & Rem. Code § 135.016 and amended by Acts 1999, 76th Leg., ch. 450, § 1.05, eff. Sept. 1, 1999. Amended by Acts 2013, 83rd Leg., ch. 134, § 1, eff. Jan. 1, 2014.

Statutes in Context
§ 166.164

Section 166.164 contains the form which the principal completes and signs to appoint an agent to make health care decisions. Note that the principal may provide individualized instructions in the section labeled "limitations of the decision-making authority of my agent." The power requires either (1) two witnesses or (2) notarization.

---

§ 166.164. Form of Medical Power of Attorney

The medical power of attorney must be in substantially the following form:
MEDICAL POWER OF ATTORNEY DESIGNATION OF HEALTH CARE AGENT.

I, _____ (insert your name) appoint:

Name:_____

Address:_____

Phone_____

as my agent to make any and all health care decisions for me, except to the extent I state otherwise in this document. This medical power of attorney takes effect if I become unable to make my own health care decisions and this fact is certified in writing by my physician.

LIMITATIONS ON THE DECISION-MAKING AUTHORITY OF MY AGENT ARE AS FOLLOWS:_____

DESIGNATION OF ALTERNATE AGENT.

(You are not required to designate an alternate agent but you may do so. An alternate agent may make the same health care decisions as the designated agent if the designated agent is unable or unwilling to act as your agent. If the agent designated is your spouse, the designation is automatically revoked by law if your marriage is dissolved.)

If the person designated as my agent is unable or unwilling to make health care decisions for me, I designate the following persons to serve as my agent to make health care decisions for me as authorized by this document, who serve in the following order:

A. First Alternate Agent

Name:_____

Address:_____

Phone_____

B. Second Alternate Agent

Name:_____

Address:_____

Phone_____

The original of this document is kept at:

_____

_____

The following individuals or institutions have signed copies:

Name:_____

Address:_____

Name:_____

Address:_____

DURATION.

I understand that this power of attorney exists indefinitely from the date I execute this document unless I establish a shorter time or revoke the power of attorney. If I am unable to make health care decisions for myself when this power of attorney expires, the authority I have granted my agent continues to exist until the time I become able to make health care decisions for myself.

(IF APPLICABLE) This power of attorney ends on the following date:_____

PRIOR DESIGNATIONS REVOKED.

I revoke any prior medical power of attorney.

ACKNOWLEDGMENT OF DISCLOSURE STATEMENT.

I have been provided with a disclosure statement explaining the effect of this document. I have read and understand that information contained in the disclosure statement.

(YOU MUST DATE AND SIGN THIS POWER OF ATTORNEY. YOU MAY SIGN IT AND HAVE YOUR SIGNATURE ACKNOWLEDGED BEFORE A NOTARY PUBLIC OR YOU MAY SIGN IT IN THE PRESENCE OF TWO COMPETENT ADULT WITNESSES.)

SIGNATURE ACKNOWLEDGED BEFORE NOTARY

I sign my name to this medical power of attorney on _____ day of _____ (month, year) at

_____

(City and State)

_____

(Signature)

_____

(Print Name)

State of Texas

County of_____

This instrument was acknowledged before me on _____ (date) by _____ (name of person acknowledging).

_____

NOTARY PUBLIC, State of Texas

Notary's printed name:

_____

My commission expires:

_____

OR

SIGNATURE IN PRESENCE OF TWO COMPETENT ADULT WITNESSES

I sign my name to this medical power of attorney on _____ day of _____ (month, year) at

_____

(City and State)

_____

(Signature)

_____

(Print Name)

STATEMENT OF FIRST WITNESS.

I am not the person appointed as agent by this document. I am not related to the principal by blood or marriage. I would not be entitled to any portion of the principal's estate on the principal's death. I am not the attending physician of the principal or an employee of the attending physician. I have no claim against any portion of the principal's estate on the principal's death. Furthermore, if I am an employee of a health care facility in which the principal is a patient, I am not involved in providing direct patient care to the principal and am not an officer, director, partner, or business office employee of the health care facility or of any parent organization of the health care facility.

Signature:_____

Print Name:_____
Date:_____
Address:_____
_____

SIGNATURE OF SECOND WITNESS.
Signature:_____
Print Name:_____
Date:_____
Address:_____
_____

Renumbered from Civ. Prac. & Rem. Code § 135.016 and amended by Acts 1999, 76th Leg., ch. 450, § 1.05, eff. Sept. 1, 1999. Amended by Acts 2013, 83rd Leg., ch. 134, § 1, eff. Jan. 1, 2014.

§ 166.165. Civil Action

(a) A person who is a near relative of the principal or a responsible adult who is directly interested in the principal, including a guardian, social worker, physician, or clergyman, may bring an action to request that the medical power of attorney be revoked because the principal, at the time the medical power of attorney was signed:

(1) was not competent; or

(2) was under duress, fraud, or undue influence.

(a-1) In a county in which there is no statutory probate court, an action under this section shall be brought in the district court. In a county in which there is a statutory probate court, the statutory probate court and the district court have concurrent jurisdiction over an action brought under this section.

(b) The action may be brought in the county of the principal's residence or the residence of the person bringing the action.

(c) During the pendency of the action, the authority of the agent to make health care decisions continues in effect unless the court orders otherwise.

Renumbered from Civ. Prac. & Rem. Code § 135.017 and amended by Acts 1999, 76th Leg., ch. 450, § 1.05, eff. Sept. 1, 1999. Subsecs. (a) & (c) amended by Acts 2013, 83rd Leg., ch. 134, § 2, eff. Sept. 1, 2013.

§ 166.166. Other Rights or Responsibilities Not Affected

This subchapter does not limit or impair any legal right or responsibility that any person, including a physician or health or residential care provider, may have to make or implement health care decisions on behalf of a person, provided that if an attending physician or health care facility is unwilling to honor a patient's advance directive or a treatment decision to provide life-sustaining treatment, life-sustaining treatment is required to be provided the patient, but only until a reasonable opportunity has been afforded for transfer of the patient to another physician or health care facility willing to comply with the advance directive or treatment decision.

Renumbered from Civ. Prac. & Rem. Code § 135.018 and amended by Acts 1999, 76th Leg., ch. 450, § 1.05,

eff. Sept. 1, 1999.

Title 4. Health Facilities

Subtitle F. Powers and Duties of Hospitals

Chapter 313. Consent to Medical Treatment Act

Statutes in Context
Chapter 313

The Texas Legislature enacted the Consent to Medical Treatment Act in 1993. This Act empowers a surrogate to make certain decisions regarding an adult's medical treatment if that person is (1) in a hospital or residing in a nursing home; (2) is comatose, incapacitated, or otherwise mentally or physically incapable of communication; and (3) has not made other arrangements for medical treatment decisions.

The Act is designed to fill the gap in the previous health care scheme which left many patients without someone with the authority to make medical treatment decisions. Thus, the Act does not apply to the following situations: (1) a decision to withhold or withdraw life-sustaining treatment from a qualified terminal patient who had executed a directive to physicians, (2) an agent's decision under a medical power of attorney, (3) a consent to medical treatment of minors under the Family Code, (4) a consent for emergency care, (5) a hospital patient transfer, and (6) a guardian's decision if the guardian has authority to make medical treatment decisions.

§ 313.001. Short Title

This chapter may be cited as the Consent to Medical Treatment Act.

Added by Acts 1993, 73rd Leg., ch. 407, § 1, eff. Sept. 1, 1993.

§ 313.002. Definitions

In this chapter:

(1) "Adult" means a person 18 years of age or older or a person under 18 years of age who has had the disabilities of minority removed.

(2) "Attending physician" means the physician with primary responsibility for a patient's treatment and care.

(3) "Decision-making capacity" means the ability to understand and appreciate the nature and consequences of a decision regarding medical treatment and the ability to reach an informed decision in the matter.

(3-a) Home and community support services agency" means a facility licensed under Chapter 142.

(4) "Hospital" means a facility licensed under Chapter 241.

(5) "Incapacitated" means lacking the ability, based on reasonable medical judgment, to understand and appreciate the nature and consequences of a treatment decision, including the significant benefits and harms of and reasonable alternatives to any proposed treatment decision.

(6) "Medical treatment" means a health care treatment, service, or procedure designed to maintain or treat a patient's physical or mental condition, as well as preventative care.

(7) "Nursing home" means a facility licensed under Chapter 242.

(8) "Patient" means a person who:

(A) is admitted to a hospital;

(B) is residing in a nursing home; or

(C) is receiving services from a home and community support services agency; or

(D) is an inmate of a county or municipal jail.

(9) "Physician" means:

(A) a physician licensed by the Texas State Board of Medical Examiners; or

(B) a physician with proper credentials who holds a commission in a branch of the armed services of the United States and who is serving on active duty in this state.

(10) "Surrogate decision-maker" means an individual with decision-making capacity who is identified as the person who has authority to consent to medical treatment on behalf of an incapacitated patient in need of medical treatment.

Added by Acts 1993, 73rd Leg., ch. 407, § 1, eff. Sept. 1, 1993. Subsec. (3-a) added by and subsec. (8) amended by Acts 2007, 80th Leg., ch. 1271, § 1, eff. Sept. 1, 2007. Amended by Acts 2011, 82nd Leg., ch. 253, § 1, eff. Sept. 1, 2011.

Statutes in Context
§ 313.003

A surrogate may not make a health care decision if one of the situations enumerated in § 313.003 is true such as the existence of a health care agent.

§ 313.003. Exceptions and Application

(a) This chapter does not apply to:

(1) a decision to withhold or withdraw life-sustaining treatment from qualified terminal or irreversible patients under Subchapter B, Chapter 166;

(2) a health care decision made under a medical power of attorney under Subchapter D, Chapter 166, or under Chapter XII, Texas Probate Code;

(3) consent to medical treatment of minors under Chapter 32, Family Code;

(4) consent for emergency care under Chapter 773;

(5) hospital patient transfers under Chapter 241; or

(6) a patient's legal guardian who has the authority to make a decision regarding the patient's medical treatment.

(b) This chapter does not authorize a decision to withhold or withdraw life-sustaining treatment.

Added by Acts 1993, 73rd Leg., ch. 407, § 1, eff. Sept. 1, 1993. Amended by Acts 1999, 76th Leg., ch. 450, § 2.01, eff. Sept. 1, 1999.

Statutes in Context
§ 313.004

Section 313.004 provides a priority order of individuals who are authorized to become a surrogate to make health care decisions.

§ 313.004. Consent for Medical Treatment

(a) If an adult patient of a home and community support services agency or in a hospital or nursing home, or an adult inmate of a county or municipal jail, is comatose, incapacitated, or otherwise mentally or physically incapable of communication, an adult surrogate from the following list, in order of priority, who has decision-making capacity, is available after a reasonably diligent inquiry, and is willing to consent to medical treatment on behalf of the patient may consent to medical treatment on behalf of the patient:

(1) the patient's spouse;

(2) an adult child of the patient who has the waiver and consent of all other qualified adult children of the patient to act as the sole decision-maker;

(3) a majority of the patient's reasonably available adult children;

(4) the patient's parents; or

(5) the individual clearly identified to act for the patient by the patient before the patient became incapacitated, the patient's nearest living relative, or a member of the clergy.

(b) Any dispute as to the right of a party to act as a surrogate decision-maker may be resolved only by a court of record having jurisdiction under Chapter V, Texas Probate Code.[1]

(c) Any medical treatment consented to under Subsection (a) must be based on knowledge of what the patient would desire, if known.

(d) Notwithstanding any other provision of this chapter, a surrogate decision-maker may not consent to:

(1) voluntary inpatient mental health services;

(2) electro-convulsive treatment; or

---

[1] V.A.T.S. Probate Code, § 72 et seq.

(3) the appointment of another surrogate decision-maker.

(e) Notwithstanding any other provision of this chapter, if the patient is an adult inmate of a county or municipal jail, a surrogate decision-maker may not also consent to:

(1) psychotropic medication;

(2) involuntary inpatient mental health services; or

(3) psychiatric services calculated to restore competency to stand trial.

(f) A person who is an available adult surrogate, as described by Subsection (a), may consent to medical treatment on behalf of a patient who is an adult inmate of a county or municipal jail only for a period that expires on the earlier of the 120th day after the date the person agrees to act as an adult surrogate for the patient or the date the inmate is released from jail. At the conclusion of the period, a successor surrogate may not be appointed and only the patient or the patient's appointed guardian of the person, if the patient is a ward under Chapter XIII, Texas Probate Code, may consent to medical treatment.

Added by Acts 1993, 73rd Leg., ch. 407, § 1, eff. Sept. 1, 1993. Subsec. (a) amended by Acts 2007, 80th Leg., ch. 1271, § 21, eff. Sept. 1, 2007. Amended by Acts 2011, 82nd Leg., ch. 253, § 2, eff. Sept. 1, 2011.

Statutes in Context
§ 313.005

A surrogate may make a health care decision only under the circumstances listed in § 313.005.

§ 313.005. Prerequisites for Consent

(a) If an adult patient of a home and community support services agency or in a hospital or nursing home, or an adult inmate of a county or municipal jail, is comatose, incapacitated, or otherwise mentally or physically incapable of communication and, according to reasonable medical judgment, is in need of medical treatment, the attending physician shall describe the:

(1) patient's comatose state, incapacity, or other mental or physical inability to communicate in the patient's medical record; and

(2) proposed medical treatment in the patient's medical record.

(b) The attending physician shall make a reasonably diligent effort to contact or cause to be contacted the persons eligible to serve as surrogate decision-makers. Efforts to contact those persons shall be recorded in detail in the patient's medical record.

(c) If a surrogate decision-maker consents to medical treatment on behalf of the patient, the attending physician shall record the date and time of the consent and sign the patient's medical record. The surrogate decision-maker shall countersign the patient's medical record or execute an informed consent form.

(d) A surrogate decision-maker's consent to medical treatment that is not made in person shall be reduced to writing in the patient's medical record, signed by the home and community support services agency, hospital, or nursing home staff member receiving the consent, and countersigned in the patient's medical record or on an informed consent form by the surrogate decision-maker as soon as possible.

Added by Acts 1993, 73rd Leg., ch. 407, § 1, eff. Sept. 1, 1993. § Subsecs. (a) & (d) amended by Acts 2007, 80th Leg., ch. 1271, § 3, eff. Sept. 1, 2007. Amended by Acts 2011, 82nd Leg., ch. 253, § 3, eff. Sept. 1, 2011.

Statutes in Context
§ 313.006

The fact that a surrogate consents to medical treatment has no effect on the identity of the persons financially liable for the costs associated with that care under § 313.006.

§ 313.006. Liability for Medical Treatment Costs

Liability for the cost of medical treatment provided as a result of consent to medical treatment by a surrogate decision-maker is the same as the liability for that cost if the medical treatment were provided as a result of the patient's own consent to the treatment.

Added by Acts 1993, 73rd Leg., ch. 407, § 1, eff. Sept. 1, 1993.

Statutes in Context
§ 313.007

A surrogate is protected from liability if the surrogate complies with § 313.007.

§ 313.007. Limitation on Liability

(a) A surrogate decision-maker is not subject to criminal or civil liability for consenting to medical care under this chapter if the consent is made in good faith.

(b) An attending physician, home and community support services agency, hospital, or nursing home or a person acting as an agent for or under the control of the physician, home and community support services agency, hospital, or nursing home is not subject to criminal or civil liability and has not engaged in unprofessional conduct if the medical treatment consented to under this chapter:

(1) is done in good faith under the consent to medical treatment; and

(2) does not constitute a failure to exercise due care in the provision of the medical treatment.

Added by Acts 1993, 73rd Leg., ch. 407, § 1, eff. Sept. 1, 1993. Subsec. (b) amended by Acts 2007, 80th Leg., ch. 1271, § 4, eff. Sept. 1, 2007.

Title 8. Death and Disposition of the Body

Subtitle A. Death

Chapter 671. Determination of Death and Autopsy Reports

Subchapter A. Determination of Death

Statutes in Context
§ 671.001

Section 671.001 provides for the determination of death by traditional means (irreversible cessation of breathing and heart beating) as well as by irreversible cessation of all spontaneous brain function (brain death).

---

§ 671.001. Standard Used in Determining Death

(a) A person is dead when, according to ordinary standards of medical practice, there is irreversible cessation of the person's spontaneous respiratory and circulatory functions.

(b) If artificial means of support preclude a determination that a person's spontaneous respiratory and circulatory functions have ceased, the person is dead when, in the announced opinion of a physician, according to ordinary standards of medical practice, there is irreversible cessation of all spontaneous brain function. Death occurs when the relevant functions cease.

(c) Death must be pronounced before artificial means of supporting a person's respiratory and circulatory functions are terminated.

(d) A registered nurse or physician assistant may determine and pronounce a person dead in situations other than those described by Subsection (b) if permitted by written policies of a licensed health care facility, institution, or entity providing services to that person. Those policies must include physician assistants who are credentialed or otherwise permitted to practice at the facility, institution, or entity. If the facility, institution, or entity has an organized nursing staff and an organized medical staff or medical consultant, the nursing staff and medical staff or consultant shall jointly develop and approve those policies. The executive commissioner of the Health and Human Services Commission [board] shall adopt rules to govern policies for facilities, institutions, or entities that do not have organized nursing staffs and organized medical staffs or medical consultants.

Acts 1989, 71ˢᵗ Leg., ch. 678, § 1, eff. Sept. 1, 1989. Amended by Acts 1991, 72ⁿᵈ Leg., ch. 201, § 1, eff. Sept. 1, 1991. Amended by Acts 1995, 74ᵗʰ Leg., ch. 965, § 8, eff. June 16, 1995. Subsec. (d) amended by Acts 2015, 84ᵗʰ Leg., ch. 1, § 3.1501, eff. Sept. 1, 2015.

§ 671.002. Limitation of Liability

(a) A physician who determines death in accordance with Section 671.001(b) or a registered nurse or physician assistant who determines death in accordance with Section 671.001(d) is not liable for civil damages or subject to criminal prosecution for the physician's, registered nurse's, or physician assistant's actions or the actions of others based on the determination of death.

(b) A person who acts in good faith in reliance on a physician's, registered nurse's, or physician assistant's determination of death is not liable for civil damages or subject to criminal prosecution for the person's actions.

Acts 1989, 71ˢᵗ Leg., ch. 678, § 1, eff. Sept. 1, 1989. Amended by Acts 1991, 72ⁿᵈ Leg., ch. 201, § 2, eff. Sept. 1, 1991. Amended by Acts 1995, 74ᵗʰ Leg., ch. 965, § 9, eff. June 16, 1995.

Subtitle B. Disposition of the Body

Chapter 691. Anatomical Board of the State of Texas

Subchapter B. Donation and Distribution of Bodies

Statutes in Context
§§ 691.024–691.030

Sections 691.024 - 691.030 regulate various matters relating to the distribution of dead bodies such as the persons who may claim the body for burial.

---

§ 691.024. Persons Who May Claim Body for Burial

(a) An officer, employee, or representative of the state, of a political subdivision, or of an institution is not required to give notice or deliver a body as required by Section 691.023 if the body is claimed for burial.

(b) A relative, bona fide friend, or representative of an organization to which the deceased belonged may claim the body for burial. The person in charge of the body shall release the body to the claimant without requiring payment when the person is satisfied that the claimed relationship exists.

(c) A claimant alleging to be a bona fide friend or a representative of an organization to which the deceased belonged must present a written statement of the relationship under which the claimant qualifies as a bona fide friend or organization representative.

(d) For purposes of this section, a bona fide friend means a person who is like one of the family, and does not include:

(1) an ordinary acquaintance;

(2) an officer, employee, or representative of the state, of a political subdivision, or of an institution having charge of a body not claimed for

burial or a body required to be buried at public expense;

(3) an employee of an entity listed in Subdivision (2) with which the deceased was associated; or

(4) a patient, inmate, or ward of an institution with which the deceased was associated.

(e) A person covered by Subsection (d) may qualify as a bona fide friend if the friendship existed before the deceased entered the institution.

Acts 1989, 71st Leg., ch. 678, § 1, eff. Sept. 1, 1989.

§ 691.025. Procedure After Death

(a) If a body is not claimed for burial immediately after death, the body shall be embalmed within 24 hours.

(b) For 72 hours after death, the person in charge of the institution having charge or control of the body shall make due effort to find a relative of the deceased and notify the relative of the death. If the person is not able to find a relative, the person shall file with the county clerk an affidavit stating that the person has made a diligent inquiry to find a relative and stating the inquiry the person made.

(c) A body that is not claimed for burial within 48 hours after a relative receives notification shall be delivered as soon as possible to the board or the board's representative.

(d) A relative of the deceased may claim the body within 60 days after the body has been delivered to an institution or other entity authorized to receive the body. The body shall be released without charge.

Acts 1989, 71st Leg., ch. 678, § 1, eff. Sept. 1, 1989.

§ 691.026. Body of Traveler

If an unclaimed body is the body of a traveler who died suddenly, the board shall direct the institution or other person receiving the body to retain the body for six months for purposes of identification.

Acts 1989, 71st Leg., ch. 678, § 1, eff. Sept. 1, 1989. Amended by Acts 2015, 84th Leg., ch. 624, § 4, eff. Sept. 1, 2015.

§ 691.027. Autopsy

Only the board may grant permission to perform an autopsy on an unclaimed body. The board may grant permission after receiving a specific request for an autopsy that shows sufficient evidence of medical urgency.

Acts 1989, 71st Leg., ch. 678, § 1, eff. Sept. 1, 1989.

§ 691.028. Donation of Body by Written Instrument

(a) An adult living in this state who is of sound mind may donate the adult's [his] body by will or other written instrument to the board, a medical or dental school, or another donee authorized by the board, to be used for the advancement of medical or forensic science.

(b) To be effective, the donor must sign the will or other written instrument and it must be witnessed by two adults. The donor is not required to use a particular form or particular words in making the donation, but the will or other instrument must clearly convey the donor's intent.

(c) Appointment of an administrator or executor or acquisition of a court order is not necessary before the body may be delivered under this chapter.

(d) A donor may revoke a donation made under this section by executing a written instrument in a manner similar to the original donation.

Acts 1989, 71st Leg., ch. 678, § 1, eff. Sept. 1, 1989. Amended by Acts 2003, 78th Leg., ch. 948, § 6, eff. Sept. 1, 2003. Amended by Acts 2003, 78th Leg., ch. 948, § 6, eff. Sept. 1, 2003. Subsec. (a) amended by Acts 2015, 84th Leg., ch. 624, § 5, eff. Sept. 1, 2015.

§ 691.029. Authority to Accept Bodies from Outside the State

The board may receive a body transported to the board from outside this state.

Acts 1989, 71st Leg., ch. 678, § 1, eff. Sept. 1, 1989.

§ 691.030. Board's Authority to Distribute Bodies and Anatomical Specimens

(a) The board or the board's representative shall distribute bodies donated to it and may redistribute bodies donated to medical or dental schools or other donees authorized by the board to:

(1) schools and colleges of chiropractic, osteopathy, medicine, or dentistry incorporated in this state;

(2) forensic science programs;

(3) search and rescue organizations or recovery teams that are recognized by the board, are exempt from federal taxation under Section 501(c)(3), Internal Revenue Code of 1986, and use human remains detection canines with the authorization of a local or county law enforcement agency;

(4) [, to] physicians;[,] and

(5) [to] other persons as provided by this section.

(b) In making the distribution, the board shall give priority to the schools and colleges that need bodies for lectures and demonstrations.

(c) If the board has remaining bodies, the board or the board's representative shall distribute or redistribute those bodies to the schools and colleges proportionately and equitably according to the number of students in each school or college receiving instruction or demonstration in normal or morbid anatomy and operative surgery. The dean of each school or college shall certify that number to the board when required by the board.

(d) The board may transport a body or anatomical specimen to an authorized recipient in another state if the board determines that the supply of bodies or anatomical specimens in this state exceeds the need for bodies or anatomical specimens in this state and if:

(1) the deceased donated his body in compliance with Section 691.028 and at the time of the donation authorized the board to transport the body outside this state; or

(2) the body was donated in compliance with Chapter 692A and the person authorized to make the donation under Section 692A.009 authorized the board to transport the body outside this state.

Acts 1989, 71ˢᵗ Leg., ch. 678, § 1, eff. Sept. 1, 1989. Amended by Acts 2003, 78ᵗʰ Leg., ch. 948, § 7, eff. Sept. 1, 2003. Subsec. (d) amended by Acts 2009, 81ˢᵗ Leg., ch. 186, § 3, eff. Sept. 1, 2009. Subsec. (a) amended by Acts 2015, 84ᵗʰ Leg., ch. 624, § 6, eff. Sept. 1, 2015.

Chapter 692.   Uniform Anatomical Gift Act

Statutes in Context
Chapter 692

Although the Uniform Anatomical Gift Act was replaced by the Revised Uniform Anatomical Gift Act in 2009, the below "orphan" provision remains because it was amended without reference to the repeal.

§ 692.003.   Manner of Executing Gift of Own Body

(d) A gift made by a document other than a will is effective on the death of the donor. The document may be a card designed to be carried by the donor or another record signed by the donor or other person making the gift. A statement or symbol in an online donor registry and authorized by the donor indicating the donor has made an anatomical gift may also serve as a document making a gift. To be effective, the document must be signed by the donor in the presence of two witnesses except as otherwise provided by Subchapter Q, Chapter 521, Transportation Code, this subsection, or other law. If the donor cannot sign the document, a person may sign the document for the donor at the donor's direction and in the presence of the donor and two witnesses. The witnesses to the signing of a document under this subsection must sign the document in the presence of the donor. Delivery of the document during the donor's lifetime is not necessary to make the gift valid. An online donation registration does not require the consent of another person or require two witnesses. The online registration constitutes a legal document under this chapter and remains binding after the donor's death.

Amended by Acts 1997, 75th Leg., ch. 165, § 30.211, eff. Sept. 1, 1997; Acts 1997, 75th Leg., ch. 225, § 3, eff. Sept. 1, 1997; Acts 2009, 81st Leg., ch. 831, § 2.

Chapter 692A.   Revised Uniform Anatomical Gift Act

Statutes in Context
Chapter 692A

Regardless of financial situation, each person has extremely valuable assets which can be transferred at death, namely the person's own body and its parts. Doctors perform over 20,000 organ transplants in the United States every year. Despite the media attention given to organ donation, organs are in short supply. As of 2011, over 111,000 people were waiting for organ transplants. Many people will find organ donation an exciting prospect because a high degree of self-satisfaction can come from the knowledge that donated organs will enhance or save lives. The American Bar Association urges all attorneys to discuss the topic of organ and tissue donations with their clients.

On the other hand, some people consider the use of their dead bodies for transplantation or research to be distasteful or contrary to their religious beliefs. In a way, organ donation is nothing more than cannibalism by technology. The argument is made that there is little difference between ingesting human flesh and having that flesh surgically inserted into the body; in both situations, part of a deceased person ends up inside a living person. A more widespread reason people refuse to donate organs is the fear that medical personnel may not work as hard to save the lives of organ donors as nondonors. The media are brimming with reports of people who were presumed dead but who were actually alive.

Organ donation has a relatively long history. Bones were first transplanted in 1878 and cornea transplants began in the 1940s. It was not until the kidney transplants of the 1950s, however, that the need for comprehensive organ donation law arose. The failure of then existing law to govern anatomical gifts uniformly and comprehensively led the National Conference of Commissioners on Uniform State Laws to approve the Uniform Anatomical Gift Act in 1968. Within five years, all fifty states and the District of Columbia substantially adopted the Act.

Many states have subsequently adopted either the 1987 or the 2006 revision. Texas resisted change and never adopted the 1987 version. However, in 2009, the Texas Legislature enacted the 2006 version. This revision modernizes the law regarding anatomical gifts and makes it easier for a donor to make a gift. For example, a donor card no longer needs two witnesses under most circumstances.

§ 692A.001.   Short Title

This chapter may be cited as the Revised Uniform Anatomical Gift Act.

Added by Acts 2009, 81st Leg., ch. 186, § 1, eff. Sept. 1, 2009.

§ 692A.002. Definitions

In this chapter:

(1) "Adult" means an individual who is at least 18 years of age.

(2) "Agent" means an individual:

(A) authorized to make health care decisions on the principal's behalf by a medical power of attorney; or

(B) expressly authorized to make an anatomical gift on the principal's behalf by any other record signed by the principal.

(3) "Anatomical gift" means a donation of all or part of a human body to take effect after the donor's death for the purpose of transplantation, therapy, research, or education.

(4) "Commissioner" means the commissioner of state health services.

(5) "Decedent" means a deceased individual whose body or part is or may be the source of an anatomical gift. The term includes a stillborn infant and, subject to restrictions imposed by law other than this chapter, a fetus.

(6) "Department" means the Department of State Health Services.

(7) "Disinterested witness" means a witness other than the spouse, child, parent, sibling, grandchild, grandparent, or guardian of the individual who makes, amends, revokes, or refuses to make an anatomical gift, or another adult who exhibited special care and concern for the individual. The term does not include a person to which an anatomical gift could pass under Section 692A.011.

(8) "Document of gift" means a donor card or other record used to make an anatomical gift. The term includes a statement or symbol on a driver's license, identification card, or donor registry.

(9) "Donor" means an individual whose body or part is the subject of an anatomical gift.

(10) "Donor registry" means a database that contains records of anatomical gifts and amendments to or revocations of anatomical gifts.

(11) "Driver's license" means a license or permit issued by the Department of Public Safety to operate a vehicle, whether or not conditions are attached to the license or permit.

(11-a) "Education" with respect to the purposes authorized by law for making an anatomical gift includes forensic science education and related training.

(12) "Eye bank" means a person that is licensed, accredited, or regulated under federal or state law to engage in the recovery, screening, testing, processing, storage, or distribution of human eyes or portions of human eyes.

(13) "Guardian" means a person appointed by a court to make decisions regarding the support, care,

education, health, or welfare of an individual. The term does not include a guardian ad litem.

(14) "Hospital" means a facility licensed as a hospital under the law of any state or a facility operated as a hospital by the United States, a state, or a subdivision of a state.

(15) "Identification card" means an identification card issued by the Department of Public Safety.

(16) "Imminent death" means a patient who requires mechanical ventilation, has a severe neurologic injury, and meets certain clinical criteria indicating that neurologic death is near or a patient for whom withdrawal of ventilatory support is being considered.

(17) "Know" means to have actual knowledge.

(18) "Minor" means an individual who is under 18 years of age.

(19) "Organ procurement organization" means a person designated by the secretary of the United States Department of Health and Human Services as an organ procurement organization.

(20) "Parent" means a parent whose parental rights have not been terminated.

(21) "Part" means an organ, an eye, or tissue of a human being. The term does not include the whole body.

(22) "Person" means an individual, corporation, business trust, estate, trust, partnership, limited liability company, association, joint venture, public corporation, government or governmental subdivision, agency, or instrumentality, or any other legal or commercial entity.

(23) "Physician" means an individual authorized to practice medicine or osteopathy under the law of any state.

(24) "Procurement organization" means an eye bank, organ procurement organization, or tissue bank.

(25) "Prospective donor" means an individual who is dead or near death and has been determined by a procurement organization to have a part that could be medically suitable for transplantation, therapy, research, or education. The term does not include an individual who has made a refusal.

(26) "Reasonably available" means able to be contacted by a procurement organization without undue effort and willing and able to act in a timely manner consistent with existing medical criteria necessary for the making of an anatomical gift.

(27) "Recipient" means an individual into whose body a decedent's part has been or is intended to be transplanted.

(28) "Record" means information that is inscribed on a tangible medium or that is stored in an electronic or other medium and is retrievable in perceivable form.

(29) "Refusal" means a record created under Section 692A.007 that expressly states an intent to

bar other persons from making an anatomical gift of an individual's body or part.

(30) "Sign" means, with the present intent to authenticate or adopt a record:

(A) to execute or adopt a tangible symbol; or

(B) to attach to or logically associate with the record an electronic symbol, sound, or process.

(31) "State" means a state of the United States, the District of Columbia, Puerto Rico, the United States Virgin Islands, or any territory or insular possession subject to the jurisdiction of the United States.

(32) "Technician" means an individual determined to be qualified to remove or process parts by an appropriate organization that is licensed, accredited, or regulated under federal or state law. The term includes an enucleator.

(33) "Timely notification" means notification of an imminent death to the organ procurement organization within one hour of the patient's meeting the criteria for imminent death and before the withdrawal of any life sustaining therapies. With respect to cardiac death, timely notification means notification to the organ procurement organization within one hour of the cardiac death.

(34) "Tissue" means a portion of the human body other than an organ or an eye. The term does not include blood unless the blood is donated for the purpose of research or education.

(35) "Tissue bank" means a person licensed, accredited, or regulated under federal or state law to engage in the recovery, screening, testing, processing, storage, or distribution of tissue.

(36) "Transplant hospital" means a hospital that furnishes organ transplants and other medical and surgical specialty services required for the care of transplant patients.

(37) "Visceral organ" means the heart, kidney, or liver or another organ or tissue that requires a patient support system to maintain the viability of the organ or tissue.

Added by Acts 2009, 81st Leg., ch. 186, § 1, eff. Sept. 1, 2009. Subsec. 11(a) added by Acts 2015, 84th Leg., ch. 624, § 9, eff. Sept. 1, 2015.

§ 692A.003. Applicability

This chapter applies to an anatomical gift or amendment to, revocation of, or refusal to make an anatomical gift, whenever made.

Added by Acts 2009, 81st Leg., ch. 186, § 1, eff. Sept. 1, 2009.

§ 692A.004. Persons Authorized to Make Anatomical Gift Before Donor's Death

Subject to Section 692A.008, an anatomical gift of a donor's body or part may be made during the life of the donor for the purpose of transplantation, therapy,

research, or education in the manner provided in Section 692A.005 by:

(1) the donor, if the donor is an adult or if the donor is a minor and is:

(A) emancipated; or

(B) authorized under state law to apply for a driver's license because the donor is at least 16 years of age and:

(i) circumstances allow the donation to be actualized prior to 18 years of age; and

(ii) an organ procurement organization obtains signed written consent from the minor's parent, guardian, or custodian as in Subdivision (3);

(2) an agent of the donor, unless the medical power of attorney or other record prohibits the agent from making an anatomical gift;

(3) a parent of the donor, if the donor is an unemancipated minor; or

(4) the donor's guardian.

Added by Acts 2009, 81st Leg., ch. 186, § 1, eff. Sept. 1, 2009.

§ 692A.005. Manner of Making Anatomical Gift Before Donor's Death

(a) A donor may make an anatomical gift:

(1) by authorizing a statement or symbol indicating that the donor has made an anatomical gift to be imprinted on the donor's driver's license or identification card;

(2) in a will;

(3) during a terminal illness or injury of the donor, by any form of communication addressed to at least two adults, at least one of whom is a disinterested witness; or

(4) as provided in Subsection (b).

(b) A donor or other person authorized to make an anatomical gift under Section 692A.004 may make a gift by a donor card or other record signed by the donor or other person making the gift or by authorizing that a statement or symbol indicating the donor has made an anatomical gift be included on a donor registry. If the donor or other person is physically unable to sign a record, the record may be signed by another individual at the direction of the donor or other person and must:

(1) be witnessed by at least two adults, at least one of whom is a disinterested witness, who have signed at the request of the donor or the other person; and

(2) state that the record has been signed and witnessed as provided in Subdivision (1).

(c) Revocation, suspension, expiration, or cancellation of a driver's license or identification card on which an anatomical gift is indicated does not invalidate the gift.

(d) An anatomical gift made by will takes effect on the donor's death whether or not the will is probated. Invalidation of the will after the donor's death does not invalidate the gift.

Added by Acts 2009, 81st Leg., ch. 186, § 1, eff. Sept. 1, 2009.

§ 692A.006. Amending or Revoking Anatomical Gift Before Donor's Death

(a) Subject to Section 692A.008, a donor or other person authorized to make an anatomical gift under Section 692A.004 may amend or revoke an anatomical gift by:

(1) a record signed by:

(A) the donor;

(B) the other person; or

(C) subject to Subsection (b), another individual acting at the direction of the donor or the other person if the donor or other person is physically unable to sign; or

(2) a later-executed document of gift that amends or revokes a previous anatomical gift or portion of an anatomical gift, either expressly or by inconsistency.

(b) A record signed pursuant to Subsection (a)(1)(C) must:

(1) be witnessed by at least two adults, at least one of whom is a disinterested witness, who have signed at the request of the donor or the other person; and

(2) state that the record has been signed and witnessed as provided in Subdivision (1).

(c) Subject to Section 692A.008, a donor or other person authorized to make an anatomical gift under Section 692A.004 may revoke an anatomical gift by the destruction or cancellation of the document of gift, or the portion of the document of gift used to make the gift, with the intent to revoke the gift.

(d) A donor may amend or revoke an anatomical gift that was not made in a will by any form of communication during a terminal illness or injury addressed to at least two adults, at least one of whom is a disinterested witness.

(e) A donor who makes an anatomical gift in a will may amend or revoke the gift in the manner provided for amendment or revocation of wills or as provided in Subsection (a).

Added by Acts 2009, 81st Leg., ch. 186, § 1, eff. Sept. 1, 2009.

§ 692A.007. Refusal to Make Anatomical Gift; Effect of Refusal

(a) An individual may refuse to make an anatomical gift of the individual's body or part by:

(1) a record signed by:

(A) the individual; or

(B) subject to Subsection (b), another individual acting at the direction of the individual if the individual is physically unable to sign;

(2) the individual's will, whether or not the will is admitted to probate or invalidated after the individual's death; or

(3) any form of communication made by the individual during the individual's terminal illness or injury addressed to at least two adults, at least one of whom is a disinterested witness.

(b) A record signed pursuant to Subsection (a)(1)(B) must:

(1) be witnessed by at least two adults, at least one of whom is a disinterested witness, who have signed at the request of the individual; and

(2) state that the record has been signed and witnessed as provided in Subdivision (1).

(c) An individual who has made a refusal may amend or revoke the refusal:

(1) in the manner provided in Subsection (a) for making a refusal;

(2) by subsequently making an anatomical gift pursuant to Section 692A.005 that is inconsistent with the refusal; or

(3) by destroying or canceling the record evidencing the refusal, or the portion of the record used to make the refusal, with the intent to revoke the refusal.

(d) Except as otherwise provided in Section 692A.008(h), in the absence of an express, contrary indication by the individual set forth in the refusal, an individual's unrevoked refusal to make an anatomical gift of the individual's body or part bars all other persons from making an anatomical gift of the individual's body or part.

Added by Acts 2009, 81st Leg., ch. 186, § 1, eff. Sept. 1, 2009.

§ 692A.008. Preclusive Effect of Anatomical Gift, Amendment, or Revocation

(a) Except as otherwise provided in Subsection (g) and subject to Subsection (f), in the absence of an express, contrary indication by the donor, a person other than the donor is barred from making, amending, or revoking an anatomical gift of a donor's body or part if the donor made an anatomical gift of the donor's body or part under Section 692A.005 or an amendment to an anatomical gift of the donor's body or part under Section 692A.006.

(b) A donor's revocation of an anatomical gift of the donor's body or part under Section 692A.006 is not a refusal and does not bar another person specified in Section 692A.004 or Section 692A.009 from making an anatomical gift of the donor's body or part under Section 692A.005 or Section 692A.010.

(c) If a person other than the donor makes an unrevoked anatomical gift of the donor's body or part under Section 692A.005 or an amendment to an anatomical gift of the donor's body or part under Section 692A.006, another person may not make, amend, or revoke the gift of the donor's body or part under Section 692A.010.

(d) A revocation of an anatomical gift of a donor's body or part under Section 692A.006 by a person other than the donor does not bar another person from making an anatomical gift of the body or part under Section 692A.005 or Section 692A.010.

(e) In the absence of an express, contrary indication by the donor or other person authorized to make an anatomical gift under Section 692A.004, an anatomical gift of a part is neither a refusal to give another part nor a limitation on the making of an anatomical gift of another part at a later time by the donor or another person.

(f) In the absence of an express, contrary indication by the donor or other person authorized to make an anatomical gift under Section 692A.004, an anatomical gift of a part for one or more of the purposes set forth in Section 692A.004 is not a limitation on the making of an anatomical gift of the part for any of the other purposes by the donor or any other person under Section 692A.005 or Section 692A.010.

(g) If a donor who is an unemancipated minor dies, a parent of the donor who is reasonably available may revoke or amend an anatomical gift of the donor's body or part.

(h) If an unemancipated minor who signed a refusal dies, a parent of the minor who is reasonably available may revoke the minor's refusal.

Added by Acts 2009, 81st Leg., ch. 186, § 1, eff. Sept. 1, 2009.

§ 692A.009. Who May Make Anatomical Gift of Decedent's Body or Part

(a) Subject to Subsections (b) and (c) and unless barred by Section 692A.007 or Section 692A.008, an anatomical gift of a decedent's body or part for the purpose of transplantation, therapy, research, or education may be made by any member of the following classes of persons who is reasonably available, in the order of priority listed:

(1) an agent of the decedent at the time of death who could have made an anatomical gift under Section 692A.004(2) immediately before the decedent's death;

(2) the spouse of the decedent;

(3) adult children of the decedent;

(4) parents of the decedent;

(5) adult siblings of the decedent;

(6) adult grandchildren of the decedent;

(7) grandparents of the decedent;

(8) an adult who exhibited special care and concern for the decedent;

(9) the persons who were acting as the guardians of the person of the decedent at the time of death;

(10) the hospital administrator; and

(11) any other person having the authority to dispose of the decedent's body.

(b) If there is more than one member of a class listed in Subsection (a)(1), (3), (4), (5), (6), (7), or (9) entitled to make an anatomical gift, an anatomical gift may be made by a member of the class unless that member or a person to which the gift may pass under Section 692A.011 knows of an objection by another member of the class. If an objection is known, the gift may be made only by a majority of the members of the class who are reasonably available.

(c) A person may not make an anatomical gift if, at the time of the decedent's death, a person in a prior class under Subsection (a) is reasonably available to make or to object to the making of an anatomical gift.

Added by Acts 2009, 81st Leg., ch. 186, § 1, eff. Sept. 1, 2009.

§ 692A.010. Manner of Making, Amending, or Revoking Anatomical Gift of Decedent's Body or Part

(a) A person authorized to make an anatomical gift under Section 692A.009 may make an anatomical gift by a document of gift signed by the person making the gift or by that person's oral communication that is electronically recorded or is contemporaneously reduced to a record and signed by the individual receiving the oral communication.

(b) Subject to Subsection (c), an anatomical gift by a person authorized under Section 692A.009 may be amended or revoked orally or in a record by any member of a prior class who is reasonably available. If more than one member of the prior class is reasonably available, the gift made by a person authorized under Section 692A.009 may be:

(1) amended only if a majority of the reasonably available members agree to the amending of the gift; or

(2) revoked only if a majority of the reasonably available members agree to the revoking of the gift or if they are equally divided as to whether to revoke the gift.

(c) A revocation under Subsection (b) is effective only if, before an incision has been made to remove a part from the donor's body or before the initiation of invasive procedures to prepare the recipient, the procurement organization, transplant hospital, or physician or technician knows of the revocation.

Added by Acts 2009, 81st Leg., ch. 186, § 1, eff. Sept. 1, 2009.

§ 692A.011. Persons that May Receive Anatomical Gift; Purpose of Anatomical Gift

(a) An anatomical gift may be made to the following persons named in the document of gift:

(1) an organ procurement organization to be used for transplantation, therapy, research, or education;

(2) a hospital to be used for research;

(3) subject to Subsection (d), an individual designated by the person making the anatomical gift if the individual is the recipient of the part;

(4) an eye bank or tissue bank, except that use of a gift of a whole body must be coordinated through the Anatomical Board of the State of Texas;

(5) a forensic science program at:

(A) a general academic teaching institution as defined by Section 61.003, Education Code; or

(B) a private or independent institution of higher education as defined by Section 61.003, Education Code; [or]

(6) a search and rescue organization or recovery team that is recognized by the Anatomical Board of the State of Texas, is exempt from federal taxation under Section 501(c)(3), Internal Revenue Code of 1986, and uses human remains detection canines with the authorization of a local or county law enforcement agency; or

(7) the Anatomical Board of the State of Texas.

(b) Except for donations described by Subsections (a)(1) through (6) [(5)], the Anatomical Board of the State of Texas shall be the donee of gifts of bodies or parts of bodies made for the purpose of education or research that are subject to distribution by the board under Chapter 691.

(c) A forensic science program that receives a donation under Subsection (a)(5) must submit a report to the Anatomical Board of the State of Texas on a quarterly basis that lists:

(1) the number of bodies or parts of bodies that the program received; and

(2) the method in which the program used the bodies or parts of bodies for education or research.

(d) If an anatomical gift to an individual under Subsection (a)(3) cannot be transplanted into the individual, the part passes in accordance with Subsection (i) in the absence of an express, contrary indication by the person making the anatomical gift.

(e) If an anatomical gift of one or more specific parts or of all parts is made in a document of gift that does not name a person described in Subsection (a) but identifies the purpose for which an anatomical gift may be used, the following rules apply:

(1) if the part is an eye and the gift is for the purpose of transplantation or therapy, the gift passes to the appropriate eye bank;

(2) if the part is tissue and the gift is for the purpose of transplantation or therapy, the gift passes to the appropriate tissue bank;

(3) if the part is an organ and the gift is for the purpose of transplantation or therapy, the gift passes to the appropriate organ procurement organization as custodian of the organ; and

(4) if the part is an organ, an eye, or tissue and the gift is for the purpose of research or education, the gift passes to the appropriate procurement organization.

(f) For the purpose of Subsection (e), if there is more than one purpose of an anatomical gift set forth in the document of gift but the purposes are not set forth in any priority, the gift must be used for transplantation or therapy, if suitable. If the gift cannot be used for transplantation or therapy, the gift may be used for research or education.

(g) If an anatomical gift of one or more specific parts is made in a document of gift that does not name a person described in Subsection (a) and does not identify the purpose of the gift, the gift may be used only for transplantation or therapy, and the gift passes in accordance with Subsection (i).

(h) If a document of gift specifies only a general intent to make an anatomical gift by words such as "donor," "organ donor," or "body donor," or by a symbol or statement of similar import, the gift may be used only for transplantation or therapy, and the gift passes in accordance with Subsection (i).

(i) For purposes of Subsections (d), (g), and (h), the following rules apply:

(1) if the part is an eye, the gift passes to the appropriate eye bank;

(2) if the part is tissue, the gift passes to the appropriate tissue bank; and

(3) if the part is an organ, the gift passes to the appropriate organ procurement organization as custodian of the organ.

(j) An anatomical gift of an organ for transplantation or therapy, other than an anatomical gift under Subsection (a)(3), passes to the organ procurement organization as custodian of the organ.

(k) If an anatomical gift does not pass pursuant to Subsections (a) through (j) or the decedent's body or part is not used for transplantation, therapy, research, or education, custody of the body or part passes to the person under obligation to dispose of the body or part.

(l) A person may not accept an anatomical gift if the person knows that the gift was not effectively made under Section 692A.005 or Section 692A.010 or if the person knows that the decedent made a refusal under Section 692A.007 that was not revoked. For purposes of this subsection, if a person knows that an anatomical gift was made on a document of gift, the person is deemed to know of any amendment or revocation of the gift or any refusal to make an anatomical gift on the same document of gift.

(m) Except as otherwise provided in Subsection (a)(3), nothing in this chapter affects the allocation of organs for transplantation or therapy.

(n) A donee may accept or reject a gift.

Added by Acts 2009, 81ˢᵗ Leg., ch. 186, § 1, eff. Sept. 1, 2009. Subsecs (a) & (b) amended by Acts 2015, 84ᵗʰ Leg., ch. 624, § 10, eff. Sept. 1, 2015.

§ 692A.012. Search and Notification

The donor card of a person who is involved in an accident or other trauma shall accompany the person to the hospital or other health care facility. The driver's license or personal identification certificate indicating an affirmative statement of gift of a person who is involved in an accident or other trauma shall accompany the person to the hospital or health care facility if the person does not have a donor card.

Added by Acts 2009, 81ˢᵗ Leg., ch. 186, § 1, eff. Sept. 1, 2009.

§ 692A.013. Delivery of Document of Gift Not Required; Right to Examine

(a) A document of gift need not be delivered during the donor's lifetime to be effective.

(b) On or after an individual's death, a person in possession of a document of gift or a refusal to make an anatomical gift with respect to the individual shall allow examination and copying of the document of gift or refusal by a person authorized to make or object to the making of an anatomical gift with respect to the individual or by a person to which the gift could pass under Section 692A.011.

Added by Acts 2009, 81ˢᵗ Leg., ch. 186, § 1, eff. Sept. 1, 2009.

§ 692A.014. Rights and Duties of Procurement Organization and Others

(a) When a hospital refers an individual at or near death to a procurement organization, the organization shall make a reasonable search of the records of the Department of Public Safety and any donor registry that it knows exists for the geographical area in which the individual resides to ascertain whether the individual has made an anatomical gift.

(b) A procurement organization must be allowed reasonable access to information in the records of the Department of Public Safety to ascertain whether an individual at or near death is a donor.

(c) When a hospital refers an individual at or near death to a procurement organization, the organization may conduct any reasonable examination necessary to ensure the medical suitability of a part that is or could be the subject of an anatomical gift for transplantation, therapy, research, or education from a donor or a prospective donor. During the examination period, measures necessary to ensure the medical suitability of the part may not be withdrawn unless the hospital or procurement organization knows that the individual expressed a contrary intent.

(d) Unless prohibited by law other than this chapter, at any time after a donor's death, the person to which a part passes under Section 692A.011 may conduct any reasonable examination necessary to ensure the medical suitability of the body or part for its intended purpose.

(e) Unless prohibited by law other than this chapter, an examination under Subsection (c) or (d) may include an examination of all medical and dental records of the donor or prospective donor.

(f) On the death of a minor who was a donor or had signed a refusal, unless a procurement organization knows the minor is emancipated, the procurement organization shall conduct a reasonable search for the parents of the minor and provide the parents with an opportunity to revoke or amend the anatomical gift or revoke the refusal.

(g) On referral by a hospital under Subsection (a), a procurement organization shall make a reasonable search for any person listed in Section 692A.009 having priority to make an anatomical gift on behalf of a prospective donor. If a procurement organization receives information that an anatomical gift to any other person was made, amended, or revoked, it shall promptly advise the other person of all relevant information.

(h) Subject to Sections 692A.011(k) and 693.002, the rights of the person to which a part passes under Section 692A.011 are superior to the rights of all others with respect to the part. The person may accept or reject an anatomical gift wholly or partly. Subject to the terms of the document of gift and this chapter, a person that accepts an anatomical gift of an entire body may allow embalming, burial, or cremation, and use of remains in a funeral service. If the gift is of a part, the person to which the part passes under Section 692A.011, on the death of the donor and before embalming, burial, or cremation, shall cause the part to be removed without unnecessary mutilation.

(i) The physician who attends the decedent at death or the physician who determines the time of the decedent's death may not participate in the procedures for removing or transplanting a part from the decedent.

(j) A physician or technician may remove a donated part from the body of a donor that the physician or technician is qualified to remove.

Added by Acts 2009, 81ˢᵗ Leg., ch. 186, § 1, eff. Sept. 1, 2009.

§ 692A.015. Coordination of Procurement and Use; Hospital Procedures

Each hospital in this state shall enter into agreements or affiliations with procurement organizations for coordination of procurement and use of anatomical gifts. Each hospital must have a protocol that ensures its maintenance of an effective donation system in order to maximize organ, tissue, and eye donation. The protocol must:

(1) be available to the public during the hospital's normal business hours;

(2) establish a procedure for the timely notification to an organ procurement organization of individuals whose death is imminent or who have died in the hospital;

(3) establish procedures to ensure potential donors are declared dead by an appropriate practitioner in an acceptable time frame;

(4) establish procedures to ensure that hospital staff and organ procurement organization staff maintain appropriate medical treatment of potential donors while necessary testing and placement of potential donated organs, tissues, and eyes take place;

(5) ensure that all families are provided the opportunity to donate organs, tissues, and eyes, including vascular organs procured from asystolic donors;

(6) provide that the hospital use appropriately trained persons from an organ procurement

organization, tissue bank, or eye bank to make inquiries relating to donations;

(7) provide for documentation of the inquiry and of its disposition in the decedent's medical records;

(8) require an organ procurement organization, tissue bank, or eye bank that makes inquiries relating to donations to develop a protocol for making those inquiries;

(9) encourage sensitivity to families' beliefs and circumstances in all discussions relating to the donations;

(10) provide that the organ procurement organization determines medical suitability for organ donation and, in the absence of alternative arrangements by the hospital, the organ procurement organization determines medical suitability for tissue and eye donation, using the definition of potential tissue and eye donor and the notification protocol developed in consultation with the tissue and eye banks identified by the hospital for this purpose;

(11) ensure that the hospital works cooperatively with the designated organ procurement organization, tissue bank, and eye bank in educating staff on donation issues;

(12) ensure that the hospital works with the designated organ procurement organization, tissue bank, and eye bank in reviewing death records; and

(13) provide for monitoring of donation system effectiveness, including rates of donation, protocols, and policies, as part of the hospital's quality improvement program.

Added by Acts 2009, 81ˢᵗ Leg., ch. 186, § 1, eff. Sept. 1, 2009.

§ 692A.016. Sale or Purchase of Parts Prohibited

(a) Except as otherwise provided in Subsection (b), a person commits an offense if the person for valuable consideration knowingly purchases or sells a part for transplantation or therapy if removal of a part from an individual is intended to occur after the individual's death. An offense under this subsection is a Class A misdemeanor.

(b) A person may charge a reasonable amount for the removal, processing, preservation, quality control, storage, transportation, implantation, or disposal of a part.

(c) If conduct that constitutes an offense under this section also constitutes an offense under other law, the actor may be prosecuted under this section, the other law, or both this section and the other law.

Added by Acts 2009, 81ˢᵗ Leg., ch. 186, § 1, eff. Sept. 1, 2009.

§ 692A.017. Other Prohibited Acts

(a) A person commits an offense if the person, in order to obtain a financial gain, intentionally falsifies, forges, conceals, defaces, or obliterates a document of gift, an amendment or revocation of a document of gift, or a refusal. An offense under this section is a Class A misdemeanor.

(b) If conduct that constitutes an offense under this section also constitutes an offense under other law, the actor may be prosecuted under this section, the other law, or both this section and the other law.

Added by Acts 2009, 81ˢᵗ Leg., ch. 186, § 1, eff. Sept. 1, 2009.

§ 692A.018. Immunity

(a) A person who acts in good faith in accordance with this chapter is not liable for civil damages or subject to criminal prosecution for the person's action if the prerequisites for an anatomical gift are met under the laws applicable at the time and place the gift is made.

(b) A person that acts in accordance with this chapter or with the applicable anatomical gift law of another state, or attempts in good faith to do so, is not liable for the act in a civil action, criminal prosecution, or administrative proceeding.

(c) A person who acts in good faith in accordance with this chapter is not liable as a result of the action except in the case of an act or omission of the person that is intentional, wilfully or wantonly negligent, or done with conscious indifference or reckless disregard. For purposes of this subsection, "good faith" in determining the appropriate person authorized to make a donation under Section 692A.009 means making a reasonable effort to locate and contact the member or members of the highest priority class who are reasonably available at or near the time of death.

(d) Neither a person making an anatomical gift nor the donor's estate is liable for any injury or damage that results from the making or use of the gift.

(e) In determining whether an anatomical gift has been made, amended, or revoked under this chapter, a person may rely on representations of an individual listed in Section 692A.009(a)(2), (3), (4), (5), (6), (7), or (8) relating to the individual's relationship to the donor or prospective donor unless the person knows that the representation is untrue.

Added by Acts 2009, 81ˢᵗ Leg., ch. 186, § 1, eff. Sept. 1, 2009.

§ 692A.019. Law Governing Validity; Choice of Law as to Execution of Document of Gift; Presumption of Validity

(a) A document of gift is valid if executed in accordance with:

(1) this chapter;

(2) the laws of the state or country where it was executed; or

(3) the laws of the state or country where the person making the anatomical gift was domiciled, had a place of residence, or was a national at the time the document of gift was executed.

(b) If a document of gift is valid under this section, the law of this state governs the interpretation of the document of gift.

(c) A person may presume that a document of gift or amendment of an anatomical gift is valid unless that person knows that it was not validly executed or was revoked.

Added by Acts 2009, 81ˢᵗ Leg., ch. 186, § 1, eff. Sept. 1, 2009.

§ 692A.020. Glenda Dawson Donate Life-Texas Registry; Education Program

(a) A nonprofit organization designated by the Department of Public Safety shall maintain and administer a statewide donor registry, to be known as the Glenda Dawson Donate Life-Texas Registry.

(b) The nonprofit organization administering the registry must include representatives from each organ procurement organization in this state.

(c) The nonprofit organization shall establish and maintain a statewide Internet-based registry of organ, tissue, and eye donors.

(d) The Department of Public Safety at least monthly shall electronically transfer to the nonprofit organization administering the registry the name, date of birth, driver's license number, most recent address, and any other relevant information in the possession of the Department of Public Safety for any person who indicates on the person's driver's license application under Section 521.401, Transportation Code, that the person would like to make an anatomical gift.

(e) The nonprofit organization administering the registry shall:

(1) make information obtained from the Department of Public Safety under Subsection (d) available to procurement organizations;

(2) allow potential donors to submit information in writing directly to the organization for inclusion in the Internet-based registry;

(3) maintain the Internet-based registry in a manner that allows procurement organizations to immediately access organ, tissue, and eye donation information 24 hours a day, seven days a week through electronic and telephonic methods; and

(4) protect the confidentiality and privacy of the individuals providing information to the Internet-based registry, regardless of the manner in which the information is provided.

(f) Except as otherwise provided by Subsection (e)(3) or this subsection, the Department of Public Safety, the nonprofit organization administering the registry, or a procurement organization may not sell, rent, or otherwise share any information provided to the Internet-based registry. A procurement organization may share any information provided to the registry with an organ procurement organization or a health care provider or facility providing medical care to a potential donor as necessary to properly identify an individual at the time of donation.

(g) The Department of Public Safety, the nonprofit organization administering the registry, or the procurement organizations may not use any demographic or specific data provided to the Internet-based registry for any fund-raising activities. Data may only be transmitted from the selected organization to procurement organizations through electronic and telephonic methods using secure, encrypted technology to preserve the integrity of the data and the privacy of the individuals providing information.

(h) In each office authorized to issue driver's licenses or personal identification certificates, the Department of Public Safety shall make available educational materials developed by the nonprofit organization administering the registry.

(i) The Glenda Dawson Donate Life-Texas Registry fund is created as a trust fund outside the state treasury to be held by the comptroller and administered by the Department of Public Safety as trustee on behalf of the statewide donor registry maintained for the benefit of the citizens of this state. The fund is composed of money deposited to the credit of the fund under Sections 502.405(b), 521.008, and 521.422(c), Transportation Code, as provided by those subsections. Money in the fund shall be disbursed at least monthly, without appropriation, to the nonprofit organization administering the registry to pay the costs of:

(1) maintaining, operating, and updating the Internet-based registry and establishing procedures for an individual to be added to the registry;

(2) designing and distributing educational materials for prospective donors as required under this section; and

(3) providing education under this chapter.

(j) Repealed by Acts 2013, 83rd Leg., R.S., Ch. 121, Sec. 6(a), eff. May 18, 2013.

(k) To the extent funds are available and as part of the donor registry program, the nonprofit organization administering the registry may educate residents about anatomical gifts. The education provided under this section shall include information about:

(1) the laws governing anatomical gifts, including Subchapter Q, Chapter 521, Transportation Code, Chapter 693, and this chapter;

(2) the procedures for becoming an organ, eye, or tissue donor or donee; and

(3) the benefits of organ, eye, or tissue donation.

(l) Repealed by Acts 2013, 83rd Leg., R.S., Ch. 121, Sec. 6(a), eff. May 18, 2013.

(m) The nonprofit organization administering the registry may:

(1) implement a training program for all appropriate Department of Public Safety and Texas Department of Transportation employees on the benefits of organ, tissue, and eye donation and the procedures for individuals to be added to the Internet-based registry; and

(2) conduct the training described by Subdivision (1) on an ongoing basis for new employees.

(n) The nonprofit organization administering the registry may develop a program to educate health care providers and attorneys in this state about anatomical gifts.

(o) The nonprofit organization administering the registry shall encourage:

(1) attorneys to provide organ donation information to clients seeking advice for end-of-life decisions;

(2) medical and nursing schools in this state to include mandatory organ donation education in the schools' curricula; and

(3) medical schools in this state to require a physician in a neurology or neurosurgery residency program to complete an advanced course in organ donation education.

(p) The nonprofit organization administering the registry may not use the registry to solicit voluntary donations of money from a registrant.

Added by Acts 2009, 81ˢᵗ Leg., ch. 186, § 1, eff. Sept. 1, 2009. Amended by Acts 2011, 82ⁿᵈ Leg., ch. 554, § 1, eff. Jan. 1, 2012. Subsec. (i) amended by Acts 2013, 83ʳᵈ Leg., ch. 161, § 10.006, eff. Jan. 1, 2014. Subsecs. (j) & (l) repealed by Acts 2013, 83ʳᵈ Leg., ch. 121, § 6, eff. Sept. 1, 2013. Subsecs. (a), (c), (d), (e), (f), (g), (i), (k), (m), (n), (o), & (p) amended by Acts 2013, 83ʳᵈ Leg., ch. 121, § 1, eff. Sept. 1, 2013.

§ 692A.021. Effect of Anatomical Gift on Advance Directive

(a) In this section:

(1) "Advance directive" means a medical power of attorney or a record signed or authorized by a prospective donor containing the prospective donor's direction concerning a health-care decision for the prospective donor.

(2) "Declaration" means a record signed by a prospective donor specifying the circumstances under which a life support system may be withheld or withdrawn from the prospective donor.

(3) "Health-care decision" means any decision made regarding the health care of the prospective donor.

(b) If a prospective donor has a declaration or advance directive and the terms of the declaration or directive and the express or implied terms of a potential anatomical gift are in conflict with regard to the administration of measures necessary to ensure the medical suitability of a part for transplantation or therapy, the prospective donor's attending physician and prospective donor shall confer to resolve the conflict. If the prospective donor is incapable of resolving the conflict, an agent acting under the prospective donor's declaration or directive, or, if the agent is not reasonably available, another person authorized by law other than this chapter to make

health-care decisions on behalf of the prospective donor, shall act on the prospective donor's behalf to resolve the conflict. The conflict must be resolved as expeditiously as possible. Information relevant to the resolution of the conflict may be obtained from the appropriate procurement organization and any other person authorized to make an anatomical gift for the prospective donor under Section 692A.009. Before resolution of the conflict, measures necessary to ensure the medical suitability of the part may not be withheld or withdrawn from the prospective donor.

(c) If the conflict cannot be resolved, an expedited review of the matter must be initiated by an ethics or medical committee of the appropriate health care facility.

Added by Acts 2009, 81ˢᵗ Leg., ch. 186, § 1, eff. Sept. 1, 2009.

§ 692A.022. Uniformity of Application and Construction

In applying and construing this chapter, consideration must be given to the need to promote uniformity of the law with respect to the subject matter of this chapter among states that enact a law substantially similar to this chapter.

Added by Acts 2009, 81ˢᵗ Leg., ch. 186, § 1, eff. Sept. 1, 2009.

§ 692A.023. Relation to Electronic Signatures in Global and National Commerce Act

This chapter modifies, limits, and supersedes the provisions of the Electronic Signatures in Global and National Commerce Act (15 U.S.C. Section 7001 et seq.), but does not modify, limit, or supersede Section 101(a) of that Act (15 U.S.C. Section 7001(a)), or authorize electronic delivery of any of the notices described in Section 103 of that Act (15 U.S.C. Section 7003(b)).

Added by Acts 2009, 81ˢᵗ Leg., ch. 186, § 1, eff. Sept. 1, 2009.

Chapter 693. Removal of Body Parts, Body Tissue, and Corneal Tissue

Statutes in Context
Chapter 693

Chapter 693 permits certain government officials to allow the removal of certain organs without the consent of the donor or the donor's family.

Subchapter A. Removal of Body Parts or Tissue

§ 693.001. Definition

In this subchapter, "visceral organ" means the heart, kidney, liver, or other organ or tissue that requires a patient support system to maintain the viability of the organ or tissue.

Acts 1989, 71st Leg., ch. 678, § 1, eff. Sept. 1, 1989.

Statutes in Context
§§ 693.002–693.004

Upon a request from a qualified organ procurement organization, the medical examiner may, if certain conditions are satisfied, permit the removal of organs from a decedent who died under circumstances requiring an inquest by the medical examiner even without the consent of a family member. See §§ 693.002 - 693.004.

---

§ 693.002. Removal of Body Part or Tissue from Decedent Who Died Under Circumstances Requiring an Inquest

(a)(1) On a request from an organ procurement organization, as defined by Section 692A.002, the medical examiner, justice of the peace, county judge, or physician designated by the justice of the peace or county judge may permit the removal of organs from a decedent who died under circumstances requiring an inquest by the medical examiner, justice of the peace, or county judge if consent is obtained pursuant to Sections 692A.005 through 692A.010 or Section 693.003.

(2) If no autopsy is required, the organs to be transplanted shall be released in a timely manner to the organ procurement organization, as defined by Section 692A.002, for removal and transplantation.

(3) If an autopsy is required and the medical examiner, justice of the peace, county judge, or designated physician determines that the removal of the organs will not interfere with the subsequent course of an investigation or autopsy, the organs shall be released in a timely manner for removal and transplantation. The autopsy will be performed in a timely manner following the removal of the organs.

(4) If the medical examiner is considering withholding one or more organs of a potential donor for any reason, the medical examiner shall be present during the removal of the organs. In such case, the medical examiner may request a biopsy of those organs or deny removal of the anatomical gift. If the medical examiner denies removal of the anatomical gift, the medical examiner shall explain in writing the reasons for the denial. The medical examiner shall provide the explanation to:

(A) the organ procurement organization; and

(B) any person listed in Section 692A.009 who consented to the removal.

(5) If the autopsy is not being performed by a medical examiner and one or more organs may be withheld, the justice of the peace, county judge, or designated physician shall be present during the removal of the organs and may request the biopsy or deny removal of the anatomical gift. If removal of the anatomical gift is denied, the justice of the peace, county judge, or physician shall provide the written explanation required by Subdivisions (4)(A) and (B).

(6) If, in performing the duties required by this subsection, the medical examiner or, in those cases in which an autopsy is not performed by a medical examiner, the justice of the peace, county judge, or designated physician is required to be present at the hospital to examine the decedent prior to removal of the organs or during the procedure to remove the organs, the qualified organ procurement organization shall on request reimburse the county or the entity designated by the county for the actual costs incurred in performing such duties, not to exceed $1,000. Such reimbursements shall be deposited in the general fund of the county. The payment shall be applied to the additional costs incurred by the office of the medical examiner, justice of the peace, or county judge in performing such duties, including the cost of providing coverage beyond regular business hours. The payment shall be used to facilitate the timely procurement of organs in a manner consistent with the preservation of the organs for the purposes of transplantation.

(7) At the request of the medical examiner or, in those cases in which an autopsy is not performed by a medical examiner, the justice of the peace, county judge, or designated physician, the health care professional removing organs from a decedent who died under circumstances requiring an inquest shall file with the medical examiner, justice of the peace, or county judge a report detailing the condition of the organs removed and their relationship, if any, to the cause of death.

(b) On a request from a tissue bank, as defined by Section 692A.002, the medical examiner may permit the removal of tissue believed to be clinically usable for transplants or other therapy or treatment from a decedent who died under circumstances requiring an inquest if consent is obtained pursuant to Sections 692A.005 through 692A.010 or Section 693.003 or, if consent is not required by those sections, no objection by a person listed in Section 692A.009 is known by the medical examiner. If the medical examiner denies removal of the tissue, the medical examiner shall explain in writing the reasons for the denial. The medical examiner shall provide the explanation to:

(1) the tissue bank; and

(2) the person listed in Section 692A.009 who consented to the removal.

(c) If the autopsy is not being performed by a medical examiner, the justice of the peace, county judge, or designated physician may permit the removal of tissue in the same manner as a medical examiner under Subsection (b). If removal of the anatomical gift is denied, the justice of the peace, county judge, or physician shall provide the written explanation required by Subsections (b)(1) and (2).

Acts 1989, 71ˢᵗ Leg., ch. 678, § 1, eff. Sept. 1, 1989. Amended by Acts 1995, 74ᵗʰ Leg., ch. 523, § 1, eff. June 13, 1995; Acts 2003, 78ᵗʰ Leg., ch. 1220, § 1, eff. July 1, 2003. Subsec. (a) amended by Acts 2009, 81ˢᵗ Leg., ch. 186, § 4, eff. Sept. 1, 2009; Subsec (b) amended by Acts 2009, 81ˢᵗ Leg., ch. 186, § 5, eff. Sept. 1, 2009.

§ 693.003. Consent Not Required in Certain Circumstances

If a person listed in Section 692A.009 cannot be identified and contacted within four hours after death is pronounced and the county court determines that no reasonable likelihood exists that a person can be identified and contacted during the four-hour period, the county court may permit the removal of a nonvisceral organ or tissue.

Acts 1989, 71ˢᵗ Leg., ch. 678, § 1, eff. Sept. 1, 1989. Amended by Acts 2009, 81ˢᵗ Leg., ch. 186, § 6, eff. Sept. 1, 2009.

§ 693.004. Persons Who May Consent or Object to Removal

The following persons may consent or object to the removal of tissue or a body part:

(1) the decedent's spouse;

(2) the decedent's adult children, if there is no spouse;

(3) the decedent's parents, if there is no spouse or adult child; or

(4) the decedent's brothers or sisters, if there is no spouse, adult child, or parent.

Acts 1989, 71ˢᵗ Leg., ch. 678, § 1, eff. Sept. 1, 1989.

§ 693.005. Immunity from Damages in Civil Action

In a civil action brought by a person listed in Section 692A.009 who did not object before the removal of tissue or a body part specified by Section 693.002, a medical examiner, justice of the peace, county judge, medical facility, physician acting on permission of a medical examiner, justice of the peace, or county judge, or person assisting a physician is not liable for damages on a theory of civil recovery based on a contention that the plaintiff's consent was required before the body part or tissue could be removed.

Acts 1989, 71ˢᵗ Leg., ch. 678, § 1, eff. Sept. 1, 1989. Amended by Acts 2003, 78ᵗʰ Leg., ch. 1220, § 1, eff. July 1, 2003. Amended by Acts 2009, 81ˢᵗ Leg., ch. 186, § 7, eff. Sept. 1, 2009.

§ 693.006. Removal of Corneal Tissue

On a request from an eye bank, as defined in Section 692A.002, the medical examiner, justice of the peace, county judge, or physician designated by the justice of the peace or county judge may permit the removal of corneal tissue subject to the same provisions that apply to removal of a visceral organ on the request of a procurement organization under Chapter 692A. The provisions of this subchapter relating to immunity and consent apply to the removal of the corneal tissue.

Added by Acts 2005, 79ᵗʰ Leg., ch. 1069, § 2, eff. Sept. 1, 2005. Amended by Acts 2009, 81ˢᵗ Leg., ch. 186, § 8, eff. Sept. 1, 2009.

Subchapter C. Eye Enucleation

§ 693.021. Definition

In this chapter, "ophthalmologist" means a person licensed to practice medicine who specializes in treating eye diseases.

Acts 1989, 71ˢᵗ Leg., ch. 678, § 1, eff. Sept. 1, 1989.

§ 693.022. Persons Who May Enucleate Eye as Anatomical Gift

Only the following persons may Enucleate an eye that is an anatomical gift:

(1) a licensed physician;

(2) a licensed doctor of dental surgery or medical dentistry;

(3) a licensed embalmer; or

(4) a technician supervised by a physician.

Acts 1989, 71ˢᵗ Leg., ch. 678, § 1, eff. Sept. 1, 1989.

§ 693.023. Eye Enucleation Course

Each person, other than a licensed physician, who performs an eye enucleation must complete a course in eye enucleation taught by an ophthalmologist and must possess a certificate showing that the course has been completed.

Acts 1989, 71ˢᵗ Leg., ch. 678, § 1, eff. Sept. 1, 1989.

§ 693.024. Requisites of Eye Enucleation Course

The course in eye enucleation prescribed by Section 693.023 must include instruction in:

(1) the anatomy and physiology of the eye;

(2) maintaining a sterile field during the procedure;

(3) use of the appropriate instruments; and

(4) procedures for the sterile removal of the corneal button and the preservation of it in a preservative fluid.

Acts 1989, 71ˢᵗ Leg., ch. 678, § 1, eff. Sept. 1, 1989.

Subtitle C. Cemeteries

Chapter 711. General Provisions Relating to Cemeteries

Subchapter A. General Provisions

Statutes in Context
§ 711.002

A significant number of individuals are deeply concerned about how their bodies will be disposed of upon death. Many people have strong preferences regarding the disposition method, that is, burial or cremation. Other individuals wish to spell out the particulars of their funeral in great detail such as the location of the burial, whether the viewing is open or closed casket, the type of religious service, the inscription on the headstone, the kind of flowers and music, and the contents of the obituary. The legal systems of the ancient Greeks and Romans gave great weight to the deceased's instructions concerning bodily disposition. However, the common-law courts recognized no property rights in a dead body. This view gained widespread acceptance in the United States and thus a person's desires regarding disposition of the body were considered to be only precatory. A growing number of states have rejected this rule and recognize a person's right to determine the final disposition of the body.

The 1993 Texas Legislature took significant action to make it easier for a person to exercise the right to control the disposition of the person's remains when it made significant changes to § 711.002. Top priority for the disposition of remains is given to the expressed directions of the decedent. The directions must be in writing and may be contained in the following documents: (1) a will, (2) a prepaid funeral contract, or (3) a signed and acknowledged written instrument.

Second priority is granted to a special agent the decedent appointed for the purpose of controlling the disposition of the decedent's remains. This is a tremendous departure from normal agency law which provides that an agent's power, even one granted in a durable power, ends upon the principal's death. The statute supplies a model fill-in-the-blank form to make it simple and inexpensive for a person to appoint an agent, successor agents, and to state any special instructions. The agency appointment document must meet the following requirements: (1) signed by the decedent, (2) contain an acknowledgment of the decedent's signature, and (3) signed by the agent before the agent acts.

If the decedent left no binding instructions and did not properly appoint an agent, the following people in the priority listed have the right and duty to dispose of the decedent's remains: (1) the decedent's surviving spouse, (2) any one of the decedent's adult children, (3) either one of the decedent's parents, (4) any one of the decedent's adult siblings, (5) the decedent's personal representative, and (6) any adult in the next degree of kinship determined as if the person died intestate.

§ 711.002. Disposition of Remains; Duty to Inter

(a) Except as provided by Subsection (l), unless a decedent has left directions in writing for the disposition of the decedent's remains as provided in Subsection (g), the following persons, in the priority listed, have the right to control the disposition, including cremation, of the decedent's remains, shall inter the remains, and in accordance with Subsection (a-1) are liable for the reasonable cost of interment:

(1) the person designated in a written instrument signed by the decedent;

(2) the decedent's surviving spouse;

(3) any one of the decedent's surviving adult children;

(4) either one of the decedent's surviving parents;

(5) any one of the decedent's surviving adult siblings; [or]

(6) any one or more of the duly qualified executors or administrators of the decedent's estate; or

(7) any adult person in the next degree of kinship in the order named by law to inherit the estate of the decedent.

(a-1) If the person with the right to control the disposition of the decedent's remains fails to make final arrangements or appoint another person to make final arrangements for the disposition before the earlier of the 6th day after the date the person received notice of the decedent's death or the 10th day after the date the decedent died, the person is presumed to be unable or unwilling to control the disposition, and:

(1) the person's right to control the disposition is terminated; and

(2) the right to control the disposition is passed to the following persons in the following priority:

(A) any other person in the same priority class under Subsection (A) as the person whose right was terminated; or

(B) a person in a different priority class, in the priority listed in Subsection (A).

(a-2) If a United States Department of Defense Record of Emergency Data, DD Form 93, or a successor form, was in effect at the time of death for a decedent who died in a manner described by 10 U.S.C. Sections 1481(a)(1) through (8), the DD Form 93 controls over any other written instrument described by Subsection (a)(1) or (g) with respect to designating a person to control the disposition of the decedent's remains. Notwithstanding Subsections (b) and (c), the form is legally sufficient if it is properly completed, signed by the decedent, and witnessed in the manner required by the form.

(a-3) A person exercising the right to control the disposition of remains under Subsection (a), other than a duly qualified executor or administrator of the decedent's estate, is liable for the reasonable cost of interment and may seek reimbursement for that cost from the decedent's estate. When an executor or administrator exercises the right to control the disposition of remains under Subsection (a)(6), the decedent's estate is liable for the reasonable cost of interment, and the executor or administrator is not individually liable for that cost.

(b) The written instrument referred to in Subsection (a)(1) may [shall] be in substantially the following form:

APPOINTMENT FOR [OF AGENT TO CONTROL] DISPOSITION OF REMAINS

I, _____,
(your name and address) being of sound mind, willfully and voluntarily make known my desire that, upon my death, the disposition of my remains shall be controlled by _____ (name of agent) in accordance with Section 711.002 of the Health and Safety Code and, with respect to that subject only, I hereby appoint such person as my agent (attorney-in-fact).

All decisions made by my agent with respect to the disposition of my remains, including cremation, shall be binding.

SPECIAL DIRECTIONS:
Set forth below are any special directions limiting the power granted to my agent:

_____

_____

AGENT:
Name: _____
Address: _____
Telephone Number: _____
Acceptance of Appointment: _____
                    (signature of agent)
Date of Signature: _____

SUCCESSORS:

If my agent or a successor agent dies, becomes legally disabled, resigns, or refuses to act, or if I divorce my agent or successor agent and this instrument does not state that the divorced agent or successor agent continues to serve after my divorce from that agent or successor agent, I hereby appoint the following persons (each to act alone and successively, in the order named) to serve as my agent (attorney-in-fact) to control the disposition of my remains as authorized by this document:

1. First Successor
Name: _____
Address: _____
Telephone Number: _____
Acceptance of Appointment: _____
                  (signature of first successor)
Date of Signature: _____

2. Second Successor
Name: _____
Address: _____

Telephone Number: _____
Acceptance of Appointment: _____
                  (signature of second successor)
Date of Signature: _____

DURATION:
This appointment becomes effective upon my death.

PRIOR APPOINTMENTS REVOKED:
I hereby revoke any prior appointment of any person to control the disposition of my remains.

RELIANCE:
I hereby agree that any cemetery organization, business operating a crematory or columbarium or both, funeral director or embalmer, or funeral establishment who receives a copy of this document may act under it. Any modification or revocation of this document is not effective as to any such party until that party receives actual notice of the modification or revocation. No such party shall be liable because of reliance on a copy of this document.

ASSUMPTION:
THE AGENT, AND EACH SUCCESSOR AGENT, BY ACCEPTING THIS APPOINTMENT, ASSUMES THE OBLIGATIONS PROVIDED IN, AND IS BOUND BY THE PROVISIONS OF, SECTION 711.002 OF THE HEALTH AND SAFETY CODE.

SIGNATURES:
This written instrument and my appointments of an agent and any successor agent in this instrument are valid without the signature of my agent and any successor agents below. Each agent, or a successor agent, acting pursuant to this appointment must indicate acceptance of the appointment by signing below before acting as my agent.

Signed this _____ day of _____, 20 [19].
_____
         (your signature)

State of _____
County of _____
This document was acknowledged before me on _____ (date) by _____ (name of principal).

_____
(signature of notarial officer)
(Seal, if any, of notary)
_____ (printed name)
My commission expires: _____

ACCEPTANCE AND ASSUMPTION BY AGENT:

I have no knowledge of or any reason to believe this Appointment for Disposition of Remains has been revoked. I hereby accept the appointment made in this instrument with the understanding that I will be individually liable for the reasonable cost of the decedent's interment, for which I may seek reimbursement from the decedent's estate.

Acceptance of Appointment:

_____

(signature of agent)

Date of Signature: _____

Acceptance of Appointment:

_____
(signature of first successor)

Date of Signature: _____

Acceptance of Appointment:

_____
(signature of second successor)

Date of Signature: _____

(c) A written instrument is legally sufficient under Subsection (a)(1) if the instrument designates a person to control the disposition of the decedent's remains, the instrument is signed by the decedent, the signature of the decedent is acknowledged, and the agent or successor agent signs the instrument before acting as the decedent's agent. Unless the instrument provides otherwise, the designation of the decedent's spouse as an agent or successor agent in the instrument is revoked on the divorce of the decedent and the spouse appointed as an agent or successor agent [wording of the instrument complies substantially with Subsection (b), the instrument is properly completed, the instrument is signed by the decedent, the agent, and each successor agent, and the signature of the decedent is acknowledged]. Such written instrument may be modified or revoked only by a subsequent written instrument that complies with this subsection.

(d) A person listed in Subsection (a) has the right, duty, and liability provided by that subsection only if there is no person in a priority listed before the person.

(e) If there is no person with the duty to inter under Subsection (a) and:

(1) an inquest is held, the person conducting the inquest shall inter the remains; and

(2) an inquest is not held, the county in which the death occurred shall inter the remains.

(f) A person who represents that the person knows the identity of a decedent and, in order to procure the disposition, including cremation, of the decedent's remains, signs an order or statement, other than a death certificate, warrants the identity of the decedent and is liable for all damages that result, directly or indirectly, from that warrant.

(g) A person may provide written directions for the disposition, including cremation, of the person's remains in a will, a prepaid funeral contract, or a written instrument signed and acknowledged by such person. A party to the prepaid funeral contract or a written contract providing for all or some of a decedent's funeral arrangements who fails to honor the contract is liable for the additional expenses incurred in the disposition of the decedent's remains as a result of the breach of contract. The directions may govern the inscription to be placed on a grave marker attached to any plot in which the decedent had the right of sepulture at the time of death and in which plot the decedent is subsequently interred. The directions may be modified

or revoked only by a subsequent writing signed and acknowledged by such person. The person otherwise entitled to control the disposition of a decedent's remains under this section shall faithfully carry out the directions of the decedent to the extent that the decedent's estate or the person controlling the disposition are financially able to do so.

(h) If the directions are in a will, they shall be carried out immediately without the necessity of probate. If the will is not probated or is declared invalid for testamentary purposes, the directions are valid to the extent to which they have been acted on in good faith.

(i) A cemetery organization, a business operating a crematory or columbarium or both, a funeral director or an embalmer, or a funeral establishment shall not be liable for carrying out the written directions of a decedent or the directions of any person who represents that the person is entitled to control the disposition of the decedent's remains.

(k) Any dispute among any of the persons listed in Subsection (a) concerning their right to control the disposition, including cremation, of a decedent's remains shall be resolved by a court of competent jurisdiction. A cemetery organization or funeral establishment shall not be liable for refusing to accept the decedent's remains, or to inter or otherwise dispose of the decedent's remains, until it receives a court order or other suitable confirmation that the dispute has been resolved or settled.

(l) A person listed in Subsection (a) may not control the disposition of the decedent's remains if, in connection with the decedent's death, an indictment has been filed charging the person with a crime under Chapter 19, Penal Code, that involves family violence against the decedent. A person regulated under Chapter 651, Occupations Code, who knowingly allows the person charged with a crime to control the disposition of the decedent's remains in violation of this subsection commits a prohibited practice under Section 651.460, Occupations Code, and the Texas Funeral Service Commission may take disciplinary action or assess an administrative penalty against the regulated person under that chapter.

Acts 1989, 71st Leg., ch. 678, § 1, eff. Sept. 1, 1989. Amended by Acts 1991, 72nd Leg., ch. 14, § 213, eff. Sept. 1, 1991. Amended by Acts 1993, 73rd Leg., ch. 634, § 2, eff. Sept. 1, 1993; Acts 1997, 75th Leg., ch. 967, § 1, eff. Sept. 1, 1997; Acts 1999, 76th Leg., ch. 1385, § 1, eff. Aug. 30, 1999. Subsec. (a-1) added by Acts 2011, 82nd Leg., ch. 95, § 1, eff. May 20, 2011. Subsec. (a-1) added by Acts 2011, Amended by 82nd Leg., ch. 532, § 2, eff. Sept. 1, 2011. Subsec. (a-1) added by Acts 2011, 82nd Leg., ch. 1336, § 2, eff. Sept. 1, 2011. Subsec. (a) amended by and subsec. (j) repealed by Acts 2011, 82nd Leg., ch. 707, § 1, eff. June 17, 2011. Subsection (a-1)as added by Acts 2011, 82nd Leg., ch. 95, § 1, redesignated as subsection (a-2) by Acts 2013, 83rd Leg., ch. 161, § 22.001(28), eff. Jan. 1, 2014. Amended by Acts 2015, 84th Leg., ch. 1103, § 1, eff. Sept. 1, 2015. Subsec. (l) amended by Acts 2015, Acts 2015, 84th Leg., ch. 619, § 2, eff. Sept. 1, 2015.

Subchapter C. Cemetery Organizations

Statutes in Context
§ 711.039

A burial plot is presumed to be the separate property of the person named as the grantee in the certificate of ownership or the deed to the plot under § 711.039. The spouse of the grantee has a vested right of interment for the spouse's remains in the plot while (1) the spouse is married to the plot owner, or (2) if the spouse is married to the plot owner at the time of the plot owner's death. Unless the spouse either (1) joins in a conveyance, or (2) consents in writing and attaches the consent to the conveyance, any attempted conveyance will not divest the spouse of the vested right of interment.

A plot owner who is interred in the plot and who wishes to transfer all rights in the plot must either (1) make a specific disposition of the plot by express reference to the plot in the plot owner's will (a gift of "all my property" would not transfer the burial plot), or (2) file and record a written declaration in the office of the cemetery organization. If the plot owner does not do so, then (1) a grave, niche, or crypt in the plot is reserved for the plot owner's surviving spouse, and (2) the plot owner's children, in order of need, have the right to be interred in any remaining locations in the plot without the consent of a person claiming an interest in the plot.

§ 711.039. Rights of Interment in Plot

(a) A plot in which the exclusive right of sepulture is conveyed is presumed to be the separate property of the person named as grantee in the certificate of ownership or other instrument of conveyance.

(b) The spouse of a person to whom the exclusive right of sepulture in a plot is conveyed has a vested right of interment of the spouse's remains in the plot while the spouse is married to the plot owner or if the spouse is married to the plot owner at the time of the owner's death.

(c) An attempted conveyance or other action without the joinder or written, attached consent of the spouse of the plot owner does not divest the spouse of the vested right of interment.

(d) The vested right of interment is terminated:

(1) on the final decree of divorce between the plot owner and the owner's former spouse unless the decree provides otherwise; or

(2) when the remains of the person having the vested right are interred elsewhere.

(e) Unless a plot owner who has the exclusive right of sepulture in a plot and who is interred in that plot has made a specific disposition of the plot by express reference to the plot in the owners will or by written declaration filed and recorded in the office of the cemetery organization:

(1) a grave, niche, or crypt in the plot shall be reserved for the surviving spouse of the plot owner; and

(2) the owner's children, in order of need, may be interred in any remaining graves, niches, or crypts of the plot without the consent of a person claiming an interest in the plot.

(f) The surviving spouse or a child of an interred plot owner may each waive his right of interment in the plot in favor of a relative of the owner or relative of the owner's spouse. The person in whose favor the waiver is made may be interred in the plot.

(g) The exclusive right of sepulture in an unused grave, niche, or crypt of a plot in which the plot owner has been interred may be conveyed only by:

(1) specific disposition of the unused grave, niche, or crypt by express reference to it in a will or by written declaration of the plot owner filed and recorded in the office of the cemetery organization; or

(2) the surviving spouse if any, and the heirs-at-law of the owner.

(h) Unless a deceased plot owner who has the exclusive right of sepulture in a plot and who is not interred in the plot has otherwise made specific disposition of the plot, the exclusive right of sepulture in the plot, except the one grave, niche, or crypt reserved for the surviving spouse, if any, vests on the death of the owner in the owner's heirs-at-law and may be conveyed by them.

Amended by Acts 1993, 73rd Leg., ch. 634, § 20, eff. Sept. 1, 1993; Acts 2001, 77th Leg., ch. 502, § 1, eff. Sept. 1, 2001.

Chapter 712. Perpetual Care Cemeteries

Subchapter B. Perpetual Care Trust Fund

Statutes in Context
Chapter 712

Chapter 712 addresses issues concerning perpetual care cemeteries.

§ 712.020. Conflict With Other Law

To the extent of any conflict between this subchapter and Subtitle B, Title 9, Property Code, this subchapter controls.

Added by Acts 2015, 84th Leg., ch. 19, § 1, eff. May. 15, 2015.

§ 712.021. Establishment and Purposes of Fund

(a) A corporation that operates a perpetual care cemetery in this state shall have a fund established with a trust company or a bank with trust powers that is located in this state. The trust company or bank may not have more than one director who is also a director of the corporation.

(b) Except as provided by Section 712.0255, the [The] principal of the fund may not be reduced voluntarily, and it must remain inviolable. The trustee shall maintain the principal of the fund separate from all operating funds of the corporation.

(c) In establishing a fund, the corporation may adopt plans for the general care, maintenance, and embellishment of its perpetual care cemetery.

(d) The fund and the trustee are governed by the Texas Trust Code (Section 111.001 et seq., Property Code).

(e) A corporation that establishes a fund may receive and hold for the fund and as a part of the fund or as an incident to the fund any property contributed to the fund.

(f) The fund and contributions to the fund are for charitable purposes. The perpetual care financed by the fund is:

(1) the discharge of a duty due from the corporation to persons interred and to be interred in its perpetual care cemetery; and

(2) for the benefit and protection of the public by preserving and keeping the perpetual care cemetery from becoming a place of disorder, reproach, and desolation in the community in which the perpetual care cemetery is located.

(g) The trustors of two or more perpetual care trust funds may establish a common trust fund in which deposits required by this chapter are made, provided that separate records of principal and income are maintained for each perpetual care cemetery for the benefit of which the common trust fund is established, and further provided that the income attributable to each perpetual care cemetery is used only for the perpetual care of that cemetery.

Acts 1989, 71ˢᵗ Leg., ch. 678, § 1, eff. Sept. 1, 1989. Amended by Acts 1993, 73ʳᵈ Leg., ch. 634, § 31, eff. Sept. 1, 1993. Subsec. (b) amended by Acts 2015, 84ᵗʰ Leg., ch. 19, § 2, eff. May 15, 2015.

§ 712.0255. Judicial Modification or Termination of Fund

(a) The commissioner may petition a court to modify or terminate a fund under Section 112.054, Property Code. In addition to the grounds described by that section, the commissioner may petition a court under that section if the income from the fund is inadequate to maintain, repair, and care for the perpetual care cemetery and another source for providing additional contributions to the fund is unavailable.

(b) If feasible, the corporation for the perpetual care cemetery and the trustee of the fund are necessary parties to an action described by this section. A court may not modify or terminate the fund without the consent of the commissioner.

(c) At the request or with the consent of the commissioner, the court may order the distribution and transfer of all or a portion of the assets in the fund to a nonprofit corporation, municipality, county, or other appropriate person who is willing to accept, continue to care for, and maintain the perpetual care cemetery. A transfer under this subsection does not limit the court's ability to modify or terminate the fund under an action described by this section.

Added by Acts 2015, 84ᵗʰ Leg., ch. 19, §3 , eff. May 15, 2015.

§ 712.030. Use of Gift for Special Care of Plot in Perpetual Care Cemetery

A trustee may take and hold property transferred to the trustee in trust in order to apply the principal, proceeds, or income of the property for any purpose consistent with the purpose of a corporation's perpetual care cemetery, including:

(1) the improvement or embellishment of any part of the perpetual care cemetery;

(2) the erection, renewal, repair, or preservation of a monument, fence, building, or other structure in the perpetual care cemetery;

(3) planting or cultivating plants in or around the perpetual care cemetery; or

(4) taking special care of or embellishing a plot, section, or building in the perpetual care cemetery.

Acts 1989, 71ˢᵗ Leg., ch. 678, § 1, eff. Sept. 1, 1989. Amended by Acts 1993, 73ʳᵈ Leg., ch. 634, § 40, eff. Sept. 1, 1993.

XII.

INSURANCE CODE

Title 7. Life Insurance and Annuities

Subtitle A. Life Insurance in General

Chapter 1103. Life Insurance Policy Beneficiaries

Subchapter D. Forfeiture of Beneficiary's Rights

Statutes in Context
§ 1103.151 & § 1103.152

Section 1103.151 provides that a beneficiary of a life insurance policy who wilfully kills the insured may not collect the proceeds and § 1103.152 explains how the contingent beneficiary in the policy is then normally entitled to the proceeds.

---

§ 1103.151. Forfeiture

A beneficiary of a life insurance policy or contract forfeits the beneficiary's interest in the policy or contract if the beneficiary is a principal or an accomplice in wilfully bringing about the death of the insured.

Added by Acts 2001, 77ᵗʰ Leg., ch. 1419, § 2, eff. June 1, 2003.

§ 1103.152. Payment of Proceeds to Contingent Beneficiary or to Relative

(a) Except as provided by Subsection (b), if a beneficiary of a life insurance policy or contract forfeits an interest in the policy or contract under Section 1103.151, a contingent beneficiary named by the insured in the policy or contract is entitled to receive the proceeds of the policy or contract.

(b) A contingent beneficiary is not entitled to receive the proceeds of a life insurance policy or contract if the contingent beneficiary forfeits an interest in the policy or contract under Section 1103.151.

(c) If there is not a contingent beneficiary entitled to receive the proceeds of a life insurance policy or contract under Subsection (a), the nearest relative of the insured is entitled to receive those proceeds.

Added by Acts 2001, 77ᵗʰ Leg., ch. 1419, § 2, eff. June 1, 2003.

Chapter 1104. Life Insurance and Annuity Contracts Issued to Certain Persons

Subchapter B. Trustee Named as Beneficiary of Life Insurance Policy

---

Statutes in Context
§§ 1104.021–1104.025

A trustee of an inter vivos trust or testamentary may be named as the beneficiary of a life insurance policy under §§ 1104.021 - 1104.025. This is consistent with Property Code § 111.004(12).

---

§ 1104.021. Trustee Named as Beneficiary in Policy

(a) An individual may make a trust agreement providing that the proceeds of a life insurance policy insuring the individual be made payable to a trustee named as beneficiary in the policy. The validity of a trust agreement or declaration of trust that is designated as a beneficiary of a life insurance policy is not affected by whether any corpus of the trust exists in addition to the right of the trustee to receive insurance proceeds.

(b) Life insurance policy proceeds described by Subsection (a) shall be paid to the trustee. The trustee shall hold and dispose of the proceeds as provided by the trust agreement.

Added by Acts 2001, 77ᵗʰ Leg., ch. 1419, § 2, eff. June 1, 2003. Subsec. (a) amended by Acts 2009, 81ˢᵗ Leg., ch. 672, § 1, eff. Sept. 1, 2009.

§ 1104.022. Trustee Named as Beneficiary in Will

(a) A life insurance policy may provide that the beneficiary of the policy be a trustee designated by will in accordance with the policy provisions and the requirements of the insurance company.

(b) Except as provided by Subsection (c), on probate of a will described by Subsection (a), the life insurance policy proceeds shall be paid to the trustee. The trustee shall hold and dispose of the proceeds as provided under the terms of the will as the will existed on the date of the testator's death and in the same manner as other testamentary trusts are administered.

(c) Except as otherwise provided by agreement with the insurance company during the life of the insured, the insurance company shall pay the life insurance policy proceeds to the executors, administrators, or assigns of the insured if, during the 18-month period beginning on the first day after the date of the insured's death:

(1) a qualified trustee does not make to the insurance company a claim to the proceeds; or

(2) the insurance company is provided satisfactory evidence showing that there is or will be no trustee to receive the proceeds.

Added by Acts 2001, 77ᵗʰ Leg., ch. 1419, § 2, eff. June 1, 2003.

§ 1104.023. Debts; Inheritance Tax

Life insurance policy proceeds received by a trustee under this subchapter are not subject to debts of the insured or to inheritance tax to any greater extent than if the proceeds were payable to a beneficiary other than the executor or administrator of the insured's estate.

Added by Acts 2001, 77ᵗʰ Leg., ch. 1419, § 2, eff. June 1, 2003.

§ 1104.024. Commingling

Life insurance policy proceeds received by a trustee under this subchapter may be commingled with any other assets properly coming into the trust.

Added by Acts 2001, 77ᵗʰ Leg., ch. 1419, § 2, eff. June 1, 2003.

§ 1104.025. Certain Prior Beneficiary Designations Not Affected

This subchapter does not affect the validity of a life insurance policy beneficiary designation made before July 1, 1967, that names as beneficiary a trustee of a trust established by will.

Added by Acts 2001, 77ᵗʰ Leg., ch. 1419, § 2, eff. June 1, 2003.

Chapter 1108. Benefits Exempt from Seizure

Statutes in Context
§ 1108.001 & § 1108.002

Sections 1108.001 - 1108.102 protect payments from many life insurance policies and annuity plans from creditors of both the insured and the beneficiary.

Subchapter A. General Provisions.

§ 1108.001. Construction with Other Law

The exemptions under this chapter are in addition to the exemptions from garnishment, attachment, execution, or other seizure under Chapter 42, Property Code.

Added by Acts 2001, 77ᵗʰ Leg., ch. 1419, § 2, eff. June 1, 2003.

§ 1108.002. Annuity Contracts

For purposes of regulation under this code, an annuity contract is considered an insurance policy or contract if the annuity contract is issued:

(1) by a life, health, or accident insurance company, including a mutual company or fraternal benefit society; or

(2) under an annuity or benefit plan used by an employer or individual.

Added by Acts 2001, 77ᵗʰ Leg., ch. 1419, § 2, eff. June 1, 2003.

Subchapter B. Exemptions from Seizure

§ 1108.051. Exemptions for Certain Insurance and Annuity Benefits

(a) Except as provided by Section 1108.053, this section applies to any benefits, including the cash value and proceeds of an insurance policy, to be provided to an insured or beneficiary under:

(1) an insurance policy or annuity contract issued by a life, health, or accident insurance company, including a mutual company or fraternal benefit society; or

(2) an annuity or benefit plan used by an employer or individual.

(b) Notwithstanding any other provision of this code, insurance or annuity benefits described by Subsection (a):

(1) inure exclusively to the benefit of the person for whose use and benefit the insurance or annuity is designated in the policy or contract; and

(2) are fully exempt from:

(A) garnishment, attachment, execution, or other seizure;

(B) seizure, appropriation, or application by any legal or equitable process or by operation of law to pay a debt or other liability of an insured or of a beneficiary, either before or after the benefits are provided; and

(C) a demand in a bankruptcy proceeding of the insured or beneficiary.

Added by Acts 2001, 77ᵗʰ Leg., ch. 1419, § 2, eff. June 1, 2003.

§ 1108.052. Exemptions Unaffected by Beneficiary Designation

The exemptions provided by Section 1108.051 apply regardless of whether:

(1) the power to change the beneficiary is reserved to the insured; or

(2) the insured or the insured's estate is a beneficiary.

Added by Acts 2001, 77ᵗʰ Leg., ch. 1419, § 2, eff. June 1, 2003. Amended by Acts 2013, 83ʳᵈ Leg., ch. 91, § 1, eff. Sept. 1, 2013.

§ 1108.053. Exceptions to Exemptions

The exemptions provided by Section 1108.051 do not apply to:

(1) a premium payment made in fraud of a creditor, subject to the applicable statute of limitations for recovering the payment;

(2) a debt of the insured or beneficiary secured by a pledge of the insurance policy or the proceeds of the policy; or

(3) a child support lien or levy under Chapter 157, Family Code.

Added by Acts 2001, 77th Leg., ch. 1419, § 2, eff. June 1, 2003. Amended by Acts 2003, 78th Leg., ch. 1276, § 10A.301(a), eff. Sept. 1, 2003.

Subchapter C. Assignment of Benefits

§ 1108.101. Assignment Generally

(a) This chapter does not prevent an insured, owner, or annuitant from assigning, in accordance with the terms of the policy or contract:

(1) any benefits to be provided under an insurance policy or annuity contract to which this chapter applies; or

(2) any other rights under the policy or contract.

(b) A benefit or right described by Subsection (a) assigned by an insured, owner, or annuitant after a child support lien notice has been filed against the insured, owner, or annuitant by the Title IV-D agency continues to be subject to the child support lien after the date of assignment. The lien continues to secure payment of all child support arrearages owed by the insured, owner, or annuitant under the underlying child support order, including arrearages that accrue after the date of assignment.

Added by Acts 2001, 77th Leg., ch. 1419, § 2, eff. June 1, 2003. Amended by Acts 2011, 82nd Leg., ch. 508, § 20, eff. Sept. 1, 2011.

§ 1108.102. Certain Assignments Void

If an insurance policy, annuity contract, or annuity or benefit plan described by Section 1108.051 prohibits a beneficiary from assigning or commuting benefits to be provided or other rights under the policy, contract, or plan, an assignment or commutation or attempted assignment or commutation of the benefits or rights by the beneficiary is void.

Added by Acts 2001, 77th Leg., ch. 1419, § 2, eff. June 1, 2003.

Chapter 1111A.   Life Settlement Contracts

Statutes in Context
Chapter 1111A

Two innovative uses of life insurance can provide valuable benefits to an insured while the insured is still alive but facing a rapidly approaching death. One technique involves a life insurance policy that requires the insurer to prepay all or a portion of the death benefit to the insured when the insured has a disabling or life threatening condition which doctors predict will cause death within a relatively short period of time. These provisions are referred to by terms such as accelerated death benefit, living needs benefit, acceleration-of-life-insurance benefit, and living payout option. The insured may then use the proceeds to offset health care expenses. Depending on the debilitating extent of the illness, the extra money also may allow the insured to enjoy the remainder of the insured's life to its fullest such as by taking a vacation before the insured becomes too ill to do so. Some policies also will provide benefits to pay for a life-saving organ transplant. State governments have been quick to authorize insurance companies to offer policies that contain accelerated benefits. By the end of 1991, the insurance commissions of all states had authorized accelerated benefits.

The other technique provides basically the same result but through a different means. In a viatical settlement, a third party purchases the life insurance policy of an insured (the viator) who has a life-threatening disease or illness. The insured receives a one-time payment which usually ranges from 50 to 80 percent of the policy's face value or the insured may elect to receive periodic payments. Most purchasers require the insured to have two years or less to live. The shorter the insured's life expectancy, the greater the purchase price will be. The purchaser becomes the owner of the policy and typically names itself as the beneficiary. The purchaser continues to pay any required premiums and receives the policy's entire face value when the insured dies.

Comprehensive provisions were enacted by the Texas Legislature to regulate viatical settlements and accelerated term life insurance benefits in 2001. These provisions were substantially revised in 2011 when the Texas Legislature repealed Chapter 1111, Subchapter A and replaced in with Chapter 1111A.

§ 1111A.001.   Short Title

This Act may be cited as the Life Settlements Act.

Added by Acts 2011, 82nd Leg., ch. 1156, § 3, eff. Sept. 1, 2011.

§ 1111A.002. Definitions

In this chapter:

(1) "Advertisement" means a written, electronic, or printed communication or a communication by means of a recorded telephone message or transmitted on radio, television, the Internet, or similar communications media, including film strips, motion pictures, and videos, published, disseminated, circulated, or placed directly before the public for the purpose of creating an interest in or inducing a person to purchase or sell, assign, devise, bequest, or transfer the death benefit or ownership of a life insurance policy or an interest in a life insurance policy under a life settlement contract.

(2) "Broker" means a person who, on behalf of an owner and for a fee, commission, or other valuable consideration, offers or attempts to negotiate a life settlement contract between an owner and a provider or estimates life expectancies for a life settlement contract. A broker who offers or attempts to negotiate a life settlement contract represents only the owner and owes a fiduciary duty to the owner to act according to the owner's instructions, and in the best interest of the owner, notwithstanding the manner in which the broker is compensated. A broker does not include an attorney, certified public accountant, or financial planner retained in the type of practice customarily performed in a professional capacity to represent the owner whose compensation is not paid directly or indirectly by the provider or any other person, except the owner.

(3) "Business of life settlements" means an activity involved in, but not limited to, offering to enter into, soliciting, negotiating, procuring, effectuating, monitoring, or tracking, of life settlement contracts.

(4) "Chronically ill" means:

(A) being unable to perform at least two activities of daily living such as eating, toileting, transferring, bathing, dressing, or continence;

(B) requiring substantial supervision to protect the individual from threats to health and safety due to severe cognitive impairment; or

(C) having a level of disability similar to that described in Paragraph (A) as determined under rules adopted by the commissioner after consideration of any applicable regulation, guideline, or determination of the United States Secretary of Health and Human Services.

(5) "Financing entity" means an underwriter, placement agent, lender, purchaser of securities, purchaser of a policy or certificate from a provider, credit enhancer, or any entity that has a direct ownership in a policy or certificate that is the subject of a life settlement contract whose principal activity related to the transaction is providing funds to effect the life settlement contract or purchase of a policy, and who has an agreement in writing with a provider to finance the acquisition of a life settlement contract. The term does not include a non-accredited investor or purchaser.

(6) "Financing transaction" means a transaction in which a licensed provider obtains financing from a financing entity including secured or unsecured financing, a securitization transaction, or a securities offering that is either registered or exempt from registration under federal and state securities law.

(7) "Fraudulent life settlement act" includes:

(A) an act or omission committed by a person who, knowingly and with intent to defraud, for the purpose of depriving another of property or for pecuniary gain, commits, or permits an employee or an agent to engage in, acts including:

(i) presenting, causing to be presented, or preparing with knowledge and belief that it will be presented to or by a provider, premium finance lender, broker, insurer, insurance agent, or any other person, false material information, or concealing material information, as part of, in support of, or concerning a fact material to one or more of the following:

(a) an application for the issuance of a life settlement contract or an insurance policy;

(b) the underwriting of a life settlement contract or an insurance policy;

(c) a claim for payment or benefit pursuant to a life settlement contract or an insurance policy;

(d) premium paid on an insurance policy;

(e) payment for and changes in ownership or beneficiary made in accordance with the terms of a life settlement contract or an insurance policy;

(f) the reinstatement or conversion of an insurance policy;

(g) in the solicitation, offer to enter into, or effectuation of a life settlement contract, or an insurance policy;

(h) the issuance of written evidence of life settlement contracts or insurance; or

(i) an application for or the existence of or any payment related to a loan secured directly or indirectly by an interest in a life insurance policy;

(ii) failing to disclose to the insurer, if the insurer has requested the disclosure, that the prospective insured has undergone a life expectancy evaluation by any person or entity other than the insurer or its authorized representatives in connection with the issuance of the policy; or

(iii) employing a device, scheme, or artifice to defraud in the business of life settlements; and

(B) acts or omissions in the furtherance of a fraud or to prevent the detection of a fraud, or acts or omissions that permit an employee or an agent to:

(i) remove, conceal, alter, destroy, or sequester from the commissioner the assets or records of a license holder or another person engaged in the business of life settlements;

(ii) misrepresent or conceal the financial condition of a license holder, financing entity, insurer, or other person;

(iii) transact the business of life settlements in violation of laws requiring a license, certificate of authority, or other legal authority for the transaction of the business of life settlements;

(iv) file with the commissioner or the chief insurance regulatory official of another jurisdiction a document containing false information or concealing information about a material fact;

(v) engage in embezzlement, theft, misappropriation, or conversion of monies, funds, premiums, credits, or other property of a provider, insurer, insured, owner, insurance policy owner, or any other person engaged in the business of life settlements or insurance;

(vi) knowingly and with intent to defraud, enter into, broker, or otherwise deal in a life settlement contract, the subject of which is a life insurance policy that was obtained by presenting false information concerning any fact material to the policy or by concealing that fact, for the purpose of misleading another, or providing information concerning any fact material to the policy, if the owner or the owner's agent intended to defraud the policy's issuer;

(vii) attempt to commit, assist, aid or abet in the commission of, or engage in conspiracy to commit the acts or omissions specified in this paragraph; or

(viii) misrepresent the state of residence of an owner to be a state or jurisdiction that does not have a law substantially similar to this chapter for the purpose of evading or avoiding the provisions of this chapter.

(8) "Insured" means a person covered under the policy being considered for sale in a life settlement contract.

(9) "Life expectancy" means the arithmetic mean of the number of months the insured under the life insurance policy to be settled can be expected to live as determined by a life expectancy company or provider considering medical records and appropriate experiential data.

(10) "Life insurance agent" means a person licensed in this state as a resident or nonresident insurance agent who has received qualification or authority to write life insurance coverage under this code.

(11) "Life settlement contract" means a written agreement entered into between a provider and an owner establishing the terms under which compensation or anything of value will be paid and is less than the expected death benefit of the insurance policy or certificate, in return for the owner's assignment, transfer, sale, devise, or bequest of the death benefit or a portion of an insurance policy or certificate of insurance for compensation; provided, however, that the minimum value for a life settlement contract must be greater than a cash surrender value or accelerated death benefit available at the time of an application for a life settlement contract. The term also includes the transfer for compensation or value of ownership or beneficial interest in a trust or other entity that owns the policy if the trust or other entity was formed or used for the principal purpose of acquiring one or more life insurance contracts that insure the life of an individual residing in this state. The term also includes:

(A) a written agreement for a loan or other lending transaction, secured primarily by an individual or group life insurance policy; and

(B) a premium finance loan made for a policy on or before the date of issuance of the policy if:

(i) the loan proceeds are not used solely to pay premiums for the policy and any costs or expenses incurred by the lender or the borrower in connection with the financing;

(ii) the owner receives on the date of the premium finance loan a guarantee of the future life settlement value of the policy; or

(iii) the owner agrees on the date of the premium finance loan to sell the policy or any portion of its death benefit on a date following the issuance of the policy.

(11-A) "Life settlement contract" does not include:

(A) a policy loan by a life insurance company under the terms of a life insurance policy or accelerated death provision contained in the life insurance policy, whether issued with the original policy or as a rider;

(B) a premium finance loan or any loan made by a bank or other licensed financial institution, provided that neither default on the loan nor the transfer of the policy in connection with the default is under an agreement or understanding with any other person for the purpose of evading regulation under this chapter;

(C) a collateral assignment of a life insurance policy by an owner;

(D) a loan made by a lender that does not violate Chapter 651, provided that the loan is not described in Subdivision (11) and is not otherwise within the definition of life settlement contract;

(E) an agreement with respect to which all the parties are closely related to the insured by blood or law or have a lawful substantial economic interest in the continued life, health, and bodily safety of the person insured, or are trusts established primarily for the benefit of the parties;

(F) a designation, consent, or agreement by an insured who is an employee of an employer in connection with the purchase by the employer, or trust established by the employer, of life insurance on the life of the employee;

(G) a bona fide business succession planning arrangement:

(i) between one or more shareholders in a corporation or between a corporation and one or more of its shareholders or one or more trusts established by its shareholders;

(ii) between one or more partners in a partnership or between a partnership and one or more of its partners or one or more trusts established by its partners; or

(iii) between one or more members in a limited liability company or between a limited liability company and one or more of its members or one or more trusts established by its members;

(H) an agreement entered into by a service recipient, or a trust established by the service recipient, and a service provider, or a trust established by the service provider, who performs significant services for the service recipient's trade or business; or

(I) any other contract, transaction, or arrangement from the definition of life settlement contract that the commissioner determines is not of the type intended to be regulated by this chapter.

(12) "Net death benefit" means the amount of the life insurance policy or certificate to be settled less any outstanding debts or liens.

(13) "Owner" means the owner of a life insurance policy or a certificate holder under a group policy, with or without a terminal illness, who enters or seeks to enter into a life settlement contract. In this chapter, the term "owner" is not limited to an owner of a life insurance policy or a certificate holder under a group policy that insures the life of an individual with a terminal or chronic illness or condition except as specifically provided. The term does not include:

(A) a provider or other license holder under this chapter;

(B) a qualified institutional buyer as defined by 17 C.F.R. Section 230.144A, as amended;

(C) a financing entity;

(D) a special purpose entity; or

(E) a related provider trust.

(14) "Patient identifying information" means an insured's address, telephone number, facsimile number, e-mail address, photograph or likeness, employer, employment status, social security number, or any other information that is likely to lead to the identification of the insured.

(15) "Policy" means an individual or group policy, group certificate, contract, or arrangement of life insurance owned by a resident of this state, regardless of whether delivered or issued for delivery in this state.

(16) "Premium finance loan" is a loan made primarily for the purposes of making premium payments on a life insurance policy that is secured by an interest in the life insurance policy.

(17) "Person" means an individual or legal entity, including a partnership, limited liability company, association, trust, or corporation.

(18) "Provider" means a person, other than an owner, who enters into or effectuates a life settlement contract with an owner. The term does not include:

(A) a bank, savings bank, savings and loan association, or credit union;

(B) a licensed lending institution or creditor or secured party pursuant to a premium finance loan agreement that takes an assignment of a life insurance policy or certificate issued pursuant to a group life insurance policy as collateral for a loan;

(C) the insurer of a life insurance policy or rider to the extent of providing accelerated death benefits or riders under Subchapter B, Chapter 1111, or cash surrender value;

(D) an individual who enters into or effectuates not more than one agreement in a calendar year for the transfer of a life insurance policy or certificate issued pursuant to a group life insurance policy, for compensation or anything of value less than the expected death benefit payable under the policy;

(E) a purchaser;

(F) any authorized or eligible insurer that provides stop loss coverage to a provider, purchaser, financing entity, special purpose entity, or related provider trust;

(G) a financing entity;

(H) a special purpose entity;

(I) a related provider trust;

(J) a broker; or

(K) an accredited investor or qualified institutional buyer as those terms are defined by 17 C.F.R. Sections 230.501 and 230.144A, respectively, as amended, who purchases a life settlement policy from a provider.

(19) "Purchased policy" means a policy or group certificate that has been acquired by a provider pursuant to a life settlement contract.

(20) "Purchaser" means a person who pays compensation or anything of value as consideration for a beneficial interest in a trust that is vested with, or for the assignment, transfer, or sale of, an ownership or other interest in a life insurance policy or a certificate issued pursuant to a group life insurance policy that has been the subject of a life settlement contract.

(21) "Related provider trust" means a titling trust or other trust established by a licensed provider or a financing entity for the sole purpose of holding the ownership or beneficial interest in purchased policies in connection with a financing transaction. In order to qualify as a related provider trust, the trust must have a written agreement with the licensed provider under which the licensed provider is responsible for ensuring compliance with all statutory and regulatory requirements and under which the trust agrees to make all records and files relating to life settlement transactions available to the department as if those records and files were maintained directly by the licensed provider.

(22) "Settled policy" means a life insurance policy or certificate that has been acquired by a provider pursuant to a life settlement contract.

(23) "Special purpose entity" means a corporation, partnership, trust, limited liability company, or other legal entity formed solely to provide either directly or indirectly access to institutional capital markets:

(A) for a financing entity or provider; or

(B) in connection with a transaction in which:

(i) the securities in the special purpose entity are acquired by the owner or by a qualified institutional buyer as defined by 17 C.F.R. Section 230.144A, as amended; or

(ii) the securities pay a fixed rate of return commensurate with established asset-backed institutional capital markets.

(24) "Terminally ill" means having an illness or sickness that can reasonably be expected to result in death not later than 24 months after the date of diagnosis.

Added by Acts 2011, 82nd Leg., ch. 1156, § 3, eff. Sept. 1, 2011.

§ 1111A.003. Licensing Requirements; Exemption

(a) A person, wherever located, may not act as a provider or broker with an owner who is a resident of this state, unless the person holds a license from the department.

(b) An application for a provider or broker license must be made to the department by the applicant on a form prescribed by the commissioner. The application must be accompanied by a fee in an amount established by the commissioner by rule. The license and renewal fees for a provider license must be reasonable and the license and renewal fees for a broker license may not exceed those established for an insurance agent, as otherwise provided by this chapter.

(c) A person who has been licensed as a life insurance agent in this state or the person's home state for at least one year and is licensed as a nonresident agent in this state meets the licensing requirements of this section and may operate as a broker.

(d) Not later than the 30th day after the first date of operating as a broker, a life insurance agent shall notify the commissioner on a form prescribed by the commissioner that the agent is acting as a broker and shall pay any applicable fee to be determined by the commissioner by rule. Notification must include an acknowledgement by the life insurance agent that the agent will operate as a broker in accordance with this chapter.

(e) An insurer that issued a policy that is the subject of a life settlement contract is not responsible for any act or omission of a broker or provider or purchaser arising out of or in connection with the life settlement transaction, unless the insurer receives compensation for the placement of a life settlement contract from the provider, purchaser, or broker in connection with the life settlement contract.

(f) A person licensed as an attorney, certified public accountant, or financial planner accredited by a nationally recognized accreditation agency, who is retained to represent the owner and whose compensation is not paid directly or indirectly by the provider or purchaser, may negotiate life settlement contracts for the owner without having to obtain a license as a broker.

(g) A license expires on the second anniversary of the date of issuance. A license holder may renew the license on payment of a renewal fee. As specified by Subsection (b), the renewal fee for a provider license may not exceed a reasonable fee.

(h) An applicant shall provide the information that the commissioner requires on forms adopted by the commissioner. The commissioner may, at any time, require an applicant to fully disclose the identity of its stockholders, except stockholders owning fewer than 10 percent of the shares of an applicant whose shares are publicly traded, partners, officers and employees, and the commissioner may, in the exercise of the commissioner's sole discretion, refuse to issue a license in the name of any person if the commissioner is not satisfied that an officer, an employee, a stockholder, or a partner of the applicant who may materially influence the applicant's conduct meets the standards of Sections 1111A.001 to 1111A.018.

(i) A license issued to a partnership, corporation, or other entity authorizes each member, officer, and designated employee named in the application and any supplement to the application to act as a license holder under the license.

(j) After the filing of an application and the payment of the license fee, the commissioner shall investigate each applicant and may issue a license if the commissioner finds that the applicant:

(1) if a provider, has provided a detailed plan of operation;

(2) is competent and trustworthy and intends to transact business in good faith;

(3) has a good business reputation and has had experience, training, or education to qualify in the business for which the license is applied;

(4) if the applicant is a legal entity, is formed or organized under the laws of this state or is a foreign legal entity authorized to transact business in this state, or provides a certificate of good standing from the state of its domicile; and

(5) has provided to the commissioner an antifraud plan that meets the requirements of Section 1111A.022 and includes:

(A) a description of the procedures for detecting and investigating possible fraudulent acts and procedures for resolving material inconsistencies between medical records and insurance applications;

(B) a description of the procedures for reporting fraudulent insurance acts to the commissioner;

(C) a description of the plan for antifraud education and training of its underwriters and other personnel; and

(D) a written description or chart outlining the arrangement of the antifraud personnel who are responsible for the investigation and reporting of possible fraudulent insurance acts and the investigation of unresolved material inconsistencies between medical records and insurance applications.

(k) The commissioner may not issue a license to a nonresident applicant unless a written designation of an agent for service of process is filed and maintained with the department or unless the applicant has filed with the department the applicant's written irrevocable consent that any action against the applicant may be commenced by service of process on the commissioner.

(l) A license holder shall file with the department not later than March 1 of each year an annual statement containing the information as the commissioner by rule prescribes.

(m) A provider may not allow any person to perform the functions of a broker unless the person holds a current, valid license as a broker, and as provided in this section.

(n) A broker may not allow any person to perform the functions of a provider unless the person holds a current, valid license as a provider, and as provided in this section.

(o) A provider or broker shall provide to the commissioner new or revised information about officers, stockholders described by Subsection (h), partners, directors, members, or designated employees within 30 days of the change.

(p) An individual licensed as a broker shall complete on a biennial basis 15 hours of training related to life settlements and life settlement transactions, as required by the commissioner. A life insurance agent who is operating as a broker under this section is not subject to the requirements of this subsection.

(q) The business of life settlements constitutes the business of insurance.

Added by Acts 2011, 82nd Leg., ch. 1156, § 3, eff. Sept. 1, 2011.

§ 1111A.004 License Suspension, Revocation, or Refusal to Renew

(a) The commissioner may suspend, revoke, or refuse to renew the license of a license holder if the commissioner finds that:

(1) there was a material misrepresentation in the application for the license;

(2) the license holder or an officer, partner, member, or director of the license holder has been guilty of fraudulent or dishonest practices, is subject to a final administrative action, or is otherwise shown to be untrustworthy or incompetent to act as a license holder;

(3) the license holder is a provider and demonstrates a pattern of unreasonably withholding payments to policy owners;

(4) the license holder no longer meets the requirements for initial licensure;

(5) the license holder or any officer, partner, member, or director of the license holder has been convicted of a felony, or of any misdemeanor with respect to which criminal fraud is an element, or has pleaded guilty or nolo contendere with respect to a felony or a misdemeanor with respect to which criminal fraud or moral turpitude is an element, regardless of whether a judgment of conviction has been entered by the court;

(6) the license holder is a provider and has entered into a life settlement contract using a form that has not been approved under this chapter;

(7) the license holder is a provider and has failed to honor contractual obligations in a life settlement contract;

(8) the license holder is a provider and has assigned, transferred, or pledged a settled policy to a person other than a provider licensed in this state, a purchaser, an accredited investor or qualified institutional buyer as defined respectively in 17 C.F.R. Section 230.144A, as amended, a financing entity, a special purpose entity, or a related provider trust; or

(9) the license holder or any officer, partner, member, or key management personnel of the license holder has violated this chapter.

(b) The commissioner may deny a license application or suspend, revoke, or refuse to renew the license of a license holder in accordance with Chapter 2001, Government Code.

Added by Acts 2011, 82nd Leg., ch. 1156, § 3, eff. Sept. 1, 2011.

§ 1111A.005 Requirements For Contract Forms, Disclosure Forms, and Advertisements

(a) A person may not use any form of life settlement contract in this state unless the form has been filed with and approved, if required, by the commissioner in a manner that conforms with the filing procedures and any time restrictions or deeming provisions for life insurance forms, policies, and contracts.

(b) An insurer may not, as a condition of responding to a request for verification of coverage or in connection with the transfer of a policy pursuant to a life settlement contract, require that the owner, insured, provider, or broker sign any form, disclosure, consent, waiver, or acknowledgment that has not been expressly approved by the commissioner for use in connection with life settlement contracts.

(c) A person may not use a life settlement contract form or provide to an owner a disclosure statement form unless the form is first filed with and approved by the commissioner. The commissioner shall disapprove a life settlement contract form or disclosure statement form if, in the commissioner's opinion, the contract or contract provisions fail to meet the requirements of Sections 1111A.011, 1111A.012, 1111A.014, and 1111A.023(b), or are unreasonable, contrary to the interests of the public, or otherwise misleading or unfair to the owner.

(d) At the commissioner's discretion, the commissioner may require the submission of advertisements.

Added by Acts 2011, 82nd Leg., ch. 1156, § 3, eff. Sept. 1, 2011.

§ 1111A.006. Reporting Requirements and Privacy

(a) For a policy settled not later than the fifth anniversary of the date of policy issuance, each provider shall file with the commissioner not later than March 1 of each year an annual statement containing the information that the commissioner prescribes by rule. In addition to any other requirements, the annual statement must specify the total number, aggregate face amount, and life settlement proceeds of policies settled during the immediately preceding calendar year, together with a breakdown of the information by policy issue year. The annual statement must also include the names of each insurance company whose policies have been settled and the brokers that have settled the policies.

(b) The information required under Subsection (a) is limited to only those transactions in which the insured is a resident of this state and may not include individual transaction data regarding the business of life settlements or information if there is a reasonable basis to find that the information could be used to identify the owner or the insured.

(c) A provider that wilfully fails to file an annual statement as required in this section, or wilfully fails to reply not later than the 30th day after the date the provider receives a written inquiry from the department about the filing of the annual statement, shall, in addition to other penalties provided by this chapter, after notice and opportunity for hearing be subject to a penalty of up to $250 for each day of delay, not to exceed $25,000 in the aggregate, for the failure to file or respond.

(d) Except as otherwise allowed or required by law, a provider, broker, insurance company, insurance agent, information bureau, rating agency or company, or any other person with actual knowledge of an insured's identity, may not disclose the identity of an insured or information that there is a reasonable basis to believe could be used to identify the insured or the insured's financial or medical information to any other person unless the disclosure is:

(1) necessary to effect a life settlement contract between the owner and a provider and the owner and insured have provided prior written consent to the disclosure;

(2) necessary to effectuate the sale of a life settlement contract, or interests in the contract, as an investment, provided the sale is conducted in accordance with applicable state and federal securities law and provided further that the owner and the insured have both provided prior written consent to the disclosure;

(3) provided in response to an investigation or examination by the commissioner or another governmental officer or agency or under Section 1111A.018;

(4) a term or condition of the transfer of a policy by one provider to another licensed provider, in which case the receiving provider shall comply with the confidentiality requirements of this subsection;

(5) necessary to allow the provider or broker or the provider's or broker's authorized representative to make contact for the purpose of determining health status provided that in this subdivision, authorized representative does not include a person who has or may have a financial interest in the settlement contract other than a provider, licensed broker, financing entity, related provider trust, or special purpose entity and that the provider or broker requires the authorized representative to agree in writing to adhere to the privacy provisions of this chapter; or

(6) required to purchase stop loss coverage.

(e) Nonpublic personal information solicited or obtained in connection with a proposed or actual life settlement contract is subject to the provisions applicable to financial institutions under the federal Gramm-Leach-Bliley Act (Pub. L. No. 106-102), and any other state and federal laws relating to confidentiality of nonpublic personal information.

Added by Acts 2011, 82nd Leg., ch. 1156, § 3, eff. Sept. 1, 2011.

§ 1111A.007. Examination

Subchapter B, Chapter 401, applies to a person engaged in the business of life settlements.

Added by Acts 2011, 82nd Leg., ch. 1156, § 3, eff. Sept. 1, 2011.

§ 1111A.008. Immunity from Liability

(a) No cause of action shall arise nor shall any liability be imposed against the commissioner, the commissioner's authorized representatives, or any examiner appointed by the commissioner for a statement made or conduct performed in good faith while carrying out this chapter.

(b) No cause of action shall arise, nor shall any liability be imposed against any person for the act of communicating or delivering information to the commissioner or the commissioner's authorized representative or examiner pursuant to an examination made under this chapter, if the act of communication or delivery was performed in good faith and without fraudulent intent or the intent to deceive. This subsection does not abrogate or modify in any way any common law or statutory privilege or immunity enjoyed by any person identified in Subsection (a).

Added by Acts 2011, 82nd Leg., ch. 1156, § 3, eff. Sept. 1, 2011.

§ 1111A.009. Investigative Authority of the Commissioner

The commissioner may investigate a suspected fraudulent life settlement act and a person engaged in the business of life settlements.

Added by Acts 2011, 82nd Leg., ch. 1156, § 3, eff. Sept. 1, 2011.

§ 1111A.010. Cost of Examinations

The reasonable and necessary cost of an examination under this chapter is to be assessed against the person being examined in accordance with Section 751.208.

Added by Acts 2011, 82nd Leg., ch. 1156, § 3, eff. Sept. 1, 2011.

§ 1111A.011 Advertising

(a) A broker or provider licensed pursuant to this chapter may conduct or participate in an advertisement in this state. The advertisement must comply with all advertising and marketing laws under Chapter 541 and rules adopted by the commissioner that are applicable to life insurers or to license holders under this chapter.

(b) Advertisements shall be accurate, truthful, and not misleading in fact or by implication.

(c) A person may not:

(1) market, advertise, solicit, or otherwise promote the purchase of a policy for the sole purpose of or with an emphasis on settling the policy; or

(2) use the words "free," "no cost," or words of similar import in the marketing, advertising, or soliciting of, or otherwise promoting, the purchase of a policy.

Added by Acts 2011, 82nd Leg., ch. 1156, § 3, eff. Sept. 1, 2011.

§ 1111A.012. Disclosures to Owners

(a) The broker, or the provider if no broker is involved in the application, shall provide in writing, in a separate document that is signed by the owner, the following information to the owner not later than the date of application for a life settlement contract:

(1) the fact that possible alternatives to life settlement contracts exist, including accelerated benefits offered by the issuer of the life insurance policy;

(2) the fact that some or all of the proceeds of a life settlement contract may be taxable and that assistance should be sought from a professional tax advisor;

(3) the fact that the proceeds from a life settlement contract could be subject to the claims of creditors;

(4) the fact that receipt of proceeds from a life settlement contract may adversely affect the recipients' eligibility for public assistance or other government benefits or entitlements and that advice should be obtained from the appropriate agency;

(5) the fact that the owner has a right to terminate a life settlement contract within 15 days of the date the contract is executed by all parties and the owner has received the disclosures described in this section, that rescission, if exercised by the owner, is effective only if both notice of the rescission is given and the owner repays all proceeds and any premiums, loans, and loan interest paid on account of the provider during the rescission period, and that if the insured dies during the rescission period, the contract is considered rescinded subject to repayment by the owner or the owner's estate of all proceeds and any premiums, loans, and loan interest to the provider;

(6) the fact that proceeds will be sent to the owner within three business days after the provider has received the insurer or group administrator's acknowledgement that ownership of the policy or interest in the certificate has been transferred and the beneficiary has been designated in accordance with the terms of the life settlement contract;

(7) the fact that entering into a life settlement contract may cause the owner to forfeit other rights or benefits, including conversion rights and waiver of premium benefits that may exist under the policy or certificate of a group policy, and that assistance should be sought from a professional financial advisor;

(8) the amount and method of calculating the compensation, including anything of value, paid or given, or to be paid or given, to the broker, or any other person acting for the owner in connection with the transaction;

(9) the date by which the funds will be available to the owner and the identity of the transmitter of the funds;

(10) the fact that the commissioner requires delivery of a buyer's guide or a similar consumer advisory package in the form prescribed by the commissioner to owners during the solicitation process;

(11) the following language: "All medical, financial, or personal information solicited or obtained by a provider or broker about an insured, including the insured's identity or the identity of family members or a spouse or a significant other, may be disclosed as necessary to effect the life settlement contract between the owner and provider. If you are asked to provide this information, you will be asked to consent to the disclosure. The information may be provided to someone who buys the policy or provides funds for the purchase. You may be asked to renew your permission to share information every two years.";

(12) the fact that the commissioner requires providers and brokers to print separate signed fraud warnings on the applications and on the life settlement contracts as follows: "Any person who knowingly presents false information in an application for insurance or a life settlement contract is guilty of a crime and may be subject to fines and confinement in prison.";

(13) the fact that the insured may be contacted by either the provider or broker or an authorized representative of the provider or broker for the purpose of determining the insured's health status or to verify the insured's address and that this contact is limited to once every three months if the insured has a life expectancy of more than one year, and not more than once per month if the insured has a life expectancy of one year or less;

(14) the affiliation, if any, between the provider and the issuer of the insurance policy to be settled;

(15) that a broker represents exclusively the owner, and not the insurer or the provider or any other person, and owes a fiduciary duty to the owner, including a duty to act according to the owner's instructions and in the best interest of the owner;

(16) the name, address, and telephone number of the provider;

(17) the name, business address, and telephone number of the independent third party escrow agent, and the fact that the owner may inspect or receive copies of the relevant escrow or trust agreements or documents; and

(18) the fact that a change of ownership could in the future limit the insured's ability to purchase future insurance on the insured's life because there is a limit to how much coverage insurers will issue on one life.

(b) The written disclosures described by Subsection (a) must be conspicuously displayed in a life settlement contract furnished to the owner by a provider, including any affiliations or contractual arrangements between the provider and the broker.

(c) A broker shall provide the owner and the provider with at least the following disclosures not later than the date on which the life settlement contract is signed by all parties and which must be conspicuously displayed in the life settlement contract or in a separate document signed by the owner:

(1) the name, business address, and telephone number of the broker;

(2) a full, complete, and accurate description of all the offers, counter-offers, acceptances, and rejections relating to the proposed life settlement contract;

(3) a written disclosure of any affiliations or contractual arrangements between the broker and any person making an offer in connection with the proposed life settlement contract;

(4) the name of each broker who receives compensation and the amount of compensation, including anything of value, paid or given to the broker in connection with the life settlement contract; and

(5) a complete reconciliation of the gross offer or bid by the provider to the net amount of proceeds or value to be received by the owner.

(d) For the purpose of this section, "gross offer or bid" means the total amount or value offered by the provider for the purchase of one or more life insurance policies, inclusive of commissions and fees.

(e) The failure to provide the disclosures or rights described in this section is an unfair method of competition or an unfair or deceptive act or practice.

Added by Acts 2011, 82nd Leg., ch. 1156, § 3, eff. Sept. 1, 2011.

§ 1111A.013. Disclosure to Insurer

(a) Without limiting the ability of an insurer to assess the insurability of a policy applicant and to determine whether to issue the policy, and in addition to other questions an insurance carrier may lawfully pose to a life insurance applicant, an insurer may inquire in the application for insurance whether the proposed owner intends to pay premiums with the assistance of financing from a lender that will use the policy as collateral to support the financing.

(b) If, as described in Sections 1111A.002(11) and (11-A), the loan provides funds that can be used for a purpose other than paying for the premiums, costs, and expenses associated with obtaining and maintaining the life insurance policy and loan, and notwithstanding any other law, the application must be rejected as a violation of Section 1111A.017.

(c) If the financing does not violate Section 1111A.017, the insurance carrier:

(1) may make disclosures, not later than the date of the delivery of the policy, to the applicant and the insured, either on the application or on an amendment to the application that include the following or substantially similar statements:

"If you have entered into a loan arrangement in which the policy is used as collateral, and the policy does change ownership at some point in the future in satisfaction of the loan, the following may be true:

(A) a change of ownership could lead to a stranger owning an interest in the insured's life;

(B) a change of ownership could in the future limit your ability to purchase future insurance on the insured's life because there is a limit to how much coverage insurers will issue on one life;

(C) should there be a change of ownership and you wish to obtain more insurance coverage on the insured's life in the future, the insured's higher issue age, a change in health status, or other factors may reduce the ability to obtain coverage or may result in significantly higher premiums; and

(D) you should consult a professional advisor, since a change in ownership in satisfaction of the loan may result in tax consequences to the owner, depending on the structure of the loan.";

(2) may require certifications, such as the following, from the applicant or the insured:

(A) "I have not entered into any agreement or arrangement providing for the future sale of this life insurance policy";

(B) "My loan arrangement for this policy provides funds sufficient to pay for some or all of the premiums, costs, and expenses associated with obtaining and maintaining my life insurance policy, but I have not entered into any agreement by which I am to receive consideration in exchange for procuring this policy"; and

(C) "The borrower has an insurable interest in the insured."

Added by Acts 2011, 82nd Leg., ch. 1156, § 3, eff. Sept. 1, 2011.

§ 1111A.014. General Rules

(a) Before entering into a life settlement contract with an owner of a policy with respect to which the insured is terminally or chronically ill, the provider must obtain:

(1) if the owner is the insured, a written statement from a licensed attending physician that the owner is of sound mind and under no constraint or undue influence to enter into a settlement contract; and

(2) a document in which the insured consents to the release of medical records to a provider, settlement broker, or insurance agent and, if the policy was issued less than two years after the date of application for a settlement contract, to the insurance company that issued the policy.

(b) An insurer shall respond to a request for verification of coverage submitted by a provider, settlement broker, or life insurance agent not later than the 30th calendar day after the date the request is received. The request for verification of coverage must be made on a form approved by the commissioner. The insurer shall complete and issue the verification of coverage or indicate in which respects the insurer is unable to respond. In the response, the insurer shall indicate whether at the time of the response, based on the medical evidence and documents provided, the insurer intends to pursue an investigation about the validity of the insurance contract.

(c) On or before the date of execution of the life settlement contract, the provider shall obtain a witnessed document in which the owner consents to the settlement contract, represents that the owner has a full and complete understanding of the settlement contract and of the benefits of the policy, acknowledges that the owner is entering into the settlement contract freely and voluntarily, and, for persons with a terminal or chronic illness or condition, acknowledges that the insured has a terminal or chronic illness and that the terminal or chronic illness or condition was diagnosed after the policy was issued.

(d) The insurer may not unreasonably delay effecting change of ownership or beneficiary with any life settlement contract lawfully entered into in this state or with a resident of this state.

(e) If a settlement broker or life insurance agent performs any of these activities required of the provider, the provider is deemed to have fulfilled the requirements of this section.

(f) If a broker performs the verification of coverage activities required of the provider, the provider is deemed to have fulfilled the requirements of Section 1111A.012.

(g) Not later than the 20th day after the date that an owner executes the life settlement contract, the provider shall give written notice to the insurer that issued that insurance policy that the policy has become subject to a life settlement contract. The notice shall be accompanied by the documents required by Section 1111A.013(c).

(h) Medical information solicited or obtained by a license holder is subject to the applicable provision of state law relating to confidentiality of medical information, if not otherwise provided in this chapter.

(i) A life settlement contract entered into in this state must provide that the owner may rescind the contract on or before 15 days after the date the contract is executed by all parties to the contract. Rescission, if exercised by the owner, is effective only if notice of the rescission is given and the owner repays all proceeds and any premiums, loans, and loan interest paid on account of the provider within the rescission period. If the insured dies during the rescission period, the contract is rescinded subject to repayment by the owner or the owner's estate of all proceeds and any premiums, loans, and loan interest to the provider.

(j) Not later than the third business day after the date the provider receives from the owner the documents to effect the transfer of the insurance policy, the provider shall pay the proceeds of the settlement into an escrow or trust account managed by a trustee or escrow agent in a state or federally chartered financial institution pending acknowledgement of the transfer by the issuer of the policy. The trustee or escrow agent shall transfer to the owner the proceeds due to the owner not later than the third business day after the date the trustee or escrow officer receives from the insurer acknowledgment of the transfer of the insurance policy.

(k) Failure to tender the life settlement contract proceeds to the owner on or before the date disclosed to the owner renders the contract voidable by the owner for lack of consideration until the time the proceeds are tendered to and accepted by the owner. A failure to give written notice of the right of rescission under this subsection tolls the right of rescission for 30 days after the date the written notice of the right of rescission has been given.

(l) A fee paid by a provider, an owner, or other person to a broker in exchange for services provided to the owner pertaining to a life settlement contract must be computed as a percentage of the offer obtained, not the face value of the policy. Nothing in this section prohibits a broker from voluntarily reducing the broker's fee to less than a percentage of the offer obtained.

(m) A broker shall disclose to the owner anything of value paid or given to a broker that relates to a life settlement contract.

(n) A person, at any time prior to or at the time of the application for, or issuance of, a policy, or during a two-year period beginning on the date of issuance of the policy, may not enter into a life settlement contract regardless of the date the compensation is to be provided and regardless of the date the assignment, transfer, sale, devise, bequest, or surrender of the policy is to occur. This prohibition does not apply if:

(1) the owner certifies to the provider that the policy was issued on the owner's exercise of conversion rights arising out of a group or individual policy, provided the total of the time covered under the conversion policy plus the time covered under the prior policy is at least 24 months; or

(2) the owner submits independent evidence to the provider that one or more of the following conditions have been met during the two-year period described by this subsection:

(A) the owner or insured is terminally or chronically ill;

(B) the owner or insured disposes of the owner's or insured's ownership interests in a closely held corporation, pursuant to the terms of a buyout or other similar agreement in effect at the time the insurance policy was initially issued;

(C) the owner's spouse dies;

(D) the owner divorces the owner's spouse;

(E) the owner retires from full-time employment;

(F) the owner becomes physically or mentally disabled and a physician determines that the disability prevents the owner from maintaining full-time employment; or

(G) a final order, judgment, or decree is entered by a court of competent jurisdiction, on the application of a creditor of the owner, adjudicating the owner bankrupt or insolvent, or approving a petition seeking reorganization of the owner or appointing a receiver, trustee, or liquidator to all or a substantial part of the owner's assets.

(o) For the purposes of Subsection (n)(1), time covered under a group policy must be calculated without regard to a change in insurance carriers, provided the coverage has been continuous and under the same group sponsorship.

(p) Copies of the independent evidence described by Subsection (n)(2) must be submitted to the insurer at the time the provider submits a request to the insurer for verification of coverage. The copies must be accompanied by a letter of attestation from the provider that the copies are true and correct copies of the documents received by the provider. This section does not prohibit an insurer from exercising its right to contest the validity of a policy.

(q) If the provider submits to the insurer a copy of independent evidence provided for Subsection (n)(2)(A) at the time the provider submits a request to the insurer to effect the transfer of the policy to the provider, the copy is deemed to establish that the settlement contract satisfies the requirements of this section.

Added by Acts 2011, 82nd Leg., ch. 1156, § 3, eff. Sept. 1, 2011.

§ 1111A.015. Authority to Adopt Rules

(a) The commissioner may adopt rules implementing this chapter and regulating the activities and relationships of providers, brokers, insurers, and their authorized representatives.

(b) The commissioner may not adopt a rule establishing a price or fee for the sale or purchase of a life settlement contract. This subsection does not prohibit the commissioner from adopting a rule relating to an unjust price or fee for the sale or purchase of a life settlement contract.

(c) The commissioner may not adopt a rule that regulates the actions of an investor providing money to a life or viatical settlement company.

Added by Acts 2011, 82ⁿᵈ Leg., ch. 1156, § 3, eff. Sept. 1, 2011.

§ 1111A.016. Conflict of Laws

(a) If there is more than one owner on a single policy, and the owners are residents of different states, the life settlement contract is governed by the law of the state in which the owner having the largest percentage ownership resides or, if the owners hold equal ownership, the state of residence of one owner agreed on in writing by all of the owners. The law of the state of the insured shall govern in the event that equal owners fail to agree in writing on a state of residence for jurisdictional purposes.

(b) A provider licensed in this state who enters into a life settlement contract with an owner who is a resident of another state that has enacted statutes or adopted rules governing life settlement contracts is governed in the effectuation of that life settlement contract by the statutes and rules of the owner's state of residence. If the state in which the owner is a resident has not enacted statutes or adopted rules governing life settlement contracts, the provider shall give the owner notice that neither state regulates the transaction on which the owner is entering. For transactions in those states, however, the provider shall maintain all records required by this chapter if the transactions were executed in this state. The forms used in those states need not be approved by the department.

(c) If there is a conflict in the laws that apply to an owner and a purchaser in any individual transaction, the laws of the state that apply to the owner shall take precedence and the provider shall comply with those laws.

Added by Acts 2011, 82ⁿᵈ Leg., ch. 1156, § 3, eff. Sept. 1, 2011.

§ 1111A.017. Prohibited Practices

(a) A person may not:

(1) enter into a life settlement contract if the person knows or reasonably should have known that the life insurance policy was obtained by means of a false, deceptive, or misleading application for the policy;

(2) engage in a transaction, practice, or course of business if the person knows or reasonably should have known that the intent of engaging in the transaction, practice, or course of business is to avoid the notice requirements of this chapter;

(3) engage in a fraudulent act or practice in connection with a transaction relating to any settlement involving an owner who is a resident of this state;

(4) issue, solicit, market, or otherwise promote the purchase of an insurance policy for the purpose of, or with an emphasis on, settling the policy;

(5) if providing premium financing, receive any proceeds, fee, or other consideration from the policy or owner in addition to the amounts required to pay principal, interest, and any reasonable costs or expenses incurred by the lender or borrower in connection with the premium finance agreement, except in event of a default, unless either the default on the loan or transfer of the policy occurs pursuant to an agreement or understanding with any other person for the purpose of evading regulation under this chapter;

(6) with respect to any settlement contract or insurance policy and to a broker, knowingly solicit an offer from, effectuate a life settlement contract with, or make a sale to any provider, financing entity, or related provider trust that is controlling, controlled by, or under common control with the broker unless the relationship is fully disclosed to the owner;

(7) with respect to any life settlement contract or insurance policy and a provider, knowingly enter into a life settlement contract with an owner if, in connection with the life settlement contract, anything of value will be paid to a broker that is controlling, controlled by, or under common control with the provider or the financing entity or related provider trust that is involved in such settlement contract, unless the relationship is fully disclosed to the owner;

(8) with respect to a provider, enter into a life settlement contract unless the life settlement promotional, advertising, and marketing materials, as may be prescribed by rule, have been filed with the commissioner, provided that in no event may any marketing materials expressly reference that the insurance is free for any period of time; or

(9) with respect to any life insurance agent, insurance company, broker, or provider, make any statement or representation to the applicant or policyholder in connection with the sale or financing of a life insurance policy to the effect that the insurance is free or without cost to the policyholder for any period of time unless provided in the policy.

(b) A violation of this section is a fraudulent life settlement act.

Added by Acts 2011, 82ⁿᵈ Leg., ch. 1156, § 3, eff. Sept. 1, 2011.

§ 1111A.018 Fraud Prevention and Control

(a) A person may not commit a fraudulent life settlement act.

(b) A person may not interfere with the enforcement of this chapter or an investigation of a suspected or actual violation of this chapter.

(c) A person in the business of life settlements may not knowingly or intentionally permit a person convicted of a felony involving dishonesty or breach of trust to participate in the business of life settlements.

(d) A life settlement contract and an application for a life settlement contract, regardless of the form of transmission, must contain the following, or a substantially similar, statement: "Any person who knowingly presents false information in an application for insurance or a life settlement contract is guilty of a crime and may be subject to fines and confinement in prison."

(e) The failure to include a statement as required in Subsection (d) is not a defense in any prosecution for a fraudulent life settlement act.

Added by Acts 2011, 82ⁿᵈ Leg., ch. 1156, § 3, eff. Sept. 1, 2011.

§ 1111A.019. Mandatory Reporting of Fraudulent Life Settlement Acts

A person engaged in the business of life settlements has a duty under Section 701.051 to report a fraudulent life settlement act.

Added by Acts 2011, 82ⁿᵈ Leg., ch. 1156, § 3, eff. Sept. 1, 2011.

§ 1111A.020. Confidentiality

(a) The documents and evidence obtained by the commissioner in an investigation of a suspected or an actual fraudulent life settlement act are privileged and confidential, are not a public record, and are not subject to discovery or subpoena in a civil or criminal action.

(b) Subsection (a) does not prohibit release by the commissioner of documents and evidence obtained in an investigation of a suspected or an actual fraudulent life settlement act:

(1) in an administrative or judicial proceeding to enforce a provision of this code or another insurance law of this state;

(2) to a federal, state, or local law enforcement or regulatory agency, to an organization established for the purpose of detecting and preventing a fraudulent life settlement act, or to the National Association of Insurance Commissioners; or

(3) at the discretion of the commissioner, to a person in the business of life settlements that is aggrieved by a fraudulent life settlement act.

(c) Release of documents and evidence under Subsection (b) does not abrogate or modify the privilege granted in Subsection (a).

Added by Acts 2011, 82ⁿᵈ Leg., ch. 1156, § 3, eff. Sept. 1, 2011.

§ 1111A.021. Other Law Enforcement or Regulatory Authority

This chapter does not:

(1) preempt the authority or relieve the duty of another law enforcement or regulatory agency to investigate, examine, and prosecute a suspected violation of law;

(2) preempt, supersede, or limit any provision of any state securities law or any rule, order, or notice issued under the law;

(3) prevent or prohibit a person from disclosing voluntarily information concerning life settlement fraud to a law enforcement or regulatory agency other than the department; or

(4) limit the powers granted by the laws of this state to the commissioner or an insurance fraud unit to investigate and examine a possible violation of law and to take appropriate action against wrongdoers.

Added by Acts 2011, 82ⁿᵈ Leg., ch. 1156, § 3, eff. Sept. 1, 2011.

§ 1111A.022. Life Settlement Antifraud Initiatives

(a) A provider or broker shall implement antifraud initiatives reasonably calculated to detect, prosecute, and prevent fraudulent life settlement acts. At the discretion of the commissioner, the commissioner may order, or a license holder may request and the commissioner may grant, a modification of the following required initiatives as necessary to ensure an effective antifraud program. A modification granted under this section may be more or less restrictive than the required initiatives so long as the modification may reasonably be expected to accomplish the purpose of this section. Antifraud initiatives must include:

(1) fraud investigators, who may be provider or broker employees or independent contractors; and

(2) an antifraud plan, which must be submitted to the commissioner and must include:

(A) a description of the procedures for detecting and investigating possible fraudulent life settlement acts and procedures for resolving material inconsistencies between medical records and insurance applications;

(B) a description of the procedures for reporting possible fraudulent life settlement acts to the commissioner;

(C) a description of the plan for antifraud education and training of underwriters and other personnel; and

(D) a description or chart outlining the organizational arrangement of the antifraud personnel who are responsible for the investigation and reporting of possible fraudulent life settlement acts and investigating unresolved material inconsistencies between medical records and insurance applications.

(b) An antifraud plan submitted to the commissioner is privileged and confidential, is not subject to disclosure under Chapter 552, Government Code, and is not subject to discovery or subpoena in a civil action.

Added by Acts 2011, 82nd Leg., ch. 1156, § 3. eff. Sept. 1, 2011.

§ 1111A.023. Injunction; Civil Remedies; Cease and Desist Orders

(a) In addition to the penalties and other enforcement provisions of this chapter, if any person violates this chapter or any rule implementing this chapter, the commissioner may seek an injunction in a court in the county where the person resides or has a principal place of business and may apply for temporary and permanent orders that the commissioner determines necessary to restrain the person from further committing the violation.

(b) The commissioner may issue a cease and desist order against a person who violates any provision of this chapter, any rule or order adopted by the commissioner, or any written agreement entered into with the commissioner, in accordance with Chapter 82.

(c) If the commissioner finds that an action in violation of this chapter presents an immediate danger to the public and requires an immediate final order, the commissioner may issue an emergency cease and desist order under Chapter 83.

(d) The provisions of this chapter may not be waived by agreement. No choice of law provision may prevent the application of this chapter to any settlement.

Added by Acts 2011, 82nd Leg., ch. 1156, § 3. eff. Sept. 1, 2011.

§ 1111A.024. Penalties

(a) It is a violation of this chapter for any person, provider, broker, or any other party related to the business of life settlements to commit a fraudulent life settlement act.

(b) A person who knowingly, recklessly, or intentionally commits a fraudulent life settlement act commits a criminal offense and is subject to penalties under Chapter 35, Penal Code.

(c) Subtitle B, Title 2, applies to a violation of this chapter.

Added by Acts 2011, 82nd Leg., ch. 1156, § 3. eff. Sept. 1, 2011.

§ 1111A.025. Applicability of Other Insurance Laws

The following laws apply to a person engaged in the business of life settlements:

(1) Chapters 82, 83, 84, 101, 481, and 701;

(2) Sections 31.002, 32.021, 32.023, 32.041, 38.001, 81.004, 86.001, 86.051, 86.052, 201.004, 401.051, 401.054, 401.151(a), 521.003, 521.004, 543.001(c), 801.056, and 862.052;

(3) Subchapter A, Chapter 32;

(4) Subchapter C, Chapter 36;

(5) Subchapter B, Chapter 404; and

(6) Subchapter B, Chapter 491.

Added by Acts 2011, 82nd Leg., ch. 1156, § 3. eff. Sept. 1, 2011.

§ 1111A.026. Applicability of Certain Provisions to Life Expectancy Estimators

(a) The following provisions do not apply to a broker who acts solely as a life expectancy estimator:

(1) Section 1111A.003(p);

(2) Section 1111A.012; and

(3) Sections 1111A.014(l) and (m).

(b) The commissioner may exempt a broker who acts only as a life expectancy estimator from other provisions of this chapter if the commissioner finds that the application of those provisions to the broker is not necessary for the public welfare.

Added by Acts 2011, 82nd Leg., ch. 1156, § 3. eff. Sept. 1, 2011.

XIII.
LOCAL GOVERNMENT CODE

Title 4.   Finances

Subtitle B.   County Finances

Chapter 118.   Fees Charged by County Officers

Subchapter C.   Fees of Clerk of County Court

§ 118.052.   Fee Schedule

Each clerk of a county court shall collect the following fees for services rendered to any person:

(1) CIVIL COURT ACTIONS

   (A) Filing of Original Action (Sec. 118.053):

      (i) Garnishment after judgment . . . $15.00

      (ii) All others . . . $40.00

   (B) Filing of Action Other than Original (Sec. 118.054) . . . $30.00

   (C) Services Rendered After Judgment in Original Action (Sec. 118.0545):

      (i) Abstract of judgment . . . $ 5.00

      (ii) Execution, order of sale, writ, or other process . . . $ 5.00

(2) PROBATE COURT ACTIONS

   (A) Probate Original Action (Sec. 118.055):

      (i) Probate of a will with independent executor, administration with will attached, administration of an estate, guardianship or receivership of an estate, or muniment of title . . . $40.00

      (ii) Community survivors . . . $40.00

      (iii) Small estates . . . $40.00

      (iv) Declarations of heirship . . . $40.00

      (v) Mental health or chemical dependency services . . . $40.00

      (vi) Additional, special fee (Sec. 118.064) . . . $ 5.00

   (B) Services in Pending Probate Action (Sec. 118.056):

      (i) Filing an inventory and appraisement as provided by Section 118.056(d) . . . $25.00

      (ii) Approving and recording bond . . . $ 3.00

      (iii) Administering oath . . . $ 2.00

      (iv) Filing annual or final account of estate . . . $25.00

      (v) Filing application for sale of real or personal property . . . $25.00

      (vi) Filing annual or final report of guardian of a person . . . $10.00

      (vii) Filing a document not listed under this paragraph after the filing of an order approving the inventory and appraisement or after the 120th day after the date of the initial filing of the action, whichever occurs first, if more than 25 pages . . . $25.00

   (C) Adverse Probate Action (Sec. 118.057) . . . $40.00

   (D) Claim Against Estate (Sec. 118.058) . . . $10.00 [$ 2.00]

   (E) Supplemental Court-Initiated Guardianship Fee in Probate Original Actions and Adverse Probate Actions (Sec. 118.067) . . . $20.00

   (F) Supplemental Public Probate Administrator Fee For Counties That Have Appointed a Public Probate Administrator (Sec. 118.068) . . . $10.00

(3) OTHER FEES

   (A) Issuing Document (Sec. 118.059): original document and one copy . . . $ 4.00

   each additional set of an original and one copy . . . $ 4.00

   (B) Certified Papers (Sec. 118.060): for the clerk's certificate . . . $ 5.00

   plus a fee per page or part of a page of . . . $ 1.00

   (C) Noncertified Papers (Sec. 118.0605): for each page or part of a page . . . $ 1.00

   (D) Letters Testamentary, Letter of Guardianship, Letter of Administration, or Abstract of Judgment (Sec. 118.061) . . . $ 2.00

   (E) Safekeeping of Wills (Sec. 118.062) . . . $ 5.00

   (F) Mail Service of Process (Sec. 118.063) . . . same as sheriff

   (G) Records Management and Preservation Fee . . . $ 5.00

   (H) Records Technology and Infrastructure Fee if authorized by the commissioners court of the county (Sec. 118.026) . . . $ 2.00

Acts 1987, 70th Leg., ch. 149, § 1. eff. Sept. 1, 1987. Amended by Acts 1989, 71st Leg., ch. 1. § 19(a), eff. Aug. 28, 1989; Acts 1989, 71st Leg., ch. 1080, § 7, eff. Sept. 1, 1989; Acts 1991, 72nd Leg., ch. 587. § 3, eff. Sept. 1, 1991; Acts 1993, 73rd Leg., ch. 554, § 3, eff. Sept. 1, 1993; Acts 1993, 73rd Leg., ch. 675, § 1, eff. Sept. 1, 1993; Acts 1995, 74th Leg., ch. 764, § 3, eff. Aug. 28, 1995; Acts 1999, 76th Leg., ch. 1001, § 1, eff. Sept. 1, 1999; Acts 2005, 79th Leg., ch. 1233, § 1, eff. Sept. 1, 2005; Acts 2007, 80th Leg., ch. 96, § 2. eff. Sept. 1, 2007; Acts 2007, 80th Leg., ch. 399, § 1, eff. Sept. 1,

2007. Amended by Acts 2013, 83rd Leg., ch. 671, § 4, eff. Jan. 1, 2014. Subsec. (2)(D) amended by Acts 2015, 84th Leg., ch. 654, § 6, eff. Sept. 1, 2015. Subsec. (3)(G) added by Acts 2015, 84th Leg., ch. 379, § 4, eff. Sept. 1, 2015.

§ 118.055. Probate Original Action

(a) The fee for "Probate Original Action" under Section 118.052(2(A)) is for all clerical duties in connection with an original action in a probate court.

(b) The fee for affidavits of heirship includes the filing of the affidavit, after approval by the judge, in the small estates records of the county clerk's office.

(c) The fee for an action involving mental health or chemical dependency services is for the services listed in Sections 571.016, 571.017, 571.018, and 574.008(c), Health and Safety Code, or services under Subchapter C or D, Chapter 462, Health and Safety Code. The fees shall be paid by the person executing the application for mental health or chemical dependency services and are due at the time the application is filed if the services requested relate to services provided or to be provided in a private facility. If the services requested relate to services provided or to be provided in a mental health facility of the Texas Department of Mental Health and Mental Retardation or the federal government, the county clerk may collect the fees only in accordance with Section 571.018(h), Health and Safety Code.

(d) Except as otherwise provided, the fees listed in this section are total fees. The fee for probate of a will with independent executor, administration with a will attached, administration of an estate, guardianship or receivership of an estate, or muniment of title is for services rendered from the initiating of the action until either an order approving the inventory and appraisement is filed or the 120th day after the date on which the action is filed, whichever occurs first.

(e) Except as provided by Subsection (c), the fee shall be paid by the party initiating the action and is due at the time the action is initiated, except that with the permission of the court the fee may be paid:

(1) at the time that the legal or personal representative of the estate qualifies; or

(2) if a Veterans Administration chief attorney is the attorney of record, at the time the legal or personal representative of the estate receives funds with which to make the payment.

(f) The fee does not apply to services for which another fee is prescribed by Section 118.052(1), 118.052(2)(B), 118.052(2)(D), or 118.052(3).

Acts 1987, 70th Leg., ch. 149, § 1, eff. Sept. 1, 1987. Amended by Acts 1991, 72nd Leg., ch. 76, § 18, eff. Sept. 1, 1991; Acts 1991, 72nd Leg., ch. 587, § 4, eff. Sept. 1, 1991; Acts 1993, 73rd Leg., ch. 174, § 2, eff. Aug. 30, 1993; Acts 1997, 75th Leg., ch. 584, § 1, eff. Sept. 1, 1997; Acts 2007, 80th Leg., ch. 96, § 3, eff. Sept. 1, 2007.

§ 118.056. Services in Pending Probate Action

(a) Except as provided by Subsection (d), the fees for "Services in Pending Probate Action" under Section 118.052(2) are for services in an action in an open probate docket rendered after the filing of an order approving the inventory and appraisement or after the 120th day after the date of the initial filing of the action, whichever occurs first.

(b) The fee for filing a document also applies to each page or part of a page for the filing of a document or exhibit filed by a movant after the filing of an original answer or response, after the filing of an order approving the inventory and appraisement, or after the 120th day after the date of the initial filing of the action, whichever occurs first, and before the filing of an adverse action, contest, suit, or pleading seeking affirmative relief.

(c) Each fee shall be paid in cash at the time of the filing or the rendering of the service and is in addition to other fees prescribed by Section 118.052.

(d) The fee for filing an inventory and appraisement under Section 118.052(2)(B)(i) applies only if the instrument is filed after the 90th day after the date the personal representative has qualified to serve or, if the court grants an extension under Section 309.051, Estates [250, Texas Probate] Code, after the date of the extended deadline specified by the court.

Acts 1987, 70th Leg., ch. 149, § 1, eff. Sept. 1, 1987. Amended by Acts 1999, 76th Leg., ch. 66, § 1, eff. Sept. 1, 1999. Subsec. (a) amended by subsec. (d) added by Acts 2007, 80th Leg., ch. 399, §2, eff. Sept. 1, 2007. Subsec. (d) amended by Acts 2015, 84th Leg., ch. 1236, § 20.021, eff. Sept. 1, 2015.

XIV.
PENAL CODE

Title 5. Offenses Against the Person

Chapter 22. Assaultive Offenses

Statutes in Context
§ 22.08

Assisted suicide arises when the person committing suicide needs help in procuring the means to commit the act such as a weapon, drugs, or Dr. Jack Kevorkian's "suicide machine." The person, however, self-administers the lethal agent by pulling the trigger, swallowing the pills, turning on the gas, or the like. If a doctor assists the person in procuring the fatal drugs, the term physician-assisted suicide is often used. Assisted suicide in general is sometimes called passive euthanasia because the euthanatizer merely supplies the means of death rather than directly causing the death. Assisted suicide can be contrasted with voluntary euthanasia in which the euthanatizer actually kills the person at that person's request. The term involuntary euthanasia is reserved for cases where the euthanatizer kills a person out of reasons of mercy but where the person did not specifically request to be killed.

Most state legislatures have enacted statutes such as § 22.08 of the Texas Penal Code which make it a crime to assist someone to commit suicide. These statutes withstood constitutional muster in the United States Supreme Court case of *Vacco v. Quill*, 117 S. Ct. 2293 (1997). The Court held that the United States Constitution does not guarantee a person the right to die and that states can prohibit assisted suicide. However, the Court indicated that a state may decide to authorize and regulate assisted suicide. As of August 2003, Oregon is the only state to permit its citizens to seek assistance in procuring the means to commit suicide.

Note that withholding or withdrawing life-sustaining procedures under a valid directive to physicians or out-of-hospital do-not-resuscitate order is not considered aiding suicide. See Health and Safety Code §§ 166.047 and 166.096.

§ 22.08. Aiding Suicide

(a) A person commits an offense if, with intent to promote or assist the commission of suicide by another, he aids or attempts to aid the other to commit or attempt to commit suicide.

(b) An offense under this section is a Class C misdemeanor unless the actor's conduct causes suicide or attempted suicide that results in serious bodily injury, in which event the offense is a state jail felony.

Acts 1973, 63rd Leg., p. 883, ch. 399, § 1, eff. Jan. 1, 1974. Amended by Acts 1993, 73rd Leg., ch. 900, § 1.01, eff. Sept. 1, 1994.

Title 7. Offenses Against Property

Chapter 32. Fraud

Subchapter D. Other Deceptive Practices

Statutes in Context
§ 32.45

Section 32.45 provides criminal penalties when a fiduciary such as an executor, administrator, trustee, or guardian misapplies property, that is, deals with the property contrary to the terms of the instrument (trust, will, etc.) or any law prescribing the custody or disposition of the property (Probate Code, Property Code, etc.). Note that the fiduciary's conduct must be intentional, knowing, or reckless. Mere negligent conduct will not give rise to a criminal offense although it may subject the fiduciary to civil liability. No actual loss to the property or gain to the fiduciary is necessary. All that must occur is that the property be handled in a manner that involves substantial risk of loss.

§ 32.45. Misapplication of Fiduciary Property or Property of Financial Institution

(a) For purposes of this section:

(1) "Fiduciary" includes:

(A) a trustee, guardian, administrator, executor, conservator, and receiver;

(B) an attorney in fact or agent appointed under a durable power of attorney as provided by Chapter XII, Texas Probate Code;

(C) any other person acting in a fiduciary capacity, but not a commercial bailee unless the commercial bailee is a party in a motor fuel sales agreement with a distributor or supplier, as those terms are defined by Section 162.001, Tax Code; and

(D) an officer, manager, employee, or agent carrying on fiduciary functions on behalf of a fiduciary.

(2) "Misapply" means deal with property contrary to:

(A) an agreement under which the fiduciary holds the property; or

(B) a law prescribing the custody or disposition of the property.

(b) A person commits an offense if he intentionally, knowingly, or recklessly misapplies property he holds as a fiduciary or property of a financial institution in a manner that involves substantial risk of loss to the owner of the property or to a person for whose benefit the property is held.

(c) An offense under this section is:

(1) a Class C misdemeanor if the value of the property misapplied is less than $100 [$20];

(2) a Class B misdemeanor if the value of the property misapplied is $100 [$20] or more but less than $750 [$500];

(3) a Class A misdemeanor if the value of the property misapplied is $750 [$500] or more but less than $2,500 [$1,500];

(4) a state jail felony if the value of the property misapplied is $2,500 [$1,500] or more but less than $30,000 [$20,000];

(5) a felony of the third degree if the value of the property misapplied is $30,000 [$20,000] or more but less than $150,000 [$100,000];

(6) a felony of the second degree if the value of the property misapplied is $150,000 [$100,000] or more but less than $300,000 [$200,000]; or

(7) a felony of the first degree if the value of the property misapplied is $300,000 [$200,000] or more.

(d) With the consent of the appropriate local county or district attorney, the attorney general has concurrent jurisdiction with that consenting local prosecutor to prosecute an offense under this section that involves the state Medicaid program.

(e) An offense described for purposes of punishment by Subsections (c)(1)-(6) is increased to the next higher category of offense if it is shown on the trial of the offense that the offense was committed against an elderly individual as defined by Section 22.04.

Acts 1973, 63rd Leg., p. 883, ch. 399, § 1, eff. Jan. 1, 1974. Amended by Acts 1991, 72nd Leg., ch. 565, § 2, eff. Sept. 1, 1991; Acts 1993, 73rd Leg., ch. 900, § 1.01, eff. Sept. 1, 1994; Amended by Acts 1997, 75th Leg., ch. 1036, § 14, eff. Sept. 1, 1997; Acts 2001, 77th Leg., ch 1047, § 1, eff. Sept. 1, 2001; Acts 2003, 78th Leg., ch. 198, § 2.137, eff. Sept. 1, 2003; Acts 2003, 78th Leg., ch. 257, § 14, eff. Sept. 1, 2003; Acts 2003, 78th Leg., ch. 432, § 3, eff. Sept. 1, 2003. Former subsec. (d) renamed as new subsec. (e) as amended by Acts 2005, 79th Leg., ch. 728, § 23.001(77), eff. Sept. 1, 2005. Subsec. (a) subdiv. (1) amended by Acts 2013, 83rd Leg., ch. 128, § 5, eff. Sept. 1, 2013. Subsec. (c) amended by Acts 2015, 84th Leg., ch. 1251, § 21, eff. Sept. 1, 2015.

---

§ 32.47
Statutes in Context

A person who fraudulently destroys, alters, or conceals a will, trust, power of attorney, or other writing may be subject to criminal liability under § 32.47.

---

§ 32.47. Fraudulent Destruction, Removal, or Concealment of Writing

(a) A person commits an offense if, with intent to defraud or harm another, he destroys, removes, conceals, alters, substitutes, or otherwise impairs the verity, legibility, or availability of a writing, other than a governmental record.

(b) For purposes of this section, "writing" includes:

(1) printing or any other method of recording information;

(2) money, coins, tokens, stamps, seals, credit cards, badges, trademarks;

(3) symbols of value, right, privilege, or identification; and

(4) universal product codes, labels, price tags, or markings on goods.

(c) Except as provided in Subsection (d), an offense under this section is a Class A misdemeanor.

(d) An offense under this section is a state jail felony if the writing:

(1) is a will or codicil of another, whether or not the maker is alive or dead and whether or not it has been admitted to probate; or

(2) is a deed, mortgage, deed of trust, security instrument, security agreement, or other writing for which the law provides public recording or filing, whether or not the writing has been acknowledged.

Acts 1973, 63rd Leg., p. 883, ch. 399, § 1, eff. Jan. 1, 1974. Amended by Acts 1993, 73rd Leg., ch. 900, § 1.01, eff. Sept. 1, 1994; Acts 2001, 77th Leg., ch. 21, § 1, eff. Sept. 1, 2001.

XV.
PROBATE CODE

Statutes in Context
Probate Code

The Texas Probate Code ceased to be effective on January 1, 2014.

The final version of the Texas Probate Code showing in red-lined format the changes made by the 2013 Legislature is available on a complimentary basis at www.ProfessorBeyer.com/Estates_Code/Texas _Probate_Code_(08-19-2013).pdf.

XVI.
PROPERTY CODE

Title 2. Conveyances

Chapter 5. Conveyances

Subchapter A. General Provisions

Statutes in Context
§ 5.001

At common law, a fee simple was granted only if the words of limitation "and his heirs" were used. Section 5.001 reverses the common law presumption so that a grant "to A" results in A receiving a fee simple.

---

§ 5.001. Fee Simple

(a) An estate in land that is conveyed or devised is a fee simple unless the estate is limited by express words or unless a lesser estate is conveyed or devised by construction or operation of law. Words previously necessary at common law to transfer a fee simple estate are not necessary.

(b) This section applies only to a conveyance occurring on or after February 5, 1840.

Acts 1983, 68th Leg., p. 3480, ch. 576, § 1, eff. Jan. 1, 1984.

§ 5.002. Failing as a Conveyance

An instrument intended as a conveyance of real property or an interest in real property that, because of this chapter, fails as a conveyance in whole or in part is enforceable to the extent permitted by law as a contract to convey the property or interest.

Acts 1983, 68th Leg., p. 3480, ch. 576, § 1, eff. Jan. 1, 1984.

§ 5.003. Partial Conveyance

(a) An alienation of real property that purports to transfer a greater right or estate in the property than the person making the alienation may lawfully transfer alienates only the right or estate that the person may convey.

(b) Neither the alienation by deed or will of an estate on which a remainder depends nor the union of the estate with an inheritance by purchase or descent affects the remainder.

Acts 1983, 68th Leg., p. 3480, ch. 576, § 1, eff. Jan. 1, 1984.

§ 5.004. Conveyance by Authorized Officer

(a) A conveyance of real property by an officer legally authorized to sell the property under a judgment of a court within the state passes absolute title to the property to the purchaser.

(b) This section does not affect the rights of a person who is not or who does not claim under a party to the conveyance or judgment.

Acts 1983, 68th Leg., p. 3480, ch. 576, § 1, eff. Jan. 1, 1984.

§ 5.005. Aliens

An alien has the same real and personal property rights as a United States citizen.

Acts 1983, 68th Leg., p. 3481, ch. 576, § 1, eff. Jan. 1, 1984.

§ 5.009. Duties of Life Tenant

(a) Subject to Subsection (b), if the life tenant of a legal life estate is given the power to sell and reinvest any life tenancy property, the life tenant is subject, with respect to the sale and investment of the property, to all of the fiduciary duties of a trustee imposed by the Texas Trust Code (Subtitle B, Title 9, Property Code)[1] or the common law of this state.

(b) A life tenant may retain, as life tenancy property, any real property originally conveyed to the life tenant without being subject to the fiduciary duties of a trustee; however, the life tenant is subject to the common law duties of a life tenant.

Acts 1993, 73rd Leg., ch. 846, § 34, eff. Sept. 1, 1993. Renumbered from § 5.008 by Acts 1995, 74th Leg., ch. 76, § 17.01(42), eff. Sept. 1, 1995.

Subchapter C. Future Estates

§ 5.041. Future Estates

A person may make an inter vivos conveyance of an estate of freehold or inheritance that commences in the future, in the same manner as by a will.

Acts 1983, 68th Leg., p. 3483, ch. 576, § 1, eff. Jan. 1, 1984.

---

[1] Property Code §111.001 et seq.

Statutes in Context
§ 5.042

Section 5.042 abolishes many of the arcane common law rules regarding conveyances such as the Rule in Shelley's case and the Doctrine of Worthier Title.

§ 5.042. Abolition of Common-Law Rules

(a) The common-law rules known as the rule in Shelley's case, the rule forbidding a remainder to the grantor's heirs, the doctrine of worthier title, and the doctrine or rule prohibiting an existing lien upon part of a homestead from extending to another part of the homestead not charged with the debts secured by the existing lien upon part of the homestead do not apply in this state.

(b) A deed, will, or other conveyance of property in this state that limits an interest in the property to a particular person or to a class such as the heirs, heirs of the body, issue, or next of kin of the conveyor or of a person to whom a particular interest in the same property is limited is effective according to the intent of the conveyor.

(c) Status as an heir or next of kin of a conveyor or the failure of a conveyor to describe a person in a conveyance other than as a member of a class does not affect a person's right to take or share in an interest as a conveyee.

(d) Subject to the intention of a conveyor, which controls unless limited by law, the membership of a class described in this section and the participation of a member in a property interest conveyed to the class are determined under this state's laws of descent and distribution.

(e) This section does not apply to a conveyance taking effect before January 1, 1964.

Amended by Acts 1999, 76th Leg., ch. 1510, § 5, eff. Sept. 1, 1999.

Statutes in Context
§ 5.043

Article I, § 26 of the Texas Constitution adopts the common law version of the Rule Against Perpetuities, that is, "a future interest not destructible by the owner of a prior interest cannot be valid unless it becomes vested at a date not more remote than twenty-one years after lives in being at the creation of such interest, plus the period of gestation. Any future interest so limited that it retains its indestructible and contingent character until a more remote time is invalid." Interpretive Commentary to Article I, § 21. The court must, however, reform or construe transfers that violate the Rule under § 5.043 to carry out the general intent and specific directives of the grantor to the extent possible without violating the Rule. The court may apply the equitable doctrine of cy

pres in this process. See also Property Code § 112.036 (indicating that the Rule does not apply to charitable trusts).

§ 5.043. Reformation of Interests Violating Rule Against Perpetuities

(a) Within the limits of the rule against perpetuities, a court shall reform or construe an interest in real or personal property that violates the rule to effect the ascertainable general intent of the creator of the interest. A court shall liberally construe and apply this provision to validate an interest to the fullest extent consistent with the creator's intent.

(b) The court may reform or construe an interest under Subsection (a) of this section according to the doctrine of cy pres by giving effect to the general intent and specific directives of the creator within the limits of the rule against perpetuities.

(c) If an instrument that violates the rule against perpetuities may be reformed or construed under this section, a court shall enforce the provisions of the instrument that do not violate the rule and shall reform or construe under this section a provision that violates or might violate the rule.

(d) This section applies to legal and equitable interests, including noncharitable gifts and trusts, conveyed by an inter vivos instrument or a will that takes effect on or after September 1, 1969, and this section applies to an appointment made on or after that date regardless of when the power was created.

Amended by Acts 1991, 72nd Leg., ch. 895, § 16, eff. Sept. 1, 1991.

Title 4. Actions and Remedies

Chapter 26. Use of a Deceased Individual's Name, Voice, Signature, Photograph, or Likeness

Statutes in Context
Chapter 26

Chapter 26 establishes that an individual has a property right in the use of the individual's name, voice, signature, photograph, or likeness after the individual's death. Chapter 26 further explains how that right may be transferred, who owns the right after the person's death, and who may exercise the right.

§ 26.001. Definitions

In this chapter:

(1) "Photograph" means a photograph or photographic reproduction, still or moving, videotape, or live television transmission of an individual in a manner that allows a person viewing the photograph

with the naked eye to reasonably determine the identity of the individual.

(2) "Property right" means the property right created by this chapter.

(3) "Name" means the actual or assumed name used by an individual which, when used in conjunction with other information, is intended to identify a particular person.

(4) "Media enterprise" means a newspaper, magazine, radio station or network, television station or network, or cable television system.

Added by Acts 1987, 70ᵗʰ Leg., ch. 152, § 1, eff. Sept. 1, 1987.

§ 26.002. Property Right Established

An individual has a property right in the use of the individual's name, voice, signature, photograph, or likeness after the death of the individual.

Added by Acts 1987, 70ᵗʰ Leg., ch. 152, § 1, eff. Sept. 1, 1987.

§ 26.003. Applicability

This chapter applies to an individual:

(1) alive on or after September 1, 1987, or who died before September 1, 1987, but on or after January 1, 1937; and

(2) whose name, voice, signature, photograph, or likeness has commercial value at the time of his or her death or comes to have commercial value after that time.

Added by Acts 1987, 70ᵗʰ Leg., ch. 152, § 1, eff. Sept. 1, 1987.

§ 26.004. Transferability

(a) The property right is freely transferable, in whole or in part, by contract or by means of trust or testamentary documents.

(b) The property right may be transferred before or after the death of the individual.

Added by Acts 1987, 70ᵗʰ Leg., ch. 152, § 1, eff. Sept. 1, 1987.

§ 26.005. Ownership After Death of Individual

(a) If the ownership of the property right of an individual has not been transferred at or before the death of the individual, the property right vests as follows:

(1) if there is a surviving spouse but there are no surviving children or grandchildren, the entire interest vests in the surviving spouse;

(2) if there is a surviving spouse and surviving children or grandchildren, one-half the interest vests in the surviving spouse and one-half the interest vests in the surviving children or grandchildren;

(3) if there is no surviving spouse, the entire interest vests in the surviving children of the deceased individual and the surviving children of any deceased children of the deceased individual; or

(4) if there is no surviving spouse, children, or grandchildren, the entire interest vests in the surviving parents of the deceased individual.

(b) The interests of the deceased individual's children and grandchildren are divided among them and exercisable on a per stirpes basis in the manner provided by Section 43, Texas Probate Code, according to the number of the deceased individual's children represented. If there is more than one child of a deceased child of the deceased individual, the share of a child of a deceased child may only be exercised by a majority of the children of the deceased child.

(c) If the property right is split among more than one person, those persons who own more than a one-half interest in the aggregate may exercise the right on behalf of all persons who own the right.

Added by Acts 1987, 70ᵗʰ Leg., ch. 152, § 1, eff. Sept. 1, 1987.

§ 26.006. Registration of Claim

(a) A person who claims to own a property right may register that claim with the secretary of state.

(b) The secretary of state shall provide a form for registration of a claim under this section. The form must be verified and must include:

(1) the name and date of death of the deceased individual;

(2) the name and address of the claimant;

(3) a statement of the basis of the claim; and

(4) a statement of the right claimed.

(c) The secretary of state may microfilm or reproduce by another technique a document filed under this section and destroy the original document.

(d) A document or a reproduction of a document filed under this section is admissible in evidence.

(e) The secretary of state may destroy all documents filed under this section after the 50ᵗʰ anniversary of the date of death of the individual whose property right they concern.

(f) The fee for filing a claim is $25.

(g) A document filed under this section is a public record.

Added by Acts 1987, 70ᵗʰ Leg., ch. 152, § 1, eff. Sept. 1, 1987.

§ 26.007. Effect of Registration

(a) Registration of a claim is prima facie evidence of a valid claim to a property right.

(b) A registered claim is superior to a conflicting, unregistered claim unless a court invalidates the registered claim.

Added by Acts 1987, 70ᵗʰ Leg., ch. 152, § 1, eff. Sept. 1, 1987.

§ 26.008. Exercise of Ownership for First Year Following Death of Individual

(a) Except as provided by Subsection (b), for the first year following the death of the individual a property right may be exercised, if authorized by law or an appointing court, by the following persons who may be appointed by a court for the benefit of the estate of the deceased individual:

(1) an independent executor;

(2) an executor;

(3) an independent administrator;

(4) a temporary or permanent administrator; or

(5) a temporary or permanent guardian.

(b) For the first year following the death of the individual, an owner of a property right may exercise that right only if the owner registers a valid claim as provided by Section 26.006.

Added by Acts 1987, 70th Leg., ch. 152, § 1, eff. Sept. 1, 1987.

§ 26.009. Exercise of Ownership After First Year Following Death of Individual

After the first year following the death of the individual, an owner of a property right may exercise that right whether or not the owner has registered a claim as provided by Section 26.006.

Added by Acts 1987, 70th Leg., ch. 152, § 1, eff. Sept. 1, 1987.

§ 26.010. Termination

A property right expires on the first anniversary of the date of death of the individual if:

(1) the individual has not transferred the right; and

(2) a surviving person under Section 26.005 does not exist.

Added by Acts 1987, 70th Leg., ch. 152, § 1, eff. Sept. 1, 1987.

§ 26.011. Unauthorized Uses

Except as provided by Section 26.012, a person may not use, without the written consent of a person who may exercise the property right, a deceased individual's name, voice, signature, photograph, or likeness in any manner, including:

(1) in connection with products, merchandise, or goods; or

(2) for the purpose of advertising, selling, or soliciting the purchase of products, merchandise, goods, or services.

Added by Acts 1987, 70th Leg., ch. 152, § 1, eff. Sept. 1, 1987.

§ 26.012. Permitted Uses

(a) A person may use a deceased individual's name, voice, signature, photograph, or likeness in:

(1) a play, book, film, radio program, or television program;

(2) a magazine or newspaper article;

(3) material that is primarily of political or newsworthy value;

(4) single and original works of fine art; or

(5) an advertisement or commercial announcement concerning a use under this subsection.

(b) A media enterprise may use a deceased individual's name, voice, signature, photograph, or likeness in connection with the coverage of news, public affairs, a sporting event, or a political campaign without consent. Any use other than the above by a media enterprise of a deceased individual's name, voice, signature, photograph, or likeness shall require consent if the material constituting the use is integrally and directly connected with commercial sponsorship or paid advertising. No consent shall be required for the use of the deceased individual's name, voice, signature, photograph, or likeness by a media enterprise if the broadcast or article is not commercially sponsored or does not contain paid advertising.

(c) A person who is an owner or employee of a media enterprise, including a newspaper, magazine, radio station or network, television station or network, cable television system, billboard, or transit ad, that is used for advertising a deceased individual's name, voice, signature, photograph, or likeness in a manner not authorized by this section is not liable for damages as provided by this section unless the person:

(1) knew that the use was not authorized by this section; or

(2) used the deceased individual's name, voice, signature, photograph, or likeness in a manner primarily intended to advertise or promote the media enterprise itself.

(d) A person may use a deceased individual's name, voice, signature, photograph, or likeness in any manner after the 50th anniversary of the date of the individual's death.

Added by Acts 1987, 70th Leg., ch. 152, § 1, eff. Sept. 1, 1987.

§ 26.013. Liability for Unauthorized Use

(a) A person who uses a deceased individual's name, voice, signature, photograph, or likeness in a manner not authorized by this chapter is liable to the person who owns the property right for:

(1) the amount of any damages sustained, as a result of the unauthorized use, by the person who owns the property right or $2,500, whichever is greater;

(2) the amount of any profits from the unauthorized use that are attributable to that use;

(3) the amount of any exemplary damages that may be awarded; and

(4) reasonable attorney's fees and expenses and court costs incurred in recovering the damages and profits established by this section.

(b) The amount of profits under Subsection (a)(2) may be established by a showing of the gross revenue attributable to the unauthorized use minus any expenses that the person who committed the unauthorized use may prove.

Added by Acts 1987, 70th Leg., ch. 152, § 1, eff. Sept. 1, 1987.

§ 26.014. Other Rights Not Affected

This chapter does not affect a right an individual may have in the use of the individual's name, voice, signature, photograph, or likeness before the death of the individual.

Added by Acts 1987, 70th Leg., ch. 152, § 1, eff. Sept. 1, 1987.

§ 26.015. Defenses to Liability

A person shall not be liable for damages under this chapter if he has acted in reliance on the results of a probate proceeding governing the estate of the deceased personality in question.

Added by Acts 1987, 70th Leg., ch. 152, § 1, eff. Sept. 1, 1987.

Title 5.   Exempt Property and Liens

Subtitle A.   Property Exempt from Creditors' Claims

Chapter 41.   Interests in Land

Subchapter A.   Exemptions in Land Defined

Statutes in Context
§ 41.001

The source of the tremendous protection granted to Texas homesteads is Article XVI, § 50 of the Texas Constitution. See *Statutes in Context* to Article XVI, § 50 for additional information.

Section 41.001(c) provides that after a homestead is sold, the proceeds remain protected for 6 months. In other words, a person who sells a homestead has 6 months to reinvest the proceeds in a new homestead.

---

§ 41.001.   Interests in Land Exempt from Seizure

(a) A homestead and one or more lots used for a place of burial of the dead are exempt from seizure for the claims of creditors except for encumbrances properly fixed on homestead property.

(b) Encumbrances may be properly fixed on homestead property for:

(1) purchase money;

(2) taxes on the property;

(3) work and material used in constructing improvements on the property if contracted for in writing as provided by Sections 53.254(a), (b), and (c);

(4) an owelty of partition imposed against the entirety of the property by a court order or by a written agreement of the parties to the partition, including a debt of one spouse in favor of the other spouse resulting from a division or an award of a family homestead in a divorce proceeding;

(5) the refinance of a lien against a homestead, including a federal tax lien resulting from the tax debt of both spouses, if the homestead is a family homestead, or from the tax debt of the owner;

(6) an extension of credit that meets the requirements of Section 50(a)(6), Article XVI, Texas Constitution; or

(7) a reverse mortgage that meets the requirements of Sections 50(k)-(p), Article XVI, Texas Constitution.

(c) The homestead claimant's proceeds of a sale of a homestead are not subject to seizure for a creditor's claim for six months after the date of sale.

Amended by Acts 1984, 68th Leg., 2nd C.S., p. 216, ch. 18, § 2(b), eff. Oct. 2, 1984. Amended by Acts 1985, 69th Leg., ch. 840, § 1, eff. June 15, 1985; Acts 1993, 73rd Leg., ch. 48, § 2, eff. Sept. 1, 1993; Acts 1995, 74th Leg., ch. 121, § 1.01, eff. May 17, 1995; Acts 1995, 74th Leg., ch. 121, § 2.01; Acts 1997, 75th Leg., ch. 526, § 1, eff. Sept. 1, 1997; Acts 2001, 77th Leg., ch. 516, § 1, eff. Sept. 1, 2001.

Statutes in Context
§ 41.002

Homesteads are classified by property type as either rural or urban. The size of the exemption depends on this classification and is set forth in Article XVI, § 51 of the Texas Constitution. See *Statutes in Context* to Article XVI, § 51.

Note that § 41.002(b) attempts to reduce the size of a rural homestead for a single adult to 100 acres. It is unclear whether the Property Code may cut back the constitutionally provided 200-acre rural homestead.

---

§ 41.002.   Definition of Homestead

(a) If used for the purposes of an urban home or as both an urban home and a place to exercise a calling or business, the homestead of a family or a single, adult person, not otherwise entitled to a homestead, shall consist of not more than 10 acres of land which may be in one or more contiguous lots, together with any improvements thereon.

(b) If used for the purposes of a rural home, the homestead shall consist of:

(1) for a family, not more than 200 acres, which may be in one or more parcels, with the improvements thereon; or

(2) for a single, adult person, not otherwise entitled to a homestead, not more than 100 acres,

which may be in one or more parcels, with the improvements thereon.

(c) A homestead is considered to be urban if, at the time the designation is made, the property is:

(1) located within the limits of a municipality or its extraterritorial jurisdiction or a platted subdivision; and

(2) served by police protection, paid or volunteer fire protection, and at least three of the following services provided by a municipality or under contract to a municipality:

(A) electric;

(B) natural gas;

(C) sewer;

(D) storm sewer; and

(E) water.

(d) The definition of a homestead as provided in this section applies to all homesteads in this state whenever created.

Amended by Acts 1985, 69th Leg., ch. 840, § 1, eff. June 15, 1985; Acts 1989, 71st Leg., ch. 391, § 2, eff. Aug. 28, 1989; Acts 1999, 76th Leg., ch. 1510, § 1, eff. Jan. 1, 2000; Acts 1999, 76th Leg., ch. 1510, § 2, eff. Sept. 1, 1999.

Statutes in Context
§ 41.0021

The 2009 Legislature provided that if a settlor transfers property to a "qualifying trust" (basically a revocable inter vivos trust) which otherwise would qualify as the homestead of the settlor or the beneficiary had it not been transferred into the trust, this property may still qualify as the settlor's or beneficiary's homestead if the person occupies and uses it as his or her homestead. Accordingly, the homestead does not lose the creditor protection it would normally have merely because the homestead property is being held in trust form.

---

§ 41.0021. Homestead in Qualifying Trust

(a) In addition to the exemption prescribed by Section 42.001, a person's right to the assets held in or to receive payments, whether vested or not, under any stock bonus, pension, annuity, deferred compensation, profit-sharing, or similar plan, including a retirement plan for self-employed individuals, or a simplified employee pension plan, an individual retirement account or individual retirement annuity, including an inherited individual retirement account or individual retirement annuity, or a health savings account, and under any annuity or similar contract purchased with assets distributed from that type of plan or account, is exempt from attachment, execution, and seizure for the satisfaction of debts to the extent the plan, contract, annuity, or account is exempt from federal income tax, or to the extent federal income tax on the person's interest is deferred until actual payment of benefits to the person under Section 223, 401(a), 403(a), 403(b),

408(a), 408A, 457(b), or 501(a), Internal Revenue Code of 1986, including a government plan or church plan described by Section 414(d) or (e), Internal Revenue Code of 1986. For purposes of this subsection, the interest of a person in a plan, annuity, account, or contract acquired by reason of the death of another person, whether as an owner, participant, beneficiary, survivor, coannuitant, heir, or legatee, is exempt to the same extent that the interest of the person from whom the plan, annuity, account, or contract was acquired was exempt on the date of the person's death. If this subsection is held invalid or preempted by federal law in whole or in part or in certain circumstances, the subsection remains in effect in all other respects to the maximum extent permitted by law.

(b) Property that a settlor or beneficiary occupies and uses in a manner described by this subchapter and in which the settlor or beneficiary owns a beneficial interest through a qualifying trust is considered the homestead of the settlor or beneficiary under Section 50, Article XVI, Texas Constitution, and Section 41.001.

(c) Amounts distributed from a plan, annuity, account, or contract entitled to an exemption under Subsection (a) are not subject to seizure for a creditor's claim for 60 days after the date of distribution if the amounts qualify as a nontaxable rollover contribution under Subsection (b).

(d) A participant or beneficiary of a plan, annuity, account, or contract entitled to an exemption under Subsection (a), other than an individual retirement account or individual retirement annuity, is not prohibited from granting a valid and enforceable security interest in the participant's or beneficiary's right to the assets held in or to receive payments under the exempt plan, annuity, account, or contract to secure a loan to the participant or beneficiary from the exempt plan, annuity, account, or contract, and the right to the assets held in or to receive payments from the plan, annuity, account, or contract is subject to attachment, execution, and seizure for the satisfaction of the security interest or lien granted by the participant or beneficiary to secure the loan.

(e) This section does not affect the rights of a surviving spouse or surviving children under Section 52, Article XVI, Texas Constitution, or Part 3, Chapter VIII, Texas Probate Code.

Added by Acts 2009, 81st Leg., ch. 984, § 1, eff. Sept. 1, 2009. Amended by Acts 2011, 82nd Leg., ch. 933, § 1, eff. June 17, 2011.

---

§ 41.003. Temporary Renting of a Homestead

Temporary renting of a homestead does not change its homestead character if the homestead claimant has not acquired another homestead.

Amended by Acts 1985, 69th Leg., ch. 840, § 1, eff. June 15, 1985.

§ 41.004. Abandonment of a Homestead

If a homestead claimant is married, a homestead cannot be abandoned without the consent of the claimant's spouse.

Added by Acts 1985, 69ᵗʰ Leg., ch. 840, § 1, eff. June 15, 1985.

§ 41.005. Voluntary Designation of Homestead

(a) If a rural homestead of a family is part of one or more parcels containing a total of more than 200 acres, the head of the family and, if married, that person's spouse may voluntarily designate not more than 200 acres of the property as the homestead. If a rural homestead of a single adult person, not otherwise entitled to a homestead, is part of one or more parcels containing a total of more than 100 acres, the person may voluntarily designate not more than 100 acres of the property as the homestead.

(b) If an urban homestead of a family, or an urban homestead of a single adult person not otherwise entitled to a homestead, is part of one or more contiguous lots containing a total of more than ten acres, the head of the family and, if married, that person's spouse or the single adult person, as applicable, may voluntarily designate not more than 10 acres of the property as the homestead.

(c) Except as provided by Subsection (e) or Subchapter B, to designate property as a homestead, a person or persons, as applicable, must make the designation in an instrument that is signed and acknowledged or proved in the manner required for the recording of other instruments. The person or persons must file the designation with the county clerk of the county in which all or part of the property is located. The clerk shall record the designation in the county deed records. The designation must contain:

(1) a description sufficient to identify the property designated;

(2) a statement by the person or persons who executed the instrument that the property is designated as the homestead of the person's family or as the homestead of a single adult person not otherwise entitled to a homestead;

(3) the name of the current record title holder of the property; and

(4) for a rural homestead, the number of acres designated and, if there is more than one survey, the number of acres in each.

(d) A person or persons, as applicable, may change the boundaries of a homestead designated under Subsection (c) by executing and recording an instrument in the manner required for a voluntary designation under that subsection. A change under this subsection does not impair rights acquired by a party before the change.

(e) Except as otherwise provided by this subsection, property on which a person receives an exemption from taxation under Section 11.43, Tax Code, is considered to have been designated as the person's homestead for purposes of this subchapter if the property is listed as the person's residence homestead on the most recent appraisal roll for the appraisal district established for the county in which the property is located. If a person designates property as a homestead under Subsection (c) or Subchapter B and a different property is considered to have been designated as the person's homestead under this subsection, the designation under Subsection (c) or Subchapter B, as applicable, prevails for purposes of this chapter.

(f) If a person or persons, as applicable, have not made a voluntary designation of a homestead under this section as of the time a writ of execution is issued against the person, any designation of the person's or persons' homestead must be made in accordance with Subchapter B.

(g) An instrument that made a voluntary designation of a homestead in accordance with prior law and that is on file with the county clerk on September 1, 1987, is considered a voluntary designation of a homestead under this section.

Added by Acts 1987, 70ᵗʰ Leg., ch. 727, § 1, eff. Aug. 31, 1987. Amended by Acts 1993, 73ʳᵈ Leg., ch. 48, § 3, eff. Sept. 1, 1993; Acts 1993, 73ʳᵈ Leg., ch. 297, § 1, eff. Aug. 1, 1993; Acts 1997, 75ᵗʰ Leg., ch. 846, § 1, eff. Sept. 1, 1997; Acts 1999, 76ᵗʰ Leg., ch. 1510, § 3, eff. Jan. 1, 2000.

§ 41.0051. Disclaimer and Disclosure Required

(a) A person may not deliver a written advertisement offering, for a fee, to designate property as a homestead as provided by Section 41.005 unless there is a disclaimer on the advertisement that is conspicuous and printed in 14-point boldface type or 14-point uppercase typewritten letters that makes the following statement or a substantially similar statement:

THIS DOCUMENT IS AN ADVERTISEMENT OF SERVICES. IT IS NOT AN OFFICIAL DOCUMENT OF THE STATE OF TEXAS.

(b) A person who solicits solely by mail or by telephone a homeowner to pay a fee for the service of applying for a property tax refund from a tax appraisal district or other governmental body on behalf of the homeowner shall, before accepting money from the homeowner or signing a contract with the homeowner for the person's services, disclose to the homeowner the name of the tax appraisal district or other governmental body that owes the homeowner a refund.

(c) A person's failure to provide a disclaimer on an advertisement as required by Subsection (a) or to provide the disclosure required by Subsection (b) is considered a false, misleading, or deceptive act or practice for purposes of Section 17.46(a), Business and Commerce Code, and is subject to action by the consumer protection division of the attorney general's office as provided by Section 17.46(a), Business and Commerce Code.

Added by Acts 2001, 77ᵗʰ Leg., ch. 341, § 1, eff. Sept. 1, 2001. Amended by Acts 2003, 78ᵗʰ Leg., ch. 1191, §§ 1

& 2, eff. Sept, 1, 2003.

§ 41.006. Certain Sales of Homestead

(a) Except as provided by Subsection (c), any sale or purported sale in whole or in part of a homestead at a fixed purchase price that is less than the appraised fair market value of the property at the time of the sale or purported sale, and in connection with which the buyer of the property executes a lease of the property to the seller at lease payments that exceed the fair rental value of the property, is considered to be a loan with all payments made from the seller to the buyer in excess of the sales price considered to be interest subject to Title 4, Finance Code.

(b) The taking of any deed in connection with a transaction described by this section is a deceptive trade practice under Subchapter E, Chapter 17, Business & Commerce Code,[1] and the deed is void and no lien attaches to the homestead property as a result of the purported sale.

(c) This section does not apply to the sale of a family homestead to a parent, stepparent, grandparent, child, stepchild, brother, half brother, sister, half sister, or grandchild of an adult member of the family.

Added by Acts 1987, 70th Leg., ch. 1130, § 1, eff. Sept. 1, 1987. Amended by Acts 1999, 76th Leg., ch. 62, § 7.84, eff. Sept. 1, 1999.

§ 41.007. Home Improvement Contract

(a) A contract for improvements to an existing residence described by Section 41.001(b)(3) must contain:

(1) the contractor's certificate of registration number from the Texas Residential Construction Commission if the contractor is required to register as a builder with the commission;

(2) the address and telephone number at which the owner may file a complaint with the Texas Residential Construction Commission about the conduct of the contractor if the contractor is required to register as a builder with the commission; and

(3) the following warning conspicuously printed, stamped, or typed in a size equal to at least 10-point bold type or computer equivalent:

"IMPORTANT NOTICE: You and your contractor are responsible for meeting the terms and conditions of this contract. If you sign this contract and you fail to meet the terms and conditions of this contract, you may lose your legal ownership rights in your home. KNOW YOUR RIGHTS AND DUTIES UNDER THE LAW."

(b) A violation of Subsection (a) of this section is a false, misleading, or deceptive act or practice within the meaning of Section 17.46, Business & Commerce Code, and is actionable in a public or private suit brought under the provisions of the Deceptive Trade Practices-Consumer Protection Act (Subchapter E, Chapter 17, Business & Commerce Code).[2]

(c) A provision of a contract for improvements to an existing residence described by Section 41.001(b)(3) that requires the parties to submit a dispute arising under the contract to binding arbitration must be conspicuously printed or typed in a size equal to at least 10-point bold type or the computer equivalent.

(d) A provision described by Subsection (c) is not enforceable against the owner unless the requirements of Subsection (c) are met.

Added by Acts 1987, 70th Leg., ch. 116, § 1, eff. Sept. 1, 1987. Renumbered from § 41.005 by Acts 1989, 71st Leg., ch. 2, § 16.01(30), eff. Aug. 28, 1989. Amended by Acts 1993, 73rd Leg., ch. 48, § 4, eff. Sept. 1, 1993. Subsec. (a) amended by and subsecs. (c) & (d) added by Acts 2007, 80th Leg., ch. 843, § 5, eff. Sept. 1, 2007

§ 41.008. Conflict With Federal Law

To the extent of any conflict between this subchapter and any federal law that imposes an upper limit on the amount, including the monetary amount or acreage amount, of homestead property a person may exempt from seizure, this subchapter prevails to the extent allowed under federal law.

Added by Acts 1999, 76th Leg., ch. 1510, § 4.

Subchapter B. Designation of a Homestead in Aid of Enforcement of a Judgment Debt

§ 41.021. Notice to Designate

If an execution is issued against a holder of an interest in land of which a homestead may be a part and the judgment debtor has not made a voluntary designation of a homestead under Section 41.005, the judgment creditor may give the judgment debtor notice to designate the homestead as defined in Section 41.002. The notice shall state that if the judgment debtor fails to designate the homestead within the time allowed by Section 41.022, the court will appoint a commissioner to make the designation at the expense of the judgment debtor.

Amended by Acts 1985, 69th Leg., ch. 840, § 1, eff. June 15, 1985; Acts 1987, 70th Leg., ch. 727, § 2, eff. Aug. 31, 1987.

§ 41.022. Designation by Homestead Claimant

At any time before 10 a.m. on the Monday next after the expiration of 20 days after the date of service of the notice to designate, the judgment debtor may designate the homestead as defined in Section 41.002 by filing a written designation, signed by the judgment debtor, with the justice or clerk of the court from which the writ of execution was issued, together with a plat of the area designated.

---

[1] Business & Commerce Code § 17.41 et seq.

[2] Business & Commerce Code § 17.41 et seq.

Amended by Acts 1985, 69th Leg., ch. 840, § 1, eff. June 15, 1985.

§ 41.023. Designation by Commissioner

(a) If a judgment debtor who has not made a voluntary designation of a homestead under Section 41.005 does not designate a homestead as provided in Section 41.022, on motion of the judgment creditor, filed within 90 days after the issuance of the writ of execution, the court from which the writ of execution issued shall appoint a commissioner to designate the judgment debtor's homestead. The court may appoint a surveyor and others as may be necessary to assist the commissioner. The commissioner shall file his designation of the judgment debtor's homestead in a written report, together with a plat of the area designated, with the justice or clerk of the court not more than 60 days after the order of appointment is signed or within such time as the court may allow.

(b) Within 10 days after the commissioner's report is filed, the judgment debtor or the judgment creditor may request a hearing on the issue of whether the report should be confirmed, rejected, or modified as may be deemed appropriate in the particular circumstances of the case. The commissioner's report may be contradicted by evidence from either party, when exceptions to it or any item thereof have been filed before the hearing, but not otherwise. After the hearing, or if there is no hearing requested, the court shall designate the homestead as deemed appropriate and order sale of the excess.

(c) The commissioner, a surveyor, and others appointed to assist the commissioner are entitled to such fees and expenses as are deemed reasonable by the court. The court shall tax these fees and expenses against the judgment debtor as part of the costs of execution.

Amended by Acts 1985, 69th Leg., ch. 840, § 1, eff. June 15, 1985; Acts 1987, 70th Leg., ch. 727, § 3, eff. Aug. 31, 1987.

§ 41.024. Sale of Excess

An officer holding an execution sale of property of a judgment debtor whose homestead has been designated under this chapter may sell the excess of the judgment debtor's interest in land not included in the homestead.

Amended by Acts 1985, 69th Leg., ch. 840, § 1, eff. June 15, 1985; Acts 1987, 70th Leg., ch. 727, § 4, eff. Aug. 31, 1987.

Chapter 42. Personal Property

Statutes in Context
Chapter 42

Chapter 42 provides that certain personal property is exempt from the claims of most creditors. This protection may continue after death as detailed in Probate Code § 281.

---

§ 42.001. Personal Property Exemption

(a) Personal property, as described in Section 42.002, is exempt from garnishment, attachment, execution, or other seizure if:

(1) the property is provided for a family and has an aggregate fair market value of not more than $100,000 [$60,000], exclusive of the amount of any liens, security interests, or other charges encumbering the property; or

(2) the property is owned by a single adult, who is not a member of a family, and has an aggregate fair market value of not more than $50,000 [$30,000], exclusive of the amount of any liens, security interests, or other charges encumbering the property.

(b) The following personal property is exempt from seizure and is not included in the aggregate limitations prescribed by Subsection (a):

(1) current wages for personal services, except for the enforcement of court-ordered child support payments;

(2) professionally prescribed health aids of a debtor or a dependent of a debtor;

(3) alimony, support, or separate maintenance received or to be received by the debtor for the support of the debtor or a dependent of the debtor; and

(4) a religious bible or other book containing sacred writings of a religion that is seized by a creditor other than a lessor of real property who is exercising the lessor's contractual or statutory right to seize personal property after a tenant breaches a lease agreement for or abandons the real property.

(c) Except as provided by Subsection (b)(4), this section does not prevent seizure by a secured creditor with a contractual landlord's lien or other security in the property to be seized.

(d) Unpaid commissions for personal services not to exceed 25 percent of the aggregate limitations prescribed by Subsection (a) are exempt from seizure and are included in the aggregate.

(e) A religious bible or other book described by Subsection (b)(4) that is seized by a lessor of real property in the exercise of the lessor's contractual or statutory right to seize personal property after a tenant breaches a lease agreement for the real property or abandons the real property may not be included in the aggregate limitations prescribed by Subsection (a).

Amended by Acts 1991, 72nd Leg., ch. 175, § 1, eff. May 24, 1991; Acts 1997, 75th Leg., ch. 1046, § 1, eff. Sept. 1, 1997. Subsecs (b) & (c) amended by and subsec. (e) added by Acts 2007, 80th Leg., ch. 444, § 1, eff. Sept. 1, 2007. Subsec. (a) amended by Acts 2015, 84th Leg., ch. 793, § 1, eff. Sept. 1, 2015.

§ 42.002. Personal Property

(a) The following personal property is exempt under Section 42.001(a):

(1) home furnishings, including family heirlooms;

(2) provisions for consumption;

(3) farming or ranching vehicles and implements;

(4) tools, equipment, books, and apparatus, including boats and motor vehicles used in a trade or profession;

(5) wearing apparel;

(6) jewelry not to exceed 25 percent of the aggregate limitations prescribed by Section 42.001(a);

(7) two firearms;

(8) athletic and sporting equipment, including bicycles;

(9) a two-wheeled, three-wheeled, or four-wheeled motor vehicle for each member of a family or single adult who holds a driver's license or who does not hold a driver's license but who relies on another person to operate the vehicle for the benefit of the nonlicensed person;

(10) the following animals and forage on hand for their consumption:

(A) two horses, mules, or donkeys and a saddle, blanket, and bridle for each;

(B) 12 head of cattle;

(C) 60 head of other types of livestock; and

(D) 120 fowl; and

(11) household pets.

(b) Personal property, unless precluded from being encumbered by other law, may be encumbered by a security interest under Subchapter B, Chapter 9, Business & Commerce Code, or Subchapter F, Chapter 501, Transportation Code, or by a lien fixed by other law, and the security interest or lien may not be avoided on the ground that the property is exempt under this chapter.

Amended by Acts 1991, 72ⁿᵈ Leg., ch. 175, § 1, eff. May 24, 1991; Acts 1993, 73ʳᵈ Leg., ch. 216, § 1, eff. May. 17, 1993; Acts 1997, 75ᵗʰ Leg., ch. 165, § 30.245, eff. Sept. 1, 1997; Acts 1999, 76ᵗʰ Leg., ch. 414, § 2.36, eff. July 1, 2001; Acts 1999, 76ᵗʰ Leg., ch. 846, § 1, eff. Aug. 30, 1999.

§ 42.0021. Additional Exemption for Certain Savings Plans

(a) In addition to the exemption prescribed by Section 42.001, a person's right to the assets held in or to receive payments, whether vested or not, under any stock bonus, pension, annuity, deferred compensation, profit-sharing, or similar plan, including a retirement plan for self-employed individuals, or a simplified employee pension plan, an individual retirement account or individual retirement annuity, including an inherited individual retirement account, individual retirement annuity, Roth IRA, or inherited Roth IRA, or a health savings account, and under any annuity or similar contract purchased with assets distributed from that type of plan or account, is exempt from attachment, execution, and seizure for the satisfaction of debts to the extent the plan, contract, annuity, or account is exempt from federal income tax, or to the extent federal income tax on the person's interest is deferred until actual payment of benefits to the person under Section 223, 401(a), 403(a), 403(b), 408(a), 408A, 457(b), or 501(a), Internal Revenue Code of 1986, including a government plan or church plan described by Section 414(d) or (e), Internal Revenue Code of 1986. For purposes of this subsection, the interest of a person in a plan, annuity, account, or contract acquired by reason of the death of another person, whether as an owner, participant, beneficiary, survivor, coannuitant, heir, or legatee, is exempt to the same extent that the interest of the person from whom the plan, annuity, account, or contract was acquired was exempt on the date of the person's death. If this subsection is held invalid or preempted by federal law in whole or in part or in certain circumstances, the subsection remains in effect in all other respects to the maximum extent permitted by law.

(b) Contributions to an individual retirement account that exceed the amounts permitted under the applicable provisions of the Internal Revenue Code of 1986 and any accrued earnings on such contributions are not exempt under this section unless otherwise exempt by law. Amounts qualifying as nontaxable rollover contributions under Section 402(a)(5), 403(a)(4), 403(b)(8), or 408(d)(3) of the Internal Revenue Code of 1986 before January 1, 1993, are treated as exempt amounts under Subsection (a). Amounts treated as qualified rollover contributions under Section 408A, Internal Revenue Code of 1986, are treated as exempt amounts under Subsection (a). In addition, amounts qualifying as nontaxable rollover contributions under Section 402(c), 402(e)(6), 402(f), 403(a)(4), 403(a)(5), 403(b)(8), 403(b)(10), 408(d)(3), or 408A of the Internal Revenue Code of 1986 on or after January 1, 1993, are treated as exempt amounts under Subsection (a). Amounts qualifying as nontaxable rollover contributions under Section 223(f)(5) of the Internal Revenue Code of 1986 on or after January 1, 2004, are treated as exempt amounts under Subsection (a).

(c) Amounts distributed from a plan, annuity, account, or contract entitled to an exemption under Subsection (a) are not subject to seizure for a creditor's claim for 60 days after the date of distribution if the amounts qualify as a nontaxable rollover contribution under Subsection (b).

(d) A participant or beneficiary of a plan, annuity, account, or contract entitled to an exemption under Subsection (a), other than an individual retirement account or individual retirement annuity, is not prohibited from granting a valid and enforceable security interest in the participant's or beneficiary's right to the assets held in or to receive payments under the exempt plan, annuity, account, or contract to secure a loan to the participant or beneficiary from the exempt plan, annuity, account, or contract, and the right to the assets held in or to receive payments from the plan, annuity, account, or contract is subject to attachment, execution, and seizure for the satisfaction of the security interest or lien granted by the participant or beneficiary to secure the loan.

(e) If Subsection (a) is declared invalid or preempted by federal law, in whole or in part or in certain circumstances, as applied to a person who has not brought a proceeding under Title 11, United States Code, the subsection remains in effect, to the maximum extent permitted by law, as to any person who has filed that type of proceeding.

(f) A reference in this section to a specific provision of the Internal Revenue Code of 1986 includes a subsequent amendment of the substance of that provision.

Added by Acts 1987, 70ᵗʰ Leg., ch. 376, § 1, eff. Sept. 1, 1987. Amended by Acts 1989, 71ˢᵗ Leg., ch. 1122, § 1, eff. Sept. 1, 1989; Acts 1995, 74ᵗʰ Leg., ch. 963, § 1, eff. Aug. 28, 1995; Acts 1999, 76ᵗʰ Leg., ch. 106, § 1, eff. Sept. 1, 1999. Title amended by Acts 2005, 79ᵗʰ Leg., ch. 130, § 1, eff. May 24, 2005. Subsecs. (a), (b) amended by Acts 2005, 79ᵗʰ Leg., ch. 130, § 2, eff. May 24, 2005. Amended by Acts 2011, 82ⁿᵈ Leg., ch. 933, eff. June 17, 2011. Subsecs. (a) and (b) amended by Acts 2013, 83ʳᵈ Leg., ch. 91, eff. Sept. 1, 2013.

§ 42.0022. Exemption for College Savings Plans

(a) In addition to the exemption prescribed by Section 42.001, a person's right to the assets held in or to receive payments or benefits under any of the following is exempt from attachment, execution, and seizure for the satisfaction of debts:

(1) any fund or plan established under Subchapter F, Chapter 54, Education Code, including the person's interest in a prepaid tuition contract;

(2) any fund or plan established under Subchapter G, Chapter 54, Education Code, including the person's interest in a savings trust account; or

(3) any qualified tuition program of any state that meets the requirements of Section 529, Internal Revenue Code of 1986, as amended.

(b) If any portion of this section is held to be invalid or preempted by federal law in whole or in part or in certain circumstances, this section remains in effect in all other respects to the maximum extent permitted by law.

Added by Acts 2003, 78ᵗʰ Leg., ch. 113, § 1, eff. Sept. 1, 2003.

§ 42.003. Designation of Exempt Property

(a) If the number or amount of a type of personal property owned by a debtor exceeds the exemption allowed by Section 42.002 and the debtor can be found in the county where the property is located, the officer making a levy on the property shall ask the debtor to designate the personal property to be levied on. If the debtor cannot be found in the county or the debtor fails to make a designation within a reasonable time after the officer's request, the officer shall make the designation.

(b) If the aggregate value of a debtor's personal property exceeds the amount exempt from seizure under Section 42.001(a), the debtor may designate the portion of the property to be levied on. If, after a court's request, the debtor fails to make a designation within a reasonable time or if for any reason a creditor contests that the property is exempt, the court shall make the designation.

Acts 1983, 68ᵗʰ Leg., p. 3524, ch. 576, § 1, eff. Jan. 1, 1984. Amended by Acts 1991, 72ⁿᵈ Leg., ch. 175, § 1, eff. May 24, 1991.

§ 42.004. Transfer of Nonexempt Property

(a) If a person uses the property not exempt under this chapter to acquire, obtain an interest in, make improvement to, or pay an indebtedness on personal property which would be exempt under this chapter with the intent to defraud, delay, or hinder an interested person from obtaining that to which the interested person is or may be entitled, the property, interest, or improvement acquired is not exempt from seizure for the satisfaction of liabilities. If the property, interest, or improvement is acquired by discharging an encumbrance held by a third person, a person defrauded, delayed, or hindered is subrogated to the rights of the third person.

(b) A creditor may not assert a claim under this section more than two years after the transaction from which the claim arises. A person with a claim that is unliquidated or contingent at the time of the transaction may not assert a claim under this section more than one year after the claim is reduced to judgment.

(c) It is a defense to a claim under this section that the transfer was made in the ordinary course of business by the person making the transfer.

Acts 1983, 68ᵗʰ Leg., p. 3524, ch. 576, § 1, eff. Jan. 1, 1984. Amended by Acts 1991, 72ⁿᵈ Leg., ch. 175, § 1, eff. May 24, 1991.

Statutes in Context
§ 42.005

In *Dryden v. Dryden*, 97 S.W.3d 863 (Tex. App. — Corpus Christi 2003, pet. denied), a parent ordered to pay child support claimed that § 42.005 violated Texas Constitution art. XVI, § 49, because it excepts individuals who owe child support from the protections afforded to debtors in other sections of the Property Code. The court determined that the parent's obligation for child support is not a true debt but actually a natural and legal duty. Accordingly, the court held that § 42.005 was constitutional.

---

§ 42.005. Child Support Liens

Sections 42.001, 42.002, and 42.0021 of this code do not apply to a child support lien established under Subchapter G, Chapter 157, Family Code.[1]

Added by Acts 1991, 72nd Leg., 1st C.S., ch. 15, § 4.07, eff. Sept. 1, 1991. Amended by Acts 1997, 75th Leg., ch. 165, § 7.56, eff. Sept. 1, 1997.

Title 6.   Unclaimed Property

Chapter 71.   Escheat of Property

Subchapter A.   General Provisions

Statutes in Context
§ 71.001

Section 71.001 provides that the property of an intestate who dies without an heir (see Probate Code §§ 38 and 45) escheats to the state.

§ 71.001.   Escheat

(a) If an individual dies intestate and without heirs, the real and personal property of that individual is subject to escheat.

(b) "Escheat" means the vesting of title to property in the state in an escheat proceeding under Subchapter B.[2]

Acts 1983, 68th Leg., p. 3585, ch. 576, § 1, eff. Jan. 1, 1984. Amended by Acts 1985, 69th Leg., ch. 230, § 2, eff. Sept. 1, 1985.

Statutes in Context
§ 71.002

With regard to the presumption of death, see Probate Code § 72.

§ 71.002.   Presumption of Death

An individual is presumed dead for the purpose of determining if the individual's real or personal property is subject to escheat if the individual:

(1) is absent from the individual's place of residence for seven years or longer; and

(2) is not known to exist.

Acts 1983, 68th Leg., p. 3585, ch. 576, § 1, eff. Jan. 1, 1984. Amended by Acts 1985, 69th Leg., ch. 230, § 3, eff. Sept. 1, 1985.

---

[1] Family Code § 157.311 et seq.

[2] Property Code § 71.101 et seq.

Statutes in Context
§ 71.003

Section 71.003 provides that a person is presumed to die intestate after 7 years if no will is recorded or probated.

§ 71.003.   Presumption of Intestacy

An individual is presumed to have died intestate if, on or before the seventh anniversary of the date of the individual's death, the individual's will has not been recorded or probated in the county where the individual's property is located.

Acts 1983, 68th Leg., p. 3585, ch. 576, § 1, eff. Jan. 1, 1984.

§ 71.004.   Presumption of Death Without Heirs

An individual is presumed to have died leaving no heirs if for the seven-year period preceding the court's determination:

(1) a lawful claim to the individual's property has not been asserted; and

(2) a lawful act of ownership of the individual's property has not been exercised.

Acts 1983, 68th Leg., p. 3585, ch. 576, § 1, eff. Jan. 1, 1984.

§ 71.005.   Act of Ownership

For the purposes of this chapter, an individual exercises a lawful act of ownership in property by, personally or through an agent, paying taxes to this state on the property.

Acts 1983, 68th Leg., p. 3585, ch. 576, § 1, eff. Jan. 1, 1984.

§ 71.006.   Review of Probate Decree

(a) If the state claims that an estate that has been administered in probate court in this state is subject to escheat, the state may have the judgment of the probate court reviewed by filing a petition in district court alleging that the administration of the estate was obtained by fraud or mistake of fact.

(b) The case shall be tried in accordance with the law for the revision and correction of a decree of the probate court.

Acts 1983, 68th Leg., p. 3585, ch. 576, § 1, eff. Jan. 1, 1984.

§ 71.007.   Identification of Real Property Subject to Escheat

The tax assessor-collector of each county shall:

(1) take all steps necessary to identify real property that may be subject to escheat; and

(2) notify the commissioner of the General Land Office and the attorney general so that they may take appropriate action.

Added by Acts 2003, 78th Leg., ch. 1276, § 13.002, eff. Sept, 1, 2003.

Subchapter B.   Escheat Proceedings

§ 71.101.   Petition for Escheat

(a) If any person, including the attorney general, the comptroller, or a district attorney, criminal district attorney, county attorney, county clerk, district clerk, or attorney ad litem is informed or has reason to believe that real or personal property is subject to escheat under this chapter, the person may file a sworn petition requesting the escheat of the property and requesting a writ of possession for the property.

(b) The petition must contain:

(1) a description of the property;

(2) the name of the deceased owner of the property;

(3) the name of the tenants or persons claiming the estate, if known; and

(4) the facts supporting the escheat of the estate.

(c) If the petition is filed by a person other than the attorney general, the person shall send to the attorney general written notice of the filing and a copy of the petition to permit the attorney general to elect to participate on behalf of the state.

(d) An action brought under this section is governed by the procedure relating to class actions provided by the Texas Rules of Civil Procedure.

(e) A petition filed under this section is not subject to an objection relating to misjoinder of parties or causes of action.

Acts 1983, 68ᵗʰ Leg., p. 3586, ch. 576, § 1, eff. Jan. 1, 1984. Amended by Acts 1985, 69ᵗʰ Leg., ch. 230, § 4, eff. Sept. 1, 1985; Acts 1991, 72ⁿᵈ Leg., ch. 153, § 1, eff. Sept. 1, 1991. Amended by Acts 1997, 75ᵗʰ Leg., ch. 1037, § 4, eff. Sept. 1, 1997; Acts 1997, 75ᵗʰ Leg., ch. 1423, § 16.01, eff. Sept. 1, 1997.

§ 71.102.   Citation

(a) If a petition is filed under this subchapter, the district clerk shall issue citation as in other civil suits to:

(1) each defendant alleged by the petition to possess or claim the property that is the subject of the petition;

(2) any person required by this chapter to be cited; and

(3) persons interested in the estate, including lienholders of record.

(b) The citation required by Subdivision (3) of Subsection (a) must be published as required for other civil suits and must:

(1) briefly state the contents of the petition; and

(2) request all persons interested in the estate to appear and answer at the next term of the court.

Acts 1983, 68ᵗʰ Leg., p. 3587, ch. 576, § 1, eff. Jan. 1, 1984. Amended by Acts 1985, 69ᵗʰ Leg., ch. 923, § 21, eff. Aug. 26, 1985.

§ 71.103.   Party to Proceeding

(a) A person who exercises a lawful act of ownership in property that is the subject of an escheat proceeding must be made a party to the proceeding by:

(1) personal service of citation if the person is a resident of this state and the person's address can be obtained by reasonable diligence; or

(2) service of citation on a person's agent if the person is a nonresident or a resident who cannot be found and the agent can be found by the use of reasonable diligence.

(b) For the purposes of this section, reasonable diligence includes an inquiry and investigation of the records of the office of the tax assessor-collector of the county in which the property sought to be escheated is located.

(c) The comptroller is an indispensable party to any judicial or administrative proceeding concerning the disposition and handling of property that is the subject of an escheat proceeding and must be made a party to the proceeding by personal service of citation.

Acts 1983, 68ᵗʰ Leg., p. 3587, ch. 576, § 1, eff. Jan. 1, 1984. Amended by Acts 1991, 72ⁿᵈ Leg., ch. 153, § 2, eff. Sept. 1, 1991. Amended by Acts 1997, 75ᵗʰ Leg., ch. 1037, § 5, eff. Sept. 1, 1997; Acts 1997, 75ᵗʰ Leg., ch. 1423, § 16.02, eff. Sept. 1, 1997.

§ 71.104.   Appearance of Claimants

Any person, whether named in the escheat petition or not, who claims an interest in property that is the subject of an escheat proceeding may appear, enter a pleading, and oppose the facts stated in the petition.

Acts 1983, 68ᵗʰ Leg., p. 3588, ch. 576, § 1, eff. Jan. 1, 1984.

§ 71.105.   Trial

(a) If a person appears and denies the state's right to the property or opposes a material fact of the petition, the court shall try the issue as any other issue of fact.

(b) The court may order a survey as in other cases in which the title or the boundary of the land is in question.

Acts 1983, 68ᵗʰ Leg., p. 3588, ch. 576, § 1, eff. Jan. 1, 1984.

§ 71.106.   Default Judgment

If citation is issued in accordance with Section 71.102 and no person answers within the period provided by the Texas Rules of Civil Procedure, the court shall render a default judgment in favor of the state.

Acts 1983, 68ᵗʰ Leg., p. 3588, ch. 576, § 1, eff. Jan. 1, 1984.

§ 71.107.   Judgment for State

(a) If the court renders a judgment for the state finding that an intestate died without heirs, the property escheats to the state and title to the property is considered to pass to the state on the date of death of the owner as established by the escheat proceeding. The court may award court costs to the state.

(b) If the judgment involves real property, the state may sell the property under the general laws governing the sale of Permanent School Fund lands, and, after the second anniversary of the date of the final judgment, the court shall issue a writ of possession for the property.

(c) If the judgment involves personal property, the court shall issue a writ of possession that contains an adequate description of the property as in other cases for recovery of personal property.

(d) When the record of an escheat proceeding reflects that a lienholder or his predecessor received actual or constructive notice of the escheat proceeding, the entry of the judgment in the escheat proceeding will either satisfy or extinguish any lien which the lienholder or his predecessor claimed or could have claimed on the escheated property at the escheat proceeding.

(e) The sheriff, constable, court clerk, or other officer appointed by the judge in an escheat proceeding shall execute a writ of possession by filing the writ with the deed or map records of the county when the escheated property relates to realty and by serving the writ on any holder, tenant, or occupant of any escheated property. Additionally, the person who executes a writ of possession shall either:

(1) post the writ for at least three consecutive weeks on the door or posting board of the county courthouse in the county where the proceeding was conducted or in the county where the property is located; or

(2) in the case of real property, post the writ for at least two consecutive weeks at a reasonably conspicuous place on the realty; or

(3) publicize the writ in any other fashion ordered by the court.

(f) After validly executing a writ of possession, the sheriff, constable, court clerk, or other appointed officer shall note the method of the execution of the writ on the writ return and shall return the writ to the clerk to be filed in the court records of the escheat proceeding.

Acts 1983, 68th Leg., p. 3588, ch. 576, § 1, eff. Jan. 1, 1984. Amended by Acts 1985, 69th Leg., ch. 230, § 5, eff. Sept. 1, 1985; Acts 1985, 69th Leg., ch. 923, § 22, eff. Aug. 26, 1985.

§ 71.108. Costs Paid by State

If the property does not escheat, the state shall pay court costs. The clerk of the court shall certify the amount of the costs, and when the certificate is filed in the office of the comptroller of public accounts, the comptroller shall issue a warrant for the amount of the costs.

Acts 1983, 68th Leg., p. 3588, ch. 576, § 1, eff. Jan. 1, 1984.

§ 71.109. Appeal; Writ of Error

A party who appeared at an escheat proceeding may appeal the judgment rendered or may file an application for a writ of error on the judgment. The attorney general or the other person acting on behalf of the state in the escheat proceeding may make an appeal or file the writ.

Acts 1983, 68th Leg., p. 3589, ch. 576, § 1, eff. Jan. 1, 1984.

Subchapter C. Disposition of Escheated Property

§ 71.201. Seizure and Sale of Personal Property

(a) If personal property escheated to the state, the court shall issue to the sheriff a writ that commands the sheriff to seize the escheated property.

(b) The sheriff shall:

(1) dispose of the personal property at public auction in accordance with the law regarding the sale of personal property under execution; and

(2) deposit into the State Treasury the proceeds of the sale, less court costs.

Acts 1983, 68th Leg., p. 3589, ch. 576, § 1, eff. Jan. 1, 1984.

§ 71.202. Disposition of Real Property

(a) Real property that escheats to the state under this title before January 1, 1985, becomes a part of the permanent school fund. Real property that escheats to the state on or after January 1, 1985, is held in trust by the Commissioner of the General Land Office for the use and benefit of the foundation school fund. The revenue from all leases, sales, and use of land held for the foundation school fund shall be deposited to the credit of the foundation school fund.

(b) Before the 91st day after the day on which a judgment that provides for the recovery of real property is rendered, the clerk of the district court rendering the judgment shall send to the Commissioner of the General Land Office:

(1) a certified copy of the judgment; and

(2) notice of any appeal of that judgment.

(c) The commissioner shall list real property as escheated foundation school fund land or permanent school land as appropriate when the commissioner receives:

(1) a certified copy of a judgment under which the property escheats to the state and from which appeal is not taken; or

(2) a certified copy of notice of the affirmance on appeal of a judgment under which the property escheats to the state.

Acts 1983, 68th Leg., p. 3589, ch. 576, § 1, eff. Jan. 1, 1984. Amended by Acts 1984, 68th Leg., 2nd C.S., ch. 28, art. II, part B, § 13, eff. Sept. 1, 1984.

§ 71.203. Account of Escheated Property

The comptroller shall keep an account of the money paid to and real property vested in this state under this chapter.

Acts 1983, 68th Leg., p. 3590, ch. 576, § 1, eff. Jan. 1, 1984.

Subchapter D. Recovery of Escheated Property

§ 71.301. Suit for Escheated Personal Property

(a) If personal property of a deceased owner escheats to the state under this chapter and is delivered to the state, a person who claims the property as an heir. devisee, or legatee of the deceased may file suit against the state in a district court of Travis County, Texas. The suit must be filed on or before the fourth anniversary of the date of the final judgment of the escheat proceeding.

(b) The petition must state the nature of the claim and request that the money be paid to the claimant.

(c) A copy of the petition shall be served on the comptroller, who shall represent the interests of the state. As the comptroller elects and with the approval of the attorney general, the attorney general, the county attorney or criminal district attorney for the county, or the district attorney for the district shall represent the comptroller.

Acts 1983, 68th Leg., p. 3590, ch. 576, § 1, eff. Jan. 1, 1984. Amended by Acts 1991, 72nd Leg., ch. 153, § 3, eff. Sept. 1, 1991. Amended by Acts 1997, 75th Leg., ch. 1037, § 6, eff. Sept. 1, 1997; Acts 1997, 75th Leg., ch. 1423, § 16.03, eff. Sept. 1, 1997.

§ 71.302. Recovery of Personal Property

(a) If in a suit filed under Section 71.301 the court finds that a claimant is entitled to recover personal property, the court shall order the comptroller to issue a warrant for payment of the claim without interest or costs.

(b) A copy of the order under seal of the court is sufficient voucher for issuing the warrant.

Acts 1983, 68th Leg., p. 3590, ch. 576, § 1, eff. Jan. 1, 1984.

§ 71.303. Suit for Escheated Real Property

(a) If real property escheats to the state under this chapter, a person who was not personally served with citation in the escheat proceedings may file suit in the district court of Travis County for all or a part of the property. The suit must be filed not later than the second anniversary of the date of the final judgment in the escheat proceedings.

(b) A copy of the petition must be served on the attorney general. who shall represent the interests of the state.

(c) To the extent the claimant is adjudged to be the owner of all or a part of the property, the state is divested of the property.

Acts 1983, 68th Leg., p. 3590, ch. 576, § 1, eff. Jan. 1, 1984. Amended by Acts 1991, 72nd Leg., ch. 153, § 4, eff. Sept. 1, 1991.

§ 71.304. State as Party in Suit for Assets

(a) A suit brought for the collection of personal property delivered to the comptroller under this chapter must be brought in the name of this state.

(b) A suit brought for the possession of real property held in trust by the Commissioner of the General Land Office under this chapter must be brought in the name of this state.

Acts 1983, 68th Leg., p. 3591, ch. 576, § 1, eff. Jan. 1, 1984. Amended by Acts 1991, 72nd Leg., ch. 153, § 4, eff. Sept. 1, 1991. Amended by Acts 1997, 75th Leg., ch. 1037, § 7, eff. Sept. 1, 1997; Acts 1997, 75th Leg., ch. 1423, § 16.04, eff. Sept. 1, 1997.

Chapter 72. Abandonment of Personal Property

Subchapter A. General Provisions

§ 72.001. Application of Chapter

(a) Tangible or intangible personal property is subject to this chapter if it is covered by Section 72.101 and:

(1) the last known address of the apparent owner, as shown on the records of the holder, is in this state

(2) the records of the holder do not disclose the identity of the person entitled to the property, and it is established that the last known address of the person entitled to the property is in this state;

(3) the records of the holder do not disclose the last known address of the apparent owner, and it is established that:

(A) the last known address of the person entitled to the property is in this state; or

(B) the holder is a domiciliary or a government or governmental subdivision or agency of this state and has not previously paid or delivered the property to the state of the last known address of the apparent owner or other person entitled to the property;

(4) the last known address of the apparent owner, as shown on the records of the holder, is in a state that does not provide by law for the escheat or custodial taking of the property or is in a state in which the state's escheat or unclaimed property law is not applicable to the property, and the holder is a domiciliary or a government or governmental subdivision or agency of this state;

(5) the last known address of the apparent owner, as shown on the records of the holder, is in a foreign nation and the holder is a domiciliary or a government or governmental subdivision or agency of this state; or

(6) the transaction out of which the property arose occurred in this state and:

(A) the last known address of the apparent owner or other person entitled to the property is:

(i) unknown; or

(ii) in a state that does not provide by law for the escheat or custodial taking of the property or in a state in which the state's escheat or unclaimed property law is not applicable to the property; and

(B) the holder is a domiciliary of a state that does not provide by law for the escheat or custodial taking of the property or a state in which the state's escheat or unclaimed property law is not applicable to the property.

(b) This chapter supplements other chapters in this title, and each chapter shall be followed to the extent applicable.

Text of subsec. (c) effective until June 1, 2003

(c) This chapter applies to property held by life insurance companies with the exception of unclaimed funds, as defined by Section 3, Article 4.08, Insurance Code, held by those companies that are subject to Article 4.08, Insurance Code.

Text of subsec. (c) effective June 1, 2003

(c) This chapter applies to property held by life insurance companies with the exception of unclaimed proceeds to which Chapter 1109, Insurance Code, applies and that are held by those companies that are subject to Chapter 1109, Insurance Code.

(d) A holder of property presumed abandoned under this chapter is subject to the procedures of Chapter 74.

(e) In this chapter, a holder is a person, wherever organized or domiciled, who is:

(1) in possession of property that belongs to another;

(2) a trustee; or

(3) indebted to another on an obligation.

(f) In this chapter, a corporation shall be deemed to be a domiciliary of the state of its incorporation.

Acts 1983, 68th Leg., p. 3592, ch. 576, § 1, eff. Jan. 1, 1984. Amended by Acts 1985, 69th Leg., ch. 230, § 7, eff. Sept. 1, 1985; Acts 1987, 70th Leg., ch. 426, § 2, eff. Sept. 1, 1987; Acts 1991, 72nd Leg., ch. 153, § 5, eff. Sept. 1, 1991; Acts 2001, 77th Leg., ch. 1419, § 30, eff. June 1, 2003.

Subchapter B. Presumption of Abandonment

Statutes in Context
§ 72.101

Section 72.101 sets forth the circumstances under which personal property is presumed abandoned.

§ 72.101. Personal Property Presumed Abandoned

(a) Except as provided by this section and Sections 72.1015, 72.1016, 72.1017, [and] 72.102, and 72.104, personal property is presumed abandoned if, for longer than three years:

(1) the existence and location of the owner of the property is unknown to the holder of the property; and

(2) according to the knowledge and records of the holder of the property, a claim to the property has not been asserted or an act of ownership of the property has not been exercised.

(b)(1) The three-year period leading to a presumption of abandonment of stock or another intangible ownership interest in a business association, the existence of which is evidenced by records available to the association, commences on the first date that either a sum payable as a result of the ownership interest is unclaimed by the owner or a communication to the owner is returned undelivered by the United States Postal Service.

(2) The running of the three-year period of abandonment ceases immediately on the exercise of an act of ownership interest or sum payable or a communication with the association as evidenced by a memorandum or other record on file with the association or its agents.

(3) At the time an ownership is presumed abandoned under this section, any sum then held for interest or owing to the owner as a result of the interest and not previously presumed abandoned is presumed abandoned.

(4) Any stock or other intangible ownership interest enrolled in a plan that provides for the automatic reinvestment of dividends, distributions, or other sums payable as a result of the ownership interest is subject to the presumption of abandonment as provided by this section.

(c) Property distributable in the course of a demutualization or related reorganization of an insurance company is presumed abandoned on the first anniversary of the date the property becomes distributable if, at the time of the first distribution, the last known address of the owner according to the records of the holder of the property is known to be incorrect or the distribution or statements related to the distribution are returned by the post office as undeliverable and the owner has not:

(1) communicated in writing with the holder of the property or the holder's agent regarding the interest; or

(2) otherwise communicated with the holder regarding the interest as evidenced by a memorandum or other record on file with the holder or its agents.

(d) Property distributable in the course of a demutualization or related reorganization of an insurance company that is not subject to Subsection (c) is presumed abandoned as otherwise provided by this section.

(e) This section does not apply to money collected as child support that:

(1) is being held for disbursement by the state disbursement unit under Chapter 234, Family Code, or a local registry, as defined by Section 101.018, Family Code, pending identification and location of the person to whom the money is owed; or

(2) has been disbursed by the state disbursement unit under Chapter 234, Family Code, by electronic funds transfer into a child support debit card account established for an individual under Section 234.010, Family Code, but not activated by the individual.

Acts 1983, 68th Leg., p. 3593, ch. 576, § 1, eff. Jan. 1, 1984. Amended by Acts 1985, 69th Leg., ch. 230, § 9, eff. Sept. 1, 1985; Acts 1987, 70th Leg., ch. 426, § 3, eff. Sept. 1, 1987; Acts 1991, 72nd Leg., ch. 153, § 6, eff. Sept. 1, 1991; Acts 1993, 73rd Leg., ch. 36, § 3.01, eff. Sept. 1, 1993. Subsec. (a), amended by Acts 2005, 79th Leg., ch. 81, § 2, eff. Sept. 1, 2005. Subsec. (e) added by Acts 2009, 81st Leg., ch. 767, § 34, eff. June 19, 2009; Subsec. (e) added by Acts 2009, 81st Leg., ch. 551, § 2, eff. June 19, 2009. Subsec. (a) amended by Acts 2011, 82nd Leg., ch. 685, § 1, eff. Sept. 1, 2011. Subsec. (a) amended by Acts 2015, 84th Leg., ch. 606, § 1, eff. Sept. 1, 2015.

§ 72.102. Traveler's Check and Money Order

(a) A traveler's check or money order is not presumed to be abandoned under this chapter unless:

(1) the records of the issuer of the check or money order indicate that it was purchased in this state;

(2) the issuer's principal place of business is in this state and the issuer's records do not indicate the state in which the check or money order was purchased; or

(3) the issuer's principal place of business is in this state, the issuer's records indicate that the check or money order was purchased in another state, and the laws of that state do not provide for the escheat or custodial taking of the check or money order.

(b) A traveler's check to which Subsection (a) applies is presumed to be abandoned on the latest of:

(1) the 15th anniversary of the date on which the check was issued;

(2) the 15th anniversary of the date on which the issuer of the check last received from the owner of the check communication concerning the check; or

(3) the 15th anniversary of the date of the last writing, on file with the issuer, that indicates the owner's interest in the check.

(c) A money order to which Subsection (a) applies is presumed to be abandoned on the latest of:

(1) the third anniversary of the date on which the money order was issued;

(2) the third anniversary of the date on which the issuer of the money order last received from the owner of the money order communication concerning the money order; or

(3) the third anniversary of the date of the last writing, on file with the issuer, that indicates the owner's interest in the money order.

Amended by Acts 1997, 75th Leg., ch. 1037, § 8, eff. Sept. 1, 1997; Acts 2001, 77th Leg., ch. 179, § 1, eff. June 1, 2004. Subsec. (c) amended by Acts 2011, 82nd Leg., ch. 685, § 3, eff. Sept. 1, 2011.

§ 72.103. Preservation of Property

Notwithstanding any other provision of this title except a provision of this section relating to a money order, a holder of abandoned property shall preserve the property and may not at any time, by any procedure, including a deduction for service, maintenance, or other charge, transfer or convert to the profits or assets of the holder or otherwise reduce the value of the property. For purposes of this section, value is determined as of the date of the last transaction or contact concerning the property, except that in the case of a money order, value is determined as of the date the property is presumed abandoned under Section 72.102(c). If a holder imposes service, maintenance, or other charges on a money order prior to the time of presumed abandonment, such charges may not exceed the amount of $1 per month for each month the money order remains uncashed prior to the month in which the money order is presumed abandoned.

Amended by Acts 1997, 75th Leg., ch. 1037, § 9, eff. Sept. 1, 1997: Acts 2001, 77th Leg., ch. 179, § 2, eff. June 1, 2002. Amended by Acts 2011, 82nd Leg., ch. 685, § 4, eff. Sept. 1, 2011.

Chapter 73. Property Held by Financial Institutions

Subchapter A. General Provisions

§ 73.001. Definitions and Application of Chapter

(a) In this chapter:

(1) "Account" means funds deposited with a depository in an interest-bearing account, or a child support debit card account established under Section 234.010, Family Code, a checking or savings account, or funds received by a depository in exchange for the purchase of a stored value card.

(2) "Depositor" means a person who has an ownership interest in an account.

(3) "Owner" means a person who has an ownership interest in a safe deposit box.

(4) "Holder" means a depository.

(5) "Check" includes a draft, cashier's check, certified check, registered check, or similar instrument.

(b) This chapter supplements other chapters in this title, and each chapter shall be followed to the extent applicable.

(c) Any property, other than an account, check, or safe deposit box, held by a depository is subject to the abandonment provisions of Chapter 72.

(d) A holder of accounts, checks, or safe deposit boxes presumed abandoned under this chapter is subject to the procedures of Chapter 74.

Acts 1983, 68th Leg., p. 3607, ch. 576, § 1, eff. Jan. 1, 1984. Amended by Acts 1985, 69th Leg., ch. 230, § 13, eff. Sept. 1, 1985; Acts 1991, 72nd Leg., ch. 153, §§ 7, 8, eff. Sept. 1, 1991. Amended by Acts 1997, 75th Leg., ch. 1037, §§ 11, 12, eff. Sept. 1, 1997. Subsec. (a-1), amended by Acts 2005, 79th Leg., ch. 81, § 5, eff. Sept. 1, 2005. Subsec. (a) amended by Acts 2009, 81st Leg., ch. 767, § 35, eff. June 19, 2009; Subsec. (a) amended by Acts 2009, 81st Leg., ch. 551, § 3, eff. June 19, 2009.

§ 73.002. Depository

For the purposes of this chapter, a depository is a bank, savings and loan association, credit union, or other banking organization that:

(1) receives and holds a deposit of money or the equivalent of money in banking practice or other personal property in this state; or

(2) receives and holds such a deposit or other personal property in another state for a person whose last known residence is in this state.

Acts 1983, 68th Leg., p. 3607, ch. 576, § 1, eff. Jan. 1, 1984. Amended by Acts 1997, 75th Leg., ch. 1037, § 13, eff. Sept. 1, 1997.

§ 73.003. Preservation of Inactive Account or Safe Deposit Box

(a) A depository shall preserve an account that is inactive and the contents of a safe deposit box that is inactive. The depository may not, at any time, by any procedure, including the imposition of a service charge, transfer or convert to the profits or assets of the depository or otherwise reduce the value of the account or the contents of such a box. For purposes of this subsection, value is determined as of the date the account or safe deposit box becomes inactive.

(b) An account is inactive if for more than one year there has not been a debit or credit to the account because of an act by the depositor or an agent of the depositor, other than the depository, and the depositor has not communicated with the depository. A safe deposit box is inactive if the rental on the box is delinquent.

(c) This section does not affect the provisions of Subchapter B, Chapter 59, Finance Code.

Acts 1983, 68th Leg., p. 3607, ch. 576, § 1, eff. Jan. 1, 1984. Amended by Acts 1984, 68th Leg., 2nd C.S., ch. 18, § 8(b), eff. Oct. 2, 1984; Acts 1985, 69th Leg., ch. 230, § 14, eff. Sept. 1, 1985; Acts 1991, 72nd Leg., ch. 153, § 9, eff. Sept. 1, 1991; Acts 1993, 73rd Leg., ch. 36, § 3.02, eff. Sept. 1, 1993. Amended by Acts 1995, 74th

Leg., ch. 914, § 11, eff. Sept. 1, 1995; Acts 1997, 75th Leg., ch. 1037, § 13, eff. Sept. 1, 1997; Acts 1999, 76th Leg., ch. 62, § 7.85, eff. Sept. 1, 1999.

Subchapter B. Presumption of Abandonment

§ 73.101. Inactive Account or Safe Deposit Box Presumed Abandoned

(a) An account or safe deposit box is presumed abandoned if:

(1) except as provided by Subsection (c), the account or safe deposit box has been inactive for at least five years as determined under Subsection (b);

(2) the location of the depositor of the account or owner of the safe deposit box is unknown to the depository; and

(3) the amount of the account or the contents of the box have not been delivered to the comptroller in accordance with Chapter 74.

(b) For purposes of Subsection (a)(1):

(1) an account becomes inactive beginning on the date of the depositor's last transaction or correspondence concerning the account; and

(2) a safe deposit box becomes inactive beginning on the date a rental was due but not paid.

(c) If the account is a checking or savings account or is a matured certificate of deposit, the account is presumed abandoned if the account has been inactive for at least three years as determined under Subsection (b)(1).

Acts 1983, 68th Leg., p. 3607, ch. 576, § 1, eff. Jan. 1, 1984. Amended by Acts 1984, 68th Leg., 2nd C.S., ch. 18, § 8(d), eff. Oct. 2, 1984; Acts 1985, 69th Leg., ch. 230, § 16, eff. Sept. 1, 1985; Acts 1991, 72nd Leg., ch. 153, §§ 11, 12, eff. Sept. 1, 1991. Amended by Acts 1997, 75th Leg., ch. 1037, § 14, eff. Sept. 1, 1997; Acts 1997, 75th Leg., ch. 1423, § 16.05, eff. Sept. 1, 1997. Amended by Acts 2011, 82nd Leg., ch. 685, § 5, eff. Sept. 1, 2011.

§ 73.102. Checks

A check is presumed to be abandoned on the latest of:

(1) the third anniversary of the date the check was payable;

(2) the third anniversary of the date the issuer or payor of the check last received documented communication from the payee of the check; or

(3) the third anniversary of the date the check was issued if, according to the knowledge and records of the issuer or payor of the check, during that period, a claim to the check has not been asserted or an act of ownership by the payee has not been exercised.

Added by Acts 1997, 75th Leg., ch. 1037, § 15, eff. Sept. 1, 1997.

Title 9.   Trusts

Subtitle A.   Provisions Generally Applicable to Trusts

Chapter 101.   Provisions Generally Applicable to Trusts

Statutes in Context
§ 101.001

Under the common law, a person became a bona fide purchaser (BFP) of trust property by (1) paying value for the property and (2) being without actual or constructive notice of the existence of the trust and the concomitant equitable interest of the beneficiary. A BFP takes free of the beneficiary's interest and may retain and transfer the property without subsequent question by the beneficiary or someone claiming through the beneficiary. Because BFP status was denied to purchasers who knew they were buying trust property or were dealing with a trustee, purchasers were prone to pay less than fair market value for trust property because of the increased risk associated with the purchase.

To alleviate this problem, § 101.001 and its counterpart § 114.082, modify the common law rule and permit a purchaser, as well as donees, to achieve protected status even if the grantee is on notice that the grantee is dealing with a trustee or buying trust property (e.g., the conveyance to the trustee reads "Tom Smith, trustee"). This modern approach permits people to deal with trustees with relative safety and permits trustees to negotiate for higher sale prices. However, the purchaser or donee will not be protected under this section if the conveyance to the trustee either (1) identifies the trust (e.g., "to Tom Smith, trustee of the Windfall Trust"), or (2) discloses the name of any beneficiary "(e.g., "to Tom Smith, trustee for Benny Fishery"). The transferee, however may still be protected by § 114.081.

Section 101.001 is not actually in the Trust Code which begins with § 111.001. The reason for this section to be outside of the Trust Code which has a virtually identical provision (§ 114.082) is that § 101.001 applies even if there is no actual trust but rather just a designation of a person as trustee (a possible resulting trust). Section 101.001 applies when the conveyance is "to a person *designated* as a trustee" (emphasis added) while § 114.082 applies when the conveyance is "to a trustee."

§ 101.001.   Conveyance by Person Designated as Trustee

If property is conveyed or transferred to a person designated as a trustee but the conveyance or transfer does not identify a trust or disclose the name of any beneficiary, the person designated as trustee may convey, transfer, or encumber the title of the property without subsequent question by a person who claims to be a beneficiary under a trust or who claims by, through, or under any undisclosed beneficiary or by, through, or under the person designated as trustee in that person's individual capacity.

Acts 1983, 68th Leg., p. 3654, ch. 576, § 1, eff. Jan. 1, 1984. Amended by Acts 1987, 70th Leg., ch. 683, § 3, eff. Aug. 31, 1987.

Statutes in Context
§ 101.002

The trustee should earmark the trust property, that is, label the property as belonging to the trust. Earmarking prevents trust property from being confused with the trustee's own property so that the trustee's personal creditors, heirs, beneficiaries, and other claimants do not take trust property under the mistaken belief that it belongs to the trustee. Section 101.002 and its Trust Code counterpart § 114.0821, provide that failure to earmark does not cause the unearmarked trust property to be liable for the trustee's personal obligations.

§ 101.002.   Liability of Trust Property

Although trust property is held by the trustee without identifying the trust or its beneficiaries, the trust property is not liable to satisfy the personal obligations of the trustee.

Acts 1983, 68th Leg., p. 3654, ch. 576, § 1, eff. Jan. 1, 1984. Renumbered from § 101.001(b) by Acts 1987, 70th Leg., ch. 683, § 3, eff. Aug. 31, 1987.

Subtitle B.   Texas Trust Code: Creation, Operation, and Termination of Trusts

Statutes in Context
Subtitle B

The owner of property may create a trust by transferring that property in a unique fashion. First, the owner must divide the title to the property into legal and equitable interests and, second, the owner must impose fiduciary duties on the holder of the legal title to deal with the property for the benefit of the holder of the equitable title. Once the owner transfers property in this manner, the property is usually referred to as the trust principal, corpus, estate, or res.

In general, a trust scenario arises when a property owner wants to bestow benefits on a worthy individual or charity but does not want to make an unrestricted outright gift. Thus, the owner transfers legal title to a reliable individual or financial institution and equitable title to the individual or charity deserving the windfall. The holder of legal title manages that property following state law requirements and the original owner's instructions as specified in the trust instrument. The trustee then makes payments to or for the benefit of the individual or charity according to the original owner's instructions. When the property is exhausted or the instructions are completed, the trust ends and, once again, title to any remaining property is unified in the hands of the individual or charity the property owner specified.

The person who creates a trust by splitting title and imposing fiduciary duties is called the settlor. You may see the settlor referred to by other terms. In old cases and statutes, the settlor may be dubbed by the archaic term, trustor. In tax-related discussions, the settlor is frequently designated as the grantor because the settlor is making a grant of the property by splitting the title. The settlor may also be called a donor because most transfers of beneficial title are actually gifts.

The person who holds the legal interest to the property is the trustee. The trustee has all of the duties, responsibilities, and liabilities associated with property ownership but the trustee receives none of the benefits of that ownership. The best the trustee can hope for is a fee for serving as the trustee. Thus, if I told you I am giving you legal title to $1 million, you would not be very happy. In fact, you would be quite upset unless you were going to get paid because I would have imposed upon you all the burdens of owning $1 million. And, it actually gets worse because you would be holding that legal title as a fiduciary. This means that you would be required to manage the property with reasonable care, avoid any type of self-dealing with the property, and be certain not to be in a position where your own personal interests could be in conflict with those of the beneficiaries. If your conduct would ever fall beneath these standards, even if the lapse were merely negligent, you could be personally responsible in a civil action for damages and could even face a criminal prosecution.

The equitable title to the trust property is held by the beneficiary. The beneficiary is entitled to enjoy the trust property but, unlike the donee of an outright gift, not in an unrestricted manner. The beneficiary may receive only the benefits from the property as the settlor specified in the trust instrument. Typically, the beneficiary has no control over the trustee or how the trustee manages the legal title to the property. However, the beneficiary has the right to sue the trustee if the trustee's conduct breaches the fiduciary duties or if the trustee does not follow the settlor's instructions as set forth in the trust instrument. You may see the beneficiary referred to by other terms. The French term cestui que trust is often used in older cases. When the emphasis is on the tax consequences of equitable title ownership, the beneficiary is typically called the grantee and when the gift element of the transfer is most important, the term donee may be used.

Trusts are an extremely powerful, useful, and advantageous estate planning technique. Some of the reasons a property owner may want to convey property in trust are summarized below.

1. Provide For and Protect Beneficiaries. The settlor's desire to provide for and protect someone is probably the most common reason for creating a trust. Although a donor could make a quick, convenient, and uncomplicated outright gift, there are many situations in which such outright gifts would not effectuate the donor's true intent.

(a) Minors. Minors lack legal capacity to manage property and usually have insufficient maturity to do so as well. A trust permits the settlor to make a gift for the benefit of a minor without giving the minor control over the property or triggering the necessity for the minor to have a court-appointed guardian to manage that property. A trust is also more flexible and allows a settlor to have greater control over how the property is used when contrasted with other methods such as a transfer to a guardian or conservator of the minor's estate or to a custodian under the Texas Uniform Transfers to Minors Act (see Property Code Chapter 141).

(b) Individuals Who Lack Management Skills. An individual may lack the skills necessary to properly manage the trust property. This deficiency could be the result of mental or physical incompetence or a lack of experience in the rigors of making prudent investment decisions. For example, persons who suddenly obtain large amounts of money, such as performers, professional athletes, lottery winners, or personal injury plaintiffs, tend to deplete these windfalls rapidly because they have never learned how to manage their money wisely. By putting the money under the control of a trustee with investment experience, the settlor increases the likelihood that the beneficiary's interests are served for a longer period of time.

(c) Spendthrifts. Some individuals may be competent to manage property but are prone to use it in an excessive or frivolous manner. By using a carefully drafted trust, a settlor may protect the trust property from the beneficiary's own excesses as well as the beneficiary's creditors. See § 112.035 (spendthrift provisions).

(d) Persons Susceptible to Influence. When a person suddenly acquires a significant amount of property, that person may be under pressure from family, friends, charities, investment advisers, and opportunistic scam artists who wish to share in the windfall. A trust can make it virtually impossible for the beneficiary to transfer trust property to these people.

2. Flexible Distribution of Assets. An outright gift, either inter vivos or testamentary, gives the donee total control over the way the property is used. With a trust, the settlor can restrict the beneficiary's control over the property in any manner the settlor desires as long as the restrictions are not illegal or in violation of public policy. This flexibility allows the settlor to determine how the trustee distributes trust benefits, such as by spreading the benefits over time, giving the trustee discretion to select who receives distributions and in what amounts, requiring the beneficiary to meet certain criteria to receive or continue receiving benefits, or limiting the purposes for which trust property may be used such as health care or education.

3. Protection Against Settlor's Incompetence. Once an individual is incompetent due to illness, injury, or other cause, the person cannot manage the person's own property. The court then needs to appoint a guardian of the estate or a conservator to manage the property. The process of judicially determining a person's incompetency may cause the person considerable private and public embarrassment and there is no guarantee the incompetent person will be happy with the guardian's decisions. Guardianships are also inconvenient and costly because guardians act under court supervision and are required to submit detailed reports on a regular basis.

A trust may be used to avoid this need for a guardian. The settlor may create a trust and maintain considerable control over the trust property by, for example, serving as the trustee, retaining the power to revoke the trust, and keeping a beneficial life interest. However, upon incompetency, the settlor's designated successor trustee would take over the administration of the trust property in accordance with the directions the settlor expressed in the trust instrument. This type of arrangement is often called a stand-by trust.

An alternative method to protect property and avoid the need for a guardian in the event of incompetency is to have the client execute a durable power of attorney for property management. See Probate Code §§ 481-506.

4. Professional Management of Property. The settlor may create a trust to obtain the services of a professional asset manager, either for the benefit of third-party beneficiaries or for the settlor as the beneficiary. Professional trustees, such as banks and trust companies, have more expertise and experience with various types of investments than most individuals. Assume that you have just inherited a wheat farm located in Kansas, an office building in New York City, an apartment building in San Francisco, U.S. Government savings bonds, corporate stock in a dozen domestic corporations, oil and gas property in Texas, and an import-export business in Italy. Would you have the skill to handle all of these different types of assets? If not, placing the assets in trust would be one way of obtaining professional management. And, there is another advantage to making a trust conveyance. If you negligently manage your own property and suffer financially as a result, there is not much you can do about it; you cannot successfully bring a law suit against yourself. However, if a trustee is negligent, you can bring suit for breach of fiduciary duties and, if successful, have a strong chance of recovery because most financial institutions and trust companies have money or other assets which can be reached to satisfy a damage award.

Professional trustees also have greater investment opportunities. For example, a bank may combine funds from several trusts into one common trust fund to take advantage of opportunities that require a large investment and to diversify, thus reducing the damage to the value of the trust when one investment turns sour.

5. Probate Avoidance. Property in a trust created during the settlor's lifetime is not part of the probate estate upon the settlor's death. The property remaining in the trust when the settlor dies is administered and distributed according to the terms of the trust; it does not pass under the settlor's will or by intestate succession. Advantages to avoiding probate include getting the property into the hands of the beneficiaries quickly, avoiding gaps in management, and evading probate publicity. These advantages, however, do not apply to a trust created in the settlor's will because the property must first pass through the probate process.

6. Tax Benefits. Another popular reason for using trusts is tax avoidance. Income taxes may be saved by transferring income-producing property to a trust which has a beneficiary who is in a lower tax bracket than the settlor. Additionally, gift taxes may be avoided by structuring the transfers to a trust to fall within the annual exclusion from the federal gift tax which, as of 2013, is $14,000 per year per donee. Likewise, if a trust is properly constructed, the trust property will not be included in the settlor's taxable estate.

7. Avoid Conflicts of Interest. A person may be unable to own certain assets outright if ownership would cause impermissible conflicts of interest. For example, the President, a governor, a mayor, or other political figure may own stocks, bonds, real property, and other investments. While carrying out the official's duties, there would be a tremendous likelihood that conflicts of interest would arise between the person's investments and political decisions. Likewise, a corporate officer may also be placed in similar conflict of interest situations. To eliminate these conflicts, the person places the assets in trust, names an independent third party as trustee, and indicates that the person has no control over the management of the assets and no authority to inquire about the exact nature of the trust investments while the person remains in office. This type of arrangement is often called a *blind trust*.

Chapter 111. General Provisions

Statutes in Context
Chapter 111

There are three main time periods of Texas trust legislation.

Prior to 1943. Only sparse codification of trust law existed prior to 1943.

Texas Trust Act. The Texas Trust Act took effect on April 19, 1943 and, as amended, remained the cornerstone of trust law in Texas for over 40 years. The Texas Trust Act was very innovative in its extensive codification of the law relating to the creation, administration, and enforcement of trusts.

Texas Trust Code. The Texas Trust Code took effect on January 1, 1984. The Code modernized and expanded the Act while retaining most of its key features. For the applicability of the Code to old trusts, see § 111.006. The Texas Trust Code was one of the major foundations for the Uniform Trust Code approved in 2000 by the National Conference of Commissioners on Uniform States Laws.

§ 111.001. Short Title

This subtitle may be cited as the Texas Trust Code.

Amended by Acts 1983, 68th Leg., p. 3332, ch. 567, art. 2, § 2, eff. Jan. 1, 1984.

Statutes in Context
§ 111.002

The Code and the Act are treated as one continuous statute. Thus, if a trust refers to the Texas Trust Act, the Code is considered as an amendment to the Act.

§ 111.002. Construction of Subtitle

This subtitle and the Texas Trust Act, as amended (Articles 7425b-1 through 7425b-48, Vernon's Texas Civil Statutes),[1] shall be considered one continuous statute, and for the purposes of any statute or of any instrument creating a trust that refers to the Texas Trust Act, this subtitle shall be considered an amendment to the Texas Trust Act.

Amended by Acts 1983, 68th Leg., p. 3332, ch. 567, art. 2, § 2, eff. Jan. 1, 1984. Amended by Acts 2005, 79th Leg., ch. 148, § 1, eff. Jan. 1, 2006.

Statutes in Context
§ 111.003

The Code applies only to express trusts. Other trust-like or trust-nominated relationships are not covered.

§ 111.003. Trusts Subject to this Subtitle

For the purposes of this subtitle, a "trust" is an express trust only and does not include:

(1) a resulting trust;

(2) a constructive trust;

(3) a business trust; or

(4) a security instrument such as a deed of trust, mortgage, or security interest as defined by the Business & Commerce Code.

Amended by Acts 1983, 68th Leg., p. 3332, ch. 567, art. 2, § 2, eff. Jan. 1, 1984.

Statutes in Context
§ 111.0035

Under former Trust Code § 111.002, the terms of the trust prevailed over conflicting Trust Code rules except that the settlor could not waive certain self-dealing duties of corporate trustees. Section 111.0035 was added to the Trust Code in 2005 and amended in 2007 to expand the list of non-waivable items and provides detailed rules with regard to the waiver of certain trustee duties.

Trust Purposes: The settlor may not change the restriction in Trust Code § 112.031 that a trust may not be created for an illegal purpose or require the trustee to commit a criminal or tortious act or an act that is contrary to public policy.

---

[1] Repealed; see, now, Property Code § 111.001 et seq.

Trustee Exculpation: In another new section enacted in 2005, § 114.007, the rules regarding trustee exculpation are recodified and expanded. The settlor is prohibited from restricting the limitations on exculpation imposed by this section.

Statute of Limitations: The settlor may not shorten the periods of limitation for commencing a judicial proceeding regarding a trust.

Trustee's Duty to Account for Irrevocable Trusts: The settlor may not limit the duty of a trustee of an irrevocable trust to respond to a beneficiary's demand for an accounting under Trust Code § 113.151 provided that the beneficiary is either (1) entitled or permitted to receive trust distributions or (2) would receive a distribution from the trust if the trust terminated at the time of the demand.

Note the settlor may restrict the trustee's duty to account in other situations such as (1) if the trust is revocable or (2) if the beneficiaries of the irrevocable trust are remote, that is they are not eligible for current distributions or a distribution if the trust were to terminate.

Trustee's Duty of Good Faith: The settlor may not limit the trustee's duty to act in good faith and in accordance with the purposes of the trust.

Court's Power: The settlor may not restrict the power of a court to take action or exercise jurisdiction. The statute provides a non-exclusive list of powers included in this restriction:

Modify, terminate, or take other action with regard to the trust under Trust Code § 112.054,

Remove a trustee under Trust Code § 113.082,

Exercise jurisdiction over the trust under Trust Code § 115.001,

Determine matters related to the trustee's bond (e.g., require, dispense with, modify, or terminate the bond),

Adjust or deny compensation to a trustee who committed a breach of trust, and

Create a forfeiture for trust contests brought in good faith and with probable cause under § 112.038.

Trustee's Duty to Keep Beneficiary Informed: The settlor may not limit the common-law duty of a trustee to keep a beneficiary of an irrevocable trust who is 25 years old or older informed if the beneficiary is entitled or permitted to receive distributions or would receive a distribution if the trust were terminated.

§ 111.0035. Default and Mandatory Rules; Conflict Between Terms and Statute

(a) Except as provided by the terms of a trust and Subsection (b), this subtitle governs:

(1) the duties and powers of a trustee;

(2) relations among trustees; and

(3) the rights and interests of a beneficiary.

(b) The terms of a trust prevail over any provision of this subtitle, except that the terms of a trust may not limit:

(1) the requirements imposed under Section 112.031;

(2) the applicability of Section 114.007 to an exculpation term of a trust;

(3) the periods of limitation for commencing a judicial proceeding regarding a trust;

(4) a trustee's duty:

(A) with regard to an irrevocable trust, to respond to a demand for accounting made under Section 113.151 if the demand is from a beneficiary who, at the time of the demand:

(i) is entitled or permitted to receive distributions from the trust; or

(ii) would receive a distribution from the trust if the trust terminated at the time of the demand; and

(B) to act in good faith and in accordance with the purposes of the trust;

(5) the power of a court, in the interest of justice, to take action or exercise jurisdiction, including the power to:

(A) modify or terminate a trust or take other action under Section 112.054;

(B) remove a trustee under Section 113.082;

(C) exercise jurisdiction under Section 115.001;

(D) require, dispense with, modify, or terminate a trustee's bond; or

(E) adjust or deny a trustee's compensation if the trustee commits a breach of trust; or

(6) the applicability of Section 112.038.

(c) The terms of a trust may not limit any common-law duty to keep a beneficiary of an irrevocable trust who is 25 years of age or older informed at any time during which the beneficiary:

(1) is entitled or permitted to receive distributions from the trust; or

(2) would receive a distribution from the trust if the trust were terminated.

Added by Acts 2005, 79ᵗʰ Leg., ch. 148, § 2, eff. Jan. 1, 2006. Subsec. (b) amended and subsec. (c) added by Acts 2007, 80ᵗʰ Leg., ch. 451, § 2, eff. June 15, 2007. . (b) amended by Acts 2009, 81ˢᵗ Leg., ch. 414, § 2, eff. June 19, 2009.

Statutes in Context
§ 111.004

Section 111.004 contains definitions of terms used throughout the Code. The definition of settlor in subsection (14) was revised in 2005 to make it clear that a person who contributes property to the trust is encompassed within the term. In other words, the Trust Code provisions effecting a person who *creates* a trust apply equally to a person who *contributes* property to an existing trust.

§ 111.004. Definitions

In this subtitle:

(1) "Affiliate" includes:

(A) a person who directly or indirectly, through one or more intermediaries, controls, is controlled by, or is under common control with another person; or

(B) any officer, director, partner, employee, or relative of a person, and any corporation or partnership of which a person is an officer, director, or partner.

(2) "Beneficiary" means a person for whose benefit property is held in trust, regardless of the nature of the interest.

(3) "Court" means a court of appropriate jurisdiction.

(4) "Express trust" means a fiduciary relationship with respect to property which arises as a manifestation by the settlor of an intention to create the relationship and which subjects the person holding title to the property to equitable duties to deal with the property for the benefit of another person.

(5) "Income" is defined in Section 116.002.

(6) "Interest" means any interest, whether legal or equitable or both, present or future, vested or contingent, defeasible or indefeasible.

(7) "Interested person" means a trustee, beneficiary, or any other person having an interest in or a claim against the trust or any person who is affected by the administration of the trust. Whether a person, excluding a trustee or named beneficiary, is an interested person may vary from time to time and must be determined according to the particular purposes of and matter involved in any proceeding.

(8) "Internal Revenue Code" means the Internal Revenue Code of 1954, as amended,[1] or any corresponding statute subsequently in effect.

(9) "Inventory value" means the cost of property purchased by a trustee, the market value of property at the time it became subject to the trust, or, in the case of a testamentary trust, any value used by the trustee that is finally determined for the purposes of an estate or inheritance tax.

(10) "Person" means:

(A) an individual;

(B) a corporation;

(C) a limited liability company;

(D) a partnership;

(E) a joint venture;

(F) an association;

(G) a joint-stock company;

(H) a business trust;

(I) an unincorporated organization;

(J) two or more persons having a joint or common interest, including an individual or a corporation acting as a personal representative or in any other fiduciary capacity;

(K) a government;

(L) a governmental subdivision, agency, or instrumentality;

(M) a public corporation; or

(N) any other legal or commercial entity.

(11) "Principal" is defined in Section 116.002

(12) "Property" means any type of property, whether real, tangible or intangible, legal, or equitable, including property held in any digital or electronic medium. The term also includes choses in action, claims, and contract rights, including a contractual right to receive death benefits as designated beneficiary under a policy of insurance, contract, employees' trust, retirement account, or other arrangement.

(13) "Relative" means a spouse or, whether by blood or adoption, an ancestor, descendant, brother, sister, or spouse of any of them.

(14) "Settlor" means a person who creates a trust or contributes property to a trustee of a trust. If more than one person contributes property to a trustee of a trust, each person is a settlor of the portion of the property in the trust attributable to that person's contribution to the trust. The terms "grantor" and "trustor" mean the same as "settlor."

(15) "Terms of the trust" means the manifestation of intention of the settlor with respect to the trust expressed in a manner that admits of its proof in judicial proceedings.

(16) "Transaction" means any act performed by a settlor, trustee, or beneficiary in relation to a trust, including the creation or termination of a trust, the investment of trust property, a breach of duty, the receipt of trust property, the receipt of income or the incurring of expense, a distribution of trust property, an entry in the books and records of the trust, and an accounting by a trustee to any person entitled to receive an accounting.

(17) "Trust property" means property placed in trust by one of the methods specified in Section 112.001 or property otherwise transferred to or acquired or retained by the trustee for the trust.

(18) "Trustee" means the person holding the property in trust, including an original, additional, or successor trustee, whether or not the person is appointed or confirmed by a court.

(19) "Employees' trust" means:

---

[1] 26 U.S.C. § 1 et seq.

(A) a trust that forms a part of a stock-bonus, pension, or profit-sharing plan under Section 401, Internal Revenue Code of 1954 (26 U.S.C.A. Sec. 401 (1986));

(B) a pension trust under Chapter 111; and

(C) an employer-sponsored benefit plan or program, or any other retirement savings arrangement, including a pension plan created under Section 3, Employee Retirement Income Security Act of 1974 (29 U.S.C.A. Sec. 1002 (1986)), regardless of whether the plan, program, or arrangement is funded through a trust.

(20) "Individual retirement account" means a trust, custodial arrangement, or annuity under Section 408(a) or (b), Internal Revenue Code of 1954 (26 U.S.C.A. Sec. 408 (1986)).

(21) "Retirement account" means a retirement-annuity contract, an individual retirement account, a simplified employee pension, or any other retirement savings arrangement.

(22) "Retirement-annuity contract" means an annuity contract under Section 403, Internal Revenue Code of 1954 (26 U.S.C.A. Sec. 403 (1986)).

(23) "Simplified employee pension" means a trust, custodial arrangement, or annuity under Section 408, Internal Revenue Code of 1954 (26 U.S.C.A. Sec. 408 (1986)).

(24) "Environmental law" means any federal, state, or local law, rule, regulation, or ordinance relating to protection of the environment.

(25) "Breach of trust" means a violation by a trustee of a duty the trustee owes to a beneficiary.

Amended by Acts 1983, 68th Leg., p. 3332, ch. 567, art. 2, § 2, eff. Jan. 1, 1984; Acts 1987, 70th Leg., ch. 741, §§ 1, 2, eff. Aug. 31, 1987; Acts 1993, 73rd Leg., ch. 846, § 28, eff. Sept. 1, 1993. Amended by Acts 1995, 74th Leg., ch. 642, § 14, eff. Sept. 1, 1995. Amended by Acts 2003, 78th Leg., ch. 659, § 2, eff. Jan. 1, 2004; Acts 2003, 78th Leg., ch. 1103, § 2, eff. Jan. 1, 2004. Subsecs. (14), (25) amended by Acts 2005, 79th Leg., ch. 148, § 3, eff. Jan. 1, 2006. Subsecs. (10) & (18) amended by Acts 2007, 80th Leg., ch. 451, § 3, eff. Sept. 1, 2007. Subsection (12) amended by Acts 2013, 83rd Leg., ch. 699, § 1, eff. Sept. 1, 2013.

§ 111.005. Reenactment of Common Law

If the law codified in this subtitle repealed a statute that abrogated or restated a common law rule, that common law rule is reestablished, except as the contents of the rule are changed by this subtitle.

Added by Acts 1983, 68th Leg., p. 3332, ch. 567, art. 2, § 2, eff. Jan. 1, 1984.

Statutes in Context
§ 111.006

The Code applies to (1) all trusts created after January 1, 1984 and (2) all transactions after January 1, 1984 involving trusts even if the trust was created before January 1, 1984.

§ 111.006. Application

This subtitle applies:

(1) to all trusts created on or after January 1, 1984, and to all transactions relating to such trusts; and

(2) to all transactions occurring on or after January 1, 1984, relating to trusts created before January 1, 1984; provided that transactions entered into before January 1, 1984, and which were subject to the Texas Trust Act, as amended (Articles 7425b-1 through 7425b-48, Vernon's Texas Civil Statutes),1 and the rights, duties, and interests flowing from such transactions remain valid on and after January 1, 1984, and must be terminated, consummated, or enforced as required or permitted by this subtitle.

Added by Acts 1983, 68th Leg., p. 3332, ch. 567, art. 2, § 2, eff. Jan. 1, 1984.

Chapter 112. Creation, Validity, Modification, and Termination of Trusts

Subchapter A. Creation

Statutes in Context
§ 112.001

Section 112.001 lists the methods which a settlor may use to create a trust. The most commonly used of these methods are discussed below.

Inter Vivos or Living Trust. A trust which the settlor creates to take effect while the settlor is still alive is referred to as an inter vivos trust or a living trust. The two basic methods a settlor may use to create an inter vivos trust are distinguished by the identity of the person who holds legal title to the trust property.

In a declaration (or self-declaration) of trust, the settlor declares him- or herself to be the trustee of specific property and then transfers some or all of that property's equitable title to one or more beneficiaries. The settlor retains the legal title and is subject to self-imposed fiduciary duties. See § 112.001(1).

In a transfer or conveyance in trust, the settlor transfers legal title to another person as trustee and imposes fiduciary duties on that person. The settlor may retain some or all of the equitable title or transfer all of the equitable title to other persons. See § 112.001(2).

Testamentary Trust. A settlor can create a trust to take effect upon the settlor's death by including a gift in trust in the settlor's will. See § 112.001(3). The split of title and the imposition of duties does not occur until the settlor dies. This type of trust is called a testamentary trust. A precondition to the validity of a testamentary trust is for the will itself to be valid. If the will fails, any testamentary trust contained in that will is also ineffective. After the will is established, the trust is examined to determine its validity. The trust is not automatically valid just because the will is valid.

§ 112.001. Methods of Creating Trust

A trust may be created by:

(1) a property owner's declaration that the owner holds the property as trustee for another person;

(2) a property owner's inter vivos transfer of the property to another person as trustee for the transferor or a third person;

(3) a property owner's testamentary transfer to another person as trustee for a third person;

(4) an appointment under a power of appointment to another person as trustee for the donee of the power or for a third person; or

(5) a promise to another person whose rights under the promise are to be held in trust for a third person.

Amended by Acts 1983, 68th Leg., p. 3332, ch. 567, art. 2, § 2, eff. Jan. 1, 1984.

Statutes in Context
§ 112.002

Trust intent is the threshold factor in determining whether or not a conveyance of property is sufficient to create an express trust. If the transferor does not manifest trust intent, no trust is created and the court will not intervene to create a trust.

A transferor of property has trust intent if the transferor (1) divides title to the property into legal and equitable components, and (2) imposes enforceable fiduciary duties on the holder of legal title to deal with the property for the benefit of the equitable title holder. See § 111.004(4) (defining "express trust").

No particular words or conduct is necessary to establish trust intent. Likewise, the mere use of trust terminology alone is insufficient to show trust intent.

§ 112.002. Intention to Create Trust

A trust is created only if the settlor manifests an intention to create a trust.

Amended by Acts 1983, 68th Leg., p. 3332, ch. 567, art. 2, § 2, eff. Jan. 1, 1984.

Statutes in Context
§ 112.003

Because a trust is a type of gratuitous property transfer, rather than a contractual arrangement, the beneficiary does not need to give consideration to the settlor for the transfer. Do not be confused when a written document creating a trust is carelessly referred to as a "trust agreement" rather than a "trust instrument." The term "agreement" in this context does not connote an agreement of any kind, contractual or otherwise, between the settlor and the beneficiary.

A promise to create a trust in the future, just like any other promise to make a gift, is not enforceable unless the promise qualifies as a contract.

§ 112.003. Consideration

Consideration is not required for the creation of a trust. A promise to create a trust in the future is enforceable only if the requirements for an enforceable contract are present.

Amended by Acts 1983, 68th Leg., p. 3332, ch. 567, art. 2, § 2, eff. Jan. 1, 1984.

Statutes in Context
§ 112.004

Generally, a trust must be in writing to be enforceable. The policy underlying the requirement that certain trusts be evidenced by a writing is to protect a transferee who actually received an outright conveyance from having those rights infringed upon by someone claiming that the transfer was actually one in trust. Thus, an alleged trustee will use the lack of a writing to raise the Statute of Frauds as a defense to a plaintiff who is trying to deprive the alleged trustee of that person's rights as the donee of an outright gift.

The writing must contain (1) evidence of the terms of the trust (e.g., identity of the beneficiaries, the property, and how that property is to be used) and (2) the signature of the settlor or the settlor's authorized agent (see Government Code § 311.005(6) defining "signed").

The normal requirements are relaxed in some situations for trusts containing personal property. Subsection (1) explains when an oral trust may be enforceable and subsection (2) provides when a writing which does not meet the standard requirements may be sufficient.

Courts may enforce an oral trust of real property if the trustee partially performs. In other words, if the alleged trustee acts, at least temporarily, as if a trust exists, the trustee may be estopped from denying the existence of a trust at a later time and claiming the property as the donee of an outright gift. For example, if the trustee permits the beneficiary to possess the land or make valuable improvements to that land, the trustee may be prohibited from later asserting that a trust did not exist.

Violating the Statute of Frauds merely makes the trust unenforceable (voidable) rather than void. Accordingly, the trustee may carry out the terms of a trust which does not comply with the statute of frauds although no one could have forced the trustee to do so.

See also § 112.051(c) which requires a trust revocation, modification, or amendment to be in writing if the settlor created the trust in writing.

§ 112.004. Statute of Frauds

A trust in either real or personal property is enforceable only if there is written evidence of the trust's terms bearing the signature of the settlor or the settlor's authorized agent. A trust consisting of personal property, however, is enforceable if created by:

(1) a transfer of the trust property to a trustee who is neither settlor nor beneficiary if the transferor expresses simultaneously with or prior to the transfer the intention to create a trust; or

(2) a declaration in writing by the owner of property that the owner holds the property as trustee for another person or for the owner and another person as a beneficiary.

Added by Acts 1983, 68th Leg., p. 3332, ch. 567, art. 2, § 2, eff. Jan. 1, 1984.

Statutes in Context
§ 112.005

A trust is a method of holding title to property. Consequently, the existence of property is essential for the initial creation and continued existence of a trust. No trust exists until it has property and a trust terminates when no property remains.

Any type of property (e.g., real, personal, tangible, intangible, legal, equitable, chose in action, claim, contract right, etc.) may be held in trust. See § 111.004(12) (defining "property") and § 111.004(17) (defining "trust property").

If a person cannot transfer the property, such as property belonging to another person, property that has valid restrictions on its transfer, or the

expectancy to inherit from someone who is still alive, then that property cannot support a trust.

Legal title to the trust property must reach the hands of the trustee. It is not enough for the settlor to sign a trust instrument, own assets that would make good trust property, and intend for that property to be in the trust. The settlor must consummate this intent by actually transferring or delivering the property.

§ 112.005. Trust Property

A trust cannot be created unless there is trust property.

Added by Acts 1983, 68th Leg., p. 3332, ch. 567, art. 2, § 2, eff. Jan. 1, 1984.

Statutes in Context
§ 112.006

Generally, property may be added to an existing trust. However, additions are not permitted if either (1) the terms of the trust prohibit the addition or (2) the property is unacceptable to the trustee (the trustee's duties may not be enlarged without the trustee's consent).

§ 112.006. Additions to Trust Property

Property may be added to an existing trust from any source in any manner unless the addition is prohibited by the terms of the trust or the property is unacceptable to the trustee.

Added by Acts 1983, 68th Leg., p. 3332, ch. 567, art. 2, § 2, eff. Jan. 1, 1984.

Statutes in Context
§ 112.007

The settlor must have the capacity to convey property to create a trust. This requirement does not impose any different standard on the settlor as the settlor would face in an outright, non-trust, transfer of the same property. If the settlor can convey property, the settlor may elect to convey that property by splitting the legal and equitable title and creating a trust. Thus, the capacity required to create an inter vivos trust is usually the same as the capacity to make an outright gift and the capacity necessary to create a testamentary trust is the same as the capacity to execute a will (see Estates Code § 251.001).

§ 112.007. Capacity of Settlor

A person has the same capacity to create a trust by declaration, inter vivos or testamentary transfer, or appointment that the person has to transfer, will, or appoint free of trust.

Added by Acts 1983, 68th Leg., p. 3332, ch. 567, art. 2,

§ 2, eff. Jan. 1, 1984.

Statutes in Context
§ 112.008

The trustee must have the ability to take, hold, and transfer title to the trust property, that is, (a) an individual trustee must be of legal age (or have had the disabilities of minority removed) and competent and (b) a corporate trustee must have the power to act as a trustee in Texas. *See* Finance Code §§ 32.001(b)(3) & 182.001(b)(3). Although the trustee may be a person unconnected with the rest of the trust arrangement, such detachment is not necessary. A trustee may also be the settlor or a beneficiary of the same trust as long as the sole trustee is not also the sole beneficiary. See § 112.034 (merger).

§ 112.008. Capacity of Trustee

(a) The trustee must have the legal capacity to take, hold, and transfer the trust property. If the trustee is a corporation, it must have the power to act as a trustee in this state.

(b) Except as provided by Section 112.034, the fact that the person named as trustee is also a beneficiary does not disqualify the person from acting as trustee if he is otherwise qualified.

(c) The settlor of a trust may be the trustee of the trust.

Added by Acts 1983, 68ᵗʰ Leg., p. 3332, ch. 567, art. 2, § 2, eff. Jan. 1, 1984.

Statutes in Context
§ 112.009

A person does not become a trustee merely because the settlor names that person as the trustee of a trust. The settlor cannot force legal title and the accompanying fiduciary duties on an unwilling person. Thus, a person must take some affirmative step to accept the position. Once acceptance occurs, the person is responsible for complying with the terms of the trust as well as applicable law.

The trustee's acceptance of the trust may be established in two main ways. First, the trustee may sign the trust instrument or a separate acceptance document. When creating an inter vivos trust, it is common practice for attorneys to have the trustee sign the trust instrument at the same time as the settlor. The signature of the trustee is conclusive evidence of acceptance. Second, the trustee's acceptance may be implied from the fact that the trustee has started to act like a trustee by exercising trust powers or performing trust duties. Note that certain acts of the trustee will not be considered acceptance such as acting

to preserve trust property under limited circumstances and inspecting the property.

If the named trustee does not accept, the trust instrument is consulted to see if the settlor named an alternate or specified a method for selecting a replacement. If this does not result in a trustee who accepts the trust, the court will appoint a trustee upon petition of an interested person. See § 111.004(7) (defining "interested person").

§ 112.009. Acceptance by Trustee

(a) The signature of the person named as trustee on the writing evidencing the trust or on a separate written acceptance is conclusive evidence that the person accepted the trust. A person named as trustee who exercises power or performs duties under the trust is presumed to have accepted the trust, except that a person named as trustee may engage in the following conduct without accepting the trust:

(1) acting to preserve the trust property if, within a reasonable time after acting, the person gives notice of the rejection of the trust to:

(A) the settlor; or

(B) if the settlor is deceased or incapacitated, all beneficiaries then entitled to receive trust distributions from the trust; and

(2) inspecting or investigating trust property for any purpose, including determining the potential liability of the trust under environmental or other law.

(b) A person named as trustee who does not accept the trust incurs no liability with respect to the trust.

(c) If the person named as the original trustee does not accept the trust or if the person is dead or does not have capacity to act as trustee, the person named as the alternate trustee under the terms of the trust or the person selected as alternate trustee according to a method prescribed in the terms of the trust may accept the trust. If a trustee is not named or if there is no alternate trustee designated or selected in the manner prescribed in the terms of the trust, the court shall appoint a trustee on a petition of any interested person.

Added by Acts 1983, 68ᵗʰ Leg., p. 3332, ch. 567, art. 2, § 2, eff. Jan. 1, 1984. Amended by Acts 2005, 79ᵗʰ Leg., ch. 148, § 4, eff. Jan. 1, 2006.

Statutes in Context
§ 112.010

Just as heirs may disclaim inheritances and beneficiaries may disclaim testamentary gifts, potential trust beneficiaries are not required to accept the proffered equitable title. The reasons a beneficiary may decide to disclaim and the requirements of the disclaimer are fundamentally the same as for an heir or beneficiary who disclaims. See Property Code Title 13 which contains the Texas Uniform Disclaimer of Property

Interests Act which took effect on September 1, 2015 replacing the previous disclaimer provisions of the Estates and Trust Codes.

§ 112.010. Presumed Acceptance [or Disclaimer] by [or on Behalf of] Beneficiary; Disclaimer

(a) Acceptance by a beneficiary of an interest in a trust is presumed.

(b) A disclaimer of an interest in or power over trust property is governed by Chapter 240 [If a trust is created by will, a beneficiary may disclaim an interest in the manner and with the effect for which provision is made in the applicable probate law].

(c) Except as provided by Subsection (c-1), the following persons may disclaim an interest in a trust created in any manner other than by will:

(1) a beneficiary, including a beneficiary of a spendthrift trust;

(2) the personal representative of an incompetent, deceased, unborn or unascertained, or minor beneficiary, with court approval by the court having jurisdiction over the personal representative; and

(3) the independent executor or independent administrator of a deceased beneficiary, without court approval.

(c-1) A person authorized to disclaim an interest in a trust under Subsection (c) may not disclaim the interest if the person in the person's capacity as beneficiary, personal representative, independent executor, or independent administrator has either exercised dominion and control over the interest or accepted any benefits from the trust.

(c-2) A person authorized to disclaim an interest in a trust under Subsection (c) of this section may disclaim an interest in whole or in part by:

(1) evidencing his irrevocable and unqualified refusal to accept the interest by written memorandum, acknowledged before a notary public or other person authorized to take acknowledgments of conveyances of real estate; and

(2) delivering the memorandum to the trustee or, if there is not a trustee, to the transferor of the interest or his legal representative not later than the date that is nine months after the later of:

(A) the day on which the transfer creating the interest in the beneficiary is made;

(B) the day on which the beneficiary attains age 21; or

(C) in the case of a future interest, the date of the event that causes the taker of the interest to be finally ascertained and the interest to be indefeasibly vested.

(d) A disclaimer under this section is effective as of the date of the transfer of the interest involved and relates back for all purposes to the date of the transfer and is not subject to the claims of any creditor of the disclaimant. Unless the terms of the trust provide otherwise, the interest that is the subject of the disclaimer passes as if the person disclaiming had predeceased the transfer and a future interest that would otherwise take effect in possession or enjoyment after the termination of the estate or interest that is disclaimed takes effect as if the disclaiming beneficiary had predeceased the transfer. A disclaimer under this section is irrevocable.

(e) Failure to comply with this section makes a disclaimer ineffective except as an assignment of the interest to those who would have received the interest being disclaimed had the person attempting the disclaimer died prior to the transferor of the interest.

Added by Acts 1983, 68th Leg., p. 3332, ch. 567, art. 2, § 2, eff. Jan. 1, 1984. Amended by Acts 1987, 70th Leg., ch. 467, § 3, eff. Sept. 1, 1987; Acts 1993, 73rd Leg., ch. 846, § 3, eff. Sept. 1, 1993. Subsecs. (c), (c-1) amended by Acts 2009, 81st Leg., ch. 672, § 2, eff. Sept. 1, 2009. Subsec. (c-3) added by Acts 2011, 82nd Leg., ch. 657, § 1, eff. Sept. 1, 2011. Amended by Acts 2015, 84th Leg., ch. 562, §§ 13, 14, & 16, eff. Sept. 1, 2015.

Subchapter B. Validity

Statutes in Context
§ 112.031

The settlor may create a trust for any purpose as long as that purpose is not illegal. In addition, the terms of the trust may not require the trustee to commit an act that is criminal, tortious, or contrary to public policy.

Courts have used two main approaches in evaluating the legality of a trust purpose. The first analysis concentrates on the settlor's intent and the effect of the trust's existence on the behavior of other persons. Under the intent approach, a trust is illegal if the existence of the trust could induce another person to commit a crime even if the trustee does not have to perform an illegal act. This is the majority approach in the United States and appears to be the one adopted by § 112.031 by its use of the word "purpose." The second approach focuses on how the trust property is actually used, rather than on the motives of the settlor.

§ 112.031. Trust Purposes

A trust may be created for any purpose that is not illegal. The terms of the trust may not require the trustee to commit a criminal or tortious act or an act that is contrary to public policy.

Amended by Acts 1983, 68th Leg., p. 3332, ch. 567, art. 2, § 2, eff. Jan. 1, 1984.

Statutes in Context
§ 112.032

The historical origin of the two components of trust intent, the split of title and the imposition of duties, is derived from the common law history of trusts. The common law precursor to a trust was called a use. Before the fifteenth century, uses were not enforceable and thus a "beneficiary" had no rights and had to hope that the "trustee" would fulfill a merely honorary obligation. This situation changed in the 1400s as uses started to be enforceable as equitable estates in property. By the 1500s, uses were common and were, from the government's point of view, often abused. Property owners were employing uses to avoid their duties of property ownership under the feudal land ownership system, especially financial obligations such as paying money (today called taxes) to the monarch (now the Internal Revenue Service), to hinder creditors and others with claims against the property, and to provide benefits for various religious organizations contrary to the Crown's wishes.

The English Parliament enacted the Statute of Uses in 1536 to end these abuses. The statute executed the use which meant that the beneficiary's equitable interest in real property was turned into a legal interest as well. Because this had the effect of eliminating the legal interest which the trustee formerly held, the beneficiary was now the owner of all title, both legal and equitable, and was fully responsible for all of the burdens of property ownership. Had the Statute of Uses been carried out exactly as written, trusts as we know them would not exist.

An important exception to the Statute of Uses developed for the active trust and is reflected in § 112.032. An active trust is an arrangement where the trustee's holding of property is not merely nominal in an attempt to gain some untoward benefit, but where the trustee actually needs legal title to the property to perform a power or duty relating to the property for the beneficiary's benefit.

Although the Texas Statute of Uses applies only to real property, a similar result would be reached for personal property because without a true split of title and imposition of duties, the definition of an express trust in § 111.004(4) would not be satisfied.

§ 112.032. Active and Passive Trusts; Statute of Uses

(a) Except as provided by Subsection (b), title to real property held in trust vests directly in the beneficiary if the trustee has neither a power nor a duty related to the administration of the trust.

(b) The title of a trustee in real property is not divested if the trustee's title is not merely nominal but is subject to a power or duty in relation to the property.

Amended by Acts 1983, 68th Leg., p. 3332, ch. 567, art. 2, § 2, eff. Jan. 1, 1984.

Statutes in Context
§ 112.033

The settlor may wish to create a trust but may also desire to retain considerable interests in and powers over the trust property. May a settlor do so and still create a valid trust? If the settlor conveys the property in trust so that the settlor and trustee are different persons, there is a clear split of title and imposition of duties. However, if the settlor makes a declaration of trust so the settlor is also the trustee, the reality of the split of title and duty imposition is less clear.

Section 112.033 which codified the result in *Westerfeld v. Huckaby*, 474 S.W.2d 189 (Tex. 1972), takes a very liberal approach by providing that the settlor may retain virtually all interests over the trust property provided there is some beneficial interest created in another person. This interest may be quite "weak" because it is contingent on some future event or is subject to revocation.

§ 112.033. Reservation of Interests and Powers by Settlor

If during the life of the settlor an interest in a trust or the trust property is created in a beneficiary other than the settlor, the disposition is not invalid as an attempted testamentary disposition merely because the settlor reserves or retains, either in himself or another person who is not the trustee, any or all of the other interests in or powers over the trust or trust property, such as:

(1) a beneficial life interest for himself;

(2) the power to revoke, modify, or terminate the trust in whole or in part;

(3) the power to designate the person to whom or on whose behalf the income or principal is to be paid or applied;

(4) the power to control the administration of the trust in whole or in part;

(5) the right to exercise a power or option over property in the trust or over interests made payable to the trust under an employee benefit plan, life insurance policy, or otherwise; or

(6) the power to add property or cause additional employee benefits, life insurance, or other interests to be made payable to the trust at any time.

Amended by Acts 1983, 68th Leg., p. 3332, ch. 567, art. 2, § 2, eff. Jan. 1, 1984.

Statutes in Context
§ 112.034

Any separation of legal and equitable title coupled with the imposition of fiduciary duties on the holder of the legal title is sufficient to satisfy the split of title requirement for a valid trust. Only if all legal and all equitable title are in the same person is a trust not created.

If all legal and equitable title becomes reunited in one person after originally being separated, merger occurs and the trust will cease to exist. In the normal course of events, this is what happens when the trust terminates and the trustee distributes the property to the remainder beneficiaries. However, merger could occur earlier either because of circumstances the settlor did not anticipate or because the trustee and beneficiary are working together to terminate the trust. A trust containing a spendthrift provision (see § 112.035) will not end via merger unless the settlor is also the beneficiary. Instead, the court will appoint a trustee to keep title split. This rule prevents the trustee and beneficiary from circumventing the settlor's intent by triggering a merger.

§ 112.034. Merger

(a) If a settlor transfers both the legal title and all equitable interests in property to the same person or retains both the legal title and all equitable interests in property in himself as both the sole trustee and the sole beneficiary, a trust is not created and the transferee holds the property as his own. This subtitle does not invalidate a trust account validly created and in effect under Chapter XI, Texas Probate Code.[1]

(b) Except as provided by Subsection (c) of this section, a trust terminates if the legal title to the trust property and all equitable interests in the trust become united in one person.

(c) The title to trust property and all equitable interests in the trust property may not become united in a beneficiary, other than the settlor, whose interest is protected under a spendthrift trust, and in that case the court shall appoint a new trustee or cotrustee to administer the trust for the benefit of the beneficiary.

Added by Acts 1983, 68th Leg., p. 3332, ch. 567, art. 2, § 2, eff. Jan. 1, 1984.

Statutes in Context
§ 112.035

A spendthrift clause is a provision of a trust which does two things. First, it prohibits the beneficiary from selling, giving away, or otherwise transferring the beneficiary's interest. Second, a spendthrift clause prevents the beneficiary's

[1] V.A.T.S. Probate Code, § 436 et seq.

creditors from reaching the beneficiary's interest in the trust. The provision permits the settlor to carry out the settlor's intent of benefiting the designated beneficiary but not the beneficiary's assignees or creditors. Settlors include spendthrift restrictions in practically every trust because they protect beneficiaries from their own improvidence and their personal creditors. Note, however, that neither the settlor nor the beneficiary must show that a beneficiary is actually incapable of prudently managing property to obtain spendthrift protection.

Spendthrift restrictions are easy to create. The settlor does not need to use any particular language as long as the settlor's intent is clear. In fact, § 112.035(b) provides that it is adequate for the settlor to simply write, "This is a spendthrift trust."

A spendthrift provision has no effect once the trustee delivers a trust distribution to the beneficiary.

Under several circumstances, courts will not enforce spendthrift provisions for public policy reasons. The following is a nonexclusive list: (1) A creditor may still reach trust property if the settlor is also the beneficiary under § 112.035(d). Note, however, that some states, such as Alaska, enforce spendthrift provisions even if the trust is self-settled. (2) The court may order the trustees of a spendthrift trust to make payments for the support of the beneficiary's child. See *Statutes in Context* to Family Code § 154.005. (3) Property in a spendthrift trust will not be protected from the beneficiary's federal tax obligations. See *United States v. Dallas Nat'l Bank*, 152 F.2d 582 (5th Cir. 1945).

Subsection (e) prevents the beneficiary of a *Crummey* trust from being deemed a settlor and thereby losing spendthrift protection if the beneficiary elects not to exercise the withdrawal right. Subsection (f) helps assure that a surviving spouse does not lose spendthrift protection under a bypass trust under specified circumstances.

An assignment that would defeat a spendthrift provision may not be made under Estates Code § 122.206.

§ 112.035. Spendthrift Trusts

(a) A settlor may provide in the terms of the trust that the interest of a beneficiary in the income or in the principal or in both may not be voluntarily or involuntarily transferred before payment or delivery of the interest to the beneficiary by the trustee.

(b) A declaration in a trust instrument that the interest of a beneficiary shall be held subject to a "spendthrift trust" is sufficient to restrain voluntary or involuntary alienation of the interest by a beneficiary to the maximum extent permitted by this subtitle.

(c) A trust containing terms authorized under Subsection (a) or (b) of this section may be referred to as a spendthrift trust.

(d) If the settlor is also a beneficiary of the trust, a provision restraining the voluntary or involuntary transfer of the settlor's beneficial interest does not prevent the settlor's creditors from satisfying claims from the settlor's interest in the trust estate. A settlor is not considered a beneficiary of a trust solely because:

(1) a trustee who is not the settlor is authorized under the trust instrument to pay or reimburse the settlor for, or pay directly to the taxing authorities, any tax on trust income or principal that is payable by the settlor under the law imposing the tax; or

(2) the settlor's interest in the trust was created by the exercise of a power of appointment by a third party.

(e) A beneficiary of the trust may not be considered a settlor merely because of a lapse, waiver, or release of:

(1) a power described by Subsection (f); or

(2) the beneficiary's right to withdraw a part of the trust property to the extent that the value of the property affected by the lapse, waiver, or release in any calendar year does not exceed the greater of the amount specified in:

(A) Section 2041(b)(2) or 2514(e), Internal Revenue Code of 1986; or

(B) Section 2503(b), Internal Revenue Code of 1986.

(f) A beneficiary of the trust may not be considered to be a settlor, to have made a voluntary or involuntary transfer of the beneficiary's interest in the trust, or to have the power to make a voluntary or involuntary transfer of the beneficiary's interest in the trust, merely because the beneficiary, in any capacity, holds or exercises:

(1) a presently exercisable power to:

(A) consume, invade, appropriate, or distribute property to or for the benefit of the beneficiary, if the power is:

(i) exercisable only on consent of another person holding an interest adverse to the beneficiary's interest; or

(ii) limited by an ascertainable standard, including health, education, support, or maintenance of the beneficiary; or

(B) appoint any property of the trust to or for the benefit of a person other than the beneficiary, a creditor of the beneficiary, the beneficiary's estate, or a creditor of the beneficiary's estate;

(2) a testamentary power of appointment; or

(3) a presently exercisable right described by Subsection (e)(2).

(g) For the purposes of this section, property contributed to the following trusts is not considered to have been contributed by the settlor, and a person who would otherwise be treated as a settlor or a deemed settlor of the following trusts may not be treated as a settlor:

(1) an irrevocable inter vivos marital trust if:

(A) the settlor is a beneficiary of the trust after the death of the settlor's spouse; and

(B) the trust is treated as:

(i) qualified terminable interest property under Section 2523(f), Internal Revenue Code of 1986; or

(ii) a general power of appointment trust under Section 2523(e), Internal Revenue Code of 1986;

(2) an irrevocable inter vivos trust for the settlor's spouse if the settlor is a beneficiary of the trust after the death of the settlor's spouse; or

(3) an irrevocable trust for the benefit of a person:

(A) if the settlor is the person's spouse, regardless of whether or when the person was the settlor of an irrevocable trust for the benefit of that spouse; or

(B) to the extent that the property of the trust was subject to a general power of appointment in another person.

(h) For the purposes of Subsection (g), a person is a beneficiary whether named a beneficiary:

(1) under the initial trust instrument; or

(2) through the exercise of a limited or general power of appointment by:

(A) that person's spouse; or

(B) another person.

Added by Acts 1983, 68ᵗʰ Leg., p. 3332, ch. 567, art. 2, § 2, eff. Jan. 1, 1984. Amended by Acts 1997, 75ᵗʰ Leg., ch. 109, § 1, eff. Sept. 1, 1997. Subsec. (e) amended by Acts 2005, 79ᵗʰ Leg., ch. 148, § 5, eff. Jan. 1, 2006. Subsec. (f) added by Acts 2005, 79ᵗʰ Leg., ch. 148, § 5, eff. Jan. 1, 2006. Subsec. (d) amended by Acts 2007, 80ᵗʰ Leg., ch. 451, § 4, eff. Sept. 1, 2007. Subsecs. (d) amended, (g) and (h) added by Acts 2013, 83ʳᵈ Leg., ch. 699, § 2, eff. Sept. 1, 2013.

Statutes in Context
§ 112.036

Article I, § 26 of the Texas Constitution adopts the common law version of the Rule Against Perpetuities, that is, "a future interest not destructible by the owner of a prior interest cannot be valid unless it becomes vested at a date not more remote than twenty-one years after lives in being at the creation of such interest, plus the period of gestation. Any future interest so limited that it retains its indestructible and contingent character until a more remote time is invalid." Interpretive Commentary to Article I, § 21.

Section 112.036 makes it clear that this rule applies to all noncharitable trusts. However, the court must reform or construe transfers that violate the Rule under Property Code § 5.043 to carry out the general intent and specific directives of the grantor to the extent possible without violating the

Rule. The court may apply the equitable doctrine of cy pres in this process.

§ 112.036. Rule Against Perpetuities

The rule against perpetuities applies to trusts other than charitable trusts. Accordingly, an interest is not good unless it must vest, if at all, not later than 21 years after some life in being at the time of the creation of the interest, plus a period of gestation. Any interest in a trust may, however, be reformed or construed to the extent and as provided by Section 5.043.

Added by Acts 1983, 68ᵗʰ Leg., p. 3332, ch. 567, art. 2, § 2, eff. Jan. 1, 1984. Amended by Acts 1984, 68ᵗʰ Leg., 2ⁿᵈ C.S., ch. 18, § 10, eff. Oct. 2, 1984.

Statutes in Context
§ 112.037

Traditionally, a trust in favor of specific animals failed for a variety of reasons such as for being in violation of the Rule Against Perpetuities because the measuring life was not human or for being an unenforceable honorary trust because it lacked a human or legal entity as a beneficiary who would have standing to enforce the trust. To get around this problem, pet owners who wanted to assure that their pets were properly cared for after they died created a traditional trust which indirectly provided pet care by instructing the trustee to help the person, the actual beneficiary of the trust, who is providing care to the pet by paying for the pet's expenses (and perhaps a fee) according to the pet owner's directions as long as the beneficiary takes proper care of the pet.

With the enactment of § 112.037 in 2005, Texas joined the growing number of states which authorize statutory pet trusts. This type of trust is a basic plan and does not require the pet owner to make as many decisions regarding the terms of the trust. The statute "fills in the gaps" and thus a simple provision in a will such as, "I leave $1,000 in trust for the care of my dog, Rover" may be effective.

§ 112.037. Trust For Care of Animal

(a) A trust may be created to provide for the care of an animal alive during the settlor's lifetime. The trust terminates on the death of the animal or, if the trust is created to provide for the care of more than one animal alive during the settlor's lifetime, on the death of the last surviving animal.

(b) A trust authorized by this section may be enforced by a person appointed in the terms of the trust or, if a person is not appointed in the terms of the trust, by a person appointed by the court. A person having an interest in the welfare of an animal that is the subject of a trust authorized by this section may request the court

to appoint a person to enforce the trust or to remove a person appointed to enforce the trust.

(c) Except as provided by Subsections (d) and (e), property of a trust authorized by this section may be applied only to the property's intended use under the trust.

(d) Property of a trust authorized by this section may be applied to a use other than the property's intended use under the trust to the extent the court determines that the value of the trust property exceeds the amount required for the intended use.

(e) Except as otherwise provided by the terms of the trust, property not required for the trust's intended use must be distributed to:

(1) if the settlor is living at the time the trust property is distributed, the settlor; or

(2) if the settlor is not living at the time the trust property is distributed:

(A) if the settlor has a will, beneficiaries under the settlor's will; or

(B) in the absence of an effective provision in a will, the settlor's heirs.

(f) For purposes of Section 112.036, the lives in being used to determine the maximum duration of a trust authorized by this section are:

(1) the individual beneficiaries of the trust;

(2) the individuals named in the instrument creating the trust; and

(3) if the settlor or settlors are living at the time the trust becomes irrevocable, the settlor or settlors of the trust or, if the settlor or settlors are not living at the time the trust becomes irrevocable, the individuals who would inherit the settlor or settlors' property under the law of this state had the settlor or settlors died intestate at the time the trust becomes irrevocable.

Added by Acts 2005, 79ᵗʰ Leg., ch. 148, § 6, eff. Jan. 1, 2006.

Statutes in Context
§ 112.038

A forfeiture clause is presumed enforceable unless the party who wants the clause to be unenforceable establishes by a preponderance of the evidence that just cause existed for bringing the action and the action was brought and maintained in good faith. The unenforceability of *in terrorem* provisions under these circumstances cannot be changed by the settlor under § 111.0035(b)(6).

§ 112.038. Forfeiture Clause

A provision in a trust that would cause a forfeiture of or void an interest for bringing any court action, including contesting a trust, is enforceable unless in a court action determining whether the forfeiture clause should be enforced, the person who brought the action contrary to the forfeiture clause establishes by a preponderance of the evidence that:

(1) just cause existed for bringing the action; and

(2) the action was brought and maintained in good faith.

Added by Acts 2009, 81ˢᵗ Leg., ch. 414, § 3, eff. June 19, 2009. Amended by Acts 2011, 82ⁿᵈ Leg., ch. 657, § 2, eff. Sept. 1, 2011. Amended by 2013, 83ʳᵈ Leg., ch. 351, § 3.01, eff. Sept. 1, 2013.

Subchapter C. Revocation, Modification, and Termination of Trusts

Statutes in Context
§ 112.051

Unlike under the law of most states, trusts are presumed revocable in Texas. A trust may, of course, be made irrevocable by its express terms.

The settlor may not enlarge the duties of the trustee without obtaining the trustee's express consent.

Subsection (c) augments § 112.004, the Statute of Frauds provision, by requiring a written trust to be revoked, modified, or amended in writing even if the trust originally would not have had to be in writing (e.g., an oral trust of personal property).

§ 112.051. Revocation, Modification, or Amendment by Settlor

(a) A settlor may revoke the trust unless it is irrevocable by the express terms of the instrument creating it or of an instrument modifying it.

(b) The settlor may modify or amend a trust that is revocable, but the settlor may not enlarge the duties of the trustee without the trustee's express consent.

(c) If the trust was created by a written instrument, a revocation, modification, or amendment of the trust must be in writing.

Amended by Acts 1983, 68ᵗʰ Leg., p. 3332, ch. 567, art. 2, § 2, eff. Jan. 1, 1984.

Statutes in Context
§ 112.052

Trusts eventually terminate unless they are charitable. Upon termination, all legal and equitable title to any remaining trust property becomes reunited in the hands of the remainder beneficiaries.

The trustee's powers do not end immediately upon trust termination. Section 112.052 permits the trustee to continue to exercise trust powers for the reasonable period of time necessary to wind up the affairs of the trust. The length of this period depends on the circumstances of each case and the type of property involved. More sophisticated investments and businesses may take longer to wrap up and transfer to the beneficiary than other assets which need a mere change in registration or physical delivery. See *Myrick v. Enron Oil & Gas Co.*, 296 S.W.3d 724 (Tex. App.—El Paso 2009, no pet.)

§ 112.052. Termination

A trust terminates if by its terms the trust is to continue only until the expiration of a certain period or until the happening of a certain event and the period of time has elapsed or the event has occurred. If an event of termination occurs, the trustee may continue to exercise the powers of the trustee for the reasonable period of time required to wind up the affairs of the trust and to make distribution of its assets to the appropriate beneficiaries. The continued exercise of the trustee's powers after an event of termination does not affect the vested rights of beneficiaries of the trust.

Amended by Acts 1983, 68ᵗʰ Leg., p. 3332, ch. 567, art. 2, § 2, eff. Jan. 1, 1984.

Statutes in Context
§ 112.053

The settlor may provide for the disposition of trust property when the trust fails, terminates, or is revoked. Note that the settlor may also use a negative provision stating how trust property may not be distributed. If the settlor does not provide for the disposition of trust property, a resulting trust will arise for the benefit of the settlor, or if the settlor is deceased, the settlor's successors in interest (heirs or beneficiaries). See *Roberts v. Squyres*, 4 S.W.3d 485 (Tex. App. — Beaumont 1999, pet. denied).

§ 112.053. Disposition of Trust Property on Failure of Trust

The settlor may provide in the trust instrument how property may or may not be disposed of in the event of failure, termination, or revocation of the trust.

Added by Acts 1983, 68ᵗʰ Leg., p. 3332, ch. 567, art. 2, § 2, eff. Jan. 1, 1984. Amended by Acts 1991, 72ⁿᵈ Leg., ch. 895, § 17, eff. Sept. 1, 1991.

Statutes in Context
§ 112.054

A court may be willing to permit the trustee to deviate from the settlor's instructions as contained in the trust instrument if the court is convinced that the settlor would have consented to the change had the settlor anticipated the current situation. Deviation typically occurs if (1) the purposes of the trust have been fulfilled, (2) the purposes of the trust have become illegal, (3) the purposes of the trust are now impossible to fulfill, or (4) because of circumstances not known to or anticipated by the settlor, the deviation will further the purposes of the trust. The grounds for deviation were greatly expanded by the 2005 Legislature when subsections (a)(3)-(5) were added and (a)(2) liberalized.

Using its deviation powers, the court may authorize a wide array of administrative revisions such as (1) changing the trustee, (2) permitting the trustee to perform acts that are not authorized or are forbidden by the trust instrument, (3) prohibiting the trustee from performing acts that the settlor mandated in the trust instrument, (4) modifying the terms of the trust, and (5) terminating the trust.

The court will not authorize a deviation from the terms of a trust that is not clearly authorized by Property Code § 112.054 even if the beneficiaries agree to the change. See *In re Willa Peters Hubberd Testamentary Trust*, 432 S.W.3d 358 (Tex. App.—San Antonio 2014, no pet.).

Although the trustee and the beneficiaries have standing to request deviation, the settlor lacks standing to do so.

§ 112.054. Judicial Modification or Termination of Trusts

(a) On the petition of a trustee or a beneficiary, a court may order that the trustee be changed, that the terms of the trust be modified, that the trustee be directed or permitted to do acts that are not authorized or that are forbidden by the terms of the trust, that the trustee be prohibited from performing acts required by the terms of the trust, or that the trust be terminated in whole or in part, if:

(1) the purposes of the trust have been fulfilled or have become illegal or impossible to fulfill;

(2) because of circumstances not known to or anticipated by the settlor, the order will further the purposes of the trust;

(3) modification of administrative, nondispositive terms of the trust is necessary or appropriate to prevent waste or avoid impairment of the trust's administration;

(4) the order is necessary or appropriate to achieve the settlor's tax objectives and is not contrary to the settlor's intentions; or

(5) subject to Subsection (d)

(A) continuance of the trust is not necessary to achieve any material purpose of the trust; or

(B) the order is not inconsistent with a material purpose of the trust.

(b) The court shall exercise its discretion to order a modification or termination under Subsection (a) in the manner that conforms as nearly as possible to the probable intention of the settlor. The court shall consider spendthrift provisions as a factor in making its decision whether to modify or terminate, but the court is not precluded from exercising its discretion to modify or terminate solely because the trust is a spendthrift trust.

(c) The court may direct that an order described by Subsection (a)(4) has retroactive effect.

(d) The court may not take the action permitted by Subsection (a)(5) unless all beneficiaries of the trust have consented to the order or are deemed to have consented to the order. A minor, incapacitated, unborn, or unascertained beneficiary is deemed to have consented if a person representing the beneficiary's interest under Section 115.013(c) has consented or if a guardian ad litem appointed to represent the beneficiary's interest under Section 115.014 consents on the beneficiary's behalf.

Added by Acts 1983, 68th Leg., p. 3332, ch. 567, art. 2, § 2, eff. Jan. 1, 1984. Amended by Acts 1985, 69th Leg., ch. 149, § 1, eff. May 24, 1985. Subsecs. (a), (b) amended by Acts 2005, 79th Leg., ch. 148, § 7, eff. Jan. 1, 2006. Subsec. (c), (d) added by Acts 2005, 79th Leg., ch. 148, § 7, eff. Jan. 1, 2006.

Statutes in Context § 112.055

Section 112.055 provides that certain charitable trusts automatically have enumerated terms statutorily provided to assist these trusts in qualifying for favorable federal tax treatment. See also § 112.056.

§ 112.055. Amendment of Charitable Trusts by Operation of Law

(a) Except as provided by Section 112.056 and Subsection (b) of this section, the governing instrument of a trust that is a private foundation under Section 509, Internal Revenue Code, as amended,[1] a nonexempt charitable trust that is treated as a private foundation under Section 4947(a)(1), Internal Revenue Code, as amended,[2] or, to the extent that Section 508(e), Internal Revenue Code,[3] is applicable to it, a nonexempt split-interest trust under Section 4947(a)(2), Internal Revenue Code, as amended,[4] is considered to contain provisions stating that the trust:

(1) shall make distributions at times and in a manner as not to subject the trust to tax under Section 4942, Internal Revenue Code;[5]

---

[1] 26 U.S.C. § 509
[2] 26 U.S.C. § 4947(a)(1)
[3] 26 U.S.C. § 508(e)
[4] 26 U.S.C. § 4947(a)(2)
[5] 26 U.S.C. § 4942

(2) may not engage in an act of self-dealing that would be subject to tax under Section 4941, Internal Revenue Code;[1]

(3) may not retain excess business holdings that would subject it to tax under Section 4943, Internal Revenue Code;[2]

(4) may not make an investment that would subject it to tax under Section 4944, Internal Revenue Code;[3] and

(5) may not make a taxable expenditure that would subject it to tax under Section 4945, Internal Revenue Code.[4]

(b) If a trust was created before January 1, 1970, this section applies to it only for its taxable years that begin on or after January 1, 1972.

(c) This section applies regardless of any provision in a trust's governing instrument and regardless of any other law of this state, including the provisions of this title.

Added by Acts 1983, 68th Leg., p. 3332, ch. 567, art. 2, § 2, eff. Jan. 1, 1984.

§ 112.056. Permissive Amendment by Trustee of Charitable Trust

(a) If the settlor of a trust that is described under Subsection (a) of Section 112.055 is living and competent and consents, the trustee may, without judicial proceedings, amend the trust to expressly include or exclude the provisions required by Subsection (a) of Section 112.055.

(b) The amendment must be in writing, and it is effective when a duplicate original is filed with the attorney general's office.

Added by Acts 1983, 68th Leg., p. 3332, ch. 567, art. 2, § 2, eff. Jan. 1, 1984.

Statutes in Context
§ 112.057

Section 112.057 allows trustees to divide or merge trusts if the result does not impair the rights of any beneficiary or adversely affect the achievement of the purposes of the original trust. Prior to January 1, 2006, such an action was allowed only if it would achieve significant tax savings.

---

§ 112.057. Division and Combination of Trusts

(a) The trustee may, unless expressly prohibited by the terms of the instrument establishing the trust, divide a trust into two or more separate trusts without a judicial proceeding if the result does not impair the rights of any beneficiary or adversely affect

achievement of the purposes of the original trust. The trustee may make a division under this subsection by:

(1) giving written notice of the division, not later than the 30th day before the date of a division under this subsection, to each beneficiary who might then be entitled to receive distributions from the trust or may be entitled to receive distributions from the trust once it is funded; and

(2) executing a written instrument, acknowledged before a notary public or other person authorized to take acknowledgements of conveyances of real estate stating that the trust has been divided pursuant to this section and that the notice requirements of this subsection have been satisfied.

(b) A trustee, in the written instrument dividing a trust, shall allocate trust property among the separate trusts on a fractional basis, by identifying the assets and liabilities passing to each separate trust, or in any other reasonable manner. The trustee shall allocate undesignated trust property received after the trustee has divided the trust into separate trusts in the manner provided by the written instrument dividing the trust or, in the absence of a provision in the written instrument, in a manner determined by the trustee.

(c) The trustee may, unless expressly prohibited by the terms of the instrument establishing a trust, combine two or more trusts into a single trust without a judicial proceeding if the result does not impair the rights of any beneficiary or adversely affect achievement of the purposes of one of the separate trusts The trustee shall complete the trust combination by:

(1) giving a written notice of the combination, not later than the 30th day before the effective date of the combination, to each beneficiary who might then be entitled to receive distributions from the separate trusts being combined or to each beneficiary who might be entitled to receive distributions from the separate trusts once the trusts are funded; and

(2) executing a written instrument, acknowledged before a notary public or other person authorized to take acknowledgments of conveyances of real estate stating that the trust has been combined pursuant to this section and that the notice requirements of this subsection have been satisfied.

(d) The trustee may divide or combine a testamentary trust after the will establishing the trust has been admitted to probate, even if the trust will not be funded until a later date. The trustee may divide or combine any other trust before it is funded.

(e) A beneficiary to whom written notice is required to be given under this section may waive the notice requirement in a writing delivered to the trustee. If all beneficiaries to whom notice would otherwise be required to be given under this section waive the notice requirement, notice is not required.

(f) Notice required under this section shall be given to a guardian of the estate, guardian ad litem, or parent

---

[1] 26 U.S.C. § 4941

[2] 26 U.S.C. § 4943

[3] 26 U.S.C. § 4944

[4] 26 U.S.C. § 4945

of a minor or incapacitated beneficiary. A guardian of the estate, guardian ad litem, or parent of a minor or incapacitated beneficiary may waive the notice requirement in accordance with this section on behalf of the minor or incapacitated beneficiary.

Added by Acts 1991, 72nd Leg., ch. 895, § 18, eff. Sept. 1, 1991. Title amended by Acts 2005, 79th Leg., ch. 148, § 8, eff. Jan. 1, 2006. Subsecs. (a), (c), (d) amended by Acts 2005, 79th Leg., ch. 148, § 9, eff. Jan. 1, 2006. Subsecs. (e) & (f) added by Acts 2011, 82nd Leg., ch. 657, § 3, eff. Sept. 1, 2011.

§ 112.058. Conversion of Community Trust to Nonprofit Corporation

(a) In this section:

(1) "Assets" means the assets of the component trust funds of a community trust.

(2) "Community trust" means a community trust as described by 26 CFR § 1.170A-9(e)(11) (1999), including subsequent amendments.

(b) A community trust with court approval may transfer the assets of the trust to a nonprofit corporation and terminate the trust as provided by this section.

(c) The community trust may transfer assets of the trust to a nonprofit corporation only if the nonprofit corporation is organized under the Texas Non-Profit Corporation Act (Article 1396-1.01 et seq., Vernon's Texas Civil Statutes) and organized for the same purpose as the community trust. The charter of the nonprofit corporation must describe the purpose of the corporation and the proposed use of the assets transferred using language substantially similar to the language used in the instrument creating the community trust.

(d) To transfer the assets of and terminate a community trust under this section, the governing body of the community trust must:

(1) file a petition in a probate court, county court, or district court requesting:

(A) the transfer of the assets of the trust to a nonprofit corporation established for the purpose of receiving and administering the assets of the trust; and

(B) the termination of the trust;

(2) send by first class mail to each trust settlor and each trustee of each component trust of the community trust who can be located by the exercise of reasonable diligence a copy of the governing body's petition and a notice specifying the time and place of the court-scheduled hearing on the petition; and

(3) publish once in a newspaper of general circulation in the county in which the proceeding is pending a notice that reads substantially similar to the following:

(NAME OF COMMUNITY TRUST) HAS FILED A PETITION IN (NAME OF COURT) OF (NAME OF COUNTY), TEXAS, REQUESTING PERMISSION TO CONVERT TO A NONPROFIT CORPORATION. IF PERMITTED TO CONVERT:

TO ALL INTERESTED PERSONS:

(1) THE (NAME OF COMMUNITY TRUST) WILL BE TERMINATED; AND

(2) THE ASSETS OF THE TRUST WILL BE:

(A) TRANSFERRED TO A NONPROFIT CORPORATION WITH THE SAME NAME AND CREATED FOR THE SAME PURPOSE AS THE (NAME OF COMMUNITY TRUST); AND

(B) HELD AND ADMINISTERED BY THE CORPORATION AS PROVIDED BY THE TEXAS NON-PROFIT CORPORATION ACT (ARTICLE 1396-1.01 ET SEQ., VERNON'S TEXAS CIVIL STATUTES).

(1) THE (NAME OF COMMUNITY TRUST) WILL BE TERMINATED; AND

(2) THE ASSETS OF THE TRUST WILL BE:

(A) TRANSFERRED TO A NONPROFIT CORPORATION WITH THE SAME NAME AND CREATED FOR THE SAME PURPOSE AS THE (NAME OF COMMUNITY TRUST); AND

(B) HELD AND ADMINISTERED BY THE CORPORATION AS PROVIDED BY THE TEXAS NON-PROFIT CORPORATION ACT (ARTICLE 1396-1.01 ET SEQ., VERNON'S TEXAS CIVIL STATUTES).

THE PURPOSE OF THE CONVERSION IS TO ACHIEVE SAVINGS AND USE THE MONEY SAVED TO FURTHER THE PURPOSES FOR WHICH THE (NAME OF COMMUNITY TRUST) WAS CREATED.

A HEARING ON THE PETITION IS SCHEDULED ON (DATE AND TIME) AT (LOCATION OF COURT).

FOR ADDITIONAL INFORMATION, YOU MAY CONTACT THE GOVERNING BODY OF THE (NAME OF COMMUNITY TRUST) AT (ADDRESS AND TELEPHONE NUMBER) OR THE COURT.

(e) The court shall schedule a hearing on the petition to be held after the 10th day after the date the notices required by Subsection (d)(2) are deposited in the mail or the date the notice required by Subsection (d)(3) is published, whichever is later. The hearing must be held at the time and place stated in the notices unless the court, for good cause, postpones the hearing. If the hearing is postponed, a notice of the rescheduled hearing date and time must be posted at the courthouse of the county in which the proceeding is pending or at the place in or near the courthouse where public notices are customarily posted.

(f) The court, on a request from the governing body of the community trust, may by order require approval from the Internal Revenue Service for an asset transfer under this section. If the court orders approval from the Internal Revenue Service, the asset transfer may occur on the date the governing body of the community trust files a notice with the court indicating that the Internal Revenue Service has approved the asset transfer. The notice required by this subsection must be filed on or before the first anniversary of the date the court's order approving the asset transfer is signed. If the notice is not filed within the period prescribed by this subsection, the court's order is dissolved.

(g) A court order transferring the assets of and terminating a community trust must provide that the duties of each trustee of each component trust fund of the community trust are terminated on the date the assets are transferred. This subsection does not affect the liability of a trustee for acts or omissions that occurred before the duties of the trustee are terminated.

Added by Acts 1999, 76th Leg., ch. 1035, § 1, eff. Sept. 1, 1999.

Statutes in Context
§ 112.059

This section was added by the 2007 Legislature to permit a trustee of a small trust (that is, under $50,000 in value) to terminate the trust if it not prudent from an economic standpoint to continue the trust.

---

§ 112.059. Termination of Uneconomic Trust

(a) After notice to beneficiaries who are distributees or permissible distributees of trust income or principal or who would be distributees or permissible distributees if the interests of the distributees or the trust were to terminate and no powers of appointment were exercised, the trustee of a trust consisting of trust property having a total value of less than $50,000 may terminate the trust if the trustee concludes after considering the purpose of the trust and the nature of the trust assets that the value of the trust property is insufficient to justify the continued cost of administration.

(b) On termination of a trust under this section, the trustee shall distribute the trust property in a manner consistent with the purposes of the trust.

(c) A trustee may not exercise a power described by Subsection (a) if the trustee's possession of the power would cause the assets of the trust to be included in the trustee's estate for federal estate tax purposes.

(d) This section does not apply to an easement for conservation or preservation.

Added by Acts 2007, 80th Leg., ch. 451, § 5, eff. Sept. 1, 2007.

Subchapter D. Distribution of Trust Principal in Further Trust

Statutes in Context
Chapter 112, Subchapter D

In 2013, Texas joined the growing number of states which have statutes granting the trustee the power to decant, that is, to distribute trust principal to another trust for the benefit of one or more of the beneficiaries of the original trust under specified circumstances.

The summary of these provisions below is adapted from William D. Pargaman, *Out With the Old [Probate Code] and In With the New [Estates Code]: 2013 Texas Estate and Trust Legislative Update* (Sept. 20, 2013), at 9-10.

This new subchapter adds statutory decanting provisions that supplement any similar provisions in a trust, unless the settlor expressly prohibits decanting. (A standard spendthrift clause is not considered such a prohibition.)

If a trustee has "full discretion" (i.e., a power that is not limited in any manner), that trustee may distribute principal to another trust for the benefit of one or more of the current beneficiaries of the first trust. If there is more than one trustee and less than all have full discretion, those trustees may exercise this power without the participation of any "limited" trustee.

If the trustee could have made an outright distribution to the beneficiary, then the trustee may give the beneficiary a power of appointment in the second trust in favor of one or more of the current beneficiaries of the first trust. The permissible appointees may be broader than the beneficiaries of the first trust.

If a trustee has "limited discretion" (i.e., a power that is limited in some way), that trustee may distribute principal to another trust so long as the current beneficiaries of both trusts are the same, and the successor and remainder beneficiaries of both trusts are the same. The distribution language of the second trust must be the same as the first trust. If a beneficiary of the first trust has a power of appointment, the beneficiary must be given the same power over the second trust. In other words, this provision really is limited to changing administrative provisions.

In either case, the trustee must act "in good faith, in accordance with the terms and purpose of the trust, and in the interests of the beneficiaries."

Notice provisions include the attorney general if a charity is involved, and allow intervention by the attorney general.

A trustee may not exercise a decanting power if it would:

(1) reduce a beneficiary's current right to a mandatory distribution or to withdraw a portion of the trust;

(2) materially impair the rights of any beneficiary;

(3) materially lessen a trustee's fiduciary duty;

(4) decrease the trustee's liability or indemnify or exonerate a trustee for failure to exercise reasonable care, diligence, and prudence;

(5) eliminate another person's power to remove or replace the trustee; or

(6) modify the perpetuities period (unless the first trust expressly permits this modification).

The decanting power is reduced to the extent it would cause any intended tax benefits, such as the annual gift tax exclusion, the marital deduction, or the charitable deduction, to be lost.

A trustee may not exercise a decanting power without court approval solely to change the trustee compensation provisions. The trustee may, however, modify the compensation provisions in conjunction with other valid reasons for decanting if the change raises the trustee's compensation to reasonable limits in accord with Texas law.

In no case is a trustee deemed to have a duty to decant.

If there are one or more current beneficiaries and one or more presumptive remainder beneficiaries who are not incapacitated, neither consent of the settlor nor court approval is required to exercise the decanting power if the trustee has sent written, descriptive notice to those beneficiaries.

A trustee may elect to petition a court to order the distribution. If a beneficiary timely objects, either the trustee or the beneficiary may petition to court to approve, modify, or deny the power.

§ 112.071. Definitions

In this subchapter:

(1) "Authorized trustee" means a person, other than the settlor, who has authority under the terms of a first trust to distribute the principal of the trust to or for the benefit of one or more current beneficiaries.

(2) "Charity" means a charitable entity or a charitable trust, as those terms are defined by Section 123.001.

(3) "Current beneficiary," with respect to a particular date, means a person who is receiving or is eligible to receive a distribution of income or principal from a trust on that date.

(4) "First trust" means an existing irrevocable inter vivos or testamentary trust all or part of the principal of

which is distributed in further trust under Section 112.072 or 112.073.

(5) "Full discretion" means the power to distribute principal to or for the benefit of one or more of the beneficiaries of a trust that is not limited or modified by the terms of the trust in any way, including by restrictions that limit distributions to purposes such as the best interests, welfare, or happiness of the beneficiaries.

(6) "Limited discretion" means a limited or modified power to distribute principal to or for the benefit of one or more beneficiaries of a trust.

(7) "Presumptive remainder beneficiary," with respect to a particular date, means a beneficiary of a trust on that date who, in the absence of notice to the trustee of the exercise of the power of appointment and assuming that any other powers of appointment under the trust are not exercised, would be eligible to receive a distribution from the trust if:

(A) the trust terminated on that date; or

(B) the interests of all beneficiaries currently eligible to receive income or principal from the trust ended on that date without causing the trust to terminate.

(8) "Principal" means property held in trust for distribution to a remainder beneficiary when the trust terminates and includes income of the trust that, at the time of the exercise of a power of distribution under Section 112.072 or 112.073, is not currently required to be distributed.

(9) "Second trust" means any irrevocable trust to which principal is distributed under Section 112.072 or 112.073.

(10) "Successor beneficiary" means a beneficiary other than a current or presumptive remainder beneficiary. The term does not include a potential appointee under a power of appointment held by a beneficiary.

Added by Acts 2013, 83rd Leg., ch. 699, § 3, eff. Sept. 1, 2013.

§ 112.072. Distribution to Second Trust: Trustee With Full Discretion

(a) An authorized trustee who has the full discretion to distribute the principal of a trust may distribute all or part of the principal of that trust in favor of a trustee of a second trust for the benefit of one or more current beneficiaries of the first trust who are eligible to receive income or principal from the trust and for the benefit of one or more successor or presumptive remainder beneficiaries of the first trust who are eligible to receive income or principal from the trust.

(b) The authorized trustee may, in connection with the exercise of a power of distribution under this section, grant a power of appointment, including a currently exercisable power of appointment, in the second trust to one or more of the current beneficiaries of the first trust who, at the time the power of appointment is granted, is eligible to receive the principal outright under the terms of the first trust.

(c) If the authorized trustee grants a power of appointment to a beneficiary under Subsection (b), the class of permissible appointees in whose favor the beneficiary may appoint under that power may be broader or different than the current, successor, and presumptive remainder beneficiaries of the first trust.

(d) If the beneficiaries of the first trust are described as a class of persons, the beneficiaries of the second trust may include one or more persons who become members of that class after the distribution to the second trust.

(e) The authorized trustee shall exercise a power to distribute under this section in good faith, in accordance with the terms and purposes of the trust, and in the interests of the beneficiaries.

Added by Acts 2013, 83rd Leg., ch. 699, § 3, eff. Sept. 1, 2013.

§ 112.073. Distribution to Second Trust: Trustee With Limited Discretion

(a) An authorized trustee who has limited discretion to distribute the principal of a trust may distribute all or part of the principal of that trust in favor of a trustee of a second trust as provided by this section.

(b) The current beneficiaries of the second trust must be the same as the current beneficiaries of the first trust, and the successor and presumptive remainder beneficiaries of the second trust must be the same as the successor and presumptive remainder beneficiaries of the first trust.

(c) The second trust must include the same language authorizing the trustee to distribute the income or principal of the trust that was included in the first trust.

(d) If the beneficiaries of the first trust are described as a class of persons, the beneficiaries of the second trust must include all persons who become members of that class after the distribution to the second trust.

(e) If the first trust grants a power of appointment to a beneficiary of the trust, the second trust must grant the power of appointment to the beneficiary in the second trust, and the class of permissible appointees under that power must be the same as the class of permissible appointees under the power granted by the first trust.

(f) The authorized trustee shall exercise a power of distribution under this section in good faith, in accordance with the terms and purposes of the trust, and in the interests of the beneficiaries.

Added by Acts 2013, 83rd Leg., ch. 699, § 3, eff. Sept. 1, 2013.

§ 112.074. Notice Required

(a) An authorized trustee may exercise a power of distribution under Section 112.072 or 112.073 without the consent of the settlor or beneficiaries of the first trust and without court approval if the trustee provides to all of the current beneficiaries and presumptive remainder beneficiaries written notice of the trustee's decision to exercise the power.

(b) For the purpose of determining who is a current beneficiary or presumptive remainder beneficiary entitled to the notice, a beneficiary is determined as of the date the notice is sent. A beneficiary includes a person entitled to receive property under the terms of the first trust.

(c) In addition to the notice required under Subsection (a), the authorized trustee shall give written notice of the trustee's decision to the attorney general if:

(1) a charity is entitled to notice;

(2) a charity entitled to notice is no longer in existence;

(3) the trustee has the authority to distribute trust assets to one or more charities that are not named in the trust instrument; or

(4) the trustee has the authority to make distributions for a charitable purpose described in the trust instrument, but no charity is named as a beneficiary for that purpose.

(d) If the beneficiary has a court-appointed guardian or conservator, the notice required to be given by this section must be given to that guardian or conservator. If the beneficiary is a minor for whom no guardian or conservator has been appointed, the notice required to be given by this section must be given to a parent of the minor.

(e) The authorized trustee is not required to provide the notice to a beneficiary who:

(1) is known to the trustee and cannot be located by the trustee after reasonable diligence;

(2) is not known to the trustee;

(3) waives the requirement of the notice under this section; or

(4) is a descendant of a beneficiary to whom the trustee has given notice if the beneficiary and the beneficiary's ancestor have similar interests in the trust and no apparent conflict of interest exists between them.

(f) The notice required under Subsection (a) must:

(1) include a statement that:

(A) the authorized trustee intends to exercise the power of distribution;

(B) the beneficiary has the right to object to the exercise of the power; and

(C) the beneficiary may petition a court to approve, modify, or deny the exercise of the trustee's power to make a distribution under this subchapter;

(2) describe the manner in which the trustee intends to exercise the power;

(3) specify the date the trustee proposes to distribute the first trust to the second trust;

(4) include the name and mailing address of the trustee;

(5) include copies of the agreements of the first trust and the proposed second trust;

(6) be given not later than the 30th day before the proposed date of distribution to the second trust; and

(7) be sent by registered or certified mail, return receipt requested, or delivered in person, unless the notice is waived in writing by the person to whom notice is required to be given.

Added by Acts 2013, 83rd Leg., ch. 699, § 3, eff. Sept. 1, 2013.

§ 112.075. Written Instrument Required

A distribution under Section 112.072 or 112.073 must be made by a written instrument that is signed and acknowledged by the authorized trustee and filed with the records of the first trust and the second trust.

Added by Acts 2013, 83rd Leg., ch. 699, § 3, eff. Sept. 1, 2013.

§ 112.076. Reference to Trust Terms

A reference to the governing instrument or terms of the governing instrument of a trust includes the terms of a second trust to which that trust's principal was distributed under this subchapter.

Added by Acts 2013, 83rd Leg., ch. 699, § 3, eff. Sept. 1, 2013.

§ 112.077. Settlor of Second Trust

(a) Except as provided by Subsection (b), the settlor of a first trust is considered to be the settlor of a second trust established under this subchapter.

(b) If a settlor of a first trust is not also the settlor of a second trust into which principal of that first trust is distributed, the settlor of the first trust is considered the settlor of the portion of the second trust distributed to the second trust from that first trust under this subchapter.

Added by Acts 2013, 83rd Leg., ch. 699, § 3, eff. Sept. 1, 2013.

§ 112.078. Court-Ordered Distribution

(a) An authorized trustee may petition a court to order a distribution under this subchapter.

(b) If the authorized trustee receives a written objection to a distribution under this subchapter from a beneficiary before the proposed effective date of the distribution specified in the notice provided to the beneficiary under Section 112.074, the trustee or the beneficiary may petition a court to approve, modify, or deny the exercise of the trustee's power to make a distribution under this subchapter.

(c) If the authorized trustee receives a written objection to the distribution from the attorney general not later than the 30th day after the date the notice required by Section 112.074 was received by the attorney general, the trustee may not make a distribution under Section 112.072 or 112.073 without petitioning a court to approve or modify the exercise of the trustee's power to make a distribution under this subchapter.

(d) In a judicial proceeding under this section, the authorized trustee may present the trustee's reasons for supporting or opposing a proposed distribution, including whether the trustee believes the distribution would enable the trustee to better carry out the purposes of the trust.

(e) The authorized trustee has the burden of proving that the proposed distribution furthers the purposes of the trust, is in accordance with the terms of the trust, and is in the interests of the beneficiaries.

Added by Acts 2013, 83rd Leg., ch. 699, § 3, eff. Sept. 1, 2013.

§ 112.079. Divided Discretion

If an authorized trustee has full discretion to distribute the principal of a trust and another trustee has limited discretion to distribute principal under the trust instrument, the authorized trustee having full discretion may exercise the power to distribute the trust's principal under Section 112.072.

Added by Acts 2013, 83rd Leg., ch. 699, § 3, eff. Sept. 1, 2013.

§ 112.080. Later Discovered Assets

To the extent the authorized trustee does not provide otherwise:

(1) the distribution of all of the principal of a first trust to a second trust includes subsequently discovered assets otherwise belonging to the first trust and principal paid to or acquired by the first trust after the distribution of the first trust's principal to the second trust; and

(2) the distribution of part of the principal of a first trust to a second trust does not include subsequently discovered assets belonging to the first trust or principal paid to or acquired by the first trust after the distribution of principal from the first trust to the second trust, and those assets or that principal remain the assets or principal of the first trust.

Added by Acts 2013, 83rd Leg., ch. 699, § 3, eff. Sept. 1, 2013.

§ 112.081. Other Authority to Distribute in Further Trust Not Limited

This subchapter may not be construed to limit the power of an authorized trustee to distribute property in further trust under the terms of the governing instrument of a trust, other law, or a court order.

Added by Acts 2013, 83rd Leg., ch. 699, § 3, eff. Sept. 1, 2013.

§ 112.082. Need for Distribution Not Required

An authorized trustee may exercise the power to distribute principal to a second trust under Section 112.072 or 112.073 regardless of whether there is a current need to distribute principal under the terms of the first trust.

Added by Acts 2013, 83rd Leg., ch. 699, § 3, eff. Sept. 1, 2013.

§ 112.083. Duties Not Covered

(a) This subchapter does not create or imply a duty for an authorized trustee to exercise a power to distribute principal, and impropriety may not be inferred as a result of the trustee not exercising a power conferred by Section 112.072 or 112.073.

(b) An authorized trustee does not have a duty to inform beneficiaries about the availability of the authority provided by this subchapter or a duty to review the trust to determine whether any action should be taken under this subchapter.

Added by Acts 2013, 83rd Leg., ch. 699, § 3, eff. Sept. 1, 2013.

§ 112.084. Certain Distributions Prohibited

(a) Except as provided by Subsection (b), an authorized trustee may not exercise a power to distribute principal of a trust otherwise provided by Section 112.072 or 112.073 if the distribution is expressly prohibited by the terms of the governing instrument of the trust.

(b) A general prohibition of the amendment or revocation of a trust or a provision that constitutes a spendthrift clause does not preclude the exercise of a power to distribute principal of a trust under Section 112.072 or 112.073.

Added by Acts 2013, 83rd Leg., ch. 699, § 3, eff. Sept. 1, 2013.

§ 112.085. Exceptions to Power of Distribution

An authorized trustee may not exercise a power to distribute principal of a trust under Section 112.072 or 112.073 to:

(1) reduce, limit, or modify a beneficiary's current, vested right to:

(A) receive a mandatory distribution of income or principal;

(B) receive a mandatory annuity or unitrust interest;

(C) withdraw a percentage of the value of the trust; or

(D) withdraw a specified dollar amount from the trust;

(2) materially impair the rights of any beneficiary of the trust;

(3) materially limit a trustee's fiduciary duty under the trust or as described by Section 111.0035;

(4) decrease or indemnify against a trustee's liability or exonerate a trustee from liability for failure to exercise reasonable care, diligence, and prudence;

(5) eliminate a provision granting another person the right to remove or replace the authorized trustee exercising the distribution power under Section 112.072 or 112.073; or

(6) reduce, limit, or modify in the second trust a perpetuities provision included in the first trust, unless expressly permitted by the terms of the first trust.

Added by Acts 2013, 83rd Leg., ch. 699, § 3, eff. Sept. 1, 2013.

§ 112.086. Tax-Related Limitations

(a) The authorized trustee may not distribute the principal of a trust under Section 112.072 or 112.073 in a manner that would prevent a contribution to that trust from qualifying for or that would reduce the exclusion, deduction, or other federal tax benefit that was originally claimed for that contribution, including:

(1) the annual exclusion under Section 2503(b), Internal Revenue Code of 1986;

(2) a marital deduction under Section 2056(a) or 2523(a), Internal Revenue Code of 1986;

(3) the charitable deduction under Section 170(a), 642(c), 2055(a), or 2522(a), Internal Revenue Code of 1986;

(4) direct skip treatment under Section 2642(c), Internal Revenue Code of 1986; or

(5) any other tax benefit for income, gift, estate, or generation-skipping transfer tax purposes under the Internal Revenue Code of 1986.

(b) Notwithstanding Subsection (a), an authorized trustee may distribute the principal of a first trust to a second trust regardless of whether the settlor is treated as the owner of either or both trusts under Sections 671-679, Internal Revenue Code of 1986.

(c) If S corporation stock is held in trust, an authorized trustee may not distribute all or part of that stock under Section 112.072 or 112.073 to a second trust that is not a permitted shareholder under Section 1361(c)(2), Internal Revenue Code of 1986.

(d) If an interest in property that is subject to the minimum distribution rules of Section 401(a)(9), Internal Revenue Code of 1986, is held in trust, an authorized trustee may not distribute the trust's interest in the property to a second trust under Section 112.072 or 112.073 if the distribution would shorten the minimum distribution period applicable to the property.

Added by Acts 2013, 83rd Leg., ch. 699, § 3, eff. Sept. 1, 2013.

§ 112.087. Compensation of Trustee

(a) Except as provided by Subsection (b) and unless a court, on application of the authorized trustee, directs otherwise, the trustee may not exercise a power under Section 112.072 or 112.073 solely to change trust provisions regarding the determination of the compensation of any trustee.

(b) An authorized trustee, in connection with the exercise of a power under Section 112.072 or 112.073 for another valid and reasonable purpose, may bring the trustee's compensation into conformance with reasonable limits authorized by state law.

(c) The compensation payable to an authorized trustee of the first trust may continue to be paid to the trustee of the second trust during the term of the second trust and may be determined in the same manner as the compensation would have been determined in the first trust.

(d) An authorized trustee may not receive a commission or other compensation for the distribution of a particular asset from a first trust to a second trust under Section 112.072 or 112.073.

Added by Acts 2013, 83rd Leg., ch. 699, § 3, eff. Sept. 1, 2013.

Chapter 113. Administration

Subchapter A. Powers of Trustee

Statutes in Context
§§ 113.002–113.028

Sections 113.002-113.028 provide an extensive list of powers which trustees automatically receive. These provisions permit settlors to draft relatively short trust instruments because they do not need to enumerate all of the powers they wish the trustees to have. Section 113.001 provides that terms of a trust instrument granting additional powers or limiting powers will trump the statutorily provided powers.

---

§ 113.001. Limitation of Powers

A power given to a trustee by this subchapter does not apply to a trust to the extent that the instrument creating the trust, a subsequent court order, or another provision of this subtitle conflicts with or limits the power.

Amended by Acts 1983, 68th Leg., p. 3332, ch. 567, art. 2, § 2, eff. Jan. 1, 1984.

Statutes in Context
§ 113.002

Section 113.002 along with § 113.024 codify the principle of implied powers, that is, a trustee is deemed to have whatever powers which the settlor must have intended the trustee to have to achieve the objectives set out in the trust instrument.

---

§ 113.002. General Powers

Except as provided by Section 113.001, a trustee may exercise any powers in addition to the powers authorized by this subchapter that are necessary or appropriate to carry out the purposes of the trust.

Amended by Acts 1983, 68th Leg., p. 3332, ch. 567, art. 2, § 2, eff. Jan. 1, 1984.

§ 113.003. Options

A trustee may:

(1) grant an option involving a sale, lease, or other disposition of trust property, including an option exercisable beyond the duration of the trust; or

(2) acquire and exercise an option for the acquisition of property, including an option exercisable beyond the duration of the trust.

Added by Acts 2005, 79th Leg., ch. 148, § 10, eff. Jan. 1, 2006.

§ 113.004. Additions to Trust Assets

A trustee may receive from any source additions to the assets of the trust.

Amended by Acts 1983, 68th Leg., p. 3332, ch. 567, art. 2, § 2, eff. Jan. 1, 1984.

§ 113.005. Acquisition of Undivided Interests

A trustee may acquire all or a portion of the remaining undivided interest in property in which the trust holds an undivided interest.

Amended by Acts 1983, 68th Leg., p. 3332, ch. 567, art. 2, § 2, eff. Jan. 1, 1984.

§ 113.006. General Authority to Manage and Invest Trust Property

Subject to the requirements of Chapter 117, a trustee may manage the trust property and invest and reinvest in property of any character on the conditions and for the lengths of time as the trustee considers proper, notwithstanding that the time may extend beyond the term of the trust.

Amended by Acts 1983, 68th Leg., p. 3332, ch. 567, art. 2, § 2, eff. Jan. 1, 1984. Amended by Acts 2003, 78th Leg., ch. 1103, § 3, eff. Sept. 1, 2003.

§ 113.007. Temporary Deposits of Funds

A trustee may deposit trust funds that are being held pending investment, distribution, or the payment of debts in a bank that is subject to supervision by state or federal authorities. However, a corporate trustee depositing funds with itself is subject to the requirements of Section 113.057 of this code.

Amended by Acts 1983, 68th Leg., p. 3332, ch. 567, art. 2, § 2, eff. Jan. 1, 1984; Acts 1984, 68th Leg., 2nd C.S., ch. 18, § 11, eff. Oct. 2, 1984.

§ 113.008. Business Entities

A trustee may invest in, continue, or participate in the operation of any business or other investment enterprise in any form, including a sole proprietorship, partnership, limited partnership, corporation, or association, and the trustee may effect any change in the organization of the business or enterprise.

Amended by Acts 1983, 68th Leg., p. 3332, ch. 567, art. 2, § 2, eff. Jan. 1, 1984.

§ 113.009. Real Property Management

A trustee may:

(1) exchange, subdivide, develop, improve, or partition real property;

(2) make or vacate public plats;

(3) adjust boundaries;

(4) adjust differences in valuation by giving or receiving value;

(5) dedicate real property to public use or, if the trustee considers it in the best interest of the trust, dedicate easements to public use without consideration;

(6) raze existing walls or buildings;

(7) erect new party walls or buildings alone or jointly with an owner of adjacent property;

(8) make repairs; and

(9) make extraordinary alterations or additions in structures as necessary to make property more productive.

Amended by Acts 1983, 68th Leg., p. 3332, ch. 567, art. 2, § 2, eff. Jan. 1, 1984.

§ 113.010. Sale of Property

A trustee may contract to sell, sell and convey, or grant an option to sell real or personal property at public auction or private sale for cash or for credit or for part cash and part credit, with or without security.

Amended by Acts 1983, 68th Leg., p. 3332, ch. 567, art. 2, § 2, eff. Jan. 1, 1984.

Statutes in Context
§ 113.-011

Section 113.011(b) authorizes the trustee to enter into a long-term lease, that is, a lease which lasts beyond the term of the trust. Long-term leases restrict the ability of the remainder beneficiary to enjoy the property because it is encumbered by the lease. On the other hand, long-term leases may permit the trustee to earn more income from the property. For example, a company may not be willing to construct a large building on the property unless the company is assured of being able to use it for a long time.

§ 113.011. Leases

(a) A trustee may grant or take a lease of real or personal property for any term, with or without options to purchase and with or without covenants relating to erection of buildings or renewals, including the lease of a right or privilege above or below the surface of real property.

(b) A trustee may execute a lease containing terms or options that extend beyond the duration of the trust.

Amended by Acts 1983, 68th Leg., p. 3332, ch. 567, art. 2, § 2, eff. Jan. 1, 1984.

§ 113.012. Minerals

(a) A trustee may enter into mineral transactions, including:

(1) negotiating and making oil, gas, and other mineral leases covering any land, mineral, or royalty interest at any time forming a part of a trust;

(2) pooling and unitizing part or all of the land, mineral leasehold, mineral, royalty, or other interest of a trust estate with land, mineral leasehold, mineral, royalty, or other interest of one or more persons or entities for the purpose of developing and producing oil, gas, or other minerals, and making leases or assignments granting the right to pool and unitize;

(3) entering into contracts and agreements concerning the installation and operation of plans or other facilities for the cycling, repressuring, processing, or other treating or handling of oil, gas, or other minerals;

(4) conducting or contracting for the conducting of seismic evaluation operations;

(5) drilling or contracting for the drilling of wells for oil, gas, or other minerals;

(6) contracting for and making "dry hole" and "bottom hole" contributions of cash, leasehold interests, or other interests towards the drilling of wells;

(7) using or contracting for the use of any method of secondary or tertiary recovery of any mineral, including the injection of water, gas, air, or other substances;

(8) purchasing oil, gas, or other mineral leases, leasehold interests, or other interests for any type of consideration, including farmout agreements requiring the drilling or reworking of wells or participation therein;

(9) entering into farmout contracts or agreements committing a trust estate to assign oil, gas, or other mineral leases or interests in consideration for the drilling of wells or other oil, gas, or mineral operations;

(10) negotiating the transfer of and transferring oil, gas, or other mineral leases or interests for any consideration, such as retained overriding royalty interests of any nature, drilling or reworking commitments, or production interests; and

(11) executing and entering into contracts, conveyances, and other agreements or transfers considered necessary or desirable to carry out the powers granted in this section, whether or not the action is now or subsequently recognized or considered as a common or proper practice by those engaged in the business of prospecting for, developing, producing, processing, transporting, or marketing minerals, including entering into and executing division orders, oil, gas, or other mineral sales contracts, exploration agreements, processing agreements, and other contracts relating to the processing, handling, treating, transporting, and

marketing of oil, gas, or other mineral production from or accruing to a trust and receiving and receipting for the proceeds thereof on behalf of a trust.

(b) A trustee may enter into mineral transactions that extend beyond the term of the trust.

Amended by Acts 1983, 68th Leg., p. 3332, ch. 567, art. 2, § 2, eff. Jan. 1, 1984.

Statutes in Context
§ 113.013

The trustee may purchase insurance not only to protect the trust but also to protect the trustee.

---

§ 113.013. Insurance

A trustee may purchase insurance of any nature, form, or amount to protect the trust property and the trustee.

Amended by Acts 1983, 68th Leg., p. 3332, ch. 567, art. 2, § 2, eff. Jan. 1, 1984.

§ 113.014. Payment of Taxes

A trustee may pay taxes and assessments levied or assessed against the trust estate or the trustee by governmental taxing or assessing authorities.

Amended by Acts 1983, 68th Leg., p. 3332, ch. 567, art. 2, § 2, eff. Jan. 1, 1984.

§ 113.015. Authority to Borrow

A trustee may borrow money from any source, including a trustee, purchase property on credit, and mortgage, pledge, or in any other manner encumber all or any part of the assets of the trust as is advisable in the judgment of the trustee for the advantageous administration of the trust.

Amended by Acts 1983, 68th Leg., p. 3332, ch. 567, art. 2, § 2, eff. Jan. 1, 1984.

§ 113.016. Management of Securities

A trustee may:

(1) pay calls, assessments, or other charges against or because of securities or other investments held by the trust;

(2) sell or exercise stock subscription or conversion rights;

(3) vote corporate stock, general or limited partnership interests, or other securities in person or by general or limited proxy;

(4) consent directly or through a committee or other agent to the reorganization, consolidation, merger, dissolution, or liquidation of a corporation or other business enterprise; and

(5) participate in voting trusts and deposit stocks, bonds, or other securities with any protective or other committee formed by or at the instance of persons holding similar securities, under such terms and conditions respecting the deposit

thereof as the trustee may approve; sell any stock or other securities obtained by conversion, reorganization, consolidation, merger, liquidation, or the exercise of subscription rights free of any restrictions upon sale otherwise contained in the trust instrument relative to the securities originally held; assent to corporate sales, leases, encumbrances, and other transactions.

Amended by Acts 1983, 68th Leg., p. 3332, ch. 567, art. 2, § 2, eff. Jan. 1, 1984.

Statutes in Context
§ 113.017

Normally, a trustee has a duty to earmark trust property as belonging to the trust. Section 113.017 permits a trustee to hold corporate stock and other securities in the name of a nominee. Note that § 16 of the Texas Trust Act permitted any property to be held in nominee form if certain requirements were satisfied.

---

§ 113.017. Corporate Stock or Other Securities Held in Name of Nominee

A trustee may:

(1) hold corporate stock or other securities in the name of a nominee;

(2) under Subchapter B, Chapter 161,[1] or other law, employ a bank incorporated in this state or a national bank located in this state as custodian of any corporate stock or other securities held in trust; and

(3) under Subchapter C, Chapter 161,[2] or other law, deposit or arrange for the deposit of securities with a Federal Reserve Bank or in a clearing corporation.

Amended by Acts 1983, 68th Leg., p. 3332, ch. 567, art. 2, § 2, eff. Jan. 1, 1984.

Statutes in Context
§ 113.018

A settlor expects the trustee to administer the trust. The settlor selected the trustee because the settlor had confidence in that person's judgment and ability to carry out the settlor's instructions. The settlor did not want someone else to be managing the trust property. However, it would be too burdensome to force a trustee to personally perform all acts necessary in the administration of the trust.

The traditional rule regarding delegation of powers was that the trustee may delegate mere ministerial duties but may not delegate discretionary acts. Although easy to state, the

---

[1] Property Code §161.021 et seq.

[2] Property Code §161.051 et seq.

application of the rule was not always easy. The extreme situations were relatively clear. The trustee could delegate ministerial acts such as secretarial and janitorial duties, record keeping, and the collection of income. But, discretionary acts such as selecting investments, deciding which beneficiary of a discretionary trust to pay and how much, and settling claims against the trust could not be delegated.

Section 113.018 adopts a different approach, that is, delegation is permissible if it is "reasonably necessary." Accordingly, the trustee may delegate responsibilities to agents if a reasonably prudent owner of that type of property holding that property for similar reasons as those of the trust, would employ outside assistance.

Section 113.018 suffers from the problem that the 2003 Legislature did not amend it to be consistent with Chapter 117 (Uniform Prudent Investor Act); the term "investment agent" is a holdover from the prior (repealed) statute. The term is no longer defined. Section 113.018 should be viewed as the general section for the hiring of agents for non-discretionary decisions with § 117.011 governing agents but only for "investment and management functions."

See also § 117.011 which permits the delegation of investment and management decisions under specified circumstances.

§ 113.018. Employment of Agents

A trustee may employ attorneys, accountants, agents, including investment agents, and brokers reasonably necessary in the administration of the trust estate.

Amended by Acts 1999, 76th Leg., ch. 794, § 1, eff. Sept. 1, 1999.

§ 113.019. Claims

A trustee may compromise, contest, arbitrate, or settle claims of or against the trust estate or the trustee.

Added by Acts 1983, 68th Leg., p. 3332, ch. 567, art. 2, § 2, eff. Jan. 1, 1984.

§ 113.020. Burdensome or Worthless Property

A trustee may abandon property the trustee considers burdensome or worthless.

Added by Acts 1983, 68th Leg., p. 3332, ch. 567, art. 2, § 2, eff. Jan. 1, 1984.

Statutes in Context
§ 113.021

The trustee should make trust distributions directly to the beneficiary if the beneficiary is a competent adult unless the settlor requires or authorizes the trustee in the trust instrument to make distributions in another manner. For example, the trust may permit the trustee to pay the beneficiary's college tuition by sending payments directly to the school.

If the beneficiary is a minor or is incapacitated and the trust does not provide distribution instructions, § 113.021(a) supplies the trustee with a variety of distribution options. Note that the trustee determines whether a beneficiary is incapacitated; neither a court nor medical determination of incapacity is necessary.

§ 113.021. Distribution to Minor or Incapacitated Beneficiary

(a) A trustee may make a distribution required or permitted to be made to any beneficiary in any of the following ways when the beneficiary is a minor or a person who in the judgment of the trustee is incapacitated by reason of legal incapacity or physical or mental illness or infirmity:

(1) to the beneficiary directly;

(2) to the guardian of the beneficiary's person or estate;

(3) by utilizing the distribution, without the interposition of a guardian, for the health, support, maintenance, or education of the beneficiary;

(4) to a custodian for the minor beneficiary under the Texas Uniform Transfers to Minors Act (Chapter 141) or a uniform gifts or transfers to minors act of another state;

(5) by reimbursing the person who is actually taking care of the beneficiary, even though the person is not the legal guardian, for expenditures made by the person for the benefit of the beneficiary; or

(6) by managing the distribution as a separate fund on the beneficiary's behalf, subject to the beneficiary's continuing right to withdraw the distribution.

(b) The written receipts of persons receiving distributions under Subsection (a) of this section are full and complete acquittances to the trustee.

Added by Acts 1983, 68th Leg., p. 3332, ch. 567, art. 2, § 2, eff. Jan. 1, 1984. Subsec. (a) amended by Acts 2005, 79th Leg., ch. 148, § 11, eff. Jan. 1, 2006.

Statutes in Context
§ 113.0211

The 2003 Texas Legislature enacted § 113.0211 which establishes a procedure for the trustee of a charitable trust to make adjustments between principal and income within certain parameters. The Legislature did not, however, correlate this section with the passage of the Uniform Principal and Income Act which also contains a procedure for making adjustments between principal and income. See Property Code

§ 116.005. Accordingly, it is unclear whether charitable trustees are restricted to § 113.0211 or whether they may use the Uniform Act procedure as well.

§ 113.0211. Adjustment of Charitable Trust

(a) In this section:

(1) "Charitable entity" has the meaning assigned by Section 123.001(1).

(2) "Charitable trust" means a trust:

(A) the stated purpose of which is to benefit only one or more charitable entities; and

(B) that qualifies as a charitable entity.

(b) The trustee of a charitable trust may acquire, exchange, sell, supervise, manage, or retain any type of investment, subject to restrictions and procedures established by the trustee and in an amount considered appropriate by the trustee, that a prudent investor, exercising reasonable skill, care, and caution, would acquire or retain in light of the purposes, terms, distribution requirements, and other circumstances of the trust. The prudence of a trustee's actions under this subsection is judged with reference to the investment of all of the trust assets rather than with reference to a single trust investment.

(c) The trustee of a charitable trust may make one or more adjustments between the principal and the income portions of a trust to the extent that the trustee considers the adjustments necessary:

(1) to comply with the terms of the trust, if any, that describe the amount that may or must be distributed to a charitable entity beneficiary by referring to the income portion of the trust; and

(2) to administer the trust in order to carry out the purposes of the charitable trust.

(d) The authority to make adjustments under Subsection (c) includes the authority to allocate all or part of a capital gain to trust income.

(e) In making adjustments under Subsection (c), the trustee shall consider:

(1) except to the extent that the terms of the trust clearly manifest an intention that the trustee shall or may favor one or more charitable entity beneficiaries, the needs of a charitable entity beneficiary, based on what is fair and reasonable to all other charitable entity beneficiaries of the trust, if any; and

(2) the need of the trust to maintain the purchasing power of the trust's investments over time.

Added by Acts 2003, 78th Leg., ch. 550, § 1, eff. Sept. 1, 2003.

§ 113.022. Power to Provide Residence and Pay Funeral Expenses

A trustee of a trust that is not a charitable remainder unitrust, annuity trust, or pooled income fund that is intended to qualify for a federal tax deduction under Section 664, Internal Revenue Code,[1] after giving consideration to the probable intention of the settlor and finding that the trustee's action would be consistent with that probable intention, may:

(1) permit real estate held in trust to be occupied by a beneficiary who is currently eligible to receive distributions from the trust estate;

(2) if reasonably necessary for the maintenance of a beneficiary who is currently eligible to receive distributions from the trust estate, invest trust funds in real property to be used for a home by the beneficiary; and

(3) in the trustee's discretion, pay funeral expenses of a beneficiary who at the time of the beneficiary's death was eligible to receive distributions from the trust estate.

Added by Acts 1983, 68th Leg., p. 3332, ch. 567, art. 2, § 2, eff. Jan. 1, 1984. Amended by Acts 1985, 69th Leg., ch. 149, § 2, eff. May 24, 1985.

§ 113.023. Ancillary Trustee

(a) If trust property is situated outside this state, a Texas trustee may name in writing an individual or corporation qualified to act in the foreign jurisdiction in connection with trust property as ancillary trustee.

(b) Within the limits of the authority of the Texas trustee, the ancillary trustee has the rights, powers, discretions, and duties the Texas trustee delegates, subject to the limitations and directions of the Texas trustee specified in the instrument evidencing the appointment of the ancillary trustee.

(c) The Texas trustee may remove an ancillary trustee and appoint a successor at any time as to all or part of the trust assets.

(d) The Texas trustee may require security of the ancillary trustee, who is answerable to the Texas trustee for all trust property entrusted to or received by the ancillary trustee in connection with the administration of the trust.

(e) If the law of the foreign jurisdiction requires a certain procedure or a judicial order for the appointment of an ancillary trustee or to authorize an ancillary trustee to act, the Texas trustee and the ancillary trustee must satisfy the requirements.

Added by Acts 1983, 68th Leg., p. 3332, ch. 567, art. 2, § 2, eff. Jan. 1, 1984.

Statutes in Context
§ 113.024

See Statutes in Context to § 113.002.

---

§ 113.024. Implied Powers

The powers, duties, and responsibilities under this subtitle do not exclude other implied powers, duties, or

---

[1] 26 U.S.C. §664.

responsibilities that are not inconsistent with this subtitle.

Added by Acts 1983, 68th Leg., p. 3332, ch. 567, art. 2, § 2, eff. Jan. 1, 1984.

Statutes in Context
§ 113.025

Section 113.025 permits the trustee to investigate trust property for potential environmental liability concerns even before accepting the trust property. This is helpful in protecting the trust and the trustee from liability under the Comprehensive Environmental Response, Compensation, and Liability Act. See 42 U.S.C. §§ 9601 et seq.

---

§ 113.025. Powers of Trustee Regarding Environmental Laws

(a) A trustee or a potential trustee may inspect, investigate, cause to be inspected, or cause to be investigated trust property, property that the trustee or potential trustee has been asked to hold, or property owned or operated by an entity in which the trustee or potential trustee holds or has been asked to hold any interest or for the purpose of determining the potential application of environmental law with respect to the property. This subsection does not grant any person the right of access to any property. The taking of any action under this subsection with respect to a trust or an addition to a trust is not evidence that a person has accepted the trust or the addition to the trust.

(b) A trustee may take on behalf of the trust any action before or after the initiation of an enforcement action or other legal proceeding that the trustee reasonably believes will help to prevent, abate, or otherwise remedy any actual or potential violation of any environmental law affecting property held directly or indirectly by the trustee.

Added by Acts 1993, 73rd Leg., ch. 846, § 29, eff. Sept. 1, 1993.

Statutes in Context
§ 113.026

Section 113.026 permits the trustee, under specified circumstances, to exercise cy pres to replace a charitable beneficiary without the necessity of obtaining a court order if the charity (1) did not exist when the interest vested, (2) ceases to exist, or (3) ceases to be charitable in nature.

---

§ 113.026. Authority to Designate New Charitable Beneficiary

(a) In this section:

(1) "Charitable entity" has the meaning assigned by Section 123.001.

(2) "Failed charitable beneficiary" means a charitable entity that is named as a beneficiary of a trust and that:

(A) does not exist at the time the charitable entity's interest in the trust becomes vested;

(B) ceases to exist during the term of the trust; or

(C) ceases to be a charitable entity during the term of the trust.

(b) This section applies only to an express written trust created by an individual with a charitable entity as a beneficiary. If the trust instrument provides a means for replacing a failed charitable beneficiary, the trust instrument governs the replacement of a failed charitable beneficiary, and this section does not apply.

(c) The trustee of a trust may select one or more replacement charitable beneficiaries for a failed charitable beneficiary in accordance with this section.

(d) Each replacement charitable beneficiary selected under this section by any person must:

(1) be a charitable entity and an entity described under Sections 170(b)(1)(A), 170(c), 2055(a), and 2522(a) of the Internal Revenue Code of 1986, as amended; and

(2) have the same or similar charitable purpose as the failed charitable beneficiary.

(e) If the settlor of the trust is living and not incapacitated at the time a trustee is selecting a replacement charitable beneficiary, the trustee shall consult with the settlor concerning the selection of one or more replacement charitable beneficiaries.

(f) If the trustee and the settlor agree on the selection of one or more replacement charitable beneficiaries, the trustee shall send notice of the selection to the attorney general. If the attorney general determines that one or more replacement charitable beneficiaries do not have the same or similar charitable purpose as the failed charitable beneficiary, not later than the 21st day after the date the attorney general receives notice of the selection, the attorney general shall request in writing that a district court in the county in which the trust was created review the selection. If the court agrees with the attorney general's determination, any remaining replacement charitable beneficiary agreed on by the trustee and the settlor is the replacement charitable beneficiary. If there is not a remaining replacement charitable beneficiary agreed on by the trustee and the settlor, the court shall select one or more replacement charitable beneficiaries. If the court finds that the attorney general's request for a review is unreasonable, the replacement charitable beneficiary is the charitable beneficiary agreed on by the trustee and the settlor, and the court may require the attorney general to pay all court costs of the parties involved. Not later than the 30th day after the date the selection is final, the trustee shall provide to each replacement charitable beneficiary selected notice of the selection by certified mail, return receipt requested.

(g) If the trustee and the settlor cannot agree on the selection of a replacement charitable beneficiary, the trustee shall send notice of that fact to the attorney general not later than the 21st day after the date the trustee determines that an agreement cannot be reached. The attorney general shall refer the matter to a district court in the county in which the trust was created. The trustee and the settlor may each recommend to the court one or more replacement charitable beneficiaries. The court shall select a replacement charitable beneficiary and, not later than the 30th day after the date of the selection, provide to each charitable beneficiary selected notice of the selection by certified mail, return receipt requested.

Added by Acts 1999, 76th Leg., ch. 63, § 1, eff. Aug. 30, 1999.

Statutes in Context
§ 113.027

Section 113.027 was added by the 2005 Legislature to remedy a potentially significant federal income tax problem that could result if the trust instrument did not expressly authorize a non-pro rata distribution. Under Rev. Rul. 69-486, 1969-2 C.B. 159, a non-pro rata distribution is treated as a pro rata distribution which is followed by exchanges between the beneficiaries. These exchanges could then subject the beneficiaries to capital gains tax.

---

§ 113.027. Distributions Generally

When distributing trust property or dividing or terminating a trust, a trustee may:

    (1) make distributions in divided or undivided interests;

    (2) allocate particular assets in proportionate or disproportionate shares;

    (3) value the trust property for the purposes of acting under Subdivision (1) or (2); and

    (4) adjust the distribution, division, or termination for resulting differences in valuation.

Added by Acts 2005, 79th Leg., ch. 148, § 12, eff. Jan. 1, 2006.

§ 113.028. Certain Claims and Causes of Action Prohibited

(a) A trustee may not prosecute or assert a claim for damages in a cause of action against a party who is not a beneficiary of the trust if each beneficiary of the trust provides written notice to the trustee of the beneficiary's opposition to the trustee's prosecuting or asserting the claim in the cause of action.

(b) This section does not apply to a cause of action that is prosecuted by a trustee in the trustee's individual capacity.

(c) The trustee is not liable for failing to prosecute or assert a claim in a cause of action if prohibited by the beneficiaries under Subsection (a).

Added by Acts 2005, 79th Leg., ch. 765, § 3, eff. June 17,

2005.

Statutes in Context
§ 113.029

The 2009 Legislature added § 113.029(a) to codify the common law rule that regardless of the extent of discretion the settlor grants to a trustee, the trustee must always act "in good faith and in accordance with the terms and purposes of the trust and the interests of the beneficiaries." Thus, even if the settlor provides that the trustee's discretion is "absolute" or "uncontrolled," the trustee's actions must still comport with fiduciary standards and are reviewable by the court.

Tax problems may result if a non-settlor beneficiary is also the trustee of a trust and is given the power to make self-distributions that are not limited by an ascertainable standard relating to health, education, support, or maintenance. A settlor may create this problem inadvertently by giving the trustee/beneficiary unrestricted discretion or may limit distributions to a standard that is not ascertainable such as for the trust/beneficiary's comfort, benefit, welfare, or well-being.

To remedy this problem, the 2009 Legislature provided that in such situations, the trustee/beneficiary's power to distribute is "cut back" to an ascertainable standard relating to health, education, support, or maintenance. Likewise, the trustee/beneficiary's power to distribute is restricted so that distributions cannot be made to satisfy a legal obligation of support that the trustee/beneficiary personally owes to another person. § 113.029(b).

If there are other trustees besides the beneficiary, a majority of the remaining trustees may exercise the power to make discretionary distributions to the "limited" trustee/beneficiary without regard to the cut-back. If there is no trustee who is not free of restrictions, the court may appoint a special fiduciary with authority to exercise the power. § 113.029(c).

The automatic cut-back will not apply if one of the following circumstances exists:

The trust was created and became irrevocable before September 1, 2009. (If the trust was created before September 1, 2009 but did not become irrevocable until September 1, 2009 or thereafter, the cut-back will apply.)

The settlor is the beneficiary/trustee. § 113.029(b)(1)

The settlor expressly indicated that the cut-back provisions of this section do not apply. § 113.029(b).

The trustee/beneficiary is the settlor's spouse and a martial deduction was previously allowed for the trust. § 113.029(d)(1).

The settlor may amend or revoke the trust. § 113.029(d)(2).

Contributions to the trust qualify for the gift tax annual exclusion. § 113.029(d)(3).

§ 113.029. Discretionary Powers; Tax Savings

(a) Notwithstanding the breadth of discretion granted to a trustee in the terms of the trust, including the use of terms such as "absolute," "sole," or "uncontrolled," the trustee shall exercise a discretionary power in good faith and in accordance with the terms and purposes of the trust and the interests of the beneficiaries.

(b) Subject to Subsection (d), and unless the terms of the trust expressly indicate that a requirement provided by this subsection does not apply:

(1) a person, other than a settlor, who is a beneficiary and trustee, trustee affiliate, or discretionary power holder of a trust that confers on the trustee a power to make discretionary distributions to or for the trustee's, the trustee affiliate's, or the discretionary power holder's personal benefit may exercise the power only in accordance with an ascertainable standard relating to the trustee's, the trustee affiliate's, or the discretionary power holder's individual health, education, support, or maintenance within the meaning of Section 2041(b)(1)(A) or 2514(c)(1), Internal Revenue Code of 1986; and

(2) a trustee may not exercise a power to make discretionary distributions to satisfy a legal obligation of support that the trustee personally owes another person.

(c) A power the exercise of which is limited or prohibited by Subsection (b) may be exercised by a majority of the remaining trustees whose exercise of the power is not limited or prohibited by Subsection (b). If the power of all trustees is limited or prohibited by Subsection (b), the court may appoint a special fiduciary with authority to exercise the power.

(d) Subsection (b) does not apply to:

(1) a power held by the settlor's spouse who is the trustee of a trust for which a marital deduction, as defined by Section 2056(b)(5) or 2523(e), Internal Revenue Code of 1986, was previously allowed;

(2) any trust during any period that the trust may be revoked or amended by its settlor; or

(3) a trust if contributions to the trust qualify for the annual exclusion under Section 2503(c), Internal Revenue Code of 1986.

(e) In this section, "discretionary power holder" means a person who has the sole power or power shared with another person to make discretionary decisions on behalf of a trustee with respect to distributions from a trust.

Added by Acts 2009, 81st Leg., ch. 672, § 3, eff. Sept. 1, 2009. Subsecs. (b) amended and (e) added by Acts 2013, 83rd Leg., ch. 699, § 4, eff. Sept. 1, 2013.

Statutes in Context
§ 113.030

The 2009 Legislature enacted this section to remedy the "orphan trust" problem as described in the analysis of S.B. 666 as follows:

The "orphan trust" or charitable foundations set up by donors who have no heirs or other family that they wish to carry out their wills, are often entrusted to lawyers or local banks who will keep the money invested in the local community. However, when an attorney retires or local banks are sold to multinational financial institutions, the foundations are no longer run by the people and banks familiar with the donors' specific wishes. The corporate trustees have wide latitude to change the way the trust operates, and to decide which charities will receive grants and thus the danger of distorting or altogether ignoring the donor's intent is increased with each transaction. Banks give fewer and smaller charitable gifts from the trusts they manage, all the while increasing the foundation's assets, and increasing administrative fees that the banks charge to foundations for the services they provide. Additionally, banks as trustees will often provide grants which serve their own interests, but that do not honor the donor's favorite causes. * * * The consequences of charitable funds being moved and used as assets and revenue streams for large financial institutions is that communities that stood to benefit from the philanthropy of their citizens are denied the good works and good will of the original donors.

The statute provides that the location of a charitable trust's administration cannot be changed to an out-of-state location other than as (1) the settlor provided in the trust or (2) the court approves under the procedure set forth in the statute. § 113.030(b).

A trustee who wants to move the location out of Texas must first give proper notice. If the settlor is alive and competent, the trustee must consult with the settlor and submit the selection to the attorney general. § 113.030(c)(1). If the settlor is dead or incapacitated, then the trustee must propose a new location and submit the proposal to the attorney general. § 113.030(c)(2).

The trustee must then file an action in the appropriate court to get permission to move the trust administration out of the Texas. § 113.030(d). The court may not authorize a relocation unless it finds that the charitable purposes of the trust will not be impaired by the move. § 113.030(e).

The statute grants the attorney general the power to enforce this section. If a trustee does not comply with the statute, the court may remove the trustee and appoint a new trustee. The court may charge the costs of the removal, including reasonable attorney's fees, against the removed trustee. § 113.030(f).

§ 113.030. Relocation of Administration of Charitable Trust

(a) In this section:

(1) "Charitable entity" has the meaning assigned by Section 123.001.

(2) "Charitable trust" means a trust:

(A) the stated purpose of which is to benefit only one or more charitable entities; and

(B) that qualifies as a charitable entity.

(3) "Trust administration" means the grant-making function of the trust.

(b) Except as provided by this section or specifically authorized by the terms of a trust, the trustee of a charitable trust may not change the location in which the trust administration takes place from a location in this state to a location outside this state.

(c) If the trustee decides to change the location in which the trust is administered from a location in this state to a location outside this state, the trustee shall:

(1) if the settlor is living and not incapacitated:

(A) consult the settlor concerning the selection of a new location for the administration of the trust; and

(B) submit the selection to the attorney general; or

(2) if the settlor is not living or is incapacitated:

(A) propose a new location; and

(B) submit the proposal to the attorney general.

(d) The trustee may file an action in the district court or statutory probate court in which the trust was created seeking a court order authorizing the trustee to change the location in which the trust is administered to a location outside this state. The court may exercise its equitable powers to effectuate the original purpose of the trust.

(e) Except as provided by Subsection (b), the location in which the administration of the trust takes place may not be changed to a location outside this state unless:

(1) the charitable purposes of the trust would not be impaired if the trust administration is moved; and

(2) a district court or statutory probate court authorizes the relocation.

(f) The attorney general may bring an action to enforce the provisions of this section. If a trustee of a charitable trust fails to comply with the provisions of this section, the district court or statutory probate court in the county in which the trust administration was originally located may remove the trustee and appoint a new trustee. Costs of a proceeding to remove a trustee, including reasonable attorney's fees, may be assessed against the removed trustee. This provision is in addition to and does not supersede the provisions of Chapter 123.

(g) This section does not affect a trustee's authority to sell real estate owned by a charitable trust.

Added by Acts 2009, 81st Leg., ch. 754, eff. Sept. 1, 2009. Redesigned from § 113.029 by Acts 2011, 82nd Leg., ch. 91, § 27.001(52), eff. Sept. 1, 2011.

Subchapter B. Duties of Trustee

Statutes in Context § 113.051

If the trust instrument and the Trust Code are both silent about a particular issue regarding trust administration, the common law rules still apply.

§ 113.051. General Duty

The trustee shall administer the trust in good faith according to its terms and this subtitle. In the absence of any contrary terms in the trust instrument or contrary provisions of this subtitle, in administering the trust the trustee shall perform all of the duties imposed on trustees by the common law.

Amended by Acts 1983, 68th Leg., p. 3332, ch. 567, art. 2, § 2, eff. Jan. 1, 1984; Acts 2005, 79th Leg., ch. 148, § 13, eff. Jan. 1, 2006.

Statutes in Context § 113.052

A trustee may not self-deal by borrowing property from the trust either for the trustee's personal use or for the use of closely related or connected persons. However, the settlor may expressly authorize these loans in the trust instrument. For example, Grandparent may establish a trust for Grandchildren naming Child as the trustee and permit Child to make educational loans to Grandchildren from trust property.

See § 111.004(1) (defining "affiliate") and § 111.004(13) (defining "relative" in a narrow fashion which excludes many close relatives, such as uncles, aunts, nephews, and nieces).

Corporate trustees are allowed to deposit trust funds with itself (that is, loan trust funds to itself) under the circumstances set forth in § 113.057.

§ 113.052. Loan of Trust Funds to Trustee

(a) Except as provided by Subsection (b) of this section, a trustee may not lend trust funds to:

(1) the trustee or an affiliate;

(2) a director, officer, or employee of the trustee or an affiliate;

(3) a relative of the trustee; or

(4) the trustee's employer, employee, partner, or other business associate.

(b) This section does not prohibit:

(1) a loan by a trustee to a beneficiary of the trust if the loan is expressly authorized or directed by the instrument or transaction establishing the trust; or

(2) a deposit by a corporate trustee with itself under Section 113.057.

Amended by Acts 1983, 68th Leg., p. 3332, ch. 567, art. 2, § 2, eff. Jan. 1, 1984.

Statutes in Context
§ 113.053

A trustee may not purchase trust assets for the trustee's personal use. Likewise, a trustee cannot sell the trustee's personal assets to the trust. A trustee cannot be expected to act fairly in these situations because as a purchaser, the trustee wants to pay as little as possible and as a seller, the trustee wants to receive a favorable price. The prohibition also applies to closely related or connected persons.

See § 111.004(1) (defining "affiliate") and § 111.004(13) (defining "relative" in a narrow fashion which excludes many close relatives, such as uncles, aunts, nephews, and nieces). Subsections (b)-(g) provide limited exceptions to the prohibition.

---

§ 113.053. Purchase or Sale of Trust Property by Trustee

(a) Except as provided by Subsections (b), (c), (d), (e), (f), and (g), a trustee shall not directly or indirectly buy or sell trust property from or to:

(1) the trustee or an affiliate;

(2) a director, officer, or employee of the trustee or an affiliate;

(3) a relative of the trustee; or

(4) the trustee's employer, partner, or other business associate.

(b) A national banking association or a state-chartered corporation with the right to exercise trust powers that is serving as executor, administrator, guardian, trustee, or receiver may sell shares of its own capital stock held by it for an estate to one or more of its officers or directors if a court:

(1) finds that the sale is in the best interest of the estate that owns the shares;

(2) fixes or approves the sales price of the shares and the other terms of the sale; and

(3) enters an order authorizing and directing the sale.

(c) If a corporate trustee, executor, administrator, or guardian is legally authorized to retain its own capital stock in trust, the trustee may exercise rights to purchase its own stock if increases in the stock are offered pro rata to shareholders.

(d) If the exercise of rights or the receipt of a stock dividend results in a fractional share holding and the acquisition meets the investment standard required by this subchapter, the trustee may purchase additional fractional shares to round out the holding to a full share.

(e) A trustee may:

(1) comply with the terms of a written executory contract signed by the settlor, including a contract for deed, earnest money contract, buy/sell agreement, or stock purchase or redemption agreement; and

(2) sell the stock, bonds, obligations, or other securities of a corporation to the issuing corporation or to its corporate affiliate if the sale is made under an agreement described in Subdivision (1) or complies with the duties imposed by Chapter 117.

(f) A national banking association, a state-chartered corporation, including a state-chartered bank or trust company, a state or federal savings and loan association that has the right to exercise trust powers and that is serving as trustee, or such an institution that is serving as custodian with respect to an individual retirement account, as defined by Section 408, Internal Revenue Code, or an employee benefit plan, as defined by Section 3(3), Employee Retirement Income Security Act of 1974 (29 U.S.C. Section 1002(3)), regardless of whether the custodial account is, or would otherwise be, considered a trust for purposes of this subtitle, may, subject to its fiduciary duties:

(1) employ an affiliate or division within a financial institution to provide brokerage, investment, administrative, custodial, or other account services for the trust or custodial account and charge the trust or custodial account for the services;

(2) unless the instrument governing the fiduciary relationship expressly prohibits the purchase or charge, purchase insurance underwritten or otherwise distributed by an affiliate, a division within the financial institution, or a syndicate or selling group that includes the financial institution or an affiliate and charge the trust or custodial account for the insurance premium, provided that:

(A) the person conducting the insurance transaction is appropriately licensed if required by applicable licensing and regulatory requirements administered by a functional regulatory agency of this state; and

(B) the insurance product and premium are the same or similar to a product and premium offered by organizations that are not an affiliate, a division within the financial institution, or a syndicate or selling group that includes the financial institution or an affiliate; and

(3) receive a fee or compensation, directly or indirectly, on account of the services performed or the insurance product sold by the affiliate, division within the financial institution, or syndicate or selling group that includes the financial institution or an affiliate, whether in the form of shared commissions, fees, or otherwise, provided that any amount charged by the affiliate, division, or syndicate or selling group that includes the financial institution or an affiliate for the services or insurance product is disclosed and does not exceed the customary or prevailing amount that is charged by the affiliate, division, or syndicate or selling group that includes the financial institution or an affiliate, or a comparable entity, for comparable services rendered or insurance provided to a person other than the trust.

(g) In addition to other investments authorized by law for the investment of funds held by a fiduciary or by the instrument governing the fiduciary relationship, and notwithstanding any other provision of law and subject to the standard contained in Chapter 117, a bank or trust company acting as a fiduciary, agent, or otherwise, in the exercise of its investment discretion or at the direction of another person authorized to direct the investment of funds held by the bank or trust company as fiduciary, may invest and reinvest in the securities of an open-end or closed-end management investment company or investment trust registered under the Investment Company Act of 1940 (15 U.S.C. § 80a-1 et seq.) if the portfolio of the investment company or investment trust consists substantially of investments that are not prohibited by the governing instrument. The fact that the bank or trust company or an affiliate of the bank or trust company provides services to the investment company or investment trust, such as those of an investment advisor, custodian, transfer agent, registrar, sponsor, distributor, manager, or otherwise, and receives compensation for those services does not preclude the bank or trust company from investing or reinvesting in the securities if the compensation is disclosed by prospectus, account statement, or otherwise. An executor or administrator of an estate under a dependent administration or a guardian of an estate shall not so invest or reinvest unless specifically authorized by the court in which such estate or guardianship is pending.

Amended by Acts 1983, 68th Leg., p. 3332, ch. 567, art. 2, § 2, eff. Jan. 1, 1984; Acts 1985, 69th Leg., ch. 974, §§ 1, 2, eff. Aug. 26, 1985; Acts 1989, 71st Leg., ch. 341, § 1, eff. Aug. 28, 1989; Acts 1993, 73rd Leg., ch. 933, § 1, eff. Aug. 30, 1993. Amended by Acts 2003, 78th Leg., ch. 1103, § 4, eff. Jan. 1, 2004. Subsec. (f) amended by Acts 2013, 83rd Leg., ch. 1337, § 1, eff. Sept. 1, 2013.

Statutes in Context
§ 113.054

A trustee may not sell property to another trust for which the trustee is also serving as the trustee. A conflict of interest arises because as the trustee of the selling trust, the trustee has a duty to get the highest price possible for the asset. However, as the trustee of the purchasing trust, the trustee has the duty to secure the most economical price. Section 113.054 provides an exception for the transfer of obligations issued or fully guaranteed by the federal government and which are sold at their current market price.

This duty may be waived by the settlor or the beneficiaries for all types of trustees. See §§ 111.0035 & 114.005(a).

§ 113.054. Sales from One Trust to Another

A trustee of one trust may not sell property to another trust of which it is also trustee unless the property is:

(1) a bond, note, bill, or other obligation issued or fully guaranteed as to principal and interest by the United States; and

(2) sold for its current market price.

Amended by Acts 1983, 68th Leg., p. 3332, ch. 567, art. 2, § 2, eff. Jan. 1, 1984.

Statutes in Context
§ 113.055

A conflict of interest arises if a trustee invests in the same securities as both a trustee and an individual. This would place the trustee in a position of making decisions for both the trustee as an individual and the trust. The best choice for the trustee may not be the best option for the beneficiaries of the trust. Accordingly, § 113.055 prohibits a trustee from being in this conflict of interest situation. Note that although a trustee may not purchase for the trust stock in corporations in which the trustee individually holds shares, a trustee may retain stock in the trust which the trust already owns when the trustee becomes the trustee as long as it is prudent to do so.

This duty may be waived by the settlor or the beneficiaries for all types of trustees. See §§ 111.0035 and 114.005(a).

§ 113.055. Purchase of Trustee's Securities

(a) Except as provided by Subsection (b) of this section, a corporate trustee may not purchase for the trust the stock, bonds, obligations, or other securities of the trustee or an affiliate, and a noncorporate trustee may not purchase for the trust the stock, bonds, obligations, or other securities of a corporation with which the trustee is connected as director, owner, manager, or any other executive capacity.

(b) A trustee may:

(1) retain stock already owned by the trust unless the retention does not satisfy the requirements prescribed by Chapter 117; and

(2) exercise stock rights or purchase fractional shares under Section 113.053.

Amended by Acts 1983, 68th Leg., p. 3332, ch. 567, art. 2, § 2, eff. Jan. 1, 1984. Amended by Acts 2003, 78th Leg., ch. 1103, § 5, eff. Jan. 1, 2004.

§ 113.056. Authorization to Make Certain Investments

(a) Unless the terms of the trust instrument provide otherwise, and subject to the investment standards provided by this subtitle and any investment standards provided by the trust instrument, the trustee may invest all or part of the trust assets in an investment vehicle authorized for the collective investment of trust funds pursuant to Part 9, Title 12, of the Code of Federal Regulations.

(b) (Repealed)

(c) (Repealed)

(d) Subject to any investment standards provided by this chapter, Chapter 117, or the trust instrument, whenever the instrument directs, requires, authorizes, or permits investment in obligations of the United States government, the trustee may invest in and hold such obligations either directly or in the form of interests in an open-end management type investment company or investment trust registered under the Investment Company Act of 1940, 15 U.S.C. § 80a-1 et seq., or in an investment vehicle authorized for the collective investment of trust funds pursuant to Part 9, Title 12 of the Code of Federal Regulations, so long as the portfolio of such investment company, investment trust, or collective investment vehicle is limited to such obligations and to repurchase agreements fully collateralized by such obligations.

Amended by Acts 1983, 68th Leg., p. 3332, ch. 567, art. 2, § 2, eff. Jan. 1, 1984; Acts 1985, 69th Leg., ch. 341, § 1, eff. June 10, 1985; Acts 1991, 72nd Leg., ch. 876, § 1, eff. June 16, 1991. Amended by Acts 2003, 78th Leg., ch. 1103, §§ 6, 7 & 17, eff. Jan. 1, 2004.

Statutes in Context
§ 113.057

The operation of § 113.057 is demonstrated by the following example. Assume that Octopus National Bank (ONB) is serving as the trustee of a trust. ONB keeps $80,000 in one of its certificates of deposit which is earning a competitive rate of interest. In addition, ONB maintains a checking account for the trust which it uses to pay expenses and make distributions to beneficiaries. Both accounts are fully insured by the federal government.

Technically, both of these accounts violate ONB's duty of loyalty. In ONB's capacity as a trustee, it is a lender, while in its capacity as a bank, it is a borrower. Thus, ONB has actually lent funds to itself. (See § 113.052.) Because it would be inefficient to force ONB to use another financial institution for banking services, § 113.057 permits certain self-deposits. The certificate of deposit is a long-term investment and thus the transaction has a significant self-dealing aspect and it would not be a great burden on ONB to search elsewhere for this type of investment. However, if the settlor authorized this type of investment, ONB may properly open the CD. (If the trust was created before January 1, 1988, a beneficiary may provide the necessary consent.) With regard to the checking account, the benefit to the trust of having fast and convenient access to trust funds outweighs the self-dealing nature of the deposit. Accordingly, § 113.057 permits self-deposits pending investment, distribution, or payment of debts under the statutorily mandated conditions.

§ 113.057. Deposits by Corporate Trustee with Itself

(a) A corporate trustee may deposit trust funds with itself as a permanent investment if authorized by the settlor in the instrument creating the trust or if authorized in a writing delivered to the trustee by a beneficiary currently eligible to receive distributions from a trust created before January 1, 1988.

(b) A corporate trustee may deposit with itself trust funds that are being held pending investment, distribution, or payment of debts if, except as provided by Subsection (d) of this section:

(1) it maintains under control of its trust department as security for the deposit a separate fund of securities legal for trust investments;

(2) the total market value of the security is at all times at least equal to the amount of the deposit; and

(3) the separate fund is marked as such.

(c) The trustee may make periodic withdrawals from or additions to the securities fund required by Subsection (b) of this section as long as the required value is maintained. Income from securities in the fund belongs to the trustee.

(d) Security for a deposit under this section is not required for a deposit under Subsection (a) or under Subsection (b) of this section to the extent the deposit is insured or otherwise secured under state or federal law.

Added by Acts 1983, 68th Leg., p. 3332, ch. 567, art. 2, § 2, eff. Jan. 1, 1984. Amended by Acts 1985, 69th Leg., ch. 149, § 3, eff. May 24, 1985.

Statutes in Context
§ 113.058

The trustee may need to post bond conditioned on the faithful performance of the trustee's duties. The court sets the amount of the bond based on the value of the trust property. The trustee may deliver that amount in cash to the court. However, the trustee typically obtains the bond from a surety company. In exchange for the payment of premiums, the surety company agrees to pay the amount of the bond to the beneficiaries if the trustee breaches the applicable fiduciary duties. Of course, if the surety is required to pay, the surety will seek reimbursement from the trustee.

Section 113.058 exempts the trustee from the bond requirement if either (1) the settlor waived bond in the trust instrument or (2) the trustee is a corporation.

§ 113.058. Bond

(a) A corporate trustee is not required to provide a bond to secure performance of its duties as trustee.

(b) Unless the instrument creating the trust provides otherwise, a noncorporate trustee must give bond:

(1) payable to the trust estate of the trust, the registry of the court, or each person interested in the trust, as their interests may appear; and

(2) conditioned on the faithful performance of the trustee's duties.

(c) The bond must be in an amount and with the sureties required by order of a court in a proceeding brought for this determination.

(d) Any interested person may bring an action to increase or decrease the amount of a bond, require a bond, or substitute or add sureties. Notwithstanding Subsection (b), for cause shown, a court may require a bond even if the instrument creating the trust provides otherwise.

(e) The trustee shall deposit the bond with the clerk of the court that issued the order requiring the bond. A suit on the bond may be maintained on a certified copy. Appropriate proof of a recovery on a bond reduces the liability of the sureties pro tanto.

(f) Failure to comply with this section does not make void or voidable or otherwise affect an act or transaction of a trustee with any third person.

Added by Acts 1983, 68th Leg., p. 3332, ch. 567, art. 2, § 2, eff. Jan. 1, 1984. Subsec. (b) amended by Acts 2005, 79th Leg., ch. 148, § 14, eff. Jan. 1, 2006. Subsecs. (b) & (d) amended by Acts 2007, 80th Leg., ch. 451, § 16, eff. Sept. 1, 2007.

Statutes in Context
§ 113.060 [repealed]

The 2005 Legislature codified the common law duty to keep the beneficiaries informed about the trust and its administration in § 113.060. Because of uncertainty regarding how a trustee may comply with this statutory duty, this section was repealed by the 2007 Legislature.

§ 113.060. Informing Beneficiaries

The trustee shall keep the beneficiaries of the trust reasonably informed concerning:

(1) the administration of the trust; and

(2) the material facts necessary for the beneficiaries to protect the beneficiaries' interests.

Added by Acts 2005, 79th Leg., ch. 148, § 15, eff. Jan. 1, 2006. Repealed by Acts 2007, 80th Leg., ch. 451, § 21, eff. June. 15, 2007.

The enactment of Section 113.060, Property Code, by Chapter 148, Acts of the 79th Legislature, Regular Session, 2005, was not intended to repeal any common-law duty to keep a beneficiary of a trust informed, and the repeal by this Act of Section 113.060, Property Code, does not repeal any common-law duty to keep a beneficiary informed. The common-law duty to keep a beneficiary informed that existed immediately before January 1, 2006, is continued in effect. Acts 2007, 80th Leg., ch. 451, § 24(b).

Subchapter C. Resignation or Removal of Trustee, and Authority of Multiple and Successor Trustees

Statutes in Context
§ 113.081

A trustee is not stuck with serving as a trustee until the trust ends or the trustee dies. The trustee may resign either by (1) following the terms of the trust or (2) petitioning the court for permission to resign. The trustee cannot just "walk away" from the job.

§ 113.081. Resignation of Trustee

(a) A trustee may resign in accordance with the terms of the trust instrument, or a trustee may petition a court for permission to resign as trustee.

(b) The court may accept a trustee's resignation and discharge the trustee from the trust on the terms and conditions necessary to protect the rights of other interested persons.

Amended by Acts 1983, 68th Leg., p. 3332, ch. 567, art. 2, § 2, eff. Jan. 1, 1984.

Statutes in Context
§ 113.082

Section 113.082 explains the circumstances under which a trustee may be removed from office. Despite the use of the word "may," Texas courts have held that they must remove a trustee for the specific reasons enumerated in the statute such as for materially violating the trust or becoming insolvent. See *Akin v. Dahl*, 661 S.W.2d 911 (Tex. 1983). The 2003 Texas Legislature changed the statute by adding the phrase "in its discretion" after the term "may" to make it clear that whether or not to remove a trustee is always a discretionary decision of the court.

The court has broad discretion to remove a trustee "for other cause." However, courts are reluctant to remove a trustee because of dissent between the trustee and the beneficiaries, especially when the settlor appointed the trustee (as compared to a court-appointed trustee). For example, the settlor may have anticipated the beneficiaries' greed and wanted the trustee to stand firm against their demands.

The Texas Supreme Court held in *Ditta v. Conte*, 298 S.W.3d 187 (Tex. 2009), that "no statutory limitations period restricts a court's discretion to remove a trustee. A limitations period, while applicable to suits seeking damages for breach of fiduciary duty, has no place in suits that seek removal rather than recovery." The court studied § 113.082(a) which grants the court broad discretion to remove a trustee for certain enumerated conduct as well for any "other cause" which the court finds sufficient to justify removal. The court stressed that a decision to remove "turns on the special status of the trustee as a fiduciary and the ongoing relationship between trustee and beneficiary, not on any particular or discrete act of the trustee."

§ 113.082. Removal of Trustee

(a) A trustee may be removed in accordance with the terms of the trust instrument, or, on the petition of an interested person and after hearing, a court may, in its discretion, remove a trustee and deny part or all of the trustee's compensation if:

(1) the trustee materially violated or attempted to violate the terms of the trust and the violation or attempted violation results in a material financial loss to the trust;

(2) the trustee becomes incapacitated or insolvent;

(3) the trustee fails to make an accounting that is required by law or by the terms of the trust; or

(4) the court finds other cause for removal.

(b) A beneficiary, cotrustee, or successor trustee may treat a violation resulting in removal as a breach of trust.

(c) A trustee of a charitable trust may not be removed solely on the grounds that the trustee exercised the trustee's power to adjust between principal and income under Section 113.0211.

Added by Acts 1983, 68th Leg., p. 3332, ch. 567, art. 2, § 2, eff. Jan. 1, 1984. Amended by Acts 2003, 78th Leg.,

ch. 550, § 2, eff. Sept. 1, 2003. Subsec. (a) amended by Acts 2005, 79th Leg., ch. 148, § 16, eff. Jan. 1, 2006.

Statutes in Context
§ 113.083

If no trustee remains (e.g., the sole or surviving trustee dies), a replacement trustee is selected by (1) the method specified in the trust instrument, (2) the court on its own motion, or (3) the court upon petition of an interested party. If at least one trustee remains, however, the court will not fill a vacancy. However, the majority of the trustees of a charitable (not private) trust may by majority vote to fill the vacancy if they so desire.

See also Finance Code §§ 274.001-274.203 (the Substitute Fiduciary Act).

§ 113.083. Appointment of Successor Trustee

(a) On the death, resignation, incapacity, or removal of a sole or surviving trustee, a successor trustee shall be selected according to the method, if any, prescribed in the trust instrument. If for any reason a successor is not selected under the terms of the trust instrument, a court may and on petition of any interested person shall appoint a successor in whom the trust shall vest.

(b) If a vacancy occurs in the number of trustees originally appointed under a valid charitable trust agreement and the trust agreement does not provide for filling the vacancy, the remaining trustees may fill the vacancy by majority vote.

Added by Acts 1983, 68th Leg., p. 3332, ch. 567, art. 2, § 2, eff. Jan. 1, 1984.

§ 113.084. Powers of Successor Trustee

Unless otherwise provided in the trust instrument or by order of the court appointing a successor trustee, the successor trustee has the rights, powers, authority, discretion, and title to trust property conferred on the trustee.

Added by Acts 1983, 68th Leg., p. 3332, ch. 567, art. 2, § 2, eff. Jan. 1, 1984.

Statutes in Context
§ 113.085

The settlor may two or more persons to serve as co-trustees. The traditional rule requires all trustees to consent before taking any action with respect to the trust unless the settlor expressly provided otherwise in the trust. Texas rejects the unanimity rule in § 113.085 and permits a majority of the trustees to make decisions regarding the trust. Under limited circumstances such as when one of two co-trustees is absent or ill, the other co-trustee may take action if it is necessary to achieve the purposes of the trust or to avoid injury to the trust property. Co-trustees also have a duty to

724

prevent breaches of trust by another co-trustee and, if a breach is discovered, to compel a redress for that breach.

The 2009 Legislature expanded the ability of co-trustees to act if a co-trustee is unable to participate in the performance of a trustee function. In addition to the previous reasons for the need for prompt action such as to carry out the purposes of the trust and to avoid injury to the trust property, two reasons were added – to achieve the efficient administration of the trust and to avoid injury to a beneficiary.

§ 113.085. Exercise of Powers by Multiple Trustees

(a) Cotrustees may act by majority decision.

(b) If a vacancy occurs in a cotrusteeship, the remaining cotrustees may act for the trust.

(c) A cotrustee shall participate in the performance of a trustee's function unless the cotrustee:

(1) is unavailable to perform the function because of absence, illness, suspension under this code or other law, disqualification, if any, under this code, disqualification under other law, or other temporary incapacity; or

(2) has delegated the performance of the function to another trustee in accordance with the terms of the trust or applicable law, has communicated the delegation to all other cotrustees, and has filed the delegation in the records of the trust.

(d) If a cotrustee is unavailable to participate in the performance of a trustee's function for a reason described by Subsection (c)(1) and prompt action is necessary to achieve the efficient administration or purposes of the trust or to avoid injury to the trust property or a beneficiary, the remaining cotrustee or a majority of the remaining cotrustees may act for the trust.

(e) A trustee may delegate to a cotrustee the performance of a trustee's function unless the settlor specifically directs that the function be performed jointly. Unless a cotrustee's delegation under this subsection is irrevocable, the cotrustee making the delegation may revoke the delegation.

Added by Acts 1983, 68th Leg., p. 3332, ch. 567, art. 2, § 2, eff. Jan. 1, 1984. Former subsecs. (1), (2) replaced by new subsecs.(a) – (e) by Acts 2005, 79th Leg., ch. 148, § 16, eff. Jan. 1, 2006. Subsec. (a) amended by Acts 2007, 80th Leg., ch. 451, § 7, eff. Sept. 1, 2007. Subsecs. (c), (d) amended by Acts 2009, 81st Leg., ch. 973, 1, eff. Sept. 1, 2009.

Subchapter E. Accounting by Trustee

Statutes in Context
§ 113.151

The trustee has a duty to keep accurate records of all transactions involving trust property and to provide accountings to the beneficiaries. This information helps the beneficiaries to determine whether the trustee is doing an acceptable job of administering the trust. Unlike some states, Texas does not require the trustee to render periodic accountings. Instead, § 113.151 provides that a trustee must account only if (1) a beneficiary makes a written demand, or (2) an interested party obtains a court order. The settlor may not waive the trustee's responsibility to provide these accountings. See *Hollenbeck v. Hanna*, 802 S.W.2d 412 (Tex. App. — San Antonio 1991, no writ).

The trustee must provide the accounting on or before the 90th day after the trustee receives the demand unless a court order provides for a longer period.

If the beneficiary is successful in a suit to compel an accounting, the court has the discretion to award all or part of the court costs and all the beneficiary's reasonable and necessary attorney's fees against the trustee in either the trustee's individual or representative capacity. Note that the section does not seem to permit the court to award only a part of the attorney's fees; it appears to be an "all or nothing" situation unlike with regard to court costs where the court has the discretion to award "all or part."

Many good reasons exist for a trustee to render an annual accounting even though not required to do so by law or under the trust. The trustee will have an easier time preparing the accounting when the transactions are fresh in the trustee's mind. The trustee may have a difficult time recalling trust events years or decades later. Accountings also have a good psychological impact on the beneficiaries. Beneficiaries like to know what is going on and voluntarily submitted annual accountings may reflect highly on the trustee's conscientiousness and candor.

§ 113.151. Demand for Accounting

(a) A beneficiary by written demand may request the trustee to deliver to each beneficiary of the trust a written statement of accounts covering all transactions since the last accounting or since the creation of the trust, whichever is later. If the trustee fails or refuses to deliver the statement on or before the 90th day after the date the trustee receives the demand or after a longer period ordered by a court, any beneficiary of the trust may file suit to compel the trustee to deliver the statement to all beneficiaries of the trust. The court may require the trustee to deliver a written statement of account to all beneficiaries on finding that the nature of the beneficiary's interest in the trust or the effect of the administration of the trust on the beneficiary's interest is sufficient to require an accounting by the trustee. However, the trustee is not obligated or required to account to the beneficiaries of a trust more frequently than once every 12 months unless a more frequent accounting is required by the court. If a beneficiary is successful in the suit to compel a statement under this section, the court may, in its discretion, award all or part of the costs of the court and all of the suing beneficiary's reasonable and necessary attorney's fees and costs against the trustee in the trustee's individual capacity or in the trustee's capacity as trustee.

(b) An interested person may file suit to compel the trustee to account to the interested person. The court may require the trustee to deliver a written statement of account to the interested person on finding that the nature of the interest in the trust of, the claim against the trust by, or the effect of the administration of the trust on the interested person is sufficient to require an accounting by the trustee.

Added by Acts 1983, 68th Leg., p. 3332, ch. 567, art. 2, § 2, eff. Jan. 1, 1984. Amended by Acts 2003, 78th Leg., ch. 550, § 3, eff. Sept. 1, 2003.

Statutes in Context
§ 113.152

Section 113.152 enumerates the items required in a trustee's accounting. A trustee may find it convenient to keep records in this format from the beginning to make it a relatively easy task to render an accounting.

§ 113.152. Contents of Accounting

A written statement of accounts shall show:

(1) all trust property that has come to the trustee's knowledge or into the trustee's possession and that has not been previously listed or inventoried as property of the trust;

(2) a complete account of receipts, disbursements, and other transactions regarding the trust property for the period covered by the account, including their source and nature, with receipts of principal and income shown separately;

(3) a listing of all property being administered, with an adequate description of each asset;

(4) the cash balance on hand and the name and location of the depository where the balance is kept; and

(5) all known liabilities owed by the trust.

Added by Acts 1983, 68th Leg., p. 3332, ch. 567, art. 2, § 2, eff. Jan. 1, 1984.

Subchapter F. Common Trust Funds

Statutes in Context
§ 113.171 & § 113.172

Sections 113.171 and 113.172 permit corporate trustees to commingle the property from several trusts into common trust funds. These funds permit trustees to diversify, lower transaction costs, and better leverage the trust property. Individual trustees do not have the option of commingling the property of different trusts. However, they can secure the same benefits by investing in regular commercial mutual funds.

§ 113.171. Common Trust Funds

(a) A bank or trust company qualified to act as a fiduciary in this state may establish common trust funds to provide investments to itself as a fiduciary, including as a custodian under the Texas Uniform Transfers to Minors Act (Chapter 141) or a uniform gifts or transfers to minors act of another state or to itself and others as cofiduciaries.

(b) The fiduciary or cofiduciary may place investment funds in interests in common trust funds if:

(1) the investment is not prohibited by the instrument or order creating the fiduciary relationship; and

(2) if there are cofiduciaries, the cofiduciaries consent to the investment.

(c) A common trust fund includes a fund:

(1) qualified for exemption from federal income taxation as a common trust fund and maintained exclusively for eligible fiduciary accounts; and

(2) consisting solely of assets of retirement, pension, profit sharing, stock bonus, or other employees' trusts that are exempt from federal income taxation.

Added by Acts 1983, 68th Leg., p. 3332, ch. 567, art. 2, § 2, eff. Jan. 1, 1984. Subsec. (a) amended by Acts 2005, 79th Leg., ch. 148, § 18, eff. Jan. 1, 2006.

§ 113.172. Affiliated Institutions

A bank or trust company that is a member of an affiliated group under Section 1504, Internal Revenue Code of 1954 (26 U.S.C. § 1504), with a bank or trust company maintaining common trust funds may participate in one or more of the funds.

Added by Acts 1983, 68th Leg., p. 3332, ch. 567, art. 2, § 2, eff. Jan. 1, 1984.

Chapter 114. Liabilities, Rights, and Remedies of Trustees, Beneficiaries, and Third Persons

Subchapter A. Liability of Trustee

Statutes in Context
§ 114.001

A trustee is accountable for any profit made by the trustee through or arising out of the administration of the trust even though the profit does not result from a breach of trust. See § 114.001(a). For example, if the trustee obtains knowledge of a good investment while working for the trust and then makes the investment for the trustee individually, the trustee will be responsible for any profit the trustee makes. In all other cases, however, the trustee must breach the trust before liability attaches. See § 114.001(b). The available remedies include:

1. Lost Value. The court may award the loss or depreciation in value to the trust property caused by the breach. The plaintiff must be able to demonstrate that the trustee's breach caused the loss but does not need to show that the trustee personally benefited from the breach. See § 114.001(c)(1).

2. Profit Made by Trustee. The trustee is responsible for any profit the trustee gained by being a trustee, except for the trustee's compensation. The trustee is liable for the profit even if the trust did not suffer a loss because of the breach. See § 114.001(c)(2).

3. Lost Profits. The court may hold the trustee liable for the profits the trust would have earned had the trustee not breached the trustee's fiduciary duties. These damages are more difficult to prove because of their speculative nature. See § 114.001(c)(3).

4. Punitive Damages. An intentional breach of duty by the trustee is considered a tort. Consequently, the court may be able to justify an award of punitive damages. See *Interfirst Bank Dallas, N.A. v. Risser*, 739 S.W.2d 882 (Tex. App. — Texarkana 1987, no writ).

The statute of limitations does not begin to run against the beneficiary until the beneficiary has notice that the trustee has repudiated the trust. The beneficiary does not have a duty to investigate until the beneficiary has knowledge of facts which are sufficient to trigger a reasonable person to inquire. In other words, the statute of limitations does not run from the date of the trustee's breach but rather from when that breach is, or should have been, discovered. See *Courseview, Inc. v. Phillips Petroleum Co.*, 312 S.W.2d 197 (Tex. 1957).

§ 114.001. Liability of Trustee to Beneficiary

(a) The trustee is accountable to a beneficiary for the trust property and for any profit made by the trustee through or arising out of the administration of the trust, even though the profit does not result from a breach of trust; provided, however, that the trustee is not required to return to a beneficiary the trustee's compensation as provided by this subtitle, by the terms of the trust instrument, or by a writing delivered to the trustee and signed by all beneficiaries of the trust who have full legal capacity.

(b) The trustee is not liable to the beneficiary for a loss or depreciation in value of the trust property or for a failure to make a profit that does not result from a failure to perform the duties set forth in this subtitle or from any other breach of trust.

(c) A trustee who commits a breach of trust is chargeable with any damages resulting from such breach of trust, including but not limited to:

(1) any loss or depreciation in value of the trust estate as a result of the breach of trust;

(2) any profit made by the trustee through the breach of trust; or

(3) any profit that would have accrued to the trust estate if there had been no breach of trust;

(d) The trustee is not liable to the beneficiary for a loss or depreciation in value of the trust property or for acting or failing to act under Section 113.025 or under any other provision of this subtitle if the action or failure to act relates to compliance with an environmental law and if there is no gross negligence or bad faith on the part of the trustee. The provision of any instrument governing trustee liability does not increase the liability of the trustee as provided by this section unless the settlor expressly makes reference to this subsection.

(e) The trustee has the same protection from liability provided for a fiduciary under 42 U.S.C. § 9607(n).

Amended by Acts 1983, 68th Leg., p. 3332, ch. 567, art. 2, § 2, eff. Jan. 1, 1984; Acts 1984. 68th Leg., 2nd C.S., ch. 18, § 13, eff. Oct. 2. 1984; Acts 1989, 71st Leg., ch. 341, § 2, eff. Aug. 28, 1989; Acts 1993, 73rd Leg., ch. 846, § 30, eff. Sept. 1, 1993. Amended by Acts 1997, 75th Leg., ch. 263, § 1, eff. Sept. 1, 1997. Amended by Acts 2003. 78th Leg., ch. 1103, § 8, eff. Jan. 1, 2004.

Statutes in Context
§ 114.002

A successor trustee is liable for a breach of a predecessor trustee under the circumstances set forth in § 114.002.

§ 114.002. Liability of Successor Trustee for Breach of Trust by Predecessor

A successor trustee is liable for a breach of trust of a predecessor only if he knows or should know of a situation constituting a breach of trust committed by the predecessor and the successor trustee:

(1) improperly permits it to continue;

(2) fails to make a reasonable effort to compel the predecessor trustee to deliver the trust property; or

(3) fails to make a reasonable effort to compel a redress of a breach of trust committed by the predecessor trustee.

Amended by Acts 1983, 68th Leg., p. 3332, ch. 567, art. 2, § 2, eff. Jan. 1, 1984.

Statutes in Context
§ 114.003

Section 114.003 permits a settlor of a charitable trust to name a *trust protector* who has the ability to direct the trustees to take (or not take) certain actions. Normally, the trustee must follow the trust protector's directives unless the trustee recognizes that to do so would be manifestly contrary to the terms of the trust or is a serious breach of the protector's duties. A trust protector of a charitable trust is presumed to be a fiduciary and must act in good faith with regard to the purposes of the trust and the interests of the beneficiaries. Liability will attach if the trust protector breaches a fiduciary duty.

Section 114.0031 deals with trust protectors in private trusts providing less restrictive rules.

§ 114.003. Powers to Direct: Charitable Trusts

(a) In this section, "charitable trust" has the meaning assigned by Section 123.001.

(a-1) The terms of a charitable trust may give a trustee or other person a power to direct the modification or termination of the trust.

(b) If the terms of a charitable trust give a person the power to direct certain actions of the trustee, the trustee shall act in accordance with the person's direction unless:

(1) the direction is manifestly contrary to the terms of the trust; or

(2) the trustee knows the direction would constitute a serious breach of a fiduciary duty that the person holding the power to direct owes to the beneficiaries of the trust.

(c) A person, other than a beneficiary, who holds a power to direct with respect to a charitable trust is presumptively a fiduciary required to act in good faith with regard to the purposes of the trust and the interests of the beneficiaries. The holder of a power to direct with respect to a charitable trust is liable for any loss that results from a breach of the person's fiduciary duty.

Amended by Acts 1983, 68th Leg., p. 3332, ch. 567, art. 2, § 2, eff. Jan. 1, 1984. Title amended by Acts 2005, 79th Leg., ch. 148, § 19, eff. Jan. 1, 2006; former section replaced by new subsecs. (a), (b), (c) by Acts 2005, 79th Leg., ch. 148, § 19, eff. Jan. 1, 2006. Amended by Acts 2015, 84th Leg., ch. 1108, § 1, eff. June 19, 2015.

Statutes in Context
§ 114.0031

Section 114.0031 was added in 2015 to provide more detailed governance for trust protectors in the private trust context.

The settlor may grant the protector any powers and authority which the settlor desires including, but not limited to, the power to remove and appoint trustees and advisors, the power to modify or amend the trust for tax purposes or to facilitate efficient trust administration, and the power to modify, expand, or restrict the terms of a power of appointment the settlor granted to a beneficiary.

By default, the trust protector is a fiduciary. However, the settlor may provide that a protector acts in a nonfiduciary capacity.

The trustee is liable for following the directions of a trust protector only if the trustee's conduct constitutes willful misconduct.

If the settlor requires the trustee to obtain the consent of a trust protector before acting, the trustee is not liable for any act taken or not taken as a result of the protector's failure to provide the required consent after being requested to do so unless the trustee's actions constitute willful misconduct or gross negligence.

Unless the settlor provided otherwise, the trustee has no duty to monitor the protector's conduct, to provide advice to or consult with the protector, or tell the beneficiaries that that the trustee would have acted differently from how the protector directed.

The trustee's actions in carrying out the protector's directions are deemed to be merely administrative actions and are not considered to be the trustee monitoring or participating in actions within the scope of the protector's authority unless there is clear and convincing evidence to the contrary.

Section 114.003 deals with trust protectors in charitable trusts providing more restrictive rules.

§ 114.0031. Directed Trusts; Advisors

(a) In this section:

(1) "Advisor" includes protector.

(2) "Investment decision" means, with respect to any investment, the retention, purchase, sale, exchange, tender, or other transaction affecting the ownership of the investment or rights in the investment and, with respect to a nonpublicly traded investment, the valuation of the investment.

(b) This section does not apply to a charitable trust as defined by Section 123.001.

(c) For purposes of this section, an advisor with authority with respect to investment decisions is an investment advisor.

(d) A protector has all the power and authority granted to the protector by the trust terms, which may include:

(1) the power to remove and appoint trustees, advisors, trust committee members, and other protectors;

(2) the power to modify or amend the trust terms to achieve favorable tax status or to facilitate the efficient administration of the trust; and

(3) the power to modify, expand, or restrict the terms of a power of appointment granted to a beneficiary by the trust terms.

(e) If the terms of a trust give a person the authority to direct, consent to, or disapprove a trustee's actual or proposed investment decisions, distribution decisions, or other decisions, the person is considered to be an advisor and a fiduciary when exercising that authority except that the trust terms may provide that an advisor acts in a nonfiduciary capacity.

(f) A trustee who acts in accordance with the direction of an advisor, as prescribed by the trust terms, is not liable, except in cases of wilful misconduct on the part of the trustee so directed, for any loss resulting directly or indirectly from that act.

(g) If the trust terms provide that a trustee must make decisions with the consent of an advisor, the trustee is not liable, except in cases of wilful misconduct or gross negligence on the part of the trustee, for any loss resulting directly or indirectly from any act taken or not taken as a result of the advisor's failure to provide the required consent after having been requested to do so by the trustee.

(h) If the trust terms provide that a trustee must act in accordance with the direction of an advisor with respect to investment decisions, distribution decisions, or other decisions of the trustee, the trustee does not, except to the extent the trust terms provide otherwise, have the duty to:

(1) monitor the conduct of the advisor;

(2) provide advice to the advisor or consult with the advisor; or

(3) communicate with or warn or apprise any beneficiary or third party concerning instances in which the trustee would or might have exercised the trustee's own discretion in a manner different from the manner directed by the advisor.

(i) Absent clear and convincing evidence to the contrary, the actions of a trustee pertaining to matters within the scope of the advisor's authority, such as confirming that the advisor's directions have been carried out and recording and reporting actions taken at the advisor's direction, are presumed to be administrative actions taken by the trustee solely to allow the trustee to perform those duties assigned to the trustee under the trust terms, and such administrative actions are not considered to constitute an undertaking by the trustee to monitor the advisor or otherwise participate in actions within the scope of the advisor's authority.

Added by Acts 2015, 84th Leg., ch. 1108, § 2, eff. June 19, 2015.

Statutes in Context
§ 114.004

Trustees are generally under an absolute and unqualified duty to make trust distributions to the correct persons. A trustee who makes an improper distribution is liable even though the trustee exercised reasonable care and made the mistake in good faith. This duty is stricter than the standard applicable to other aspects of trust management because the beneficiary is the owner of the equitable title and is thus entitled to the trust distributions according to the terms of the trust.

Section 114.004, however, provides protection for a trustee who makes a distribution without actual knowledge or written notice of a fact impacting distribution such as the beneficiary's marriage, divorce, attainment of a certain age, or the performance of educational requirements. The trustee still has a duty to seek recovery of the mistaken payment and the beneficiary who received the mistaken payment has a duty to repay it. See § 114.031.

---

§ 114.004. Actions Taken Prior to Knowledge or Notice of Facts

A trustee is not liable for a mistake of fact made before the trustee has actual knowledge or receives written notice of the happening of any event that determines or affects the distribution of the income or principal of the trust, including marriage, divorce, attainment of a certain age, performance of education requirements, or death.

Amended by Acts 1983, 68th Leg., p. 3332, ch. 567, art. 2, § 2, eff. Jan. 1, 1984.

Statutes in Context
§ 114.005

A beneficiary may give prior approval to the trustee for actions that would otherwise be in breach of trust. Likewise, the beneficiary may ratify breaches of trust which have already occurred. Section 114.005 provides the requirements for a release.

---

§ 114.005. Release of Liability by Beneficiary

(a) A beneficiary who has full legal capacity and is acting on full information may relieve a trustee from any duty, responsibility, restriction, or liability as to the beneficiary that would otherwise be imposed on the trustee by this subtitle, including liability for past violations.

(b) The release must be in writing and delivered to the trustee.

Amended by Acts 1983, 68th Leg., p. 3332, ch. 567, art. 2, § 2, eff. Jan. 1, 1984. Amended by Acts 2007, 80th Leg., ch. 451, § 8, eff. Sept. 1, 2007.

Statutes in Context
§ 114.006

Generally, co-trustees are jointly and severally liable to the beneficiaries. Section 114.006 explains how a dissenting trustee may attempt to be protected from liability for the acts of the majority.

---

§ 114.006. Liability of Cotrustees for Acts of Other

(a) A trustee who does not join in an action of a cotrustee is not liable for the cotrustee's action, unless the trustee does not exercise reasonable care as provided by Subsection (b).

(b) Each trustee shall exercise reasonable care to:

(1) prevent a cotrustee from committing a serious breach of trust; and

(2) compel a cotrustee to redress a serious breach of trust.

(c) Subject to Subsection (b), a dissenting trustee who joins in an action at the direction of the majority of the trustees and who has notified any cotrustee of the dissent in writing at or before the time of the action is not liable for the action.

Amended by Acts 1983, 68th Leg., p. 3332, ch. 567, art. 2, § 2, eff. Jan. 1, 1984. Title amended by Acts 2005, 79th Leg., ch. 148, § 20, eff. Jan. 1, 2006; former subsecs. (a), (b) replaced by new subsecs. (a), (b), (c) by Acts 2005, 79th Leg., ch. 148, § 20, eff. Jan. 1, 2006.

Subchapter B.   Liability of Beneficiary

Statutes in Context
§ 114.007

The settlor is, for the most part, the master of the trust and thus may provide for things to be handled differently than the Trust Code indicates. The terms of the trust trump the Trust Code except as provided in § 111.0035.

The settlor may include an exculpatory clause to excuse breaches of the standard of care or to permit transactions that would otherwise be self-dealing or create a conflict of interest.

The 2003 and 2005 Texas Legislatures codified the rules regarding the enforceability of exculpatory clauses in trusts. A settlor is prohibited from relieving a trustee of liability for a breach of trust committed (1) in bad faith, (2) intentionally, or (3) with reckless indifference to the interest of the beneficiary. In addition, the settlor may not permit the trustee to retain any profit derived from a breach of trust. An exculpatory clause is ineffective to the extent the provision was included in the trust because of an abuse by the trustee of a fiduciary duty to or confidential relationship with the settlor.

Note, however, that exculpatory provisions in Chapter 142 management trusts (Property Code §§ 142.001 – 142.009) and Section 867 trusts (Probate Code 867) will be enforceable only if the following two requirements are satisfied.

The exculpatory provision is limited to specific facts and circumstances unique to the property of that trust and is not applicable generally to the trust.

The court creating or modifying the trust makes a specific finding that there is clear and convincing evidence that the exculpatory provision is in the best interests of the beneficiary of the trust.

This new requirement for Chapter 142 and Section 867 trusts is a reaction to the Texas Supreme Court opinion in *Texas Commerce Bank, N.A. v. Grizzle*, 96 S.W.3d 240 (Tex. 2002), in which the court enforced a boilerplate exculpatory clause in a Chapter 142 trust.

§ 114.007.   Exculpation of Trustee

(a) A term of a trust relieving a trustee of liability for breach of trust is unenforceable to the extent that the term relieves a trustee of liability for:

(1) a breach of trust committed:

(A) in bad faith;

(B) intentionally; or

(C) with reckless indifference to the interest of a beneficiary; or

(2) any profit derived by the trustee from a breach of trust.

(b) A term in a trust instrument relieving the trustee of liability for a breach of trust is ineffective to the extent that the term is inserted in the trust instrument as a result of an abuse by the trustee of a fiduciary duty to or confidential relationship with the settlor.

(c) This section applies only to a term of a trust that may otherwise relieve a trustee from liability for a breach of trust. Except as provided in Section 111.0035, this section does not prohibit the settlor, by the terms of the trust, from expressly:

(1) relieving the trustee from a duty or restriction imposed by this subtitle or by common law; or

(2) directing or permitting the trustee to do or not to do an action that would otherwise violate a duty or restriction imposed by this subtitle or by common law.

Added by Acts 2005, 79th Leg., ch. 148, § 21, eff. Jan. 1, 2006.

Statutes in Context
§ 114.008

Section 114.008 was added by the 2005 Legislature to provide a non-exclusive listing of possible remedies for a breach of trust.

§ 114.008. Remedies for Breach of Trust

(a) To remedy a breach of trust that has occurred or might occur, the court may:

(1) compel the trustee to perform the trustee's duty or duties;

(2) enjoin the trustee from committing a breach of trust;

(3) compel the trustee to redress a breach of trust, including compelling the trustee to pay money or to restore property;

(4) order a trustee to account;

(5) appoint a receiver to take possession of the trust property and administer the trust;

(6) suspend the trustee;

(7) remove the trustee as provided under Section 113.082;

(8) reduce or deny compensation to the trustee;

(9) subject to Subsection (b), void an act of the trustee, impose a lien or a constructive trust on trust property, or trace trust property of which the trustee wrongfully disposed and recover the property or the proceeds from the property; or

(10) order any other appropriate relief.

(b) Notwithstanding Subsection (a)(9), a person other than a beneficiary who, without knowledge that a trustee is exceeding or improperly exercising the trustee's powers, in good faith assists a trustee or in good faith and for value deals with a trustee is protected from liability as if the trustee had or properly exercised the power exercised by the trustee.

Added by Acts 2005, 79th Leg., ch. 148, § 21, eff. Jan. 1, 2006.

Statutes in Context
§ 114.031

A beneficiary is generally not in a position to breach the trust and is not liable for breaches of trust committed by the trustee. Under the circumstances listed in § 114.031, however, a beneficiary may be liable for a loss to the trust.

§ 114.031. Liability of Beneficiary to Trustee

(a) A beneficiary is liable for loss to the trust if the beneficiary has:

(1) misappropriated or otherwise wrongfully dealt with the trust property;

(2) expressly consented to, participated in, or agreed with the trustee to be liable for a breach of trust committed by the trustee;

(3) failed to repay an advance or loan of trust funds;

(4) failed to repay a distribution or disbursement from the trust in excess of that to which the beneficiary is entitled; or

(5) breached a contract to pay money or deliver property to the trustee to be held by the trustee as part of the trust.

(b) Unless the terms of the trust provide otherwise, the trustee is authorized to offset a liability of the beneficiary to the trust estate against the beneficiary's interest in the trust estate, regardless of a spendthrift provision in the trust.

Added by Acts 1983, 68th Leg., p. 3332, ch. 567, art. 2, § 2, eff. Jan. 1, 1984.

Statutes in Context
§ 114.032

Section 114.032 provides for limited virtual representation so that a release may bind beneficiaries who did not actually agree because, for example, they are minors, unborn, or unascertained. Note that this provision may not be used to modify or terminate the trust. See § 115.013 (judicial virtual representation).

§ 114.032. Liability for Written Agreements

(a) A written agreement between a trustee and a beneficiary, including a release, consent, or other agreement relating to a trustee's duty, power, responsibility, restriction, or liability, is final and binding on the beneficiary and any person represented by a beneficiary as provided by this section if:

(1) the instrument is signed by the beneficiary;

(2) the beneficiary has legal capacity to sign the instrument; and

(3) the beneficiary has full knowledge of the circumstances surrounding the agreement.

(b) A written agreement signed by a beneficiary who has the power to revoke the trust or the power to appoint, including the power to appoint through a power of amendment, the income or principal of the trust to or for the benefit of the beneficiary, the beneficiary's creditors, the beneficiary's estate, or the creditors of the beneficiary's estate is final and binding on any person who takes under the power of appointment or who takes in default if the power of appointment is not executed.

(c) A written instrument is final and binding on a beneficiary who is a minor if:

(1) the minor's parent, including a parent who is also a trust beneficiary, signs the instrument on behalf of the minor;

(2) no conflict of interest exists; and

(3) no guardian, including a guardian ad litem, has been appointed to act on behalf of the minor.

(d) A written instrument is final and binding on an unborn or unascertained beneficiary if a beneficiary who has an interest substantially identical to the interest of the unborn or unascertained beneficiary signs the instrument. For purposes of this subsection, an unborn or unascertained beneficiary has a substantially identical interest only with a trust beneficiary from whom the unborn or unascertained beneficiary descends.

(e) This section does not apply to a written instrument that modifies or terminates a trust in whole or in part unless the instrument is otherwise permitted by law.

Added by Acts 1999, 76th Leg., ch. 794, § 3, eff. Sept. 1, 1999.

Subchapter C.   Rights of Trustee

Statutes in Context
§ 114.061

At common law, a trustee was presumed to serve without compensation unless the trust instrument expressly provided otherwise. The policy behind this rule was that a trustee should not earn a profit by serving in a fiduciary capacity. Otherwise, the trustee might take certain actions which were not necessary or not in the best interest of the trust merely to increase the compensation.

Section 114.061 provides that a trustee is entitled to reasonable compensation unless the trust expressly provides that the trustee is not to be paid or provides a method for determining compensation. The following factors may be considered in determining the amount of compensation which is reasonable: (1) The amount of time the trustee spent working on trust matters; (2) the gross income of the trust; (3) the appreciation in value of trust property; (4) the trustee's unusual or special skills or experience (e.g., being an attorney or accountant); (5) the trustee's degree of fidelity or disloyalty to the trust; (6) the amount of risk and responsibility the trustee assumed; (7) the fees charged by other trustees in the local community for similar services; (8) the character of the trustee's work, that is, did it involve skill and judgment or was it merely routine or ministerial; and (9) the trustee's own estimate of the value of the services.

The trustee may then take this amount from the trust without court approval. If a beneficiary or co-trustee believes the fee is excessive, that person may seek judicial review. See § 115.001(a)(9). The court may deny compensation to a trustee who commits a breach of trust. See § 114.061(b).

§ 114.061. Compensation

(a) Unless the terms of the trust provide otherwise and except as provided in Subsection (b) of this section, the trustee is entitled to reasonable compensation from the trust for acting as trustee.

(b) If the trustee commits a breach of trust, the court may in its discretion deny him all or part of his compensation.

Added by Acts 1983, 68th Leg., p. 3332, ch. 567, art. 2, § 2, eff. Jan. 1, 1984.

Statutes in Context
§ 114.062

See Statutes in Context to § 114.083.

§ 114.062. Exoneration or Reimbursement for Tort

(a) Except as provided in Subsection (b) of this section, a trustee who incurs personal liability for a tort committed in the administration of the trust is entitled to exoneration from the trust property if the trustee has not paid the claim or to reimbursement from the trust property if the trustee has paid the claim, if:

(1) the trustee was properly engaged in a business activity for the trust and the tort is a common incident of that kind of activity;

(2) the trustee was properly engaged in a business activity for the trust and neither the trustee nor an officer or employee of the trustee is guilty of actionable negligence or intentional misconduct in incurring the liability; or

(3) the tort increased the value of the trust property.

(b) A trustee who is entitled to exoneration or reimbursement under Subdivision (3) of Subsection (a) is entitled to exoneration or reimbursement only to the extent of the increase in the value of the trust property.

Added by Acts 1983, 68th Leg., p. 3332, ch. 567, art. 2, § 2, eff. Jan. 1, 1984.

Statutes in Context
§ 114.063

Section 114.063 codifies the trustee's reimbursement rights.

§ 114.063. General Right to Reimbursement

(a) A trustee may discharge or reimburse himself from trust principal or income or partly from both for:

(1) advances made for the convenience, benefit, or protection of the trust or its property;

(2) expenses incurred while administering or protecting the trust or because of the trustee's holding or owning any of the trust property; and

(3) expenses incurred for any action taken under Section 113.025.

(b) The trustee has a lien against trust property to secure reimbursement under Subsection (a).

(c) A potential trustee is entitled to reimbursement from trust principal or income or partly from both for reasonable expenses incurred for any action taken under Section 113.025(a) if:

(1) a court orders reimbursement or the potential trustee has entered into a written agreement providing for reimbursement with the personal representative of the estate, the trustee of the trust, the settlor, the settlor's attorney-in-fact, the settlor's personal representative, or the person or entity designated in the trust instrument or will to appoint a trustee; and

(2) the potential trustee has been appointed trustee under the terms of the trust instrument or will or has received a written request to accept the trust from the settlor, the settlor's attorney-in-fact, the settlor's personal representative, or the person or entity designated in the trust instrument or will to appoint a trustee.

Added by Acts 1983, 68th Leg., p. 3332, ch. 567, art. 2, § 2, eff. Jan. 1, 1984. Amended by Acts 1993, 73rd Leg., ch. 846, § 31, eff. Sept. 1, 1993.

Statutes in Context
§ 114.064

The court may award costs and attorneys' fees to any party in a trust action. Thus, all parties should request fees so the court may make an equitable and just award.

---

§ 114.064. Costs

(a)[1] In any proceeding under this code the court may make such award of costs and reasonable and necessary attorney's fees as may seem equitable and just.

Added by Acts 1985, 69th Leg., ch. 149, § 4, eff. May 24, 1985.

Subchapter D. Third Persons

Statutes in Context
§§ 114.081–114.082

Section 114.081, along with § 114.082, explains when a person who deals with a trustee may obtain protection akin to that of a bona fide purchaser.

---

§ 114.081. Protection of Person Dealing with Trustee

(a) A person who deals with a trustee in good faith and for fair value actually received by the trust is not liable to the trustee or the beneficiaries of the trust if the trustee has exceeded the trustee's authority in dealing with the person.

(b) A person other than a beneficiary is not required to inquire into the extent of the trustee's powers or the propriety of the exercise of those powers if the person:

(1) deals with the trustee in good faith; and

(2) obtains:

(A) a certification of trust described by Section 114.086; or

(B) a copy of the trust instrument.

(c) A person who in good faith delivers money or other assets to a trustee is not required to ensure the proper application of the money or other assets.

(d) A person other than a beneficiary who in good faith assists a former trustee, or who in good faith and for value deals with a former trustee, without knowledge that the trusteeship has terminated, is protected from liability as if the former trustee were still a trustee.

(e) Comparable protective provisions of other laws relating to commercial transactions or transfer of securities by fiduciaries prevail over the protection provided by this section.

Added by Acts 1983, 68th Leg., p. 3332, ch. 567, art. 2, § 2, eff. Jan. 1, 1984. Amended by Acts 2007, 80th Leg., ch. 451, § 8, eff. Sept. 1, 2007.

Statutes in Context
§ 114.082

See Statutes in Context to § 101.001.

---

§ 114.082. Conveyance by Trustee

If property is conveyed or transferred to a trustee in trust but the conveyance or transfer does not identify the trust or disclose the names of the beneficiaries, the trustee may convey, transfer, or encumber the title of the property without subsequent question by a person who claims to be a beneficiary under the trust or who claims by, through, or under an undisclosed beneficiary.

Added by Acts 1983, 68th Leg., p. 3332, ch. 567, art. 2, § 2, eff. Jan. 1, 1984. Amended by Acts 1987, 70th Leg., ch. 683, § 4, eff. Aug. 31, 1987.

Statutes in Context
§ 114.0821

See Statutes in Context to § 101.002.

---

§ 114.0821. Liability of Trust Property

Although trust property is held by the trustee without identifying the trust or its beneficiaries, the trust property is not liable to satisfy the personal obligations of the trustee.

Added by Acts 1983, 68th Leg., p. 3332, ch. 567, art. 2, § 2, eff. Jan. 1, 1984. Renumbered from § 114.082(b) by Acts 1987, 70th Leg., ch. 683, § 4, eff. Aug. 31, 1987.

---

[1] As in enrolled bill; there is no (b).

Statutes in Context
§ 114.083

A trustee may commit a tort during the administration of the trust. For example, the trustee may negligently injure someone or may convert the property of another believing it belongs to the trust. The trustee also may be liable for the tortious acts of the trustee's employees and agents which are committed in the scope of their work for the trust under normal respondeat superior rules. At common law, a tort plaintiff was required to sue the trustee personally and could not reach the trust property directly by suing the trustee in the trustee's representative capacity. The trustee could seek indemnification or reimbursement from the trust only if the trustee had not engaged in willful misconduct. If the trust property was inadequate, the trustee was stuck with the loss. Courts justified this strict rule on the grounds that it encouraged trustees to exercise a high level of care for fear of being personally liable and protected trust property from tort claimants.

The trustee is still personally liable for torts committed by the trustee or the trustee's agents/employees. See § 114.083(c). However, § 114.083(a) permits plaintiffs to sue the trustee in the trustee's representative capacity and to recover directly against trust property in three situations: (1) the tort is a common incident of the business activity in which the trust was properly engaged (e.g., the trust owns a grocery store in which a customer slips, falls, and is injured because an employee negligently failed to clean up a spill); (2) the trustee is not personally at fault because the tort is based on strict liability; and (3) the tort actually increased the value of trust property, such as conversion. In these same three situations, the trustee is entitled to exoneration or reimbursement from trust property under § 114.062. Because the trustee remains personally liable for amounts the trust cannot reimburse or exonerate, the trustee should purchase insurance. See § 113.013.

§ 114.083. Rights and Liabilities for Committing Torts

(a) A personal liability of a trustee or a predecessor trustee for a tort committed in the course of the administration of the trust may be collected from the trust property if the trustee is sued in a representative capacity and the court finds that:

(1) the trustee was properly engaged in a business activity for the trust and the tort is a common incident of that kind of activity;

(2) the trustee was properly engaged in a business activity for the trust and neither the trustee nor an officer or employee of the trustee is guilty of actionable negligence or intentional misconduct in incurring the liability; or

(3) the tort increased the value of the trust property.

(b) A trust that is liable for the trustee's tort under Subdivision (3) of Subsection (a) is liable only to the extent of the permanent increase in value of the trust property.

(c) A plaintiff in an action against the trustee as the representative of the trust does not have to prove that the trustee could have been reimbursed by the trust if the trustee had paid the claim.

(d) Subject to the rights of exoneration or reimbursement under Section 114.062, the trustee is personally liable for a tort committed by the trustee or by the trustee's agents or employees in the course of their employment.

Added by Acts 1983, 68th Leg., p. 3332, ch. 567, art. 2, § 2, eff. Jan. 1, 1984.

Statutes in Context
§ 114.084

A trustee frequently enters into contracts in the performance of the trustee's investment and managerial duties. For example, the trustee may contract with an attorney to provide legal services or with a janitorial service to maintain an office building that is part of the trust corpus. Unless the trustee takes special steps to avoid liability, the trustee is personally liable for any breach of contract. See § 114.084(a). To recoup damages paid to a contract claimant, the trustee must prove that the trustee properly entered into the contract for the benefit of the trust and then seek reimbursement from the trust property. See § 114.063. The trustee would be stuck with any loss that results if the trust does not have adequate property to make a complete reimbursement.

At common law, a contract plaintiff could not sue the trustee in the trustee's representative capacity and could not recover directly against trust property. The common law courts did not take notice of the trust relationship and thus did not recognize the trustee as an individual as being a separate entity from the trustee in a representative capacity. Section 114.063, however, permits contract plaintiffs to reach the trust property directly by proceeding against the trustee in the trustee's fiduciary capacity.

A trustee will usually want to take steps to prevent the trustee's exposure to personal liability on contracts entered into for the benefit of the trust. The trustee should include a provision in the contract which expressly excludes the trustee's personal liability. See § 114.084(a). Instead, if the trustee only signs in a representative capacity (e.g., "as trustee"), the trustee may still be personally liable but the signature acts as prima facie evidence of an intent to exclude the trustee from personal liability. See § 114.084(b).

§ 114.084. Contracts of Trustee

(a) If a trustee or a predecessor trustee makes a contract that is within his power as trustee and a cause of action arises on the contract, the plaintiff may sue the trustee in his representative capacity, and a judgment rendered in favor of the plaintiff is collectible by execution against the trust property. The plaintiff may sue the trustee individually if the trustee made the contract and the contract does not exclude the trustee's personal liability.

(b) The addition of "trustee" or "as trustee" after the signature of a trustee who is party to a contract is prima facie evidence of an intent to exclude the trustee from personal liability.

(c) In an action on a contract against a trustee in the trustee's representative capacity the plaintiff does not have to prove that the trustee could have been reimbursed by the trust if the trustee had paid the claim.

Added by Acts 1983, 68th Leg., p. 3332, ch. 567, art. 2, § 2, eff. Jan. 1, 1984.

§ 114.085. Partnerships

(a) To the extent allowed by law, a trustee who takes the place of a deceased partner in a general partnership in accordance with the articles of partnership is liable to third persons only to the extent of the:

(1) deceased partner's capital in the partnership; and

(2) trust funds held by the trustee.

(b) A trustee who contracts to enter a general partnership in its capacity as trustee shall limit, to the extent allowed by law, the trust's liability to:

(1) the trust assets contributed to the partnership; and

(2) other assets of the trust under the management of the contracting trustee.

(c) If another provision of this subtitle conflicts with this section, this section controls. This section does not exonerate a trustee from liability for negligence.

Added by Acts 1983, 68th Leg., p. 3332, ch. 567, art. 2, § 2, eff. Jan. 1, 1984.

§ 114.086. Certification of Trust

(a) As an alternative to providing a copy of the trust instrument to a person other than a beneficiary, the trustee may provide to the person a certification of trust containing the following information:

(1) a statement that the trust exists and the date the trust instrument was executed;

(2) the identity of the settlor;

(3) the identity and mailing address of the currently acting trustee;

(4) one or more powers of the trustee or a statement that the trust powers include at least all the powers granted a trustee by Subchapter A, Chapter 113;

(5) the revocability or irrevocability of the trust and the identity of any person holding a power to revoke the trust;

(6) the authority of cotrustees to sign or otherwise authenticate and whether all or less than all of the cotrustees are required in order to exercise powers of the trustee; and

(7) the manner in which title to trust property should be taken.

(b) A certification of trust may be signed or otherwise authenticated by any trustee.

(c) A certification of trust must state that the trust has not been revoked, modified, or amended in any manner that would cause the representations contained in the certification to be incorrect.

(d) A certification of trust:

(1) is not required to contain the dispositive terms of a trust; and

(2) may contain information in addition to the information required by Subsection (a).

(e) A recipient of a certification of trust may require the trustee to furnish copies of the excerpts from the original trust instrument and later amendments to the trust instrument that designate the trustee and confer on the trustee the power to act in the pending transaction.

(f) A person who acts in reliance on a certification of trust without knowledge that the representations contained in the certification are incorrect is not liable to any person for the action and may assume without inquiry the existence of the facts contained in the certification.

(g) If a person has actual knowledge that the trustee is acting outside the scope of the trust, and the actual knowledge was acquired by the person before the person entered into the transaction with the trustee or made a binding commitment to enter into the transaction, the transaction is not enforceable against the trust.

(h) A person who in good faith enters into a transaction relying on a certification of trust may enforce the transaction against the trust property as if the representations contained in the certification are correct. This section does not create an implication that a person is liable for acting in reliance on a certification of trust that fails to contain all the information required by Subsection (a). A person's failure to demand a certification of trust does not:

(1) affect the protection provided to the person by Section 114.081; or

(2) create an inference as to whether the person has acted in good faith.

(i) A person making a demand for the trust instrument in addition to a certification of trust or excerpts as described by Subsection (e) is liable for damages if the court determines that the person did not act in good faith in making the demand.

(j) This section does not limit the right of a person to obtain a copy of the trust instrument in a judicial proceeding concerning the trust.

(k) This section does not limit the rights of a beneficiary of the trust against the trustee.

Added by Acts 2007, 80th Leg., ch. 451, § 10, eff. Sept. 1, 2007.

Chapter 115. Jurisdiction, Venue, and Proceedings

Subchapter A. Jurisdiction and Venue

Statutes in Context
§ 115.001

Jurisdiction over trust matters is typically in the district court. See § 115.001(a). However, if the county also has a statutory probate court, the statutory probate court also has jurisdiction. See § 115.001(d). See also Estates Code Chapter 32.

Section 115.001(a) provides an extensive non-exclusive list of actions over which the court has jurisdiction such as to construe a trust instrument, determine the applicable law, appoint or remove a trustee, ascertain beneficiaries, make fact determinations, require the trustee to account, determine the powers, responsibilities, duties, and liability of a trustee, review trustee fees, and settle interim or final accounts.

Of particular importance is § 115.001(a)(8), the ultimate escape clause. The court has the ability to relieve a trustee from any duty, limitation, or restriction which is imposed by the trust instrument or the Trust Code. Thus, a trustee in breach of trust who has an equitable argument that the breach should be forgiven, may "beg" the court for "mercy."

Subsection (b) provides that the court has all of the powers of a court of equity such as the ability to apply cy pres, issue injunctions, and appoint receivers.

The court does not have continuing supervision over the trust unless the court order expressly so provides. See § 115.001(c).

An arbitration clause in a trust requiring the beneficiaries to arbitrate any dispute with the trustees is enforceable. *Rachal v. Reitz*, 403 S.W.3d 840 (Tex. 2013).

§ 115.001. Jurisdiction

(a) Except as provided by Subsection (d) of this section, a district court has original and exclusive jurisdiction over all proceedings by or against a trustee and all proceedings concerning trusts, including proceedings to:

(1) construe a trust instrument;

(2) determine the law applicable to a trust instrument;

(3) appoint or remove a trustee;

(4) determine the powers, responsibilities, duties, and liability of a trustee;

(5) ascertain beneficiaries;

(6) make determinations of fact affecting the administration, distribution, or duration of a trust;

(7) determine a question arising in the administration or distribution of a trust;

(8) relieve a trustee from any or all of the duties, limitations, and restrictions otherwise existing under the terms of the trust instrument or of this subtitle;

(9) require an accounting by a trustee, review trustee fees, and settle interim or final accounts; and

(10) surcharge a trustee.

(a-1) The list of proceedings described by Subsection (a) over which a district court has exclusive and original jurisdiction is not exhaustive. A district court has exclusive and original jurisdiction over a proceeding by or against a trustee or a proceeding concerning a trust under Subsection (a) whether or not the proceeding is listed in Subsection (a).

(b) The district court may exercise the powers of a court of equity in matters pertaining to trusts.

(c) The court may intervene in the administration of a trust to the extent that the court's jurisdiction is invoked by an interested person or as otherwise provided by law. A trust is not subject to continuing judicial supervision unless the court orders continuing judicial supervision.

(d) The jurisdiction of the district court is exclusive except for jurisdiction conferred by law on:

(1) a statutory probate court;

(2) a court that creates a trust under Section 867, Texas Probate Code;

(3) a court that creates a trust under Section 142.005;

(4) a justice court under Chapter 27, Government Code;

(5) a small claims court under Chapter 28, Government Code; or

(6) a county court at law.

Amended by Acts 1983, 68th Leg., p. 3332, ch. 567, art. 2, § 2, eff. Jan. 1, 1984. Amended by Acts 1997, 75th Leg., ch. 1375, § 5, eff. Sept. 1, 1997. Subsecs. (c), (d) amended by Acts 2005, 79th Leg., ch. 148, § 22, eff. Jan. 1, 2006. Subsec. (a) & (d) amended by and subsec. (a-1) added by Acts 2007, 80th Leg., ch. 451, § 11, eff. Sept. 1, 2007. Subsec. (d)(6) added by Acts 2011, 82nd Leg., ch. 657, § 4, eff. Sept. 1, 2011 with the notation that the amendment is "intended to clarify rather than change existing law."

Statutes in Context
§ 115.002

Proper venue for a trust action is determined by § 115.002. Different rules apply if there is (1) a single noncorporate trust, (2) multiple individual trustees, (3) any trustee is a corporation, or (4) the settlor is deceased and an administration of the settlor's estate is pending.

§ 115.002. Venue

(a) The venue of an action under Section 115.001 is determined according to this section.

(b) If there is a single, noncorporate trustee, an action shall be brought in the county in which:

(1) the trustee resides or has resided at any time during the four-year period preceding the date the action is filed; or

(2) the situs of administration of the trust is maintained or has been maintained at any time during the four-year period preceding the date the action is filed.

(b-1) If there are multiple noncorporate trustees and the trustees maintain a principal office in this state, an action shall be brought in the county in which:

(1) the situs of administration of the trust is maintained or has been maintained at any time during the four-year period preceding the date the action is filed; or

(2) the trustees maintain the principal office.

(b-2) If there are multiple noncorporate trustees and the trustees do not maintain a principal office in this state, an action shall be brought in the county in which:

(1) the situs of administration of the trust is maintained or has been maintained at any time during the four-year period preceding the date the action is filed; or

(2) any trustee resides or has resided at any time during the four-year period preceding the date the action is filed.

(c) If there are one or more corporate trustees, an action shall be brought in the county in which:

(1) the situs of administration of the trust is maintained or has been maintained at any time during the four-year period preceding the date the action is filed; or

(2) any corporate trustee maintains its principal office in this state.

(c-1) Notwithstanding Subsections (b), (b-1), (b-2), and (c), if the settlor is deceased and an administration of the settlor's estate is pending in this state, an action involving the interpretation and administration of an inter vivos trust created by the settlor or a testamentary trust created by the settlor's will may be brought:

(1) in a county in which venue is proper under Subsection (b), (b-1), (b-2), or (c); or

(2) in the county in which the administration of the settlor's estate is pending.

(d) For just and reasonable cause, including the location of the records and the convenience of the parties and witnesses, the court may transfer an action from a county of proper venue under this section to another county of proper venue:

(1) on motion of a defendant or joined party, filed concurrently with or before the filing of the answer or other initial responsive pleading, and served in accordance with law; or

(2) on motion of an intervening party, filed not later than the 20th day after the court signs the order allowing the intervention, and served in accordance with law.

(e) Notwithstanding any other provision of this section, on agreement by all parties the court may transfer an action from a county of proper venue under this section to any other county.

(f) For the purposes of this section:

(1) "Corporate trustee" means an entity organized as a financial institution or a corporation with the authority to act in a fiduciary capacity.

(2) "Principal office" means:

(A) if there are one or more corporate trustees, an office of a corporate trustee in this state where the decision makers for the corporate trustee within this state conduct the daily affairs of the corporate trustee; or

(B) if there are multiple trustees, none of which is a corporate trustee, an office in this state that is not maintained within the personal residence of any trustee, and in which one or more trustees conducts the daily affairs of the trustees.

(2-a) The mere presence of an agent or representative of a trustee does not establish a principal office as defined by Subdivision (2). The principal office of a corporate trustee or the principal office maintained by multiple noncorporate trustees may also be but is not necessarily the same as the situs of administration of the trust.

(3) "Situs of administration" means the location in this state where the trustee maintains the office that is primarily responsible for dealing with the settlor and beneficiaries of the trust. The situs of administration may also be but is not necessarily the same as the principal office of a corporate trustee or the principal office maintained by multiple noncorporate trustees.

Amended by Acts 1983, 68th Leg., p. 3332, ch. 567, art. 2, § 2, eff. Jan. 1, 1984; Amended by Acts 1999, 76th Leg., ch. 344, § 4.026, eff. Sept. 1, 1999; Acts 1999, 76th Leg., ch. 933, § 1, eff. Sept. 1, 1999. Subsec. (c-1) added by Acts 2011, 82nd Leg., ch. 657, § 5, eff. Sept. 1, 2011. Subsecs. (b-1), (b-2) added and (c), and (f) amended by Acts 2013, 83rd Leg., ch. 699, § 5, eff. Sept. 1, 2013.

Subchapter B. Parties, Procedure, and Judgments

Statutes in Context
§ 115.011

An interested person has standing to bring a trust action. See § 111.004(7) (defining "interested person").

Section 115.011(b) enumerates the parties who are necessary to a trust action.

Subsection (c) references the requirement that the attorney general be notified of any action involving a charitable trust. See *Statutes in Context* to § 123.001.

A trust beneficiary has the right to intervene in an action against a trustee in contract or tort. See § 115.015 (requiring tort and contract plaintiffs to give notice to beneficiaries).

§ 115.011. Parties

(a) Any interested person may bring an action under Section 115.001.

(b) Contingent beneficiaries designated as a class are not necessary parties to an action under Section 115.001. The only necessary parties to such an action are:

(1) a beneficiary of the trust on whose act or obligation the action is predicated;

(2) a beneficiary of the trust designated by name, other than a beneficiary whose interest has been distributed, extinguished, terminated, or paid;

(3) a person who is actually receiving distributions from the trust estate at the time the action is filed; and

(4) the trustee, if a trustee is serving at the time the action is filed.

(c) The attorney general shall be given notice of any proceeding involving a charitable trust as provided by Chapter 123 of this code.

(d) A beneficiary of a trust may intervene and contest the right of the plaintiff to recover in an action against the trustee as representative of the trust for a tort committed in the course of the trustee's administration or on a contract executed by the trustee.

Amended by Acts 1983, 68th Leg., p. 3332, ch. 567, art. 2, § 2, eff. Jan. 1, 1984. Amended by Acts 1995, 74th Leg., ch. 172, § 1, eff. Sept. 1, 1995. Subsec. (b) amended by Acts 2005, 79th Leg., ch. 148, § 23, eff. Jan. 1, 2006. Subsec. (b) amended by Acts 2011, 82nd Leg., ch. 657, § 6, eff. Sept. 1, 2011.

§ 115.012. Rules of Procedure

Except as otherwise provided, all actions instituted under this subtitle are governed by the Texas Rules of Civil Procedure and the other statutes and rules that are applicable to civil actions generally.

Amended by Acts 1983, 68th Leg., p. 3332, ch. 567, art. 2, § 2, eff. Jan. 1, 1984.

Statutes in Context
§ 115.013

Section 115.013 provides for virtual representation under specified circumstances so that a court order may bind beneficiaries who did not actually agree because, for example, they are minors, unborn, or unascertained. See § 114.032 (limited nonjudicial virtual representation).

§ 115.013. Pleadings and Judgments

(a) Actions and proceedings involving trusts are governed by this section.

(b) An affected interest shall be described in pleadings that give reasonable information to an owner by name or class, by reference to the instrument creating the interest, or in other appropriate manner.

(c) A person is bound by an order binding another in the following cases:

(1) an order binding the sole holder or all coholders of a power of revocation or a presently exercisable general power of appointment, including one in the form of a power of amendment, binds other persons to the extent their interests, as objects, takers in default, or otherwise are subject to the power;

(2) to the extent there is no conflict of interest between them or among persons represented:

(A) an order binding a guardian of the estate or a guardian ad litem binds the ward; and

(B) an order binding a trustee binds beneficiaries of the trust in proceedings to review the acts or accounts of a prior fiduciary and in proceedings involving creditors or other third parties;

(3) if there is no conflict of interest and no guardian of the estate or guardian ad litem has been appointed, a parent may represent his minor child as guardian ad litem or as next friend; and

(4) an unborn or unascertained person who is not otherwise represented is bound by an order to the extent his interest is adequately represented by another party having a substantially identical interest in the proceeding.

(d) Notice under Section 115.015 shall be given either to a person who will be bound by the judgment or to one who can bind that person under this section, and notice may be given to both. Notice may be given to unborn or unascertained persons who are not represented under Subdivision (1) or (2) of Subsection (c) by giving notice to all known persons whose interests in the proceedings are substantially identical to those of the unborn or unascertained persons.

Amended by Acts 1983, 68th Leg., p. 3332, ch. 567, art. 2, § 2, eff. Jan. 1, 1984. Subsec. (d) amended by Acts 2009, 81st Leg., ch. 672, § 4, eff. Sept. 1, 2009.

Statutes in Context
§ 115.014

The court may appoint a guardian and/or an attorney ad litem to represent the interests of a minor, incapacitated, unborn, unascertained, etc., beneficiary.

§ 115.014. Guardian or Attorney Ad Litem

(a) At any point in a proceeding a court may appoint a guardian ad litem to represent the interest of a minor, an incapacitated, unborn, or unascertained person, or person whose identity or address is unknown, if the court determines that representation of the interest otherwise would be inadequate. If there is not a conflict of interests, a guardian ad litem may be appointed to represent several persons or interests.

(b) At any point in a proceeding a court may appoint an attorney ad litem to represent any interest that the court considers necessary, including an attorney ad litem to defend an action under Section 114.083 for a beneficiary of the trust who is a minor or who has been adjudged incompetent.

(c) A guardian ad litem may consider general benefit accruing to the living members of a person's family.

(d) A guardian ad litem is entitled to reasonable compensation for services in the amount set by the court to be taxed as costs in the proceeding.

(e) An attorney ad litem is entitled to reasonable compensation for services in the amount set by the court in the manner provided by Section 114.064.

Amended by Acts 1983, 68th Leg., p. 3332, ch. 567, art. 2, § 2, eff. Jan. 1, 1984. Subsec. (c) added by Acts 2005, 79th Leg., ch. 148, § 24, eff. Jan. 1, 2006. Heading amended by Acts 2009, 81st Leg., ch. 672, § 5, eff. Sept. 1, 2009; Subsec. (b) amended and subsecs. (d), (e) added by Acts 2009, 81st Leg., ch. 672, § 6, eff. Sept. 1, 2009.

Statutes in Context
§ 115.015

Contract and tort plaintiffs have an obligation to notify the beneficiary before being entitled to a judgment against the trustee. Section 115.015 explains the timing of the notice and how the plaintiff may obtain a list of beneficiaries and their addresses from the trustee. The purpose of the notice is to alert the beneficiary that something may be "wrong" with the trust administration. Once notified, the beneficiary may decide to exercise the right to intervene under § 115.011(d).

Note that § 115.015(a)(2) requires that the attorney general be given notice only in contract cases, not tort cases. This anomaly is traceable to Texas Trust Act § 21 which was written before Texas abolished charitable immunity. See *Howle*

v. Camp Amon Carter, 470 S.W.2d 629 (Tex. 1971) (abolishing charitable immunity as of March 9, 1966); but see Charitable Immunity and Liability Act, Civil Practice & Remedies Code, ch. 84. The attorney general may nonetheless be entitled to notice under Property Code ch. 123.

§ 115.015. Notice to Beneficiaries of Tort or Contract Proceeding

(a) A court may not render judgment in favor of a plaintiff in an action on a contract executed by the trustee or in an action against the trustee as representative of the trust for a tort committed in the course of the trustee's administration unless the plaintiff proves that before the 31st day after the date the action began or within any other period fixed by the court that is more than 30 days before the date of the judgment, the plaintiff gave notice of the existence and nature of the action to:

(1) each beneficiary known to the trustee who then had a present or contingent interest; or

(2) in an action on a contract involving a charitable trust, the attorney general and any corporation that is a beneficiary or agency in the performance of the trust.

(b) The plaintiff shall give the notice required by Subsection (a) of this section by registered mail or by certified mail, return receipt requested, addressed to the party to be notified at the party's last known address. The trustee shall give the plaintiff a list of the beneficiaries or persons having an interest in the trust estate and their addresses, if known to the trustee, before the 11th day after the date the plaintiff makes a written request for the information.

(c) The plaintiff satisfies the notice requirements of this section by notifying the persons on the list provided by the trustee.

Amended by Acts 1983, 68th Leg., p. 3332, ch. 567, art. 2, § 2, eff. Jan. 1, 1984.

§ 115.016. Notice

(a) If notice of hearing on a motion or other proceeding is required, the notice may be given in the manner prescribed by law or the Texas Rules of Civil Procedure, or, alternatively, notice may be given to any party or to his attorney if the party has appeared by attorney or requested that notice be sent to his attorney.

(b) If the address or identity of a party is not known and cannot be ascertained with reasonable diligence, on order of the court notice may be given by publishing a copy of the notice at least three times in a newspaper having general circulation in the county where the hearing is to be held. The first publication of the notice must be at least 10 days before the time set for the hearing. If there is no newspaper of general circulation in the county where the hearing is to be held, the publication shall be made in a newspaper of general circulation in an adjoining county.

Added by Acts 1983, 68th Leg., p. 3332, ch. 567, art. 2,

§ 2, eff. Jan. 1, 1984.

§ 115.017. Waiver of Notice

A person, including a guardian of the estate, a guardian ad litem, or other fiduciary, may waive notice by a writing signed by the person or his attorney and filed in the proceedings.

Added by Acts 1983, 68ᵗʰ Leg., p. 3332, ch. 567, art. 2, § 2, eff. Jan. 1, 1984.

Chapter 116.   Uniform Principal and Income Act

Statutes in Context
§ Chapter 116

The settlor may grant certain beneficiaries the right to trust income (income beneficiaries) and other beneficiaries the right to the principal when the trust terminates (remainder beneficiaries). This arrangement places these two types of beneficiaries in conflict. The income beneficiaries want the trust corpus invested in property which generates high rates of return such as corporate bonds and mutual funds. On the other hand, remainder beneficiaries want the trustee to invest in property which appreciates in value such as real property and growth stocks. Many investments that are good for one type of beneficiary will not benefit another. For example, assume that the trustee invested in a government insured certificate of deposit earning 7 percent interest. The income beneficiaries will be elated because the rate of return is relatively high and the investment is extremely safe. However, the remainder beneficiaries will be furious. The CD will not grow in value because the trustee will get back the same amount the trustee invested when the CD matures. In addition, because of inflation, the buying power of the proceeds will shrink to less than the amount invested so the remainder beneficiaries will actually incur a loss. To resolve this problem, a trustee either selects investments that earn both income and appreciate in value, such as rental real property and certain types of stock, or diversifies trust investments to balance investments that earn income and investments which increase in value.

A trustee also needs to know how to categorize property received from the trust assets to carry out the trustee's duty to be fair and impartial to both the income and remainder beneficiaries. Likewise, the trustee must determine whether to reduce income or principal when the trustee pays trust expenses. The trustee has three ways to determine how to allocate receipts and expenses between income and principal. First, the settlor may have provided instructions in the trust instrument. These instructions may state specific allocation rules or may merely give the trustee discretion to make the allocation. See § 116.004(a)(1)-(2). Second, if the instrument is silent, the trustee must follow the rules in Chapter 116 which is the Texas adoption of the 1997 version of the Uniform Principal and Income Act. See § 116.004(a)(3). Third, if neither the instrument nor the statute specifies the proper method of allocation, the trustee must allocate to principal. See § 116.004(a)(4).

The Texas adoption of the 1997 UPIA took effect on January 1, 2004. Prior to this time, Texas followed the 1962 version. Many of the provisions of the 1997 version are significantly different from prior law. Perhaps the most controversial change is the trustee's ability to adjust between principal and income under § 116.005.

Subchapter A.   Definitions, Fiduciary Duties, and Other Miscellaneous Provisions

§ 116.001. Short Title

This chapter may be cited as the Uniform Principal and Income Act.

Added by Acts 2003, 78ᵗʰ Leg., ch. 659, § 1, eff. Jan. 1, 2004.

Statutes in Context
§ 116.002

Section 116.002 provides definitions used throughout Chapter 116. Note that these definitions do not apply to other Trust Code chapters.

§ 116.002. Definitions

In this chapter:

(1) "Accounting period" means a calendar year unless another 12-month period is selected by a fiduciary. The term includes a portion of a calendar year or other 12-month period that begins when an income interest begins or ends when an income interest ends.

(2) "Beneficiary" includes, in the case of a decedent's estate, an heir, legatee, and devisee and, in the case of a trust, an income beneficiary and a remainder beneficiary.

(3) "Fiduciary" means a personal representative or a trustee. The term includes an executor, administrator, successor personal representative, special administrator, and a person performing substantially the same function.

(4) "Income" means money or property that a fiduciary receives as current return from a principal asset. The term includes a portion of receipts from a

sale, exchange, or liquidation of a principal asset, to the extent provided in Subchapter D.

(5) "Income beneficiary" means a person to whom net income of a trust is or may be payable.

(6) "Income interest" means the right of an income beneficiary to receive all or part of net income, whether the terms of the trust require it to be distributed or authorize it to be distributed in the trustee's discretion.

(7) "Mandatory income interest" means the right of an income beneficiary to receive net income that the terms of the trust require the fiduciary to distribute.

(8) "Net income" means the total receipts allocated to income during an accounting period minus the disbursements made from income during the period, plus or minus transfers under this chapter to or from income during the period.

(9) "Person" has the meaning assigned by Section 111.004.

(10) "Principal" means property held in trust for distribution to a remainder beneficiary when the trust terminates.

(11) "Remainder beneficiary" means a person entitled to receive principal when an income interest ends.

(12) "Terms of a trust" means the manifestation of the intent of a settlor or decedent with respect to the trust, expressed in a manner that admits of its proof in a judicial proceeding, whether by written or spoken words or by conduct.

(13) "Trustee" has the meaning assigned by Section 111.004.

Added by Acts 2003, 78th Leg., ch. 659, § 1, eff. Jan. 1, 2004. Subsecs. (9) & (13) amended by Acts 2007, 80th Leg., ch. 451, § 12, eff. Sept. 1, 2007.

§ 116.003. Uniformity of Application and Construction

In applying and construing this Uniform Act, consideration must be given to the need to promote uniformity of the law with respect to its subject matter among states that enact it.

Added by Acts 2003, 78th Leg., ch. 659, § 1, eff. Jan. 1, 2004.

Statutes in Context
§ 116.004

The trustee has three ways to determine how to allocate receipts and expenses between income and principal. First, the settlor may have provided instructions in the trust instrument. These instructions may state specific allocation rules or may merely give the trustee discretion to make the allocation. See § 116.004(a)(1)-(2). Second, if the instrument is silent, the trustee must apply the rules in Chapter 116. See § 116.004(a)(3). Third, if neither the instrument nor the statute specifies the

proper method of allocation, the trustee must allocate to principal. See § 116.004(a)(4). Note that this last rule is a significant departure from prior law which provided that the trustee must allocate in a "reasonable and equitable" manner if both the instrument and statute were silent.

An allocation in accordance with the UPIA's rules by a trustee who has discretionary authority is presumed to be fair and reasonable to all beneficiaries. See § 116.004(b).

§ 116.004. Fiduciary Duties; General Principles

(a) In allocating receipts and disbursements to or between principal and income, and with respect to any matter within the scope of Subchapters B and C, a fiduciary:

(1) shall administer a trust or estate in accordance with the terms of the trust or the will, even if there is a different provision in this chapter;

(2) may administer a trust or estate by the exercise of a discretionary power of administration given to the fiduciary by the terms of the trust or the will, even if the exercise of the power produces a result different from a result required or permitted by this chapter;

(3) shall administer a trust or estate in accordance with this chapter if the terms of the trust or the will do not contain a different provision or do not give the fiduciary a discretionary power of administration; and

(4) shall add a receipt or charge a disbursement to principal to the extent that the terms of the trust and this chapter do not provide a rule for allocating the receipt or disbursement to or between principal and income.

(b) In exercising the power to adjust under Section 116.005(a) or a discretionary power of administration regarding a matter within the scope of this chapter, whether granted by the terms of a trust, a will, or this chapter, a fiduciary shall administer a trust or estate impartially, based on what is fair and reasonable to all of the beneficiaries, except to the extent that the terms of the trust or the will clearly manifest an intention that the fiduciary shall or may favor one or more of the beneficiaries. A determination in accordance with this chapter is presumed to be fair and reasonable to all of the beneficiaries.

Added by Acts 2003, 78th Leg., ch. 659, § 1, eff. Jan. 1, 2004.

Statutes in Context
§ 116.005

Section 116.005 is the most innovative provision of the 1997 UPIA. Consider the following example: Settlor created a testamentary trust requiring trust income to be paid to Daughter for life with the remainder to Granddaughter. The trust corpus consists primarily of real estate which is appreciating in value at about 15 percent per year due to its proximity to the edge of a growing city. The land is still subject to a multiple-year lease which Settlor signed with Tenant many years ago. The rent Tenant pays is significantly below market value and is insufficient to support Daughter as Settlor intended. May Trustee sell part of the land and allocate a portion of the profits to income?

Under traditional trust rules, Trustee could not allocate any of the profits from the sale of the real estate to income. Granddaughter has a right to the principal and appreciation belongs to the principal. However, § 116.005 grants the trustee the power to adjust between principal and income under specified circumstances. The adjustment power section is quite lengthy and requires Trustee to consider a variety of factors such as the settlor's intent and the identity and circumstances of the beneficiaries. In this example, it appears that Settlor established the trust to provide for Daughter and Settlor's intent would be frustrated if Trustee did not allocate some of the profits to income to provide Daughter with an appropriate level of support.

The adjustment power has proven to be an extremely controversial aspect of the 1997 Act because of its tremendous departure from traditional law, the fear that trustees may abuse the power, and the potential of a beneficiary suing a trustee if the trustee does not exercise the adjustment power in the beneficiary's favor. Accordingly, many of the states enacting the 1997 version of the Act have omitted the adjustment provisions or have altered or restricted them in some way.

---

§ 116.005. Trustee's Power to Adjust

(a) A trustee may adjust between principal and income to the extent the trustee considers necessary if the trustee invests and manages trust assets as a prudent investor, the terms of the trust describe the amount that may or must be distributed to a beneficiary by referring to the trust's income, and the trustee determines, after applying the rules in Section 116.004(a), that the trustee is unable to comply with Section 116.004(b). The power to adjust conferred by this subsection includes the power to allocate all or part of a capital gain to trust income.

(b) In deciding whether and to what extent to exercise the power conferred by Subsection (a), a trustee shall consider all factors relevant to the trust and its beneficiaries, including the following factors to the extent they are relevant:

(1) the nature, purpose, and expected duration of the trust;

(2) the intent of the settlor;

(3) the identity and circumstances of the beneficiaries;

(4) the needs for liquidity, regularity of income, and preservation and appreciation of capital;

(5) the assets held in the trust; the extent to which they consist of financial assets, interests in closely held enterprises, tangible and intangible personal property, or real property; the extent to which an asset is used by a beneficiary; and whether an asset was purchased by the trustee or received from the settlor;

(6) the net amount allocated to income under the other sections of this chapter and the increase or decrease in the value of the principal assets, which the trustee may estimate as to assets for which market values are not readily available;

(7) whether and to what extent the terms of the trust give the trustee the power to invade principal or accumulate income or prohibit the trustee from invading principal or accumulating income, and the extent to which the trustee has exercised a power from time to time to invade principal or accumulate income;

(8) the actual and anticipated effect of economic conditions on principal and income and effects of inflation and deflation; and

(9) the anticipated tax consequences of an adjustment.

(c) A trustee may not make an adjustment:

(1) that reduces the actuarial value of the income interest in a trust to which a person transfers property with the intent to qualify for a gift tax exclusion;

(2) that changes the amount payable to a beneficiary as a fixed annuity or a fixed fraction of the value of the trust assets;

(3) from any amount that is permanently set aside for charitable purposes under a will or the terms of a trust unless both income and principal are so set aside;

(4) if possessing or exercising the power to make an adjustment causes an individual to be treated as the owner of all or part of the trust for income tax purposes, and the individual would not be treated as the owner if the trustee did not possess the power to make an adjustment;

(5) if possessing or exercising the power to make an adjustment causes all or part of the trust assets to be included for estate tax purposes in the estate of an individual who has the power to remove a trustee or appoint a trustee, or both, and the assets would not be included in the estate of the individual if the trustee did not possess the power to make an adjustment;

(6) if the trustee is a beneficiary of the trust; or

(7) if the trustee is not a beneficiary, but the adjustment would benefit the trustee directly or indirectly.

(d) If Subsection (c)(4), (5), (6), or (7) applies to a trustee and there is more than one trustee, a cotrustee to whom the provision does not apply may make the adjustment unless the exercise of the power by the remaining trustee or trustees is not permitted by the terms of the trust.

(e) A trustee may release the entire power conferred by Subsection (a) or may release only the power to adjust from income to principal or the power to adjust from principal to income if the trustee is uncertain about whether possessing or exercising the power will cause a result described in Subsections (c)(1)-(5) or Subsection (c)(7) or if the trustee determines that possessing or exercising the power will or may deprive the trust of a tax benefit or impose a tax burden not described in Subsection (c). The release may be permanent or for a specified period, including a period measured by the life of an individual.

(f) Terms of a trust that limit the power of a trustee to make an adjustment between principal and income do not affect the application of this section unless it is clear from the terms of the trust that the terms are intended to deny the trustee the power of adjustment conferred by Subsection (a).

Added by Acts 2003, 78th Leg., ch. 659, § 1, eff. Jan. 1, 2004. Subsec. (c) amended by Acts 2005, 79th Leg., ch. 148, § 25, eff. Jan. 1, 2006. Amended by Acts 2011, 82nd Leg., ch. 91, § 21.002, eff. Sept. 1, 2011 and Acts 2011, 82nd Leg., ch. 657, § 7, eff. Sept. 1, 2011.

Statutes in Context
§116.006

Section 116.006 provides the trustee with the option of seeking court approval of an adjustment between principal and income under § 116.005. The Texas version of this section differs from the uniform version in that it includes additional protections for the beneficiaries.

§ 116.006. Judicial Control of Discretionary Power

(a) The court may not order a trustee to change a decision to exercise or not to exercise a discretionary power conferred by Section 116.005 of this chapter unless the court determines that the decision was an abuse of the trustee's discretion. A trustee's decision is not an abuse of discretion merely because the court would have exercised the power in a different manner or would not have exercised the power.

(b) The decisions to which Subsection (a) applies include:

(1) a decision under Section 116.005(a) as to whether and to what extent an amount should be transferred from principal to income or from income to principal; and

(2) a decision regarding the factors that are relevant to the trust and its beneficiaries, the extent to which the factors are relevant, and the weight, if any, to be given to those factors in deciding whether and to what extent to exercise the discretionary power conferred by Section 116.005(a).

(c) If the court determines that a trustee has abused the trustee's discretion, the court may place the income and remainder beneficiaries in the positions they would have occupied if the discretion had not been abused, according to the following rules:

(1) to the extent that the abuse of discretion has resulted in no distribution to a beneficiary or in a distribution that is too small, the court shall order the trustee to distribute from the trust to the beneficiary an amount that the court determines will restore the beneficiary, in whole or in part, to the beneficiary's appropriate position;

(2) to the extent that the abuse of discretion has resulted in a distribution to a beneficiary which is too large, the court shall place the beneficiaries, the trust, or both, in whole or in part, in their appropriate positions by ordering the trustee to withhold an amount from one or more future distributions to the beneficiary who received the distribution that was too large or ordering that beneficiary to return some or all of the distribution to the trust; and

(3) to the extent that the court is unable, after applying Subdivisions (1) and (2), to place the beneficiaries, the trust, or both, in the positions they would have occupied if the discretion had not been abused, the court may order the trustee to pay an appropriate amount from its own funds to one or more of the beneficiaries or the trust or both.

(d) If the trustee of a trust reasonably believes that one or more beneficiaries of such trust will object to the manner in which the trustee intends to exercise or not exercise a discretionary power conferred by Section 116.005, the trustee may petition the court having jurisdiction over the trust, and the court shall determine whether the proposed exercise or nonexercise by the trustee of such discretionary power will result in an abuse of the trustee's discretion. The trustee shall state in such petition the basis for its belief that a beneficiary would object. The failure or refusal of a beneficiary to sign a waiver or release is not reasonable grounds for a trustee to believe the beneficiary will object. The court may appoint one or more guardians ad litem or attorneys ad litem pursuant to Section 115.014. If the petition describes the proposed exercise or nonexercise of the power and contains sufficient information to inform the beneficiaries of the reasons for the proposal, the facts upon which the trustee relies, and an explanation of how the income and remainder beneficiaries will be affected by the proposed exercise or nonexercise of the power, a beneficiary who challenges the proposed exercise or nonexercise has the burden of establishing that it will result in an abuse of discretion. The trustee shall advance from the trust principal all costs incident to the judicial determination, including the reasonable attorney's fees and costs of the trustee, any beneficiary or beneficiaries who are parties to the action and who retain counsel, any guardian ad litem, and any attorney ad litem . At the conclusion of the proceeding, the court may award costs and reasonable and necessary attorney's fees as provided in Section 114.064, including, if the court considers it appropriate, awarding part or all of such costs against the trust principal or income, awarding part or all of such costs against one or more beneficiaries or such beneficiary's or beneficiaries' share of the trust, or awarding part or all of such costs against the trustee in the trustee's individual capacity, if the court determines that the trustee's exercise or nonexercise of discretionary power would have resulted in an abuse of discretion or that the trustee did not have reasonable grounds for believing one or more beneficiaries would object to the proposed exercise or nonexercise of the discretionary power.

Added by Acts 2003, 78th Leg., ch. 659, § 1, eff. Jan. 1, 2004. Subsec. (d) amended by Acts 2009, 81st Leg., ch. 672, § 7, eff. Sept. 1, 2009.

Statutes in Context
§ 116.007

To avoid the accounting hassle of allocating receipts and expenses between the income and remainder interests, as well as to reduce the inherent conflict of interest between current and future beneficiaries, some settlors adopt a unitrust or total return approach. The current beneficiary of a unitrust is entitled to receive a fixed percentage of the value of the trust property annually. The current beneficiary may or may not also be entitled to additional distributions. For example, the trust could provide: "Trustee shall distribute 5 percent of the value of the trust property to Current Beneficiary on January 10 of every year. Trustee has the discretion to make additional distributions to Current Beneficiary for Current Beneficiary's health, education, and support. Upon Current Beneficiary's death, Trustee shall deliver all remaining trust property to Remainder Beneficiary."

Under a unitrust, both beneficiaries have the same goal — they want the value of the property in the trust to increase. It does not matter to them whether the increase in value is due to receipts traditionally nominated income (e.g., interest or rent) or principal (i.e., appreciation). All increases inure to the benefit of all beneficiaries. Likewise, all beneficiaries share in the expenses regardless of their usual characterization.

Because of the enhanced ability of trustees to make productive investments when they are concerned only about total return rather than balancing the interests of income and principal beneficiaries, the use of unitrusts is seen by courts and legislatures as desirable. Section 116.007 applies only to noncharitable unitrusts and is included primarily for tax purposes. The UPIA does not contain an equivalent provision.

§ 116.007. Provisions Regarding Noncharitable Unitrusts

(a) This section does not apply to a charitable remainder unitrust as defined by Section 664(d), Internal Revenue Code of 1986 (26 U.S.C. Section 664), as amended.

(b) In this section:

(1) "Unitrust" means a trust the terms of which require distribution of a unitrust amount.

(2) "Unitrust amount" means a distribution mandated by the terms of a trust in an amount equal to a fixed percentage of not less than three or more than five percent per year of the net fair market value of the trust's assets, valued at least annually. The unitrust amount may be determined by reference to the net fair market value of the trust's assets in one year or more than one year.

(c) Distribution of the unitrust amount is considered a distribution of all of the income of the unitrust and shall not be considered a fundamental departure from applicable state law. A distribution of the unitrust amount reasonably apportions the total return of a unitrust.

(d) Unless the terms of the trust specifically provide otherwise, a distribution of the unitrust amount shall be treated as first being made from the following sources in order of priority:

(1) from net accounting income determined as if the trust were not a unitrust;

(2) from ordinary accounting income not allocable to net accounting income;

(3) from net realized short-term capital gains;

(4) from net realized long-term capital gains; and

(5) from the principal of the trust estate.

Added by Acts 2003, 78th Leg., ch. 659, § 1, eff. Jan. 1, 2004.

Subchapter B. Decedent's Estate or Terminating Income Interest

---

Statutes in Context
§ 116.051

Section 116.051 provides guidance to the trustee for determining and distributing net income after (1) a decedent dies or (2) an income interest in a trust ends. In a significant departure from prior law, unpaid pecuniary gifts in a will (either outright or in trust) begin to earn interest one year after the decedent dies rather than one year after the court grants letters testamentary. The trustee may allocate interest on estate taxes to either principal or income rather than only against principal.

---

§ 116.051. Determination and Distribution of Net Income

After a decedent dies, in the case of an estate, or after an income interest in a trust ends, the following rules apply:

(1) A fiduciary of an estate or of a terminating income interest shall determine the amount of net income and net principal receipts received from property specifically given to a beneficiary under the rules in Subchapters C, D, and E which apply to trustees and the rules in Subdivision (5). The fiduciary shall distribute the net income and net principal receipts to the beneficiary who is to receive the specific property.

(2) A fiduciary shall determine the remaining net income of a decedent's estate or a terminating income interest under the rules in Subchapters C, D, and E which apply to trustees and by:

(A) including in net income all income from property used to discharge liabilities;

(B) paying from income or principal, in the fiduciary's discretion, fees of attorneys, accountants, and fiduciaries; court costs and other expenses of administration; and interest on death taxes, but the fiduciary may pay those expenses from income of property passing to a trust for which the fiduciary claims an estate tax marital or charitable deduction only to the extent that the payment of those expenses from income will not cause the reduction or loss of the deduction; and

(C) paying from principal all other disbursements made or incurred in connection with the settlement of a decedent's estate or the winding up of a terminating income interest, including debts, funeral expenses, disposition of remains, family allowances, and death taxes and related penalties that are apportioned to the estate or terminating income interest by the will, the terms of the trust, or applicable law.

(3) A fiduciary shall distribute to a beneficiary who receives a pecuniary amount outright the interest or any other amount provided by the will, the terms of the trust, or applicable law from net income determined under Subdivision (2) or from principal to the extent that net income is insufficient. If a beneficiary is to receive a pecuniary amount outright from a trust after an income interest ends and no interest or other amount is provided for by the terms of the trust or applicable law, the fiduciary shall distribute the interest or other amount to which the beneficiary would be entitled under applicable law if the pecuniary amount were required to be paid under a will. Unless otherwise provided by the will or the terms of the trust, a beneficiary who receives a pecuniary amount, regardless of whether in trust, shall be paid interest on the pecuniary amount at the legal rate of interest as provided by Section

302.002, Finance Code. Interest on the pecuniary amount is payable:

(A) under a will, beginning on the first anniversary of the date of the decedent's death; or

(B) under a trust, beginning on the first anniversary of the date on which an income interest ends.

(4) A fiduciary shall distribute the net income remaining after distributions required by Subdivision (3) in the manner described in Section 116.052 to all other beneficiaries even if the beneficiary holds an unqualified power to withdraw assets from the trust or other presently exercisable general power of appointment over the trust.

(5) A fiduciary may not reduce principal or income receipts from property described in Subdivision (1) because of a payment described in Section 116.201 or 116.202 to the extent that the will, the terms of the trust, or applicable law requires the fiduciary to make the payment from assets other than the property or to the extent that the fiduciary recovers or expects to recover the payment from a third party. The net income and principal receipts from the property are determined by including all of the amounts the fiduciary receives or pays with respect to the property, whether those amounts accrued or became due before, on, or after the date of a decedent's death or an income interest's terminating event, and by making a reasonable provision for amounts that the fiduciary believes the estate or terminating income interest may become obligated to pay after the property is distributed.

(6) A fiduciary, without reduction for taxes, shall pay to a charitable organization that is entitled to receive income under Subdivision (4) any amount allowed as a tax deduction to the estate or trust for income payable to the charitable organization.

Added by Acts 2003, 78th Leg., ch. 659, § 1, eff. Jan. 1, 2004.

Statutes in Context
§ 116.052

Section 116.052 explains how a trustee is to determine the appropriate amount of trust income to distribute to the residuary and remainder beneficiaries once the income interest ends.

---

§ 116.052. Distribution to Residuary and Remainder Beneficiaries

(a) Each beneficiary described in Section 116.051(4) is entitled to receive a portion of the net income equal to the beneficiary's fractional interest in undistributed principal assets, using values as of the distribution date. If a fiduciary makes more than one distribution of assets to beneficiaries to whom this section applies, each beneficiary, including one who does not receive part of the distribution, is entitled, as of each distribution date, to the net income the fiduciary has received after the date of death or terminating event or earlier distribution date but has not distributed as of the current distribution date.

(b) In determining a beneficiary's share of net income, the following rules apply:

(1) The beneficiary is entitled to receive a portion of the net income equal to the beneficiary's fractional interest in the undistributed principal assets immediately before the distribution date, including assets that later may be sold to meet principal obligations.

(2) The beneficiary's fractional interest in the undistributed principal assets must be calculated without regard to property specifically given to a beneficiary and property required to pay pecuniary amounts not in trust.

(3) The beneficiary's fractional interest in the undistributed principal assets must be calculated on the basis of the aggregate value of those assets as of the distribution date without reducing the value by any unpaid principal obligation.

(4) The distribution date for purposes of this section may be the date as of which the fiduciary calculates the value of the assets if that date is reasonably near the date on which assets are actually distributed.

(c) If a fiduciary does not distribute all of the collected but undistributed net income to each person as of a distribution date, the fiduciary shall maintain appropriate records showing the interest of each beneficiary in that net income.

(d) A fiduciary may apply the rules in this section, to the extent that the fiduciary considers it appropriate, to net gain or loss realized after the date of death or terminating event or earlier distribution date from the disposition of a principal asset if this section applies to the income from the asset.

Added by Acts 2003, 78ᵗʰ Leg., ch. 659, § 1, eff. Jan. 1, 2004.

Subchapter C. Apportionment at Beginning and End of Income Interest

Statutes in Context
Subchapter C

Subchapter C explains the amounts to which an income beneficiary is entitled both when the trust begins and when the trust terminates. Note that inter vivos and testamentary trusts have different rules. In addition, the applicable rule may depend on the precise type of asset involved (e.g., a periodic payment such as rent or interest, a corporate distribution, etc.).

§ 116.101. When Right to Income Begins and Ends

(a) An income beneficiary is entitled to net income from the date on which the income interest begins. An income interest begins on the date specified in the terms of the trust or, if no date is specified, on the date an asset becomes subject to a trust or successive income interest.

(b) An asset becomes subject to a trust:

(1) on the date it is transferred to the trust in the case of an asset that is transferred to a trust during the transferor's life;

(2) on the date of a testator's death in the case of an asset that becomes subject to a trust by reason of a will, even if there is an intervening period of administration of the testator's estate; or

(3) on the date of an individual's death in the case of an asset that is transferred to a fiduciary by a third party because of the individual's death.

(c) An asset becomes subject to a successive income interest on the day after the preceding income interest ends, as determined under Subsection (d), even if there is an intervening period of administration to wind up the preceding income interest.

(d) An income interest ends on the day before an income beneficiary dies or another terminating event occurs, or on the last day of a period during which there is no beneficiary to whom a trustee may distribute income.

Added by Acts 2003, 78ᵗʰ Leg., ch. 659, § 1, eff. Jan. 1, 2004.

§ 116.102. Apportionment of Receipts and Disbursements when Decedent Dies or Income Interest Begins

(a) A trustee shall allocate an income receipt or disbursement other than one to which Section 116.051(1) applies to principal if its due date occurs before a decedent dies in the case of an estate or before an income interest begins in the case of a trust or successive income interest.

(b) A trustee shall allocate an income receipt or disbursement to income if its due date occurs on or after the date on which a decedent dies or an income interest begins and it is a periodic due date. An income receipt or disbursement must be treated as accruing from day to day if its due date is not periodic or it has no due date. The portion of the receipt or disbursement accruing before the date on which a decedent dies or an income interest begins must be allocated to principal and the balance must be allocated to income.

(c) An item of income or an obligation is due on the date the payer is required to make a payment. If a payment date is not stated, there is no due date for the purposes of this chapter. Distributions to shareholders or other owners from an entity to which Section 116.151 applies are deemed to be due on the date fixed by the entity for determining who is entitled to receive the distribution or, if no date is fixed, on the declaration date for the distribution. A due date is periodic for receipts or disbursements that must be paid at regular intervals under a lease or an obligation to pay interest or if an entity customarily makes distributions at regular intervals.

Added by Acts 2003, 78ᵗʰ Leg., ch. 659, § 1, eff. Jan. 1, 2004.

§ 116.103. Apportionment When Income Interest Ends

(a) In this section, "undistributed income" means net income received before the date on which an income interest ends. The term does not include an item of income or expense that is due or accrued or net income that has been added or is required to be added to principal under the terms of the trust.

(b) When a mandatory income interest ends, the trustee shall pay to a mandatory income beneficiary who survives that date, or the estate of a deceased mandatory income beneficiary whose death causes the interest to end, the beneficiary's share of the undistributed income that is not disposed of under the terms of the trust unless the beneficiary has an unqualified power to revoke more than five percent of the trust immediately before the income interest ends. In the latter case, the undistributed income from the portion of the trust that may be revoked must be added to principal.

(c) When a trustee's obligation to pay a fixed annuity or a fixed fraction of the value of the trust's assets ends, the trustee shall prorate the final payment if and to the extent required by applicable law to accomplish a purpose of the trust or its settlor relating to income, gift, estate, or other tax requirements.

Added by Acts 2003, 78ᵗʰ Leg., ch. 659, § 1, eff. Jan. 1, 2004.

Subchapter D. Allocation of Receipts During Administration of Trust

Part 1. Receipts from Entities

Statutes in Context
§ 116.151

Section 116.151 explains the allocation of distributions from corporations, partnerships, and other entities. Generally, cash dividends belong to income while stock dividends go to principal. The logic behind the latter rule is that the trust owns the same proportion of the corporation both before and after the stock dividend. The trust may own a greater number of shares but because all other stock holders also own proportionately the same number of additional shares, the stock dividend did not improve the trust's position. Consequently, it would be unfair to allocate stock dividends to income.

---

§ 116.151. Character of Receipts

(a) In this section, "entity" means a corporation, partnership, limited liability company, regulated investment company, real estate investment trust, common trust fund, or any other organization in which a trustee has an interest other than a trust or estate to which Section 116.152 applies, a business or activity to which Section 116.153 applies, or an asset-backed security to which Section 116.178 applies.

(b) Except as otherwise provided in this section, a trustee shall allocate to income money received from an entity.

(c) A trustee shall allocate the following receipts from an entity to principal:

(1) property other than money;

(2) money received in one distribution or a series of related distributions in exchange for part or all of a trust's interest in the entity;

(3) money received in total or partial liquidation of the entity; and

(4) money received from an entity that is a regulated investment company or a real estate investment trust if the money distributed is a capital gain dividend for federal income tax purposes.

(d) Money is received in partial liquidation:

(1) to the extent that the entity, at or near the time of a distribution, indicates that it is a distribution in partial liquidation; or

(2) if the total amount of money and property received in a distribution or series of related distributions is greater than 20 percent of the entity's gross assets, as shown by the entity's year-end financial statements immediately preceding the initial receipt.

(e) Money is not received in partial liquidation, nor may it be taken into account under Subsection (d)(2), to the extent that it does not exceed the amount of income tax that a trustee or beneficiary must pay on taxable income of the entity that distributes the money.

(f) A trustee may rely upon a statement made by an entity about the source or character of a distribution if the statement is made at or near the time of distribution by the entity's board of directors or other person or group of persons authorized to exercise powers to pay money or transfer property comparable to those of a corporation's board of directors.

Added by Acts 2003, 78ᵗʰ Leg., ch. 659, § 1, eff. Jan. 1, 2004.

§ 116.152. Distribution from Trust or Estate

A trustee shall allocate to income an amount received as a distribution of income from a trust or an estate in which the trust has an interest other than a purchased interest, and shall allocate to principal an amount received as a distribution of principal from such a trust or estate. If a trustee purchases an interest in a trust that is an investment entity, or a decedent or donor transfers an interest in such a trust to a trustee, Section 116.151 or 116.178 applies to a receipt from the trust.

Added by Acts 2003, 78ᵗʰ Leg., ch. 659, § 1, eff. Jan. 1, 2004.

Statutes in Context
§ 116.153

A trustee may maintain separate accounting records to determine the income of trust property which is held as a business or farm under § 116.153. Instead of using the UPIA rules, the trustee computes income in accordance with generally accepted accounting principles (GAAP). The trustee may wish to hire an accountant or CPA to assist in this process. See § 113.018.

---

§ 116.153. Business and Other Activities Conducted by Trustee

(a) If a trustee who conducts a business or other activity determines that it is in the best interest of all the beneficiaries to account separately for the business or activity instead of accounting for it as part of the trust's general accounting records, the trustee may maintain separate accounting records for its transactions, whether or not its assets are segregated from other trust assets.

(b) A trustee who accounts separately for a business or other activity may determine the extent to which its net cash receipts must be retained for working capital, the acquisition or replacement of fixed assets, and other reasonably foreseeable needs of the business or activity, and the extent to which the remaining net cash receipts are accounted for as principal or income in the trust's general accounting records. If a trustee sells assets of the business or other activity, other than in the ordinary course of the business or activity, the trustee shall account for the net amount received as principal in the trust's general accounting records to the extent the trustee determines that the amount received is no longer required in the conduct of the business.

(c) Activities for which a trustee may maintain separate accounting records include:

(1) retail, manufacturing, service, and other traditional business activities;

(2) farming;

(3) raising and selling livestock and other animals;

(4) management of rental properties;

(5) extraction of minerals and other natural resources;

(6) timber operations; and

(7) activities to which Section 116.177 applies.

Added by Acts 2003, 78ᵗʰ Leg., ch. 659, § 1, eff. Jan. 1, 2004.

Part 2.   *Receipts Not Normally Apportioned*

Statutes in Context
§ 116.161

Section 116.161 enumerates the receipts which are considered principal. Note that when the trustee sells an asset, both the return of the investment and the profit (capital gain) are allocated to principal. See § 116.161(2).

---

§ 116.161.   Principal Receipts

A trustee shall allocate to principal:

(1) to the extent not allocated to income under this chapter, assets received from a transferor during the transferor's lifetime, a decedent's estate, a trust with a terminating income interest, or a payer under a contract naming the trust or its trustee as beneficiary;

(2) money or other property received from the sale, exchange, liquidation, or change in form of a principal asset, including realized profit, subject to this subchapter;

(3) amounts recovered from third parties to reimburse the trust because of disbursements described in Section 116.202(a)(7) or for other reasons to the extent not based on the loss of income;

(4) proceeds of property taken by eminent domain, but a separate award made for the loss of income with respect to an accounting period during which a current income beneficiary had a mandatory income interest is income;

(5) net income received in an accounting period during which there is no beneficiary to whom a trustee may or must distribute income; and

(6) other receipts as provided in Part 3.

Added by Acts 2003, 78ᵗʰ Leg., ch. 659, § 1, eff. Jan. 1, 2004.

Statutes in Context
§ 116.162

Generally, receipts from rental real or personal property are income under § 116.162. The section also explains that certain receipts are principal, such as a refundable security deposit.

---

§ 116.162.   Rental Property

To the extent that a trustee accounts for receipts from rental property pursuant to this section, the trustee shall allocate to income an amount received as rent of real or personal property, including an amount received for cancellation or renewal of a lease. An amount received as a refundable deposit, including a security deposit or a deposit that is to be applied as rent for future periods, must be added to principal and held subject to the terms of the lease and is not available for distribution to a beneficiary until the trustee's

748

contractual obligations have been satisfied with respect to that amount.

Added by Acts 2003, 78ᵗʰ Leg., ch. 659, § 1, eff. Jan. 1, 2004.

Statutes in Context
§ 116.163

The trustee should allocate interest received on money lent (e.g., a certificate of deposit) to income under § 116.163. In a change from prior law, a trustee no longer may allot to income the increase in value of a bond which pays no interest but appreciates in value (e.g., U.S. Series E savings bonds and other zero-coupon bonds) unless its maturity date is within one year after acquisition.

---

§ 116.163. Obligation to Pay Money

(a) An amount received as interest, whether determined at a fixed, variable, or floating rate, on an obligation to pay money to the trustee, including an amount received as consideration for prepaying principal, must be allocated to income without any provision for amortization of premium.

(b) A trustee shall allocate to principal an amount received from the sale, redemption, or other disposition of an obligation to pay money to the trustee more than one year after it is purchased or acquired by the trustee, including an obligation whose purchase price or value when it is acquired is less than its value at maturity. If the obligation matures within one year after it is purchased or acquired by the trustee, an amount received in excess of its purchase price or its value when acquired by the trust must be allocated to income.

(c) This section does not apply to an obligation to which Section 116.172, 116.173, 116.174, 116.175, 116.177, or 116.178 applies.

Added by Acts 2003, 78ᵗʰ Leg., ch. 659, § 1, eff. Jan. 1, 2004.

Statutes in Context
§ 116.164

Section 116.164 provides that life insurance proceeds are generally allocated to principal.

---

§ 116.164. Insurance Policies and Similar Contracts

(a) Except as otherwise provided in Subsection (b), a trustee shall allocate to principal the proceeds of a life insurance policy or other contract in which the trust or its trustee is named as beneficiary, including a contract that insures the trust or its trustee to a trust asset. The trustee shall allocate dividends on an insurance policy to income if the premiums on the policy are paid from income, and to principal if the premiums are paid from principal.

(b) A trustee shall allocate to income proceeds of a contract that insures the trustee against loss of occupancy or other use by an income beneficiary, loss of income, or, subject to Section 116.153, loss of profits from a business.

(c) This section does not apply to a contract to which Section 116.172 applies.

Added by Acts 2003, 78ᵗʰ Leg., ch. 659, § 1, eff. Jan. 1, 2004.

Part 3. Receipts Normally Apportioned

Statutes in Context
§ 116.171

Under many circumstances, § 116.171 frees the trustee from the obligation of allocating insubstantial amounts. Instead, the entire amount is allocated to principal. The section, however, does not define "insubstantial." Thus, a $1,000 receipt could be substantial for some trusts but insubstantial for others depending on the size of the trust corpus.

---

§ 116.171. Insubstantial Allocations Not Required

If a trustee determines that an allocation between principal and income required by Section 116.172, 116.173, 116.174, 116.175, or 116.178 is insubstantial, the trustee may allocate the entire amount to principal unless one of the circumstances described in Section 116.005(c) applies to the allocation. This power may be exercised by a cotrustee in the circumstances described in Section 116.005(d) and may be released for the reasons and in the manner described in Section 116.005(e).

Added by Acts 2003, 78ᵗʰ Leg., ch. 659, § 1, eff. Jan. 1, 2004.

Statutes in Context
§ 116.172

Section § 116.172 provides guidance for a trustee when allocating receipts from deferred compensation plans, annuities, and similar arrangements such as IRAs. Generally, each year, receipts are allocated to income until they total 4 percent of the asset's fair market value. Amounts in excess of 4 percent are allocated to principal. This plan, however, is problematic given Rev. Ruling 2006-26 which indicates that if this type of provision controls, the qualified plan or IRA may not qualify for marital deduction treatment. Accordingly, the 2009 Legislature amended § 116.172 to include a marital deduction savings clause which, in summary, requires the trustee to determine the internal income of these assets which qualify for the marital deduction.

§ 116.172. Deferred Compensation, Annuities, and Similar Payments

(a) In this section:

(1) "Future payment asset" means the asset from which a payment is derived.

(2) "Payment" means a payment that a trustee may receive over a fixed number of years or during the life of one or more individuals because of services rendered or property transferred to the payer in exchange for future payments. The term includes a payment made in money or property from the payer's general assets or from a separate fund created by the payer.

(3) "Separate fund" includes a private or commercial annuity, an individual retirement account, and a pension, profit-sharing, stock-bonus, or stock-ownership plan.

(b) To the extent that the payer characterizes a payment as interest or a dividend or a payment made in lieu of interest or a dividend, a trustee shall allocate it to income. The trustee shall allocate to principal the balance of the payment and any other payment received in the same accounting period that is not characterized as interest, a dividend, or an equivalent payment.

(c) If no part of a payment is characterized as interest, a dividend, or an equivalent payment, and all or part of the payment is required to be made, a trustee shall allocate to income the part of the payment that does not exceed an amount equal to:

(1) four percent of the fair market value of the future payment asset on the date specified in Subsection (d); less

(2) the total amount that the trustee has allocated to income for all previous payments received from the future payment asset during the same accounting period in which the payment is made.

(d) For purposes of Subsection (c)(1), the determination of the fair market value of a future payment asset is made on the later of:

(1) the date on which the future payment asset first becomes subject to the trust; or

(2) the last day of the accounting period of the trust that immediately precedes the accounting period during which the payment is received.

(e) For each accounting period a payment is received, the amount determined under Subsection (c)(1) must be prorated on a daily basis unless the determination of the fair market value of a future payment asset is made under Subsection (d)(2) and is for an accounting period of 365 days or more.

(f) A trustee shall allocate to principal the part of the payment described by Subsection (c) that is not allocated to income.

(g) If no part of a payment is required to be made or the payment received is the entire amount to which the trustee is entitled, the trustee shall allocate the entire payment to principal. For purposes of Subsection (c) and this subsection, a payment is not "required to be made" to the extent that it is made only because the trustee exercises a right of withdrawal.

(h) Subsections (j) and (k) apply and Subsections (b) and (c) do not apply in determining the allocation of a payment made from a separate fund to:

(1) a trust to which an election to qualify for a marital deduction under Section 2056(b)(7), Internal Revenue Code of 1986, has been made; or

(2) a trust that qualifies for the marital deduction under Section 2056(b)(5), Internal Revenue Code of 1986.

(i) Subsections (h), (j), and (k) do not apply if and to the extent that a series of payments would, without the application of Subsection (h), qualify for the marital deduction under Section 2056(b)(7)(C), Internal Revenue Code of 1986.

(j) The trustee shall determine the internal income of the separate fund for the accounting period as if the separate fund were a trust subject to this code. On request of the surviving spouse, the trustee shall demand of the person administering the separate fund that this internal income be distributed to the trust. The trustee shall allocate a payment from the separate fund to income to the extent of the internal income of the separate fund, and the balance to the principal. On request of the surviving spouse, the trustee shall allocate principal to income to the extent the internal income of the separate fund exceeds payments made to the trust during the accounting period from the separate fund.

(k) If the trustee cannot determine the internal income of the separate fund but can determine the value of the separate fund, the internal income of the separate fund shall be four percent of the fund's value, according to the most recent statement of value preceding the beginning of the accounting period. If the trustee can determine neither the internal income of the separate fund nor the fund's value, the internal income of the fund shall be the product of the interest rate and the present value of the expected future payments, as determined under Section 7520, Internal Revenue Code of 1986, for the month preceding the accounting period for which the computation is made.

Added by Acts 2003, 78th Leg., ch. 659, § 1, eff. Jan. 1, 2004. Subsecs. (c), (d) amended by Acts 2005, 79th Leg., ch. 148, § 26, eff. Jan. 1, 2006. Acts 2007, 80th Leg., ch. 451, § 13, eff. Sept. 1, 2007. Subsec. (a) amended by Acts 2009, 81st Leg., ch. 672, § 8, eff. Sept. 1, 2009; Subsec. (h) amended and subsecs. (i), (j), (k) added by Acts 2009, 81st Leg., ch. 672, § 9, eff. Sept. 1, 2009.

Statutes in Context
§ 116.173

A liquidating or wasting asset is one which goes down in value as it is used to produce income beyond what would be considered mere depreciation from normal use and age. For example, the patent on the 8-track tape was very valuable in the 1970s but has little value today.

Likewise, a royalty interest in today's blockbuster motion picture may have little value 50 years from now. The trustee needs to allocate a portion of the proceeds from liquidating assets to principal to compensate for the depletion of the principal which occurs as the proceeds are generated. Section 116.173 governs assets such as leaseholds, patents, copyrights, and royalties. The trustee must allocate 10 percent of each receipt to income and the remaining 90 percent to principal. This allocation is significantly different from prior Texas law which provided that receipts up to 5 percent of the asset's value each year were income with any excess being principal.

§ 116.173. Liquidating Asset

(a) In this section, "liquidating asset" means an asset whose value will diminish or terminate because the asset is expected to produce receipts for a period of limited duration. The term includes a leasehold, patent, copyright, royalty right, and right to receive payments during a period of more than one year under an arrangement that does not provide for the payment of interest on the unpaid balance. The term does not include a payment subject to Section 116.172, resources subject to Section 116.174, timber subject to Section 116.175, an activity subject to Section 116.177, an asset subject to Section 116.178, or any asset for which the trustee establishes a reserve for depreciation under Section 116.203.

(b) A trustee shall allocate to income 10 percent of the receipts from a liquidating asset and the balance to principal.

(c) The trustee may allocate a receipt from any interest in a liquidating asset the trust owns on January 1, 2004, in the manner provided by this chapter or in any lawful manner used by the trustee before January 1, 2004, to make the same allocation.

Added by Acts 2003, 78th Leg., ch. 659, § 1. eff. Jan. 1, 2004.

Statutes in Context
§ 116.174

Traditionally under Texas law, oil and gas royalties were allocated 72.5 percent to income and 27.5 percent to principal. These percentages were based on former federal income tax rules which used these percentages for depletion allowances. The UPIA gives only 10 percent to income with the remaining 90 percent to principal. (Note how unfair this would be to a beneficiary who is receiving 72.5 percent and then discovers that the new law cuts the percentage way down to 10 percent.) Texas deviates from the UPIA in § 116.174 by requiring the trustee to allocate these receipts "equitably." In addition, the trustee may use the prior allocation percentages if the trust owned the natural resource on January 1, 2004.

It is irrelevant whether or not any natural resources were being taken from the land at the time the property was placed in trust. In other words, the open mine doctrine is not followed in a trust context. See § 116.174(c).

§ 116.174. Minerals, Water, and Other Natural Resources

(a) To the extent that a trustee accounts for receipts from an interest in minerals or other natural resources pursuant to this section, the trustee shall allocate them as follows:

(1) If received as delay rental or annual rent on a lease, a receipt must be allocated to income.

(2) If received from a production payment, a receipt must be allocated to income if and to the extent that the agreement creating the production payment provides a factor for interest or its equivalent. The balance must be allocated to principal.

(3) If received as a royalty, shut-in-well payment, take-or-pay payment, or bonus, the trustee shall allocate the receipt equitably.

(4) If an amount is received from a working interest or any other interest not provided for in Subdivision (1), (2), or (3), the trustee must allocate the receipt equitably.

(b) An amount received on account of an interest in water that is renewable must be allocated to income. If the water is not renewable, the trustee must allocate the receipt equitably.

(c) This chapter applies whether or not a decedent or donor was extracting minerals, water, or other natural resources before the interest became subject to the trust.

(d) The trustee may allocate a receipt from any interest in minerals, water, or other natural resources the trust owns on January 1, 2004, in the manner provided by this chapter or in any lawful manner used by the trustee before January 1, 2004, to make the same allocation. The trustee shall allocate a receipt from any interest in minerals, water, or other natural resources acquired by the trust after January 1, 2004, in the manner provided by this chapter.

(e) An allocation of a receipt under this section is presumed to be equitable if the amount allocated to principal is equal to the amount allowed by the Internal Revenue Code of 1986 as a deduction for depletion of the interest.

Added by Acts 2003, 78th Leg., ch. 659, § 1, eff. Jan. 1, 2004. Subsec. (a) amended by Acts 2007, 80th Leg., ch. 451, § 14, eff. Sept. 1, 2007.

Statutes in Context
§ 116.175

Timber is unlike other natural resources because it is renewable; the trees will grow back. The time it will take the trees to regrow, however, depends on the type of trees. For example, some varieties of pine trees may be ready to harvest in 20 years while other trees such as redwoods may take over a century. Consequently, it is difficult to create a precise allocation rule. Section 116.175 explains that receipts are income if the timber removed does not exceed the rate of new growth but receipts become principal if they are from timber in excess of the regrowth rate. This provision provides more guidance than prior law which merely instructed the trustee to do what was reasonable and equitable.

§ 116.175. Timber

(a) To the extent that a trustee accounts for receipts from the sale of timber and related products pursuant to this section, the trustee shall allocate the net receipts:

(1) to income to the extent that the amount of timber removed from the land does not exceed the rate of growth of the timber during the accounting periods in which a beneficiary has a mandatory income interest;

(2) to principal to the extent that the amount of timber removed from the land exceeds the rate of growth of the timber or the net receipts are from the sale of standing timber;

(3) to or between income and principal if the net receipts are from the lease of timberland or from a contract to cut timber from land owned by a trust, by determining the amount of timber removed from the land under the lease or contract and applying the rules in Subdivisions (1) and (2); or

(4) to principal to the extent that advance payments, bonuses, and other payments are not allocated pursuant to Subdivision (1), (2), or (3).

(b) In determining net receipts to be allocated pursuant to Subsection (a), a trustee shall deduct and transfer to principal a reasonable amount for depletion.

(c) This chapter applies whether or not a decedent or transferor was harvesting timber from the property before it became subject to the trust.

(d) If a trust owns an interest in timberland on January 1, 2004, the trustee may allocate a net receipt from the sale of timber and related products in the manner provided by this chapter or in any lawful manner used by the trustee before January 1, 2004, to make the same allocation. If the trust acquires an interest in timberland after January 1, 2004, the trustee shall allocate net receipts from the sale of timber and related products in the manner provided by this chapter.

Added by Acts 2003, 78th Leg., ch. 659, § 1, eff. Jan. 1, 2004.

Statutes in Context
§ 116.176

The trustee should not retain property that does not earn income absent express permission in the trust instrument unless it is prudent to retain

it under Chapter 117. Although some nonproductive assets, such as collectible items and unleased land, may have the potential of significantly appreciating in value, the retention of nonproductive property usually would violate the trustee's duty of fairness to the income beneficiaries. Under prior law, the trustee was required to promptly sell underproductive property which meant property that did not earn at least 1 percent of its value per year, assuming the trustee was under a duty to sell either according to the terms of the trust or because it was imprudent to retain the property. Once the trustee sold the underproductive property, the trustee was often required to allocate a portion of the sale proceeds to income as delayed income to make up for the income the trust should have earned had this portion of the trust been placed in income-producing investments.

Section 116.176(b) dispenses with the allocation of delayed income. Now, the proceeds from the sale or other disposition of a trust asset are principal without regard to the amount of income the asset produced. However, § 116.176(a) does retain the duty to make property productive for marital deduction trusts to make certain they continue to qualify for favored tax treatment.

§ 116.176. Property Not Productive of Income

(a) If a marital deduction is allowed for all or part of a trust whose assets consist substantially of property that does not provide the spouse with sufficient income from or use of the trust assets, and if the amounts that the trustee transfers from principal to income under Section 116.005 and distributes to the spouse from principal pursuant to the terms of the trust are insufficient to provide the spouse with the beneficial enjoyment required to obtain the marital deduction, the spouse may require the trustee to make property productive of income, convert property within a reasonable time, or exercise the power conferred by Section 116.005(a). The trustee may decide which action or combination of actions to take.

(b) In cases not governed by Subsection (a), proceeds from the sale or other disposition of an asset are principal without regard to the amount of income the asset produces during any accounting period.

Added by Acts 2003, 78th Leg., ch. 659, § 1, eff. Jan. 1, 2004.

§ 116.177. Derivatives and Options

(a) In this section, "derivative" means a contract or financial instrument or a combination of contracts and financial instruments which gives a trust the right or obligation to participate in some or all changes in the price of a tangible or intangible asset or group of assets, or changes in a rate, an index of prices or rates, or other market indicator for an asset or a group of assets.

(b) To the extent that a trustee does not account under Section 116.153 for transactions in derivatives, the trustee shall allocate to principal receipts from and disbursements made in connection with those transactions.

(c) If a trustee grants an option to buy property from the trust, whether or not the trust owns the property when the option is granted, grants an option that permits another person to sell property to the trust, or acquires an option to buy property for the trust or an option to sell an asset owned by the trust, and the trustee or other owner of the asset is required to deliver the asset if the option is exercised, an amount received for granting the option must be allocated to principal. An amount paid to acquire the option must be paid from principal. A gain or loss realized upon the exercise of an option, including an option granted to a settlor of the trust for services rendered, must be allocated to principal.

Added by Acts 2003, 78th Leg., ch. 659, § 1, eff. Jan. 1, 2004.

§ 116.178. Asset-Backed Securities

(a) In this section, "asset-backed security" means an asset whose value is based upon the right it gives the owner to receive distributions from the proceeds of financial assets that provide collateral for the security. The term includes an asset that gives the owner the right to receive from the collateral financial assets only the interest or other current return or only the proceeds other than interest or current return. The term does not include an asset to which Section 116.151 or 116.172 applies.

(b) If a trust receives a payment from interest or other current return and from other proceeds of the collateral financial assets, the trustee shall allocate to income the portion of the payment which the payer identifies as being from interest or other current return and shall allocate the balance of the payment to principal.

(c) If a trust receives one or more payments in exchange for the trust's entire interest in an asset-backed security in one accounting period, the trustee shall allocate the payments to principal. If a payment is one of a series of payments that will result in the liquidation of the trust's interest in the security over more than one accounting period, the trustee shall allocate 10 percent of the payment to income and the balance to principal.

Added by Acts 2003, 78th Leg., ch. 659, § 1, eff. Jan. 1, 2004.

Subchapter E. Allocation of Disbursements During Administration of Trust

---

Statutes in Context
§ 116.201

Section 116.201 enumerates disbursements which are deducted from income. The 2013 Legislature made a significant change with respect to the allocation of trustee compensation. Rather than being required to allocate trustee compensation equally between income and principal, the trustee may now allocate in any manner as long as it is consistent with the trustee's fiduciary duties.

---

§ 116.201. Disbursements from Income

A trustee shall make the following disbursements from income to the extent that they are not disbursements to which Section 116.051(2)(B) or (C) applies:

(1) one-half of the regular compensation of the trustee and of any person providing investment advisory or custodial services to the trustee unless, consistent with the trustee's fiduciary duties, the trustee determines that a different portion, none, or all of the compensation should be allocated to income;

(2) one-half of all expenses for accountings, judicial proceedings, or other matters that involve both the income and remainder interests;

(3) all of the other ordinary expenses incurred in connection with the administration, management, or preservation of trust property and the distribution of income, including interest, ordinary repairs, regularly recurring taxes assessed against principal, and expenses of a proceeding or other matter that concerns primarily the income interest; and

(4) recurring premiums on insurance covering the loss of a principal asset or the loss of income from or use of the asset.

Added by Acts 2003, 78th Leg., ch. 659, § 1, eff. Jan. 1, 2004. Amended by Acts 2013, 83rd Leg., ch. 1337, § 2, eff. Sept. 1, 2013.

Statutes in Context
§ 116.202

Section 116.202 enumerates the expenditures which the trustee must charge against the principal of the trust.

---

§ 116.202. Disbursements from Principal

(a) A trustee shall make the following disbursements from principal:

(1) the remaining one-half of the disbursements described in Section 116.201(1) unless, consistent with the trustee's fiduciary duties, the trustee determines that a different portion, none, or all of those disbursements should be allocated to income, in which case that portion of the disbursements that

are not allocated to income shall be allocated to principal;

(1-a) the remaining one-half of the disbursements described in Section 116.201(2);

(2) all of the trustee's compensation calculated on principal as a fee for acceptance, distribution, or termination, and disbursements made to prepare property for sale;

(3) payments on the principal of a trust debt;

(4) expenses of a proceeding that concerns primarily principal, including a proceeding to construe the trust or to protect the trust or its property;

(5) premiums paid on a policy of insurance not described in Section 116.201(4) of which the trust is the owner and beneficiary;

(6) estate, inheritance, and other transfer taxes, including penalties, apportioned to the trust; and

(7) disbursements related to environmental matters, including reclamation, assessing environmental conditions, remedying and removing environmental contamination, monitoring remedial activities and the release of substances, preventing future releases of substances, collecting amounts from persons liable or potentially liable for the costs of those activities, penalties imposed under environmental laws or regulations and other payments made to comply with those laws or regulations, statutory or common law claims by third parties, and defending claims based on environmental matters.

(b) If a principal asset is encumbered with an obligation that requires income from that asset to be paid directly to the creditor, the trustee shall transfer from principal to income an amount equal to the income paid to the creditor in reduction of the principal balance of the obligation.

Added by Acts 2003, 78th Leg., ch. 659, § 1, eff. Jan. 1, 2004. Subsection (a) amended by Acts 2013, 83rd Leg., ch. 1337, § 3, eff. Sept. 1, 2013.

Statutes in Context
§ 116.203

A trustee may make transfers from income to principal to compensate for the depreciation of the principal. Under prior law, however, a trustee was required to make a reasonable allowance for depreciation.

---

§ 116.203. Transfers from Income to Principal for Depreciation

(a) In this section, "depreciation" means a reduction in value due to wear, tear, decay, corrosion, or gradual obsolescence of a fixed asset having a useful life of more than one year.

(b) A trustee may transfer to principal a reasonable amount of the net cash receipts from a principal asset

that is subject to depreciation, but may not transfer any amount for depreciation:

(1) of that portion of real property used or available for use by a beneficiary as a residence or of tangible personal property held or made available for the personal use or enjoyment of a beneficiary;

(2) during the administration of a decedent's estate; or

(3) under this section if the trustee is accounting under Section 116.153 for the business or activity in which the asset is used.

(c) An amount transferred to principal need not be held as a separate fund.

Added by Acts 2003, 78th Leg., ch. 659, § 1, eff. Jan. 1, 2004.

§ 116.204. Transfers from Income to Reimburse Principal

(a) If a trustee makes or expects to make a principal disbursement described in this section, the trustee may transfer an appropriate amount from income to principal in one or more accounting periods to reimburse principal or to provide a reserve for future principal disbursements.

(b) Principal disbursements to which Subsection (a) applies include the following, but only to the extent that the trustee has not been and does not expect to be reimbursed by a third party:

(1) an amount chargeable to income but paid from principal because it is unusually large, including extraordinary repairs;

(2) a capital improvement to a principal asset, whether in the form of changes to an existing asset or the construction of a new asset, including special assessments;

(3) disbursements made to prepare property for rental, including tenant allowances, leasehold improvements, and broker's commissions;

(4) periodic payments on an obligation secured by a principal asset to the extent that the amount transferred from income to principal for depreciation is less than the periodic payments; and

(5) disbursements described in Section 116.202(a)(7).

(c) If the asset whose ownership gives rise to the disbursements becomes subject to a successive income interest after an income interest ends, a trustee may continue to transfer amounts from income to principal as provided in Subsection (a).

Added by Acts 2003, 78th Leg., ch. 659, § 1, eff. Jan. 1, 2004.

Statutes in Context
§ 116.205

Section 116.205 governs whether taxes are paid by income or principal. For example, regular income taxes are charged against income while a capital gains tax, although called an income tax, is charged against principal.

§ 116.205. Income Taxes

(a) A tax required to be paid by a trustee based on receipts allocated to income must be paid from income.

(b) A tax required to be paid by a trustee based on receipts allocated to principal must be paid from principal, even if the tax is called an income tax by the taxing authority.

(c) A tax required to be paid by a trustee on the trust's share of an entity's taxable income must be paid:

(1) from income to the extent that receipts from the entity are allocated only to income;

(2) from principal to the extent that receipts from the entity are allocated only to principal;

(3) proportionately from principal and income to the extent that receipts from the entity are allocated to both principal and income; and

(4) from principal to the extent that the tax exceeds the total receipts from the entity.

(d) After applying the other provisions of this section, the trustee shall adjust income or principal receipts to the extent that the trust's taxes are reduced because the trust receives a deduction for payments made to a beneficiary.

Added by Acts 2003, 78th Leg., ch. 659, § 1, eff. Jan. 1, 2004. Subsecs. (c) & (d) amended by Acts 2011, 82nd Leg., ch. 657, § 8, eff. Sept. 1, 2011.

Statutes in Context
§ 116.206

Section 116.206 provides for equitable adjustments between principal and income because of taxes under enumerated circumstances.

§ 116.206. Adjustments Between Principal and Income Because of Taxes

(a) A fiduciary may make adjustments between principal and income to offset the shifting of economic interests or tax benefits between income beneficiaries and remainder beneficiaries which arise from:

(1) elections and decisions, other than those described in Subsection (b), that the fiduciary makes from time to time regarding tax matters;

(2) an income tax or any other tax that is imposed upon the fiduciary or a beneficiary as a result of a transaction involving or a distribution from the estate or trust; or

(3) the ownership by an estate or trust of an interest in an entity whose taxable income, whether or not distributed, is includable in the taxable income of the estate, trust, or a beneficiary.

(b) If the amount of an estate tax marital deduction or charitable contribution deduction is reduced because a fiduciary deducts an amount paid from principal for income tax purposes instead of deducting it for estate tax purposes, and as a result estate taxes paid from principal are increased and income taxes paid by an estate, trust, or beneficiary are decreased, each estate, trust, or beneficiary that benefits from the decrease in income tax shall reimburse the principal from which the increase in estate tax is paid. The total reimbursement must equal the increase in the estate tax to the extent that the principal used to pay the increase would have qualified for a marital deduction or charitable contribution deduction but for the payment. The proportionate share of the reimbursement for each estate, trust, or beneficiary whose income taxes are reduced must be the same as its proportionate share of the total decrease in income tax. An estate or trust shall reimburse principal from income.

Added by Acts 2003, 78th Leg., ch. 659, § 1, eff. Jan. 1, 2004.

Chapter 117. Uniform Prudent Investor Act

Statutes in Context
Chapter 117

The trustee is responsible for investing trust property to make it productive while simultaneously protecting that property from undue risk. A trustee is not an insurer of the trust's success and consequently is personally liable for losses only if the trustee's conduct falls beneath the applicable standard of care.

Until January 1, 2004, the propriety of the trustee's investments were judged according to the prudent person standard. A trustee was required to exercise the degree of care and level of skill that a person of ordinary prudence would exercise in dealing with that person's own property. The trustee was required to consider three main factors in selecting an investment. First, the trustee examined the safety of the investment. Risky or speculative investments were not allowed. Second, the trustee determined the investment's potential to appreciate in value. Third, the trustee evaluated the income which the investment was expected to generate. Prior law also contained a portfolio-type provision in that the determination of whether a trustee acted prudently was based on a consideration of how all the assets of the trust were invested collectively rather than by examining each investment individually.

The Texas version of the Uniform Prudent Investor Act took effect on January 1, 2004. Under this "total asset management" approach, the appropriateness of investments is based on the performance of the entire trust portfolio. A prudent investor could decide that the best investment strategy is to select some assets that appreciate and others that earn income, as well as some investments that are rock-solid balanced with some that have a reasonable degree of risk. In selecting investments, the trustee should incorporate risk and return objectives that are reasonably suited to the trust. Different trusts may call for different investment approaches depending on the trustee's abilities, the trust's purposes, the beneficiary's needs, and other circumstances. See § 117.004.

§ 117.001. Short Title

This chapter may be cited as the "Uniform Prudent Investor Act."

Added by Acts 2003, 78th Leg., ch. 1103, § 1, eff. Jan. 1, 2004.

§ 117.002. Uniformity of Application and Construction

This chapter shall be applied and construed to effectuate its general purpose to make uniform the law with respect to the subject of this chapter among the states enacting it.

Added by Acts 2003, 78th Leg., ch. 1103, § 1, eff. Jan. 1, 2004.

Statutes in Context
§ 117.003

The prudent investor rule is the default standard of care for trustees under § 117.003(a). However, § 117.003(b) authorizes the settlor to provide for a higher or lower standard of care.

---

§ 117.003. Prudent Investor Rule

(a) Except as otherwise provided in Subsection (b), a trustee who invests and manages trust assets owes a duty to the beneficiaries of the trust to comply with the prudent investor rule set forth in this chapter.

(b) The prudent investor rule, a default rule, may be expanded, restricted, eliminated, or otherwise altered by the provisions of a trust. A trustee is not liable to a beneficiary to the extent that the trustee acted in reasonable reliance on the provisions of the trust.

Added by Acts 2003, 78th Leg., ch. 1103, § 1, eff. Jan. 1, 2004.

Statutes in Context
§ 117.004

Section 117.004 is the key provision which explains how the prudent investor rule operates. Subsection (c) enumerates the factors a trustee must consider when making investment and management decisions. Note that no particular type of property is categorically improper and that some risk or speculation may be prudent. See

§ 117.004(e). A trustee who has or represents as having more skill than a prudent investor has a duty to exercise those additional skills. See § 117.004(f).

---

§ 117.004. Standard of Care; Portfolio Strategy; Risk and Return Objectives

(a) A trustee shall invest and manage trust assets as a prudent investor would, by considering the purposes, terms, distribution requirements, and other circumstances of the trust. In satisfying this standard, the trustee shall exercise reasonable care, skill, and caution.

(b) A trustee's investment and management decisions respecting individual assets must be evaluated not in isolation but in the context of the trust portfolio as a whole and as a part of an overall investment strategy having risk and return objectives reasonably suited to the trust.

(c) Among circumstances that a trustee shall consider in investing and managing trust assets are such of the following as are relevant to the trust or its beneficiaries:

(1) general economic conditions;

(2) the possible effect of inflation or deflation;

(3) the expected tax consequences of investment decisions or strategies;

(4) the role that each investment or course of action plays within the overall trust portfolio, which may include financial assets, interests in closely held enterprises, tangible and intangible personal property, and real property;

(5) the expected total return from income and the appreciation of capital;

(6) other resources of the beneficiaries;

(7) needs for liquidity, regularity of income, and preservation or appreciation of capital; and

(8) an asset's special relationship or special value, if any, to the purposes of the trust or to one or more of the beneficiaries.

(d) A trustee shall make a reasonable effort to verify facts relevant to the investment and management of trust assets.

(e) Except as otherwise provided by and subject to this subtitle, a trustee may invest in any kind of property or type of investment consistent with the standards of this chapter.

(f) A trustee who has special skills or expertise, or is named trustee in reliance upon the trustee's representation that the trustee has special skills or expertise, has a duty to use those special skills or expertise.

Added by Acts 2003, 78th Leg., ch. 1103, § 1, eff. Jan. 1, 2004.

Statutes in Context
§ 117.005

Section 117.005 codifies the trustee's duty to diversify to spread the risk so that if one investment goes bad, the entire trust does not suffer. However, the trustee is not required to diversify if the circumstances demonstrate that the purposes of the trust would be better served without diversifying. For example, assume that Settlor created a trust containing Settlor's heirloom jewelry and a 20,000 acre farm that has been in Settlor's family for almost 200 years. At the termination of the trust, all remaining trust property passes to Settlor's children. Should Trustee sell some of this property to create a balanced portfolio of investments? Retaining all trust property in two assets of this type is certainly not a proper diversification. On the other hand, it is reasonable to conclude that Settlor wanted the heirloom jewelry and the farm to remain in the trust so they would pass to Settlor's children and thus Trustee may retain the assets without diversification.

§ 117.005. Diversification

A trustee shall diversify the investments of the trust unless the trustee reasonably determines that, because of special circumstances, the purposes of the trust are better served without diversifying.

Added by Acts 2003, 78th Leg., ch. 1103, § 1, eff. Jan. 1, 2004.

Statutes in Context
§ 117.006

The trustee must review trust assets within a reasonable time after accepting the trust or receiving trust property under § 117.006. The trustee must then bring the trust property into compliance with the prudent investor rule. This is a significant change from prior Texas law which permitted the trustee to retain the initial trust property without diversification and without liability for loss or depreciation.

§ 117.006. Duties at Inception of Trusteeship

Within a reasonable time after accepting a trusteeship or receiving trust assets, a trustee shall review the trust assets and make and implement decisions concerning the retention and disposition of assets, in order to bring the trust portfolio into compliance with the purposes, terms, distribution requirements, and other circumstances of the trust, and with the requirements of this chapter.

Added by Acts 2003, 78th Leg., ch. 1103, § 1, eff. Jan. 1, 2004.

Statutes in Context
§ 117.007

Section 117.007 codifies the principle that the trustee's loyalty is to the beneficiaries. Accordingly, social investing may be problematic, especially if the returns from a "politically correct" investment are lower than from other investments. Social investment refers to the consideration of factors other than the monetary safety of the investments and their potential to earn income and appreciate. Examples of these types of factors include a company's handling of environmental matters, whether a company does business with countries with policies that do not protect human rights, whether a company employs and pays substandard wages to workers in foreign countries, and the political party affiliation of the company's leadership.

§ 117.007. Loyalty

A trustee shall invest and manage the trust assets solely in the interest of the beneficiaries.

Added by Acts 2003, 78th Leg., ch. 1103, § 1, eff. Jan. 1, 2004.

Statutes in Context
§ 117.008

The trustee must act impartially and not favor one beneficiary over another under § 117.008. This is especially important in the context of income and principal allocations under Chapter 116.

§ 117.008. Impartiality

If a trust has two or more beneficiaries, the trustee shall act impartially in investing and managing the trust assets, taking into account any differing interests of the beneficiaries.

Added by Acts 2003, 78th Leg., ch. 1103, § 1, eff. Jan. 1, 2004.

Statutes in Context
§ 117.009

The trustee must minimize investment costs under § 117.009.

§ 117.009. Investment Costs

In investing and managing trust assets, a trustee may only incur costs that are appropriate and reasonable in relation to the assets, the purposes of the trust, and the skills of the trustee.

Added by Acts 2003, 78th Leg., ch. 1103, § 1, eff. Jan. 1, 2004.

Statutes in Context
§ 117.010

A trustee's compliance with the prudent investor rule is measured by the facts and circumstances existing at the time of the trustee's action under § 117.010. In other words, a trustee's conduct is not judged with the benefit of hindsight (no "Monday morning quarterbacking").

§ 117.010. Reviewing Compliance

Compliance with the prudent investor rule is determined in light of the facts and circumstances existing at the time of a trustee's decision or action and not by hindsight.

Added by Acts 2003, 78th Leg., ch. 1103, § 1, eff. Jan. 1, 2004.

Statutes in Context
§ 117.011

The traditional rule regarding delegation of powers is that the trustee may delegate mere ministerial duties but may not delegate discretionary acts. Investment of trust property was deemed a discretionary act and thus was not subject to delegation.

In 1999, Texas altered this rule and allowed the trustee to delegate investment decisions to an investment agent. The statute required the trustee to send written notice to the beneficiaries at least 30 days before entering into an agreement to delegate investment decisions to an investment agent. Generally, the trustee remained responsible for the agent's investment decisions. However, the trustee could have avoided liability for the investment agent's decisions if all of the relatively strenuous criteria specified in the statute were satisfied.

Section 117.011 takes a very different approach. The trustee may delegate any investment or management decision provided a prudent trustee of similar skills could properly delegate under the same circumstances. Of course, the trustee must exercise reasonable care, skill, and caution in selecting and reviewing the agent's actions. In the usual case, the trustee is not liable to the beneficiaries or the trust for the decisions or actions of the agent. See § 117.011(c).

§ 117.011. Delegation of Investment and Management Functions

(a) A trustee may delegate investment and management functions that a prudent trustee of comparable skills could properly delegate under the circumstances. The trustee shall exercise reasonable care, skill, and caution in:

(1) selecting an agent;

(2) establishing the scope and terms of the delegation, consistent with the purposes and terms of the trust; and

(3) periodically reviewing the agent's actions in order to monitor the agent's performance and compliance with the terms of the delegation.

(b) In performing a delegated function, an agent owes a duty to the trust to exercise reasonable care to comply with the terms of the delegation.

(c) A trustee who complies with the requirements of Subsection (a) is not liable to the beneficiaries or to the trust for the decisions or actions of the agent to whom the function was delegated, unless:

(1) the agent is an affiliate of the trustee; or

(2) under the terms of the delegation:

(A) the trustee or a beneficiary of the trust is required to arbitrate disputes with the agent; or

(B) the period for bringing an action by the trustee or a beneficiary of the trust with respect to an agent's actions is shortened from that which is applicable to trustees under the law of this state.

(d) By accepting the delegation of a trust function from the trustee of a trust that is subject to the law of this state, an agent submits to the jurisdiction of the courts of this state.

Added by Acts 2003, 78th Leg., ch. 1103, § 1, eff. Jan. 1, 2004.

Statutes in Context
§ 117.012

Section 117.012 indicates that certain phrases in trust instruments are deemed to trigger the prudent investor standard. Note that some of these phrases which invoke the prudent investor standard clearly appear to invoke a much different standard (e.g., "prudent person rule").

§ 117.012. Language Invoking Standard of Chapter

The following terms or comparable language in the provisions of a trust, unless otherwise limited or modified, authorizes any investment or strategy permitted under this chapter: "investments permissible by law for investment of trust funds," "legal investments," "authorized investments," "using the judgment and care under the circumstances then prevailing that persons of prudence, discretion, and intelligence exercise in the management of their own affairs, not in regard to speculation but in regard to the permanent disposition of their funds, considering the probable income as well as the probable safety of their capital," "prudent man rule," "prudent trustee rule," "prudent person rule," and "prudent investor rule."

Added by Acts 2003, 78th Leg., ch. 1103, § 1, eff. Jan. 1, 2004.

Subtitle C. Miscellaneous Trusts

Chapter 121. Employees' Trusts

Statutes in Context
Chapter 121

Chapter 121 sets forth the special rules which govern pension trusts and death benefits payable under employees' trusts.

Subchapter A. Pension Trusts

§ 121.001. Pension Trusts

(a) For the purposes of this subchapter, a pension trust is an express trust:

(1) containing or relating to property;

(2) created by an employer as part of a stock-bonus plan, pension plan, disability or death benefit plan, or profit-sharing plan for the benefit of some or all of the employer's employees;

(3) to which contributions are made by the employer, by some or all of the employees, or by both; and

(4) created for the principal purpose of distributing to the employees, or the successor to their beneficial interest in the trust, the principal or income, or both, of the property held in trust.

(b) This subchapter applies to a pension trust regardless of when the trust was created.

Acts 1983, 68th Leg., p. 3691, ch. 576, § 1, eff. Jan. 1, 1984.

§ 121.002. Employees of Controlled Corporations

For the purposes of this subchapter, the relationship of employer and employee exists between a corporation and its own employees, and between a corporation and the employees of each other corporation that it controls, by which it is controlled, or with which it is under common control through the exercise by one or more persons of a majority of voting rights in one or more corporations.

Acts 1983, 68th Leg., p. 3691, ch. 576, § 1, eff. Jan. 1, 1984.

§ 121.003. Application of Texas Trust Code [Act]

The Texas Trust Code (Chapters 111 through 117) applies to a pension trust.

Acts 1983, 68th Leg., p. 3691, ch. 576, § 1, eff. Jan. 1, 1984. Amended by Acts 2005, 79th Leg., ch. 148, § 27, eff. Jan. 1, 2006.

§ 121.004. Rule Against Perpetuities

A pension trust may continue for as long as is necessary to accomplish the purposes of the trust and is not invalid under the rule against perpetuities or any other law restricting or limiting the duration of a trust.

Acts 1983, 68th Leg., p. 3691, ch. 576, § 1, eff. Jan. 1, 1984.

§ 121.005. Accumulation of Income

Notwithstanding any law limiting the time during which trust income may be accumulated, the income of a pension trust may be accumulated under the terms of the trust for as long as is necessary to accomplish the purposes of the trust.

Acts 1983, 68th Leg., p. 3692, ch. 576, § 1, eff. Jan. 1, 1984.

Subchapter B. Death Benefits Under Employees' Trusts

§ 121.051. Definitions

(a) In this subchapter:

(1) "Death benefit" means a benefit of any kind, including the proceeds of a life insurance policy or any other payment, in cash or property, under an employees' trust or a retirement account, a contract purchased by an employees' trust or a retirement account, or a retirement-annuity contract that is payable because of an employee's, participant's, or beneficiary's death to or for the benefit of the employee's, participant's, or beneficiary's beneficiary.

(2) "Employee" means a person covered by an employees' trust or a retirement account that provides a death benefit or a person whose interest in an employees' trust or a retirement account has not been fully distributed.

(3) "Employees' trust" means:

(A) a trust forming a part of a stock-bonus, pension, or profit-sharing plan under Section 401, Internal Revenue Code of 1954 (26 U.S.C.A. Sec. 401 (1986));

(B) a pension trust under Chapter 111; and

(C) an employer-sponsored benefit plan or program, or any other retirement savings arrangement, including a pension plan created under Section 3, Employee Retirement Income Security Act of 1974 (29 U.S.C.A. Sec. 1002 (1986)), regardless of whether the plan, program, or arrangement is funded through a trust.

(4) "Individual retirement account" means a trust, custodial arrangement, or annuity under Section 408(a) or (b), Internal Revenue Code of 1954 (26 U.S.C.A. Sec. 408 (1986)).

(5) "Participant" means a person covered by an employees' trust or a retirement account that provides a death benefit or a person whose interest in an employees' trust or a retirement account has not been fully distributed.

(6) "Retirement account" means a retirement-annuity contract, an individual retirement account, a

simplified employee pension, or any other retirement savings arrangement.

(7) "Retirement-annuity contract" means an annuity contract under Section 403, Internal Revenue Code of 1954 (26 U.S.C.A. Sec. 403 (1986)).

(8) "Simplified employee pension" means a trust, custodial arrangement, or annuity under Section 408, Internal Revenue Code of 1954 (26 U.S.C.A. Sec. 408 (1986)).

(9) "Trust" and "trustee" have the meanings assigned by the Texas Trust Code (Chapters 111 through 115), except that "trust" includes any trust, regardless of when it is created.

(b) References to specific provisions of the Internal Revenue Code of 1954 (26 U.S.C.A.) include corresponding provisions of any subsequent federal tax laws.

Acts 1983, 68th Leg., p. 3692, ch. 576, § 1, eff. Jan. 1, 1984. Amended by Acts 1987, 70th Leg., ch. 741, § 3, eff. Aug. 31, 1987.

Statutes in Context
§ 121.052

Section 121.052 permits the employee to pour over the death benefits to a trust. The result is similar to a pour-over will provision under Probate Code § 58a although there are some significant differences. For example, the benefits are governed by the terms of the trust as they exist on the date of the employee's death while testamentary pour-overs are governed by the terms of the trust including amendments made after the testator's death.

§ 121.052. Payment of Death Benefit to Trustee

(a) A death benefit is payable to a trustee of a trust evidenced by a written instrument or declaration existing on the date of an employee's or participant's death, or to a trustee named or to be named as trustee of a trust created under an employee's or participant's will, if the trustee is designated as beneficiary under the plan containing the employees' trust or under the retirement account.

(b) A trustee of a testamentary trust may be designated under Subsection (a) prior to the execution of the will.

(c) A death benefit under a will is not payable until the will is probated.

(d) The trustee shall hold, administer, and dispose of a death benefit payable under this section in accordance with the terms of the trust on the date of the employee's death.

(e) A death benefit is payable to a trustee of a trust created by the will of a person other than the employee if:

(1) the will has been probated at the time of the employee's death; and

(2) the death benefit is payable to the trustee to be held, administered, and disposed of in accordance with the terms of the testamentary trust.

Acts 1983, 68th Leg., p. 3693, ch. 576, § 1, eff. Jan. 1, 1984. Amended by Acts 1987, 70th Leg., ch. 741, § 4, eff. Aug. 31, 1987.

§ 121.053. Validity of Trust Declaration

The validity of a trust agreement or declaration is not affected by:

(1) the absence of a corpus other than the right of the trustee to receive a death benefit as beneficiary;

(2) the employee's reservation of the right to designate another beneficiary of the death benefit; or

(3) the existence of authority to amend, modify, revoke, or terminate the agreement or declaration.

Acts 1983, 68th Leg., p. 3693, ch. 576, § 1, eff. Jan. 1, 1984.

§ 121.054. Unclaimed Benefits

If a trustee does not claim a death benefit on or before the first anniversary of the employee's or participant's death or if satisfactory evidence is provided to a trustee, custodian, other fiduciary, or other obligor of the employees' trust, contract purchased by the employees' trust, or the retirement account before the first anniversary of the employee's or participant's death that there is or will be no trustee to receive the death benefit, the death benefit shall be paid:

(1) according to the beneficiary designation under the plan, trust, contract, or arrangement providing the death benefit under the employees' trust or retirement account; or

(2) if there is no designation in the employees' trust or retirement account, to the personal representative of the deceased employee's or participant's estate.

Acts 1983, 68th Leg., p. 3693, ch. 576, § 1, eff. Jan. 1, 1984. Amended by Acts 1987, 70th Leg., ch. 741, § 5, eff. Aug. 31, 1987.

§ 121.055. Exemption from Taxes and Debts

Unless the trust agreement, declaration of trust, or will provides otherwise, a death benefit payable to a trustee under this subchapter is not:

(1) part of the deceased employee's estate;

(2) subject to the debts of the deceased employee or the employee's estate, or to other charges enforceable against the estate; or

(3) subject to the payment of taxes enforceable against the deceased employee's estate to a greater extent than if the death benefit is payable, free of trust, to a beneficiary other than the executor or administrator of the estate of the employee.

Acts 1983, 68th Leg., p. 3694, ch. 576, § 1, eff. Jan. 1, 1984.

§ 121.056. Commingling of Assets

A trustee who receives a death benefit under this subchapter may commingle the property with other assets accepted by the trustee and held in trust, either before or after the death benefit is received.

Acts 1983, 68th Leg., p. 3694, ch. 576, § 1, eff. Jan. 1, 1984.

§ 121.057. Prior Designations Not Affected

This subchapter does not affect the validity of a beneficiary designation made by an employee before April 3, 1975, that names a trustee as beneficiary of a death benefit.

Acts 1983, 68th Leg., p. 3694, ch. 576, § 1, eff. Jan. 1, 1984.

§ 121.058. Construction

(a) This subchapter is intended to be declaratory of the common law of this state.

(b) A court shall liberally construe this subchapter to effect the intent that a death benefit received by a trustee under this subchapter is not subject to the obligations of the employee or the employee's estate unless the trust receiving the benefit expressly provides otherwise.

(c) A death benefit shall not be included in property administered as part of a testator's estate or in an inventory filed with the county court because of a reference in a will to the death benefit or because of the naming of the trustee of a testamentary trust.

Acts 1983, 68th Leg., p. 3694, ch. 576, § 1, eff. Jan. 1, 1984.

Chapter 123. Attorney General Participation in Proceedings Involving Charitable Trusts

Statutes in Context
Chapter 123

The attorney general of Texas has standing to enforce charitable trusts. To increase the likelihood that the attorney general is aware of lawsuits involving charitable trusts, Chapter 123 requires that the party initiating the action give notice to the attorney general. This notice is by certified or registered mail within 30 days of filing but not less than 25 days before a hearing and must include a copy of the petition. See § 123.003. Section 123.001(3) provides an extensive list of proceedings to which the attorney general is entitled to notice.

If the attorney general does not receive notice, any judgment or settlement is voidable. In other words, the attorney general may set aside any judgment or settlement at any time. No grounds are required other than the fact that the attorney general did not receive notice. See § 123.004.

It is significant to note the broad definition given to the term "charitable trust" in § 123.001(2). The term encompasses any inter vivos or testamentary gift to a charitable entity in addition to traditional charitable trusts. An attorney perusing the statutes might read the caption to Chapter 123 which contains the term "charitable trusts" and not realize that the chapter applies to all charitable gifts, whether they be in trust or outright. Likewise, the term "charitable trusts" includes any charitable entity, even if not run as a trust.

§ 123.001. Definitions

In this chapter:

(1) "Charitable entity" means a corporation, trust, community chest, fund, foundation, or other entity organized for scientific, educational, philanthropic, or environmental purposes, social welfare, the arts and humanities, or another civic or public purpose described by Section 501(c)(3) of the Internal Revenue Code of 1986 (26 U.S.C. § 501(c)(3)).

(2) "Charitable trust" means a charitable entity, a trust the stated purpose of which is to benefit a charitable entity, or an inter vivos or testamentary gift to a charitable entity.

(3) "Proceeding involving a charitable trust" means a suit or other judicial proceeding the object of which is to:

(A) terminate a charitable trust or distribute its assets to other than charitable donees;

(B) depart from the objects of the charitable trust stated in the instrument creating the trust, including a proceeding in which the doctrine of cy-pres is invoked;

(C) construe, nullify, or impair the provisions of a testamentary or other instrument creating or affecting a charitable trust;

(D) contest or set aside the probate of an alleged will under which money, property, or another thing of value is given for charitable purposes;

(E) allow a charitable trust to contest or set aside the probate of an alleged will;

(F) determine matters relating to the probate and administration of an estate involving a charitable trust; or

(G) obtain a declaratory judgment involving a charitable trust.

(4) "Fiduciary or managerial agent" means an individual, corporation, or other entity acting either as a trustee, a member of the board of directors, an officer, an executor, or an administrator for a charitable trust.

Added by Acts 1987, 70th Leg., ch. 147, § 4, eff. Sept. 1, 1987. Amended by Acts 1995, 74th Leg., ch. 172, § 2, eff. Sept. 1, 1995.

§ 123.002. Attorney General's Participation

For and on behalf of the interest of the general public of this state in charitable trusts, the attorney general is a proper party and may intervene in a proceeding involving a charitable trust. The attorney general may join and enter into a compromise, settlement agreement, contract, or judgment relating to a proceeding involving a charitable trust.

Added by Acts 1987, 70th Leg., ch. 147, § 4, eff. Sept. 1, 1987.

§ 123.003. Notice

(a) Any party initiating a proceeding involving a charitable trust shall give notice of the proceeding to the attorney general by sending to the attorney general, by registered or certified mail, a true copy of the petition or other instrument initiating the proceeding involving a charitable trust within 30 days of the filing of such petition or other instrument, but no less than 25 days prior to a hearing in such a proceeding. This subsection does not apply to a proceeding that is initiated by an application that exclusively seeks the admission of a will to probate, regardless of whether the application seeks the appointment of a personal representative, if the application:

(1) is uncontested; and

(2) is not subject to Section 83, Texas Probate Code.

(b) Notice shall be given to the attorney general of any pleading which adds new causes of action or additional parties to a proceeding involving a charitable trust in which the attorney general has previously waived participation or in which the attorney general has otherwise failed to intervene. Notice shall be given by sending to the attorney general by registered or certified mail a true copy of the pleading within 30 days of the filing of the pleading, but no less than 25 days prior to a hearing in the proceeding.

(c) The party or the party's attorney shall execute and file in the proceeding an affidavit stating the facts of the notice and shall attach to the affidavit the customary postal receipts signed by the attorney general or an assistant attorney general.

Added by Acts 1987, 70th Leg., ch. 147, § 4, eff. Sept. 1, 1987. Amended by Acts 1995, 74th Leg., ch. 172, § 3, eff. Sept. 1, 1995. Subsecs. (a), (b) amended by Acts 2005, 79th Leg., ch. 1017, § 1, eff. Sept. 1, 2005 Subsec. (a) amended by Acts 2007, 80th Leg., ch. 451, § 15, eff. Sept. 1, 2007.

§ 123.004. Voidable Judgment or Agreement

(a) A judgment in a proceeding involving a charitable trust is voidable if the attorney general is not given notice of the proceeding as required by this chapter. On motion of the attorney general after the judgment is rendered, the judgment shall be set aside.

(b) A compromise, settlement agreement, contract, or judgment relating to a proceeding involving a charitable trust is voidable on motion of the attorney general if the attorney general is not given notice as required by this chapter unless the attorney general has:

(1) declined in writing to be a party to the proceeding; or

(2) approved and joined in the compromise, settlement agreement, contract, or judgment.

Added by Acts 1987, 70th Leg., ch. 147, § 4, eff. Sept. 1, 1987.

§ 123.005. Breach of Fiduciary Duty; Venue; Jurisdiction

(a) Venue in a proceeding brought by the attorney general alleging breach of a fiduciary duty by a charitable entity or a fiduciary duty by a fiduciary or managerial agent of a charitable trust shall be a court of competent jurisdiction in Travis County or in the county where the defendant resides or has its principal office. To the extent of a conflict between this section and any provision of the Texas Probate Code providing for venue of a proceeding brought with respect to a charitable trust created by a will that has been admitted to probate, this section controls.

(b) A statutory probate court of Travis County has concurrent jurisdiction with any other court on which jurisdiction is conferred by Section 4A, Texas Probate Code, in a proceeding brought by the attorney general alleging breach of a fiduciary duty with respect to a charitable trust created by a will that has been admitted to probate.

Added by Acts 1987, 70th Leg., ch. 147, § 4, eff. Sept. 1, 1987. Amended by Acts 1995, 74th Leg., ch. 172, § 4, eff. Sept. 1, 1995. Amended by Acts 2009, 81st Leg., ch. 133, § 1, eff. Sept. 1, 2009; Amended by Acts 2009, 81st Leg., ch. 1351, §12(h), eff. Sept. 1, 2009. Amended by Acts 2011, 82nd Leg., ch. 91, § 21.003, eff. Sept. 1, 2011. Subsec. (b) added by Acts 2011, ch. 401, § 1, eff. June 17, 2011.

§ 123.006. Attorney's Fees

(a) In a proceeding subject to Section 123.005, the attorney general, if successful in the proceeding, is entitled to recover from the charitable entity or fiduciary or managerial agent of the charitable trust actual costs incurred in bringing the suit and may recover reasonable attorney's fees.

(b) In a proceeding in which the attorney general intervenes under this chapter, other than a proceeding subject to Section 123.005, a court may award the attorney general court costs and reasonable and necessary attorney's fees as may seem equitable and just.

Added by Acts 2009, 81st Leg., ch. 133, § 2, eff. Sept. 1, 2009.

Chapter 124. Partition of Mineral Interests of Charitable Trust

§ 124.001. Definitions

In this chapter:

(1) "Charitable entity" means a corporation, trust, community chest, fund, foundation, or other entity organized for scientific, educational, philanthropic, or environmental purposes, social welfare, the arts and humanities, or another civic or public purpose described by Section 501(c)(3), Internal Revenue Code of 1986.

(2) "Charitable trust" means a charitable entity, a trust the stated purpose of which is to benefit a charitable entity, or an inter vivos or testamentary gift to a charitable entity.

(3) "Mineral interest" means an interest in oil, gas, or other mineral substance in place or that otherwise constitutes real property without regard to the depth at which such mineral substance is found.

Added by Acts 2013, 83rd Leg., ch. 480, § 1, eff. Sept. 1, 2013.

§ 124.002. Compulsory Divestment Prohibited

In a suit or other judicial proceeding the object or effect of which is to compel the partition of a mineral interest owned or claimed by a charitable trust, a sale or other action that would divest the charitable trust of the trust's ownership of a mineral interest may not be ordered unless the trust has refused to execute a mineral lease, the terms of which are fair and reasonable, to the plaintiff or petitioner in the proceeding.

Added by Acts 2013, 83rd Leg., ch. 480, § 1, eff. Sept. 1, 2013.

Title 10. Miscellaneous Beneficial Property Interests

Subtitle A. Persons Under Disability

Chapter 141. Transfers to Minors

Statutes in Context
Chapter 141

Individuals who wish to make gifts or other transfers to minors need to select the method used to transfer the property. Transferors have several techniques available to them. First, the transferor could simply make the transfer directly to the minor. In many circumstances, direct transfers will necessitate the appointment of a guardian of the minor's estate. An estate guardianship requires extensive court involvement and thus is costly and time-consuming. In addition, the minor will receive the property outright at age 18, possibly before the young adult has acquired the maturity to handle the property prudently. Second, the transfer could be placed in trust for the benefit of the minor. A trust will avoid the necessity of a guardianship and will give the transferor the ability to designate how the property is to be managed and distributed. Significant transaction costs may be incurred, however, such as attorneys' fees to draft the trust and trustees' fees to manage the trust. In addition, certain transferors, such as creditors, are not able to take advantage of this technique. Third, the transferor may transfer the property to a custodian for the minor. Although not achieving all the benefits of a trust, transfers to a custodian are cost-effective, relatively simple to make, and are available to a wide range of transferors.

Until September 1, 1995, transfers to a custodian for a minor were governed by the Texas Uniform Gifts to Minors Act (TUGMA) and its various amendments. The 1995 Texas Legislature enacted the Texas Uniform Transfers to Minors Act (TUTMA) as a replacement for the outdated TUGMA.

§ 141.001. Short Title

This chapter may be cited as the Texas Uniform Transfers to Minors Act.

Acts 1983, 68th Leg., p. 3698, ch. 576, § 1, eff. Jan. 1, 1984. Amended by Acts 1995, 74th Leg., ch. 1043, § 1, eff. Sept. 1, 1995. Renumbered from Property Code § 1 by Acts 1997, 75th Leg., ch. 165, § 31.01(72), eff. Sept. 1, 1997.

Statutes in Context
§ 141.002

The transferee must be a minor at the time of the transfer. The age at which minority status is lost is 21, not 18 as under the TUGMA. See § 141.002(11). There is no requirement that the minor and the transferor be related.

§ 141.002. Definitions

In this chapter:

(1) "Adult" means an individual who is at least 21 years of age.

(2) "Benefit plan" means a retirement plan, including an interest described by Sections 111.004(19)-(23).

(3) "Broker" means a person lawfully engaged in the business of effecting transactions in securities or commodities for the person's own account or for the account of another.

(4) "Court" means a court with original probate jurisdiction.

(5) "Custodial property" means:

(A) any interest in property transferred to a custodian under this chapter; and

(B) the income from and proceeds of that interest in property.

(6) "Custodian" means a person designated as a custodian under Section 141.010 or a successor or substitute custodian designated under Section 141.019.

(7) "Financial institution" means a bank, trust company, savings institution, or credit union chartered and supervised under state or federal law.

(8) "Guardian" means a person appointed or qualified by a court to act as general, limited, or temporary guardian of a minor's property or a person legally authorized to perform substantially the same functions.

(9) "Legal representative" means an executor, independent executor, administrator or independent administrator of a decedent's estate, an obligor under a benefit plan or other governing instrument, a successor legal representative, or a person legally authorized to perform substantially the same functions.

(10) "Member of the minor's family" means the minor's parent, stepparent, spouse, grandparent, brother, sister, uncle, or aunt, whether of whole or half blood or by adoption.

(11) "Minor" means an individual who is younger than 21 years of age.

(12) "Transfer" means a transaction that creates custodial property under Section 141.010.

(12-a) "Qualified minor's trust" means a trust to which a gift is considered a present interest under Section 2503(c), Internal Revenue Code of 1986.

(13) "Transferor" means a person who makes a transfer under this chapter.

(14) "Trust company" means a financial institution, corporation, or other legal entity authorized to exercise general trust powers.

Acts 1983, 68th Leg., p. 3698, ch. 576, § 1, eff. Jan. 1, 1984. Amended by Acts 1995, 74th Leg., ch. 1043, § 1, eff. Sept. 1, 1995. Renumbered from Property Code § 2 by Acts 1997, 75th Leg., ch. 165, § 31.01(72), eff. Sept. 1, 1997. Subsec. (2) amended by and subsec. (12-a) added by Acts 2007, 80th Leg., ch. 451, § 16, eff. Sept. 1, 2007.

§ 141.003. Scope and Jurisdiction

(a) This chapter applies to a transfer that refers to the Texas Uniform Transfers to Minors Act in the designation under Section 141.010(a) by which the transfer is made if at the time of the transfer, the transferor, the minor, or the custodian is a resident of this state or the custodial property is located in this state. The custodianship created under Section 141.010 remains subject to this chapter despite a subsequent change in residence of a transferor, the minor, or the custodian or the removal of custodial property from this state.

(b) A person designated as custodian under this chapter is subject to personal jurisdiction in this state with respect to any matter relating to the custodianship.

(c) A transfer that purports to be made and that is valid under the Uniform Transfers to Minors Act, the Uniform Gifts to Minors Act, or a substantially similar act of another state is governed by the law of the designated state and may be executed and is enforceable in this state if at the time of the transfer, the transferor,

the minor, or the custodian is a resident of the designated state or the custodial property is located in the designated state.

Acts 1983, 68th Leg., p. 3700, ch. 576, § 1, eff. Jan. 1, 1984. Amended by Acts 1995, 74th Leg., ch. 1043, § 1, eff. Sept. 1, 1995. Renumbered from Property Code § 3 by Acts 1997, 75th Leg., ch. 165, § 31.01(72), eff. Sept. 1, 1997.

Statutes in Context
§ 141.004

A person who has the right to designate the recipient of property which is transferable when a future event occurs (e.g., the death of the person) may revocably nominate a custodian to receive the property for a minor beneficiary upon the occurrence of that event. Examples of prospective transfer arrangements included in the scope of this section are wills, trusts, deeds, life insurance policies, annuity contracts, retirement plans, trust accounts, and P.O.D. accounts. This type of designation does not actually create a custodianship relationship until the nominating instrument becomes irrevocable or the transfer to the nominated custodian occurs.

---

§ 141.004. Nomination of Custodian

(a) A person having the right to designate the recipient of property transferable on the occurrence of a future event may revocably nominate a custodian to receive the property for a minor beneficiary on the occurrence of that event by naming the custodian followed in substance by the words: "as custodian for (name of minor) under the Texas Uniform Transfers to Minors Act." The nomination may name one or more persons as substitute custodians to whom the property must be transferred, in the order named, if the first nominated custodian dies before the transfer or is unable, declines, or is ineligible to serve. The nomination may be made in a will, a trust, a deed, an instrument exercising a power of appointment, or in a writing designating a beneficiary of contractual rights, including the right to receive payments from a benefit plan, that is registered with or delivered to the payor, issuer, or other obligor of the contractual rights.

(b) A custodian nominated under this section must be a person to whom a transfer of property of that kind may be made under Section 141.010(a).

(c) The nomination of a custodian under this section does not create custodial property until the nominating instrument becomes irrevocable or a transfer to the nominated custodian is completed under Section 141.010. Unless the nomination of a custodian has been revoked, the custodianship becomes effective on the occurrence of the future event, and the custodian shall enforce a transfer of the custodial property under Section 141.010.

Acts 1983, 68th Leg., p. 3702, ch. 576, § 1, eff. Jan. 1,

1984. Amended by Acts 1995, 74th Leg., ch. 1043, § 1, eff. Sept. 1, 1995. Renumbered from Property Code § 4 by Acts 1997, 75th Leg., ch. 165, § 31.01(72), eff. Sept. 1, 1997. Subsec. (a) amended by Acts 2007, 80th Leg., ch. 451, § 17, eff. Sept. 1, 2007.

Statutes in Context
§ 141.005

The donor of an outright irrevocable inter vivos gift may transfer the gifted property to a custodian for a minor donee. The donee of a power of appointment may exercise it irrevocably in favor of a custodian for the benefit of a minor appointee.

---

§ 141.005. Transfer by Gift or Exercise of Power of Appointment

A person may make a transfer by irrevocable gift to, or the irrevocable exercise of a power of appointment in favor of, a custodian for the benefit of a minor under Section 141.010.

Acts 1983, 68th Leg., p. 3704, ch. 576, § 1, eff. Jan. 1, 1984. Amended by Acts 1995, 74th Leg., ch. 1043, § 1, eff. Sept. 1, 1995. Renumbered from Property Code § 5 by Acts 1997, 75th Leg., ch. 165, § 31.01(72), eff. Sept. 1, 1997.

Statutes in Context
§ 141.006

A will may authorize the personal representative to make distributions to a custodian for a minor beneficiary. Likewise, a trust may authorize the trustee to distribute to a minor's custodian.

---

§ 141.006. Transfer Authorized by Will or Trust

(a) A legal representative or trustee may make an irrevocable transfer under Section 141.010 to a custodian for a minor's benefit as authorized in the governing will or trust.

(b) If the testator or settlor has nominated a custodian under Section 141.004 to receive the custodial property, the transfer must be made to that person.

(c) If the testator or settlor has not nominated a custodian under Section 4, or all persons nominated as custodian die before the transfer or are unable, decline, or are ineligible to serve, the legal representative or the trustee shall designate the custodian from among those persons eligible to serve as custodian for property of that kind under Section 141.010(a).

Acts 1983, 68th Leg., p. 3704, ch. 576, § 1, eff. Jan. 1, 1984. Amended by Acts 1985, 69th Leg., ch. 149, § 5, eff. May 24, 1985. Amended by Acts 1995, 74th Leg., ch. 1043, § 1, eff. Sept. 1, 1995. Renumbered from Property Code § 6 by Acts 1997, 75th Leg., ch. 165, § 31.01(72), eff. Sept. 1, 1997.

Statutes in Context
§ 141.007

Under certain circumstances, fiduciaries may make transfers to a custodian for a minor's benefit even without express authorization from the original owner of the property. These fiduciaries include the administrator of an intestate, the executor of a will, the trustee of a trust, and the guardian of a ward. See also § 113.021(a)(4).

---

§ 141.007. Other Transfer by Fiduciary

(a) Subject to Subsections (b) and (c), a guardian, legal representative, or trustee may make an irrevocable transfer to another adult or trust company as custodian for a minor's benefit under Section 141.010 in the absence of a will or under a will or trust that does not contain an authorization to do so.

(b) With the approval of the court supervising the guardianship, a guardian may make an irrevocable transfer to another adult or trust company as custodian for the minor's benefit under Section 141.010.

(c) A transfer under Subsection (a) or (b) may be made only if:

(1) the legal representative or trustee considers the transfer to be in the best interest of the minor;

(2) the transfer is not prohibited by or inconsistent with provisions of the applicable will, trust agreement, or other governing instrument; and

(3) the transfer is authorized by the court if it exceeds $25,000 [$10,000] in value.

Acts 1983, 68th Leg., p. 3706, ch. 576, § 1, eff. Jan. 1, 1984. Amended by Acts 1995, 74th Leg., ch. 1043, § 1, eff. Sept. 1, 1995. Renumbered from Property Code § 7 by Acts 1997, 75th Leg., ch. 165, § 31.01(72), eff. Sept. 1, 1997. Subsec. (c) amended by Acts 2015, 84th Leg., ch. 622, § 1, eff. Sept. 1, 2015.

Statutes in Context
§ 141.008

A person who either holds property of or owes a liquidated debt to a minor who does not have a guardian may transfer the property to a custodian for the minor's benefit. Examples of these type of transferors include a tort judgment debtor, a bank holding a joint account on which the minor has the right of survivorship, and a life insurance company holding proceeds due a minor beneficiary.

---

§ 141.008. Transfer by Obligor

(a) Subject to Subsections (b) and (c), a person who is not subject to Section 141.006 or 141.007 and who holds property, including a benefit plan of a minor who does not have a guardian, or who owes a liquidated debt to a minor who does not have a guardian may make an irrevocable transfer to a custodian for the benefit of the minor under Section 141.010.

(b) If a person who has the right to nominate a custodian under Section 141.004 has nominated a custodian under that section to receive the custodial property, the transfer must be made to that person.

(c) If a custodian has not been nominated under Section 141.004, or all persons nominated as custodian die before the transfer or are unable, decline, or are ineligible to serve, a transfer under this section may be made to an adult member of the minor's family or to a trust company unless the property exceeds $25,000 [$15,000] in value.

Acts 1983, 68th Leg., p. 3707, ch. 576, § 1. eff. Jan. 1, 1984. Amended by Acts 1995, 74th Leg., ch. 1043, § 1, eff. Sept. 1, 1995. Renumbered from Property Code § 8 by Acts 1997, 75th Leg., ch. 165, § 31.01(72). eff. Sept. 1, 1997. Subsecs. (a) & (c) amended by Acts 2007, 80th Leg., ch. 451, § 18, eff. Sept. 1, 2007. Subsec. (c) amended by Acts 2015, 84th Leg., ch. 622, § 2, eff. Sept. 1, 2015.

§ 141.009. Receipt for Custodial Property

A written acknowledgment of delivery by a custodian constitutes a sufficient receipt and discharge for custodial property transferred to the custodian under this chapter.

Acts 1983, 68th Leg., p. 3708, ch. 576, § 1, eff. Jan. 1, 1984. Amended by Acts 1995, 74th Leg., ch. 1043, § 1, eff. Sept. 1, 1995. Renumbered from Property Code § 9 by Acts 1997, 75th Leg., ch. 165, § 31.01(72), eff. Sept. 1, 1997.

§ 141.010. Manner of Creating Custodial Property and Effecting Transfer; Designation of Initial Custodian; Control

(a) Custodial property is created and a transfer is made when:

(1) an uncertificated security or a certificated security in registered form is:

(A) registered in the name of the transferor, an adult other than the transferor, or a trust company, followed in substance by the words: "as custodian for (name of minor) under the Texas Uniform Transfers to Minors Act"; or

(B) delivered if in certificated form, or any document necessary for the transfer of an uncertificated security is delivered, with any necessary endorsement to an adult other than the transferor or to a trust company as custodian, accompanied by an instrument in substantially the form set forth in Subsection (b);

(2) money is paid or delivered, or a security held in the name of a broker, financial institution, or its nominee is transferred, to a broker or financial institution for credit to an account in the name of the transferor, an adult other than the transferor, or a trust company, followed in substance by the words: "as custodian for (name of minor) under the Texas Uniform Transfers to Minors Act";

(3) the ownership of a life or endowment insurance policy or annuity contract is:

(A) registered with the issuer in the name of the transferor, an adult other than the transferor, or a trust company, followed in substance by the words: "as custodian for (name of minor) under the Texas Uniform Transfers to Minors Act"; or

(B) assigned in a writing delivered to an adult other than the transferor or to a trust company whose name in the assignment is followed in substance by the words: "as custodian for (name of minor) under the Texas Uniform Transfers to Minors Act";

(4) an irrevocable exercise of a power of appointment or an irrevocable present right to future payment under a contract is the subject of a written notification delivered to the payor, issuer, or other obligor that the right is transferred to the transferor, an adult other than the transferor, or a trust company, whose name in the notification is followed in substance by the words: "as custodian for (name of minor) under the Texas Uniform Transfers to Minors Act";

(5) an interest in real property is conveyed by instrument recorded in the real property records in the county in which the real property is located to the transferor, an adult other than the transferor, or a trust company, followed in substance by the words: "as custodian for (name of minor) under the Texas Uniform Transfers to Minors Act";

(6) a certificate of title issued by a department or agency of a state or of the United States that evidences title to tangible personal property is:

(A) issued in the name of the transferor, an adult other than the transferor, or a trust company, followed in substance by the words: "as custodian for (name of minor) under the Texas Uniform Transfers to Minors Act"; or

(B) delivered to an adult other than the transferor or to a trust company, endorsed to that person followed in substance by the words: "as a custodian for (name of minor) under the Texas Uniform Transfers to Minors Act"; or

(7) an interest in any property not described in Subdivisions (1)-(6) is transferred to an adult other than the transferor or to a trust company by a written instrument in substantially the form set forth in Subsection (b).

(b) An instrument in the following form satisfies the requirements of Subsections (a)(1)(B) and (7):

TRANSFER UNDER THE TEXAS UNIFORM
TRANSFERS TO MINORS ACT

I, _____ (name of transferor or name and representative capacity if a fiduciary) hereby transfer to _____ (name of custodian), as custodian for _____ (name of minor) under the Texas Uniform Transfers to Minors Act, the following: (insert a description of the custodial property sufficient to identify it).

Dated: _____

_____ (Signature)

_____ (name of custodian) acknowledges receipt of the property described above as custodian for the minor named above under the Texas Uniform Transfers to Minors Act.

Dated: _____

_____ (Signature of Custodian)

(c) A transferor shall place the custodian in control of the custodial property as soon as practicable.

Acts 1983, 68th Leg., p. 3708, ch. 576, § 1, eff. Jan. 1, 1984. Amended by Acts 1995, 74th Leg., ch. 1043, § 1, eff. Sept. 1, 1995. Renumbered from Property Code § 10 by Acts 1997, 75th Leg., ch. 165, § 31.01(72), eff. Sept. 1, 1997.

Statutes in Context
§ 141.011

Only one person may be named as a transferee or custodian.

§ 141.011. Single Custodianship

A transfer may be made only for one minor, and only one person may be the custodian. All custodial property held under this chapter by the same custodian for the benefit of the same minor constitutes a single custodianship.

Acts 1983, 68th Leg., p. 3709, ch. 576, § 1, eff. Jan. 1, 1984. Amended by Acts 1995, 74th Leg., ch. 1043, § 1, eff. Sept. 1, 1995. Renumbered from, Property Code § 11 by Acts 1997, 75th Leg., ch. 165, § 31.01(72), eff. Sept. 1, 1997.

§ 141.012. Validity and Effect of Transfer

(a) The validity of a transfer made in a manner prescribed by this chapter is not affected by the:

(1) transferor's failure to comply with Section 141.010(c) concerning possession and control;

(2) designation of an ineligible custodian, except designation of the transferor in the case of property for which the transferor is ineligible to serve as custodian under Section 141.010(a); or

(3) death or incapacity of a person nominated under Section 141.004 or designated under Section 141.010 as custodian or the disclaimer of the office by that person.

(b) A transfer made under Section 141.010 is irrevocable, and the custodial property is indefeasibly vested in the minor. The custodian has all the rights, powers, duties, and authority provided in this chapter, and the minor or the minor's legal representative does not have any right, power, duty, or authority with respect to the custodial property except as provided by this chapter.

(c) By making a transfer, the transferor incorporates all the provisions of this chapter in the disposition and grants to the custodian, or to any third person dealing with a person designated as custodian, the respective powers, rights and immunities provided by this chapter.

Acts 1983, 68th Leg., p. 3709, ch. 576, § 1, eff. Jan. 1, 1984. Amended by Acts 1995, 74th Leg., ch. 1043, § 1, eff. Sept. 1, 1995. Renumbered from Property Code § 12 by Acts 1997, 75th Leg., ch. 165, § 31.01(72), eff. Sept. 1, 1997.

Statutes in Context
§ 141.013

The custodian must "observe the standard of care that would be observed by a prudent person dealing with property of another." The custodian is not limited by any other Texas law which restricts investments by fiduciaries. If a custodian has a special skill or other expertise (e.g., a professional custodian or trust company), the custodian must exercise that skill or expertise. However, the custodian may retain any property received from a transferor without liability for failing to invest that property in a more productive manner or to diversify.

§ 141.013. Care of Custodial Property

(a) A custodian shall:

(1) take control of custodial property;

(2) register or record title to custodial property if appropriate; and

(3) collect, hold, manage, sell, convey, invest, and reinvest custodial property.

(b) In dealing with custodial property, a custodian shall observe the standard of care that would be observed by a prudent person dealing with property of another and is not limited by any other statute restricting investments by fiduciaries. If a custodian has a special skill or expertise, the custodian shall use that skill or expertise. However, a custodian, in the custodian's discretion and without liability to the minor or the minor's estate, may retain any custodial property received from a transferor.

(c) A custodian may invest in or pay premiums on life insurance or endowment policies on the life of:

(1) the minor only if the minor or the minor's estate is the sole beneficiary; or

(2) another person in whom the minor has an insurable interest only to the extent that the minor, the minor's estate, or the custodian in the capacity of the custodian is the irrevocable beneficiary.

(d) A custodian at all times shall keep custodial property separate and distinct from all other property in a manner sufficient to identify it clearly as custodial property of the minor. Custodial property consisting of an undivided interest is so identified if the minor's interest is held as a tenant in common and is fixed. Custodial property subject to recordation is so identified if it is recorded, and custodial property subject to registration is so identified if it is registered, or held in an account designated, in the name of the custodian

followed in substance by the words: "as custodian for
_____ (name of minor) under the Texas
Uniform Transfers to Minors Act."

(e) A custodian shall keep records of all transactions
with respect to custodial property, including
information necessary for the preparation of the minor's
tax returns, and shall make the records available for
inspection at reasonable intervals by a parent or legal
representative of the minor or by the minor if the minor
is at least 14 years of age.

*Acts 1983, 68th Leg., p. 3710, ch. 576, § 1, eff. Jan. 1,
1984. Amended by Acts 1995, 74th Leg., ch. 1043, § 1,
eff. Sept. 1, 1995. Renumbered from, Property Code
§ 13 by Acts 1997, 75th Leg., ch. 165, § 31.01(72), eff.
Sept. 1, 1997.*

Statutes in Context
§ 141.014

The custodian has all the rights, powers, and
authority over the custodial property that an
unmarried adult owner has over his or her own
property. The custodian may exercise these rights,
powers, and authority only in a custodial capacity.

§ 141.014. Powers of Custodian

(a) A custodian, acting in a custodial capacity, has
all the rights, powers, and authority over custodial
property that unmarried adult owners have over their
own property, but a custodian may exercise those rights,
powers, and authority in that capacity only.

(b) This section does not relieve a custodian from
liability for breach of Section 141.013.

*Acts 1983, 68th Leg., p. 3710, ch. 576, § 1, eff. Jan. 1,
1984. Amended by Acts 1995, 74th Leg., ch. 1043, § 1,
eff. Sept. 1, 1995. Renumbered from Property Code § 14
by Acts 1997, 75th Leg., ch. 165, § 31.01(72), eff. Sept.
1, 1997.*

Statutes in Context
§ 141.015

The custodian has the power to (1) deliver or
pay custodial property directly to the minor and (2)
expend custodial property for the minor's benefit.
The custodian is not limited by any standard (e.g.,
support, education, or medical care) in making
distributions as long as the distribution is for the
use or benefit of the minor. The custodian need
not obtain a court order before making
distributions. In addition, the custodian may use
custodial property for the minor even if (1) the
custodian personally has a duty or the ability to
support the minor, (2) another person has a duty
or the ability to support the minor, and (3) the
minor has other income or property which could be
used instead.

A minor who is at least 14 years old and any
interested person may petition to the court to force
the custodian to distribute custodial property. The
court may order distribution of as much of the
property as the court considers advisable for the
use and benefit of the minor.

Distributions of custodial property are in
addition to, not in substitution for, and do not affect
any obligation which a person may have to support
the minor.

§ 141.015.   Use of Custodial Property

(a) A custodian may deliver or pay to the minor or
expend for the minor's benefit as much of the custodial
property as the custodian considers advisable for the use
and benefit of the minor, without court order and
without regard to:

(1) the duty or ability of the custodian
personally or of any other person to support the
minor; or

(2) any other income or property of the minor
that may be applicable or available for that purpose.

(b) On petition of an interested person or the minor
if the minor is at least 14 years of age, the court may
order the custodian to deliver or pay to the minor or
expend for the minor's benefit as much of the custodial
property as the court considers advisable for the use and
benefit of the minor.

(b-1) A custodian may, without a court order,
transfer all or part of the custodial property to a
qualified minor's trust. A transfer of property under
this subsection terminates the custodianship to the
extent of the property transferred.

(c) A delivery, payment, or expenditure under this
section is in addition to, not in substitution for, and does
not affect any obligation of a person to support the
minor.

*Added by Acts 1995, 74th Leg., ch. 1043, § 1, eff. Sept.
1, 1995. Renumbered from Property Code § 15 by Acts
1997, 75th Leg., ch. 165, § 31.01(72), eff. Sept. 1, 1997.
Subsec. (b-1) added by Acts 2007, 80th Leg., ch. 451,
§ 19, eff. Sept. 1, 2007.*

Statutes in Context
§ 141.016

The custodian is normally entitled to charge
reasonable compensation for the custodian's
services. The custodian must affirmatively elect to
receive compensation each year or else the right
lapses. A custodian who was the donor of an
irrevocable gift or who exercised a power of
appointment may not take compensation.

§ 141.016. Custodian's Expenses, Compensation, and Bond

(a) A custodian is entitled to reimbursement from custodial property for reasonable expenses incurred in the performance of the custodian's duties.

(b) Except for one who is a transferor under Section 141.005, a custodian has a noncumulative election during each calendar year to charge reasonable compensation for services performed by the custodian during that year.

(c) Except as provided by Section 141.019(f), a custodian is not required to give a bond.

Added by Acts 1995, 74th Leg., ch. 1043, § 1, eff. Sept. 1, 1995. Renumbered from Property Code § 16 by Acts 1997, 75th Leg., ch. 165, § 31.01(72), eff. Sept. 1, 1997.

§ 141.017. Exemption of Third Person from Liability

A third person, in good faith and without court order, may act on the instructions of or otherwise deal with any person purporting to make a transfer or act in the capacity of a custodian and, in the absence of knowledge, is not responsible for determining the:

(1) validity of the purported custodian's designation;

(2) propriety of, or the authority under this chapter for, any act of the purported custodian;

(3) validity or propriety under this chapter of any instrument or instructions executed or given by the person purporting to make a transfer or by the purported custodian; or

(4) propriety of the application of the minor's property delivered to the purported custodian.

Added by Acts 1995, 74th Leg., ch. 1043, § 1, eff. Sept. 1, 1995. Renumbered from Property Code § 17 by Acts 1997, 75th Leg., ch. 165, § 31.01(72), eff. Sept. 1, 1997.

§ 141.018. Liability to Third Person

(a) A claim based on a contract entered into by a custodian acting in a custodial capacity, an obligation arising from the ownership or control of custodial property, or a tort committed during the custodianship may be asserted against the custodial property by proceeding against the custodian in the custodian's custodial capacity, whether or not the custodian or the minor is personally liable for the claim.

(b) A custodian is not personally liable:

(1) on a contract properly entered into in the custodian's custodial capacity unless the custodian fails to reveal that capacity and to identify the custodianship in the contract; or

(2) for an obligation arising from control of custodial property or for a tort committed during the custodianship unless the custodian is personally at fault.

(c) A minor is not personally liable for an obligation arising from ownership of custodial property or for a tort committed during the custodianship unless the minor is personally at fault.

Added by Acts 1995, 74th Leg., ch. 1043, § 1, eff. Sept. 1, 1995. Renumbered from Property Code § 18 by Acts 1997, 75th Leg., ch. 165, § 31.01(72), eff. Sept. 1, 1997.

§ 141.019. Renunciation, Resignation, Death, or Removal of Custodian; Designation of Successor Custodian

(a) A person nominated to serve as a custodian under Section 141.004 or designated to serve as a custodian under Section 141.010 may decline to serve as custodian by delivering written notice to the person who made the nomination or to the transferor's legal representative. If the event giving rise to a transfer has not occurred and no substitute custodian who is able, willing, and eligible to serve was nominated under Section 4, the person who made the nomination may nominate a substitute custodian under Section 4; otherwise the transferor or the transferor's legal representative shall designate a substitute custodian at the time of the transfer, in either case from among the persons eligible to serve as custodian for that kind of property under Section 141.010(a). A substitute custodian designated under this section has the rights of a successor custodian.

(b) A custodian at any time may designate as successor custodian a trust company or an adult other than a transferor under Section 141.005 by executing and dating an instrument of designation before a subscribing witness other than the successor. If the instrument of designation does not contain or is not accompanied by the custodian's resignation, the designation of the successor does not take effect until the custodian resigns, dies, becomes incapacitated, or is removed.

(c) A custodian may resign at any time by delivering:

(1) written notice to the successor custodian and to the minor if the minor is at least 14 years of age; and

(2) the custodial property to the successor custodian.

(d) If a custodian is ineligible, dies, or becomes incapacitated without having effectively designated a successor and the minor is at least 14 years of age, the minor may designate as successor custodian an adult member of the minor's family, a guardian of the minor, or a trust company in the manner prescribed by Subsection (b). If the minor is younger than 14 years of age or fails to act within 60 days after the ineligibility, death, or incapacity of the custodian, the minor's guardian becomes successor custodian. If the minor has no guardian or the minor's guardian declines to act, the transferor, the legal representative of the transferor or of the custodian, an adult member of the minor's family, or any other interested person may petition the court to designate a successor custodian.

(e) As soon as practicable, a custodian who declines to serve under Subsection (a) or resigns under Subsection (c), or the legal representative of a deceased or incapacitated custodian, shall put the custodial

769

property and records in the possession and control of the successor custodian. The successor custodian by action may enforce the obligation to deliver custodial property and records and becomes responsible for each item as received.

(f) A transferor, the legal representative of a transferor, an adult member of the minor's family, a guardian of the person of the minor, the guardian of the minor, or the minor if the minor is at least 14 years of age may petition the court to:

(1) remove the custodian for cause and designate a successor custodian other than a transferor under Section 141.005; or

(2) require the custodian to give appropriate bond.

Added by Acts 1995, 74th Leg., ch. 1043, § 1, eff. Sept. 1, 1995. Renumbered from Property Code § 19 by Acts 1997, 75th Leg., ch. 165, § 31.01(72), eff. Sept. 1, 1997.

§ 141.020. Accounting by and Determination of Liability

(a) A minor who is at least 14 years of age, the minor's guardian of the person or legal representative, an adult member of the minor's family, a transferor, or a transferor's legal representative may petition the court for:

(1) an accounting by the custodian or the custodian's legal representative; or

(2) a determination of responsibility, as between the custodial property and the custodian personally, for claims against the custodial property unless the responsibility has been adjudicated in an action under Section 141.018 to which the minor or the minor's legal representative was a party.

(b) A successor custodian may petition the court for an accounting by the predecessor custodian.

(c) The court, in a proceeding under this chapter or in any other proceeding, may require or permit the custodian or the custodian's legal representative to account.

(d) If a custodian is removed under Section 141.019(f), the court shall require an accounting and order delivery of the custodial property and records to the successor custodian and the execution of all instruments required for transfer of the custodial property.

Added by Acts 1995, 74th Leg., ch. 1043, § 1, eff. Sept. 1, 1995. Renumbered from Property Code § 20 by Acts 1997, 75th Leg., ch. 165, § 31.01(72), eff. Sept. 1, 1997.

Statutes in Context
§ 141.021

The custodianship terminates and the custodian must transfer the custodial property to the minor or the minor's estate when the first of the following events occurs: (1) the minor reaches age 21, if the property was transferred by gift, exercise of power of appointment, will, or trust (If the

custodianship was created before September 1, 1995, it will still terminate when the minor reaches age 18.); (2) the minor reaches age 18, if the property was transferred by a fiduciary or an obligor; or (3) the minor dies.

§ 141.021. Termination of Custodianship

The custodian shall transfer in an appropriate manner the custodial property to the minor or to the minor's estate on the earlier of the date:

(1) the minor attains 21 years of age, with respect to custodial property transferred under Section 141.005 or 141.006;

(2) the minor attains the age of majority under the laws of this state other than this chapter, with respect to custodial property transferred under Section 141.007 or 141.008; or

(3) the minor's death.

Added by Acts 1995, 74th Leg., ch. 1043, § 1, eff. Sept. 1, 1995. Renumbered from Property Code § 21 by Acts 1997, 75th Leg., ch. 165, § 31.01(72), eff. Sept. 1, 1997.

§ 141.022. Applicability

Except as provided by Section 141.025, this chapter applies to a transfer within the scope of Section 141.003 made after September 1, 1995, if:

(1) the transfer purports to have been made under the Texas Uniform Gifts to Minors Act; or

(2) the instrument by which the transfer purports to have been made uses in substance the designation "as custodian under the Uniform Gifts to Minors Act" or "as custodian under the Uniform Transfers to Minors Act" of any other state, and the application of this chapter is necessary to validate the transfer.

Added by Acts 1995, 74th Leg., ch. 1043, § 1, eff. Sept. 1, 1995. Amended by Acts 1997, 75th Leg., ch. 221, § 1, eff. Sept. 1, 1997. Renumbered from Property Code § 22 by Acts 1997, 75th Leg., ch. 165, § 31.01(72), eff. Sept. 1, 1997.

§ 141.023. Effect on Existing Custodianships

(a) Any transfer of custodial property under this chapter made before September 1, 1995, is validated notwithstanding that there was no specific authority in this chapter for the coverage of custodial property of that kind or for a transfer from that source at the time the transfer was made.

(b) Sections 141.002 and 141.021, with respect to the age of a minor for whom custodial property is held under this chapter, do not apply to custodial property held in a custodianship that terminated because the minor attained the age of 18 after August 26, 1973, and before September 1, 1995.

Added by Acts 1995, 74th Leg., ch. 1043, § 1, eff. Sept. 1, 1995. Renumbered from Property Code § 23 by Acts 1997, 75th Leg., ch. 165, § 31.01(72), eff. Sept. 1, 1997.

§ 141.024. Uniformity of Application and Construction

This chapter shall be applied and construed to effect its general purpose, to make uniform the law with respect to the subject of this chapter among states enacting that law.

Added by Acts 1995, 74ᵗʰ Leg., ch. 1043, § 1, eff. Sept. 1, 1995. Renumbered from Property Code § 23 by Acts 1997, 75ᵗʰ Leg., ch. 165, § 31.01(72), eff. Sept. 1, 1997.

§ 141.025. Additional Transfers to Custodianships in Existence Before Effective Date of Act

(a) This section applies only to a transfer within the scope of Section 141.003 made after September 1, 1995, to a custodian of a custodianship established before September 1, 1995, under the Texas Uniform Gifts to Minors Act.

(b) This chapter does not prevent a person from making additional transfers to a custodianship described by Subsection (a). On the direction of the transferor or custodian, custodial property that is transferred to the custodianship shall be commingled with the custodial property of the custodianship established under the Texas Uniform Gifts to Minors Act. The additional transfers to the custodianship shall be administered and distributed on termination of the custodianship, as prescribed by this chapter, except that for purposes of Section 141.021, the custodian shall transfer the custodial property to:

(1) the beneficiary on the date the beneficiary attains 18 years of age or an earlier date as prescribed by Section 141.021; or

(2) the beneficiary's estate if the individual dies before the date prescribed by Subdivision (1).

Added by Acts 1997, 75ᵗʰ Leg., ch. 221, § 2, eff. Sept. 1, 1997. Amended by Acts 1997, 75ᵗʰ Leg., ch. 165, § 31.01(72), eff. Sept. 1, 1997. Renumbered from Property Code § 25 by Acts 1999, 76ᵗʰ Leg., ch. 62, § 19.01(91), eff. Sept. 1, 1999.

Chapter 142. Management of Property Recovered in Suit by a Next Friend or Guardian Ad Litem

Statutes in Context
Chapter 142

Chapter 142 provides for the management of property recovered on behalf of a minor or incapacitated person by a next friend or guardian ad litem. Of particular importance is § 142.005 which allows for the court to create a trust to manage the property.

§ 142.001. Management by Decree

(a) In a suit in which a minor or incapacitated person who has no legal guardian is represented by a next friend or an appointed guardian ad litem, the court,

on application and hearing, may provide by decree for the investment of funds accruing to the minor or other person under the judgment in the suit.

(b) If the decree is made during vacation, it must be recorded in the minutes of the succeeding term of the court.

Acts 1983, 68ᵗʰ Leg., p. 3711, ch. 576, § 1, eff. Jan. 1, 1984. Amended by Acts 1984, 68ᵗʰ Leg., 2ⁿᵈ C.S., ch. 18, § 14(b), eff. Oct. 2, 1984; Acts 1999, 76ᵗʰ Leg., ch. 195, § 2, eff. Sept. 1, 1999.

§ 142.002. Management by Bonded Manager

(a) In a suit in which a minor or incapacitated person who has no legal guardian is represented by a next friend or an appointed guardian ad litem, the court in which a judgment is rendered may by an order entered of record authorize the next friend, the guardian ad litem, or another person to take possession of money or other personal property recovered under the judgment for the minor or other person represented.

(b) The next friend, guardian ad litem, or other person may not take possession of the property until the person has executed a bond as principal that:

(1) is in an amount at least double the value of the property or, if a surety on the bond is a solvent surety company authorized under the law of this state to execute the bond, is in an amount at least equal to the value of the property;

(2) is payable to the county judge; and

(3) is conditioned on the obligation of the next friend, guardian ad litem, or other person to use the property under the direction of the court for the benefit of its owner and to return the property, with interest or other increase, to the person entitled to receive the property when ordered by the court to do so.

Acts 1983, 68ᵗʰ Leg., p. 3711, ch. 576, § 1, eff. Jan. 1, 1984. Amended by Acts 1984, 68ᵗʰ Leg., 2ⁿᵈ C.S., ch. 18, § 14(c), eff. Oct. 2, 1984; Amended by Acts 1999, 76ᵗʰ Leg., ch. 195, § 3, eff. Sept. 1, 1999.

§ 142.003. Compensation and Duties of Managers

(a) A person who manages property under Section 142.001 or 142.002 is entitled to receive compensation as allowed by the court.

(b) The person shall make dispositions of the property as ordered by the court and shall return the property into court on the order of the court.

Acts 1983, 68ᵗʰ Leg., p. 3711, ch. 576, § 1, eff. Jan. 1, 1984.

§ 142.004. Investment of Funds

(a) In a suit in which a minor or incapacitated person who has no legal guardian is represented by a next friend or an appointed guardian ad litem, any money recovered by the plaintiff, if not otherwise managed under this chapter, may be invested:

(1) by the next friend or guardian ad litem in:

(A) a higher education savings plan established under Subchapter G, Chapter 54, Education Code, or a prepaid tuition program [the Texas tomorrow fund] established under [by] Subchapter H [F], Chapter 54, Education Code; or

(B) interest-bearing time deposits in a financial institution doing business in this state and insured by the Federal Deposit Insurance Corporation; or

(2) by the clerk of the court, on written order of the court of proper jurisdiction, in:

(A) a higher education savings plan established under Subchapter G, Chapter 54, Education Code, or a prepaid tuition program [the Texas tomorrow fund] established under [by] Subchapter H [F], Chapter 54, Education Code;

(B) interest-bearing deposits in a financial institution doing business in this state and insured by the Federal Deposit Insurance Corporation;

(C) United States treasury bills;

(D) an eligible interlocal investment pool that meets the requirements of Sections 2256.016, 2256.017, and 2256.019, Government Code; or

(E) a no-load money market mutual fund, if the fund:

(i) is regulated by the Securities and Exchange Commission;

(ii) has a dollar weighted average stated maturity of 90 days or fewer; and

(iii) includes in its investment objectives the maintenance of a stable net asset value of $1 for each share

(b) If the money invested under this section may not be withdrawn from the financial institution without an order of the court, a next friend or guardian ad litem who makes the investment is not required to execute a bond with respect to the money.

(c) When money invested under this section is withdrawn, the court may:

(1) on a finding that the person entitled to receive the money is no longer under the disability, order the funds turned over to the person; or

(2) order management of the funds under another provision of this chapter.

(d) Interest earned on an account invested by the clerk of the court shall be paid in the same manner as interest earned on an account under Chapter 117, Local Government Code.

(e) If money is invested under Subsection (a)(2)(E), the court may waive any bonding requirement.

Amended by Acts 1997, 75th Leg., ch. 505, § 22, eff. Sept. 1, 1997; Acts 1999, 76th Leg., ch. 94, § 1, eff. May 17, 1999; Acts 1999, 76th Leg., ch. 195, § 4, eff. Sept. 1, 1999; Acts 2001, 77th Leg., ch. 1420, § 17.002, eff. Sept. 1, 2001. Subsec. (a) amended by Acts 2015, 84th Leg.,

ch. 1211, § 1, eff. Sept. 1, 2015.

Statutes in Context
§ 142.005

Section 142.005 permits the court to create a trust to manage the property of a minor or incapacitated person recovered by a guardian ad litem or next friend. Only a trust company or bank may serve as the trustee. The trust must contain the provisions listed in this section. Note that a trust created on behalf of a minor may continue past age 18 but must end no later than the minor's twenty-fifth birthday. A trust for an incapacitated individual ends when the individual regains capacity.

The court may include provisions to have the trust qualify as a special needs trust under 42 U.S.C. § 1396(d)(4)(A) so the trust will not prevent the beneficiary from qualifying for Medicaid.

The 2003 Texas Legislature added § 142.005(j) to provide that an exculpatory provision in a Chapter 142 management trust will be enforceable only if both of the following two requirements are satisfied:

- The exculpatory provision is limited to specific facts and circumstances unique to the property of that trust and is not applicable generally to the trust.
- The court creating or modifying the trust makes a specific finding that there is clear and convincing evidence that the exculpatory provision is in the best interests of the beneficiary of the trust.

This new requirement is a reaction to the Texas Supreme Court opinion in *Texas Commerce Bank, N.A. v. Grizzle*, 96 S.W.3d 240 (Tex. 2002), in which the court enforced a boilerplate exculpatory clause in a Chapter 142 trust.

---

§ 142.005. Trust for Property

(a) Any court of record with jurisdiction to hear a suit involving a beneficiary may, on application and on a finding that the creation of a trust would be in the best interests of the beneficiary, enter a decree in the record directing the clerk to deliver any funds accruing to the beneficiary under the judgment to a financial institution, except as provided by Subsections (m) and (n).

(b) The decree shall provide for the creation of a trust for the management of the funds for the benefit of the beneficiary and for terms, conditions, and limitations of the trust, as determined by the court, that are not in conflict with the following mandatory provisions:

(1) The beneficiary shall be the sole beneficiary of the trust.

(2) The trustee may disburse amounts of the trust's principal, income, or both as the trustee in the trustee's sole discretion determines to be reasonably necessary for the health, education, support, or maintenance of the beneficiary. The trustee may conclusively presume that medicine or treatments approved by a licensed physician are appropriate for the health of the beneficiary.

(3) The income of the trust not disbursed under Subdivision (2) shall be added to the principal of the trust.

(4) If the beneficiary is a minor, the trust shall terminate on the death of the beneficiary, on the beneficiary's attaining an age stated in the trust, or on the 25th birthday of the beneficiary, whichever occurs first, or if the beneficiary is an incapacitated person, the trust shall terminate on the death of the beneficiary or when the beneficiary regains capacity.

(5) A trustee that is a financial institution shall serve without bond.

(6) The trustee shall receive reasonable compensation paid from trust's income, principal, or both on application to and approval of the court.

(7) The first page of the trust instrument shall contain the following notice:

NOTICE: THE BENEFICIARY AND CERTAIN PERSONS INTERESTED IN THE WELFARE OF THE BENEFICIARY MAY HAVE REMEDIES UNDER SECTION 114.008 OR 142.005, PROPERTY CODE.

(c) A trust established under this section may provide that:

(1) distributions of the trust principal before the termination of the trust may be made from time to time as the beneficiary attains designated ages and at designated percentages of the principal; and

(2) distributions, payments, uses, and applications of all trust funds may be made to the legal or natural guardian of the beneficiary or to the person having custody of the beneficiary or may be made directly to or expended for the benefit, support, or maintenance of the beneficiary without the intervention of any legal guardian or other legal representative of the beneficiary.

(d) A court that creates a trust under this section has continuing jurisdiction and supervisory power over the trust, including the power to construe, amend, revoke, modify, or terminate the trust. A trust created under this section is not subject to revocation by the beneficiary or a guardian of the beneficiary's estate. If the trust is revoked by the court before the beneficiary is 18 years old, the court may provide for the management of the trust principal and any undistributed income as authorized by this chapter. If the trust is revoked by the court after the beneficiary is 18 years old, the trust principal and any undistributed income shall be delivered to the beneficiary after the payment of all proper and necessary expenses.

(e) On the termination of the trust under its terms or on the death of the beneficiary, the trust principal and any undistributed income shall be paid to the beneficiary or to the representative of the estate of the deceased beneficiary.

(f) A trust established under this section prevails over any other law concerning minors, incapacitated persons, or their property, and the trust continues in force and effect until terminated or revoked, notwithstanding the appointment of a guardian of the estate of the minor or incapacitated person, or the attainment of the age of majority by the minor.

(g) Notwithstanding any other provision of this chapter, if the court finds that it would be in the best interests of the beneficiary for whom a trust is established under this section, the court may omit or modify any terms required by Subsection (b) if the court determines that the omission or modification is necessary or appropriate to allow the beneficiary to be eligible to receive public benefits or assistance under a state or federal program. This section does not require a distribution from a trust if the distribution is discretionary under the terms of the trust.

(h) A trust created under this section is subject to Subtitle B, Title 9.

(i) Notwithstanding Subsection (h), this section prevails over a provision in Subtitle B, Title 9, that is in conflict or inconsistent with this section.

(j) A provision in a trust created under this section that relieves a trustee from a duty, responsibility, or liability imposed by this section or Subtitle B, Title 9, is enforceable only if:

(1) the provision is limited to specific facts and circumstances unique to the property of that trust and is not applicable generally to the trust; and

(2) the court creating or modifying the trust makes a specific finding that there is clear and convincing evidence that the inclusion of the provision is in the best interests of the beneficiary of the trust.

(k) In addition to ordering other appropriate remedies and grounds, the court may appoint a guardian ad litem to investigate and report to the court whether the trustee should be removed for failing or refusing to make distributions for the health, education, support, or maintenance of the beneficiary required under the terms of the trust if the court is petitioned by:

(1) a parent of the beneficiary;

(2) a next friend of the beneficiary;

(3) a guardian of the beneficiary;

(4) a conservator of the beneficiary;

(5) a guardian ad litem for the beneficiary; or

(6) an attorney ad litem for the beneficiary.

(l) A person listed in Subsection (k) shall be reimbursed from the trust for reasonable attorney's fees, not to exceed $1,000, incurred in bringing the petition.

(m) If the value of the trust's principal is $50,000 or less, the court may appoint a person other than a financial institution to serve as trustee of the trust only if the court finds the appointment is in the beneficiary's best interests.

(n) If the value of the trust's principal is more than $50,000, the court may appoint a person other than a financial institution to serve as trustee of the trust only if the court finds that:

(1) no financial institution is willing to serve as trustee; and

(2) the appointment is in the beneficiary's best interests.

(o) In this section:

(1) "Beneficiary" means:

(A) a minor or incapacitated person who:

(i) has no legal guardian; and

(ii) is represented by a next friend or an appointed guardian ad litem; or

(B) a person with a physical disability.

(2) "Financial institution" means a financial institution, as defined by Section 201.101, Finance Code, that has trust powers, exists, and does business under the laws of this or another state or the United States.

Acts 1983, 68th Leg., p. 3712, ch. 576, § 1, eff. Jan. 1, 1984. Amended by Acts 1984, 68th Leg., 2nd C.S., ch. 18, § 14(e), (f), eff. Oct. 2, 1984. Amended by Acts 1997, 75th Leg., ch. 128, § 1, eff. Sept. 1, 1997. Amended by Acts 2003, 78th Leg., ch. 1154, § 3, eff. Sept. 1, 2003. Subsecs. (a), (d) amended by Acts 2005, 79th Leg., ch. 148, § 28, eff. Jan. 1, 2006. Subsecs. (a), (b), and (g) amended by and subsecs. (k)-(o) added by Acts 2007, 80th Leg., ch. 451, § 20, eff. Sept. 1, 2007.

§ 142.006. Claims Against Property

If any person claims an interest in property subject to management under this chapter, the court having authority over the property may hear evidence on the interest and may order the claim or the portion of the claim found to be just to be paid to the person entitled to receive it.

Acts 1983, 68th Leg., p. 3714, ch. 576, § 1, eff. Jan. 1, 1984.

§ 142.007. Incapacitated Person

For the purposes of this chapter, "incapacitated person" means a person who is impaired because of mental illness, mental deficiency, physical illness or disability, advanced age, chronic use of drugs, chronic intoxication, or any other cause except status as a minor to the extent that the person lacks sufficient understanding or capacity to make or communicate responsible decisions concerning his person.

Added by Acts 1984, 68th Leg., 2nd C.S., ch. 18, § 14(g), eff. Oct. 2, 1984.

§ 142.008. Structured Settlement

(a) In a suit in which a minor or incapacitated person who has no legal guardian is represented by a next friend or an appointed guardian ad litem, the court,

on a motion from the parties, may provide for a structured settlement that:

(1) provides for periodic payments; and

(2) is funded by:

(A) an obligation guaranteed by the United States government; or

(B) an annuity contract that meets the requirements of Section 142.009.

(b) The person obligated to fund a structured settlement shall provide to the court:

(1) a copy of the instrument that provides funding for the structured settlement; or

(2) an affidavit from an independent financial consultant that specifies the present value of the structured settlement and the method by which the value is calculated.

(c) A structured settlement provided for under this section is solely for the benefit of the beneficiary of the structured settlement and is not subject to the interest payment calculations contained in Section 117.054, Local Government Code.

Added by Acts 1999, 76th Leg., ch. 195, § 5, eff. Sept. 1, 1999.

§ 142.009. Annuity Contract Requirements for Structured Settlement

(a) An insurance company providing an annuity contract for a structured settlement as provided by Section 142.008 must:

(1) be licensed to write annuity contracts in this state;

(2) have a minimum of $1 million of capital and surplus; and

(3) be approved by the court and comply with any requirements imposed by the court to ensure funding to satisfy periodic settlement payments.

(b) In approving an insurance company under Subsection (a)(3), the court may consider whether the company:

(1) holds a industry rating equivalent to at least two of the following rating organizations:

(A) A.M. Best Company: A + + or A+;

(B) Duff & Phelps Credit Rating Company Insurance Company Claims Paying Ability Rating: AA-, AA, AA+, or AAA;

(C) Moody's Investors Service Claims Paying Ability Rating: Aa3, Aa2, Aa1, or aaa; or

(D) Standard & Poor's Corporation Insurer Claims-Paying Ability Rating: AA-, AA, AA+, or AAA;

(2) is an affiliate, as that term is defined by Article 21.49-1, Insurance Code, of a liability insurance carrier involved in the suit for which the structured settlement is created; or

(3) is connected in any way to person obligated to fund the structured settlement.

Added by Acts 1999, 76th Leg., ch. 195, § 5, eff. Sept. 1, 1999. Amended by Acts 2001, 77th Leg., ch. 96, § 2, eff.

Sept. 1, 2001.

Subtitle B. Fiduciaries

Chapter 163. *Management, Investment, and Expenditure of Institutional Funds*

Statutes in Context
Chapter 163

The 2007 Legislature enacted the Uniform Prudent Management of Institutional Funds Act (UPMIFA) replacing the Uniform Management of Institutional Funds Act passed in 1989. UPMIFA provides statutory guidelines for the management, investment, and expenditure of endowment funds held by charitable institutions. It expressly provides for diversification of assets, pooling of assets, and total return investment to implement whole portfolio management. This brings the law governing charitable institutions in line with modern investment and expenditure practice as is done in the trust context by the Uniform Prudent Investor Act (see Statutes in Context to Chapter 117).

§ 163.001. Short Title

This chapter may be cited as the Uniform Prudent Management of Institutional Funds Act.

Acts 2007, 80th Leg., ch. 834, § 1, eff. Sept. 1, 2007.

§ 163.002. Legislative Findings and Purpose

(a) The legislature finds that:

(1) institutions organized and operated exclusively for a charitable purpose perform essential and needed services in the state;

(2) uncertainty exists regarding the prudence standards for the management and investment of charitable funds and for endowment spending by institutions described by Subdivision (1); and

(3) the institutions, their officers, directors, and trustees, and the citizens of this state will benefit from removal of the uncertainty regarding applicable prudence standards and by permitting endowment funds to be invested for the long-term goals of achieving growth and maintaining purchasing power without adversely affecting the availability of funds for current expenditure.

(b) The purpose of this chapter is to provide guidance and authority through modern articulations of prudence standards for the management and investment of charitable funds and for endowment spending by institutions organized and operated exclusively for a charitable purpose in order to provide uniformity and remove uncertainty regarding those standards.

Acts 2007, 80th Leg., ch. 834, § 1, eff. Sept. 1, 2007.

§ 163.003. Definitions

In this chapter:

(1) "Charitable purpose" means the promotion of a scientific, educational, philanthropic, or environmental purpose, social welfare, the arts and humanities, or another civic or public purpose described by Section 501(c)(3) of the Internal Revenue Code of 1986.

(2) "Endowment fund" means an institutional fund or part thereof that, under the terms of a gift instrument, is not wholly expendable by the institution on a current basis. The term does not include assets that an institution designates as an endowment fund for its own use.

(3) "Gift instrument" means a record or records, including an institutional solicitation, under which property is granted to, transferred to, or held by an institution as an institutional fund.

(4) "Institution" means:

(A) a person, other than an individual, organized and operated exclusively for charitable purposes;

(B) a government or governmental subdivision, agency, or instrumentality, to the extent that it holds funds exclusively for a charitable purpose; and

(C) a trust that had both charitable and noncharitable interests, after all noncharitable interests have terminated.

(5) "Institutional fund" means a fund held by an institution exclusively for charitable purposes. The term does not include:

(A) program-related assets;

(B) a fund held for an institution by a trustee that is not an institution; or

(C) a fund in which a beneficiary that is not an institution has an interest, other than an interest that could arise upon violation or failure of the purposes of the fund.

(6) "Person" means an individual, corporation, business trust, estate, trust, partnership, limited liability company, association, joint venture, public corporation, government or governmental subdivision, agency, or instrumentality, or any other legal or commercial entity.

(7) "Program-related asset" means an asset held by an institution primarily to accomplish a charitable purpose of the institution and not primarily for investment.

(8) "Record" means information that is inscribed on a tangible medium or that is stored in an electronic or other medium and is retrievable in perceivable form.

Acts 2007, 80th Leg., ch. 834, § 1, eff. Sept. 1, 2007.

§ 163.004. Standard of Conduct in Managing and Investing Institutional Fund

(a) Subject to the intent of a donor expressed in a gift instrument, an institution, in managing and investing an institutional fund, shall consider the charitable purposes of the institution and the purposes of the institutional fund.

(b) In addition to complying with the duty of loyalty imposed by law other than this chapter, each person responsible for managing and investing an institutional fund shall manage and invest the fund in good faith and with the care an ordinarily prudent person in a like position would exercise under similar circumstances.

(c) In managing and investing an institutional fund, an institution:

(1) may incur only costs that are appropriate and reasonable in relation to the assets, the purposes of the institution, and the skills available to the institution; and

(2) shall make a reasonable effort to verify facts relevant to the management and investment of the fund.

(d) An institution may pool two or more institutional funds for purposes of management and investment.

(e) Except as otherwise provided by a gift instrument, the following rules apply:

(1) In managing and investing an institutional fund, the following factors, if relevant, must be considered:

(A) general economic conditions;

(B) the possible effect of inflation or deflation;

(C) the expected tax consequences, if any, of investment decisions or strategies;

(D) the role that each investment or course of action plays within the overall investment portfolio of the fund;

(E) the expected total return from income and the appreciation of investments;

(F) other resources of the institution;

(G) the needs of the institution and the fund to make distributions and to preserve capital; and

(H) an asset's special relationship or special value, if any, to the charitable purposes of the institution.

(2) Management and investment decisions about an individual asset must be made not in isolation but rather in the context of the institutional fund's portfolio of investments as a whole and as a part of an overall investment strategy having risk and return objectives reasonably suited to the fund and to the institution.

(3) Except as otherwise provided by law other than this chapter, an institution may invest in any kind of property or type of investment consistent with this section.

(4) An institution shall diversify the investments of an institutional fund unless the institution reasonably determines that, because of special circumstances, the purposes of the fund are better served without diversification.

(5) Within a reasonable time after receiving property, an institution shall make and carry out decisions concerning the retention or disposition of the property or to rebalance a portfolio, in order to bring the institutional fund into compliance with the purposes, terms, and distribution requirements of the institution as necessary to meet other circumstances of the institution and the requirements of this chapter.

(6) A person that has special skills or expertise, or is selected in reliance upon the person's representation that the person has special skills or expertise, has a duty to use those skills or that expertise in managing and investing institutional funds.

Acts 2007, 80th Leg., ch. 834, § 1, eff. Sept. 1, 2007.

§ 163.005. Appropriation for Expenditure or Accumulation of Endowment Fund; Rules of Construction

(a) Subject to the intent of a donor expressed in the gift instrument and to Subsections (d) and (e), an institution may appropriate for expenditure or accumulate so much of an endowment fund as the institution determines is prudent for the uses, benefits, purposes, and duration for which the endowment fund is established. Unless stated otherwise in the gift instrument, the assets in an endowment fund are donor-restricted assets until appropriated for expenditure by the institution. In making a determination to appropriate or accumulate, the institution shall act in good faith, with the care that an ordinarily prudent person in a like position would exercise under similar circumstances, and shall consider, if relevant, the following factors:

(1) the duration and preservation of the endowment fund;

(2) the purposes of the institution and the endowment fund;

(3) general economic conditions;

(4) the possible effect of inflation or deflation;

(5) the expected total return from income and the appreciation of investments;

(6) other resources of the institution; and

(7) the investment policy of the institution.

(b) To limit the authority to appropriate for expenditure or accumulate under Subsection (a), a gift instrument must specifically state the limitation.

(c) Terms in a gift instrument designating a gift as an endowment, or a direction or authorization in the gift instrument to use only "income," "interest," "dividends," or "rents, issues, or profits," or "to preserve the principal intact," or words of similar import:

(1) create an endowment fund of permanent duration unless other language in the gift instrument limits the duration or purpose of the fund; and

(2) do not otherwise limit the authority to appropriate for expenditure or accumulate under Subsection (a).

(d) Except as provided in Subsection (f), appropriation for expenditure in any year of an amount greater than seven percent of the fair market value of an endowment fund with an aggregate value of $1 million or more, calculated on the basis of market values determined at least quarterly and averaged over a period of not less than three years immediately preceding the year in which the appropriation for expenditure was made, creates a rebuttable presumption of imprudence. For an endowment fund in existence for fewer than three years, the fair market value of the endowment fund must be calculated for the period the endowment fund has been in existence. This subsection does not:

(1) apply to an appropriation for expenditure permitted under law other than this chapter or by the gift instrument; or

(2) create a presumption of prudence for an appropriation for expenditure of an amount less than or equal to seven percent of the fair market value of the endowment fund.

(e) For an institution with an endowment fund with an aggregate value of less than $1 million, a rebuttable presumption of imprudence is created if more than five percent of the fair market value of the endowment fund is appropriated for expenditure in any year, calculated on the basis of market values determined at least quarterly and averaged over a period of not less than three years immediately preceding the year in which the appropriation for expenditure was made. For an endowment fund in existence for fewer than three years, the fair market value of the endowment fund must be calculated for the period the endowment fund has been in existence. This subsection does not:

(1) apply to an appropriation for expenditure permitted under law other than this chapter or by the gift instrument; or

(2) create a presumption of prudence for an appropriation for expenditure of an amount less than or equal to five percent of the fair market value of the endowment fund.

(f) This subsection applies only to a university system, as defined by Section 61.003(10), Education Code. The appropriation for expenditure in any year of any amount greater than nine percent of the fair market value of an endowment fund with an aggregate value of $450 million or more, calculated on the basis of market values determined at least quarterly and averaged over a period of not less than three years immediately preceding the year in which the appropriation for expenditure was made, creates a rebuttable presumption of imprudence. For an endowment fund in existence for fewer than three years, the fair market value of the endowment fund must be calculated for the period the endowment fund has been in existence. This subsection does not:

(1) apply to an appropriation for expenditure permitted under law other than this chapter or by the gift instrument; or

(2) create a presumption of prudence for an appropriation for expenditure of an amount less than or equal to nine percent of the fair market value of the endowment fund.

(g) If an institution pools the assets of individual endowment funds for collective investment, this section applies to the pooled fund and does not apply to individual endowment funds, including individual endowment funds for which the nature of the underlying asset or donor restrictions preclude inclusion in a pool but which are managed by the institution in accordance with a collective investment policy.

Acts 2007, 80th Leg., ch. 834, § 1, eff. Sept. 1, 2007.

§ 163.006. Delegation of Management and Investment Functions

(a) Subject to any specific limitation set forth in a gift instrument or in law other than this chapter, an institution may delegate to an external agent the management and investment of an institutional fund to the extent that an institution could prudently delegate under the circumstances. An institution shall act in good faith, with the care that an ordinarily prudent person in a like position would exercise under similar circumstances, in:

(1) selecting an agent;

(2) establishing the scope and terms of the delegation, consistent with the purposes of the institution and the institutional fund; and

(3) periodically reviewing the agent's actions in order to monitor the agent's performance and compliance with the scope and terms of the delegation.

(b) In performing a delegated function, an agent owes a duty to the institution to exercise reasonable care to comply with the scope and terms of the delegation.

(c) An institution that complies with Subsection (a) is not liable for the decisions or actions of an agent to which the function was delegated.

(d) By accepting delegation of a management or investment function from an institution that is subject to the laws of this state, an agent submits to the jurisdiction of the courts of this state in all proceedings arising from or related to the delegation or the performance of the delegated function.

(e) An institution may delegate management and investment functions to its committees, officers, or employees as authorized by law of this state other than this chapter.

Acts 2007, 80th Leg., ch. 834, § 1, eff. Sept. 1, 2007.

§ 163.007. Release or Modification of Restrictions on Management, Investment, or Purpose

(a) If the donor consents in a record, an institution may release or modify, in whole or in part, a restriction contained in a gift instrument on the management, investment, or purpose of an institutional fund. A release or modification may not allow a fund to be used for a purpose other than a charitable purpose of the institution.

(b) The court, upon application of an institution, may modify a restriction contained in a gift instrument regarding the management or investment of an institutional fund if the restriction has become impracticable or wasteful, if it impairs the management or investment of the fund, or if, because of circumstances not anticipated by the donor, a modification of a restriction will further the purposes of the fund. Chapter 123 applies to a proceeding under this subsection. To the extent practicable, any modification must be made in accordance with the donor's probable intention.

(c) If a particular charitable purpose or a restriction contained in a gift instrument on the use of an institutional fund becomes unlawful, impracticable, impossible to achieve, or wasteful, the court, upon application of an institution, may modify the purpose of the fund or the restriction on the use of the fund in a manner consistent with the charitable purposes expressed in the gift instrument. Chapter 123 applies to a proceeding under this subsection.

(d) If an institution determines that a restriction contained in a gift instrument on the management, investment, or purpose of an institutional fund is unlawful, impracticable, impossible to achieve, or wasteful, the institution, 60 days after receipt of notice by the attorney general, may release or modify the restriction, in whole or part, if:

(1) the institutional fund subject to the restriction has a total value of less than $25,000;

(2) more than 20 years have elapsed since the fund was established; and

(3) the institution uses the property in a manner consistent with the charitable purposes expressed in the gift instrument.

(e) The notification to the attorney general under Subsection (d) must be accompanied by a copy of the gift instrument and a statement of facts sufficient to evidence compliance with Subsections (d)(1), (2), and (3).

Acts 2007, 80th Leg., ch. 834, § 1, eff. Sept. 1, 2007.

§ 163.008. Reviewing Compliance

Compliance with this chapter is determined in light of the facts and circumstances existing at the time a decision is made or action is taken, and not by hindsight.

Acts 2007, 80th Leg., ch. 834, § 1, eff. Sept. 1, 2007.

§ 163.009. Relation to Electronic Signatures in Global and National Commerce Act

This chapter modifies, limits, and supersedes the provisions of the Electronic Signatures in Global and National Commerce Act (15 U.S.C. Section 7001 et seq.) but does not modify, limit, or supersede Section 101 of that Act (15 U.S.C. Section 7001(a)) or authorize electronic delivery of any of the notices described in Section 103 of that Act (15 U.S.C. Section 7003(b)).

Acts 2007, 80th Leg., ch. 834, § 1, eff. Sept. 1, 2007.

§ 163.010. Uniformity of Application and Construction

In applying and construing this chapter, consideration must be given to the need to promote uniformity of the law with respect to the subject matter of this chapter among states that enact a law substantially similar to this chapter.

Acts 2007, 80th Leg., ch. 834, § 1, eff. Sept. 1, 2007.

§ 163.011. Applicability of Other Parts of Code

Subtitle B, Title 9 (the Texas Trust Code), does not apply to any institutional fund subject to this chapter.

Acts 2007, 80th Leg., ch. 834, § 1, eff. Sept. 1, 2007.

Subtitle C. Powers of Appointment

Chapter 181. Powers of Appointment

Statutes in Context
Chapter 181

A power of appointment is the right to designate the new owner of property. You have this power with respect to the property you own because you may give anything you own to another person. The power to name a new owner of your property is one of the things you take for granted as accompanying property ownership.

You may sever this power of appointment from the ownership of the property itself. When this happens, the following relationships are created. The owner of property (the person who is severing) is the donor of the power, the person with the power to appoint the property is the donee, and the prospective new owners are the objects of the power. When the donee actually exercises the power, the new owners are called the appointees. If the donee fails to exercise the power, the property passes to the default takers. If the donor failed to name default takers, the property reverts to the donor or the donor's estate.

The donor can create a power of appointment in an inter vivos document, such as a deed or trust, or in a separate power of appointment instrument. The donor can also create a power of appointment by will.

Powers of appointment are generally categorized in one of two ways. First, the power of appointment may be general, meaning that there are no restrictions or conditions on the donee's exercise of the power. Thus, the donee could even appoint the donee's own self as the new owner. In many aspects, the donee of a general power of appointment is like the actual owner of the property. Second, the power may be specific, special, or limited, i.e., the donor may specify certain individuals or groups as the objects of the power which do not include the donee, the donee's creditors, the donee's estate, or the creditors of the donee's estate. In addition, the donor may make the donee's exercise of the power conditional on whatever factors, within legal bounds, the donor desires, for example, only for the appointees' health-related and educational expenses.

The donee of a power of appointment does not have title, either legal or equitable, to the subject property. Instead, the donee only has a power to appoint. The appointees take title from the donor, not the donee.

The donee has no duty to exercise the power of appointment in favor of the hopeful appointees. Unlike a trustee, a donee is not a fiduciary and has no duty to manage the property or to distribute the property. A power of appointment is also not an agency relationship; the donee is not the donor's agent.

The donor may dictate the method the donee must use to exercise the power of appointment. For example, the power may be an inter vivos power indicating that the donee must exercise it while alive. Alternatively, it may be a testamentary power which the donee may only exercise by will. The donor also may permit the donee to exercise the power in both ways.

Although the donor may create a power of appointment in anyone, powers of appointment are typically used with trusts. Trustees often have the power to decide which beneficiaries will receive distributions and in what amounts. Settlors of trusts also may give powers of appointment over trust property to the beneficiaries.

Subchapter A. General Provisions

§ 181.001. Definitions

In this chapter:

(1) "Donee" means a person, whether or not a resident of this state, who, either alone or in conjunction with others, may exercise a power.

(1-a) "Object of the power of appointment" means a person to whom the donee is given the power to appoint.

(2) "Power" means the authority to appoint or designate the recipient of property, to invade or consume property, to alter, amend, or revoke an instrument under which an estate or trust is created or held, and to terminate a right or interest under an estate or trust, and any authority remaining after a partial release of a power.

(3) "Property" means all property and interests in property, real or personal, including parts of property, partial interests, and all or any part of the income from property.

(4) "Release" means a renunciation, relinquishment, surrender, refusal to accept, extinguishment, and any other form of release, including a covenant not to exercise all or part of a power.

Acts 1983, 68th Leg., p. 3723, ch. 576, § 1, eff. Jan. 1, 1984. Amended by Acts 2003, 78th Leg., ch. 551, § 1, eff. Sept. 1, 2003.

§ 181.002. Application

(a) Except as provided by Subsection (b), this chapter applies:

(1) to a power or a release of a power, regardless of the date the power is created;

(2) to a vested, contingent, or conditional power; and

(3) to a power classified as a power in gross, a power appurtenant, a power appendant, a collateral power, a general, limited, or special power, an exclusive or nonexclusive power, or any other power.

(b) This chapter applies regardless of the time or manner a power is created or reserved or the release is made and regardless of the time, manner, or in whose favor a power may be exercised.

(c) This chapter does not apply to a power in trust that is imperative.

Acts 1983, 68th Leg., p. 3723, ch. 576, § 1, eff. Jan. 1, 1984.

§ 181.003. Chapter Not Exclusive

The provisions of this chapter concerning the release of a power are not exclusive.

Acts 1983, 68th Leg., p. 3724, ch. 576, § 1, eff. Jan. 1, 1984.

§ 181.004. Construction

This chapter is intended to be declarative of the common law of this state, and it shall be liberally construed to make all powers, except imperative powers in trust, releasable unless the instrument creating the trust expressly provides otherwise.

Acts 1983, 68th Leg., p. 3724, ch. 576, § 1, eff. Jan. 1, 1984.

Subchapter B. Release of Powers of Appointment

§ 181.051. Authority of Donee to Release Power

Unless the instrument creating the power specifically provides to the contrary, a donee may at any time:

(1) completely release the power;

(2) release the power as to any property subject to the power;

(3) release the power as to a person in whose favor a power may be exercised; or

(4) limit in any respect the extent to which the power may be exercised.

Acts 1983, 68th Leg., p. 3724, ch. 576, § 1, eff. Jan. 1, 1984.

§ 181.052. Requisites of Release

(a) A partial or complete release of a power, with or without consideration, is valid if the donee executes and acknowledges, in the manner required by law for the execution and recordation of deeds, an instrument evidencing an intent to make the release, and the instrument is delivered:

(1) to the person or in the manner specified in the instrument creating the power;

(2) to an adult, other than the donee releasing the power, who may take any of the property subject to the power if the power is not exercised or in whose favor it may be exercised after the partial release;

(3) to a trustee or cotrustee of the property subject to the power; or

(4) to an appropriate county clerk for recording.

(b) An instrument releasing a power may be recorded in a county in this state in which:

(1) property subject to the power is located;

(2) a donee in control of the property resides;

(3) a trustee in control of the property resides;

(4) a corporate trustee in control of the property has its principal office; or

(5) the instrument creating the power is probated or recorded.

Acts 1983, 68th Leg., p. 3724, ch. 576, § 1, eff. Jan. 1, 1984.

§ 181.053. Release by Guardian

If a person under a disability holds a power, the guardian of the person's estate may release the power in the manner provided in this chapter on the order of the court in this state in which the guardian was appointed or in which the guardianship proceeding is pending.

Acts 1983, 68th Leg., p. 3725, ch. 576, § 1, eff. Jan. 1, 1984.

§ 181.054. Effect of Release on Multiple Donees

Unless the instrument creating a power provides otherwise, the complete or partial release by one or more donees of a power that may be exercised by two or more donees, either as an individual or a fiduciary, together or successively, does not prevent or limit the exercise or participation in the exercise of the power by the other donee or donees.

Acts 1983, 68th Leg., p. 3725, ch. 576, § 1, eff. Jan. 1, 1984.

§ 181.055. Notice of Release

(a) A fiduciary or other person in possession or control of property subject to a power, other than the donee, does not have notice of a release of the power until the original release or a copy is delivered to the fiduciary or other person.

(b) A purchaser, lessee, or mortgagee of real property subject to a power who has paid a valuable consideration and who is without actual notice does not have notice of a release of the power until the instrument releasing the power is filed for record with the county clerk of the county in which the real property is located.

Acts 1983, 68th Leg., p. 3725, ch. 576, § 1, eff. Jan. 1, 1984.

§ 181.056. Recording

(a) A county clerk shall record a release of a power in the county deed records, and the clerk shall index the release, with the name of the donee entered in the grantor index.

(b) The county clerk shall charge the same fee for recording the release of a power as the clerk is authorized to charge for recording a deed.

Acts 1983, 68th Leg., p. 3725, ch. 576, § 1, eff. Jan. 1, 1984.

§ 181.057. Effect of Failure to Deliver or File

Failure to deliver or file an instrument releasing a power under Sections 181.052 and 181.055 does not affect the validity of the release as to the donee, the person in whose favor the power may be exercised, or any other person except those expressly protected by Sections 181.052 and 181.055.

Acts 1983, 68th Leg., p. 3726, ch. 576, § 1, eff. Jan. 1, 1984.

§ 181.058. Restraints on Alienation or Anticipation

The release of a power that otherwise may be released is not prevented merely by provisions of the instrument creating the power that restrain alienation or anticipation.

Acts 1983, 68th Leg., p. 3726, ch. 576, § 1, eff. Jan. 1, 1984.

Statutes in Context
Subchapter C

The 2003 Legislature codified various aspects of the law governing the exercise of powers of appointment when it added Subchapter C. Unless the power of appointment expressly provides otherwise, the donee of a power of appointment may do the following things when exercising the power:

(1) Appoint present, future, or both present and future interests.

(2) Impose conditions and limitations on the appointment.

(3) Impose restraints on alienation.

(4) Appoint interests to a trustee for the benefit of one or more objects of the power.

(5) Create any right existing under the common law.

(6) Grant the objects of the power of appointment the power to appoint the property provided that these powers of appointment must be exercisable only in favor of the objects of the power who would have been permissible objects under the original donee's power.

(7) If the donee has the power to appoint outright to the object of the power, exercise the power to give a power of appointment to the object of the original power. The donee of the original power becomes the donor of the second-generation power. There are no restrictions on the identity of the objects of the second-generation power; in other words, these objects do not have to be permissible objects of the original power of appointment.

Subchapter C. Exercise of Powers of Appointment

§ 181.081. Extent of Power

Unless an instrument creating a power expressly provides to the contrary, a donee may exercise a power in any manner consistent with this subchapter.

Added by Acts 2003, 78th Leg., ch. 551, § 2, eff. Sept. 1, 2003.

§ 181.082. General Exercise

In exercising a power, a donee may make an appointment:

(1) of present, future, or present and future interests;

(2) with conditions and limitations;

(3) with restraints on alienation;

(4) of interests to a trustee for the benefit of one or more objects of the power; and

(5) that creates any right existing under common law.

Added by Acts 2003, 78th Leg., ch. 551, § 2, eff. Sept. 1, 2003.

§ 181.083. Creating Additional Powers

(a) In exercising a power, a donee may make appointments that create in the objects of the power additional powers of appointment. The additional powers of appointment must be exercisable in favor of objects of the power who would have been permissible objects under the original donee's power.

(b) In exercising a power, a donee who may appoint outright to an object of the power may make appointments that create in the object of the power powers exercisable in favor of persons that the original donee may direct, even though the objects of the secondary power of appointment may not have been permissible objects of the original donee's power.

Added by Acts 2003, 78th Leg., ch. 551, § 2, eff. Sept. 1, 2003.

Title 13. Disclaimer of Property Interests

Chapter 240. Texas Uniform Disclaimer of Property Interests Act

Statutes in Context
Chapter 240

The 2015 Texas Legislature enacted the Uniform Disclaimer of Property Interests Act to replace the provisions in the Estate Code and the Trust Code.

Under modern law, an heir, will beneficiary, life insurance beneficiary, or beneficiary of a survivorship agreement may disclaim or renounce the person's interest. In the normal course of events, heirs and beneficiaries do not disclaim. Most people like the idea of getting something for free. However, there are many good reasons why a person may desire to forego the offered bounty. Four of the most common reasons are as follows: (1) the property may be undesirable or accompanied by an onerous burden (e.g., littered with leaky barrels of toxic chemical waste or subject to back taxes exceeding the value of the land); (2) the heir or beneficiary may believe that it is wrong to benefit from the death of another and refuse the property on moral or religious grounds; (3) an heir or beneficiary who is in debt may disclaim the property to prevent the property from being taken by the person's creditors; and (4) the heir or beneficiary may disclaim to reduce the person's transfer tax burden (a "qualified disclaimer" under I.R.C. § 2518).

The heir or beneficiary may "pick and choose" which assets to disclaim but if the person accepts the property, the right to disclaim is waived. Even a relatively small exercise of dominion or control over the property may prevent disclaimer. See *Badouh v. Hale*, 22 S.W.3d 392 (Tex. 2000) (holding that a beneficiary who used property she expected to receive under a will as collateral for a loan prior to the testator's death could not disclaim because such a use was the exercise of dominion and control).

"[T]o be effective, a disclaimer of an inheritance is enforceable against the maker only when it has been made with adequate knowledge of that which is being disclaimed." *McCuen v. Huey*, 255 S.W.3d 716, 731 (Tex. App.—Waco 2008, no pet.).

Once a valid disclaimer is made, the disclaimant is treated as predeceasing the person from whom the disclaimant is taking. The disclaimed property then passes under intestacy, the will, or the contract as if the disclaimant had died first. The disclaimant cannot specify the new owner of the disclaimed property. See *Welder v. Hitchcock*, 617 S.W.2d 294 (Tex. Civ. App. — Corpus Christi 1981, writ ref'd n.r.e.) (holding that the disclaimed property passes as if the disclaiming person is dead vis-à-vis the disclaimed property, not the entire estate). A disclaimer may be effective even if the disclaimant is mistaken about to whom the disclaimed property would pass. *Nat'l Cas. Co. v. Doucette*, 817 S.W.2d 396 (Tex. App.—Fort Worth 1991, writ denied).

Once made, a disclaimer is irrevocable.

Disclaimers are an effective method for a debtor to prevent property to be inherited, received under a will, or taken under a survivorship agreement from falling into the hands of a creditor. The disclaimer is not a fraudulent conveyance and thus it may not be set aside by the disclaimant's creditors.

There are, however, two important exceptions. First, the United States Supreme Court held that a disclaimer will not defeat a federal tax lien. *Drye v. United States*, 528 U.S. 49 (1999). Second, an heir or will beneficiary may not disclaim property if that person is in arrears in paying child support.

For a comprehensive discussion of the Uniform Act, see Glenn M. Karisch, Thomas M. Featherston, Jr., & Julia E. Jonas, *Disclaimers Under the New Texas Uniform Disclaimer of Property Interests Act*, available at http://texasprobate.com/index/2015/6/9/the-new-texas-uniform-disclaimer-of-property-interests-act.html.

Subchapter A. General provisions

§ 240.001. Short Title

This chapter may be cited as the Texas Uniform Disclaimer of Property Interests Act.

Added by Acts 2015, 84th Leg., ch. 562, § 15, eff. Sept. 1, 2015.

§ 240.002. Definitions

In this chapter:

(1) "Current beneficiary" and "presumptive remainder beneficiary" have the meanings assigned by Section 112.071.

(2) "Disclaim" means to refuse to accept an interest in or power over property, including an interest or power the person is entitled to:

(A) by inheritance;

(B) under a will;

(C) by an agreement between spouses for community property with a right of survivorship;

(D) by a joint tenancy with a right of survivorship;

(E) by a survivorship agreement, account, or interest in which the interest of the decedent passes to a surviving beneficiary;

(F) by an insurance, annuity, endowment, employment, deferred compensation, or other contract or arrangement;

(G) under a pension, profit sharing, thrift, stock bonus, life insurance, survivor income, incentive, or other plan or program providing retirement, welfare, or fringe benefits with respect to an employee or a self-employed individual; or

(H) by an instrument creating a trust.

(3) "Disclaimant" means:

(A) the person to whom a disclaimed interest or power would have passed had the disclaimer not been made;

(B) the estate to which a disclaimed interest or power would have passed had the disclaimer not been made by the personal representative of the estate; or

(C) the trust into which a disclaimed interest or power would have passed had the disclaimer not been made by the trustee of the trust.

(4) "Disclaimed interest" means the interest that would have passed to the disclaimant had the disclaimer not been made.

(5) "Disclaimed power" means the power that would have been possessed by the disclaimant had the disclaimer not been made.

(6) "Disclaimer" means the refusal to accept an interest in or power over property.

(7) "Estate" has the meaning assigned by Section 22.012, Estates Code.

(8) "Fiduciary" means a personal representative, a trustee, an attorney in fact or agent acting under a power of attorney, or any other person authorized to act as a fiduciary with respect to the property of another person.

(9) "Guardian" has the meaning assigned by Section 1002.012, Estates Code.

(10) Notwithstanding Section 311.005, Government Code, "person" means an individual, corporation, including a public corporation, business trust, partnership, limited liability company, association, joint venture, governmental entity, including a political subdivision, agency, or instrumentality, or any other legal entity.

(11) "Personal representative" has the meanings assigned by Sections 22.031 and 1002.028, Estates Code.

(12) "State" means a state of the United States, the District of Columbia, Puerto Rico, the United States Virgin Islands, or any territory or insular possession subject to the jurisdiction of the United States. The term includes an Indian tribe or band, or Alaskan native village, recognized by federal law or formally acknowledged by a state.

(13) "Survivorship property" means property held in the name of two or more persons under an arrangement in which, on the death of one of the persons, the property passes to and is vested in the other person or persons. The term includes:

(A) property held by an agreement described in Section 111.001, Estates Code;

(B) property held by a community property survivorship agreement defined in Section 112.001, Estates Code; and

(C) property in a joint account held by an agreement described in Section 113.151, Estates Code.

(14) "Trust" has the meaning assigned by Section 111.003.

(15) "Ward" has the meaning assigned by Section 22.033, Estates Code.

Added by Acts 2015, 84th Leg., ch. 562, § 15, eff. Sept. 1, 2015.

§ 240.003. Applicability of Chapter

This chapter applies to disclaimers of any interest in or power over property, whenever created.

Added by Acts 2015, 84th Leg., ch. 562, § 15, eff. Sept. 1, 2015.

§ 240.004. Chapter Supplemented by Other Law

(a) Unless displaced by a provision of this chapter, the principles of law and equity supplement this chapter.

(b) This chapter does not limit any right of a person to waive, release, disclaim, or renounce an interest in or power over property under a statute other than this chapter.

Added by Acts 2015, 84th Leg., ch. 562, § 15, eff. Sept. 1, 2015.

§ 240.005. Uniformity of Application and Construction

In applying and construing this chapter, consideration must be given to the need to promote uniformity of the law, with respect to the subject matter of this chapter, among states that enact a law based on the uniform act on which this chapter is based.

Added by Acts 2015, 84th Leg., ch. 562, § 15, eff. Sept. 1, 2015.

§ 240.006. Power to Disclaim by Person Other Than Fiduciary

(a) A person other than a fiduciary may disclaim, in whole or in part, any interest in or power over property, including a power of appointment.

(b) A person other than a fiduciary may disclaim an interest or power under this section even if the creator of the interest or power imposed a spendthrift provision or similar restriction on transfer or a restriction or limitation on the right to disclaim.

Added by Acts 2015, 84th Leg., ch. 562, § 15, eff. Sept. 1, 2015.

§ 240.007. Power to Disclaim Power Held in Fiduciary Capacity by Person Designated to Serve as or Serving as Fiduciary

(a) Subject to Subsection (b) and except to the extent the person's right to disclaim is expressly restricted or limited by a law of this state or by the instrument creating the fiduciary relationship, a person designated to serve or serving as a fiduciary may disclaim, in whole or in part, any power over property, including a power of appointment and the power to disclaim, held in a fiduciary capacity.

(b) If a power being disclaimed under Subsection (a) by a person designated to serve or serving as a trustee affects the distributive rights of any beneficiary of the trust:

(1) the person may disclaim only on or after accepting the trust;

(2) the disclaimer must be compatible with the trustee's fiduciary obligations; and

(3) if the disclaimer is made on accepting the trust, the trustee is considered to have never possessed the power disclaimed.

(c) A person designated to serve or serving as a fiduciary may disclaim a power under this section even if the creator of the power imposed a spendthrift provision or similar restriction on transfer.

Added by Acts 2015, 84th Leg., ch. 562, § 15, eff. Sept. 1, 2015.

§ 240.008. Power to Disclaim by Fiduciary Acting in Fiduciary Capacity

(a) Subject to this section and except to the extent the fiduciary's right to disclaim is expressly restricted or limited by a law of this state or by the instrument creating the fiduciary relationship, a fiduciary acting in a fiduciary capacity may disclaim, in whole or in part, any interest in or power over property, including a power of appointment and the power to disclaim, that would have passed to the ward, estate, trust, or principal with respect to which the fiduciary was acting had the disclaimer not been made even if:

(1) the creator of the interest or power imposed a spendthrift provision or similar restriction on transfer or a restriction or limitation on the right to disclaim; or

(2) an instrument other than the instrument that created the fiduciary relationship imposed a restriction or limitation on the right to disclaim.

(b) Except as provided by Subsection (c), (d), or (f), a disclaimer by a fiduciary acting in a fiduciary capacity does not require court approval to be effective unless the instrument that created the fiduciary relationship requires court approval.

(c) The following disclaimers by a fiduciary acting in a fiduciary capacity are not effective unless approved by a court of competent jurisdiction:

(1) a disclaimer by a personal representative who is not an independent administrator or independent executor;

(2) a disclaimer by the trustee of a management trust created under Chapter 1301, Estates Code;

(3) a disclaimer by the trustee of a trust created under Section 142.005; or

(4) a disclaimer that would result in an interest in or power over property passing to the person making the disclaimer.

(d) A trustee acting in a fiduciary capacity may not disclaim an interest in property that would cause the interest in property not to become trust property unless:

(1) a court of competent jurisdiction approves the disclaimer; or

(2) the trustee provides written notice of the disclaimer in accordance with Section 240.0081.

(e) In the absence of a court-appointed guardian, without court approval, a natural guardian as described by Section 1104.051, Estates Code, may disclaim on behalf of a minor child of the natural guardian, in whole or in part, any interest in or power over property, including a power of appointment, that the minor child is to receive solely as a result of another disclaimer, but only if the disclaimed interest or power does not pass to or for the benefit of the natural guardian as a result of the disclaimer.

(f) Unless a court of competent jurisdiction approves the disclaimer, a disclaimer by a fiduciary acting in a fiduciary capacity must be compatible with the fiduciary's fiduciary obligations. A disclaimer by a fiduciary acting in a fiduciary capacity is not a per se breach of the fiduciary's fiduciary obligations.

(g) Possible remedies for a breach of fiduciary obligations do not include declaring an otherwise effective disclaimer void or granting other legal or equitable relief that would make the disclaimer ineffective.

Added by Acts 2015, 84th Leg., ch. 562, § 15, eff. Sept. 1, 2015.

§ 240.0081. Notice Required by Trustee Disclaiming Certain Interests in Property; Effect of Notice

(a) A trustee acting in a fiduciary capacity may disclaim an interest in property that would cause the interest in property not to become trust property without court approval if the trustee provides written notice of the disclaimer to all of the current beneficiaries and presumptive remainder beneficiaries of the trust.

(b) For the purpose of determining who is a current beneficiary or presumptive remainder beneficiary entitled to the notice under Subsection (a), a beneficiary is determined as of the date the notice is sent.

(c) In addition to the notice required under Subsection (a), the trustee shall give written notice of the trustee's disclaimer to the attorney general if:

(1) a charity is entitled to notice;

(2) a charity entitled to notice is no longer in existence;

(3) the trustee has the authority to distribute trust assets to one or more charities that are not named in the trust instrument; or

(4) the trustee has the authority to make distributions for a charitable purpose described in the trust instrument, but no charity is named as a beneficiary for that purpose.

(d) If the beneficiary has a court-appointed guardian or conservator, the notice required to be given by this section must be given to that guardian or conservator. If the beneficiary is a minor for whom no guardian or conservator has been appointed, the notice required to be given by this section must be given to a parent of the minor.

(e) The trustee is not required to provide the notice to a beneficiary who:

(1) is known to the trustee and cannot be located by the trustee after reasonable diligence;

(2) is not known to the trustee;

(3) waives the requirement of the notice under this section; or

(4) is a descendant of a beneficiary to whom the trustee has given notice if the beneficiary and the beneficiary's ancestor have similar interests in the trust and no apparent conflict of interest exists between them.

(f) The notice required under Subsection (a) must:

(1) include a statement that:

(A) the trustee intends to disclaim an interest in property;

(B) if the trustee makes the disclaimer, the property will not become trust property and will not be available to distribute to the beneficiary from the trust;

(C) the beneficiary has the right to object to the disclaimer; and

(D) the beneficiary may petition a court to approve, modify, or deny the disclaimer;

(2) describe the interest in property the trustee intends to disclaim;

(3) specify the earliest date the trustee intends to make the disclaimer;

(4) include the name and mailing address of the trustee;

(5) be given not later than the 30th day before the date the disclaimer is made; and

(6) be sent by personal delivery, first-class mail, facsimile, e-mail, or any other method likely to result in the notice's receipt.

(g) A beneficiary is not considered to have accepted the disclaimed interest solely because the beneficiary acts or does not act on receipt of a notice provided under this section.

(h) If the trustee makes the disclaimer for which notice is provided under this section, the beneficiary does not lose the beneficiary's right, if any, to sue the trustee for breach of the trustee's fiduciary obligations in connection with making the disclaimer. Section 240.008(g) applies to remedies sought in connection with the alleged breach.

Added by Acts 2015, 84ᵗʰ Leg., ch. 562, § 15, eff. Sept. 1, 2015.

§ 240.009. Power to Disclaim; General Requirements; When Irrevocable

(a) To be effective, a disclaimer must:
(1) be in writing;
(2) declare the disclaimer;
(3) describe the interest or power disclaimed;
(4) be signed by the person making the disclaimer; and
(5) be delivered or filed in the manner provided by Subchapter C.

(b) A partial disclaimer may be expressed as a fraction, percentage, monetary amount, term of years, limitation of a power, or any other interest or estate in the property.

(c) A disclaimer is irrevocable on the later of the date the disclaimer:
(1) is delivered or filed under Subchapter C; or
(2) takes effect as provided in Sections 240.051-240.056.

(d) A disclaimer made under this chapter is not a transfer, assignment, or release.

Added by Acts 2015, 84ᵗʰ Leg., ch. 562, § 15, eff. Sept. 1, 2015.

Subchapter B. Type and Effect of Disclaimer

§ 240.0501. Definition

In this subchapter, "future interest" means an interest that:
(1) takes effect in possession or enjoyment, if at all, later than the time at which the instrument creating the interest becomes irrevocable; and
(2) passes to the holder of the interest at the time of the event that causes the taker of the interest to be finally ascertained and the interest to be indefeasibly vested.

Added by Acts 2015, 84ᵗʰ Leg., ch. 562, § 15, eff. Sept. 1, 2015.

§ 240.051. Disclaimer of Interest in Property

(a) This section and Sections 240.0511 and 240.0512 apply to a disclaimer of an interest in property other than a disclaimer subject to Section 240.052 or 240.053.

(b) If an interest in property passes because of the death of a decedent:
(1) a disclaimer of the interest:
(A) takes effect as of the time of the decedent's death; and
(B) relates back for all purposes to the time of the decedent's death; and
(2) the disclaimed interest is not subject to the claims of any creditor of the disclaimant.

(c) If an interest in property passes because of an event not related to the death of a decedent:
(1) a disclaimer of the interest:
(A) takes effect:
(i) as of the time the instrument creating the interest became irrevocable; or
(ii) in the case of an irrevocable transfer made without an instrument, at the time of the irrevocable transfer; and
(B) relates back for all purposes to the time the instrument became irrevocable or the time of the irrevocable transfer, as applicable; and
(2) the disclaimed interest is not subject to the claims of any creditor of the disclaimant.

(d) A disclaimed interest passes according to any provision in the instrument creating the interest that provides for:
(1) the disposition of the interest if the interest were to be disclaimed; or
(2) the disposition of disclaimed interests in general.

(e) If the instrument creating the disclaimed interest does not contain a provision described by Subsection (d) and:
(1) if the disclaimant is not an individual, the disclaimed interest passes as if the disclaimant did not exist; or
(2) if the disclaimant is an individual:
(A) except as provided by Section 240.0511, if the interest is passing because of the death of a decedent, the disclaimed interest passes as if the disclaimant had died immediately before the time as of which the disclaimer takes effect under Subsection (b); or
(B) except as provided by Section 240.0512, if the interest is passing because of an event not related to the death of a decedent, the disclaimed interest passes as if the disclaimant had died immediately before the time as of which the disclaimer takes effect under Subsection (c).

(f) A disclaimed interest that passes by intestacy passes as if the disclaimant died immediately before the decedent.

Added by Acts 2015, 84ᵗʰ Leg., ch. 562, § 15, eff. Sept.

1, 2015.

§ 240.0511. Disposition of Interest Passing Because of Decedent's Death and Disclaimed by Individual

(a) Subject to Subsection (b):

(1) if by law or under the instrument creating the disclaimed interest the descendants of a disclaimant of an interest passing because of the death of a decedent would share in the disclaimed interest by any method of representation under Section 240.051(e)(2)(A), the disclaimed interest passes only to the descendants of the disclaimant who survive the decedent; or

(2) if the disclaimed interest would have passed to the disclaimant's estate under Section 240.051(e)(2)(A), the disclaimed interest instead passes by representation to the descendants of the disclaimant who survive the decedent.

(b) If no descendant of the disclaimant survives the decedent, the disclaimed interest passes to those persons, including the state but excluding the disclaimant, and in such shares as would succeed to the transferor's intestate estate under the intestate succession law of the transferor's domicile had the transferor died immediately before the decedent, except that if the transferor's surviving spouse is living but remarried before the decedent's death, the transferor is considered to have died unmarried immediately before the decedent's death.

(c) On the disclaimer of a preceding interest, a future interest held by a person other than the disclaimant takes effect as if the disclaimant had died immediately before the decedent, but a future interest held by the disclaimant is not accelerated in possession or enjoyment.

Added by Acts 2015, 84th Leg., ch. 562, § 15, eff. Sept. 1, 2015.

§ 240.0512. Disposition of Interest Passing Because of Event Other Than Decedent's Death and Disclaimed by Individual

(a) Subject to Subsection (b):

(1) if by law or under the instrument creating the disclaimed interest the descendants of a disclaimant of an interest passing because of an event not related to the death of a decedent would share in the disclaimed interest by any method of representation under Section 240.051(e)(2)(B), the disclaimed interest passes only to the descendants of the disclaimant living at the time of the event that causes the interest to pass; or

(2) if the disclaimed interest would have passed to the disclaimant's estate under Section 240.051(e)(2)(B), the disclaimed interest instead passes by representation to the descendants of the disclaimant living at the time of the event that causes the interest to pass.

(b) If no descendant of the disclaimant is living at the time of the event described by Subsection (a)(1), the disclaimed interest passes to those persons, including the state but excluding the disclaimant, and in such shares as would succeed to the transferor's intestate estate under the intestate succession law of the transferor's domicile had the transferor died immediately before the event described by Subsection (a)(1), except that if the transferor's surviving spouse is living but remarried before the event, the transferor is considered to have died unmarried immediately before the event.

(c) On the disclaimer of a preceding interest, a future interest held by a person other than the disclaimant takes effect as if the disclaimant had died immediately before the time the disclaimer takes effect under Section 240.051(c)(1)(A), but a future interest held by the disclaimant is not accelerated in possession or enjoyment.

Added by Acts 2015, 84th Leg., ch. 562, § 15, eff. Sept. 1, 2015.

§ 240.052. Disclaimer of Rights in Survivorship Property

(a) On the death of a holder of survivorship property, a surviving holder may disclaim, in whole or in part, an interest in the property of the deceased holder that would have otherwise passed to the surviving holder by reason of the deceased holder's death.

(b) If an interest in survivorship property is disclaimed by a surviving holder of the property:

(1) the disclaimer:

(A) takes effect as of the time of the deceased holder's death; and

(B) relates back for all purposes to the time of the deceased holder's death; and

(2) the disclaimed interest is not subject to the claims of any creditor of the disclaimant.

(c) An interest in survivorship property disclaimed by a surviving holder of the property passes as if the disclaimant predeceased the holder to whose death the disclaimer relates.

Added by Acts 2015, 84th Leg., ch. 562, § 15, eff. Sept. 1, 2015.

§ 240.053. Disclaimer of Interest by Trustee

(a) If a trustee disclaims an interest in property that otherwise would have become trust property:

(1) the interest does not become trust property;

(2) the disclaimer:

(A) takes effect as of the time the trust became irrevocable; and

(B) relates back for all purposes to the time the trust became irrevocable; and

(3) the disclaimed interest is not subject to the claims of any creditor of the trustee, the trust, or any trust beneficiary.

(b) If the instrument creating the disclaimed interest contains a provision that provides for the disposition of the interest if the interest were to be disclaimed, the disclaimed interest passes according to that provision.

(c) If the instrument creating the disclaimed interest does not contain a provision described by Subsection (b), the disclaimed interest passes as if:

(1) all of the current beneficiaries, presumptive remainder beneficiaries, and contingent beneficiaries of the trust affected by the disclaimer who are individuals died before the trust became irrevocable; and

(2) all beneficiaries of the trust affected by the disclaimer who are not individuals ceased to exist without successor organizations and without substitution of beneficiaries under the cy pres doctrine before the trust became irrevocable.

(d) Subsection (c) applies only for purposes of determining the disposition of an interest in property disclaimed by a trustee that otherwise would have become trust property and applies only with respect to the trust affected by the disclaimer. Subsection (c) does not apply with respect to other trusts governed by the instrument and does not apply for other purposes under the instrument or under the laws of intestacy.

Added by Acts 2015, 84th Leg., ch. 562, § 15, eff. Sept. 1, 2015.

§ 240.054. Disclaimer of Power of Appointment or Other Power Not Held in Fiduciary Capacity

(a) If a holder disclaims a power of appointment or other power not held in a fiduciary capacity, this section applies.

(b) If the holder:

(1) has not exercised the power, the disclaimer takes effect as of the time the instrument creating the power becomes irrevocable; or

(2) has exercised the power and the disclaimer is of a power other than a presently exercisable general power of appointment, the disclaimer takes effect immediately after the last exercise of the power.

(c) The instrument creating the power is construed as if the power had expired when the disclaimer became effective.

Added by Acts 2015, 84th Leg., ch. 562, § 15, eff. Sept. 1, 2015.

§ 240.055. Disclaimer by Appointee of, or Object or Taker in Default of Exercise of, Power of Appointment

(a) A disclaimer of an interest in property by an appointee of a power of appointment takes effect as of the time the instrument by which the holder exercises the power becomes irrevocable.

(b) A disclaimer of an interest in property by an object or taker in default of an exercise of a power of appointment takes effect as of the time the instrument creating the power becomes irrevocable.

Added by Acts 2015, 84th Leg., ch. 562, § 15, eff. Sept. 1, 2015.

§ 240.056. Disclaimer of Power Held in Fiduciary Capacity

(a) If a person designated to serve or serving as a fiduciary disclaims a power held or to be held in a fiduciary capacity that has not been exercised, the disclaimer takes effect as of the time the instrument creating the power becomes irrevocable.

(b) If a person designated to serve or serving as a fiduciary disclaims a power held or to be held in a fiduciary capacity that has been exercised, the disclaimer takes effect immediately after the last exercise of the power.

(c) A disclaimer subject to this section is effective as to another person designated to serve or serving as a fiduciary if:

(1) the disclaimer provides that it is effective as to another person designated to serve or serving as a fiduciary; and

(2) the person disclaiming has the authority to bind the estate, trust, or other person for whom the person is acting.

Added by Acts 2015, 84th Leg., ch. 562, § 15, eff. Sept. 1, 2015.

§ 240.057. Tax Qualified Disclaimer

(a) In this section, "Internal Revenue Code" has the meaning assigned by Section 111.004.

(b) Notwithstanding any other provision of this chapter, if, as a result of a disclaimer or transfer, the disclaimed or transferred interest is treated under the Internal Revenue Code as never having been transferred to the disclaimant, the disclaimer or transfer is effective as a disclaimer under this chapter.

Added by Acts 2015, 84th Leg., ch. 562, § 15, eff. Sept. 1, 2015.

§ 240.058. Partial Disclaimer by Spouse

A disclaimer by a decedent's surviving spouse of an interest in property transferred as the result of the death of the decedent is not a disclaimer by the surviving spouse of any other transfer from the decedent to or for the benefit of the surviving spouse, regardless of whether the interest that would have passed under the disclaimed transfer passes because of the disclaimer to or for the benefit of the surviving spouse by the other transfer.

Added by Acts 2015, 84th Leg., ch. 562, § 15, eff. Sept. 1, 2015.

Subchapter C. Delivery or Filing

§ 240.101. Delivery or Filing Generally

(a) Subject to applicable requirements of this subchapter, a disclaimant may deliver a disclaimer by personal delivery, first-class mail, facsimile, e-mail, or any other method likely to result in the disclaimer's receipt.

(b) If a disclaimer is mailed to the intended recipient by certified mail, return receipt requested, at an address the disclaimant in good faith believes is likely to result in the disclaimer's receipt, delivery is considered to have occurred on the date of mailing regardless of receipt.

Added by Acts 2015, 84th Leg., ch. 562, § 15, eff. Sept. 1, 2015.

§ 240.102. Disclaimer of Interest Created Under Intestate Succession or Will

In the case of an interest created under the law of intestate succession or an interest created by will, other than an interest in a testamentary trust:

(1) a disclaimer must be delivered to the personal representative of the decedent's estate; or

(2) if no personal representative is then serving, a disclaimer must be filed in the official public records of any county in which the decedent:

(A) was domiciled on the date of the decedent's death; or

(B) owned real property.

Added by Acts 2015, 84th Leg., ch. 562, § 15, eff. Sept. 1, 2015.

§ 240.103. Disclaimer of Interest in Testamentary Trust

In the case of an interest in a testamentary trust:

(1) a disclaimer must be delivered to the trustee then serving;

(2) if no trustee is then serving, a disclaimer must be delivered to the personal representative of the decedent's estate; or

(3) if no trustee or personal representative is then serving, a disclaimer must be filed in the official public records of any county in which the decedent:

(A) was domiciled on the date of the decedent's death; or

(B) owned real property.

Added by Acts 2015, 84th Leg., ch. 562, § 15, eff. Sept. 1, 2015.

§ 240.104. Disclaimer of Interest in Inter Vivos Trust

In the case of an interest in an inter vivos trust:

(1) a disclaimer must be delivered to the trustee then serving, or, if no trustee is then serving, a disclaimer must be filed:

(A) with a court having jurisdiction to enforce the trust; or

(B) in the official public records of the county in which:

(i) the situs of administration of the trust is maintained; or

(ii) the settlor is domiciled or was domiciled on the date of the settlor's death; and

(2) if a disclaimer is made before the time the instrument creating the trust becomes irrevocable, a disclaimer must be delivered to the settlor of a revocable trust or the transferor of the interest.

Added by Acts 2015, 84th Leg., ch. 562, § 15, eff. Sept. 1, 2015.

§ 240.105. Disclaimer of Interest Created by Beneficiary Designation

(a) In this section, "beneficiary designation" means an instrument, other than an instrument creating a trust, naming the beneficiary of:

(1) an annuity or insurance policy;

(2) an account with a designation for payment on death;

(3) a security registered in beneficiary form;

(4) a pension, profit-sharing, retirement, or other employment-related benefit plan; or

(5) any other nonprobate transfer at death.

(b) In the case of an interest created by a beneficiary designation that is disclaimed before the designation becomes irrevocable, the disclaimer must be delivered to the person making the beneficiary designation.

(c) In the case of an interest created by a beneficiary designation that is disclaimed after the designation becomes irrevocable:

(1) a disclaimer of an interest in personal property must be delivered to the person obligated to distribute the interest; and

(2) a disclaimer of an interest in real property must be recorded in the official public records of the county where the real property that is the subject of the disclaimer is located.

Added by Acts 2015, 84th Leg., ch. 562, § 15, eff. Sept. 1, 2015.

§ 240.106. Disclaimer by Surviving Holder of Survivorship Property

In the case of a disclaimer by a surviving holder of survivorship property, the disclaimer must be delivered to the person to whom the disclaimed interest passes.

Added by Acts 2015, 84th Leg., ch. 562, § 15, eff. Sept. 1, 2015.

§ 240.107. Disclaimer by Object or Taker in Default of Exercise of Power of Appointment

In the case of a disclaimer by an object or taker in default of an exercise of a power of appointment at any time after the power was created:

(1) the disclaimer must be delivered to the holder of the power or to the fiduciary acting under the instrument that created the power; or

(2) if no fiduciary is then serving, the disclaimer must be filed:

(A) with a court having authority to appoint the fiduciary; or

(B) in the official public records of the county in which the creator of the power is domiciled or was domiciled on the date of the creator's death.

Added by Acts 2015, 84ᵗʰ Leg., ch. 562, § 15, eff. Sept. 1, 2015.

§ 240.108. Disclaimer by Certain Appointees

In the case of a disclaimer by an appointee of a nonfiduciary power of appointment:

(1) the disclaimer must be delivered to the holder, the personal representative of the holder's estate, or the fiduciary under the instrument that created the power; or

(2) if no fiduciary is then serving, the disclaimer must be filed:

(A) with a court having authority to appoint the fiduciary; or

(B) in the official public records of the county in which the creator of the power is domiciled or was domiciled on the date of the creator's death.

Added by Acts 2015, 84ᵗʰ Leg., ch. 562, § 15, eff. Sept. 1, 2015.

§ 240.109. Disclaimer by Certain Fiduciaries

In the case of a disclaimer by a fiduciary of a power over a trust or estate, the disclaimer must be delivered as provided by Section 240.102, 240.103, or 240.104 as if the power disclaimed were an interest in property.

Added by Acts 2015, 84ᵗʰ Leg., ch. 562, § 15, eff. Sept. 1, 2015.

§ 240.110. Disclaimer of Power by Agent

In the case of a disclaimer of a power by an agent, the disclaimer must be delivered to the principal or the principal's representative.

Added by Acts 2015, 84ᵗʰ Leg., ch. 562, § 15, eff. Sept. 1, 2015.

§ 240.111. Recording of Disclaimer

If an instrument transferring an interest in or power over property subject to a disclaimer is required or authorized by law to be filed, recorded, or registered, the disclaimer may be filed, recorded, or registered as that instrument. Except as otherwise provided by Section 240.105(c)(2), failure to file, record, or register the disclaimer does not affect the disclaimer's validity between the disclaimant and persons to whom the property interest or power passes by reason of the disclaimer.

Added by Acts 2015, 84ᵗʰ Leg., ch. 562, § 15, eff. Sept. 1, 2015.

Subchapter D. Disclaimer Barred or Limited

§ 240.151. When Disclaimer Barred or Limited

(a) A disclaimer is barred by a written waiver of the right to disclaim.

(b) A disclaimer of an interest in property is barred if any of the following events occur before the disclaimer becomes effective:

(1) the disclaimant accepts the interest sought to be disclaimed by:

(A) taking possession of the interest; or

(B) exercising dominion and control over the interest;

(2) the disclaimant voluntarily assigns, conveys, encumbers, pledges, or transfers the interest sought to be disclaimed or contracts to do so; or

(3) the interest sought to be disclaimed is sold under a judicial sale.

(c) The acceptance of an interest in property by a person in the person's fiduciary capacity is not an acceptance of the interest in the person's individual capacity and does not bar the person from disclaiming the interest in the person's individual capacity.

(d) A disclaimer, in whole or in part, of the future exercise of a power held in a fiduciary capacity is not barred by the previous exercise of the power.

(e) A disclaimer, in whole or in part, of the future exercise of a power not held in a fiduciary capacity is not barred by the previous exercise of the power unless the power is exercisable in favor of the disclaimant.

(f) A disclaimer of:

(1) a power over property that is barred by this section is ineffective; and

(2) an interest in property that is barred by this section takes effect as a transfer of the interest disclaimed to the persons who would have taken the interest under Subchapter B had the disclaimer not been barred.

(g) A disclaimer by a child support obligor is barred as to disclaimed property that could be applied to satisfy the disclaimant's child support obligations if those obligations have been:

(1) administratively determined by the Title IV-D agency as defined by Section 101.033, Family Code, in a Title IV-D case as defined by Section 101.034, Family Code; or

(2) confirmed and reduced to judgment as provided by Section 157.263, Family Code.

(h) If Subsection (g) applies, the child support obligee to whom child support arrearages are owed may enforce the child support obligation against the disclaimant as to disclaimed property by a lien or by any other remedy provided by law.

Added by Acts 2015, 84ᵗʰ Leg., ch. 562, § 15, eff. Sept. 1, 2015.

XVII.
TAX CODE

Title 1. Property Tax Code

Subtitle C. Taxable Property and Exemptions

Chapter 11. Taxable Property and Exemptions

Subchapter B. Exemptions

Statutes in Context
§ 11.13

Section 11.13 provides a tax exemption for homesteads. Note that § 11.13(j) permits the settlor of a trust in which the settlor placed the settlor's homestead to claim the exemption for tax purposes under certain circumstances. For an analogous provision regarding creditor protection for a homestead in trust, see Prop. Code § 41.0021.

§ 11.13. Residence Homestead

(a) A family or single adult is entitled to an exemption from taxation for the county purposes authorized in Article VIII, Section 1-a, of the Texas Constitution of $3,000 of the assessed value of his residence homestead.

(b) An adult is entitled to exemption from taxation by a school district of $25,000 [$15,000] of the appraised value of the adult's residence homestead, except that only $5,000 [$10,000] of the exemption applies [does not apply] to an entity operating under former Chapter 17, 18, 25, 26, 27, or 28, Education Code, as those chapters existed on May 1, 1995, as permitted by Section 11.301, Education Code.

(c) In addition to the exemption provided by Subsection (b) of this section, an adult who is disabled or is 65 or older is entitled to an exemption from taxation by a school district of $10,000 of the appraised value of his residence homestead.

(d) In addition to the exemptions provided by Subsections (b) and (c) of this section, an individual who is disabled or is 65 or older is entitled to an exemption from taxation by a taxing unit of a portion (the amount of which is fixed as provided by Subsection (e) of this section) of the appraised value of his residence homestead if the exemption is adopted either:

(1) by the governing body of the taxing unit; or

(2) by a favorable vote of a majority of the qualified voters of the taxing unit at an election called by the governing body of a taxing unit, and the governing body shall call the election on the petition of at least 20 percent of the number of qualified voters who voted in the preceding election of the taxing unit.

(e) The amount of an exemption adopted as provided by Subsection (d) of this section is $3,000 of the appraised value of the residence homestead unless a larger amount is specified by:

(1) the governing body authorizing the exemption if the exemption is authorized as provided by Subdivision (1) of Subsection (d) of this section; or

(2) the petition for the election if the exemption is authorized as provided by Subdivision (2) of Subsection (d) of this section.

(f) Once authorized, an exemption adopted as provided by Subsection (d) of this section may be repealed or decreased or increased in amount by the governing body of the taxing unit or by the procedure authorized by Subdivision (2) of Subsection (d) of this section. In the case of a decrease, the amount of the exemption may not be reduced to less than $3,000 of the market value.

(g) If the residence homestead exemption provided by Subsection (d) of this section is adopted by a county that levies a tax for the county purposes authorized by Article VIII, Section 1-a, of the Texas Constitution, the residence homestead exemptions provided by Subsections (a) and (d) of this section may not be aggregated for the county tax purposes. An individual who is eligible for both exemptions is entitled to take only the exemption authorized as provided by Subsection (d) of this section for purposes of that county tax.

(h) Joint, community, or successive owners may not each receive the same exemption provided by or pursuant to this section for the same residence homestead in the same year. An eligible disabled person who is 65 or older may not receive both a disabled and an elderly residence homestead exemption but may choose either. A person may not receive an exemption under this section for more than one residence homestead in the same year.

(i) The assessor and collector for a taxing unit may disregard the exemptions authorized by Subsection (b), (c), (d), or (n) of this section and assess and collect a tax pledged for payment of debt without deducting the amount of the exemption if:

(1) prior to adoption of the exemption, the unit pledged the taxes for the payment of a debt; and

(2) granting the exemption would impair the obligation of the contract creating the debt.

(j) For purposes of this section:

(1) "Residence homestead" means a structure (including a mobile home) or a separately secured and occupied portion of a structure (together with the land, not to exceed 20 acres, and improvements used in the residential occupancy of the structure, if the structure and the land and improvements have identical ownership) that:

(A) is owned by one or more individuals, either directly or through a beneficial interest in a qualifying trust;

(B) is designed or adapted for human residence;

(C) is used as a residence; and

(D) is occupied as the individual's principal residence by an owner, by an owner's surviving spouse who has a life estate in the property, or, for property owned through a beneficial interest in a qualifying trust, by a trustor or beneficiary of the trust who qualifies for the exemption.

(2) "Trustor" means a person who transfers an interest in real or personal property to a qualifying trust, whether during the person's lifetime or at death, or the person's spouse.

(3) "Qualifying trust" means a trust:

(A) in which the agreement, will, or court order creating the trust, an instrument transferring property to the trust, or any other agreement that is binding on the trustee provides that the trustor of the trust or a beneficiary of the trust has the right to use and occupy as the trustor's or beneficiary's principal residence residential property rent free and without charge except for taxes and other costs and expenses specified in the instrument or court order:

(i) for life;

(ii) for the lesser of life or a term of years; or

(iii) until the date the trust is revoked or terminated by an instrument or court order that describes the property with sufficient certainty to identify it and is recorded in the real property records of the county in which the property is located; and

(B) that acquires the property in an instrument of title or under a court order that:

(i) describes the property with sufficient certainty to identify it and the interest acquired; and

(ii) is recorded in the real property records of the county in which the property is located.

(k) A qualified residential structure does not lose its character as a residence homestead if a portion of the structure is rented to another or is used primarily for other purposes that are incompatible with the owner's residential use of the structure. However, the amount of any residence homestead exemption does not apply to the value of that portion of the structure that is used primarily for purposes that are incompatible with the owner's residential use.

(l) A qualified residential structure does not lose its character as a residence homestead when the owner who qualifies for the exemption temporarily stops occupying it as a principal residence if that owner does not establish a different principal residence and the absence is:

(1) for a period of less than two years and the owner intends to return and occupy the structure as the owner's principal residence; or

(2) caused by the owner's:

(A) military service inside or outside of the United States as a member of the armed forces of the United States or of this state; or

(B) residency in a facility that provides services related to health, infirmity, or aging.

(m) In this section:

(1) "Disabled" means under a disability for purposes of payment of disability insurance benefits under Federal Old-Age, Survivors, and Disability Insurance.

(2) "School district" means a political subdivision organized to provide general elementary and secondary public education. "School district" does not include a junior college district or a political subdivision organized to provide special education services.

(n) In addition to any other exemptions provided by this section, an individual is entitled to an exemption from taxation by a taxing unit of a percentage of the appraised value of his residence homestead if the exemption is adopted by the governing body of the taxing unit before July 1 in the manner provided by law for official action by the body. If the percentage set by the taxing unit produces an exemption in a tax year of less than $5,000 when applied to a particular residence homestead, the individual is entitled to an exemption of $5,000 of the appraised value. The percentage adopted by the taxing unit may not exceed 20 percent.

(n-1) The governing body of a school district, municipality, or county that adopted an exemption under Subsection (n) for the 2014 tax year may not reduce the amount of or repeal the exemption. This subsection expires December 31, 2019.

(o) For purposes of this section, a residence homestead also may consist of an interest in real property created through ownership of stock in a corporation incorporated under the Cooperative Association Act (Article 1396-50.01, Vernon's Texas Civil Statutes) to provide dwelling places to its stockholders if:

(1) the interests of the stockholders of the corporation are appraised separately as provided by Section 23.19 of this code in the tax year to which the exemption applies;

(2) ownership of the stock entitles the owner to occupy a dwelling place owned by the corporation;

(3) the dwelling place is a structure or a separately secured and occupied portion of a structure; and

(4) the dwelling place is occupied as his principal residence by a stockholder who qualifies for the exemption.

(p) Exemption under this section for a homestead described by Subsection (o) of this section extends only to the dwelling place occupied as a residence homestead and to a portion of the total common area used in the residential occupancy that is equal to the percentage of the total amount of the stock issued by the corporation that is owned by the homestead claimant. The size of a residence homestead under Subsection (o) of this section, including any relevant portion of common area, may not exceed 20 acres.

(q) The surviving spouse of an individual who qualifies for an exemption under Subsection (d) for the residence homestead of a person 65 or older is entitled to an exemption for the same property from the same taxing unit in an amount equal to that of the exemption for which the deceased spouse qualified if:

(1) the deceased spouse died in a year in which the deceased spouse qualified for the exemption;

(2) the surviving spouse was 55 or older when the deceased spouse died; and

(3) the property was the residence homestead of the surviving spouse when the deceased spouse died and remains the residence homestead of the surviving spouse.

(r) An individual who receives an exemption under Subsection (d) is not entitled to an exemption under Subsection (q).

(s) Expired.

Acts 1979, 66th Leg., p. 2234, ch. 841, § 1, eff. Jan. 1, 1980. Amended by Acts 1981, 67th Leg., 1st C.S., p. 127, ch. 13, § 31, eff. Jan. 1, 1982; Acts 1983, 68th Leg., p. 4822, ch. 851, § 6, eff. Aug. 29, 1983; Acts 1985, 69th Leg., ch. 301, § 1, eff. June 7, 1985; Acts 1987, 70th Leg., ch. 547, § 1, eff. Jan. 1, 1988; Acts 1991, 72nd Leg., ch. 20, § 18, eff. Aug. 26, 1991; Acts 1991, 72nd Leg., ch. 20, § 19(a), eff. Jan. 1, 1992; Acts 1991, 72nd Leg., ch. 391, § 14; Acts 1993, 73rd Leg., ch. 347, § 4.08, eff. May 31, 1993; Acts 1993, 73rd Leg., ch. 854, § 1, eff. Jan. 1, 1994; Acts 1995, 74th Leg., ch. 76, § 15.01, eff. Sept. 1, 1995; Acts 1995, 74th Leg., ch. 610, § 1, eff. Jan. 1, 1996; Acts 1997, 75th Leg., ch. 194, § 1, eff. Jan. 1, 1998; Acts 1997, 75th Leg., ch. 592, § 2.01; Acts 1997, 75th Leg., ch. 1039, § 6, eff. Jan. 1, 1998; Acts 1997, 75th Leg., ch. 1059, § 2, eff. June 19, 1997; Acts 1997, 75th Leg., ch. 1071, § 28, eff. Sept. 1, 1997; Acts 1999, 76th Leg., ch. 1199, § 1, eff. June 18, 1999; Acts 1999, 76th Leg., ch. 1481, § 1, eff. Jan. 1, 2000; Acts 2003, 78th Leg., ch. 240, § 1, eff. June 18, 2003. Subsec. (j)(3) amended by Acts 2005, 79th Leg., ch. 159, § 1, eff. Jan. 1, 2006. Subsec. (j) amended by Acts 2013, 83rd Leg., ch. 699, § 6, eff. Sept. 1, 2013. Subsec. (b)

amended and subsec. (n-1) added by Acts 2015, 84th Leg., ch. 465, § 1, eff. only if the constitutional amendment proposed by S.J.R. 1 takes effect. Subsec. (j)(1)(D) amended by Acts 2015, 84th Leg., ch. 391, § 1, eff. Jan. 1, 2016. Subsec. (l)(2)(A) amended by Acts 2015, 84th Leg., ch. 400, § 1, eff. June 10, 2015.

§ 11.131. Residence Homestead of 100 Percent or Totally Disabled Veteran.

(a) In this section:

(1) "Disabled veteran" has the meaning assigned by Section 11.22.

(2) "Residence homestead" has the meaning assigned by Section 11.13.

(3) "Surviving spouse" means the individual who was married to a disabled veteran at the time of the veteran's death.

(b) A disabled veteran who receives from the United States Department of Veterans Affairs or its successor 100 percent disability compensation due to a service-connected disability and a rating of 100 percent disabled or of individual unemployability is entitled to an exemption from taxation of the total appraised value of the veteran's residence homestead.

(c) The surviving spouse of a disabled veteran who qualified for an exemption under Subsection (b) when the disabled veteran died, or of a disabled veteran who would have qualified for an exemption under that subsection if that subsection had been in effect on the date the disabled veteran died, is entitled to an exemption from taxation of the total appraised value of the same property to which the disabled veteran's exemption applied, or to which the disabled veteran's exemption would have applied if the exemption had been authorized on the date the disabled veteran died, if:

(1) the surviving spouse has not remarried since the death of the disabled veteran; and

(2) the property:

(A) was the residence homestead of the surviving spouse when the disabled veteran died; and

(B) remains the residence homestead of the surviving spouse.

(d) If a surviving spouse who qualifies for an exemption under Subsection (c) subsequently qualifies a different property as the surviving spouse's residence homestead, the surviving spouse is entitled to an exemption from taxation of the subsequently qualified homestead in an amount equal to the dollar amount of the exemption from taxation of the former homestead under Subsection (c) in the last year in which the surviving spouse received an exemption under that subsection for that homestead if the surviving spouse has not remarried since the death of the disabled veteran. The surviving spouse is entitled to receive from the chief appraiser of the appraisal district in which the former residence homestead was located a written certificate providing the information necessary to determine the amount of the exemption to which the surviving spouse is entitled on the subsequently qualified homestead.

Added by Acts 2009, 81ˢᵗ Leg., ch. 1405, § 1(a), eff. Jan. 1, 2010. Amended by Acts 2011, 82ⁿᵈ Leg., ch. 1222, §§ 1-2. eff. Jan. 1, 2012. Subsec. (c) amended by Acts 2015, 84ᵗʰ Leg., ch. 702, § 1, eff. Jan. 1, 2016, but only if the constitutional amendment authorizing the legislature to provide for an exemption from ad valorem taxation of all or part of the market value of the residence homestead of the surviving spouse of a 100 percent or totally disabled veteran who died before the law authorizing a residence homestead exemption for such a veteran took effect is approved by the voters.

§ 11.132. Donated Residence Homestead of Partially Disabled Veteran

(a) In this section:

(1) "Charitable organization" means an organization that is exempt from federal income taxation under Section 501(a), Internal Revenue Code of 1986, as an organization described by Section 501(c)(3) of that code.

(2) "Disability rating" and "disabled veteran" have the meanings assigned by Section 11.22.

(3) "Residence homestead" has the meaning assigned by Section 11.13.

(4) "Surviving spouse" has the meaning assigned by Section 11.131.

(b) A disabled veteran who has a disability rating of less than 100 percent is entitled to an exemption from taxation of a percentage of the appraised value of the disabled veteran's residence homestead equal to the disabled veteran's disability rating if the residence homestead was donated to the disabled veteran by a charitable organization at no cost to the disabled veteran.

(c) The surviving spouse of a disabled veteran who qualified for an exemption under Subsection (b) of a percentage of the appraised value of the disabled veteran's residence homestead when the disabled veteran died is entitled to an exemption from taxation of the same percentage of the appraised value of the same property to which the disabled veteran's exemption applied if:

(1) the surviving spouse has not remarried since the death of the disabled veteran; and

(2) the property:

(A) was the residence homestead of the surviving spouse when the disabled veteran died; and

(B) remains the residence homestead of the surviving spouse.

(d) If a surviving spouse who qualifies for an exemption under Subsection (c) subsequently qualifies a different property as the surviving spouse's residence homestead, the surviving spouse is entitled to an exemption from taxation of the subsequently qualified residence homestead in an amount equal to the dollar amount of the exemption from taxation of the former residence homestead under Subsection (c) in the last year in which the surviving spouse received an exemption under that subsection for that residence homestead if the surviving spouse has not remarried since the death of the disabled veteran. The surviving spouse is entitled to receive from the chief appraiser of the appraisal district in which the former residence homestead was located a written certificate providing the information necessary to determine the amount of the exemption to which the surviving spouse is entitled on the subsequently qualified residence homestead.

Added by Acts 2013, 83ʳᵈ Leg., ch. 122, § 1, eff. Jan. 1, 2014.

§ 11.13_3_2. Residence Homestead of Surviving Spouse of Member of Armed Services Killed in Action

(a) In this section:

(1) "Residence homestead" has the meaning assigned by Section 11.13.

(2) "Surviving spouse" means the individual who was married to a member of the armed services of the United States at the time of the member's death.

(b) The surviving spouse of a member of the armed services of the United States who is killed in action is entitled to an exemption from taxation of the total appraised value of the surviving spouse's residence homestead if the surviving spouse has not remarried since the death of the member of the armed services.

(c) A surviving spouse who receives an exemption under Subsection (b) for a residence homestead is entitled to receive an exemption from taxation of a property that the surviving spouse subsequently qualifies as the surviving spouse's residence homestead in an amount equal to the dollar amount of the exemption from taxation of the first property for which the surviving spouse received the exemption under Subsection (b) in the last year in which the surviving spouse received that exemption if the surviving spouse has not remarried since the death of the member of the armed services. The surviving spouse is entitled to receive from the chief appraiser of the appraisal district in which the first property for which the surviving spouse claimed the exemption was located a written certificate providing the information necessary to determine the amount of the exemption to which the surviving spouse is entitled on the subsequently qualified homestead.

Added by Acts 2013, 83ʳᵈ Leg., ch.138, § 1, eff. Jan. 1, 2014. Renumbered by Acts 2015, 84ᵗʰ Leg., ch.1238 , § 21.001(44), eff. Sept. 1, 2015.

Title 2.   State Taxation

Subtitle J.   Inheritance Tax

Chapter 211.   Inheritance Taxes

Subchapter B. Inheritance Taxes: Federal Estate Tax Credit and Generation-Skipping Transfer Tax Credit

Statutes in Context
§§ 211.051–211.055

Manny states impose a tax on at-death transfers. These taxes fall into three main categories. The approach previously adopted by Texas in §§ 211.051 - 211.055 was the pick-up tax, also called the sponge, sop, or soak-up tax. Under this type of tax, the state estate tax is set at the maximum amount of credit which the decedent's estate could claim for paying state death taxes. A pick-up tax is a cost-free tax. The amount of the state death tax is the same as the amount of the federal credit; if the state did not impose the tax, the decedent's estate would owe more tax to the federal government. The decedent's personal representative simply sends two checks, one to the I.R.S. and one to the state government, totaling the same amount that would be owed to the I.R.S. alone if the state did not have an estate tax.

The amount of the federal death tax credit decreased rapidly and it no longer existed as of 2005 (instead, there is a deduction for state death taxes). Thus, Texas effectively has had *no* estate tax since 2005. The 2015 Legislature made it "official" by repealing these sections.

States may impose two other types of taxes on at-death transfers which may be in place of or in addition to the pick-up tax. The first of these is an estate tax imposed on the privilege of transferring property at death. State estate taxes operate in a similar fashion to the federal estate tax although the property included in the gross estate and the types and amounts of deductions and credits may differ significantly. The second type is an inheritance tax imposed on the heir's or beneficiary's privilege of receiving property. Typically, the closer that the heir or beneficiary is related to the decedent, the lower the rate of tax and the greater the number and size of exemptions.

§ 211.051. Tax on Property of Resident

(a) A tax equal to the amount of the federal credit is imposed on the transfer at death of the property of every resident.

(b) If the estate of a resident is subject to a death tax imposed by another state or states for which the federal credit is allowable, the amount of the tax due under this section is reduced by the lesser of:

(1) the amount of the death tax paid the other state or states and that is allowable as the federal credit; or

(2) an amount determined by multiplying the federal credit by a fraction, the numerator of which is the value of the resident's gross estate less the value of the property of a resident, as defined by Section (c) of this section, that is included in the gross estate and the denominator of which is the value of the resident's gross estate.

(c) Property of a resident includes real property having an actual situs in this state whether or not held in trust; tangible personal property having an actual situs in this state; and all intangible personal property, wherever the notes, bonds, stock certificates, or other evidence, if any, of the intangible personal property may be physically located or wherever the banks or other debtors of the decedent may be located or domiciled; except that real property in a personal trust is not taxed if the real property has an actual situs outside this state.

Amended by Acts 1981, 67th Leg., p. 2759, ch. 752, § 6(a), eff. Jan. 1, 1982. Repealed by Acts 2015, 84th Leg., ch.1888 , § 1. eff. Sept. 1, 2015.

§ 211.052. Tax on Property of Nonresident

(a) A tax is imposed on the transfer at death of the property located in Texas of every nonresident.

(b) The tax is an amount determined by multiplying the federal credit by a fraction, the numerator of which is the value of the property located in Texas that is included in the gross estate and the denominator of which is the value of the nonresident's gross estate.

(c) Property located in Texas of a nonresident includes real property having an actual situs in this state whether or not held in trust and tangible personal property having an actual situs in this state, but intangibles that have acquired an actual situs in this state are not taxable.

Amended by Acts 1981, 67th Leg., p. 2759, ch. 752, § (a), eff. Jan. 1, 1982. Repealed by Acts 2015, 84th Leg., ch.1888 , § 1, eff. Sept. 1, 2015.

§ 211.053. Tax on Property of Alien

(a) A tax is imposed on the transfer at death of the property located in Texas of every alien.

(b) The tax is an amount determined by multiplying the federal credit by a fraction, the numerator of which is the value of the property located in Texas that is included in the gross estate and the denominator of which is the value of the alien's gross estate.

(c) Property located in Texas of an alien includes real property having an actual situs in this state whether or not held in trust; tangible personal property having an actual situs in this state; and intangible personal property if the physical evidence of the property is located within this state or if the property is directly or indirectly subject to protection, preservation, or regulation under the law of this state, to the extent that the property is included in the decedent's gross estate.

Amended by Acts 1981, 67th Leg., p. 2759, ch. 752, § 6(a), eff. Jan. 1, 1982. Repealed by Acts 2015, 84th

Leg., ch.1888 , § 1, eff. Sept. 1, 2015.

§ 211.054. ~~Tax on Property Included in Generation-Skipping Transfer~~

~~(a) A tax is imposed on every generation-skipping transfer.~~

~~(b) The tax is an amount determined by multiplying the generation-skipping transfer tax credit by a fraction, the numerator of which is the value of the property located in Texas included in the generation-skipping transfer and the denominator of which is the value of all property included in the generation-skipping transfer.~~

~~(c) Property located in Texas includes real property having an actual situs in this state whether or not held in trust; tangible personal property having an actual situs in this state; and tangible personal property owned by a trust having its principal place of administration in this state at the time of the generation-skipping transfer.~~

Amended by Acts 1981, 67th Leg., p. 2759, ch. 752, § 6(a), eff. Jan. 1, 1982. Repealed by Acts 2015, 84th Leg., ch.1888 , § 1, eff. Sept. 1, 2015.

§ 211.055. ~~Maximum Tax~~

~~The amount of tax imposed by this chapter may not exceed the amount of the imposed under Section 2001, Internal Revenue Code, reduced by the unified credit provided under Section 2010, Internal Revenue Code.~~

Amended by Acts 1981, 67th Leg., p. 2759, ch. 752, § 6(a), eff. Jan. 1, 1982; Acts 2001, 77th Leg., ch. 1263, § 73, eff. Sept. 1, 2001. Repealed by Acts 2015, 84th Leg., ch.1888 , § 1, eff. Sept. 1, 2015.

XVIII.

TRANSPORTATION CODE

Title 7. Vehicles and Traffic

Subtitle A. Certificates of Title and Registration of Vehicles

Chapter 501. Certificate of Title Act

Subchapter B. Certificate of Title Requirements

Statutes in Context
§ 501.031

Section 501.031 requires certificates of title for motor vehicles to contain a right of survivorship agreement. The inclusion of this language makes it easier for individuals, especially spouses, to hold a motor vehicle in survivorship form. The vehicle will then pass directly to the survivor rather than to will beneficiaries or intestate heirs. The vehicle is a nonprobate asset and would not be listed on the estate inventory.

---

§ 501.031. Rights of Survivorship Agreement

(a) The department shall include on each title an optional rights of survivorship agreement that:

(1) provides that if the agreement is between two or more eligible persons, the motor vehicle will be owned by the surviving owners when one or more of the owners die; and

(2) provides for the acknowledgment by signature, either electronically or by hand, of the persons.

(b) If the vehicle is registered in the name of one or more of the persons who acknowledged the agreement, the title may contain a:

(1) rights of survivorship agreement acknowledged by all the persons; or

(2) remark if a rights of survivorship agreement is on file with the department.

(c) Ownership of the vehicle may be transferred only:

(1) by all the persons acting jointly, if all the persons are alive; or

(2) on the death of one of the persons, by the surviving person or persons by transferring ownership of the vehicle, in the manner otherwise required by law, with a copy of the death certificate of the deceased person.

(d) A rights of survivorship agreement under this section may be revoked only if the persons named in the agreement file a joint application for a new title in the name of the person or persons designated in the application.

(e) A person is eligible to file a rights of survivorship agreement under this section if the person:

(1) is married and the spouse of the person is the only other party to the agreement;

(2) is unmarried and attests to that unmarried status by affidavit; or

(3) is married and provides the department with an affidavit from the person's spouse that attests that the person's interest in the vehicle is the person's separate property.

(f) The department may develop an optional electronic rights of survivorship agreement for public use.

Acts 1995, 74th Leg., ch. 165, § 1, eff. Sept. 1, 1995. Amended by Acts 1997, 75th Leg., ch. 165, § 30.39(a), eff. Sept. 1, 1997. Amended by Acts 1999, 76th Leg., ch. 62, § 17.05, eff. Sept. 1, 1999; Acts 1999, 76th Leg., ch. 241, § 1, eff. Sept. 1, 1999. Amended by Acts 2011, 82nd Leg., ch. 1296, § 20, eff. Jan. 1, 2012. Subsecs. (a) & (c) amended by Acts 2013, 83rd Leg., ch. 1135, § 46, eff. Sept. 1, 2013.

Subtitle B. Driver's Licenses and Personal Identification Cards

Chapter 521. Driver's Licenses and Certificates

Subchapter Q. Anatomical Gifts

Statutes in Context
§§ 521.401–521.405

Sections 521.401 - 521.405 explain the inter-relationship between anatomical gifts and driver's license designations. Over the past several years, there has been considerable debate as to whether a statement indicating that person is an organ donor on a driver's license would be effective. The law has changed several times with the most recent being in 2005 when the driver's license method was once again authorized after being deauthorized in 1997.

---

§ 521.401. Statement of Gift

(a) A person who wishes to be an eye, tissue, or organ donor may execute a statement of gift.

(b) The statement of gift may be shown on a donor's driver's license or personal identification certificate or by a card designed to be carried by the donor to evidence the donor's intentions with respect to organ, tissue, and eye donation. A donor card signed by the donor shall be given effect as if executed pursuant to 692A.005, Health and Safety Code.

(c) Donor registry information shall be provided to the department and the Texas Department of Transportation by organ procurement organizations, tissue banks, or eye banks, as those terms are defined in Section 692A.002, Health and Safety Code, or by the Glenda Dawson Donate Life-Texas Registry operated under Chapter 692A, Health and Safety Code. The department, with expert input and support from the nonprofit organization administering the Glenda Dawson Donate Life-Texas Registry, shall:

(1) provide to each applicant for the issuance of an original, renewal, corrected, or duplicate driver's license or personal identification certificate who applies in person, by mail, over the Internet, or by other electronic means:

(A) the opportunity to indicate on the person's driver's license or personal identification certificate that the person is willing to make an anatomical gift, in the event of death, in accordance with Section 692A.005, Health and Safety Code; and

(B) an opportunity for the person to consent to inclusion in the statewide Internet-based registry of organ, tissue, and eye donors and release to procurement organizations in the manner provided by Subsection (c-1); and

(2) provide a means to distribute donor registry information to interested individuals in each office authorized to issue driver's licenses or personal identification certificates.

(c-1) The department shall:

(1) specifically ask each applicant only the question, "Would you like to register as an organ donor?"; and

(2) if the applicant responds affirmatively to the question asked under Subdivision (1), provide the person's name, date of birth, driver's license number, most recent address, and other information needed for identification purposes at the time of donation to the nonprofit organization contracted to maintain the statewide donor registry under Section 692A.020, Health and Safety Code, for inclusion in the registry.

(d) An affirmative statement of gift on a person's driver's license or personal identification certificate executed after August 31, 2005, shall be conclusive evidence of a decedent's status as a donor and serve as consent for organ, tissue, and eye removal.

(e) The department shall distribute at all field offices Donate Life brochures that provide basic donation information in English and Spanish and include a contact phone number and e-mail address. The department shall include the question required under Subsection (c)(1)(B) and information on the donor registry Internet website in renewal notices.

Acts 1995, 74th Leg., ch. 165, § 1, eff. Sept. 1, 1995. Amended by Acts 1997, 75th Leg., ch. 225, § 1, eff. Sept. 1, 1997. Subsecs. (b), (c), (d) amended by Acts 2005, 79th Leg., ch. 1186, § 1, eff. June 18, 2005. Subsec. (c) amended and Subsec (e) added by Acts 2009, 81st Leg., ch. 831, § 4, eff. Sept. 1, 2009; Subsecs. (b), (c) amended by Acts 2009, 81st Leg., ch. 186, § 9, eff. Sept. 1, 2009. Subsec. (c) amended and (c-1) add by Acts 2011, 82nd Leg., ch. 554, § 5, eff. Jan. 1, 2012.

§ 521.402. Revocation of Statement of Gift

(a) To revoke an affirmative statement of gift on a person's driver's license or personal identification certificate, a person must apply to the department for an amendment to the license or certificate.

(b) The fee for an amendment is the same as the fee for a duplicate license.

(c) To have a person's name deleted from the statewide Internet-based registry of organ, tissue, and eye donors maintained as provided by Chapter 692A, Health and Safety Code, a person must provide written notice to the nonprofit organization selected under that chapter to maintain the registry directing the deletion of the person's name from the registry. On receipt of a written notice under this subsection, the organization shall promptly remove the person's name and information from the registry.

Acts 1995, 74th Leg., ch. 165, § 1, eff. Sept. 1, 1995. Amended by Acts 1997, 75th Leg., ch. 225, § 1, eff. Sept. 1, 1997. Amended by Acts 2005, 79th Leg., ch. 1186, § 2, eff. June 18, 2005. Amended by Acts 2011, 82nd Leg., ch. 554, § 6, eff. Jan. 1, 2012.

XIX.

UNITED STATES CODE

Title 10. Armed Forces

Subtitle A. General Military Law

Part II. Personnel

Chapter 53. Miscellaneous Rights and Benefits

Statutes in Context
§ 1044d

Section 551 of the Floyd D. Spence National Defense Authorization Act for Fiscal Year 2001 (codified as 10 U.S.C. § 1044d) provides that a military testamentary instrument is exempt from all state law formalities and has the same legal effect as a will prepared and executed under local state law. The statute sets forth the requirements for military testamentary instruments and how to make them self-proved. The motivating factor behind this legislation is that the military lawyers should not be required to learn the law of 50 states to prepare wills for military personnel. With this new legislation, all military lawyers may follow the same procedure without regard to the domicile of their clients. This is especially important when many wills have to be prepared quickly during major military operations.

This legislation could be challenged on Tenth Amendment grounds because succession matters were not delegated to the United States by the Constitution and thus are reserved to the states. On the other hand, matters regarding the wills of service personnel are tightly connected with the federal government's right to maintain the military. The case to watch for is one in which the will is valid under the federal law but not under state law and the heirs contest the will.

§ 1044d. Military Testamentary Instruments: Requirement for Recognition by States

(a) Testamentary Instruments To Be Given Legal Effect. — A military testamentary instrument —

(1) is exempt from any requirement of form, formality, or recording before probate that is provided for testamentary instruments under the laws of a State; and

(2) has the same legal effect as a testamentary instrument prepared and executed in accordance with the laws of the State in which it is presented for probate.

(b) Military Testamentary Instruments. — For purposes of this section, a military testamentary instrument is an instrument that is prepared with testamentary intent in accordance with regulations prescribed under this section and that —

(1) is executed in accordance with subsection (c) by (or on behalf of) a person, as a testator, who is eligible for military legal assistance;

(2) makes a disposition of property of the testator; and

(3) takes effect upon the death of the testator.

(c) Requirements for Execution of Military Testamentary Instruments. — An instrument is valid as a military testamentary instrument only if —

(1) the instrument is executed by the testator (or, if the testator is unable to execute the instrument personally, the instrument is executed in the presence of, by the direction of, and on behalf of the testator);

(2) the instrument is executed in the presence of a military legal assistance counsel acting as presiding attorney;

(3) the instrument is executed in the presence of at least two disinterested witnesses (in addition to the presiding attorney), each of whom attests to witnessing the testator's execution of the instrument by signing it; and

(4) the instrument is executed in accordance with such additional requirements as may be provided in regulations prescribed under this section.

(d) Self-Proving Military Testamentary Instruments. — (1) If the document setting forth a military testamentary instrument meets the requirements of paragraph (2), then the signature of a person on the document as the testator, an attesting witness, a notary, or the presiding attorney, together with a written representation of the person's status as such and the person's military grade (if any) or other title, is prima facie evidence of the following:

(A) That the signature is genuine.

(B) That the signatory had the represented status and title at the time of the execution of the will.

(C) That the signature was executed in compliance with the procedures required under the regulations prescribed under subsection (f).

(2) A document setting forth a military testamentary instrument meets the requirements of this paragraph if it includes (or has attached to it), in a form and content required under the regulations prescribed under subsection (f), each of the following:

(A) A certificate, executed by the testator, that includes the testator's acknowledgment of the testamentary instrument.

(B) An affidavit, executed by each witness signing the testamentary instrument, that attests to the circumstances under which the testamentary instrument was executed.

(C) A notarization, including a certificate of any administration of an oath required under the regulations, that is signed by the notary or other official administering the oath.

(e) Statement To Be Included. — (1) Under regulations prescribed under this section, each military testamentary instrument shall contain a statement that sets forth the provisions of subsection (a).

(2) Paragraph (1) shall not be construed to make inapplicable the provisions of subsection (a) to a testamentary instrument that does not include a statement described in that paragraph.

(f) Regulations. — Regulations for the purposes of this section shall be prescribed jointly by the Secretary of Defense and by the Secretary of Homeland Security with respect to the Coast Guard when it is not operating as a service in the Department of the Navy.

(g) Definitions. — In this section:

(1) The term "person eligible for military legal assistance" means a person who is eligible for legal assistance under section 1044 of this title.

(2) The term "military legal assistance counsel" means —

(A) a judge advocate (as defined in section 801(13) of this title); or

(B) a civilian attorney serving as a legal assistance officer under the provisions of section 1044 of this title.

(3) The term "State" includes the District of Columbia, the Commonwealth of Puerto Rico, the Commonwealth of the Northern Mariana Islands, and each possession of the United States.

Added Pub. Law 106-398, Sec. 1 ((div. A), title V, Sec. 551(a)), Oct. 30, 2000, 114 Stat. 1654, 1654A-123; amended by Pub. Law. 107-296, Sec. 1704(b)(1), Nov. 25, 2002, 116 Stat. 2314.

Title 26. *Internal Revenue Code*

Subtitle B. *Estate and Gift Taxes*

Chapter 11. *Estate Tax*

Subchapter C. *Miscellaneous*

Statutes in Context
§ 2206 & § 2207

Federal law mandates that life insurance beneficiaries and recipients of property under powers of appointment shoulder their fair share of transfer taxes. See I.R.C. §§ 2206 and 2207. These apportionment statutes are designed to carry out the decedent's presumed intent. Congress believes that most decedents would want the recipients of these transfers to be responsible for their share of the tax rather than for the heirs or the residuary beneficiaries to bear the entire tax burden. If the testator does not agree, the testator may provide otherwise in the will and those instructions will prevail over the apportionment statutes. See also Probate Code § 322A.

§ 2206. Liability of Life Insurance Beneficiaries

Unless the decedent directs otherwise in his will, if any part of the gross estate on which tax has been paid consists of proceeds of policies of insurance on the life of the decedent receivable by a beneficiary other than the executor, the executor shall be entitled to recover from such beneficiary such portion of the total tax paid as the proceeds of such policies bear to the taxable estate. If there is more than one such beneficiary, the executor shall be entitled to recover from such beneficiaries in the same ratio. In the case of such proceeds receivable by the surviving spouse of the decedent for which a deduction is allowed under section 2056 (relating to marital deduction), this section shall not apply to such proceeds except as to the amount thereof in excess of the aggregate amount of the marital deductions allowed under such section.

Aug. 16, 1954, ch. 736, 68A Stat. 402; Oct. 4, 1976, Pub. Law 94-455, title XX, Sec. 2001(c)(1)(H), 90 Stat. 1852.

§ 2207. Liability of Recipient of Property Over which Decedent Had Power of Appointment

Unless the decedent directs otherwise in his will, if any part of the gross estate on which the tax has been paid consists of the value of property included in the gross estate under section 2041, the executor shall be entitled to recover from the person receiving such property by reason of the exercise, nonexercise, or release of a power of appointment such portion of the total tax paid as the value of such property bears to the taxable estate. If there is more than one such person, the executor shall be entitled to recover from such persons in the same ratio. In the case of such property received by the surviving spouse of the decedent for which a deduction is allowed under section 2056 (relating to marital deduction), this section shall not apply to such property except as to the value thereof reduced by an amount equal to the excess of the aggregate amount of the marital deductions allowed under section 2056 over the amount of proceeds of insurance upon the life of the decedent receivable by the surviving spouse for which proceeds a marital deduction is allowed under such section.

Aug. 16, 1954, ch. 736, 68A Stat. 402; Oct. 4, 1976, Pub. Law 94-455, title XX, Sec. 2001(c)(1)(I), 90 Stat. 1852.

Statutes in Context
§ 2207A

The following example demonstrates the application of I.R.C. § 2207A. Assume that Husband's will provided that property valued at $300,000 was to be placed in trust with all the income payable to Wife annually. Upon Wife's death, the corpus of the trust was to be distributed to Husband's children from other partners. Husband's estate elected to take the marital deduction treating the entire $300,000 as qualified-terminable interest property (Q-TIP). Wife has just died and the value of the trust property is $1,000,000. Wife's gross estate will include the trust property at its date of death value of $1,000,000. However, the personal representative is entitled to charge this property with the estate tax triggered by the inclusion of the property in Wife's gross estate at the highest marginal rate. This prevents the beneficiaries of the surviving spouse's estate from shouldering the burden of the taxes on the Q-TIP property.

---

§ 2207A. Right of Recovery in the Case of Certain Marital Deduction Property

(a) Recovery with respect to estate tax

(1) In general - If any part of the gross estate consists of property the value of which is includible in the gross estate by reason of section 2044 (relating to certain property for which marital deduction was previously allowed), the decedent's estate shall be entitled to recover from the person receiving the property the amount by which -

(A) the total tax under this chapter which has been paid, exceeds

(B) the total tax under this chapter which would have been payable if the value of such property had not been included in the gross estate.

(2) Decedent may otherwise direct - Paragraph (1) shall not apply with respect to any property to the extent that the decedent in his will (or a revocable trust) specifically indicates an intent to waive any right of recovery under this subchapter with respect to such property.

(b) Recovery with respect to gift tax - If for any calendar year tax is paid under chapter 12 with respect to any person by reason of property treated as transferred by such person under section 2519, such

person shall be entitled to recover from the person receiving the property the amount by which -

(1) the total tax for such year under chapter 12, exceeds

(2) the total tax which would have been payable under such chapter for such year if the value of such property had not been taken into account for purposes of chapter 12.

(c) More than one recipient of property - For purposes of this section, if there is more than one person receiving the property, the right of recovery shall be against each such person.

(d) Taxes and interest - In the case of penalties and interest attributable to additional taxes described in subsections (a) and (b), rules similar to subsections (a), (b), and (c) shall apply.

Added Pub. Law 97-34, title IV, Sec. 403(d)(4)(A), Aug. 13, 1981, 95 Stat. 304; amended Pub. Law 105-34, title XIII, Sec. 1302(a), Aug. 5, 1997, 111 Stat. 1039.

Chapter 12. Gift Tax

Subchapter B. Transfers

Statutes in Context
§ 2518

An heir or beneficiary may disclaim property to reduce the person's transfer tax burden. If a disclaimer meets the requirements of a qualified disclaimer under I.R.C. § 2518, then the heir/beneficiary is treated as if the person never owned the property. Thus, the heir/beneficiary is not considered to have made a gift when the property passes to another person and the property is not part of the heir or beneficiary's estate.

Compare Property Code Title 13 (Uniform Disclaimer of Property Interests Act).

---

§ 2518. Disclaimers

(a) General rule - For purposes of this subtitle, if a person makes a qualified disclaimer with respect to any interest in property, this subtitle shall apply with respect to such interest as if the interest had never been transferred to such person.

(b) Qualified disclaimer defined - For purposes of subsection (a), the term "qualified disclaimer" means an irrevocable and unqualified refusal by a person to accept an interest in property but only if -

(1) such refusal is in writing,

(2) such writing is received by the transferor of the interest, his legal representative, or the holder of the legal title to the property to which the interest relates not later than the date which is 9 months after the later of -

(A) the day on which the transfer creating the interest in such person is made, or

(B) the day on which such person attains age 21,

(3) such person has not accepted the interest or any of its benefits, and

(4) as a result of such refusal, the interest passes without any direction on the part of the person making the disclaimer and passes either -

(A) to the spouse of the decedent, or

(B) to a person other than the person making the disclaimer.

(c) Other rules - For purposes of subsection (a) -

(1) Disclaimer of undivided portion of interest - A disclaimer with respect to an undivided portion of an interest which meets the requirements of the preceding sentence shall be treated as a qualified disclaimer of such portion of the interest.

(2) Powers - A power with respect to property shall be treated as an interest in such property.

(3) Certain transfers treated as disclaimers - A written transfer of the transferor's entire interest in the property -

(A) which meets requirements similar to the requirements of paragraphs (2) and (3) of subsection (b), and

(B) which is to a person or persons who would have received the property had the transferor made a qualified disclaimer (within the meaning of subsection (b)), shall be treated as a qualified disclaimer.

Added Pub. Law 94-455, title XX, Sec. 2009(b)(1), Oct. 4, 1976, 90 Stat. 1893; amended Pub. Law 95-600, title VII, Sec. 702(m)(1), Nov. 6, 1978, 92 Stat. 2935; Pub. Law 97-34, title IV, Sec. 426(a), Aug. 13, 1981, 95 Stat. 318; Pub. Law 97-448, title I, Sec. 104(e), Jan. 12, 1983, 96 Stat. 2384.

Title 31. Money and Finance

Subtitle III. Financial Management

Chapter 37. Claims

Subchapter II. Claims of the United States Government

Statutes in Context
§ 3713

See *Statutes in Context* for Probate Code § 320.

§ 3713. Priority of Government Claims

(a)(1) A claim of the United States Government shall be paid first when —

(A) a person indebted to the Government is insolvent and —

(i) the debtor without enough property to pay all debts makes a voluntary assignment of property;

(ii) property of the debtor, if absent, is attached; or

(iii) an act of bankruptcy is committed; or

(B) the estate of a deceased debtor, in the custody of the executor or administrator, is not enough to pay all debts of the debtor.

(2) This subsection does not apply to a case under title 11.

(b) A representative of a person or an estate (except a trustee acting under title 11) paying any part of a debt of the person or estate before paying a claim of the Government is liable to the extent of the payment for unpaid claims of the Government.

Pub. Law 97-258, Sept. 13, 1982, 96 Stat. 972.

TABLE OF CASES

CPSIA information can be obtained at www.ICGtesting.com
Printed in the USA
LVOW09s0829281215

468070LV00001B/1/P